Final Cut Pro® 4 Bible

Zed Saeed, J.J. Marshall, and Jeffrey Chong

WILEY

Wiley Publishing, Inc.

Final Cut Pro® 4 Bible

Published by
Wiley Publishing, Inc.
10475 Crosspoint Boulevard
Indianapolis, IN 46256
www.wiley.com

Copyright © 2004 by Wiley Publishing, Inc., Indianapolis, Indiana

Published simultaneously in Canada

Library of Congress Control Number is available from the publisher.

ISBN: 0-7645-4053-X

Manufactured in the United States of America

10 9 8 7 6 5 4 3 2 1

1O/SQ/QR/QU/IN

WILEY

About the Authors

Zed Saeed is the Senior Post Production Consultant at Digital Film Tree in Los Angeles; he specializes in editing, compositing, and workflow issues. Zed served as a senior post-production consultant for Apple Computer and Oxygen Media on Final Cut Pro and digital-video workflow design and with Media 100 and Adobe Systems on video-related products. He has also worked as an editor, producer, compositing artist, and broadcast designer for Showtime Channels, Sundance Channel, and ESPN Classics. Zed has written articles on digital media technologies for magazines and has served on the faculty of NYU Graduate School, Parsons School of Design, and New School University. Zed has written, produced, and edited videos that have received awards and recognition by the Academy of Television Arts and Sciences and the American Film Institute.

J.J. Marshall lives in New York City, where he makes his living as a digital video editor, designer, teacher, and consultant. Most recently, he wrote the *After Effects 5 Bible* (published by Wiley) right after assisting with the development of a nationwide broadband news-on-demand network called The FeedRoom. Prior to that, J.J. helped introduce Oxygen Media to the joys of Final Cut Pro and After Effects while editing a weekly two-hour show. In addition to teaching Motion Graphics at the School of Visual Arts, his recent freelance efforts have included projects for the New York New Media Association (NYNMA), Avon, and the Center for Neurobiology and Behavior at Columbia University, as well as numerous documentary productions.

Jeffrey Chong is a freelance film and television editor who has worked in commercial production for the past 20 years. His passion for Macintosh computers and the do-it-yourself attitude of an auteur made him, almost by definition, a prime candidate for working with Apple's Final Cut Pro since its first release. He currently lives, works, and teaches in New York City.

Credits

Acquisitions Editor
Tom Heine

Project Editor
Elizabeth Kuball

Technical Editor
Will Cox

Editorial Manager
Rev Mengle

Vice President & Executive Group Publisher
Richard Swadley

Vice President and Executive Publisher
Bob Ipsen

Vice President and Publisher
Joseph B. Wikert

Executive Editorial Director
Mary Bednarek

Project Coordinator
Kristie Rees

Graphics and Production Specialists
Andrea Dahl
Sean Decker
Brian Drumm
Lauren Goddard
Joyce Haughey
Jennifer Heleine
LeAndra Hosier
Lynsey Osborn
Heather Ryan

Quality Control Technicians
Carl William Pierce
Brian H. Walls

Permissions Editor
Laura Moss

Media Development Specialist
Travis Silvers

Proofreading and Indexing
TECHBOOKS Production Services

Preface

Why edit? Well, I think that editing is a human need. Books are edited, films are edited, conversations are edited, music is edited, and some would argue that even reality is edited. (Okay, so maybe that last bit was a stretch.)

My concern in this book of course is the editing of moving images. The idea of editing shots together to form a coherent narrative has been around for a long time. However, for much of that time, the editing technologies have been the domain of the few and the technologically privileged.

Thanks to the advent of computers, the entire scene of video editing has changed. Final Cut Pro is an application that takes this revolution a step farther. It is no surprise that this revolution originates from Apple Computer. Over the last few years, Apple has taken on the task of demystifying multimedia technologies and making the complex accessible to most. Final Cut Pro is a major shot across the bow of the old stodgy and limited thinking that existed in the digital nonlinear editing world.

I can easily say that working with Final Cut Pro has been the most fun I've ever had. The world of digital video itself is a heck of a lot of fun actually. Okay, so I'm a bit of a pointy-head, and that's probably why I say that. But there's a good chance that if you've picked up this book (and managed to get even this far into it), that there's a bit of a pointy-head in you too. And so, I think you'll have just as much fun as I've had working with digital video.

In this book, I've worked hard to add information above and beyond the use of the application itself. In doing so, I tried to cobble together under one roof a whole host of relevant information about video. I hope that you find that useful.

Over the last few years, my work with Apple Computer on Final Cut Pro has been an immensely rewarding and satisfying experience. Being part of the development process of Final Cut Pro was an experience in watching the world change forever. Some very dedicated and talented people have put in an enormous amount of work to make Final Cut Pro a great experience and a useful tool for its users. I hope this application brings you all the fun and usefulness that it has brought me.

Onward with the revolution!

Acknowledgments

A book of this size and magnitude is rarely a result of one person's work. It takes many people working very hard to create a book such as this.

Zed Saeed — My gratitude to the entire Final Cut Pro team at Apple Computer for their help, especially Will Stein, Bill Hudson, Brian Meaney, Dave Black, Erin Skitt, Alex Mera, Eric Lin, and others.

From Aurora Video Systems, I was given invaluable support by Darryl Hock, Tim MacMahon, Mike Stroven, and Adam Berman.

Special thanks to Matt Hutchinson, Donna Suhl, and Carol Whisker of Sony Corporation. I am also grateful for the assistance of Jayne Scheckla of Tektronix.

My eternal gratitude to my mentor Dirk Van Dall, and to John Gunther for being my first teacher in video technologies.

J.J. Marshall — All my love and thanks to my beautiful wife, Christine.

Jeffrey Chong — I could not have accomplished this Sisyphean task were it not for my wife and son, whose unwavering love, support, smiles, laughter, hugs, and constant supply of chocolate-chip cookies saw me through this challenging project. To them, I owe my gratitude and love.

Contents at a Glance

Contents

Part V: Color Correcting in Final Cut Pro   787

Part IX: Appendixes   1089

Final Cut Pro 4 QuickStart

C H A P T E R

♦ ♦ ♦ ♦

In This QuickStart

Creating a project

Creating and editing a sequence of clips

Advanced sequence editing

Compositing in Final Cut Pro

Adding and editing audio tracks in a sequence

Exporting a QuickTime movie

♦ ♦ ♦ ♦

First of all, welcome to Final Cut Pro 4.0. Since Apple's first released version of their professional nonlinear editing software, Final Cut Pro has been dazzling editors with its intuitive interface, professional tool set and incredible price value. With the release of Version 4.0, Final Cut Pro has expanded and improved even more. The latest version of Final Cut Pro is truly big news, and it's a testament to the efforts of a development team that has created an elegant and cost-effective video editing solution that is simple to learn and, frankly, a lot of fun to use. As a result, its use is becoming more and more common in professional broadcast environments. So the message here is simple: A little investment of your time toward mastering the application is a good idea, because Final Cut Pro skills are growing in demand.

This chapter assumes that you've purchased, or have access to, the application and are now sitting at your desk, wanting to see what happens when you put the pedal to the metal. If that's the case, then you have come to the right place, because in this Quick Start you're going to start editing a sequence almost immediately. In the process of creating a basic video edit, you're going to take a brief look at many of Final Cut Pro's features. When you've finished this chapter, you'll have a good idea of what Final Cut Pro can do for you after you've spent a little time getting familiar with the program.

For the purpose of this exercise, we will be working with DV media in NTSC (National Television Standards Committee) format. This media has already been acquired with Final Cut Pro and is located on the DVD-ROM that accompanies this book. This chapter assumes that you've successfully installed Final Cut Pro with the NTSC (as opposed to the PAL) option.

I've put all the media that you need for this chapter on the DVD-ROM that accompanies this book. You'll need to copy the folder called Mountain Biking Tutorial to your hard drive before you can begin working.

Creating a Project

Not surprisingly, your first step in working with Final Cut Pro is to open the application. Follow these steps to begin your first project:

1. **Double-click the Final Cut Pro icon to launch the program.**

   When the program opens, you should see the Browser, the Viewer, the Canvas, and the Timeline.

2. **All of the windows are probably empty, so open the Mountain Biking project.**

3. **If you haven't yet copied the Mountain Biking Tutorial folder from this book's DVD-ROM to your hard drive, do so at this time.**

4. **In Final Cut Pro, choose File ⇨ Open.**

5. **Navigate to the folder on your hard drive where you copied the project and open the project file called Mountain Biking.fcp.**

   If you want to save the project with a different name or create a backup copy of it, choose File ⇨ Save Project As.

In your future work, creating a new project from scratch is as easy as choosing File ⇨ New Project. From there, you simply choose File ⇨ Save Project As to create a project file in exactly the same manner as you just did with the Mountain Biking project.

Creating a project is the first step in working with Final Cut Pro. In the next section, I'll show you how to create a sequence in Final Cut Pro. Sequences are Timelines that contain your edited clips and transitions.

Creating and Editing a Sequence of Clips

A sequence in Final Cut Pro is a series of clips that are edited together in a program or program segment. A single project can have many sequences. To create a new sequence in the Mountain Biking project, choose File ⇨ New ⇨ Sequence. This step creates a new numbered sequence in the Browser. The text to the right of the sequence is highlighted (see Figure QS-1), indicating that you can type in the name that you want to give this new sequence. Type **Mountain Biking First Draft** and then double-click the new name. The new sequence reveals a tab in both the Canvas and the Timeline, but because you haven't added any media yet, both of these windows are empty.

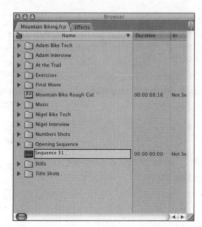

Figure QS-1: Sequence 1 is highlighted in black, indicating that you can type a new name to rename it.

Tip   Quickly double-clicking a sequence in the Browser opens that sequence in the Canvas and the Timeline. Slowly double-clicking (for example, click once, wait a moment, and then click again) a sequence's name or bin name allows you to rename it. Just type in your desired name and finish the task by pressing Return.

In the Browser window, click the arrow to the left of the bin called Nigel Interview. This arrow is a *disclosure triangle,* and after you click it, the triangle points down and the contents of that bin are revealed, as shown in Figure QS-2.

Nigel Interview bin

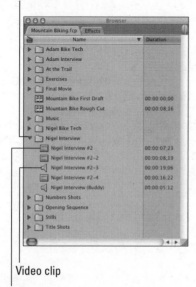

Figure QS-2: The disclosure triangle next to the Nigel Interview bin is pointed down, and you can see its contents listed underneath.

Video clip

Audio clip

Playing and navigating a clip

Double-click the Nigel Interview #2 clip, and it appears in the Viewer as shown in Figure QS-3. You can play the clip by clicking the Play button in the View window or by pressing the spacebar on your keyboard. Press the spacebar again to stop the playback. Most editors prefer to use the spacebar for the sake of speed, but the interface buttons are elegantly intuitive and easier to use when you're first learning the program.

Shuttle Control   Jog Control

Figure QS-3: The Nigel Interview #2 clip is displayed in the Viewer.

The number in the upper-right corner of the Viewer indicates the source timecode of the clip. The source timecode is the timecode on the tape from which the clip was taken. The number in the upper-left corner tells you the duration of the clip. Timecodes are displayed in hours:minutes:seconds:frames. You can navigate to specific locations in a clip by entering numeric timecodes with your keyboard. For example, if you type 00064900, you can jump directly to 00:06:49:00 in the clip.

You can also use the jog and shuttle controls to navigate through a clip. The shuttle control is in the lower-left corner of the Viewer. Click and drag it left or right, and you see that you can move slowly or quickly through a piece of media. For even tighter control, you can use the jog control disk in the lower-right portion of the Viewer. Clicking and dragging the jog control lets you get to specific frames in a clip more easily than with the shuttle.

Adding a clip to a sequence

Now that you have a sequence named Mountain Biking First Draft, you'll add the Nigel Interview #2 clip to it. First, you'll trim both the head and the tail of the clip a little bit by marking it with both In and Out points before adding Nigel's Interview #2 clip to the sequence. On this particular clip, you will place an In point at the spot where Nigel begins speaking and place your Out point where he finishes talking about starch in his diet. Follow these steps to mark an In and Out point on this clip and to add it to the sequence:

1. **Make sure that the Viewer is the active window by clicking on it and that the Nigel Interview #2 clip is loaded into it.**

2. **Press Home on the keyboard to park the playhead on the first frame of the clip.**

   Alternatively you can use the up-arrow key to move your playhead at the beginning of the clip as well. The up-arrow key is generally located on the lower-right side of your Mac keyboard.

3. **Go forward exactly 1 second by holding down the Shift key and pressing the right arrow key once.**

   The timecode in the upper-right-hand corner should read 00:06:46;02.

4. **Press the *I* key to mark an In point.**

   The In point is indicated by an icon in both the picture frame and in the white line, or *scrubber bar area,* representing the clip duration in the Viewer (see Figure QS-4).

5. **Press the End key to go to the end of the clip.**

   Alternatively you can use the down-arrow key to move your playhead at the beginning of the clip as well. The down-arrow key is generally located on the lower-right side of your Mac keyboard.

6. **Using the numeric keypad, type –100 to go back 1 second.**

7. **Press the O (as in Out) key on your keyboard to mark an Out point.**

   An Out point icon should appear at 00:06:54;09.

8. **Now that you've marked In and Out points for the clip, position the mouse anywhere over the video image, and click and drag the image to the right toward the Canvas window.**

   A thumbnail version of the clip image moves with the mouse pointer as you drag it.

In Point icon

Figure QS-4: An In point has been set in the Nigel Interview #2 clip.

In Point icon

9. **As you drag the clip over to the Canvas window, there are a few options visible. Release the mouse button while the Overwrite option is highlighted as shown in Figure QS-5.**

Overwrite edits are a kind of edit that writes over any other items present at an edit point in the Timeline and are just one of the many edit types available in Final Cut Pro.

Figure QS-5: Drag the clip over the Overwrite option in the Canvas and then release the mouse button.

Drag the clip from Viewer to either location to overwrite clip into the sequence

After releasing the clip to the Canvas window, the appearance of both the Canvas and the Timeline window changes. The Timeline displays the new clip that you've just dropped into the sequence, and the Canvas shows you added the trimmed clip, Nigel Interview #2, in the sequence as well. You can play the sequence by using the controls in the Viewer. The playheads of the Canvas window and the Timeline window move in tandem because they are both marking the passage of time in the same sequence. The sequence clip displayed in the Canvas contains only the portion of the clip that was trimmed.

You can add additional pieces of media to the sequence by using the same steps. To add another clip:

1. **Double-click the Adam – Interview Pt.#1 clip in the Browser.**

   This clip loads into the Viewer.

2. **Set an In point at 00:13:11;01 in Adam – Interview Pt.#1 clip by moving your playhead to the timecode location in the Viewer and pressing the *I* key.**

3. **Click the Timeline to make it active and press End to park the playhead at the end of the sequence.**

4. **Click and drag the Adam – Interview Pt.#1 clip from the Viewer to the Canvas using either the Overwrite or Insert option when releasing the mouse button.**

   The Timeline should now look something like Figure QS-6.

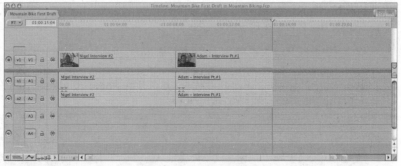

Figure QS-6: The Timeline shows the two clips you've added to the sequence.

Note

If things don't look right after you perform an edit, you can undo your last action by choosing Edit ➪ Undo, or press Command+Z. If you are a big fan of the undo feature, you can configure Final Cut Pro to let you undo your last 99 actions!

In the last four steps, you have added a second clip to the Timeline. A common step after adding some clips to a Timeline is the process of trimming them. Much like the pruning of trees, trimming is the process of eliminating portions of the clips that have been edited into the Timeline. The next section will show you how to trim a clip in the Timeline.

Trimming a clip in the Timeline

In the previous section you learned how to trim a clip by setting In and Out points in the Viewer using the Selection tool. You can also trim clips in the Timeline. You do this by using the Razor Blade tool in the Tools palette shown in Figure QS-7.

— Selection tool

Razor Blade tool
⌐

Razor Blade Tool – b

Figure QS-7: The Tools palette provides you with a variety of editing tools.

If the Tools palette is not visible on-screen, choose Window ➪ Tools. Now you are ready to trim the Adam – Interview Pt.#1 clip in the Timeline. To trim the clip, follow these steps:

1. **Click in the Timeline window to make it active and then press the End key to park the playhead at the end of the sequence.**

2. **Using the numeric keypad, type –100 to go back 1 second.**

3. **Select the Razor Blade tool either by clicking it in the Tools palette or by pressing the B key on the keyboard.**

4. **Hover the Razor Blade over the playhead in the Timeline.**

   As you bring the Razor Blade tool over the clip, your pointer becomes a small Razor Blade icon as shown in Figure QS-8. The Razor Blade snaps to the location of the playhead as you bring it closer.

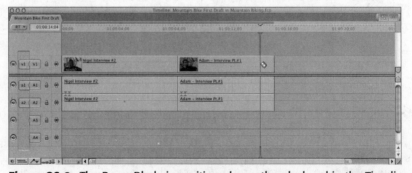

Figure QS-8: The Razor Blade is positioned over the playhead in the Timeline.

5. **Click once, and a cut line appears at the playhead.**

6. **Choose the Selection tool from the Tools palette.**

7. **Select the end section you just cut from the clip in the Timeline by clicking it.**

   The section becomes highlighted.

8. **Press the Delete key and the selected portion disappears.**

The last section showed you just one of the many ways you can trim clips in Final Cut Pro. Placing clips in the sequence and trimming them are basic functions of editing. Next, I will show you how to perform some advanced editing functions in Final Cut Pro. You may want to make sure you have your seat belts on.

Performing Advanced Edits

Trimming clips and adding them to sequences are among the most basic forms of edits you perform in Final Cut Pro. But you perform many advanced edits on a regular basis, as well. You may need to sharpen your edits, add transitions between clips, and more. The next two sections introduce you to two common advanced editing techniques. First, you fine-tune edits in the Timeline, and then you add a basic transition.

Fine-tuning edits in the Timeline

You may often find that, after editing a clip into a sequence, some aspect of the timing is not exactly right. The clip may start too soon, end too early, play too long, or have a variety of other problems that you want to correct. You can fix such problems by using Final Cut Pro's Slip, Slide, Ripple, and Roll tools. Each tool has a unique purpose:

✦ **Slip tool:** This tool changes the portion of a master clip that appears between In and Out points. The length of the editing clip doesn't change, nor does the clip's location in the sequence.

✦ **Slide tool:** This tool maintains the location of In and Out points on a clip, while changing In or Out points of adjacent clips in a sequence as you slide the clip one way or the other.

✦ **Ripple tool:** This tool lets you change the In or Out point on a clip. All clips after the clip being edited are moved, or rippled, in relation to the change.

✦ **Roll tool:** This tool changes the In and Out points of abutting clips as the edit point, or the point where two consecutive clips meet, is adjusted forward or back in the Timeline.

Cross-Reference The Slip, Slide, Ripple, and Roll tools are described in detail in Chapter 13.

The best way to learn how to use each of these editing tools is to experiment with them. For now, try out a Ripple edit on the sequence you created earlier:

1. **Press the N key on your keyboard to turn off snapping.**

   Snapping is a behavior in Final Cut Pro that allows clips to have gravity to one another and the playhead. Snapping is useful for making sure your clips are aligned correctly to one another.

2. **Select the Ripple Edit tool by clicking and holding the Roll tool in the Tools palette , then select the second tool option, the Ripple Edit tool, as shown in Figure QS-9.**

Figure QS-9: Click and hold the Roll tool in the Tools Palette and choose the Ripple Edit tool.

3. **Position the Ripple tool over the left edge of the Nigel Interview #2 clip in the Timeline (see Figure QS-10), then click and drag the tool to the left until you've shortened the Nigel Interview #2 clip by 30 frames, or 1 second.**

Ripple Tool

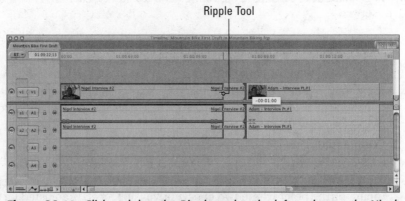

Figure QS-10: Click and drag the Ripple tool to the left to shorten the Nigel Interview #2 clip.

As you follow Step 3 above, look at the Canvas window. The window on the left shows you the *last* frame of the *outgoing* clip at the edit point, and the window on the right shows you the *first* frame of the *incoming* clip. Figure QS-11 shows what your Canvas window may look like. This feature helps you see the precise frames of each clip at the edit point.

Last frame of outgoing clip

First frame of incoming clip

Figure QS-11: When using the Ripple tool, the Canvas window shows you what's actually happening at the edit point.

Adding and adjusting transitions

Editors often use transitions to move visually from one clip to the next. Transitions avoid subjecting the audience to a jarring experience as they follow a visual narrative from one shot to the next. The best transitions are generally the ones that viewers don't notice, so keep this point in mind when creating transitions in your own projects. Some situations may call for a colorful or noisy transition, but these types of transitions are generally the exception, not the rule. I say that because you may feel numb when you see the large number of transitions provided in Final Cut Pro, and some of these are best avoided for their garish look and that special 1980s late-night, paid-programming look.

Experiment by adding a common transition to the Mountain Biking project that you have been working on throughout this QuickStart. A dissolve is one of the most common types of transitions used between clips, and when a transition is viewed, it looks like one shot fades in while the old shot dissolves away. To add a dissolve transition, use these steps:

1. **Click the Effects tab in the Browser to bring it to the front.**

2. **Twirl down the disclosure triangle next to the Video Transitions bin and then twirl down the triangle next to the Dissolve bin.**

3. **Click and drag the Cross Dissolve transition from the Browser directly to the center of the edit point between two clips in the Timeline, as shown in Figure QS-12.**

Transition

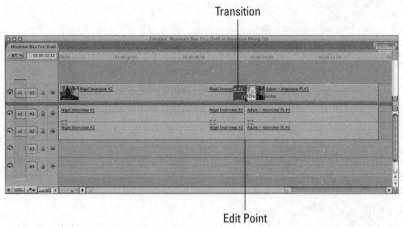

Edit Point

Figure QS-12: Click and drag the Cross Dissolve transition to an edit point in the Timeline and release the mouse.

4. **Release the mouse.**

When you release the mouse, the render bar indicator above the transition in the Timeline is colored red. This indicator tells you that the transition needs to be rendered before it can be played or mastered to tape.

Note

Final Cut Pro 4's new software-based real-time effects architecture, called RT Extreme, allows you to play back clips with effects and filters without the need to render. Depending on your CPU's speed, the number of simultaneous effects applied, and the Real Time settings selected in the RT pop-up menu in the upper-left-hand corner of the Timeline patch panel, a clip's render bar might be a color other than red. Clips and transitions with render bars colored other than red will play back at various resolutions and qualities without requiring rendering. For more information about render bar indicator colors and RT settings, see Chapter 18.

5. **Double-click the Cross Dissolve transition that you just added to the Timeline.**

The transition opens in the View window, as shown in Figure QS-13. As you can see in this figure, the outgoing clip begins to fade out and the incoming clip begins to fade in 15 frames before the edit point, and the transition is complete 15 frames after the edit point. Therefore, the transition is a total of 30 frames, or 1 second long.

Duration of transition   Handle of outgoing clip

Outgoing clip

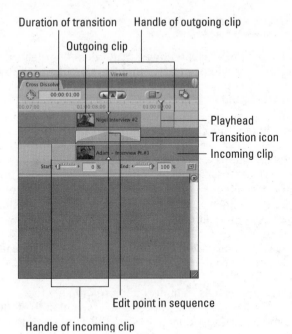

— Playhead
— Transition icon
— Incoming clip

Edit point in sequence

Handle of incoming clip

Figure QS-13: The View window shows the inner workings of the Cross Dissolve transition.

Caution

Transitions only work if the clips at the edit point have extra footage beyond what's visible in the Timeline. This extra footage is called *pad* or a clip's *handles* by editors in the trade. Make sure that you have adequate handles at the edit points of each clip if you want to be able to add transitions.

6. **Click the Timeline to make it the active window and choose Sequence ⇨ Render ⇨ Both.**

A dialog box appears showing the rendering progress. The process of rendering creates a render cache file. This cache file consists of new media created that contains the portions of the clips and the transitions used. This render cache file plays during the transition for a seamless playback of shots and transition.

There you are! Now you have progressed quite a bit into this tutorial. So far you've added a few clips into the sequence, trimmed them, and gone so far as to add a transition. Let's move on to another of Final Cut Pro's fabulous features—compositing. Layering clips and stills to create multilayered video is commonly known as compositing in the video industry. In the next section, I will show you the basics of creating multilayered clips in Final Cut Pro.

Cross-Reference

To learn more about rendering and working with transitions, see Chapter 16.

Compositing in Final Cut Pro

Final Cut Pro's strengths lie in its powerful editing capabilities. The elegance of its design enables you to sequence a visual narrative that is unmatched by anything on the market, both in its own price range and beyond. Among Final Cut Pro's many capabilities is the ability to layer video, stills, and graphics together in a process called *compositing*. Although this program is not designed solely for compositing, like Adobe's After Effects, the compositing capabilities in Final Cut Pro are very good.

This section helps you build a multilayered composite for the opening of your Mountain Biking sequence. The tutorial is meant to get you started using these features. You finish the composite on your own by adding your own design touches. To see an example, refer to the sequences I created in the bin called Opening Sequence in the Mountain Biking project on the DVD-ROM.

 Cross-Reference This composite is somewhat complicated if you're just starting to become familiar with Final Cut Pro. For more on compositing, see Chapter 17.

Your first step in creating a composite is to import a Photoshop file that I created for the title sequence. This Photoshop file has several layers, and in the following steps, you will animate some of the individual layers as well as place video tracks on top of some of the still images. To create a basic composite, use these steps:

1. **Choose File ⇨ Import ⇨ File, and import the file called Nigel Pass – Title_v04.psd from the folder called Photoshop File in the Mountain Biking folder you copied to your hard drive from the DVD-ROM.**

2. **In the Browser, double-click the newly imported Nigel Pass – Title_v04.ps to open it up in the Timeline.**

   You can rename the sequence if you like.

3. **In the Timeline, click the different layers to select them.**

   As you do so, look at the Canvas window to see which layers refer to the various parts of the composite.

The first task you need to do is fade the background image of Nigel on his bike. Additionally, you make the image black and white and restore its color over a period of time. To fade the background, use these steps:

1. **Double-click the Image layer located on track V1 in the Timeline window.**

   This layer opens in the Viewer.

2. **In the Viewer, click the Motion tab and bring the playhead back to the beginning of the clip.**

3. **Twirl down the arrow next to the Opacity settings so that your Viewer looks similar to Figure QS-14.**

Keyframe Navigation arrows   Duration of clip in sequence

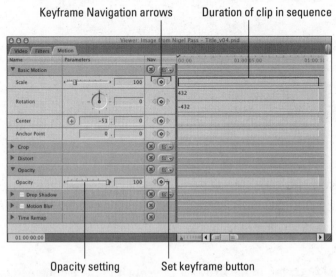

Opacity setting   Set keyframe button

Figure QS-14: Here is the Motion tab of the View window with the Opacity settings visible.

4. **Click the set keyframe button next to Opacity to set an opacity keyframe at the first frame.**

5. **Move the playhead forward in the clip about 4 seconds and set another opacity keyframe.**

   For more precision, hold down the Shift key as you press the right-arrow key four times.

6. **Using the arrows to the left and right of the set keyframe button, navigate to the first keyframe.**

7. **Click and drag the Opacity slider to zero.**

   The image of Nigel is now set so that it fades up from black over a 4-second period. The View window should resemble Figure QS-15.

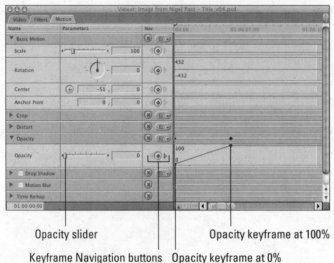

Opacity slider   Opacity keyframe at 100%

Keyframe Navigation buttons   Opacity keyframe at 0%

Figure QS-15: The Viewer shows the new opacity keyframes.

Now add the Proc Amp filter to fade color into the image over time by following these steps:

1. **Click the Effects tab in the Browser to bring it to the front, open the Video Filters bin, and then open the Image Control bin.**

2. **Click and drag the Proc Amp filter from the Browser and drop it directly on the Image layer in the Timeline, as shown in Figure QS-16.**

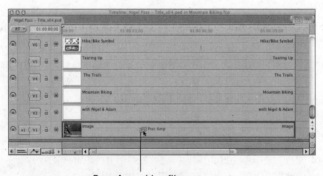

Proc Amp video filter

Figure QS-16: Drag the Proc Amp filter from the Browser and drop it onto the Image layer in the Timeline.

3. **Return to the Viewer and click the Filters tab.**

The Proc Amp filter has been added to the Image layer.

4. **Move the playhead forward 2 seconds in the View window, set a chroma keyframe, and set another chroma keyframe at 10 seconds.**

5. **Navigate back to the keyframe you set at 2 seconds and drag the Chroma slider to 0 to completely desaturate the image.**

Your Viewer should look similar to Figure QS-17.

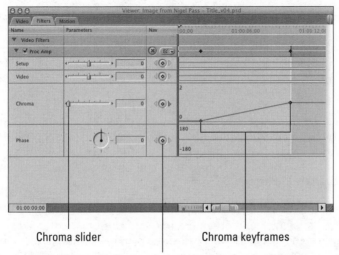

Chroma slider   Chroma keyframes

Green diamond indicates playhead is parked on keyframe

Figure QS-17: The Viewer shows the new Proc Amp filter animation.

To preview the changes you've made, turn off visibility for all the layers of video in the Timeline except V1. To turn off visibility for a track, click the green visibility indicators at the left edge of the Timeline as shown in Figure QS-18. (Option+clicking will mute all other tracks except that track, also known as soloing.) After all the layers except V1 are turned off, render the sequence by choosing Sequence ➪ Render All ➪ Both. When the rendering is complete, play the Timeline to see what your edits look like.

Note

Final Cut Pro 4's new software-based real time effects architecture, called RT Extreme, allows you to play back clips with effects and filters without the need to render them. Depending on your CPU's speed, the number of simultaneous effects applied, and the Real Time settings selected in the RT pop-up menu in the upper-left of the Timeline patch panel, a clip's render bar might be a color other than red. Clips and transitions with render bars colored other than red will play back at various resolutions and qualities without requiring rendering. For more information about render bar indicator colors and RT settings, see Chapter 18.

Track visibility is off

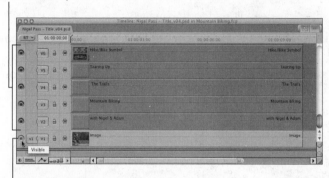

Track visibility is on

Figure QS-18: Turn off the visibility of video tracks in the Timeline by clicking the green switches.

Whew! Compositing and animating clips is fun but it can seem quite complex. Of course, you'll be happy to know that I've devoted many pages in this book to the process of creating layered video in Final Cut Pro. (If you're curious, check out Chapter 17 on multilayering and compositing, and Chapter 26 on working with Photoshop and After Effects.)

Working with audio is a crucial task in any editing application. You may want to work with music, voiceover, and other audio to add clarity and drama to your edited sequence. In the next section, I will show you how to add audio clips and edit audio in your sequence.

Adding and Editing Audio in Your Sequence

Adding and editing audio, if done well, is usually what separates great editors from good ones. Research has shown that the human brain favors hearing over seeing, and an audience can handle blurred or obscured visuals as long as they can hear what's happening in the action of a given cut. The converse of that statement can be an editor's undoing; specifically, great visuals on top of garbled or otherwise unclear audio is a sure way to lose viewers' interest.

Always make sure that your editing never disregards the most important aspect of a story as it is being told. The main voice track should always be audible over ambient sound and music soundtracks, but not overbearing. When you cut between clips, you must take care to avoid pops or scratches, however minor they may seem. A viewer may not be able to articulate why he or she doesn't like a certain presentation even though it *appears* flawless, but the odds are high that such opinions are based on poor audio.

Use the following steps to create a new sequence, add interview clips and music to that sequence, and edit the audio levels over time. Use material from the Mountain Biking Project folder on the DVD-ROM that accompanies this book. If you haven't done so already, copy this folder to your hard drive. To build the sequence, use the following clips:

✦ From the Nigel Interview bin:

   • Nigel Interview #2-4

   • Nigel Interview (Buddy) (*Note:* This is an audio-only clip.)

✦ From the At the Trail bin:

   • Nigel & Adam Pass

   • Nigel & Adam Trailhead4

✦ From the Adam Bike Tech bin:

   • Adam – Tire Blooper

   • Adam – Tire Blooper-2

✦ From the Music bin:

   • Ntracks_J&E2_59.aif (*Note:* This is an audio-only clip.)

After you have the files copied to your hard drive, you're ready to create a new sequence and edit some audio into it:

1. **Choose File ⇨ New ⇨ Sequence and rename it Audio Editing — QuickStart or any other name you'd prefer.**

2. **Double-click the new sequence to open it in the Timeline.**

3. **In the Timeline, add two audio tracks by choosing Sequence ⇨ Insert Tracks.**

4. **Enter 2 in the Insert Audio Tracks field so that you have six total tracks.**

5. **In the Browser, hold down the Command key and click the following clips in the order in which they are listed:**

   • Nigel Interview #2-4

   • Nigel & Adam Pass

   • Nigel & Adam Trailhead4

   • Adam – Tire Blooper

   • Adam – Tire Blooper-2

6. **Make sure the target tracks are V1, A1, and A2 and then drag the selected clips from the Browser to the Canvas and release them by using the Overwrite option.**

7. **Press the N key to make sure that snapping is turned on and then drag the Nigel Interview (Buddy) clip directly to the Timeline in tracks A3 and A4.**

8. **Place the clip's right edge even with the right edge of the Nigel & Adam Pass clip in the tracks above it.**

   When the clip snaps into place, release the mouse.

9. **Place the Ntracks_J&E2_59.aif clip even with the end of the sequence in tracks A5 and A6.**

   The sequence should now resemble Figure QS-19.

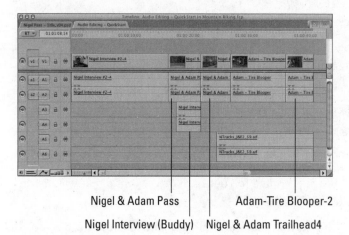

Nigel & Adam Pass   Adam-Tire Blooper-2

Nigel Interview (Buddy)   Nigel & Adam Trailhead4

Figure QS-19: Your Audio Editing – QuickStart sequence should look something like this.

Caution

The Ntracks_J&E2_59.aif clip has an In point that you must not change as you follow the steps listed here.

10. **Before editing the audio, cut the first 11 seconds off the first clip Nigel Interview #2-4 by using the Razor Blade tool.**

11. **Cut the last three and a half seconds off the Adam-Tire Blooper clip.**

12. **Cut the first second off the Adam Tire Blooper-2 clip.**

13. **Shift the position of the Ntracks_J&E2_59.aif clip back in time by dragging it in the Timeline so that the clip's right edge is once again even with the edge of the last clip in tracks V1, A1, and A2.**

   Your sequence should now resemble Figure QS-20.

You've cut the first 11
seconds off this clip

You've cut the first seconds off this clip

You've cut the last 3.5 seconds off this clip

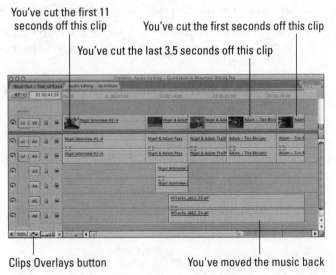

Clips Overlays button   You've moved the music back

Figure QS-20: The Audio Editing – QuickStart sequence is
progressing toward completion.

14. Turn Clip Overlays on so that you can see the audio levels.

Alternately you can also use the shortcut of Command+W to turn the Clip
Overlays on. (Press Command+W again to toggle them off.)

15. Choose Sequence ⇨ Settings to open the Sequence Settings dialog box.

Before selecting this menu option, be sure to check that the Timeline window
is selected, otherwise the option may be grayed out and not available to you.
You can select the Timeline window by simply clicking on it.

**16. Click the Timeline Options tab and click the Show Audio Waveforms option
to enable it.**

Note that, instead of going through the menus, you can use the keyboard
shortcut of Command+Option+W to turn on the waveform display in the
Timeline. (Use the same command again to toggle the display off.)

17. Click OK to close the dialog.

Audio waveforms let you *see* the audio, making editing and synchronizing
audio easier.

**18. Zoom in your view of the critical moments of both the music and the tire
explosion by using the handles in the lower-right portion of the Timeline
window.**

19. Click and drag the music track to the right until it sets up the tire explosion.

Your enlarged Timeline will probably end up looking like Figure QS-21. I moved the music track about 3 seconds downstream to achieve the desired effect.

Tire explosion

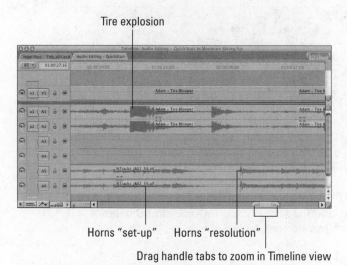

Horns "set-up"   Horns "resolution"

Drag handle tabs to zoom in Timeline view

Figure QS-21: The enlarged view of the Timeline with Audio Waveforms visible makes audio editing much simpler.

Note   The music track for this exercise was provided by Narrator Tracks. Go to their Web site at www.narratortracks.com to listen to samples of their great music.

20. Zoom out your view of the Timeline by pressing Shift+Z so that you can adjust the levels in the sequence to round it all out.

This command makes the contents of your sequence fit to fill the available space.

21. Trim the end off the music clip so that it's even with the end of the last clip (Adam-Tire Blooper-2) in tracks V1, A1, and A2.

22. Select the Pen tool from the bottom of the Tools Palette and again zoom in on the Timeline, focusing on the music track.

23. Position the Pen tool over the audio levels at the beginning of the music clip and click once to set an initial audio keyframe.

The keyframe looks like two dots at the beginning of the music track.

24. **Create another audio keyframe roughly 2 seconds later in the music track.**

25. **Move the Pen tool back over the first keyframe you set so that the pointer's appearance changes into a small crosshair.**

26. **Click and drag all the way down to the bottom of the music track until the level reads – ∞ as shown in Figure QS-22.**

Use Crosshair cursor to drag down keyframe to -∞ (silence)

Figure QS-22: Use the Pen tool in the Timeline to set audio keyframes and adjust audio levels.

27. **To finish the audio edit, add two more keyframes at the end of the music track so that it starts to fade out before Adam says, "That was psycho!"**

Working with audio filters

In the Mountain Biking project, you've probably noticed that Nigel's interview clips all contain a hum that makes his clips audibly different from Adam's interview clips. Hum and extraneous noise is something you should always try to avoid in production, but sometimes that's not an option. Avoid promising that you can "fix it in post" as the saying goes. Starting with consistent audio is always preferable, but often you have to play the hand you're dealt. As an editor, you will often be given footage without having had any influence on it prior to its being unceremoniously dumped in your lap. This is certainly the case here, because the media on the DVD-ROM was already shot, logged, and acquired before you copied it to your hard drive to follow the steps in this QuickStart.

Applying an audio filter to a clip

Final Cut Pro contains an arsenal of tools to help you deal with a problem such as the hum in Nigel's interview clips. Open the Effects tab in the Browser and look at the contents of the bin called Audio Filters. Here, you see two bins of audio filters — one called Apple, and the other labeled Final Cut Pro. In the Final Cut Pro audio filters bin you will find the Hum Remover filter. To practice using this filter, start by creating a sequence that only contains a single clip from the Nigel Interview bin. Follow these steps to apply the audio filter:

1. **Choose File ⇨ New ⇨ Sequence and name your new sequence Hum Remover – Quickstart or any other name you prefer.**

2. **Add the Nigel Interview #2 clip to the sequence.**

   Play the sequence and listen carefully.

3. **On the Effects tab, open the Audio Filters bin.**

4. **Drag and drop the Hum Remover filter on the Nigel Interview #2 clip in the sequence.**

5. **Double-click the clip in the sequence to open it in the Viewer, and in the Viewer, click the Filters tab.**

   The Viewer should look similar to Figure QS-23.

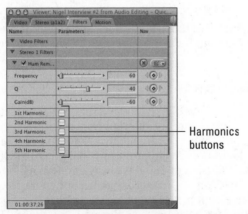

Figure QS-23: The View window shows the inner workings of the Hum Remover audio filter.

You need to remove the hum in the audio, but you don't know what these sliders and buttons do. Don't worry. Experiment a little. You can learn a lot by pushing buttons and seeing what happens.

Exporting a Sequence

After you finish editing a project, what happens next? The answer to this question depends on your needs. Whom are you editing for? If you're in a professional broadcast environment, chances are you'll lay your final edits onto a high-quality tape format like Sony's Betacam SP. Other projects may be laid to DV tape formats. You may even export your final sequence to a broadband Web audience by using a high bit rate setting in QuickTime. To export in this last format, follow these steps:

1. **Select your final sequence in the Browser, or double-click the sequence so that it opens in the Timeline and choose File ⇨ Export ⇨ Using QuickTime Conversion.**

2. **In the bottom pull-down menu marked with the word Use, choose DSL/ Cable – High, and save it to the desktop.**

3. **When you're done saving the clip, double-click the file to play your project and see what you have created.**

Congratulations! You made it. Keep in mind that all concepts introduced in this QuickStart are explored in detail in the chapters that follow. If any of the topics introduced here have provoked your interest, use the book as a desktop reference and refer to the detailed explanations. If Final Cut Pro is relatively new to you, I can personally guarantee that you'll have a much different appreciation of the skills you were just exposed to in this QuickStart if you hunt down the related information in the later chapters. This is, after all, the *Final Cut Pro 4 Bible*.

✦   ✦   ✦

Getting to Know Final Cut Pro

What Is Final Cut Pro?

I am an impatient man. If you're like me, you just want to get on with editing. You purchased Final Cut Pro, you bought this book and brought it home, and you made your way through the QuickStart. Now you just want to edit your documentary or the dream piece you've been shooting as your calling card in Hollywood. But wait a minute — hold your horses, Buckaroo.

If you've had some basic experience with nonlinear editing in the past, you may be tempted to skip this chapter. Don't do it. I specially finagled this chapter into the book. Even though most nonlinear editing systems are based on similar principles, Final Cut Pro has its own way of dealing with video editing principles, and understanding the subtle differences are crucial to your success.

In the QuickStart, I walked you through editing a short sequence. If that were all you needed to do, this book would be much thinner. But this book is fat for a good reason — it covers a lot of information. For example, in the QuickStart, I never explained the relationship of project files to media files to clips, and so on. In this chapter, I cover the basics of video editing as well as numerous other concepts that you should know about to successfully edit your video projects. Get yourself a cup of coffee, sit back, relax, and read this chapter. Hollywood has waited for you all these years — it can wait another half-hour.

Reviewing the Fundamentals of Video Editing

My work consists of consulting for companies who are having problems with their digital editing process. I am called in to help editors and producers who have rushed into projects without having a firm grasp of the basic concepts of digital editing. Final Cut Pro can make digital editing look so simple and easy. And in some ways, the program is that — and so much more. But when problems occur on a two-hour show that you spent weeks working on, you'll wish that you had taken the time to understand the fundamentals of digital video.

Comparing analog and digital video

Before you get into actual editing, you need to understand the difference between analog and digital signals. Today, the word *digital* is bandied about with reckless abandon. What does it mean, and how does it differ from *analog?*

Analog signals consist of varying voltage. An analog value can occupy any location along the signal voltage. Most televisions are analog devices. The video you see on a television is sent as an analog signal, either through wires or through the air.

Digital signals, on the other hand, use computer-based binary language and can only be represented by discrete values. Binary language consists only of *zeros* and *ones,* also known as *off* and *on* states. Think of a sloping ramp as an analog signal and a series of stair steps as a digital signal. Tossing a coin on the sloping ramp can land it anywhere on the slope. On a series of steps however, the coin can land only on discrete steps. Figure 1-1 illustrates how an analog signal compares to a digital signal. For a digital file to represent an analog signal, the analog file must first go through a process called *digitizing*.

The main disadvantage of analog signals is their capacity for deterioration, or atten-uation. As a videotape is copied, the signal noise increases and the quality of the picture decreases. Make more copies of a VHS tape for a few generations, and you'll soon find the picture unviewable. A digital tape, such as the popular DV format, shows no signal loss when transferred over a digital path (such as FireWire), no matter how many times it has been copied.

Cross-Reference   For more information on the DV format and FireWire, see Chapter 2.

Analog signals are also harder to manipulate than digital signals. Analog signals can have any value along the signal voltage. Digital signals always have discrete values. Making applications based on mathematical schemes that can manipulate discrete values is far easier than making infinitely variable analog ones. Final Cut Pro works with digital files and must have analog video converted to a digital signal before any work can be started.

Be aware that the previous few paragraphs have been an exercise in gross oversim-plification. There's a heck of a lot more to both analog and digital signals than I have addressed here. When an analog signal is *digitized,* or converted to a digital signal, a host of issues comes into play, issues that I cover in the next few chapters. Some of these issues are about the conversion of color and brightness information. For now, keep in mind that the popular DV format is entirely digital, making each copy as good as the original.

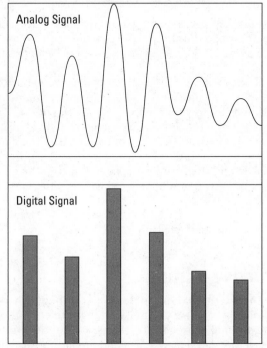

Figure 1-1: Analog signals consist of varying voltage. Digital signals consist of discrete values.

Understanding linear and nonlinear editing

Digital computer editing, as done by Final Cut Pro, performs *nonlinear* editing on your material, whereas tape-based editing is usually *linear*. The best way to illustrate the difference between linear and nonlinear editing is to use the classic analogy of a typewriter versus a word processor. Both can be used to write a letter, but a typewriter uses linear editing while a word processor uses nonlinear editing. With a nonlinear editing system, you can quickly perform edits in the middle of a document and move material around with just a few mouse clicks. With a linear editor, you can only type in a linear fashion — one word at a time followed by the next word. Inserting paragraphs is difficult, as is making most any changes to the document.

In the not-too-distant past, video editing and re-editing were time-consuming and complex processes. The tape editing process often had me working through the following steps (often over and over again): Place the titles, edit the shots, then die a small death after the producer asked me to switch shots two and three and move other scenes around. I still remember breaking out in a cold sweat when a producer asked for the slightest change.

Then I heard about nonlinear editing. A guy was moving around shots on the screen with a mouse and changing their order and duration in the timeline with a click or two. I remember people gasping. The rest is a bit foggy because I was crying so hard.

The concept of nonlinear editing is based on the fact that you've captured your video on tape and moved it into your computer. Final Cut Pro's capture ability enables you to easily move video from your camcorder to your computer. After you do, you have a virtual representation of a timeline—the timeline is also called *sequence* in Final Cut Pro—and you can move this shot anywhere you want. You can trim the shot, copy it, and paste it. The shot is nonlinear; therefore, you can work in any order that you like. You can edit the middle first and then copy and paste it next to the ending later, with just a few mouse clicks. And if you don't like what you did, just undo it with a keyboard command. Hallelujah!

Cross-Reference   Editing in the timeline is explained in more detail in Chapter 11.

Performing nondestructive editing

Nondestructive editing is another *non-* term that I should explain. Editing with a program like Final Cut Pro is *nondestructive* because you make changes to your clips in the program without affecting the original source file on the disk. The clips in the Final Cut Pro are merely pointers to the actual media files and are not the actual media files. You can trim clips, apply effects to them, and so on and still have the original source clip safe, sound, and unchanged on your hard drive. Even if you delete the clips from within Final Cut Pro, your source media file is still on your disk.

Tip   If you delete a clip from the browser, you can drag and drop the media file back into the browser from the hard drive, or import it back into a project by using the Import command.

Here I should point out two small but very significant exceptions to nondestructive editing in Final Cut Pro. These two exceptions are:

✦ Changing the reel number of the clips

✦ Changing a clip's timecode

If you make either of these changes to a clip, they will be saved to the media file.

Evaluating the pros and cons of digital video editing

I don't want to oversell digital nonlinear editing. Many production houses still choose to maintain their linear editing systems, because in certain cases it is the most effective way to go. As magical as nonlinear and nondestructive editing sounds, editing in the digital domain does have its pros and cons. I'll briefly cover a few of them here.

The pros

Don't be fooled by this shortlist of pros — though few in number, the following points have huge implications.

✦ **Changes are easier.** The ease of making changes is perhaps the most significant advantage of digital editing. The freedom to explore various edits, try different effects, and create new effects without fear of lengthy re-edits is stupefying compared to the limitations of linear editing. Final Cut Pro provides up to 99 levels of undo. The levels of undo mean that if you're not happy with what you just did, you can undo the action up to *your past 99 edits.* That kind of power is unheard of in linear, tape-based editing. In fact, that's way more power than I *ever* need. I can't even remember what I did 5 edits ago, much less 99, but that may just mean that I'm growing old. In Final Cut Pro, the Undo command shortcut is Command+Z. You can keep pressing that for additional undos.

✦ **You have more editing options.** Digital editing is a whole universe unto itself. With Final Cut Pro, you can mix Photoshop layouts and audio files with video to create a final video program. You can use effects, add plug-ins to extend the functionality of the program, exchange digital files between applications, create movie files for streaming on the Web, and more — all within this one application. Tape-based systems require stand-alone equipment to do effects. Final Cut Pro is an editor and an effects engine, all in one.

✦ **Quality remains consistent.** In a completely digital environment, no *generational* loss occurs. With analog video, each copy of a tape is said to have gone down one generation. Every copy, no matter how many copies of a copy it is, will look the same as long as the format and signal path remain digital. For example, with Final Cut Pro, a DV camera with FireWire, and a G4 computer, you can capture, edit, and then send the final edit back to tape without losing a single generation. In analog video, the simple act of editing from the play deck to the record deck makes you lose one generation and, with it, some quality.

✦ **It's cheaper.** A digital editing setup based on Final Cut Pro costs a lot less than a tape-based editing system. In fact, with some care, you can put together a very respectable Final Cut Pro and DV-based editing system for under $5,000.

✦ **It's a lot more fun.** I must admit, fun makes it a huge pro for me. The fact that I have the freedom to edit, create, and explore on my Powerbook while flying across the country is something few editors could have dreamed of just a few years ago.

The cons

As digital nonlinear editing has become the industry standard, its disadvantages are not so much irrelevant, but acceptable drawbacks to be dealt with. Still, they are worth considering, and so I list them here.

✦ **Changes are easier.** "Wait," you say, "I just read that under 'The pros.'" Well, editing ease is both a blessing and a curse. The fact that changes are so much easier causes a new disease you probably haven't heard before. This disease comes from having too many options and too many versions. One time, a producer made me do 25 completely separate versions of a 30-second spot because she wanted to "explore" her options. Freedom, as the saying goes, is its own punishment.

✦ **It can be more time-consuming.** I think that one of the biggest myths that came out of the digital editing world was that it was going to be so much faster and save you so much time that you wouldn't know what to do with all that leisure time on your hands. According to this myth, everyone goes home promptly at five o'clock, having magically met all their deadlines. Alas, that turned out not to be the case. What people forgot was that, in tape-based editing, there was no digitizing time, no repeated system crashes, no rendering time, no corrupt files, no re-digitizing, and no layback to tape. I've worked in completely digital production houses, but they still needed a tape-based editing system because it was the fastest and most efficient method for some projects. It is possible to save time with digital editing, but doing so requires planning and shrewd management skills.

✦ **There's more to know.** The knowledge base required to successfully navigate through the thicket of digital nonlinear editing tools is quite significant. However, the unlimited options and the advent of digital video revolutionized the world of media and made it accessible to more people than ever before, making the efforts worthwhile.

✦ **More problems can occur.** When digital video works well, nothing compares. It's like being in calm repose in some video heaven with angels running their fingers through your hair and harps playing in the background. However, when you run into problems, it's like descending into a circle of Hell even Dante could not have imagined.

✦ **Analog video is still relevant.** In the future full of flying cars, roads made of glass, and people dressed in silver suits with zippers, there will be no analog video. Presently, however, you will continue to manage your video in a world that is a hybrid of digital and analog. In fact, that is one of the reasons that life in the digital domain is full of pitfalls. As you work on your digital video project, you'll see how interactions between Final Cut Pro and analog video produce complex issues and require an in-depth understanding of the conversion process from analog to digital formats. In short, despite the hoopla around DVDs and the death of VHS, analog videotapes are not about to become obsolete anytime soon. You can save that silver suit for another day and age.

Editing your video: Offline or online?

You may hear these terms when working with nonlinear editing. However, both concepts of *online* and *offline* editing come from the tape-to-tape analog editing world. In the past, big production houses usually had separate online rooms and offline rooms. Online rooms were bigger, had more expensive equipment, and had more options for effects than the offline room counterparts, so consequently they cost more to operate and use. Offline rooms were small and had just enough equipment for basic editing. Offline editing rooms are also cheaper to rent. The idea was that editors first edited a project in the offline room, making decisions about what to edit to get a basic cut. ***Remember:*** You can't just cut and paste shots; it's time-consuming and quite a chore to try different cuts when you're editing offline. As a result, offline editing saved money while allowing producers to use the online editing later in the process to explore options — like gee-whiz effects that weren't even available in the offline rooms — and experiment with different cuts.

After an acceptable cut was obtained in the offline room, the project then moved to an online room for addition of effects and more complete audio work. Some online rooms looked like the bridge of the *Starship Enterprise.* These rooms had more buttons, knobs, levers, decks, lights, and blinking LEDs than you could count. It was quite something to be an editor in one of these rooms. It used to be badge of honor to say, "I am an online editor," but now people just laugh at you, because the technological advancements in digital technology over the last 20 years enable you to do virtually all that an online room ever could from a modest desktop computer!

When digital video editing first appeared, the new computer systems were only capable of working with low-resolution video that was not acceptable for a final broadcast. Thus, early digital editing systems were utilized as offline systems only. Editors would digitize at low resolution and edit a basic cut. After the basic cut was created, an Edit Decision List (EDL) was generated. An EDL is a list of timecodes that shows the order of the shots, the reels they came from, and the portions that were used. The EDL was then taken to an online tape-to-tape editing room and the show was recut at a higher resolution — usually for broadcast — using the original source tapes. Online edit rooms could import EDLs and perform the edits automatically. Because most of the work was already done, the low-resolution digital offline editing system effectively saved time and money. Figure 1-2 shows a simple EDL.

Cross-Reference
Edit Decision Lists (EDLs) are covered in Chapter 22.

Computer-based digital editing systems rival and, in some cases, surpass the quality of tape-based editing systems. However, high-quality video takes up a lot of disk space and most nonlinear editing systems have limited disk space. When space is limited, video is first digitized at a low resolution. Low resolution allows more media to be stored on the drives than media digitized at a high resolution. The first offline cut is done this way. Having more media on the drives provides for more explorations and more choices. These days, the term *offline* generally means digitizing material at a low resolution into digital editing systems and creating an acceptable edited video program.

```
TITLE: My Final Edit
FCM: DROP FRAME

FCM: NON-DROP FRAME
001          AX AA/V  C        01:00:06:04 01:00:15:00 01:00:00:00 01:00:08:26

002  REEL5      V    C        04:08:41:07 04:08:51:19 01:00:08:26 01:00:19:08
FINAL CUT PRO REEL: REEL 5 REPLACED BY: REEL5

003          AX AA/V  C        01:00:00:00 01:00:24:22 01:00:20:11 01:00:45:03

004          AX V    C        01:00:00:00 01:00:16:00 01:00:45:03 01:01:01:05
004          AX V    D    030 01:00:11:10 01:00:24:22 01:01:01:05 01:01:14:17
* EFFECT NAME: CROSS DISSOLVE

005  REEL3      V    C        03:12:05:29 03:12:08:20 01:01:14:17 01:01:17:08
FINAL CUT PRO REEL: REEL 3

006          AX V    C        00:00:03:18 00:00:05:02 01:01:17:08 01:01:18:22

007          AX AA/V  C        01:00:00:00 01:00:24:22 01:01:18:22 01:01:43:14

008          AX V    C        00:00:03:18 00:00:05:02 01:01:43:14 01:01:44:28

009  REEL5      V    C        04:10:55:14 04:11:09:06 01:01:44:28 01:01:58:20
FINAL CUT PRO REEL: REEL 5 REPLACED BY: REEL5

010  REEL1      V    C        03:11:45:14 03:11:53:13 01:01:58:20 01:02:06:21
FINAL CUT PRO REEL: REEL 1 |

011  REEL3      V    C        03:12:08:20 03:12:10:04 01:02:06:21 01:02:08:05
FINAL CUT PRO REEL: REEL 4
```

Figure 1-2: An Edit Decision List (EDL) is a text file that gives the order of shots, reel numbers, and in and out points that can be exchanged between tape-based edit systems and nonlinear edit systems. This EDL text file is also another way of exchanging edits between two nonlinear edit systems.

Then, after the final cut is performed, the low-resolution media is deleted and the program is recaptured at the highest-quality settings. This recapture process is very efficient because you capture only what will be used in the final program. For this process to work correctly, it is imperative that the following conditions be met:

✦ You must have the correct reel numbers.

✦ You should not have timecode breaks.

✦ You must be able to control the transport functions of your video deck via the computer, and this control must be *frame accurate*.

Final Cut Pro has a first-rate device control that is compatible with most video decks, as well as many other functions designed to help you do an offline edit in low resolution and then recapture your material, or online it, at high resolution.

Note Having a clip *offline* in Final Cut Pro is entirely different from *offline editing.* In the Final Cut Pro program, an offline clip is simply a clip that fails to link to the original media file, which usually happens when the media file is moved or deleted.

Understanding How Final Cut Pro Works

Now that you've mastered the fundamentals of video editing, you need to look at some basics that are specific to Final Cut Pro. If you feel that you already know the basics, take a moment to review this section anyway. The meanings of terms change, and I may use them differently than you expect. Not only are the terms crucial to understanding nonlinear editing in general, but these terms also apply to Final Cut Pro specifically.

Defining clips, sequences, bins, and project files in Final Cut Pro

Every computer program has its own jargon and terms associated with it, and Final Cut Pro is no exception. Some terms you need to know include the following:

✦ **Clip:** A clip is an individual component in your project. Audio files, video shots, and still photographs are all imported as clips.

✦ **Sequence:** A *sequence,* or *timeline,* is a series of clips placed together on tracks, the sum of which forms a video program. A sequence contains your audio and video tracks, dissolves, effects, text, and so on. You can have unlimited sequences in your project.

✦ **Bin:** *Bins* are folders in your project that enable you to store shots. Bins are essential for keeping what often becomes a countless number of clips organized. You can have bins within bins, and you can also label and color-code them as you choose.

✦ **Project file:** A *project file* holds all your clips, sequences, and any and all other files in your program. You can have more than one project open at the same time.

Figure 1-3 shows how these items appear in the Final Cut Pro program.

Cross-Reference I explain sequences, project files, and clips in more detail in Chapter 10.

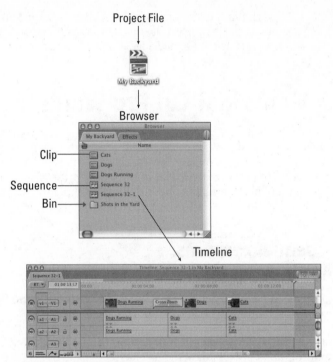

Figure 1-3: Project files contain clips, sequences, and bins. Clips are the video clips, audio files, or stills used in the project. Bins are used to organize the clips. A sequence opens into a timeline where all these elements are arranged.

Comparing media files to clips and project files

The first phase in working with Final Cut Pro is capturing shots from tape to your computer. Media files are the actual digital video files that you capture and store on your hard drive. Clips in Final Cut Pro are merely representations, or pointers, of these media files inside the editing program. Figure 1-4 illustrates this relationship.

The project file My Backyard has an icon that looks like a movie slate and holds all the clips, information about the clips, and information about the edits that you create. The project file also contains all the bins and sequences. Clips first appear in the Final Cut Pro Browser and can then be used in the timeline. In Figure 1-4, Dogs Running is the original media file digitized to disk. It appears in the Browser, and it was used twice in the timeline. All three occurrences of Dogs Running (one in the Browser, two in the timeline) are linked to the same media file. You can manipulate, trim, and make changes to the clips in the Browser or the timeline without affecting the original media files on the disk, because your edits are stored and saved in the project file.

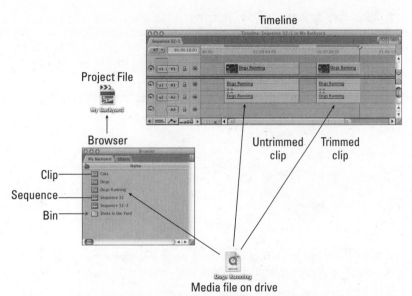

Timeline

Project File

Browser

Clip

Sequence

Bin

Untrimmed clip

Trimmed clip

Media file on drive

Figure 1-4: Project files hold the information about the clips and edits you create. Clips in the Browser or timeline are merely virtual representations of the actual media files that are stored on the disk. Editing allows for manipulation of the clips while leaving your media files untouched.

Caution

If you delete the media file from the disk, all clips linked to it in the project lose their reference. In short, they'll be blank. Nada.

In the sample project shown in Figure 1-4, notice that I used the clip Dogs Running in the timeline twice. In the second occurrence of that clip, I've shortened it a bit, which you can see by the difference in the length of the two clips. The first copy will play in its entirety, and the second occurrence will only play a part of the clip. All that has taken place is that the application has sent a command to the media file to first play in full, and the second time to play only up to a certain point.

Digitizing video

The term *digitizing* can have many different meanings, but generally this term refers to the conversion of an analog signal to a digital signal. The computer that you're using only understands the digital, also known as *binary,* language. Anything you want to bring into your computer, such as video or still images, has to be digitized into your computer. For instance, you have an old still photograph of Grandma Edith that you want to bring into the computer, airbrush a bit, and e-mail over to Cousin Bobby. Grandma Edith's photograph is considered analog because it is printed on a paper with color dyes and emulsions. To convert the photograph to a digital image, you must first digitize it with a scanner. After the scanner digitizes it, you can open the picture in a graphics program, such as Photoshop, and airbrush it to your heart's content, as I've illustrated in Figure 1-5. The digital file of Grandma can now be sent via e-mail, another digital-format medium, to Bobby.

Grandma Edith's Picture   Scanner   Computer

Analog   Digitizing   Digital

Figure 1-5: Digitizing is the process of converting an analog signal into a digital one because computers only understand digital (also known as *binary*) language.

Cross-Reference

Complete your digitizing, or capturing, of video by using the Log and Capture window in Final Cut Pro. The Log and Capture window is explained in detail in Chapter 7.

Digitizing an analog format

To digitize video from an analog format, say a Betacam SP tape, you need a digitizing card. These cards, also referred to as *capture cards,* are available from many manufacturers and can be installed easily in your computer's PCI slot. These cards often have numerous video and audio input points, and after the outputs of the Betacam deck are connected to these points, you can play your tape, digitize it, and play and edit it in Final Cut Pro.

Cross-Reference

To learn about installing a capture card in your computer's PCI slot, see Chapter 3.

Like a scanner, capture cards offer numerous controls for managing color and brightness. These controls appear within Final Cut Pro for calibration of color bars to ensure accurate color reproduction during digitizing. These cards can also convert the digital signal back into an analog one, meaning that, after you've edited your video inside your computer, you can send it back out through the card to an analog deck of your choice, such as a VHS recorder.

After you've installed a capture card and its appropriate drivers (a *driver* is a tiny piece of software that helps the added-on card talk to your Macintosh and Final Cut Pro), all of its functions and settings are accessible within Final Cut Pro. You never have to leave Final Cut Pro to accomplish tweaking, calibrating, controlling, and digitizing of your video.

The performance and price of capture cards vary widely, depending on their quality and interface features. A basic card, which only has a composite input for VHS, costs considerably less than a card with component interfaces for a Betacam SP deck. Apple has certified numerous video cards for use with Final Cut Pro, and I cover them later in this book. You can also go to Apple's Final Cut Pro Web site (www.apple.com/finalcutpro) to find a list of approved cards.

Cross-Reference

Digitizing cards is covered in Chapter 3.

Using Final Cut Pro to capture your digital format

When it comes to capturing a digital format (such as the ever-popular DV format) into your computer via Final Cut Pro, no actual digitizing is involved, because the video signal is already digital on the tape. You're basically just copying a digital file from the tape to your computer.

If you're working with a digital tape format, all you need is a digital path to move the data from the digital camera to your computer. The most common path is known as *FireWire* (see Figure 1-6). FireWire is the Apple trade name for the technical designation of IEEE-1394, which is the much more boring but "official" name for this technology. It is also called iLink on some Sony cameras. FireWire, originally developed by Apple, is a high-performance digital serial bus and is in wide use with DV formats. Almost all DV cameras have a FireWire port on them. All new Apple computers, such as G-5's, G4's, iMacs, iBooks and Powerbooks come with built-in FireWire ports. Figure 1-6 shows two FireWire cable connectors. FireWire ports are recognized worldwide by a sort of nuclear-looking symbol. Don't worry; it's not really dangerous. This symbol is just Apple's way of letting you know that something very fast and cool is happening.

Note

Recently, Apple has implemented its new FireWire protocol called FireWire 800, technically known as IEEE-1394b. This new protocol can deliver up to 800Mbs of data—twice that of the current FireWire, now retro-named FireWire 400. FireWire 400 and 800 are covered in detail in Chapter 2.

To capture material into your computer, you attach a FireWire cable between your DV camera and the FireWire port on your computer. Rather than digitizing DV footage, you're actually transferring video and sound that is already digital on the tape to the computer's hard drive. If you really want to sound sophisticated, you can say that you're *bit copying* the video. The process of bit copying is like moving the binary zeros and ones from one location to another. Think of copying a simple text file inside your computer — that's a bit copy. Figure 1-7 shows the capture of analog versus digital material. Again, all this happens in real time.

Tip

For basic analog formats such as VHS, you can also use a Sony DA-2 converter to convert the analog signal to a DV signal. Keep in mind, though, that doing so turns your analog signal into DV at the DV data and compression rate. This approach may be okay for formats such as VHS or Hi-8, but it may not be the right approach for Betacam SP or higher-resolution formats.

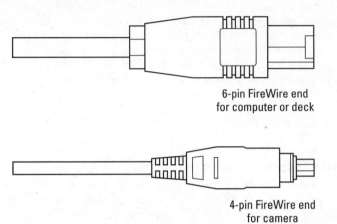

6-pin FireWire end
for computer or deck

4-pin FireWire end
for camera

Figure 1-6: FireWire, also known as IEEE-1394 and iLink, is a digital, high-speed serial connection developed by Apple. With a cable between a DV camera and a computer with a FireWire port, you can capture your video into the computer by using Final Cut Pro.

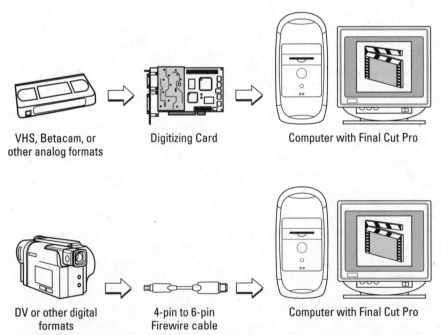

VHS, Betacam, or
other analog formats

Digitizing Card

Computer with Final Cut Pro

DV or other digital
formats

4-pin to 6-pin
Firewire cable

Computer with Final Cut Pro

Figure1-7: Capture of analog material requires a digitizing card. Digital formats, such as DV, simply require a FireWire cable and a port to move the data from the tape to the computer.

Managing data rates

One key difference between scanning a single photograph and digitizing video is easy to discover. Whereas a photograph is just one picture, you have to remember that video has 30 pictures per second! Video runs at 29.97 frames per second (fps), and capturing each of these frames is similar to scanning a picture. To be able to play and edit video on the computer, each frame must be captured completely and accurately. The capture process occurs in real time as the video is played.

You must be extremely careful not to "drop," or skip, frames while capturing the video, or your clips will stutter and skip when you're playing them back. Also, it's important that your clips maintain a constant data rate. The *data rate* measures how much material per second goes through the pipeline of a computer. This *pipeline* is limited by the bus speed of the CPU and other factors, such as the speed of the hard disk. If the pipeline is too small, you'll wind up with dropped frames and stuttering video.

Another consideration is the sheer size of a video stream. Just one second of video, if captured uncompressed, can fill approximately 20MB of space! Yes, that's 20 *megabytes* — the big ones. To capture video at such a high data rate, you not only need a very fast drive but also a big one. For every minute of uncompressed video, you'll need over 1 gigabyte (GB) of disk space. These numbers are approximations, but they give you an idea of just how much data you're dealing with when you capture video. Bear in mind that the data rate is affected by hardware and not necessarily software such as Final Cut Pro. Final Cut Pro can handle uncompressed video just fine. The responsibility for adequate data rate falls on the hardware, including your hard drives and capture card. Often the basic drives that a computer is purchased with are not sufficient to capture high-end video. To sustain data rates when you edit digital video, you must use the best equipment you can afford and use capture settings that make optimum use of the hardware you have.

The average drive in a Macintosh is simply unable to handle data rates required when working with high-quality video. Your video will refuse to play and stall or fall out of sync. Somehow, you have to find a way to make this data rate manageable. Of course, the ideal solution is to work with fast drives.

 Note The drives that new G4 Macs ship with are considered sufficient to support the data rate of DV video. However, for safety and additional space you may want to install more internal drives into your G4, or better yet, get yourself one of the newer external FireWire drives — they seem to be getting cheaper and faster every month!

Compression and decompression

One solution to the data rate conundrum is compression. To make the data rates acceptable during the process of digitizing, you usually have to apply compression to your video. *Compression* is the act of reducing the size of a video file inside the computer. The trick is to find a balance that makes the files small enough to optimize data rates and storage space without making visible sacrifices in quality.

Because of the enormous amounts of data that a stream of video contains, compression is necessary. During the capture of video through a card, the video is compressed in real time and stored as movie files or *media files* in the computer. The file is decompressed during playback. Most compression and decompression in video cards occurs in real time and is handled by *codecs.* The term *codec* comes from a shortening of *compression/decompression,* just as the word *modem* is short for *modulation/demodulation.* Codecs can be software- or hardware-based. Common codecs include MJPEG and DV (now regarded as DV25); Sorensons are also codecs, except that they're not used for capture but for delivery, such as on CD-ROMs or in Web streaming.

Compression technology is a very sophisticated science and has been an area of tremendous development in the past few years. However, its basic principles generally remain the same. Compression is based on the fundamentals of human vision. For example, it turns out that the human eye is more sensitive to changes in luminance values than changes in chrominance values. That's just a pointy-headed way of saying that human beings notice changes in brightness much more than they notice changes in color values. Thus, many compression techniques are based on throwing away more color values from the video being captured while retaining more of the brightness values. When I say "throwing away" you might imagine your color video turning into black and white after being captured into the computer, but that's just not so. Information that is discarded during the capture process is usually not noticeable to the human eye.

As a Final Cut Pro user, compression affects you by determining the quality of your video. A video that is highly compressed looks jaggy, or artifacted and has low resolution. It does, however, take up less storage space than a high-resolution video that utilizes less compression. Keep these formulas in your head:

> *More* compression = *smaller* data rates = *smaller* files = *lower* quality
>
> *Less* compression = *higher* data rates = *larger* files = *better* quality

Figure 1-8 illustrates the relationship between compression, data rates, file sizes, and image quality.

Compression in the DV domain

More and more these days, you're probably seeing video cameras that have the DV symbol on them. They use small, compact videotapes that also have the DV symbol on them. This new format is known as the *DV format.* The tapes and the cameras look somewhat like the 8mm or the Hi-8 camcorders that came out years before. However, you'll find one very significant difference: The picture quality of a DV format video is superior to the quality of Hi-8 or VHS analog video.

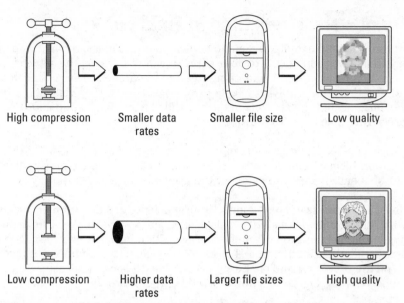

Figure 1-8: A high level of compression produces smaller data rates, small file sizes, and low-quality images. Low compression gives higher data rates, large file sizes, and higher quality pictures.

The DV format and compression is discussed in much more detail in Chapter 2.

The most common version of the DV format is the MiniDV, but you also find variations, such as DVCAM and DVC-PRO, and most recently, DVCPRO50. Another variation of the DV format is the Digital 8 format, which is basically a DV signal recorded onto a Hi-8 tape. The quality on these different types of tapes is essentially the same.

Why does DV video look as good as it does? The simple answer is that the picture is encoded digitally to the tape by using a very efficient compression scheme called DV compression. The codec is called the DV codec.

In the case of DV, a hardware codec is built into the camera that compresses the picture. The data rate of DV is 3.6MB per second (including DV audio), significantly lower than the 20MB per second data rate for uncompressed video. Even the basic drives that accompany a G4 or an iMac can handle that kind of data rate. In other words, with an Apple G4 computer, Final Cut Pro, a basic DV camera, and a FireWire cable, you can have an editing system.

Rendering versus real time in Final Cut Pro

Final Cut Pro can handle numerous audio and video layers in a sequence, and you can apply transitions and effects to your clips. However, because the software is relying mostly on the power of your computer and the processor to make calculations and play the video, applying effects to video can exceed the capacity of the computer. Imagine juggling six balls in the air while trying to eat soup and wipe your nose at the same time. That probably exceeds your capacity.

If your video sequence involves cuts only, you can play it in real time in Final Cut Pro with no problems. But if you add a transition or an effect to a clip, you have to *render* the sequence before you can view the transition or effect smoothly.

Rendering is the process of combining your original media files with the transitions or effects to create a *render media file,* also called a *render cache file.* This is the file that plays during the duration of an effect or transition between two clips. The process of rendering takes a bit of time, but after the transition is complete, it takes the pressure off the processor and enables your timeline to play seamlessly without glitches and skipping. Figure 1-9 shows how this process works.

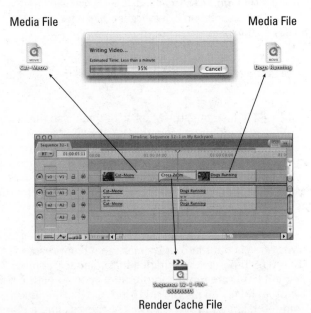

Render Cache File

Figure 1-9: When Final Cut Pro displays a Writing Video status bar, it is making a *render cache file,* in this case for a *dissolve*—a type of transition. This cache file plays during the playback of the dissolve area in the timeline.

Since version 2.0, Final Cut Pro has been built on a *real-time architecture,* meaning certain video cards approved by Apple allow certain effects to display in real time, without the need for rendering. Not content to sit on its laurels, Apple has retooled Final Cut Pro's render engine, dubbed *RT Extreme,* which now yields even more real-time effects and previews over FireWire, *without* the need for any additional hardware.

New Feature

Although real-time playback is limited to using Apple's DV and Offline codecs, the number of real-time effects you can display is only limited by the speed of your system's processor. In other words, the faster your CPU (and dual processor G4's reign supreme in this area), the more simultaneous real-time effects you can preview.

Cross-Reference

Rendering is explained in greater detail in Chapter 18.

Before you start jumping for joy at the mention of real time, consider this: The reality of real time is subject to the limitations of any nonlinear editing system. Final Cut Pro, for example, can have 99 layers of video. So, does the implementation of real time in Final Cut Pro allow you to play these 99 layers without rendering? Well, do pigs fly? Whether real-time playback is software-based or hardware-based, you can expect it will have some limitations. For example, only certain transitions may be real time while other effects will still have to be rendered. Some real-time systems, like Final Cut Pro's RT Extreme, will only work within the DV format.

Know your needs and then scrutinize closely what the cards offer in real time before you run out and buy one. Real-time effects, like anything else in digital video, are full of exceptions and small print.

Workflow considerations

Workflow is the process or order in which you perform editing tasks. It's like remembering to put underwear on *before* the pants and not after. To be honest, if some video editors I know dressed like they work, they'd have their underwear *outside* their pants. I'm here to save you from that fate.

Before proceeding with a project in Final Cut Pro, you must evaluate your workflow from beginning to end. Earlier in this chapter, I mentioned that more errors occur in the digital domain. Keep that rule about errors in mind as you move forward. Here are the four basic steps you should follow whenever you're working in Final Cut Pro:

1. **Gather your media.**

2. **Edit the media.**

3. **Process the media.**

4. **Output your program.**

Gather your media

When you edit with Final Cut Pro, you'll be working with many different types of media. If you have the right hardware setup, you can capture a variety of video formats into Final Cut Pro. The most common format, DV, can be captured with a FireWire interface. For other formats you may require video capture cards. You need to consider your format choices. What tape and video formats are you bringing in? DV? Betacam? Digital Beta? High Definition? Each format can have a variety of paths into Final Cut Pro, and you need to consider which path is best.

You can also import a variety of other digital media formats, such as audio, still graphics, and QuickTime files into Final Cut Pro. These should all be considered carefully because some of these file formats need conversion, while others have to be formatted and created correctly to avoid distortion when used with video. For example, files created in Photoshop or other such programs can suffer slight distortion after being mixed with video unless they're prepared properly.

 Cross-Reference   See Chapter 26 for working with Final Cut Pro and other applications.

Another acquisition step that you'll take part in is logging. *Logging* is a process that consists of viewing your tapes carefully and making selections by jotting down accurate timecodes and reel numbers. With the advent of nonlinear editing, some producers and editors got a bit lazy about logging their tapes. Being able to just digitize hours and hours of material at low resolution, play around with it for days, get a program you're happy with, and then just re-digitize it in high resolution for output to tape seemed too good to be true. Logging seemed like a thing of the past.

Careful logging and preparation for editing is more relevant now than ever before, and I have the scars to prove it. As a naive and innocent nonlinear editor, I too believed the utopian promise of such an ideal scenario. I learned the hard way about disk storage limitations, timecode breaks, inconsistencies in reel numbering, and other fiascos that made my life difficult. Digitizing a whole lot of material can turn out to be an organizational nightmare. I found that even the best of drives can be bogged down with too much material and slow my project to a crawl.

Be vigilant about careless digitizing. Even if you have seemingly unlimited disk space, failure to log can have unanticipated consequences. For example, with too much media on your drives, you can have slowdowns in your system, and your drives may not work at their advertised efficiency. And it is a lot harder to go back after the fact and delete unused media. Start right, and you'll be a happy camper. I've seen enough teary-eyed campers in my time to be able to relay that message.

Logging has never been easier than it is in Final Cut Pro. With some ingenuity, you can set up a Final Cut Pro–based logging system where you view your tapes and mark your selections for later digitizing. This is also a good stage to determine if you have enough material for your edit. Do you have all the shots and cutaways you need per your script?

Cross-Reference

Logging is covered in Chapter 7.

Editing the media

Editing is the most obvious step in your workflow, and you'll spend a majority of your time doing this step. Some editors like to start with a basic rough cut and leave the effects and transitions for later. Others work with refined edits from the very start, pausing at each stage to finalize their edits. You can choose what method works best for you, but remember the considerations of rendering time. For example, if you work with low-resolution media and create a timeline where you've rendered out numerous effects and transitions, when you recapture that timeline in high resolution, all those effects have to be re-rendered in high resolution. This process is automatic, but it takes time nevertheless.

Note

High resolution versus low resolution is not an issue if you're working strictly with DV media and the DV Codec. The DV format and the DV Codec always remain at their set resolution.

Process the media

You can add some snazzy effects to your edit. Some editors also leave the audio work for after the basic edit is done. Final Cut Pro offers a practically unlimited choice of effects, transitions, and filters for this part of the workflow. You can also add third-party effects or make your own by using the Final Cut Pro's FX Builder.

Some people still prefer to do their effects and compositing in programs, like After Effects (you can use a lot of After Effects filters within Final Cut Pro). If this sounds like you, make sure that you answer these questions:

✦ Do you know the correct settings to export the video for After Effects?

✦ Do you have the correct settings for creating a composite in After Effects and rendering back the video for Final Cut Pro?

If I have any doubts that I have used the correct settings, I do a short test of the entire workflow. For example, if the After Effects artist needs video exported by me that they will render back to me through After Effects, I often do a small test by sending the artist a short piece from Final Cut Pro and then asking them to send me the final render. If I do this well in advance of the actual project, I identify any potential problem and resolve it before it becomes a crisis.

Cross-Reference

Turn to Chapter 26 for more information on working with After Effects.

Output your program

Finally, you've wrapped up your work. How are you going to output your final edit? Is the final output going to be back to tape? Is it for Web streaming, CD-ROM or DVD playback? Fear not. Final Cut Pro accommodates all these options and then some with Apple's addition of its brand-new video-compression application called Compressor. However, as I said at the top, plan carefully in advance. A whole host of choices you make at the acquisition, editing, or processing stage can affect your distribution stage. Read this book carefully and be prepared. Sleep with this book next to you if you need to.

Cross-Reference   Turn to Chapter 23 for more information about working with Compressor.

Separating Final Cut Pro from Other Nonlinear Editing Systems

I've spent a lot of time in this chapter talking about nonlinear editing systems and how wonderful they are. Nonlinear editing systems have revolutionized the world of editing and postproduction. They've caused people to drool and have opened up a whole new world of digital effects previously unthinkable. They've made people laugh. They've made people cry. However, even within the wonderful world of nonlinear editing systems, Final Cut Pro represents a revolution of sorts. It has turned some of the most well-known rules of the digital-editing world on their heads. And the beneficiaries of this revolution are people like you and me, the average Joe and Jane editors of the world.

Final Cut Pro is very different from other digital editing systems. Some of these differences may simply be of academic value, while others will affect you quite dramatically.

Final Cut Pro is not tied to proprietary hardware

Before Final Cut Pro arrived on the scene, if you wanted to go and buy an editing system, your choices were quite limited. The most well-known brand — let's call it Edit Composter — was pretty much your only choice. When you bought an Edit Composter, you had to buy an entire editing system — and I mean a *system*. It wasn't just a box of software that said Edit Composter. You had to buy the computer, usually a Macintosh, the video cards, the software, the drives, the monitors, and even the cables, all as one big Edit Composter package.

These systems cost anywhere from $80,000 to $500,000, and some of the cables cost over $200. If you didn't buy its cables, the company insisted that it couldn't guarantee the performance of the system. Similarly, the drives were expensive. Yet drives were nothing more than generic industry drives, put in a nice plastic box with a really cool Edit Composter logo. This hardware was known as *proprietary* hardware. Big resellers sold these systems to big companies with big money. A troop of people showed up to deliver and install the system. Bills ran into the hundreds of thousands of dollars.

For ordinary editors like me, owning systems like Edit Composter was unthinkable. Digital editing was strictly the domain of big editing houses and commercial production facilities with millions of dollars.

More choices appeared on the market, but the formula remained generally the same. A nonlinear editing system was not just any piece of software you ran on your computer. You had to buy the whole "turnkey" package: their video card, their drives, their cables, and their software. Most editing software was tied to very particular hardware, and it was unthinkable to run it on anything other than what the company wanted to sell you. For example, you couldn't just buy the software from our mythical company Edit Composter and run it on hardware sold by another company. Doing so was considered insane.

Then along came Final Cut Pro. Here was a piece of editing software made by Apple, a company famous for its commitment to multimedia and creative professionals. Best of all, it was not tied to proprietary hardware. If you had a FireWire-capable Mac, Final Cut Pro, and a DV camera, you had yourself an edit system.

Apple's continued philosophy and dedication to keep Final Cut Pro a premium, software-based, nonlinear editor is evident in version 4.0, which includes more than 300 added features — none requiring a stitch of additional hardware in order to function. The most obvious example of this is the Final Cut Pro 4.0 RT Extreme render engine that adds preview output and dozens of real-time effects right out of the box.

So, with the right hardware and Final Cut Pro, you can pretty much edit anything you want. What's different is that Apple is not tying its software to its own video card and drives sold to you at a vastly inflated price. It also continues to keep Final Cut Pro open to third-party developers. Many companies now sell cards that are compatible with Final Cut Pro, and a vast variety of drives work with the program as well.

Note   A complete list of compatible cards and drives is available at the Apple Web site.

Final Cut Pro provides all kinds of options previously not available. For example, you can now edit with Final Cut Pro on your Powerbook while you're on the road. These edits can be brought back to the edit facility, where another high-end system configured with Final Cut Pro can recapture and output a high-resolution version to tape. In fact, I know an editor in Hollywood who edits portions of his films this way. This kind of portability was unthinkable in the pre–Final Cut Pro days.

 Cross-Reference   You can find information on film editing with Final Cut Pro in Chapter 27.

Final Cut Pro works with many formats and standards

Most nonlinear edit systems, despite their big price tags, work with a limited number of formats and standards. For example, if you have an edit system from our mythical company, Edit Composter, you can edit broadcast-quality video from Betacam SP. But to capture DV, you often have to buy another card as an add-on. And if you want to work in a different frame rate or aspect ratio, good luck. Edit Composter only supports one frame rate and one aspect ratio. Only spending thousands of additional dollars will give you the new capability, if at all.

Final Cut Pro is dramatically different. To paraphrase the Final Cut Pro designers in Apple's Cupertino campus, Final Cut Pro works with everything from DV to HDTV. With the proper drive and hardware support, you can use Final Cut Pro to edit almost any frame rate, aspect ratio, and standard. Some of the formats that Final Cut Pro works with include

✦ **DV format with FireWire.** This includes the MiniDV, DVCAM, DVCPRO and DVCPRO50 cameras, decks, and tapes.

✦ **NTSC and PAL.** Apple-approved third-party cards are required to work with NTSC and PAL video with composite, component, and serial digital (SDI) signal paths.

✦ **QuickTime standard file formats.** These include MJPEG (a popular video codec), Sorensen, and Cinepak, among others. Final Cut Pro also supports numerous frame rates, compression schemes, and aspect ratios.

✦ **24 fps film.** Final Cut Pro has 24 fps support for film editing. Numerous films have been edited by using Final Cut Pro. Big Hollywood releases, such as *George Washington, Bo Jangles, Full Frontal,* and *Rules of Attraction,* were edited with Final Cut Pro.

✦ **HDTV.** Recently Apple showed Final Cut Pro systems being used to edit High-Definition Television (HDTV). High-Definition Television is the wave of the future. HDTV delivers high-quality video at many different aspect ratios and frame rates. Final Cut Pro supports all the major HDTV standards.

Next we'll see how other important technologies converged to popularize Final Cut Pro.

Other Technologies and Final Cut Pro

Timing, as they say, is everything. This phrase is true in comedy as well as making history. Final Cut Pro appeared at a very appropriate time. Final Cut Pro relies heavily on a whole host of technologies such as FireWire and DV that were in development for many years. These technologies matured just in time for Final Cut Pro to materialize. This convergence, illustrated in Figure 1-10, is one the reasons for Final Cut Pro's popularity.

Steve Jobs, Apple's CEO, has referred to digital video as "the next big thing." Whenever Steve says something like that, the world listens. This statement also reflects Apple's deep commitment to digital video and multimedia. Apple has led the way in the development of many of the technologies used by Final Cut Pro. In the next few sections I briefly cover the technologies used in the making of Final Cut Pro so that you can see what the big deal is and why I'm as excited as a kid in a candy store.

The G4 processor

Final Cut Pro is an editing program that relies heavily on the computer processor to do all its calculations. The G4 processor, developed by Motorola, has become the central processor in most of the recent Apple PowerMac computers. Without the G4 processor, Final Cut Pro would be hard-pressed to perform its miracles. This processor contains several key features:

✦ **The G4 performs in the gigaflop range.** A *gigaflop* is one billion calculations per second. Processing digital video, even DV with its lean data rate, is extremely calculation-intensive. Final Cut Pro is specially optimized to take advantage of all the benefits offered by the G4.

✦ **The G4 Processor is ideally suited for multimedia.** The instruction set for the G4 chip shows its biggest gains in the area of multimedia performance. Numerous software companies have offered G4 plug-ins to speed up their software. The Final Cut Pro team continues to revise the code for its software to take advantage of the G4 instruction set.

✦ **The architecture of the G4 supports multiprocessor configurations.** The G4 is designed to support multiprocessing. This allows for more than one processor to work in tandem. The older processors in the Apple Macintosh were not well suited to multiprocessing. Apple now offers *dual processor* G4s that include two of these processors. Rumors persist of quad (four processors) and dual-quad (eight processors) machines in the future. This development bodes well for Final Cut Pro.

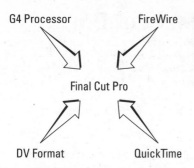

G4 Processor   FireWire

Final Cut Pro

DV Format   QuickTime

Figure 1-10: Final Cut Pro capitalizes on a convergence of technologies that matured at just the right time. Apple Computer led the way for development of many of these technologies.

FireWire

FireWire is Apple's brand name for the technology also known as IEEE-1394. Those people at Apple are masters at coming up with zippy names for fancy technologies, aren't they? Sony calls this technology iLink on its cameras. FireWire offers many important features to the Final Cut Pro editor:

Note   Recently, Apple has implemented its new FireWire protocol called FireWire 800, technically known as IEEE-1394b. This new protocol can deliver up to 800Mbs of data — twice that of the current FireWire, now retro-named FireWire 400. FireWire 400 and 800 are covered in detail in Chapter 2.

✦ **It is the fastest I/O standard.** IEEE-1394 is the fastest serial input/output standard ever developed. This allows for very high data rate transfers and is especially useful for video, audio, or other data transfers that need to occur between computer hardware. You can currently purchase FireWire scanners, cameras, and hard drives, among other items. Hopefully, FireWire will one day replace the older SCSI standard.

Note   The SCSI standard is an older data transfer standard that allows you to connect high-speed drives to the computer for fast data rate transfers. Despite being a major pain in the neck to use, it's still the most reliable and the speediest hard-drive bus for high-quality video editing. Ultra-fast and wide SCSI RAIDs (Redundant Arrays of Independent Disks) are still a favorite industry workhorse in commercial production facilities. See Chapter 4 for more details about disk drives and RAIDs.

✦ **It allows integration of consumer electronics with personal computers.** A few years ago, a camcorder was a camcorder and a computer was a computer. The idea of plugging a camera into a computer was pretty far-fetched. With FireWire, a new bridge has been built between computers and electronics such as video cameras.

✦ **It's hot-pluggable!** I don't know how many people appreciate this, but writing these words brought tears to my eyes. If you've ever lived with SCSI drives and connectors and have spent hours fiddling with huge connectors that look like bear paws that skin your knuckles, and have constantly had to restart your computer to mount SCSI drives, you'll be very happy to read this. Being *hot-pluggable* means that you don't have to power down your computer to "mount" a FireWire component. Just plug it in and it shows up on your desktop. And the FireWire cable connectors are no bigger than a phone jack and are just as easy to plug in. No more cursing as you switch drives at the back of your computer!

✦ **There are no IDs to set.** In SCSI-based drives, you had to set ID numbers for each SCSI item, which caused numerous conflicts and problems. And then there was the whole termination issue. SCSI chains had to be physically terminated with a termination plug or switch or else they caused massive headaches for users. Occasionally the terminator plugs used for this purpose would be of low quality and cause even further problems. FireWire handles all these ID and termination conflicts automatically.

✦ **It supports numerous devices.** FireWire can handle up to 63 devices on a single port.

A word on Apple and Macintosh

If you're a longtime Mac user, this sidebar may not be all that relevant to you. But if you're a PC or Windows user, and for some bizarre reason you find yourself holding this book, you may want to read on.

Final Cut Pro is designed and sold by Apple Computers and only works in Apple's machines. Final Cut Pro does not work on any machines running DOS, Windows, Windows NT, or UNIX variants. The true irony is that Final Cut Pro started out its early days as a Windows application over at Macromedia, the makers of Flash and other wonderful products. It used to be called Key Grip. (I know, I know . . . like I said earlier, Apple people are much better at finding snappy names for their products.) However, Steve Jobs bought it from Macromedia and turned it into an entirely Apple product. Apple also renamed it Final Cut Pro. (What the heck does a *key grip* have to do with editing videos anyway?)

Final Cut Pro is so heavily dependent on Apple technologies that I cannot foresee a day when it may be available on Windows. However, even as I write this, I realize that much stranger things have come to pass. If you're a Windows owner and have plans to work with digital video, I strongly suggest buying an Apple Mac capable of running Final Cut Pro. If you can't or don't want to buy a Mac, buy this book. Take it home and read it from cover to cover. Then put your best thinking hat on and ponder this question: Can *your* nonlinear editing system do everything Final Cut Pro can do?

QuickTime

Steve Jobs once remarked that QuickTime was the best thing Apple ever did. I agree. QuickTime is considered a kind of Swiss army knife of multimedia. Most users may be familiar with the QuickTime Player and QuickTime Movies, but what they may not know is that QuickTime is an enabling technology and a sophisticated architecture that allows for multimedia management, programming, and delivery. Enabling technologies work in the background and allow other programs to work faster, better, and stronger. QuickTime also happens to be the backbone of Final Cut Pro. Final Cut Pro can work with so many different types of media on the input side as well as output all kinds of different formats. Advantages of QuickTime include

✦ **QuickTime enables many formats.** QuickTime works with video, audio, MIDI music, 3-D files, and virtual-reality files. This aspect of the program allows for flexibility and exchangeability with many applications. Countless multimedia applications, such as Adobe's After Effects and Adobe Premiere, are based on QuickTime.

✦ **QuickTime is generally transparent to the user.** Users of QuickTime may not always know that it made your program better. However, chances are that if you're doing any kind of multimedia work on an Apple Macintosh with any kind of an application, you're being helped by QuickTime. For example, when you're exporting or importing files in Final Cut Pro, QuickTime is being employed in this process, it's just working unseen in the background.

✦ **QuickTime is easy to use.** As transparent as it may be, occasionally you need to interact with QuickTime and understand how it works. QuickTime is easy to use and understand. For example, using the QuickTime player, you can view and export movies. The player is a great example of how easy a technology QuickTime can be.

DV

One of the key reasons for Final Cut Pro's popularity is its high level of compatibility with the DV format. The DV recording format has exploded in popularity in the last few years, boosting Final Cut Pro's own popularity. I do advise you to keep in mind that Final Cut Pro can work with far more than just the DV format, but this format does offer a variety of advantages:

✦ **DV is a recording format *and* a compression standard.** For this reason DV is seen as a tape format for DV-compatible cameras as well as a software codec that is used for compression and decompression when working on a computer in multimedia applications.

✦ **DV is digital and has no generational loss.** DV is a digital method of recording the video signal on the tape. The signal is recorded in the computer's binary language of zeros and ones. Analog formats store the signal as a fluctuation of a voltage signal. A DV signal, when transferred over a digital path, remains free of any deterioration. Having a clean signal is one of the most important advantages of DV.

✦ **DV requires a relatively low data rate.** The biggest hurdle for working with digital video is its data rate. However, DV25's data rate of 3.6MB per second and DVCPRO50's data rate of 7MB per second are relatively lean. Even the basic drive in a Macintosh computer can handle this data rate.

✦ **DV is high resolution.** Low data rate mostly equates with low-quality video. However, DV compression maintains a very high image and sound quality, despite the low data rate. Video in DV is almost twice as sharp as a VHS. Some people say it rivals Sony's Betacam SP format. I am not one of those people.

✦ **DV blurs the line between professional- and consumer-level video.** Despite the raging debate over whether DV rivals Betacam SP or whether it's as good as other reigning formats, undoubtedly DV blurs the line between professional-level video and consumer-level camcorders. The fact that a *debate* exists reveals how superior the DV format is to its predecessors. I never remember hearing any debate over whether my VHS-C Handycam was as good as a Betacam SP deck. As a result of DV's high quality, numerous documentaries, network programs, and even feature films are being shot in DV format. DV has gained acceptance in many networks and broadcast houses.

✦   ✦   ✦

Video and DV

In Chapter 1, I stated that despite the popularity of digital video, analog video is still a formidable industry standard that will not disappear any time soon. In this chapter, I'll cover some of the ways that video travels between components and the connections it uses. The chapter explores different types of video, and then takes an in-depth look at the DV format and all the implications it has for you as an editor using Final Cut Pro.

Getting to Know Video Types

Many Final Cut Pro users shoot in DV, edit in DV, and then output back to DV. Life for these editors is just peachy. Generally speaking DV users only have to concern themselves with FireWire cables. However, many people have to work with other formats, such as VHS, Betacam SP, and the like. Each of these formats can use different kinds of video signals. Video equipment, such as decks, monitors, and cameras often use a combination of signal types. Consumer equipment usually has the fewest signal choices, whereas professional-grade equipment offers a better variety of signals for higher quality. That's why professional equipment costs more, too.

Bear in mind that if you need to capture high-quality analog material in Final Cut Pro, you'll need a digitizing card, also known as a capture card. (You also need high-speed drives to sustain an appropriate data rate.) The capture card should have the same interface as your deck or camera outputs because capture card prices vary depending on the type of interface they offer. For example, a card that offers composite inputs is going to be a lot cheaper than one that offers component inputs. Check your decks to see what type of interface they use. If you have component outputs on your deck or camera, purchasing a card with component inputs is best. (If you don't know what *component* and *composite* mean, read on.)

Cross-Reference   Capture cards that are approved by Apple for use with Final Cut Pro are covered in Chapter 4.

Composite

If you've ever connected the Video Out port on your home VCR to the Video In port on another device (such as a TV monitor), you were most likely using a *composite* signal. Composite is the most basic kind of video signal path. Usually a composite signal uses an RCA-type or BNC-type connector. Figure 2-1 shows these types of connectors.

A composite signal sends the *luminance* and the *chrominance* (that's just a fancy way of saying brightness and color) portions of a video signal over a single pair of wires. The drawback to composite is that often these signals interfere with each other and result in noise and artifacts. These artifacts manifest themselves as noisy edges, crawl of color into neighboring areas, and rainbow effects. Highly saturated colors flicker. If you see old news footage from the 1980s, you'll see these artifacts. You may see what looks like a color from someone's shirt bleeding into his coat. Newsrooms at the time used an old video format called ¾-inch Umatic, which was a composite tape format. When Sony first released the Umatic format, it caused a sensation — it was a portable format for Sony deck, and it looked really good for its time.

Note   Formats such as VHS do record their color and brightness information on separate tracks on the tape. Unfortunately, after this signal gets on the composite path, color and brightness are mixed back together, which causes interference and results in noise and colors that bleed.

Composite signal is also frequently sent via coaxial cable. In a coaxial cable even the audio signal is sent along in the same wires along with color and brightness information. The audio information can interfere with the picture with nasty results. Coaxial cable is often used to connect cable boxes to home televisions.

Artifacts and noise are not just visual annoyances. Because of these drawbacks in composite signals, achieving an effect such as blue-screening is difficult if not altogether impossible. *Blue-screening* is the effect where objects are shot in front of a blue screen, and then the blue color is removed during editing and filled in with a different background. You see this effect daily during the weather portion of any newscast. Your local weatherperson is really just pointing at a big blue wall (and feeling quite silly, I bet) while the techies at the TV station replace the blue wall with a weather map.

So in short, composite signal is not a very high-quality signal to say the least. But it is very common and the one you are most likely to encounter. Capture cards that have composite inputs are the most basic kinds of cards you'll find. They're also the most affordable.

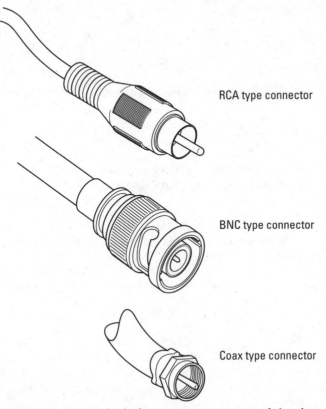

RCA type connector

BNC type connector

Coax type connector

Figure 2-1: Composite is the most common type of signal used in analog video. It uses an RCA-type or a BNC-type plug. A coaxial cable is sometimes used as well.

S-Video

S-Video is a solution to the drawbacks of composite signals. The S-Video signal is better because it separates color and brightness information across two separate pairs of wires. This causes less interference between the two signals, resulting in a sharper image. S-Video is not a perfect solution however because the color signals can still interfere with each other. Figure 2-2 shows an S-Video connector. S-Video connectors are also known as Y/C connectors. The letter *Y* in video terminology often represents luminance or brightness, and the *C* stands for chroma or color.

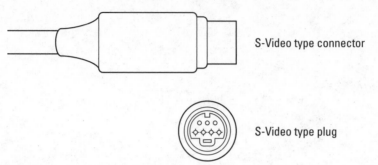

S-Video type connector

S-Video type plug

Figure 2-2: An S-Video connector sends the luminance and chrominance signals on two separate pairs of wires, reducing interference and giving a sharper and cleaner signal.

Note   The S-Video connector looks very much like the old Macintosh ADB connector that was used to connect keyboards to the computer. In fact, I've heard stories that, in a pinch, people have used a Macintosh keyboard cable as an S-Video cable. I recommend you stay away from that, unless you feel a deep need to fry your equipment.

The S-Video connector is often associated with S-VHS, and people sometimes use these two terms interchangeably; that is incorrect. S-VHS is a tape format that is a variant of the basic VHS tape that people use in their home VCRs to watch movies. S-VHS provides slightly better quality than VHS due to its ability to handle a higher luminance signal. An S-VHS format VCR may very well have an S-Video connector but they aren't the same. S-Video connectors are also found on decks other than S-VHS decks.

Even formats such as VHS show improvement in picture quality when carried over S-Video cables. However, despite S-Video's cleaner and sharper signal, it's still considered a consumer-level or a prosumer level signal. (The term *prosumer* is a combination of *consumer* and *professional* and describes that in-between market that has arisen in recent years.)

Component

The next step up the food chain of analog video is *component* video. Component is considered the best way to get the cleanest possible signal in the analog video world. The idea behind a component signal is to break up the color and the brightness information completely across three wires. Component connectors usually consist of three separate BNC-type connectors; a variety of other connectors have been implemented over the years but have never fully supplanted the three BNC-type connectors. Figure 2-3 shows a set of component connectors and plugs.

Component video is commonly relied upon in big networks and production houses. The Component format offers very high quality and, despite the rise of digital video, is not about to go away anytime soon.

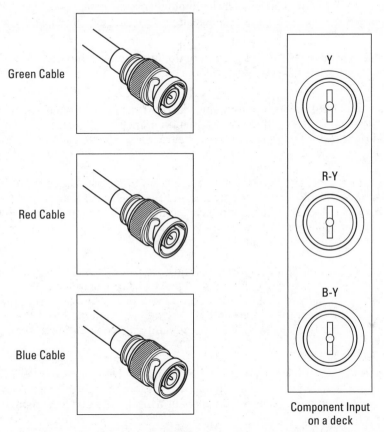

Green Cable

Red Cable

Blue Cable

Y

R-Y

B-Y

Component Input
on a deck

Figure 2-3: A component video signal is broken down and sent over three separate wires. This is considered the best way for an analog signal to travel.

Video cameras have historically captured images in the RGB (red, green, blue) mode. This means that they break down the incoming image into its red, green, and blue portions or components. These components are later mixed back together to see a full-color image. In fact, a normal tube television has three light guns, one for red, one for green, and one for blue, which create the final color image.

The video signal in a component interface is sent across three wires. These wires are colored red, green, and blue, but the colors of the wires don't really indicate what's traveling through them. Each wire carries a unique signal:

✦ **Green wire:** This wire carries just the luminance (also called the *brightness information*) portion of the entire image. If you could view this signal by itself, it would look like a black-and-white image.

✦ **Red wire:** This carries the red portion of the image *minus* the brightness information. This wire is labeled *R-Y* (pronounced "R minus Y"), meaning red minus its brightness.

✦ **Blue wire:** The third wire, colored blue, carries the blue portion of the image, minus (you got it) the brightness information. Hence, it is labeled *B-Y* for "blue minus brightness." The red and blue signals are also known as the *color difference* signals.

Wait, you say, how is the green color generated? I knew you'd ask. Green is produced by combining the two color difference signals and the brightness value. When you look at the back of a deck that has component inputs, you'll see inputs for Y, R-Y, and B-Y. The green cable goes into the connector marked Y, the red cable goes into the input marked R-Y, and the blue cable connects to B-Y.

Even within the fairly standardized format of the component signal, there are variations. The most common type of component signal is called Component YUV. A newer variation has emerged that is called Component RGB. This new variation is found in some of the latest televisions and other video equipment, but YUV is still the type of component signal you're likely to encounter as you work with analog video.

Note Component YUV is also known by the technically correct term *Component Y Cr Cb*. Some newer literature and equipment may use this term, but don't let it fool you. For all practical purposes, consider Component Y Cr Cb the same as Component YUV.

You may also encounter component connections with a fourth BNC cable. This extra cable provides a *sync* signal that can synchronize timing between professional-level video equipment, such as between two cameras or two decks. Most pro-level decks and cameras have a sync input marked Genlock or Ref. Some video capture cards also have this input to allow for synchronization.

Decks and equipment that have component interfaces are quite expensive. Capture cards that offer this interface are also quite a bit higher in price. However, if you're working with a high-quality format such as Betacam SP, you should consider a component signal-based setup. Nearly all Betacam SP decks have a component output and are well worth the money.

FireWire

I cover FireWire in depth in Chapter 1, but it's worth glancing at one more time in discussing the various signal types. FireWire is also known as IEEE-1394 or iLink. Apple Computer helped originate and develop this standard, and a FireWire port appears on nearly all new Macintosh computers. Figure 2-4 shows a FireWire cable.

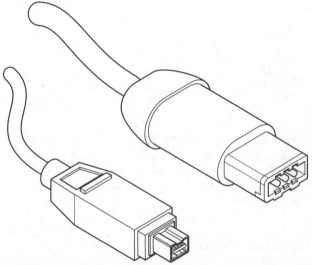

Figure 2-4: FireWire cables can have 6-pin and 4-pin connectors. Cameras often use a 4-pin connector, while computers and other peripherals tend to use 6-pin connectors.

FireWire allows for a high data-rate transfer. Most video equipment, such as cameras and decks, use a 4-pin FireWire connector, while FireWire ports on computers usually use a 6-pin connector. By connecting a 6-pin-to-4-pin FireWire cable between a Mac and a DV camera, you can capture video and audio into your computer quickly and easily using Final Cut Pro. Note that there is no difference in the quality of the video signal between a 4-pin and a 6-pin FireWire cable.

FireWire's technical specification for maximum transfer of data is 400 Mbps (megabits per second). Not fast enough? Apple's recent release and implementation of its new FireWire protocol can deliver 800 Mbps — *twice* as much data as the current FireWire standard! Appropriately named FireWire 800, this next generation of FireWire has all the attributes of the original FireWire, now renamed FireWire 400, plus total backward compatibility with all FireWire 400 hardware. In other words, the hot swappable, plug-and-play, daisy-chain connective up to 63 devices, affordable, and fast I/O (input/output) standard just got faster! The device connector is a 9-pin FireWire cable, shown in Figure 2-5.

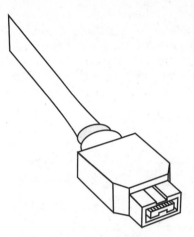

Figure 2-5: FireWire 800 cables have 9-pin connectors shown here, but they also can have 4-pin or 6-pin FireWire 400 connectors on one end for backward compatibility of devices.

Many people confuse FireWire with the DV format. It's easy to see why — most DV cameras use a FireWire cable to capture video into a computer — however, FireWire and DV are two separate standards. FireWire is a fast serial I/O standard that can be used with DV as well as scanners, hard drives, and CD-ROM burners. DV is a digital tape format and compression standard.

Serial Digital Interface (SDI)

Serial Digital Interface (SDI), sometimes called *Serial Digital Interconnect,* is a friendlier name for the technical specification SMPTE 259M. SDI is an extremely high-quality standard used to transfer uncompressed digital video. Of course, like I do, you probably expect this awesome digital connection to utilize some huge- looking switch that looks like a prop from a sci-fi show. Alas, the SDI connector looks like nothing more than a humble BNC connector (terribly disappointing if you ask me). Figure 2-6 shows an SDI connector. Despite the similarity of appearance, you should not use the SDI cable with a BNC interchangeably.

One benefit of SDI is its ability to send signals long distance across a cable. SDI is particularly robust and suffers little loss across distances, even when sent as far as 600 feet. It is therefore used in many networks and production houses to send high-quality digital video from one edit room to another or from a studio to an edit room.

SDI-capable decks include D1 and D5 tape formats. Another place an SDI interface is found is on a Digital Betacam deck. Digital Betacam is a digital version of the well-known Betacam SP format and is extremely high quality. DVCAM and DVCPRO decks often have SDI interface as well. Both Sony and Panasonic have their own versions of SDI. Sony calls its standard QSDI while CSDI is Panasonic's version.

To be able to work with SDI video in Final Cut Pro, you need some pretty expensive hardware. You need a capture card with an SDI interface, as well as high-speed disk drives able to sustain the large transfer rates SDI is capable of.

Cross-Reference For more information on video formats such as D1 and D5 rates, see Chapter 3.

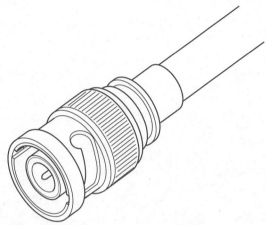

Figure 2-6: Serial Digital Interconnect (SDI) is a high-quality path for sending uncompressed digital video signals.

Analyzing Audio Connectors

Now that you're familiar with the various video connectors you may encounter when working with video, this section covers what some common audio connectors look like. Some of the connectors described in this section might be quite familiar to you. Some look suspiciously like the connectors on your headsets. Be sure to match the *impedance* of your audio connectors. Impedance is a measure of how well the two ends of a connection match electrically. Mismatch in impedance causes distortion or low audio signal. Figure 2-7 shows some of the most common audio connectors.

Although many of these connectors may seem familiar to you, there are a few key things to remember when working with audio cables. Many of the connectors shown in Figure 2-7 are found on computers' audio ports as well as numerous types of audio equipment. However, some of these may not be used interchangeably, *even* if the connector looks the same. Ratings of audio plugs are described as dBV (decibels voltage) and dBu (decibels power dissipation). For instance, you must know beforehand whether your audio connection is rated for an impedance of +4dBV or for −10dBu. The most common type of audio connection found on home stereo equipment, the RCA plug, is generally rated for −10dBu. These −10dBu RCA plugs are also known as *unbalanced audio*.

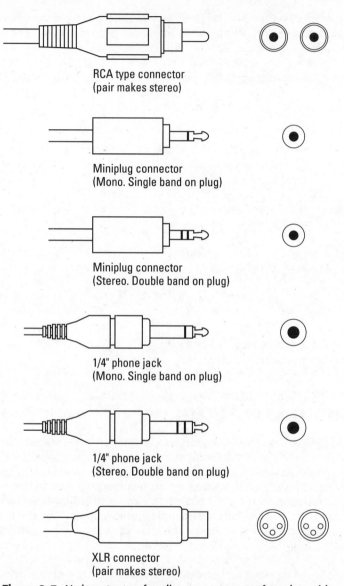

RCA type connector
(pair makes stereo)

Miniplug connector
(Mono. Single band on plug)

Miniplug connector
(Stereo. Double band on plug)

1/4" phone jack
(Mono. Single band on plug)

1/4" phone jack
(Stereo. Double band on plug)

XLR connector
(pair makes stereo)

Figure 2-7: Various types of audio connectors are found on video equipment, decks, and digitizing cards. Matching the impedance of these connectors with your equipment is important to avoid distortion or a low signal.

Balanced connectors, such as the XLR connector, are rated for +4dBV. Sending a –10dBu output into a +4dBV input will result in a very low signal level, and you'll find yourself turning the volume way up. On the other hand, sending a +4dBV output into a –10dBu input will cause distortion. This will sound like flies are buzzing around in someone's mouth as they speak. Needless to say, you don't want that.

Be sure to check the ratings on your inputs and outputs before you plug these connections into each other.

 Note   If you must create a mismatch between a +4dBV and –10dBu plugs, you can purchase a matching transformer from an electronics store.

Also, keep an eye on whether you're working with mono or stereo connections. The mini plugs and the ¼-inch jacks are mono if they have just one band across their plug and stereo if they have two bands across.

Capture cards that have unbalanced audio I/O (input/output) are generally cheaper than ones with balanced I/O. Check your equipment to see what you need before you buy a card.

Understanding the DV format

Having covered some of the common video formats and connectors, I'll turn to the DV format, which is currently becoming quite popular. After years of living with 8mm, Hi-8, and monstrous VHS camcorders, DV represents a revolution in the world of independent video. DV is significant enough that I devote the rest of this chapter to it.

DV is significant because it makes high-quality video obtainable and affordable for a greater number of people. In the not-so-distant past, if you had an old VHS camcorder, you could not expect your video to be accepted by networks. VHS, Hi-8, and 8mm formats were considered strictly consumer formats due primarily to their quality. They were good enough to shoot your baby's birthday or a family trip to the local park, but not good enough to be aired on prime time. Granted, occasionally a documentary or two would show up that were shot in VHS, but the quality was miserable, the picture dark as mud, and tape hiss nearly drowned out any other sound or voice.

For years if you needed to do video for broadcast or another application where high quality was demanded, the choice was a professional format such as Betacam SP. The cameras, decks, and editing systems for such formats cost an arm and a leg, and perhaps even a tooth or two. They were cumbersome and generally lousy for low-light situations.

The emergence of DV camcorders transformed this bleak and badly lit video scene. The most significant difference between DV and the various formats that came before it is that DV is a digital standard based on a binary code of zeros and ones, while most previous formats were analog signals that deteriorated and suffered generational loss, noise, and degradation problems. Theoretically, DV faces no such shortcomings.

A technology that helped make DV possible is the Charged Coupled Device (CCD). The cost for CCDs was finally low enough to be used in video cameras as replacements for video pickup tubes. Some of the older video cameras used pickup tubes that required a lot of light and caused streaking and *comet tailing,* the old 1970s effect where a pan across a light makes it look like Halley's Comet just arrived on the set.

CCDs are, to put it simply, image sensors that work as pickups for the light coming through the camera lens. CCDs capture the incoming image electronically, converting light to electrical energy. The quick response and low-light capacity of CCDs is quite impressive compared to video pickup tubes.

CCD-equipped DV cameras have infused new life into the video scene. Numerous documentaries have been shot entirely on the DV format. Networks and broadcast houses have come to accept DV, though some networks still have reservations about the format. I would not describe the current situation as an open-arm embrace of DV, but rather a grudging and reluctant acceptance of sorts. Networks and broadcast houses in general don't have the stomach for innovative new upstart technologies, and for good reason: They have deadlines to meet and their workflow to consider. Networks tend to stay with what has proven to work rather than grab hold of the latest miracle.

Figure 2-8 shows the Sony DSR-40 DV deck. This deck is designed for DV playback and DVCAM recording and playback.

DV has reinvigorated the independent film market. More and more feature films have been shot on DV, and the trend is becoming more popular. Later these "films" get transferred to real celluloid film and released in the theatre. Don't get me wrong; they still look like DV transferred to film. But it is significant that DV makes such work possible. And perhaps best of all, most DV cameras are not that much more expensive than Hi-8 and other analog formats. The quality of DV format is far superior to that of Hi-8, 8mm, and other analog video formats.

If you're working with Final Cut Pro, chances are pretty good that you're using the DV format. It's not a stretch to suggest that DV's popularity has contributed to Final Cut Pro's acceptance and its stature as one of the most popular editing programs.

Note   Despite the focus on DV technology, don't forget that Final Cut Pro can work with just about any format and any type of video, given the right hardware. In techno-speak, this is known as *scalability.* As they say at Apple, Final Cut Pro works with everything from DV to HDTV.

Figure 2-8: Sony's DSR-40 is one of the highest-rated DV and DVCAM decks on the market.

Photo courtesy of Sony Corp., Inc.

The history of the DV format

The DV format was launched in 1995. DV is a set of specifications and a standard created by a consortium of 55 different companies. It is both a new video recording format as well as a compression standard. In other words, DV describes a particular way of capturing *and* compressing video. The advent of DV has created a whole new market for video makers to create broadcast-quality video on surprisingly low budgets. Sony, Canon, and Panasonic have created numerous cameras, decks and other peripherals based on the DV format. These cameras are often inexpensive and deliver high-quality video. The resolution of DV is roughly twice that of VHS videotape.

One of the truly remarkable things about the DV format is that engineers created a format with a data stream lean enough that desktop computers can handle it, while maintaining a remarkably high picture quality. A common misconception about DV is that it is an "uncompressed" format. This is quite untrue. DV is a compressed signal. Later in this chapter, you'll get into the details of this compression and see how it affects you.

Another major advantage of the DV format is that it has digital audio tracks. This represents a quantum leap forward from the noisy analog tracks of old analog camcorders. Despite the fact that the DV format compresses video, it does not compress audio. DV can record two channels of 16-bit audio at 48 kHz sampling rate, or four channels of 12-bit at 32 kHz audio. Most DV camcorders allow the operator to select between the sampling rates. I strongly suggest you try to use the 16-bit or 48 kHz setting as often as possible and avoid the 12-bit or 32 kHz setting. The compromise in audio quality can pose problems later when you may export audio or mix and match sampling rates.

Sampling rate refers to the number of samples a digitizing circuit takes of an audio signal. Audio samples are usually taken at 32,000, 44,100, or 48,000 times per second, resulting in the terms 32 kHz, 44.1 kHz, and 48 kHz. 44.1 kHz is considered CD quality, because that is the sampling rate of audio tracks on a compact disc.

For more information on audio sampling rates see Chapter 14.

Variations of the DV format

As I mentioned, DV is both a recording format and a compression standard. First consider the tape format. This is likely to be your first contact with DV, particularly if you just bought a DV camera and have been shooting with it. Some common types of DV format tapes are discussed in the following sections.

MiniDV

MiniDV is the most common manifestation of the DV format and it was the first to arrive on the video scene. Often referred to as *Consumer DV,* these tapes are the smallest of the DV format tapes and are used in most of the DV camcorders currently available. MiniDV tapes can record up to 60 minutes of video. Virtually all MiniDV camcorders have a FireWire (IEEE-1394) interface. However, in many PAL-format cameras (PAL is a format for video equipment in Europe and other parts of the world; the Americas use NTSC-format equipment), the FireWire *input* to the camera is bled. Don't ask me why, but apparently there's some worry in Europe that people will start dubbing movies and sell them on MiniDV tape. I have no idea why people would do that in Europe but not in the United States!

Despite the high quality of digital audio, MiniDV uses unlocked audio (as opposed to the locked variety in DVCAM and DVCPro tapes). This is a problem when editing tape-to-tape with a MiniDV tape. Some edits can produce an audible audio pop.

Chip or no chip

While shooting in the field, the camera operator can mark shots and scenes on a DVCAM tape as OK or NG (no good.) During the logging and capturing phase, only the shots marked OK can be loaded in. Sony calls this function ClipLink, and this function is accomplished with the help of a tiny chip inside the Sony DVCAM cassette. This memory chip has a capacity of 16 kilobits, but it is enough to store the *Mark In* and *Mark Out* timecode, *OK/NG* status, reel number, scene number, and take numbers for up to 198 scenes.

When purchasing MiniDV tapes, you have the option of selecting cassettes with the memory chip. Also bear in mind that, on a MiniDV tape, the chip has a memory of 4 kilobits, big enough for information for 45 scenes.

Note   Locked versus unlocked audio in DV format refers to the fact that in an unlocked audio format the number of samples for audio are not tightly synchronized to each video frame. Often a frame is off by a few samples of audio, and during an edit this can produce an audible pop.

MiniDV-based camcorders usually have consumer-level audio hookups such as audio mini jacks or RCA-type connectors. Many videographers purchase XLR-based kits and expensive microphones to enhance their audio capabilities, so check any camcorder you plan to buy to ensure it has the types of connectors you'll need.

When MiniDV tapes (see Figure 2-9) came out, video people went wild over them. The quality was good, MiniDV camcorders were affordable, and the audio was superb. The success of the DV format took manufacturers by surprise. However, many of the early MiniDV tapes did not stand up to the rigors of tape-to-tape editing and shuttling. People started noticing dropouts, problems with insert editing, and other general quality issues. To rectify this, the DVCPro format was created by Panasonic. Sony followed with their DVCAM standard. These tape formats are discussed next.

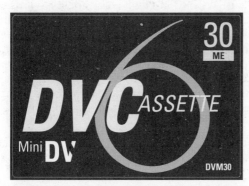

Figure 2-9: The MiniDV format is the most common format for DV tapes.

DVCPro

DVCPro is a DV format developed by Panasonic for its professional DV equipment. DVCPro was created to address the shortcomings of the MiniDV format. DVCPro's quality and compression is exactly the same as MiniDV. The difference between MiniDV and DVCPro is the size of the tape shell, better tracks on DVCPro for insert editing, and in general a more robust construction for DVCPro tapes. DVCPro equipment also usually has Serial Digital Interface (SDI) connections. MiniDV-based equipment, on the other hand, most often has FireWire connections.

Cross-Reference   SDI video, also known by its technical specification SMPTE 259M, is described earlier in this chapter.

On a DVCPro tape, the track pitch is 18 microns, compared to 10 microns for MiniDV. This helps make the tape perform better during shuttling and tape-to-tape editing. DVCPro tapes are formulated with metal particles, and they have an analog cue and control track. On the cue track is an additional audio track, which is used during shuttle functions. This allows for "scrubbing" of audio while the deck is in a search mode. The control track on the DVCPro tapes allows for better playback and keeps pre-roll times short. DVCPro decks have the additional advantage of being able to play MiniDV and DVCAM tapes as well as DVCPro tapes. Figure 2-10 shows the track layout of a DV tape.

A variant of DVCPRO is DVCPRO50. DVCPRO50 is a codec that uses a similar compression scheme as DV, but with some very significant differences. DVCPRO50 has a fixed data rate of 7MB per second compared to DV's 3.6MB per second data rate. The higher data rate translates to less compression and ultimately better video quality. 7MB per second is still a very lean throughput that will not necessarily require a Redundant Array of Independent Disks (RAID) setup for capture and playback.

The boon for broadcast professionals is DVCPRO50's high-color fidelity — it uses 4:2:2 color sampling instead of DV's 4:1:1 (color sampling is covered in detail later in this chapter). This is the same color sampling rate used by Beta SP and Digital Beta, but with the distinct advantage of DV's smaller and less-expensive equipment. That being said, DVCPRO50 is a codec that requires cameras, playback decks, and editing stations that are DVCPRO50 capable. Final Cut Pro 4.0 natively supports Panasonic DVCPRO50. Because DVCPRO50 uses the same tape format and stock as DVCPRO, most DVCPRO50 playback and recording decks can also play regular DVCPRO recordings.

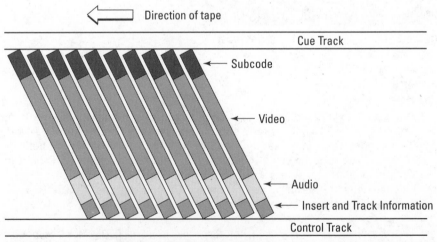

Figure 2-10: A single frame of NTSC video laid out across ten helical tracks of DV tape. The Insert and Track information portion handles tracking and playback synchronization. The Subcode area contains timecode and edit information.

DVCAM

Panasonic has its own format for its line of professional equipment, and so does Sony. Sony's proprietary format is DVCAM. The difference between the DVCAM and MiniDV is the size of the tape shell and the size of the tracks as they are laid on the tape. The compression and the image quality on DVCAM are exactly the same as MiniDV. DVCAM equipment also usually has Serial Digital Interface (SDI) video interface. DVCAM tapes generally do not play in other DV equipment. However, DVCAM equipment can play consumer MiniDV tapes. DVCAM tapes, like the ones shown in Figure 2-11, can record up to 180 minutes worth of video.

Figure 2-11: DVCAM is Sony's format for its line of professional DV tapes and equipment.

Photos courtesy of Sony Corp., Inc.

In DVCAM tapes, the width of a track is increased to 15 microns (MiniDV's track width is 10 microns). The wider track reduces the recording time somewhat and it reduces dropouts. DVCAM (like DVCPro) uses locked audio. This means that the audio samples are tightly synchronized with each video frame. Additionally, a very tiny cross fade is added at each edit to maintain alignment.

Each DVCAM tape shell has an embedded 16k memory chip that stores information about timecode and when a "cue" button was pressed. These cue marks can be used as markers to shuttle the tape. DVCAM tapes also have the capacity to store a small picture of each shot (see the sidebar, "Chip or no chip").

DV25 turns 50

With the emergence of DVCPRO50, also known as DV50, the original DV format has been retro-named DV25. This designation was derived from their respective data rates — 50Mbps for DV50 and 25Mbps for DV25. DV50 retains many attributes of DV25 in addition to even higher video quality and color sampling while keeping the data rate relatively low and manageable. The transfer rate of DV50 is fixed at 7MB per second, with a compression of only 3.3:1 and it can also be carried over FireWire. However, acquisition, editing, and outputting of DV50 does require professional-grade equipment that few but commercial production houses or broadcast facilities can afford. Until the cost of DVCPRO50-enabled equipment is dramatically reduced, DV25 will remain a viable and thriving format. For this reason, the DV issues covered in this chapter and elsewhere in this book pertain mainly to DV25 — although many apply to DV50 as well.

Some DVCAM videotape recorders (VTRs) support a 4X transfer. Therefore, a 20-minute DVCAM tape can be captured in five minutes. This is a major benefit in that it speeds up the capture process, which usually works in real time.

Note   Bear in mind that even though technically there's no difference between the quality and compression of MiniDV and DVCAM or DVCPro, the cameras that support DVCAM and DVCPro tend to be of better quality and produce a better picture. They also tend to be more expensive because DVCAM and DVCPro equipment is sold as professional-grade equipment.

Much like MiniDV, DVCAM allows you to record in 12-bit, 32 kHz or 16-bit, 48 kHz mode. However, DVCAM records the sound in the Audio Lock mode, as opposed to the MiniDV's unlocked audio mode. The Audio Lock mode assigns a precise number of audio samples to be linked with each video frame. Consumer-level DV devices use the less-accurate unlocked mode, which allows the sample number to vary slightly. The precision of the variation depends on the recorder's internal oscillator circuit. The Audio Lock mode in DVCAM assures absolute synchronization between the audio and the video on the tape. This synchronization allows for seamless insert edits. However, this distinction has a side effect you must know about. *You cannot make digital dubs from consumer-level DV devices to professional level DVCAM VTRs.* Although both the DV and the DVCAM devices have the same interface, the layout of the audio bits is different and incompatible.

Digital 8

Digital 8 was introduced by Sony in 1998, and it represents a bridge between the analog 8mm, Hi-8, and the new DV tapes. The Digital 8 format uses the same video compression scheme as DV. Digital 8 camcorders use 8mm or Hi-8 tapes to record DV material on them. Digital 8 camcorders also have the added flexibility of being able to play the old 8mm and Hi-8 tapes. These camcorders often have analog and FireWire inputs and outputs much like many DV camcorders.

Understanding DV compression

A stream of uncompressed video contains a huge amount of data, approximately 20MB per second. Most computer hard drives cannot handle a data rate this high. When digitizing a video signal into the computer, the data rate must be made manageable without sacrificing too much quality. To achieve just the right combination, compression is applied. Note that I use the word *manageable* and the phrase *too much;* the meanings have been the subject of many heated debates among video editors on the Internet, the likes of which I've never seen. People have an almost religious zeal in their arguments when they speak about compression and quality. I will try to avoid foaming at the mouth and simply show you some of the issues you should be aware of. From past experience, however, I know that no amount of diplomacy is going to save me from the slings and arrows of the digital video gurus.

The compression and decompression of a video in DV is achieved by something called a *codec* (short for compression/decompression). There are many different kinds of codecs. Some of these codecs reside in your computer. Some are hardware-based codecs, others are software-based. The DV codec is just one of the many codecs in your computer. The QuickTime Compression Settings dialog box is one place in the Mac OS where you can find a bunch of codecs. Figure 2-12 shows the Compression Settings dialog box and some of the codecs you'll find there.

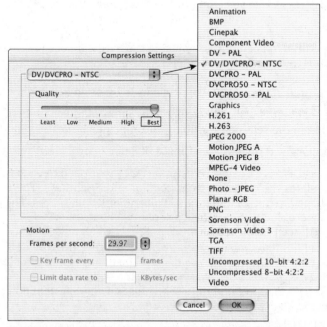

Figure 2-12: This QuickTime dialog box contains a list of codecs, which you can see on the right. Codecs are compression/ decompression tools that allow you to reduce the data rate of a video stream while maintaining an acceptable level of quality.

Some codecs are variable; they can handle different rates of compression. The DV codec is not variable. It works at a fixed rate of compression. This is both an advantage and a disadvantage. The advantage is that a fixed rate of compression keeps the data rate steady at 3.6MB per second. At this rate, DV takes up 1GB for every 4.5 minutes of video. An hour of DV captured into your computer will fill 13GB worth of disk space. It's hard to believe that the tiny 60-minute MiniDV tape is holding 13GB of digital data!

If you calculate this against the data rate of uncompressed video (generally considered to be around 18 to 20MB per second, or even higher depending on how much of the signal is being digitized and what format it is) that works out to a 5:1 compression ratio for DV. This ratio allows for a very manageable data rate that even the basic Macintosh hard drives can support.

Details of DV compression

The science of image compression is a complex and sophisticated one. Compression technologies have many faces and variations, but the basic idea behind compression is always the same: Compress the image down to an acceptable size, but make sure the image still looks good. Behind that statement lies a whole host of issues. Image-compression schemes are based on the fact that you throw away data that isn't discernable to the human eye. Then you can apply techniques that reduce large areas of similar color and brightness into small numbers. These areas are then decoded back into the image.

When a DV frame is captured, it is compressed inside the hardware of the camera. Here's what happens in NTSC-format DV:

1. Each frame is captured at the size of 720 pixels wide by 480 pixels high.

2. Every other pixel of color is discarded to get a resulting sampling of 4:1:1. (I explain this later, in the section describing chrominance issues.)

3. The resulting frame is next divided into blocks of 8 pixels by 8 lines.

4. A process known as Discrete Cosine Transform (DCT) is applied to each frame. This process calculates the common areas of color and brightness. The resulting values are grouped to form a total of 1,350 macro, or larger, blocks. The data in each of these macroblocks is stored as a separate value.

This entire process occurs in real time of course, while capturing video at 29.97 frames per second (fps). For PAL it works at 25 fps and the macroblocks are sized a little differently. When DV is played back, this compression scheme is reversed and the image re-created. At DV's compression ratio of 5:1 this is a very efficient compression scheme and results in a very high-quality picture.

Is it really 5:1?

Okay, I'm about to say something here that I'm sure will earn me some flames and nasty e-mails, but I have to say it. Throughout this book, I keep saying that the compression for DV is 5:1. If you read DV literature and information sites, they all say the same thing. But is this really correct?

One of the processes that occurs inside the camera when DV is captured is that every other chroma, or color pixel, is discarded. When manufacturers say that DV is 5:1, they're measuring the compression *before* the chroma is discarded. If you measure it *after,* the compression works out to be almost 7:1. (That's how most other digital formats are measured, such as Digital Betacam.) Okay, in all fairness, what does it matter if the compression is 7:1 or 5:1 or that 50 percent of an image's chroma is thrown away? The picture of DV looks quite good. However, you're not just concerned with capturing and playing back a DV tape. You'll be processing the video as well. You'll be editing it, adding dissolves and layers to it, and performing myriad other changes.

The macroblock scheme that DV uses is limited in its flexibility, and on repeated compressions you start to see artifacts and breakdown of the image. DV compression also results in a fixed frame size, although other compression schemes are more generous. When DV captures an image, it assigns a fixed amount of data to each block, depending on what the image is. Areas of low detail get less data. Areas of more detail get more. In a postproduction environment, if a high-quality graphic is added and the DV image is recompressed, which it must be to merge the graphic, the relationship of low detail areas and high detail areas changes because of the overlay of the graphic. The result of all this is that if you add a graphic or recompress the DV image, it has to work with the same amount of data as it had when it was without the graphic, and thus you lose detail in the graphic.

Titles can also cause problems. Adding a title can cause a number of these macroblocks to suddenly need more data than they did before the title was overlaid. The space requirement for this additional data is created at the cost of heavily compressing other sections of the frame. At times, this compression can become noticeable to the human eye.

Note
> The degradation of DV video when overlaid with titles was particularly visible when using the standard DV codec provided by Apple. This was the old codec, and it rendered titles like mud. Apple's programmers now swear that this issue is gone, so the new standard Apple DV codec should not pose this issue. And of course, you can always purchase and use a codec made by another vendor.

Considering other DV issues in a postproduction environment

There are a few other issues you should consider when working with DV. These issues relate to aspect ratio and color issues, among other things. The next few sections describe some issues you need to consider.

Aspect ratios

All video formats have a frame aspect ratio and a pixel aspect ratio. The *frame aspect ratio* is the height versus the length of the frame, and the *pixel aspect ratio* describes the height and length of individual pixels. DV's frame aspect ratio is 720 × 480 pixels, which means that a frame is 720 pixels long and 480 pixels wide. Its pixel aspect ratio is slightly rectangular and is known as D1 pixel aspect ratio. Figure 2-13 illustrates frame and pixel aspect ratios.

The frame aspect ratio for broadcast signals is usually 720 × 486, and an aspect ratio of 640 × 480 is sometimes used on computers. 720 × 486 formats tend to have a D1 pixel aspect ratio whereas 640 × 480 ones generally have a square pixel aspect ratio. Note that DV's aspect ratio and pixel aspect ratio add a third set of specifications, which differs from the other two specifications of broadcast or computer-based video. Some reformatting and reprocessing is almost always necessary when mixing and matching these frame and pixel aspect ratios in a project. You need to keep this in mind when working with After Effects or other programs and plan accordingly. Adobe's After Effects is a standard compositing program used in the industry to create video graphics.

Cross-Reference   Chapter 26 covers working with After Effects and Final Cut Pro.

Color gamut conversion

Color space is a term used to describe systems that define the range, strength, and coding of color. DV formats utilize a color space known as YUV color space. This color space, also called a *gamut,* is ideal for video use. Computers utilize a color space known as RGB. When converting from one color space to another, slight color shifts occur.

Programs such as After Effects use RGB filters rather than YUV. You'll see a slight color shift if you render DV in After Effects and bring it back to play in Final Cut Pro.

Blue-screening with DV

Blue-screening is a process where people or objects are shot against a blue screen. Later, the blue is removed and other background material is filled in. This is also sometimes known as the *weatherperson effect,* because you see it on your daily news. There's actually no map back there; the weatherperson is actually gesturing at a blue screen (or possibly green). This blue screen is replaced with the weather map during the news using expensive switchers. However, in situations other than live broadcast this kind of color replacement is done during post-edit work. Final Cut Pro has a blue-screening filter that allows you to perform this effect, which is sometimes also called *keying*.

Due to its 4:1:1 chroma ratio, DV (DV25) is not the ideal format for keying. You can get away with it, but in general it's considered a weak format for keying. If it's a big enough job and an important enough project, try shooting the blue-screen shot with as high a format as your budget will allow, such as DVCPRO50, Beta SP, or Digital Beta.

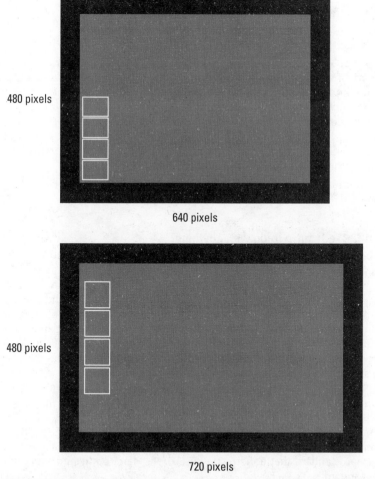

Figure 2-13: Frame aspect ratios define the height versus the width of a frame. Pixel aspect ratios are the aspect ratios of the individual pixels. The pixel aspect ratio in DV is rectangular and is called D1.

Capturing DV as MJPEG

DV could in many ways be considered a better acquisition format than a postproduction format. This means that DV's image quality may lend itself extremely well to capturing high-quality video, but in a postproduction environment DV tends to show its weaknesses when recompressed and reprocessed with other elements. Often, production houses shoot DV and use Final Cut Pro to edit their video, but they don't capture the video via FireWire. They may use a digitizing board and the component or S-Video input to capture DV into their system using the MJPEG codec. This is a codec that is used in many high-end digitizing boards and is considered to be extremely high quality. Keep in mind that, at this point, your video is no longer DV but has been converted to MJPEG. You can no longer simply master it back to tape using a FireWire cable and a DV deck. But the MJPEG route can help you get around the graphics overlay problem if you encounter it.

Chrominance issues with DV compression

Chrominance refers to the color part of the video signal. It's nothing more than a video-geek's way of saying *color*. What I want to look at is how color is treated during DV compression and what effect this compression has. Let me take a moment to explain a few terms you may have heard around the fireside. For example, if you've studied the specifications of video equipment, you've often seen the term Component 4:2:2 or 4:1:1. You may wonder what that number means. I'm going to talk about what some of the specifications relating to chrominance mean, and in the process I'll also consider DV's treatment of color and its implications.

Cross-Reference   Component video is explained earlier in this chapter.

What does ITU-R BT.601 have to do with anything?

There was a big international committee called the International Radio Consultative Committee (CCIR). (I know, CCIR does not spell out the name, but that's because the original name is in French and in that language CCIR does spell out the name.) In 1992, this committee merged with another committee called ITU, and this new conglomeration is now called ITU-R. Why am I going on this major tangent on international committees? Because this committee is very important to us. This international committee is not dedicated to world peace (which wouldn't be a such a bad thing, by the way) but to setting standards. ITU-R has set a technical standard on how analog video should be converted to digital form and then back. This standard is known as ITU-R BT.601. Almost everybody that makes professional-level video equipment must conform to these standards, which have a major effect on image quality.

Note   By the way, this standard is sometimes known as CCIR-601, or just the 601 standard, which is the older name for it. It's also sometimes called the D-1 standard. D-1 is a tape standard that adheres to the 601 standard, but it's incorrect to call the 601 standard D-1.

Understanding the 601 standard is very important, because it affects everyone working with digital video, and makers of video cards work hard to adhere to these standards. Video formats such as Betacam SP, Digital Betacam, and others are also based on this standard. The 601 standard states that digital coding of the video signal should be based on sampling the color values at half the rate of luminance sampling, in effect 4:2:2. Chapter 1 told you that the human eye is much more sensitive to changes in brightness values than color values. The 601 standard takes that into account and gives the brightness information twice as much data space as the color information.

In this ratio 4:2:2, the 4 refers to the data used to store the luma or brightness information and the first 2 refers to the red color difference signal. The last 2 refers to the blue color difference signal, thus resulting in 4:2:2. The 601 standard sets the specifications based on the component method of signal transfer. Because of this style of bit sampling, the 601 video standard is also known as 8-bit video.

Note   In computer terminology *bit* is the smallest unit of information. It's a single digit, 0 or 1, off or on (the word *bit* is short for *binary digit,* if you really must know). Eight bits make 1 *byte.* 1 byte is what a computer needs to make up one unit of display. The character *X* for example takes up 1 byte of storage or memory space on the computer. 1,024 bytes make 1 *kilobyte,* and 1,024 kilobytes (KB) makes 1 megabyte (MB). 1024MB makes 1 gigabyte (GB). Now you know.

Cross-
Reference   CCIR 601 video is also known as 8-bit video. This is the most commonly used video in the world of digital postproduction. Another form of video, 10-bit video, is becoming increasingly popular. For information on 10-bit video, see Chapter 3.

Video is coded in the manner specified by the 601 standard for some very fine reasons. During the phase of analog transmissions, 601 video takes up less bandwidth than it would otherwise and, more importantly to you, it saves disk space used for storage of your digitized signal. Figure 2-14 illustrates how different sampling schemes work.

Compared to the broadcast 4:2:2 video signals, DV25 discards a percent of the chroma information present in every frame before the image is compressed. This results in the DV standard sampling of 4:1:1, as shown in Figure 2-13. DV allows the same amount of data for the luminance part of the video but allows *half* as much for the color part. Again, DV does this to make its data rate smaller, and this is how DV achieves a very lean data rate of 3.6MB per second.

Note   The 4:1:1 sampling method applies to NTSC DV only. In the PAL version of DV, another way of sampling, known as the *co-sited* 4:2:0, works a bit differently.

Represents one
luminance sample

Represents one red and
one blue sample

4:4:4

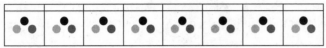

The 4:4:4 format is rarely seen in true 601 compliant video boards and relies
on a fudge of sorts. This sampling is used in the RGB computer domain
or for storage or transmission of digital video media.

4:2:2

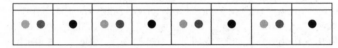

The 601 standard is used in most 601 compliant formats. Betacam
SP and Digital Beta are just some of the formats that use this standard.

4:1:1

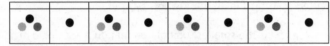

NTSC DV uses the 4:1:1 sampling.

Cosited 4:2:0

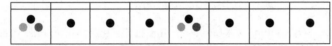

PAL uses a Cosited 4:2:0 sampling.

Figure 2-14: Video sampling determines the quality of the video. In a
4:2:2 arrangement, two samples are taken of the luminance for every
one sample of chrominance. Betacam SP, DVCPRO50 and Digital Betacam
use this sampling method. DV in NTSC, now also called DV25 NTSC,
uses the 4:1:1 arrangement.

Keep in mind that whatever the DV compression does with its chroma, it is still a
very good-looking signal. So why am I bothering you with these details? Well, for
three reasons:

✦ Even though DV looks good, the 4:1:1 has an effect on our work.

✦ This information can help you evaluate the digital video specifications.

✦ I think it's fun to talk about these things. It encourages a better understanding of what you're working with and stimulates discussion in the video editing community.

Whether DV's 4:1:1 sampling will affect your work depends on the kind of work you're doing. If you're a documentary maker and you shoot hours and hours of video on DV, and then edit it together using Final Cut Pro, you have no reason to worry. However, if you're a fancy artist type who's going to capture DV into your computer, do multilayering, blue-screening, and all kinds of other operations that merge layers, heed this warning: The 4:1:1 sampling of DV will result in less-than-acceptable results. You'll see softening of images and visual artifacts. And if graphics are placed over DV during post-production and then recompressed with the DV codec, you'll see some reduction in the chrominance of the overall picture, including the graphic.

To the fancy artist types with aspirations of layering, keying, and graphics animation, I suggest looking for ways to capture DV through analog inputs or not use DV at all.

Luminance clamping in DV or what hath the DV codec wrought

The previous section mentioned that 601 video is also called 8-bit video because it consists of 8 separate bits. A *bit* is a single element of binary language in either an on or off state. Within 8 bits (remember, 8 bits = 1 byte) the possible on and off combinations number 256. Thus, in the 8 bits that this signal consists of, luminance or brightness is counted in values of 0 to 255. However, in DV as well as other digital-video formats that use the YUV color space, the values that are actually used are 16 to 235. A value of 16 is considered black and 235 is considered white. In the color space for a computer, called RGB, values range from 0 to 255. In RGB color space, 0 is black and 255 is white. Figure 2-15 illustrates this luminance correlation.

The values from 1 to 15 are reserved for blacker-than-black and the values from 235 to 254 are reserved for whiter-than-white. (The end values of 0 and 255 are used for internal synchronization and are not relevant.) These ranges are also known as *footroom* and *headroom,* respectively. I must admit that I have rarely seen anyone use the term *footroom,* but it seems to get the idea across. The footroom provides accommodation for shots that may have black that is less than 16, and the headroom allows for whites that may be hotter than 235, such as glare off of glass or a light source in the shot. Even some bright white objects can be bright enough to end up in the 235 to 254 range. For example, a white chair standing in the bright sun can register as brighter than white.

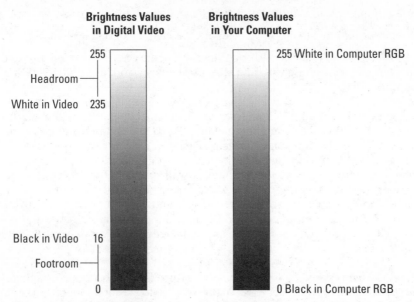

Figure 2-15: Digital video luminance values range from 16 to 235, leaving footroom and headroom for blacker-than-black and whiter-than-white values. Your computer's RGB color space counts luminance in values from 0 to 255.

A problem occurs when the DV codec handles luminance in the headroom and footroom of YUV video. All DV codecs work a little differently, but some codecs map video's 16 to a computer RGB value of 0 and video's 235 to a computer RGB value of 255. Therefore, if you had super whites and super blacks that lay below 15 and above 235, the DV codec is simply going to clip them off as shown in Figure 2-16. If you had shot of a white chair sitting in the sun in your backyard, the brightest parts of the chair would get clipped into a flat blob.

Note   In analog video engineering, another scale, known as the IRE scale, is used. This scale is commonly measured using waveform monitors. Although IRE and waveforms belong in the analog world, they're also a presence when working with nonlinear editing systems such as Final Cut Pro. Whites on the IRE scale lie at 100 IRE and often go up to 110 IRE. However, whites above 100 IRE are generally considered "illegal" for broadcast and are discouraged. Don't worry, no one's going to break your door down and arrest you. But it is advised that you use a good waveform monitor to make sure your whites don't exceed 100 IREs. In NTSC Video, 100 IREs translate to 235 on the video scale and 16 translates to 7.5 IREs. In PAL, 16 translates to 0 IRE.

Cross-Reference   For more information on waveform monitors, see Chapter 3.

Bear in mind that some of the YUV values above 235 may very well fall beyond the legal limits of broadcast. However, the fact remains that cameras capture images with luminance values that fall between 1 and 15 and between 235 and 254 all the time.

The problem of losing certain YUV luminance values upon conversion to RGB is known as luma clamping and is usually associated with DV codecs. Luma clamping appears when bright highlights that a camera captured turn into white blotches without any detail. This problem gives DV a bad name, but unfairly so because there are many versions of DV codecs that allow the full mapping of YUV luminance values. Some DV codecs even give you a choice.

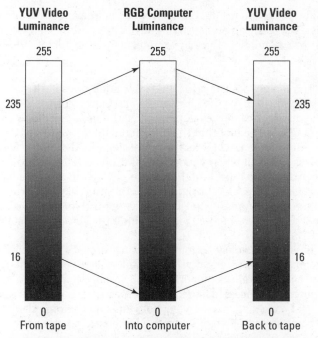

Figure 2-16: YUV video, which is the basis for digital video, measures its luminance on a scale of 16 to 235 while leaving headroom and footroom for brighter or darker images. A luma clamping DV codec will map a YUV value of 16 to a computer's RGB value of 0 and a YUV of 235 to a computer's RGB of 255, essentially clamping any luminance information that lies in the headroom or footroom. This process is reversed when going from your computer back to tape. Newer DV codecs do not have the luma clamping problem.

Luma clamping generally manifests as a slight darkening of super white areas. Most often the clamping is visible during a dissolve between two clips because the clip will suddenly darken during the transition period.

Luma clamping was really a big deal in the early days of DV because the early DV codec that Apple gave out with its QuickTime modules had the problem, and this codec was used to convert the values while you worked with Final Cut Pro. This codec, in a word, stank. I don't mean for this to reflect on the fine people over at Apple—they're the cheeriest and most talented lot I've ever worked with—but the early DV codec from Apple was an unmitigated disaster. It clamped out highlights, was slow in rendering, and dealt with colors rather poorly, too.

Since the release of Final Cut Pro 2.0 in 2001, the DV codec is free and clear of the dreaded luma clamping issue. Other manufacturers have either addressed clamping in their codecs or given you a choice between clamping and using full luminance mapping.

This luma clamping issue is mainly of historical value now, but it does illustrate a few issues that are still relevant to you. DV video, as simple and easy to use as it may be, has issues that can bite you at times. For example, one of the most insidious manifestations of luma clamping was the fact that the clamped whites would not be seen on your Macintosh computer screen. As far as the computer's RGB monitor was concerned, everything was fine. But when you looked at it on an NTSC video monitor, or worse, sent your program to tape, and then someone looked at it, the luma clamping issue stuck out like a sore, albeit bright white, thumb. This is instructive because although the luma clamping issue has been largely resolved, there is still no replacement for previewing your video on an NTSC monitor before releasing it.

Note   Chroma clamping is an issue similar to luma clamping, except that it involves chrominance, or color. There are certain values of colors that component YUV video contains that cannot be represented in the RGB world. When video is captured into the computer and processed into RGB color space, some YUV colors will be crushed and a slight darkening may be seen. Both luma and chroma clamping occur because the computer's RGB color space and luminance range is less than video's YUV space.

Cross-Reference   Starting with Final Cut Pro 1.2.5, you are allowed to render in YUV space instead of the default RGB space. I show you how to do this in Chapter 24.

All DV codecs are different

Keep in mind that there is not just a single DV codec out there. Many companies make their own codecs. DV compression is a set of specifications agreed upon by many manufacturers. This standard is known as the Blue Book standard. (Apparently the cover of the report that specifies these specs is blue!) Although it is a specification, the Blue Book standard does allow for a lot of flexibility. Apple has its version of the DV codec, and there are many others. Some are built for speed, others for accuracy. Some DV codecs are ideal for playback but not for compressing graphics. These codecs are made by companies such as Pinnacle Systems, DPS, FireMax, and others. Promax offers a DV toolkit that provides a flexible and very useful DV codec.

If you're using your basic Mac OS on a G4 or an iMac (flat panel G4) with a DV camera and Final Cut Pro, you're most likely working with the Apple DV codec. Apple has made numerous changes in their codec to improve color, luminance handling, compression, and decompression. For all intents and purposes, you can use the current Apple DV codec without worrying about the clamping issues I just described.

The Future of DV

The original DV standard is more specifically known as DV25. The 25 stands for the data rate of DV, which is 25Mbps. That's 25 mega*bits* per second, which works out to 3.6 mega*bytes* per second (remember, 8 bits = 1 byte, 1,024 bytes = 1 kilobyte, and 1,024 kilobytes = 1 megabyte).

Two emerging DV standards are known as DV50 and DV100. Both the 50 and the 100 signify the data rate of these future standards. The DV50 standard uses the 4:2:2 sampling rate and, due to its high data rate, has a compression ratio of 3:1. The DV100 standard is for use in High-Definition Television (HDTV), an emerging standard for broadcast that is of extremely high quality.

Two years ago, this book forecasted a bright and shiny future for the burgeoning DV format. Since then, DV has not only become ubiquitous, but the continued advances in hardware, software, and supporting infrastructure protocols seem to foreshadow more than just consumer popularity. DV in all its variant forms has become a force to reckon with. Is it indeed safe to say DV is here to stay?

✦   ✦   ✦

Understanding Broadcast Video

Without a doubt, digital video is taking over. Much of the post-production world has switched to nonlinear editing. However, analog video is not dead quite yet. For many practical and valid reasons, analog formats are still a large presence in the world of video production. In fact, most video-tape formats these days are still analog. With few exceptions, like DV and Digital Betacam, most broadcast work is still done in analog formats such as Betacam SP, VHS, and U-Matic.

There are two important reasons to continue to care about analog video:

+ **Analog video is still around.** For users starting out their video careers on nonlinear editing applications such as Final Cut Pro, analog video presents a puzzle of sorts. DV decks are quite different from analog decks such as a Betacam SP unit.

+ **Different though digital and analog video may be, there are still many areas of overlap between these two types of video.** The recent revolution in digital video started with analog video, and understanding the basics of analog video is a huge help when you have to troubleshoot video problems. Many of the concepts of digital video have evolved from analog video. For example, color bars were originally invented for analog video, and are still used in digital video. Color bars are just one concept of analog video that has crossed over into digital. This and other crossover concepts will be discussed in this chapter.

This chapter provides a refresher of sorts on the technical aspects of the video signal. Over the years, some misconceptions and misunderstandings have arisen over what the video signal consists of and some of the criteria used to compare various signals. This chapter provides coverage that helps you understand the key concepts.

◆ ◆ ◆ ◆

In This Chapter

Understanding interlaced and progressive scanning

Working with different tape formats

Using color bars

Understanding waveform and vectorscope

Using high-end video cards

◆ ◆ ◆ ◆

Understanding Interlaced and Progressive Scanning

Video signals can be divided into two categories based on how they are scanned. Video signals are either *interlaced* or *progressively scanned* (progressive scanning is sometimes called *non-interlaced scanning*). In interlaced scanning, each frame of video consists of two fields that are drawn on the TV screen in two passes. With progressive scanning, however, the entire video frame is drawn from top to bottom in a single pass. Video using NTSC, PAL, or SECAM standards uses interlaced scanning. NTSC is the video standard used in North America, while PAL and SECAM are used in Europe and other parts of the world. Computer screens, on the other hand, use progressive scanning. Figure 3-1 illustrates the difference between interlaced and progressive scanning.

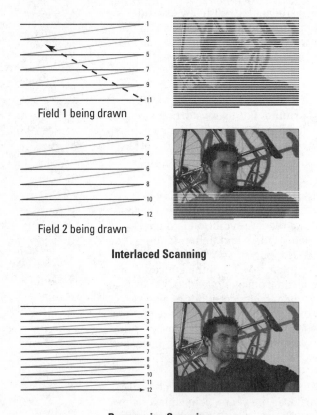

Field 1 being drawn

Field 2 being drawn

Interlaced Scanning

Progressive Scanning

Figure 3-1: Interlaced scanning draws a frame of video in two passes. Progressive scanning draws a frame of video in a single pass.

The interlaced scanning process is relatively simple to understand. A video frame is made up of many horizontal scan lines. The first field is drawn from top to bottom. In between each scan line, the beam is turned off. This is known as the *horizontal blanking interval.* The horizontal blanking period is indicated by the light-gray lines in Figure 3-1. After finishing the first field, the beam is turned off again as it goes back to the top to draw the second field. This period is known as the *vertical blanking interval.* The dashed arrow indicates the vertical blanking interval.

In NTSC video, there are a total of 525 scan lines, drawn in two fields of 262.5 lines each. For every *second* of NTSC, there are 29.97 frames, resulting in 59.94 fields per second, and a total of 15,734 scan lines per second. Thus, in NTSC video, a single field displays for approximately 1/60th of a second. PAL and SECAM video have a frame rate of 25 fps, so the fields are displayed for 1/50th of a second each.

Why, you may be asking, did the engineers and scientists come up with such a fiendishly complicated system? Good question. Interlaced scanning, which may seem like a curse, was actually invented as an ingenious solution to two problems: the limitations of early television technology, and the phenomena of the persistence of human vision.

Video and film pictures are nothing more than a series of images being flickered fast enough to give the illusion of motion. If you don't believe me, look closely at a piece of film; it's just a series of still pictures. In order for a series of still pictures to appear in motion to human vision, the rate of the frames has to be fast enough to achieve *persistence of vision* without a flicker. If you were ever in gradeschool, you may have made a flip-book in one of your science or art classes. You can see persistence of vision at work with one of those novelty flip-books that have a series of images drawn on them. If you flip the pages of the book fast enough, the image appears to be in perfect motion without any flicker. Any slower, and the flicker increases and the images appear to be static.

Early NTSC-standard televisions were only able to show 30 *frames* per second, which isn't quite fast enough to completely achieve persistence of vision. The solution was interlaced fields. Interlacing two fields created an effective rate of 60 *fields* per second and took care of the persistence of vision issue as well. The number 60 (as opposed to, say, 50 or 70) is derived from the fact that electricity in the United States is based on a 60 Hz power cycle.

Interlacing was also invented to take care of the maddening issue of phosphor fading. Early TV screens used phosphor on the inside surface of the picture tube. The phosphor glowed when struck with the electron beam. That principle is still used today, though phosphor technology has advanced considerably. But the problem with progressive scanning on earlier phosphor picture tubes was that, by the time the electron beam reached the bottom of the frame, the top part of the frame had lost its glow and appeared darker. Interlaced scanning made the picture tube evenly bright at all times. Finally, interlacing requires much lower bandwidth to transmit a signal than progressive scanning.

Europeans use electricity that is based on a 50 Hz power cycle. Thus, they have a 50 field per second rate, resulting in a frame rate of 25 frames per second.

Understanding field order

Video formats and codecs are designed to accept the top or the bottom field as their first field. When working with video, you should always know which field is accepted first. For example, DV video always uses Field 1 (the bottom field) as its dominant field. Thus, DV video is considered lower-field dominant. If you are preparing files in Adobe's After Effects or other third-party applications and you render a DV movie using an upper-field-dominant codec, you get reversed fields. Objects moving across the screen do a nasty back-and-forth jig and have a comb-like image break up as shown in Figure 3-2.

Figure 3-2: A frame of DV video shows field breakup when played back with reversed field order.

In Final Cut Pro, you encounter two options for field dominance:

✦ **Upper:** This means that Field 2 is dominant, or that the second field is drawn first. This setting is commonly used in systems that use the frame size 640 × 480.

✦ **Lower:** Field 1 is dominant, or the first field is drawn first. Systems that use 720 × 486 or 720 × 480 (such as DV) are lower-field based.

Caution When you export a still from Final Cut Pro you see the "comb" effect on moving objects. You can remove this comb effect by applying deinterlacing. For example, in Adobe's Photoshop you can use Filter ➪ Video ➪ Deinterlace to get rid of this comb effect. The Deinterlace filter removes one of the fields from the image (you can choose which field).

A very important issue you should keep in mind is that because computer monitors are progressively scanned, they are not ideal for solving field problems. If you are working with reversed fields or movie files with other field issues, you should always attempt to look at your video on an NTSC monitor or TV that displays interlaced video.

Note A video that may appear to play fine on your computer's RGB monitor might flicker when played on an NTSC monitor.

Understanding video standards

The three common video standards are NTSC, PAL, and SECAM. Other variations exist, but these are the three big ones. Final Cut Pro is currently compatible with NTSC and PAL standards. NTSC is the video standard for North America, while PAL and SECAM are commonly used in Europe and other parts of the world. Converting between standards is done using specialized equipment.

The differences between the three dominant video standards are based on the frame rate, lines of resolution, and the sub-carrier frequency used to encode color and brightness information. For example, NTSC's higher frame rate produces less flicker than PAL or SECAM, but the better color sub-carrier frequency gives PAL and SECAM an edge over NTSC when it comes to color and hue reproduction. Table 3-1 shows the basic differences between NTSC, PAL, and SECAM.

Table 3-1		
Comparison of Video Standards		
Standard	*Frame/Field Rate*	*Lines of Resolution*
NTSC	29.97/59.94	525
PAL	25/50	625
SECAM	25/50	625

As you can see in Table 3-1, both PAL and SECAM have over 100 more lines of resolution than NTSC. (See the sidebar "Vertical versus horizontal resolution.") This translates into better resolution. However, each system has its own merits and drawbacks. The next few sections describe the strengths and weaknesses of each standard.

NTSC

NTSC stands for *National Television Standards Committee*. The NTSC standard is used in the United States, Canada, Japan, Puerto Rico, the Philippines, and other countries. Advantages of NTSC video include:

✦ **Higher frame rate:** The higher frame rate of NTSC results in reduced flicker.

✦ **Better signal-to-noise ratio:** NTSC video equipment has a better signal-to-noise ratio than PAL. This means less noise in the video signal.

NTSC has some disadvantages as well. These include:

✦ **Color and hue shifts:** Due to differences in sub-carrier frequencies, NTSC is more prone to color and hue fluctuations. (Some engineers jokingly say that NTSC stands for Never The Same Color.)

✦ **Fewer scan lines:** Fewer scan lines mean less resolution. Many people easily perceive the better picture resolution of PAL video.

✦ **Less contrast:** Due to technical specifications, NTSC has slightly less contrast than PAL or SECAM.

PAL

PAL is an acronym for *Phase Alternating Line;* it is used in Western Europe, Australia, Yemen, Malaysia, Ghana, and other countries. Advantages of PAL include:

✦ **More scan lines:** PAL has 100 more scan lines than NTSC. This results in better resolution.

✦ **Simpler frame rate:** PAL's 25 fps rate is simpler to work with. Filmmakers who shoot in video for later transfer to film prefer the PAL standard. It is much easier to transfer the 25 fps rate of PAL to film's 24 fps than it is to accomplish the same with the NTSC's odd rate of 29.97 fps.

✦ **Better brightness:** Due to better sub-carrier frequencies, PAL has slightly better brightness levels and contrast.

✦ **Stable colors and hues:** PAL has better and more-stable colors and hues.

As with NTSC, there are a few disadvantages to PAL as well. They include:

✦ **Slower frame rate:** PAL's 25 fps rate is more prone to flicker.

✦ **More noise:** PAL video equipment generally has less signal-to-noise ratio, resulting in more noise in the video signal.

Vertical versus horizontal resolution

Vertical resolution for video is determined by its scan rate. The bandwidth of the video signal determines its horizontal resolution. The scan rate of NTSC video signal draws approximately 525 lines across a TV screen; hence, that is the vertical resolution on an NTSC video signal.

Bandwidth of a video signal is the frequency range of the video signal—the higher the bandwidth, the higher the resulting horizontal resolution of a video signal.

Both vertical and horizontal resolutions are a measure of the resolving capacity of a video signal. Since vertical resolution of video is determined by its scan rate, there is no real way to improve that. (I guess the only way to improve the vertical resolution might be to redesign the entire broadcast system.) You will rarely find yourself reading about *vertical* resolution of video, since it is all the same for a given scan rate.

Horizontal resolution on the other hand is what matters and is shown as lines per inch. Manufacturers determine the horizontal resolution of equipment by using a chart with a series of patterns of lines. Cameras and other video equipment are tested with these charts and their "resolving power" determined. Note that these lines on the chart are drawn on the chart *vertically;* hence, you may find yourself staring at a *horizontal* resolution of a camera described as 500 *vertical* lines per inch. Don't let this confuse you. I'm still talking about horizontal resolution.

SECAM

SECAM stands for *Sequential Couleur Avec Memoire* (Sequential Color with Memory). This system is widely used in France and Eastern Europe. Many other countries, such as Egypt, Greece, and Syria, also use SECAM systems. The advantages of SECAM include:

✦ **More scan lines:** Like PAL, SECAM has 100 more scan lines than NTSC. This results in better resolution.

✦ **Stable colors and hues:** SECAM has better and more-stable colors and hues. In fact, its color rendition is considered superior to PAL.

The disadvantages of SECAM are:

✦ **Slower frame rate:** Like PAL's 25 fps rate, SECAM is more prone to flicker.

✦ **Too many variations:** There are different, often politically inspired, versions of SECAM. These versions are generally incompatible with one another.

Working with Different Tape Formats

Do you remember the VHS versus Betamax war? There was a time when JVC's VHS format and Sony's Betamax format competed for the hearts and minds of American consumers. Today, the format war is a distant memory. JVC's VHS tapes, for a variety of marketing reasons, won out over Betamax. Sony's format was *technically* superior, which goes to show you that just because some technology is better doesn't mean it is going to prevail. Marketing has just as much, if not more, to do with which technology prevails.

Note

Another reason Sony's Betamax format may have lost is due to the fact that the early Betamax tapes were one hour long — too short for a movie. The two-hour VHS format was ideally suited for movies.

These days there are more tape formats than you can count. Starting with the basic VHS, we now have S-VHS (Super VHS), VHS-C (a smaller version of VHS), as well as 8mm, Hi-8, and industrial formats such as ¾-inch Umatic and ¾-inch Umatic SP. In the professional market, by far the most dominant format is the Sony Betacam SP.

Various digital formats have also tried to dominate the format market. Before the advent of mini-DV, DVCAM, and DVCPRO, there were the D-1, D-2, D-3, and D-5 format tapes (there was never a D-4 format). There are even some consumer digital camcorders that use a format called Digital8, which records DV-format video on Hi-8 tapes. Some of the more-common formats are listed in Table 3-2, along with factors in which they differ, such as tape width, signal type, and lines of resolution. (See the sidebar "Lines aren't everything.")

Table 3-2 Tape Format Details			
Tape Format	**Tape Width**	**Signal Type**	**Horizontal Resolution in Lines**
8mm	8mm	Composite	260
Hi-8	8mm	Y/C	400
VHS	½ inch	Composite	250
S-VHS	½ inch	Y/C	400
¾-inch Umatic	¾ inch	Composite	280
¾-inch Umatic-SP	¾ inch	Composite	340
Betacam	½ inch	Component	300
Betacam SP	½ inch	Component	340
M-II	½ inch	Component	340
1-Inch-C	1 inch	Composite	360

Tape Format	Tape Width	Signal Type	Horizontal Resolution in Lines
D-1	¾ inch	Component-Digital	460
D-2	¾ inch	Composite-Digital	450
D-3	½ inch	Composite-Digital	450
D-5	½ inch	Component-Digital	450
DV	½ inch	Digital	500
DV-CAM	¼ inch	Digital	Over 500
DVC-PRO	¼ inch	Digital	Over 500
Digital-S	½ inch	Digital	Over 500
Betacam-SX	½ inch	Digital	Over 500

Cross-Reference

In case you're wondering why DVCPRO50 is not included in the preceding table, remember that DVCPRO50 is a broadcast-quality *codec,* not a tape format. DVCPRO50-capable cameras and decks use DVCPRO metal tape stock. Chapter 2 covers codecs and tape formats in detail.

The following is a more detailed look at each of the common tape formats that you may encounter:

✦ **VHS:** VHS is the dominant format for home video. It is omnipresent and useful for production workflow. Making VHS copies of high-end tape formats with timecode burn-ins (also known as *window dubs*) is general practice. VHS uses a composite signal and offers poor quality for shooting just about anything.

✦ **S-VHS:** Super VHS was invented to address the shortcomings of VHS. S-VHS has better resolution and luminance ranges and performs better than VHS. S-VHS VTRs (*video tape recorder* is the professional jargon for VCR, or *video cassette recorder*) can play VHS tapes as well. Both S-VHS and Hi-8 tape formats have the reputation for being the first *prosumer* formats. (Prosumer is a commercially coined term for products that fall between professional and consumer quality, features and cost.) With a high-priced S-VHS camcorder you could get some decent looking footage. Figure 3-3 shows the VHS and the S-VHS format tapes.

✦ **8mm:** This format has a slightly better quality than VHS, but not by much. 8mm is almost never used for TV production. This format was convenient because the tapes were smaller and the 8mm camcorders were small and easy to use.

✦ **Hi-8:** Sony came up with this format and caused a wave of excitement among independent videographers. The quality of Hi-8 was superior to that of VHS and 8mm and was used in producing many documentaries. Hi-8 tapes are also used by Digital8 camcorders. Figure 3-4 shows the Hi-8 format tapes.

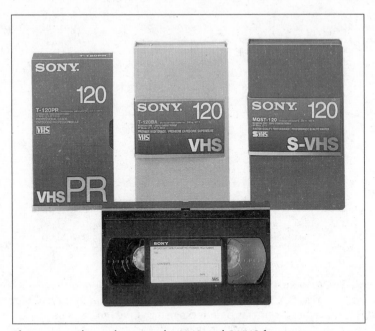

Figure 3-3: Shown here are the VHS and S-VHS format tapes.
Photo courtesy of Sony

Figure 3-4: The Hi-8 format tapes are shown in this figure.
Photo courtesy of Sony

✦ **¾-inch Umatic:** Umatic format (see Figure 3-5) was a Sony professional standard that became popular in the 1970s and 1980s that is still used in many production houses and cable channels today. The tape shell for a Umatic tape is quite large and cumbersome. A later development of an SP version of the ¾-inch format produced better resolution and color and brightness quality.

Figure 3-5: The Umatic format tapes from Sony.
Photo courtesy of Sony

✦ **Betacam SP:** Betacam SP is the dominant analog standard in the current professional and broadcast market. It has managed to hold up fairly well in the face of the DV onslaught. The popularity of this format can be seen in the fact that the DV format is most often compared to Betacam SP. Many production houses that hoped to save their budgets by investing in DV equipment and facilities instead of Betacam SP were disappointed. In 1993, Sony introduced the Digital Betacam format. This is an expensive format but its quality is exceptional. The Betacam-SP-format tapes are shown in Figure 3-6.

✦ **M-II:** This format was invented by Panasonic Corporation to compete with Sony's Betacam SP. M-II has a comparable quality to Betacam SP but costs a bit less than Sony's Betacam SP equipment.

✦ **1-Inch-C:** The 1-Inch-C format, shown in Figure 3-7, became famous during the Los Angeles and Seoul Olympic Games. The 1-Inch-C format is known for its ultra-smooth slow-motion and freeze-frame capabilities. Other higher- end formats, such as Betacam-SP, have displaced this format. These days the 1-Inch-C format is only used for its superior freeze-frame and slow-motion capabilities. Use of the 1-inch-C format is mostly reserved for sporting events.

Figure 3-6: Sony's Betacam SP format is a long-standing broadcast standard.

Photo courtesy of Sony

Figure 3-7: The 1-Inch-C format tapes are used in sports for their ultra-smooth slow-motion capabilities.

Photo courtesy of Sony

✦ **D-1:** D-1 format (see Figure 3-8) is a component-digital format introduced by Sony around 1986. The image quality is good but D-1 tapes and VTRs are expensive, large, and cumbersome. Some Sony D-1 VTRs cost upward of $100,000. Ouch!

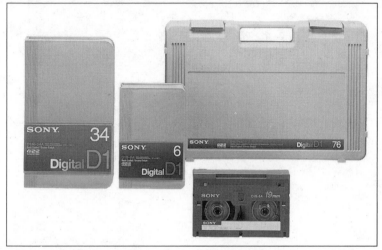

Figure 3-8: The D-1 format is a component digital format from Sony.
Photo courtesy of Sony

✦ **D-2:** This is a digital format created by Ampex. It is limited by being a composite format. Like D-1, D-2 is large, cumbersome, and expensive. Figure 3-9 shows the D-2 format tapes.

✦ **D-3:** Not wanting to be left behind, Panasonic introduced the D-3 format in 1991. Unlike the D-1 and D-2 formats which use a ¾-inch wide tape, D-3 uses a ½-inch-wide tape. This makes the tapes for D-3 smaller and the VTRs more manageable in size. The size of the D-3 also makes it possible to have D-3 camcorders for professional use.

✦ **D-4:** There is no D-4. (Rumor has it that Japanese consider 4 an unlucky number.)

✦ **D-5:** Panasonic improved on D-3 and introduced the D-5 format. This is a digital format that uses a 10-bit Component 4:2:2 path, and its picture is better than D-3.

✦ **DV, DVCAM:** DV is the digital format that revolutionized the "prosumer" market. The picture quality is excellent and the size of the tapes and cameras makes it possible for the format to be used as a first-rate acquisition format. DVCAM and DVCPRO are larger-size versions of mini-DV that were invented to address the shortcomings of the mini-DV format in the post-production environment. Shown in Figure 3-10 are the DVCAM tapes from Sony.

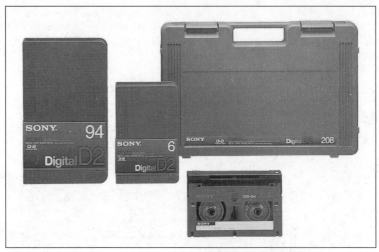

Figure 3-9: The D-1 format is a composite signal format.
Photo courtesy of Sony

Figure 3-10: The DVCAM format has the same compression and image quality as the consumer mini-DV tapes.
Photo courtesy of Sony

Cross-Reference   For more on the DV format, see Chapter 2.

✦ **Digital 8:** This format is worth mentioning here because it is quite popular these days. Sony created Digital 8 to provide a cost-effective alternative to mini-DV and for reasons of backward compatibility. Digital 8 format is recorded on analog 8mm or Hi-8 tapes. However, the signal uses the same compression and quality as the DV format. In short, you can record DV on an 8mm or a Hi-8 tape in a Digital 8 camcorder. Digital 8 camcorders also play 8mm and Hi-8 tapes. You can record 60 minutes of DV material on a 120-minute 8mm or Hi-8 tape when using a Digital 8 camcorder. Sony recommends that if you are using 8mm tapes, for best results, you should record and play-back on the same camcorder.

✦ **Betacam SX:** Even though Digital Betacam is fast becoming the preferred tape standard for post-production, the tapes are expensive and the decks (and cameras, too) are prohibitively expensive for all but post-production houses. Betacam SX (see Figure 3-11) was developed as an alternative to Digital Betacam; it is an unusual format that uses MPEG-2 compression for its tape. Betacam SX allows users to not only play, but record on regular Betacam SP tapes. However, when recording on analog Betacam SP tapes, you get a digital signal that can only be read back on an SX format deck. By making the SX decks cheaper than the SP decks, Sony is hoping to get a bigger share of the professional digital market.

Figure 3-11: The DVCAM format has the same compression and image quality as the consumer mini-DV tapes.

Photo courtesy of Sony

✦ **HDCAM:** Sony's HDCAM format was created to fulfill the needs of the new and emerging DTV (Digital Television) market, including HDTV (High-Definition Television). HDCAM format tapes (see Figure 3-12) use the same physical characteristics as that of a Betacam SP tapes, which makes them portable and easy to manage. The HDCAM format records four channels of uncompressed audio and uses the Dolby-E-type audio format. Dolby-E-format audio is the emerging standard for digital surround-sound production and its use in the HDCAM format results in an effective eight channels of editable audio channels.

Figure 3-12: The HDCAM format tapes are used for recording HDTV (High-Definition Television) video.

Photo courtesy of Sony

Working with Betacam SP

If you work in a high-end post house where you do lots of commercials, you may be intimately familiar with the D-series VTRs. On the other hand, you may have invested less than $10,000 in hardware and work from production to post entirely in the DV world. Ultimately, the choice of which format you work in is dictated primarily by your own pocketbook. For example, the D-series digital tapes are top quality, but their extremely high costs keep most users away from them. A basic D-2 machine can run upward of $70,000!

Lines aren't everything

Just because a format has more lines of resolution, that does not automatically make it superior. Many other factors can influence the overall picture quality. If you just look at the number of lines it may seem like the picture quality of ¾-inch Umatic rivals that of Betacam SP, but in reality this is not the case. Other factors to consider are signal-to-noise ratios, and the frequency used to encode the color and brightness signals. Signal-to-noise ratios describe the relationship of valid signal to the electronic noise present in the video. Betacam SP also uses a component signal rather than the composite signal of ¾-inch Umatic. Component signals are far superior to composite in terms of quality and color purity. Likewise, some of the D formats have fewer lines of resolution than DV, but some of these D formats are uncompressed and produce unparalleled picture quality.

Another point to consider is that even though the 720 × 480 frame size may make it seem like DV has 720 lines of resolution, the process required to extrapolate a true horizontal resolution from a frame size number brings this down to around 500. Even then most DV cameras are hard-pressed to capture anywhere near 400 lines. The Canon XL-1, GL-2, and the Sony DSR-PD150 are three exceptions because they are DV cameras that come near to, or exceed, capturing 500 lines of resolution.

On the other end of the spectrum, VHS tapes are cheap but low quality. The ¾-inch Umatic format dominated the production market for decades, but it has been fading in recent years. The one contender that is strong in the professional market is the Sony Betacam SP format. Because Betacam SP is one of the most widely used formats in the professional market, this chapter covers it in a bit more depth. However, it avoids the Betacam-SP-versus-DV debate and focuses instead on covering the Betacam SP format here because so many users of Final Cut Pro run into it and don't know enough about it.

Note   Betacam SP is *one* of the variations of the Betacam format. The others are Digital Betacam and Betacam SX. The tape shells for Betacam are similar to the old Sony Betamax format, the one that lost out to VHS in the home format wars.

The *SP* in Betacam stands for *Superior Performance.* The SP version is vastly superior to the original Betacam format. The Betacam SP format uses metal oxide tapes, which are superior to the original Betacam's oxide tapes because they have better frequency carriers and improved picture quality. The SP version also has superior hi-fi sound.

Betacam SP has managed to maintain its grip on the professional and broadcast industry for many reasons. One of those reasons is that Betacam SP uses a *component signal.* This means that the chroma and luma information is recorded on separate paths on the tape, giving a far superior picture. The Achilles heel of the basic

composite signal is the leakage of luminance information and chrominance information into one another. By separating the recording and travel paths, Betacam SP provides a better picture. A component signal also travels over separate wires meant
for luma and chroma. This produces a superior color and brightness. Component
signals also make Betacam SP ideal for effects processing and other post-production needs. Figure 3-13 shows the track layout for Sony's Betacam SP tape format.

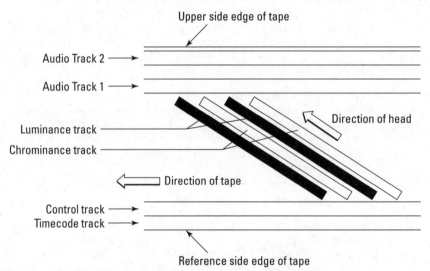

Figure 3-13: Track layout for Sony's Betacam SP tape format.

Cross-
Reference   For more information on the component video signal, see Chapter 2.

Betacam SP tapes come in two shell sizes: small and large. Most Betacam SP VTRs
handle both sizes of SP tapes. The small size SP tapes come in running times of
5 to 30 minutes, whereas the large-sized tapes come in the lengths of 5 to 90 minutes.
The Betacam SP tapes have reusable record-prevention tabs. These tabs are red
and are located along the bottom edge of the SP tapes. Pressing them in prevents
accidental erasure. Pulling them out allows recording. Figure 3-14 shows the two
Betacam SP tape sizes and the location of their record-prevention tabs.

Because Betacam SP records brightness and color information on separate tracks
using separate heads, it has a much larger bandwidth to work with and much greater
accuracy for recording and playback reliability. What is incredible about Betacam
SP is that despite being an analog format, it handles multigenerational loss quite
well. When making dubs, loss of chrominance and luminance, as well as dot-crawl,
cross color, and other issues, are minimized.

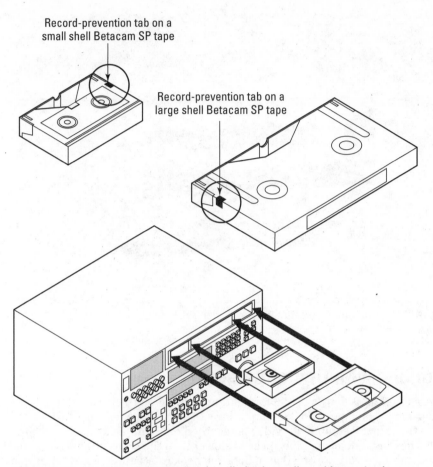

Record-prevention tab on a
small shell Betacam SP tape

Record-prevention tab on a
large shell Betacam SP tape

Figure 3-14: Most Betacam SP VTRs handle both small- and large-sized tapes.
Record-prevention tabs are located along the bottom edge of Betacam SP tapes.

Betacam SP VTRs cover a wide range of levels and prices. The original SP VTR series
is the BVW-series. In 1993, Sony began the UVW and then later the PVW-series of
Betacam SP decks. The BVW models for SP are the most expensive and have the
most features. A BVW model deck can cost as much as $75,000. Sony introduced the
UVW-series Betacam SP decks as a more affordable line of VTRs. These decks can
cost from $5,000 to $7,000. The UVW-series decks often lack high-end features such
as dynamic motion control and Hi-Fi audio tracks. Figure 3-15 shows the UVW-1800
Betacam SP deck from Sony.

Figure 3-15: The Sony Betacam SP deck model UVW-1800.
Photo courtesy of Sony

Working with Digital Betacam

Digital Betacam is Sony's digital format that is based on the basic mechanics of Betacam SP. The tapes and decks for Sony's Digital Betacam format look quite similar to Betacam SP equipment. Video is recorded on Digital Betacam in a digital format. The Digital Betacam tape speed is slower than the conventional Betacam SP decks, but the heads for the Digital Betacam deck rotate three times faster than the regular Betacam SP. Digital Betacam tapes are durable and can handle a huge number of passes before showing any significant degradation.

Note   Digital Betacam is often known by the terms D-Beta or Digibeta as well.

This format employs expensive tapes and decks, but the quality of video on Digital Betacam is extremely high. It is commonly used in situations where the only previous alternative was the D-1 format. For example, one of the more common uses of Digital Betacam is to use it for telecine transfers from film.

Digital Betacam uses DCT (Discrete Cosine Transform) and BRR (Bit Rate Reduction) for recording its signal. Using DCT compression, the redundant data from the video is compressed and then re-created on the fly for playback. Most current video formats are based on 8-bit systems. Digital Betacam is a 10-bit system. An 8-bit system, such as D-1, is limited to producing 250 values for brightness. A Digital Betacam format, with its 10-bit image system, can replicate 1,000 values of brightness. The 10-bit feature is what makes the Digital Betacam format the choice of telecine houses when transferring film to tape because Telecine units work in 10-bit mode.

Digital Betacam also has four independent channels of uncompressed audio. This format uses 20-bit audio, an improvement over the 16-bit audio used by some systems. Figure 3-16 shows the basic track layout of Sony's Digital Betacam format. Note that audio tracks in this format have been placed in the center of the tape. This prevents edge damage and avoids tracking problems caused by stretching of the tape.

Digital Betacam decks, or "Digi-Beta" decks as they are affectionately called by their users, are reasonably versatile. Digital Betacam decks have digital inputs, such as SDI (Serial Digital Interface). SDI is also known by the official title SMPTE 259M. An SDI signal consists of an uncompressed digital-video signal and four discrete digital channels of audio. However, these decks do not have FireWire inputs or outputs. Digital Betacam decks also have analog component inputs and outputs. The combination of component and digital is a boon for post houses. For post-production facilities, component transfers are the best way to go, and keeping the signal digital is an added bonus.

Heads up

When a Betacam SP tape is inserted into a VTR, the tape gets pulled out and wrapped around the video head assembly as shown here.

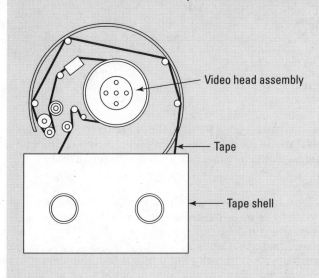

Video head assembly

Tape

Tape shell

Continued

Continued

In a Betacam SP tape, the video signal is recorded by separating the color information from the brightness information. The Y symbol represents the luminance or brightness, and the C symbol is used to indicate the color information. The C head records the color information, while the Y head records the brightness information. The ½-inch tape of the Betacam SP format goes around the head of the VTR, and the information is recorded on the tape as shown here.

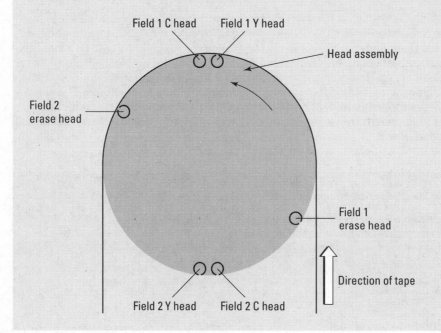

Field 1 C head   Field 1 Y head

Head assembly

Field 2 erase head

Field 1 erase head

Direction of tape

Field 2 Y head   Field 2 C head

Many third-party video cards that can be used with Final Cut Pro have an SDI interface. These cards can connect directly to Digital Betacam decks. In lieu of SDI, you can also use a card with a component video interface to connect to a Digital Betacam deck.

On some Digital Betacam decks, it is possible to play back regular Betacam SP tapes. However, these decks tend to be more expensive than ones that simply play Digital Betacam tapes. A Digital Betacam deck that plays back analog SP tapes has the letter *A* in its model number. The DVW-A500 is one of these decks. The simpler DVW-500 cannot play SP tapes. Figure 3-17 shows a Sony Digital Betacam deck.

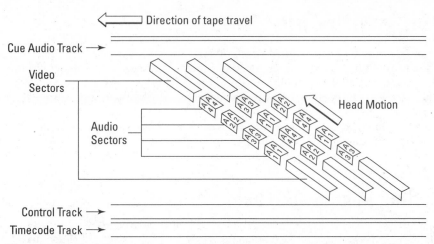

Figure 3-16: Track layout for Sony's Digital Betacam format places the audio in the center of the tape.

Figure 3-17: The Sony Digital Betacam deck model DVW-A500.
Photo courtesy of Sony

Working with Color Bars

Color bars are at once the most common and the most misunderstood aspect of video production. Color bars are used in professional and broadcast environments for calibration. While shooting footage in the field, color bars are placed at the head of tapes. These bars are used as references when digitizing footage into a nonlinear editing system. This ensures accurate color, hue, and brightness while capturing. While making a layback to tape of your final edit, these bars are again placed at the head of the master tape. Production facilities use the bars on your master tape to make accurately calibrated dubs for color and other information.

Getting to know the bars

This section takes a closer look at the bars: what they are and what they tell you. Figure 3-18 shows the SMPTE color bars. The SMPTE bars are also known as *split field bars*. You may see a few other color bar patterns in your work, but the SMPTE pattern is the most common.

Section 1

Section 2

Section 3

Figure 3-18: A split-field SMPTE color bar pattern has three basic sections.

The SMPTE bars can be broken down into three sections. These sections are:

✦ **Section 1:** The top two-thirds section of a color bar pattern includes seven strips. These strips consist of white and six primary colors at 75 percent amplitude and 100 percent saturation. The order of the strips is white, yellow, cyan, green, magenta, red, and blue.

✦ **Section 2:** The middle section of the narrow small bars represents the color pattern in Section 1 but with two differences. The sequence of colors in Section 1 is reversed and the green color is removed. The color order for Section 2 is blue, black, magenta, black, cyan, black, and blue.

✦ **Section 3:** The left portion of this section contains pure –I and +Q signals. These two signals were originally designed to calibrate NTSC color, but IQ type color encoding is no longer used, so you can safely ignore them. The right portion of Section 3 contains the PLUGE line or *picture line-up generation equipment* line. PLUGE is a set of three black strips. The center strip is black, while the one on the left is slightly darker than black and the one on the right is slightly brighter than black. IRE values (described in the next section) are used to precisely set the brightness levels of the PLUGE. The PLUGE line is used to adjust the brightness and contrast of a monitor.

Figure 3-19 illustrates the section breakdown of the SMPTE color bars.

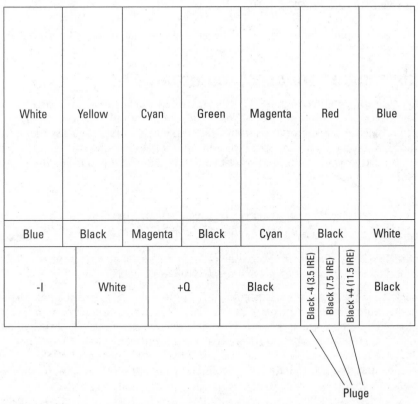

Figure 3-19: Each portion of the SMPTE color bar pattern has a specific purpose.

Understanding IREs

Luminance (also called *brightness*) values of a video image are measured in IREs. IRE is an acronym for *Institute of Radio Engineers.* IREs describe the amplitude of a video signal. On the IRE scale, 100 represents absolute white while 7.5 IRE represents pure black in the American NTSC video standard. NTSC in Japan uses 0 IRE to describe pure black. PAL also uses 0 IRE for pure black.

When working with video for broadcast, you should try to keep your brightness values between 7.5 and 100 IREs for American NTSC. Color bars, when generated by professional-grade equipment, are calibrated to precise IRE values. Waveform monitors show the IRE values for a video signal.

The issue of brightness values has gotten a bit murky lately due to the popularity of DV. DV camcorders often record *super whites* (signals that are above the "legal" 100 IRE limit are called super whites and include bright lights and highlights). If you are preparing your program for American broadcast, take care to maintain the brightness levels between 7.5 IRE and 100 IREs.

Cross-Reference   For more information on legal and illegal brightness values, see Chapter 2.

Calibrating a broadcast monitor

When calibrating a video signal, ideally you should work with a Waveform monitor and Vectorscope. If you don't have those items, your monitor becomes the reference to rely upon. This should be your first step when working with video. If the NTSC or PAL monitor you are using for editing or checking shots in the field is not calibrated properly for color and brightness, it could cause you to misjudge your exposure and color values.

Life behind bars

Besides the SMPTE-style color bars, you may often find yourself staring at other color bar patterns. Don't worry. These variations are rare and are easily explained.

First of all, keep in mind that color bars come in 75 percent or 100 percent amplitude versions. The percentage refers to the *amplitude* of the signal, not the *saturation* of the colors. The 100 percent variations are only found in full-field bars, which are bars that cover the full screen with long strips of color bars. SMPTE color bars, which are split-field color bars, are always 75 percent. Whenever possible use 75 percent amplitude, split-field, or SMPTE color bars for calibration. These are the most reliable and have the most checks and balances built into them. Other types of color bars include:

✦ **EIA Color Bars:** EIA Stands for Electronic Industries Association. The EIA bars consist of eight full-field color bars with black, white, and the six primary colors. All the bars except black are at 75 percent amplitude and 100 percent saturation. EIA color bars like the ones shown here are most often used with NTSC video.

✦ **EBU Color Bars:** EBU is an acronym for European Broadcast Union. The EBU bars are exactly the same as the EIA bars, with one exception; the white bar at the far left is at 100 percent amplitude. EBU bars, as you may have guessed from the name, are commonly used with the PAL standard video. An EBU-style color bar pattern is shown here.

Continued

Continued

✦ **Luma Step Patterns:** You may occasionally see five-step or ten-step luma patterns. These patterns should appear on a monitor as a smooth transition between black and white. No coloration should be visible. On a waveform monitor, these step patterns appear as a stair-step. For this reason luma bars like the ones shown here are also known as stair step bars.

5 Step luma pattern

10 Step luma pattern

Caution   The calibration steps in this section apply to the TV or broadcast monitor you are using to view your video, *not* your computer monitor.

Calibrating your broadcast monitor ensures that you are viewing accurate colors and brightness levels on your monitor. To calibrate your monitor using color bars:

1. Turn on your monitor and let it warm up for about 10 to 15 minutes.

Calibrating a monitor from a cold start is not recommended.

2. **Feed the color bars through your monitor.**

I strongly suggest that if you have professional color bar generating equipment, you should use that to feed color bars into your monitor. Otherwise, you can use Final Cut Pro's bars to feed them into the monitor. To use bars from Final Cut Pro, start up Final Cut Pro, and in the View window select Bars and Tone (NTSC) from the pull-down menu (marked with a small film-strip icon and the letter *A*) on the lower-right corner of the window. Make sure these bars appear in your monitor.

3. **Turn the Chroma or color knob on your monitor *all the way down*.**

This step is important for true brightness and contrast adjustment.

4. **First adjust the brightness of the monitor.**

Look at the PLUGE line as you adjust the brightness. The PLUGE line, shown in Figure 3-20, consists of three black strips in the lower-right portion of the color bars. The middle strip is black, while the one on the left is slightly darker than black and the one on the right is slightly brighter than black. As you adjust the brightness, the middle and the left bar should merge into one another, while the right side bar remains barely visible.

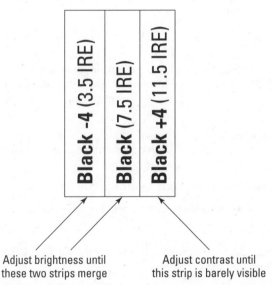

Adjust brightness until these two strips merge

Adjust contrast until this strip is barely visible

Figure 3-20: Adjust the brightness and contrast on your monitor using the PLUGE portion of the color bars. Make sure that the color is turned all the way down before making this adjustment.

5. Now adjust the contrast.

Turn the contrast up on your monitor so that the right PLUGE bar becomes bright. Then turn the contrast down until this bar goes back to being barely visible. This is your correct contrast setting.

Another way to adjust your contrast is to turn up the contrast until the white patch on the lower-left side of the color bars spills over to the neighboring bars. Then turn the contrast back down until it does not spill over anymore.

6. The next step is to adjust the hue and chroma of your monitor.

To do so you must have a Blue Only setting on your monitor. The Blue Only setting uses only the blue gun of the monitor and turns the color bars into a black-and-white pattern. If you have a Blue Only setting on your monitor, turn it on.

If you do not have a Blue Only setting on your monitor, you can use a blue filter. A Wratten 47B blue filter is available from professional photo stores. Look at the monitor through the filter while adjusting for hue.

7. While the Blue Only setting is on, adjust the hue (may also be marked phase or tint) on your monitor until the third bar from the left (cyan) and third bar from the right (magenta) appear to match the brightness and contrast of the small bars under them.

The bars appear as shades of gray at this point, but just go ahead and match them as best as possible.

8. While the Blue Only setting is on, adjust the color (may also be labeled chroma) until the outermost bars (white on the far left and blue on the far right) appear to match the brightness and contrast of the small bars under them.

The bars appear as shades of gray at this point, but just go ahead and match these as best as possible. Figure 3-21 illustrates the adjustment procedure for hue and color.

9. Turn off the Blue Only setting on your monitor.

Your monitor should now be calibrated for accurate brightness, contrast, hue, and color.

It is important that you adjust your monitor in the proper order. Start with brightness, then contrast, hue, and finally color.

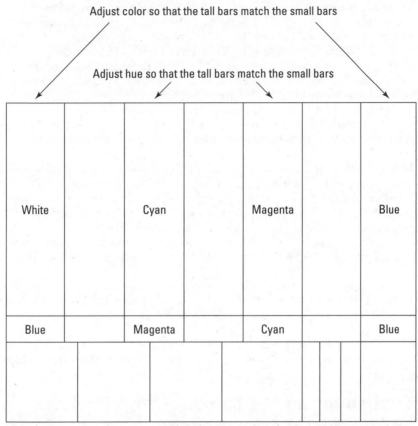

Figure 3-21: Adjust the hue and color on your monitor using color bars. Make sure the Blue Only setting on your monitor is on for this adjustment.

Working with Waveform Monitors and Vectorscopes

For a professional broadcast setup, the integrity of the video signal is a constant concern. Shots in the field and in the studio can often exceed "legal" brightness and color values. Using NTSC or PAL picture monitors to judge the absolute values of brightness levels in a video image is unreliable to say the least.

In today's broadcast environment, images for video can also originate from software applications such as Adobe Photoshop, Illustrator, or After Effects. None of these programs was specifically designed for a broadcast environment. It is very easy to have colors and brightness values in images created in these programs that far exceed the "legal" NTSC values as set by the Federal Communications Commission (FCC). The FCC has set stringent technical standards for brightness and color values of video signals that can be broadcast in the United States. If you flaunt these rules, you may find that many broadcast houses return your master tape and refuse to broadcast it until it meets the FCC technical standards. This is one of the areas where it really pays to know what you are putting out as defined by NTSC.

In a professional broadcast environment *Waveform monitors* and *Vectorscopes* are used to check the luminance and chrominance values of a video signal. Waveform monitors display the brightness information, while Vectorscopes are used to check the color and hue of a video signal. A Waveform monitor can actually tell you a lot more about a video signal than just the brightness. But for now, this section focuses on the topics that are important to you as you prepare video from Final Cut Pro. The infinite details of a Waveform monitor are enough to fill a book of their own.

Waveform monitors and Vectorscopes are instruments that overlap in function and usually complement each other, so they are often placed side by side in editing setups. Figure 3-22 shows a Waveform monitor and a Vectorscope.

Cross-Reference Final Cut Pro has a built-in Waveform monitor and Vectorscope. See Chapter 7 for more on using Final Cut Pro's built-in Waveform monitor and Vectorscope.

Configuring analog hardware for Waveform and Vectorscope monitoring

If you have a separate Waveform monitor and Vectorscope, you need to set up your hardware properly to check the brightness and color values of your video signal. Even though Final Cut Pro has a built-in Waveform monitor and Vectorscope, these are only good for basic use. For any high-end professional and broadcast work, you should have a separate Waveform monitor and Vectorscope connected to your video editing setup.

A processing amplifier is commonly added along with the Waveform monitor and Vectorscope. Adding a processing amplifier allows you to control the brightness and the color information of your video signal while viewing it on the Waveform monitor and Vectorscope. Figure 3-23 shows a basic setup using a third-party analog video card with Final Cut Pro.

In an analog setup, the video output on the analog VTR is fed into a processing amplifier. Processing amplifiers (also called a *Proc Amp* by "in the know" professionals) allow you to control the brightness, contrast, hue, and chroma of a video signal. In some cases, TBCs (Time Base Correctors) also have built-in controls for adjusting similar settings for a video signal.

Waveform monitor

Vectorscope

Figure 3-22: Waveform monitors are used to check the luminance values of your video image. Vectorscopes are used for monitoring hue and color values.
Images courtesy of Tektronix

The output of the processing amplifier should be fed into the analog capture card you are using in your computer. The output of the analog card feeds the NTSC or PAL monitor you are using. Most professional-level monitors have a *loop-through* feature. The loop-through feature allows you to input video into the monitor and pass the same video signal back out, as well. You can take the output of the monitor and feed the Waveform monitor and Vectorscope with it. Most Waveform monitors and Vectorscopes have loop-through features as well.

Cross-Reference In the absence of a processing amplifier, Final Cut Pro's own image adjustment controls can be used. To find out more information about Final Cut Pro's image adjustment controls, see Chapter 7.

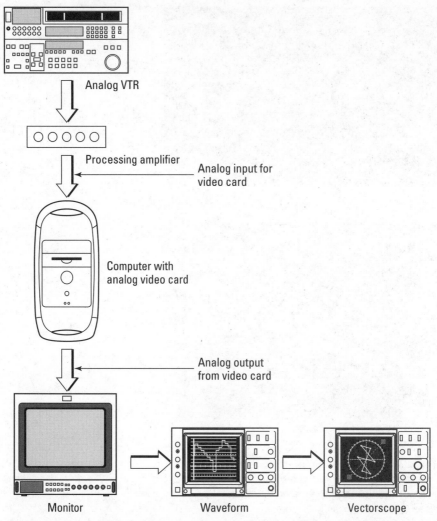

Figure 3-23: A possible hardware configuration using a third-party video card in a Final Cut Pro workstation is shown here.

Configuring DV hardware for Waveform and Vectorscope monitoring

Working with a DV setup using a FireWire signal path presents an interesting challenge for Final Cut Pro users. In most cases, you do not require a Waveform monitor and Vectorscope because they do not apply when capturing DV material via FireWire.

The image adjustment controls under the Clip Settings tab of the Log and Capture window are also inactive when capturing DV with a FireWire connection. The reason for this behavior is the nature of DV and FireWire. When capturing DV with FireWire, you are not "digitizing" as you do when converting analog video into digital. With DV all you are doing is a "bit copy" of your material via the FireWire cable and connector.

However, there is a complicating issue that may require a DV setup to have a Waveform monitor and Vectorscope. If you plan to capture DV via FireWire but you expect to master your edited program to analog tape for broadcast, then you must use a Waveform monitor and Vectorscope to check your signal during the output stage.

When you output DV material using FireWire, Final Cut Pro outputs black colors at the industry standard of 16 (between the video brightness level values from 16 to 235). When you master to a DV-based deck, your black values are fine. However, if you output to an analog deck you cannot be certain of the black value. Some DV decks have analog outputs that place this black value of 16 at the 7.5 IRE setting, which is correct for the NTSC system in the United States. However, some DV decks place this 16 value at 0 IREs, which is wrong for NTSC in the United States. This distinction may seem small but it can cause major problems if your plan is to broadcast from an analog tape. In this case you should use a hardware setup as shown in Figure 3-24.

What is a Time Base Corrector?

When working with analog video, mechanical variations and imperfections of the playback devices cause various problems on the tape playback. These problems can manifest themselves as slight skews at the bottom of the picture. These errors are known as *time base errors,* because they are produced by errors in the playback timing of the tape. A Time Base Corrector (TBC) can grab each frame of video on the fly and correct the time base error. In addition to correcting skews on the video image, some TBCs have controls for adjusting hue, chroma, black level, and other image settings. These settings can allow the TBC to serve the function of a processing amplifier.

Some TBCs are standalone devices that can be quite expensive. However, knowing that analog formats are susceptible to time base errors, many professional level VTR makers offer built-in TBCs in their decks. TBCs are often seen in some Betacam SP decks.

If you are digitizing ¾-inch Umatic material into Final Cut Pro or any other nonlinear editing system, you may find yourself begging for some kind of TBC. Old ¾-inch Umatic tapes and VTRs exhibit some of the worst tape skew I have ever seen. Many digital decks, such as DVCAM and DVCPRO decks also have TBCs whose entire function is image adjustment, rather than adjusting time base errors.

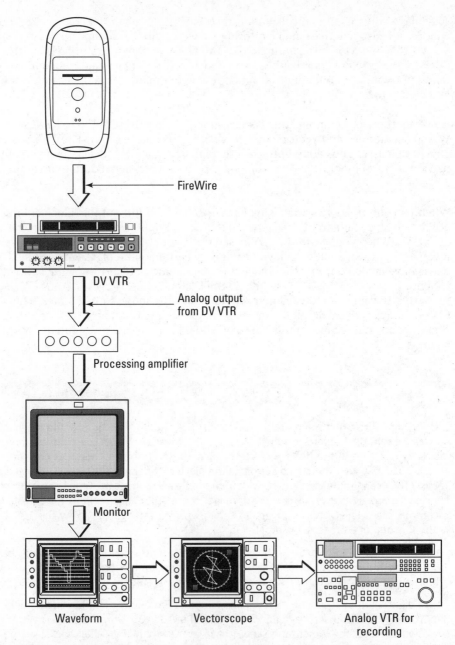

FireWire

DV VTR

Analog output
from DV VTR

Processing amplifier

Monitor

Waveform

Vectorscope

Analog VTR for
recording

Figure 3-24: Here is a possible configuration for converting DV to analog from a
Final Cut Pro workstation.

In the hardware setup shown in Figure 3-24, the FireWire cable connects the computer to the DV VTR. Connect the analog output of the DV VTR to the processing amplifier, and then loop it through the NTSC monitor, Waveform monitor, and Vectorscope. Loop the output of the Vectorscope into the analog deck. Using this setup, you can view the output of your DV material through a Waveform monitor and Vectorscope and use the processing amplifier to make adjustments to the brightness and color.

Reading a Waveform monitor

The Waveform monitor is a very sophisticated piece of equipment. It is generally used to view the luminance or brightness values of your incoming video signal. The display on the Waveform monitor has two parts: the *graticule* and the *trace*. The screen of a Waveform monitor has markings and numbers. These are known as *graticule* and are used to measure the parameters of an incoming video signal. The *trace* is the actual video signal that draws a green waveform on the display itself.

The graticule on a Waveform monitor is displayed in IRE units and ranges from –40 IRE to 100 IRE. You also notice horizontal markings and a scale at the 0 line. This scale is used for timing purposes on a waveform. Figure 3-25 shows a Waveform monitor's graticule with the trace of a color bar signal.

When first using a Waveform monitor, you should feed a color bar signal into it. When a color bar signal is fed into a Waveform monitor, you see a green waveform appear over the graticule. Figure 3-26 shows a color bar signal as it appears on a Waveform monitor.

The Waveform monitor provides a great deal of information:

✦ **Field 1 of the frame:** The waveform in Figure 3-26 is in a 2-H view. In this view, the two fields of video are shown. The first field is on the left, while the second field is on the right. Each of these fields consists of 262.5 scan lines, for a total of 525 lines for one frame of NTSC video.

✦ **Field 2 of the frame:** The second half of the waveform shows the second field.

✦ **White at 100 IRE:** The brightest section of the color bars appears at the 100 IRE mark.

✦ **Color burst:** The color burst carries reference information for the color and is inserted before each horizontal scan line.

✦ **Black at 7.5 IRE:** All the black that has an IRE value of 7.5 should be lined up along the dashed 7.5 IRE line on the Waveform monitor.

✦ **Blanking at 0 IRE:** Between drawing each scan line the electron gun is turned off or *blanked*. This is the blanking signal.

✦ **Sync Pulse:** Between the drawing of the two fields, the electron gun is turned off. The Sync Pulse controls the synchronization of the electron gun. The Sync pulse starts at 0 IRE and dips down to –40.

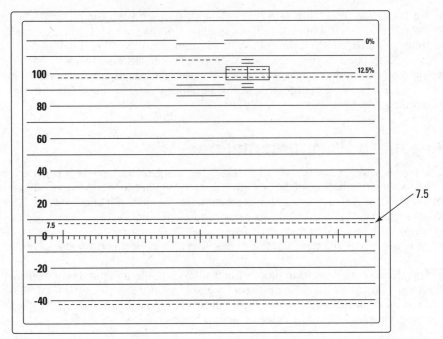

Figure 3-25: The brightness scale, or graticule, of a Waveform monitor ranges from −40 IRE to 100 IRE.

In Figure 3-26, you're actually looking at both the brightness and luminance information. If the color information were turned off, the waveform for one field would look like the one shown in Figure 3-27.

In Figure 3-27, you can see how the color bars appear as brightness values on the waveform. Note that the brightest white in the bars should be aligned precisely at 100 IRE. Note also that bars that have a black value of 7.5 IRE all appear along the same 7.5 IRE line on the graticule. The PLUGE appears as small notches at 3, 7.5, and 11.5 IREs.

There are many brands of Waveform monitors on the market. You should read the accompanying documentation for your monitor to figure out how to make precise adjustments with it. The steps below describe generally the method to use a Waveform monitor.

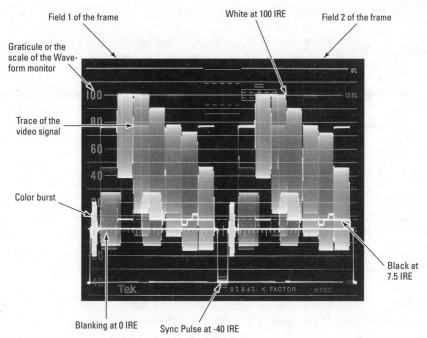

Field 1 of the frame

White at 100 IRE

Field 2 of the frame

Graticule or the scale of the Waveform monitor

Trace of the video signal

Color burst

Black at 7.5 IRE

Blanking at 0 IRE

Sync Pulse at -40 IRE

Figure 3-26: A carefully calibrated color bar signal appears like this on a Waveform monitor.

Photo courtesy of Tektronix

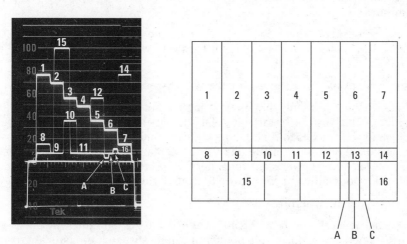

Figure 3-27: The Color information has been turned off, leaving just the brightness peaks for each color bar in the waveform.

Photo courtesy of Tektronix

To use a Waveform monitor, follow these steps:

1. **Set up your hardware so that the Waveform monitor and processing amplifier are active and are part of the signal path as described earlier in this chapter.**

    Remember that Waveform monitors do not alter any part of a video signal. The Waveform monitor is merely a measuring device. Any changes to the actual video signal must be made on a processing amplifier. This processing amplifier can be purchased as a separate unit. Some high-end analog and digital decks have built-in processing amplifiers.

2. **Feed a color bar signal into the system.**

    Make sure the color bars appear on your Waveform monitor.

3. **Align the blanking to 0 IRE. Do this using the position knob on your Waveform monitor.**

    Position knobs on most Waveform monitors move the displayed waveform up and down on the graticule. This gives you a starting reference because the blanking should *always* lie at 0 IRE.

4. **Adjust the pedestal or black level setting on your processing amplifier so that the black level, also called "set up," lines up at 7.5 IRE.**

    On most Waveform monitors, there is a dashed line on the graticule to indicate the 7.5 IRE location.

5. **Adjust the Gain setting on your processing amplifier to make sure that the 100% white patch of bars lines up to the 100 IRE setting on the Waveform monitor.**

    Sometimes you may get a "hot" signal where the whites go past 100 IRE. Figure 3-28 shows a "hot" set of color bars with whites that are topping above 100 IREs.

6. **Next, look at the Sync Pulse on your Waveform monitor.**

    The Sync Pulse is a long, thin dip that is seen between fields on the Waveform monitor. The Sync Pulse starts at the 0 IRE mark and dips down to –40. After adjusting your blacks to 7.5 IRE and whites to 100 IRE, the bottom of the sync pulse should line up automatically at the –40 mark. If the sync pulse is a few IREs off, see if your processing amplifier has a setting for *sync amplitude* adjustment. If it does, adjust it so that the bottom of the sync pulse lines up at –40.

7. **Review your final settings.**

    The black level should be at 7.5 IRE, white at 100 IRE, and the sync pulse's bottom lined up at –40. At this point you can be sure that the bars are reading correctly in the Waveform monitor.

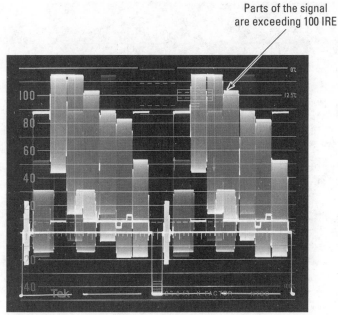

Figure 3-28: This "hot" color bars signal has some whites that exceed 100 IREs.

Photo courtesy of Tektronix

After you have checked your bars and calibrated your system, you can now capture video into your system with confidence. You should keep your eye on the Waveform monitor as you select your shots and capture them. As you play your video, the Waveform monitor draws a luminance picture of your video signal. As objects move in your video shots, the waveform changes to reflect the values. No whites should be registering above 100 IREs on your waveform and no blacks should be below 7.5 IRE.

Reading the Vectorscope

Just as the Waveform monitor is used to check the absolute brightness values of your video signal, the Vectorscope is used to check the color and hue values of your video. When you send a color bar signal through a Vectorscope, each bar makes a dot on the display. There are small boxes drawn on the scope's graticule. These boxes represent the targets for those dots. Think of this as an old-fashioned video game. The position of the dots relative to the target boxes and the alignment of the *color burst* signal indicate how "true" your color signal is. Color burst is a reference signal that carries color information. Figure 3-29 shows the display for a Vectorscope with the trace for SMPTE color bars.

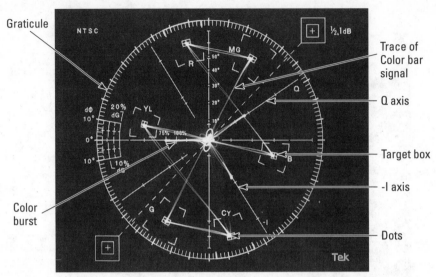

Figure 3-29: The trace of a color bar signal on a Vectorscope looks like this. Note that all the dots are located in their target boxes, and the color burst is placed correctly on the horizontal axis.

Photo courtesy of Tektronix

The Vectorscope checks two attributes of the color signal. It checks the *chroma gain* (the amount of color) and *chroma phase* (the hue of the color). The following is what the Vectorscope display shows you:

✦ **Graticule:** The graticule for a Vectroscope is a full circle, with markings all around it in 2- and 10-degree increments. The center point of this circle is the reference mark for centering the trace. Note that the –I and Q axis are also located in the graticule.

✦ **Color burst:** The color burst is a color reference signal that is sent for every line of video. This burst should always be aligned along the horizontal axis at the 9 o'clock position on the Vectorscope.

✦ **Trace of color bars signal:** The color bars signal makes a trace that includes dots for each color and a color burst signal.

✦ **Target box:** Within the circle of the Vectorscope, you see six target *brackets*, each containing smaller, sectioned box shapes. The smaller box shapes are where each dot of the color bars signal should fall if the chroma gain and phase are adjusted properly. Each box is marked with a shortened name for the colors red, magenta, blue, cyan, green, and yellow.

✦ **Dots:** Each color bar's trace makes a dot on the graticule. These dots have to be positioned in the appropriate target box.

Caution

In Figure 3-29, the color bars are making very small dots. In reality, dots that are so small that they fall completely within the small target boxes are only created by a very-low-noise signal, such as — you guessed it — a signal directly from a color bars generator. Normally, you can expect the dots to be much larger and fuzzier on signals from VTRs and tapes.

Just like a Waveform monitor, the Vectorscope does not alter the video signal in any way. It is merely used to measure the signal. You need a processing amplifier to change the settings on your video signal. There are many different brands of Vectorscopes on the market. You should read the documentation that came with your Vectorscope to learn how to make precise adjustments on it. To use a Vectorscope, use these steps to guide you:

1. **Configure your hardware so that the Vectorscope and processing amplifier are active and are part of the signal path as described earlier in this chapter.**

   Some high-end analog and digital decks have built-in processing amplifiers.

2. **Feed a color bars signal through the Vectorscope.**

   The bars should make a trace on the scope. The presence of the color burst signal along the horizontal axis is a good reference point to start. If you do not see the color burst signal lined up along the horizontal axis at the 9 o'clock position, adjust the phase control on the Vectorscope until it does.

3. **Adjust the hue or phase knob on your processing amplifier.**

   You notice that the dots turn left and right along the circle. Move the hue or phase setting until the dots are aligned in the proper boxes. Make sure that the color burst signal is still aligned at the 9 o'clock position. If the phase is incorrect, your color hues are going to be off. Peoples' faces may appear green or blue. Figure 3-30 shows a color bars signal that is out of phase on the Vectorscope.

4. **Turn the chroma gain or color knob on your processing amplifier so that the dots for the bars fall within the target boxes.**

   As you adjust the chroma setting, the dots go farther out of the boxes or closer to the center. The signal shown in Figure 3-31 has too much chroma. The dots are far outside the target boxes.

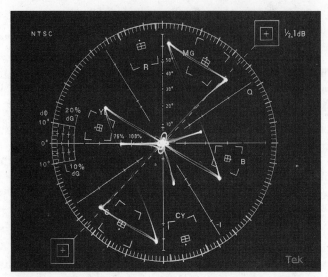

Figure 3-30: If the phase is misaligned, the dots for the color bars are rotated incorrectly in relation to the color burst.

Photo courtesy of Tektronix

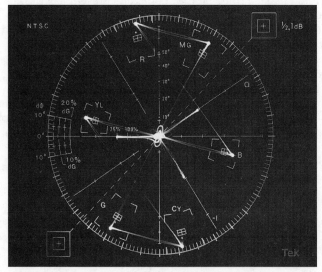

Figure 3-31: If the chroma gain is too high, the dots for the color bars fall outside of the target boxes.

Photo courtesy of Tektronix

5. **You may need to go back and forth between the chroma gain and phase adjustments to line up the dots in the target boxes correctly.**

   When you are done, you have calibrated your system for accurate color display and capture. Your Vectorscope should look like Figure 3-31.

After you have calibrated the brightness and color values for your video signal, you can capture or record material to and from tape. Of course, if you are preparing to capture from tape, you should be adjusting your system to the color bars that were placed on the beginning of the tape. As you play back and capture from the tape, you see the Vectorscope respond to the colors of your tape. The trace your video shots make will never be as defined and precise as the ones made by the set of color bars. That is because your color bars have a very precise color and amplitude. Shots of objects and images on tape have a wide mixture of colors.

As you work with graphics, you can keep an eye on the scope as well. If colors seem to go past the target areas, you are probably working with NTSC "illegal" colors. You can adjust your processing amplifier to bring the color down while checking your adjustments on the Vectorscope.

Working with High-Definition (HD) Video

Final Cut Pro was designed by its engineers to be a DV-to-HDTV solution. This is also known as being *scalable,* because Final Cut Pro is a resolution-independent application that can "scale up," or expand, as your needs and projects may demand. For example, when your client wants to produce his next project in Digital Betacam instead of DV, Final Cut Pro is more than capable of editing in this format if you add an appropriate capture card and disk drives to your setup.

In the past, Apple Computer has positioned Final Cut Pro as the perfect solution for DV-based editing. If you are setting up a digital editing studio based on the DV format and FireWire hardware, Apple promotional literature told you that you couldn't make a better choice than Final Cut Pro.

 Cross-Reference For more information on working with DV and FireWire-based setups with Final Cut Pro, see Chapter 4.

However, with the implementation of Unix-based OS X and Final Cut Pro's new architecture and feature set, Final Cut Pro has stepped up to the plate to fulfill the second part of that DV-to-HDTV phrase. The fact is, Final Cut Pro is an excellent choice for working with a wide range of video formats (including 24 fps video for film match-back). The high-end HD (High Definition) solutions that are possible with Final Cut Pro are of staggering quality, and even though they may strike the DV crowd as expensive, bear in mind that just a few years ago the same solutions would cost you five to ten times more. If you want to see how Final Cut Pro can change the world, you should look at the HD solutions that are possible with this application.

Understanding High-Definition (HD) video

HD is the new all-encompassing term used to describe the advent of high-definition television technologies. Think of HDTV this way: Your standard NTSC format (also known as SD, for *Standard Definition*) can display up to 720 × 486 pixels. HD can have a resolution of up to 1920 × 1080 pixels. That is almost six times more pixels than the SD video signal.

The amount of data to be managed with HD video is incredibly high. Standard Definition, or SD video, can average around 20MB/sec when used uncompressed. HD video can require a data throughput rate of over 160MB/sec. (On top of that you still need to allow throughput for audio streams and system overhead.) One terabyte (1000GB) of disk space will hold approximately 12 hours of SD video. The same amount of disk space will only contain around two hours of HD. A new emerging standard of high-speed SCSI drives, known as *SCSI 160,* is commonly used for HD video.

Cross-Reference   For more information on SCSI drives, see Chapter 4.

Learning about High-Definition (HD) formats

The list of standard HD formats can be quite confusing. The Advanced Television Systems Committee (ATSC) has defined the ATSC DTV (for Digital Television) specifications that include a list of 18 picture-compression formats. Only six of these formats qualify for the HD label.

Table 3-3 shows the 18 formats specified by the ATSC.

Table 3-3 HD Format Details				
DTV Format	*Scan Lines*	*Horizontal Pixels*	*Aspect Ratio*	*Picture Rate (i =interlaced, p=progressive)*
HDTV	1080	1920	16:9	60 i, 30p, 24p
HDTV	720	1280	16:9	60p, 30p, 24p
SDTV	480	704	16:9	60p, 60 i, 30p, 24p
SDTV	480	704	4:3	60p, 60 i, 30p, 24p
SDTV	480	640	4:3	60p, 60 i, 30p, 24p

When faced with these formats, you should try to remember two items. First, that the ATSC formats also encompass the SD (Standard Definition) formats. Only six formats are considered HD. Second, most of the DTV formats defined by the ATSC are meant for transmission and broadcast. Even then, not all broadcasters are going to send out transmissions in all 18 formats. For example, NBC and CBS have committed to 1080i while ABC and FOX will transmit in 720p.

For post-production needs, only a few important HD formats come into play. These relevant formats are the six interlaced (i) and progressive (p) variations of 1080 × 1920 and 720 × 1280.

Working with high-end video capture cards

Because Final Cut Pro 4.0 operates exclusively on OS X, makers of third-party capture cards have had to write new drivers for their products currently working with earlier versions of Final Cut Pro running on OS 9. If you didn't already know, *drivers* are those small bits of software that enable communication between the capture card and the Mac computer. Some companies have even developed new product lines exclusively for OS X. Although not all are currently approved by Apple, there are many reports of successful integrations with these high-end capture cards delivering broadcast-quality output in conjunction with Final Cut Pro. These capture cards fit in the PCI bus slot of the computer and have connectors or breakout boxes (BOBs) that can interface with your video deck using basic video connectors. Using these cards in tandem with Final Cut Pro, you can capture high-quality video, edit the video, and lay your edited program back to tape. Some of these cards also support HD (High Definition) formats discussed in the previous section.

When using these types of cards, you should be aware that *high quality* also translates to *high data rates*. For this reason, you should familiarize yourself with the needs for high-speed drives and other requirements.

For more information on data rates, drives, and hardware, see Chapter 4.

Currently, there are five major players who are making high-end video capture cards for use with Final Cut Pro:

- ✦ Aurora Video Systems
- ✦ Pinnacle Systems
- ✦ Digital Voodoo
- ✦ AJA Video Systems
- ✦ Blackmagic

Drooling in real time

I am not one of those people who starts drooling at the mere mention of the phrase *real time.* I've lived too long and seen too much in the world of digital video to respond with unrestrained glee when I hear that phrase. The general understanding that users have of real time is that you do not have to render transitions and effects. The idea behind a real-time system is that you place a transition in between two shots, back up your playhead, and just play the transition in real time. No rendering is required, and there is no waiting time. Ideally, you should also be able to play the transition back to tape in real time as well as without rendering. Ideally.

Things quickly get complicated when you look closer at the real-time claims from card-makers. For example, are effects and filters in real time as well? All of them, or some of them? What about text? Animated text?

Different manufacturers also use different definitions of *real time.* Sometimes it gets downright bizarre. I know one video card maker whose definition of *real time* means that a transition that is 1 second long takes 1 second to render. Pardon?

Some real-time systems provide only a limited set of transitions that work in real time, others have limits on text, graphics, and motion effects, and yet other cards simply cannot handle a few real-time functions when placed in a row in the Timeline. For example, if a real-time system promises transitions in real time, placing a few of these next to each other may require rendering some of them because the throughput and the calculations required exceed the real-time capacity of the card.

There are also real-time systems that require you to render every "real time" effect before you can master them to tape. Sure you can look at them in real time while working, but you have to *render* before you go to tape. The idea is that, when working in situations where clients are watching over your shoulders, you don't have to twiddle your thumbs while rendering, and your client doesn't have to stand there tapping on the table and counting the time in dollars.

When dealing with cards and systems that try to sell you the real-time dream, look very carefully at *exactly* what it is that the system or the card promises in real time. Then go to discussion boards and Web sites that review the cards. Don't just believe every word that any manufacturer says about the performance of their real-time systems.

Using the Aurora Systems cards for Final Cut Pro

Aurora Video Systems makes some of the most popular video cards for Final Cut Pro. The engineers at Aurora Systems have worked on cards and software exclusively for the Macintosh for years. The Aurora Systems' Igniter card has been updated for OS X and is now called IgniterX. Some of the features of the Aurora Igniter system are:

✦ **Variable compression:** The Aurora IgniterX system uses MJPEG-A video compression for its video. (The higher-end cards use SDI or are uncompressed.) MJPEG-A is an ideal compression format because it is high quality and allows a variable data rate. Using an Igniter system, you can use a compression of

1.5:1 (almost uncompressed) to 50:1 (highly compressed). This variable compression allows you to capture vast amounts of video at low quality to cut your show. Later you can recapture the edited Timeline at a high setting.

Use of MJPEG-A also presents another very significant advantage. This type of compression is readily available on most Apple computers. That means that anyone with a Macintosh computer can render a movie for use in a Final Cut Pro workstation based on the Aurora Igniter card.

In addition to Aurora's MJPEG codec, IgniterX is now able to capture uncompressed video at a data rate of 20MB/sec. This feature allows you a huge workflow advantage when recapturing a final edit done at offline compression. What this means is that you can recapture a sequence as uncompressed video on the same workstation that the offline edit was done on. Of course, this depends on whether you have a fast enough RAID, enough hard-disk space, and a fast enough CPU to accommodate the heavy stream of u data of uncompressed video.

✦ **Affordable film-editing option:** Aurora's IgniterX also has a film option you can purchase. Using this option, you can remove 3:2 pulldown on the fly from film-to-tape transfers and convert the video to true 24 fps files. You can edit the film using these files within Final Cut Pro.

✦ **Scalable architecture:** The Igniter card is a "scalable" card. This means that a basic Igniter card has composite input and output along with unbalanced audio interface. However, there is a simple and logical upgrade path that allows you to add many options to the basic Igniter card. Option packages from Aurora include:

  • **Aurora IgniterX:** This is the basic card offering composite and Y/C analog capture while using unbalanced audio connectors. This card takes up one PCI slot on your computer and comes with cables that are used to connect the video and audio signals. IgniterX now supports the following real time effects: Brightness and Contrast, Desaturate, Gamma, Correction, Proc Amp, SL Balance, Color Corrector 3-way, Invert, Mask Shape, Widescreen and Uncompressed Overlays. As mentioned previously, IgniterX is also capable of capturing uncompressed video as well as compressed MJPEG.

  • **Aurora IgniterX Pro:** An upgrade that utilizes a "daughter card" and a breakout box (or BOB). The daughter card connects to the basic Aurora IgniterX card. This avoids having to use up another PCI slot in your computer. (All Igniter upgrades use daughter-card architecture, saving PCI slots.) The junction box has inputs and outputs for component, composite, Y/C, and balanced XLR connectors. The component option also has a timecode read/write capability. This feature allows you to write the timecode from your Final Cut Pro Timeline to your tape. Alternately, you can use the timecode output to connect other devices, such as a synchronizer for a ProTools digital audio workstation (DAW). IgniterX Pro now includes the Film Feature that adds real-time reverse telecine capture capabilities and real-time 3:2 pulldown on playback from a 24-frame sequence.

• **Aurora IgniterX SDI:** You can purchase the Aurora 10-bit SDI option and upgrade your Igniter card to work with the Serial Digital Interface. You also get an AES/EBU digital audio interface. AES/EBU audio is the type of digital audio used with the Serial Digital Interface. The Film Feature is now included with this option as well.

• **Aurora Igniter Studio:** The Aurora Igniter Studio is the premium upgrade that bundles the IgniterX card with the Pro and SDI options, and the Film Feature.

Cross-Reference   For more information on video signal types and audio connectors, see Chapter 2.

For a Final Cut Pro-based setup that is being designed for long-form program editing and high-quality analog work (with a future eye toward digital) the Aurora System's IgniterX card (shown in Figure 3-32) is worth consideration. It allows variable analog compression with extremely high quality and versatility. The upgrade options also make this system attractive.

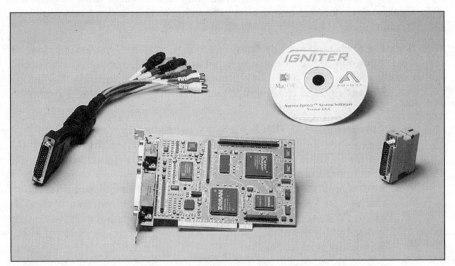

Figure 3-32: The Aurora Systems Igniter card is a versatile and scalable card with options that can change its quality and options.
Photo courtesy of Aurora Video Systems, Inc.

Cross-Reference   For more information on the Aurora Systems Igniter card, see Chapter 21.

Working with the Pinnacle Systems CinèWave card for Final Cut Pro

Pinnacle Systems' CinèWave card, shown in Figure 3-33, is a true high-end card. This card has a scalable architecture that provides various upgrade options that allow you to work with DV, SD (Standard Definition) video, and even HDTV (High-Definition Television). The CinèWave card is extremely high quality and works with uncompressed video. The data rate for uncompressed video is very high and so are the storage requirements. At about 27MB/sec worth of throughput, you need fast drives and lots of storage, but if you want to work with uncompressed video, this card can handle it. Some of the features that make Pinnacle Systems' CinèWave a standout are:

Figure 3-33: The Pinnacle System's CinèWave card is shown here.

Photo courtesy of Pinnacle Systems, Inc.

✦ **Ideal quality for high-end graphics:** Many production houses prefer the Pinnacle CinèWave for its high-quality video. Users capture from Betacam SP, Digital Betacam, and D-1 into the CinèWave cards and use the video for effects' creation and processing. Effects such as blue-screening and rotoscoping demand the highest quality video and the CinèWave delivers.

✦ **Flexible design:** This card offers flexible processing in 4:2:2 or 4:4:4:4 digital formats. You can choose between 4:3 or 16:9 aspect ratios, and the Pinnacle CinèWave card supports frame rates of 24, 25, or 29.97. You can also remove the 3:2 pulldown on the fly for converting film transfer on tape back to 24 fps and edit in Final Cut Pro at the true film rate.

✦ **Scalable architecture:** The design of the Pinnacle CinèWave system is scalable to literally cover everything from DV to HDTV. You can start out with a basic package and later add options.

The basic package from Pinnacle is the Targa Cinè Engine. This package includes the Targa CinèWave card, which is the main driving engine behind the CinèWave system. It has two Digital Tether port connections that are used to connect a variety of breakout boxes, which provide many different types of interfaces. These options are known as the Digital Tether I/O options. The four Tether options available from Pinnacle are:

- **Pro Analog Option:** This option gives you analog composite, component, and S-Video options. The audio interface has both balanced and unbalanced connections. All connections are located on a breakout junction box (shown in Figure 3-34) that comes as part of this option.

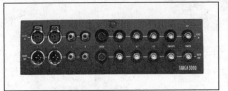

Figure 3-34: The breakout box for Pinnacle's Pro Analog Option for the CinèWave card.

Photo courtesy of Pinnacle Systems, Inc

- **Pro Digital Option:** This option (shown in Figure 3-35) consists of an SDI (Serial Digital Interface), also known by its official name SMPTE 259 M.

Figure 3-35: The Pro Digital Option for Pinnacle's CinèWave card.

Photo courtesy of Pinnacle Systems, Inc.

- **Pro Digital and Analog Option:** This option (shown in Figure 3-36) consists of a large breakout junction box with numerous connectors. These connectors allow you to input and output analog S-Video, composite, and component video. You also get an SDI option built into the junction box. Audio capabilities include four in and six out analog balanced audio, and four in and four out for AES/EBU digital audio.

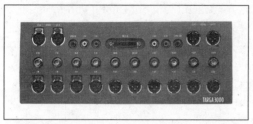

Figure 3-36: The breakout box for the Pro Digital and Analog Option for Pinnacle's CinèWave card.
Photo courtesy of Pinnacle Systems, Inc.

• **Pro HD Digital Option:** This option (shown in Figure 3-37) includes a high-definition (HD) SDI interface. Using this option, you can work with HDTV at the following standards: 1080i, 60p, 1080p/24, and 720p. The specifications for HDTV have multiple formats that are divided between interlaced (i) and progressive (p) designations. 1080 and 720 refer to the frame size of the format, while 60 and 24 are the frame rates.

Figure 3-37: A Pro HD Digital Option for Pinnacle's CinèWave card.
Photo courtesy of Pinnacle Systems, Inc.

Pinnacle's CinèWave is an extremely high-quality card. If you plan to work with uncompressed video and process film special effects, this is your card. The HDTV capability makes this card extremely attractive for filmmakers and production houses working with the HDTV format. The data rate of high-end digital video can be very high and the space requirements astronomical, but for users who demand the finest quality, the Pinnacle CinèWave is the answer.

Working with the Digital Voodoo D1 Desktop 64RT card for Final Cut Pro

A few years back, Apple declared the Digital Voodoo card "the highest quality QuickTime card on the planet." Since then, other manufacturers have joined the high-end capture board market for Macintosh, but Digital Voodoo still ranks high in capture quality and price value. The Digital Voodoo D1 64RT is a 10-bit card that represents a vast quality improvement over the standard 8-bit cards. Even though Aurora and Pinnacle also offer 10-bit options, Digital Voodoo's image quality is considered extremely high quality.

The D1 64RT card from Digital Voodoo, shown in Figure 3-38, stands apart because of the following features:

✦ **High quality:** The Digital Voodoo card provides 10-bit uncompressed video. This results in a high data rate but also very-high-quality video. The 10-bit video allows for unprecedented brightness levels and smooth color transitions.

✦ **Uncompressed or SDI:** You can choose to work with SDI or uncompressed 10-bit or 8-bit 4:2:2 digital video. Both types of video are high quality but demand fast drives and high storage requirements. Your drives should be capable of a minimum of 30MB/sec of throughput.

✦ **Strong audio features:** The D1 64RT Digital Voodoo card features impressive audio capabilities that were previously found on the D1 64AV model. This card has six channels of AES/EBU digital audio available at 48 KHz or 96KHz sampling rate. Each of these audio channels work at 24-bit depth (switchable to 20- or 16-bit). These six channels of audio allow the Digital Voodoo card to provide support for 5.1 surround-sound channels.

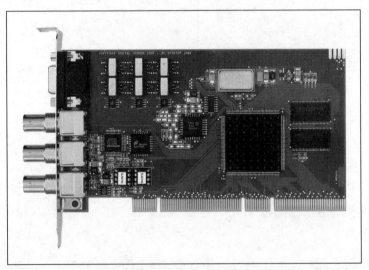

Figure 3-38: The Digital Voodoo D1 64RT card can capture and play back 10-bit uncompressed video in real time.
Photo courtesy of Digital Voodoo

The Digital Voodoo card is used by production houses that specialize in producing short duration and high-impact motion graphics. The 10-bit processing allows for very high video quality.

Working with the AJA Kona-SD card for Final Cut Pro

The Kona-SD (Standard Definition) card made by AJA is thought by many to be the perfect uncompressed-video capture card for Final Cut Pro. Designed from the ground up for Mac OS X, the Kona card, shown in Figure 3-39, is a joint development between AJA, the manufacturer of the physical card, and Blackmagic Design, developers of the codec and QuickTime drivers.

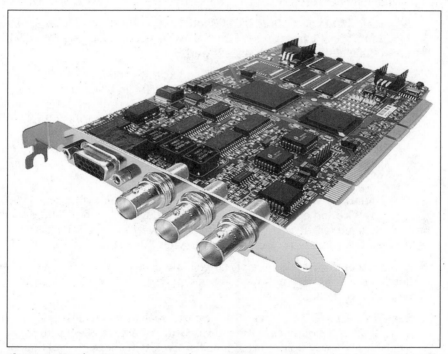

Figure 3-39: The AJA Kona-SD card can capture uncompressed 10-bit and 8-bit video, as well as variable JPEG formats.
Photo courtesy of AJA Video Systems

An impressive aspect about this 10-bit SDI card is that it offers many features of its competitors, but it's packaged all on one PCI board. If you add to this its operation stability, AJA's client responsiveness and, to date, free software upgrades sold at a very competitive mid-level price range (around $3,300 or more), you might begin to understand why so many people are smitten with the Kona card. Some of its many features are:

✦ **Uncompressed 10-bit and 8-bit capture and playback:** Using the SDI In and Out ports, you can capture uncompressed 10-bit or 8-bit video for the highest possible quality. As great as uncompressed looks, don't forget the enormous amount of disk space that's required to capture this much data.

✦ **Offline codecs:** Like Aurora's IgniterX, the Kona card can perform capture and playback using a variety of lossy codecs. This is an incredible workflow enhancement when you have a limited amount of hard disk space (who doesn't?) to rough-cut a project that will ultimately be recaptured as uncompressed, or at least at a higher resolution.. The codecs that work with Kona-SD are:

  • **Final Cut Pro's Offline RT:** A Photo JPEG codec that only requires 1 MB/sec at a frame size of 320 × 240. This codec is used primarily for offline editing a project on a PowerBook.

  • **Kona JPEG:** like Aurora's MJPEG codec, the Kona JPEG is a variable lossy codec that supports 4:2:2 color sampling. It can be used for offline, and at its highest quality setting is passable online (but why would you when you're currently using a premiere uncompressed board capture card?). In addition to its compression versatility, the Kona JPEG codec is a Photo-JPEG-based format that is found on most Macintosh computers, thus allowing any user to view, edit, or create content for a project using the Photo-JPEG codec.

  • **KonaDV:** Using the KonaDV codec, you can capture your media via FireWire and output your DV project through SDI with real-time effects. No need for the extra FireWire to SDI converter — the Kona card will output your DV projects directly to your SDI-enabled tape deck.

✦ **KonaFilm option:** Added *free of charge* in their recent version 2.1 software update, the Kona card now captures and plays back true 24p *(progressive)* footage in real time.

✦ **Real-Time effects:** The Kona card supports dual-stream real-time effects for both 10-bit and 8-bit uncompressed video. The real-time effects currently available are 3-way Color Correction, dissolves, and image control that include Brightness and Contrast, Gamma Correction, Proc Amp, Sepia, and Tint. More effects are said to be in the offing, but the current set seems to cover the lion's share of effects most used by professional editors on a daily basis. Unfortunately, you cannot stack any of these effects without having to render, but single layered effects will still output in real time with no, I repeat, absolutely *no* rendering required for Edit to Tape output. Currently, this is the only uncompressed real-time card that does not require render before tape output.

✦ **Digital Audio In and Out:** Kona-SD can handle up to six channels of AES and SDI embedded audio channels.

If there is a shortcoming of the AJA Kona-SD card, it might be the lack of any breakout box (BOB) for analog input and output. However, not only does AJA makes excellent standalone video digital/analog converters, there are many other brands of digital/analog converters fully compatible with the Kona card. Some have even argued the *advantages* of having separate digital/analog converters: mobility and accessibility of converters for other workstations, cost-effectiveness of discrete converters instead of brand-dedicated on-board converters, and de facto noise isolation of standalone converters that are away from the torrent of possible signal noise inside a CPU chassis. These are all good, but noncrucial, points that do not outweigh any consideration that the AJA Kona-SD board is of the highest quality and price value for editing high-quality video with Final Cut Pro.

8-bits and 10-bits

Working with 10-bit systems instead of 8-bit systems has some important advantages for production facilities that do special effects and compositing work. Both the range of colors and the brightness increase dramatically when working with 10-bit systems. This increase is crucial for achieving clean "keys" when blue-screening and multilayering video.

Computer graphic images on the Macintosh have 8 bits of information for each RGB channel. Because there are 8 bits for the red channel, 8 bits for green, 8 bits for blue, and another 8 bits for the alpha channel, you can have up to 16 million possible colors represented by a combination of the RGB channels. In addition, the 8-bit Alpha channel means you can have 256 possible values for transparency.

For most situations, 16 million colors are plenty. However, there are times when even 16 million colors are not enough. You see this shortcoming most clearly in "banding" that appears when one color is drawn as a smooth ramp into another. On the other hand, 10-bit color provides 1,024 possible color values for each channel. This gives over 1 billion possible colors. When working in 10-bit mode, so many colors are available that the banding problems do not manifest themselves.

Some high-end digital video animation and compositing systems, such as the Quantel Henry and Discrete Logic's Flame, work at the 10-bits-per-pixel level. The Digital Betacam format also works in 10-bit mode. All telecine suites that transfer film to tape also use the 10-bit mode.

Working in 10-bit also allows 1,024 levels of gray, and 1,024 levels of transparency for the Alpha channel. The added values in the range of transparency are a boon for special-effects compositing work. You get cleaner layering of video elements. The 10-bit grays give you superior brightness values as well.

Continued

Continued

The increase in brightness values is very important for a critical reason. Computer imagery is stored in the RGB color gamut, whereas video commonly works in the YCrCb gamut. In the video color gamut, Y represents luminance, whereas Cr and Cb are the color signals. When brightness levels are converted between the RGB and the YCrCb modes, there are "rounding" errors. That's because not all brightness values translate precisely from YCrCb to RGB and back. Adding the extra 2 bits provides four times the brightness level values possible with an 8-bit system. An 8-bit system can contain 250 brightness values, whereas a 10-bit system can have 1,000 brightness levels. The following figure illustrates this concept.

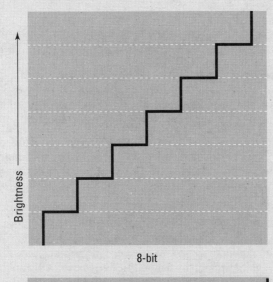

8-bit

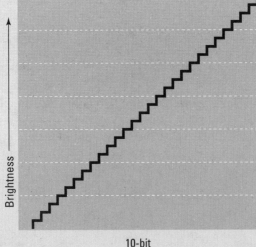

10-bit

Working with the Blackmagic Design DeckLink card for Final Cut Pro

Not to be outdone by their AJA partners, Blackmagic offers their own line of high-end PCI capture cards, called DeckLink. Through innovative design and manufacturing choices, the Blackmagic DeckLink card, shown in Figure 3-40, is able to capture and deliver 10-bit uncompressed video at an unprecedented low price, and is quickly becoming the darling of many production houses that edit with Final Cut Pro.

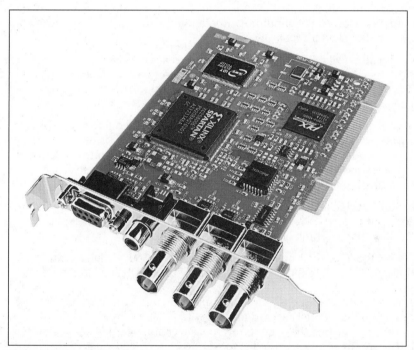

Figure 3-40: The Blackmagic DeckLink card is one of the most affordable capture card capable of capturing uncompressed 8-bit, 10-bit, JPEG and DV.
Photo courtesy of Blackmagic Design

There are three DeckLink standard-definition (SD) capture card models; all have the same basic feature set, which includes:

✦ **Variable video qualities:** DeckLink can capture and playback, in real time, 10-bit uncompressed video, 8-bit uncompressed video, Blackmagic's Online JPEG, DV/DVCPRO and DVCPRO 50, as well as Final Cut Pro's OfflineRT codec.

✦ **Digital audio:** DeckLink supports eight channels of SDI audio that is carried with SDI video. A separate SPDIF connector is provided for digital audio output or monitoring

✦ **Codec compatibility:** Not only are Blackmagic's QuickTime codecs known to deliver fantastic quality, Blackmagic has written them to be fully compatible with other systems. For example, Blackmagic DV10 codec is fully compatible with Digital Voodoo's uncompressed 10-bit codec, while its Uncompressed 8 bit 2Vuy codec is based on the same QuickTime standard as Pinnacle's CineWave uncompressed 8-bit codec. Because Blackmagic wrote the drivers and codecs for the AJA Kona cards, all of the Kona SD codecs will work with DeckLink. Blackmagic's coded versatility allows more options for editing and finishing a project on multiple edit stations —. even edit stations that are using a competition's capture card. The Blackmagic codecs are free to download on their website, `www.decklink.com`, allowing anyone with these installed codecs to render an view (throughput notwithstanding) video files using these codecs, without the need for a hardware codec.

✦ **Real-time effects:** Decklink offers the same real-time effects written for the Kona card. As more become available, real-time filters and plug-ins will be free to download from their website. Decklink also supports Final Cut Pro's RT (Real Time) Extreme architecture.

✦ **Real-time SDI monitoring:** Full resolution, 10-bit uncompressed SDI video is always available for playback monitoring or mastering. Using the Video Desktop option, you can view any opened file on a broadcast monitor connected to the DeckLink monitor output. This is ideal for checking non-QuickTime files, such as Photoshop or Power Point, for broadcast quality.

✦ **Built-in deck control:** The built-in RS-422 connector enables you to connect and control any RS-422 deck, eliminating the need for a USB-serial adapter card or dongle. Think of it as a free deck controller.

✦ **DV bridge:** Like the Kona card, DeckLink can output native DV projects through SDI with real-time effects, directly to an SDI-enabled tape deck.

One of the ways Blackmagic is able to manufacture and sell DeckLink cards at such a low price point is by offering card models with different Input/Output (I/O) connectors, thereby eliminating the need to buy a basic capture card *and then* purchase separate hardware (or software) add-ons to work with high-end video. This *non-scalable* approach might seem anachronistic in this era of modular design, until you realize that the features and capabilities of DeckLink cards leave you nowhere to scale up to! With DeckLink cards, you're pretty much at the high end of high-end video capture cards. The three standard definition DeckLink models to choose from are:

✦ **DeckLink:** Designed specifically for SDI video deck and system connectivity, the standard DeckLink card has SDI I/O connectors, a separate SDI output for video monitoring on a SDI-capable monitor, and one SPDIF (an RCA connector port used for digital audio) for audio monitoring. If you've ever had to sort through a jungle of cables connected to your analog capture card, you'll truly appreciate this streamlined I/O interface.

✦ **DeckLink Pro:** The DeckLink Pro is an enhanced version of the standard DeckLink model. While it has similar connections, it also includes genlock input, high-quality YUV/NTSC/PAL monitoring via XLR connectors, and four SPDIF monitoring outputs for eight channel audio monitoring. All of the connectors are bundled into a seven-foot break-out cable for direct connection to equipment while using only a single cable to the Decklink Pro card.

✦ **DeckLink SP:** Because the DeckLink SP is designed to work with professional analog video decks, it does *not* have any SDI inputs. Instead, the DeckLink SP uses industry-standard XLR connectors for analog video component I/Os, and separate XLR connectors for balanced stereo I/O. The DeckLink SP's full-resolution, 10-bit output for video monitoring can also be connected to a SDI-capable deck for mastering back to tape, thus avoiding analog conversion for final delivery. The DeckLink SP uses the same break-out cable design as the DeckLink Pro for all connections.

Blackmagic also offers a HD card, DeckLink HD, which is switchable between HD and SD. That means it delivers all the features of DeckLink Pro *and* HD for less than the cost of many competitor's SD capture cards — but this is a topic for another time. Given the incredible feature set and cost value of Blackmagic DeckLink, I think it's fair to say that Blackmagic DeckLink is setting the standard for digital video acquisition and delivery.

✦　　✦　　✦

Using Final Cut Pro with and without DV Hardware

Although Final Cut Pro is a truly powerful piece of software, it's just one component of a complete editing system. That system consists of the Final Cut Pro software, your Macintosh computer, and your video gear. If you want to produce high-quality video, you need not only the best possible editing software but also the best possible hardware. This chapter looks at some of the hardware issues that affect the quality of your video. It reviews hard drives, analog video converters, and the hardware and operating system configuration of your Mac. The chapter also looks at device control, a feature that allows you to maintain necessary control over your video gear using Final Cut Pro.

Selecting the Right Drive

Digital video takes up lots of disk space in your computer. Before the advent of digital video, a 350MB drive seemed huge, but now that's just a drop in the bucket. Choosing a hard drive to use with Final Cut Pro is probably the most important hardware choice you'll make for your setup. Your choice can determine the ease with which you're able to work, and if you make the wrong decision, your life as an editor could be a nightmare. I suggest not skimping on money when it comes to buying hard drives. Most people try to get the most space for their money, and that's fine. However, you don't want to focus on getting massive storage space at the expense of all other hard-drive considerations. Try to find a middle ground between sheer space and the quality of the drives. A gazillion jigabyte drive is not going to do you any good if it won't play your masterpiece without dropping frames. You may as well use it as a doorstop at that point (in fact, I once did just that).

If you own a Macintosh G4 or an iMac G4, the drive that it came with is sufficient to capture and play DV video. Editors do this all the time. They use the basic drive their Mac G4 comes with as their primary drive for capture and storage of media. However, I strongly advise that you not do that. Any computer on which you use Final Cut Pro should have a separate drive dedicated to media captured from tape. Besides, you probably want more space than is available on your boot hard drive anyway. Likewise, if you're working with uncompressed MJPEG video, you have to plan for higher data rates, and this means selecting much faster drives.

Caution   Users often partition their main system drive into two and use one for their media capture needs. This is ill-advised. These partitions are *virtual,* residing on the same internal drive, and the media is still going to the same *physical* drive. This can cause crashes and various other problems with the system drive.

In the past, Apple's site posted a list of approved ATA drives that could be used with Final Cut Pro. Because most, if not all, of today's drives are faster than those of even a few years ago and are sufficient for capturing and playing low data rate codecs, like a simple DV project, this posting has disappeared. Apple still does not fully endorse the use of FireWire drives for video capture and playback, but they have conceded that current FireWire drives, in addition to being useful as a medium for transporting media files, can also be used for low data rate projects like DV.

Caution   If you have more than one drive hooked up to your computer, do not use similar names for them. A drive name should not contain the entire name of another drive, such as Media and Media 1. Final Cut Pro won't like that. During capture, you can have problems, such as crashes and media ending up in the wrong place. Give completely individual names to your drives, like Curly, Moe, and Larry. Cartoon characters and fruit names are very popular for drive names. In a pinch, consult a book on selecting baby names.

Keep in mind when choosing a drive that many vendors sell the same drives in different plastic containers. For example, Seagate makes drive mechanisms that are sold through many different vendors by packaging them in different-colored plastic containers with vendors' logos on them. Be wise and collect information about the mechanism rather than the brand name, unless of course you really need a particularly colored plastic box to match your curtains.

Choosing between internal and external drives

Hard drives can be located either inside your computer case *(internal),* or outside the CPU housed in an external box that connects to your Mac using a cable *(external).* The main advantage of internal drives is their convenience. They fit inside your computer — no muss, no fuss. Internal drives also tend to be cheaper. Having drives inside the main computer case also cuts down on the noise. However, the expansion capacity of the computer limits the type and size of drives you can have inside the case.

Heat can also become an issue with internal drives. For example, in the G4 tower, you can have up to four internal drives. However, the heat generated from these drives (not to mention the heat of the CPU itself) makes this a risky proposition. Despite the fact that Apple Authorized Resellers may offer up to four additional drives in a G4, you should avoid having more than two additional internal drives (not counting the main Macintosh hard drive) in your G4.

External drives are generally more expensive, but they also offer more flexibility. Usually external drives can easily be moved from room to room. This makes it very easy to move projects around from one machine to another. External drives are often noisier because they have their own fans, but at least they don't add heat to the inside of your computer. External drives also allow far more choices of speed, transfer rates, and prices. Figure 4-1 shows the Micronet Genesis drives.

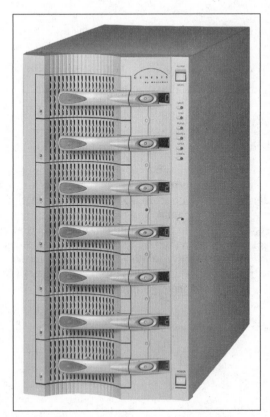

Figure 4-1: Shown here is a Micronet Genesis external drive system with a slide-out feature. This drive can be slid out from its bay and inserted into a bay located in another edit suite. These kinds of external drives are common in production houses where moving from room to room during projects is common.

Image courtesy of Micronet

Determining your data rates

Before you select a drive, know the data rate that you'll need. For example, if you're working with DV only, your rate is going to be 3.6MBps. If you're using an Apple-approved video capture card and MJPEG video, your data rate can be anywhere from 1MB per second (for offline) to 12MB per second (for online) and up. If you're planning to work with uncompressed video, expect a data rate of around 20 to 24MB per second. Whatever your needs, make sure that any drives you select offer an adequate data rate. Also, always allow for overhead. Try to get a drive that performs at least 50 percent above the data rate you'll actually need.

Determining your space requirements

I made a commitment to myself to avoid any complicated math and fancy formulas in this book. However, I have allowed myself basic math. (Hey, I'm just as bad at math as anyone else.) Figuring out your disk space requirements involves just some basic math if you know your data rate. For example, if you're working with DV, your data rate is 3.6MB per second:

> 3.6MB per second × 60 seconds = 216MB per minute. DV takes up 216MB for every minute.

> To store 10 minutes worth of video and audio, 216 × 10 minutes = 2,160MB.

> To convert megabytes to gigabytes, divide that number by 1,024.

> So 2,160 ÷ 1,024 = 2.1GB.

Hey! This is so simple, even I can figure it out.

Table 4-1 contains a basic chart to help you work out disk-space requirements. However, there's a bit more to it than simply multiplying the data rate. So far we've only calculated the size of the video we plan to capture. As you'll see throughout this book, Final Cut Pro also generates render, cache, and other important files. These files can take up a lot of disk space, too. In fact, Apple recommends that you multiply the total storage space you'll need for video by 5 to get an estimate of what you'll actually need. So, if you estimate that you'll need 2.1GB of space for captured video, multiply that amount by 5 to get 10.5GB. I think that this factor of five may be a bit of overkill, but a factor of two or three is a must!

	Table 4-1 Estimating Disk Space				
Video Format	Data Rate	1 Minute	10 Minutes	60 Minutes
Offline RT (Photo JPEG)	300 to 500KB per second	18 to 30MB	180 to 300MB	1 to 1.8GB
DV25	3.6MB per second	216MB	2.10GB	13GB
DV50	7.2MB per second	216MB	2.10GB	13GB
MJPEG (Low Resolution)	1MB per second	60MB	600MB	3.5GB
MJPEG (Medium Resolution)	7MB per second	420MB	4.1GB	24.6GB
MJPEG (High Resolution)	12MB per second	720MB	7GB	42GB
Uncompressed 601 SD Video.	20MB per second	1.20GB	12.0GB	72.0GB

Reading drive specifications

Before you can evaluate the specifications of a drive you intend to buy, you need to understand just what exactly a drive is. Figure 4-2 illustrates what the inside of a typical hard drive looks like. Basically, a drive consists of a bunch of platters on a spindle that turns very, very fast. Data is stored on the platters, and each platter is divided into tracks and sectors. Each platter has a pair of read/write heads connected to an arm that reads and writes data on the sectors of the drive. The size, density, and number of platters determine the amount of data the drive can hold.

Note In most designs, the read/write head doesn't actually touch the platter but flies a thousandth of a millimeter above it due to the slight aerodynamic design and the (very slight) flow of air created by the spin of the drives.

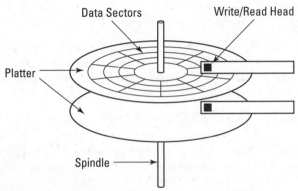

Figure 4-2: Data is stored in a hard drive on magnetic coatings on the disk platters.

There are three issues to consider when evaluating drive specifications for Final Cut Pro. These issues are sustained transfer speed, seek time, and spindle speed. The next few sections describe these terms and what to look for. However, keep in mind that most of the numbers reported on a drive's spec sheet are *computed* rather than taken from real-world experience. Whenever possible, read tests and reports on Web sites (and not just the company's site) and in magazines for any drive you're considering buying. Numerous Web sites devoted to digital video have forums where users can share their experiences with various drives.

Sustained transfer speed

Sustained transfer speed is the amount of data that can be written to your drives per second. This speed is also known as the data rate. Sustained transfer speed is usually expressed as MB/sec (megabytes per second).

Note   MB/sec denotes megabytes per second. Be advised that in product literature transfer speeds are sometimes expressed in Mbps (or mega*bits* per second). Keep an eye out for that lowercase *b* versus the uppercase *B*. *A byte is eight times larger than a bit.* If you read the data rate as Mb, then divide by 8 to get an approximate MB rate. With MB, *multiply* the rate by 8 to get an approximate Mb rate.

If you're working with DV, the situation is straightforward. DV's data rate is 3.6MB/sec and DV50's is 7MB/sec and is constant. It never varies. However, if you use a video capture card such as the Aurora Igniter, then you use a type of compression called MJPEG. With MJPEG, you can vary the quality of your compression. In this case, the higher the sustained transfer speed of your drives, the higher the quality of the video you can write to it.

Another factor is that with MJPEG and other kinds of high-end video compression schemes, the data rate is not always constant. MJPEG, even if it's told to work at 8MB/sec, can often have much lower or much higher data rates. That's because MJPEG compression schemes are *adaptive* — the amount of compression varies according to a frame's image complexity. An image with large areas of the same color and little visual detail can be compressed into a smaller file than a full-range image containing tons of color and minute details. DV, on the other hand, maintains a constant data rate of 3.6MB/sec regardless of the image being compressed.

Note   MJPEG compression always allows the ability to lock the data rate, giving you more control. However, locking the data rate can be wasteful of disk space because the MJPEG codec cannot adapt higher compression to certain kinds of video.

Here's a bucket of cold water for you: Data transfer rates, as reported for most drives in their spec sheets and literature, usually consist of computed values rather than the actual data rate you'll get when using the drive in the real world. The term *throughput* is used interchangeably with *sustained transfer rate*. Throughput measures the actual useful data that is being moved, which is always lower than the sustained transfer rate. Sometimes it's a lot lower. That's because there's a lot more than just the movie media file being sent around. The drive is also communicating with the operating system, and this creates overhead. There are also many choke points for the throughput. It's limited by the bus speed of your computer as well as the operating system's ability to feed the data to Final Cut Pro.

The whole issue of throughput does not mean that you can't trust the numbers being quoted to you in the drive spec literature; just don't haggle over a few MB to save some money. When reviewing sustained transfer speed, allow a substantial overhead. If you're planning to work with a data rate of around 6MB/sec, allow at least twice that.

Spindle speed or RPM

Spindle speed is the speed at which the spindle — and the platters attached to it — spin. This speed directly affects sustained transfer rate. If all other factors are the same, the higher the spindle speed of the drive, the higher the sustained transfer rate. Spindle speed is measured in revolutions per minute (RPM). When looking at spindle speed, a higher RPM is better. A drive meant for multimedia will often run at 7,200RPM or higher.

A high RPM also means more heat will be generated by the drive. Most external high-speed drives have built-in fans for cooling. However, you should carefully consider ventilation before you locate a high-speed drive inside your main computer case.

Seek time

Seek time indicates how fast the data stored on the drive can be accessed, or *seeked*. Seek time is measured in *ms* or milliseconds. The read/write head races across the platters seeking the data that it needs to play out. When you capture material in Final Cut Pro or render media, the data can end up spread out over the drive on any of the data sectors on any of its platters. While playing a movie, hundreds of media files have to be sought and played back without dropping a frame. Seek time measures the speed at which the read/write head can race across the platters and locate the necessary data. When looking at seek time, a lower number is better.

Considering the various kinds of drives

Up to now, I've been speaking about computer disk drives in general. But many different kinds of disk drives, both internal and external, are available for your Macintosh. Most of the drives that will be suitable for you to store digital media on are hard drives, but there are also drives that use removable storage media such as Zip drives, CD-ROM drives, and others. The next few sections describe the various kinds of disk drives available to you and show you which ones are best for working with digital video.

Zip drives or CD-ROMs

Zip drives, created by Iomega, were very popular for storage and transfer of graphic files. However, a Zip drive, or any removable media drive for that matter, is not going to work for the playback of your media. These drives just don't have the seek time or transfer rate needed for capture or playback of digital video. The same goes for CD-ROMs. Recordable CDs (CD-Rs) are very popular for storing large files, but they cannot seek or transfer data fast enough to allow video editing without dropped frames. Even DV's relatively tame data rate is too much for Zip or CD-ROM drives.

These drives are, however, ideal for moving broadcast-quality media from one computer to another. Once captured onto an approved drive, you can use Zip or CD-R disks to copy these files and move them from room to room. I do say that with some reservations, though. In my limited experience with removable media disks, I have found that they're best suited for graphics or other files. Copying a video file from a hard drive to a removable drive and then back to another drive is a slow process at best, and it also creates potential for corruption in those files. The file-corruption issue is anecdotal, but my personal experience has shown me never to rely on these drives to move around video files.

FireWire drives

FireWire-based drives for digital video? They said it couldn't be done. And they were right *at the time.*

The story of FireWire's initial difficulties travels along the boulevard of broken dreams. The FireWire standard was announced with much fanfare by Apple, and it seemed like it was destined to replace overnight many of the awkward, older technologies, like SCSI (described later in this chapter). The first-generation FireWire drives stuttered, hiccupped, and dropped frames during video capture and playback—an unmitigated disaster that portended the end before FireWire's beginning.

Much of the problem wasn't with FireWire itself, but with its theoretical transfer rate of 400 Mbps. Many of the causes included poorly written FireWire drivers, slow drive mechanisms, and largely, the bridge circuit that translates and transfers the data between FireWire and the drive mechanism, usually an ATA drive. So Apple rolled up its sleeves and revamped its FireWire drivers while hard disk drive technology pushed the envelope with faster *and* cheaper drive units. But a major contributor to FireWire's recovery from its childhood woes was the introduction of the Oxford 911 bridge chipset used in FireWire drives. This new ATA-FireWire bridge increases transfer rate from real-world rates of 13MB/sec to more than 29MB/sec, allowing for multiple channels of streaming data and RAID options that can push data rates up to 75MB/sec and higher.

Today it seems you can't throw a stick without hitting a FireWire drive (see Figure 4-3). FireWire seems as ubiquitous as the personal computer. Manufacturers of professional video equipment, such as Sony, Panasonic, and JVC, have begun to include FireWire ports on their high-end broadcast video decks and cameras. Peripheral equipment from scanners and printers to CD and DVD burners now offer a FireWire interface. With the recent release of FireWire 800 — doubling the throughput capability of the original protocol — FireWire seems to have emerged from its long and painful role as the ugly duckling.

Note

FireWire is also known as IEEE-1394, a standard originated and developed by Apple Computer. Numerous cameras use this to transfer DV to the computer. Sony labels the FireWire as iLink. FireWire is also used for scanners, disk drives, and other peripherals.

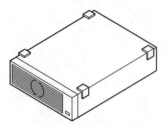

Figure 4-3: Club Mac offers FireWire disk drives, but they are not capable of capturing most formats of digital video.

A Club Mac FireWire drive

There is just one problem with using FireWire drives to capture video: *Apple has not approved any FireWire drive for use with Final Cut Pro.* This means that Apple does not guarantee you'll be able to capture to or play back from a FireWire drive for all but the least demanding of codecs (like DV) while using Final Cut Pro. You're likely to drop frames and have other issues.

Let's examine for a moment what Apple's lack of approval really means. Deep in some inner sanctum of the Apple campus in Cupertino, California, resides a testing station. On this station is a Final Cut Pro timeline that Apple uses to test all FireWire drives. Apple engineers have fashioned a standard project and a timeline in Final Cut Pro. If this timeline plays fine on a given FireWire drive, then that drive will be considered for approval. When testing a FireWire drive, an engineer copies the project and the media onto it and then plays it from the drive. The drive skips frames like mad, and the engineer shakes his head in a dejected fashion. Another one bites the dust. The engineer unplugs the drive and drops it into the trash bucket on the way out the door of the lab.

Before you write off all FireWire drives, consider the sequence that Apple engineers use to test drives. The sequence has eight audio tracks, as well as numerous places where more than one video track is used. The sequence contains many examples of compositing or multilayering. Most FireWire drives currently available fail to perform adequately using this sequence. But what if you're working with a sequence that contains just two tracks of audio and barely any multilayering? When I tested a Club Mac FireWire drive under this limited scenario, it produced very acceptable results. This means that if you're planning projects that won't go on for hours, you're planning simple audio work, and you don't use a lot of multilayered sequences, you can very successfully hook up one of these Club Mac FireWire drives to your G4 and digitize and edit. Just keep in mind that Apple has not approved these drives, so use them at your own risk.

All FireWire-based drives are, however, ideal for moving media and projects around. Some people I know use these drives for backing up their media as well. There are even pocket-size FireWire drives that power off the computer's FireWire port, through the same data cable, thus eliminating the need for an external power source or cord. What I really love about them is that as soon as you hook them up, they show up on your desktop. There's no need to restart your computer. The files also copy quite fast.

EIDE or Ultra ATA drives

The terms EIDE (Enhanced Integrated Drive Electronics) and Ultra ATA (AT Attachment, a term based on an old IBM PC drive specification) are used interchangeably to refer to a type of hard drive that is common in personal computers. EIDE drives are ideal drives for DV video, and many Final Cut Pro editors use them. EIDE drives with the ATA-33 designation have a data rate of 33MB/sec, and ATA-66 drives have a calculated throughput of 66MB/sec. The latest generation of EIDE drives, ATA-100 and ATA-133, are even fast enough to be used for low- to moderate-quality MJPEG projects. Apple G4s have ATA-100 drives.

EIDE drives have no problem handling DV's fixed data rate of 3.6MB/sec. These drives are small and are installed internally on G4 and G3 computers. Many editors use these internal drives for media capture for Final Cut Pro. Apple, however, strongly discourages the use of main system drives for media capture. Apple recommends that if you're considering purchasing additional EIDE drives to add to your workstation, they meet the following specifications:

✦ Sustained transfer rate of 8MB/sec or faster

✦ Average seek time less than 9ms

✦ Spindle speed of at least 5,400RPM

Modern EIDE drives that meet these specifications are the norm today, and best of all, they're usually quite affordable. This makes EIDE drives ideally suited for the Final Cut Pro user, especially if you're working with content that uses DV compression.

To install an EIDE drive inside your computer, you need an ATA interface. This consists of a PCI card that takes up one of the PCI slots in your G4. Apple G4s already have an ATA interface built in. If you need to install an ATA interface card, make sure that you have a vacant PCI slot available. The Mac OS allows you to run up to four ATA drives off one ATA interface. You may also need a special bracket that allows you to install more than two drives inside the G4 case.

Caution Many Apple resellers offer G4s with up to four ATA drives installed internally. This can raise your storage space as high as 1TB! Yep that's right, a full 1,000GB (4 x 250GB drives) or more, depending on the size of each drive, and this much storage space can be tempting. However, experience suggests that the heat generated by four hard drives in an enclosed space such as a G4 case, along with the heat of the processor itself, is not ideal for the life of the drives. I strongly suggest limiting yourself to two additional internal ATA drives giving you a total of three.

SCSI drives

SCSI stands for *Small Computer Systems Interface* and is commonly pronounced *scuzzy*. SCSI is a standard that has been around for a while and is used for everything from scanners to disk drives. Anyone who has used SCSI devices knows that they usually mean a hornet's nest of connectors, cables, IDs, and terminators. As far as I'm concerned, SCSI won't die fast enough. In this day and age of plug-and-play toys like the tiny VST FireWire drives that hold a gazillion gigabytes of video and slip into my shirt pocket, SCSI is an old and painfully cumbersome standard that is an annoyance in virtually every way.

SCSI stinks like mad in every way but one: It is by far the best and the most reliable way to work with digital video. Despite all the talk about FireWire and fancy arrays of IDEs, SCSI is still the mother of all drives and shows no sign of slowing down. SCSI is an old standard and, over the years, it has spawned numerous variations: SCSI-1, SCSI-2 (fast), Ultra SCSI, and so on. (I keep waiting for the low-fat SCSI.) The current reigning SCSI standard is Ultra2-LVD SCSI and Ultra160 SCSI and recently, Ultra 320 SCSI. Ultra2-LVD SCSI is capable of sustained data rates of up to 80MB/sec; 160M SCSI up to 160MB/sec; and Ultra 320, you guessed it, is rated to have a maximum data rate up to 320MB/sec. Speed such as this is what makes SCSI drives so well suited to digital video work.

SCSI drives are often designed to be used externally, connecting to your computer through a SCSI cable. As mentioned earlier in this chapter, external drives help you avoid heat-related problems inside your computer case. In order to run a SCSI drive, you need a SCSI interface. As with EIDE interfaces, SCSI interface cards are usually PCI-based cards that reside in a PCI slot in your computer. The two most well known SCSI card makers are ATTO and Adaptec.

Theoretically, you can daisy-chain up to 14 SCSI drives off of one interface card, but you'd have to be out of your mind to do so. I strongly recommend that you not daisy-chain more than four SCSI devices off of one interface card, because configuring and managing those devices will be a lot easier. The last drive in the chain must be terminated, and this is accomplished with a special device called a *terminator*. Many newer SCSI devices have a built-in termination feature, controlled using a switch on the back of the device. Figure 4-4 illustrates a typical SCSI chain with three devices.

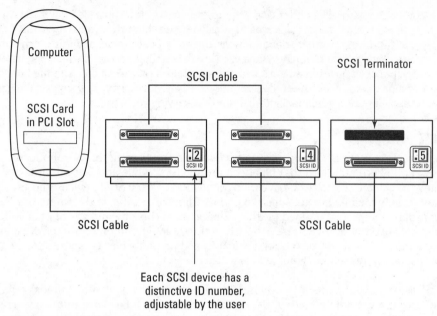

Figure 4-4: SCSI is an older but fast and reliable standard for disk drives and peripherals. Multiple SCSI devices can be daisy-chained as shown here.

Each device on a SCSI chain must also have a unique ID number. These ID numbers are user selectable by switches on the back of the SCSI device. If your Mac has a SCSI drive as its main internal drive, that drive usually has an ID number of 0. If the CD-ROM drive in your Mac is a SCSI device, its ID is most likely 3. Keep this in mind when setting ID numbers on other SCSI devices.

Caution   SCSI chains are very sensitive to cable lengths. Try to keep the total length of all the SCSI cable in a chain to under 20 feet. Keep the length of cable *between* SCSI devices down to 18 to 24 inches.

Despite the advent of FireWire and the promise of an end to the SCSI nightmare, SCSI is thriving. In fact, new standards are emerging on the SCSI scene. Ultra 320 SCSI is a new standard that boosts data rates up to 320MB/sec. When Apple engineers want to test Final Cut Pro with HDTV (High Definition Television), they hook up a new SCSI 320 interface and strap themselves in with seat belts. The data rate of HDTV can exceed 160MB/sec! That makes anything else look like a trickle from a leaky tap. The full 10-bit 60i standard is 161MB/sec!

RAID

The acronym RAID stands for *Redundant Arrays of Independent Disks.* RAID is a method of combining multiple disk drives into a single unit, creating an array of redundant drives that improves the performance and the reliability of the data and the throughput. There are many types of RAID that are defined as levels. RAID Level5 (RAID 5) is considered ideal for video capture. This level delivers both high performance and data redundancy. Data redundancy is created by copying your data on hidden portions of the other disks in the array. That way if you lose your data from one drive, you can recover it from another. RAID Level 3 is also used by many productions. Like RAID 5, RAID 3 reads and writes data across multiple disks for increase throughput, but it does not write redundant files for data backup. The advantage of using RAID 3 over RAID 5 is simple mathematics: Because you are not writing data files twice for backup protection, you can capture twice the amount of video to the RAID.

RAIDs are a reliable, secure, and expensive way of working with digital video. If you're planning a small edit facility or a large production setup, you should seriously consider RAID drives.

Medea drives

If you're considering drives for a setup that you'll be using with video that has a higher data rate than DV, you may want to consider Medea drives. Medea is a company that specializes in video storage solutions and has had well-deserved success because its drives are cheap and easy to set up. Medea makes VideoRaid disk arrays in stand-alone modules of two, four, or six drives. Figure 4-5 shows two of their drives.

Figure 4-5: Medéa is the maker of some very popular drives for storing digital video, such as these VideoRaid models.

Drives come in single modules of up to 160GB and offer data rates as high as 55MB/sec. They are extremely easy to hook up and the basic Mac disk utility is used to format them. You can daisy-chain Medea drives into modules of up to 2 terabytes! (1 terabyte equals 1,000GB.)

Converting Analog Video to FireWire

Although Final Cut Pro is most often associated with digital video, you may also have to work with analog formats such as VHS. Or you may simply need to output your video program to VHS. Generally speaking you need a video capture card when working with analog sources, but sometimes that's overkill. For something as low-resolution as VHS or an old 8mm tape, a video card may not be necessary. A simpler solution for converting analog video sources is an external device that converts analog video to FireWire and vice versa. These analog-to-DV converters are made by many companies including Sony, Canopus, Datavideo, and Formac. Figure 4-6 shows a picture of the Sony DVMC-DA2 unit.

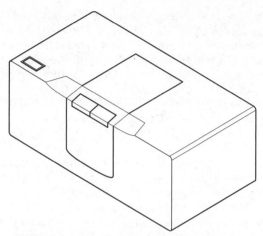

Figure 4-6: The Sony DVMC-DA2 allows you to convert analog video to DV and visa versa.

This small and easy-to-operate converter has both analog and FireWire inputs and outputs. You can simply plug in your video and audio outputs from your VHS deck into the converter's video and audio in ports (the unit has both S-Video and composite inputs), and then connect the converter's FireWire Out port to the FireWire port into your computer. When you play the VHS tape, it's converted to DV and captured into your computer using FireWire. A DV signal can be sent back to the analog VHS recorder just as easily by reversing the wire connections.

An analog-to-digital converter is ideal for converting basic analog formats such as VHS and 8mm to DV. However, keep in mind that it only has S-Video and composite video interfaces as well as unbalanced audio inputs. For formats such as Betacam or higher, you should consider a video card approved by Apple for use with Final Cut Pro. These cards offer component video interfaces as well as balanced professional-level audio interfaces.

Cross-Reference

For more on component video and balanced audio connectors, see Chapter 2.

Using Device Control

Device control is a crucial concept in digital video editing. The concept of Device Control is based on the interface of hardware, such as video decks, with nonlinear editors, such as Final Cut Pro. Part of device control is having the proper connections, and the other part is software being able to talk to the hardware in order for Final Cut Pro to work properly with the video deck or camera. For example, the device control must receive timecode and transport control cues *from* the tape deck, and at the same time relay timecode and deck control instructions from Final Cut Pro *back* to the deck. Using device control, Final Cut Pro will be able to control the playback, rewind, and fast-forward functions on your deck. This is important because it allows you to mark In and Out points for your shots and cue them up for capturing. Properly configured device control also allows Batch Capture. This is the ability to automatically line up a bunch of clips on tape and capture them all at once.

Batch Capturing with Final Cut Pro is covered in Chapter 7.

Precise device control is critical because without 100-percent frame-accurate control, you can't expect to recapture successfully. If you're working offline by capturing analog video at low resolution and plan to recapture the final edited sequence later at high resolution, you must have device-control reliability, or else your timecode will be unreliable, and you'll end up with the wrong shots. You'll encounter two kinds of device control when working in Final Cut Pro: FireWire device control for FireWire components, and Serial RS-232 or RS-422 device control for professional decks.

FireWire device control

In the case of DV-based cameras and decks, device-control information (along with the timecode) is sent through the FireWire cable. An important thing to note about DV-based device control is that it is *not* 100-percent frame accurate. Even though timecode on DV tapes is displayed in the SMPTE format of hours:minutes:seconds:frames, it is still technically not timecode that conforms fully to Society of Motion Picture and Television Engineers (SMPTE) specifications. This generally does not affect you if you're working strictly with DV (beyond the fact that it isn't 100-percent reliable), but it does affect you if you're working in a cross-format environment.

For more information on working with timecode see Chapter 9.

FireWire device control can be used successfully to control the transport functions such as play, rewind, and fast-forward on your DV camcorder. However, this wears out the mechanism of your camcorder. I strongly recommend that you purchase a basic DV deck if you're going to be logging and capturing DV for hours on end. Avoid using your camera as a logging and capturing deck.

Final Cut Pro allows two types of FireWire-based device control:

✦ Apple FireWire
✦ Apple FireWire Basic

The default in Final Cut Pro and for most cameras and decks should be Apple FireWire. However, DV devices vary in their compliance to the full set of specifications in the FireWire device-control protocol. In the case of a device that does not fully comply with the protocol, Apple offers the Apple FireWire Basic device control. Apple FireWire Basic works with a wider variety of gear than Apple FireWire. Chapter 5 shows you how to select specific device controls.

Caution A common mistake is to leave a DV camera in Camera mode while trying to capture clips. Be sure to switch your DV camcorder to VCR mode before capturing clips. On DV-based decks there may also be a Local and Remote selection button. Local setting allows manual control from the deck itself. Switch to Remote if you're using device control.

Serial RS-232 and RS-422 device control

Nearly all professional-level analog camcorders and decks use serial device control. Numerous prosumer- and professional-level DV devices also offer this type of device control. Serial device control is facilitated by a special cable connected to a 9-pin connector on the back of a video deck and to the serial port on your computer. Figure 4-7 illustrates a 9-pin serial connector. The serial device control cable only sends and receives the timecode and transport cue information. Video and audio signals are transmitted through other cables, such as composite, S-Video, or component connectors.

RS-232 and RS-422 are generally the same except that RS-232 is an older protocol and found on less-expensive decks and devices. RS-422 is a much more common protocol today, and it offers a more robust form of serial device control.

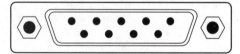

Figure 4-7: The RS-422 is a 9-pin device control connector that appears on numerous professional-level video decks.

To use serial device control you need to connect the 9-pin port on the back of your deck to the serial port of your computer. However, for many years now, Macs have replaced the serial port in favor of a USB (Universal Serial Bus) port. You will need to add a 9-pin connector to your G4 using either a USB serial adapter cable, or, a Serial card that installs into one of your computer's PCI slots. Currently, Keyspan is the only Apple-approved manufacturer of Serial interfaces for use with Final Cut Pro 4.

Tip   You can check for Apple-approved hardware that will work properly with Final Cut Pro on their website at www.apple.com/finalcutpro/qualification.html.

Device-control protocols supported by Final Cut Pro

Final Cut Pro supports a variety of device-control protocols. Check your hardware to ensure that it supports one of the following protocols:

✦ **Apple FireWire and Apple FireWire Basic:** Used with DV- and FireWire-based devices

✦ **Sony RS-422:** The most current professional serial device-control protocol

✦ **Sony RS-232:** Final Cut Pro supports many variations of this protocol

✦ **Sony VISCA:** An older Sony protocol, seen mostly as a small 8-pin connector and sometimes used by S-VHS decks

✦ **Sony LANC:** An older and somewhat limited protocol; you'll need an Addenda RS-4/L adapter for this

✦ **Panasonic RS-232 and RS-422:** Panasonic's version of serial device-control protocols

✦ **JVC RS-232:** JVC decks commonly use this serial protocol

Capturing from devices without device control

If you have a deck that doesn't support device control (such as a VHS home VCR), you're still able to capture clips with Final Cut Pro by disabling device control (see Chapter 5 for details). However, any material captured without device control should always be done with the understanding that you cannot expect to recapture it again later at a higher resolution, meaning you won't be able to do offline editing with this material.

Setting Up Your Hardware

You want to hook up your camera or deck to your computer to capture or play back your footage. But there is more to this process than knowing the difference between In and Out ports. You may want to use a TV or a monitor to view your work and a set of external speakers to hear your audio. There are many variations to how you can set up your editing station, depending on whether you want a strictly DV-based setup or you want to use an Apple-approved third-party video card. Your setup will also vary depending on the type of device control you plan to use. And of course, you have to decide what kind of disk drive you're going to store all your video on. Let's look at a few scenarios for how you may set up your video editing hardware.

If you're unfamiliar with video and audio connectors and what they look like, see Chapter 2.

A basic DV setup

The most basic setup you can have is to simply connect your camera to the computer. All that's required is that both your computer and your DV camera have FireWire ports (labeled iLink on some cameras). A 6-pin-to-4-pin FireWire cable is needed for this setup. The camera gets the 4-pin end of the cable while the computer gets the 6-pin plug.

This simple camera-to-FireWire setup (shown in Figure 4-8) is the most basic hardware configuration you can use. It allows you to capture footage from your DV camera and bring it into the computer using Final Cut Pro. You can edit the footage and send the final program back to the tape on camera using the same FireWire cable. All video, audio, and timecode information travels over the FireWire cable. Device control is also accomplished via FireWire, and you can monitor your audio through the computer speakers.

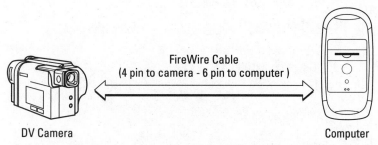

FireWire Cable
(4 pin to camera - 6 pin to computer)

DV Camera   Computer

Figure 4-8: The most basic hardware setup you can use with Final Cut Pro involves simply connecting a camera to your computer using a FireWire interface.

An intermediate DV setup

If you have slightly more ambitious plans and expect to spend many days capturing and editing, you may want to bring your hardware setup to the next level. In this case, you should get a DV deck, which saves wear and tear on the transport mechanism of your camera. A monitor is important because it allows you to view your DV picture in full resolution and NTSC colors. A set of external speakers allows you to listen to your audio for careful work, and some additional storage space will allow you to capture more material. Device control is accomplished with an RS-422 or RS-232 (depending on your deck) port and a Stealth Serial Adapter. Video and audio information still travel in the FireWire cable. And in the case of a DV deck, you'll probably need a 6-pin-to-6-pin FireWire cable, because most DV decks use a 6-pin FireWire port. Figure 4-9 shows such a setup.

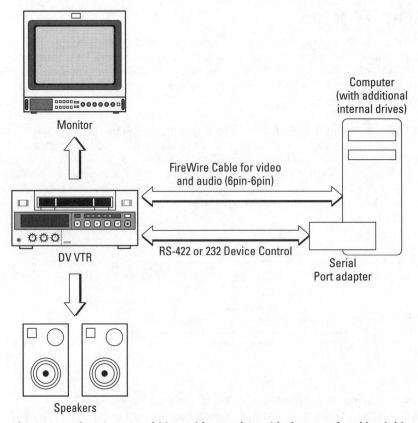

Figure 4-9: If you're an ambitious videographer with dreams of making it big, then you need a setup like the one shown here.

An advanced DV setup

For advanced, professional-level DV editing you'll want to add storage space. This probably means adding SCSI-based external drives. To connect SCSI drives to your computer, you'll need an SCSI controller card, which will occupy a PCI slot on your computer. Another feature you may want in an advanced DV setup is an analog to DV converter such as the Sony DVMC-DA2 converter. This allows you to easily import video from analog formats such as VHS or Hi8 and export your completed programs to VHS tape. Figure 4-10 illustrates an advanced DV setup like the one described here.

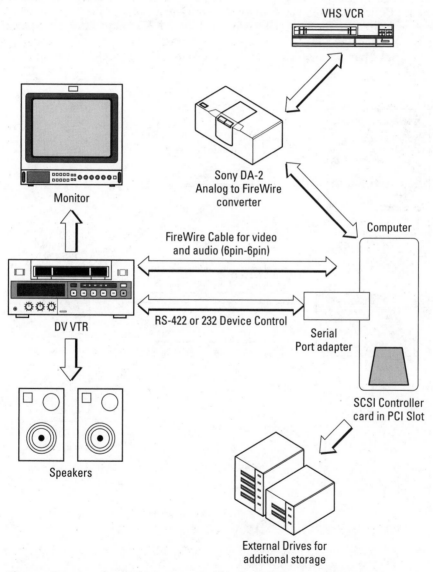

Figure 4-10: An advanced DV setup could include a Sony DA2 converter for converting basic analog signals to DV, as well as extra storage in the form of external SCSI drives.

A possible analog setup

If you plan to edit a lot of analog content along with DV content, an Apple-approved digitizing card is required. This card will occupy a PCI slot in your computer. Consider this when purchasing a computer for your setup to ensure that there is a vacant PCI slot available. Additionally, a sync generator may also be a good idea when working with professional analog decks and Final Cut Pro. A sync generator provides a signal used for synchronization of the deck with the video card. Figure 4-11 shows a hardware setup for Final Cut Pro that accommodates analog video sources.

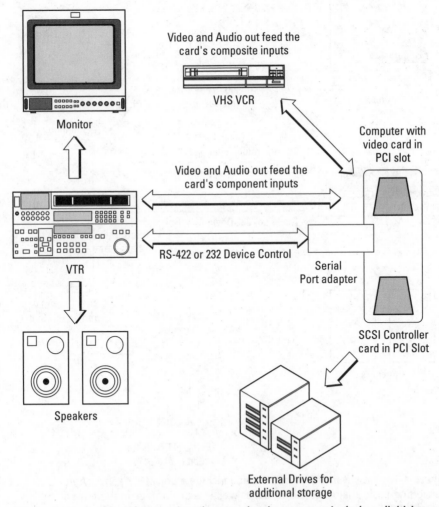

Figure 4-11: Analog video requires that your hardware setup include a digitizing card and possibly a sync generator.

Optimizing Final Cut Pro's Performance

Final Cut Pro can be a finicky application. It requires love and care for best performance. Part of this is due to the program's amazing flexibility and the fact that it can place huge demands on your computer system. Final Cut Pro is flexible enough to work on anything from a modest iMac G4 to the latest dual processor G4 tower.

For Final Cut Pro to do its job correctly, you have to watch out for a few details. The next few sections show you some of the settings and controls that you need to check to ensure the best possible performance from your system.

Cross-Reference   If you haven't yet installed Final Cut Pro, see Appendix A.

Allocating memory to Final Cut Pro

When you open a file on a Mac, it's loaded into the computer memory, called RAM (short for *Random Access Memory*). Computers ship with different amounts of RAM pre-installed. In addition to the data of the file being opened, the application running the file requires RAM, too. The operating system, extensions, and other utilities all take their own bite out of the computer's total RAM as well.

To use Final Cut Pro, Apple recommends that you have a minimum of 384MB of RAM installed on your computer. To run Soundtrack and RT Extreme, 512MB are recommended. However, for real-world use, 1GB or more is preferable.

"Why so much memory?" you might ask. In order for Final Cut Pro to perform its feats of editing magic, it requires a fast CPU, hence the G4 minimum processor requirement, and *tons* of RAM. But there is another very important reason to install as much RAM as you can mortgage: Final Cut Pro has never run smoothly when virtual memory is enabled in the OS System Preferences — it still doesn't. But under the required Mac OS X10.2 or higher, there is no longer an option to turn off virtual memory or allocate RAM for most native OS X applications. In Final Cut Pro, however, you can set a *percentage* of unused RAM allocated to Final Cut Pro at startup, which can prevent the Mac OS from using virtual memory unnecessarily. To set RAM allocation for Final Cut Pro:

1. **Start Final Cut Pro.**

2. **Go to System Settings under the menu heading Final Cut Pro (or press Shift+Q).**

3. **Click on the Memory & Cache tab (shown in Figure 4-12).**

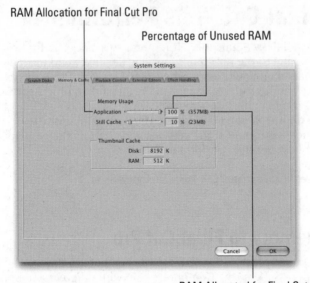

RAM Allocation for Final Cut Pro

Percentage of Unused RAM

RAM Allocated for Final Cut Pro

Figure 4-12: The Memory & Cache preference setting allows
you to allocate RAM for Final Cut Pro.

4. **If the Application slider is not at 100 percent (that is, all the way to the right), set it there.**

   Alternatively, you can click in the Application percentage field, type **100,** and hit Enter.

   Note the amount of unused RAM currently available in parentheses to the right of the slider. This tells you how much RAM you currently have allocated to Final Cut Pro less the RAM used by the OS.

5. **Move the Application slider to the left to allocate less RAM to Final Cut Pro when it starts up.**

   Allow for some unexpected RAM overhead and one or two smaller applications to run concurrently with Final Cut Pro. If the total amount of RAM used by Final Cut Pro and the other applications does not exceed the total amount of unused RAM available as noted in Step 4 earlier, then virtual memory will not be used, or at worst, used minimally.

Note   The minimum RAM needed to run Final Cut Pro is 125MB. If you have less than this available, the slider will be dimmed.

6. **Click the OK button to accept changes.**

7. **Save your project by pressing Command+S.**

8. **Quit Final Cut Pro.**

   Your RAM allocation changes will be used at the next restart of Final Cut Pro.

Final Cut Pro and Internet surfing

Some people say you shouldn't use your digital editing workstation for Web surfing. Some experts recommend that you get two separate computers, one for Final Cut Pro work and another for Internet access.

This view is not entirely accurate. If you want to surf the Web, you can. OS X has all but negated the issue of disabling all non-essential system extensions, such as TCP/IP for Internet connection, when Final Cut Pro is in use because of its implementation of true Preemptive Multitasking. However, being a true professional can sometimes be synonymous with being a paranoid, and I, for one, still advise that you not be logged on or using a network to access the Internet while working with Final Cut Pro.

A related, but more insidious problem is file sharing while using Final Cut Pro. Enabling your computer to be shared on a network, whether through AppleTalk, TCP/IP, or FTP can have serious impact on Final Cut Pro's performance. This is especially true while capturing media or laying programs back to tape. Even basic playback and rendering performance can be adversely affected if your computer is being accessed by others. Simply put: Turn file sharing off.

Choosing an initial setup for FCP

The first time you start Final Cut Pro, you'll be asked to choose an initial setup by the Choose Setup dialog box (shown in Figure 4-13). This box contains two crucial startup settings that affect the way Final Cut Pro operates on your system—you should choose your setup carefully:

Summary of selected Preset

Presets pull-down menu

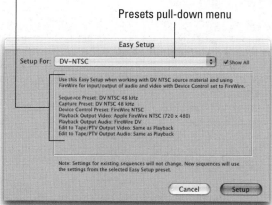

Figure 4-13: The Choose Setup box is presented to you the first time you start up Final Cut Pro.

✦ **Setup For:** This pull-down menu contains a list of what are known in Final Cut Pro as *Easy Setups*. An Easy Setup is a collection of settings that affect how Final Cut Pro is configured. Some commonly used Easy Setups are provided for you as presets, but you can make your own. Since Final Cut Pro can work with so many types of video formats, device-control protocols, and capture settings, an Easy Setup is a good way to create setups based on the specific settings that you'll be working with in Final Cut Pro.

Below the Setup For pull-down menu is a brief summary of the setup. You'll find detailed information about the Sequence and Capture presets, as well as the device-control protocol that you'll be using with this setup.

Checking the Show All checkbox will show you *all* the presets in the pull-down menu Setup For. There are 36 presets from Apple, but you'll only see 4 presets plus the option for a Custom Setup if you keep this option unchecked. The four basics are: DV-NTSC, DV-PAL, Offline-RT NTSC, and Offline-PAL.

✦ **Primary Scratch Disk:** Use this pop-up menu to select from available volumes currently mounted on the desktop in the Finder. This is only an initial selection that can be changed later. However, always select a disk drive designed for video capture and playback that is connected to your computer by a hardwire cable, not mounted through a local area network (*LAN*). Most LAN transfer rates fall well short of even DV requirements.

By default, Final Cut Pro chooses the disk where the application was installed as the Primary Scratch Disk. In most cases, this will be your Macintosh system hard drive. It is strongly advised that you use a separate disk for capturing media.

For more on customizing Final Cut Pro, see Chapter 6.

Troubleshooting startup errors

One of the most common errors you'll encounter when starting Final Cut Pro is the External Video error shown in Figure 4-14. The beauty of this error message (unlike some others) is that it tells you exactly why it showed up and what you should do to fix it. This error generally appears because your hardware is not connected to the computer properly or the external decks or cameras are not turned on.

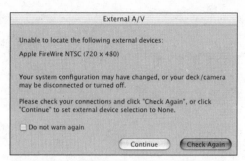

Figure 4-14: This error message may appear when starting up Final Cut Pro if your external hardware is not ready.

When you see this message, check all your cables, power connections, and power switches. When you think everything is ready, click Check Again.

If you don't care about the DV device being hooked up right now, just click Continue to close the message.

At this stage, you're done setting up for Final Cut Pro. It's now time to have a closer look at the Final Cut Pro interface. For that, you have to turn to the next chapter.

✦   ✦   ✦

Touring Final Cut Pro's Interface

The previous chapter covered a number of hardware issues that need to be addressed as you set up your editing system for Final Cut Pro. This chapter discusses the actual Final Cut Pro software. Why, you may ask, do I not dive right into editing and doing fancy effects with Final Cut Pro? You'll soon find that actually editing in Final Cut Pro is not all that difficult. The interface was *designed* to be mastered in a relatively short time. And if you have experience with other non-linear editing systems, you'll pick it up in no time. However, inside the Final Cut Pro interface lie some key differences that you may not find on your own. These differences may not affect you much at first, but rest assured they *will* affect you at some time during your work.

Of course, if you're brand new to nonlinear editors this chapter is important as well. This chapter provides an overview of all the menus and the most common windows that make up Final Cut Pro. You'll also find out about built-in help resources in Final Cut Pro, and it shows you how to customize and save the Final Cut Pro window to meet your own preferences.

Touring the Final Cut Pro Interface

The Final Cut Pro interface follows many of the conventions set forth over the years by the Macintosh operating system as well as other nonlinear editing programs. Its features are organized into systems of menus, windows, palates, keyboard shortcuts, and context menus. An understanding of the Final Cut Pro interface is required before you can perform any meaningful work in the program. The next few sections look at the various parts of this interface, beginning with the menus.

Using menus

Like nearly all Macintosh programs, Final Cut Pro includes a lot of menus. These menus are not your typical menus. Instead of chicken cutlets, salads, and burgers, these menus contain all the commands you need to edit in Final Cut Pro. Need to mark an In point? Pull down the Mark menu and choose the Mark In command. Need to quit? Pull down the File menu and choose Quit. Need a milkshake? Sorry, not on these menus. You may be familiar with the Mac OS menus and their behaviors, but a basic refresher may still be in order. To open a menu, click a menu name at the top of the screen while Final Cut Pro is active. Figure 5-1 shows the Modify menu in Final Cut Pro.

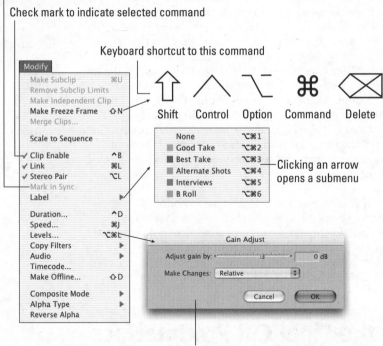

Dimmed menu items not available in the current window

Check mark to indicate selected command

Keyboard shortcut to this command

Clicking an arrow opens a submenu

Choosing a command with ellipses opens a dialog box

Figure 5-1: Each menu in Final Cut Pro is broken down into subcategories that are separated by gray lines. Keyboard shortcuts are listed to the right of commands whenever applicable.

As you can see in Figure 5-1, the menus can contain many options. Features to look for in menus include the following:

✦ **Submenus:** If a menu item has an arrow (black triangle) next to it, click the item to open a submenu of additional options.

✦ **Keyboard shortcuts:** Many functions have keyboard shortcuts. If a menu item has a corresponding shortcut, the shortcut is indicated to the right of the item.

Tip

If you have assigned, or reassigned a keyboard shortcut using Final Cut Pro 4.0's new remappable keyboard feature, the first keystroke assigned will be visible next to the item in the menu. (You can assign more than one keystroke shortcut to a command.)

Cross-Reference

Customizing your keyboard for Final Cut Pro is covered in detail in Appendix B.

✦ **Selected options:** Clicking a menu item one time selects it. The selection is confirmed with a check mark that appears in the menu. To toggle the selection on or off, reselect the item.

✦ **Dialog boxes:** Menu items that lead to dialog boxes have ellipses (. . .) after them.

Final Cut Pro menus are divided into eleven menu headings — Final Cut Pro, File, Edit, View, Mark, Modify, Sequence, Effects, Tools, Window, and Help. The next few sections briefly cover each of these menus.

Cross-Reference

See Appendix B for a detailed list of all keyboard shortcuts in Final Cut Pro.

Final Cut Pro menu

Under the new Aqua interface requirements of OS X, all native programs now have a new menu item titled with the application's name. Here you'll always find the application's Preference Settings, Quit command, and options previously found in OS 9's Application Switcher, like Hide application and Show All. Because Final Cut Pro has many Preference settings, this OS-required consolidation is a welcome change. Figure 5-2 shows the Final Cut Pro menu.

Figure 5-2: The Application menu shows you the currently active Application and rounds up most Preferences settings.

Another benefit of this new menu implementation is the ability to quickly and easily figure out which application of all the ones currently open on your computer is the currently active one—its name is the only one in bold type in the menu bar, which is right next to the aqua Apple icon.

File menu

The File menu enables you to create new Projects, Sequences, and Bins. Figure 5-3 shows the File menu. The File menu also enables you to open files that may be stored on your disk drive. Use this menu for saving files as well as importing and exporting most items to and from Final Cut Pro. Two important commands here are:

✦ **Log and Capture:** Leads to the Log and Capture window, used to capture media into Final Cut Pro.

✦ **Print to Video:** Allows you to play back your edited program to tape.

The list of recent projects has been moved from the bottom of this menu to the sub-menu named Open Recent.

Edit menu

The Edit menu (shown in Figure 5-4) contains common editing commands such as Cut, Copy, and Paste, which you know and love from many other Mac programs. These commands generally work much like they do in a word processor. The Copy command copies a clip and the Paste command pastes that clip to a new location. The Undo command is used to undo the last action taken. You can repeat Undo up to 99 times, undoing the last 99 actions (if your preferences are set for it). The lower part of this menu provides access to Properties information about individual items, as well as Project Properties for setting timecode display options and Comment Column Heading names.

Figure 5-3: The File menu contains commands for creating and managing projects.

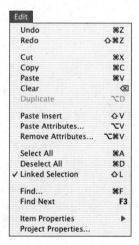

Figure 5-4: The Edit menu contains common editing commands.

View menu

The View menu (see Figure 5-5) controls the views of various windows. Commands for zooming, viewing overlays, and other view-related items are contained in this menu. The commands for viewing Wireframes are used when creating animations for clips and graphics. At the bottom part of this menu are a few options for playback, such as looping and audio scrubbing. Scrubbing enables you to shuttle through your audio while being able to hear it faster than real time, enabling you to locate specific audio portions of your content. External Video settings let you control the viewing of video on an external TV or monitor.

Figure 5-5: Changing the views of various windows is the task of some of the commands in the View menu.

Mark menu

Commands for marking clips in all kinds of ways are found in the Mark menu, shown in Figure 5-6. You can mark In and Out points on clips and in the timeline by using options from this menu. You can also use commands in the Mark menu to create split edits. *Split edits* are edits where either audio or video leads before the other. At the bottom of this menu are numerous choices for playing clips and navigating through your work.

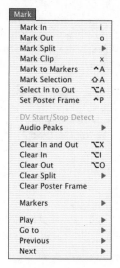

Figure 5-6: Marking In and Out points on clips is accomplished through the Mark menu. At the bottom of this menu are navigation commands.

Modify menu

The Modify menu (shown in Figure 5-7) could perhaps have a better name. This menu provides a hodgepodge of commands. Some of these commands do modify clips by changing the speed or duration, or by changing the Composite or Alpha assignment of clips. The menu also has some view-related commands, such as Clip Visibility, renamed Clip Enable, and Link. The Clip Enable command toggles the visibility of a clip in the Timeline without needing to delete it. The Link command is used to toggle the linking of the video portion of a clip with the audio portion.

Figure 5-7: Most of the commands in the Modify menu allow you to change many different attributes of a clip, such as Duration, Speed, and Timecode.

Sequence menu

The most important commands in the Sequence menu are the Render commands. These commands, as shown in Figure 5-8, tell Final Cut Pro to render effects or transitions you may have placed in your sequence. The Insert Tracks command enables you to add video and audio tracks to your Timeline.

Figure 5-8: The Sequence menu consists of commands that allow you to render sequences, trim edits, extend edits, lift clips, or add transitions.

Effects menu

The Effects menu contains commands and choices for controlling transitions and filters. This menu, as shown in Figure 5-9, is roughly divided into video transitions, video filters, audio transitions, and audio filters, with choices for setting favorites for each. The Effects menu has many submenus containing further options relating to transitions and filters.

Figure 5-9: The Effects menu is where you control transitions and filters.

Tools menu

The Tools menu, as shown in Figure 5-10, is where you'll find some of Final Cut Pro 4.0's coolest new features. From here you can access the real-time Audio Mixer, the Voice Over tool for adding narration directly into your sequences as it plays, as well as the Video Scopes. You can remap and create new keyboard shortcuts with your own set of hotkeys using the Keyboard Layout window, or add shortcut buttons to most windows using the Button List.

Figure 5-10: The Tools menu contains some new and useful tools for customizing your interface, recording a voiceover track, doing media analysis, as well as managing rendered files.

The Analyze Movie tool from previous versions remains indispensable for troubleshooting and finding out detailed information about individual clips, while the Render Manager enables you to clear up disk space by deleting old render files. This menu also has commands for accessing the FXBuilder, which enables you to create your own effects plug-ins for Final Cut Pro.

Window menu

The primary purpose of the Window menu (shown in Figure 5-11) is to help you manage window layouts. Managing your window layouts is important because placing your windows willy-nilly on the screen can adversely affect your playback and editing abilities in Final Cut Pro. You should get into the habit of using the Window ⇨ Arrange submenu to select from the many window layouts available to you. Doing so ensures skip-free performance from Final Cut Pro. This menu also allows you to bring up any window in the Final Cut Pro editing interface.

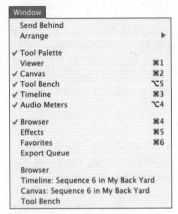

Figure 5-11: The Window menu allows windows management, which is quite important for optimizing your playback performance.

Help menu

The Help menu is possibly the most underrated of all Final Cut Pro menus. Figure 5-12 illustrates this deceivingly small but useful, some even say life-saving menu. Because the help files are now PDF (Adobe Acrobat's Portable Document Format) files, all Help files are searchable. The Final Cut Pro help system is described later in this chapter.

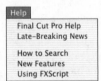

Figure 5-12: When you're screaming for help, the Help menu is the place to go.

Context sensitivity in Final Cut Pro menus

I am a longtime Mac user, and I have grown familiar with the behavior of windows and menus in the Macintosh Operating System. Mac makes adapting to different applications easy because their windows, menus, and other components follow the conventions of the Mac OS. One feature of Final Cut Pro that you may not be familiar with, however, is the context sensitivity of menus in the program.

For example, when you try to use some menus, you'll find that options are grayed out. There seems to be no obvious reason for it. You'll be ripping out your hair trying to figure out why. All Final Cut Pro menus limit the available options, depending on what window is highlighted or active at the time. The following figure illustrates two examples of the Mark menu; note that in one case many options are grayed out, and in the other, more options are available.

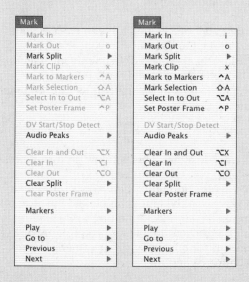

Final Cut Pro menus are context-sensitive because their appearance varies depending on the context in which they're used. Sometimes, this context can be difficult to ascertain. If you ever get frustrated trying to figure out why a certain command is not available, check to make sure that the right window is selected. The next figure illustrates what a window looks like when it's selected and when it isn't. As you can see, a selected window's title bar is lighter, and it has clearly delineated window controls in the upper-left corner.

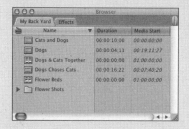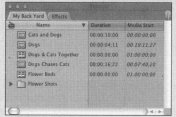

Keep the context sensitivity of Final Cut Pro's menus in mind as you work. If a command you need isn't available, make sure that the correct window or item is selected!

Taking the grand tour of windows and palettes

After you're familiar with Final Cut Pro's menus, it's time for a grand tour of the program's various windows. Like tourists in a new town, we don't have time to look at every detail of every window, so for now you'll just have a quick look at the essential landmarks. This section marks the essentials and shows the main sections. Like all enlightened tourists, however, you'll recognize that there's much more to this fascinating town of Final Cut Pro than these landmarks.

Despite the depth of Final Cut Pro's interface and menus, you'll spend most of your time in four main windows. The Browser, Viewer, Canvas, and Timeline windows make up the main part of your editing world. You also use a Tool palette for selecting various editing tools as well as an audio meter for monitoring audio levels. In the next few sections, you'll have the opportunity to look at those items as well as some other important windows that are a regular part of the Final Cut Pro experience.

Log and Capture window

The Log and Capture window is found in the File menu. This window performs two main functions. First, it allows you to *log* clips, which means entering information about them from the tapes that they're on. This information can consist of a clip's name, the reel name, and the In and Out points on the tape. The second function of this window is to capture the logged clips into your disk for editing with Final Cut Pro. The Log and Capture window includes a preview area where you can preview video on tape and includes transport controls for controlling your camera or deck. Figure 5-13 shows a view of the Log and Capture window.

Preview area for viewing tape footage   Field for logging information

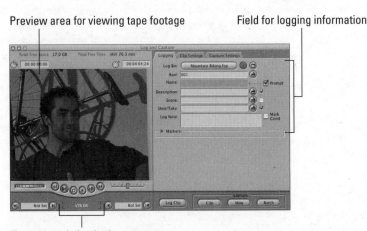

Tape controls for deck or camera

Figure 5-13: The Log and Capture window is primarily used to log information about clips on tape and capture them to the drive on your computer.

Tip If you don't have device control, the transport controls won't show up. You can still capture your material without device control; just press Play on your deck and click the Capture Now button, located in the lower-right corner.

Browser window

The Browser is your friend. When it comes to nonlinear editing, you can use all the friends you can get. The Browser is a place to store and organize all your source media and your Timelines (also called *sequences*). Each project has a tab in the Browser window. On each tab, you can find all the files for that project. You can have multiple projects open and move files between them as you choose.

The Browser also shows an incredible 45 columns of information about each item in it. This information is not only crucial for editing and organizing, but it serves as a basic database for troubleshooting. You can often find answers to you problems in Final Cut Pro by carefully looking at the Browser columns for the clips that may be creating trouble for you. The Browser also contains an Effects tab. All the effects and transitions live here. Each Browser has only one Effects tab. Figure 5-14 shows a typical Browser.

Each project has a separate tab in the Browser

The Browser has numerous sortable columns of information

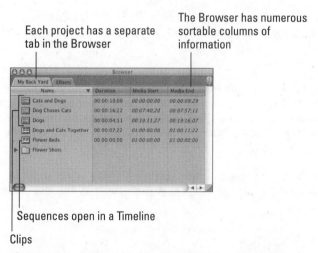

Sequences open in a Timeline

Clips

Figure 5-14: Make a friend of your Browser. The fields of information shown here tell you important information about your clips and sequences, helping you organize and troubleshoot your media.

Viewer window

In the Viewer window, you look at your unedited clips. You can load clips into the Viewer by double-clicking them in the Browser or on a Timeline. Figure 5-15 shows three different tabs of the Viewer window. This window has controls for playing and navigating in a clip as well as for marking selections or In and Out points. Timecode fields indicate the current timecode as well as the duration of selections.

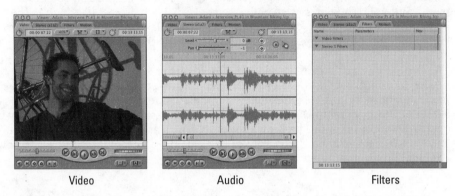

| Video | Audio | Filters |

Figure 5-15: The Viewer window is a versatile window used mainly for viewing source clips. The Audio, Filters, and Motion tabs in the Viewer window allow you to access various functions.

In addition to viewing and marking clips from the Browser or Timeline, the Viewer is where you can also create video media such as color bars, color mattes, blank filler clips called *slugs,* as well as text and titles. These types of video media are called generators and can be accessed from the Generator pop-up button in the lower-right corner of the video tab.

Note

The Viewer window is context-sensitive. For example, if there is no audio for a video clip, there will be no audio tab when that clip is loaded into the viewer. Smart, huh?

Canvas window

While the Viewer window shows source clips, the Canvas window shows clips as they are edited in sequences. Figure 5-16 shows a Canvas window. Many of the controls of the Canvas window are similar to controls in the Viewer window. The Canvas and the Timeline are closely related. Each sequence, when opened, opens a Timeline and a corresponding Canvas window. The Canvas window gives you a visual of what is playing in the sequence. If you find yourself confused by all that, read on and the relationships of the windows will become clearer to you.

Name of sequence being viewed in the Canvas window

Figure 5-16: The Final Cut Pro designers want you to feel like an artist so they named this window the Canvas window. This window is used to perform edits and to view edited sequences.

Timeline window

The Timeline window displays your video and audio tracks in a hierarchal order and is where you lay out your edits and arrange transitions. A Timeline window opens whenever you double-click a sequence in the Browser. A Timeline can have up to 99 video and 99 audio tracks. The base video track is labeled V1. However, any video track above another gets priority, meaning that the topmost track is seen first. Clips placed in the Timeline appear as colored strips that lie within tracks. By default, you'll see the first frame of the clip in the Timeline and the name of the clip. These clips can be moved in the Timeline to change their order.

The Timeline serves as a chart of what appears in the Canvas window. When you play the Timeline, your clips play in the Canvas window in the edited order. A thin gray line with a yellow triangle on top represents the playhead. The Canvas window displays the frame over which the line of the playhead is currently positioned. This line moves across the Timeline as it is played. Figure 5-17 shows a Timeline.

Browser window

Canvas window

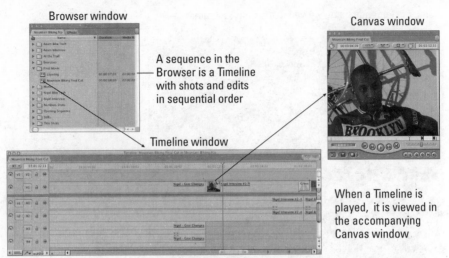

A sequence in the Browser is a Timeline with shots and edits in sequential order

Timeline window

When a Timeline is played, it is viewed in the accompanying Canvas window

Figure 5-17: A Timeline window shows the layout of your clips, transitions, effects, audio, and track information in the timeline. As the Timeline plays, it will be displayed in the Canvas window.

Cross-Reference Editing directly within the Timeline is covered in Chapter 11.

Trim Edit Window

Trimming is generally a term reserved in editing for fine adjustment of the edit points between clips in a Timeline. In common usage, simply adjusting an In or Out point of a single clip is also referred to as trimming. Final Cut Pro provides numerous tools and keyboard shortcuts to help you perform trimming. The Trim Edit window is a more advanced tool for trimming between two clips. The Trim Edit window can be seen in Figure 5-18. Double-clicking on an edit point between clips brings up the Trim Edit window. The window shows both sides of your edit and has many features to fine-tune the edit points and preview them.

Cross-Reference The Trim Edit window is covered in detail in Chapter 13.

The Tool palette

The Tool palette is a toolbox that contains all the editing tools available to you. Tools in this palette are used for selecting tracks, trimming clips, distorting, zooming, and more. Click and hold a tool to see additional tools as shown in Figure 5-19. If the Tool palette is not in view, choose Window ➪ Tools.

Clip A   Clip B

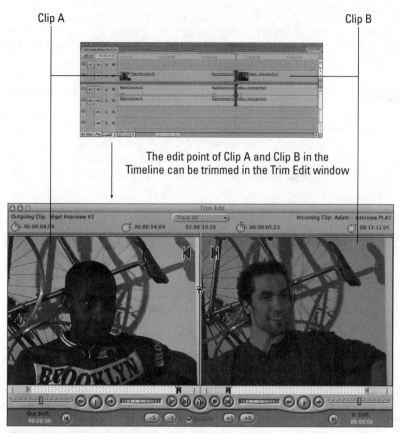

The edit point of Clip A and Clip B in the
Timeline can be trimmed in the Trim Edit window

Figure 5-18: The Trim Edit window allows fine adjustment of In and Out
points between two clips.

Press and hold to view other choices

Arrow tool —— A
Group tool —— G
Track tool —— T
Roll tool —— R
Slip tool —— S
Blade tool —— B
Zoom tool —— Z
Crop tool —— C
Pen tool —— P

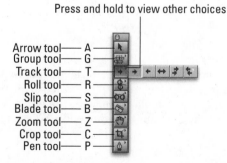

Figure 5-19: The Tool palette contains the
tools you'll need to crop, zoom, or perform
a variety of other edits to your clips.

Tip   Forget the name of a particular button in the Tool palette? Float your cursor over the button and a small yellow Tooltip appears naming the button. For buttons in button submenus, click and hold on the button for two seconds, and the name will be revealed.

Audio Meter

The floating Audio Meter is a dynamic indicator for audio levels played in any window. When audio is played, the LED type indicators light up and down this meter. The meter monitors audio levels during logging, during editing, or during playback to tape. If the meter is hiding or missing for some reason, choose Window ➪ Audio Meter to bring it back again. Figure 5-20 shows what the Audio Meter looks like.

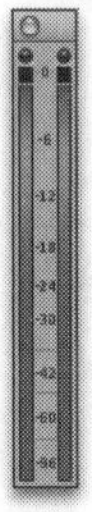

Figure 5-20: The Audio Meter is useful for monitoring your audio levels when working in Final Cut Pro.

One drawback to the Audio Meter is that the numbers are hard to read. I think Apple believes that everyone working with Final Cut Pro has 20/20 vision. Old geezers like me who cannot find their keys without glasses are left squinting, their noses an inch from the computer screen.

Cross-Reference   There are also audiometers in Final Cut Pro's new Audio Mixer tool. These Track level meters display the audio level of clips in tracks of the active Timeline only. For more details about audiometers and the Audio Mixer, see Chapter 14.

Print to Video window

The Print to Video command is found in the File menu.

The Print to Video window enables you to send your edited material to videotape. In this window, you have a choice of adding leader elements to the video such as color bars, tone, or a countdown. You can also add a black trailer at the end of your piece so that the tape does not abruptly end when your program ends. You can also choose to loop your footage. A key advantage of the Print to Video window is that Device Control is not required to play back your program to tape. This can be helpful in situations where you're playing back your program to a VHS home VCR and have no device control of the VCR. Figure 5-21 shows a Print to Video window.

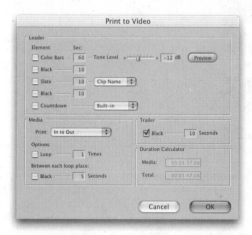

Figure 5-21: The Print to Video window helps you control playing back your material to tape, even when you do not have device control with your equipment.

Edit to Tape window

The Edit to Tape is accessed from the Tools menu.

If you have Device Control with your equipment, you'll use the Edit to Tape window instead of the Print to Video window to play back material to tape. The Edit to Tape window gives more control over the playback process. It allows you to insert edits on tape and control the timecode on the tape where the program will be mastered. This window looks and works like the Canvas window. However, unlike the Canvas window, where clips are edited into the Timeline, in the Edit to Tape window, clips are edited to tape. You can drag and drop entire sequences over this window for laying them back to tape with a precise timecode. Figure 5-22 shows the Edit to Tape window.

Choose video or audio for insert editing

Insert, assemble, or preview edit choices

Figure 5-22: The Edit to Tape window is used to play back edited material to tape. The Edit to Tape window requires Device Control, and as a result it has more features.

Media Manager window

This window is accessed from the File menu.

Material that you capture or import into a project gets stored in the Browser. However, the actual files are not really in the Browser. The media files go to your Scratch Disk. Clips in the Browser are merely links to the media files. The Media Manager window enables you to move and manage media files with options that can be especially helpful for large projects. You can gather media for a project, including the render files if you want, and move them to another folder while keeping them online in your project. This tool should be used with *extreme* caution because it can make permanent changes to your media and projects. Figure 5-23 shows the Media Manager window.

Render Manager window

To access the Render Manager, choose Tools ➪ Render Manager.

When you render a transition or effect, Final Cut Pro creates a render media file. This media file plays for the duration of the effect. However, if you delete this effect from the Timeline, the render cache file created for it remains and takes up disk space. The Render Manager window helps you delete unwanted render files. This window is seen in Figure 5-24.

Tip

The first five layouts saved to disk are added to the bottom of the Arrange menu and can be selected by clicking on them or pressing their default shortcut keystrokes, which are Control+Shift+(6,7,8,9,0).

To save a custom layout in Final Cut Pro:

1. **Lay out all your windows the way you'd like them.**

   Be sure there aren't any overlapping windows on the screen.

2. **Position your Tool Palette and the Audio Meter.**

3. **Hold down the Option key and choose Window ⇨ Arrange ⇨ Set Custom Layout 1 or Custom Layout 2.**

Tip

The resolution of your monitor at the time you make a custom layout will be the minimum resolution for that custom layout.

To select a custom layout after it's been saved, choose Window ⇨ Arrange ⇨ Custom Layout 1 or Custom Layout 2.

If you need more than the two Custom Layouts that are saved in Final Cut Pro, or if you want to use a custom layout for another workstation, you'll need to save it to your hard drive:

1. **Lay out all your windows the way you'd like them.**

   Be sure there aren't any overlapping windows on the screen.

2. **Position your Tool Palette and the Audio Meter.**

3. **Choose Window ⇨ Arrange ⇨ Save Window Layout.**

4. **Navigate to your desired folder to store your layouts.**

5. **Name your Custom Layout and click Save.**

Note

Final Cut Pro defaults to the folder location: `System Folder/Preferences/ Final Cut Pro User Data/Window Layout`.

To select a custom layout after it has been saved to disk, or import another's Custom Layout:

1. **Choose Window ⇨ Arrange ⇨ Restore Window Layout.**

2. **In the Open dialog box, navigate to the location of your custom layout.**

3. **Select the desired layout and click Open.**

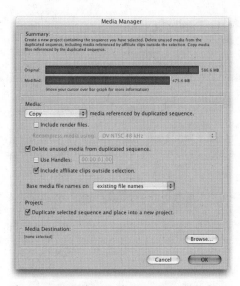

Figure 5-23: The Media Manager window enables you to locate and manage media, including render files, and copy or move them to other folders.

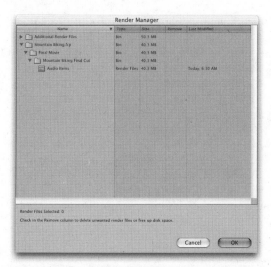

Figure 5-24: The Render Manager helps you free up disk space by deleting render files that are no longer in use.

Using keyboard and button shortcuts

The life of an editor using Final Cut Pro is made far easier by the existence of keyboard shortcuts. If all editing functions were performed using the menus, very little work would get done. With Final Cut Pro 4.0, you can assign any and every command to a keystroke. Keyboard shortcuts help you exploit the speed and the ease of use of Final Cut Pro. Mac users should be quite familiar with keyboard shortcuts.

Note   Don't forget about Final Cut Pro's context sensitivity. Keyboard shortcuts apply to the currently selected window. If a keyboard shortcut doesn't work, make sure you've selected the right window.

Menus list keyboard shortcuts for various commands with the appropriate modifier key listed in front of the command. Figure 5-25 illustrates how shortcut and modifier keys are listed in Final Cut Pro menus. To use a shortcut key, hold down the modifier key and press the appropriate shortcut key. For example, if you want to use the Make Freeze Frame command shown in Figure 5-25, hold down the Shift key on your keyboard and press the N key.

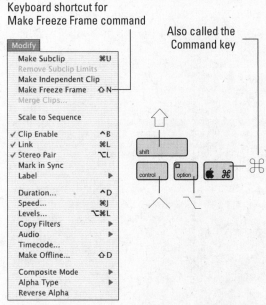

Figure 5-25: Keyboard shortcuts are listed across from the command in each menu.

Cross-Reference   Appendix B provides a detailed list of all default keyboard shortcuts and how to use the Customize Keyboard Layout window to assign or reassign keyboard shortcuts.

If you can't give up your mouse, there is another type of shortcut more in keeping with Mac's Graphic User Interface (GUI). This comes in the form of shortcut buttons. You can create clickable icon buttons that can perform any command found in Final Cut Pro's menus. Shortcut buttons are added to the button bar at the top of any Final Cut Pro main window. You can create as many as you want and even duplicate buttons in whatever configuration you find most efficient for your workflow. The window that the shortcut button is located on doesn't need to be active for you to use the button. Figure 5-26 shows two shortcut buttons I've added to my Timeline.

Shortcut buttons Close Gap and Two Up window layout added to Timeline window

Figure 5-26: Here I've added two Shortcut Buttons to the Timeline.

Harnessing the power of contextual menus

Starting with OS 8, Mac users got fabulous new tools called pop-up or *contextual Control key menus.* To see a pop-up menu, press and hold down the Control key and then click and hold down with your mouse anywhere on your Mac's desktop. A small menu appears containing commands that you can choose. These menus are called *contextual* because when you Control+click different items, different menus pop up that relate to that item. Pop-up menus change based on the context in which they're used.

Tip   Many editors, myself included, find contextual menus to be such a quick and efficient way to edit that they've surrendered their beloved Mac mouse and replaced it with a two-button (PC-style—ugh!) mouse. The left button on this mouse performs the standard click operation; however, clicking the right button is equivalent to a Control+click—all done with one finger on one hand. Contextual menus are truly just one click away. This is also called *right-clicking* in software manuals that address both Mac and PC products.

Many applications use contextual menus. However, Final Cut Pro has taken pop-up menus to another art form. Control+clicking on various places in Final Cut Pro produces numerous handy contextual menus. Figure 5-27 shows two of them.

Control+clicking on an item give you a contextual menu of commands specific to that item.

Control+clicking within the Browser gives you a contextual menu of commands specific to the Browser.

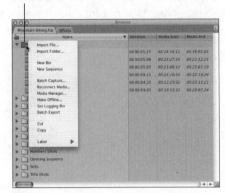
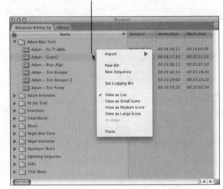

Figure 5-27: Contextual menus galore reside in Final Cut Pro. Press the Control key and click with your mouse on windows and items to bring up menus that have numerous useful commands. Try it. You'll love it.

Note   If no menu appears when you Control+click, there probably isn't a menu for that context.

Utilizing ToolTips

Final Cut Pro may very well have one of the busiest interfaces you've ever seen. Apple programmers have packed it with features, options, and speedy functions. This results in a profusion of buttons, controls, and places to click. When starting out, it can be quite hard to remember all the functions of all the controls. A feature called *ToolTips* allows you to see the function of a button when you place your cursor right on top of the button without clicking it. Just hover the mouse pointer over a button that you're curious about, hold the mouse still for a moment, and a ToolTip describing the button appears as shown in Figure 5-28. ToolTips also show you the keyboard equivalent for buttons.

Note   ToolTips may not be activated on your system. To activate ToolTips, choose Final Cut Pro ➪ User Preferences and place a check mark next to Show ToolTips.

Figure 5-28: ToolTips bring up a small yellow indicator labeling the function of a button when you point to it.

Understanding tabbed-window behavior

Final Cut Pro uses tabs to organize its many windows. Having dozens of separate little windows open at one time can be confusing. The tabbed windows of Final Cut Pro greatly reduce screen clutter and make the program easier to use. Each project, for example, has its own tab in the Browser. In the Viewer, tabs allow you to access functions such as audio and effects. Figure 5-29 shows several tabbed windows. The three most frequently used windows are:

✦ **Viewer window:** The Viewer window tabs vary according to the assets of a clip. For example, the Viewer does not have an audio tab if the clip is without audio.

✦ **Canvas window:** Each open sequence has its own tab in the Canvas windows. Click a sequence tab to bring its Timeline forward.

✦ **Browser window:** Projects have individual tabs in the Browser window. Click a tab to bring that project forward.

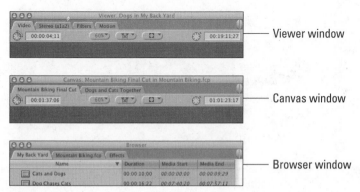

Figure 5-29: Tabs help Final Cut Pro organize the profusion of windows that make up its interface.

Remember that you can drag a tab away into a separate window from the main window where it originates. Of course, the last thing you may want are more windows on your screen. Screen real-estate management is a full-time job when working with Final Cut Pro. Many editors add a second monitor to their computer so that they can keep more windows open. To return a separated tab to its original window, just drag it back.

Note   To close a tab in any window, but not the window itself, press the Control key and click with your mouse on any tab to select Close Tab from the contextual menu. Selecting this option closes the tab.

Using the Help System

Final Cut Pro Help has a new format. In previous versions, the Help was written in a file format for Apple's own HTML-like application, Help Viewer. Although Help Viewer is still used by OS X and other OS X–native programs, Final Cut Pro's Help is now delivered as a PDF file. This format makes it easier to access, share, and navigate through this incredibly well documented and lengthy tome (more than 1,600 pages!). Using Adobe's free Acrobat Reader, Final Cut Pro's Help is word-searchable and easily navigated with thumbnail or outline-structured bookmark links. Figure 5-30 shows the main window of the Final Cut Pro Help system.

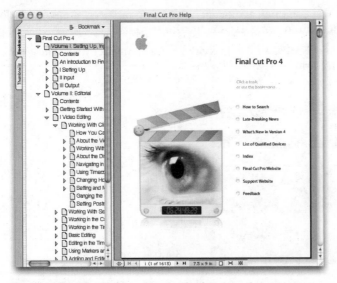

Figure 5-30: The Help system in Final Cut Pro is a treasure trove of information.

If you don't feel like whipping out the printed manual (or this book) every time you have a question, the help system can walk you step-by-step through many operations. The help system can be activated by choosing Help ➪ Final Cut Pro Help.

Customizing and Saving Your Work Screen Layout

You can lay out your windows in Final Cut Pro many ways. More often than not, you'll be working with the default Standard layout with the Browser on the left, the Viewer window in the center and the Canvas to the right, the Timeline below the Canvas, and the Browser to the left of it. Figure 5-31 shows the position of the windows in this layout. Final Cut Pro has preset layouts built you can choose from for various tasks. I suggest that you explore them all to see which layout works best for you.

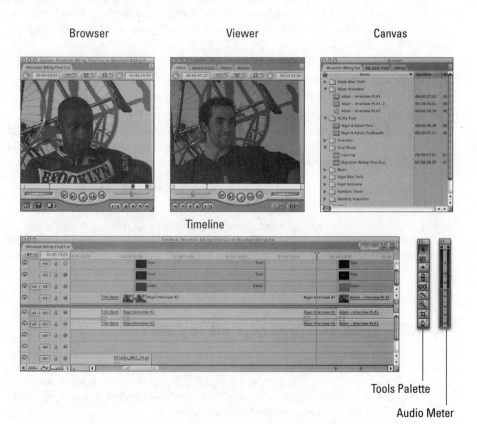

Figure 5-31: Shown here is a common working layout for windows in Final Cut Pro.

Final Cut Pro also allows you to make custom layouts of windows to best suit your own style and workflow. You can save your custom layouts for future use, call them up when you need them, export them for others to use or for you own use on another workstation, and even import custom layouts from another user.

Tip   New to Final Cut Pro 4.0 is the ability to resize multiple windows at the same time. Simply position your cursor on the edge of any abutting windows until it changes to a resize tool, then click and drag to resize. All adjoining windows will resize in the direction you drag.

Choosing a Preset window layout

You can select screen layouts under Window ➪ Arrange, then select the custom or preset layout needed for your current task. The preset layouts are

✦ **Audio Mixing:** This layout has the Viewer in the top left side, the Canvas window to the right and center, and opens the Tool Bench window with the Audio Mixer tool loaded on the right-top of the screen. Below these three windows from left to right are the Browser, Timeline, and Tools palette and Audio Meters.

✦ **Color Correction:** This is the same layout as the Audio Mixer, but with the Video Scopes and Frame Viewer loaded into the Tool Bench window instead of the Audio Mixer, for obvious reasons.

✦ **Standard:** The Standard layout gives maximum real estate to the Timeline. In this layout, the Timeline takes up the entire width of your screen down at the bottom. The Viewer and the Canvas windows are small in this layout and move to the right to make room for the Browser, which moves up to the top-left side of the monitor. This setting also has the convenient keyboard short-cut of Control+U, and I find myself using it often to clean up my windows if I've been moving things around too much.

✦ **Two Up:** Windows are laid out evenly with Viewer to the left, Canvas to the right, and Browser and Timeline down below. The Tool Palette and the Audio Meter are placed in lower right in this arrangement. This layout a favorite of many editors, because it displays larger Viewer and Canvas windows for easy watching of media on your computer monitor.

Working with custom screen layouts

If you have your own idea of how you think the screen should be laid out, create your own custom layout and save it for later use. You can save two Custom Layout settings, as well as save additional custom layouts to your hard drive. Even if you have a two-monitor setup, the custom layouts will remember the position of windows and palettes on the second monitor, too.

Cleaning up your windows

It pays to keep your windows clean in Final Cut Pro. Of course, these windows don't get dirty with dirt, but they have their own way of needing to be cleaned. Final Cut Pro, despite being a fun and versatile application, can be finicky and temperamental. Here you have an editing workstation based on nothing more than a G4 and a DV camera. In a world where you can expect anything of technology, Final Cut Pro can sometimes ask too much of the hardware that is available. Unless you respect some settings and layout issues, Final Cut Pro will misbehave. In terms of layout, be careful of the following two situations:

✦ **Make sure that video you're playing will fit in the Viewer window. You** can check this by looking to see if there are scroll bars for the viewing area. Adjust the magnification in the Viewer window until the scrollbars are gone.

✦ **Don't let windows overlap, especially the Viewer and Canvas windows.** Doing so can result in skipping or stuttering during playback, reduced video quality, and/or reduced amount of real-time effects that can be played back in real time. Move the windows around so that they aren't overlapping.

Both these issues are seen in Figure 5-32.

These scroll bars indicate image size is bigger than the window and can cause your clips to stutter or not play at all

Overlapping windows, such as these, can cause playback problems and dropped frames

Figure 5-32: Avoid overlapping windows or scroll bars in your Viewer window. This will cause your playback to skip, and clips may stutter during playback.

✦   ✦   ✦

Customizing Final Cut Pro Preferences, Easy Setup, and Presets

CHAPTER

6

One of the primary strengths of Final Cut Pro is the fact that it's an extremely versatile program. As mentioned earlier in this book, this amazing program can edit everything from DV to HDTV. Final Cut Pro's ability to customize and expand its capabilities is known as *scalability*, because it can scale up or down as your project and budget allowances change. In order to take full advantage of Final Cut Pro's scalable architecture, you will have to set up user interface and media handling options, which can be found in Final Cut Pro's Preferences and Presets windows.

As you might have expected, Final Cut Pro's ever-increasing capabilities means more preferences and presets have been implemented, which, in turn, means that there's more for you to control. In fact, the Preferences and Presets, which were once contained in one window with five tabs, are now found in four separate windows, each with as many tabs as the original. Thankfully, the Mac OS X requires all native OS X applications to locate all preferences under the Applications menu item, which is where you'll find the four that belong to Final Cut Pro.

This chapter will look at setting program preferences, as well as describing how to work with Easy Setups and Presets in Final Cut Pro.

Setting Your Preferences

Just about every computer program you'll ever use has a list of preferences you can set to adjust the application to your own needs. These preferences usually consist of groups of settings that control the behavior of the application. Final Cut Pro is no exception. It also has numerous preferences you can control, but unlike some other programs where the preferences are often cosmetic, in Final Cut Pro, some preference settings can have a major effect on the performance of the program.

There are two types of Final Cut Pro Preferences, each located in separate preference windows — User Preferences and System Settings. The settings in User Preferences affect general user features, behavior, and application defaults used *within* Final Cut Pro's user environment, like Timeline features options, default freeze frame durations, dropped frame notification, and Auto Render, to name just a few. System Settings, on the other hand, control general functions of Final Cut Pro *outside* its editing interface, where Final Cut Pro interacts with the computer OS and hardware. Examples of this would be scratch disk destination, Memory Usage (RAM), and selecting other applications to edit imported media files (external editors). I'll cover User Preferences first.

Note   By virtue of Mac OS X's User Log In structure, all Final Cut Pro User Preferences and System Settings are saved separately with each user's files. This means your preferences and settings are safe from being changed by other users of the same computer, as long as you are working under your own secured User account. See Chapter 29 for details about using Final Cut Pro in Mac OS X.

Understanding User Preferences

The User Preferences window is divided into five tabs. Each tab can be accessed by clicking on the tab name. These five tabs are General, Labels, Timeline Options, Render Control, and Audio Output. To begin setting preferences in Final Cut Pro:

1. **Choose Final Cut Pro ➪ User Preferences, or use the keyboard shortcut Option+Q.**

2. **Click on one of the tabs and adjust settings as needed.**

3. **Click the OK button to finish.**

In other software applications that you have used, going into the Preferences might have been a rare occurrence, but in Final Cut Pro, it's something you'll probably do on a regular basis. The next few sections walk you step by step through each User Preference setting in Final Cut Pro and describe to you what they mean.

General preferences

General preferences are just that, general. These cover a wide range of functions and behaviors in Final Cut Pro. Figure 6-1 shows the General preferences tab. This section covers each setting.

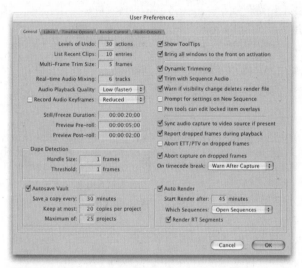

Figure 6-1: General preferences cover a wide range of settings that affect the way you work with the Final Cut Pro interface.

Levels of Undo

In the Levels of Undo field, you enter the number of actions that can be undone. The command for undoing an action is accessed by selecting Edit ⇨ Undo, or by using the common keyboard shortcut Command+Z. The default setting is 10 levels of undo. The highest number of undos possible in Final Cut Pro is 99. Before you set this number too high, I should warn you that raising the levels of available undo commands uses up valuable memory. The more memory you have for Final Cut Pro, the higher this number can be set.

Cross-Reference   See Chapter 4 to learn how to change the Memory Usage for Final Cut Pro.

I know editors who rely on the Undo command as a major editing tool. They set this preference very high and freely make changes in their sequences and edits. Then they wear out their keyboards using the Command+Z function to go back many steps and then try something else. Although the Undo command can provide a useful way to test theories or correct mistakes, I strongly discourage you from relying too heavily on it. Besides using up precious memory, it is often difficult to remember precisely what you did in the last 20 actions. You may find yourself undoing one or two steps that you wanted to keep. Instead, try working on a copy of your sequence, preserving the original should you decide against the many modifications made to the copy.

Undo actions are window-sensitive, remembering which Final Cut Pro window an action occurred in, and will make that window active before undoing that action. For example, if you deleted a transition in the Timeline and then deleted a bin in the Browser, selecting Undo once will restore the deleted clip in the Browser, leaving the Browser active. Performing Undo again will restore the transition in the Timeline while leaving the Timeline window active.

List Recent Clips

The List Recent Clips setting determines the number of recently opened clips that you can access via the Recent Clips pop-up menu (described in Chapter 9) in the View window. The default for this setting is 10 but it can be set as high as 20. This is a handy feature of the View window, and it even displays the clips in the order in which they were looked at in the Viewer.

Multi-Frame Trim Size

The Multi-Frame Trim Size setting affects the Trim Edit window. This window is used to fine- tune edits between clips. The frame size affects how far back or forward the edit moves when the Trim Back or Trim Forward buttons in the Trim Edit window is pressed. You can go up to as high as 99 frames in this setting. This number also appears alongside the plus and minus buttons in the Trim Edit window. The default value of 5 is generally acceptable for most work.

Cross-Reference   To learn more about the Trim Edit window, see Chapter 13.

Real-Time Audio Mixing

When the amount of calculations required to play back the audio tracks of a Timeline exceeds the capacity of your computer, you must render your audio tracks and other effects. The Real-Time Audio Mixing setting allows you to specify the number of audio tracks that you can mix in real time without rendering. The default setting is 8 and Apple literature says you can set this as high as 99. However, just changing the number in here is not going to allow you to mix 99 tracks of audio in real time. Your ability to play back a number of audio tracks in real time is determined by your processor speed, the amount of effects and filters you have applied to clips in the Timeline, as well as the amount of memory allocated to Final Cut Pro and the speed of your drives.

If your computer is having playback issues, such as your audio dropping out or audible popping or clicking noise, known as *pops*, reduce the number in the Real-Time Audio Mixing setting. You'll have to render your audio if you have more than the specified number of tracks, but it will avoid audio dropouts and pops.

Audio Playback Quality

Use this pop-up to select the quality of audio resampling when playing clips with a sample rate different from that of the sequence. The three choices are:

✦ **Low (faster):** This is the default setting, good for general editing because it allows you maximum real-time audio mixing capabilities.

✦ **Medium and High:** Select either of these for higher audio fidelity when you're mixing or finishing audio, at the expense of fewer tracks of audio you can play in real time without rendering. High setting allows for the highest audio quality and the lowest number of tracks you can simultaneously mix in real time.

Tip

If you are using the High setting and experiencing dropped frames during playback, try using the Mixdown render command by selecting Sequence ➪ Render Only ➪ Mixdown.

Note

Final Cut Pro always uses the highest audio playback quality when rendering, mixing down audio, editing to tape, printing to video or exporting to OMF, regardless of the setting in the Audio Playback Quality pop-up menu.

Record Audio Keyframes

Check this option to record keyframes automatically whenever adjustments are made to the audio level or panning control in the Audio Mixer or slider controls of a sequence clip loaded in the Viewer. There are three options in the pop-up menu that control the number of keyframes recorded onto a clips audio overlay:

✦ **All:** Selecting this setting will record the maximum number of keyframes whenever a level, pan, or filter parameter fader or slider is adjusted. Although this will give you the most accurate representation of your adjustment, the sheer number of keyframes in the audio overlay could make editing the overlay difficult.

✦ **Reduced:** Fewer keyframes are created with this setting selected when the level, pan, or filter parameter fader or slider is adjusted. This is the most commonly used setting because the levels set are usually accurate enough while allowing for relatively easy editing of the audio clips overlay using the Pen or Selection tool.

✦ **Peaks Only:** This option records the minimum number of keyframes when the level, pan, or filter parameter fader or slider is adjusted, representing only the highest and lowest adjustments made. This setting is used when you want the fewest keyframes created, knowing you will edit the overlay later.

As you can see, the actual number of keyframes created by the All and Reduced settings are relative to each other. Suffice it to say, All will record clusters of keyframes for most adjustments, whereas the Reduced setting will produce a fairly accurate re-creation of your moves with fewer keyframes than All, and still allow you enough space between overlay keyframes to easily edit.

Note   The checkbox to enable Record Audio Keyframes in the General tab of the User Preferences window is effectively the same button located in the Audio Mixer window. Enabling or disabling either of these controls will be mirrored in the other window.

Still/Freeze Duration

The Still/Freeze Duration setting has two functions. First, it affects the length of imported still images. When you import a still image into Final Cut Pro, the default length that is given to it is 10 seconds. You can change the length of any imported still image at an alter point. However, if you are importing multiple stills that you want to lay out in your Timeline to play and you know the duration you want them to play for, this is the setting to change.

Secondly, Still/Freeze Duration affects the length of a freeze frame you can make in Final Cut Pro. You can make a freeze frame out of any frame of a clip by placing the playhead over the frame you want, then selecting Modify ⇨ Make Freeze Frame, or pressing Shift+N.

Preview Pre-roll

Used by the Play Around Current control, the Preview Pre-roll setting determines how far the playhead will jump back from the current frame before playing up to the current frame. I generally keep this setting between 1 and 2 seconds. The Play Around Current control is found with the transport controls in the Viewer, Canvas, and Trim Edit windows. Pressing the \ (backslash key) also invokes the Play Around Current command.

Preview Post-roll

Like the Preview Pre-roll setting, the Preview Post-roll setting is related to the Play Around Current command in Final Cut Pro. This setting determines how far forward you want the playhead to play after the current location when the Play Around Current command is invoked.

Dupe Detection

When Show Duplicate Frames indicators are enabled for any sequence, the Dupe Detection Handle Size and Threshold settings affect when the indicators appear in the Timeline.

✦ **Handle Size:** This is the number of frames added before and after a clip's In and Out point when comparing clips in a sequence for duplicate frames used. An invaluable application of this feature is for film matchback, where additional frames for negative cutting and gluing are needed and must not be used by another clip. The default setting for this setting is 0.

✦ **Threshold:** This is the minimum number of frames that must be duplicated before duplicate frames indicators will appear. The default setting for this is 0, so any instances of duplicate frames will display an indicator. The maximum setting for this field is 99 frames.

Autosave Vault

Click the Autosave Vault checkbox to enable it. Final Cut Pro will automatically save incremental project files of your project at set timed intervals. This allows you to select from a series of earlier versions of your work stored in a default folder, known as the Autosave Vault folder. Be aware that your original project file is not saved until you use the Save command, so saving often is still the reigning motto. Also, autosave projects are not saved again if no changes have been made to the project since the last autosave. The options for the Autosave Vault are:

✦ **Save a copy every *x* minutes:** Enter the amount of time between Autosave executions.

✦ **Keep at *most x copies* per project:** Enter the maximum number of autosave copies to store before deleting the oldest version to make room for the newest (first-in-first-out principle).

✦ **Maximum of *x* projects:** Enter the maximum number of projects you want to keep in the Autosave Vault, both opened and closed. If, however, the number of projects opened at the same time is greater than the amount entered her, then *all* open projects are autosaved.

When the maximum number of copies of a project is exceeded, Final Cut Pro replaces the oldest autosaved file with the new autosave copy. This is known as the first-in-first-out scheme, which guarantees that you always have the latest copies of backed up projects. All projects or folders removed from the Autosave Vault are never deleted; instead, they're moved to the trash where they are still available until you manually empty the trash.

To open an autosaved project file, use the Restore Project command in the File menu. See Chapter 8 for more details.

Show ToolTips

Checking the Show ToolTips setting enables short descriptions of controls to appear in Final Cut Pro when you hover your cursor over them for a moment. Keyboard shortcuts are displayed as well. ToolTips, like the one shown in Figure 6-2, are very handy when you are just starting out with Final Cut Pro.

Figure 6-2: ToolTips can help identify controls and tools when you hover your mouse over an item.

To learn more about ToolTips, see Chapter 5.

Bring All Windows to the Front on Activation

When this option is selected and Final Cut Pro is in the background, clicking one Final Cut Pro window brings all Final Cut Pro windows to the front at the same time. If this option is not selected, then clicking on a Final Cut Pro window when it is in the background activates Final Cut Pro and brings only the selected program window to the front, leaving all other Final Cut Pro windows in the background until each is selected.

Dynamic Trimming

Selecting this option enables the Dynamic Trimming feature in the Trim Edit window. When using Dynamic Trimming, the edit point between the two clips in the Trim Edit window will follow the playhead.

For more details about using Dynamic Trim, see Chapter 13.

Warn If Visibility Change Deletes Render Files

If I asked you if you wanted a warning if a doomsday meteor were about to hit Earth, most likely your answer would be "Yes." The Warn If Visibility Change Deletes Render Files setting is a doomsday warning of sorts, but it merely portends the disappearance of some of your editing work rather than humanity itself.

In Final Cut Pro, you can have more than one track of video. You can apply effects and filters to each track as well as animate them. You also can choose to make tracks visible or invisible. Unfortunately, when you make a track invisible in Final Cut Pro its render files are deleted. Ouch! This can really bite you if you've spent a long time rendering those files. This setting gives you a warning before those render files are deleted. Check to make sure this option is on right now, and leave it on. Losing your render files may not be as cataclysmic as a meteor striking the Earth, but it may feel like it when you're working toward a tight deadline.

Prompt for Settings on New Sequence

Each sequence in Final Cut Pro can have its own aspect ratio, compression scheme, and resolution. If you have the Prompt for Settings on New Sequence option checked, you'll have the option to choose a Preset for every new sequence. If you usually work with the same types of clips and compression, it is best to leave this option unchecked. You only want it enabled if you frequently jump back and forth between various compressions, codecs, and resolutions.

Pen Tools Can Edit Locked Item Overlays

In Final Cut Pro, you can change your animation keyframes for effects and filters in the Timeline itself. Checking the Pen Tools Can Edit Locked Item Overlays option allows such modification even when the tracks are locked.

Sync Audio Capture to Video Source If Present

When capturing audio from a device-controllable deck that will be used with video captured separately to make a merged clip, accurate audio sync can only be guaranteed if the audio deck is genlocked to your computer's video capture board. You must select this option to ensure accurate audio sync when capturing from a genlocked audio deck.

Report Dropped Frames during Playback

During playback, it may not seem like such a bad occurrence to occasionally have a stutter or two. With the Report Dropped Frames during Playback option enabled, you'll see a warning message, shown in Figure 6-3, about dropped frames every time it happens; playback will stop altogether until you click the OK button in the warning dialog box. You may be tempted to uncheck this option, but keep in mind that this warning also applies when sending your edited sequence to tape. That is one place you do not want to drop frames because then the tape will record the sequence with stutters and skips.

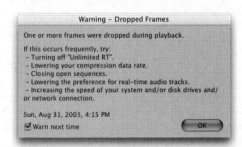

Figure 6-3: When the Report Dropped Frames option is enabled, this message box appears if frames are dropped during playback.

The best course of action is to keep this setting enabled, and if the big, nasty error message does appear, do what it says. If you work your way down the list and follow every direction it gives you, you may very well solve your issue and not have dropped frames during playback. Dropped frames during playback are usually the result of hardware issues, and following the advice of this message, you can rid yourself of the problem.

Abort ETT/PTV on Dropped Frames

Checking this option instructs Final Cut Pro to cancel any further output to tape during Edit to Tape (ETT) or Print to Video (PTV) if dropped frames are detected during output playback. This option should always be selected to ensure stutter-free, skip-free playback of your output on tape. Dropped frames at any stage of editing can be difficult and frustrating to resolve, but if you are able to watch *where* the playhead is in the Timeline when the Edit to Tape, or Print to Video process aborts, you'll at least have a localized starting point to begin your troubleshooting.

Abort Capture on Dropped Frames

When the Abort Capture on Dropped Frames option is checked, dropped frames during capture will present a warning and stop the capture. All media captured before the dropped frame is timecode-accurate and saved to the Browser. This new feature of saving the captured portion of the clip not only saves you the time of having to recapture the whole clip after you track down the source of the dropped frame, it basically tells you where the dropped frame is because the clip's last frame is the frame before the dropped frame.

This is a critical preference that you should leave on while capturing. It is one thing to drop frames during playback because the media files are intact, but dropping frames during *capture* means the frames won't be there in the first place. Once a clip is captured with dropped frames, there is no way to fix it except to recapture the clip. Always abort capture if you drop frames, solve the issue that is causing them to drop, and then proceed with capturing.

On Timecode Break

Inconsistent timecode on your source tapes, known as timecode breaks, can pose many problems during the capture process. Such problems range from your deck not being able to locate a specified timecode on your source tape, to finding the wrong shot with duplicate timecode on your tape, to incorrect timecode written to clips with timecode break. This new option gives you three options in the pop-up menu to deal with timecode breaks encountered during capture:

✦ **Make New Clip:** This option is Final Cut Pro's innovative method of capture *around* timecode breaks during capture. When a timecode break is encountered during capture, Final Cut Pro saves the captured clip up to the timecode break but then continues to capture from the first frame *after the timecode break* as a new and separate file. The first clip has the original name of the logged clip; each subsequent clip after a timecode break is named with the original name plus a dash and an incremented number. Using this method, clips captured before and after the timecode break are timecode accurate and in sync.

Note

As of this writing, the Make New Clip option works with DV only.

✦ **Abort Capture:** Selecting this option results in action by Final Cut Pro that is similar to that of the Abort Capture on Dropped Frames option. When a time-code break is encountered during capture, the capture process is immediately stopped. All media captured before the timecode break are timecode accurate and saved to the Browser.

✦ **Warn After Capture:** Selecting this option allows Final Cut Pro to continue capturing when a timecode break is encountered. A warning message is displayed after capture is finished, and the resulting clip is saved to the Browser. It is strongly advised that you do not use such a clip if you plan to recapture the clip at a later time, or export an EDL, because the clip's timecode accuracy is not guaranteed for frames after the timecode break.

Auto Render

The Auto Render option has to be the next best thing to real-time effects. Enabling this option by clicking on the Auto Render checkbox will result in automatic rendering of open sequences when you are not editing. The time required before auto rendering is invoked is the idle time of Final Cut Pro, not the idle time of your computer system. This means you can be working in another application on the same computer while still accruing idle time in your open Final Cut Pro project for auto rendering in the background. Because of Mac OS X's true preemptive multi-tasking ability, chances are you won't even realize rendering is happening. There are three settings for Auto Rendering:

✦ **Start Render After:** Enter the number of minutes of idle time before Final Cut Pro starts automatically renders open sequences.

✦ **Which Sequences:** This pop-up menu has three options:

- **Open Sequences:** Choose this option to render all open sequences in the Timeline.

- **Current Only:** Choose this option to render only the currently selected sequence tab in the Timeline.

- **Open Except Current:** Choose this option to render all open sequences *except* the currently selected sequence tab in the Timeline.

✦ **Render RT Segments:** Select this option to render real-time effects in auto-rendered sequences. Deselect this option to save rendering time for effects capable of playing in real-time without rendering.

When Final Cut Pro begins auto rendering, there is actually a series of render passes done using the following hierarchal protocol:

✦ If Autosave is enabled, the project is saved before rendering begins.

✦ The first render is any selected region or items in the currently opened sequence.

✦ The second render is all red render bar (non-real-time) sections of the currently opened sequence.

✦ The third render is all audio of the currently opened sequence.

✦ The fourth render is all yellow, orange, and blue sections of the Timeline.

✦ The fifth render, if the Render Real Time Segments is selected, is all green sections of the currently opened sequence.

✦ The sequence is Autosaved.

✦ At this point, if Open Sequence is selected in the Which Sequence pop-up menu, the render cycle from first pass to autosave is applied to each open sequence.

Note   Final Cup Pro renders all offline clips as static video clips with the words *Media Offline* and the clip's name. Be aware of this if you have an open sequence with offline clips and Auto Render is enabled, as render cache files of offline media will use valuable disk drive space.

Labels

The Labels tab (see Figure 6-4) of the Preferences dialog box allows you to edit the name of colored labels you can apply to your clips. Clips can be color-coded in the Browser. These labels can be used to sort clips in the Browser, locate them using the Find command, or just visually identify them while you work. To label your clips in the Browser, Control+click on one or more clips and select the label from the Label submenu that appears in the context menu.

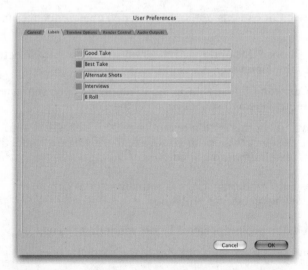

Figure 6-4: Labels can help you organize clips in the Browser.

Note   The default label of all items in the Browser is set to None, with no label color.

Timeline Options

The preferences in the Timeline Options tab (see Figure 6-5) allow you to change display settings relating to your sequences. However, keep in mind that these settings only affect new sequences created in a project. After you create a sequence, you can only change its Timeline settings using the Timeline Options tab in the Sequence ⇨ Setting command.

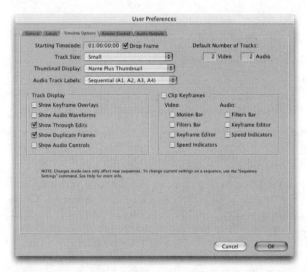

Figure 6-5: Timeline Options determine Timeline settings for new sequences you create in a project.

The Timeline Options tab has a number of important options. They include:

✦ **Starting Timecode:** Determine the starting timecode for your sequences here. The default setting is 1:00:00:00, or one hour, but you can change this to suit other editing needs. For example, you might be working on the second hour of a program and want to set the starting timecode of your sequence to 2:00:00:00, or 2 hours. You might be putting together a sequence that has to be edited to a location on tape where the timecode is 1:10:00:00. In that case, you can set the same timecode as a starting timecode in your sequence. This option will help you align your settings.

✦ **Drop Frame:** Uncheck this box if you want to see your sequence in non-drop-frame mode timecode. Bear in mind that this is different from the "dropped frames" I often refer to, which are a problem in capturing or playing back video. Drop-frame versus non-drop-frame is simply a different way to label timecode. Drop Frame is only used in NTSC format and is the default setting for NTSC settings.

✦ **Default Number of Tracks:** You can set the default number of tracks on your Timeline. You can have up to 99 tracks of video *and* 99 tracks of audio on a Timeline. However, for most assembling of new sequences, you will probably use only 1 to 2 tracks of each. More tracks can be created later for multilayered video of video, text, and other graphics.

✦ **Track Size:** This drop-down menu lets you choose Reduced, Small, Medium, or Large track sizes. This setting determines how thick or thin video and audio tracks appear in the timeline.

Note   If Reduced is selected, thumbnails and waveforms will not be displayed in Timeline tracks.

✦ **Thumbnail Display:** This setting determines how your clips appear in the timeline. Name displays the name only, Name Plus Thumbnail shows the first frame of each clip, and Filmstrip shows a series of images from the clip.

✦ **Audio Track Labels:** This allows you to choose how your audio tracks will be labeled. If you choose Sequential, tracks are labeled A1, A2, A3, and so on. If you choose Paired, tracks are labeled A1a, A1b, A2a, A2b, and so on.

✦ **Show Keyframe Overlays:** This setting enables display of opacity or audio levels keyframe overlays in a new Timeline. Black opacity lines will display over video portions of clips in the Timeline, and red audio levels lines will appear over audio clips in audio tracks. After a sequence is created, the keyframes overlays can be toggled to display or hide by clicking on the Clip Keyframes control at the bottom of the Timeline.

✦ **Show Audio Waveform:** Audio clips appear as plain green bars in the Timeline. However, checking this option will show the waveform for all the audio clips in the Timeline. This can be an extremely useful tool for cutting and timing purposes. However, this feature slows down the display and the redraw time of the sequence. I recommend you keep this setting off, but remember that the handy keyboard shortcut Command+W allows you to toggle waveforms on and off.

✦ **Show Though Edits:** Select this option to display through edit indicators in Timeline clips. A through edit indicator is represented by two red triangles on either side of an edit point, indicating an edit has been added to a clip without any modification to clips on either side of the edit point. A through edit is shown in Figure 6-6.

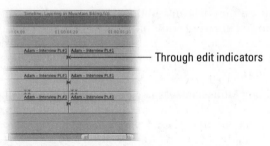

Through edit indicators

Figure 6-6: A through edit is indicated by two red triangles on both sides of an edit.

Because a through edit consists of consecutive frames that contain no missing or additional frames between them, the clips on either side of a through edit can be joined and then edited as a single clip by Control+clicking on the through edit and selecting Join Through Edit, as shown in Figure 6-7.

Figure 6-7: Connecting clips on both sides of a through edit through the contextual menu displayed when you Control+click on the edit point.

✦ **Show Duplicate Frames:** Select this option to show color bar indicators at the bottom of video clips that have been used more than once in the same Timeline. The user-defined settings for determining when duplicate frame indicators appear are set in the General tab of User Preferences.

✦ **Show Audio Controls:** Selecting this control displays the mute and solo controls in the patch panel of the Timeline. The default setting for this option is not selected. After a sequence is created, these audio controls can be displayed or hidden by clicking on the Audio Controls button at the bottom of the Timeline.

✦ **Clip Keyframes:** This option adds an additional area in the Timeline below each video and audio track, where additional controls are displayed. These controls can be shown or hidden separately for video and audio tracks, allowing you to customize your Timeline to your editing needs. The controls that can appear in the Clip Keyframes area are:

- **Motion bars:** If any Motion effects have been applied to the clip, a blue bar will appear just below the filter bar. Black, diamond-shaped keyframe indicators appear if you have added any keyframes. You can edit keyframes on the motion bar with the Selection tool. Because audio portions of clips cannot have motion effects (like scale or position, for example), the motion bar is only displayed in video tracks.

- **Filter bars:** If any filters have been applied to the clip, a green bar will appear at the top of this space. Black, diamond-shaped keyframe indicators appear if you have added any keyframes. You can edit keyframes on the filter bar with the Selection tool.

- **Keyframe editor:** The Keyframe editor is a graph of the keyframes for motion or filter effects. It is identical to the keyframe graph found in a clip's motion and filter tab in the Viewer. The Keyframe editor allows you to edit keyframes with the pen and selection tools directly in the Timeline; however, only one keyframe graph can be displayed at a time. To select a parameter to edit, Control+click anywhere in the Keyframe editor space and select a parameter from the contextual menu.

- **Speed indicator:** Speed indicators display the speed of clips in the sequence using tic marks. The spacing and color of the tic marks represent the speed and direction of playback of the clip. There is no user control for this indicator. See Chapter 17 for more about changing the speed of a clip.

Cross-Reference
To learn how to work with Filter and Motion bars, see Chapter 17.

Render Control

Final Cut Pro enables you to customize and save render options using the Render Control window, shown in Figure 6-8. Here you can select or deselect processor-intensive effects, thus speeding up your workflow. The options selected in the Render Control tab affect real-time playback, rendering, video, and QuickTime output. All settings made to the Render Control tab in the User Preferences will affect apply only to newly created sequences. If you wish to change the Render Control settings of an existing sequence, you must make the changes in the Render Control tab in the sequence's Sequence Settings window.

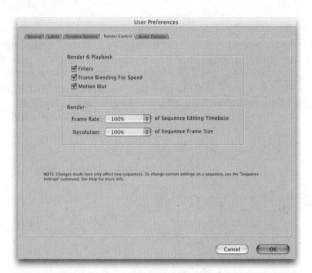

Figure 6-8: The Render Control tab window is identical in Sequence Settings and User Preferences windows but affects different sequences.

The settings in the Render Control window are:

✦ **Filters:** Check this box to allow filters to be processed when rendering or during playback. If this option not select, all unrendered filters are ignored.

✦ **Frame Blending for Speed:** Check this box to enable frame blending for rendering or playback. This setting works with clips that have speed modifications applied to them.

✦ **Motion Blur:** Check this option to enable motion blur for rendering or playback.

✦ **Frame Rate:** Use this pop-up menu to select a lower frame rate of rendered effects. Lower frame rates can greatly reduce rendering time, with the trade-off of lower playback quality. The setting for this control is a percentage of the Timeline frame rate. For example, setting 50 percent in a DV NTSC Timeline will play back effects rendered at 15 frames per second.

✦ **Resolution:** Use this pop-up menu to select a lower resolution of rendered effects. Lower resolution can greatly reduce rendering time, with the trade-off of lower playback quality. The setting for this control is a percentage of the Sequence frame size. For example, setting 50 percent in a DV NTSC Sequence of 720 × 480 will play back effects rendered at 360 × 240, interlaced. When the rendered effect is played back, they are still displayed full frame, but at the reduced resolution that will appear less sharp and non-interlaced. At a lower-resolution percentage, Final Cut Pro has to process fewer pixels and thus rendering is faster. The resolution is set as a percentage of the current frame size of the sequence.

Audio Outputs

The Audio Outputs tab, shown in Figure 6-9, is where you can create, delete, and ultimately assign a preset that defines the number of audio output channels that sequences have available for an external audio interface connected to the computer. An external audio interface is the physical pathway on which audio is output from your computer, such as the audio outputs of a third-party video capture card, a dedicated audio In/Out (I/O) card, or the audio channels of your FireWire connection.

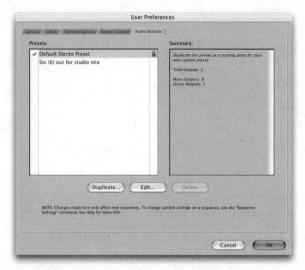

Figure 6-9: In the Audio Outputs tab, you can create, modify, delete and assign presets of audio output channels for your sequences.

The selection made in the Audio Outputs tab of User Preferences is applied to all new sequences. To change the Audio Outputs selection of an existing sequence, you must make the necessary settings modification in the Audio Outputs tab in the Sequence Settings window.

Note   The Audio Outputs settings allows you to set up the number of audio channels of your sequence, regardless of the actual number of output channels of your computer's external audio interface. To configure your external audio interface, use the A/V Devices tab in the Audio/Video Settings window after the interface hardware and any software drivers are properly installed.

For most projects, a single set of stereo outputs is all that is needed. However, you can set up a multichannel output for tracks isolation. One application for isolated tracks, or *splits,* are projects slated for foreign distribution that require dialog, music, and sound effects on separate output tracks for dubbing or music replacement.

Tip

Using Final Cut Pro's multichannel outputs, you can audio mix your sequence tracks using a hardware mixing console. By configuring the audio outputs as dual mono outputs, you can assign each sequence audio track to a dedicated track strip of a connected mixing board, using the external mixers' controls for panning, EQ, and levels.

As noted earlier, the number of Audio Output channels is a sequence setting, and is not restricted by the number of audio channels of the computer's external audio interface. This means you can assign more audio channel outputs to a sequence than you currently have hardware capability for, a handy option allowing you to preconfigure your audio outputs bound for another system with more audio output capabilities. When a project is opened on another computer, all sequence settings, including the audio output settings, are retained for each sequence regardless of the number of audio channels supported on that system.

If you create more output channels than are available on your external audio interface, you are presented with a warning dialog box when you create a new sequence, as shown in Figure 6-10.

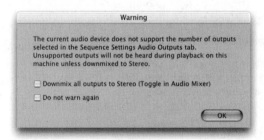

Figure 6-10: This warning dialog box tells you there are more audio output channels assigned to this sequence than are available on the current system.

As indicated in the warning message, you must select Downmix All Output to Stereo in order to hear all audio tracks. If you do not select this option, tracks that correspond to the audio output channels exceeding the computer's external audio interface will not be heard during playback or output. Downmixing to stereo means all odd-numbered tracks are output together to the left channel, and all even-numbered channels are output to the right channel. When the Downmix option is selected, each audio channel's output level is reduced by the dB amount set in the Downmix pop-up menu in the Audio Output preset.

Note

Selecting the Downmix All Output to Stereo option is effectively the same as the Downmix control in the Audio Mixer. Selecting this option in this dialog box will be reflected in the Downmix control being selected in the Audio Mixer.

The Audio Outputs tab

The Audio Output tab works more like a Presets tab in the Audio/Video Settings windows than the line item setting used in the rest of User Preferences. To configure the Audio Outputs, select a preset from a list of available ones, or create a customized preset to suit your project requirements.

Relatively spare and simple to use, the Audio Output tab contains the following controls:

✦ **Presets:** This is a list of available presets from which you make your selection. To select a preset, simply click in the column to the left of its name. A checkmark will appear, indicating it is the selected preset. A lock icon in the column to the right of a preset indicates it cannot be modified or deleted.

✦ **Summary:** The summary section displays a description of the preset currently highlighted in the Presets list. A highlighted preset need not be selected with a check mark; it is highlighted by clicking on it once. This allows you to review the any presets before selecting one.

✦ **Duplicate button:** With a preset highlighted, click this button to create a copy of it. You then can edit and rename this copy to create a new preset.

✦ **Edit button:** With a preset highlighted, click this button to open the Audio Outputs Presets Editor window, where you can modify preset settings. If you select a locked Preset and click the Edit button, a dialog box appears informing you that a copy of this locked preset will be created for you to edit. Click OK.

✦ **Delete button:** Highlight a preset you want to delete, and then click this button. Neither a locked preset nor a preset currently in use (indicated with a checkmark next to its name) can be deleted. If you try to delete either of these types of presets, you will see that the Delete button will remain dimmed and inactive. To delete a preset currently in use, first make another preset active by clicking in the column to the left of its name in the Presets list, and then highlight the inactive preset you want to delete. You will notice the Delete button is no longer dimmed. Click Delete.

Settings of an Audio Outputs preset

When you select an Audio Outputs preset and click the Edit button, an Audio Outputs Presets Editor window opens. This Editor window, shown in Figure 6-11, is where you can modify the preset's settings:

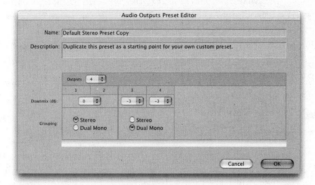

Figure 6-11: The Audio Outputs Preset Editor is used for modifying or creating new presets.

✦ **Name:** Enter a new name for your preset in this field. The name entered here will appear in the available Presets list in the Audio Outputs tab.

✦ **Description:** Enter a brief description of the preset's intended use in this field. This may include the name of the external audio interface it will be used with and the number of outputs assigned. The text entered here will be displayed in the Summary area in the Audio Outputs tab when the preset is highlighted.

✦ **Outputs pop-up:** Use this pop-up menu to set the number of audio outputs you want to assign to your sequence. *Remember:* The number of audio outputs selected here can be greater or less than the number of output channels of your current external audio interface. The default setting is two channels of output for stereo. Because you can only select outputs in pairs, the maximum number of 24 outputs will display as 12 pairs of outputs.

✦ **Channel number:** Identifies the channel pair the other controls will affect.

✦ **Downmix (dB) pop-up menu:** Use this pop-up to set the amount the outputs will be lowered or raised, in dB values, when the Downmixed to Stereo option is selected; the Downmix setting affects audio output during playback of sequence, Print to Video, Export to Tape, and exporting QuickTime or audio files. The dB range that can be selected in the pop-up menu is +10 dB to –10 dB; it can be set to off (0 db) as well.

✦ **Grouping buttons:** Select one of these radio buttons to define the pair of audio output channel type:

- **Stereo:** Sequence tracks that are assigned to stereo pair outputs have stereo panning enabled. Stereo pairs have only one Downmix pop-up menu that controls both channels, set to a default value of 0 dB.

- **Mono:** Sequence tracks assigned to mono outputs have no stereo output, so the stereo panning slider in the Audio Mixer is disabled. For mono pairs of audio outputs, there are two Downmix pop-up menus, one for each channel, each with a default value of −3 dB. Both types of channel types are shown in separate audio pairs in Figure 6-11.

Turn down the Downmix

When you Downmix multiple audio output channels, you're not only combining the content of all the audio channels, you're also adding together their audio levels. The final stereo output level increases with every audio channel of a Downmix and can result in distortion if the combined signal level exceeds the maximum level of 0 dB. This cumulative effect is more pronounced when Downmixing dual mono channels because, unlike stereo channels that are *divided evenly between* left and right outputs according to their pan/spread setting, *each* mono channel is applied *in full* to both left and right output channels of the final stereo output. This means Downmixing a pair of dual mono audio channels will produce a mixed audio signal with a level that is double each of the original. For this reason, Final Cut Pro assigns a default value of −3 dB to the Downmix levels control of all dual mono output channels. You can modify this control setting to decrease (or increase) a channel's output when Downmixing for playback, output to tape, or exporting audio files.

A simplified way to understand this concept is to envision two audio signals as two streams of water flowing through two separate pipes; the pipes that carry the water are like the audio channels that carry the audio signals. All is fine when the streams are flowing in their own pipes until you combine (downmix) the streams into a single pipe. Now, twice the water must flow through the single pipe, resulting in higher water pressure. This higher water pressure is analogous to the increased signal level of a Mixdown audio channel—too much pressure and pipe may burst. Well, your audio channel won't break, but what will happen is audio levels (pressure) that exceed 0 dB will result in distortion of your audio output. The Downmix levels controls are like valves on each of the water pipes, which you use to lower the water flow (and resulting pressure) before its stream enters the mix.

Understanding System Settings

The System Settings window is divided into five tabs that control how Final Cut Pro works with your computer system and other applications. Each tab can be accessed by clicking on the tab name. The five tabs are Scratch Disks, Memory & Cache, Playback Control, External Editors, and Effects Handling. System Settings can be access by selecting Final Cut Pro ➪ System Settings, or by pressing Shift+Q.

Scratch Disks tab

The scratch disk is where captured and imported media files, render files, and other files related to your editing work are stored. The default scratch disk is the same hard disk where Final Cut Pro is installed. If this is also your startup disk, you should use the Scratch Disk tab in the System Settings to select a different, media-capable disk. The Scratch Disk tab (shown in Figure 6-12) in the System Settings window offers many options and controls for specifying scratch disks for a variety of tasks. You can set up to 12 scratch disks.

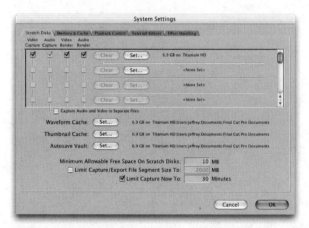

Figure 6-12: The Scratch Disk tab allows you to set the destination disk for your captured media, render, and cache files.

Caution You should avoid using your main system hard disk as the scratch disk. Using the startup disk for your scratch disk, although not impossible, is highly discouraged by Apple because accessing the same drive for both OS commands, applications commands, and now disk-intensive media read/write tasks can seriously degrade the performance of all operations. This rule applies even if you have partitioned your drive into two or more volumes. Apple suggests that you dedicate a separate drive to the single purpose of media capture.

Choosing a scratch disk

Choosing a scratch disk is easy. All you have to do is follow these steps:

1. **Choose Final Cut Pro ⇨ System Settings.**

2. **Click on the Scratch Disk tab to bring it to the front.**

3. **Click the checkboxes directly under Video Capture, Video Render, and Audio Render (refer to Figure 6-7) to select them.**

Do not check the Capture Audio and Video to Separate Files box. That option is reserved for a few specific situations when working with high-data-rate video. Never use this option with DV video.

4. **Click on the uppermost Set button.**

   A dialog box similar to the one shown in Figure 6-13 appears.

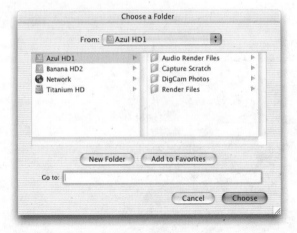

Figure 6-13: Highlight the disk you'd like to use as your destination disk and click the Select button below.

5. **Select the desired disk and click the Select button.**

   The Select button displays the name of the highlighted drive on it.

The disk you selected, along with the free space available on it, will now be listed next to the Set button on the Scratch Disks tab. You can specify up to 12 disks this way using the other select buttons. Final Cut Pro will use them in order of most available space first, regardless of the order of the disks as listed in the Scratch Disk tab.

To remove a particular drive as a scratch disk, simply click the Clear button next to its listing on the Scratch Disks tab.

Caution   If you have more than one drive hooked up to your computer, do not use similar names for them. A drive name should not contain the entire name of another drive, such as Media and Media 1. Otherwise, Final Cut Pro can get confused during capture and send the media to the wrong disk. To be safe, name your drives with completely different names, such as Apple, Orange, or Banana.

You can also use the Scratch Disks tab to specify custom locations for your waveform and thumbnail cache, and Autosave Vault folders. Click the Set button next to the item you want to specify and follow the preceding steps to select a drive. Other settings in the Scratch Disk tab are:

✦ **Minimum Allowable Free Space on Scratch Disks:** This setting determines the amount of free space you want Final Cut Pro to leave on each scratch disk before it moves on to the next disk. Always set the minimum no lower than 10 to 20MB to ensure best system and disk performance, and don't forget to allow more for render cache files that will be generated as your project progresses.

✦ **Limit Capture/Export File Segment Size To:** In previous versions of Final Cut Pro, users were confronted with a file size limit of 2GB. (This was a holdover from the old Mac OS days when no file could be larger than 2GB!) Even though the later versions of Mac OS and Final Cut Pro are now free from this limit, you may work with third-party software that still has this limit. If you find yourself in this situation (check the documentation for your other multimedia software), make sure no capture or export from Final Cut Pro exceeds 2GB (the default setting of 2000MB is close enough to 2GB). If a file should exceed that limit, Final Cut Pro will make two separate, but linked files.

✦ **Limit Capture Now To:** Capture Now is a setting in the Log and Capture window that tells Final Cut Pro to start capturing immediately. However, how "immediate" this is can be a delay from seconds into many minutes depending on the size of your specified capture disk. Use the Limit Capture Now To setting to limit the Capture Now length, because the length of most of your capture now clips will range anywhere from 30 minutes to 2 hours (the length of most video tapes). This will prevent the pause as Final Cut Pro prepares the drive for capture.

Dealing with Unavailable Scratch Disks

Scratch disks can become unavailable for a variety of reasons: They might be turned off, disconnected from the computer, or temporarily unmounted. Also, if the scratch disk folder is moved, deleted, or renamed, Final Cut Pro might not be able to recognize the scratch disk. When a scratch disk becomes unavailable, then the next time you open Final Cut Pro, you will see a dialog box with the following options:

✦ **Quit:** Clicking this button quits Final Cut Pro without changing the scratch disk preference.

✦ **Set Scratch Disk:** Clicking this button will automatically open the Scratch Disk preference tab so you can select another scratch disk. Any unavailable scratch disks are removed from the list. You must select at least one scratch disk to continue.

✦ **Check Again:** Clicking this button after you have started up or reconnected the scratch disk drive, instructs Final Cut Pro to scan the drive buses again for selected scratch disks.

Memory & Cache Tab

The settings in this tab control the amount of RAM and disk space for cache files used by Final Cut Pro and is shown in Figure 6-14.

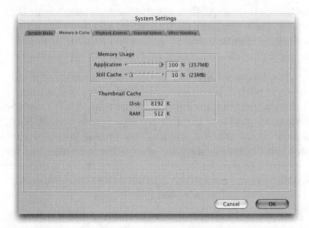

Figure 6-14: The Memory & Cache tab has controls for setting the amount of RAM used by Final Cut Pro and disk space for cache files.

Memory Usage settings

These settings are used to set the amount of available RAM to use for running Final Cut Pro. Your computer's available RAM is the amount of RAM not used by Mac OS X and any other running applications. Limiting the amount of RAM that Final Cut Pro uses can prevent, or at least minimize, Mac OS X's dynamic use of virtual memory, which can impede Final Cut Pro's performance.

✦ **Application:** Use this slider to set the percentage of available RAM used by Final Cut Pro. The total amount of RAM in megabytes is shown to the right. The minimum amount of RAM you can allocate to Final Cut Pro is 125MB. If the available amount of RAM is less than this, the slider is dimmed.

✦ **Still Cache:** Use this slider to set the percentage of excessive RAM allocated to Final Cut Pro used to hold still images for real-time playback. As you might expect, the more memory allocated to the Still Cache, the more still images can be played back in real time in the currently selected sequence. If your computer is not real-time capable, or there is no excess RAM available, this slider is dimmed.

Thumbnail Cache settings

Each clip in Final Cut Pro has a small thumbnail image that is drawn for it. The thumbnail usually shows the first frame of the clip. These thumbnails are stored as Thumbnail Cache files so that they don't have to be redrawn every time you view it in the Browser or sequence. You can choose the disk and the size of this storage space. The destination disk for the Thumbnail Cache is set in the Scratch Disk preferences. There are two settings for thumbnail cache:

✦ **Disk:** Sets the amount of hard disk space used for holding thumbnail cache files.

✦ **RAM:** Sets the amount of RAM to use for displaying and scrubbing preview of larger browser video icons.

Enter the desired cache size directly in the fields for each setting. You may want to allocate more disk space if you have a large number of clips you want to view with thumbnails or large Browser icons.

Increasing the amount of RAM allocated to the thumbnail cache can optimize the playback quality of large Browser icons when scrubbed.

Playback Control tab

As its name denotes, the Playback Control tab is where you set the playback quality of sequences in Final Cut Pro. What its name cannot tell you is that these settings also control Final Cut Pro's playback *capability* as well—namely, the amount of real-time effects you can play simultaneously using Final Cut Pro's software-based real-time architecture, RT Extreme. For example, choosing a high quality playback setting by deselecting Unlimited RT option and selecting High in the Playback Video Quality setting also means you will be able to play fewer real-time effects without rendering. On the other end of the scale, if you choose the Unlimited RT option and lower Playback Video Quality, you will now be able to play more real-time effects than your system is capable of, with the trade-off of possible dropped frames during playback. The Playback Control tab is shown in Figure 6-15.

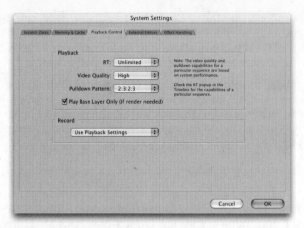

Figure 6-15: The Playback Control tab has settings for determining playback quality and real-time effects of your sequences.

Note

The settings in the Playback Control tab are the same controls in the Real-Time Effects (RT) pop-up menu in the Timeline, and are system-wide settings that affect all sequences and projects opened on that computer.

The settings for the Playback Control tab are:

✦ **Unlimited RT:** Selecting this option allows Final Cut Pro to play more real-time effects than the computer system is capable of without dropping frames. This might be sufficient if you need to see a preview of a complex effects composite, knowing that 100-percent frame playback is not guaranteed. Deselecting this option limits Final Cut Pro to play back only real-time effects your system is capable of without dropping frames.

Note

When setting this control in the RT pop-up in the Timeline, selecting Safe RT option is the same as *deselecting* the Unlimited RT option in the Playback Control tab.

✦ **Base Layer When Needs Render:** If this option is selected, Final Cut Pro ignores all effects processing (this does not include effects already rendered—rendered effects will still play back). Motion effects or filters applied to clips are ignored and only the source video is played. Speed adjustments are still applied to keep the duration of your sequence accurate but will still display the Unrendered screen in the canvas when played back. For multilayered tracks, only the base video layer will play without any transitions or effects. If this option is not checked, all effects that need to be rendered will display an Unrendered screen when played back.

✦ **Playback Video Quality:** If the codec you are using supports multiple resolutions, like DV, you can choose from the three quality settings in this pop-up menu. The higher the video quality selected, the more system overhead is required to play it back, resulting in fewer simultaneous real-time effects that can be played. The three quality levels are:

- **High:** This setting ensures full-frame, full-resolution video playback. Video interlacing is preserved.

- **Medium:** This setting plays a high-quality quarter-frame resolution video, which is not interlaced.

- **Low:** This setting plays a low-quality quarter-frame resolution video, which is not interlaced.

✦ **Pulldown Pattern:** When you are working with a 23.97 timebase sequence and want to output it to an NTSC video via FireWire, you can choose one of three *pull-down insertion* patterns. Pull-down insertion is the method of converting 23.97 fps to NTSC/29.97 fps by inserting additional frames into the footage using a very precise pattern. For more information, see Chapter 27. The three pull-down insertion patterns available in the Pulldown Pattern pop-up menu are:

- **3:2:3:2** This is the most commonly supported pull-down pattern for NTSC devices and is well suited for SD TV, MPEG-2, or high-end finishing systems. This method of pull-down insertion is the most processor-intensive but results in the highest quality NTSC output.

- **2:3:3:2** Using this option for recording or displaying video on DV equipment that supports this insertion pattern can deliver higher image quality than the 3:2 pull-down method. You can still record the output using 2:3:3:2 pull-down on any NTSC device, but at a lower quality than the 3:2 pull-down method.

- **2:2:2:4** This option is the least processor-intensive method of adding pull-down and is ideal for previewing playback with as many real-time effects as possible. This is also a good choice when working on an older, slower computer that suffers dropped frames when you try to output using the 3:2 or 2:3 method. Keep in mind that the output quality is significantly lower than the 3:2 pull-down method, and should be used for previewing or rough-cut outputs only.

✦ **Record settings:** The pop-up options under Record allow you to control the video output quality when using Print to Video or Edit to Tape commands. There are two options to choose from:

- **Full Quality:** When Full Quality is selected, video is always output to tape at the highest quality. This means any effects in your sequence that don't play back at full resolution are forced to render before output to tape.

- **Use Playback Settings:** Choosing the option, Final Cut Pro will use the Real-Time Effects settings selected in the RT pop-up menu when outputting to tape. This means your sequence will output at its current playback quality, including any real-time effects with less-than full-resolution due to selecting the RT Unlimited option. If there are any effects that will output at less than full resolution, a warning dialog box is displayed when you output to tape using Edit to Tape or Print to Video.

Tip   The Pulldown Pattern options will display in the Timeline RT pop-up menu only in sequences with a 23.97 fps timebase.

External Editors tab

One of Final Cut Pro's strengths lies in its ability to work with a wide variety of media formats. From still images, to computer-generated graphics, to the many QuickTime movie and audio file formats, Final Cut can import and play a seemingly untold number of media types. In the course of editing with these many file types in Final Cut Pro, you may need to change a clip or file with an application other than Final Cut Pro. Using the options in the External Editors tab allows you to assign specific applications to open for editing of these clips.

The four types of files for which you can set external editors are still images, video, audio, and LiveType movies. For example, you can have all imported still images open in Photoshop for image modifications; or perhaps you want your video files to open in After Effects instead of the default QuickTime Player. After you have made your modifications in the external editor and saved these changes, Final Cut Pro will update all the clips in your project that use this modified file.

Selecting an external editor is easy:

1. **Choose Final Cut Pro ⇨ System Settings.**

2. **In the System Settings window, click the External Editors tab to select it and bring it forward.**

3. **Next to the file type you wish to set an external editor for, click the Set button.**

   The Choose a File dialog box opens.

4. **Navigate to the application you wish to select, click on it to select it, and then click the Choose button.**

   When the Choose a File dialog box closes, you will see the pathname of the selected application next to the file type in the External Editors tab window, shown in Figure 6-16.

Figure 6-16: Use the External Editors tab to select other applications to modify clips already in a Final Cut Pro project.

To remove an assign external editor:

1. **Choose Final Cut Pro ⇨ System Settings.**

2. **In the System Settings window, click the External Editors tab to select it and bring it forward.**

3. **Next to the file type you wish to remove the external editor assigned, click the Clear button.**

When you want to open a clip in an external editor, there are two ways to do so:

✦ **Control+click on the clip in the Browser or Timeline and select Open in Editor from the contextual menu, shown in Figure 6-17.**

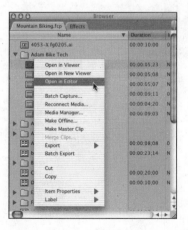

Figure 6-17: Open a clip in an external editor by Control+clicking on it and selecting Open in Editor in the contextual menu.

✦ **Select the clip in the Browser or Timeline, or display it in an active Viewer or Canvas window, then select View ⇨ Clip in Editor.** The clip will open in the external editor application that is assigned to its file type. After you make your modifications to the clip, save your changes and Final Cut Pro will update all occurrences of the modified clip throughout your project. It is extremely important that you save your modified clip without changing the filename, file format, or scratch disk location. If any of these file parameters are changed, Final Cut Pro may not be able to keep the link to the clips, resulting in offline clips when you return to Final Cut Pro.

Note   If no external editor has been assigned to handle that type of media file, indicated by the default <None Set> in the External Editor tab window, then the application that would open that particular file in the Mac OS X Finder is used.

Effects Handling tab

The Effects Handling tab is where you select how real-time effects are handled for clips using a real-time capable codec. With Final Cut Pro's software-based real-time architecture, the codecs that are real-time capable include NTSC and PAL DV, DVCPRO, DVCPRO-50, and Photo JPEG. The Effects Handling tab is shown in Figure 6-18.

Figure 6-18: In the Effects Handling tab you can choose how real-time effects are processed.

If you've installed a third-party capture card that supports real-time effects of any of these codecs, you can reassign real-time handling to your hardware card, instead of Final Cut Pro. In addition, any codec used by your third-party card that has been installed on your system and is real-time capable, will appear in the list of codecs.

To select the real-time handler of a specific codec:

1. **Select Final Cut Pro ⇨ System Settings.**

2. **Click on the Effects Handling tab to bring it to the front of the window.**

3. **In the pop-up menu of the codec you want to set, choose from the options:**

   • **None:** Selecting None disables all real-time effects for that codec.

   • **Final Cut Pro:** This is the default selection. Selecting this option processes real-time effects for that codec using Final Cut Pro real-time software.

Note If a third-party card has been installed on your system and is real-time capable with a particular codec, the card will appear in the pop-up menu as well.

Working with Easy Setups

Final Cut Pro's versatility makes it stand head and shoulders above any other non-linear editing application on the market. All video formats and aspect ratios have been accommodated. All frame rates and compressions are allowed as options. The fact that one nonlinear editing application covers so many bases makes Final Cut Pro a hornet's nest of settings, presets, and choices. No other nonlinear editing application seems to have this issue because they are generally designed to work with one compression, one aspect ratio, and one frame rate.

To help simplify the editing process by consolidating choices and settings, Final Cut Pro uses Easy Setups. An Easy Setup is actually a group of presets, and each preset represents a list of specific settings. Figure 6-19 illustrates how groups of presets combine to make an Easy Setup. Easy Setups make it easy to switch settings for different formats of video, or when switching hardware. Final Cut Pro arrives configured with some commonly used Easy Setups. Of course, you can create new Easy Setups or modify an existing one.

Note Easy Setups are most useful if you frequently switch between different kinds of video and various types of hardware. If you plan to stick with one kind of video (such as DV) and you won't be switching hardware very often, you will rarely change Easy Setups.

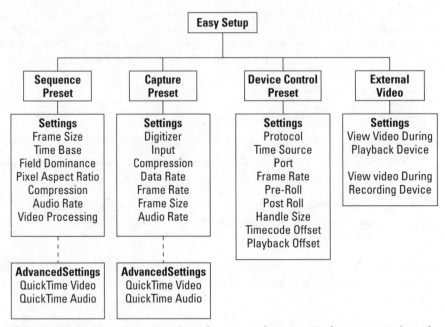

Figure 6-19: An Easy Setup consists of a group of presets. Each preset consists of a list of settings.

Selecting an Easy Setup

When you start Final Cut Pro for the first time, you'll be asked to choose an Easy Setup as well as a scratch disk. Figure 6-20 shows the Choose Setup screen.

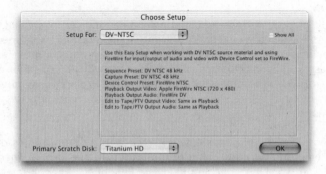

Figure 6-20: The Choose Setup window is presented to you the first time you start Final Cut Pro.

Although you choose an Easy Setup when you first launch the program, you can choose a different one anytime. Switching the Easy Setup changes your presets and settings to accommodate new hardware or video, adjusting device control, capture, sequence presets, external video settings, and more. To select an Easy Setup in Final Cut Pro:

1. **Choose Final Cut Pro ➪ Easy Setup.**

2. **Choose an Easy Setup from the Setup For pop-up menu.**

3. **Click the Setup button when you are done.**

This new Easy Setup will apply to all new projects and sequences you create. Existing projects and sequences are not affected. Figure 6-21 shows the Easy Setup selection window.

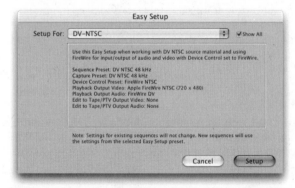

Figure 6-21: The Easy Setup window lets you select Easy Setups that accommodate various kinds of video and hardware.

Removing Apple-provided Easy Setups

When you first install Final Cut Pro, there are a few Easy Setups already available. Some of them may not be relevant to you. For example, if you are in the Americas, you may never work with PAL video, or if you're in Europe you may never use NTSC video. You can easily remove presets that you have no intention of using:

1. **Quit Final Cut Pro.**

2. **Locate the Custom Setting folder along the following directory path:**
   Startup Volume/Library/Application Support/Final Cut Pro System Support/ Custom Settings.

3. **In the Custom Settings folder, you will find the preset files for all Easy Setups. Remove any that you do not want to appear in the Easy Setup menu.**

   As a precaution, save any removed preset in a different folder and label the folder Unused Presets in case you need to restore the presets at some later time.

4. **Locate the Final Cut Pro Preferences file and delete it by moving to Trash and then emptying the trash.**

   If you do not delete the Preferences file, the Easy Setup will still appear in the Easy Setup and the Choose Setup windows. Final Cut Pro Preferences are saved to the OS X logged in User's Preferences folder, located at the following directory path: `Home/Library/Preferences/Final Cut Pro User Data`.

5. **Restart Final Cut Pro.**

   The preset is no longer available in the Easy Setup choice menu. If you moved the Easy Setup preset to a holding folder as suggested in Step 3, you should have no problem restoring an Easy Setup by simply dragging the Easy Setup file back to the Custom Settings folder. You can follow these same steps to add an Easy Setup provided by a third party.

Creating Easy Setups

If the preexisting Easy Setups don't exactly meet your needs, you may want to create your own. Easy Setups can be customized to your needs with specific changes that suit your setup and hardware. Modifying presets is described later in this chapter. To create a custom Easy Setup:

1. **Choose Final Cut Pro ⇨ Audio/Video Settings.**

2. **In the Summary tab, choose the presets you want using the pop-up menus.**

   You can also modify presets and individual audio and video settings within them to create entirely new presets.

3. **Click the Create Easy Setup button.**

   You'll see the Easy Setup Name and Description box.

4. **Enter a name and description for the Easy Setup you want to create.**

5. **Click the Create button.**

   A dialog box opens prompting you to save the Easy Setup file. Be sure that the new file is saved in the Custom Settings folder found in this directory path: `Startup Volume/Library/Application Support/Final Cut Pro System Support/ Custom Settings`.

6. Click Save.

The new Easy Setup appears in the Easy Setup selection box. You can check this by selecting Final Cut Pro ➪ Easy Setup and clicking on the pop-up menu. Your new Easy Setup will be listed in the pop-up menu.

Note   To delete a custom Easy Setup, follow the steps for deleting a preinstalled Easy Setup.

Working with Presets

As described earlier, Easy Setups are actually collections of presets. A preset in Final Cut Pro is a group of specific settings, and it helps you change many common settings with minimal effort. There are three main kinds of presets in Final Cut Pro:

✦ **Sequence Presets:** These contain settings about the sequences you create. These settings include the frame size of the video, the pixel aspect ratio of the video, the frame rate, and other audio and video settings.

✦ **Capture Presets:** These settings pertain to the media you are capturing and are dependent on the kind of video and the hardware you use. Like the Sequence Presets, these settings determine frame size, pixel aspect ratio, and other settings. Ideally, the main settings for the Capture Presets should be the same as the Sequence Presets.

✦ **Device Control Presets:** These determine the control protocol that you will use to control your video device, be it a deck or camera. A control protocol is a language that devices use to speak to each other. Common device controls are FireWire, RS-422, and RS-232. Final Cut Pro can accommodate these and many others. Device Control settings vary with each protocol and sometimes within protocols.

Cross-Reference   For more information on Device Control, see Chapter 4.

It is very important that some of the primary Sequence Preset settings match your Capture Preset settings. Otherwise, your captured clips will not play properly in the sequence. For example, if the Capture Preset setting for the frame size is 720 × 480 pixels, and the Sequence Preset frame size is 720 × 486 pixels, the captured clip will display a red line above it.

Note   You might be wondering why the last tab in the Audio/Video Settings window is not included here with the other three. Although it does control the destination of audio and video output, the controls are not considered a preset because its settings are hardware-based to your computer system's setup rather than Final Cut Pro's operational functions or options. Fear not, as the A/V Devices tab is covered later in this chapter.

Picking and choosing presets

When you select an Easy Setup a group of presets is chosen for you. These presets are Sequence, Capture, and Device Control. External Video and External Audio settings, which determine the output device for your video, are also chosen. You can review the presets in the Easy Setup dialog box after you have chosen a setup, as shown in Figure 6-22.

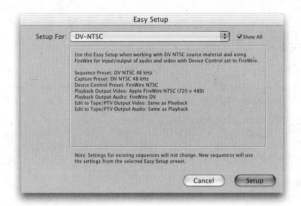

Figure 6-22: Each Easy Setup choice activates a specific set of presets.

You may not want the precise setup choices that are made for you. For example, you may want to switch from PAL video to NTSC, or you may want to deactivate Device Control if you are working with a camera or deck that does not support Device Control. To choose different presets:

1. **Choose Final Cut Pro ⇨ Audio/Video Settings.**

2. **On the Summary tab, select the desired presets using the pop-up menus as shown in Figure 6-23.**

3. **Click the OK button to close the Audio/Video Settings dialog box.**

Note   Each preset has its own tab in the Audio/Video Settings dialog box. If you want to review or change individual settings within each preset, click the corresponding tab.

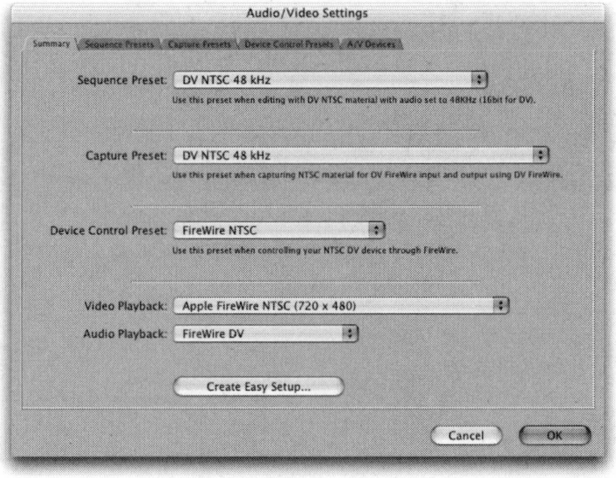

Figure 6-23: The Summary tab displays the active presets for the current Easy Setup.

Making a new preset

You may find that none of the existing presets satisfies your needs. In this case, creating a new preset would be a good idea. The best way to do that is to duplicate an existing preset and modify it to suit your needs. To create a new preset:

1. **Choose Final Cut Pro ➪ Audio/Video Settings.**

2. **Click the preset tab for which you want to create a new preset.**

   This may be the Sequence, Capture, Device Control, or A/V Devices tab.

3. **Select the preset you'd like to copy and click the Duplicate button.**

   In Figure 6-24, I'm about to duplicate and edit a Capture preset.

Highlight the preset you want to edit

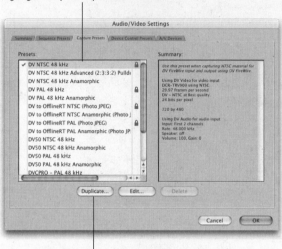

Click Duplicate to make a copy of the preset

Figure 6-24: Select a preset you want to copy and click Duplicate.

4. **In the Capture Preset Editor window that appears (see Figure 6-25), enter a name for the new preset.**

Make the name clear and descriptive.

5. **Enter a description for this preset.**

This description will appear as a summary when you call up this preset, so include as much helpful information as possible.

6. **Modify the audio and video capture settings that you want to change.**

7. **Click OK to finish editing the preset.**

Note   You can delete a preset by highlighting it in the Preset window (select another preset to make sure there's no check mark next to the one you want to delete) and clicking the Delete button. Just make sure that a current sequence isn't using the preset, or playback problems could result.

Enter a description for your preset

Enter a name for your new preset

Modify video and audio settings

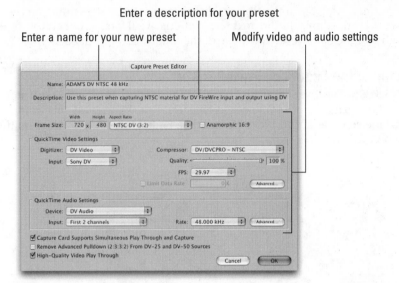

Figure 6-25: The Capture Preset Editor window allows you to edit presets.

Adjusting preset settings

Easy Setups, as explained earlier in this chapter, consist of groups of Sequence, Capture, and Device Control presets, and an A/V Device setting. Each preset is itself a group of many individual settings that affect the way Final Cut Pro works. Once you understand how Easy Setups, presets, and settings relate to each other, changing individual settings in presets is easy and fast:

1. **Choose Final Cut Pro ⇨ Audio/Video Settings.**

2. **Click the tab containing the settings you want to access.**

3. **Select a preset and click Edit.**

Note

You cannot edit a locked preset. You must first duplicate it as described earlier. A locked preset is indicated by a padlock symbol next to its listing in the Audio/Video Settings window. Currently active presets, indicated by a check mark next to the preset's name, also cannot be edited. If you double-click on a locked preset, you get a box that says, "The selected preset is locked and cannot be modified. A copy will be made for editing." Click the OK button and you will be presented the Preset Editor window.

4. **In the Preset Editor window, give the preset a name and description, and edit the desired settings.**

5. **Click OK to save the preset.**

The settings available in the Preset Editor window differ depending on the type of preset you are editing. In the next few sections, we'll look at the editor for each preset tab and break down the purpose of the unique settings in each one.

Details of the Sequence Preset Editor

Figure 6-26 shows the Sequence Preset Editor window. Here you'll find settings that control the behavior of sequences in Final Cut Pro. Notice that this window has two tabs, labeled General and Video Processing. First, look at the settings on the General tab:

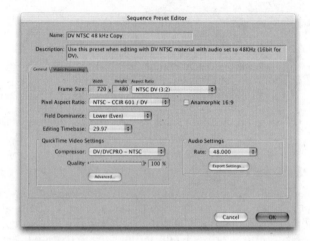

Figure 6-26: The Sequence Preset Editor contains settings that control the way sequences operate.

✦ **Name:** Enter a name here for your preset. This name will appear in the Audio/Video Settings window in two places: the Sequence Preset pop-up menu in the Summary tab, and the list of presets in the Sequence Presets tab.

✦ **Description:** Enter a brief description, or summary, of the preset's intended use.

✦ **Frame Size:** Choose a specific frame size from the Aspect Ratio pop-up menu, or choose Custom and then enter a nonconstrained frame size manually. Figure 6-26 shows NTSC-DV from the pull-down menu. DV-NTSC's frame size is 720 × 480 pixels.

✦ **Pixel Aspect Ratio:** This is the aspect ratio of the pixels that make up the frame size. All formats have their own pixel aspect ratios. Some video frame sizes are associated with particular pixel aspect ratios. Figure 6-26 shows NTSC-CCIR 601/DV. This is a non-square pixel used in DV video.

As a general rule of thumb, the only frame size that uses a square pixel aspect ratio is 640 × 480. This is a common frame size for computer-based multimedia and some older video capture cards. Almost all current broadcast video frame sizes use a CCIR-601 non-square pixel aspect ratio.

✦ **Anamorphic 16:9.** This is the box to check if you are capturing footage with a 16:9 aspect ratio. This letterboxed or widescreen look is very popular these days and is based on the aspect ratio of most cinematic films. When viewing clips in your sequence on your computer monitor with this option selected, you'll see the frame as a rectangle with black bars on top and bottom. This check box should only be used for footage that was originally captured at a 16:9 aspect ratio.

> **Cross-Reference**
>
> To learn more about working with 16:9 media, see Chapter 24.

✦ **Field Dominance.** Video for broadcast is *interlaced*. That is, each individual frame consists of two fields that are interlaced to make one frame. Each *field* contains half the resolution lines needed to make the frame. All video is either upper-field dominant or lower-field dominant. That is, either the upper field starts the frame or the lower field starts it. DV video is always lower-field dominant. Computer-based multimedia work does not have multiple fields for each frame and is called *progressive*. For progressive media, you'll choose the None setting.

✦ **Editing Timebase:** This is the frame rate for your sequence. Even though we commonly say that video's frame rate is 30 frames per second (fps), the actual rate for NTSC video is 29.97 fps. PAL works at 25 fps. This menu contains a number of frame rates to accommodate a variety of media formats, including film and HDTV.

✦ **Compressor (under QuickTime Video Settings):** Here you get to choose the codec you will be using for your video. There are many codecs to choose from. Note that except for the more generic codecs like DV-NTSC, names of codecs usually correspond to the names of capture card manufacturers. Make sure you choose a codec that matches your hardware.

> **Cross-Reference**
>
> For more information on codecs and compression, see Chapter 22.

✦ **Quality (under QuickTime Video Settings):** This slider is related to the Compressor setting. With some codecs like DV/DVCPRO, for example, the compression and data rate are fixed — any adjustment to the Quality control will have not effect. A higher setting on this slider applies a *lower* compression, giving you *better* quality but making the file size *larger*. A *lower* setting on this slider applies a *high* compression, giving you much *lower* quality and *smaller* files.

✦ **Advanced (under QuickTime Video Settings):** Clicking on this button will take you to additional QuickTime settings. The options found here will vary depending on your capture card. In most cases, you do not need to go into the Advanced settings area.

✦ **Rate (under QuickTime Audio Settings):** This controls the audio sampling rate. There are a few standard rates, which represent the number of times per second that digital audio is sampled. DV format is almost always recorded at 32 kHz (12-bit) or 48 kHz (16-bit). 48 kHz (kilohertz) means that the audio is sampled 48,000 times per second. CD-Audio is recorded at 44.1 kHz.

✦ **Advanced (under QuickTime Audio Settings):** This button takes you to the advanced section of the QuickTime Audio dialog box. Here you get many more choices of audio sampling rates. Unless you are specifically working with lower sampling rates, I strongly suggest not using sampling rates any lower than 32 kHz. Lower rates will create distortion and pops in your audio.

The second tab in the Sequence Preset Editor is the Video Processing tab, shown in Figure 6-27. Here you choose settings that have to do with the color space and luminance conversion of your chosen compression. Settings include:

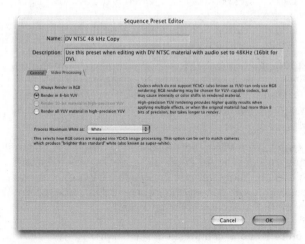

Figure 6-27: The Video Processing tab of the Sequence Preset Editor allows you to control color space rendering and luminance options.

✦ **Always Render in RGB:** This option forces the codec to render in RGB instead of YCrCb. Using this option may cause occasional shifts in color intensity. The reason for this shift is that some codecs that normally process color in YCrCb color space will be forced to process in the RGB color space. However, in some cases you may use this setting to achieve consistent colors.

For example, if you are using filters for Adobe After Effects (some of which process in RGB) in combination with Final Cut Pro's filters (which work in the YCrCb color space) selecting this option will give you consistent colors.

✦ **Render in 8-bit YUV:** This option will render media in 8-bit YUV color space. This is the most common option that is appropriate for DV footage and third-party capture card that capture in 8-bit video in YUV using a YUV compatible codec.

✦ **Render 10-bit material in high-precision YUV:** This option enables 10-bit rendering in YUV color space of 10-bit media files using a YUV compatible codec. Final Cut Pro can process 10-bit video with much more precision and latitude than 8-bit video.

✦ **Render all YUV material in high-precision YUV:** This option enables 10-bit rendering in YUV, even using 8-bit source clips. Although this will not improve or alter the original color space of an 8-bit YUV media clip, it does allow for improved quality of the render file of an 8-bit source clip that has multiple filters applied to it. The trade-off to this option is longer render times than with 8-bit YUV rendering.

✦ **Process Maximum White As:** This option will only appear if Always Render in RGB is unchecked. Here you are able to match RGB brightness values to YUV clips using super-white. *Super-white* is a term used for whites that are brighter than the NTSC "legal" brightness of 100 IREs. IRE is a unit of measurement for brightness in NTSC video, and waveform monitors are often used to monitor the IRE levels of video. The choices are either White or Super-White. Generally, you select the brightness according to the following:

  • Choose White if you are sure that you do not have any super-bright spots in your video that go above the 100 IRE as defined by a waveform monitor.

  • Choose Super-White if you have areas of brightness that may exceed the 100 IRE safe level set by NTSC.

  • DV camcorders often record video that is above the "safe" level of 100 IREs. If you have such spots, set this to Super-White.

Cross-Reference

For more information on RGB and YUV luminance, see Chapter 24.

Details of the Capture Preset Editor

The Capture Preset (see Figure 6-28) is a series of settings that determine how your media is captured. These settings depend largely on the type of video you are capturing and the hardware you are using to capture it. If you are installing a video capture card or advanced capture hardware, it will come with detailed documentation that should recommend the best capture settings to use. Some of these settings, including the Frame Size and Compressor settings, are similar to settings in the sequence presets. Other unique settings in this editor include:

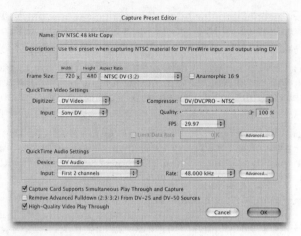

Figure 6-28: The Capture Preset Editor window adjusts capture presets for various kinds of video.

✦ **Digitizer (under QuickTime Video Settings):** This allows you to select the capture interface. For DV and FireWire, set this to DV Video. If there is no FireWire device attached, you'll see [Missing] DV Video in this setting.

✦ **Input (under QuickTime Video Settings):** When using DV, set this to DV. However, some video capture cards have multiple inputs, such as composite or component. This setting allows you to choose a specific input.

✦ **FPS (under QuickTime Video Settings):** For NTSC video, always set this to 29.97 fps. PAL video has a frame rate of 25 fps.

✦ **Limit Data Rate to X K/Second:** DV has a fixed data rate of 3.6MB/sec so this option does not apply to DV video. However, MJPEG and other compression-based codecs allow choices of data rates. Low-quality MJPEG generally has a data rate of about 1MB/sec (1000KB/sec). Medium-quality MJPEG compression runs at around 7MB/sec (7000 KB/sec), and high-quality video often has a data rate of about 12 to 13MB/sec (13,000 KB). Before you set this number, check the specifications of your card and drives to see the maximum data rate they support.

Cross-Reference   For more information on data, rates see Chapter 1.

✦ **Device (under QuickTime Audio Settings):** Choose DV audio if you are connected with FireWire. When FireWire is not available, this setting reverts to [Missing] DV Audio. Other choices include Built-In and None. When you install a capture card and its software driver, other choices will appear in the menu that relate to your card. Check the documentation that came with your card.

✦ **Input (under QuickTime Audio Settings):** DV devices can have up to four audio tracks. However, you can only capture two of these at a time. This menu gives you a choice of First 2 Channels, Second 2 Channels, or Mix 4 Channels. Mixing channels will capture all four channels as one stereo pair.

✦ **Capture Card Supports Simultaneous Play Through and Capture:** Some video capture cards allow you to view video on an external NTSC monitor while the Log and Capture window is open in Final Cut Pro; other cards do not. Check the documentation for your card to determine this setting.

✦ **Remove Advanced Pulldown (2:3:3:2) from DV-25 and DV-50 Sources:** Select this option if you are capturing from a DV source that used the 2:3:3:2 pull-down insertion method to capture 24P (short for *24 fps/Progressive scan*) video at 23.97 fps onto 29.97 fps DV NTSC frame rate. Removing the extra frames allows you to edit in 24 (actually 23.97) fps progressive timebase.

✦ **High Quality Video Play Through:** Selecting this option will display DV-format video at a higher quality in the Log and Capture window.

Details of the Device Control Preset Editor

The Device Control Preset (shown in Figure 6-29) is a series of settings that determine how Final Cut Pro controls your video deck or camera. DV devices generally use FireWire as their device-control protocol. Some DV decks and other video equipment use RS-422 or RS-232 device control. In this window, you can choose the type of protocol as well as other settings that are important to accurate and reliable device control. Settings to review in this preset are:

Figure 6-29: In the Device Control Preset Editor, you can adjust settings that determine the device control functionality of your equipment.

✦ **Name:** Enter a name here for your preset. This name will appear in the Audio/Video Settings window in two places: the Device Control Preset pop-up menu in the Summary tab, and the list of presets in the Device Control Presets tab.

✦ **Description:** Enter a brief description, or summary, of the preset's intended use.

✦ **Protocol:** Select the protocol your video device uses. DV cameras frequently use Apple FireWire or Apple FireWire Basic. The Basic is a modified and simpler version of the FireWire protocol for some cameras and decks that may not fully conform to the Apple FireWire Device control specifications. Analog and other professional decks use different protocols. Check the documentation for your equipment to determine the type of protocol to use.

Cross-Reference

For more information on Device Control, see Chapter 4.

✦ **Audio Mapping:** Use this pop-up menu to choose an audio track configuration for the device-controllable video or audio deck you will be recording audio to when using the Edit to Tape command. The options available in this pop-up menu depend on the device control protocol selected. For FireWire device control, this option is dimmed because of FireWire's set protocol of two channels of 16-bit resolution, or four channels at 12-bit resolution. The most common device control protocol, Sony RS-422, can output more than two channels of audio for tape assembly or insert. Because the Audio Mapping option cannot detect the number of channels available on the audio recording device to which you will be outputting, you must select the number of channels manually using this pop-up menu.

✦ **Time Source:** Your choices here are LTC, VITC, LTC+ VITC, Timer, and DV Time. If you are using DV and FireWire, set this to DV Time. This is DV's version of timecode. Keep in mind that this timecode is not 100-percent frame accurate. If you need frame accuracy, you should use a DV deck that supports RS-422 or RS-232 type protocol. LTC (Longitudinal Timecode) and VITC (Vertically Interleaved Timecode) are common types of timecode used on analog tapes. When using an analog deck, it is best to use the LTC+ VITC setting, because then Final Cut Pro looks for both. Many tapes have both timecodes on them. Timer is a basic clock-based timecode.

✦ **Port:** Device control is facilitated by a cable connecting the device control port of the video deck to the computer's serial or USB port. This menu allows you to choose the port that you are using. When using the FireWire protocol, this choice is disabled.

✦ **Frame Rate:** Choose the frame rate you are working with. 29.97 fps is the rate for most NTSC video. PAL is 25 fps.

✦ **Use Desk Search Mechanism:** When using a deck that uses RS-422 or RS-232 device control, you can check this box if you want to use the deck's internal search mechanism to locate timecode. You may want to check this off if the deck is having trouble locating the precise timecode.

✦ **Capture Offset:** Occasionally, you will find a slight discrepancy between the timecode on tape and the timecode that appears in captured clips in Final Cut Pro. This setting allows you to adjust for such discrepancies.

Cross-Reference I show you how to calibrate your capture offset in Chapter 24.

✦ **Handle Size:** This is the extra footage, or *handle,* you may want captured with your clips. *Handles* are the extra frames captured and added automatically to the beginning and the end of clips.

✦ **Playback Offset:** This setting affects the way your edited sequence is laid back to tape. When using analog decks with RS-422 device control, Final Cut Pro will often lay down a black frame before the first frame of video or start a frame late into the video. This setting allows you to adjust for that. This could be an issue when doing insert edits onto tapes.

Cross-Reference For more on calibrating and adjusting Playback Offset, see Chapter 24.

✦ **Pre-roll:** This setting determines how far back the deck starts playing the tape before the actual In point that was set by you. For example, if you set this to 2 seconds, and your In point on the tape is located at 1:04:12:15, then the deck will roll back to 1:04:10:15 and start playing the tape before it begins capture at 1:04:12:15. Decks require pre-roll time to synchronize their internal mechanism and get their playheads up to speed. A setting of 3 seconds is best. Change this to a lower number if you have a timecode break just before the shot In point. Increase it if your deck is having trouble getting up to speed.

✦ **Post-roll:** This setting is used to determine how much past the current point the video plays. This is used in the Viewer and Canvas window during Play Around Current command, and it is also used to preview edits to tape in the Edit to Tape window. In this window, you can perform a preview edit, which shows you how the edit is going to be performed without actually doing it. The Post-roll setting determines how far the deck continues to play after the edit ends.

✦ **Auto Record and PTV After:** If this option is selected when you use the Print to Video command, Final Cut Pro will automatically engage your DV camcorder or deck in Record mode, pause for the time specified, and begin print to video. If this option is not selected and you use the Print to Video command, you will be prompted to insert a tape and click Record.

Note   This option only works with DV camcorders and decks; it will not work with serial device control.

External Video and Audio setting

The settings in the A/V Devices tab control how your video will be shown on your deck, camcorder, TV, or monitor. This tab is shown in Figure 6-30. In addition to the A/V Devices tab, there are other places where you can select external video and audio settings:

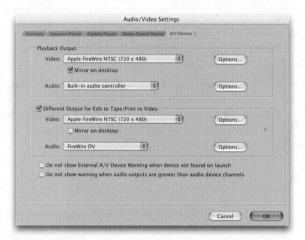

Figure 6-30: The A/V Devices tab adjusts how you view your video on an external monitor, TV, camcorder, or deck.

✦ **Summary tab in the Audio/Video Settings window:** In the Summary tab, you can select, independently, the video and audio destinations for video playback.

✦ **A/V Devices tab:** This tab, located in the Audio/Video Settings window, has more controls for specifying external audio and video output during playback, as well as controls for redirecting playback to a second destination for Edit to Tape and Print to Video commands.

✦ **View menu:** The view menu allows you to turn viewing on an external monitor on or off, as well as play back render options for the external monitor not found in the two Audio/Video Settings tabs.

Choosing an External Video and Audio Setting in the Summary tab

Although an External Video and Audio setting is assigned with every Easy Setup, you can change the selection in the Audio/Video Settings widows. The quickest way to do this is in the Summary tab:

1. **Choose Final Cut Pro ➪ Audio/Video Settings.**

2. **At the bottom of the Summary tab, select an option from the Video Playback pop-up menu.**

   The options for this pop-up include:

   - **None:** This turns off any external video output. You cannot see anything you play out to your deck, camcorder, TV, or monitor.

   - **Apple FireWire NTSC (720 × 480):** If you are using a DV-based setup, and have an NTSC camcorder or deck connected to your computer via FireWire, video playback will be available to the connected device. If your camcorder or the DV deck is hooked up to a monitor, you'll be able to see the video you play in the Timeline on this monitor, too.

   - **Apple FireWire PAL (720 × 576):** This settings works just like Apple FireWire NTSC (720 × 480), except it is designed for PAL video and devices.

See Chapter 4 for information on hooking up your DV camcorder to your Final Cut Pro workstation.

   - **Other available video interface:** Depending on your hardware setup and the video capture card you are using, any third-party capture card will be available to you in this menu. Select the card to view playback video on a device connected to the card.

3. **At the bottom of the Summary tab, select an option from the Audio Playback pop-up menu.**

   The options in this pop-up include:

   - **Built-in audio controller:** This is your computer's built-in audio interface—this plays audio through your computer speakers. This is the default setting if you don't have an external audio interface, camera, or deck connected to your computer.

   - **FireWire DV:** If you are connected to a DV camcorder or deck, this option is the default setting.

   - **Other available audio interface:** If you installed a third-party capture card or audio interface, it will be available to you in this menu. Choose the interface where audio will output to during playback.

Choosing an External Video and Audio Setting in the A/V Devices tab

In this tab, there are more options and controls for defining the video and audio playback selections than in the Summary tab. Any modifications and selections in this tab window are automatically reflected in the Summary tab, and vice versa. To select an external video and audio:

1. **Choose Final Cut Pro ➪ Audio/Video Settings.**
2. **Select the A/V Devices tab by clicking on it.**
3. **Make your selections in the Playback Output section.**

   The choices for the video and audio pop-ups are the same as the options in the Summary tab with a few additional options:

   - **Mirror on desktop:** Checking this option enables video playback in the viewer and Canvas windows along with video playback to the external monitor. If this option is not selected, video playback will only output to the external monitor during playback, and not in the Viewer or Canvas windows. By not mirroring playback in Final Cut Pro program windows during playback, processor overhead is considerably reduced. If None is selected, or there is no detected external interface, or the interface selected in not available (indicated with a [Missing] label in the pop-up menus), this option is either ignored or not displayed.

   - **Options (for Video):** Depending on your computer's hardware setup, video playback might require decompressing frames when viewing video on an external monitor. Click Options, to select Decompress after Compress. This option is not available when using FireWire. If you're using a third-party capture card, check the documentation that came with the card to see if you should use this option.

   - **Options (for Audio):** Clicking this button will open a dialog box with three pop-up menus allowing you more additional control when defining your external audio output. The available selections for audio options may vary, depending on your computer's hardware setup. The three options are Channels, Bit Depth, and Sample Rate (Hz).

     In Channels, select the number of audio channels your external audio interface is capable of outputting.

     Caution   The channels selected in this pop-up menu are the output channels to which sequence tracks are assigned using the Audio Outputs options in the Timeline and Audio Mixer.

     In Bit Depth, select a resolution of 16-bit for most applications. Use 24-bit for high resolution mixing or exports. In Sample Rate (Hz), select a sample rate for your audio playback. For professional audio applications, 44.1 kHz (CD quality) and 48 kHz (DV quality) are used.

   - **Different Output for Edit to Tape/Print to Video:** Check this box to redirect playback output to the specified video and audio interfaces when using Edit to Tape or Print to Video commands. Of course, this only works if you have more than one external video or audio interface for your computer. When you select this option, all controls in this section become available. These controls are identical to those appearing in the Playback Output section, noted earlier.

Note

If this option is not selected, all video and audio playback is output to the video and audio interfaces specified in the Playback Output controls — even when the Edit to Tape and Print to Video commands are used.

- **Do Not Show External A/V Device Warning When Device Not Found on Launch:** Select this option if you don't want the warning message "Unable to locate the external video device" to appear when Final Cut Pro starts up and no external interface is detected. With this option selected, Final Cut Pro will still search for external video device at each start up; it just won't display the warning message when none are found.

Note

Selecting the Don't Show Again option in the Warning message dialog box also selects this Do Not Show External A/V Device Warning, in this tab.

- **Do Not Show Warning When Audio Outputs Are Greater Than Audio Device Channels:** Select this option to disable the warning, "The selected external audio device does not support outputs. Unsupported outputs will be ignored during playback on this machine." This warning message appears if you assign more audio output channels to a sequence than are currently available on the selected audio interface.

Note

Assigning more audio output channels to a sequence than are currently available on your selected external audio interface can be useful in preparation for mixing on another system with more audio outputs. For more on setting up Audio Output channels, see Settings of an Audio Outputs preset in the "Understanding User Preferences" section located earlier in this chapter.

✦　　✦　　✦

Capturing and Organizing Media in Final Cut Pro

Capturing Media for Your Projects

Your first step in editing projects in Final Cut Pro is capturing media. After all, you must have something to edit before you can edit it, right?

Getting media onto your computers' drives from videotapes involves the process of *logging* and *capturing*. Logging is the process of marking the beginning and end, or In and Out points, of selections from your footage and saving this information as clips *without* capturing the media from your tape. The *capturing* stage is where the video files of logged clips are brought into the computer.

For Log and Capture in Final Cut Pro 4.0, there are some impressive new features adding to an already solid and intuitive interface. One of the more innovative enhancements is the ability to capture footage from a tape with timecode breaks without interruption while ensuring all resulting clips are timecode-accurate and in sync. Used in tandem with the new DV scene detection that automatically identifies and places markers for later subclip creation, Final Cut Pro can now capture a complete tape easily and efficiently.

You can capture many different kinds of media into Final Cut Pro, including video, audio, and stills. Though you spend most of your time capturing video, this chapter also explains many other types of media that can be brought into Final Cut Pro.

Before you capture media, you should make sure that you're familiar with Final Cut Pro basics and that you have your hardware and Final Cut Pro application settings configured to capture your media properly. If you haven't done so already, review the previous chapters (especially Chapter 6) before you start capturing media.

Getting Familiar with the Log and Capture Window

The Log and Capture window is where you perform all logging and capturing of footage from tapes. Here you control almost all aspects of logging, controlling, and capturing clips from your videotape. Before opening this window, make sure that your hardware and connections are set up properly, as described in Chapter 4. To open the Log and Capture window, choose File ➪ Log and Capture or use the keyboard shortcut Command+8. The Log and Capture window appears as shown in Figure 7-1.

Figure 7-1: The Log and Capture window is the place where you log all your shots and capture them into your computer.

The preview and marking area, on the left, is where you'll watch your video to determine the beginning and end of each shot. This area also contains transport controls for you to operate your playback device, as well as controls for marking In and Out points of your tape. These transport controls look very much like the playback controls in the Viewer or the Canvas windows in Final Cut Pro. However, in the Log and Capture window, they control the functions of your playback device using device control. Details of the Preview area are shown in Figure 7-2.

Note   Keep your eye on the VTR status indicator area in the Log and Capture window. There you'll see the current status of your playback device. If the communication is good, you'll see VTR OK. Otherwise, you may see NO COMMUNICATION if there's a problem with the connection between your playback device and your computer. If no tape is inserted in the VTR you may see a NOT THREADED message.

Preview area for video

Duration of selection

Available space and time on scratch drive

Current Timecode field

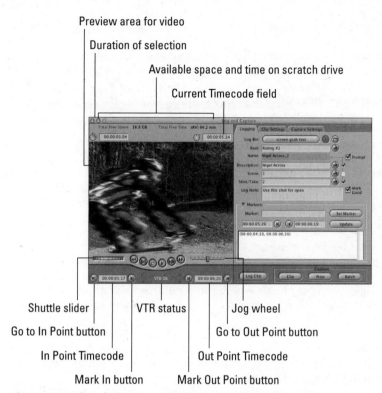

Shuttle slider   VTR status   Jog wheel

Go to In Point button   Go to Out Point button

In Point Timecode   Out Point Timecode

Mark In button   Mark Out Point button

Figure 7-2: The playback and marking area of the Log and Capture window is devoted to controlling the playback of your deck and marking In and Out points as you choose.

Note   The playback controls will not appear if device control is not active or your VTR does not support it. However, you will be prompted by a dialog box that tells you that you'll still be able to log offline clips (creating uncaptured clips for later capture).

Logging Clips

The Log and Capture window has a Logging information tab where you enter pertinent information for your shots. The Logging tab allows for entry of useful information that stays with your clips from then on. This logging information is seen in the Browser columns as well as other locations throughout Final Cut Pro and is used to organize your clips and projects.

By far the most important entry in the Logging tab is the Reel number. This number is how Final Cut Pro identifies tapes when you're recapturing media or generating an Edit Decision List (EDL) for working elsewhere with your project. Number your tapes if they aren't numbered already, and work out a system of organizing your source tapes before you proceed to logging. Keep the numbers consistent and you'll be spared a lot of headache.

In my own work, I tend to use short and to-the-point reel numbering schemes. For example, on a fictitious project, such as a short documentary about my backyard, I would label my reels as "MB#1," "MB#2," and so on. Short reel numbers are important because there are many fields where these numbers will appear within Final Cut Pro, and not all of them accommodate long reel numbers well.

Tip   If you plan to export an Edit Decision List (EDL) of your project for high-quality recapturing and finishing, or film matchback, be aware that many EDL formats have strict requirements for reel name length and characters. For more details about creating EDLs, see Chapter 22.

You can use bins in Final Cut Pro to organize your clips. Bins are represented by folder icons and can be used to store clips. A Logging Bin is a specific bin that you designate where logged clips are stored once they are entered in the Log and Capture window. The Logging tab has controls to make and select Log Bins, as shown in the detailed view of the Logging tab in Figure 7-3.

Caution   Before attempting to log, be sure to calibrate Final Cut Pro for any timecode offset you may have on your system. This is particularly important if 100 percent frame-accurate timecode is required for the purposes of recapturing or creating an accurate EDL (Edit Decision List). Bear in mind that DV timecode is not a frame-accurate protocol. This calibration generally applies to RS-422 or RS-232 type device control.

Cross-Reference   See Chapter 24 for more on calibrating timecode.

Reel, Name, and other shot description fields

Indicates current Log Bin

Up button selects previous bin in Browser

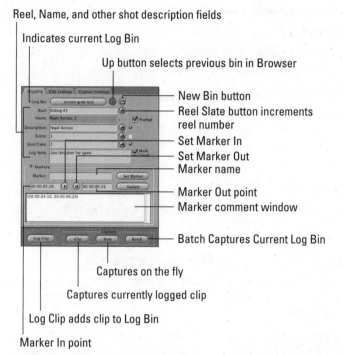

New Bin button

Reel Slate button increments reel number

Set Marker In

Set Marker Out

Marker name

Marker Out point

Marker comment window

Batch Captures Current Log Bin

Captures on the fly

Captures currently logged clip

Log Clip adds clip to Log Bin

Marker In point

Figure 7-3: The Logging tab in the Log and Capture window is used to enter information about your clip. The most important setting here is the Reel number for your tape. Final Cut Pro references this Reel number when recapturing footage.

Logging in Final Cut Pro

Logging clips by using the Log and Capture window is simple. Make sure that your hardware is connected, turned on, and working properly, and then perform the following:

1. **Choose File ⇨ Log and Capture.**

2. **Use the transport controls to play and move around on your tape.**

   Use the Shuttle or Jog controls to precisely locate a shot you want to capture. The Shuttle control is the slider located just below the preview image area to the left of the playback controls. The Jog control is the wheel located to the right of the playback controls, just under the image preview area.

3. **Enter a Reel name/number in the Logging tab.**

4. **Enter a shot description.**

   If the small check box next to the Description field is selected, this description is entered in the Name field automatically. Uncheck the box if you don't want this Description to be entered in the Name field.

> **Note**   You cannot enter any data directly into the shaded Name field. The Name of the clip is a *concatenation* (linking together) of the Description, Scene, and Take fields, if they are checked, and it appears in the Name field after data is entered into each selected field.

5. **Enter a Scene or a Take.**

   If the small check boxes next to the Scene or Take fields are checked, this information will be entered in the Name field automatically. Uncheck the boxes if you don't want this information entered into the Name field.

6. **Click the Marker In button to mark an In point for your shot.**

   You can read the In point timecode in the Marker In Point timecode field. You may have to click on the small disclosure triangle, located next to the Markers label, to open the Marker controls.

7. **Play the shot on your tape until you reach the desired end of the shot and click the Marker Out button.**

   This will mark an Out point for your shot. To capture a shot, you need an In point, determining the start location of the capture, and an Out point to indicate the end point of the capture for that shot.

8. **Click the Go to In Point button under the playback area of the Log and Capture window.**

   Final Cut Pro should roll your VTR to the place where you marked your In point. This allows you to confirm the location of your In point.

9. **Read the duration of your selection in the duration field in the upper-left corner of the playback area and confirm that it looks correct.**

10. **Click the Log Clip button to log your clip.**

The clip will appear in the Logging Bin of your browser with a red line across it, indicating that your clip is ready to be captured, but for now is *offline*. You've just set an In and an Out point and logged a clip. Later, you can batch-capture this and other clips that you've logged.

Speed-logging the wizard's way

In the previous section, we logged the old-fashioned way. That method works fine, but the whole business of clicking the In and Out buttons and dragging the shuttle slider around grows old surprisingly fast. Thankfully, there is a faster way. I like to call this way the "Wizard's Way." Here's how you do it:

1. **Press Command+8 to bring up the Log and Capture window if it isn't already open.**

2. **Manually enter the Reel name.**

   This is the only time you will use the mouse in this logging method.

3. **Instead of using the Shuttle slider or the transport controls, use the JKL keys on your keyboard to move the tape back and forth:**

   - **J:** Moves the tape backward. Repeatedly pressing J moves your tape backward faster and faster.

   - **K:** Pauses the tape.

   - **L:** Moves the tape forward. Pressing the L key repeatedly moves it forward faster and faster.

   This may take a bit of practice to get used to your deck's device-control response, but within minutes your fingers will be flying.

4. **Instead of using the Jog wheel to fine-tune your exact frame of the shot, use the arrow keys on the right side of your Mac keyboard.**

   The left arrow moves the tape backward one frame at a time. The right arrow moves it forward one frame at a time. Add the Shift key to move in increments of one second.

5. **When you find the In point on the tape, press the I key to mark the In point.**

6. **Use the O key to mark an Out point.**

   Tip

   If you want to navigate to the In or Out points that you've just marked, press Shift+I to go to the In point and Shift+O to go to the Out point. If you want to play just the selection between the In and Out points, press Shift+\.

7. **When you're ready to log your clip, press the F2 key on your keyboard.**

   If the Prompt box is checked, you'll get a Log Clip box. (I suggest leaving this box checked so that you can enter your name for the clip and not allow Final Cut Pro to use its naming system.)

8. **Enter the name of the clip in the Log Clip window (see Figure 7-4).**

Figure 7-4: The Log Clip window is where you enter a name for a clip and add a note for it.

9. **Press the Tab key on your keyboard to move the cursor down to the Log Note field in the Log Clip box.**

Enter a note for this shot if desired.

10. **When you're done, press the Enter key on your keyboard to close the box.**

Working with logging bins

Logging bins are folders where your logged clips reside in the Browser. Logging bins are important organizational tools, and the bin for a project is usually the folder for the main project. However, you can make new folders or bins and designate them as Logging Bins. Any clips you log will appear in this new Logging Bin. This may save you trouble and work later as you organize clips. To select a Logging Bin:

1. **In the Browser window choose New ⇨ Bin from the File menu (or use the keyboard shortcut Command+B).**

A new folder appears in your Browser with its name highlighted.

2. **Change this name to your liking.**

For example, the name could be the number of the reel you're about to log. The bins will be listed in the alphabetical order of their names. These bins will tend to mix with other items in the Browser. You can add a space before the name of every bin to group them at the top of the list in the Browser.

3. **Select this new folder and choose File ⇨ Set Logging Bin.**

A small slate appears next to it, indicating this folder as the current logging bin.

You've just set your new folder as the current Logging Bin. Final Cut Pro will keep putting all logged clips in this folder until you decide to change it.

Note

Final Cut Pro also references the Logging Bin for Batch Capture commands (capturing more than one clip at a time), so it's crucial to know where Final Cut Pro is looking for clips to be captured.

Understanding offline clips

In Final Cut Pro, you'll often encounter the terms *offline* and *online* in reference to clips. These terms can have various meanings. When a clip is logged, it'll appear in the Browser as a "logged" clip. Nothing has been captured; the clip has simply been logged. The associated media for the clip remains on the tape and has not been captured to the hard drive. A clip that has been logged but not captured will have a red slash line that appears on it in the Browser, as shown in the following figure, and is referred to as an *offline* clip. Once you capture the clip, the red line goes away, and the clip becomes an *online* clip. That means the media for the clip is now available on the drives.

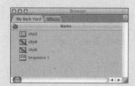

Final Cut Pro has another use for the terms *online* and *offline*. Any captured clip, still, or audio file imported into the Browser is not moved or copied into the Project file or the Final Cut Pro folder. The files remain on the hard drive wherever they may be located. Each Browser clip icon only represents a *link* to the original media file on the drive. These linked files are considered online. Clips that become unlinked from their media are called offline.

It is thus vital to retain these links. Removing, renaming, or deleting the media files can break a link. Therefore, it is very important to organize the media files you plan to import into your Browser. If you plan to import a series of stills or audio files, organize them into a folder and place the folder in a location that you will not tamper with. Avoid leaving files on the desktop and dragging and dropping them into the Browser. If you move these files to a different location later on, Final Cut Pro will lose its link to that file, and the clip will become offline.

You can use the File ➪ Reconnect Media command to relink an offline clip to its media file, *if the media file is still around*. If the media file was deleted, you can recapture it using the offline clip, since the timecode and reel information is still intact on an offline clip.

Changing preferences in the Log and Capture window

During the Log and Capture phase, you may decide to change your capture preferences. For example, you may want to switch the type of device control from FireWire to RS-422 or change your scratch disk to another drive. You can use the Capture Settings Tab in the Log and Capture window to do that:

1. **In the Log and Capture window, click on the Capture Settings tab.**

2. **Use the Device Control pop-up menu to select the device control you want to start using.**

3. **Use the Capture/Input pop-up menu to select the type of capture preset you want to switch to.**

Note   The selections available in the Device Control pop-up menu and the Capture/Input pop-up menu correspond to the presets available when you select the menu item Final Cut Pro ⇨ Audio/Video Settings. If you create more presets to reflect your hardware and settings, these presets will be available through Device Control and Capture/Input pop-up menus as well.

4. **In the Capture Settings tab, Final Cut Pro displays the amount of free space available on the drive that is currently selected as your scratch disk.**

   If necessary, click the Scratch Disk button to go to the Scratch Disk Preferences tab to change the drive you're currently using as a scratch disk.

Caution   If you have more than one hard disk or partitions you're using as capture scratch drives, make sure they don't have similar names. For example, a common convention is to name your media drives "Media 1," "Media 2," and so on. Try selecting completely distinct names, such as "Adam," "Alice," or "Zoe," in order to minimize the risk of confusing you or Final Cut Pro as to which disk to capture to.

Calibrating capture settings with bars and tone

Color Bars are used in the world of video to calibrate the video signal. A set of color bars is recorded onto a tape in the field that is being shot with a camera. Later this tape is digitized using a capture card into a Final Cut Pro–based system. Before the digitizing process occurs it is important to calibrate the video-capture card to the color bars from the tape. This ensures that no undue shift in the brightness and color values of the tape occurs during the digitizing process. A waveform monitor and vectorscope are two pieces of equipment that are used in the professional video world to calibrate the color bar's signal.

The image quality controls in the Clip Settings tab, located in the Log and Capture window, are used to ensure the bars are coming in with correct color and brightness. This process is reversed when Final Cut Pro is used to lay the video back to tape. Color bars are added to the beginning of the tape before a program is laid down on it.

Note   DV Video, when captured with FireWire, does not require adjustment for bars and tone. The color and brightness controls are inactive in the Clip Settings tab when you're capturing DV with FireWire because there is no "digitizing" process. In the case of DV with FireWire, you're basically just performing a "bit copy" of the video. *Digitizing* is the process of converting analog video to digital, but DV is digital already.

Waveform and vectorscope

Analog video in broadcast and professional environments is monitored with waveform monitors and vectorscopes. These are scopes or monitors that allow you to look at and calibrate an incoming video signal for accurate brightness and color values. A waveform represents the incoming signal's brightness values, whereas a vectorscope is used to check its color and hue. Waveform monitors and vectorscopes are stand-alone items that are usually quite expensive.

A standard set of color bars is used as a reference signal to be adjusted with a waveform monitor and a vectorscope. This ensures proper brightness and color values for the incoming video signal. Final Cut Pro has a built-in waveform monitor and a vectorscope that can be used as substitutes for the real thing. Bear in mind that software-based monitoring equipment can rarely compare with expensive hardware units. However, this will do for most cases, and it's a good way to illustrate how they work. To use Final Cut Pro's waveform and vectorscope to calibrate color bars:

1. **Choose File ➪ Log and Capture to open the Log and Capture window.**

2. **Make sure that your tape has color bars on it. Cue up the tape to see the color bars through the Preview area of the Log and Capture window.**

3. **Click the Clip Settings tab in the Log and Capture window.**

4. **Click the Waveform and Vectorscope button.**

   You'll get the Waveform and Vectorscope display shown in Figure 7-5.

5. **Click the Targets check box to make sure that the purple targets are displayed.**

6. **The Waveform Monitor shows the color bars as a series of brightness steps.**

   Each color in the bars shows up as one of these steps. The object is to adjust the brightness and the contrast so that the bars, which show up as green markers, match the ideal targets, which appear in purple.

> **Note**
>
> If you're using a composite or S-Video input on your digitizing card, you'll only be able to adjust the Hue, Saturation, Brightness, and Contrast sliders. Black Level and White Level sliders will be inactive. If you're using a component input, then you'll be able to adjust the Black Level and White Level sliders.

If you're capturing using Composite or S-Video input, adjust the Brightness and Contrast sliders in the Clip Settings by following these steps:

1. Adjust the Brightness so that the green markers at the top of each color bar lie on their corresponding purple targets.

2. Adjust the Contrast so that the top and the bottoms of the bars stay within the boundaries set by both top and bottom targets.

3. Continue to adjust both Brightness and Contrast until you have a range of brightness between the 100 and 7.5 IRE targets.

Brightness
values

Color
values

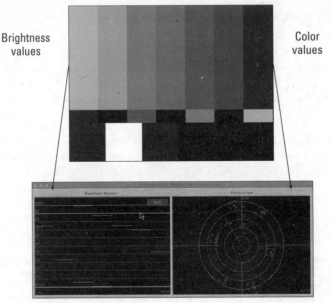

Figure 7-5: The Waveform Monitor is used to monitor brightness values of the color bars and the video signal. The Vectorscope is used to calibrate the color and hue of the signal.

If you're capturing using Component video, adjust the Black Level and White Level sliders by following these steps:

1. Adjust the Black Level so that the third bar from the left touches the 7.5 IRE target.

2. Adjust the White Level so that the second bar from the left touches the 100 IRE target.

7. **Begin to adjust the Vectorscope by clicking the Lines check box to make sure the lines appear to connect the dots on the Vectorscope.**

The Vectorscope, located to the left of the Waveform monitor, shows the color values of the video frame as a point graph. Each point you see on the circular graph represents one of the color bars. In the Vectorscope, the color bars are reflected as points that are connected by green lines.

8. **Adjust the Hue and the Saturation sliders to match the purple target circles.**

Hue will rotate your lines. Saturation will tend to spread the lines out or in. Adjust them as close to the purple target circles as possible.

Cross-Reference

In order for you to correctly align your bars in the Waveform and Vectorscope window of Final Cut Pro, I would advise you to learn more about the theory behind the color bars and what a Waveform and Vectorscope do. For more information on color bars and calibration see Chapter 20.

Calibrating a video signal without color bars

In some cases, you may not have a set of color bars on tape. In a pinch, you can sometimes get decent results calibrating your video signal for accurate flesh tones. This is a commonly used technique for analog video. To calibrate the signal using flesh tones:

1. **Find a section of your tape where you have a large area of flesh tone.**

   Faces are ideal for this calibration.

   On the Vectorscope, there is a purple line extending from the center outward toward the 11 o'clock position. This is the target for the flesh tone. You should see a white spike, or trace, next to it. This white spike represents your flesh tone as seen on tape.

2. **Adjust the hue and saturation until the white line matches the flesh tone target and orientation.**

   Figure 7-6 shows this process.

Flesh tone target

Trace

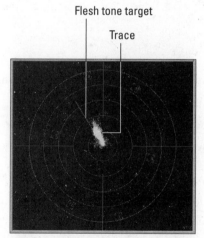

Figure 7-6: The white trace made by the flesh tone on the Vectorscope should be lined up with the purple target line representing flesh tone.

3. **Check the shot after you've calibrated using the flesh tone.**

   The shot should have improved in color and hue. If not, find another area of flesh tone and make the adjustment again.

Note Adjusting colors by flesh tone is not a perfect science. (For example, *whose* flesh tone are we talking about?) Using flesh tone to adjust colors is a judgment call at best and can work under certain special circumstances.

Calibrating audio levels

Just as color bars are used to calibrate the video signal, an audio tone is used to calibrate the audio inputs before digitizing. Along with the bars, a reference tone is generally recorded on tapes. This is the annoying loud beep that you hear when you're playing the color bars on a tape. It is also known as the 1 kHz reference tone, and it is set to play at 0 db (decibels) on analog systems. This 0 db analog tone is equivalent to –12 db in digital systems. If your tape was recorded properly, all the audio should have been recorded in relation to this reference tone. If you set this tone at the appropriate mark on the Final Cut Pro audiometer, you should be able to count on undistorted and clean audio.

Note When capturing DV audio via FireWire, you cannot use the gain slider to adjust the level of the incoming audio for the same reason that only limited controls are available when capturing DV video footage: The audio file coming in over the FireWire is already in binary digital format, which you're basically transferring to the computer drive.

To check and set audio levels in Final Cut Pro:

1. **Choose File ⇨ Log and Capture to bring up the Log and Capture window.**

2. **Click the Clip Settings tab.**

3. **Bring up the audio meters by choosing Window ⇨ Audio Meters.**

4. **Play the tone on your tape so that it plays through the Log and Capture window.**

   You can do that by pressing the Play button in the Log and Capture window.

5. **Adjust the Gain slider in the Clip Settings tab (see Figure 7-7) so that the tone rises in the audio meter to –12 db.**

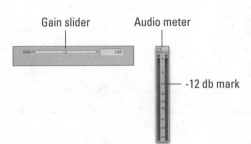

Gain slider   Audio meter

-12 db mark

Figure 7-7: A 0 db analog tone should be adjusted to –12 db on the Final Cut Pro audio meter. Adjust the Gain slider in the Clip Settings tab of the Log and Capture window to set audio levels.

6. **Play your tape at different places to check that the audio peaks do not rise above −3 db.**

Your peaks should remain between −12 db and −3 db. Your audio levels should not hit the 0 db mark too often, if at all, or else the audio will distort.

Note

It is a common scenario that the reference tone recorded on a tape will have no relationship to the audio recorded on the rest of the tape. Even though the reference tone is a good place to start, you should always review your tape through the Log and Capture window while keeping an eye on the audio meters. "Healthy" levels should generously rise up to −3 db often but should not remain there. Also, listen to the audio content itself. A person speaking in a room will show audio levels different from a scene on the street with passing cars and other ambient noise.

Understanding Clip Settings

We've been visiting the Clip Settings tab in the Log and Capture window to adjust our incoming video and audio signals. This window has some other controls that need some explanation as well. These controls can affect you during log and capture as well as when performing batch capture. Figure 7-8 shows the details of the Clip Settings tab. Table 7-1 describes the settings you'll find here.

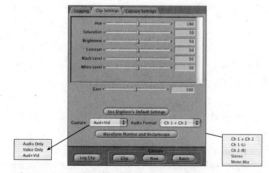

Figure 7-8: The Clip Settings tab in the Log and Capture window is used to adjust the incoming video and audio.

Table 7-1
Details of the Settings Tab in the Log and Capture Window

Control	Description
Image Quality Control Sliders	Use to adjust the brightness and the color of incoming video signal, but only when using a digitizing card. When using DV video with FireWire connections, this setting is inactive.
Gain Slider	Use to adjust the level of the incoming audio signal. This works with digitizing cards. When using DV with FireWire cables, this slider is inactive.
Use Digitizer Default Settings	Your capture card, if any, has predefined settings for Image Quality Control. To restore the Image Quality Sliders to the default settings, click this button.
Capture Format Pull-down Menu	Allows selection of capturing Video only, Audio only, or Video + Audio. If you wanted to record just the audio or just the video from a tape, this is where you'd switch these settings.
Audio Format Pull-down Menu	Choose the channels you'd like to record. This affects how audio is captured into your system, not tracks from your tape.
Channel 1+ Channel 2	This captures both channels but does not tie Channel 1 and Channel 2 as a stereo pair. This affects you two ways: When you open a clip that was captured this way in the Viewer, you will get separate Audio tabs for Ch 1 and Ch 2. Also, level and pan changes applied to one of these channels in the timeline will not automatically affect the other. Only use this setting if the two channels of audio on your tape are totally discrete channels that you want to adjust separately.
Channel (L)	This setting captures only Channel 1, or the left channel, of your tape. Stereo pan of the incoming clip is set to center. This is not an option for DV.
Channel (R)	This setting captures only Channel 2, or the right channel, of your tape. Stereo pan of the incoming clip is set to center. This is not an option for DV.
Stereo	This captures both channels and ties Channel 1 and Channel 2 as a stereo pair. This affects you two ways: When you open a clip that was captured this way in the Viewer, you'll get only one audio tab with Channel 1 and Channel 2 displayed as two tracks of waveforms. Also, level and pan changes applied to one of these channels in the Timeline will automatically affect the other. Use this setting when capturing mixed stereo tracks from tape that have no audio separation between the channels.

When logging clips, all the settings in the Clip Setting window are saved with each clip. For example, if you change the brightness for Clip 1 and the hue for Clip 2 before logging them, these clips will be saved with the log information. When you batch-capture these clips, each clip will be captured with its properly adjusted setting (adjusted brightness and hue in the cases of Clip 1 and Clip 2, respectively). What's more, if during the logging process you left the Audio Format selectors to some undesired setting or overlooked the fact that you had mistakenly selected Audio Only in the Capture Format pull-down menu, Final Cut Pro will attempt to capture the logged clips as Audio only when you invoke Batch Capture.

Final Cut Pro remembers all the settings in the Clip Settings window for each clip and attempts to use them for Batch Capture. This is an excellent feature. It means that each clip can have its own image-control settings, as well as audio gain and audio-format selections. But it also means that if you change your mind about certain settings you'll have to go back and modify them before capturing the clip. Here's how:

1. **Choose File ➪ Log and Capture and click the Clip Settings tab.**

2. **Modify the settings to reflect how you want to capture a previously logged clip.**

3. **Close the Log and Capture window.**

4. **Choose File ➪ Batch Capture.**

5. **In the Batch Capture dialog box, uncheck the Use Logged Clip Setting Options check box.**

    Final Cut Pro will ignore the originally logged clip settings and use the ones in the current Clip Settings tab.

Note   An easy way to change your audio track selection on a logged clip is to Control+click on the Tracks column in the Browser window for that clip and choose from the selections that appear. Now you can Batch Capture the clip with the new audio track choice.

Capturing Media for Your Projects

Media is a term that everyone seems to be using these days. When I say *capturing media,* I don't mean kidnapping the local news anchor. In this book *media* is the footage you'll record from tape into your computer. Media may also be stills you made in a graphics program such as Adobe Photoshop, or it could be audio tracks you imported from CD directly into your project. Captured footage, imported stills, audio, and other files are all referred to as *media* when we work with Final Cut Pro.

In the last section, you learned how to log clips. After you've logged your clips, the next step is to capture them. The easiest way to capture a large number of logged clips is to batch-capture them. *Batch-capturing* is the process of capturing one or more clips (a batch of them) all at once. Final Cut Pro uses device control to automatically find the In and Out points that you logged for the footage and captures the clips into your computer for you. Device control is required to perform batch captures, but you can still capture media (just not as efficiently) from devices that don't support device control.

Capturing video with device control

Capturing clips with hardware that uses device control is easy. If you're not sure whether your hardware supports device control, check out Chapter 4. Before you begin capturing video, make sure all your cables and devices are hooked up, turned on, and ready to go. If you just want to capture a single clip, and you haven't already logged it, follow these steps:

1. **Choose File ➪ Log and Capture.**

2. **Play your tape using the transport controls at the bottom of the Log and Capture window.**

   Locate the shot you want to capture from your tape.

3. **Enter a Reel name in the Log tab of the Log and Capture window.**

   Be sure that the Prompt box is checked next to the Name field.

4. **Click the Mark In button to mark an In point for your shot.**

5. **Play the shot on your tape and click the Mark Out button when you're sure you want to end capturing the shot.**

   This action marks an Out point for your shot.

6. **Click the Capture Clip button in the Logging tab of the Log and Capture window.**

   The Log Clip dialog box appears.

7. **Enter a Name and Log Notes for the clip, and then click OK.**

Final Cut Pro will use device control to roll back a few seconds before the In point of your clip, and then the shot will be captured up to the Out point you set. Once captured, the clip will appear in your Browser.

Caution   The amount that Final Cut Pro rolls back before the In point is called the *pre-roll* and is set in the Device Control Presets. If you have a timecode break just before your In point, this may interfere with the pre-roll. Changing the pre-roll time to a shorter length in the Device Control Presets Editor tab in the Audio/Video Settings panels should resolve this problem; however, most playback decks require a minimum of 2 seconds pre-roll for proper operation.

Capturing video without device control

If you don't have device control, you can still capture clips in Final Cut Pro. You can't use the Batch Capture feature, but you can capture one clip at a time. This is a common situation when capturing material from a home VHS VCR, which does not support device control. But be aware: Because you'll be capturing manually without deck controls, you won't be able to recapture the same clips frame-accurately later. Whenever working without device control, be sure to capture your material at the highest resolution you'll need for your final program. To capture a clip without device control:

1. **Choose File ⇨ Log and Capture.**

2. **If you haven't already deactivated device control, select the Capture Settings tab in the Log and Capture window and select Non-Controllable Device from the Device Control pull-down menu.**

   This will deactivate device control and also simplify your Log and Capture window.

3. **Click the Logging tab and enter any information you require.**

4. **Click on the Clip Settings tab and adjust settings as needed.**

5. **Press the Play button on your VCR or video deck.**

6. **Click the Capture Now button when the shot you need appears in the Preview area of your Log and Capture window.**

   To give the deck a few seconds to roll to speed, it is often helpful to start playing the tape a few seconds before your shot. There's also a slight delay between the moment you press the Capture Now button and the moment that Final Cut Pro actually starts the capture. You should compensate for this delay as you proceed.

7. **Press the Esc key on the upper-left corner of your keyboard to stop capturing.**

   The captured clip appears in a separate Viewer window. *Note that this clip has not been saved into your project yet, nor has its media been saved to your disk. The next step is crucial for saving this clip properly.*

8. **Drag the clip from the Viewer to the Browser by dragging the image of the clip from the Viewer and dropping it into the Browser.**

   A Save File dialog box appears.

9. **Enter a name that follows your organizing scheme, and save the clip into the scratch disk of your choice.**

   Of course, take care not to store the clip just anywhere but in an appropriate folder. The clip's media is saved to disk, and the clip will appear in the Browser.

Note   The Capture Now option can also be used when using Device Control. You'll find a slight delay between the time you press the Capture Now button and the time that Final Cut Pro will start capturing. Keep this delay in mind as you capture with the Capture Now option.

Batch-capturing video clips

Batch-capture is the automated process of capturing one or more clips that you've logged. Device control is required for batch-capturing and can work only if you use tapes that have valid timecode so that the tape can find the correct In and Out points. For this reason, timecode breaks usually wreak havoc during batch-capture and should be avoided as much as humanly possible. *Timecode break* is a jump or skip in the timecode of the source videotape. For example, a tape might start out having a timecode of 3:00:00:00 (some people use the hour code to specify the reel number on tapes in the field) but then after the break, the timecode switches to 1:00:00:00. This confuses the batch-capture process.

Final Cut Pro 4.0's new feature that automatically handles capturing from tapes with timecode breaks might very well be the end of your timecode break woes. You enable this feature in the General tab of the User Preferences settings. Choose Make New Clip in the pop-up field for On timecode break: option. When a timecode break is encountered during capture, Final Cut Pro will save the clip up to the timecode break and then continue capturing from the frame after the dropped timecode as a separate file. The first clip has the original name of the logged clip with each subsequent clip after a timecode break named with the original name plus a dash and an incremented number.

Cross-Reference   As of this writing, the Make New Clip option works with DV only. Other options in the User Preferences for handling timecode breaks during capture are covered in detail in Chapter 6.

Before you begin a batch capture, make sure that your scratch disk is set correctly and that there's enough space to capture the material. Also, take time to look through your clips to weed out duplicate names and change them as needed. Now you're ready to batch-capture your clips:

1. **Select the clips in the Browser you want to batch-capture.**

   To select more than one clip, lasso adjacent clips by clicking and dragging the arrow tool around the clips, or select nonadjacent, or noncontiguous clips by Command+clicking clips.

2. **Choose File ➪ Batch Capture.**

   The Batch Capture dialog box appears.

3. **Review the settings and click OK.**

These settings are described in the next section. The Insert Reel box appears asking you for all the reels (tapes) needed for this batch.

4. **Click on one of the reels, insert that reel into your VTR, and click Continue.**

Final Cut Pro will batch-capture the shots from that reel for you.

Caution

Editors often click on the Batch Capture button in the Logging tab of the Log and Capture window to batch-capture clips. Bear in mind that this starts to batch-capture the clips in the logging bin that is currently designated. This can cause confusion because you'll be asked for reels and shots you may not intend to capture right now. The method described in the preceding steps provides a simpler and much safer way to control your batch-capture.

Reviewing options in the Batch Capture dialog box

The Batch Capture dialog box will appear every time you start a batch-capture process. This box, shown in Figure 7-9, controls many options that affect the way your batch capture is conducted. You'll also get a summary of the total minutes of media time you're about to capture. Table 7-2 describes the details of the Batch Capture dialog box.

Figure 7-9: In the Batch Capture dialog box, you select options that can affect your batch capture, review a summary of the preset you're going to use, and see the length of the media you're about to capture.

Table 7-2
Details of the Batch Capture Dialog Box

Setting	Description
Capture	The most common choice here is All Selected Items, as shown in Figure 7-9. If you invoked the Batch Capture command in the Log and Capture window, this setting will relate to your logging bin.
Use Logged Clip Settings	Selecting this box will use the individual settings saved with each clip. These were the settings you chose in the Clip Settings tab, in the Log and Capture window, while logging clips. If you want to capture the clips using the current settings in the Clip Settings tab, uncheck this box.
Add Handles	This amount is added to the In and Out point of your clips. Check this option and enter a time in the field if you want all your clips to be captured with a few extra frames or seconds, or "handles" at each end.
Capture Preset	This pull-down menu allows you to change your capture preset. These choices are the same ones that you have in the Capture Presets tab of the Audio/Video Settings dialog box.
Media Time	Shows the total time of all the clips you're about to batch-capture.
Total Disk Space	Indicates the amount of disk space needed for this batch as well as the amount of disk space available on your current scratch disk.

To successfully perform a batch-capture, there are a few points you should keep in mind:

✦ **Check your critical settings before you start.** Always check the Abort Capture on Dropped Frames option in the General tab of the Preferences window. You don't want to waste time capturing clips with dropped frames.

✦ **Do a test batch-capture.** When I start the day with a lot of batch-captures on the agenda, I will first take a minute to batch-capture one clip from one reel. Then I play that captured clip in the viewer, checking the sound and picture to make sure all the settings are correct before I go ahead and spend the whole day capturing clips. This confirms that my batch-capture settings are good, and that there are no issues with hardware that will cause capture problems.

✦ **Keep it simple.** Sort the Browser by reel name and capture one reel at a time. Don't be overly ambitious and try to batch-capture 120 shots at once. As wonderful as Final Cut Pro is, it isn't a magic box. Things can go wrong. Proceed with care and take frequent breaks to check the progress and quality of your clips.

✦ **Don't leave the batch-capture unattended.** Some editors believe too strongly in the "magic" of batch-capture. They start a batch-capture and then go off for a long lunch. It's an automated process — what can possibly go wrong? If time is important to you, try not to leave the batch unattended. There are many issues that can stop a batch-capture. If you're there, you can fix the issue and continue capturing.

✦ **Keep an eye on the Batch Capture Status window.** During a batch capture, Final Cut Pro shows a large window on your computer monitor displaying a preview of the shots that it is capturing. A small gray window just below the preview window shows the status of the batch-capture. Figure 7-10 shows this small window.

In this figure you can see that Final Cut Pro is cueing up the tape to start capturing the clip. The clip it is about to capture is called "Band1" and this clip's duration is 3 seconds, 19 frames. You can also see that "Band1" is only one of the two clips in this batch capture, and you can see the remaining capture time left on this reel. This window can help you spot which clip Final Cut Pro is having a problem with if an error occurs.

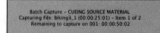

Figure 7-10: This gray window appears when Final Cut Pro is batch-capturing clips.

✦ **Avoid timecode breaks.** Avoid timecode breaks like the plague. If you have any influence on the source tapes you get, insist that they be as free from timecode breaks as possible. This is *critical* if you're batch-capturing at low resolution with plans to recapture at higher resolution after the program is edited. If, for whatever reason, Make New Clip is not selected in the User Preference panel and Final Cut Pro captures a clip with a timecode break, the timecode on the captured clip *will be incorrect from the timecode break onwards*. You cannot expect to successfully recapture the portions after that timecode break. Luckily the option of On timecode break: Make New Clip is the default selection. Unless you have a very specific reason for not using this excellent feature, leave it set there.

Note   As of this writing, the Make New Clip option works with DV only.

✦ **Read any error messages that appear.** I know this sounds silly, but often users simply don't pay attention to the messages they get when using Final Cut Pro. For example, if there have been timecode breaks during a batch-capture, Final Cut Pro will open a window at the end and provide you with a list of names of the clips that had timecode breaks in them. Save this list so that you can work around the problem later.

✦ **Use the Browser to troubleshoot your batch-capture problems.** If you get errors and batch-capturing is generally unsuccessful, use the Browser to find the problem clip. Sort the logged clips by duration. See if an incorrect time-code entry is causing erroneous durations. Also check to see if there's enough pre-roll before the problem clip's In point on the tape.

Note   Final Cut Pro does not like duplicated filenames. If two of your clips have similar names, the batch-capture process will present a dialog box for you to change the name of the clip before proceeding.

Working with batch lists

Batch lists are lists you can create in any spreadsheet program such as AppleWorks or Microsoft Excel. These lists consist of logging information, such as reel numbers, shot names, and in and out timecodes. These batch lists can be imported into Final Cut Pro, which converts the text into logged clips. You can then capture these clips using batch-capture.

Batch lists are a powerful way of working with Final Cut Pro. For instance, you can log your tapes on a home VCR if you can see the timecode with a *burn in,* also known as a *window dub.* Window dubs on VHS are often made from Betacam and other tape formats for editors or producers to view at home and make shot selections. If you create your batch list using a spreadsheet program, you can easily import the list into Final Cut Pro to create a list of offline clips for capturing. To prepare a batch list in a spreadsheet program:

1. **Open a spreadsheet program such as Microsoft Excel.**

2. **Create a new file and save it with the name of your batch (such as "Reel 1").**

3. **The minimum data columns necessary are Reel, Media Start, and Media End.**

    However, I always add a Name column as my first column. Create these columns in your spreadsheet and enter data in the appropriate fields, as shown in Figure 7-11.

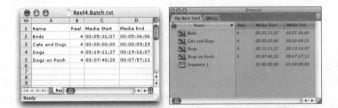

Figure 7-11: Batch lists can be created in any spreadsheet program. This Excel document, when imported into Final Cut Pro as a batch list, creates offline clips that can be batch captured. The window on the right shows how the clips identified in the batch list appear when captured into the Browser.

4. **When you're done, choose File ⇨ Save As in the spreadsheet program and name the file.**

5. **In the Save As dialog box, use the Save File as Type pull-down menu to select the Text (Tab Delimited) option.**

6. **Click Save to save the file.**

Exporting batch lists from Final Cut Pro

Another way to work with batch lists is to export a batch list from Final Cut Pro and open this list in a spreadsheet program. This exported list will have an extensive selection of data columns. You can modify this spreadsheet to your needs and later import it back into Final Cut Pro. This saves you from having to type in column headings and other information you may want to keep. To export a batch list from Final Cut Pro:

1. **Open any project in Final Cut Pro that has a few clips in it.**

2. **While the Browser is active, choose View ⇨ Browser Items ⇨ As List.**

   This will display your Browser in the List View mode.

3. **Set up the columns in the Browser the way you want them in your batch list.**

   For example, if you don't want a certain column, Control+click on that column heading and choose Hide Column from the contextual menu that appears. If you want to see certain columns that aren't there, Control+click again on any column heading and select the hidden column heading you'd like to add from the contextual menu. The contextual menu will only show you the names of the columns that are hidden.

4. **Choose File ⇨ Export ⇨ Batch List.**

5. **Select a destination in the dialog box that is presented to you and give the file a name.**

6. **Choose Tabbed Text in this window as an export option.**

7. **Click Save.**

8. **Drag and drop the batch file onto the application icon for your spreadsheet program (such as Microsoft Excel) to open it.**

   You'll see a spreadsheet that you can edit and modify as you see fit. Don't modify any of the column names.

9. **When you're done editing the list, choose File ⇨ Save As and give the file a name.**

10. **In the Save As dialog box, use the Save File As Type pull-down menu to select the Text (Tab Delimited) option.**

11. **Click Save.**

Tip

Don't be misled and choose Batch Export under the File menu. This command is to export multiple media files from your project, not a batch *list*.

Note

Batch lists are freely exchanged between nonlinear editing systems such as Avid, Media 100, Adobe Premiere, and Final Cut Pro. The only caution is to minimize the number of columns between systems and find out in advance what terminology some other systems may prefer. For example, Final Cut Pro uses Media Start and Media End as the In and Out designation in the batch. Other systems may use terms such as *In* or *Out*. For Final Cut Pro to import a batch successfully, it must at least have Reel, Media Start, and Media End columns. A clever trick to understand each system's preference is to first export a batch out of any of these systems and save the batch as a text file. Open this file, and you'll be able to see what the batch preferences of that system are.

Caution

Make sure that the batch list has been saved with the Text (Tab Delimited) option while saving in Excel or another spreadsheet program. If you don't do this, Final Cut Pro may not recognize the file as a batch list.

Caution

Final Cut Pro cannot import a batch list saved as a Rich Text Format (RTF) file. If you need to import a RTF batch list, open it first in a text editor application and save it as a plain text document.

Creating a batch list with a text editor

You really don't even need a spreadsheet program to generate a batch list. If you're careful, you can create a batch list using a text editor such as SimpleText. The SimpleText file will *look* messier than a spreadsheet file for a large batch, and it's easier in this messy looking file to add an errant space, but if you create the file properly, the batch will work just fine.

The trick is to separate all the fields with a tab on your keyboard. So, in SimpleText you could type

```
Reel<TAB>Media Start<TAB>Media End<RETRUN>
```

And on the next line type

```
4<TAB>01:14:14:15<TAB>01:14:26:00<RETURN>
```

This code creates a tab-delimited file. **Remember:** Don't type any spaces between fields, just tabs, and press Return at the end of each line.

Importing Other Media for Your Project

The most basic media that you gather is the video and audio clips from your tapes. However, when working with a project in Final Cut Pro, you can import many other kinds of files. These files include still images, QuickTime video files, AIFF and WAV sound files, and others. Importing these files does not bring the actual media into your Browser. The files appear as clips in your Browser, and they're linked to the actual media on your drives.

The beauty of this process is that, because Final Cut Pro is based on QuickTime, you can incorporate just about any kind of QuickTime-compatible file into your project. QuickTime recognizes numerous still, audio, and video file formats. Keep in mind that you still have to be concerned about resolution, aspect ratio, and other issues. But nevertheless, QuickTime happens to be one of the more popular architectures for computer-based media. This allows you to import numerous kinds of media and file types into your Final Cut Pro projects.

The following sections describe some of the issues relating to the various kinds of media you can import, but the process for importing them is the same:

1. **Locate the files you want to import into your project.**

   If they are on a DVD-ROM, copy them to your hard drive. It is a good idea to consolidate your files into a single folder if they are currently located in different folders and drives.

2. **Open your project in Final Cut Pro and make the Browser window active by clicking on it.**

3. **Choose File ⇨ Import ⇨ Files.**

4. **Locate and select a file in the dialog box that appears.**

5. **Click Open.**

   This file you opened appears as a clip in your Browser.

Tip

You can also import files using the time honored drag-and-drop method. Just drag a media file from a desktop folder onto the Browser to import it. If you try to drop a file in the Browser that is not compatible with Final Cut Pro, such as a text file, an error message will appear.

Importing QuickTime video files

It is important to note that when you capture any material from your tape via the Log and Capture window, these files are converted and kept as QuickTime media files on your hard drive. These QuickTime media files appear as clips in your Browser.

Video compressions and QuickTime file exchange

QuickTime video files can be saved with a variety of compression schemes. When you place a QuickTime video file into a sequence that doesn't have the same compression scheme as that file, you need to render the QuickTime file before it can be played in your timeline. It is much easier to use the correct codec in the first place to compress your QuickTime files so that you can avoid rendering time.

QuickTime files on a stock footage DVD-ROM may use an *Animation* codec. This codec is often misunderstood to be used only on animations in computer graphics. However, Animation is actually an excellent codec for video files because it doesn't have limitations on data rate, color choices, or alpha channels.

The figure shows the QuickTime compression dialog box accessible through all QuickTime compatible applications, such as Final Cut Pro.

If you use the Animation codec with the QuickTime quality slider set to Best, as shown in the figure, this codec renders at "uncompressed" quality and data rate. This may be undesirable if your system is not set up to support uncompressed data rates. If necessary, bring down the quality slider to Medium to reduce the data rate.

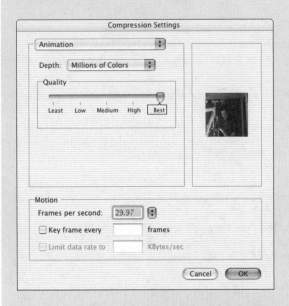

Of course, there's more to making QuickTime files compatible with your Timeline than just the compression. You need to match the frame rate, frame size, pixel aspect ratio, and field dominance of the video. If these options don't match, a red bar will appear over the clip when you drop it in the Timeline, and you'll need to render the clip before you can play it. Check your current sequence preset and note the preceding information in case you need to pass it on to other people who are preparing QuickTime files for your sequence.

You can bring in other types of QuickTime video files as well. These files may be QuickTime footage captured on another workstation, stock footage from a DVD-ROM, 3-D animation clips rendered as QuickTime movie files, or a movie rendered as a QuickTime-compatible file.

Importing stills

Final Cut Pro allows you to import stills in a wide variety of image formats. These stills can be prepared in image editing programs such as Adobe Photoshop or Illustrator. You can also import graphics, titles, and stills that you have prepared or obtained from a DVD-ROM of stock images. Stills must be rendered when placed in a Timeline. Final Cut Pro can import a variety of still formats, including:

✦ **PICT:** This is a very popular image format on the Mac OS platform. It's easy to handle and view on a Mac. Even basic programs such a SimpleText can open a PICT file.

✦ **Photo JPEG:** JPEG stands for the *Joint Photographic Experts Group*. This is a very common image format. It produces small file sizes on very-high-quality images. This format does not allow Alpha channels, however, meaning you cannot superimpose JPEG files over video images. JPEG files are commonly found on the Internet.

For more information on Alpha channels, see Chapter 15.

✦ **TIFF:** Tagged Image File Format is a format developed by Aldus, and is found on Mac and Windows machines. This format is often used for printing.

✦ **TGA:** Also known as *Targa file format,* this format uses no compression, meaning the file sizes are often very large. TGA files are found on Windows machines, Macs, Silicon Graphics machines, and others.

Extending the duration of a still image

When Final Cut Pro imports a still image, it's given a default duration of ten seconds. There are many ways to change this duration. If you're going to be importing a bunch of stills and know that you need them all to be five seconds, you should change the default duration of stills to five seconds in the General tab of the Final Cut Pro preferences dialog box, as described in Chapter 6. That way, all the stills you import will have this desired duration. You can also change the duration of stills after you've imported them into the Browser:

1. **Double-click the number in the Duration column for a still in the Browser.**

2. **Enter a new duration.**

3. **Press Enter when you're done.**

Numbered image sequences

Animators often create numbered image sequences for their animation. These are a series of still images that, when played together, create an animation. Final Cut Pro allows you to import a sequence of numbered images and use the sequence in the timeline as an animation. Each image is essentially one frame of video, so before you import them you'll probably want to change the default still duration in the Final Cut Pro Preferences dialog to one frame. Then you can import the numbered image sequence:

1. **Prepare a folder containing your images and make sure that they are marked correctly.**

   Numbered images should have the same name except for the number itself. For example, a series of stills for an animation of a cat smiling might have the name "Cat1," "Cat2," "Cat3," and so on. Store them all in a folder called "Cat Smiling."

   Tip

   To keep numbered images in correct order, use leading zeros in the name, like "Cat01", "Cat02", "Cat03." This is necessary because the Browser sorts all numbers in the Name field as text, sorting all clips with the same leading number first. For example, in the Browser, Cat1 would be followed by Cat10 and Cat11 before Cat2.

2. **Open your project in Final Cut Pro and make the Browser window active.**

3. **Choose menu item Final Cut Pro ➪ User Preferences.**

4. **In the General tab, change the Still/Freeze Duration to a duration of your choice by highlighting the field and entering a new value.**

   Each of the stills in your numbered image sequence will be this length when they are imported. Enter **1** frame if that is what you want the length of each of your stills to be.

5. **Click the OK button when you are done.**

6. **Choose File ➪ Import ➪ Folder.**

   Tip

   You can also drag and drop a folder containing your numbered image sequence from your desktop into the Browser.

7. **In the Select a Folder dialog box, locate and highlight the folder that contains your numbered image sequence.**

8. **Click the Select button at the bottom of your dialog box.**

   This button should also contain the name of the folder that you are about to import.

Final Cut Pro quickly checks the files and brings the entire folder into your Browser. Later, you can drag and drop the *entire folder* from the Browser into the Timeline. The images from the folder will appear in the Timeline in the order they were sorted in the Browser.

A sequence of stills dropped in a Timeline will appear in the order they were sorted in the Browser. Use the Name column heading to make sure your stills are in the correct numbering order before you lay them in the Timeline.

Working with multilayered Photoshop files

Final Cut Pro has another great still import feature. You can import multilayered files prepared in Adobe Photoshop. Photoshop is the most popular image editing program available and is used widely for artwork and photo editing.

When a Photoshop file is imported, Final Cut Pro automatically creates a sequence with all the layers of the Photoshop file composited as separate video layers in the sequence. The frame size of the sequence will be the same as the original Photoshop image size. You can drag and drop a multilayered Photoshop file from the desktop to the Browser like any other still file. If your images were created in Photoshop 3.0 and later, these images will maintain certain settings from the original file. These settings include opacity, composite modes, layer order, and layer name. Masks are ignored, however. If you want to import a multilayered Photoshop file as one image, you must first flatten it in Photoshop.

You can open a Photoshop file from within Final Cut Pro by selecting a layer in a Photoshop sequence and choosing View ➪ Clip in Editor. This layer will open in Photoshop along with all the other layers of the original file. You can make adjustments to any of the layers as long as you don't add, delete or re-order any layer. After saving your modifications, Final Cut Pro automatically updates the Photoshop sequence in your project with your changes.

The ability to open a file in its originating or designated application is set in the External Editors tab in System Settings, covered in detail in Chapter 6.

Although you can modify a Photoshop file once it is imported into Final Cut Pro, you should never add or delete layers in the original file. Doing so almost always causes unpredictable results rendering your Photoshop sequence unusable. As a rule of thumb, don't move or change *any* media files unless absolutely necessary once they are in use in Final Cut Pro. If you have to add or delete layers from a Photoshop file after it is in your project, save another modified version of it and re-import it into your project.

Working with Alpha channels

Most images in the digital domain consist of three channels: red, green, and blue (RGB). A lesser-known fourth channel called an *Alpha channel* is also often included on an image. While red, green and blue channels determine the final color of an image, Alpha channels determine the transparency of the image. That means that if an image of a flower in Photoshop was created with an Alpha channel around it, the image of the flower will *key over,* or superimpose itself over, another video track in Final Cut Pro, showing the image of the lower track through any areas of transparency as defined by alpha channel of the flower file. Many books about image editing say that you can think of an Alpha channel as a cutout around the image. This can be a bit misleading in that Alpha channels are versatile and have many uses besides being a cutout. However, this analogy will suffice for our purposes here.

When you import a still image or a video file with an Alpha channel, Final Cut Pro automatically recognizes it. This image, if layered above others, can be composited over a background layer. Ideally, you can place a movie or a still with an Alpha channel in the V2 track above the V1 track in your sequence. If you have a video layer in V1, the image with the Alpha channel will superimpose itself over the video file.

Cross-Reference   For more information on Alpha channels, see Chapter 15.

Working with audio files

There are many ways to work with audio files in Final Cut Pro. You can separate the audio portion of a clip from its video part after you have captured them. You can also import audio files from sound effects CDs or music CDs. Often you may want to import a track from an audio CD to add to your program. I have a collection of sound effects and stock music CDs and I am always importing fun effects to use in my programs.

It is important to keep the sampling rate of your imported audio files set to 44.1 kHz or above. This is the standard rate for audio files on CDs as well. Sampling rates lower than 44.1 kHz are not recommended for video work and are generally reserved for files destined for the Web or for DVD-ROM playback.

You can import AIFF and WAV audio files into Final Cut Pro as well. This is handy because most sound facilities now work with digital audio and often use the AIFF format to distribute the final mixes, voiceovers, and music on DVD-ROMs. AIFF, or Audio Interchange File Format, is supported on many platforms. WAV is a common audio format on Windows platforms. You can drag and drop AIFF or WAV audio files into the Browser directly (be sure to copy the files from the DVD-ROM to the drive first), or import them like any other media using File ➪ Import ➪ Files.

Note   Final Cut Pro does not support MP3 (short for MPEG-Level 3) audio files. MP3s are very popular for distributing music on the Web. You have to convert MP3 files to AIFF before you can import them into Final Cut Pro. You can use the QuickTime player and other utilities to convert MP3 files to AIFF.

Cross-Reference   For more information on working with audio in Final Cut Pro, see Chapter 14.

Because OS X now recognizes music CD track format, or .ccda files, you can import tracks directly into Final Cut Pro without having to convert them first. Hurray! Just drag and drop, or import them like any other digital file using File ⇨ Import ⇨ Files. Once an audio file has been brought into your project Brower, it will display as a speaker icon, shown in Figure 7-12.

Figure 7-12: Audio files have small speaker icons in the Browser. Here "Track 6 Movie" was imported from a CD. You can rename the file by double-clicking the filename.

Caution

In your elated state, don't forget to copy the CD audio tracks to your hard disk before you import them into Final Cut Pro, or else the files will become *offline* when the CD is ejected.

Converting sample rates for playback

When you import an audio track from a CD into your Browser, the default sampling rate is 44.1 kHz. However, you may be working in sequences that are based on 48 kHz audio. You may have done this if your DV tape has audio recorded at 48 kHz.

When you drop a 44.1 kHz CD audio file into a 48 kHz sequence, you do not need to render the file. Final Cut Pro will "up-sample" the 44.1 kHz file to 48 kHz on the fly as you play it. You will not notice anything different. However, this conversion on the fly does require some processor overhead and will reduce the number or quality of effects that can be played in real time without rendering.

It is generally a good idea not to mix sampling rates in a sequence. For example, if you are mixing a 32 kHz audio file in a sequence that is based on a 48 kHz preset, then that 32 kHz file will be "up-sampled." Even Apple does not recommend a 32 kHz-to-48 kHz on-the-fly conversion. This adds noticeable overhead and can result in audio dropouts and occasionally dropped frames.

Tip

If you intend to export audio files as Open Media Format (OMF), all audio clips in your sequence should use the same sample rate in order for the OMF export to operate correctly.

If you have imported a CD track, it comes in at the default rate of 44.1 kHz. You should convert the file to a 48 kHz sampling rate and then re-import the file into Final Cut Pro, as described here:

1. **In the Browser, select the audio file you want to convert.**

2. **Choose File ⇨ Export ⇨ Using QuickTime Conversion.**

3. **Select AIFF from the Format pull-down menu in the dialog box.**

4. **Click the Options button to bring up the Sound Settings dialog box.**

5. **In the Rate field type** 48.000 **or select that rate from the pull-down menu located to the right of the field.**

   Make sure the 16 bit and Stereo options are selected. Click OK when you are done (see Figure 7-13).

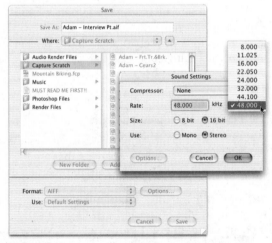

Figure 7-13: Converting audio sample rate using QuickTime Movie Conversion.

6. **Click Save and the file will be saved with the new sampling rate.**

7. **Re-import the file back into the Browser by dragging it from your Finder into the Browser.**

   Your file now has a sampling rate of 48 kHz.

Note

In general, you should always try to choose the 16-bit, 48 kHz sound setting on your DV cameras and decks when recording.

✦   ✦   ✦

Managing Your Projects with the Browser Window

You usually keep everything you own in your home. Your bed, your furniture, your food, and your clothes are all there. And you probably keep all your things organized. You know where your socks are and where your sneakers are. You use closets and wardrobes and shelves to organize all your possessions. Similarly, the Browser is home to your projects and material in Final Cut Pro. Everything you capture goes into the Browser and is kept organized there. This chapter is all about using the Browser and other tools to keep your video "stuff" organized and feeling at home in Final Cut Pro, as well as using the Browser to troubleshoot your video.

Understanding How Final Cut Pro Organizes Your Material

The main organizational element in Final Cut Pro is the project file. The icon for a project file looks like the movie slate, and within this file is *everything* relating to your project. *Everything* includes clips, Browser settings, sequences, effects, transitions, In and Out points, and everything else connected to your project. All these pieces of information are stored *within* the project file.

Other nonlinear editing systems, such as Media 100, follow a different organizational scheme. In Media 100, bins and sequences exist both within a project file *and* outside the file as their own elements. This makes organizing material in Media 100 cumbersome, but it can also protect against data loss in case the project file gets corrupted. Of course, the media itself is not part of the project file in Final Cut Pro, but still if you lose your edits you'll lose a lot of work.

However, Final Cut Pro's organizational structure and project integrity has been vastly enhanced since the AutosaveVault feature was implemented in the previously released version.

Figure 8-1 illustrates the general organizational structure of Final Cut Pro.

Tip   Do not rely solely on the Autosave feature for your project's backups. Making the effort to make backup copies of your project files on a daily basis is not only a prudent practice, it is also a professional habit you might not truly appreciate until you have lost a day or more of work to a system crash or corrupted file. For added security, keep the backup copy on a separate disk from the main disk you're working from.

As shown in Figure 8-1, a project file contains many different elements. When you double-click a project file, it opens in the Browser. Separate projects are represented as individual tabs within the Browser. The project file contains:

  ✦ **Clip:** A clip is an individual piece of media. It can be a video clip, an audio file, a still, or a graphics file. The clip is not the actual media but rather a link to the media file, which is stored on your scratch disk drive.

  ✦ **Bin:** A bin is Final Cut Pro's version of a folder. You can make new bins, name them, and have bins within bins. You use bins to store and organize items in a project. You can have bins for video clips, bins for stills, and bins for audio clips. You can separate sequences by keeping them in bins of their own.

  ✦ **Sequences:** Sequences contain the Timeline where your clips and media are organized into an edited program. You can have many sequences within a project.

  ✦ **Effects:** Each Browser window has an Effects tab, where all the effects are kept. Effects are applied to clips, and their settings can be animated. All information about effects and their application is saved in the Project file.

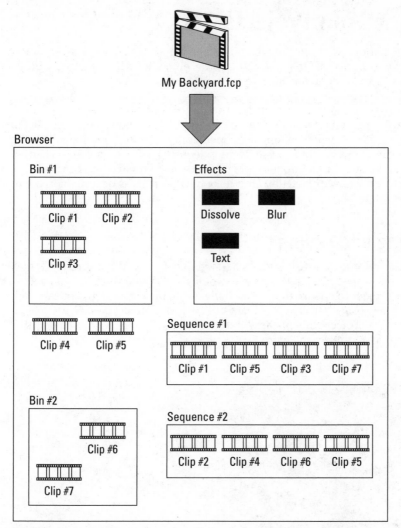

Figure 8-1: A Final Cut Pro project file contains all the information about your project.

Managing Your Projects

When you work in Final Cut Pro, you'll manage your projects from within the browser. One of the most important things to remember when working with your projects is to keep them manageable and organized.

When a project grows to a large size, with hundreds of clips, scores of folders, and innumerable media files, you may notice a slowdown in the performance of Final Cut Pro. The project will take longer to open, longer to save, and longer to quit. Everything about Final Cut Pro will begin to feel sluggish. To avoid this, I advise you to break up longer shows into multiple projects, one for each segment of the show. To do this, you'll have to start by creating a new project, as described in the next section.

Creating and saving projects

Every time you want to start work on a new project in Final Cut Pro, you'll have to create a new project file. And of course, when you're done working, you will want to save your project to ensure that your changes will be available to you later on. Creating a new project is easy. In Final Cut Pro, just choose File ➪ New Project. A new untitled project will appear within the Browser window with an empty sequence in it, as shown in Figure 8-2.

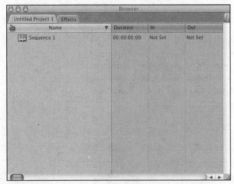

Figure 8-2: A new project appears as an untitled project tab. The project will always include a blank sequence.

Saving a project is also easy. When you're done working, choose File ➪ Save Project. You can also use the keyboard shortcut Command+S. If you have not yet named the Project, you will get a dialog box asking you to name your project and choose a location to save it in. You can safely save project files on your main Macintosh hard drive. I save my projects in a folder called Projects-Do Not Delete as shown in Figure 8-3.

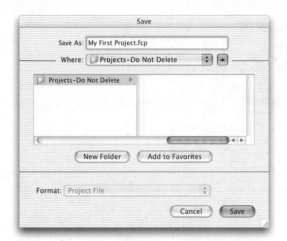

Figure 8-3: Use this dialog box to name your project file and choose a location to save it.

Note   To save all open projects, use File ⇨ Save All or use the Option+Command+S keyboard shortcut.

Final Cut Pro can help you save your valuable project even when you don't. Although the Autosave Vault concept is not an original innovation of Apple's, it is a security feature that can save you hours, if not days, of work that might otherwise be lost if your computer system crashes and you forgot to save the changes to your project. With the Autosave Vault feature enabled in the User Preferences, Final Cut Pro will automatically save incremental project files of your project at set timed intervals. This means you have many files of your project from each Autosave execution, allowing you to open an earlier version of your work (from the "vault") instead of just the last saved version.

Cross-Reference   The settings for Autosave Vault are detailed in Chapter 6.

When you're done editing and want to close a project, Control+click on the project's tab in the Browser and choose Close Tab from the small menu that appears (see Figure 8-4). You can also close a project by using the keyboard shortcut Command+W, but be aware that this will close *all* opened projects because you're really telling Final Cut Pro to close the Browser window containing the opened projects within it. Instead, press Control+W to close just the project that's currently active (its tab will be forward-most in the Browser).

If you try to close a project that you've made changes to but have not yet saved, Final Cut Pro will present a dialog box asking you if you want to save the changes before closing the project. Figure 8-5 shows this dialog box.

Figure 8-4: To close a project, Control+click its tab and choose Close Tab.

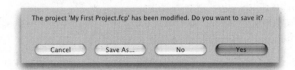

Figure 8-5: If you attempt to close a modified but unsaved project, Final Cut Pro presents a box to allow you to save these changes before closing the project.

Opening projects

When you want to continue working on a project you saved earlier, all you have to do is open the project file again. To do so, choose File ➪ Open. Locate the project file in the dialog box that appears and open it.

Note   Another way to open a Final Cut Pro project is simply to double-click on the Project file in the Finder or a folder window. Project files have a movie slate icon.

Tip   If you start your Final Cut Pro application without opening a project file, Final Cut Pro will default to open the last projects with all window positions, window states, and sequences as they were when last saved.

Opening projects created in Final Cut Express and previous versions of Final Cut Pro

You can open projects created in Final Cut Express and earlier versions of Final Cut Pro in Final Cut Pro 4.0. However, the projects must be updated to take advantage of Final Cut Pro's ability to render in YCrCb (also known as YUV) color space, and the new Master/Affiliated clip relationship. Figure 8-6 shows the dialog box you might see when a project from an earlier version of Final Cut Pro is opened.

Figure 8-6: Projects created in earlier versions of Final Cut Pro might need to be converted to an updated format when first opened. This is the dialog box for that option. If you choose NO, opening the project will be cancelled.

Some things to keep in mind when opening and converting these projects:

✦ **It's always a good practice to make a backup copy of the project file before updating it with any application.** In case you want to make changes to the file with the previous version of the application, you can with the unaltered original project file. Updating a file usually precludes it from being compatible with the earlier, original version of the application.

✦ **Unless your project is primarily in RGB color space (computer-generated media, for example), you will want to choose "Update sequences for improved color fidelity" when presented with this option in the updating project dialog box.** This sets all Sequence Settings in the project to render in YUV space while maximum whites are set to Super-White values.

✦ **If your project uses an unknown codec and you want to render in YUV color space, you will have to first select a codec that supports YUV rendering, like DV/DVCPRO in the Sequence Settings, and then manually select YUV rendering by deselecting "Always Render in RBG" option in the Video Processing tab.**

✦ **You will need to manually render all effects that are in sequences that have been converted.**

✦ **There is an option to Keep Existing Render Files when updating a project.** You may choose to keep existing render files if you do not require high color fidelity and want to re-edit without having to re-render the project sequences.

✦ **To create the master/affiliate clip relationship for projects created in Final Cut Pro 3.0 and earlier, choose Tools ⇨ Create Master Clips once the project has been updated and opened.**

Note

Final Cut Pro 4.0 can open iMovie 3 projects, but all sequences will need to be rendered after they are opened. Projects created in iMovie 2 or earlier cannot be opened by Final Cut Pro 4.0.

Opening a project file with Revert Project

At some point you might want to forget all the changes you have just tried and decide that you want to start over again with the last saved version of your project. The fastest and easiest way is to use the Revert Project command under the File menu. This will return your project to the last saved state. When you select Revert Project, you will see a dialog box, shown in Figure 8-7, warning you that all current changes since the last save will be lost. Click OK to revert to your saved project.

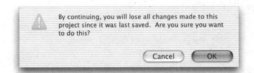

Figure 8-7: The Revert Project dialog box warns you that you are about to lose all changes since the last save.

Opening a project with Restore Project

Like Revert project, using the Restore Project command allows you to quickly go back to an earlier saved version of your project, but with the choice of all saved versions in the Autosave Vault. This is particularly essential if you need to retrieve a version of your project that is *not* your last saved version. Say your client suddenly decides that the best version of the commercial you're cutting for him was *yesterday's* cut. If you didn't have incremented files from the Autosave Vault, you might be stuck with only the last saved version. Autosave Vault to the rescue! Here's how to use it:

1. **In the Browser window, click on the tab of the project you wish to Restore.**

   Because you can have many projects open at the same time, you need to select which project to Restore. When Restore Project is selected, Final Cut Pro will display only files in the Autosave Vault folder of the currently active project. The project currently active is the tabbed window that is forward most and displayed in the Browser window.

2. **Choose File ⇨ Restore Project**

   A dialog box will appear with the Autosave files available. Figure 8-8 shows this dialog. Notice that the time and date of the files helps you to choose the best version.

3. **Select the version of the Autosave project file you want to open.**

4. **When a message appears warning you that all current changes to the project will be lost since it was saved, click OK.**

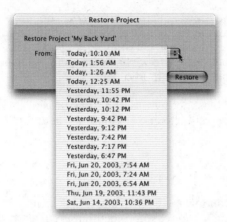

Figure 8-8: Restore Project lets you select and open a previously saved version of your project from the Autosave Vault.

Note   The restored project is a separate file from the original project and is reflected by its Autosave filename. If you want to continue the Autosave features of the original project, you need to use Save Project As and rename the restored project exactly as you did the original.

Cross-Reference   Autosave Vault settings are covered in detail in Chapter 6.

Understanding the Browser Window

The Browser serves three important functions in Final Cut Pro: organization, information, and troubleshooting. Organization is perhaps the most important function of the Browser window. Your clips can be sorted in bins that you create and name. You can label, rename, and color-code your media and bins. The Browser holds sequences that contain your edits and transitions. You can name and rename these sequences, duplicate them, and mix them together.

The second primary function of the Browser is to provide information. In the Browser, you can see the file size of your clips, the start and end time of clips, reel numbers, frame size, pixel aspect ratio, data rate, and the names of the clips. Of the more than 50 columns available, the Browser can show up to 41 of these. If that sounds like more information than you'll ever want to know, just wait until you have been editing for a while. You'll probably find that you use most, if not all, of the information in the Browser at one time or another. The Browser is also searchable. Using the Find feature, you can locate one or more items based on specific criteria you choose.

The third important function of the Browser is that of a troubleshooting tool. You'll often find that you can use the Browser to identify problems and technical glitches in Final Cut Pro. Knowing what to look for and carefully sorting and searching will often lead to solutions for problems such as to why an errant clip is misbehaving in a project, or why a sequence doesn't play properly.

The most common method of troubleshooting with the Browser is to simply scan the columns of information for an errant clip and compare the settings to other non-errant clips.

Details of the Browser window

The basic details of the Browser window are easy to master. As mentioned earlier, the Browser window has a separate tab for each project that is currently open. The Browser also has an Effects tab where your effects reside. Click on the tabs to switch between them. Figure 8-9 shows the Browser window.

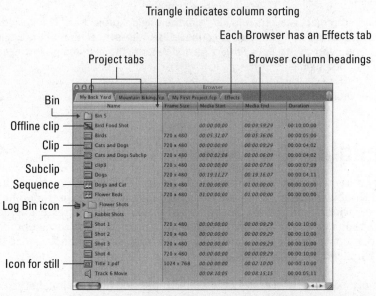

Figure 8-9: The Browser window is the central repository for your projects. It contains your media, sequences, bins, and effects.

Customizing the Browser display

The Browser can be displayed using one of four different views. The views are the List, Small Icon, Medium Icon, and Large Icon views. List view shows the most information, whereas the Small, Medium, and Large Icon views show clip thumbnails. A thumbnail is the first frame of a clip. To switch between the different views:

1. **Click the Browser window to make it active.**

2. **Choose View ➪ Browser Items.**

3. **Choose As List, As Small Icons, As Medium Icons, or as Large Icons as needed.**

Tip   A handy keyboard shortcut for switching views is Shift+H. Repeat this command to cycle through the List view, Small Icon view, and Large Icon view in the Browser.

The Small Icon view is not terribly useful, but the Medium and Large Icon and List views are very useful. The next sections describe those views in detail.

Working with Large Icon view

The Large Icon view of previous versions of Final Cut Pro has been renamed Medium Icon to make room for the even larger Large Icon designed for use with monitors of 20 inches or larger. Therefore, the Medium and Large Icon views have the same advantages and disadvantages, and I will hereafter refer to both as the Large Icon view.

The Large Icon view for the Browser is handy in a few situations. It allows you to view and scrub through the thumbnails of your clips and arrange the thumbnails as a storyboard. Often when you use the Large Icon view in the Browser, the clips will be spread all over the place like a drawer full of disorganized socks. You can clean up this view before you begin to work by making the Browser active and choosing View ➪ Arrange. Final Cut Pro will clean up the mess and organize items in alphabetical order, left-to-right and top-to-bottom, according to the current size of your Browser window. Resize the window if you wish, and use the View ➪ Arrange command again to rearrange the clips for the new window size.

Tip   In the Large Icon view, you can make a storyboard by arranging your shots left to right and top to bottom. You can then press Command+A to select all your clips and drag them to a sequence. They will be dropped into the sequence in the order in which they were arranged in the Browser.

One major advantage of the Large Icon view is poster frames. When the Browser is in the Large Icon view, thumbnails are shown for each clip. For video clips the first frame of the clip is the one that appears. This is called the *poster frame.* You can choose to show a different poster frame for a clip:

1. **Select the Scrub Video.**

   This tool is shown in Figure 8-10.

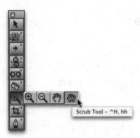

Figure 8-10: The Scrub Video tool allows you to scrub through thumbnails of video clips in the Large Icon view of the Browser.

2. **With the Scrub Video tool, click and hold on the clip icon in the Browser while scrubbing, or moving the mouse left or right, through the clip.**

3. **When you find the frame you want to use as the new poster frame, press the Control key on the keyboard.**

   The new poster frame appears for the clip.

Tip   When the Scrub Video tool is selected, you can hold down the Command or the Shift key to temporarily switch it to the Selection tool. This will allow you to move the clip around in the Browser.

Working with List view

The List view is often the most useful of the three available views in the Browser. It presents the most information about clips, while using less screen "real estate" than either of the Icon views. In List view, the Browser can display up to 41 columns of information. You can resize the columns, change their order, and decide which ones you want to see and which ones you don't. The only column you can't move or hide is the Name column, which always appears on the far-left side of the Browser window.

Tip   The Browser is highly interactive. If you Control+click in a column, you'll get a contextual menu offering choices relating to the type of information found in that column.

Working with Standard or Logging columns

The Browser window has two ways to display columns in the List view mode. Columns can be viewed as *Standard columns* or *Logging columns*. Standard Columns is the default view and is best suited to editing. Logging Columns view shows information that is useful during logging. Be advised that it is often hard to tell the difference between these two column views in the List view. Final Cut Pro has its own idea of how column headings should appear in either Standard or Logging views:

✦ **Standard Columns:** This is the default view. Standard columns appear in the following order: Duration, In, Out, Media Start, Media End, Tracks, Good, Log Note, Label, Label 2, Audio, Frame Size, Video Rate, Compressor, Data Rate, Audio Rate, Audio Format, Alpha, Reverse Alpha, Composite Pixel Aspect, Anamorphic, Field Dominance, Description, Scene, Shot/Take, Reel, Master Comment 1, Master Comment 2, Comment A, Comment B, Maser Clip, Offline, Last Modified, and Film Safe.

✦ **Logging Columns:** This view eliminates information that is not relevant to logging. By default the Logging columns appear in the following order: Media Start, Media End, In, Out, Duration, Good, Capture, Description, Scene, Shot/Take, Reel, Log Note, Master Comment 1, Master Comment 2, Master Comment 3, Master Comment 4, Comment A, Comment B, Pixel Aspect, Anamorphic, Vid Rate, Frame Size, Aud Rate, Aud Format, Compressor, and Data Rate, Maser Clip, Film Safe.

To switch between Standard and Logging Columns, Control+click on any column heading and choose Standard Columns or Logging Columns from the menu that appears (see Figure 8-11). Personally, I find that many of the Logging Columns are very useful in the Standard view. That's okay, because columns can easily be added, removed, or moved around as described later in this chapter.

Figure 8-11: Control+click on a column heading to choose between Standard Columns or Logging Columns.

Saving and using custom column layouts

After you have selected and arranged the columns of your Browser window, you can save your customized column arrangement for later use. This new feature of Final Cut Pro 4 is extremely useful because all new projects are created with Standard columns as the default layout for the Browser's List view. Unless the Standard columns layout happens to be your ideal Browser layout, you'll have to manually reconfigure the Browser *every time* you create a new project. Thankfully, reconfiguring your Browser layout is now as simple as choosing from a list of saved custom layouts. To save a column layout:

1. **Arrange the Browser columns in a layout that best suit your workflow.**

   Any column can be moved, hidden, or displayed except for the Name column. The Name column cannot be hidden or moved and is always displayed in the first column on the left of the Browser.

2. **Control+click on any column heading, except the Name column, and select Save Column Layout from the pop-up contextual menu.**

3. **In the Save dialog box that appears, type in a name for the custom layout and click the Save button.**

   The default location of saved custom layouts is: Users/*User's name*/Library/ Preferences/Final Cut Pro User Data/Custom Layouts.

All custom column layout files in the Custom Layouts folder will be displayed in the pop-up contextual menu that appears when you Control+click on any Browser column heading, except the Name column.

When you want to apply a custom column layout to your project, simply Control+ click on any Browser column heading, except the Name column, and select the name of the layout you want to use from the pop-up contextual menu.

Sorting items in columns

Items in the Browser can be sorted by any column heading. For example, you can sort using the name column to show the clips in descending alphabetical order (descending means A-to-Z). You can reverse sort the items to see the names in ascending alphabetical order (so that items appear Z-to-A). To sort items using any column heading, click the heading. An arrow pointing downward will appear, in the column heading indicating that this column is sorted in descending order, as shown in Figure 8-12. Click the heading again to make the arrow point up, indicating that the items are sorted in ascending order, as shown in Figure 8-13.

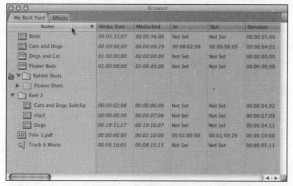

Figure 8-12: A small arrow pointing down in the column heading represents a column sorted in descending order.

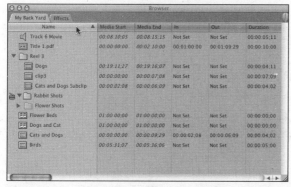

Figure 8-13: When the small arrow points up, it means the column is sorted in ascending order.

Performing multiple sorts

You can further sort Browser columns by performing multiple sorts. For example, suppose you sort your items alphabetically using the Name column. You can then perform a secondary sort, to arrange clips by Duration. You can have up to eight different sort levels. This can often be helpful for cross-referencing clips. To perform multiple sorts:

1. **Click on a column heading to perform the primary sort.**

   This sort is indicated by a small arrow in the column heading.

2. **Shift+click on another column heading to perform a second level sort.**

This sort will be indicated by another small arrow. Repeat for up to eight total sort columns. All secondary sorts are indicated by arrows but the column head will remain darkened, unlike the primary sort column that has a sort triangle and a lighter column heading. This is shown in Figure 8-14.

Primary sorted column

Secondary sorted column

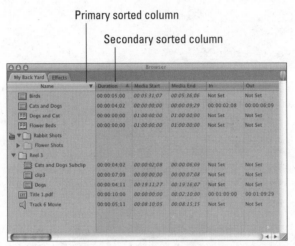

Figure 8-14: Second level sort of the Browser is indicated by sort triangles in the column heading, but with darker columns than the primary sorted column.

Organizing column headings

You have a lot of control over how your Browser columns are organized. You can resize the columns to see more information. You can reorder the columns and decide which you want to be visible. You may often find yourself working in projects where you require certain column information but not others. For example, you may find that the Pixel Aspect or Data Rate columns are not relevant to your current project, while the Duration column may be very important. You can hide the columns you don't want and reorder the columns so that the Duration column is right next to the Name column for easy access. As you hide certain columns, don't forget that you still have *all* columns available to you if you want them!

To resize a column, hold the cursor over a column border between two column headings. The cursor will turn into a double-headed arrow, as shown in Figure 8-15. Click and hold the mouse button and drag the column left or right to a new size.

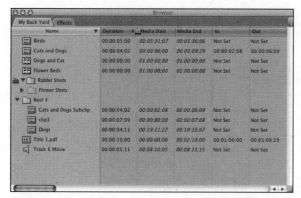

Figure 8-15: Drag the edge of any column to resize it.

To change the order of columns, you simply click and drag column headings to new locations. As you click and hold down the mouse button on a heading, the cursor turns to a bar and a double-headed arrow, as shown in Figure 8-16. Drag the column to a new location.

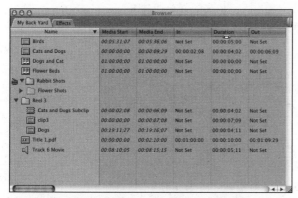

Figure 8-16: Click and drag a column heading to move it to a new location in the Browser. In this figure, the Duration column is being moved.

If you want to hide a column, Control+click on the column heading and choose Hide Column from the contextual menu that appears (see Figure 8-17).

Figure 8-17: Choose Hide Column from the contextual menu to hide a column.

To restore a hidden column back to view, Control+click any column heading and choose a menu name from the context menu. All currently hidden columns will appear in the menu, as shown in Figure 8-18.

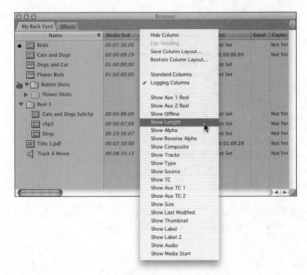

Figure 8-18: Control+click on any column heading and choose a column that you want to see from the contextual menu.

Tip

Instead of dragging a column from one side of the Browser to the other, when I want to move a column more than screen's width in distance, and *quickly*, I simply hide the column I want to move, scroll to the place where I want to place it, then Control+click to select and show it again. It's a variation of cut and paste with columns.

Browser column descriptions

As mentioned earlier, the List view of the Browser has over 50 possible columns of information, up to 41 of them can be shown. It is important to understand what all the column headings mean in order to make good use of the Browser. Some of these headings may not be relevant to a project you're working with right now, but it's good to know what is available, because you never know when the need for a certain kind of information will arise. Below is a list of all columns and a brief description of what you will find in each one:

✦ **Name:** This is the name of your clip and the Media file as you entered it in the Logging tab of the Log and Capture window. This column always appears in the far left of the Browser. This column cannot be hidden or reordered, but it can be sorted. You can change a name by clicking once on the name, pausing for a second or two, and then clicking once again. A traditional double-click will open this clip in the Viewer rather than let you rename it. Changing the name of a clip will not change the filename of the Media file.

✦ **Alpha:** Shows the type of alpha channel present on the clip. Choices are None/Ignore, Straight, Black, or White. Final Cut Pro automatically recognizes alpha channels on files and sets the type. You can change the type by Control+clicking on the Alpha type of the clip.

✦ **Anamorphic:** A check mark here denotes that the clip was captured with the anamorphic 16:9 aspect ratio. Final Cut Pro will automatically recognize clips that were shot anamorphically.

✦ **Aud Format:** Shows the format of the audio file. Indicates the bit depth and the kind of file, whether mono or stereo.

✦ **Aud rate:** Indicates the sampling rate of the audio file. This is where you get to see if your file is 32Khz, 44.1Khz, or 48Khz. This is a good column to check to ensure you aren't mixing audio sampling rates in your sequence.

✦ **Aux TC1:** This is one of the two auxiliary timecode tracks offered by Final Cut Pro for each clip. Every clip, besides having the original source timecode track, can also have two auxiliary timecode tracks. You're free to assign the timecode for these tracks. These can be very useful if you need to sync your clips with other timecode sources, such as a DAT tape with music on it. DAT tapes are often used in the field to play back or record audio on location. DAT tapes can have their own timecodes.

✦ **Aux TC2:** This is the second of the two auxiliary timecode tracks. These tracks can also be used for multiple camera-angle edits, where each camera tape may have its own timecode track.

✦ **Capture:** Shows the current capture status of a clip. Indicators include Not Yet, OK (meaning the clip has already been captured), Queued, or Aborted. More importantly, if you drop frames during the capture of a clip, this column will indicate a red Error status. This is handy for checking if you dropped frames while capturing a clip.

✦ **Comment A-B:** Two additional columns for adding comments to your shots. You can edit the content in the Browser or Item Properties window.

✦ **Composite:** This indicates the *composite mode* of clips in Final Cut Pro. The composite mode dictates how the colors of the clip interact visually with the clip below it when placed in the Timeline. There are 13 composite modes that include Normal, Add, Travel Matte-Alpha, and Travel Matte-Luma.

✦ **Compressor:** Indicates the type of compression, or codec, used for a clip. This is an important column and is good for troubleshooting, because your compression choice in the Capture preset should match that in the Sequence preset. This column allows you to quickly see what the codec was for a captured clip.

✦ **Data Rate:** This is another very important column to keep your eyes on. This column indicates the rate of data per second required for the clip. If you're working with DV, your rate will read 3.6Mbps and you have little to worry about. However, in cases where you're using a video capture card, the Data Rate column is a good place to confirm what data rate your clips were captured at. The data rate is set by you in the Capture preset. If a clip has stutters and skips in it, check the Data Rate column to see if it was captured or rendered at an unusually high rate.

✦ **Description:** Displays the description you entered for a clip in the Logging tab of the Log and Capture window.

✦ **Duration:** Indicates the duration of the clip between its In and Out points. This is not the full length of a clip, *just the time between its marked In and Out points.*

✦ **Film Safe:** When checked, telecined clip will be trimmed with a 4- to 5-frame boundary when Media Manager is used to insure full frames are intact when matched back to film.

✦ **Frame Size:** Shows the video frame size of clips in pixels. For a sequence, the pixel size is based on the sequence's presets.

✦ **Good:** Indicates with a check mark clips you marked Good while in the Logging tab of the Log and Capture window.

✦ **In:** Indicates the marked In point of the clip. This may not necessarily be the beginning of the clip, just where it was marked with an In point.

✦ **Out:** Indicates the marked Out point of the clip. This may or may not be the end of the clip, just where it was marked with an Out point.

✦ **Label:** Labels are color-coded descriptions for any item in the Browser. You can mark them None, Good Take, Best Take, Alternate Shots, Interviews, and B-Roll. Control+click on this column to get the choices in the contextual menu, or Control+click on the clip itself and select the Labels submenu to see the choices. Each of these labels has a color associated with them, and clips are easily identifiable by these colors in the Browser and the Timeline. You can also modify the descriptions for the colors by choosing User Preferences and then selecting the Labels tab.

✦ **Label 2:** You can edit this field to enter your own second label. Double-click the column space in front of the clip to enter text.

✦ **Last Modified:** Shows the date and time of the last modification. For a sequence, this column indicates the last time a change was made.

✦ **Length:** Indicates the total length of a clip's media file.

✦ **Log Note:** Shows text you entered for a clip in the Log Note field in the Logging tab of the Log and Capture window.

✦ **Master:** This column is checked if this is a master clip.

✦ **Master Comment 1-4:** You have four columns for adding comments to your shots. You can edit the comment headings. Control+click on any Master Comment heading and choose Edit Heading from the contextual menu. This allows you to give the column your own label. You can also edit these headings in the Project Properties window found under the Edit menu.

✦ **Media Start:** Indicates the first frame of the clip. This is different from the In point of the clip. It represents the source timecode for the first frame of the media file as captured to disk.

✦ **Media End:** Indicates the last frame of the clip. This is different from the Out point of the clip. It represents the source timecode for the last frame of the media file as captured to disk.

✦ **Offline:** Indicates the offline status of the clip. A check mark represents that the clip is offline. Offline can indicate that this is a logged clip for which a media file has not yet been captured, or it can represent a clip for which the media file has been deleted or moved.

✦ **Pixel Aspect:** Indicates the pixel aspect ratio of your captured clip. Various video formats and capture cards use pixels that are square. Other more-common formats use non-square pixels. Indications in this column are Square, NTSC-CCIR601 (NTSC non-square), and PAL CCIR 601.

✦ **Reel:** This shows the Reel name you entered in the Log and Capture window for the clip. A very handy Control+click menu on this column brings up the list of all the Reels you've used in this project. This is great if you captured 14 clips without switching the Reel number from Reel 3 to Reel 5. Select the 14 clips and Control+click on the Reel column. You'll see the Reel names in the contextual menu.

Caution

Changing the Reel name of a clip also changes the Reel name of the Media file on the drive.

✦ **Reverse Alpha:** Various applications use different ways to indicate the opaque and transparent parts of an image with an alpha channel. This column allows you to reverse the alpha channel display method if needed. If you see an image whose transparent part should be opaque and an opaque part that should be transparent, try clicking in this column to reverse the alpha channel.

✦ **Scene:** Shows the Scene entered for a clip in the Logging tab of the Log and Capture window. Double-click on the field to change it or enter new information.

✦ **Shot/Take:** Indicates the Shot/Take as entered in the Logging tab of the Log and Capture window. Double-click on the field to change it or enter new information.

✦ **Size:** Shows the file size of the clip in megabytes (MB) as it exists on the hard drive. This field provides a good quick way to find out the size of your files on the drive. Using this column you can identify large unused files that can be deleted to save space, or you may decide to recapture smaller portions of them.

✦ **Source:** Indicates the path to the clip's source media file. The path reads `Media Disk/Capture Scratch/Media File Name.mov`. This field provides a fast way to locate the media file for any clip in the Browser.

✦ **TC:** This shows the current timecode tracks shown in the View window. The default setting for this column is Source, which means the timecode comes from the original source timecode of the clip. Control+click on the column to switch to Aux 1 or Aux 2 timecode tracks if you have them enabled.

✦ **Thumbnail:** By default, this column shows the first frame of the clip as a thumbnail. The thumbnail can be changed as described earlier in this chapter. The big downside of having thumbnails shown in List view is that it slows down the redraw of the Browser window. Also, bringing up the thumbnails wastes precious Browser real estate. Only use this column for special needs where you must see the thumbnails.

Tip

Press Control+Shift and drag through the thumbnail. Locate a new frame that you want to set as the thumbnail and release the keys.

✦ **Tracks:** This is a very important column. It indicates whether you captured video alone, video and two channels of audio, or video and one channel of audio. Indicators here include 1V for video only, 1V, 2A for video with two audio tracks, and 1V, 1A for video and one audio track. Sequences use this column to show how many tracks of video and audio they have as well.

✦ **Type:** Indicates the type of item. Indicators are Clip, Bin, Sub Clip, Sequence, Merge Clip, or Effect.

✦ **Vid Rate:** Indicates the frame rate of the item. For a clip, this is the frame rate it was captured at. For a sequence, this indicates the Sequence Preset setting, which can be modified.

Tip

All Browser column information is interactive. Control+click on any column entry to bring up a contextual menu, and you will get options tailored specifically for that item.

Decoding icons in the Browser window

When the Browser is in the List view mode, you will see icons in the left side of the window. Each of these icons represents something different within Final Cut Pro. Learning to quickly identify these icons will help you work faster and efficiently. Table 8-1 explains what each icon represents.

	Table 8-1 Details of the Browser Window	
Icon	**Name**	**Description**
	Clip	Represents a media file. This can be a video clip with audio, just video, or graphics.
	Audio Clip	An audio media file. This file can be different formats, such as AIFF or WAV.
	Sub Clip	A subsection of a longer clip. More than one subclip can be created from a single "master" clip. Subclips still refer to the same media file as the master clip.
	Offline Clip	A clip for which the media has not been captured. This can also represent a clip for which media has been deleted or moved.
	Sequence	A Timeline where the clips have been edited together with transitions, audio, and other information.

Continued

Table 8-1 (continued)

Icon	Name	Description
	Bin	Bins are like folders and are used to organize clips. You can have bins within bins as well.
	Open Bin	A bin that is open in a window of its own.
	Locked Bin	You cannot move or delete effects from a locked bin.
	Video Transition	A transition effect, such as a dissolve, is applied to two overlapping video clips in a video track.
	Video Filter	An effect filter that is applied to a video clip.
	Audio Transition	A transition effect, such as a cross-fade, that is applied between two overlapping audio clips in an audio track.
	Audio Filter	An effect filter that is applied to an audio clip.
	Video Generator	Generators are effects "slugs" or internally generated clips that create color gradients, audio tones, and text.
	Marker	A reference marker on a clip, indicating points of interest.
	Still	Icon for an imported still in Final Cut Pro.

Selecting items in the Browser

In many ways, selecting items in the Browser is a lot like selecting items in other Macintosh areas such as the Finder. However, some of the selection behavior is a bit different and worth looking into even if you're already familiar with the Mac file system. When you want to select an item, click somewhere in the Browser window to make sure it's active, and then:

✦ **To select a single item,** click it.

✦ **To select multiple adjacent items,** click and drag a box around all the items you want to select if they're next to each other. Alternatively, select the first item in a group of adjacent items you want to select, hold down the Shift key on your keyboard, and click the last item in the list. The two items you clicked on, as well as everything between them, will be selected, as shown in Figure 8-19.

Figure 8-19: Clicking one item and Shift+clicking on another item selects those two items and all the items between them.

✦ **To select multiple nonadjacent items,** hold down the Command key on your keyboard and click once on each item you want to select. The result will look similar to Figure 8-20.

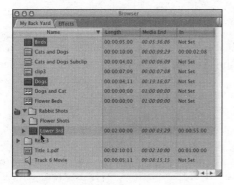

Figure 8-20: Hold down the Command key and click on nonadjacent items you want to select.

You can select an item in the Browser by quickly typing the first few letters of its name. Or you can use the up or down arrow keys on your keyboard to select the next item up or down.

Renaming items in the Browser

You'll probably find that you rename items in the Browser on a regular basis. To rename something, click on the name of the item you want to rename. After a brief pause, click it again. This will highlight the name of the item (this is just a slower version of a Macintosh double-click). You can now rename this item by typing a new name. You can rename clips, sequences, and bins by using this method in the Browser. Renaming items is shown in Figure 8-21.

Caution   Renaming items in the Browser does not rename the media files they're associated with. Renaming the media files in the Finder will make the associated clip offline in the Browser. You'll have to relink the clip in the Browser to the media file by selecting the offline clip and choosing File ➪ Reconnect Media.

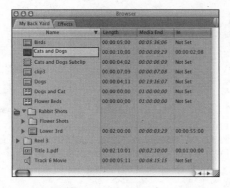

Figure 8-21: To rename items, click on the name of an item and, after a brief pause, click it again.

Tip   Another easy way to rename an item in the Browser is to select it and press the Enter key. The name will highlight, indicating that it's ready for you to type in a new name. Don't use the Return key—this will open the item, equivalent to a double-click.

Working with master and affiliate clips

The first time a clip appears in the project Browser, usually by capturing or importing, it is called a *master clip*. When a master clip is used in a sequence, or duplicated in the Browser, an *affiliated* copy of the master clip is created. There is a relationship between a master clip and all clips affiliated with it: Change to certain properties of a master clip will automatically change in all affiliated clips. Properties shared by a master and affiliated clips are:

✦ **Clip Name**

✦ **Reel Name**

✦ **TC**

✦ **Media Start and Media End**

✦ **Good**

✦ **Log Note**

✦ **Label and Label 2**

- ✦ **Anamorphic**
- ✦ **Capture**
- ✦ **Offline**
- ✦ **Scene**
- ✦ **Shot/Take**
- ✦ **Master comments 1-4**

However, change to the master clip's In and Out points, filters, and motion effects will not change in affiliated clips. This same relationship holds true in the reverse direction — changes made to shared properties of an affiliated clip automatically update in its master clip and all other affiliated clips.

The master/affiliate relationship also works with the online/offline state of affiliated clips. For example, reconnecting an offline master clip will automatically reconnect all affiliated clips as well. This is a huge time saver when you're relinking an offline project because it eliminates the need to manually reconnect the same clip in every sequence and bin it's used.

Note The master/affiliate clip relationship works only with clips within the same project. If you copy and paste a clip from another project into your own, these new clips are considered master clips with no connection to any previous affiliated clips.

Identifying master clips in the Browser

When your Browser bins become filled with master and affiliated clips from your project, you may need to know which clips are which. There are two ways to identify master clips:

- ✦ **Use the Master Clip column in the Browser list.** This column indicates a master clip with a checkmark and an affiliated clip with no checkmark.

- ✦ **Use the Reveal Master Clip command in the View menu.** Select a clip in the Browser and click on the View menu to see its drop-down menu of command options. If the Reveal Master Clip command in the View menu is dimmed, then the selected clip is a master clip (that is, it's already revealed). If, however, the Reveal Master Clip is not dimmed, the active state of the command indicates that the selected clip is an affiliated clip. If you then select the Reveal Master Clip command, the master clip of the selected affiliate clip is found and highlighted in the Browser.

Creating master clips

Master clips are automatically created when you log, capture, or importing clips into the Browser. In addition, master clips can also be created the following ways:

✦ **Create subclips, merged clips, or freeze frame clips.** Clips created as sub-clips, merged clips, or freeze frames (stills) are master clips with no connection to the clips they were made from.

✦ **Import an EDL.** An EDL imported into your project Browser will contain a bin named "Master Clips for *(sequence name)*," containing all the master clips used in the named sequence, which was also imported in the EDL.

✦ **Use the Make Master Clip command.** To make an affiliated clip into a master clip, select the clip in the Browser and choose Modify ➪ Make Master Clip. The selected clip is now a master clip and no longer has any affiliation with the original master clip.

✦ **Use the Duplicate as New Master Clip command.** If you simply copy and paste, or duplicate a master clip, the new clip will be an affiliated clip. In order to create a duplicate master clip, you must use the Duplicate as New Master Clip command. To do this:

1. **Select a master clip in the Browser.**

2. **Select Modify ➪ Duplicate as New Master Clip**

An identically named master clip will appear in the Browser. You may alternatively Control+Click on a master clip in the Browser and select Duplicate as New Master Clip from the contextual menu.

Deleting a master clip

If you delete a master clip, you will see the warning: "One or more of the clips you have selected are Master clips. By deleting them you will break their relationship to any clip or item associated with them. Do you want to continue?" If you click OK, the master clip is deleted, all occurrences of that clip used in your project sequences will become independent, and all copies of that clip in the Browser will become master clips.

Creating merged clips

Final Cut Pro 4 allows you to create merged clips by linking together separate video and audio files, and then edit them as a single clip. Merged clips are commonly used when synchronizing a video picture shot on film to its corresponding audio that was recorded separately on a sound recorder. (Recording synchronized picture and sound to separate media is called a *double system* because of the two separate recording mediums of picture on film and sound on tape.) To create a merged clip in the Browser:

1. **Select the video and audio clips you wish to link.**

You can Command+click to select multiple clips that aren't adjacent to each other in the Browser. You can merge a maximum of one video file with as many as 12 stereo or 24 mono items. You don't need any video for a merged clip, but the number of total audio files remains the same.

2. **Choose Modify ⇨ Merge Clips.**

   Of course, the Merge Clips command is also available in the contextual menu that appears when you Control+click on any of your selected items.

3. **In the Merge Clips dialog box that appears, select the option by which you want the clips synchronized.**

   If the sources (Auxiliary 1 or Auxiliary 2 timecodes of the clips) are identical, select one of these options to synchronize the clips. If the timecodes aren't identical, then you need to manually preset the In or Out point of each clip to a sync reference frame, before you select either the In points or Out points method to synchronize the selected clips. If no In or Out point is set in the clips, then the first and last frame of the clips are used for In and Out points, respectively.

4. **Click OK.**

   A new clip appears in the Browser with the name of the video clip and the word Merged added to the end. If no video item is used in the merged clip, the name of the topmost selected audio clip is used.

Tip   You can also create a merged clip by selecting items you have linked in the Timeline and dragging them into the Browser. The new merged clip that appears in the Browser is now the master clip of the linked items in the Timeline. See Chapter 11 for more on linking clips in the Timeline.

Working with bins

If the Browser were your home, bins would be the closets and wardrobes you'd use to keep your possessions organized. Bins are just like folders in the Macintosh operating system. You can use bins to organize your clips and separate them as you see fit. You can rename the bins to reflect the items you store in them. You can have bins within bins and open bins either in the Browser window or within windows of their own. Depending on the project, you may want to make bins to separate shots from different reels, or make bins to sort interviews with different subjects.

Bins are organizational elements that exist strictly within Final Cut Pro project files. No amount of sorting, renaming, and moving clips around in bins will have any effect on the actual media files that are stored on disk. You can also create, move, rename, and delete bins with no effect on your media files whatsoever.

To create a new bin in your project, make sure the Browser window is active and choose File ⇨ New ⇨ Bin. You can also use the handy keyboard shortcut Command+B (for Bin). A new bin will appear in your Browser. Type a name for the bin, as shown in Figure 8-22. If you want to rename a bin that you created earlier, click once on the bin, pause for a moment, and click it again.

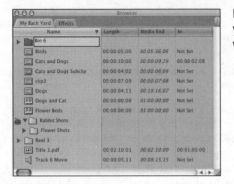

Figure 8-22: To name a new bin that you've just created, simply begin typing when the bin's name is highlighted.

Tip   Another quick method for making a new bin is to Control+click in the Name column of the Browser window and choose New Bin from the contextual menu that appears.

Like folders, bins can be opened and closed. Closing bins you aren't currently working in saves precious screen real estate, and they're easy to open again when you need to. Each bin has a small arrow to the right of it. Click on this arrow to twirl it downward and open the bin. The bin's contents will be listed in the Browser. Click the arrow again to close the bin. You can also open a bin in its own window by double-clicking it. You can then dock the open bin window with its own tab in the Browser by dragging and dropping the Bin by its title tab over the Browser window. Figure 8-23 shows a bin in its own tab window in the Browser.

Bin opened in separate tab

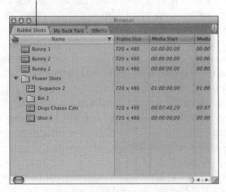

Figure 8-23: Bins can be opened in their own window. They can then be docked in the Browser, too.

Tip   Press the right arrow on your keyboard to open a highlighted bin. The left arrow closes the bin.

Searching in the Browser

On a large project, the Browser window can become full and cluttered like a closet in your home. You can have bins upon bins full of clips, and sorting through all this material for a particular item can get difficult. This is where the Browser's Search function comes in handy. You can use the Search function in Final Cut Pro to find clips based on the same criteria found in column headings. Of course, the most common use of the Search function is to find clips by name. To conduct a search by name:

1. **Choose Edit ➪ Find (or press Command+F).**

   The Find window appears, as shown in Figure 8-24.

Figure 8-24: The Find window lets you search for clips in your projects and bins.

2. **Select the name of your project in the Search pull-down menu.**

3. **Select All Media in the For menu.**

4. **In the two pull-down menus at the bottom, select Name and Contains.**

5. **Enter the text string you want to search for in the lower-right corner.**

6. **Click the Find Next button.**

7. **The Find window will close, and the first clip in the Browser matching the search string will be highlighted.**

8. **Choose Edit ➪ Find Next or press F3 to find the next clip based on your original criteria.**

   Every time you use Command+G, the next clip matching your search will be found and highlighted in the Browser window without opening the Find dialog box.

Caution Find Next will search for the next clip forward from its current location in the Browser and will not start from the beginning (top) once it reaches the end of the project. If you think the clip you are searching for might be before the current location in the Browser, use the Find All option instead.

If you want to locate every clip that matches a certain criteria, click the Find All button in the Find window instead of the Find Next button. All the clips matching your criteria and search string will appear in the Find Results window, as shown in Figure 8-25. To view one of the results in the Browser, select it and click Show in Browser.

Highlight an item and click Show in Browser to see item in Browser

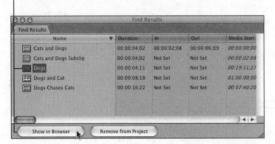

Figure 8-25: When searching for multiple items, the Find Results window shows all items found that match the required criteria.

From the Find Results Window, you can do more than find a clip's location in the Browser. You can manipulate items in the Find Results window as you would clips in the Browser, including move or copy to another bin, delete, rename, sort, change any column parameter that is editable, and even edit them directly into a sequence.

Troubleshooting with the Browser

Because of all the information it can display, the Browser window is an extremely useful troubleshooting tool. For instance, if you're working with MJPEG compression you can use the Data Rate column to check data rates on captured clips. If a clip has an unusually high data rate, you can then check it for dropped frames or other similar problems with the Analyze Clip command in the Tools menu. This is just one example of the kind of troubleshooting you can perform in the Browser. The next few sections look at a few more ways you can take advantage of the Browser's power and versatility to troubleshoot your media.

Spotting batch-capture trouble with the Browser

Batch-capture trouble can often be spotted by looking for offline clips in the Browser. A common batch-capturing problem is that the program does not stop at the Out point but continues capturing. If this occurs, simply stop the batch-capture and check offline clips for correct Duration, Media In, and Media Out columns.

Occasionally you'll find that errors in a manual timecode entry or other factors cause the errors. Figure 8-26 shows how an erroneous timecode can cause the duration to last hours when it should only be a few minutes.

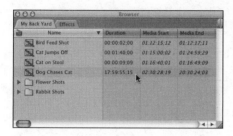

Figure 8-26: The Browser can be used to find batch-capture problems. In this case, the *Dog Chases Cat* clip has an incorrect duration of over 17 hours due to an error in a timecode entry.

Checking errant clips with the Browser

You might find yourself facing a red line (or other colors depending on your RT settings and system speed) on top of a clip when you drop it into a sequence. This line appears over transitions and effects when they need to be rendered. However, when this line appears over clips dropped into the Sequence (see Figure 8-27), it indicates that the sequence settings do not match the capture settings you used for your clip.

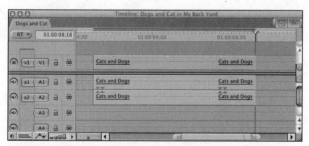

Figure 8-27: A red line above an entire clip means that the sequence settings do not match the capture settings for that clip.

In Figure 8-27 a clip named *Cats on Porch* was dropped into a sequence called *Dogs and Cats in My Backyard*. A red line appears over the clip, indicating that the sequence settings do not match the capture settings of the *Cats on Porch* clip. You can review information in the Browser to determine which settings don't match up. In Figure 8-28, you can see that the codec, frame size, and pixel aspect ratio of the *Cats on Porch* clip do not match the *Cats and Dogs* sequence. To use the clip, a new sequence would have to be created with settings that match the clip. Or you can modify the settings for the current sequence.

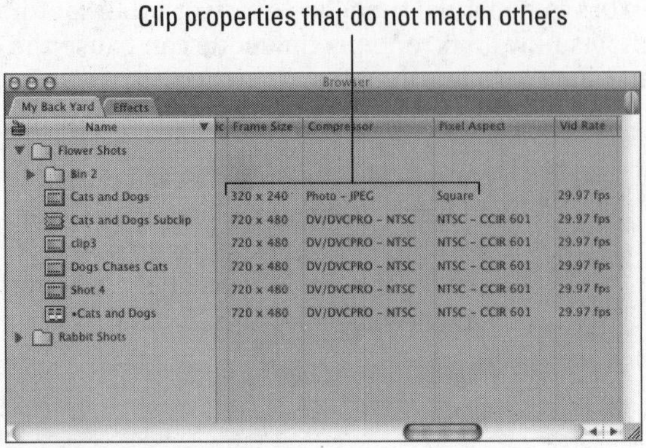

Clip properties that do not match others

Name		Frame Size	Compressor	Pixel Aspect	Vid Rate
▼ ☐ Flower Shots					
▶ ☐ Bin 2					
☐ Cats and Dogs		320 x 240	Photo – JPEG	Square	29.97 fps
☐ Cats and Dogs Subclip		720 x 480	DV/DVCPRO – NTSC	NTSC – CCIR 601	29.97 fps
☐ clip3		720 x 480	DV/DVCPRO – NTSC	NTSC – CCIR 601	29.97 fps
☐ Dogs Chases Cats		720 x 480	DV/DVCPRO – NTSC	NTSC – CCIR 601	29.97 fps
☐ Shot 4		720 x 480	DV/DVCPRO – NTSC	NTSC – CCIR 601	29.97 fps
☐ •Cats and Dogs		720 x 480	DV/DVCPRO – NTSC	NTSC – CCIR 601	29.97 fps
▶ ☐ Rabbit Shots					

Figure 8-28: The Browser can be used to identify discrepancies between clips and sequences.

Caution

If you place a clip in the Timeline and are presented with the render indication that should not be there, you might have to match the sequence settings to the capture settings of the clip. However, even after the settings are matched, you'll have to delete the clip from the sequence and replace it to make the render line go away.

✦   ✦   ✦

Learning to Edit with Final Cut Pro

Touring the Viewer Window

When you edit, you manipulate reality. You get to re-arrange real life by cutting out the slow and awkward parts and make the action appear smooth and exciting. It's interesting to observe how the world has come to accept editing as part of everyday life. We readily accept when an actor on TV looks away and the next shot depicts his point of view (POV, if you want to talk in cool editor lingo). Even though it looks natural to the viewer, those two shots could have been done many miles and many weeks apart. Accomplished editors learn to make these edits seamless. Final Cut Pro gives you tools and functions to make each edit smooth, so that viewers are unaware that what they're watching is a deeply manipulated and enhanced version of what actually occurred. One of the most important tools for creating a sequence of edits with Final Cut Pro is the Viewer window. This chapter explores the features of this window.

Cross-Reference Many of the tasks here can also be performed using the Timeline. See Chapter 11 for more on working with the Timeline.

Looking at the Features of the Viewer Window

It pays to get to know the Viewer window. You'll be spending a lot of your time here, as it becomes the center of your editing universe. The Viewer window is used for viewing clips, setting In and Out points for clip selections, placing markers, manipulating audio, and controlling effects.

Figure 9-1 shows the Viewer window with an In and Out point set, and the playhead is parked at a current timecode of 00:13:14;15. That means that the clip's source timecode on the tape was 13 minutes, 14 seconds, and 15 frames at the current location. You can move the playhead around with your mouse to "scrub" through the clip. Scrubbing allows you to move through the clip more quickly than just playing it in real time.

Figure 9-1: The Viewer window allows you to open and play your clips as well as work with audio and effects.

As mentioned earlier, the Viewer window is a richly detailed window. Table 9-1 shows the details of the Viewer window, and this chapter takes you through how to use them.

Table 9-1
Details of the Viewer window

Button	Name	Description
Video Audio Filters Motion	Function Tabs	Select tabs to viewer Video, Filters, Audio, or the Motion Properties of a Clip. Clips without audio will not have an Audio Tab.
00:00:08:20	Duration	Shows the duration of selected shot in hours:minutes:seconds: frames format. This is the time between the In and Out points.
109% ▼	Zoom Control	Click and select higher or lower magnification for viewing.
▐X▌ ▼	Playhead Sync	Enables playhead in the Viewer to lock to the playhead in the Canvas. This is called *ganging*.
⟨ ⟩ ▼	Viewer Choices	Click and select Title Safe and Wireframe Modes.
01:00:13:00	Current Timecode	Shows the current location of the playhead. Click and type in new timecode to move the playhead to a specific point.
	In Point Indicator	Press I on your keyboard to mark an In point on your clip. This represents the start point for your clip in an edit.
	Playhead	Indicates current frame displayed in the Canvas window. You can scrub through a clip by using your mouse to drag this indicator back and forth.
	Out Point Indicator	Press O on your keyboard to mark an Out point on your clip. This represents the end point for your clip in an edit.
	Shuttle Control	Click down with the mouse and drag in either direction. The further your drag the faster the clip plays through.

Continued

Table 9-1 *(continued)*

Button	Name	Description
	Previous Edit	Jumps playhead backward to the preceding edit point. This is the clip's In point, or if the playhead is already at the In point of a sequence clip, then the playhead will jump to the preceding edit point in the Timeline. The clip to the right of the edit point automatically loads into the Viewer window.
	Play In to Out	Moves the playhead to the In point of the clip and plays through to the Out point of the clip.
	Play	Plays the clip. You can also use the Spacebar to play a clip.
	Play Around Current Frame	Plays the clip around the Current frame. This play function is based on the Previewer Pre-Roll and Previewer Post-Roll settings in the General tab of the User Preferences.
	Next Edit	Jumps playhead forward to the next edit point This is the clip's Out point, or if the playhead is already at the Out point of a sequence clip, then the playhead will jump to the next edit point in the Timeline. The clip to the right of the edit point automatically loads into the Viewer window.
	Jog Control	Use to move a few frames at a time. Ideal for locating specific frames.
	Match Frame	Click to locate the current frame in the Viewer with the same frame in the sequence clip and Canvas window. Used for locating precise edits and syncing audio.

Button	Name	Description
	Mark Clip	Sets the In and Out points at the outermost points of a clip (that is, selects the full length of the clip).
	Add Keyframe	Adds a keyframe at the current time. A *keyframe* is a kind of a marker that locks the value of an effect to the current time. Keyframes are required for animating effects. This button is one quick way to set keyframes.
	Add Marker	Adds a marker to the clip at the current time. Markers are useful to locate important spots in a clip. You can name markers and add notes to them.
	Mark In	Marks an In point on the clip at the current location of the playhead. This represents the start point for your clip in an edit. You can also use the I key to mark an In point.
	Mark Out	Click this to mark an Out point on the clip at the current location of the playhead. This represents the end point for your clip in an edit. You can also use the O key to mark an Out point.
	Recent Clips	Click down on this menu to select a clip from the list of recently used clips. The number of clips displayed in this menu is set in the General tab of the User Preferences.
	Generators	Generators in FCP are Text, Mattes, Bars and Tone, and so on. This menu allows you to select a Generator and add it to the Timeline.

Cross-Reference   For a detailed list of keyboard shortcuts, see Appendix B.

The Viewer window tabs

The Viewer window is densely packed with features that go above and beyond simply viewing clips. It has several tabs that organize the various features of the
Viewer. In Figure 9-2, the Audio window has come forward after clicking the Audio
tab in the Viewer window. Note that you can still view the In and Out point locations, and the playhead is parked at the same timecode of 00:13:14;15, as it was
when viewing under the Video tab.

Figure 9-2: Clicking on the Audio tab reveals
the audio waveform for the current clip.

Keep in mind that if a clip does not have audio, the Audio tab will not appear. So
don't panic if you don't see one in your Viewer window. Tabs in the Viewer window
include the following:

✦ **Video tab:** This tab displays the video portion of your clip. Use the Video tab
to play your clips and set In and Out points. This tab is always the default
viewer for any video clip.

✦ **Audio tab:** This tab shows you the audio part of your clip, if any. If there's no
audio track with your clip, there will be no Audio tab. If the clip has two channels of audio, you will get two Audio tabs. Use this tab to mark In and Out
points on your audio as well as adjust volume and spread on your clips.

✦ **Filters tab:** This tab will show you any filters that you may have applied to you clips. This tab is used to set and adjust effects and filters.

To learn about filters and effects, see Chapter 16.

✦ **Motion tab:** Here you apply and modify motion effects for the clip.

✦ **Control tab:** This tab appears when changing parameters for a generator, such as text.

Tabs for a given clip can be separated. For example, you can click on the Audio tab for a clip and drag it away as a separate window. These two windows will remain in sync so there's no reason to click back and forth between them as tabs. You can put them side-by-side and edit away. When you're done, you can drag the tab back to merge it with the main Viewer window again.

Opening and playing clips in the Viewer

For exercises in this chapter use the Mountain Biking Tutorial project folder from the DVD-ROM. Drag the Mountain Biking Tutorial folder onto your internal drive and open the project up by double-clicking on the Mountain Biking.fcp icon. This will launch Final Cut Pro and set the windows for you.

The Viewer window is used to play your clips. The Viewer enables you to view what you have in your Browser. Simply double-click any clip in the Browser window to load it into the Viewer. To play the clip, do one of the following:

✦ **Click the Play button to start play.** Click the Play button again to stop play. If you hold down the Shift key when you click the Play button, the clip will play in reverse from the playhead's current position.

✦ **Press the spacebar on your keyboard.** Press the spacebar again to stop playback. If you hold down the Shift key when you press the spacebar, the clip will play in reverse from the playhead's current position.

✦ **Use the J, K, and L keys on you keyboard**. Pressing the J key will play your audio backward, pressing K pauses the playback, and pressing the L key plays the audio forward. If you repeatedly press the J or L keys, the playback speed increases by factors of 1X, 2X, 4X, and 8X.

You can load multiple clips in the Viewer at the same time. Select a number of clips in the Browser by holding down the Command key and clicking on each clip that you want to select, and then drag them into the Viewer window. You can then choose which clip to view using the Recent Clips pull-down menu in the Viewer window. The default number of clips you can store in this menu is ten. However, you can increase this number in the General tab of the User Preferences. You can set the number of clips in List Recent Clips up to a maximum of 20.

Ganging the Viewer and Canvas windows

There is a great new addition to Final Cut Pro 4.0, and that is the ability to lock together the playheads of the Viewer and Canvas windows. This is known as *ganging*. Ganging can be used to trim a clip in the Viewer by the duration of markers, action, or another clip in the Timeline. Another use for ganging is when you're adjusting the Color Correction filter of a clip in a sequence. By ganging the Viewer, with the Color Correction filter tab selected, to the Canvas, you can be sure that you're adjusting the filter of the same clip that is in the Canvas.

To select different ganging options, use the Playhead sync pop-up menu located at the top of the Viewer (and Canvas) window, shown in Figure 9-3. The Playhead sync pop-up menus on the Viewer and Canvas windows are the same controls, just in different locations. If you select a ganging option in one, the same option will be selected in the other, too. In other words, the ganging controls will be ganged.

Figure 9-3: The Playhead sync pop-up menu on the Viewer and Canvas windows is used to select a ganging option.

There are a few options for ganging that change the way ganging operates:

✦ **Off:** Ganging of Viewer and Canvas is disabled. The playheads of the two windows play independently of each other. This is the default setting.

✦ **Follow:** Viewer playhead is ganged to the Canvas playhead, but *only when a sequence clip is loaded into the Viewer.* When you scrub the playhead in the Timeline, the sequence clip in the Viewer moves in sync, showing the exact same frame, and vice versa.

Note   If no sequence clip is loaded into the Viewer, the playheads will not be ganged even if this option is selected. Also, ganging does not happen when the Timeline playhead is not over the corresponding sequence clip in the Timeline.

✦ **Open:** This is the same as Follow, except that sequence clips are automatically opened and loaded into the Viewer window as the playhead in the Timeline moves over them. This option is handy when you're color-correcting a series of clips in the Timeline. Because sequence clips are opened in the Viewer in the same tab that is currently selected, you can move from one clip to another while keeping the Color Correction filter tab open and be assured that you're working on the corresponding clip that is in the Canvas.

✦ **Gang:** Viewer and Canvas playheads are ganged with any offset difference between their current position maintained. This option allows you to track and time any clip in the Viewer with an action or event in the Timeline, such as an actor's movement or dialog. If you need to reset the place where the clips are synced, first turn off the ganging option, reposition the playheads to the desired frame for syncing, then reselect the Gang option.

Note Another ideal use for using the Gang option is for editing multi-camera footage. Edit the clip from camera A into your Timeline, load the footage from camera B into the Viewer, find a sync frame using timecode if the two clips have synchronous timecode (if they don't, find the sync points manually); select Gang from the Playhead sync pop-up menu, and play the two clips ganged together. Great, right? Hang on a minute. Unfortunately, Final Cut Pro does not play both ganged windows concurrently. The playheads will follow each other, frame accurately, when you *scrub* through clips, and will jump to the corresponding frame in the non-playing window when play is stopped, but play of both video streams is not supported. Real time play happens only in the selected window.

Marking selection In and Out points on a clip

Usually when you capture material, you take in more than what you're really going to use. You'll keep the best material and cut the rest, and that's what editing is all about. Playing a clip and selecting what portions of that clip you want to use is the very first step of the editing process. The start of your selection is called the *In point* and the end of the selection is called the *Out point*. When you mark In and Out points, only the selection between those points is used. In and Out points can always be adjusted, even after the clip is edited in a sequence.

Note When you make a selection by marking In and Out points on a clip, the portions of the clip before the In point and after the Out point are made inactive. However, these portions are always available to you whenever you want to return to the same clip and make a different selection.

Creating In and Out points is easy. If you don't have your own clip to work on, use Nigel & Adam Pass in the Mountain Biking.fcp project and follow the steps here. This clip has a section in the beginning that you'll eliminate by placing an In point in the clip.

1. **Load the Nigel & Adam Pass clip into the Viewer by double-clicking it.**

   This clip is located in the At the Trail folder in the Mountain Biking.fcp project.

2. **Press the Home key located on the upper-right side of your keyboard to return the playhead to the beginning of the clip.**

   Play the clip in the viewer by pressing the spacebar. In the beginning of the shot, the two bikers are too far away from the camera.

3. **Play the clip until the first biker enters the middle of the frame.**

   Press the I key on your keyboard or click the In point button in the Viewer window. This should be around 00:00:52;20. A small triangle pointing to the right appears in the scrub area in the Viewer, indicating the In point you just set.

4. **Continue to play the clip, and at the point where you'd like to stop using this clip, click the Out point button, or press the O key on your keypad.**

   This marks the Out point of the clip. Figure 9-4 shows the clip in the Viewer widow with its In and Out points set.

Figure 9-4: The Viewer window is an ideal place to set a clip's initial In and Out points.

If you place this clip in the Timeline after setting In and Out points, only the portion you have selected with the In and Out points will be used. The portion of the clip before the In point will not be shown (but is still there and available should you need it later).

Cross-Reference   To learn about placing clips in the Timeline see Chapter 10.

Marking split edits in the Viewer

Generally speaking when you mark In and Out points on a clip, the points work for both the video and the audio portion of the clip. Most of the time, this is exactly what you need. Sometimes, however, it's necessary to set the audio In and

Out points in different places than for the video. This is known as a *split edit* or an *L-cut*.

If you've watched two people talking in a television program, you've probably seen a split edit. In a common scenario where two people are talking, you often hear and see Character A start talking, and then the video cuts to Character B while the voice from Character A continues over the visual of Character B. In a split edit, either the audio or the video can lead. Many edits in a scene or sequence can sometimes seem choppy when you make simple cuts back and forth. Creating split edits can sometimes smooth out these choppy edits. Marking split edits in the Viewer window is easy:

1. **Load the Nigel Interviewer #2 into the viewer by double-clicking it.**

   This clip is located in the Nigel Interviewer bin in the Mountain Biking.fcp project.

2. **Play the clip and pause the playhead at the point in the clip just before Nigel says, "The night before a big ride. . . ."**

   Pause the playback just before this sentence by pressing the spacebar. This point in the clip should be around 00:06:46;17.

3. **Choose Mark ⇨ Mark Split ⇨ Audio In (Command+Option+I).**

   This marks an Audio In point for your clip. Your audio in this selection of the clip will start here.

4. **Play the clip up to where Nigel says, "I like to Carbo load."**

5. **After the word *load*, stop your playhead by pressing the spacebar and choose Mark ⇨ Mark Split ⇨ Video In (Control+I).**

   This will now be the In point of your video.

6. **Continue to play the clip until you reach the point where Nigel says, ". . . eat foods that are high. . . ."**

7. **Park your playhead at this spot and choose Mark ⇨ Mark Split ⇨ Video Out (Control+O).**

   This will be the Out point of your video.

8. **Play the clip until the end of the sentence, ". . . in carbohydrates."**

9. **Select Mark ⇨ Mark Split ⇨ Audio Out (Command+Option+O).**

Instead of the usual In and Out points in the Viewer scrub area, you'll see staggered split markers. Audio will now lead video in the beginning of the shot, and audio will remain after the video Out point. This allows you to place cover shots over the beginning and the end of the audio. Figure 9-5 shows what the edit looks like in the Viewer and the Timeline.

Audio In

Video In   Video Out

Audio Out

Video In   Audio Out

Audio In   Video Out

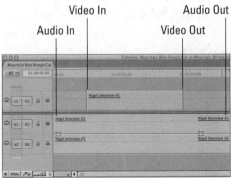

Figure 9-5: A split edit as seen in the Viewer and in the Timeline.

 Cross-Reference   Split edits can also be made directly in the Timeline. Chapter 14 shows you how.

Navigating with Timecode in the Viewer

Learning to navigate clips and projects with timecode is crucial to working in Final Cut Pro. When recording video on a DV or Beta tape for example, a timecode track is recorded along with the picture. Clips are digitized with this timecode track, and this provides a great way to locate clips and specific spots within clips. Timecode is always recorded in hours, minutes, seconds, and frames format. For example, a timecode of 01:20:12:13 indicates 1 hour, 20 minutes, 12 seconds, and 13 frames from the beginning.

The Viewer window has two places where you can view or enter a timecode:

✦ **The Duration field:** Located in the upper-left side of the Viewer window, this field always shows the duration between the marked In and Out points on the clip. In absence of In and Out points, this field shows the total duration of the clip.

✦ **The Current Time field:** Located in the upper-right side of the Viewer window, this field indicates the timecode of the playhead's position in the clip. If you Command+click in the Current Time field, a contextual menu will display the options for viewing timecode in this field, shown in Figure 9-6. The time-code viewing options are:

 • **Drop Frame, Non-Drop Frame, or Frames:** Select one of these three options to display timecode in that format. This is a viewing option only, which does not change the timecode of the clip itself. The timecode format with which the clip was captured will be in bold type.

 • **Clip Time or Source Time:** Clip time is the clip's consecutive timecode from the first frame to the last. If any speed changes have been applied to the clip, Clip Time recalculates frames added or subtracted before consecutively numbering all the frames of the clip. Source Time is the exact timecode as captured from the original recorded source, such as a tape, regardless of any speed changes to the clip. Source Time is always shown in italics.

Figure 9-6: Control+clicking in the Viewer's Current Time field will display a contextual menu showing viewing options of timecode.

Tip

If you have Auxiliary Timecode defined for a clip, this too will be shown in the options when you Control+click in the Current Time field. Up to two Auxiliary Timecodes can be added to a clip by selecting the clip in any main window and then selecting Modify ⇨ Timecode.

Cross-Reference

For more on using timecode in Final Cut Pro, see Chapter 24.

Locating a specific timecode on your clip

Timecode is the basic unit of measure in video. Every frame of video has its own individual timecode. Producers, editors, and others use the timecode to make log notes and perform edits. No matter what you use Final Cut Pro for, you'll likely use timecode to navigate your clips on a regular basis.

1. **Load the Adam-Tire Blooper clip into the viewer by double-clicking it in the Browser.**

   This clip is located in the Adam Bike Tech folder in the Mountain Biking.fcp project.

2. **Press the spacebar on your keyboard to play the clip.**

   Watch the Current Timecode field change in the upper-right side of the Viewer window as the clip plays through.

3. **Stop playback by pressing the spacebar again.**

4. **While the Viewer window is active, type 00:23:13:17. (You aren't required to highlight the timecode field, nor do you have to type the colons or the leading zeros.)**

   Final Cut Pro locates the timecode for you. This location is the precise spot where Adam's tire explodes with a loud bang! You can also confirm this by clicking on the Audio tab in the Viewer window and looking at the waveform of the tire explosion.

Using the method just described, locate the following timecodes on the following clips:

✦ 00:07:50:15 on clip Nigel Interviewer #2-4 (in the Nigel Interviewer folder). If you have located the right spot, Nigel will say, "And then after that, I am basically set to go."

✦ 00:19:58:17 on clip Adam-Tire Pump (in the Adam Bike Tech folder). If you have located the right spot, this will be the location where Adam begins to work the pump.

Tip

You do not have to type in the colons while entering the timecode. If you highlight the Current Timecode field and type **03115003,** Final Cut Pro will still take you to timecode 03:11:50:03. If you have trouble keeping track of all those figures, you can enter periods between pairs of numbers as opposed to colons.

Going forward or backward using timecode

Often you'll need to jump forward or backward a specific amount of time in a clip while editing in Final Cut Pro. You can jump ahead or back using the numeral keys on your keyboard. To move forward or backward in a clip:

1. **If you don't have a clip open in the Viewer window, open the Nigel & Adam Trailhead4 clip (in the At the Trail folder, located in the Mountain Biking.fcp project) used in the previous section.**

   Press the Home key on the upper-right side of your keyboard to make sure the playhead is located at the beginning of the clip.

2. **Enter** +15 **on the numeric keypad.**

   Your playhead jumps 15 frames forward in the clip.

3. **Type** +115, **and press Enter.**

   This action jumps your playhead forward by 1 second and 15 frames. At this frame Nigel and Adam should just be ready to emerge from frame left. Similarly, you can also enter a negative number, such as –115, to go back 1 second and 15 frames.

Tip

Keep in mind that timecode assumes there are 30 frames per second. The last field in the timecode goes up to :29 before it rolls over to :00 again. So entering **130** for timecode will translate to 2 seconds and entering **2135** will translate to 22 seconds and 5 frames. Learning to count in units of 30 rather than units of 60 will help you keep better track of timecode.

Getting friendly with timecode

If you're an editor like I have been for many years, timecode is something you live with on a daily basis. It is the unit of measurement for us video geeks like the inch, point, or pica is for print and design people. Timecode is displayed in the following format:

HOURS:MINUTES:SECONDS:FRAMES

Final Cut Pro uses colons between the seconds and frames fields to display Non Drop Frame Timecode and semicolons are used for Drop Frame. Drop Frame Timecode does not actually "drop" any frames; it just skips the frame numbering by a certain order to resolve a known discrepancy between real clock time versus timecode time.

Use of drop-frame timecode is standard in TV broadcast where the final running time of programs needs to be precisely in sync with clock time. Non-drop-frame type timecode is common in non-broadcast situations where precise matching to clock-time is not critical. Non-drop-frame timecode is also commonly used for projects that will be matched back to film and require contiguous timecode.

Continued

Continued

Again, bear in mind that just the *frame numbers* are skipped, or "dropped," not the frames themselves. Think of Drop Frame as a sort of Leap Year system for timecode, except in this case, frame numbers are removed rather than added.

A common misunderstanding that I've heard is that Drop Frame timecode is 29.97 fps (frames per second) whereas Non Drop Frame timecode is 30 fps. This is not true. In NTSC system video *always* runs at 29.97 fps. Drop and Non Drop are simply two different ways of marking frames of video with timecode. In Drop Frame timecode, frame numbers 0 and 1 are skipped on the first second of every minute, except for every tenth minute.

Almost everything you digitize into Final Cut Pro will have a timecode track to it, and FCP engineers were aware of this fact. They built in many different ways to enter timecode and work with it in FCP. Timecode features in FCP include the following:

✦ **You don't have to type those annoying colons.** To get to 01:14:15:23, just type **01141523**.

✦ **You don't have to enter leading zeros.** To get to 00:00:12:15, type in **1215**.

✦ **Skip back and forth with timecode difference.** Want to skip forward by 13 seconds? Type **+1300**. To skip backward by 10 seconds, type **–1000**.

✦ **FCP converts any frames value from 30 to 99 into seconds.** Since there are 30 frames to a second in timecode, entering **+45** will skip the playhead forward by 1 second and 15 frames (45 frames = 1 second 15 frames).

✦ **If the hour and minute don't change, you don't have to enter them.** If you're at 02:24:12:15 and want to get to 02:24:16:00, just type in **1600**. Skip the hour and minute entry because they don't change.

✦ **Substitute a period (.) for every two zeros.** You don't have to enter all those trailing zeros. You can simply substitute a period (.) for every two zeros. For example, to get to 00:14:00:00 type in **14..** (period, period).

✦ **You don't have to highlight the Current Timecode field.** If you have the Viewer selected, there's no need to highlight the Current Timecode field. Just start typing a new timecode.

✦ **Set a new Out point by entering a duration.** In your Viewer window, you can set a new Out point by entering a duration in the Duration Timecode field.

✦ **Copy and paste timecode.** You can highlight timecode in one field and use Command+C to copy it. Then highlight the field you want to paste it into and use Command+V to paste it.

✦ **Option+Drag timecode.** Press the Option key on your keyboard while dragging the timecode from one field to another. Try it, you'll love it!

These shortcuts work anywhere that timecode is used in Final Cut Pro, including the Log and Capture window, the Viewer, and the Timeline.

Organizing Your Material with Subclips

Subclips are "virtual" short clips that you create from longer clips. For example, suppose you capture long portions of an interview and you want to break up the good bites and store them as separate clips. Subclips break the large clip into more manageable chunks, saving you time and effort later on.

Subclips have icons that look like regular clip icons, except they have jagged edges that make them look like they've been cut out from a larger piece (get it?). Final Cut Pro automatically places subclips in the same bin as the main clip with the *Subclip* added to the original name, and numbered sequentially if more than one subclip is made from the master clip. You can rename these subclips at any time, and use them like any other clip in the Timeline.

Cross-Reference   See Chapter 8 for more on renaming and working with clips in the Browser.

The following is a short exercise to make a subclip from Nigel Interviewer #2-4 clip, located in the Nigel Interviewer folder in the Mountain Biking.fcp project. Nigel says the following dialog in this clip:

> I also do a check on the shifting to make sure that they are shifting correctly, so when I apply a lot of torque to the bike it's not going to slip on me. And after that I am basically set to go. I throw on my helmet, my shoes and I am ready to have fun.

In this exercise, you will make a subclip that isolates just the following part of his dialog:

> I throw on my helmet, my shoes and I am ready to have fun.

Our producer loves this line and he or she would like us to save it for future use. To do this, follow these steps:

1. **Load Nigel Interviewer #2-4 into the Viewer window by double-clicking it in the Browser.**

2. **Press the spacebar to play the clip.**

3. **Mark an In point on this clip just before Rob says, "I throw on my helmet. . . ."**

   Use the I key to mark the In point.

4. **Mark an Out point, using the O key just after Rob says, ". . . my shoes and I am ready to have fun."**

5. **Select Modify ⇨ Make Subclip or use the keyboard shortcut Command+U.**

   You'll see a new clip in the Browser called Nigel Interviewer #2-4 Subclip. The name of this subclip is highlighted for you to edit it.

6. Click on the clip's name, wait a second, and then click it again.

The name is highlighted. You can rename it to something like, "Nigel: I am ready to go."

You've just saved a portion of Nigel's lines as a subclip. When the time comes to use the subclip, simply reach for it in the Browser and use it in the Timeline. An example of master clip and subclips is shown in Figure 9-7.

Master clip

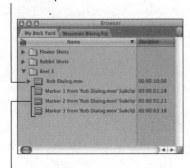

Figure 9-7: Subclips are shorter clips created from longer ones. They are used for organizing and for saving useful portions of longer clips.

Subclips

 Caution   You can make many subclips from a single master clip. Remember, all the subclips are linked to the same media file as the master clip. Deleting this media file will make all subclips as well as the master clip offline.

Locating the master clip for a subclip

Often, while working with a subclip, you'll need to go back to the master clip. You can very easily go back to a subclip's master clip by following these steps.

1. Load the subclip in the Viewer by double-clicking it.

2. Select View ➪ Reveal Master Clip, or use the keyboard shortcut Shift+F.

The master clip will be loaded into the viewer, at the current frame you were on in the subclip when you selected the View ➪ Reveal Master Clip command.

Removing subclip limits

At times you may want to remove the subclip limits and restore a clip to the same length as the original master clip. Follow these steps:

1. **Open the subclip in the Viewer.**

2. **Select Modify ⇨ Remove Subclip Limits.**

   Your subclip will be restored to the same length as the original master clip it came from.

Cross-Reference

It is possible to "truncate" media files so that only the portion of the media file used for the subclip is saved. This is helpful because you may have a long master clip from which you are only using a few seconds. I show you this technique using Media Manager in Chapter 12.

Adjusting the Viewer Display

The Viewer window gives you a variety of options for adjusting the display. You can adjust the magnification used during playback, show or hide important editing tools such as title and action safe boundaries and overlays, and change the way the background appears. These choices can help you tailor Final Cut Pro to your current needs and the material you're working with.

Using magnification in the Viewer window

Final Cut Pro's interface can seem a bit crowded at times. Sometimes it is necessary to adjust magnification to view your video or allow all the Final Cut Pro windows to fit on your desktop. At other times you may want to increase magnification to view a detail in a shot. The Viewer window gives you many ways to adjust magnification.

Caution

It is not advisable to keep the Viewer window at a high magnification such as 200 percent or 400 percent while playing a clip. This will cause stutter during playback and drop frames. You should only magnify the Viewer beyond the fit to window size percent when working on effects and adjusting effect points. This is not an issue of how large Final Cut Pro can play footage but rather how much will fit into the viewer window.

You can adjust the Viewer's display magnification using the Zoom Magnification drop-down menu. As you can see in Figure 9-8, it is located in the top center part of the Viewer window. This menu offers a number of choices:

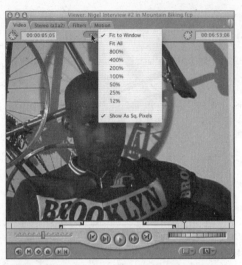

Figure 9-8: The Zoom Magnification drop-down menu in the Viewer window allows you to view your clips at various magnifications. However, setting this menu higher than 100 percent during playback can cause your playback to stutter. If the footage in the viewer is magnified beyond the size of the window, you will see the common scroll bars on the right side and/or bottom of the viewer window. If you see these blue bars, the footage will not play back properly and you should use the fit to window feature described in this section.

✦ **Fit to Window:** Fits all the video into the window, even when you resize the Viewer window. Magnification is adjusted dynamically to fit the entire clip within the display area. This useful command has the keyboard shortcut of Shift+Z.

✦ **Fit All:** Fits all the video in the window at its current size, but will not change magnification if the Viewer window is resized.

✦ **12%–800%:** This allows various magnification choices along the scale. Keep this at 100 percent to viewer your clip at actual size. Reduce it if you're encountering stuttering during playback.

✦ **Show As Sq. Pixels:** Certain kinds of video formats are composed of rectangular pixels. Images from such formats will appear distorted on your computer monitor because it uses square pixels. This effect is most visible when circles appear squashed wide. This setting allows you to view any non-square pixel clips on your computer monitor as square pixels by eliminating the distortion. This is strictly a viewing setting and does not alter any part of the image.

Tip
A quick and easy way to zoom in on the window is to use Command+ +(Plus sign) for zooming in and Command+ - (Minus) to zoom out. Each time you use the shortcut, the magnification zooms up or down the list of magnification choices (12% to 800%) in the menu.

Cross-Reference
To learn more about pixel aspect ratios in video formats, see Chapter 26.

Besides zooming in on the entire image, you can also zoom in on specific parts of the image. Select the Zoom tool (the small magnifying glass with the plus sign in it) in the Tools palette and drag a marquee on the part of the image you want to zoom in on. Figure 9-9 shows the Zoom In tool being used. Holding down the Option key while the Zoom In tool is selected will convert it to the Zoom Out tool, which is indicated by the minus sign in the magnifying glass.

 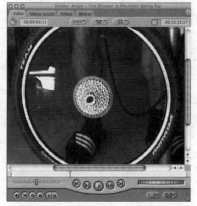

Figure 9-9: Using the Zoom In tool to enlarge or reduce the magnification view of the clip in the Viewer window can easily be selected by pressing the Z key.

Viewing title and action-safe boundaries

Television is not perfect (you probably already know that if you've seen some of the stuff that passes for programming on TV). All TVs have something called *overscan* on their screen, where portions of the image at the edges of the screen are cut off. This malady causes all TVs to show a slightly different image. Usually this is too minor to be important. However, to prevent text or important action from getting lost, video and TV engineers have come up with *Action Safe* and *Title Safe* areas. This allows editors to place their titles and important action on-screen without having to worry that a television with a bad case of overscan will cause some of the text to fall off the edges of the screen.

The Viewer window in Final Cut Pro can help you identify the Action Safe and Title Safe boundaries for your video. With the Viewer window selected, pull down the Viewer menu and select Title Safe. Two boxes will appear in the Viewer window, as shown in Figure 9-10. The outer box is the Action Safe area. No action of importance should be placed outside this area. The inner box shows the Title Safe area. No titles should be placed outside the Title Safe box. Figure 9-10 shows the Title Safe and Action Safe boundaries.

Action Safe area

Title Safe area

Choose Title Safe from the View Choices menu

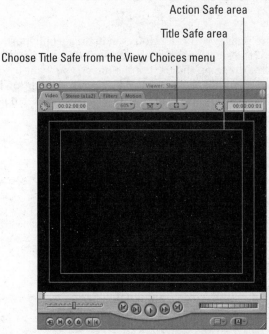

Figure 9-10: No important action should lie outside the Action Safe area. All titles should be placed within the Title Safe area.

If you are editing for computer playback or for the Web, then you need not concern yourself with title and action safety. When you play a QuickTime movie on your computer, no edges are cut off. However, if the program you're editing is meant to be played back on a television set, then you should use the Title Safe viewer in the Viewer window.

Note   In the past, editors often paid little attention to the information outside the action-safe area of the screen because it was extremely unlikely that anyone would ever see it. That is no longer the case. Flat-panel LCD and plasma televisions, which are increasingly available and affordable, will display the entire screen from the outer-most edges.

Viewing overlays

Final Cut Pro has some pretty nifty tools that show you lots of information about your material. Overlays are tools that simply "overlay" symbols and icons on the Viewer (and Canvas) windows to convey some extremely useful information about clips and edits. Editors often don't understand overlays or they ignore overlays altogether, at their own peril. They can provide crucial information about your projects and make your work easier.

To turn on overlays, select the Viewer window, open the Viewer menu and choose Overlays. Table 9-2 lists the overlays that are available in Final Cut Pro.

Table 9-2
Overlays in the Viewer Window

Overlay	Name	Description
	In Point	Appears when the playhead is at the In point frame.
	Out Point	Indicates that you are at the Out point frame.
	Start of Edit	Appears when the playhead is positioned at the start of an edit. This overlay indicates the first frame of the incoming clip. This is seen only in the Canvas window.
	End of Edit	Appears when the playhead is positioned at the end of an edit. This overlay indicates the last frame of the outgoing clip This is seen only in the Canvas window.
	Split Edit-Audio In	Indicates a split edit Audio In point.
	Split Edit-Video In	Indicates a split edit Video In point.
	Split Edit-Video Out	Indicates a split edit Video Out point.
	Split Edit-Audio Out	Indicates a split edit Audio Out point.

Continued

Table 9-2 *(continued)*		
Overlay	*Name*	*Description*
	Marker Overlay	These appear when the playhead is located on a Marker. Shows the name of the Marker if it has been labeled.
	Start/End of Media	When this appears on the left side of the window, it indicates the beginning of your media. On the right side, this indicates the end of your media file.
	End of program	Indicates the last frame in the program.

Viewing with different backgrounds

The Viewer Choices menu in the Viewer window has several options available for choosing different backgrounds. For example, you may want to choose a white background if you are creating black text. This will save you a lot of squinting. The checkerboard backgrounds are useful for adjusting transparency for layers that have Alpha channels.

Cross-
Reference   Alpha channels are created in stills and QuickTime movies for creating transparency. For more information on Alpha channels and transparency, see Chapter 17.

Using other choices in the Viewer menu

Besides the choices discussed in the previous sections, there are a few other options in the Viewer Choices menu. Mostly these relate to working with graphics and using transparency in those graphics to composite them over video. Figure 9-11 shows other choices available to you in the Viewer Choices menu. They include

✦ **Image:** Shows the video image only.

✦ **Image+Wireframe:** Shows the video image and draws a wireframe around the outer boundaries of the clip. A *wireframe* consists of a very bare outline of your graphic. This option must be on to do motion animation.

✦ **Wireframe:** Displays only the wireframe of the outer edges of the clip without a video image. This view can be useful for previewing complex animations without having to render a video image.

✦ **Show Timecode Overlays:** Displays overlay windows showing clips' In and Out points, current timecode of clips' video and audio tracks, as well as color coding of all tracks that are in sync with another track for quick visual checking of sync.

✦ **Show Excess Luma:** Displays "zebra stripes" of marching lines over areas that are near and over 100% value (broadcast legal). Red zebras indicate luma value over 100%, while green zebras indicate areas of luma values between 90 and 100%. A yellow exclamation-point icon indicates the presence of luma values that are too high. A green check-mark icon indicates there are no luma values in the frame over 100%, while the same green checkmark icon with an arrow pointing upward indicates the presence of luma values of 90 to 100%, but none in excess of 100%.

✦ **RGB:** Displays the image only. This means you just see your video or the RGB colors if it is a graphic.

✦ **Alpha:** Displays any alpha channel that the image may have. Alpha channels are created to control and manage image transparency. In this display mode, black represents transparency, white represents opaque, and levels of gray indicate varying levels of semi-transparency.

✦ **RGB+Alpha:** Displays the image and any Alpha channel it may have together. The Alpha channel will appear as a red overlay.

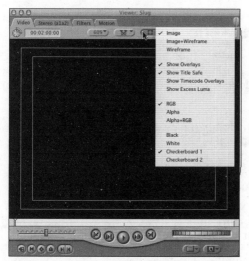

Figure 9-11: Viewer options make it easy to work with text or image transparency.

Keep in mind that if an image (such as a captured video clip) is in the Viewer, it will have no Alpha channel. Choosing the Alpha option will show only a white display.

Cross-Reference   For a discussion of Alpha channels, graphics, and compositing, see Chapter 17.

Working with Markers

Markers help you move around in and keep track of your material by allowing you to label spots on your clips. Markers are like little sticky notes you can place on your clips, such as "Tire explosion here" or "Fix the color here." They show up as text overlays on your clips when the playhead is located on them. You can edit and label these markers and quickly navigate to them. I often use markers to mark spots and leave notes for my fellow editors who might be working on the same project.

In Figure 9-12, you can see what a marker looks like when added to a clip in the Viewer window. It appears as a small red arrow in the scrub area as well as an overlay on the video clip. The marker turns yellow when the playhead is directly over it, giving you a quick, visual confirmation that you are parked on a frame with a marker.

Figure 9-12: Markers appear as small red arrows in the Viewer scrub area (left) and as overlays (right). They are handy for labeling clips.

Adding and deleting markers

You can add markers in the Viewer window while parking the playhead at the frame of your choice and selecting Mark ➪ Markers ➪ Add. After adding just one marker, you'll realize that this is a foolishly long way to do things. Follow these steps for a speedier process:

1. **Load any clip in the Mountain Biking.fcp project into the Viewer by double-clicking on it in the Browser window.**

2. **Play this clip by pressing the spacebar.**

   At a point where you'd like to add a marker, stop the playback by pressing spacebar again.

3. **Click the Add Marker button in the Viewer window (or just press the M key).**

   An overlay of Marker 1 appears over your clip in the Viewer. Note that you can also add markers on the fly without pausing playback.

4. Shift+click the Add Marker button to edit the marker.

The Edit Marker window opens as shown in Figure 9-13. (Or press the M key again to open the Edit Marker box.)

Figure 9-13: Shift+click the Add Marker button to open the Edit Marker window. Use this window to name the marker and add comments.

5. Rename the marker if you like and add a comment for it.

The name and comment will appear as overlays.

As you might have guessed, there are also several ways to delete a marker The key thing here is to remember to have the playhead parked on the frame with the marker you want to delete. Once you've done that, then you can

✦ Press M to open the Edit Marker dialog box and click the Delete button.

✦ Option+click the Add Marker button at the bottom of the Viewer window.

✦ Choose Mark ⇨ Markers ⇨ Delete.

✦ Press Command+` (accent-mark key).

To delete all markers simply choose Mark ⇨ Markers ⇨ Delete All, or use the keyboard shortcut of pressing Control+` (accent-mark key). The playhead does not need to be on any marker to delete all.

Editing markers

In addition to the text note you can add to a marker, there are now three additional types of markers' tags available in the Edit Marker dialog box. These markers can be exported with the clips and used to navigate or flag important areas of the clip in other applications:

✦ **Chapter Marker** can be used by DVD Studio Pro to create a navigable chapter point. Chapter markers are also seen by Quicktime as a chapter item that you can jump to using a pop-up menu. Chapter markers appear in the Comment field as <CHAPTER>.

✦ **Compression Marker** can be used by compression applications to identify changes in the clip's properties that might affect compression, such as an abrupt change in scene brightness or subject motion. Compression markers appear in the Comment field as <COMPRESSION>.

✦ **Scoring Marker** is an embedded audio scoring marker that is visible when the clip is opened with an Apple scoring application like Soundtrack. Scoring markers appear in the Comment field as <SCORING>.

When you export your movie, you can select which markers you want to export using File ⇨ Export ⇨ Quicktime Movie. Figure 9-14 shows the markers that can be exported with your Quicktime movie.

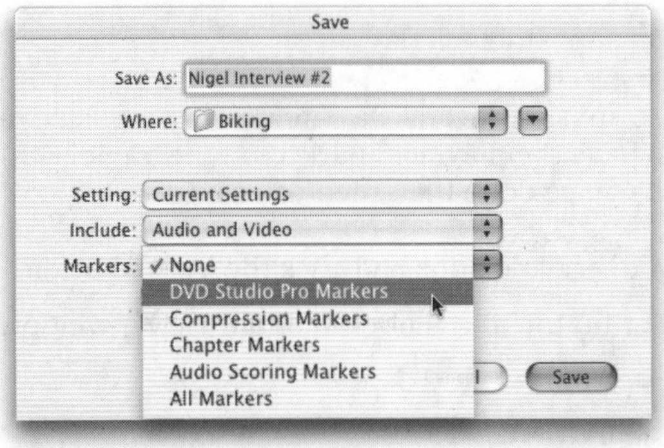

Figure 9-14: Markers that can be exported with your Quicktime movie are selected in the Export ⇨ Quicktime Movie's Save dialog box.

The various marker types that you can export are straightforward, except for DVD Studio Pro Markers. Did I miss these in the Edit Marker options? No, selecting DVD Studio Pro Markers will export all Chapter *and* Compression markers, while the other three marker options will export only that selected marker type.

Caution When exporting sequences with Chapter, Compression, or Audio markers, the markers must be added on the Timeline ruler or Canvas, and not to individual clips.

Cross-Reference Chapter markers are discussed more in Chapter 27 where I discuss creating movies for DVD Studio Pro. Compression markers are discussed in Chapter 23 where I take a look at Apple's new Compressor application.

Moving and extending markers

Moving markers is both easy and not so easy. For some inexplicable reason, Final Cut Pro has never offered an easy way to move an existing marker to an earlier position (to the left) in a clip or sequence, but it does have a variety of ways to move a marker to a later position (to the right). If you need to move a marker up earlier in a clip, here's how:

1. **Locate the playhead over a marker.**
2. **Press the M key to open the Edit Marker dialog box.**
3. **Enter a new timecode in the Start field.**

   Enter in an earlier timecode, or type in a negative frame or seconds amount you wish to move the marker.

4. **Click OK.**

   The marker will jump to its new position. Of course, this would work if you wanted to move the marker to a later position. Just type in a positive amount of frames or seconds for it to move.

When you want to move a marker "downstream," to the right, position the playhead where you want the marker to relocate and do one of the following:

✦ **Select Mark ➪ Marker ➪ Reposition.** If there are multiple markers, only the nearest marker to the left of the playhead will jump to the playhead's position.

✦ **Press Shift+` (accent-mark key).**

Markers can also be extended (again, only to the right) to show a selection of frames. The marker will have a thin extension arm from the original marker to the last frame of the marker's duration. When the playhead is positioned over any part of an extended marker, the marker's overlay in the Viewer will be visible. An extended marker is shown in Figure 9-15.

Extended Marker

Figure 9-15: Markers can be extended to
cover a selection of frames.

To extend a marker using timecode:

1. **Locate the playhead over a marker.**

2. **Press the M key to open the Edit Marker dialog box.**

3. **Enter a new timecode in the Duration field.**

   The frames or seconds amount you enter will extend the duration of the
   marker only to the right of its current position. Negatives durations entered
   are ignored.

4. **Click OK.**

   The marker's arm will extend to its new position.

You can extend a marker to the playhead by doing one of the following (once the
playhead is in the desired position—it must be to the right of the marker):

✦ **Select Mark ⇨ Marker ⇨ Extend.** If there are multiple markers, only the
   nearest marker to the left of the playhead will extend to the playhead's
   position.

✦ **Press Option+` (accent-mark key).**

Navigating to markers

Often it is necessary to navigate precisely to markers that you've placed in your clips. There are many ways to do that. In all cases the playhead jumps to the marker. Here are a few ways to navigate using markers:

✦ **Menu Choices:** Use Mark ⇨ Next ⇨ Marker or Mark ⇨ Previous ⇨ Marker to jump to markers.

✦ **Keyboard Shortcuts:** The keyboard shortcut Shift+Down Arrow key will jump you to the next marker, while Shift+Up Arrow will jump you to the previous marker.

✦ **Contextual Menu:** Control+click on the Current Timecode field, and a contextual menu will appear listing all markers with names. Select one to navigate to it. Figure 9-16 shows this.

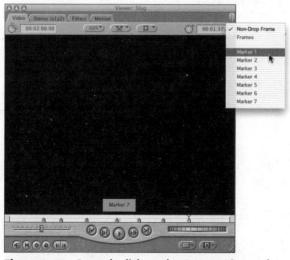

Figure 9-16: Control+click on the Current Timecode field to bring up a contextual menu with a listing of markers. Select one to jump the playhead to that marker.

Using DV Start and Stop Detect to place markers

If you've shot a DV tape with numerous starts and stops, these scenes delimited by you starting and stopping the camera can be detected and turned into markers. This can be convenient because the starts and stops on a DV tape are often good markers for shot changes.

If you shoot a DV tape with the idea of turning the start and stop points into markers, be sure to avoid any timecode breaks on the tape. You might ask, "But what about Final Cut Pro's new feature of making a new clip when a timecode break is encountered during Capture?" First, it's just good, professional practice to avoid timecode breaks as if there were no workaround solution. This approach will make clip organization and selection easier and faster during editing. Secondly, the Make New Clip at Timecode Break option will make a new *separate* clip, which means you have no scene change for DV Start/Stop to detect. To detect starts and stops on DV to place markers:

1. **Capture a lengthy DV clip from a tape that has numerous start and stop points on it.**

2. **Double-click this clip to open it in the Viewer.**

3. **Select Mark ⇨ DV Start/Stop Detect.**

For each start and stop on the clip, you'll get a marker. You can now navigate to these markers for easy identification of shot changes.

Making subclips from markers

It is also possible to make subclips based on markers. This technique can be combined with the technique mentioned previously to automate the process of creating subclips from each "scene" on a DV tape. If you have created markers with DV Start/Stop, or manually set your own, follow these steps to turn them into subclips:

1. **Be sure the Browser is in List Viewer mode by selecting the Browser and selecting View ⇨ Browser Items ⇨ As List.**

   Any clip with markers appears with a small triangle next to it in the Browser.

2. **Click the triangle open to see all markers.**

3. **Label markers if you like by clicking on the marker name with a slow double-click.**

   This name will be used later for the subclips you will create.

4. **Select all the markers by clicking and dragging them, as shown in Figure 9-17.**

5. **Select Modify ⇨ Make Subclip.**

   Video between the markers will now appear as subclips in the Browser. Note that the subclips will themselves be free of any markers or overlays.

Figure 9-17: Select markers by dragging a box around them. You can now turn these markers into locations for creating subclips by selecting Modify ➪ Make Subclip.

Deleting markers

To delete a marker you are currently on, select Mark ➪ Markers ➪ Delete, or use the keyboard shortcut Command+ ` (accent key). To delete all markers, select Mark ➪ Markers ➪ Delete All, or press Control+ ` (accent key).

Alternatively, you can Control+click on any marker in the Browser window and select Edit Marker from the contextual menu. You will be presented with the Edit Marker window. Click on the Delete button in the window to delete the currently selected marker.

Tip

Markers work anywhere in Final Cut Pro, not just in the Viewer window. The information you learn about markers in this section can be used in the Sequences and Canvas windows as well.

Working with Audio in the Viewer Window

Audiences are funny creatures. Show them poor video quality, shaky camera work, grainy footage, or badly composed shots and they'll sit there and watch it. Give them one shot with bad audio and you've lost them. This is a long known fact that viewers will accept almost any image quality, depending on the circumstances, but will rarely put up with bad audio.

Digital video editing applications exist mainly to edit video. In most cases the audio editing facilities that come with video editing programs are fairly limited. However, if you have done a lot of editing you know that audio editing is as critical a part of the editing process as video editing.

Cross-Reference

For more on working with audio in Final Cut Pro, including the new Audio Mixer tool, see Chapter 14.

Figure 9-18 illustrates the Audio tab of the Viewer window. Notice that the transport controls at the bottom of the Audio tab remain the same as other Viewer window tabs. Most of these controls should be familiar to you from previous sections in this chapter. I'll concentrate on the top portion of the Audio tab, which includes the audio manipulation controls and the waveform display area.

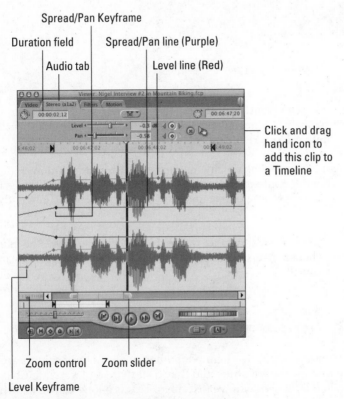

Spread/Pan Keyframe

Duration field   Spread/Pan line (Purple)

Audio tab   Level line (Red)

Click and drag hand icon to add this clip to a Timeline

Zoom control   Zoom slider

Level Keyframe

Figure 9-18: The audio tab of the Viewer window lets you edit and manipulate audio and pan levels.

Settings in the Audio tab

The Audio tab of the Viewer window contains a number of important settings to help you play and edit your audio tracks. Settings include

✦ **Level slider:** Use this to adjust the volume level of the clip in decibels (dB). The Add Keyframe button to the right of the Level slider is used to set keyframes to modify audio levels across time. You can also enter the dB value numerically in the box to the right of the slider.

Note

Keyframes are used to lock values of properties, such as audio and effects, to a particular location in time. By setting multiple keyframes with different values across time, you can animate properties such as audio levels and effect attributes.

✦ **Spread slider:** This slider is used to change the stereo panning. A value of –1 (minus one) will send the left channel to the left and the right to the right. A setting of 0 will send both channels to both channels equally. A setting of +1 will swap left with right channels. Again, the Add Keyframe box to the right of the Spread slider allows you to set keyframes and modify the spread setting across time.

✦ **Pan slider:** This appears only for non-stereo files. Use it to pan sound from one channel to another.

✦ **Hand on Speaker icon:** Drag this if you want to add the current clip to the Timeline. This is tricky. Because you can drag a video clip from the Viewer to the Timeline by dragging from the image, you may be tempted to drag from the audio waveform. While in the Audio tab however, you must click the Hand on Speaker icon and drag the clip to the Timeline.

✦ **X (reset) button:** This button deletes all keyframes and resets the level and spread to the original settings.

✦ **Level line:** This red line shows the volume or amplitude level of the clip. You can simply drag it up or down to raise or lower the audio level for the entire clip.

✦ **Spread line:** Appears as a purple line and indicates the spread of the clip. You can raise or lower this line to change the spread of the audio clip.

✦ **Zoom slider:** Dragging the ends of this slider changes the size of the slider. This causes the viewer to shrink or grow as you desire. Dragging the middle part of the slider will move the viewer around to different parts of the clip.

Working with audio waveforms in the Viewer

On the DVD-ROM

For exercises in this chapter, use the Mountain Biking Tutorial project folder from the DVD-ROM. Drag the Mountain Biking Tutorial folder onto your internal drive, and open the project by double-clicking on the Mountain Biking.fcp icon. This will launch Final Cut Pro and set the windows for you.

Audio waveforms are visual representations of the audio signal. Waveforms are extremely beneficial to editing and manipulating audio. For example, waveforms allow you to see where a phrase of a person's speech or a note of music may lie. Often, editors find it easier to place markers or edit points by simply "looking" at the audio. Keep in mind that when you set an In point while viewing the audio, you also set one for the video that is synced with it. To display audio waveforms in the Viewer window, follow these steps:

1. **Double-click Adam-Tire Blooper-2 in the Browser to load it into the Viewer.**

   This clip is located in the Adam Bike Tech folder located in the Mountain Biking.fcp project.

2. **Click the Audio tab to display the audio waveform.**

   Keep in mind that for clips without audio, there will be no audio tab, like a recorded voiceover or music clip.

3. **Press the Home key, located on the upper-right portion of your keyboard, to return to the beginning of the clip, and press the spacebar to play it.**

   You'll hear the words, "Ha! Ha! Ha! Ha! That was psycho!" This is Adam's reaction to the tire exploding.

4. **Move your playhead to the beginning of the "Ha! Ha! Ha! Ha!"**

   This should be around 00:23:29:22 on the Current Timecode setting.

5. **Try locating your playhead at the beginning of this phrase and press the spacebar to play it.**

6. **You can mark an In point by pressing the I key and an Out point using the O key.**

   These In and Out points now apply to the selection you've made based on viewing and listening to the audio waveform. Figure 9-19 shows the waveform for Adam-Tire Blooper-2.

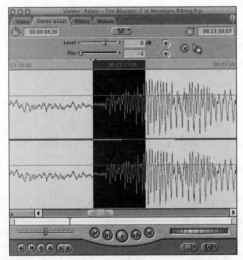

Figure 9-19: The Audio tab of the Viewer window shows the audio waveform. Waveforms allow visual editing of audio media.

The Audio tab conundrum

In order for you to look at the waveform for your audio, you can double-click a clip to open it into the Viewer and click on the Audio tab. However, you should know that, depending on how you captured your audio, the details of the Audio tab could look quite different. What format your audio was captured in is decided in the Audio Format pull-down menu. This menu is located in the Clip Settings tab of the Log and Capture window that can be found under the File menu. The following figure shows the Audio Format selection menu.

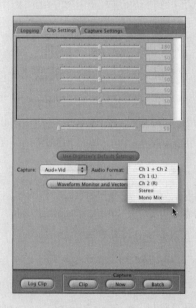

You should only consider capturing your audio in the Ch1+Ch2 format when you have a clear separation between your two audio tracks on tape. For example, if Channel 1 on your tape is ambience from the camera mike, and Channel 2 has the interviewer's audio recorded on a lavaliere microphone, the Ch1+Ch2 format is ideal. Otherwise, lacking separate tracks on tape, you should attempt to capture your audio in the Stereo format.

If you capture a clip as a Stereo clip, you will have one tab and it will be labeled Audio followed by the audio channels designation (a1a2, for example). Clicking on this tab will show the waveforms for both the left and right channels. Any changes applied to the level or spread of one channel will automatically be applied to both. The Spread slider will appear with a default value of −1. This means that the audio from the left channel will be sent to the left channel output and the audio from the right channel will be sent to right channel output. A setting of 0 in the Spread slider sends both the channels to both the outputs, in a sense creating a "mono" output. A setting of +1 in the Spread slider swaps the left and right channels. The following figure shows how a Stereo clip appears in the Audio tab.

Continued

Continued

If you capture a clip using the Channel 1 or Channel 2 setting, you will find two Audio tabs in the Viewer. These will be labeled Ch1 and Ch2. Each tab will show a waveform for that channel only and any changes applied to one channel will not be applied to the other one. This can create considerably more work. The sliders in this case will be Level and Pan. The Pan for each of the channels will be set to 0. A setting of –1 sends that channel to the left output and a setting of +1 sends that channel to the right. The following figure shows how a Channel 1 and Channel 2 clip appears in the Audio tab.

Waveforms serve another function that I've found to be quite useful: They serve as a quick and handy way of checking your audio levels. Over time, I've learned how to glance quickly at a waveform and see if I have a good level or a distorted or weak one. In Figure 9-20, you see an example of low, average, and distorted signals. A good, or "healthy," level should look like the waveforms fit inside the window well without getting clipped at the top and the bottom.

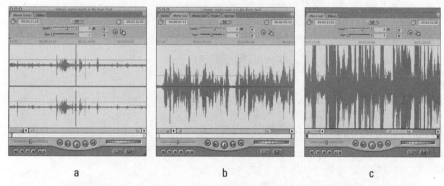

a   b   c

Figure 9-20: Waveforms provide a quick way to check the audio quality of your captures. In these three views, *a* has very low levels, *b* is audio with good levels, and *c* is distorted.

Waveforms that are tiny represent audio that is perhaps too low. Of course, all of this depends on what it is that you're looking at. For example, if Figure 9-20c was a person talking, the audio would be severely distorted. However, if Figure 9-20a represented a person talking, it may just be okay. So consider your source, and play your clip to make a judgment. Still, the waveforms are a fairly reliable way of checking your audio signal's integrity.

Adjusting audio in the Viewer

You will frequently find yourself adjusting the audio levels for a clip. This can be done a few different ways. You can modify the audio level for the entire clip, or you can use keyframes to dynamically change the audio levels across the clip.

Adjusting audio levels for a clip in the Viewer

Load a clip that contains audio in the Viewer if it is not already loaded, and click the Audio tab to view the audio waveform for the clip. By placing the arrow cursor at the Level line graph, you can click and drag the Level line up or down as shown in Figure 9-21. Another way to accomplish this is to simply drag the Level slider to the left or right.

Figure 9-21: Audio level can be adjusted by clicking and dragging the red Level line up or down in the Viewer window. Your cursor will automatically turn to the drag cursor when placed near the red Level line.

Tip   Holding down the Command key *after* you've started dragging the volume or the pan lines with the mouse will result in a "gear down," where the changes will occur in much smaller and more precise increments.

Adjusting the pan for a clip in the Viewer

Pan refers to the separation of sound between the left and right channels. By changing this setting, you can determine whether you want your sound to be centered, left heavy, or right heavy. To adjust pan, use the Pan slider or click and drag the purple Pan graph line up or down. Drag the line up to pan right or down to pan left.

Note   Stereo clips will have a Spread setting because this allows you to spread out the left and right channels. The Pan slider will only be shown in non-stereo clips.

Adjusting the spread for a stereo clip in the Viewer

The Spread slider allows stereo panning. This means that if you set the slider to –1, then the left channel will go to the left side and the right to the right. Setting this slider to 0 sends both channels equally to both sides so that the sound is centered. A setting of +1 swaps the channels and sends the left channel to the right side and the right to the left.

You can adjust the spread using several methods. You can manually enter a setting in the Spread box, you can use the slider, or you can drag the purple Spread line in the Viewer window.

Note If your clip was captured with the Channel 1 and Channel 2 setting in the Audio Format menu within the Log and Capture window, the stereo Pan will be centered at 0 by default. You can modify this value between −1 and 1. For a clip that was captured as a Stereo Pair, the Spread will default to −1, which means it is sending the left audio track to the left channel and the right audio track to the right channel.

Using keyframes to adjust audio

All the methods described in the previous sections adjust the settings for the duration of the entire clip. What if you want to raise and lower the audio levels and spread at specific points within the clip? This is a common scenario when adding a music track because this track has to rise and fall along with other audio in the program. In that case, we will use the Keyframe buttons (see Figure 9-22) in the Viewer window.

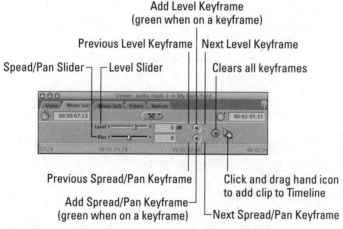

Figure 9-22: The Keyframes section in the Audio tab allows you to set and navigate to keyframes in a clip. Keyframes are used to dynamically modify the level, pan, or spread of an audio clip.

 Caution It is crucial that you use the Next and Previous keyframe buttons to navigate from one keyframe to another, and you have to be sure that the Set Keyframe button is green while modifying a keyframe. Otherwise you might create a new keyframe that could cause a glitch in your audio.

Keyframes let you lock a setting to a particular point in time. You can set multiple keyframes in a clip and adjust audio settings between keyframes, and Final Cut Pro will play these settings on the fly. To see this in action, let's use keyframes to create a simple one-second fade-up on our audio.

1. **Load an audio file into the Viewer.**

   If you don't have a file to work with, use the Ntracks_J&E2_59.aif music audio file. This file is located in the Music folder in the Mountain Biking.fcp project.

2. **Press the Home key to go to the beginning of the audio file, and press the spacebar to play it.**

   You'll hear the music play. Play up to around 13:08 into the music. Click on the Audio tab to see the audio controls for this clip.

3. **Click the top Set level Keyframe button.**

   The button turns green indicating that you're located on a keyframe. Also, a small diamond-shaped icon appears on the red Level line. That icon represents a keyframe you just set.

4. **Drag the Level slider all the way left to a reading of –60 dB.**

   This will make the audio levels go out completely.

5. **Go forward to around 14:16 into the clip and click the Set Level Keyframe button again. Raise the Levels slider to 0 db.**

   You should see two keyframes, and the red line appears to make a curve up, as shown in Figure 9-23. You've just created a fade up to your music track.

Second Level keyframe

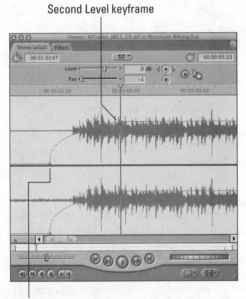

First Level keyframe

Figure 9-23: Keyframes allow you to dynamically change the audio and pan levels across a clip. This clip has a fade up of music.

Note The music track for this exercise was provided by Narrator Tracks. Go to their Web site at www.narratortracks.com to listen to samples of their great music.

6. **Play the clip, and then stop it where you want to adjust the levels. Click the Set level Keyframe button again.**

7. **Instead of using the slider, click and drag the keyframe itself.**

   This action turns your cursor into a cross that will allow you to move the keyframe up or down. You can also drag the keyframe off the window to delete it.

Tip Hold down the Shift key and then drag on the red audio levels overlay line to raise or lower all keyframes simultaneously. Additionally, you can hold down the Option key to get the Pen tool and use it to add keyframes by clicking with it on the red Level line.

Using the steps described earlier, you can also adjust the Pan and Spread settings using keyframes.

Tip Holding down the Option key while moving the cursor closer to the Level or Spread lines will turn the pointer to the Pen tool. You can click on the line with this tool to set a keyframe. However, holding down the Option key and locating the pointer over an already existing keyframe will turn the pointer into a Pen Delete tool. You can use this tool to delete keyframes.

Subframe audio editing in the Viewer window

Even though the shortest distance the playhead can move is one frame, you can actually edit audio in the Viewer window at the subframe level. Subframe precision is editing audio in increments that are smaller than one frame. Some audio pops or other problems are often less than one frame in length, so subframe editing allows you to edit out small audio problems. Figure 9-24 shows the playhead with its one frame shadow, along with some subframe keyframes that I've set. To perform subframe audio editing:

1. **Load the Nigel-Rear Tire3 CU in the Viewer by double-clicking it.**

   This clip is located in the Nigel Bike Tech folder located in the Mountain Biking.fcp project.

2. **Move the playhead to 00:11:44:21 in the clip.**

   There is a tire squeal of a very short duration at this point in the clip.

3. **Click the Audio tab and zoom in using Command+ + (Plus sign).**

   Zoom in as far as possible, remembering that the shadow next to the playhead represents one frame of video.

4. **Select the Pen tool from the tools palette.**

   Alternatively, hold down the Option key to get the Pen tool.

5. **Create two keyframes by clicking with the Pen tool, within the shadow of the playhead.**

   Click and drag on the second keyframe to make a fast dip in the audio to bring down the level of the tire squeal. You've just created a sub-frame audio edit. Bear in mind that the shadow of the playhead represents one frame of video, while audio edits are possible to within much smaller sections — 1/100th, actually — of the video frame.

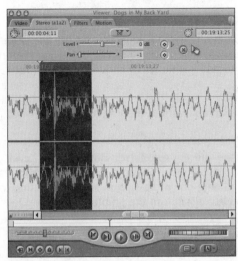

Figure 9-24: Subframe editing is useful for getting out small pops and doing micro-level audio editing. The black shadow represents one video frame, however keyframes can be set on a subframe level using the Pen tool down to 1/100th of a frame.

Tip   Control+click on any keyframe and choose Clear from the contextual menu that appears to delete individual keyframes.

Toggling scrubbing in the Viewer window

Scrubbing is an old audio term that comes from editors dragging audiotape against the tape playheads by hand to hear the audio. Scrubbing allowed them to listen to audio at faster- or slower-than real-time speeds, making it easier and quicker to find editing spots.

In the Viewer window, you can have scrubbing on or off. To enable scrubbing, select View ➪ Audio Scrubbing. If the check mark is there, then the audio scrubbing has been enabled. Select it again to get rid of the check mark and disable scrubbing.

Audio Scrubbing can also be toggled on and off using the keyboard shortcut of Shift+S. While Scrubbing is on, drag your playhead through the audio clip and hear what scrubbing sounds like. It will make your audio sound like you're dragging your ears against a grate while someone is talking to you! Still, it's helpful because you don't have to play your audio in real time; you can just scroll through it to find important spots.

Scrubbing also works when you use the J, K, and L keys on you keyboard for playing audio. ***Remember:*** The J key will play your audio backward, while K pauses the playback and L plays the audio forward. Repeatedly pressing the J or the L keys increments this playback in factors of 1X, 2X, 4X, and 8X.

However, often you want to hear just a frame or two at the current playhead. Holding down the K key while you tap on the J or the L key will move the playhead one frame in either direction, while scrubbing the audio. Holding down the K key at the same time with the J or the L key will play the audio in either direction at one-third speed.

Tip   When you zoom in to maximum magnification on an audio waveform for sub-frame editing, you can hold down the Shift key and drag the playhead shadow for subframe audio scrubbing in 1/100th of a frame increment.

✦   ✦   ✦

Editing the Final Cut Pro Way

In many respects, Final Cut Pro has a lot in common with other nonlinear editing systems. Over the years I have worked with many different editing systems. When Final Cut Pro came on the scene, I could see that the designers of this application had taken a close look at the other systems when they began the design process. They had taken some of the best features of these nonlinear editing systems and incorporated them into Final Cut Pro. Final Cut Pro 4.0 has now refined many of these standard features while also adding a host of new tools to one of the most flexible and intuitive nonlinear editing systems.

One of the more important features that Final Cut Pro designers integrated into the application is the ability to edit two shots together using a variety of techniques. On the surface, this may not seem like a major revelation, but the Final Cut Pro team knew that editors are a diverse and varied bunch. Some editors like to rely heavily on keyboard shortcuts, while others love scurrying around with the mouse, selecting tools, dragging, and clicking at controls and knobs. Final Cut Pro accommodates almost any editing style.

Of course, the Final Cut Pro team also wanted editors who were using other popular editing applications to run away from their edit stations and buy a copy of Final Cut Pro right away, so they provided workflow methods that make it easy to migrate to Final Cut Pro from other editing systems.

Whether you're new to nonlinear editing systems, or you're one of those who are migrating from another editing system, this chapter will help you get comfortable with Final Cut Pro's editing process. This chapter describes the editing process and looks at concepts such as sequences and performing basic edits. You'll find out how to troubleshoot some common problems that can occur when you first start editing.

Understanding the Editing Process

The main Final Cut Pro interface has four windows. These windows are the Browser, the Viewer, the Canvas, and the Timeline. You will routinely use these windows as you edit your projects. The basic editing cycle, illustrated in Figure 10-1, is a four-step process:

1. Select a clip.

In the Browser you select a clip that you'd like to add to your sequence.

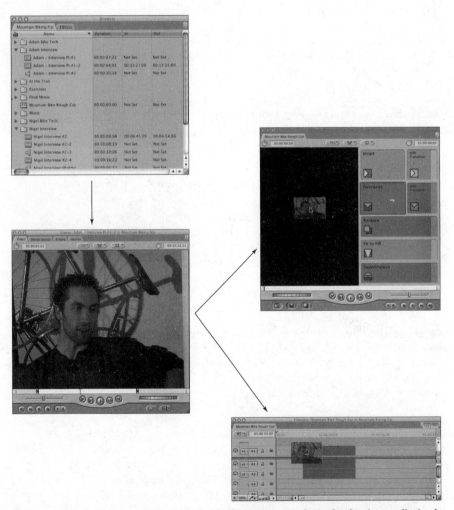

Figure 10-1: The basic edit process in Final Cut Pro consists of selecting a clip in the Browser, opening it in the Viewer, marking In and Out points, and editing the selection into the Canvas or Timeline.

2. Open the clip.

Double-click the clip that you have selected to open it in the Viewer. Play the clip and familiarize yourself with it.

3. Mark In and Out points.

In the Viewer, set an In point and an Out point on the clip to identify the portion you would like to edit.

4. Edit the clip into the Canvas, or to the Timeline.

Edit the selected portion of your clip to the Canvas or directly into the Timeline.

Of course, there are many variations and exceptions to the four steps just described, but this is the basic model of the editing process for most of your work in Final Cut Pro.

Working with Sequences

When working in Final Cut Pro, all your edits reside together in *sequences*. You can have as many sequences in a project as you like. This is an important point because, in the past, some editing applications only allowed one sequence per project. Being able to have multiple sequences provides far greater flexibility in the editing process.

Double-clicking a sequence in the Browser opens a Timeline and a Canvas window. The Timeline is where clips, transitions, audio tracks, and effects are arranged. The playhead in the Timeline works in tandem with the playhead in the Canvas. When the playhead is moved in the Timeline, the Canvas window shows the edited clips in the Timeline.

Note   New in Final Cut Pro 4.0 is the ability to have the Viewer follow, or track frame for frame, the playhead in the Timeline as it moves. This is useful if you are editing footage from a multiple-camera shoot. However, by default, the Viewer window plays source clips independently from the Timeline.

Cross-Reference   The Viewer window is covered in Chapter 9.

A sequence called *Sequence 1* is automatically created when you start a new project, as shown in Figure 10-2. You can create additional sequences in a project by choosing File ➪ New ➪ Sequence (Command+N). Sequence settings such as frame size, compressor, and pixel aspect ratio are based on your default Sequence Presets in the Audio/Video Settings. Timeline options such as the starting Timecode and default number of tracks are set in the Timeline Options tab of the User Preferences dialog box. Both these items are shown in Figure 10-3, and both can easily be changed:

✦ To set a different Sequence Preset, choose Final Cut Pro ➪ Audio/Video Settings, click on the Sequence Presets tab and make a selection. Any new sequences will now be made with this preset.

✦ To change Timeline options for future sequences, choose Final Cut Pro ➪ User Preferences and click on the Timeline Options tab.

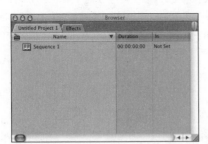

Figure 10-2: A sequence automatically appears when you make a new project.

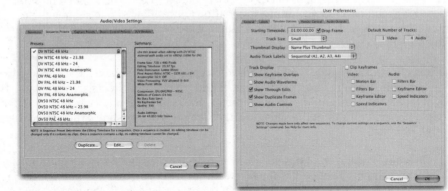

Figure 10-3: Use the Sequence Settings tab in the Audio/Video Settings and the Timeline Options tab in User Preferences to set default settings for new sequences.

Cross-Reference   See Chapter 6 for more details on Sequence Presets and Timeline Options settings.

Unless you make changes in your hardware setup and the type of video you are capturing, chances are you won't have to change your default Sequence Preset. Remember that changing either the Sequence Preset or the Timeline Options in the User Preferences will only affect *future* sequences you create, and not the current sequence. If you want to change Settings for *only* the current sequence:

1. **Select a sequence in the Browser or click in the open Timeline sequence you want to change.**

2. **Choose Sequence ⇨ Settings, or press Command+0 (zero).**

   The Sequence Settings dialog box appears with the name of your sequence in the Name field. In Figure 10-4, you can see the Sequence Settings dialog box for a sequence called *Flower Beds*.

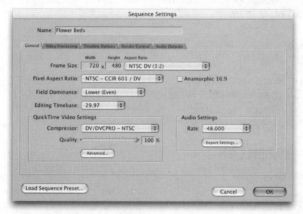

Figure 10-4: Choose Sequence ⇨ Settings (Command+0) while in an open sequence to change settings in the Sequence Settings dialog box.

3. **Select the General, Timeline Options, Video Rendering, Render Control, or Audio Outputs tab to adjust settings.**

Cross-Reference

See Chapter 6 for more details on the settings available here.

4. **Click the OK button to accept changes.**

   All changes selected will be applied *only* to the selected Sequence. All future new Sequences will still be based on Sequence Settings selected in the Audio/Video Settings and User Preferences.

Caution   Settings in the General tab of the Sequence Settings dialog box should match the settings at which the video clips were captured. If frame size, editing timebase, and the codec are mismatched between the sequence settings and the clip, the clip will have to be rendered before being played in the sequence.

Note that the Editing Timebase choice for frame rate will not be available if you already have some clips in the current sequence. You cannot alter the timebase of a sequence if you have clips in it.

Creating and deleting sequences

As mentioned earlier, you can have multiple sequences in a project. You can create new sequences for different parts of your program, or just to experiment with some edits, and then delete sequences that you don't plan to use. Creating sequences and deleting unwanted ones is easy:

✦ To create a new sequence, choose File ➪ New ➪ Sequence, or press Command+N.

✦ To delete a sequence, select the desired sequence in the Browser and press the Delete key on your keyboard. Alternatively, you can Control+click on the sequence in the Browser and choose Cut from the contextual menu.

Duplicating sequences

It is often necessary to duplicate a sequence in Final Cut Pro. You can duplicate sequences to create different versions of a program that may require different ending or minor variations for different clients. You can also use duplicate sequences to test out various edits. Some editors prefer to experiment with edits in their main sequence and just use the Undo command (Edit ➪ Undo or Command+Z) to get rid of edits they don't like. However, the undo feature can take up a lot of memory and slow down your system, especially if you set the levels of available "undos" to greater than 20.

Simply creating a duplicate sequence provides more editing freedom and keeps your system running efficiently. To duplicate a sequence:

1. **Select the sequence you want to duplicate in the Browser.**

2. **Choose Edit ➪ Duplicate, or press Option+D.**

   A copy of your sequence appears in the Browser with the word *copy* at the end of the original name.

3. **Rename the new sequence as you see fit.**

Dealing with multiple clip occurrences

Because clips in Final Cut Pro are not the actual media files that are captured to your scratch disk, but are only reference pointers to the media files, a clip can occur multiple times in a Project. Although this is a powerful and versatile aspect of nonlinear editing, the ability to have duplicate clips can be confusing and sometimes problematic. Luckily, Final Cut Pro has tools for helping you deal with multiple-use clips.

A clip brought into the project Browser for the first time, by either capturing or importing it, is called a *master clip*. When a master clip is used in a sequence or duplicated in the Browser an *affiliated* copy of the master clip is created. There is a relationship between a master clip and all clips affiliated with it. Changes made to certain properties of a master clip will automatically be reflected in all affiliated clips. Clip Name, Reel Number, or Timecode are properties that master and affiliated clips share. However, changes to the master clip's In and Out points, filters, and motion effects will not change in affiliated clips. This same relationship holds true in the reverse direction — changes made to shared properties of an affiliated clip automatically update its master clip and any other affiliated clips.

Master/affiliated clips are covered in detail in Chapter 8.

With multiple clips in your project, you have to be careful about which clip you're working on. If you want to change the original clip *(master clip)* in the Browser, be sure to double-click it in the Browser. If you want to modify a clip that is already in a sequence, called a *sequence clip,* then you need to double-click the occurrence of that clip in the sequence and not the Browser.

How can you tell if you have the master clip or the sequence clip loaded into the Viewer? There is a visual indicator in Final Cut Pro that marks this difference. Clips that are loaded from the Browser have a plain scrub area in the Viewer. Clips loaded from a sequence have a scrub area marked with a sprocket hole track on it. Figure 10-5 illustrates this difference.

Plain Scrub bar   Scrub bar with sprocket track

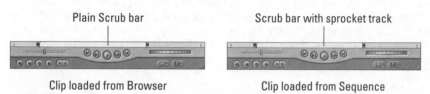

Clip loaded from Browser   Clip loaded from Sequence

Figure 10-5: Clips loaded into the Viewer from the Browser have a plain scrub bar. Clips loaded from a sequence have sprocket holes in the scrub bar.

But what about clips that appear more than once in the *same* sequence? This is critical for projects that are destined for film matchback with Cinema Tools, or output to an EDL (Edit Decision List) for tape-to-tape online finishing. To deal with this, Final Cut Pro now has Duplicate Frames indicators that flag you when a clip is reused in the same sequence. When a clip appears more than once in a sequence, a color bar is displayed across the bottom part of the clip in a sequence. Figure 10-6 shows a clip that is has been used more than once in the sequence and has a Duplicate Frames indicator.

Duplicate Frames indicator bar

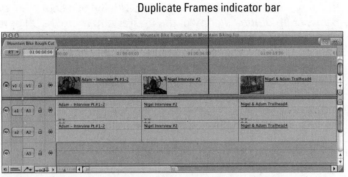

Figure 10-6: The Duplicate Frames indicator flags a clip that is being used more than once in the same sequence.

There are six different colors indicating the number of occurrences of the duplicate frames in the sequence: green, red, blue, white, black, and purple. You can set Duplicate Frames tolerances and handles in the General tab of User Preferences. Duplicate Frames indicators are enabled in the Timeline Options tab of User Preferences and Sequence Settings.

Note   If a duplicate clip in the Timeline has variable speed (Time Remap) applied to it, no Duplicate Frames indicator will appear.

If you Control+click on a clip with a Duplicate Frames indicator, you'll see in the submenu a list of all occurrences of duplicate frames. If you select an occurrence from the submenu, the sequence playhead will move to the first frame of the selected occurrence. Figure 10-7 shows a list of Duplicate Frames occurrences.

Figure 10-7: The contextual menu of a duplicate clip will show you a list of all other occurrences of the reused frames.

Performing Basic Edits

On the DVD-ROM

For this section, locate the Mountain Biking Tutorial folder on the DVD-ROM. Drag this folder to your drive. After it finishes copying, locate the Mountain Biking.fcp project file and double-click to open it in Final Cut Pro.

Throughout the early chapters of this book, you've found a lot of information on preparing yourself, your hardware, and Final Cut Pro for editing. Well, now it's time to actually start editing. One of the most basic editing tasks is placing clips in a sequence. The following steps describe how to do this using the Mountain Biking.fcp project from the DVD-ROM, but you can follow these steps using your own material as well:

1. **Open the Mountain Biking-Rough Cut sequence by double-clicking on it.**

   This sequence is located in the Exercises folder in the Mountain Biking.fcp project. The playhead should be automatically located at the beginning of the sequence. If not, press the Home key, located on the upper-right side of your keyboard, to bring the playhead back to the beginning of the sequence.

2. **Double-click the Adam - Interview Pt.#1 clip to load it into the Viewer.**

   This clip is located in the Adam Interview folder in the Mountain Biking.fcp project.

3. **Press the spacebar to play the clip.**

4. **Mark an In point just before Adam starts to say, "I like to eat grease . . ." by pressing the I key.**

   This point should be around 00:13:11;02 on this clip.

5. **Mark an Out point by pressing the O key after he finishes saying, " . . . because you need fluids."**

   This point should be around 00:13:16;22 on this clip.

6. **Drag the Adam - Interview Pt.#1 clip from the Viewer to the Canvas window by clicking and dragging on the image.**

7. **As you hold the clip over the Canvas window, you'll see the Edit Overlay controls appear over the Canvas window.**

   This overlay shows the type of edits that are possible. Hold the clip over the Overwrite overlay so that a red rectangle appears around the overlay as shown in Figure 10-8. Release the mouse button to drop the clip on the Overwrite.

   The Adam - Interview Pt.#1 clip now appears in the timeline starting at the point where the playhead was placed. The playhead will move to the end of this clip.

8. **Double-click the Nigel Interview #2 clip to load it into the Viewer.**

   This clip is located in the Nigel Interview folder.

9. **Press the spacebar to play the clip.**

10. **Mark an In point at 00:06:46;12 by pressing the I key.**

11. **Mark an Out point at 00:06:50;12 by pressing the O key.**

12. **Drag the Nigel Interview #2 clip from the Viewer to the Canvas window by clicking and dragging on the image.**

13. **Drop the clip on the Overwrite overlay, just as you did with the first clip.**

    The Nigel Interview #2 clip now appears in the timeline starting after the Adam - Interview Pt.#1 clip. The playhead's current location is used as the In point for the sequence. If you locate the playhead at another place, the new location will be used as the In point for the next incoming clip.

Cross-Reference Overwrite edits, as well as other types of edits, are described later in this chapter in the section "Understanding the Seven Types of Edits in Final Cut Pro."

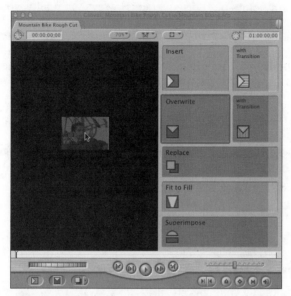

Figure 10-8: The Edit Overlay controls appear over the Canvas window when a clip is dragged from the Viewer to the Canvas.

14. **Make sure the Sequence window is selected, and then press the Home key on your keyboard to return the playhead to the beginning of the sequence.**

15. **Press the spacebar to play the sequence you've just created.**

Tip You aren't locked to the In and Out points you set in a clip after the clip is moved to the Timeline. Edit points for the clips can be extended in the Timeline by dragging the clip boundaries. Placing the pointer at the clip ends converts the pointer to a trim tool that allows you to extend the boundaries of the shots if the media is online.

Mastering three-point editing concepts

In the previous section, you performed what is known as a *three-point edit*. In an edit, there are technically *four* edit points to consider: The In and Out points on the source, and the In and Out points on the sequence. However, in reality, you just have to calculate any *three* of these points. Final Cut Pro calculates the fourth point for you. For instance, in the edit performed in the previous section, the In and Out points for the Adam - Interview Pt.#2 clip were set in the Viewer, and the third point, the sequence In point, was determined by the position of the playhead in the Timeline when the clip was dropped onto the Canvas. The sequence Out point was calculated automatically.

The rule to remember is that in the absence of a marked In or Out point in the sequence, the playhead's position is used as the In point. One exception to this is the Fit to Fill edit. The Fit to Fill edit in Final Cut Pro modifies the speed of the source clip to fit the In and Out points set in the sequence. For this type of edit you need to specify all four edit points.

Cross-Reference   Fit to fill type edits are covered later in this chapter.

Editing by setting points in the sequence

As described earlier, In and Out points for a clip can be set in the Viewer, and the sequence In point is usually determined by the playhead's position on the Timeline. You can also set editing points directly in the sequence. To set edit points in a sequence:

1. **Open the Mountain Biking-Rough Cut sequence in the Mountain Biking.fcp project used earlier in this chapter.**

   Delete any clips present in the sequence by selecting them (you can use Command+A to Select All) and pressing the Delete key on your keyboard.

2. **Drag the Adam - Interview Pt.# 1 clip (located in the Adam Interview folder) from the Browser directly into the Timeline.**

   Make sure there are no In or Out point points set on the clip. If there are, double-click the clip into the View window and press Option+X to remove any In or Out point.

3. **Press the spacebar to play the clip in the Timeline.**

4. **At the point after Adam says, " . . . because it's good, haha!" set an In point by pressing the I key.**

   An In point triangle will appear in the sequence in the time ruler area.

5. **Double-click the Adam-Gears2 clip (from the Adam Bike Text folder) to load it into the Viewer and select an In point at around 00:23:27;14.**

   Mark this point by pressing the I key. This point should be in the very beginning of this clip.

6. **Mark an Out point in the Adam-Gears2 clip at 23:31;18.**

   Press the O key to mark the Out point.

7. **Drag the Adam-Gears2 clip from the Viewer to the Canvas and drop it on the Overwrite overlay that appears when you hold the clip over the Canvas window.**

   The Adam-Gears2 overwrites the Adam - Interview Pt.#1 in the Timeline. Notice that the In point you set on the Adam-Gears2 lines up with the In point you marked in the sequence. The Out point you marked in the Adam-Gears2 is used as the Out point in the sequence. The In point that you marked in the sequence will automatically be erased.

The Three-Point Protocol

No, the Three-Point Protocol is not the name of a Robert Ludlum spy novel. Instead, it refers to the basic rules of three-point editing. Understanding and following these rules will serve you well:

✦ When no edit point has been set in the Viewer, the entire length of the clip will be used. The beginning of the clip will be considered the In point, and the end of the clip will be the Out point.

✦ If no edit point has been set in the sequence, then the location of the playhead will become the In point for the sequence.

✦ If you only set an In point for a clip in the Viewer, the end of the clip will be used as its Out point. In addition, if you only set an Out point for a clip in the Viewer, the clip's beginning will be used as the In point.

✦ When you only set an In point in the Canvas, the end of the incoming clip will be used as the Out point in the Canvas.

✦ If you only set an Out point in the sequence, Final Cut Pro will backtime the edit and match the Out point in the sequence with the Out point of the clip in the Viewer.

All of these rules have exceptions, of course. (What would a rule be without exceptions?)

✦ If you are doing a Replace edit, any edit points set in the Viewer are not used. Final Cut Pro simply uses the current clip in the Timeline (over which your playhead is located) as the In and Out points for replacement.

✦ Fit to Fill edits, which modify the speed of the shot, require all four points.

✦ When you drag a clip directly from the Viewer into the Timeline, any points set in the sequence are ignored.

Understanding the Seven Types of Edits in Final Cut Pro

Quite unlike the seven deadly sins are the seven major types of edits you can perform in Final Cut Pro. The two most common types of edits you will perform will be the Insert and the Overwrite edits. However, the other five edit types have their place as well. Some of these edits are actually lifesavers in certain tight situations. The seven edit types in Final Cut Pro are:

✦ **Overwrite:** This is the default edit type in Final Cut Pro. When you drag a clip from the Viewer into the Canvas, the Overwrite overlay will be highlighted by default. When you make an overwrite edit, any clips that may be in the video track you are editing onto will be overwritten by the incoming clip. Figure 10-9 shows an Overwrite edit.

Shots 1, 2, and 3 in the Timeline before edit

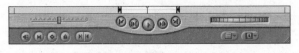

Shot 4 in the Viewer   Overwrite edit

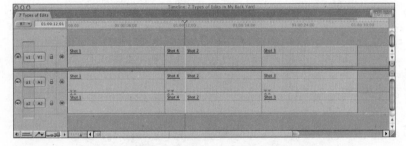

Shots 1, 2, and 3 in the Timeline after Overwrite edit

Figure 10-9: Overwrite edits appear in the Timeline as shown here.

In Figure 10-9, Shots 1, 2, and 3, which are of equal duration, are in the Timeline. The playhead positioned between Shots 1 and 2 indicates the In point in the sequence for the next incoming clip. When Shot 4 (which is shorter in duration) is edited into the sequence using an Overwrite edit, it replaces a portion of Shot 2 equal to the duration of Shot 4.

✦ **Overwrite with Transition:** This is the same as the regular Overwrite edit except that it adds a default transition between the source clip and the clip before it in the Timeline. Figure 10-10 shows an Overwrite with Transition edit.

When first installed, Final Cut Pro uses Cross Dissolve as the default transition. You can change this by selecting a different transition in the Effects tab and choosing Effects ➪ Set Default. The new default transition will be underlined in the Effects tab.

Shots 1, 2, and 3 in the Timeline before edit

Shot 4 in the Viewer

Overwrite with transition edit

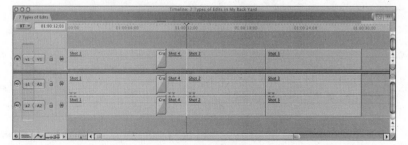

Shots 1, 2, 3, and 4 in the Timeline after Overwrite with transition edit

Figure 10-10: An Overwrite with Transition edit adds a transition between the incoming clip and the clip just before it.

✦ **Insert:** With an insert edit, all clips in the Timeline get cut at the In point in the sequence and moved forward by the length of the incoming clip. Figure 10-11 shows an Insert edit.

✦ **Insert with Transition:** This is the same as an Insert edit, except that it adds a default transition between the source clip and the clip just before it in the timeline. Figure 10-12 shows an Insert with Transition edit.

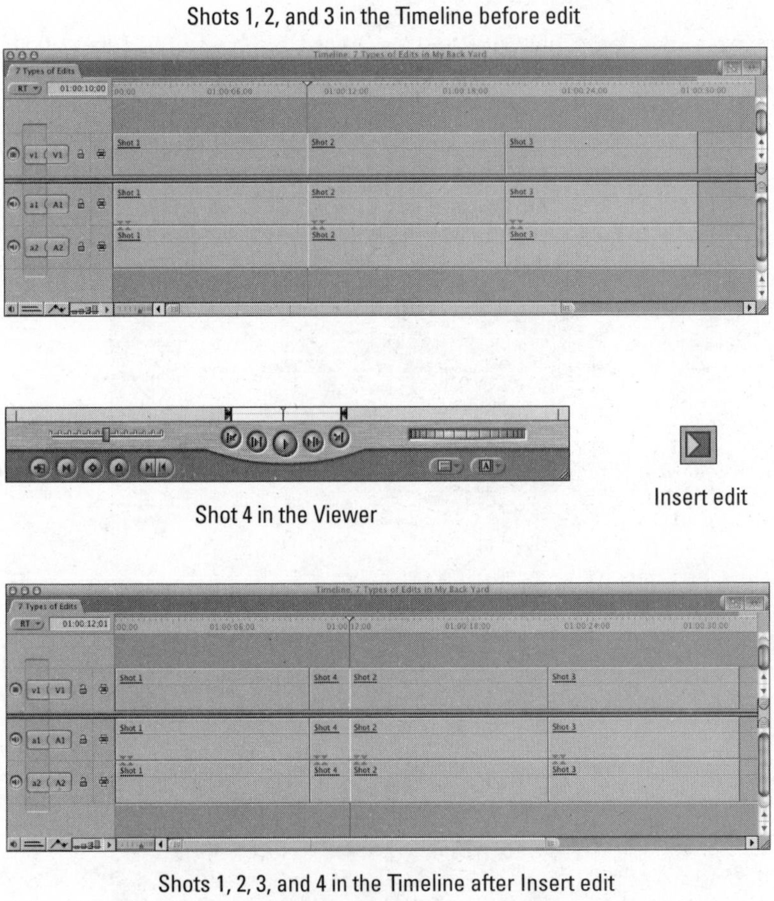

Shots 1, 2, and 3 in the Timeline before edit

Shot 4 in the Viewer

Insert edit

Shots 1, 2, 3, and 4 in the Timeline after Insert edit

Figure 10-11: An Insert edit cuts the clips at the edit point and moves them forward by the length of the incoming clip.

Shots 1, 2, and 3 in the Timeline before edit

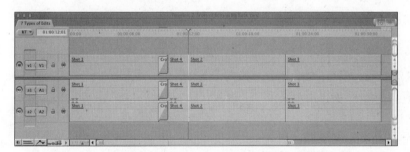

Shot 4 in the Viewer

Insert with
transition edit

Shots 1, 2, 3, and 4 in the Timeline after Insert with transition edit

Figure 10-12: An Insert with Transition edit is like an Insert edit, except that it also adds a transition between the incoming clip and the clip before it.

✦ **Replace:** In a Replace edit, the incoming clip will replace the clip currently in the sequence. However, it will do so by matching the position of the playhead in the Viewer with the position of the playhead in the sequence. This means that the frame of the playhead position in the Viewer is matched to the frame of the playhead in the Timeline. A Replace edit ignores any In or Out points set in the Viewer. Instead, it uses the limits of the clip in the sequence upon which you placed the playhead. Figure 10-13 shows a Replace edit.

Shots 1, 2, and 3 in the Timeline before edit

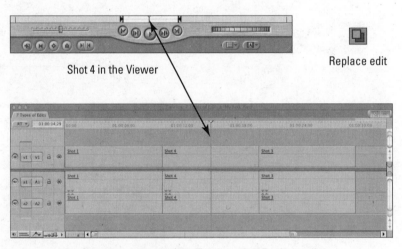

Shot 4 in the Viewer

Replace edit

Shots 1, 2, 3, and 4 in the Timeline after Replace edit

Figure 10-13: A Replace edit replaces the clip in the Sequence with the clip in the Viewer by matching the current frame in the Viewer to the current frame in the Timeline.

The Replace edit is an extremely useful edit for matching shots to underlying audio tracks. For example, if the underlying audio clip uses a word that you want to match with the video, you can line up the playhead above the audio phrase in the sequence, call up the video clip in the Viewer, and move the playhead in the Viewer to the desired video frame. At this point, making a Replace edit will replace the video clip in the Timeline with the clip from the Viewer by precisely matching the frames.

Tip

The source clip in the Viewer must have enough media both before and after the matched frame where the playhead sits to replace all the media before and after the matched frame of the clip to be replaced in the Timeline. If there aren't enough frames, you will see an error message: "Insufficient content for edit."

✦ **Fit to Fill:** This is the one type of edit that requires all four edit points. This edit requires In and Out points in the Viewer as well as In and Out points in the sequence. In absence of an In point, Final Cut Pro assumes that you want to replace the clip over which the playhead is currently parked.

When you perform a Fit to Fill edit, the Viewer clip is slowed down or sped up to fill the space in the sequence. A red bar appears over the clip if it needs to be rendered, and the speed change percentage will be shown next to the clip's name in the sequence. Figure 10-14 shows a Replace edit. In this figure there are no In or Out points set in the sequence. Final Cut Pro thus assumes that I want to replace the clip over which the playhead is parked (the playhead is on the first frame of Shot 2). Shot 2 is thus replaced with the incoming Shot 4 by automatically extending or reducing the duration of Shot 4 to fit the space left by Shot 2. Here Shot 4 is slowed down to 21 percent in order to fill the space.

✦ **Superimpose:** This edits the video and the audio above and below the specified points in the sequence. The Superimpose edit is used for laying video tracks in layers to prepare for multilayering effects. Figure 10-15 shows a Superimpose edit.

The Superimpose command will place the source media above and below the selected destination tracks, creating additional tracks if none are there, and moving any existing clips to a higher track to make room. A small tip when using Superimpose is setting an In point in the Timeline where you want the new clip to start before using the Superimpose command. This is shown in the first Timeline in Figure 10-15. If there is no In point set, the duration of the clip beneath the playhead is used and is the minimum amount of media needed from the source clip for the Superimpose to work. This doesn't work for superimposing clips *after* the edit point of the lower track. Alternately, you can drag the clip from the Viewer into the Timeline and drop it in the track above your destination track. If you drop the clip in the area above the tracks where there are no tracks currently, new tracks will automatically be made for the clip.

Shots 1, 2, and 3 in the Timeline before edit

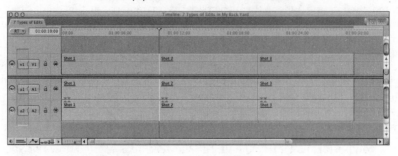

Shot 4 in the Viewer   Fit to Fill edit

Speed change is indicated in the percentage

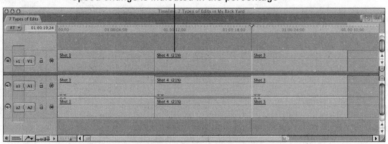

Shots 1, 3, and 4 in the Timeline after Fit to Fill edit

Figure 10-14: A Fit to Fill edit requires four edit points.

Shots 1, 2, and 3 in the Timeline before edit

Shot 4 in the Viewer

Superimpose edit

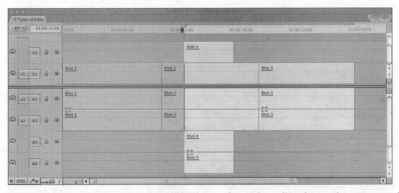

Figure 10-15: A Superimpose edit places the video clip above the current clip in the sequence and places the new audio tracks below the current audio tracks.

The three ways to skin a cat

They say there is more than one way to skin a cat. Despite the macabre image that flashes through my head every time I hear that, I have to agree with the general idea of that wise utterance. Leaving my feline friend Toby aside for the moment, there are at least three ways to perform all seven types of edits in Final Cut Pro:

Continued

Continued

✦ **Use the Edit Overlay Controls:** When you drag a clip onto the Canvas window the Edit Overlay controls appear. Dropping your clip on any of the seven edit types in the controls will perform the desired edit for you. Remember that you can drag more than one clip at a time directly from the Browser.

✦ **Use the Edit buttons:** There are three edit buttons located at the bottom left of the Canvas window, as shown in the following figure. While a clip is loaded in the Viewer, you can either click any of these edit buttons, or drag a clip from the Viewer or the Browser onto one of these edit buttons. The last of these three buttons is customizable. Click and hold on the small arrow to the right of the third button to get additional choices of edit types. Select one of these choices to change the edit type for the third button.

Tip   Don't forget, you can also assign these Edit buttons commands — any Final Cut Pro menu command, in fact — to customized shortcut buttons that can then be added to the menu bar at the top of all main application windows. For more details about creating shortcut buttons, see Appendix B.

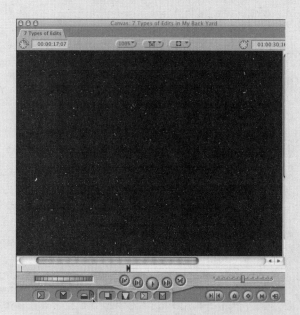

✦ **Use Keyboard Shortcuts:** This is the fastest way to perform edits. Each of the seven edit types has a corresponding keyboard shortcut. Use the following shortcuts to perform the edits:

Edit Type	Keyboard Shortcut
Insert	F9
Insert with Transition	Shift+F9
Overwrite	F10
Overwrite with Transition	Shift+F10
Replace	F11
Fit to Fill	Shift+F11
Superimpose	F12

Personally, I can never remember the keyboard shortcuts for all the seven types of edits. Some of them are just too much alike. If you have the same problem, float your cursor over one of the edit buttons for a moment to bring up the ToolTip. The ToolTip (see the following figure) is a small yellow box that shows the type of edit and its keyboard shortcut.

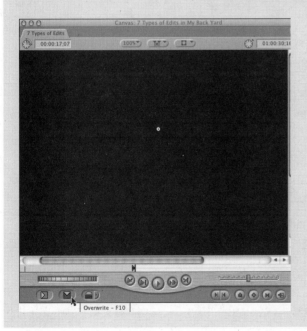

Working with Target Tracks

On the DVD-ROM   For this section, locate the Mountain Biking Tutorial folder on the DVD-ROM. Drag this folder to your drive. After it finishes copying, locate the Mountain Biking.fcp project file and double-click to open it in Final Cut Pro.

A clip generally consists of one video track and two audio tracks. However, when you edit a clip into the Timeline, you may not want all these source tracks. For example, you may want to edit the video portion of a clip into the Timeline and omit the audio portion. The tracks in the Timeline that you want to edit your clips into are *target tracks*. The tracks from the clip you are editing into the Timeline are called *source tracks*. Assigning the destination of source tracks to target tracks in the Timeline is done in with the Source and Destination controls located in the patch panel on the left side of the Timeline window. These controls are shown in Figure 10-16.

Source control buttons

Destination control buttons

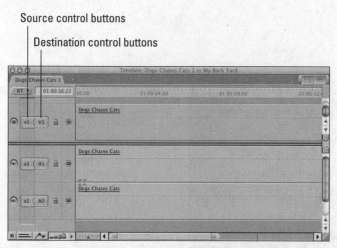

Figure 10-16: Source and destination controls determine which tracks from a clip are edited into the Timeline.

To select a target track, do one of the following:

✦ **Click on a track's destination control button.** The nearest source track will jump to that track.

✦ **Option+click on a track destination control button.** This will select the nearest source track below the selected target track.

✦ **Click and drag a source control button to the desired target track destination.**

When you select a target track, make sure the source and destination control buttons are joined together. Track targeting can be turned off when you want only certain tracks of a clip edited into a Timeline. For example, you might want to edit in just the audio tracks of a clip with no video. You can toggle this control on or off by clicking on a target track's destination control button. The Source and Destination control buttons will appear open if the track targeting is off (assigned) or closed if track targeting is on (assigned). As you would expect, this works identically for audio track targeting. Figure 10-17 shows the track targeting turned off for video track V1, but left on for audio tracks A1 and A2.

Note   You might be wondering how Final Cut Pro's new feature of Auto Select affects targeting tracks when adding clips to a Timeline. It does not come into play here because, as its name suggests, it is a tool for *selecting* clips already in the Timeline.

Cross-Reference   Auto Select is covered in Chapter 11.

Open control buttons indicate track targeting is off

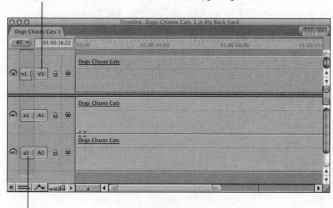

Closed control buttons indicate track targeting is on

Figure 10-17: Track targeting using the Source and Destination controls can be turned off when you want to add only video or audio portions of a clip. Track targeting for V1 is turned off, while audio tracks A1 and A2 remain assigned.

The number of Source controls that appear in the Timeline patch panel area is automatically matched to the number of tracks contained by the clip currently loaded into the Viewer. For instance, if the video clip in the Viewer is linked to four audio tracks, then four Source controls will appear in the Timeline opposite of the track Destination controls.

Note   Final Cut Pro 4 allows you to link up to 1 video and 24 audio items in the Timeline. Linking clips are covered in Chapter 11.

Target track assignments remain active until you reassign them or deactivate them. To perform an edit on specific target tracks:

1. **Double-click the Nigel Interview #2-4 clip (located in the Nigel Interview folder) to load it into the Viewer.**

2. **Create an In point just before Nigel starts saying ". . . I also do a check" (around 00:07:41;16) and create an Out point after he says, ". . . slip on me" (around 00:07:50;06.)**

   You can use the I key to mark an In point and the O key to mark an Out point.

3. **Double-click the Mountain Biking-Rough Cut sequence to open it and press the Home key to bring the playhead to the beginning of the sequence.**

   Delete any clips present in the sequence by using Command+A to select them and then pressing the Delete key.

4. **Press the F10 key to make an Overwrite edit into the Timeline.**

5. **Now play the clip in the Timeline.**

6. **After Nigel says, "I also do a check through on the shifting . . . " stop the playback by pressing the spacebar.**

7. **Press the I key to mark an In point in the sequence.**

   This spot will function as your In point for the next edit. The location of the playhead does not matter when you have specified an In point in the sequence.

8. **Double-click the Nigel-GearChanges clip into the Viewer.**

9. **Mark an In point at 00:16:50;28, where you can see the gears shift as Nigel tests his bike, and then mark an Out point around 00:16:55;00.**

   The Nigel-GearChanges clip has both audio and video, but we just want to edit its video track into the Timeline over the remainder of Adam's sentence.

10. **In the Mountain Biking-Rough Cut, click the source or destination control button of audio tracks A1 and A2 to toggle them to the disconnected state.**

    Now the only active target track is the video track, V1. This is indicated by V1 having the only source and destination controls joined.

11. **Press the F10 key to perform an Overwrite edit.**

Note   It is a common oversight to leave target tracks off and then wonder why some of the tracks from an edited clip do not appear in the Timeline. Double-check to make sure all desired tracks are selected as target tracks *and* that their source and destination controls are not disconnected.

The *Nigel-GearChanges* clip will overwrite the video portion of Nigel's dialog for a few seconds, but his audio will be heard under the *Nigel-GearChanges* clip. When the *Nigel-GearChanges* clip finishes in the Timeline, you will go back to Nigel to hear him finish his sentence. Be sure to turn the audio tracks in *Mountain Biking-Rough Cut* back on as target tracks after you've made the edit. This way the next clip will have both its audio and video edited into the sequence.

Note If you want to maintain the audio and video for both clips, Control+click in the blank gray area below A2 audio track and select Add Track from the contextual menu. Add two more tracks using this method. These will be labeled A3 and A4. Then perform Steps 7 through 10, except choose A3 and A4 as your audio target tracks.

Tip To move your playhead from edit to edit in the sequence, use the Up and Down arrow keys on your keyboard. The Up and Down arrow keys move you backward or forward in the sequence, skipping along edit points.

Working with Storyboards

The Browser window has four views. These views are List view, Small Icon view, Medium Icon view, and Large Icon view. These views can be selected by choosing View ➪ Browser Items and selecting the appropriate view from the submenu that appears. In the Large or Medium Icon view, a large thumbnail of the video, also called the *poster frame,* represents the clips. This poster frame is usually the first frame of the video, but it can be changed to be any frame in the clip.

Tip To set a poster frame, make sure that you have selected View ➪ Browser Items ➪ As Large Icons (or Medium Icons). To load any clip into the Viewer, locate a frame you would like to use as a poster frame and select Mark ➪ Set Poster Frame (Control+P).

You can make a storyboard of your clips by arranging them in a sequential order in the Browser. Set the view in the Browser to Large or Medium Icons by choosing View ➪ Browser Items ➪ As Large Icons, and then arrange your clips in the desired order. The poster frames of each clip will serve as a storyboard for your sequence. If you then select all your clips and drag them into a sequence, they will be inserted in the sequence in the order (left-to-right and top-to-bottom) that they were arranged in the browser. This can be very useful for quickly creating a rough cut for your edit for later refinement.

Troubleshooting Early Editing Problems

When you begin editing in Final Cut Pro, there are a couple of common problems you might run into. Offline clips can cause a great deal of confusion if you aren't careful about preserving media files used by your projects. Other common problems include poor playback quality and clips that have a different format from the rest of your sequence. The next two sections look at these two potential problems.

Fixing mismatched clips and sequences

One of the more common problems you'll encounter as you start editing in Final Cut Pro is that some of your clips may have a red line appear along the top of the clip, as shown in Figure 10-18. This red line commonly appears over transitions when they need to be rendered. It also appears over clips if any effects or filters have been applied to them that require rendering. However, when a clip is simply edited into a sequence and this red line appears, it generally means there's a conflict between the clip and the sequence, which you should resolve. If you see the red line, you should stop right there and troubleshoot the problem before you do any more work. (I use the red render color here to mean any color render bar — the main idea is that there should be *no* rendering required for clips that match sequence settings.)

Render line will appear across the length of the clip

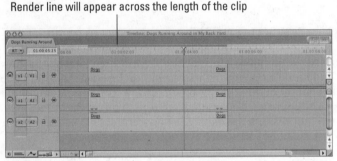

Figure 10-18: A red line above a clip you just edited into the timeline may indicate a settings conflict between the clip and the sequence.

When a render bar appears over a clip that you've just edited into the Timeline, it usually indicates a mismatch between the settings of the clip and the settings you are using for the sequence. To fix this problem:

1. **Select the clip in the Browser and choose Tools ➪ Analyze ➪ Clip.**

   You will see a short Movie Analysis report showing some of the settings for the clip. Figure 10-19 shows this report.

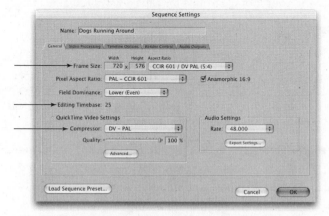

```
000                  Movie Analysis for Dogs
Filename: Dogs
Duration: 00:00:04;11
Average Data Rate: 3700k/sec
Audio Shape: Stereo

Video Track 1 (15.0 MB)
  Duration: 00:00:04;11
→ Frame Size: 720 x 480
  Color Depth: 24-bit Color
→ Codec: DV - NTSC at Most Quality
→ Frame Rate: 29.97 fps
  Average Data Rate: 3512k/sec (117k/frame)

Audio Track 1 (Stereo, 819.6 K)
  Duration: 00:00:04;11
  Average Data Rate: 188k/sec
  Format: 16-bit, Stereo
  Sampling Rate: 48.000 khz

Timecode Track Source TC
  Timecode: 00:19:11;27
  Reel: 4
```

Figure 10-19: The Movie Analysis report presents critical information about a clip.

2. **Note the Frame Size, Codec, and Frame Rate for the clip from the Movie Analysis report.**

   Move the Movie Analysis report to the right side of your display monitor to make room for the next window.

3. **Highlight the sequence in the Browser and choose Sequence ⇨ Settings.**

   The Sequence Settings dialog box appears, as shown in Figure 10-20. Compare the settings in this dialog box with the displayed settings in the Movie Analysis report for your clip.

Figure 10-20: The Sequence Settings dialog shows settings for your sequence.

In the General tab of the Sequence Settings window, the following items should match your clip settings:

✦ **Frame Size:** Make sure the clip was captured at the same frame size that is being used in the sequence. If they are not the same, change the frame size for the sequence.

✦ **Frame Rate:** Match the Editing Timebase of the sequence with the clip's frame rate. All NTSC video is 29.97 fps, whereas the sequence's Editing Timebase may be set to 30 fps or a number other than your clip's frame rate. Note that you will *not* be able to change the Editing Timebase of a sequence if it contains a clip. Delete any clips from the sequence and adjust the Editing Timebase.

✦ **Compressor:** Make sure that the sequence and the clip use the same compression scheme (codec). If not, change the sequence's codec setting.

Note   Changing settings in the Sequence Settings dialog box will only affect the settings for the current sequence. To change the settings for all future sequences you create, choose Final Cut Pro ➪ Audio/Video Settings and change your Sequence Preset selection or create a new preset.

Forcing high-quality display for DV footage

One other common problem you may run into deals with DV video clips. At times, they may look a little "soft" on your computer monitor. Playback quality will vary depending on the speed of the computer you are using. A faster machine such as a newer, dual-processor G4 or one of the new blazing-fast G5s will have better display quality than an older, slower single-processor G4, for instance. Fortunately, this is merely a *display* issue. Your footage from a DV tape always remains at best quality, and when you view it on an external video monitor you will see the best video quality at all times.

It is possible to force Final Cut Pro to always display DV video at the highest quality, although doing so can appreciatively affect the performance of Final Cut Pro. While you will get better quality playback on your computer, you may experience other playback problems such as dropped frames or fewer real-time effects without rendering. To force high-quality playback:

1. **Click on the Real-Time Effects (RT) pop-up menu in the upper-left corner of your sequence.**

   Figure 10-21 shows the RT pop-up menu.

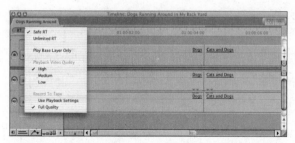

Figure 10-21: The Real-Time Effects (RT) pop-up menu is used to set a sequences display quality and output resolution.

2. Select High under the Video Playback Quality category.

This option forces Final Cut Pro to play back all clips at full resolution, full frame with video interlacing preserved. This also means, fewer real-time effects will be available without needing to render them first.

3. Click on the Real-Time Effects (RT) pop-up menu again and deselect Unlimited RT.

This is the same as selecting Safe RT, if this option is available. Safe RT makes sure your sequence plays smoothly without dropping frames, again at the expense of fewer real-time effects than can be played without rendering.

Note   Settings in the Real-Time pop-up menu are also in the Playback Control tab in the System Settings window and are system-wide settings that affect all sequences opened on this computer.

Cross-Reference   More options regarding real-time rendering are covered in Chapter 18.

Again, while it is possible to force high-quality playback on your computer monitor, a better solution is to use an external video monitor connected to the Video Out port on your video card, deck, or camera. To enable external video in Final Cut Pro, choose View ➪ External Video ➪ All Frames. Figure 10-22 shows the menu options. The External Video menu options are only going to be available if the Playback Options are selected in the A/V Devices in the Audio/Video Settings panel.

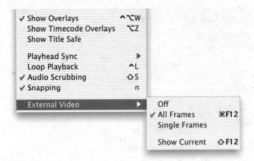

Figure 10-22: You must select All Frames from the menu View ➪ External Video to see playback on your external monitor.

When you have external video enabled, Final Cut Pro will sacrifice playback quality on your computer monitor when memory and CPU resources are strained in order to preserve playback quality on the external monitor. Frame rate and quality may be reduced to maintain the integrity of playback on the external monitor.

Caution

When working with a DV-based setup and an external monitor, enabling External Video to view All Frames disables audio output to the computer speakers. You will only be able to hear the audio through your DV device, camera, or other external playback device that is hooked up to your computer. Final Cut Pro is designed so that audio playing from a DV device will sync up *only* with video playing from the same device. If you watch the DV video on the computer monitor but listen to the sound coming from the DV camera, you will notice a sync offset. This does not mean your footage is out of sync but is due to the time difference between Final Cut Pro playback and that of the preview video stream sent over FireWire, into your deck and out to the display monitor. You should only preview your audio and video from the same monitor device.

✦   ✦   ✦

Editing in the Timeline

The previous chapter covered the "party line" on editing in Final Cut Pro. The workflow outlined in the previous chapter works just fine when you are learning the basics of a program and performing simple, "by the book" edits.

However, editing in the real world is rarely done "by the book." Editing in the real world often occurs in less-than-ideal situations and with severe time constraints. Although many stages are involved in the editing process, the basic steps remain the same as described in Chapter 10: Grab a clip, mark In and Out points, and drop the clip in a sequence. These are the steps you will repeat thousands of times when editing. The true measure of an editing system is its ability to perform these very steps in the fastest and least tedious way possible. One test of a productive editing program is its ability to perform quick, efficient work within the Timeline. Final Cut Pro passes this test with flying colors.

As Final Cut Pro has gained popularity over the past few years, I have talked to many editors who have migrated from other editing. When asked their opinion about Final Cut Pro, nearly every editor had a pet peeve or two about this program, however, almost all of them agreed on one point: When it comes to working in the editing interface, there is no equal to Final Cut Pro. Its interface allows flexibility and speed unparalleled by any other editing system. Many of Final Cut Pro 4.0's new features further enhance workflow in the Timeline with customizable interface setups, as well as new tools. This chapter introduces you to editing in the Timeline, a skill you will use almost every time you edit in Final Cut Pro.

Editing in the Timeline

A Timeline appears when you double-click a sequence in the Browser. A Timeline is where you arrange all your shots, transitions, and audio clips. Each sequence has its own tab in the Timeline, and you can switch to a different sequence by clicking on the appropriate tab. Timelines have video and audio tracks where you arrange video and audio clips. Each Timeline has an accompanying Canvas window where you can see video played from the Timeline. Figure 11-1 shows a few details of a Timeline.

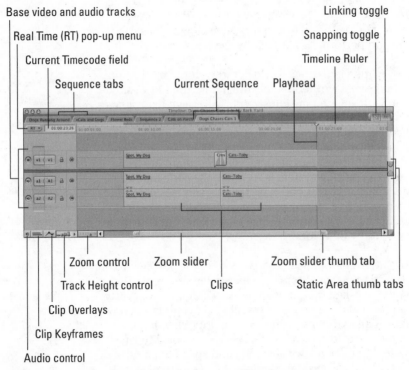

Base video and audio tracks

Real Time (RT) pop-up menu

Current Timecode field

Sequence tabs

Current Sequence   Playhead

Linking toggle

Snapping toggle

Timeline Ruler

Zoom control   Zoom slider

Track Height control   Clips

Zoom slider thumb tab

Static Area thumb tabs

Clip Overlays

Clip Keyframes

Audio control

Figure 11-1: A Timeline window has many editing features.

Mastering the details of the Timeline

Timelines have richly detailed interfaces (refer to Figure 11-1). Various features of Timelines are covered throughout this chapter as well as this entire book, but a few key features common to most Timelines include the following:

✦ **Current sequence:** Displays in the Timeline window's title bar the name of the currently active sequence.

✦ **Project name:** Indicates in the Timeline window's title bar the name of the project that contains the currently active sequence.

✦ **Base video and audio tracks:** Video and audio tracks are separated by a center divider. Above the divider are the video tracks and below are the audio tracks. By default, sequences appear with one video and two audio tracks. You can change this by choosing Final Cut Pro ⇨ User Preferences (Option + Q), and in the Timeline Options tab changing the Default Number of Tracks setting.

✦ **Clips:** Each clip looks like a colored bar in the tracks. The colors indicate various states of a clip. If a clip has audio and video, the clip's audio tracks will lie in the audio base tracks. To display additional details with each clip, choose Final Cut Pro ⇨ User Preferences (Option + Q), and then choose the Timeline Options tab to set additional view options.

✦ **Sequence tabs:** All open sequences have their own tabs. Click on a tab to make that sequence active. Corresponding tabs also appear in the Canvas window.

✦ **Playhead:** This indicates the current frame in the Timeline. The playhead in the Timeline is synchronized and locked with the playhead in the Canvas window.

✦ **Current timecode display:** This display always shows the timecode at the current position of the playhead. This is the timecode of the Timeline, not the timecode of individual clips.

✦ **Real Time (RT) pop-up menu:** Here you choose the playback quality of real-time effects. Selecting various options here allows you to determine if you would rather favor high image quality playback over the amount of real-time effects that can be played, or alternatively, view more real-time effects at the expense of the visual quality of the playback.

✦ **Track visibility control:** Click on this to toggle a track's visibility on or off. If a track's visibility is off, it will not be displayed in the canvas, external monitor, nor will it be rendered or output to tape with the sequence.

Caution

Turning off a track's visibility will sever the connection of any render files to the clips on that track. Turning the track's visibility back on will not restore the render files. Thankfully, using the Undo command (Command+Z) will restore previous renders.

✦ **Mute and Solo control:** These buttons toggle on or off the audio playback of audio tracks. These controls affect only monitoring and will not disable audio when a sequence is output to tape or exported as a movie. To disable an audio track from output, turn off the track's visibility. By default, these controls are hidden, but they can be displayed when the Audio Control button is clicked on.

✦ **Source and Destination control:** Source and Destination control are used for assigning, or targeting, the tracks from an incoming (source) clip to the desired tracks in the Timeline (destination). The number of Source controls is automatically matched to the number of tracks in the source clip currently loaded into the Viewer.

✦ **Auto Select control:** This control is used to select tracks for editing using In and Out points in the Timeline. Note that whereas the Source and Destination control are used for targeting clips to be edited *into* the Timeline, the Auto Select control enables the editing of sequence clips on selected tracks that are *already* in the Timeline.

✦ **Zoom slider:** This slider provides an odd but very smart way of controlling the zoom setting of the Timeline. Drag the thumb tabs on the side to adjust the zoom setting, then drag the center of this slider to move around the Timeline. After you get the hang of the zoom slider, you'll love it.

✦ **Zoom control:** Click on the various increments to find an appropriate zoom setting for the Timeline, or slide the zoom control pointer.

✦ **Audio Controls:** Click on this button to display the mute and solo buttons of each track. By default, these controls are hidden.

✦ **Clip Keyframes Control:** This indicator toggles an additional area in the Timeline below each video and audio track. There are four additional controls available.

   • **Filter bars:** If any filters have been applied to the clip, a green bar will appear at the top of this space. Black, diamond-shaped keyframe indicators appear if you have added any keyframes.

   • **Motion bars:** If any Motion effects have been applied to the clip, a blue bar will appear just below the filter bar. Black, diamond-shaped keyframe indicators appear if you have added any keyframes. Because audio portions of clips cannot have motion effects (like scale or position, for example), the motion bar will only show in video tracks.

   • **Keyframe editor:** The Keyframe Editor is a graph of the keyframes for motion or filter effects. It is identical to the keyframe graph found in a clip's motion and filter tab in the Viewer. The Keyframe editor allows you to edit keyframes with the pen and selection tools directly in the Timeline; however, only one keyframe graph can be displayed at a time. To select a parameter to edit, Control+click anywhere in the Keyframe editor space and select a parameter from the contextual menu.

   • **Speed indicator:** Speed indicators display the speed of clips in the sequence using tic marks. The spacing and color of the tic marks represent the speed and direction of playback of the clip. There is no user control for this indicator. See Chapter 17 for more about changing the speed of a clip.

✦ **Clip Overlays Control:** Clicking on this indicator adds two overlay lines to your clips. It adds a black line over the video section of clips, indicating opacity of the clips' images, and a red line over the audio section of clips indicating volume levels of the audio. Both of these lines can be edited in the Timeline.

✦ **Track layout menu:** This menu allows you to select track heights and track display options, and save and load custom track layouts. These settings can also be accessed in the Timeline Options tab of the Sequence Settings window.

✦ **Track Height Control:** Clicking on the bar icons allows you to select various track heights for the video and audio tracks. The size that is currently being used is indicated with blue. When selecting track height this way, all track heights are reset and any custom track height that was previously set is overridden. If you want to keep the relative track height of individually sized tracks while resizing, press the Option key while choosing a new height with this control. The height settings are called Reduce, Small, Medium, and Large. When using the Reduced track size, thumbnails and waveforms cannot be displayed.

✦ **Snapping toggle:** Click this button to turn the Snapping toggle on or off. Snapping is when clips and other items "snap" to important areas such as In or Out points of a clip or the playhead. Clips will snap to these locations when you drag them using the mouse. The Snapping toggle is a handy control because it enables quick and easy placement of clips next to each other without accidentally overlapping them and overwriting frames, or leaving a gap between clips. If the Snapping button is green, then Snapping is on, and if it's gray, then it's off. Be forewarned, the button is very small, and with the muted color palette of OS X graphics, now it's even more difficult to see than in earlier versions.

✦ **Link toggle:** This control turns Linked Selection on and off. When turned on, a clip that has synchronized video and audio tracks will work as one clip in the Timeline. If you click and drag the clip, all synchronized tracks will be selected and moved. With the Linked Selection toggle off, each track will be separate. This indicator is a green chain link when Linked Selection is on and gray when Linked Selection is off. Like the Snapping toggle, the Link toggle is very tiny (see Figure 11-2) and can be a challenge to see. In general, you should keep linking on to make sure your audio and video remain linked and in sync.

I should point out that I don't like the implementation of this feature because it turns the linking on and off *for all the clips in a sequence.* That is rarely necessary, and in a complex sequence it can cause some serious problems. The sidebar "Links that bite" later in this chapter describes some of the problems that unlinking all clips in a sequence can cause.

Snapping toggle

Link toggle

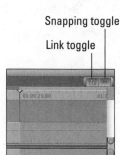

Figure 11-2: Although small, the Link and Snapping toggles will indicate if On or Off. Both Link and Snapping toggles are shown in the On state.

Links that bite

Split edits are edits in which the In or Out points for the video and audio tracks are in different positions. This is a very common editing technique and is frequently used when editing dialog. Person A starts talking on camera, and we continue to play Person A's voice while we cut to video of Person B.

To achieve a split edit, editors often turn the Linking between synchronized audio and video off to be able to trim the audio or video tracks independently. They unlink the tracks by clicking the Link toggle to turn it off. However, when you turn off the Link toggle, it unlinks every clip in the sequence, which is rarely what the editor has in mind.

The Option shortcut provides a more efficient, trouble-free way to achieve a split edit. If you hold down the Option key and drag-trim the video track, only the video track will be trimmed for a linked clip. The Option+drag-trim method works for trimming audio tracks as well.

Note: When you place your pointer at the edge of a clip in a Timeline, the pointer turns into a Trim tool. Use this Trim tool you can interactively trim the In or Out point of a clip in the Timeline.

Another fast way to unlink the video and audio tracks of a clip is to select the clip and press Command+L. This unlinks the video from the audio tracks, but only for that clip, not for the entire sequence. Note that if the audio portion of the clip was captured as Channel 1 and Channel 2, then the audio clips are also unlinked from one another. The following figure shows what a clip looks like when its video track is unlinked from its audio track. The clip name in the video track is no longer underlined when unlinked from the audio tracks.

Audio clips that are captured as a stereo pair have two pairs of triangles, which indicate linked audio clips. Clips that are captured as Channel 1 and Channel 2 do not have these indicators. If you need to unlink stereo audio tracks from one another, select the audio tracks and press Option+L to unlink the audio tracks from one another. The triangle indicators will disappear as shown in the following figure.

 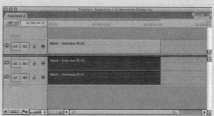

Keep in mind that if you unlink tracks and move one track in relation to the clip's other tracks, the clip will be out of sync. You will see red rectangles on out-of-sync clips showing you the number of frames by which the tracks are out of sync with one another, as shown in the following figure.

If a track is ahead of its related sync track a + (plus sign) appears. If the track is behind its related sync track a – (minus sign) appears. Control+click on the red sync marker to view choices for resyncing:

✦ **Move into Sync:** Moves the selected track back in sync, if there is space in the track.

✦ **Slip into Sync:** This choice does not move the physical relationship of the tracks that are out of sync. Instead, it *slips* the clip back in sync if there is enough media to accommodate this.

Understanding item colors in the Timeline

Clips in the Timeline are color-coded based on their function and state. It is helpful to know what these clip colors indicate because the colors can tell you a lot about a clip with just a quick glance. Colors you will find in the Timeline include:

✦ **Cyan:** Video clips

✦ **Green:** Audio clips

✦ **White:** Offline clips

✦ **Half light grey and half dark gray:** Transitions

✦ **Aquamarine:** Video graphics

✦ **Purple:** Video sequences (Yes! You can have sequences within sequences.)

✦ **Light green:** Audio sequences

Note You can color-code any clip in a sequence. To do this Control+click on a clip to bring up a contextual menu, choose Logging Info from the Item Properties sub-menu, and Control+click on the Label 1 field to see and select from a list of labeling options. Labels in this menu have their own unique colors; however, these colors only show up around the clip's name and thumbnail, *not the entire clip.* Because of the new master/affiliated clip relationship, change to a clip's label in the Timeline will also change the label and color code of its master clip in the Browser. In the Browser, the corresponding color of the label fills the master clip icon and not the clip name, or any other column data.

Customizing your Timeline display

The Timeline has numerous display options that you can customize. Choose Final Cut Pro ⇨ User Preferences and click the Timeline Options tab to make your choices. Choices made on this tab will be reflected in all new sequences you create.

If you want to change Timeline options for a sequence that you've already created, open the sequence, choose Sequence ⇨ Settings, and click the Timeline Options tab. Changes here will only apply to the currently opened sequence. Alternatively, you can Control+click on a sequence in the Browser and select Settings from the contextual menu. Click on the Timeline Options tab when the Sequence Settings window appears.

Cross-Reference For an explanation of the settings in the Timeline Options tab, see Chapter 6.

Performing edits in the Timeline

On the DVD-ROM If you don't have your own material to work with, open the Mountain Biking.fcp on your DVD-ROM and work in that project. This project is located in the Mountain Biking Tutorial folder. Be sure to drag the entire folder to your computer drive before opening the Mountain Biking.fcp project.

After many years of working as a video editor, also training and supervising other editors using Final Cut Pro, I've come to a startling conclusion: The key to speed and efficiency in editing is to skip the Viewer window, at least initially. You can perform edits by dragging clips directly into the Timeline from the Browser (you can also drag clips directly from the Viewer into a sequence, bypassing the Canvas window).

Performing an overwrite edit in the Timeline

Dragging a clip directly into the Timeline allows you to perform overwrite, insert, and superimpose edits (see Chapter 10 for more on these edit types). This section begins by performing an overwrite edit, where you overwrite one clip over a portion of another. Here's how to perform an overwrite edit:

1. **Open the project Mountain Biking.fcp.**

   You can find the project on the DVD-ROM that accompanies this book.

2. **Create a new sequence by using the Command+N keyboard shortcut.**

3. **In the Numbered Shots bin in the Browser, select Shots 1, 2, and 3 and drag them into the beginning of your new sequence.**

   These shots will lay into the sequence in the order they were sorted in the Browser. The sequence should now look like Figure 11-3.

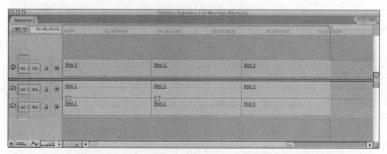

Figure 11-3: Three clips have been dropped into the sequence.

4. **Now perform an overwrite edit by dragging Shot 4 from the Browser into the Timeline.**

   (You may want to trim it a bit in the Viewer window to make it shorter than Shots 1, 2, and 3 to be able to re-create the situation in the figures.) But wait, don't just drop it anywhere. Drag it toward the middle of *Shot 2* and drop it on the *lower two-thirds of the video track.* If you look closely, you will see a subtle dividing line in the video track one-third of the way down from the top of the track. Figure 11-4 shows just where the clip should be dropped and what the cursor should look like. When you are about to perform an overwrite edit, the cursor looks like a downward pointing arrow.

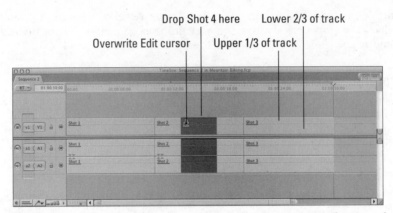

Figure 11-4: During an overwrite edit, the cursor turns into a downward pointing arrow as you drag and drop a clip into the Timeline.

You have just performed an overwrite edit in the Timeline. Shot 4 has "written over" Shot 2 for the duration of Shot 4. Figure 11-5 shows how the Timeline looks after the edit has been performed.

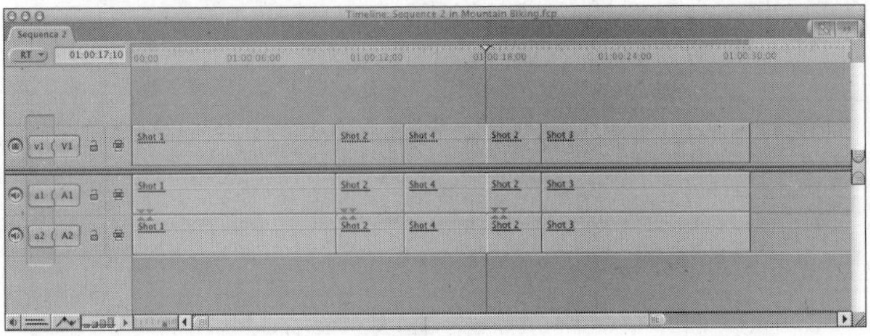

Figure 11-5: Shot 4 has overwritten part of Shot 2 as the result of an overwrite edit.

Performing an insert edit in the Timeline

In the previous section, you performed an overwrite edit, where you dropped a clip into the Timeline to *overwrite* part of an existing clip. You can also *insert* clips into a Timeline without overwriting portions of existing clips. In an insert edit, a clip is squeezed into the Timeline, pushing everything after it back to make room. To perform an insert edit, do the following:

1. **Drag Shots 1, 2, and 3 into Sequence2 from the Browser of Mountain Biking.fcp.**

If you are following along from the previous section, simply undo the last action (Command+Z) to undo your overwrite edit.

2. **Drag Shot 4 from the Browser to the middle of Shot 2 in the Timeline and drop it on the upper one-third of the video track.**

   If you look closely, you see a subtle dividing line in the video track one-third of the way down from the top of the track. Figure 11-6 shows where it should be dropped. When performing an insert edit, the cursor should look like an arrow pointing to the right.

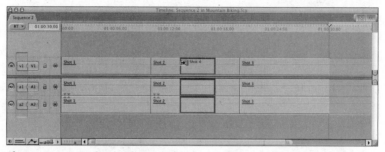

Figure 11-6: During an insert edit, the cursor turns into an arrow pointing to the right.

Note   The 1/3 track rule that determines overwrite or insert edit when dragging clips into the Timeline doesn't work for the smallest track size setting, Reduced. At this track size, all drag and drop edits are overwrites.

You have just performed an insert edit in the Timeline. Shot 4 has been "inserted" into the middle of Shot 2. The remaining parts of Shot 2 and Shot 3 have been moved over to make room for Shot 4. Figure 11-7 shows how the Timeline looks after an insert edit has been performed.

Figure 11-7: Shot 4 inserted into the middle of Shot 2 on the Timeline.

Performing a superimpose edit in the Timeline

Another kind of edit you can perform in the Timeline is a superimpose edit. With a superimpose edit, clips are superimposed, or stacked, over each other. Superimpose edits are used to layer clips. Later you can control the opacity and animate each layer separately. Superimpose edits are also used to place titles over clips. To perform a superimpose edit:

1. **Drag Shot 1, Shot 2, and Shot 3 into Sequence 2 from the Browser of Mountain Biking.fcp.**

   If you performed an insert edit in the previous section, press Command+Z to undo it.

2. **Drag Shot 4 from the Browser near the middle of Shot 2 and drop it on the clear space above the video track in the Timeline.**

   Your cursor will point downward, just as it does during an overwrite edit, but it is where you drop the shot on the Timeline that determines whether it is a superimpose or an overwrite edit. Figure 11-8 shows where it should be dropped. New tracks will be added to the Timeline to accommodate the incoming clip.

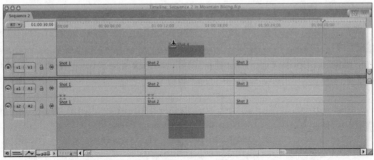

Figure 11-8: To do a superimpose edit, drop a clip up in the clear area above the main track.

This is a superimpose edit in the Timeline. The video for Shot 4 has been superimposed above Shot 2. The audio tracks for Shot 4 have been laid below the audio tracks for Shot 2. New tracks are automatically created. Figure 11-9 shows how the Timeline looks after the edit has been performed.

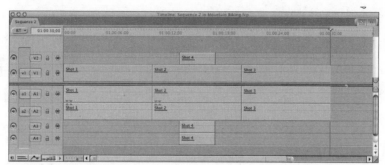

Figure 11-9: Timeline after Shot 4 has been superimposed over Shot 2.

Note

Making a superimpose edit by dragging a clip directly into the Timeline has many advantages over using the Canvas window's Superimpose command. Dragging into the Timeline is a what-you-see-is-what-you-get edit that works regardless of the playhead's position or target track assignment, and it does not use the target clip's duration for the Superimpose clip's duration, forcing the incoming Superimpose clip to cover *all* of the target clip below it. Wherever you see the shadow outline of a clip that you've dragged into the Timeline is where it will go when you release the mouse. It's that simple.

The magic of the Option key

The Option key can work magic when editing in the Timeline. It is used, as the Apple manual says, "for a great many things." You know it's very serious when an *Apple* manual says that—those writers are usually quite restrained. To get great results with the Option key, you must know *when* to press it. Some examples include the following:

✦ To make a copy of a clip that is in the Timeline, press and hold down the Option key when the cursor is over a clip *that is already selected* in the Timeline. The cursor will become a move tool (a four-arrowed diamond shape) with a small + (plus sign) indicating a duplicate of the clip will be made when dragged to another location.

✦ Hold down the Option key *before* selecting a clip in the Timeline to temporarily toggle the Link Selection setting. For instance, if the audio and video tracks for a clip are currently linked, holding the Option key when you select the clip will unlink those tracks. This is useful if you only want to select the video or audio track of a clip. If Linking is turned off, selecting a linked clip with the Option key pressed will select both the linked video and audio of a clip.

✦ Holding down the Option key *after* you start dragging a clip in the Timeline allows you to perform an insert edit in the Timeline. For example, start dragging away a clip in the Timeline and then press and hold down the Option key. Move this clip over another one and you will see a curved arrow pointing downward. Release the clip to perform an insert edit at that spot. Without the Option key you would get an overwrite edit rather than an insert edit.

Understanding track targeting

In the previous exercises, you added clips to the sequence by dragging them from the Viewer or Browser and dropping them into the Timeline. This is a very fast and easy way to place your clips. However, to place a shot precisely into the Timeline, use the Canvas overlay edit commands or edit buttons. Canvas edit commands use the Timeline In and Out points, or if none are set, then Timeline playhead position, and *track targeting* to determine where to place the incoming tracks. The tracks in the Timeline that you want to edit your clips into are *target tracks*. The tracks from the clip you are editing into the Timeline are called *source tracks*. Assigning the destination of source tracks to target tracks in the Timeline is called track targeting and is done in the Source and Destination controls located in the patch panel on the left side of the Timeline window. These controls are shown in Figure 11-10.

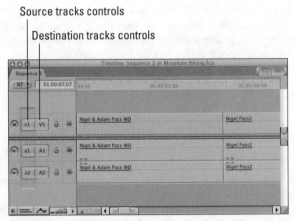

Figure 11-10: Source and Destination controls determine which tracks of a source clip are edited into the Timeline.

To select a target track, do one of following:

✦ **Click on a track Destination control button.** The nearest source track will jump to that track.

✦ **Option+click on a track Destination control button.** This will select the nearest source track *below* the selected target track.

✦ **Click and drag a Source control button to the desired target track destination.**

When you select a target track, look carefully to make sure the Source and Destination control buttons are joined together. Track targeting can be turned off when you want to omit tracks of a clip edited into a Timeline. For example, you might want to edit in just the audio tracks of a clip while omitting the video portion. You can toggle this control on or off by clicking on a target track's Destination control button. The Source and Destination control buttons will appear open if the track targeting is off (unassigned), and closed if tracks targeting is on (assigned). This works identically for audio track targeting. Figure 11-11 shows the track targeting turned on for video track V1, but turned off for audio tracks A1 and A2.

Closed Source and Destination buttons

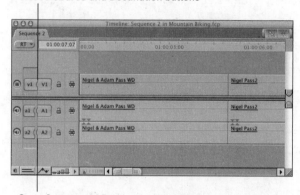

Open Source and Destination buttons

Figure 11-11: Track targeting using the Source and Destination controls can be turned off when you want to add only video or audio portions of a clip. Track targeting for V1 is turned on, while audio tracks A1 and A2 are off, or unassigned.

The number of Source controls that appear in the Timeline patch panel area is automatically matched to the number of tracks contained by the clip currently loaded into the Viewer. For instance, if the video clip in the Viewer is linked to four audio tracks, then four Source controls will appear in the Timeline opposite the track Destination controls.

Rules of the clip-drag with Target tracks

Rules, rules, rules! Why do we have to have so many rules? Rules cause editors to scream and yell at their computers (always a losing proposition) when they don't get what they expected when making an edit. That's because the editors do not know the rules. You have to watch closely where and how you are dragging your clips and what the cursor looks like while you do it. Minor differences in indicators cause vastly different results. Final Cut Pro has more rules than you can imagine. By understanding these rules, you can make Final Cut Pro dance with your fingers.

Target tracks are tracks you select in the Timeline for editing. For example, if the video track's Source and Destination control is turned on (closed buttons) and the audio Source and Destination control is turned off (open buttons), then editing clips into the Timeline via dragging the clip from the Viewer to the Canvas window only edits the video portion of that clip. The following figure shows the results of this track targeting and editing using the Canvas overlay command Overwrite.

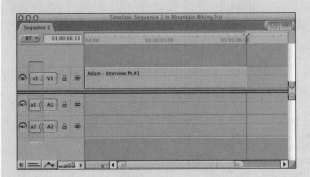

However, when dragging clips directly into the Timeline, the Target tracks also have influence. Here are the rules of their behavior:

✦ If the Video Target track is off (open buttons) then dragging the clip directly to the *audio tracks* results in no video track for this clip.

> **Note:** You must make sure to drag this clip into the audio track area. The rules for insert and overwrite still apply as far as dragging it into the upper one-third (for insert) or the lower two-thirds (for Overwrite) of the track area is concerned.

✦ If the Target tracks for audio are turned off (open buttons) then dragging the clip directly to the *Video track* results in no audio being added.

✦ If the Video track is turned off, dragging the clip into the *Video track* results in both video and audio being edited into the Timeline.

✦ If the Audio tracks are turned off, then dragging the clip to the *audio track* portion results in both audio and video being edited into the Timeline.

In short, Final Cut Pro watches where you drag and drop clips, and allows you to override the Target track selections by following the preceding rules.

Working with the Canvas two-up display

When you perform insert or overwrite edits in the Timeline as described in the previous sections, it may seem that there is no way to know exactly where you are dropping your shots. Well, fear not. Those hotshot developers at Apple thought of everything. When you drag a shot into the Timeline for an edit, your Canvas window switches to a "Two-Up" display as shown in Figure 11-12.

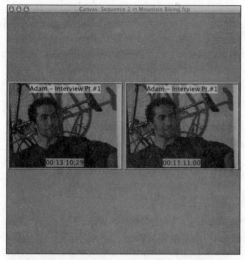

Figure 11-12: The Two-Up display appears in the Canvas window when you drag a shot into the Timeline.

The views that appear in the Two-Up display depend on what type of edit you are making:

✦ **Overwrite Edit:** When you perform an overwrite edit, the Two-Up display shows the frame just before and just after the clip to be edited in to the sequence.

The timecodes of the individual frames are displayed as well. Note that the timecode for the frame on the right is the timecode of the frame on the left *plus the duration of the clip being edited in.*

✦ **Insert Edit:** During an insert edit the Two-Up display will show the two frames that will be adjacent to the clip you are editing in. Because insert edits slice the clip and move it over, the timecodes in the left and the right window will be consecutive.

✦ **Superimpose Edit:** During a superimpose edit, the Two-Up display shows black frames.

Note   If you edit a clip into an empty track of the Timeline, the Two-Up display will be black.

Tip   For precise placement of your shots in the Timeline, hold down your mouse as you place a shot to be able to read the timecodes in the Canvas Two-Up display.

Locating a match frame

When you're editing in the Timeline, it is sometimes necessary to locate the original clip in the Browser. This is often so that you can view the full clip from the Browser, as opposed to its edited version in the sequence. The Match Frame function is used to locate the original clip from the Browser. The original clip is loaded into the Viewer and its current frame matched to the current frame of the clip in the sequence. To use the Match Frame function:

1. **Open the Mountain Biking.fcp (from the DVD-ROM) and double-click Mountain Biking Final Cut sequence to open it.**

2. **Play the sequence and pause playback at any point on the clip.**

3. **Press the letter F key on your keyboard for the Match Frame command.**

    The original source clip for the clip in the sequence will be called up from the Browser and loaded into the Viewer. If the Timeline playhead is parked on layered tracks of multiple clips, the clip on the lowest numbered track *with Auto Select enabled* is used for Match Frame operation.

After you perform a Match Frame operation, the playhead in the Viewer will match the location of the Timeline playhead located on the sequence clip. Also, the same In and Out points on the clip in the sequence will be marked on the clip that is loaded into the Viewer. At this point, you could select another portion of the clip in the Viewer and perform a Replace edit into the sequence. Bear in mind that Replace edits match the locations of the playhead from the Viewer to the Timeline and ignore any In and Out points set in the Viewer. Instead, the In and Out points of the clip in the sequence are used. By using the Match Frame and Replaced edit function, it is possible to choose a different section of a clip that has already been edited into the Timeline.

The Match Frame operation is common action taken by editors to locate a precise frame. The matching is done by Final Cut Pro automatically by locating the master clip, loading it into the Viewer and placing the playhead at the precise frame over which you had first located your playhead in the edited sequence.

Tip   Match Frame works in reverse if you have a sequence clip loaded into the Viewer: Click on the Match Frame button in the bottom-left corner of the Viewer window, or press the F key, and the Timeline playhead will move to the exact same frame in the sequence clip that is currently displayed in the Viewer. Pressing Shift+F when either the Viewer or Timeline is selected will find and highlight its Master clip in the Browser.

Color indicators for the Render Bar

The Render Bar (shown in Figure 11-13) is the area just above the timecode ruler in the Timeline. This area shows you the render status of items in the Timeline. If you have added effects or filters to an audio or video clip, the Render Bar will indicate whether the audio or video needs to be rendered.

Audio Render indicator bar

Video Render indicator bar

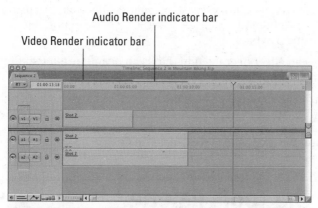

Figure 11-13: The Render Bar indicates the render status of your clips.

The Render Bar actually has two portions. The top part of the bar indicates the render status for the video portions of a clip, while the bottom portion shows the render status for the audio portions of a clip. The color of the Render Bar indicates the status of the clip:

✦ **Light gray:** There is no clip under the Render Bar.

✦ **Dark gray:** The clip does not need to be rendered.

✦ **Steel or purplish gray:** Effects or transitions that needed to be rendered have been rendered.

✦ **Dark green:** This indicates a transition or an effect that can be played and output to video at high quality in real time without being rendered.

✦ **Medium green:** This indicates a transition or an effect that can be played in real time on the computer. When played back on a third-party real-time card or output over Firewire on a fast enough computer, a lower quality playback of motion effects and scaling is displayed.

✦ **Yellow:** This indicates an effect or transition that will display an approximation of the effect during real-time playback. Some filter controls might be ignored in order to play this effect or transition in real-time. You can preview the effect, but it must be rendered before you output it to tape at full resolution. The final effect is visible when play is stopped or when scrubbing.

✦ **Dark yellow:** This indicates an effect or transition has been rendered at a lower quality than the settings in the Render Control tab of the Sequence settings. These render files are preserved even if Render Controls are changed back to 100%.

✦ **Orange:** This indicates an effect or transition that exceeds the real-time playback capabilities of your computer system but is enabled to play anyway because Unlimited RT is selected in the Real-Time Effects (RT) pop-up menu in the Timeline. Unlimited RT allows you to play more effects and transitions than your computer is inherently capable of at the expense of possible dropped frames during playback.

✦ **Blue**: This indicates an effect or transition that is an unsupported real-time enabler file that might drop frames during playback.

✦ **Red**: An effect or transition needs to be rendered before playback is possible at selected quality.

Rendering in Final Cut Pro is covered in more detail in Chapter 18.

Understanding the Tools Palette

The Tools Palette contains tools for selecting and working with items throughout the Final Cut Pro interface. The Tools Palette provides an incredible array of editing choices. You can use the tools to perform selections, edits, image manipulation, magnification, and effects adjustment. The categories of tools found in the Tools Palette include:

✦ **Selection:** Some tools allow selection of items and tracks.

✦ **Adjust Edit Point:** There are tools for adjusting your edits and their points.

✦ **Image Manipulation:** Some tools allow you to crop or distort images.

✦ **Scale and Zoom:** These allow you to zoom and scale your Timeline and images.

✦ **Keyframe:** Pen tools allow you to add and edit keyframes for effects.

Figure 11-14 shows the Tools Palette in its fully expanded glory. Of course, you won't normally see it like this; usually you'll just see one section at a time as you click and hold on a tool's tiny arrow.

To select a tool, you can just click it with your mouse. To select the other tool options, click and hold on the small arrow in the upper-right corner of each tool. A short menu containing additional choices will extend out. Table 11-1 describes each tool in the Tools Palette.

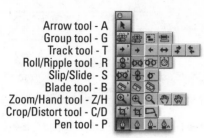

Arrow tool - A
Group tool - G
Track tool - T
Roll/Ripple tool - R
Slip/Slide - S
Blade tool - B
Zoom/Hand tool - Z/H
Crop/Distort tool - C/D
Pen tool - P

Figure 11-14: This blowout diagram shows the entire Tools Palette. Click and hold on any tool to see the other options.

Tip

Leaving the pointer over a tool brings up a ToolTip that shows the name of the tool as well as its keyboard shortcut. Make sure that the Show ToolTips option is checked on the General tab of the User Preferences window. Choose Final Cut Pro ➪ User Preferences for this window.

Table 11-1
Details of the Tools Palette

Tools for Selection

Tool	Name	Description
	Selection	Used for selecting individual items.
	Edit Selection	Drag and draw a marquee with this tool. Selects only edit points in the Timeline area within the marquee you draw. Only one edit per track is selected and the Trim window automatically comes up to allow you to trim this edit point.
	Group Selection	Selects entire clips or groups of clips in the Timeline even if the marquee you draw with this tool covers only part of the clip or clips.
	Range Selection	Selects partial clips or just the area inside the selection area drawn by this tool.
	Track Forward Select	Selects all the items forward (to the right) in a track from the point where you click this tool in the track.

Continued

Table 11-1 *(continued)*

Tool	Name	Description
←	Track Backward Select	Selects all the items backward (to the left) in a track from the point where you click this tool in the track.
↔	Track Select	Selects all items, backward and forward, in a single track.
→	All Tracks Forward Select	Selects all items in all tracks forward (right) of the point where this tool is used.
←	All Tracks Backward Select	Selects all items in all tracks backward (left) of the point where this tool is used.

Tools for Editing

Tool	Name	Description
8	Roll Tool	Rolls the edit points of two adjoining clips. This tool adjusts the location of the Out point of the first clip and the In point of the second clip in a Timeline. It can also be used for transitions and multiple clips.
ф	Ripple Tool	Ripples edit points. Ripple edit adjusts the location of either the Out point just before, or the In point just after, an edit point. This tool allows adjustment of the length of the clip to the left or the right of the edit point.
фф	Slip Tool	Slips a clip's In and Out points. This tool adjusts the In and Out points of a clip, without changing its duration or location.
фф	Slide Tool	Slides a clip in between two clips in a sequence. Using this tool, you can move a clip that is located between two shots. The Out point of the clip to the left and the In point of the clip to the right move together. The duration is not changed for all clips.
🕐	Time Remap Tool	The Time Remap Tool allows you to make variable speed changes to clips in the Timeline quickly.
▱	Razor Tool	Cuts a single clip into two.
▱	All Razor Tool	Cuts all clips in all tracks in two where clicked.

Tools for Viewing

Tool	Name	Description
	Zoom In	Zooms closer to an image, or enlarges the view in the Timeline.
	Zoom Out	Zooms farther out from an image, or reduces the view in the Timeline.
	Hand	Moves around in the Timeline or an image.
	Scrub Video	Allows scrubbing of video for clips in a Browser that is in the Large Thumbnail view.

Tools for Image Manipulation

Tool	Name	Description
	Crop	Crops an image.
	Distort	Distorts an image.

Tools for Keyframing

Tool	Name	Description
	Pen-Add Keyframe	Adds a keyframe.
	Pen-Delete Keyframe	Deletes a keyframe.
	Pen-Smooth Keyframe	Smoothes a keyframe's "interpolation" or the velocity between two keyframes.

Navigating in the Timeline

Whenever I go into a new town, the most frustrating experience I have is getting lost. Sure there are maps in the rental car, but where am I on the map?

Locating yourself accurately in a Final Cut Pro Timeline is no less important. In larger projects, Timelines can get long and complicated. You need to be able to move around in a Timeline in a rapid and reliable fashion. Shots, like unfamiliar streets, start to look alike and names don't mean much after a while. A key skill for editing in the Timeline is navigation. The next few sections show you a few techniques that may help you move around more efficiently and locate yourself in a Timeline.

Navigating with the J, K, and L keys

Of course, you can just drag your playhead around in the Timeline or click anywhere in the time ruler area to move the playhead to that location. But you can also shuttle through your Timeline using the J, K, and L keys (see Figure 11-15), which are conveniently located right next to each other on your keyboard. Here's how they work:

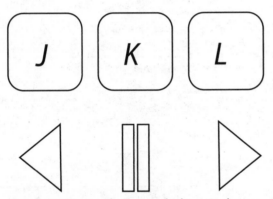

Figure 11-15: Use the J, K, and L keys to play your Timeline forward and backward and to stop it.

>   ✦ **J key:** Plays backward at 1X (*1X* stands for one times normal speed).
>
>   ✦ **K key:** Pauses playback.
>
>   ✦ **L key:** Plays forward at 1X.

You can move forward and backward using the J and L keys at varying speeds as well. Consecutively press the J or the L key up to four times to select between 1X, 2X, 4X, and 8X speeds. If you press the J key four times so that you're playing backward at 8X speed, and then you press the L key, the backward playback speed will be cut in half to 4X. If you keep pressing the L key, the speed will continue to be halved until it then starts playing forward again at 1X.

Another handy variation of these keys is the ability to play at one-third normal speed. This can be useful for closely monitoring your edits in the Timeline as you play. For one-third speed playback, hold the K key down and then hold down either the J or the L key at the same time. Playback will occur at one-third normal speed in either direction.

Note

> While using the J, K, or L method of moving at one-third speed, you will be unable to mark In or Out points using the I or O keys. Use the / (forward slash) key and the * (asterisk) key on the numeric keypad to mark In and Out points when working at one-third speed. Of course, you can use these keys any other times as well. They even work in the Viewer window to mark In and Out points.

It is also possible to move one frame at a time using key commands. Press and hold the K key and tap on the J or the L key to move one frame at a time in either direction.

Using other techniques for moving in the Timeline

Several other ways for moving around in the Timeline can be very useful. Various methods are described in the next few sections, but here are some handy keyboard shortcuts you can use:

✦ **Home and End keys:** The Home key will take you to the beginning of the Timeline, and the End key will take you to the end of the last clip in a Timeline.

✦ **Shift+Page Up and Shift+Page Down:** If your Timeline is long and you need to scroll through, try Shift+Page Up and Shift+Page Down. These commands scroll through the Timeline rapidly, one screen width at a time.

✦ **Up and Down arrow keys:** The Up arrow moves you backward in the Timeline, skipping from edit point to edit point. The Down arrow moves the playhead from edit point to edit point, going forward in the Timeline.

✦ **Left and Right arrow keys:** The Left and Right arrow keys move you one frame at a time in the Timeline. Adding the Shift key to the Left and Right arrow keys will move you one second at a time in the appropriate direction rather than just one frame.

Navigating in the Timeline using timecode

Each Timeline has a timecode ruler at the top that displays the timecode for that Timeline. You can set a specific starting timecode for a Timeline in the Timeline Options tab of the User Preferences window (Final Cut Pro ⇨ User Preferences).

The playhead always displays the current frame in the Canvas window. The playhead's current position in the Timeline is shown in the Current Timecode field, located in the top-left corner of the Timeline window. This timecode is also seen in the Canvas window's Current Timecode field, located in the upper-right corner of the Canvas window.

You can use the following methods to navigate in the Timeline using timecode:

✦ **Using absolute timecode:** Enter a timecode and then press the Enter key to move your playhead to that timecode. The timecode you enter must be present in your Timeline, of course. For example, to navigate to 1:12:13:00, enter **1.12.13.00** on the numeric keypad and press the Enter key (you don't have to enter leading zeros, and you can use the period key instead of colons). This will take the playhead to 1 hour, 12 minutes, 13 seconds, and 00 frames in the Timeline. Note that you do not have to highlight the Current Timecode field in the Timeline to use this method. Just start typing the timecode.

✦ **Using relative timecode entry:** Type a + or a - and then enter a timecode. The playhead will jump forward or backward by that amount. For example, entering **+100** will jump the playhead forward by 1 second. Entering **-15.00** will move the playhead backward by 15 seconds.

Cross-Reference

For more on timecode shortcuts and tips see the "Getting friendly with timecode" sidebar in Chapter 9.

Moving items using timecode

Final Cut Pro is intuitive and context sensitive. When you enter a timecode to move the playhead, if any item is selected that item will be moved instead of the playhead. It is important to pay attention to this behavior. For example, you may want to move a clip forward by 15 seconds. Select the clip and enter **+15.00** in the Current timecode field to move the clips forward by 15 seconds, if there is space available.

If you have a complex Timeline, you might have a difficult time determining if any items are selected in the Timeline. Here are two ways to confirm that nothing is selected:

✦ Press Command+Shift+A to deselect any items that might currently be selected. If no items are selected, this command will do no harm.

✦ When you enter a timecode, look in the Timeline to see where this timecode entry shows up. If your timecode entry shows up in the Current Timecode field of the Timeline, you are about to move the playhead. If your timecode entry shows up in the upper-center portion of the Timeline, with the word *Move* next to it, as shown in Figure 11-16, you are about to move an item.

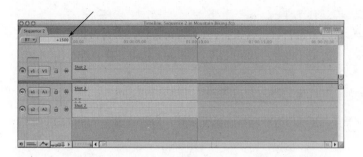

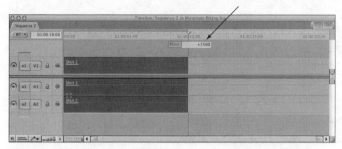

Figure 11-16: If your timecode entry appears in the Current Timecode field of the Timeline, you are about to move the playhead. If the timecode entry appears in the upper-center part of the Timeline, you are about to move an item in the Timeline.

Zooming in on the Timeline

At various times when you edit in the Timeline you will need to zoom in and out on the Timeline itself. Zooming out gives you an overall view of your Timeline when you need it, but you can still zoom in close when you need to see more detail. You can use one of several methods to zoom in or out on the Timeline:

✦ **Press Option++ (plus sign) to zoom in on the Timeline, or press Option+- (minus sign) to zoom out.** Note that this works if you use the + (plus) or - (minus) keys on the numeric keypad or on your main keyboard layout. Figure 11-17 shows a Timeline before and after I zoomed into the Timeline. When zooming using keyboard shortcuts, the center of a Timeline zoom will focus around the *currently visible* items using the following priority:

  • Selected clips in the Timeline, first

  • The Timeline playhead, second

  • The currently visible area of the Timeline if either the playhead or selected items are *not* visible, last

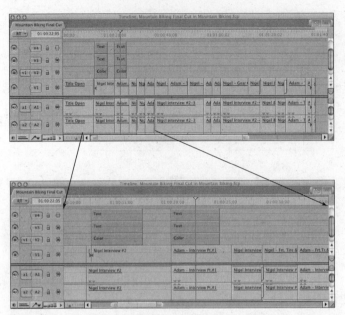

Figure 11-17: There are many ways to zoom the view of the Timeline. The most common method is Option++ (plus sign). Option+- (minus sign) zooms view out.

✦ **Click and drag on the thumb tabs on the Zoom slider at the bottom of the Timeline.** Drag the tabs to the magnification level of your choice. Once you have done this, you can drag the center part of the Zoom slider to move around in your sequence. Zooming this way always keeps the currently visible area of the sequence as the center of the zoom. If you hold down the Shift key and drag the thumb tab of the Zoom slider, the Timeline will zoom in that direction while keeping the other tab locked in place. The visible area of the Timeline will move in the same direction as your dragging.

✦ **Select the Timeline window and choose View ⇨ Level.** Select a magnification level from the submenu.

✦ **Click and drag the Zoom control tab to zoom in or out of the Timeline.** This method has a distinct advantage of always jumping to and zooming around the Timeline playhead whether or not it is currently visible in the Timeline.

✦ **Press Shift+Z to fit your entire edited program in the size of the Timeline window.**

✦ **Click and drag a section with the Zoom tool from the tools palette.** The Timeline will zoom to the necessary magnification to show all items that were lassoed with the Zoom tool. Pressing the Z key will select the Zoom tool.

A zoom too far

Zooming with the zoom slider and the menus is not an exact science and often results in less-than-perfect zooms. You can often find yourself zooming in on the wrong window. I found myself endlessly struggling with the magnification until I took the time to find the best method for zooming in and out on the Timeline.

By far the best method for zooming in on the Timeline is to press Option+-(minus sign) to zoom out, and Option++ (plus sign) to zoom in. Sure, you can also use the Command++ (plus) or Command+- (minus) shortcuts to do the zooming, as is common in many other applications. The only problem with the Command-key method is that you have to make sure that the Timeline window is selected. If the Viewer window or Canvas window is selected, the Command key method will zoom *that* window instead. Using the Option modifier key, on the other hand, will zoom *only* the Timeline, even if another window is selected.

Another tricky aspect of zooming in the Timeline is knowing *where* zooming will center around. As detailed in the previous section, the area or item used as the center of the zoom depends on which method you employ, and in one case, which element is visible at the time of zooming. In summary, using the Zoom control always zooms around the playhead. Using the Zoom slider will center the zoom on the currently visible area of the Timeline. Using the keyboard (or menu) commands for zooming will center on either a visibly selected clip or the playhead, if either is visible.

Tip   Press Shift+Option+Z to fill the full width of the Timeline with just the clips that have been selected. This is a great new feature that I've wanted since working with the first version of Final Cut Pro. It's a combination of the Fit to Fill command and the zoom tool.

✦ **Press Shift+Page Up or Shift+Page Down to move left and right in the Timeline by one screen width at a time.** For finer positioning of the visible Timeline area, use the Hand tool and drag anywhere in the Timeline when you see the Hand tool cursor. Press the H key to select the Hand tool.

Tip   You can always locate the position of the Timeline playhead, even when it is not currently visible in the Timeline — it's the purple line in the Zoom Slider scroll bar.

Searching in the Timeline window

Final Cut Pro has a very handy built-in search function for the Timeline window. You can use this function to search any open sequence. The search can be based on clip names, text you may have entered for markers, and timecode values. The search feature is very useful because, in larger projects, the Timeline gets crowded and very fast. To search in the Timeline:

1. **Open a Sequence by double-clicking it.**

2. **Choose Edit ➪ Find or press Command+F.**

   The Find window appears, as shown in Figure 11-18. You can search for text based on names you've used for items, or text you may have entered for markers. You can also search for specific timecodes.

3. **Enter the text or the timecode you want to search for in the Find: field.**

4. **Select either the Names/Markers or Timecode option from the Search: pull-down menu.**

   Selecting Timecode automatically switches the Find field to a numerical value.

5. **Choose the tracks you want to search in the Where: pull-down menu.**

   To limit your search area, you can mark In and Out points in the sequence and select From In to Out in the Where: menu.

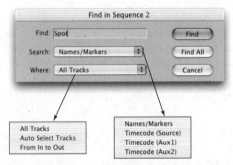

Figure 11-18: The Find window allows you to search your sequences.

6. **Click Find.**

   Final Cut Pro will take you to the next item it can locate based on your criteria.

   If you click Find All in the Find window, Final Cut Pro will highlight all the clips found in the Timeline based on your criteria rather than just the first item.

Tip   If you are searching for an item based on text, you can skip to the next item by pressing Command+G for Find Next. This allows you to find multiple occurrences of text in the Timeline.

Working with Clips and Gaps in the Timeline

While editing in the Timeline, there are various ways to select, copy, paste, and delete clips. Of course, selecting and working with clips is nothing new; every video editing program available offers this capability. But the ability to select gaps is unique to Final Cut Pro. This concept is so intuitive and obvious, that I often wonder why other software companies haven't thought of this before for their editing applications.

Selecting clips

Just about every time you perform an edit in Final Cut Pro, you'll be selecting clips in the Timeline. Sometimes you'll only select one clip, and other times you'll select several. You can manually select as many or as few clips as you like, using one of these techniques:

✦ **Selecting individual clips:** You can select individual clips by simply clicking on them with the pointer tool.

✦ **Selecting multiple clips:** Multiple clips can be selected by holding down the Command key and clicking on each clip you want to select. Selected clips do not have to be contiguous (adjacent) to one another.

✦ **Selecting a range of clips:** A range of contiguous (adjacent) clips can be selected by using one of the following two methods:

• Select the first clip of a range, and then, holding down the Shift key, click on the last clip you want to select. All clips between these two clips will be selected too.

• Use the Range Selection Tool from the tools palette. Click *inside* a clip and drag until all the clips you want to select are highlighted. With this tool, you can select portions of a clip without selecting the entire clip. Figure 11-19 shows a range of clips with only parts of the first and last clips selected.

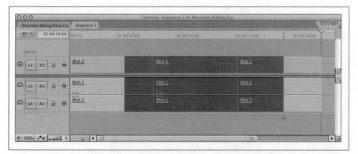

Figure 11-19: The Range Selection tool can select many clips on the same track and can even select parts of clips, as shown here.

Tip

In order for the Range Selector tool to work, you must click *inside* the first clip before dragging for the rest of the selection. The cursor for this tool is a crosshair that can deceive you into thinking that you should click and drag *around* the clips, as is done for any other manual selecting. Clicking outside a clip with the Range Selector tool will not select anything.

✦ **Selecting a group of clips:** Use the Group Select tool by choosing it in the Tools Palette, and then draw a marquee around the clips you want to select.

✦ **Selecting all items between an In and an Out point:** Set In and Out points in the sequence using the I and O keys. Then choose Mark ➪ Select In to Out. All items between the In and Out points — including *partial sections* of clips that fall within the In and Out points — and on tracks with Auto Select control enabled, will be selected. The keyboard shortcut for this command is Option+A.

Tip   You can delete portions of a clip by marking In and Out points and using the Option+A command; only the portions between the In and Out points will be deleted.

✦ **Selecting All Items:** Press Command+A to select all items in the Timeline.

✦ **Deselecting Items:** Press Command+Shift+A to deselect any and all selected items in the Timeline.

Using Auto Select control

Auto Select control is a new feature in Final Cut Pro 4 and is used to enable tracks for selection and editing via the In and Out points set in the Timeline. Each track has its own Auto Select control, which looks like two intersecting rectangles and is located to the right of the Track Lock icon. To toggle Auto Select on or off, click its icon. The center of the icon will fill with dark gray when Auto Select is enabled and will remain clear, light gray when disabled. You can enable Auto Select on as many tracks as you want. When In and Out points are set in the Timeline, and no single clip is currently selected, any clips in tracks with Auto Select Control enabled will be highlighted; clips in tracks with Auto Select not enabled remain slightly darker, as shown in Figure 11-20.

Auto Select control for track toggled on

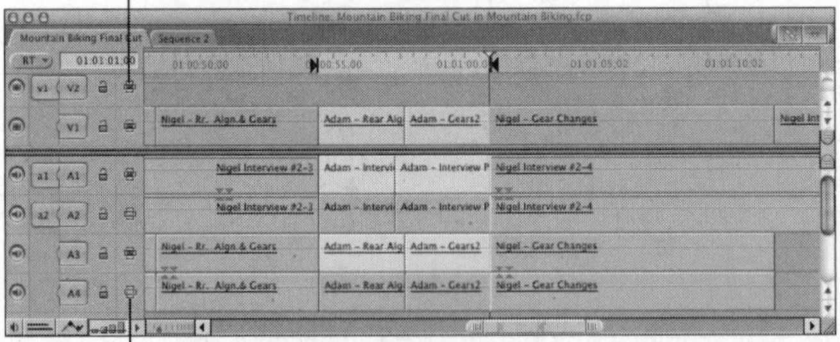

[Screenshot: Timeline: Mountain Biking Final Cut in Mountain Biking.fcp]

Auto Select control for track toggled off

Figure 11-20: Auto Select controls allow you to select tracks to edit using In and Out points set in the Timeline. Tracks with Auto Select enabled appear darker than tracks not enabled.

Only the tracks with Auto Select enabled will be affected by operations of cut, copy, and delete. Selection with Auto Select enabled lets you select portions of clips that fall within the In and Out points set in the Timeline, like the Range Selection tool. However, using Auto Select has the advantage of being able to select clips and portions of clips that are on different tracks.

Editing and pasting clips

After you have selected some clips, it's time to do something with your selection. If you have used word processors or other computer programs, you're probably accustomed to cutting, copying, and pasting pictures, words, sentences, e-mail addresses, and other kinds of data. You can perform the same kinds of actions on clips in Final Cut Pro:

✦ **Cutting a clip:** To cut a clip for pasting elsewhere, select the clip and choose Edit ➪ Cut or press Command+X. The clip will be cut from its current location.

✦ **Copying a clip:** To copy a clip for pasting elsewhere, choose Edit ➪ Copy or press Command+C.

✦ **Pasting a clip:** To paste a clip that you have cut or copied, choose Edit ➪ Paste or press Command+V. The clip will be pasted at the current location of the playhead, overwriting any material on the target tracks if present.

✦ **Paste inserting a clip:** To paste insert a clip choose Edit ➪ Paste Insert or press Shift+V. This will paste the clip at the current playhead position while moving any adjacent clips over to the right.

Control+click on any clip in the Timeline to bring up a contextual menu with various choices, including Copy, Cut, or Paste.

Deleting clips

There are many ways to remove clips from the Timeline in Final Cut Pro. However, the results may be different depending on how you delete the clips. You can perform a simple Lift Delete, where a clip is deleted and the gap in the Timeline created by its absence is left in place. You can also perform a Ripple Delete, which closes the Timeline gap created by the just-deleted clip. The following steps guide you through a lift delete:

1. **Select a clip in the Timeline.**

2. **Choose Sequence ➪ Lift, or just press the Delete key on your keyboard.**

Remember, deleting clips from the Timeline does not affect the master clips in the Browser, nor does it in any way affect the media file for the clip located on your drive.

When you perform a Lift Delete, a gap will remain in the Timeline where the clip was before you deleted it. This is often necessary when you are deleting portions of a program where you do not want to move anything while deleting a few clips. In a complex Timeline, you may have clips and shots synchronized to voice over audio clips or music, and you may just want to delete a few clips while not disturbing the overall relationship of the other clips and tracks. If these issues are not a concern, you can perform a Ripple Delete:

1. **Select the clip you want to delete in the Timeline.**

2. **Choose Sequence ⇨ Ripple Delete or press Shift+Delete on your keyboard.**

The clip will be deleted, and any gap created by its absence will automatically be closed. Ripple Delete is good to use when you are just doing a rough assemble of a Timeline. This can be a very tricky delete to use when you have a complex Timeline with many clips and tracks because Ripple will attempt to close the gap and may change the relationships between various clips. Try to only use Ripple Delete for simple Timelines and rough cuts. For complex projects, think before you use Ripple Delete.

Working with gaps

Gaps are a fact of editing. When you edit in the Timeline, move clips around, and perform edits you inevitably create gaps, or empty spaces, between clips. Some gaps are easy to spot. They are large empty spaces between clips. But other gaps may only be a few frames or so and can be hard to find. These tiny gaps are bad because though you may not see them, if you output the Timeline to tape, the gaps will show up as black flashes in the program. This is bad, very bad.

Final Cut Pro provides many ways to deal with gaps in your Timelines. But before you can get rid of your gaps, you must locate them:

1. **If you want to start at the top, press the Home key to go to the beginning of your sequence.**

   Otherwise, you can start searching for gaps from the current location of the playhead.

2. **Choose Mark ⇨ Next ⇨ Gap.**

The playhead will jump to the next gap in the Timeline. You can also use the keyboard shortcut Shift+G to navigate to the next gap. Option+G will take you to the previous gap. After you have located a gap, you should determine how long it is. This will help you figure out how much space you need to fill or account for. To determine the duration of a gap:

1. **Place your playhead anywhere in the gap.**

2. **Choose Mark ⇨ Mark Clip.**

   This will mark your gap in the Timeline with an In and an Out point. You can also press the X key on your keyboard to achieve the same results, as this is the shortcut for the Mark Clip command. Note that this marking process works only in the selected target track and not in various tracks in a given Timeline.

You can now read the gap's duration in the Duration Timecode field in the Canvas window. This is located in the upper-left side of the Canvas window.

Tip   You can select other items in the sequence and press Shift+A to mark In and Out points based around the selection. Then you can read off the duration of the selection in the Duration Timecode field of the Canvas. This is a handy shortcut for finding out the duration of portions of your sequence.

After you've determined the duration of a gap, it's time to do something about it. You could fill the gap by extending the clips adjacent to it, or you could insert a new clip into the gap. And of course, you can also just delete the gap. To delete a gap:

1. **Select the gap by clicking on it.**

2. **Press Delete to rid your Timeline of the offensive gap.**

   Keep in mind that this command might not work if there is another clip in the Timeline that overlaps the gap.

Tip   If you Control+click on a gap, a contextual menu will appear that includes a Close Gap command. Note that closing a gap is the same as deleting a gap.

Working with Tracks in the Timeline

By default, sequences have one base track of video and two base tracks of audio. You can alter this default using the Timeline Options tab when you choose Final Cut Pro ⇨ User Preferences. Within a Timeline that has already been created, there are a number of ways to work with tracks. You can quickly add or delete tracks, you can lock tracks to keep them from being changed inadvertently, and you can select or hide entire tracks.

Adding tracks to the Timeline

Final Cut Pro gives you a number of options for adding tracks to the Timeline. The fastest way to add a new track is to do it while you are dragging a clip from the Browser or the Viewer to the Timeline. If you drag a clip to the unused area above the video track and drop it there, you will automatically get a new track. Figure 11-21 shows this.

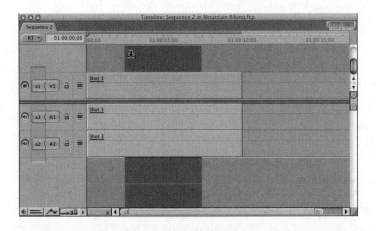

Figure 11-21: Dragging a clip to the empty area above the video track will automatically add a new track.

You can also add tracks to the Timeline using a contextual menu. Control+click on the track header area just above an existing track, or in any empty space of the Patch Panel, to get a contextual menu. Choose Add Track from the contextual menu that appears as shown in Figure 11-22. This works for both video and audio tracks.

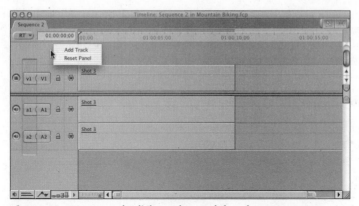

Figure 11-22: Control+click on the track header area to get a contextual menu choice for adding tracks.

Finally, you can also add tracks to the Timeline using the Sequence menu:

1. **Choose Sequence ➪ Insert Tracks.**

   The Insert Tracks dialog box appears as shown in Figure 11-23.

2. **Choose the number of tracks you want for video and audio, and choose where you want them in relation to the main tracks.**

3. **Click OK to close the dialog box and add the tracks.**

Figure 11-23: The Insert Tracks dialog box appears when you choose Sequence ➪ Insert Tracks.

Resizing tracks

In addition to resizing Timeline tracks collectively using the Track Height control, Final Cut Pro now allows you to resize the height of a single track, all tracks of the same type (video or audio), or all tracks (video *and* audio) in the Timeline by dragging the boundaries of a track.

✦ **To resize a single track:** Drag the upper boundary of a video track in the patch panel area. For an audio track, drag the lower boundary in the patch panel area to resize. The cursor becomes a resize tool when placed over a track's boundary, shown in Figure 11-24.

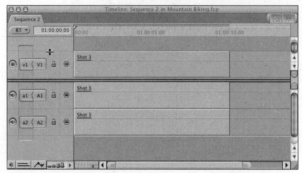

Figure 11-24: Drag a track's boundary when the cursor becomes a resize tool to change the track's height.

✦ **To resize all tracks of the same type:** Hold down the Option key while you drag the boundary of a video track. All video tracks will resize together. If you resize an audio track while holding down the Option key, all audio tracks will resize together.

✦ **To resize all tracks in the Timeline:** Hold down the Shift key while you drag the boundary of *any* track, and all tracks in the Timeline will resize by the same amount. This is the same as using the Track Height control.

Note   Any resizing of multiple tracks will reset track heights previously set to individual tracks. This is true for resizing by dragging track boundaries or using the Track Height control. If you want to save customized track heights, save the layout before collectively resizing tracks. You will then be able to reload your customized layout later.

Tip   You might need to resize the Timeline window to show more of your tracks. Don't forget Final Cut Pro 4.0's new ability to resize all windows at the same time. Simply position your cursor on the edge of any abutting windows until it changes to a resize tool, then click and drag to resize. All adjoining windows will resize in the direction you drag.

Saving and reloading track layouts

Once you've created a customized track layout, you can save it and use it again later. You can apply saved layouts to any Sequence opened in the Timeline. Saving and reloading (called *restoring* in Final Cut Pro) saved layouts is done through the

Track Layout menu, located at the bottom of the Timeline patch panel area. Up to 40 saved track layouts can be displayed here. Figure 11-25 shows the Track Layout menu.

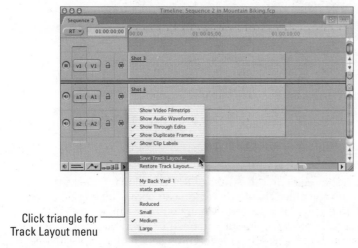

Click triangle for
Track Layout menu

Figure 11-25: In the Track Layout menu, you can select track display options, including Save and Restore custom track layouts.

✦ **To save a track layout:** After you have set the height of the tracks to your liking, select Save Track Layout from the Track Layout menu, located at the bottom of the Timeline patch panel area. Navigate to a location on your hard drive to save your layout, name your layout and click Save.

✦ **To reload a saved custom layout:** Select Restore Track Layout from the Track Layout menu. In the Open dialog box that appears, navigate to the location of the saved layout, select it, and click Open.

Cross-Reference

All options in the Track Layout menu except the Save Track Layout and Restore Track Layout commands can be selected in the Timeline Options tab of Sequence Settings, and are covered in detail in Chapter 6.

Deleting tracks

Tracks are pretty easy to delete from the Timeline. You can delete tracks by Control+clicking on the header area for any track, or in any empty space of the Patch Panel, and choosing Delete Track from the Contextual menu as shown in Figure 11-26. A quick way to delete more than one track at a time is to choose Sequence ➪ Delete Tracks. A Delete Tracks dialog box will appear. This box looks similar to the Insert Tracks dialog box but, as the name suggests, it deletes tracks rather than inserts them.

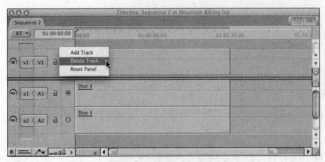

Figure 11-26: Control+click on any track's header area to get a contextual menu to delete the track.

Creating a static region

You can create a static region in the center of the Timeline for tracks that you always want to remain visible. The static region can show video and audio, just video, or just audio tracks. This is useful when you have numerous video or audio tracks that you must scroll through, but you need to always see the base tracks for reference. This is much like a freeze pane feature used in many spreadsheet applications, except the static region in the Timeline is not scrollable and can only be set from the lowest track upward. In other words, you couldn't set the static region to display only the topmost video tracks without showing all the video tracks below it starting from V1. A Timeline with a static region is shown in Figure 11-27.

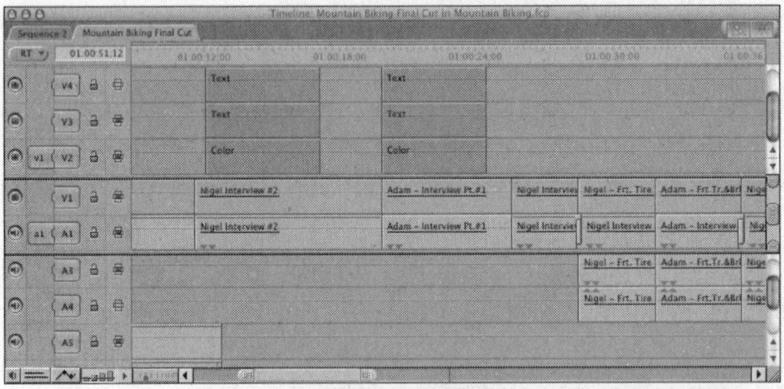

Figure 11-27: The static region of a Timeline is used to keep base tracks visible at all times.

✦ **To create a static region:** Drag the upper thumb tab in the Timeline scroll bar area up to include tracks of video. Drag the lower thumb tab down to include tracks of audio. When you drag a thumb tab, a dark gray line will snap to track boundaries, showing you which tracks will be included in the static region when you release the mouse.

✦ **To reposition the static region in the Timeline window:** Drag the center thumb tab in the static region scrollbar area. This looks deceptively like a scrolling thumb tab, but you will find that it only repositions the static region between the video and audio panes.

✦ **To eliminate the static region:** Drag the thumb tab back to the center until it overlaps the center thumb, then release it.

Locking tracks in a Timeline

If you want to prevent accidental edits or deletions of a track you want to keep, you can lock it by clicking on the small padlock icon to the left of the track. When locked, this icon will be dark gray and show a closed lock. Locked tracks will also have a crosshatch pattern across the entire track. You cannot make any changes to a locked track. Click on the lock again to unlock the track. The small lock icon will open up and the crosshatch pattern will disappear. Figure 11-28 illustrates the locked and unlocked states of tracks in the Timeline.

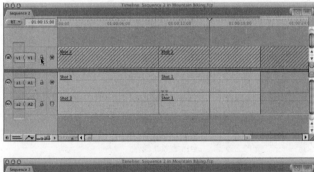

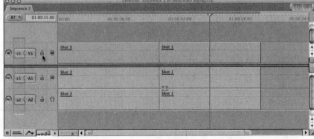

Figure 11-28: Click on the small lock icon to lock a track. Click on it again to unlock the track.

Tip

You can quickly lock all tracks of the same type by pressing the Option key when clicking a track lock. This causes all same-type tracks (audio or video) to lock, except for the track you've just selected. This is known as *soloing* the track because it is currently the only track available for editing—it's solo. If you want to lock this solo track as well, just click on its lock icon without the Option key to add it to the locked tracks. Clicking on the solo track with the Option key pressed will toggle the Solo mode off and unlock all tracks.

Working with track visibility

Entire tracks on a Timeline can be made invisible in Final Cut Pro. Invisible tracks differ from locked tracks in that they are hidden and do not show up when the Timeline is played, but they can still be edited even if they are not visible. Click on the green visibility toggle button to the left of a track to make it invisible. Green on the visibility toggle means visible, gray means invisible. Invisible tracks also have a dark overlay in the Timeline, as shown in Figure 11-29.

Tip   You can toggle track visibility by pressing the Option key when you select a track's visibility control. Option+clicking the soloed button again will turn on all tracks' visibility.

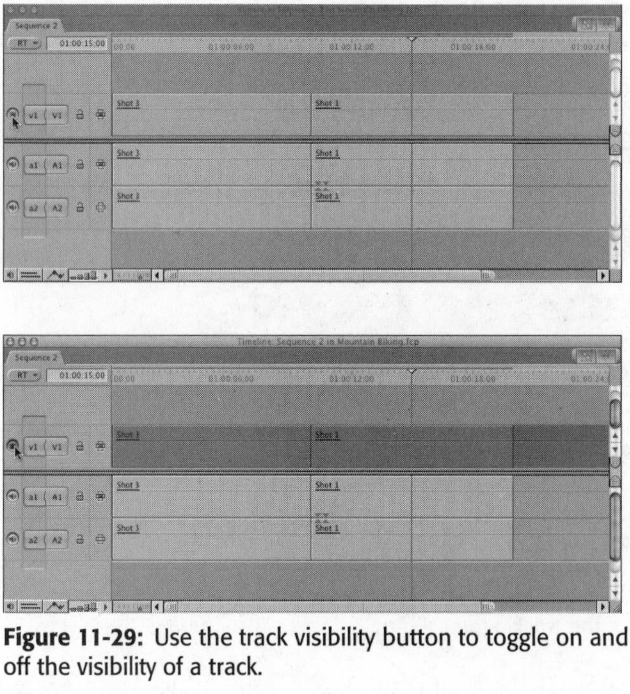

Figure 11-29: Use the track visibility button to toggle on and off the visibility of a track.

Keep in mind that making tracks invisible can have grave unintended consequences. Most of the time, multiple video tracks are used for layering. You can layer other video tracks above the base track and animate these layers in relation to other tracks. However, if you want to turn off the visibility of these tracks with the toggle button, take heed. Turning off the visibility for a track will lose all the render files for it. Turning it back on does not bring them back. To avoid this unfortunate situation, turn on the Warn If Visibility Change Deletes Render Files option in the General Preferences tab. Choose Final Cut Pro ➪ User Preferences to see this tab. Then, at least, you will be warned if you are about to delete render files by turning off the visibility of a track.

Tip   When a track's visibility is turned off, or *shied,* any render files for clips on the shied track are not actually deleted. Rather, the connection between clips and the render files is broken. If you Undo by pressing Command+Z, the shying of a track, as well as the link to all render files, is restored as well. It's a great trick when you want to preview a sequence with a shied track and then make the shied track visible again without having to re-render any previously rendered clips or transitions.

Using Mute and Solo Controls

Mute and solo controls enable you to monitor the playback of audio tracks in the Timeline. By default they are hidden, but they can be toggled to display when the Audio Control button is clicked on — it's the small speaker icon in the lower-left corner of the Timeline window. The two controls that appear to the left of the Track Visibility Control button are shown in Figure 11-30.

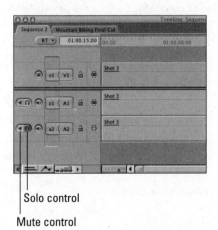

Figure 11-30: Mute and Solo controls enable audio track monitoring.

Solo control

Mute control

✦ **Mute:** The speaker icon on the left is the Mute control. When enabled, the Mute icon will highlight in orange, and audio clips on this track will not be heard on the computer or external monitor when you play down the Timeline. Muting a track only affects monitoring and does not change any properties of the audio clips. You can toggle mute on or off for any number of tracks.

✦ **Solo:** The headset icon to the right of the Mute button is the Solo control button. Enabling Solo by clicking on its button will highlight it red. When you solo a track, all other tracks will be muted, making it easy to hear in a Sequence with multiple audio tracks. You can actually enable more than one track for soloing, which might seem a contradiction in terms but can be useful when you want to hear only a few audio tracks while keeping the rest muted — don't forget you can have up to 99 tracks on audio in a Final Cut Pro sequence!

Caution

Mute and Solo controls affect playback monitoring only. If you want to prevent audio tracks from being output to tape or exported with a Movie file, you should disable the "visibility" of those tracks.

Working with Markers in the Timeline

Markers are little indicators that you can place in a sequence. When markers are added, they appear as small green pointers on the Timeline ruler. You can name markers and add notes to them. Markers added to a sequence appear as text overlays in the Canvas window. These overlays show the name of the marker and any notes that you have added. You can use markers to mark beats in your music, leave notes for a fellow editor, or simply note down important locations in your sequence.

Besides serving as virtual sticky notes for marking important locations on your clips and sequences, markers can also serve as navigation aids. It is possible to jump from marker to marker and select individual markers to jump to as well. You can even snap markers to other items, including other markers.

Cross-Reference

Working with markers in the Timeline and in sequences is virtually identical to working with markers in the Viewer window. To learn more about using markers with the Viewer, see Chapter 9.

Adding a marker to a sequence is easy:

1. **Play a sequence until the playhead is at the point where you want to add a marker.**

   Make sure that no clips under the playhead are selected.

2. **Choose Mark ➪ Markers ➪ Add.**

   You can also press the letter M on your keyboard to add a marker. A small green marker appears in the sequence's timecode ruler, as shown in Figure 11-31.

Tip

Be sure that no clip is selected in the sequence before you begin adding markers, otherwise, the marker will be added to the selected clip rather than Timeline ruler where the playhead is currently positioned. Press Command+Shift+A to make sure that nothing is selected before you add markers to the sequence.

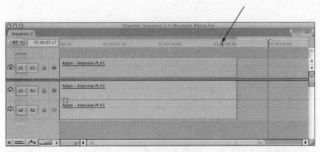

Figure 11-31: A sequence-based marker can be added by pressing the M key or by choosing Mark ⇨ Markers ⇨ Add.

There might be times when you want to add a marker to a selected clip rather than to the sequence itself. This is important because you may want a marker to stay with a specific clip rather than at a particular point in the sequence. To add a marker to a clip:

1. **Select a clip in the sequence to which you want to add a marker.**

2. **Position the playhead over the selected clip, at a spot where you want to add a marker.**

3. **Choose Mark ⇨ Markers ⇨ Add.**

    You can also press the letter M on your keyboard as a shortcut to add a marker. A small marker will appear on your clip, as shown in Figure 11-32.

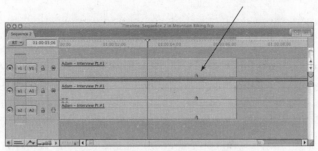

Figure 11-32: Markers can be added to individual clips in a sequence as well.

Note that if a clip is not selected, the marker will be added to the Timeline ruler instead of the clip. If you want to play a few clips in a row and add markers to them as you go along, Shift+click to select the clips you want to play, then play through them, pressing the M key where you want to add markers.

Editing markers

As mentioned earlier, you can customize markers by adding names and notes to them. This feature makes markers much more versatile and useful in Final Cut Pro. To add a name or note to a marker:

1. **Position the playhead directly over a marker in the sequence.**

   Ensure that you are right on the marker. (You should see the marker overlay in the Canvas window. If you don't see it, make sure the Overlay option is turned on for the Canvas window in the Viewer Choices pull-down menu of the Canvas window.)

2. **Press the M key to bring up the Edit Marker window.**

3. **Add a name and a comment for this marker.**

Tip   It is easier to add notes and names for markers when you create the marker in the first place. Pressing the M key twice (M+M) adds a marker and brings up the Edit Marker window to add a name and note for that marker.

In addition to the text note that you can add to a marker, there are now three additional types of marker tags available in the Edit Marker dialog box. These markers can be exported with the Sequence and used to navigate or flag important areas of the movie in other applications:

✦ **Chapter Markers** can be used by DVD Studio Pro to create a navigable chapter point. Chapter markers are also seen by QuickTime Player as a chapter item that you can jump to using a pop-up menu. Chapter markers appear in the Comment field as <CHAPTER>.

✦ **Compression Markers** can be used by compression applications to identify changes in the movie's properties that might affect compression, such as an abrupt change in scene brightness or subject motion. Compression markers appear in the Comment field as <COMPRESSION>.

✦ **Scoring Markers** are embedded audio scoring markers that are visible when the movie is opened with an Apple scoring application like Soundtrack. Scoring markers appear in the Comment field as <SCORING>.

When you export your movie, you can select which markers you want to export using File ➪ Export ➪ QuickTime Movie. Figure 11-33 shows the markers that can be exported with your QuickTime movie.

When you're exporting, the various marker types are straightforward, except for the DVD Studio Pro Marker option. Selecting DVD Studio Pro Markers will export all Chapter *and* Compression markers, while the other three marker options will export only the selected marker type.

Figure 11-33: Markers that can be exported with your QuickTime movie are selected from the Export ➪ QuickTime Movie's Save dialog box.

Caution

When exporting sequences with Chapter, Compression, or Audio markers, the markers must be added on the Timeline ruler or Canvas, and not to individual clips.

Cross-Reference

Chapter markers are discussed more in Chapter 27 where creating movies for DVD Studio Pro is covered. Compression markers are discussed in Chapter 23 where I cover Apple's new Compressor application.

Moving and extending markers

Moving a marker once it is created can be a challenge in Final Cut Pro. Like clip markers that you set in the Viewer, there is only one way to move an existing marker to an earlier position (to the left) in a Sequence (using timecode entry), but several ways to move a marker to a later position (to the right). If you need to move a marker up, that is to say, earlier in the Timeline, this is the only way to do it:

1. **Locate the playhead on the marker.**

2. **Press the M key to open the Edit Marker dialog box.**

3. **Enter a new timecode in the Start field.**

    Enter in an earlier timecode, or type in a negative frame or seconds amount you wish to move the marker.

4. **Click OK.**

    The marker will jump to its new position. Of course, this method would also work if you wanted to move the marker to a later position, just type in a positive amount of frames or seconds for it to move in that direction.

When you want to move a marker "downstream," to the right, position the playhead where you want the marker to be, then do either of the following:

✦ **Select Mark ⇨ Marker ⇨ Reposition.**

✦ If there are multiple markers, the nearest marker to the left of the playhead will jump to the playhead's current position.

✦ **Press Shift+` (accent mark key).**

You can also add a duration to a marker in the Edit Marker window. This will extend the marker as a green line in your Timeline, and the marker will appear as an overlay for that duration. Markers can be extended only to the right to show the marker's duration. When the playhead is positioned over any part of an extended marker, the marker's overlay in the Canvas will be visible. An extended marker is shown in Figure 11-34.

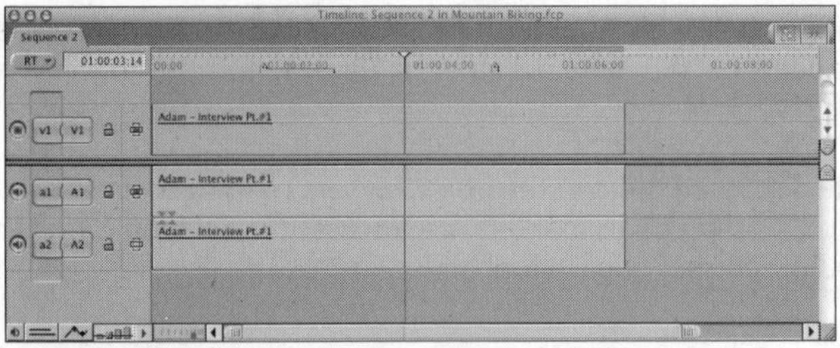

Figure 11-34: Markers can be extended to designate a selection of frames.

To extend a marker using timecode:

1. **Locate the playhead over a marker.**

2. **Press the M key to open the Edit Marker dialog box.**

3. **Enter a new timecode in the Duration field.**

   The amount you enter will extend the duration of the marker to the right of its current position. Negative durations entered are ignored.

4. **Click OK.**

   The marker's arm will extend to its new position.

You can extend a marker to the playhead by doing one of the following once the playhead is in the desired position (it must be to the right of the marker):

✦ **Select Mark ⇨ Marker ⇨ Extend.** If there are multiple markers, only the nearest marker to the left of the playhead will extend to the playhead's position.

✦ **Press Option+` (accent mark key).**

Note Only Sequence markers are displayed in the Canvas window. Markers placed on clips in the Timeline can only be seen by in the Viewer window. Double-click the clip with markers to load it into the Viewer window, then position the Viewer playhead on a marker to view the name and the comment of the clip-based marker.

Navigating to markers

Besides providing information about locations in clips and sequences, you can also use markers as navigation tools in Final Cut Pro. You can navigate using markers in one of several ways. Two easy methods include the following:

✦ To move to the next marker, press Shift+Up Arrow (the old keystroke shortcut, Shift+M, still works, too).

✦ To move to the previous marker, press Shift+ Down Arrow (the old keystroke shortcut, Option+M, still works, too).

Markers have gravity when Snapping is turned on. When Snapping is on, simply dragging the playhead around will snap it to the markers. You can also quickly jump to a specific marker for fast navigation:

1. **Control+Click anywhere on the Timeline ruler.**

2. **At the bottom of the contextual menu that appears, you'll see a selection of the markers in that sequence or clip. Select a marker from the list to move your playhead to that marker.**

   If you have added names for the markers, these names will appear in the contextual menu.

Tip You can also Control+click on the Current Timecode field of the Canvas menu (this field is in the upper-right corner of the Canvas window) to get a list of the markers in the sequence. Selecting one will move your playhead to that marker.

Snapping with markers

Because you can use clip markers to indicate important edit points or timing events within a clip, it would be ideal if clip markers could snap to items that clip edges snap to. Happily, you can. If you click and drag a sequence clip by its marker, that marker will now snap to edit points, the playhead, and even other clip and sequence markers in the Timeline. The head and tail of the clip that is usually used in snapping clips is ignored. The top Timeline in Figure 11-35 shows a clip marker snapping to an edit point. The bottom Timeline shows the result after the mouse is released — notice the exact alignment of the clip marker with the end point of the first clip.

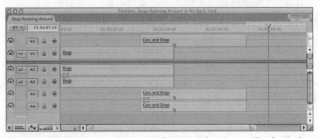

Figure 11-35: Snapping to a clip's marker is easily done by dragging the clip by its marker.

Deleting markers

Because it is not too easy to move markers back, earlier in the Timeline, it is often easier to set a new marker at the earlier position and delete the original marker. Or maybe you just don't need the marker any longer. In either case, to delete a single marker from a clip or sequence:

1. **Park your playhead over a marker.**

2. **Choose Mark ➪ Markers ➪ Delete.**

   The marker is deleted. You can also press Command+` (the accent key) to delete the marker.

If you want to delete all markers in a sequence, simply choose Mark ➪ Markers ➪ Delete All. All markers are deleted. You can also press Control+` (the accent key) to delete all markers.

Caution   To delete markers on a clip, you must locate your playhead over the clip, select the clip, and use the Command+` (accent key) to remove a single marker or Control+` (accent key) to remove all markers.

Working with Nested Sequences

A great feature of Final Cut Pro since its first released version is its ability to use a sequence within another sequence. This is possible because Final Cut Pro allows you to use a sequence like a clip, which means you can select, view, move, trim, even animate any sequence the same as you would a clip. A sequence edited within another sequence is called a *nested sequence;* the sequence containing a nested sequence is called the *parent sequence.* Figure 11-36 shows an example of nested sequences.

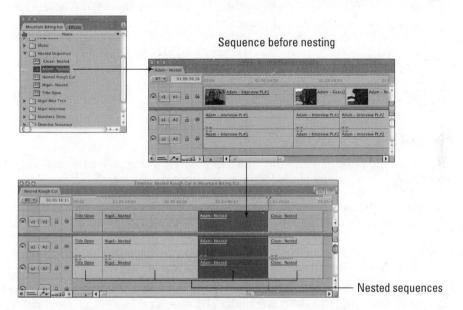

Sequence before nesting

Parent sequence holds nested sequences

Figure 11-36: A nested sequence is a sequence used within another sequence, just as you would use a clip.

There are many uses for nested sequences, such as:

✦ **Edit smaller sections of a large project in separate sequences and then nest them together into a master sequence.** This common workflow practice can help you separate, organize and streamline smaller parts of a large project. If you've ever had to work on a project of any length, you know how difficult it is to work with all the material of a project in one Timeline. For me, Final Cut Pro's ability to use nested sequences was indispensable when I was editing a two-hour weekly television show.

✦ **Use nested sequences to preserve render files. When** you render a sequence with video and audio effects and then nest this sequence into another, all the render files of the nested sequence are preserved even if you change its In or Out points in the parent sequence. Using nested sequences in this way can virtually eliminate the need to re-render effects applied within a nested sequence.

Tip

In order to preserve render files of a nested sequence, you must render effects applied to clips *within* the nested sequence. Rendering effects applied *to* a nested sequence in the parent sequence does not have the same effect and won't preserve its render file if the nested sequence's In or Out point is moved.

✦ **Use nested sequences to affect the render order of applied effects.** If you need to force the render order of effects, you can render all the effects applied to clips inside a nested sequence, then apply additional effects to the nested sequence. Affects applied to a nested sequence will then affect the total content of the nested sequence as if it were a single clip.

Note

A sequence cannot be nested into itself.

Nesting sequences

A sequence can be edited into the Timeline, creating a nested sequence, just as you would a clip by using one of the following methods:

✦ **Drag a sequence from the Browser and drop it directly into an open sequence in the Timeline.** As you drag the sequence over the Timeline, a gray-shaded image of the nested sequence will appear showing its position and duration. Use the 1/3–2/3 rule of dropping clips onto the upper or lower part of a track to affect an insert or overwrite edit.

✦ **Drag a sequence from the Browser and drop it into the Viewer. Set In and Out points, and then edit it into the Timeline as you would a clip loaded in the Viewer.** You can drag and drop the sequence from the Viewer to the Timeline, as you would from the Browser, or use the Canvas window Edit commands.

✦ **Copy a sequence in the Browser by selecting it and choosing Edit ⇨ Copy, then paste it into an open sequence in the Timeline by choosing Edit ⇨ Paste.** Before pasting the sequence, position the Timeline playhead where you want the nested sequence to be inserted. Don't forget to set destination tracks to target the placement of the video and audio tracks of the nested sequence you're pasting.

Tip

The standard Paste command, using the menu item Edit ⇨ Paste, or pressing Command+V, will perform an overwrite edit at the playhead position. If you need to insert edit a copied item, choose Edit ⇨ Paste Insert, or press Shift+V instead.

You can also select clips in an open sequence and nest them in their own sequence with the nested sequence replacing the selected clips in the Timeline. To do this, you use the Nested Item(s) command in the Sequence menu:

1. **In the Timeline, select a range of clips to be nested.**

   All linked items of a selected clip are also selected, as shown with the linked audio of the clips in Figure 11-37.

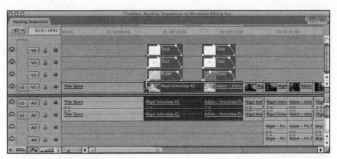

Figure 11-37: Select clips in a sequence that you want to move into their own sequence.

2. **Choose Sequence ⇨ Nested Item(s), or press Option+C.**

3. **In the Nested Items dialog box that appears, enter a new name for the nested sequence that will be created.**

   It is best to use a name different from the parent sequence name to avoid any confusion later on. It's not a bad idea to use the word "Nested" somewhere in the name of a nested sequence, shown in Figure 11-38.

Figure 11-38: This dialog box appears when you select Sequence ⇨ Nest Item(s), offering options for the nested sequence you're creating.

4. **Choose the frame dimensions of the nested sequence by using the default settings in the Aspect Ratio pop-up menu, or enter a custom size directly into the Width and Height fields.**

   If you choose a frame size different from the frame size of the parent sequence, you may have to render it before it can be played back in the parent sequence.

5. **Select the checkbox in front of Keep Effects, Markers, and Audio Levels with Clip to move these items with the selected clips, into the nested sequence.**

6. **Select the checkbox in front of Mixdown Audio to automatically render all audio in the nested sequence.**

7. Click OK.

The selected items in the Timeline will be replaced by a nested sequence containing those same items, shown in Figure 11-39. The nested sequence also appears in the same Browser bin where the parent sequence is located.

Figure 11-39: The selected clips are moved into the nested sequence which replaces the clips in the parent sequence.

All nested sequences contain only one video track, but will have the same number of audio tracks as audio output channels set in the Audio Outputs tab in the Sequence Settings of the nested sequence.

Cross-Reference   See Chapter 6 for details on setting audio outputs on the Audio Outputs tab.

If you nest a sequence in its entirety without setting In or Out points in the nested Timeline, changing its total duration by adding or subtracting media in the nested sequence will be automatically update and ripple all clips after the nested sequence in the parent sequence. If In or Out points are set in the nested sequence, or if the nested sequence is trimmed or has a transition applied to it in the parent sequence, changes to the overall length of the original nested sequence will have no effect on the nested sequence's duration in the parent sequence. To re-edit a nested sequence, simply double-click on it in the parent sequence; it will open in its own tabbed window in the Timeline.

✦   ✦   ✦

Using the Media Management Tools

◆ ◆ ◆ ◆

In This Chapter

Understanding
scratch disk behavior

Understanding links
between clips and
media files

Working with the
Media Manager

◆ ◆ ◆ ◆

There is a popular sound effect that is used to signify the sudden interruption of a blissful moment in movies and commercials. It is the sound of a record stylus being dragged rudely across a vinyl record. A young man and woman are about to kiss when the loud, scratch-across-the-vinyl-record sound invades their moment and a bottle of the latest sugared water is thrust into their hands, or some such interruption.

This chapter is, in a way, that scratching vinyl sound. I am going to interrupt your flow of editing bliss in Final Cut Pro with this chapter on media management. But rest assured; I am interrupting for a purpose much more important than to sell you some sugared water.

If editing were all there is to working with Final Cut Pro, this book would be a lot different. But the fact is that putting shots together, adding transitions, and manipulating audio tracks are just parts of the many responsibilities of the intrepid Final Cut Pro editor. A significant part of your work involves media management. Media management is so important that this chapter needs to come before chapters about more-fun topics like audio editing and working with transitions and effects. Each time you capture a shot into Final Cut Pro, a digital media file for the shot is stored on a disk drive. The clips that appear in your Browser are pointers to the media files on disk. As you render transitions and effects, even more media files are created.

Media management is the process of organizing and managing your source media and render files. This may sound like a simple process. However, the realities of editing make this process a complex one. Fortunately, Final Cut Pro offers various media management tools to help you stay organized.

Understanding Scratch Disk Behavior

Your first adventure with media management is going to involve the Scratch Disk settings. A Scratch Disk in Final Cut Pro parlance is the disk you have chosen as the place where all your captured source media, render files, and cache files are sent. Scratch Disk settings can be accessed by choosing Final Cut Pro ⇨ System Settings, or Shift+Q. The Scratch Disk tab is the default tab when you first open System Settings.

Cross-Reference Apple strongly recommends that you specify a Scratch Disk immediately after installing Final Cut Pro. Using your main system drive as a scratch disk is strongly discouraged. To learn how to set Scratch Disk Preferences see Chapter 6.

A thorough understanding of how files are saved on your Scratch Disks is critical to managing and organizing your files. When you specify a disk as your Scratch Disk, Final Cut Pro automatically creates the following five folders on the disk as shown in Figure 12-1:

✦ **Capture Scratch:** Holds all the captured media

✦ **Render Files:** Holds all the render files

✦ **Waveform Cache Files:** Holds the cache files for waveforms

✦ **Thumbnail Cache Files:** Holds the cache files for clip thumbnails

✦ **Audio Render Files:** Holds the audio render files

Note that these folders may have been created earlier during the course of another project. In that case, Final Cut Pro will use the preexisting folders. If the folders do not exist, then Final Cut Pro will create these folders from scratch.

Figure 12-1: Final Cut Pro automatically creates capture scratch folders on your assigned Scratch Disk.

When you start a new project, Final Cut Pro does more than just create the five scratch folders. As you create, capture, or render files, Final Cut Pro creates folders named for your project in the Capture Scratch, Render Files, and Audio Render Files folders. As you can see in Figure 12-2, Final Cut Pro has created these folders for a project called My Backyard.fcp. All capture and render files associated with this project will be stored in these folders.

Figure 12-2: Each scratch folder contains separate folders for each project.

Additional folders are created every time you start a new project. In Figure 12-3 you can see that a second project called Rabbits.fcp has been created. Appropriate folders for this project are created in the Capture Scratch, Render Files, and Audio Render Files folders. Even though there is more than one project, the thumbnail and waveform cache files for all projects are mixed together in the same folder.

Figure 12-3: Multiple Projects get folders with their names in the Scratch Folders. These folders are where Audio, Capture and Render files are diverted, depending on which project is active.

This process may seem simple enough, but things can get complicated when you rename a project as you work. If you save another version of your current project, Final Cut Pro will start another set of folders with the new name, and it will start sending files to those folders. As you can see in Figure 12-4, a second version of the My Backyard.fcp project called My Backyard v2.fcp has been created.

Final Cut Pro maintains this automatic folder-creation behavior when you retrieve a project from the Autosave Vault. The Save a Copy Every X Minutes in the Autosave Vault options is a feature in Final Cut Pro that automatically saves a backup file of your project at the time interval you set. The Autosave Vault feature is found under Final Cut Pro ⇨ User Preferences, in the General tab. I highly recommend saving your work often by using the Command+S shortcut, and *not* relying on the automatic-save feature as a foolproof, life-saving device. The automatic-save feature has some eccentricities that can burn you.

Figure 12-4: Saving a second version of a project causes Final Cut Pro to create another set of scratch folders.

When Final Cut Pro performs an automatic save, it creates a copy of your project with date and time added to the end of the name. Suppose that disaster strikes and you try to recover the auto-saved version of My Backyard.fcp. When you recover My Backyard.fcp_*mm_dd_yy_hrmn,* Final Cut Pro creates another set of scratch folders for this project. The cycle starts all over again if you have the auto-save feature enabled while working on My Backyard.fcp_*mm_dd_yy_hrmn,* and so on. The result of this house-of-mirrors effect is a dizzying collection of strangely named folders on your scratch disk, making the task of organizing your projects a true challenge.

To avoid entering this hall of mirrors, save often and try to work without saving *any* renamed versions of a project. If you can work through the entirety of your project without changing its name, your media will stay organized.

Cross-Reference   To learn more about the Autosave Vault feature in Final Cut Pro, see Chapter 6.

Understanding Links between Clips and Media Files

When shots are captured through the Log and Capture window in Final Cut Pro, these shots appear as clips in your Browser. However, these clips in the Browser are just part of the whole story. The captured shots exist as source media files on your Scratch Disk. The clips that appear in the Browser are simply pointers to these media files. This fact does not affect your ability to edit and work with these clips, but the fact that clips in the Browser are *not* the actual source media files does affect your management of media on your drives. Clips in the Browser are merely linked to the original media files, and if you move or delete a media file, those links will be broken.

Locating media files

Identifying the location of media files is pretty easy. You can use the Browser window or the Item Properties window to identify the source media files for your clips. This may be necessary for a variety of reasons. You may be trying to locate the source media file for an errant clip in the Timeline, or you may simply want to locate it to check the media's attributes and settings. You can see some of this information in the Browser, but there are times where you need to locate the actual source media file for a clip. To find the location of media files using the Browser:

1. **Click on the Browser window to make it active and choose View ⇨ Browser Items ⇨ As List. Resize the Browser window if necessary.**

2. **Control+click on a column heading and choose Show Source from the contextual menu that appears.**

   The directory path of the media file appears in the Show Source column for clips in the Browser as shown in Figure 12-5. You may have to resize the column to see the entire path.

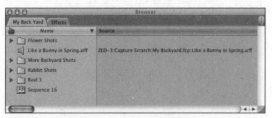

Figure 12-5: The directory path for a clip's source media file can be seen in the Browser window under the Source column.

I find that it's easier to read the directory path backward. For example, in Figure 12-5 the file Like a Bunny in Spring.aiff is located in a folder called My Backyard.fcp, which is located in a folder called Capture Scratch on the drive named ZED-3. The Macintosh operating system uses colons to indicate directories, which by the way is the reason you can't use colons in filenames.

Another way to find the location of a media file is with the Item Properties window for an individual clip. Here's how:

1. **Select a clip in the Browser whose media file path you want to see.**

2. **Choose Edit ➪ Item Properties ➪ Format.**

   You can also press Command+9 or Control+click on the clip in the Browser.

   The Item Properties window appears as shown in Figure 12-6, with the directory path of the media file indicated in the Source field of the Format tab.

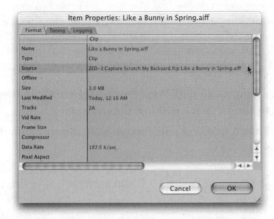

Figure 12-6: The Item Properties window shows the directory path to the media file for a clip.

In Figure 12-6, you can see that the source media file for the audio clip Like a Bunny in Spring.aiff is located in folder called My Backyard.fcp, which is located in the Capture Scratch folder on the drive named ZED-3.

Understanding offline clips

Because clips are linked to source media files by their location, moving the source media files to another drive or folder will break the link between the clips and their respective source media files. Renaming or deleting source media files will also break this link. Clips with broken links to their media files are called *offline* clips and appear in the Browser with a red slash across their icons. Offline clips can also be clips that are logged but not yet captured.

Relinking files automatically

You can relink media files automatically, or you can relink the files manually. To automatically relink media files and clips:

1. **Open a project that has broken links between clips and source media or render files.**

   If there are broken links, the Offline Files box automatically appears when you open the project as shown in Figure 12-7.

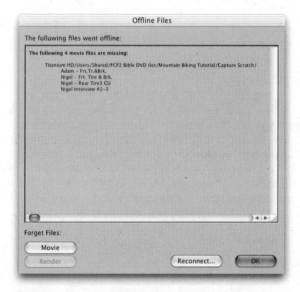

Figure 12-7: The Offline Files dialog box shows a list of offline files in the project.

For more on working with the Offline Files dialog box, see the section "Understanding the Offline Files dialog box" later in this chapter.

2. **If there are some files types you don't want to relink, click Movie or Render under *Forget Files*.**

   Depending on which type of file you want to forget, the list of files you choose to forget is eliminated from the Offline Files window. Do not check the Select Files Manually option unless you want to perform the search yourself; otherwise, Final Cut Pro will search for the missing source files.

3. Click Reconnect to relink the remaining clips in the list.

You see the Reconnect Options box as shown in Figure 12-8. The options available here vary depending on what you chose to "forget" in the previous window.

Figure 12-8: The Reconnect Options dialog box allows you to choose the types of files you'd like to reconnect.

4. Choose the kind of files you want to reconnect, then click OK.

Final Cut Pro automatically searches for the offline files by name and provides a dialog box to help you identify the files. Note that you can even select the Online option to link clips to files other than their original source media files. This should be done with great forethought and caution because it changes the clips' media across the board and you may find yourself with edits whose images have changed in the Timeline. If Final Cut Pro finds the file, it is highlighted in the dialog box shown in Figure 12-9.

Figure 12-9: Select the appropriate media file and click Select.

5. **Select the correct file and click Select.**

   Final Cut Pro relinks the file and continues through the list.

Manually reconnecting files

Clips and media files can also be manually reconnected as you work in Final Cut Pro. Here's how:

1. **In the Browser window, select a clip (or multiple clips) and choose File ➪ Reconnect Media.**

   You can also Control+click on a clip and choose Reconnect Media from the contextual menu. The Reconnect Options dialog box appears.

2. **Select the type of files you'd like to reconnect and click OK.**

   Final Cut Pro searches for the files and presents them in a dialog box like the one shown in Figure 12-9. If the file wasn't found, you can also use this dialog box to find the files yourself.

3. **Highlight the appropriate file and click Select to reconnect the file.**

Tip

When you reconnect a file in the Browser using the contextual menu's Reconnect Media option, because of Final Cut Pro's new master/affiliate clip relationship, all offline affiliated clips in the Browser and Sequences will also be reconnected.

Understanding the Offline Files dialog box

When you double-click on a Final Cut Pro project file to open it, Final Cut Pro automatically checks links between clips and media files. If media files or render files have been moved, deleted, or renamed, Final Cut Pro warns you with the Offline Files dialog box shown in Figure 12-10. Note that if you move or rename media files using the Mac OS Finder while a project is open, the Offline Files dialog box will appear when you return to the project.

The Offline Files dialog box provides a lot of useful information about your offline clips. This information includes:

✦ **The following (movie/render) file is missing:** This section of the Offline Files dialog box indicates the movie and render files that are offline for the current project. By *movie,* Final Cut Pro means source media files. This section shows you information about the missing files such as how many of each are missing, what their previous file path was, and what their names are. In the case of missing render files, this section indicates the name of the sequence in which the render files were generated.

✦ **Forget Files:** Click one of these buttons if you want Final Cut Pro to forget about missing movie or render files. Final Cut Pro "forgets" that these files are offline. If you return to this project later you will *not* get the Offline Files dialog box for the files you chose to forget. You can always relink the files later, even if you choose to forget them at this stage.

One thing to keep in mind is that source media files (the *movie* files here) are much more important to reconnect than the render files. After you have the source media files relinked, you can always generate new render files for an effect or a transition by re-rendering it.

✦ **Reconnect:** Click this button to make Final Cut Pro search for the missing files by name. When a file with the correct name is found, select it in the dialog box that appears. Just make sure that you are reconnecting to the right file. If you are working in a complex project with similarly named files, you'll have to use caution when selecting a file. Linking to the wrong files can change your edits and the images for your clips in the Browser and the Timeline.

✦ **OK:** An explanation of the OK button may seem odd, but it is necessary here. If you click on the OK button, you are choosing to bypass the reconnecting process for now. However, Final Cut Pro will *remember* the missing files for the current project. The next time you open the same project, the Offline Files dialog box will come up again with the same list of offline files.

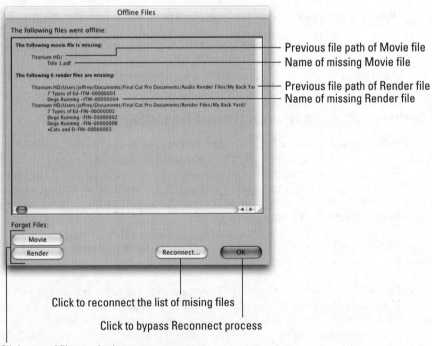

Figure 12-10: The Offline Files dialog box automatically comes up when Final Cut Pro detects missing media files for clips used in the project.

Selecting files to reconnect

When you try to reconnect an offline clip or render file, a file selection dialog box like the one shown in Figure 12-11 helps you search for and select media files to relink to. This file selection dialog box looks and works like most Mac OS X file dialog boxes. You can navigate through folders and directories with the pull-down menu at the top of the window, or click on folders to navigate to a specific location.

Just below the directory display window is the filename of the source media file you are looking for. This name is important because after searching for a bit you may not remember the exact name of the file you're looking for. Keep in mind that the name indicated here is *always* the name of the *source media file* and may not be the name of the clip you are attempting to relink. If, by chance, you renamed the clip in the Browser, when you attempt to relink the clip, the name that appears in the file selection dialog box might be different.

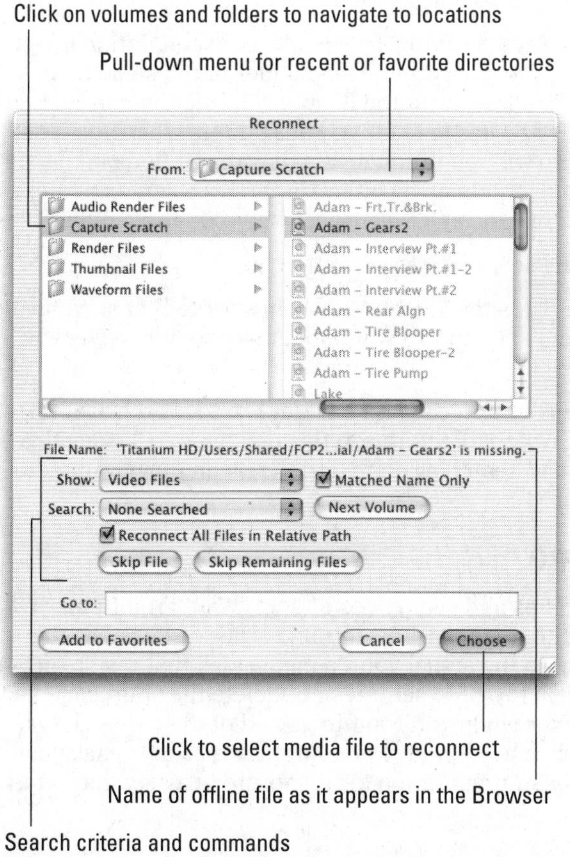

Click on volumes and folders to navigate to locations

Pull-down menu for recent or favorite directories

Click to select media file to reconnect

Name of offline file as it appears in the Browser

Search criteria and commands

Figure 12-11: The Mac OS X–style file dialog box lets you select files for reconnecting.

Although this file selection dialog box may seem familiar, there are some details that are unique to the relinking process. Details you want to pay attention to here include:

✦ **Show:** The Show pull-down menu allows you to choose which file types are displayed for relinking. The All Files choice shows you every file in the current directory or folder. Other choices in the menu are Video Files, Sound Files and Still Image Files. Choosing any of these options limits the type of files shown in the dialog box.

✦ **Match Name Only:** Another way to refine your viewing options is to enable this option. If you have many similarly named files, this option only shows files that match the current filename.

✦ **Search:** Shows the path of the media file linked to the currently selected clip.

✦ **Next Volume:** This could easily be named Find. Clicking this button searches the next volume for the media clip, and can research the current volume when it finishes with all available volumes.

✦ **Reconnect All Files in Relative Path:** This is a very useful option if you're trying to relink several clips to their source media files at the same time. If you selected more than one offline file in the Browser for reconnecting, and then checked the Reconnect All Files in Relative Path option, when you reach this dialog box, Final Cut Pro will relink any media files that it finds in this directory to any selected clips that may be offline in the Browser. Using this option avoids having to relink one file at a time from a set of multiple offline files.

✦ **Skip File:** This skips the search for the current clip.

✦ **Skip Remaining Files:** Skips the search for all clips. Note that skipping files does not "forget" them. Final Cut Pro will remember the offline files for the next time.

✦ **Find Again:** Clicking this button causes Final Cut Pro to search again. This is useful if you manually switch directories in this dialog box. Clicking this button will cause Final Cut Pro to search again to find the file in the new directory.

Making clips offline

You can intentionally make clips and sequences offline. "Wait!" You think. "Why in the world would I ever want to do that?" Recall from earlier discussions that clips in the Browser are merely links to the actual source media files that reside on your hard drive. Deleting clips from the Browser does not delete the source media files from the drive. There are times when you want to get rid of the clip and its related source media file to free up space on your drive. Another reason to make clips and sequences offline may be in preparation for recapture of a sequence at a higher resolution.

Making clips offline breaks the link between the media files on the Scratch Disk and the clips in the Browser. Making clips offline also breaks any reference to clips used in the sequence or subclips. To make a sequence offline:

1. **Select the clips in the Browser or the sequence that you may want to make offline.**

2. **Choose Modify ⇨ Make Offline.**

   You can also Control+click on the items to choose Make Offline from the contextual menu. The Make Offline dialog box appears, as shown in Figure 12-12.

Figure 12-12: The Make Offline dialog box provides options for dealing with source media files after making their respective clips offline.

3. **Choose one of the three options listed and click OK.**

Note   You can also select clips in an open sequence and choose Modify ⇨ Make Offline to make the clip offline for recapture. Later you can Control+click on the offline clip in the sequence and choose Capture to recapture the clip at a different resolution setting.

The Make Offline dialog box has one purpose: It makes your selected clip offline. However, you need to understand the choices presented in the Make Offline dialog box: The options tell Final Cut Pro what to do after it breaks the link between the clips and their respective source media files. The options are:

✦ **Leave Them on the Disk:** Choosing this option breaks the link between the clips and their respective source media files. The source media files are left alone.

✦ **Move Them to the Trash:** If you select this option, the source media files are moved to the Trash. Selecting this option brings up a threatening looking message at the bottom of the dialog box that says: "Warning: Deleting or Moving Files To Trash will make all clips based on these files offline, even if they are not selected or are in a project currently not open." As the warning suggests, all clips that are based on these media files in all your projects, open or not, will be offline.

Caution Be aware that the Move Them to the Trash option is not undoable, meaning that you can't just press Control+Z and undo the action. You also can't use the handy Mac OS shortcut Command+Y to "put away" the source files from the Trash back to their original locations. You can, however, drag the files from Trash back to the hard drive and manually relink them back to the clips.

✦ **Delete Them from the Disk:** This option deletes the source media files from the disk entirely. This action is also undoable. Command+Z will not undo this action, and once you have executed this option the files are gone. You can't even recover from the Trash. If you want the media files back, you'll have to recapture them. You will however get the "Warning: Deleting or Moving Files To Trash will make all clips based on these files offline, even if they are not selected or are in a project currently not open" message when you select this option.

Using a combination of the Make Offline dialog box and the Find feature in Final Cut Pro, you can do some creative media management as well. (See the sidebar "Deleting unused media.")

Deleting unused media

Many times you will face a situation where you have a very large project with numerous clips and media. In many cases, you may want to delete all unused media from your project. For example, you may have created two sequences in the course of editing your project but wish to delete any extraneous and unused media not used in those two sequences.

Using a combination of the Find feature in Final Cut Pro and the Make Offline dialog box, you can do this in a few easy steps.

1. Select the sequence or sequences in your project for which you want to delete unused media.

2. Select Edit ⇨ Find (Command+F).

The Find dialog box appears, shown here.

3. Select Unused Media in the For pop-up menu.

Be sure that the In Selected Sequences option box is checked.

4. **Click on the Find All button in the Find dialog box.**

   The Find Results window will be presented to you. In the Find Results window, you are shown all the clips that are unused in the sequences you selected.

5. **Select the clip(s) and Control+click on them to bring up the contextual menu.**

6. **Select Make Offline from the contextual menu, as shown in the next figure.**

7. **In the Make Offline dialog box, select Move Them to the Trash option and click the OK button.**

Before you empty the Trash, open and check your sequences to make sure no files have been inadvertently deleted — there should be no offline clips in your sequences. In case of any problem, you can manually move the files back to your drives and relink them. Otherwise, you can feel free to empty your trash and delete the unused media files.

Understanding the Media Manager

The Media Manager is the ultimate Final Cut Pro tool for managing your media. This manager allows you to copy and move your clips and sequences along with their related source media and render files. What use might this feature be? There are many uses for the Media Manager, including the following:

✦ **In a large, complex project, you can use the Media Manager to copy and move just one sequence and its related source media and render files to a separate folder or drive.** Doing so allows you to single out any and all items related to a sequence and save them separately.

✦ **You can use the Media Manager to delete all unused media from a project, keeping just the media files that you actually need.**

✦ You can use the Media Manager to create an offline duplicate of a sequence so that you can recapture just the duplicate sequence at a higher-resolution setting.

✦ You can use the Media Manager to copy and recompress an entire project using a different codec for editing on a Powerbook.

 Note   Media Manager uses only the source timecode of clips and ignores Aux 1 or Aux 2 if any have been added.

Using the Media Manager

The Media Manager provides many options and settings. To begin using the Media Manager, follow these steps:

1. **Select clips or a sequence.**

   You can simply click on a closed sequence in the Browser, select individual clips in the Browser, or select items within an open sequence. To run the Media Manager on an open sequence, make sure that its tab in the Timeline is selected.

2. **Choose File ⇨ Media Manager.**

   You can also Control+click on an item in the browser or in an open sequence then select Media Manager from the context menu that appears. The Media Manager window appears.

3. **Select the options you need.**

   The options in the Media Manager are described in the next section.

4. **If you're saving files to another location, click the Browse button in the Media Destination section, select a location, and enter a filename.**

5. **Click OK in the Media Manager dialog box to continue.**

   Final Cut Pro processes the files and options. A status bar in the Processing Files status box will show you the progress.

Understanding options in the Media Manager

A thorough understanding of the options in the Media Manager is necessary before you can use the Media Manager to its fullest potential. The Media Manager is a powerful tool, and for projects that involve complex media management, this tool can greatly enhance your productivity. Figure 12-13 shows the Media Manager window and the options available in it.

Summary of selections and operations

Bar graph showing media file size

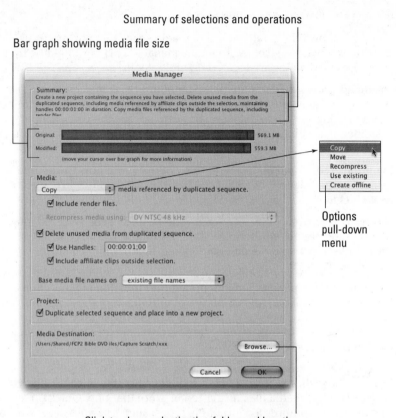

Options
pull-down
menu

Click to choose destination folder and location

Figure 12-13: Options in the Media Manager allow you to copy and move clips, sequences, and their related source media and render files.

Before you start managing your media with the Media Manager, be aware that you can get widely varying results from your options and selections. Mixing and matching options in the desired combinations will give you the results you want. Even the wording on these options and settings will vary depending on what you selected in the Browser and what settings you have enabled in the Media Manager window. Mix and match options with great care. The options include:

✦ **Summary of selections and choices:** The options and choices can often leave you confused as to what *exactly* the result of all the choices selected in the Media Manager will be. The summary area provides a narrative in clear English of what it is you're about to do. The summary description will dynamically change with each option that you choose in the Media Manager. Carefully read the summary before you click OK.

The graphic summary displays two bars:

- Original, shows the total amount of media space on your drives used by the items you have selected to media manage. This bar might be fragmented if media files are located on multiple disks.

- Modified, shows an estimate of the amount of disk space that will be used by the selected items *after* the Media Manager operations are performed using the currently selected options. Like the text summary, the Modified bar will dynamically change to reflect any options that affect media size, like deleting unused media and recompressing media.

✦ **Media options pull-down menu:** Selections here dictate how the source media files for the selected items will be handled by Final Cut Pro. Choices in this menu include:

- **Copy:** This option copies the source media files of the selected items to another location of your choice. This option leaves the original source media files alone and does not alter them in any way.

- **Move:** The Move option takes the *original* source media files and moves them from their present location to another location of your choice. As opposed to the Copy option, the Move option alters the original source media files. If the Remove Unused Media from Duplicated Items option is enabled along with this option, the source media files will be truncated to just the necessary portions.

- **Recompress Media Using:** This option is like the Copy option, except you can now choose from a list of sequence presets or the codec you want your new media files formatted in. Note that only QuickTime movies are recompressed; other file types, such as Photoshop, WAV, or AIFF files, are only copied.

Note   You cannot convert NTSC to PAL, or vice versa, using the Recompress option. Media Manager will convert the frame size, but the frame rate will remain the same as the original.

Caution   The Recompress option may fail with clips using a codec based on temporal compression, like Cinepak or Sorenson.

- **Use Existing:** This option creates new source media files. The old source media files are deleted. Note that any items that were not selected before invoking the Media Manager will go offline if you choose to proceed. This option is a great way to reduce the media down to what you're using in the selected items, but using it incorrectly can spell doom because you can't undo it. Command+Z will not allow you to go back a step after using this option.

- **Create Offline:** Selecting this option will create an offline version of the selected clips or sequences. New offline items will have no links to any previous source media files and can be recaptured. This option is helpful if you want to recapture sequences at a higher resolution.

✦ **Include Render Files:** Choose this to include any render files. This option is here because you could, if you wanted, not copy or move any render files. You can always re-render the effects and transitions to get your render files back. All it costs you is time. But it can save time at this stage, and it saves disk space depending on how many renders are in your selected items.

Note

The Include Render Files option is only available for copy and move operations.

✦ **Delete Unused Media from Selected Items:** This option removes any media not used in the selected items. Media outside the In and Out points for selected items will be removed. The wording of this setting will also vary depending on your selections in the Browser and other choices here. This option only works with QuickTime files. AIFF and WAV files are only copied in their entirety.

  • **Use Handles:** This option allows you to leave extra media around the In and Out points of the clips from which you have chosen to remove unused media. This option will not be available unless you have selected Delete Unused Media from Duplicated Items. Enter duration here for the size of the handles you want. Handles are a good idea because they provide some flexibility later for creating transitions and other adjustments.

  • **Include Affiliate Clips outside This Selection:** This option allows you to include master or affiliated clips of clips in the current selection, even if those affiliate clips are not in the current selection (they can be in another sequence, for example).

Note

Selecting Include Affiliate clips increases the amount of disk space needed for Media Manager operations, but it also insures you'll have enough media for editing choices later. The portion of a master clip that will be included is determined by the In point, Out point, or both; the media that falls between two unconnected clips from the same master clip; or any affiliate clip used in another sequence.

✦ **Base Media File Names On:** This pop-up menu allows you to select how media clips will be named when they are shortened using the Delete Unused Media option. You can select:

  • **Existing File Names:** This is the name of the source file as it appears on your hard drive.

  • **Clip Names:** This might not be the same as the source file when you captured it if you manually renamed it in your project.

✦ **Duplicate Selected Items and Place into a New Project:** Checking this option will create a new project file with copies of the selected sequences or clips. Leaving this option unchecked will not provide a copy of the project file. The wording of this setting may vary depending on your selections in the Browser and other choices here.

✦ **Media Destination:** The Media Destination section at the bottom of the Media Manager window shows the current folder to which your files will be moved or copied. If you want to save your media files in different location, click the Browse button to select a new directory and create a new folder for your operation.

Copying sequences with the Media Manager

You can perform a wide variety of tasks with the Media Manager by varying the combinations of settings and options in the Media Manager window. One of the more common tasks involves copying a sequence and its related media files into a new project. At the end of your project, it might be necessary to copy merely one sequence and the related media for it for saving purposes. Follow these steps:

1. **Select a sequence in the Browser you want to copy.**

2. **Choose File ➪ Media Manager.**

   You can also Control+click on a sequence and choose Media Manager from the contextual menu as shown in Figure 12-14. The Media Manager window appears.

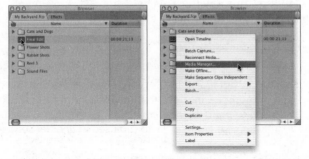

Figure 12-14: Control+click on the sequence you want to copy and choose Media Manager from the contextual menu.

3. **Choose Copy from the pull-down menu for media referenced by duplicated items if you want to leave your original source media files alone and create new copies for them.**

4. **Enable the Include Render Files option if you want to save any render files that are linked to your sequence.**

   After you've selected the options listed earlier, your Media Manager window should look similar to Figure 12-15.

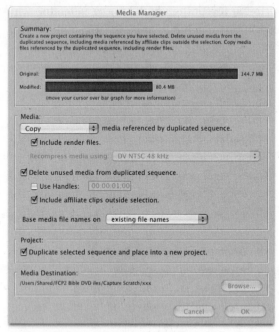

Figure 12-15: The Media Manager window is ready to copy a sequence.

5. **Enable the Delete Unused Media from Duplicated Items option, if you only want to include the media for that sequence; otherwise, deselect this option.**

6. **Select Add Handles if desired.**

   Enter the amount of time of additional media you think you'll need for fine-tuning edits and transitions.

7. **Select Include Affiliate Clips outside This Selection to include master or affiliate clips of selected items, even if affiliate clips are not a part of the current selection.**

   Selecting this option usually require considerably more disk space but allows for more flexibility when editing later.

8. **Choose existing filenames or clip names from the pop-up menu for the new media files for the naming of the new media clips.**

9. **Check the Duplicate Selected Items and Place into a New Project check box.**

10. **Click the Browse button to select a destination for the copy the sequence and its media.**

11. **To create a new folder, click the New Folder button.**

12. **Click the Choose button at the bottom of the folder selection window (see Figure 12-16) when you have highlighted the desired folder.**

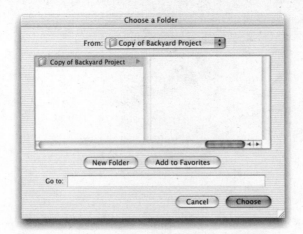

Figure 12-16: Select the drive and folder to which you want to copy your sequence and media files.

13. **Click OK in the Media Manager dialog box.**

You'll be asked to name your duplicate project.

14. **Enter a name and click Save as shown in Figure 12-17.**

Figure 12-17: Enter a name for your new duplicate project.

Final Cut Pro displays a progress bar as it copies your sequence and associated media files into the new project. When finished, the new project automatically opens in its own tab in the Browser, along with a bin named Master Clips. Media and render file folders are also created on your Scratch Disk, as shown in Figure 12-18.

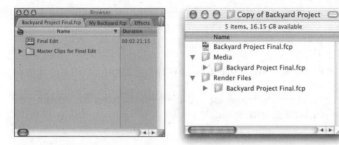

Figure 12-18: At left, Final Cut Pro automatically opens the newly duplicated project in the Browser. At right, new folders for media and render files are created on the selected drive.

Caution   Do not switch to the Finder while Media Manager is in progress.

If at this stage you find yourself having problems or the Media Manager presenting you with the "Media Manager File Copy Failed" error message, you should read the rest of this chapter and especially the sidebar, "Deep inside the Media Manager," later in this chapter. The sidebar explains the step-by-step process of the Media Manager's behavior and will help you troubleshoot your problems.

Using the Media Manager for Common Tasks

There are two good reasons for this section in a chapter on media management. First, the Media Manager is a spectacularly useful tool in Final Cut Pro. And yet, at the same time, or perhaps because of it, it is also one that can get you into trouble. You may find yourself creating some difficult situations for yourself if you select the incorrect settings for performing a task at hand.

Even though previously in this chapter I have carefully explained each function in the Media Manager window, you may still find yourself struggling to create the precise effect you are looking for.

Beyond understanding the settings, you will find there are some common tasks you will find yourself attempting with the Media Manager. For example, you may want to remove just the unused media from a project to help you clear up some disk space. At another time, you may look for a method to copy an entire project and its associated media to another disk.

For the two reasons I just cited, I have decided to give you a quick and dirty guide to performing some of the most common media management tasks in Final Cut Pro.

Removing unused media from your project

Because editing is a reductive process, you will always have more media captured than is actually used in the final edit. For example, you may have captured three hours of material from your tapes but only used an hour in your project.

To remove unused media from your project, follow these steps.

1. **In the Browser, select a sequence, or multiple sequences for which you want to remove unused media from.**

2. **Select File ⇨ Media Manager.**

3. **Select the following settings:**

    • **Choose Use Existing from the pop-up menu.**

    • **Click the Delete Unused Media from Selected Items box to select the option.** If desired, check Use Handles and enter a duration amount for the handles.

    • **Make sure the Duplicate Selected Sequence option is deselected (not checked).**

Figure 12-19 shows the proper settings for removing unused media from your project. Your source media files are shortened to include only the media used in the selected sequences, plus any handles, if you elected to include any.

Caution   Whenever you choose the Use Existing choice from the pop-up menu, you should think twice before you click on the OK button to proceed. Once the Media Manager process begins with the Use Existing setting active, the source media files are deleted *immediately* and no amount of canceling, Command+Z Undo, or prayers will bring them back.

Creating a copy of your sequence into a new project for recapture

If you have a ton of media to capture, it is not uncommon to capture and edit with low-resolution media clips; after editing to your satisfaction, you then can make a copy of this sequence into a new project to recapture at high resolution. Making a new project will also allow you to separate the media for the low resolution and the high-resolution projects.

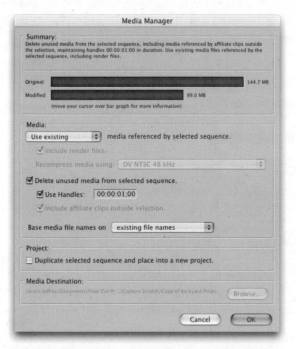

Figure 12-19: Shown in this figure are the correct settings for removing unused media in a project using the Media Manager.

To create a copy of your sequence for recapture, follow these steps:

1. **In the Browser, select the sequence you want to copy.**

2. **Select File ⇨ Media Manager.**

3. **Select the following settings:**

   • **Choose Create Offline from the pop-up menu.**

   • **Select the Delete Unused Media from Duplicated Items box.** If desired, check Use Handles and enter a duration amount for the handles.

   • **Check the Duplicated Selected Items and Place into New Project setting to select it.**

4. **At the prompt, enter a name and location for your new project file.**

   The Media Manager creates a copy of your sequence in this new project. All the clips in this sequence will be offline, and you can simply select the sequence and recapture it via the File ⇨ Batch Capture command.

Figure 12-20 shows the proper settings for creating a copy of your sequence into a new project file in preparation for recapture.

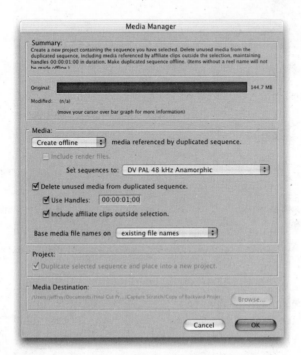

Figure 12-20: This screen shot shows the correct settings in the Media Manager for making an offline copy of your sequence into a new project file, in preparation for recapture.

Moving media for an entire project

There may be situations in which the media for a project has been captured to multiple media drives, and at some stage of your project, you may decide to move the entire media for a project into a new location. Use the Media Manager to move all your captured and rendered files from wherever they may be across multiple locations to a new single drive location.

To move media for a project to a new location, follow these steps.

1. Select all clips and sequences in the Browser window.

You can use the Command+A shortcut to achieve this result.

2. Select File ⇨ Media Manager.

3. Select the following settings:

- **Choose Move from the pop-up menu.**

- **Click the Include Render Files box to make it active.**

- **Don't select Delete unused media.** This ensures all of your source media is preserved in the move.

- **Don't select Duplicate Selected Items and Place in a New Project.** In this example, you want to consolidate the media files but still use your existing project.

Figure 12-21 shows the proper settings for moving all the media for a project to a single location. Using these settings, the Media Manager moves all the source media and render files for your project into a new location.

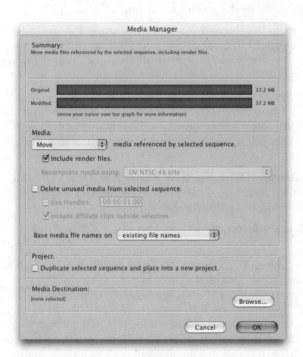

Figure 12-21: Proper settings for moving the entire media for a project to a new location are shown here.

Recompressing a project

If you ever have to edit a project on a PowerBook after you've captured and started your editing on a workstation, using Media Manager's Recompress option is a godsend. With Recompress, you can move all necessary media and sequences, while at the same time rewrite the media files to another codec or frame size, say Final Cut Pro's OfflineRT format, all in one fell swoop.

To Recompress a project and its media to a new location, follow these steps:

1. **Select all clips and sequences you want in the Browser.**

   You can use the Command+A shortcut to select all items in the Browser.

2. **Select File ⇨ Media Manager.**

3. **Choose the following settings:**

   • **Choose Recompress from the pull-down menu.**

   • **Choose a codec from the Recompressed media using the pull-down menu.** For this example, choose OfflineRT NTSC (Photo JPEG) preset. There are 30 presets offered in the pull-down menu, or create your own media by choosing Custom.

   • **Select the Delete Unused Media option.** Select Use Handles and enter the desired amount to ensure sufficient media for editing. Include affiliate clips outside the selection for more available source media flexibility, but keep in mind that this could add significantly to disk space required for the new media.

   • **Select existing filenames from the Base Media File Names On pull-down menu.** This is important if you need to relink your new project back to the original files on your workstation.

   • **Select the Duplicate Selected Items and Place into a New Project setting.**

   • **Click the Browse button to navigate to a hard disk drive you will be using as your media's scratch disk.** You can even select your PowerBook if it is connected and selected in Media Destination.

When you click OK, Media Manager will copy your project file and any media associated with it. Figure 12-22 shows the correct settings for Recompressing a project file and any media associated with it to a new location of your choice.

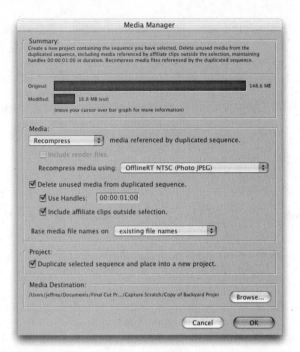

Figure 12-22: Select the settings as shown for copying a project file and its media to a new location of your choice.

Deep inside the Media Manager

Have you always wondered what goes on deep inside the mind of the Media Manager? I have and I've found that there is a reason why the Media Manager behaves the way it does. Most operations involving the Media Manager can be broken down into a ten-step process. Those steps are:

1. **If you have chosen to duplicate items, the Media Manager will ask you for a name and location for the new project file.**

2. **If you elect to remove unused media for selected items, and you choose the Move or Use Existing processing options, the Media Manager checks other clips and items in your projects (including ones you did *not* select before opening the Media Manager) to see if they are linked to the same source file.**

   If so, you will get a message like the one shown here. You can choose to add these items to the current selection, make the newly discovered items offline, or abort the process altogether.

Continued

Continued

3. **The Media Manager checks to see if you have enough space on the disk you have chosen.**

   If you don't, you get a message like the one shown below giving you the option to abort or browse for a new disk or directory that *does* have enough room.

4. **If in Step 2 you chose to make some items offline, these items are now made offline by the Media Manager.**

5. **Media Manager moves or copies the source media files to the new location.**

   Any unused media is removed if the Remove Unused Media option was checked on.

6. **If the Include Affiliated Clips outside Selection option is selected, these additional media files are preserved.**

7. **If you elected to include render files, those are copied or moved over.**

8. **If you chose to make a new project file, the new project file is created and the sequence or clips are copied into it.**

9. **The Media Manager creates links between the clips or sequences in your new project and the copied or moved media files.**

10. **Your new project opens up in the Browser window.**

✦   ✦   ✦

Modifying Your Edits

After you've placed your shots in the Timeline, the next step is often to play them back and review your edits. Sometimes you won't like what you see. The clip might be better if you pulled up a shot here, and loosened some cuts over there. Modifications you make to your edits could be as drastic as changing shots around in the Timeline, adding new shots, and deleting existing ones.

Usually your edit modifications will amount to fine-tuning of the work you've already done. You may want to just trim a few frames off one shot, or bring in the audio a bit earlier under another shot. Even seemingly minor trimming can be very challenging depending on the complexity of the sequence and the relationship of the clips to one another.

This chapter looks at the process of editing your edits, showing you how to do it effectively and without damaging the work you've already done.

Understanding Trimming

Trimming is the process of adding or removing frames from your clips to fine-tune your edits. Fortunately, performing basic trimming on your material in Final Cut Pro is fairly easy. When you have a clip in the Timeline, you can quickly modify or "trim" its In or Out points.

Tip

Tracks that are locked will not be affected by any trim operations. This can be helpful. You can lock the tracks that you don't want affected. Click on the small lock icon to the left of a track in the Timeline window to lock a track. A closed, dark lock icon indicates a locked track. An open lock icon indicates an unlocked track.

The most common tool you use for trimming is the resize cursor. You don't have to select any tool for this. If you have the basic Arrow Selection tool (the pointer) selected and you place this tool near the edges of a clip, the arrow selection cursor will turn to a Resize cursor. You can click and drag at the In or Out point of a clip in the Timeline with this cursor, as shown in Figure 13-1.

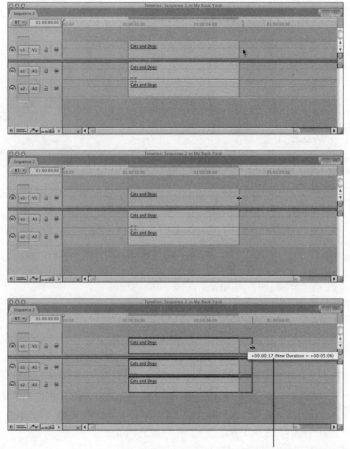

Pop-up yellow box indicates the amount of
the trim and the new duration of the clip

Figure 13-1: Placing your pointer near the In or Out point of a clip turns the pointer into a Resize cursor. Click and drag to trim the In or Out point with this cursor.

Whistle while you cut: Cutting clips in the Timeline

One of the more common editing tasks I accomplish when working in the Timeline is to cut a clip rather than trim it. When a clip is cut, it is actually split into two separate portions. The unused portion can then be deleted from the Timeline. I prefer this method of editing clips because I find that the timing is easier to control and it generally requires fewer steps. This may not be the "conventional" method for trimming clips in Final Cut Pro, but you might find it effective. To cut clips in the Timeline:

1. **Open a sequence and drag a clip directly from the Browser into the Timeline.**

   Make sure Auto Select is enabled on both the video and audio Timeline tracks where you've placed your clip. Auto Select tells Final Cut Pro which tracks to operate on when there aren't any items selected. The Auto Select control is the icon of intersecting-rectangles in the Timeline patch panel. When enabled (toggled On), the center is dark gray; when disabled (toggled Off), the center is light gray.

2. **Press the spacebar to play the clip.**

3. **When you get to the spot where you want to set an In point, press the spacebar to stop playback.**

4. **Press Control+V to cut the clip.**

   The clip will be cut at the current playhead position.

5. **Select the portion of the clip you don't want and press the Delete key.**

   The unwanted portion will be deleted. You can also press Shift+Delete. This will delete the unwanted portion of the clip and close any gaps created by its absence from the Timeline.

6. **Press the spacebar again to continue the playback.**

7. **Stop the playback by pressing the spacebar at the location where you want to mark the end of your clip.**

8. **Press Control+V again to place a cut at the current location of the playhead.**

9. **Press the X key to mark the portion of the clip you do not want.**

   The X keyboard shortcut selects the portion of the clip forward of the current playhead position.

10. **Press Shift+X to delete the unwanted section.**

    Shift+X is the shortcut for "Ripple Cut to Clipboard," which cuts the marked shot for pasting at a later location, but I like using this shortcut to simply get rid of a clip.

With just a quick combination of keyboard shortcuts, you can take many clips from the Browser into the Timeline and trim them down to useable sections before refining your edits. The shortcuts Control+V, Control+X, and Shift+X lie within easy reach of left-hand fingers, and after some practice they can be invoked very quickly.

As you drag with the Resize cursor, you get live feedback from Final Cut Pro. A small yellow box appears and shows you the status of your trim. The yellow box has two displays. The first part of the display, on the left side, specifies the amount of material you're trimming, indicated with a minus sign if you're dragging left, or a plus sign if you're dragging right. The other half of the display in the yellow box indicates the new duration of the clip. Also, as you drag with the resize cursor in the Timeline, the current frame at the edit point appears in the Canvas window.

Tip   If you want to adjust just the audio or video track independently, hold down the Option key while using the Resize cursor. This allows you to make split edits in the Timeline.

Understanding the Basic Trim Tools

The Tools palette contains some important trimming tools. A few of these tools are dedicated to selecting clips or edit points, while others allow you to make adjustments. If the Tools palette is not visible on your desktop, choose Window ⇨ Tools to bring it up. Trim tools in the palette include the following:

✦ **Tools for selection:** Certain tools in the Tools Palette are used to make selections in preparation for trimming. The main selection tool is the default arrow that you work with most of the time. This tool can select individual items such as a clip, an edit point, or a transition. Press the *A* key to select this tool.

• The Edit, Group, and Range selections tools allow you to select multiple items. You use these tools by selecting them in the Tools palette and dragging them to draw a marquee in the Timeline. Figure 13-2 shows the Edit, Group, and Range selection tools. The Edit selection tool selects only edit points at the head or tail of clips, the Group selection tool selects complete groups of clips in their entirety, even if only part of the clip falls in the selection marquee, while the Range selection tool selects only those portions of clips that fall within the marquee drawn with the Range tool. The keyboard shortcut to cycle through these three tools is the keyboard letter G.

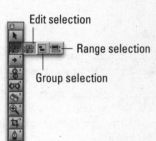

Edit selection

Range selection

Group selection

Figure 13-2: Draw a marquee in the Timeline around clips you want to edit, with the Edit, Group, and Range selection tools.

Cross-Reference

For more on the Tools Palette, see Chapter 11.

• The Track selection tools are another set of selection tools available in the Tools Palette (see Figure 13-3). To use these tools, select one and then click in the tracks of your Timeline. Track selection tools allow selection of entire tracks, single tracks, or all tracks. The tools can also select forward or backward from their point of use. Press T on your keyboard to cycle though these tools.

Single track forward select

Single track select

All tracks backward select

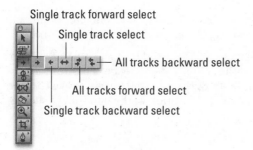

All tracks forward select

Single track backward select

Figure 13-3: Track selection tools allow you to select all items in a track forward or backward from the point in the Timeline where you use tools.

✦ **Tools for modifying edits:** These tools help you modify your selections of clips and edits. Press the R key repeatedly on your keyboard to cycle through these tools:

• The Roll tool (see Figure 13-4) moves the edit point of two adjoining clips. This tool adjusts the location of the Out point of the first clip and the In point of the second clip simultaneously, without affecting the duration of sequence.

• The Ripple tool (see Figure 13-4) can adjust the location of either the In or Out point just before, or the In point just after, an edit point. After a clip is shortened or lengthened with the Ripple tool, all clips following are moved, or *rippled,* by the same amount trimmed from the clip, thus changing the overall duration of the sequence.

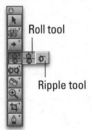

Roll tool

Ripple tool

Figure 13-4: Roll and Ripple tools can be selected by repeatedly pressing the R key on your keyboard.

- The Slip tool (see Figure 13-5) adjusts the In and Out points of a clip together without changing the clip's duration or location.

- The Slide tool (see Figure 13-5) is used to move, or *slide,* a clip already edited between two other clips in a sequence. The Out point of the clip to the left and the In point of the clip to the right move together. Neither the In or Out points, nor the duration of the clip that is sliding, is changed.

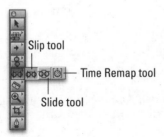

Slip tool

Time Remap tool

Slide tool

Figure 13-5: Slip and Slide tools adjust the relationship of multiple clips to each other.

Cross-Reference

The new Time Remap tool is in the Slip and Slide Tools Palette. As cool as this feature is, it is less of a trimming tool and more of an effect, covered in detail in Chapter 19.

Adjusting Settings That Affect Trimming

There are a few settings you should know about before you trim an edit. These settings can affect the results you get when trimming clips in the Timeline. If you plan to perform a lot of trim edits in the Timeline, you should learn the shortcuts to quickly turn these settings on and off because you may need them in some situations but not in others. Settings that affect trimming include the following:

✦ **Snap To:** If snapping is activated while you drag or trim, you automatically snap to important locations such as markers, edit points, and the playhead. This can complicate trimming when you're trying to make precise adjustments. When snapping is activated, you'll see a set of small triangle shadows when the clip or the edit is snapping to an item (see Figure 13-6). Check the snapping indicator on the far right side of the Timeline (also shown in Figure 13-6) and, if necessary, click it to toggle snapping off. You can also turn snapping on and off simply by pressing the N key on your keyboard. Toggling snapping on or off with the keyboard shortcut can be done on the fly while dragging clips. Snapping does perform a very useful function while moving clips around, but for precise trimming, you'll probably want it off.

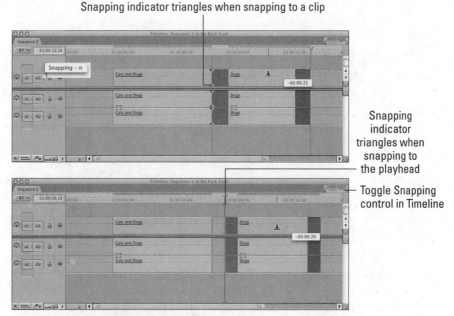

Snapping indicator triangles when snapping to a clip

Snapping indicator triangles when snapping to the playhead

Toggle Snapping control in Timeline

Figure 13-6: Snapping can complicate the process of making precision trims in the Timeline.

Tip

To "gear down" or slow down the scale of movement while dragging an edit point with the mouse, hold down the Command key while you make the adjustment. This will make finer incremental changes easier.

✦ **Linked Selection:** The linked selection setting controls how multitrack clips behave in the Timeline. If you have a captured clip with one video and two audio tracks, these tracks will automatically be linked when placed in the Timeline. Selecting any one of these tracks will select the whole clip. You can override the linked selection setting by pressing the Option key as you select a track for a clip. This modifier key reverses the current linked selection setting. The linked selection setting can be toggled with the linked selection control located to the left of the snapping control on the top right of the Timeline window. Or, if you're like me and find that the control is too small to click, press Shift+L to toggle the linked selection setting. When enabled, the linked selection control is green, and when it's off the control is gray. See Figure 13-7 for an illustration.

Linked selection is On and highlighted green when active

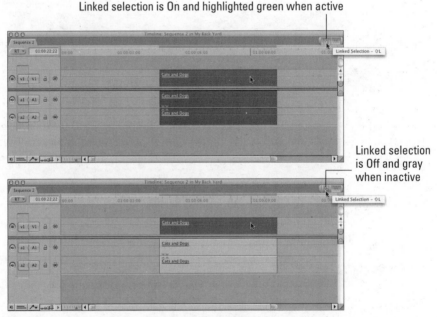

Linked selection is Off and gray when inactive

Figure 13-7: The linked selection setting controls how tracks within a clip are linked in the Timeline.

Whether you choose to have the Linked Selection on or off during trimming depends entirely on the circumstances. For example, if you just want to trim the synced audio portion of a video clip or vice versa, you should have the Linked Selection off. However, if you want to trim the video and audio tracks together for a clip, the Linked Selection should be left on.

Cross-Reference See the sidebar "Links That Bite" in Chapter 11 for more on the Linked Selection setting.

Trimming Edits in the Timeline

To follow along in the next few sections, you can find these four dummy *Numbered Shots* in the Mountain Biking.fcp project on the DVD-ROM that accompanies this book. Drag the Mountain Biking Tutorial folder from the DVD-ROM to your hard drive, and then start up the Mountain Biking.fcp project. The *Numbered Shots* clips are prepared for a DV setup. You must have your sequence and hardware settings configured for DV video to properly view and use these shots.

Trimming operations in the Timeline are performed using various edit types. These edits are roll, extend, ripple, lift, slip, slide, and swap. Each edit type can be important to you as you modify your edits. In order to explain these edit types more effectively, the examples shown in this section do not include typical video footage. Instead, the shots used are simply black video with white type. The type says Shot 1, Shot 2, Shot 3, and Shot 4. The name of each clip reflects the text that can be found in it. Over each shot is a timecode readout in white text. This may seem overly simplified, but it best serves to illustrate the various editing types.

Lift edits are covered in Chapter 11.

Selecting edit points

Before performing any trim functions you have to select one or more edit points to trim. Trimming is always done on edit points or clips that you've selected. With Final Cut Pro, you can select single or multiple edit points.

Selecting a single edit point

The most basic kind of trim is one that is performed between two clips. A single edit point can be selected for a trim operation. If Linked Selection is on, then all tracks for this clip will be selected. If Linked Selection is off, then only the track you click on will have its edit point selected. To select an edit point, click with the pointer tool to select an edit. You have to click right on the edit point between two clips to make this selection. Figure 13-8 shows a single selected edit in the Timeline.

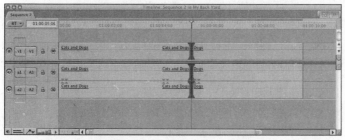

Figure 13-8: Click with the pointer tool to select a single edit.

Tip   Press the V key on your keyboard to jump the playhead to the *nearest* edit point and automatically select it.

Note   Double-clicking on an edit with the basic selection tool will bring up the Trim Edit window.

Selecting multiple edit points

Often you will need to select multiple edit points for trimming purposes. The Shift+select method will not work in this case. There are two ways you can select multiple edit points:

✦ **Command+click on multiple edit points with the Arrow Selection, Ripple, or Roll tool.**

✦ **Use the Edit Selection tool.**

To select multiple edit points using the Edit Selection tool, do the following:

1. **Choose the Edit Selection tool from the Tools Palette.**

2. **Click and drag a marquee around the edits you want to select as shown in Figure 13-9.**

   Only the edit points are selected when using the Edit Selection tool. However, be aware that only one edit per track will be selected. Trimming does not allow you to select multiple edits on the same track.

Note   The Trim Edit window automatically opens up when a selection is made with the Edit Selection tool.

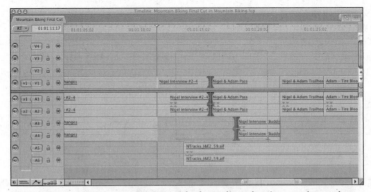

Figure 13-9: Draw a marquee with the Edit Selection tool to select multiple edits.

And now, on with the edits.

Roll edits

A roll edit relocates the edit point between two clips. In a roll edit, the Out point of Shot 1 and the In point of Shot 2 are simultaneously moved together in the direction you choose. The duration of each individual shot changes during a roll edit, *but the total duration of the sequence remains the same.*

Performing roll edits in the Timeline

Roll edits are ideal for adjusting matched action between two clips. You might face a situation where a person is raising his arm in a long shot, and want to match this action to another shot of the same person raising his arm in a tight shot. After you've edited the two shot together by matching the action of the Out point frame of the first clip to the In point frame of the second clip, you then can use the Roll Edit tool to adjust the edit point and find the precise moment the cut from the first shot to the second shot will happen. To illustrate a basic roll edit, we'll use our numbered Shots:

1. **Load Shot 1 into the Viewer by double-clicking it and set its Out point at 6:00, or 6 seconds.**

   You'll be able to see this in the white type on-screen as well as in the current timecode display in the Viewer window.

2. **Edit this clip into the sequence by pressing the F10 key.**

   This makes an overwrite edit into the Timeline.

3. **Load Shot 2 into the Viewer and set its In point at 3 seconds (3:00) into the clip.**

   Notice that the In and Out points set in the two sample clips provide additional media to "roll" over. Without extra media past the In or Out point, you cannot perform a roll edit, nor many other types of edits.

4. **Edit Shot 2 into the sequence by pressing the F10 key to make an overwrite edit.**

   You should now have Shot 1 and Shot 2 edited into the sequence.

5. **Select the Roll Edit tool in the Tools Palette as shown in Figure 13-10.**

   If the Tools Palette is not visible, choose Window ➪ Tools to bring it up.

Tip   You can also select the Roll Edit tool by pressing the R key on your keyboard.

Figure 13-10: Select the Roll Edit tool from the Tools Palette or press the R key on your keyboard.

6. **Select the edit point between the clips by clicking on it with the Roll Edit tool.**

7. **Drag the edit in either direction with the Roll Edit tool.**

As you drag with the Roll Edit tool, the Canvas window provides a "two-up" display. Shot 1 appears on the left side of the two-up display, and Shot 2 appears on the right (see Figure 13-11). The name of each clip and the current timecode frame for the shots appear in the two-up display. As you use the Roll Edit tool in the Timeline, you'll also see a small yellow box similar to the one in the lower graphic in Figure 13-11 indicating the amount you've rolled your edit. If you cannot drag any farther, you've probably reached the end of available media.

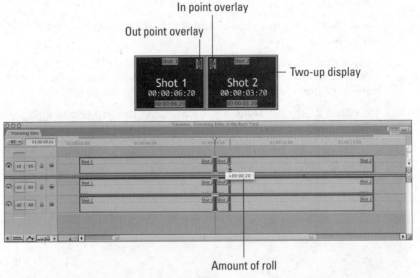

Figure 13-11: When performing a roll edit, a two-up display in the Canvas window shows the current frames for both clips at the current edit point. In and Out point overlays appear over each clip. In the Timeline, a small yellow box indicates the amount of time that the edit point is being rolled.

Tip

You can also type a + (plus) or a – (minus) sign followed by the number of frames or seconds to add or subtract from the current edit point. Press Return to enter the new value. What's great about this feature is that you don't have to have the Roll Edit tool selected. Simply select an edit with the Selection tool and start typing the amount of frames to roll edit.

Making a split edit with the Roll Edit tool

Split edits are edits where the In and Out points of the various tracks for a clip are offset. For example the video of Shot 1 can extend over audio from Shot 2, or the audio could lead the cut, and so on. Split edits are a common method for smoothing cuts. Dialog sequences between two characters often employ split edits.

To make a split edit with the Roll Edit tool, follow the steps in the previous section but with one crucial difference: Hold down the Option key while dragging with the Roll Edit tool. If you drag the video track while holding down the Option key, only the video track will roll. If you select and drag the audio track, just the audio portion of the clip will roll.

Tip

Selecting clips or edit points while pressing the Option modifier key temporarily reverses the Linked Selection state currently set in the Timeline. For example, if you're working with the Link Selection turned off, then Option+selecting will select both the video *and* audio of linked clips. Most of the time, you'll work with the Linked Selection on, so Option+selecting will select only the part of a linked clip you clicked on.

Extend edits

In an extend edit, you move an edit point to the current location of the playhead in the Timeline. Proper placement of the playhead is important when performing this type of an edit. An extend edit does not affect the total duration of your edited sequence. You don't have to select any tool to perform an extend edit.

Performing extend edits in the Timeline

Extend edits are a quick, handy way of moving an edit point to the current location of your playhead. For instance, if you're playing an edit, you might pause playback at the point to where you want to move the edit. The playhead is in the right spot, so all you have to do is tell the edit point to follow the playhead. To perform an extend edit:

1. **Load Shot 1 into the Viewer by double-clicking it and set its Out point at 6:00, or 6 seconds.**

   You'll be able to see this timecode in the white type on-screen as well as in the current timecode display in the Viewer window.

2. **Edit Shot 1 into the sequence by pressing F10.**

   This performs an overwrite edit into the Timeline.

3. **Drag and drop Shot 2 into the Timeline without setting any In or Out points on it.**

   There should be an edit point between Shot 1 and Shot 2.

4. **Play your edit and let the playhead go one or two seconds past the edit point.**

5. **Pause playback by pressing the spacebar.**

6. **Select the edit point between the clips.**

7. **Choose Sequence ⇨ Extend Edit (or press the E key on your keyboard).**

   The highlighted edit will extend itself to the playhead, as shown in Figure 13-12. Carefully note that the extend edit of Shot 1 *overwrites* Shot 2.

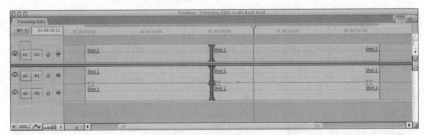

Before an extend edit

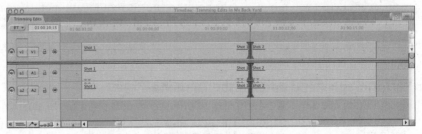

After an extend edit

Figure 13-12: Extend edit (which is a type of overwrite edit) extends the selected edit point to the current location of the playhead.

Error! Error! on the wall: Understanding error messages while trimming

There are two kinds of messages that Final Cut Pro displays if you try to perform a trim edit that isn't possible. The first is the "Insufficient content for edit" message shown below.

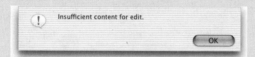

You'll get this message when there is no additional media available for a clip that is part of the trim process. When you mark In and Out points on a clip before placing it in the Timeline, any additional media on either side of these points is made inactive. However, that media is still there and available for use. Clips in the Timeline can *only* be trimmed if there is additional media available that is currently inactive, as shown below.

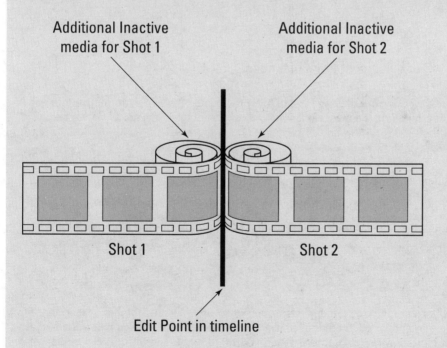

Additional Inactive media for Shot 1

Additional Inactive media for Shot 2

Shot 1

Shot 2

Edit Point in timeline

If there is no additional media and the clips are already extended to their full media file length, as shown below, then no trim is possible.

Continued

Continued

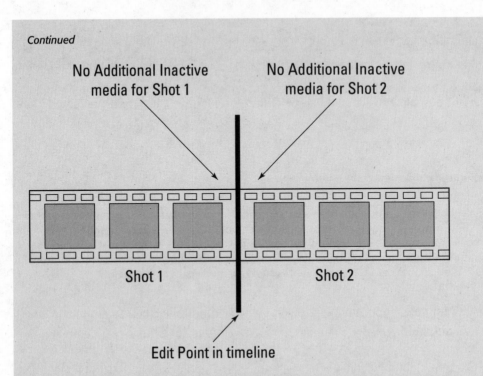

No Additional Inactive media for Shot 1

No Additional Inactive media for Shot 2

Shot 1

Shot 2

Edit Point in timeline

The second type of error message you're likely to encounter while performing a trim edit is the Media Limit error. It appears in a small yellow box in the Timeline, as shown below.

Media Limit Indication

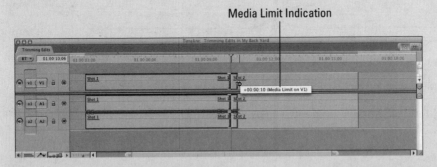

The Media Limit indicator can appear for one of several reasons. The first reason that this message may appear is if there is insufficient media available for the edit, as described earlier. This indication can also appear when you try to move an edit or a clip and there is some item, such as another clip, in the way of your intended move. For example, if you select a clip and try to move it by entering a timecode, but an adjoining clip prevents this move, you will see the Media Limit indicator.

The only problem with the Media Limit indicator is that it's easy to overlook, as you wonder why your edit is not working. It's really quite small, actually, especially compared to the large warning boxes that Final Cut Pro usually displays when there is a problem.

Making split edits using the extend edit feature

As with roll edits, you can make split edits using the extend edit feature. A split edit smoothes a cut and is a good way to make your edit "invisible" when cutting a dialog between characters on-screen. To perform a split edit during an extend edit:

1. **Load Shot 1 into the Viewer and set its Out point at 6:00, or 6 seconds.**

2. **Edit Shot 1 into the sequence by pressing F10.**

   This makes an overwrite edit into the Timeline.

3. **Drag and drop Shot 2 into the Timeline without setting any In or Out points on it.**

4. **Move your playhead back and play the edit you just created. Allow the playhead to go about one or two seconds past the edit point.**

5. **Pause playback by pressing the spacebar.**

6. **Turn off Linked Selection.**

   You can do this by choosing Edit ⇨ Linked Selection or press Shift+L.

7. **Select the edit point between the clips.**

   If you want to extend the video portion of the edit, select the edit point in the video track. If you want to extend the audio portion of the edit, select the audio portion of the track. This is only possible when linked selection is off.

8. **Choose Sequence ⇨ Extend Edit (or press the E key on your keyboard).**

   The edit point in the track you selected will extend itself over to the playhead, as shown in Figure 13-13.

Ripple edits

A ripple edit relocates either the Out point of the first shot in an edit point or the In point of the second shot. During a ripple edit, all shots following the edit point are moved over, or *rippled.* This edit changes the overall duration of an edited sequence of clips.

Another type of ripple edit is called a *ripple delete* edit. This allows you to delete a clip while closing the gap created by it. Ripple delete edits are described in Chapter 11.

Ripple edits are used when you have an entire edited sequence of clips and you just want to change the Out point of a clip without changing any other edit points in the sequence. A ripple edit can be used to extend the Out point of a clip *without overwriting any clips,* as is done in the extend edit.

Turn linked selection off

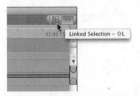

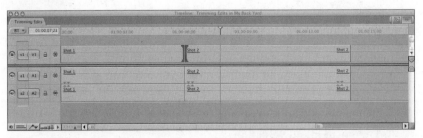

Figure 13-13: With linked selection off, you can select one of the tracks for a clip and use the extend edit feature to make a split edit.

To perform a ripple edit:

1. **Place Shots 1, 2, 3, and 4 in order in the Timeline.**

   Make sure there are no In or Out points set on any of these shots and that they're extended to their full ten-second duration.

2. **Select the Ripple Edit tool in the Tools Palette (see Figure 13-14).**

   If the Tools Palette is not visible, choose Window ➪ Tools to bring it up.

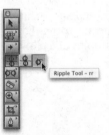

Figure 13-14: The Ripple Edit tool can be selected in the Tools Palette.

3. Click on the edit point between Shot 2 and Shot 3.

Notice that you cannot select *both* the points of an edit with this tool. You'll only be able to select *either* the Out point of Shot 2 or the In point of Shot 3 around the edit point itself.

4. Click on the either side of the edit point line to select one or the other point.

Note that your cursor will change to the Ripple Edit tool icon when dragged over the edit point. When it is over the Out point for Shot 2, the "hook" or the "film feed" portion of the icon points left. If the cursor is held over the In point of Shot 3, the hook points right. This can help you determine where your selection is located.

5. Select the Out point of Shot 2 with the Ripple Edit tool.

Your selection highlight should appear to the *left* of the edit point line.

6. Click and drag to the left with the Ripple Edit tool.

A small yellow box appears indicating the amount of ripple, and the two-up display in the Canvas window shows the current frames, names, and timecode in the window, as shown in Figure 13-15.

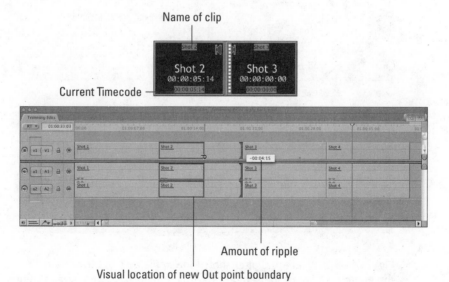

Figure 13-15: The Canvas window shows the frame, clip name, and current timecode of the frames around the current edit point. Dragging an In or Out point with the Ripple Edit tool brings up a small yellow box indicating the amount of ripple you're creating.

As with other edit types, when performing a ripple edit you may be limited by the amount of media you have. In Figure 13-15, the Out point of Shot 2 is being rippled back by 4 seconds and 15 frames. This is indicated by the -4:15 reading in the small yellow box that appears while the ripple is performed.

Upon releasing the mouse button, the Out point of Shot 2 has been trimmed by 4:15. Shots 3 and 4 have also moved to the left by the same amount. The before and after effects of such a ripple can be seen in Figure 13-16.

Tip   If you have trouble making precise adjustments, hold down the Command key to "gear down" the mouse movement. Also, try turning off snapping by pressing the N key on the keyboard.

Caution   When working in a complex Timeline with numerous audio and music tracks, you should think carefully before performing a ripple edit. Ripple edits can seriously affect the relationships of voiceovers and other audio tracks to the video in your Timeline.

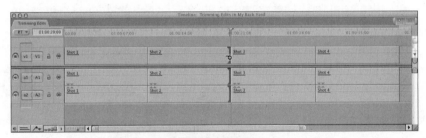

Before a ripple edit

After a ripple edit

Figure 13-16: Before and after shots for a ripple edit. In the second illustration, the entire duration of the sequence has been affected by the size of the ripple.

Asymmetrical trim edits

A type of ripple edit, asymmetrical trimming is a new feature of Final Cut Pro 4 that allows you ripple edit the video and audio of an edit point in opposite directions at the same time. Although this is an easy way to create split edits, be extremely careful with this because it is also an easy way to throw your sequence tracks out of sync. Remember, like all ripple edits, this will change the position of all clips on the same tracks after the trimmed edit point. To perform an asymmetrical trim edit, I'll use our numbered Shots:

1. **Load Shot 1 into the Viewer and set its Out point at 6:00, or 6 seconds.**

2. **Edit Shot 1 into the sequence by pressing F10.**

   This makes an overwrite edit into the Timeline.

3. **Drag and drop Shot 2 into the Timeline without setting any In or Out points.**

   Edit Shot 2 directly after Shot 1 in the Timeline. There mustn't be any gap between the two shots.

4. **Select the Ripple tool.**

   Select the Ripple tool by clicking on it in the Tools Palette, or simply press the R key twice (RR).

5. **Hold down the Option key and select the video Out point of Shot 1.**

   Adding the Option key when selecting an item in the Timeline temporarily toggles the Link Selection to the opposite state (in this case, Off) and allows you to select just the video or audio portion of a linked clip.

6. **Hold down the Option *and* Command keys and select the audio In point of Shot 2.**

   Press the Command key while selecting an item to add it to your current selection.

7. **Release the Option and Command keys, click on the selected Out point of Shot 1 video with the Ripple tool, and trim the edit point back (left) 1 second.**

   Watch the Tooltip info window in the Timeline as you drag left until you it reads –00:01:00, and the left frame of the two-up display in the Canvas window reads 5:00

8. **Release the mouse.**

   While the video Out point of shot 1 is rippled back 1 second, the audio In point of Shot 2 is rippled *forward* 1 second. This is evident by the fact that Shot 1 audio is not shortened as the video was, yet Shot 2 audio *was* shortened by 1 second in order to keep it in sync with its linked video.

Slipping edits

The Slip Edit tool allows you to "slip" a shot's In and Out points together without changing its duration. The media for the clip slips backward or forward, but the overall duration of the edited sequence and the clip is not affected. Slipping a shot is illustrated in Figure 13-17.

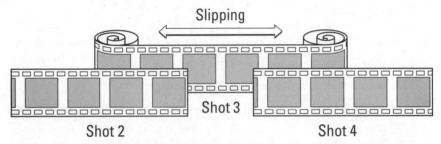

Figure 13-17: Slipping a shot allows you to change the shot's In and Out point selection together without changing its location in the Sequence in relation to the other clips.

When slipping Shot 3 in Figure 13-17, it is as if the shot moves *behind* Shot 2 and Shot 4. The In and Out points of Shot 3 change, but not the distance between those points. The overall duration of the edited sequence remains the same, as does the location of the edit points on Shot 2 and Shot 4. To perform a slip edit:

1. **Edit Shot 1 into the Timeline with no In or Out points set on it.**

2. **Edit Shot 2 into the Timeline with no In or Out points set on it.**

3. **Double-click Shot 3 to load it into the Viewer window, and set its In point at 3 seconds and its Out point at 6 seconds.**

4. **Edit Shot 3 into the Timeline.**

5. **Edit Shot 4 into the Timeline without setting any In or Out points on it.**

6. **Select the Slip tool from the Tools Palette as shown in Figure 13-18.**

   If the Tools Palette is not visible, choose Window ➪ Tools to bring it up.

Tip   You can also select the Slip tool by pressing the S key on your keyboard.

7. **Click on Shot 3 with the Slip tool and drag it to the left or the right.**

   A small yellow box appears indicating the amount of slip, and the two-up display in the Canvas window shows the current frames, names, and timecode in the window (see Figure 13-19). Note that during a slip edit the two-up display will show you *the new In and Out points for Clip 3 only,* because that is what's being changed.

Figure 13-18: The Slip tool can be selected in the Tools Palette.

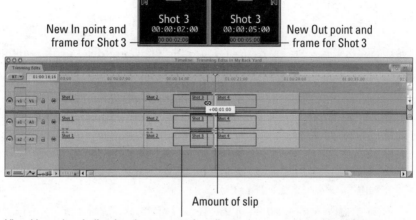

New In point and
frame for Shot 3

New Out point and
frame for Shot 3

Amount of slip

Visual boundary indicating the amount of media you have on either side of Shot 3

Figure 13-19: Dragging to the left or the right on Shot 3 with the Slip tool indicates the amount of slip in the small yellow box in the Timeline. The two-up display in the Canvas window shows the frame, the clip name, and the current timecode of the new In and Out frames for Shot 3.

8. **Release the clip to complete the slip edit.**

Tip

You can also select a clip with the Slip tool and enter + (plus) or – (minus) followed by a number to slip the clip by the amount you type in either direction.

Sliding edits

The Slide tool moves a shot *between* two others that are adjacent to it. It does so by adjusting where the middle shot places itself in relation to the clips around it. In our example, Shot 3 moves between Shot 2 and Shot 4. The duration and the In and Out points of Shot 3 remains unaffected. The durations of Shot 2 and Shot 4 change, but without changing the overall duration of the sequence. In this respect, you could think of a slide edit (see Figure 13-20) as the opposite of a slip edit.

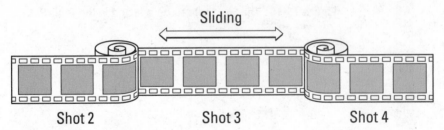

Figure 13-20: The theory behind the sliding process.

To perform a slide edit:

1. **Edit Shot 1 into the Timeline with no In or Out points set on it.**

2. **Double-click Shot 2 to load it into the Viewer and set its In point at 3 seconds. Set its Out point at 6 seconds.**

3. **Edit Shot 2 into the Timeline.**

4. **Double-click Shot 3 to load it into the Viewer and set its In point at 3 seconds and its Out point at 6 seconds.**

5. **Edit Shot 3 into the Timeline.**

6. **Double-click Shot 4 to load it into the Viewer and set its In point at 5:00.**

7. **Edit Shot 4 into the Timeline.**

8. **Select the Slide tool from the Tools Palette as shown in Figure 13-21.**

   If the Tools Palette is not visible, choose Window ⇨ Tools to bring it up.

 Tip   You can also select the Slide tool by pressing the S key on your keyboard *twice*.

Figure 13-21: The Slide tool can be selected in the Tools Palette.

9. **Click on Shot 3 with the Slide tool and drag it to the left.**

   A small yellow box appears indicating the amount of slide, and the two-up display in the Canvas window shows the current frames, names, and timecode (see Figure 13-22). Note that during a slide edit the two-up display will show you the new *Out point for Shot 2 and the new In point for Shot 4,* because that is what's being altered.

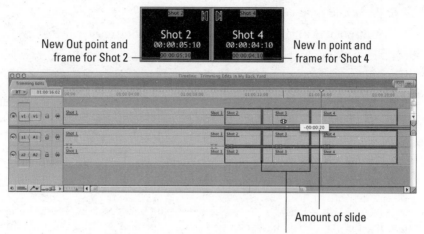

New Out point and frame for Shot 2

New In point and frame for Shot 4

Amount of slide

Visual boundary indicating the new In and Out points for Shot 3

Figure 13-22: The Timeline and the two-up display in the Canvas during a slide edit.

10. **Release the clip when you're satisfied with your change.** Shot 3 has moved to its new location while modifying the adjacent points for Shot 2 and Shot 4.

Tip

It is usually easier to do a slide if you have snapping off and you use the Command key while dragging to gear down your mouse movements.

Swap edits

Another type of edit you can perform is a swap edit. The swap edit feature is limited in that it only works with single clips. Nevertheless, when needed, the swap feature does make life very easy. The only trick to swap edits is learning the proper sequence of events while practicing your dexterity with the Option key. No tool selection is required in a swap edit. Holding down the Option key *at the proper time* will turn your pointer into a swap cursor.

Swap edits are ideal when you want to swap *adjacent* clips. That is not a requirement, but it is the best use of a swap edit. To perform a swap:

1. **Edit Shots 1, 2, 3, and 4 into the Timeline, making sure that there are no In or Out points set on any of the shots.**

    All four shots should have a duration of 10 seconds each.

2. **Click and drag Shot 3 back over Shot 2.**

    You want to align the In point of Shot 3 with the In point of Shot 2. This alignment is easier if you have snapping turned on.

3. Press and hold down the Option key.

Your pointer will turn into a downward-pointing curved arrow as shown in Figure 13-23.

 Figure 13-23: Hold down the Option key to turn the pointer into the swapping tool shown here.

4. Release Shot 3.

Shot 3 will swap with Shot 2.

 Note

A swap edit inserts the clip you are dragging between two other clips while closing the gap left behind by the moved clip, thus keeping the duration of the sequence unchanged. That being said, the swap edit does not actually swap the position of the clip you are dragging with the clip you are inserting it before. In Figure 13-24, you can see that, after doing a swap edit of Shot 4 ahead of Shot 2, Shot 2 and Shot 3 were moved right, filling the gap left by Shot 4. Shot 2 did not literally swap positions with Shot 4.

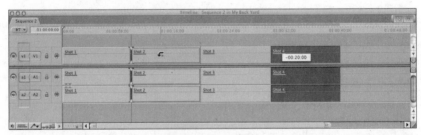

Before a swap edit

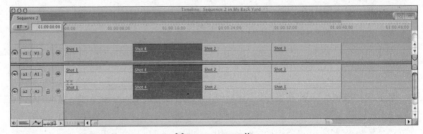

After a swap edit

Figure 13-24: Swap Edit will insert moved clips and close the gap left behind, keeping the sequence duration unchanged. However, Shot 2 did not literally swap positions with Shot 4; it just moved down.

Using the Trim Edit Window

If you're looking for precision while trimming your edits, then the Trim Edit window is what you seek. The Trim Edit window shows a large two-up display with both the outgoing and the incoming clips. The outgoing clip fills the screen on the left, and the incoming clip fills the window on the right. Below these main displays are numerous buttons that control the transport and trimming functions. The playback controls in the lower-center part of the window allow you to play your trimmed edit.

Above each clip are green bars. These bars indicate the type of trim function that is available to you. You can perform both ripple and roll edits in the Trim Edit window. You can bring up the Trim Edit window by double-clicking on an edit point between two clips in the Timeline. In Figure 13-25, you can see the Trim Edit window as it looks after double-clicking between Shot 1 and Shot 2 in a sequence I am working on. Shot 1 represents the outgoing clip, and Shot 2 represents the incoming clip.

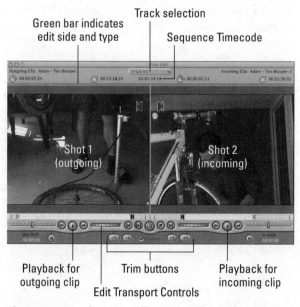

Figure 13-25: The Trim Edit window is used to precisely adjust edits.

Note Clicking on an edit point with the Selection, Roll, or Ripple Edit tools can also open the Trim Edit window. However, *what* tool you used to click with and *where* you clicked on the edit point will determine the type of trim you can perform. You can press the U key on your keyboard to switch between Ripple Outgoing, Ripple Incoming, or Rolling trim types.

The Trim Edit window has many features that you should familiarize yourself with. Table 13-1 lists the details of the Trim Edit window.

Table 13-1
Details of the Trim Edit Window

Main Controls

Control	Name	Description
 Track V1	Track Selection Menu	Allows choice of tracks to be viewed. When you select multiple edit points to be trimmed, the top track is shown here.
	Green Bar	Over both clips, the green bar indicates a roll edit. When the green bar is just over Shot 1, it indicates a ripple edit on the Out point of Shot 1. When the green bar is over Shot 2, it indicates a ripple edit on the In point of Shot 2. You can click on the side of the window you want to work on and the green bar appears.
 01:00:57;20	Sequence Timecode	Indicates the current timecode of the edit point in the sequence.
 ☑ Dynamic	Dynamic Trim checkbox	Toggles on and off Dynamic Trimming using JKL keys.

Edit Transport Controls

Control	Name	Description
 ⏮	Previous Edit	Click to move to the previous edit in your sequence. This new edit will be loaded into the Trim Edit window.

Control	Name	Description
	Play In to Out	This button plays the entire duration from the In point of Shot 1 to the Out point of Shot 2.
	Play Around Edit	Jumps the playhead back from the current location and plays forward past the current time. The timing for this setting is based on the Pre Roll and Post Roll setting in the General tab of the User Preference window.
	Stop	Stops playback.
	Next Edit	Click to move to the next edit in your sequence. The new edit will be loaded into the Trim Edit window.

Playback Controls for Clips

Control	Name	Description
	Previous Frame in Clip	Moves the view back one frame. Does not alter the In or Out points.
	Play Clip	Plays the clip.
	Next Frame in Clip	Moves the view forward one frame. Does not alter the In or Out points.

Continued

Table 13-1 (continued)

Trim Buttons

Control	Name	Description
(-5) (-1)	Trim Backward	Subtracts frames from the trim.
(+1) (+5)	Trim Forward	Adds frames to the trim.

Details of the Outgoing Clip Side

Control	Name	Description
Outgoing Clip: Adam - Rear Algn.	Clip Name	Name of outgoing clip.
00:00:03;07	Clip Duration	Duration between the In and Out points of Shot 1.
00:23:06;23	Current Timecode	Indicates the source timecode for Shot 1 at the current playhead position.
Out Shift: 00:00:00	Out Shift	Shows the amount by which the Out point has been adjusted.
	Mark In Button	Sets a new In point for Shot 2 at the current playhead position.
	Out Point	The left-pointing triangle indicates the current Out point for Shot 1.
	Playhead	Playhead for Shot 1.

Details of the Incoming Clip Side

Control	Name	Description
Incoming Clip: Adam - Gears2	Clip Name	Name of incoming clip.
00:00:03;08	Clip Duration	Duration between the In and Out points of Shot 2.

Control	Name	Description
00:23:55;01	Current Timecode	Indicates the source timecode for Shot 2 at the current playhead position.
In Shift: 00:00:00	In Shift	Shows the amount by which the in point has been adjusted.
(Mark Out Button icon)	Mark Out Button	Sets a new Out point for Shot 1 at the current playhead position.
(In Point icon)	In Point	The right-pointing arrow indicates the current in point for Shot 2.
(Playhead icon)	Playhead	Playhead for Shot 2.

Working with the Trim Edit window

The Trim Edit window is best used for refining certain trims on your edits. It can be especially useful in situations where edits must be carefully matched with each other. One situation in which I find this window handy is when I'm editing a narrative piece where I have to match action on various cuts. For example, if I have a medium shot of an actor sitting at a table and raising his glass, and I want to cut to a wide shot, *on action,* then I have to match the action in the two shots. On this match cut, the action remains continuous when I cut between the medium shot and the wide shot. In an edit like this, the Trim Edit window is indispensable.

One major enhancement to the Trim Edit window is the ability to do dynamic trim edits using the JKL keys — now you can press J to play backwards, K to stop, and L to play forward. This enables you to play back and forth over the edit point (some call this "rock-'n'-roll") and have the edit point move to the frame where you stop play. This truly is "what-you-see-is-what-you-get"! I'll get to the details in a while.

First I'll attack the basics, including using the Trim Edit in its heretofore traditional way (that is, without the Dynamic Trimming). The Trim Edit window is full of controls and timecode fields, but in principle, it is quite straightforward. You invoke the Trim Edit window by double-clicking on an edit point. The clip on the left of the edit in the Timeline fills the left side of the Trim Edit window, and the clip on the right of the edit in the Timeline fills the right side.

For the next few sections, you'll need four sample shots from the DVD-ROM that comes with this book. The shots consist of black video with white type and are located in the Numbered Shots folder on the DVD-ROM. Drag the Numbered Shots folder to your hard drive (if you haven't done so already), and then drag and drop it into your Browser window for use. These shots are prepared for a DV setup. You must have your sequence and hardware settings configured for a DV setup to properly view and use these shots.

It's very easy to get lost in the functions of the Trim Edit window. I suggest using the black video clips with white text shots used in the previous exercises to practice using the Trim Edit window. The first task you'll perform is setting up your shots for editing in the Trim Edit window. To get the shots ready:

1. **Double-click Shot 1 to load it into the Viewer and set the clip's Out point at 8 seconds.**

2. **Edit Shot 1 into the Timeline.**

3. **Double-click Shot 2 to load it into the Viewer and set the clip's In point at 4 seconds and its Out point at 6 seconds.**

4. **Edit Shot 2 into the Timeline.**

5. **Edit Shot 3 into the Timeline.**

6. **Edit Shot 4 into the Timeline.**

   There is no need to trim Shot 3 and Shot 4.

7. **Using the basic Selection arrow tool, double-click the edit between Shot 1 and Shot 2.**

   The Trim Edit window appears.

At this point, you're ready to work in the Trim Edit window. As the next few sections indicate, there are many kinds of trim edits you can perform in the Trim Edit window. Read on.

Performing a ripple edit in the Trim Edit window

After you have a couple of clips edited into the Timeline and the Trim Edit window open, you're ready to start performing edits. One of the most common edits you'll do in the Trim Edit window is a ripple edit. To perform a ripple edit on the sample clips:

1. **Move your pointer over the Shot 1 image.**

   The pointer turns into a Ripple Left tool, and you can ripple left with the cursor. If you hold the pointer over Shot 2, the pointer turns into a Ripple Right tool.

2. **Click on the Shot 1 image.**

   The green bar above Shot 1 lights up, indicating that you can now perform a ripple-left edit. If you clicked on Shot 2 instead of Shot 1, the green bar would light up over Shot 2, indicating that you were ready to perform a ripple-right edit.

3. **To perform a ripple-left edit, use your ripple-left tool to drag at the Out point indicator in the scrub bar area of Shot 1.**

   The Out point marker moves, and your clips in the Timeline ripples left. This action allows you to extend or trim back the Out point of Shot 1 while rippling Shots 2, 3, and 4. The overall duration of the edited sequence will change to accommodate your trim.

4. **To perform a ripple edit by the numbers, you can also trim back and forth using the Trim buttons.**

   The Trim buttons work to trim your edit back or forth by 1 frame or 5 frames. The multiple frames to be trimmed can be changed in the User Preference dialog box in the Multi-Frame Trim Size field and can be set up to 99 frames.

Performing a roll edit in the Trim Edit window

Roll edits can also be performed easily in the Trim Edit window. To perform a roll edit:

1. **Move your pointer to the line in the center of the two images.**

   Your cursor turns into a roll cursor.

2. **Click with the Roll cursor on the middle line.**

   The green bars over both windows light up, indicating that you can roll the current edit.

3. **To perform a roll edit, drag either the In point of Shot 2 or the Out point of Shot 1 in the scrub areas.**

   The Out point on Shot 1 and the In point on Shot 2 move together during the roll edit. The overall duration of the edited sequence does not change.

   To perform a roll edit by the numbers, you can also trim back and forth using the trim buttons. The trim buttons also work to trim your edit back or forth by 1 frame or 5 frames. The multiple frames to be trimmed can be changed in the User Preferences dialog box in the Multi-Frame Trim Size field and can be set up to 99 frames.

After trimming your edits in the Trim Edit window, it's helpful to be able to play back your changes. The next section shows you how to play back your edits to review them.

Tip   A handy keyboard shortcut for invoking the trim buttons is the [(left bracket) key for one frame back,] (right bracket) key for one frame forward, or Shift+[for five frames back and Shift+] for five frames forward (or however many frames you set in User Preferences for multiple frames trimming).

Dynamic trimming in the Trim Edit Window

As I've already noted, many editors prefer to complete most tasks using keyboard shortcuts instead of "mousing around." If you spend enough time in front of a computer, you'll eventually realize how much time this saves. Using the JKL keys for playback ranks high on the must-use keyboard controls. With Final Cut Pro 4, JKL controlling has been fully implemented along with dynamic trimming in the Trim Edit window. Pressing the L key plays the edit forward, pressing K pauses the playback, and pressing J plays backward. Pressing the J or the L keys repeatedly moves you faster in that direction. Pressing the K key while tapping or holding down the J or K key plays in that direction one frame at a time. When dynamic trimming is enabled, the edit point is automatically moved to the position of the Timeline playhead wherever you stop play.

To see better how this works, you'll use the sequence with the numbered shots you just set up for the basic Trim Edit explanation:

1. **Open the sequence with the numbered shots.**

2. **Using the basic Selection arrow tool, double-click the edit between Shot 1 and Shot 2.**

   The Trim Edit window appears.

Tip   If you see audio icons (speakers) in the preview windows indicating that you double-clicked on an Audio edit of a linked clip, simply click and hold on the Track Selection Menu at the top of the Trim Edit Window to see all the tracks that have been selected. Select Track V1 in this example, to see your clips in the Trim Edit preview windows.

3. **Check to see if Dynamic Trimming is enabled.**

   Click the "Dynamic" checkbox located just below the Play Around Edit Loop button if it's not checked.

4. **Move your cursor over Shot 1.**

   You'll see the Play control button below Shot 1 (highlighted blue), indicating that the JKL controls will now operate this window.

Note   The resting position of your cursor determines which Trim Edit window the JKL keys will control.

Tip   You can always tell which window controls are activated in the Trim Edit window by looking for the blue highlighted play button on the active controls.

5. **Position the cursor between the two clip windows, or anywhere over the controls area in the lower-center of the Trim Edit window.**

   The Play Around Loop button highlights blue. You don't need to click anything in order to activate a window's JKL control.

6. **Play the edit by pressing the J or L key to play the edit backward or forward, respectively, from the edit point.**

   Play forward and backward over the edit by alternately pressing the J and K keys until you find, or "feel," the right edit point.

7. **Press the K key to stop Play and dynamically set a new edit point.**

   When you stop play by pressing the K key, Dynamic Trimming will set the new edit point at the playhead position.

Note You can start play in the Trim Edit window by pressing the tried-and-true spacebar, but *dynamic trimming only functions if you start and stop using the JKL keys.* If you start or stop using the spacebar, it has the same effect as clicking on the Play Around Edit Loop button with no dynamic trimming function.

As always, be *extremely careful* when you are making a ripple edit because, by definition, this type of trimming will change the position of all clips on the track after the edit point you're trimming, which can throw your sequence out of sync.

Reviewing your Trim edits

To review your edits, you can use the Play In to Out button. Click this button, or simply press the spacebar, to play the first and second clips in their entirety as they are trimmed in the Timeline. You can also use the Play Around Edit Loop button to play around the edit you just trimmed, as shown in Figure 13-26.

Dynamic trim enabled

Play Around Edit controls activated

Figure 13-26: The Trim Edit window playing an edit with JKL control and Dynamic Trimming enabled.

Getting some useful hints for the Trim Edit window

When using the Trim Edit window, you have many controls to employ and perform your trims. Here are some helpful hints to remember as you use the tools in this window:

✦ **Remember the three basic trim modes and their indications.** The three trim modes are Roll, Ripple Left, and Ripple Right. You can also toggle between them by pressing the U key. The mode is indicated by the green bars that light up at the top of the Trim Edit window. If both green bars are on, you're about to perform a roll edit. The left green bar alone indicates a ripple-left edit, and the right green bar alone indicates a ripple-right edit.

✦ **Keep an eye on your shots in the Timeline.** If you find yourself getting lost as you make precise changes, you should arrange your windows so that you can simultaneously see your Trim Edit window and the shots you're trimming in the Timeline. As you make selections and changes in the Trim Edit window, your shots will adjust accordingly in the Timeline. For example, if you get confused as to which trim mode you're in, you can look at your edit in the Timeline to see which portion of the edit is highlighted. If the entire edit is highlighted, you're performing a roll edit, and if just one side of the edit is highlighted you're performing a ripple edit.

✦ **Use audio scrubbing to locate new edit points.** Press Shift+S to toggle the audio scrub setting. When audio scrub is on, using the J, K, and L keys you can hear the audio play faster or slower in the Trim Edit window. Scrubbing helps you locate edit points based on audio. For example, holding down the K key and the L key simultaneously will play forward by one-third of the real-time speed. With audio scrubbing on, this helps you locate precise edit points based on audio. Holding down the K key and tapping the J key will move the playhead back one frame at a time while playing the audio at that current frame. These shortcuts work in either direction.

✦ **Drag the edit points in the scrub area.** You can also relocate edit points by dragging them in the scrub area. Just make sure the green bar is active above that clip window, then simply click, and drag on the edit point in the scrub area to find a new edit point.

✦ **Use the playback controls to mark points.** You can use the individual playback controls for either clip and mark new In or Out points on the fly. Use the I key to mark an In point and the O key to mark an Out point. The edit in the Timeline is updated as you make changes.

✦ **Use the timecode fields to learn your offsets.** The In Shift and the Out Shift fields show you the amount of time by which you have modified the edits. The Duration, Current Clip Timecode, and Current Sequence Timecode fields, located at the top of the Trim Edit window, also update as changes are made.

Trimming Edits in the Viewer Window

Besides being able to trim edits in the Timeline and the Trim Edit window, there is yet another place where you can trim your edits. That place is the Viewer window. The next few sections cover how to perform certain trim operations in the Viewer window.

Cross-Reference To learn more about using the Viewer window, turn to Chapter 9.

Trim, trim, trim: Why so many trims?

For crying out loud, you're probably saying, *how many places can I trim these shots?* Well, you can trim shots in more places than you can trim a hedge. Let's take a moment to see why you'd choose one window over another to trim your shots:

✦ **Timeline:** Trimming in the Timeline is the speediest method. You get immediate feedback and you can view all kinds of information about your trims. You may find the viewing scale in the Timeline a bit difficult to work with while trimming. However, if you're fast with toggling snapping on and off (with the N key) and using the Command key to gear down your increments, you'll find yourself trimming in the Timeline more than anywhere else. There is one drawback to trimming in the Timeline, however. The size of the two-up display that you get in the Canvas window during trim operations in the Timeline may not be sufficient for you. The images are tiny and they only stay up there while you drag. (I wish Apple had provided a way to lock the Canvas window in a two-up display mode, but they didn't.)

✦ **Viewer:** The advantage of trimming in the Viewer is simply the size of the window. You can see a much bigger picture of your shot and you'll be able to view audio waveforms. These are handy if you're choosing your edit points based on the audio. You can quickly double-click your edit from the Timeline into the Viewer and make your changes there.

✦ **Trim Edit Window:** The Trim Edit window is best saved for refined trimming in special circumstances. It's a full-featured window and on some types of programs, such as a narrative show with lots of match-on-action cuts, you'll find yourself using the Trim Edit window much of the time. But the rest of the time, I find that the other methods are quicker.

Resizing a clip using the Viewer window

One of the simplest edits you'll make is to trim the In and Out points of a clip that has already been placed in the Timeline. The advantage of trimming a clip in the Viewer is that the image is large (as opposed to the Canvas two-up display where the images are tiny) and you have access to the audio waveforms for placing more accurate In or Out points. To resize a clip in the Timeline using the Viewer window:

1. **Double-click a clip in the Timeline to load it into the Viewer window.**

   Notice the sprocket hole graphics in the scrub area, which indicate that this clip is from the Timeline and not the Browser. (A clip loaded into the Viewer from the Browser has a plain, clean scrub area.)

2. **Locate a new In or Out point by playing the clip.**

   If you try to drag the In or Out point past another clip's boundary in the Timeline, you'll get a Media Limit message.

3. **Mark the new In or Out point using the I or the O key, respectively.**

   The clip resizes itself in the Timeline.

Performing a roll edit in the Viewer window

Resizing a clip does not allow you to "roll" over an existing adjacent clip in the Timeline. For that you need to perform a roll edit. To perform a roll edit on a clip in the Timeline using the Viewer window:

1. **Double-click a clip in the Timeline.**

   The clip loads into the Viewer window.

2. **Select the Roll Edit tool in the Tools Palette.**

   You can also press the R key repeatedly to select the Roll Edit tool.

3. **Drag the In or Out point of the clip in the Viewer scrub bar area to roll this edit.**

   You're able to see your progress in the Timeline. Note that a rolling edit overwrites the adjacent clip by adjusting its In or Out point in the opposite direction of your rolling, but it does not alter the overall duration of the edited sequence.

In a roll edit, the adjacent clip is overwritten. Thus, the overall duration of the edited sequence remains the same. The next type of edit, the ripple edit actually extends or shortens the duration of the sequence. I'll show you how to perform a ripple edit next.

Performing a ripple edit in the Viewer window

The ripple edit is a close relative of the roll edit. In a ripple edit the adjacent clips are not overwritten but are rippled (moved) over in the Timeline. To perform a ripple edit on a clip in the Timeline using the Viewer window:

1. **Double-click a clip in the Timeline.**

   The clip loads into the Viewer window.

2. **Select the Ripple Edit tool in the Tools Palette.**

3. **Drag the In or Out point of the clip in the Viewer scrub bar area to ripple this edit.**

   You're able to see your progress in the Timeline. You can also play your clip and mark a new In or Out point using the I or the O key. Note that a rippling edit does not overwrite the adjacent clip, but it does alter the overall duration of the edited sequence by rippling all following clips over.

Rippling edits is a common type of action taken by editors to trim their edits while modifying the overall duration of the sequence. You do have to be careful with ripple edits because if you have music or voiceover tracks that you're working with, rippling can move the video clips out of time with these tracks. So look before you leap.

Performing a slip edit in the Viewer window

Slipping an edit is the process of finding a new In and Out point for a clip that is located between two other clips. Slipping does not alter the overall duration of the edited sequence or of the clip being slipped. To perform a slip edit on a clip in the Timeline using the Viewer window:

1. **Double-click a clip in the Timeline that you want to slip.**

   The clip loads into the Viewer window.

2. **Select the Slip Edit tool in the Tools palette.**

   You can also press the S key repeatedly to select the Slip Edit tool.

3. **Drag either the In or Out point of the clip in the Viewer scrub bar area to slip the clip.**

   As you drag the in or out point, *both* points move together to a new location.

You can check your new selection by pressing Command + \ (backslash) key to invoke the Play In to Out command. This action plays your new selected section from the In point to the Out point.

✦   ✦   ✦

Working with Sound in Final Cut Pro

Hearing is one of the more sensitive of all the human senses. Yet, sound often takes a backseat in the world of video production, despite the fact that video and film experts acknowledge the integral importance of sound. It is a generally accepted tenet of the production world that audiences are far more forgiving of poor picture quality than they are of bad sound. Give the audience a shaky camera or grainy video and they'll still sit through it. But put some static in the soundtrack or make the dialogue inaudible and you've lost your viewers.

Sound is often undervalued because the money and effort spent on it is less apparent. If you don't have a lot of editing experience, it can be hard to imagine the effort and technology that goes into the creation of soundtracks for films and television shows. Yet, when you watch a Hollywood film, every sound — all footsteps, closing doors, passing cars, and even the rustling of clothing — was added as sound effects during the editing process. They are not production sounds recorded on location, but re-created sound effects added during the sound editing and mixing phase of post-production. Unknown to most audience, most movies contain dialog that was *looped,* or recorded after by actors in a sound studio as they watch their takes on a screen.

This chapter is all about sound, or *audio* as it is also called in post-production, and gives this subject some much-deserved attention. You'll learn the fundamentals of sound, and then you'll look at how to work with sound in Final Cut Pro.

Understanding the Nature of Sound

Before you can work with sound, you must have an understanding of the fundamentals, so I am going to talk about some basics of sound in this section. If your eyes start to glaze over because you've seen these terms described a thousand times, you can skip past some of these basics. (Though you may want to stick around anyway. When was the last time you had a refresher?)

Sound is defined as waves created by the pressure and rarefaction of air molecules. When these waves reach a listener's eardrums, the eardrums vibrate in response. The vibrations are carried to the brain through nerves. Those nerves are sensitive to vibrations, and these vibrations are perceived as sound by the brain.

Microphones are based on principles similar to human ears. Microphones have a *diaphragm,* a thin metal plate that vibrates in response to a sound wave striking it. These vibrations are converted to electrical voltage. This constantly varying voltage is then recorded onto a magnetic tape to make a sound recording.

Note   Speakers reverse the principle of microphones. Speakers take the electrical signals sent to them and convert those signals to vibrations of their cones. The vibrations from the speaker's cone travel through the air as sound waves, which then can be heard by listening eardrums.

Understanding frequency

As described in the preceding section, sound travels though the air as a pressure wave and causes eardrums or microphone diaphragms to vibrate. The number of times these vibrations occur is known as the *frequency* of the sound. Frequency is measured in Hertz (Hz), which represents one complete vibration cycle per second. One Hertz as a basic unit is too small for human aural perception, so a larger unit, kilohertz (kHz), is used. One kHz equals 1,000 cycles, or 1,000 Hz. The capability of human aural perception ranges anywhere from 20 Hz to 20 kHz, and this aural range varies with age and environment.

Frequency can be used to describe the nature of a sound. For instance, a sound that has a frequency of 440 Hz is the musical note A. Musical instruments have specific frequency ranges, as does human voice. A piano, for example, has a frequency range from 28 Hz to 4.2 kHz. The frequency range of human voice varies greatly. The frequency range of my voice, for example, is considerably less than that of Luciano Pavarotti's.

Understanding decibels

Besides frequency, another important measurement of sound is its loudness or amplitude. The loudness of a sound is measured in relative ratios, and the unit of measure used for loudness is called *decibels* (dB). The threshold of human hearing is placed at 0dB. Jet engines can be as loud as 150dB. Human ears can adjust to a surprisingly wide range of loudness. Keep in mind that decibels are a *logarithmic* scale, which means that the 150dB sound of a jet taking off is not just 150 times louder than the threshold of human hearing of 0dB. The sound of that jet is many millions of times louder. Each rise in the dB level signifies a substantial loudness change.

Note   Over the years many variants of the decibel scale have emerged. There is the basic dBm (magnetic) used in most VU meters. But there are also dBv (voltage), dBa (acoustic), and dBu (unterminated). Digital audio uses dBfs (full scale), and any dB settings mentioned for Final Cut Pro refer to the dBfs scale.

Understanding the dynamic range of sound

Dynamic range of sound is the difference between the loudest and the softest sound in a sound signal. For example, orchestras typically play between 25 and 115dB. Thus their dynamic range is 90dB. A sound that varies more between soft and loud sounds has a greater dynamic range, such as an orchestra. A sound with less of a dynamic range, such as a human voice, will vary little between its loudest and softest sounds.

Understanding the signal-to-noise ratio

The signal-to-noise ratio is the relational difference between the useful sound of your subject and any electronic background noise in a sound signal. For example, if your audio has background hiss that is as loud as the voice of the person talking on camera, then you can say that the signal-to-noise ratio, or *s/n,* is very low. In a strong, clean recording where you can hear your subject well and clear above any background noise or hiss, the s/n is considered high. You should always strive for a high s/n. You can ensure a high s/n by properly placing the microphone, selecting quiet locations for sound recording, and performing careful adjustments of recording levels on location.

Understanding sound in a digital environment

Analog signals consist of infinitely variable voltages, whereas digital signals are encoded in the binary language of zeros and ones. An analog signal does not have to have a discrete value; the value can lie anywhere on an analog curve. A binary signal, however, can only have on and off states. Figure 14-1 illustrates the difference between analog and digital signals.

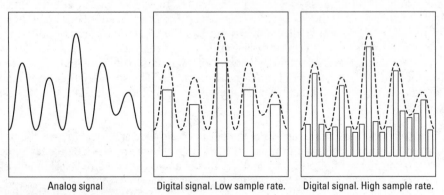

Analog signal   Digital signal. Low sample rate.   Digital signal. High sample rate.

Figure 14-1: Analog signals consist of varying voltage. Digital signals consist of discrete values. Here is an example of digital samples taken of an analog waveform. As you can see, the digital signal cannot exactly replicate the analog signal, but with a higher sampling rate it can come close.

In the early days of digital technology, a debate raged over the conversion of analog audio into digital. Analog "audiophiles" pointed to the low quality of digital audio and said it lacked "warmth" and "depth." Fans of digital audio responded by calling them Ludites, or people in fear of new technologies. The science and technology of digital audio has come a long way since then, and the debate has faded away. It was soon realized that digital audio was infinitely more practical for the emerging world of digital post-production. This practicality was especially obvious in cases where media was copied many times between its original recording and final release. Copies of analog recordings pick up hiss and lose higher frequencies with each copy, or *generation*. Even the simple act of playing analog tapes deteriorates their sound quality as the tapes wear against the playheads of the deck.

In digital audio, there is no generational loss. Copies maintain the same quality as the original no matter how many generations old they are. This makes digital formats ideal for post-production editing where copying is a way of life. The process of bringing in a camera master tape, editing it, recording the final program back to tape, and distributing copies of it requires numerous copy generations. With analog signals, each of these generations presents a slight deterioration of the audio signal. Theoretically, digital audio can be copied and reproduced infinitely without losing any quality.

Making sense of sampling rates

The quality of digital audio is defined by its sampling rate and bit depth. In order to convert analog sounds into digital signals, the smooth and infinitely variable voltage signal of an analog sound must be converted into discrete binary values. The *sampling rate* of a digital audio file measures the number of times a digital circuit measures the analog audio signal. Figure 14-1 illustrates how higher sampling rates can take a more accurate picture of analog audio.

One of the more common sampling rates for digital audio is 44.1 kHz. At this sampling rate, 44,100 samples are taken *every second.* Of course, the more samples that are taken, the more definition can be provided to the audio signal, resulting in better quality. All other things being equal, audio sampled at 44.1 kHz will sound better than audio sampled at 22.050 kHz, and audio sampled at 48 kHz will sound better than 44.1 kHz audio.

A few standard sampling rates are used in the world of digital audio. Sampling rates of 22.225 kHz and below should be restricted to use with multimedia and CD-ROM-based material. These sampling rates should never be used for video work. Sampling rates of 32 kHz and 48 kHz are commonly used in the DV recording format. Of these, the 48 kHz rate is preferred. Tracks on music CDs are recorded at a sampling rate of 44.1 kHz.

Understanding bit depth for audio

Each digital sample that is taken of an audio signal is limited in how many possible values it can represent. The number of bits assigned to each sample sets the limitation on the possible values. A *bit* is the smallest possible unit of the binary language. The value of a bit can be *zero* or *one,* also called *off* or *on.* The number of bits assigned to each digital sample is the audio's *bit depth.* The more bits you assign to each audio sample, the more discrete values that sample can represent. For example, in 16-bit audio, it is possible to represent 65,536 different values.

Bit depth directly affects the fidelity of the audio signal. The higher the bit depth, the richer and higher quality the sound. Common bit depths in the DV video world are 12-bit and 16-bit. Professional audio work is rarely done below 16-bit. Low bit depth results in noisy audio and artifacts, such as pops or static. Avoid the 12-bit setting on your DV device as much as possible.

Bit depth also affects the dynamic range of audio. *Dynamic range* is the ratio between the loudest and the softest sound containable in an audio signal. The larger the dynamic range, the better the sound quality. A 12-bit signal allows a dynamic range of 72dB. A 16-bit signal allows a dynamic range of 96dB. The dynamic range of 16-bit audio comes close to the limits of human hearing.

In the real world, the relationship between bit depth and dynamic range rarely works out so perfectly. Video capture cards and other processing circuits that work with 16-bit audio often deliver considerably less than 96dB. Due to overhead and quantization errors, the 16-bit depth is probably being worked down to around 14- or even 12-bit levels. So, in the real world, a 16-bit digital circuit usually delivers more like 72dB of dynamic range, and thus a 12-bit digital circuit delivers considerably less than 72dB of dynamic range. Again, it is best to avoid bit-depth settings below 16 bit.

Note   Even if your goal is to prepare media for Web delivery, you should still record the original audio at the best rate possible. You can compress the audio down at a later stage. Final Cut Pro allows you to export audio and video using a variety of compressions and qualities.

Sound in the DV format

Camcorders of yesteryear used formats such as VHS and other analog variants. Audio on these tapes was recorded in analog tracks along the tape. Making copies of these tapes (which could be the simple act of editing from the source tape to the record tape) magnified tape hiss, and the signal-to-noise ratio deteriorated rapidly.

The emergence of DV-based cameras and recorders has helped to eliminate the problems of analog recordings. Sound on DV tapes is recorded digitally and is comparable to the sound quality of music CDs. Sampling rates of 32 kHz and 48 kHz are commonly used on the DV tape format. DV devices sometimes display these rates as settings of 12 bit (for 32 kHz) and 16 bit (for 48 kHz). You should attempt to work with the 48 kHz setting as much as possible.

When you capture DV footage into Final Cut Pro, you should make sure that your capture sampling rates match the sampling rates of your original recording on tape. For example, if your tape is recorded at 32 kHz and you set your capture sampling rates in Final Cut Pro to 48 kHz, you will get occasional distortion in the form of static and audio pops.

In Final Cut Pro, each sequence can have its own audio sampling rate. You should always make sure that the sampling rate for your sequence matches the sampling rate used during capture.

Cross-Reference   To learn how to check your audio capture settings and audio sampling rates for sequences, see Chapter 6.

Apple engineers approve the mixing and matching 44.1 kHz (such as you would get when importing a track from a CD) and 48 kHz audio files in a 48 kHz-based sequence. Final Cut Pro can upsample the 44.1 kHz audio on the fly, and you should have no issues such as audio skips or pops — according to Apple. However, based on my own personal experience I would recommend the following:

✦ **Always shoot your DV tapes at 48 kHz, or the 16-bit setting.** Despite the fact that the 12-bit (or the 32k Hz) setting allows you to record four tracks of audio on some DV devices (as opposed to two tracks at 48 kHz) I strongly advise that you avoid the 32 kHz setting.

✦ **Never mix sampling rates in a sequence.** Even though Apple says it is okay, don't mix sampling rates. If you have imported CD tracks, they will have a sampling rate of 44.1 kHz. Convert these to 48 kHz before you use them in a sequence that is based on the 48 kHz sampling rate. Final Cut Pro does upsample well, but the upsampling places an overhead on the processor. I have seen audio dropouts and distortion result from mixing sampling rates. Also, if you plan on exporting your project's audio as OMF files for audio mixing on a digital audio workstation (DAW), you can't have audio with different sample rates in your sequences for OMF export to work properly.

To learn how to import CD audio and convert the sampling rates, see Chapter 7.

Getting Audio into Your Projects

There are many ways to bring audio into your projects with Final Cut Pro. The most basic method is to simply capture it along with video from a tape. It is also possible to capture *just* the audio portion from your videotape. Audio-only capture is accomplished by using the audio format selectors located on the Clip Settings tab of the Log and Capture window.

You can also import music or sound effects tracks from audio CDs. This type of import is useful because it allows you to use music tracks and sound effects in your program. Importing CD tracks is now simplified because OS X recognizes audio CD track files as an AIFF-compatible format. This means you can now import CD audio files by simply copying your chosen files to your hard drive and then dragging and dropping those files from your hard disk to the Browser, or select File ⇨ Import File.

To learn more about the format selectors for capturing audio, or about capturing audio tracks from audio CDs, see Chapter 7.

You can even record narration directly into your Timeline using the Voice Over tool. This handy gadget has been a boon for workflow continuity because it allows you to make a quick reference track, called a *scratch track* in many post-production houses, for timing sequences without having to wait for the final voiceover tape.

Setting up Final Cut Pro for capturing audio

No matter which method you plan to use to capture audio, there are a few basic settings you should check before you proceed. Before you start to capture, do the following:

✦ **Check the audio settings on your tape.** Check your tapes to see what the audio sampling rate was while shooting. Many DV devices display the sample rate setting when you play a tape in them. If you are shooting on DV tapes, you should always make sure that you are capturing audio at a sampling rate of 48 kHz (this setting is also called 16-bit audio on some devices). Numerous DV cameras offer the choice of being able to record four tracks of audio if you use the 12-bit/32 kHz setting. I strongly suggest avoiding the 12-bit/32 kHz setting unless you are desperate to have four tracks of audio.

If you are using a third-party video or audio card (instead of the FireWire port on your Macintosh), the sampling rate of your original tape may be somewhat irrelevant. On an analog tape such as a Betacam SP or VHS, there is no sampling rate. You can simply set your card to capture at 48 kHz.

If you have doubts about the audio sampling rate of a clip, check the *Aud Rate* column in the Browser for your clip. The *Aud Rate* column displays the sampling rate of the audio in your clip.

✦ **Check the audio settings for other captured audio.** If you are using tracks imported from an audio CD, the sampling rate of these files will be the native sampling rate of audio CDs of 44.1 kHz. Apple engineers have stated that it is okay to mix 44.1 kHz audio into a sequence based on a 48 kHz sampling rate. I not only disagree, I strongly suggest that you *never* mix and match sampling rates if possible. On long programs with six to eight tracks of audio tracks with mixed sampling rates, you can get audio dropouts and other problems. It's better to get into the habit of converting all CD tracks to 48 kHz before using them.

To learn how to convert CD audio from 44.1 kHz to 48 kHz, see Chapter 7.

✦ **Check the audio settings in the Capture Presets.** By default, Final Cut Pro sets your Capture Preset to an audio sampling rate of 48 kHz. Apple designers assume that most people will use a DV-based setup with Final Cut Pro. If you are using a DV-based setup and your tapes were shot at the 48 kHz sampling rate, then you have little reason to be concerned. But if by chance you have any tapes that used the 32 kHz setting for audio capture, then you must edit the capture preset to change the audio setting from 48 kHz to 32 kHz before you capture clips from your DV tape. Figure 14-2 shows where to edit the sample rate for your capture.

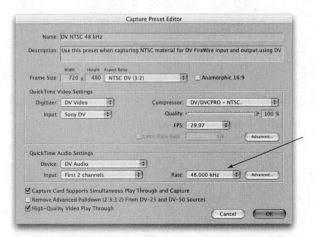

Figure 14-2: Check the sampling rate in your Capture Preset before capturing. To change this setting choose Final Cut Pro ➪ Audio/Video Settings and click the Capture Presets tab. You'll have to select a Capture Preset and click on the Edit button to enter the Capture Preset Editor.

To learn more about editing Capture Presets, see Chapter 6.

✦ **Check the Clip Settings tab in the Log and Capture window and make sure that your audio settings are correct.** In the Clip Settings tab, you can choose whether you want to capture just the audio from your tape, or both audio and video as is commonly the case. In the Clip Settings tab, you can also choose whether to capture your audio as connected stereo pairs or as separate tracks of audio labeled Channel 1 and Channel 2. Figure 14-3 shows these two selectors in the Clips Settings tab of the Log and Capture window.

See Chapter 7 for more details on the Log and Capture window's Clip Settings tab and its settings.

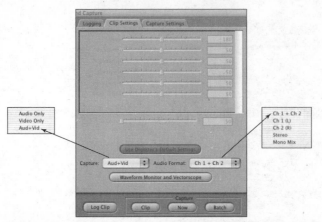

Figure 14-3: Check the two audio selectors in the Clip Settings of the Log and Capture window before capturing audio.

✦ **Check the audio settings in the Sequence Preset settings.** Sequences in Final Cut Pro are Timelines where you perform edits and arrange your edited clips. Each sequence can have its own frame size, compression and audio sample rate settings, among other settings. You should match the audio sampling rate for your sequence to that of the incoming captured audio. If you are capturing audio from a DV tape recorded at 48 kHz, and if your Capture Preset uses a 48 kHz sampling rate, then your sequence should also have the 48 kHz sampling rate. If these settings do not match, then you will experience problems such as noise, static, audio pops, or audio dropouts. Figure 14-4 shows where to edit the settings for the Sequence Preset.

To learn more about Sequence Presets, see Chapter 6.

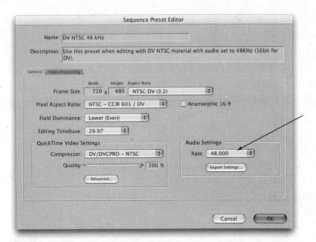

Figure 14-4: Check your sampling rate under the Sequence Presets settings by choosing Final Cut Pro ⇨ Audio/Video Settings and clicking the Sequence Presets tab. You'll have to select a Capture Preset and click on the Edit button to enter the Sequence Preset Editor.

Setting proper audio levels for capture

Before you attempt to capture clips from your tapes, you should calibrate and adjust the audio levels.

Note   The extended discussion I am about to get into is not all that relevant to you if you are working with a DV-based setup and are using a FireWire cable to capture your material. In that case, the audio Gain slider in the Clip Settings tab of the Log and Capture window will be disabled, as shown in Figure 14-5. The Gain slider is one of the controls needed for calibrating analog audio for capture.

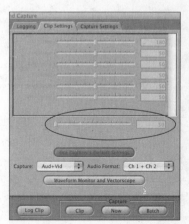

Figure 14-5: When you capture DV-format video using FireWire, the gain slider is grayed out and has no effect on the levels for the incoming audio.

Why is the Gain slider disabled when you capture audio using FireWire? When capturing from DV tape via a FireWire connector, you are not digitizing the video or audio because it is already in a digital format. You are simply performing a bit copy of the content on tape, much like a simple file copy from one disk on your computer to another.

If you are capturing content from an analog source using a third-party video or audio capture card, you *are* digitizing it. In this case, the audio levels need to be carefully calibrated to ensure the best possible audio quality. The following sections show you what to look for.

Understanding calibration with reference tone

Audio calibration relies on a *reference tone*. When you play a tape that has color bars and a shrieking tone at the beginning, you are hearing a reference tone. The reference tone is laid down on tapes either in the field (some cameras allow the operator to lay down a reference tone on tape), or during a post-production dub or edit. The reference tone is usually a 1 kHz tone recorded at the analog level of 0dB.

In the world of broadcast and professional video, all audio levels on a tape are calibrated and mixed in relation to this reference tone. When preparing for capture or layback to tape, you play the reference tone through your system so that the tone is visible in the audio meters. You adjust the audio input level so that it lies at a *reference location* on each audio meter. When the audio is calibrated to the appropriate reference location, you can proceed with capture or layback to tape.

If the tone was recorded at 0dB, you may be tempted to think that it should be matched to the 0dB setting on your audio meters in Final Cut Pro. But this is not the case. On a digital system, the reference location for an analog 0dB tone can be –12dB, –18dB, or –20dB. Which location on the meters should you use? Read on.

Understanding Volume Unit (VU) meters and Peak Program meters (PPMs)

As mentioned earlier, the unit of measure for loudness is decibels. In a post-production environment the audio levels are measured in *Volume Units,* or VUs. If you look at an analog VU meter, you'll see two scales. The top scale (generally indicating –120dB to +3dB) is for recordings on tape. The lower scale (which reads 0 to 100) is a percentage modulation reading used for broadcasts and is not relevant to our discussion.

Figure 14-6 shows two analog VU meters. Both an old-style dial indicator and the new style LED VU meters are shown. Although the two meters in Figure 14-6 *look* different, their function and behavior is exactly the same.

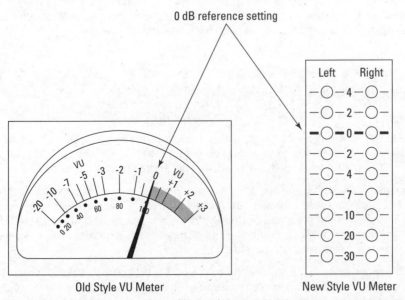

Figure 14-6: Analog VU meters indicate Volume Unit measurements of audio.

A VU meter always gives you an *average* sound level reading. VU meters generally indicate a strong audio signal between 0dB and +3dB. However, VU meters ignore the peaks that occur in the sound signal. A VU meter, be it the older dial type or the

LED type, responds too slowly to show instantaneous peaks. On average it takes an indicator on a VU meter one-third of a second to reach 0dB when provided with a 0dB signal. That's much too slow. To account for this slow response, some dial indicator VU meters have a Peak Level LED that lights up when indicating peaks. *Peaks* are short, high-level audio moments that may clip or distort the sound.

Caution

Carefully calibrated VU meters are expensive, so most "VU" meters built into consumer VCRs and other devices are often nothing more than "volt meters." These voltmeters are generally reliable for the steady tones of 0dB tone but are lousy at displaying the fast peaks and averages of a complex audio signal.

Another type of audio meter is called the PPM (Peak Program meter). A PPM is used in professional gear to indicate audio peaks. PPMs rise almost 30 times faster than VU meters. The PPM ignores the average loudness and gives you just the peaks. PPMs are commonly found on DAT (Digital Audio Tape) equipment.

If you are using a PPM, keep in mind that the readings are going to appear higher for a given sound clip than they would if you were using a VU meter for the same clip. VU and PPM readings can show a difference of as much as 12dB. That's huge, so be aware of what you are looking at when reading from either kind of meter. Because of the usefulness of both types of audio meters, special audio meters have begun to appear that use features of both VU and PPM meters.

To dB or not to dB: Where in the world is 0dB in a digital environment?

If you are reading carefully, you will notice that I have danced around the subject of where exactly a 0dB analog reference tone should be placed on the audio meters of Final Cut Pro. Alas, a specific recommendation is still not forthcoming. There are many reasons why.

When working with analog VU meters, it is common to adjust recording levels so that the majority of audio peaks reside between 0dB and +3dB, and the average loudness is kept below 0dB. This is common practice even though VU meters are marked in red in the 0dB to +3dB range. This area between 0dB and +3dB represents the *headroom* for overdriven signals that analog devices must accommodate.

Digital audio devices do not have any headroom. A signal at 0dB on a digital audio meter is a distorted signal. This is why a zero reference tone that appears at 0dB on a VU meter should be calibrated to a much lower setting on a digital audio meter. On a digital audio meter the analog reference tone is usually set to one of three standard locations: –20dB, –18dB, or –12dB. Any one of these settings is specified on digital decks such as Sony's Digital Betacam line. Networks generally specify a –20dB average loudness setting with peaks limited to less than –10dB.

But which reference point should you use? That will depend largely on the incoming audio. The most common choice is to set this incoming tone's location at −12dB. But why isn't there one perfect spot to which you can calibrate the reference tone? The answer is determined in large part by the dynamic range of your recorded audio. If you recorded the tape in a studio with a person doing a voiceover in a consistent, carefully controlled situation, you can set the 0dB VU tone to −12dB digital. However, if you have someone yelling on tape in a less controlled recording environment, then you may want to set the level of this tone to −18dB digital. Just remember that digital audio has no headroom. This is why, as you can see in the figure, the 0dB hash mark lies at the *top* of a digital audio meter, whereas it lies halfway down on most analog VU meters.

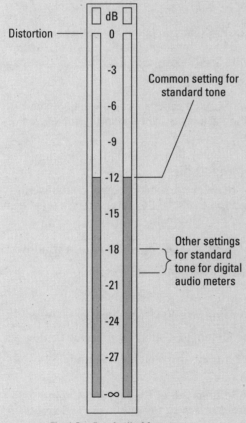

Final Cut Pro Audio Meters

Dealing with limitations of the reference tone method

Tapes from the field seldom have reference tones that you can truly rely on as you start to capture audio into Final Cut Pro. Unless there was a qualified sound person on the shooting crew monitoring and manipulating the audio, the reference tone method may be of little use. To account for this, I start by using the tone (if one is provided on the tape) to set my starting reference point. Then I shuttle though the shots I am about to capture and make adjustments to my gain slider while watching the Audio Meters in Final Cut Pro. Besides using this technique, there are a couple of other rules you can follow to ensure better audio:

✦ When recording in the field, maintain average levels between –3dB and 0dB on your analog VU meter. Keep the peaks and rises between 0dB and +3dB. If possible, lay down a 1 kHz 0dB tone at the beginning of each tape.

✦ When digitizing audio into Final Cut Pro that you know has been properly set up and recorded, keep your average level between –20dB and –12dB. Keep the peaks and rises between –12dB and –6dB. Before capturing, line up the analog 0dB tone at –12dB on the Final Cut Pro audio meters.

Note

When all else fails, just make sure that all audio peaks stay below the 0dB mark in the Final Cut Pro Audio Meters. If the Peak lights light up on the meter, you've clipped your audio.

Calibrating Audio Meters for incoming audio

If you are capturing audio from a tape with color bars and a reference tone at the beginning, use this tone to calibrate Final Cut Pro's Audio Meters before you begin to capture. Here's how:

1. **Choose File ⇨ Log and Capture to bring up the Log and Capture window.**

   Pressing Command+8 also brings up the Log and Capture window.

2. **Click the Clip Settings tab.**

3. **Bring up the Audio Meters by choosing Window ⇨ Audio Meters.**

   Alternatively, you can toggle Audio Meters to display by pressing Option+4.

4. **Play the tone on your tape so that it plays through the Log and Capture window.**

5. **Adjust the Gain slider in the Clip Settings tab of the Log and Capture window so that the tone rises in the Audio Meters to –12db (see Figure 14-7).**

6. **Now, cue your tape to the loudest section of audio that you plan to capture.**

7. **Play the tape and adjust the Gain slider to ensure that the average levels register at around –12dB on the Audio Meters.**

   The meters are colored green up to the –12dB mark.

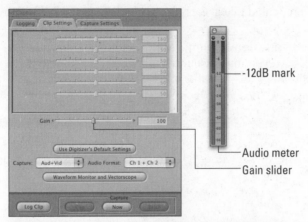

Figure 14-7: A 0db analog tone should be adjusted to −12db on the Final Cut Pro floating audio meters. Adjust the Gain slider in the Clip Settings tab of the Log and Capture window to set audio levels.

8. Use the Gain slider to keep audio peaks between −12dB and −3dB.

The section between −12dB and −3dB is colored yellow in the Audio Meters. Try not to let any audio go above 0dB. Audio above 0dB will be distorted.

To be on the safe side, you may want to capture a clip or two using the previous method, and then check the waveforms of the captured clips in the Viewer window. The waveform will give you a clearer indication of whether the captured audio stays within the desired levels.

 To learn more about using waveforms in the Viewer window, see Chapter 9.

Recording audio with the Voice Over tool

The Voice Over tool allows you to record a narration track directly into your sequence while it plays back. Although this method of recording narration is not a replacement for professionally recorded voiceovers, it is a handy addition to the tool set that can keep your editing moving forward by enabling you to record a temporary scratch track in lieu of the final voiceover recording. This is extremely appealing to those editing on-location on a PowerBook. The Voice Over Tool has many features:

✦ As you record, you can monitor the existing tracks in the sequence for timing your voiceover.

✦ Using In and Out points set in the Timeline, you can define the duration and placement of your recorded take.

✦ You can record repeated takes; each take's clip is automatically placed on its own track in the Timeline.

✦ The Voice Over tool records with "handles" before and after your Mark In and Mark Out points, preventing any clipping of your track should it run longer than the selection.

✦ After you are finished recording, clips created with the Voice Over tool can be edited as you would any audio clip in Final Cut Pro.

To open the Voice Over tool, select Tools ➪ Voice Over, or use the keyboard short-cut Option+0 (zero). The Voice Over tool will open in the Tool Bench window, shown in Figure 14-8.

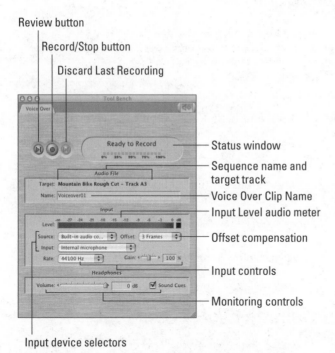

Figure 14-8: The Voice Over tool enables you to record a voiceover narration directly into your sequence as it plays back.

As you can see, the Voice Over tab has input controls, headset monitoring controls, and visual indicators to help you record a voiceover track. Table 14-1 breaks down the details of the Voice Over tool window.

Table 14-1
Details of the Voice Over Tool Window

Control	Description
Record/Stop	Click this button to start recording audio into the Timeline. Clicking this button again will stop recording and place any audio recorded after the Mark In point in the Timeline.
Review	Click to play back the Timeline portion selected with In and Out points *without* recording. Use this for rehearsing and timing of the voiceover script.
Discard Last Recording	Click to delete the clip and media file of the last take. This button is dimmed until the first voiceover track is recorded. **Note:** This operation cannot be undone.
Status window	This window displays messages indicating the current operating state of the Voice Over tool. Below the status messages is a progress bar that shows the percentage of the Timeline selection that has been recorded.
Target	Displays the name of the Sequence and the track number where the next voiceover will be placed. The target track is automatically incremented after every recorded take, moving down to the next available track.
Name	The name you type here will be used for the voiceover clip in the sequence and the media file saved to your hard disk. The filename automatically increments after every take.
Level meter	This audio level meter displays the incoming audio signal strength, controlled with the Gain slider at the bottom of the Input panel.
Source	A pop-up menu for selecting the source of the audio input device. The options here will display any external input devices connected to your computer.
Offset	This allows you to compensate for any recording latency caused by computer processing time.
Input	If the audio input device selected in the Source field has multiple inputs, you can select which one to use with this pop-up menu.
Rate	You can select an audio sampling rate for your recorded voiceover with this pop-up menu. Only rates supported by your input device will be available. Try to match the sample rate of your sequence. If a matching sample rate is not possible, select the highest rate available.
Gain	Use this slider to adjust the input level of the incoming signal. Alternatively, you can type in a percentage of gain in the field to the right of the slider to numerically set the Gain level.
Volume	This slider controls the playback volume to your headphones. Enter a decibel level in the field to the right of the slider to set the volume level numerically.
Sound Cues	Check this box if you want to hear cue beeps in your headphones during recording. The cue beeps will not be recorded in the voiceover track.

Setting up for voiceover recording

Before you begin recording your voiceover, there are a few preliminary configurations that you need to set up:

✦ **Connect your audio input device to the computer.** This is the hardware interface that will capture the audio into your computer. This includes PCI capture cards, USB audio devices, or even your DV camera.

If you select a DV camera as the input device, you might get a warning message stating you cannot record using DV audio. If this happens, simply turn off External Video by selecting View ➪ External Video ➪ Off. You can now record using your DV camera's mics.

✦ **Connect microphones to your input device.**

✦ **Configure the Input panel of the Voice Over tool.** Open the Voice Over tool by selecting Tools ➪ Voice Over, or press Option+0 (zero). Select your input device from the Source pop-up menu, microphone selection from Input pop-up, and the sample rate available for your input device in the Rate pop-up.

✦ **Calculate any offset of your audio device.** Because of the time it takes audio to be processed from the microphone to the input device and then to the computer, there is usually a time delay, or *latency,* between your recorded voiceovers and where they are placed in the Timeline. You could manually slide your voiceover track to compensate for this difference, but this can be done automatically with the Offset option in the Voice Over tool window. To determine the amount of offset of your setup (offset varies with different hardware configurations), do the following:

1. **Open a new Sequence.**

   This is only for the Offset calculation and can be discarded afterward.

2. **Set an In point at 10:00 and Out point at 20:00 in the Timeline.**

   Drag the playhead in the Timeline ruler to the 10-second position, or type in **1000** in the Current Timecode field and press Enter. Set an In point by pressing the letter I key. Then drag the playhead in the Timeline ruler to the 20-second position, or type in **2000** in the Current Timecode field and press Enter. Set an Out point by pressing the letter O key.

3. **Hold the microphone of your input device close to your computer's speaker.**

4. Select Tools ⇨ Voice Over, and then click the Record button.

You want to record the Voice Over tool's sound cues to check for offset. When the recording is finished, the new voiceover clip will appear in the Timeline in the target track.

5. In the Timeline, enable waveform overlays by clicking the Clip Overlays button at the bottom of the Timeline, or press Command+ Option+W.

6. Drag out the end of the voiceover clip with the resize cursor to see the 2 seconds recorded after the Out Mark.

This is shown in Figure 14-9.

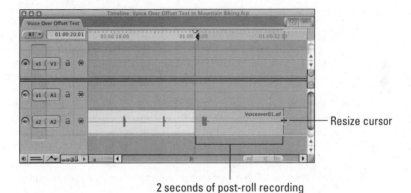

Figure 14-9: Use the resize cursor to drag out and see 2 seconds of post-roll recording

7. Compare the waveform position of the final beep with the Out point of the Timeline.

The first frame of the final sound cue beep should ideally be located at the Out point set in the Timeline. The difference between the position of the final sound beep in the clip and the Out point set in the Timeline is the offset amount. Figure 14-10 shows an example of a 5-frame offset.

Out point   Final sound cue beep

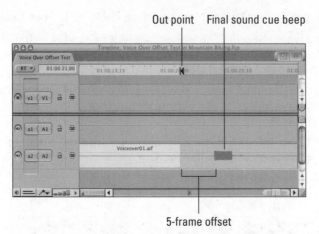

5-frame offset

Figure 14-10: The difference between the Out point in the Sequence and the position of the final beep of the Voice Over tools sound cue is the offset amount.

8. **Count the number of frames between the Out point of the Timeline and the first frame of the final sound cue beep.**

   Select this number in the Offset pop-up menu. It's a good ideal to repeat this with the new offset to confirm compensation.

✦ **Connect your headphones to the computer's headphone jack.**

Now that the Voice Over tool is ready, you have to set up the Sequence you will record the voiceover into.

1. **Set In and Out points in the Timeline for the section you wish to record voiceover.**

   The Voice Over tool plays the Sequence selection and records for the duration set between the In and Out points. It also records during the 5-second pre-roll and 2-second post-roll in case any part of the voiceover reading falls outside the In or Out points. This media is available in voiceover clips as unused media on either side of the clip's In and Out points. If no In or Out point is set in the Timeline, then recording begins at the current position of the playhead and will continue until the end of the Sequence, defined by the last clip in the Timeline.

2. Set the target track.

The Voice Over tool uses the track assigned to channel 2 (destination control a2) as the target track for the voiceover clip. The current target track is displayed after the Sequence name in the Target field in the Voice Over tool window. Setting the target track is straightforward enough, but there are a few additional guidelines you should know:

- If there are any clips on the target track in the selection between the In and Out points, then the next track below will become the target track.

- If, however, there are also audio clips on the track below the a2 target track, a new track will automatically be created and inserted below the current target track. All lower tracks are moved down one track level. New track creation is indicated in the Target field of the Voice Over window with the target track number preceded by the word *New* in parentheses, as shown in Figure 14-11.

Figure 14-11: If the assigned target track already contains audio clips, the Voice Over tool will create a new track, indicated by the *(New)* before the track label in the Target field.

- Similarly, a new target track will be created if there is no existing track below the target track already containing media.

- After recording a voiceover take, the target track will automatically increment, moving down to the next available track.

Note

From the rules listed here, it seems clear the Voice Over tool was designed to prevent any overwriting of any existing audio clips. Thankfully, that's one less thing to worry about.

Recording with the Voice Over tool

Now that you've connected the audio input device, configured the Voice Over Tool, and set a selection in your Timeline, recording the voiceover track is relatively simple. To record with the Voice Over tool:

1. **Set In and Out points in the Timeline.**

   This selection will be played back during recording and also determines the duration of the recorded voiceover track.

2. **Select a target track in the Timeline.**

   Track assigned to audio channel 2 (a2) is the default target track for the Voice Over tool. See additional rules in the preceding section.

3. **Open the Voice Over Tool by selecting Tools ⇨ Voice Over, or pressing Option+0 (zero).**

4. **Confirm the target track, input settings and headphone monitoring levels in the Voice Over window.**

5. **Click the Record button.**

   As the sequence begins pre-roll playing, the status window in the Voice Over tool will display "Starting" with a 5-second pre-roll countdown.

6. **Start speaking or reading the voiceover script when the status window displays "Recording" after the 1-second countdown mark.**

   You will hear a signal beep at 15 seconds before the Mark Out, and countdown cues during the last 5 seconds of recording. the final cue beep is longer and lower in tone.

   The sound cues are audible only through the headphone jacks when headphones are attached to the computer and are not recorded with the voiceover track.

   When the duration of the Timeline selection is finished playing, the Voice Over tool continues to record for an additional 2 seconds of post-roll. The status window will display "Finishing" and then "Saving" as it saves the clip to the hard disk. The new audio clip is inserted into the target track in your Sequence.

7. **If you wish to record additional takes, mute the new voiceover track first.**

   Figure 14-12 shows a Sequence with three takes of audio recorded with the Voice Over tool.

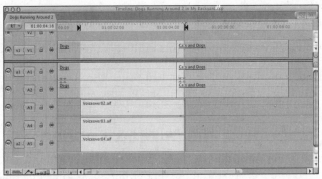

Figure 14-12: The Voice Over tool allows you to record multiple takes, each on its own track. Here, three voiceover takes have been recorded.

Note The Voice Over tool records the audio to RAM before writing it to the hard disk. The amount of RAM needed for audio recording varies, depending on the sample rate and bit depth of the digital audio signal. DV audio of 16-bit/48Mhz requires only 6MB per minute. Although this isn't much RAM relative to the requirements of Final Cut Pro itself, making as much RAM available as possible by quitting idle or unnecessary applications is always prudent.

Working with Audio in the Viewer Window

After you've captured audio, you can work with it in the Viewer or the Timeline. Whether you use the Timeline or the Viewer depends on what you are trying to accomplish as well as your editing style. The only rule I seem to follow is that most basic track work and audio adjustment can be performed right in the Timeline. However, for careful editing of sounds such as words, breaths, and other delicate work that requires a magnified view and more precise control, I prefer the Viewer window.

An important feature of the Viewer window is the ability to perform "sub-frame" audio editing. Using the Viewer window, you can make audio edits down to the level of 1/100th of a video frame. The Viewer window allows you to view the waveform in much greater detail, and it allows you to change the volume and pan levels of the audio portion or your clips. You can also set keyframes in the Viewer window to dynamically adjust audio settings for your clips. Still, you'll probably find that most audio editing is easier to perform using the Timeline.

Cross-Reference To learn more about the "sub-frame" audio editing and other details of working in the Viewer window, see Chapter 9.

Working with Audio in the Timeline

Throughout this book, I have mentioned that editing in the Timeline is the fastest and the most efficient way to work with video. Final Cut Pro also has many options for working with audio in the Timeline. You can adjust the volume and the pan levels, make edits, and apply transitions and filters to audio clips in the Timeline.

Rendering audio with the Mixdown option

If you attempt to play more tracks than what is specified in the Real-Time Audio Mixing setting, a red line will appear in the render bar above the clips that cannot be played in real time. This red line means that you must render your audio before you can play all the audio tracks in your sequence. If you try to play without rendering, you will hear a regular 1 kHz beep throughout the playback. To render only the audio portion of a clip, select the clips and choose Sequence ⇨ Render Only ⇨ Item Level.

Caution   Keep in mind that adding effects and transitions have track costs as well. For example, the track cost of a simple audio effect, such as a filter, is three tracks. This means that if your Final Cut Pro hardware setup is capable of playing eight audio tracks in real time, then adding a simple filter will drop the real-time playback capability down to five. Some filters can cost you up to six tracks of real-time playback.

If you have multiple audio tracks in your sequence with a lot of transitions and effects applied to them, you can use Final Cut Pro's Mixdown feature to consolidate your audio into a single preview file. This allows you to play through the sequence without dropping frames. Mixing down audio doesn't change the arrangement of your audio tracks or alter any edits. The mixdown occurs behind the scenes, and all it does is help Final Cut Pro generate a preview file.

To mix down audio tracks, open a sequence with multiple audio tracks and filters and choose Sequence ⇨ Render Only ⇨ Mixdown, or press Command+Option+R. The Writing Audio status bar will appear and display the mixing down of your audio. Final Cut Pro will mix down your audio so that it can play your sequence without dropping frames. If you make any changes in your audio clips, this includes moving *any* clips with audio in the Timeline, and you will need to select Mixdown again to create a new audio render file for the Sequence to play back.

Note   If the mixdown has been performed and you go back to the Sequence ⇨ Render Only ⇨ Mixdown menu choice, it will be grayed out and there will be a small check mark to the left of it. If mixdown has *not* occurred, this command will be available to you and there will be no check mark in the menu.

Cache the wave: Audio waveforms in the Timeline

The Waveforms in the Timeline window can be extremely useful. You can view the beats of a piece of music and spot silent portions of edits and voiceover tracks. Being able to view the waveforms of audio and beats makes it easy to locate edit points. However, when you turn on the audio waveforms for a Timeline, whether through the Command+Option+W shortcut or via the menu option, Final Cut Pro will take some time to draw the waveform of the audio clips currently in view in the Timeline window. Final Cut Pro actually renders the display of these waveforms and stores them as Waveform Cache.

If you head over to a section of a Timeline that Final Cut Pro has not cached, it will have to render the cache before showing you the waveform. This cache render is just a slight delay but annoying enough to slow you down. Each time you change the display of these waveforms, such as changing the size of the tracks and so on, the waveforms will have to be cached again.

After Final Cut Pro has cached a certain section of the waveform, the draw time for the screen speeds up rapidly if you head back into that section.

I just avoid keeping waveforms on at all times by remembering the extremely handy keyboard shortcut of Command+Option+W. Used once this shortcut turns the waveforms on. Used again it turns them off. I use this shortcut to quickly turn my waveform display on and then off after I am done.

Organizing audio tracks

In a complex Timeline, you should organize your tracks as much as possible. If you consistently have two main audio tracks with your video clips, another two tracks for music, and two more tracks devoted to voiceovers or effects, be sure to use these tracks consistently. In other words, don't take a shortcut and use your voiceover track for music or something else that doesn't "belong" in the track.

Generally speaking, track priority goes from top down. The main tracks get audio tracks 1 and 2. Assign tracks 3 and 4 as music tracks, and leave 5 for voiceovers and 6 for effects. Of course, the final arrangement depends on your priorities, but the idea is to keep track organization consistent. Organizing tracks is helpful for many reasons, including:

✦ When mixing, it is easier to identify which tracks contain what kind of audio.

✦ If you plan to output to a video deck that allows multitrack layback, you can easily separate audio tracks during layback so that they can be sent to a professional mix session at a sound facility. It is easier for everyone involved if the music from your program is laid back to Channels 3 and 4 of a Digital Betacam tape, and the voiceover is consistently on Channel 1.

✦ Final Cut Pro allows relative adjustment of audio levels for multiple clips simultaneously. If your tracks are organized, it will be easier to select an entire audio track and raise the levels of all the clips that are in it.

Moving audio clips across tracks

As you edit audio, you'll sometimes need to move clips from one track to another. You can easily move clips from one track to another, even if you don't want to change the location of the clip on the Timeline. To move a clip from one track to another without changing its place in time:

1. **Click on an audio clip that you want to move.**

   Don't move it yet, just hold down the mouse and get ready to move it.

2. **Press and hold the Shift key and drag the clip up or down with the mouse.**

   When you move the clip up or down to another track, the clip will be restricted only to vertical movements so long as you keep holding down the Shift key. The clip will not slip horizontally and thus not become misaligned in time. Figure 14-13 shows what this procedure looks like in the Timeline.

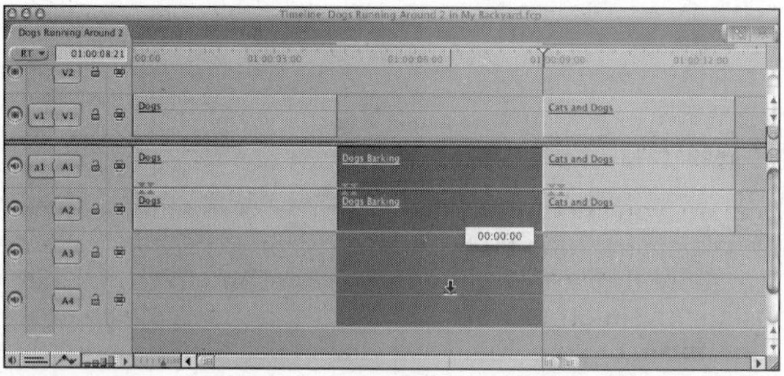

Figure 14-13: Hold down the Shift key while you move a clip across tracks to restrict clip movement in the vertical plane.

When you move clips using the Shift+drag method, you should also keep an eye on the small yellow box that appears next to the cursor as you move it. If the timecode in this small yellow box reads 00:00:00:00, then you are not displacing this clip in time. However, if it reads +5, –1, or any other timecode reading, then you are moving the clip in time.

Tip   Alternatively, you can select either the video or audio section of a clip, use Option+click to select separate parts of a linked clip, then hold down the Option key while you press the Up arrow or Down arrow key. The selected clip will move up or down a track level if there is no other clip overlapping the same space on the next track.

Adjusting audio volume in the Timeline

A common editing action in the Timeline is the adjustment of the volume level of an audio clip. Working in the Timeline, you can adjust the volume of any clip in any audio track. I often use this method to adjust the audio of music tracks in relation to main dialog tracks. There is more than one method to adjust volume for an audio clip, but adjusting it in the Timeline can be done quickly and efficiently. Here's how:

1. **Double-click a sequence in the Browser to open it.**

2. **Press Option+W to activate clip overlays.**

   You can also activate clip overlays by clicking the Clip Overlays button in the bottom-left corner of the Timeline. Red lines appear on every audio clip. This red line is the volume level overlay for that clip.

3. **Click and drag the red volume level overlay up or down to raise or lower the volume of the clip.**

   (If the clip is selected the red volume line will appear green.) As you drag the red volume level line up and down, you also get a small yellow box that indicates the current decibel level. Figure 14-14 shows how to drag the volume level overlay.

Adjust Line Segment pointer

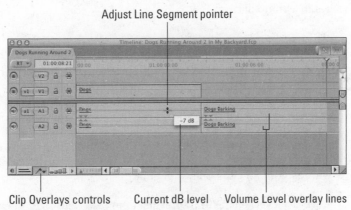

Clip Overlays controls   Current dB level   Volume Level overlay lines

Figure 14-14: Drag the red volume overlay line up or down to raise or lower the volume of a clip.

4. **You can quickly play the area around the clip by using the Play Around Current command.**

   The keyboard shortcut for the Play Around Current command is the \ (backslash) key. Use this shortcut to check your volume adjustment.

Adjusting the volume for multiple clips simultaneously

Sometimes you'll need to raise or lower the volume of a group of clips. This often happens to me when I have mixed a Timeline and decide that I want to raise the level of the voiceover just a little bit *throughout* the Timeline. In a complex Timeline, there could be as many as 60 clips for which volume would need to be adjusted. In earlier versions of Final Cut Pro, it was a major chore to adjust each clip one by one. Luckily, Final Cut Pro now lets you accomplish this tedious task in one fell swoop:

1. **Open a sequence and select all the clips whose volume you want to adjust.**

2. **Choose Modify ⇨ Levels.**

   The Gain Adjust dialog box appears as shown in Figure 14-15.

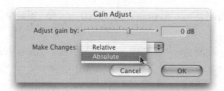

Figure 14-15: The Gain Adjust dialog box is used to make relative or absolute audio level changes to a group of clips.

3. **Enter a number or use the Adjust Gain By slider to choose a setting.**

4. **Choose Relative or Absolute in the Make Changes pull-down menu and click OK.**

The *Relative* setting changes each track's level relative to what it was before your change. If you enter +5dB Relative, a clip that had a level of 5dB will now have a level of 10dB, and a clip that previously had a level of 0dB will now have a level of 5dB. The *Absolute* setting changes all the clips to the same volume level. Entering +5dB Absolute will result in all clips being set at 5dB.

Tip   You can change clip levels on the fly by pressing Control++(Plus sign) or Control+- (Minus) as you play clips in the Timeline. Each time you press the keyboard shortcut, your clip's volume will be changed by 1db, plus or minus. This shortcut will affect the clip that your playhead is currently passing over. There will be a slight pause each time you use this shortcut, but after the pause the clip will continue to play. For a +3db level adjustment, press Control+} (right bracket) and to lower levels −3db, press Control+{ (left bracket). You can also use these keyboard shortcuts for relative level adjustments to multiple clips selected in the Timeline.

Adjusting Pan in the Timeline

Pan is the audio control that sends the sound of your clip to the left or right channel. In the Timeline, you can adjust Pan to center, *hard left* (meaning fully to the left side), or hard right. You cannot make finer adjustments than this in the Timeline, but the Viewer window does allow you to make finer Pan adjustments. Normally this lack of fine control is not a big deal because hard adjustments are the most common adjustments made to Pan anyway.

Cross-Reference

To learn how to use the Viewer to make changes in the Pan setting of a clip, as well as learn more about working with stereo pairs and Channel 1/Channel 2 audio clips, see Chapter 9.

Adjusting Pan settings for a clip in the Timeline is easy; just follow these steps:

1. **Open a sequence and select a clip or clips for which you want to adjust Pan settings.**

2. **Choose Modify ⇨ Audio and then choose the desired Pan setting from the submenu.**

   Pan Left pans the audio track to the left channel of a stereo output. Pan Center centers the track so that it outputs equally to stereo output channels. Pan Right sends the track to the right stereo output.

Using keyframes to make dynamic audio adjustments

Most of the audio adjustments described thus far in this chapter have affected entire clips. Often you will want to adjust the levels or Pan of a clip dynamically. For instance, you may want to fade in to a piece of music, gradually bring it up to a higher volume, and then fade out again at a spot later in the clip. To make dynamic changes throughout a clip, you can use keyframes. Here's how:

1. **Open a sequence and press Option+W to activate the Clip Overlays control.**

   A red volume level overlay appears across your audio clips in the sequence.

2. **If the Tools palette is not visible, choose Window ⇨ Tools to bring it up.**

3. **Select the Pen-Add Keyframe tool from the Tools palette.**

   You can also press the P key to select the Pen tool. (To go back to the arrow pointer press the A key.) The Pen tool is used to add, delete, and modify keyframes. You can press the P key repeatedly on your keyboard to select between the different Pen tools. Figure 14-16 shows the Pen tool choices.

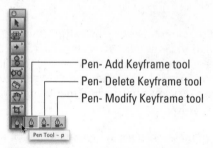

Pen- Add Keyframe tool
Pen- Delete Keyframe tool
Pen- Modify Keyframe tool

Figure 14-16: The Pen tool is used to
add, delete, and modify keyframes.

4. **Move the Pen tool to a point in the clip where you want to add a keyframe and click on the red Volume level overlay.**

   This adds a red, diamond-shaped keyframe at the current point in time.

5. **After the keyframe is added, the Pen tool turns into a crosshair pointer (make sure you leave the Pen tool above the new keyframe you just added or the crosshair pointer won't appear).**

   Use this crosshair pointer to drag a keyframe up or down and along the Timeline while reading the decibel setting in the small yellow box that appears. To create a fade out, drag the crosshair in an arc down and to the right on the Timeline. To create a fade in, drag the arc down and to the left. Figure 14-17 shows these steps.

Tip   You don't have to choose the Pen tool from the Tools Palette to make keyframes. Simply press and hold the Option key to turn the arrow pointer to a Pen tool when you place it near a volume level line.

Monitoring audio in the Timeline

While working with audio in the Timeline, you can use the floating Audio Meters to monitor your levels. Final Cut Pro provides a variety of methods for mixing together various audio tracks. You can also use filters and audio transitions to further control your audio levels.

While preparing your final mix in the Timeline, you should closely monitor the floating Audio Meters. When editing in Final Cut Pro, the ultimate goal is to *never* let audio peaks in the final mix exceed the 0dB hash mark. In general, the loudest sounds in your sequence should not rise much above the –3dB mark in the Final Cut Pro Audio Meters.

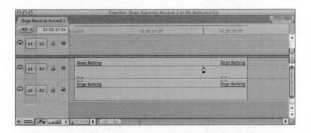

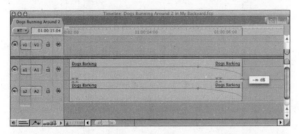

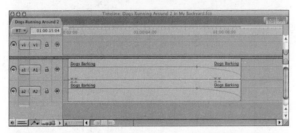

Figure 14-17: (Top) Click with the Pen tool on the volume level overlay to add a keyframe. The crosshair pointer automatically appears. Use this crosshair pointer to drag the keyframe down or up to set a new level at this current point (middle). The music clip at the bottom now has a fade out.

Tip   If you are sending your final mix to an analog deck, try to make sure that your average audio levels do not rise above +3dB on the analog deck's VU meter.

As described earlier, when you are setting digital audio levels in Final Cut Pro, you'll usually choose a reference point of –12dB, –18dB, or –20dB. You must be aware of this level as you output audio to tape, because the reference point will determine how much headroom you have. *Headroom* is the difference between your reference point and the loudest audio you can have before distortion occurs. If your reference point is –12dB, the headroom is 12dB because it lies between –12dB and 0dB. Some broadcast houses limit their dynamic range to around 6dB, so if you are outputting to such a house you should keep your sound levels between –12dB and –6dB. Figure 14-18 shows the headroom for the various digital reference standards.

Caution   If the Peak lights at the top of the Final Cut Pro Audio Meters light up, it means you are clipping your audio. These peak lights stay on and provide a good way to check for and avoid distortion.

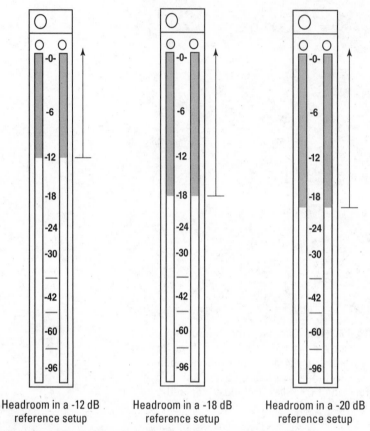

Headroom in a -12 dB   Headroom in a -18 dB   Headroom in a -20 dB
reference setup   reference setup   reference setup

Figure 14-18: Headroom is the decibel range you have between the reference point and the highest peak you can have without distortion. On a −12dB reference, the headroom is between −12dB and 0dB.

Using the Audio Mixer Tool

Every editor would agree that mixing multiple audio tracks is best done in real time as the sequence plays. This is not "real-time envy" or snobbery, but founded on the principle that judging and adjusting an audio track should be made relative to all other audio that is currently playing. For example, it is not uncommon to have a music track, a voiceover track, and a sound effects track, layered and playing at the same time. Level adjustment to any one of these audio tracks will not be an absolute value, but rather, a relative value influenced by the current levels of the other audio tracks.

Real-time adjustment of audio tracks is now possible in Final Cut Pro with the new Audio Mixer tool. The Audio Mixer tool allows you to adjust levels and panning of clips on individual tracks and control the overall audio output of the sequence, or *master mix*. Another powerful feature of this tool is its ability to record, in real time, dynamic adjustments to your audio tracks as you are making them. These dynamic adjustments are recorded as keyframes on the overlays of individual clips in the sequence and can be modified later in the Timeline or Viewer.

Although the Audio Mixer is not a replacement for the precise control available in the Viewer, or with clip overlays in the Timeline, when you're ready to mix multiple audio tracks as they are played in your sequence, you'll want to employ the Audio Mixer. To use the Audio Mixer, choose Tools ➪ Audio Mixer, or press Option+6. The Audio Mixer will appear in its own tab in the Tool Bench window, as shown in Figure 14-19.

Figure 14-19: The new Audio Mixer tool lets you make real-time adjustments as your sequence is playing.

Tip Final Cut Pro has a preset windows layout that will neatly move over the Viewer and Canvas windows to the upper-left side of your monitor to make room for the Tool Bench window *as well as* open the Audio Mixer tool at the same time. Select Window ➪ Arrange ➪ Audio Mixing.

Getting to know the Audio Mixer controls

The interface of the Audio Mixer tool is based on the controls layout of a hardware mixing board. It can be broken down into three main sections: track selection, track strips, and Master level controls, shown in Figure 14-20.

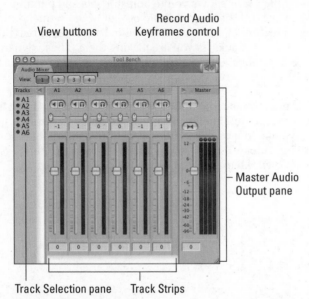

Figure 14-20: The Audio Mixer tool is laid out similarly to a hardware mixing board, consisting of three main sections of controls.

Track Selection pane

The controls found in this pane are used to help organize the track strips by showing or hiding tracks in the center Track Strip pane. You can hide or reveal the Track Selection pane by clicking on the disclosure triangle at the top of the Track Selection pane, shown in Figure 14-21.

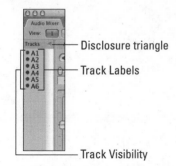

Figure 14-21: Click the disclosure triangle at the top of the Tracks to hide or show the Track Selection pane.

Disclosure triangle

Track Labels

Track Visibility

✦ **Track visibility control:** Click on this button, the little dot in front of each track label, to show or hide the corresponding track in the Audio Mixer. Hiding a track strip does not mute or disable the track in the Timeline. This is merely an Audio Mixer *viewing* option. When a track is hidden, it is removed from the Track Strip and all tracks to the right will slide left to fill the gap.

✦ **Track Label:** This is the name and number corresponding to the track in the current sequence, also shown above its track strip in the center pane of the Audio Mixer.

✦ **Output Channel shortcut menu:** Control+click on a track label to see a contextual menu allowing you to assign that audio track to one of the available audio output channels specified in the Audio Outputs tab in the current sequence's Settings.

Note Audio output assignment can also be set by Control+clicking on the mute or solo buttons of an audio track in the Timeline patch panel, and choosing Audio Outputs. For more detail on settings in the Audio Outputs tab, see Chapter 6.

Track Strip pane

Controls in the track strip are used to adjust levels and panning of tracks in the currently selected Timeline. You can also mute and solo the playback of each track. There is one corresponding track strip in the Audio Mixer for every track in the currently selected Timeline, even if there are no clips in the Timeline track. As shown in Figure 14-22, each Track Strip contains the following controls:

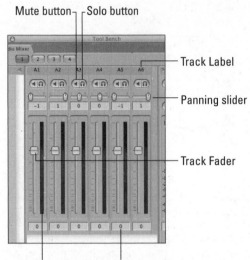

Figure 14-22: The Track Strip pane contains controls for adjusting individual tracks in your sequence.

✦ **Track Label:** This is the track name and number corresponding to the track in the current Timeline and Track Selection pane.

✦ **Mute button:** Click this button to toggle off or on playback of that track. This mutes the monitoring of the audio playback only. A muted track will still be included in output when Print to Video or Edit to Tape is used, or a movie or audio file is exported. The mute button in the Audio Mixer is the same mute button on the corresponding audio track in the Timeline, displaying the same toggle status in both windows. Muting a track does not affect any existing levels or panning adjustments.

✦ **Solo button:** Click this button to mute all other tracks that do not have solo enabled. Enabling solo on a few selected tracks allows you to quickly select and hear just those tracks while muting all others. Like the mute button, soloing only affects playback and does not disable a track from output with Print to Video, Edit to Tape, or Export movie file commands.

✦ **Panning slider:** Use this slider to control a clip's panning setting. This control operates identically to the pan slider in the Audio tab of the Viewer window. You can also enter the pan setting numerically in the field below the slider.

✦ **Track Fader:** Faders are vertical slider controls for adjusting the audio level of the clip that is currently beneath the Timeline playhead. The logarithmic scale of the fader allows you to make smooth adjustments over its range of +12dB to −∞dB (or silence). The fader control snaps to 0dB by default, unless you hold down the Control key while dragging. Any changes made with the fader can be seen in the overlay of the sequence clip (if Clip Overlay is enabled).

When the sequence is played back, the faders will animate as they follow the levels of the clips in corresponding tracks. You can also enter numeric level values directly into the field below each track fader.

Tip For more precise control, you can increase the effective resolution of a track fader by increasing its height. To do this, simply make the Audio Mixer window taller by pulling down on its resize tab in the bottom-right corner of the Tool Bench window.

✦ **Track level meter:** Each track has its own track level meter showing the audio level of the clips in that track as they are played in the sequence. Unlike hardware audio meters that only read levels when audio is playing, the audio meters in Final Cut Pro display levels whenever an audio clip is beneath the playhead, even when play is paused.

Note You might have noticed the range of the track level meter extends above 0dB, or *Digital Full Scale,* to +12dB. Although digital audio levels above 0dB will clip and distort when audio is output, the track level meters in the Audio Mixer represent Final Cut Pro's internal mixing at 32-bit floating-point resolution of individual audio tracks, in which levels above 0dB are acceptable as long as they do not exceed 0dB on the Master meters.

Audio Master pane

Use the controls in this pane to adjust the master level of all the tracks in the currently selected Timeline. You can also mute and mix down the audio of all sequence tracks. The controls of the Audio Master pane cannot be automated. You can hide or reveal the Audio Master pane and its controls by clicking on the disclosure triangle at the top of the Audio Master pane, as shown in Figure 14-23.

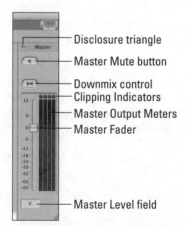

Figure 14-23: To hide or show the Audio Master Pane and its control, click on the disclosure triangle at the top of the Audio Master pane.

✦ **Master Mute button:** Clicking this button toggles on or off the muting of all tracks in the Timeline during playback. The Master Mute button affects playback monitoring only and does not disable any tracks when using Print to Video, Edit to Tape, or exporting a movie or audio file.

✦ **Downmix control:** Selecting this control forces all output channels to mix down to a single stereo pair of outputs. All odd-numbered audio outputs are assigned to the left channel, while even-numbered audio outputs are assigned to the right channel. Each output channel is reduced by the dB amount set in the Audio Output tab of the current Sequence Settings. This option might be useful when you need to monitor or output audio as a single stereo pair, say for Web delivery or to VHS tape, without having to change your output setup for multi-channel output.

Note   You may need to decrease the levels of your output channels when downmixing to prevent the mixed levels from peaking (exceeding 0 dB). This is set in the Audio Outputs tab of the Sequence Settings. See Chapter 6 for more on Downmix and Downmix levels control.

✦ **Master fader:** The Master fader controls the output of all tracks simultaneously. This control does not affect or change any levels overlay of clips in the Timeline. This control cannot be automated. Levels changes made by the Master fader affect audio output of playback, output to tape, or export of movie or audio files.

✦ **Master output audio meters:** The Master audio meter displays one audio meter (a color levels indicator) for each audio output specified in the Audio Output tab in the Sequence Setting of the current Timeline. If, for example, you have selected six audio outputs to an external audio interface, then six Master audio meters will show the audio mix of each output. Above each Master audio meter is a clipping indicator that will light when an output channel's signal level exceeds 0dB, causing distortion. Once the clipping indicator lights up, it will stay lit until play is stopped and then restarted.

Note   Unlike Final Cut Pro's floating audio meters, the Master audio meters display a range above the distortion level of 0dB. While the maxim that digital audio signal *output* will distort above 0dB still applies, the extra +12dB of "clipping room" allows you to see how much above the distortion threshold an audio output is clipping, and the amount you need to reduce the output mix in order that it not exceed the clipping threshold.

Additional controls in the Audio Mixer

There are two additional controls outside the main panes of the Audio Mixer tool: View buttons and the Record Audio Keyframes button, shown in Figure 14-24.

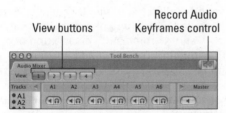

Figure 14-24: View buttons and Record Audio Keyframes controls are shown above.

✦ **View buttons:** The four View buttons above the track strips allow you to save customized displays of your visible track selection. This can be very useful when you want to streamline the Audio Mixer interface when mixing only certain tracks and want to minimize the clutter of displaying all other tracks. This is also handy when you have more audio tracks than the Audio Mixer tab can display at once. To save track selections to a specific View number, simply select the View number button and make your track visibility selection in the Track Selection pane. Track visibility is automatically saved to the current view whenever any track visibility is modified.

> **Note**
>
> Any new track added to the current Sequence is added to all Audio Mixer Views, including those views that have been customized. To hide new tracks, select the View and "shy" the track by clicking its visibility control in the Track Selection pane.

✦ **Record Audio Keyframes control:** Click this button to toggle on or off automatic creation of keyframes in sequence clips when Audio Mixer track controls are adjusted during sequence playback. New keyframes are added to the clip overlay of sequence clips. In addition to track faders and Pan sliders in the Audio Mixer, Level and Pan slider controls in the Audio tab of the Viewer can also be use to set keyframes when automatic keyframe creation is enabled. However, if the Record Audio Keyframes option is not enabled, adjusting Audio Mixer controls with clips that have no keyframes will affect only overall clip settings, and with clips containing keyframes, modify the existing keyframes without creating any new ones.

Making overall audio adjustments with the Audio Mixer

When you begin an editing project, you'll probably need to make only general, overall level adjustments to your audio, leaving the fine-tuning and keyframing until the final mix. In order to take advantage of controlling individual tracks of audio with the Audio Mixer, it is a good idea to organize your tracks with all similar types of sound clips placed on dedicated tracks. For example, Timeline audio tracks A1 and

A2 might be dedicated to original video sound (called *nat sound,* by some editors because it is the natural ambient sound recorded at the time of video shooting), tracks A3 and A4 to voiceover, and tracks A5 and A6 to music. This method of organizing tracks in the Audio Mixer makes adjustments consistent and efficient. Using the Audio Mixer to set overall levels is simple and straightforward:

1. **With your sequence opened and selected in the Timeline, open the Audio Mixer by choosing Tools ⇨ Audio Mixer.**

   The Audio Mixer tool will open in its own tab in the Tool Bench window. Or better yet, you can open the Audio Mixer and have all windows resized and neatly arranged with one command by selecting Window ⇨ Arrange ⇨ Audio Mixer.

2. **Select track visibility and monitoring controls.**

   If you want to hide tracks that you will not be modifying, simply click on the corresponding track visibility control in the Track Selection pane. You can also mute any tracks you don't want to hear during playback, or solo one or more tracks while muting all other tracks. Click on the mute or solo controls at the top of each track section to toggle them on or off.

Tip   You can toggle or adjust any Audio Mixer controls while the sequence is playing without interrupting playback. This tool really is real-time capable.

Note   Remember, mute and solo controls affect the playback monitoring only. Tracks with mute or solo selected will still be included when using Print to Video, when using Edit to Tape, or when exporting a movie or audio file of the sequence. To disable a track when outputting to tape or exporting a movie or audio file, toggle the track visibility control to Off in the Timeline.

3. **Make sure Record Audio Keyframes is off.**

   The button for this option is highlighted green when enabled. Because we want to set general levels without creating new keyframes, make sure this control is not highlighted, indicating it is off. If it is on, click on it to toggle it off.

4. **Play your sequence or sequence selection.**

   As the sequence plays back, you will hear all enabled audio tracks, and see track faders move to the levels set in the clip currently playing in that track. Muted tracks will show no signal in its track meter; however, the fader will still move to reflect current Levels of the current clip. You can play just a selection of your sequence by setting In and Out points in the Timeline and then clicking the Play In to Out button in the Canvas window, or use the keyboard shortcut by pressing Shift+\ (forward slash).

Tip

If you need to repeat a selected portion of your sequence multiple times, for setting levels of multiple layered audio tracks for instance, you can loop the playback of your selection by choosing View ➪ Loop Playback. Mark your selection to playback by setting In and Out points in the Timeline and then use Play In to Out.

5. **Make your adjustment using the track fader or panning slider as your sequence is playing.**

You will hear immediate, real-time changes as you move track fader or panning slider. The track fader will adjust the signal level of only the clip that is directly under the playhead and not the levels of all the clips on that track. If you want to modify the level of a particular clip in the Timeline with the Audio Mixer track fader, you must position the playhead directly over the clip before making adjustments. With Clip Overlays enabled in the Timeline, any adjustments to levels will be reflected in the clip overlays *after* play has stopped. You may also modify track levels by entering a numeric value in the field directly below the track audio meter.

If you are adjusting the track fader of a stereo audio clip, as you might expect, the track faders are locked together and will move as one. If, however, the audio clip is a linked pair of mono clips, audio tracks of merged clips for example, then track faders work separately, allowing you control of each track. A track's Pan slider control in the Audio Mixer behaves similarly, if the tracks have been assigned as a stereo pair in the Audio Outputs tab in the current sequence's Settings. Stereo pair clips on adjacent tracks assigned as stereo output channels will move inversely to each other, while the Pan setting of mono clips can be set independently.

You can make clip adjustments with the Audio Mixer while the sequence is playing or paused. Either way, as long as the Record Audio Keyframes option is off *and* the clip you are modifying contains no keyframes, the changes you make in the Audio Mixer will be for the duration of the whole clip.

Here are a few tips for working with track faders in the Audio Mixer tool:

✦ Track faders, by default, snap to the 0dB detent. To temporarily toggle off this snapping action, hold down the Command key as you drag the fader.

✦ To reset a fader to 0dB, hold down the Option key as you click on the fader.

✦ To reset all faders in the Audio Mixer to 0dB, Contol+click just above any track audio meter and select Reset All from the contextual menu.

Using the Audio Mixer tool for mixer automation

When the Record Audio Keyframes control in the Audio Mixer tool is enabled, all adjustments to the Audio Mixer's faders and pan sliders during playback are recorded as keyframes onto the sequence clips overlays. This ability of the Audio

Mixer tool to create keyframes and record dynamic changes to audio levels and pan settings is called *mixer automation.* The number of keyframes created during mixer automation can be set in the General tab of User Preferences. In Figure 14-25, you can see the three options in the pop-up menu for Record Audio Keyframes in the User Preferences.

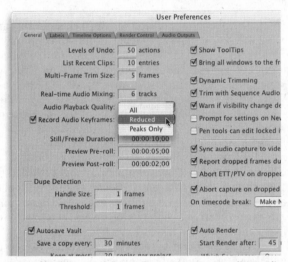

Figure 14-25: Set the number of keyframes the Audio Mixer will record in the General tab of the User Preferences.

✦ **All:** This options records the maximum number of keyframes possible when adjustments are made with the track fader or pan slider. This gives you the most accurate reproduction of your dynamic adjustments at the expense of many keyframes that might make modification difficult later.

✦ **Reduced:** A smaller number of keyframes are recorded during mixer automation, allowing for easier modification later. This is the most commonly used setting.

✦ **Peaks Only:** This option records the minimum number of keyframes during mixer automation, using only the lowest and highest values of adjustments made during playback. The minimum number of keyframes recorded with this option will give an approximation of the levels settings recorded during playback and is usually refined later in the Viewer or Timeline overlays.

With the Record Audio Keyframes control enabled, mixer automation begins from the time the mouse is pressed down on a track fader or pan slider, and continues until the mouse is released. All movements of the control while the mouse is still pressed will be recorded with newly created keyframes in the clip directly under the Timeline playhead during playback. For this reason, it is common practice to mix groupings of consecutive clips in the same track at the same time. To record the fader of panning slider automation:

1. **Enable Record Audio Keyframes control.**

   The button for this option is in the upper-right corner of the Audio Mixer tab window and is highlighted green when enabled.

2. **Play your sequence or sequence selection.**

   You can play a selection of your sequence by setting In and Out points in the Timeline and then clicking the Play In to Out button in the Canvas window, or use the keyboard shortcut by pressing Shift+\ (forward slash).

Tip

If you need to repeat a selected portion of your sequence multiple times, for setting levels of multiple layered audio tracks for instance, you can loop the playback of your selection by choosing View ⇨ Loop Playback. Mark your selection to playback by setting In and Out points in the Timeline and then use Play In to Out.

3. **Position your cursor over the track fader or pan slider you wish to adjust, then click the mouse.**

   Keyframe recording will begin from the this point.

4. **Hold the mouse down as you make levels of panning adjustments while the Timeline plays back.**

   You will hear immediate, real-time changes as you move the controls. Keyframes are created in the clips directly beneath the playhead for as long as you hold down the mouse. If Clip Overlays is enabled in the Timeline, newly created keyframes will be displayed in the clip overlays after play has stopped. You can also modify track levels or pan settings by entering a numeric value in the corresponding field.

5. **Release the mouse to stop keyframe recording.**

Note

If you want to redo any keyframe recording, simply repeat the above procedure — any new changes using mixer automation will overwrite older keyframes previously set.

If keyframe recording stops before the end of a clip is reached, the audio level or panning setting for the remaining duration of that clip will depend on the prior existence of any keyframes in that clip. If there are no keyframes in the clip prior to automated keyframe recording, the levels or panning settings will remain at the last recorded keyframe level for the remaining duration of the clip, as shown in Figure 14-26.

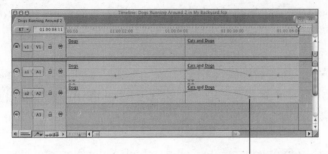

Last Recorded Keyframe level

Figure 14-26: Keyframe recording was stopped before the end of Cats and Dogs clip finished playback. Because that last clip had no previous levels keyframes, the level of the last recorded keyframe is used for the remaining duration of the clip.

If the clip contained keyframes prior to the automated keyframe recording, then the last recorded keyframe will be used to interpolate to the next (existing) keyframe level, as shown in Figure 14-27.

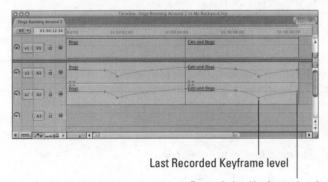

Last Recorded Keyframe level

Pre-existing Keyframe level

Figure 14-27: Keyframe recording was stopped before the Cats and Dogs clip finished playback. This time, however, the last clip contained previously existing levels keyframes, causing an interpolation from the last automated recorded keyframe to the next keyframe in the clip.

Modifying clips with previously existing keyframes

Using the Audio Mixer, you can modify clips that already have levels or panning keyframes, but the results will differ depending on if you have the Record Audio Keyframes control enabled or disabled.

✦ **If Record Audio Keyframes control is enabled:** A new set of keyframes is created, overwriting any previously existing keyframes. If the playhead is stopped, any changes will insert a new keyframe at the playhead position.

✦ **If Record Audio Keyframes control is disabled:** Changes to the levels or pan setting will not create new keyframes but will modify levels set with the fader or pan slider. If the playhead is directly over an existing keyframe, then the level of that keyframe is adjusted. If the playhead is located between two existing keyframes, then the level of the whole section between the two keyframes is set to the level made with the Audio Mixer controls.

You can make further modification to levels overlays in the Timeline and in the Viewer window with a sequence clip loaded into it, however, the panning keyframes overlay is only available in the Audio tab of the Viewer window.

Cross-Reference For more detail on working with audio in the Viewer, see Chapter 9.

Deleting keyframes created with mixer automation

You can easily remove all level and panning keyframes from a clip using the Remove Attributes command. To do this:

1. **Select the desired clip, or clips, in the sequence.**

2. **Select Edit ▷ Remove Attributes.**

   Or, you can Control+click on the selected clips and choose Remove Attributes from the contextual menu. The Remove Attributes dialog box, shown in Figure 14-28, will appear.

Figure 14-28: Use the Remove Attributes command to delete keyframes from selected clips.

3. **Select either Levels, Pan, or both.**

4. **Click OK to have selected keyframes removed from the selected clips overlays.**

   All keyframes of the selected attribute will be removed and reset to its default value—0dB for levels and –1 pan for stereo clips.

Adjusting the master level

The Master fader in the Audio Mixer tool controls the output level of all audio tracks in your sequence simultaneously. This master control is usually left at the default setting of 0dB and is adjusted only *after the final audio mix* to set the overall mix level prior to final output of the sequence. Also, when setting up at the beginning of a project, the volume of the monitor speakers is adjusted to an adequate level using a reference tone played through your editing station. Once set, it is important that neither the master level nor the monitor volume setting be adjusted so that individual track levels can be evaluated and adjusted relative to the levels of the other audio tracks, and not unduly offset by any changes made to the master mix level or monitor volume.

Exporting Audio in Final Cut Pro

Although Final Cut Pro allows audio editing and provides many mixing and filtering options, many users prefer to leave their final audio mix to professional audio facilities. Some users are content with a final audio mix prepared in Final Cut Pro, but the quality of a professional sound mix and a cleanup at the hands of a qualified sound engineer is incomparable to the basic mix you can achieve within Final Cut Pro. Professional sound mixes can be expensive but are worth every penny. Editors using Final Cut Pro will often work with scratch voice tracks and fill because they are leaving the final mix up to the audio engineers. When the final video program is mastered to tape, arrangements are made to export the audio tracks to a professional sound facility for a final mix.

Two main options exist within Final Cut Pro to export the audio information of your tracks to an audio facility that uses digital audio workstations. These options are:

✦ **Edit Decision List (EDL) export:** EDLs are simple tab-delimited text files that include information about the timecodes and reel numbers of your edits. Many digital audio workstations can import EDLs and capture audio from the original tapes. EDL export works best when you have a basic edit that consists of sync dialog and ambience track, all captured from timecoded tape material.

You should observe a few cautions when exporting EDLs. Most EDL options do not allow more than four tracks of audio. If you have more than four tracks, you should export more than one EDL, one for each audio track. Also be aware that if you have sounds such as CD music tracks or sound effects that you imported directly from the CD-ROM drive of your computer, these tracks will have no timecode reference and thus are hard to re-create and time correctly in the final edits. For best results, output any music or sound effects to a timecoded videotape and capture the sound from that tape.

Cross-Reference

See Chapter 18 for more on exporting EDLs.

✦ **Split audio tracks on tape:** Another common method for transporting audio track information is to master your program to tape while "splitting" your audio tracks. Splitting means that you have each audio track from your sequence or Timeline recorded back to a separate channel of your tape. The sound engineer can then capture these individual tracks into their digital audio workstations for the mix. In order to split audio tracks, you must make sure that sync sound goes to a separate channel on the tape from music. You can ensure this split by keeping tracks organized so that sync sound remains on channels 1 and 2 and your music remains on channels 3 and 4. Before mastering to tape you should also hard pan (maximum pan spread settings of 1 or –1) your tracks to left or right and make sure your audio channels in the hardware mixer, if any, are also hard split to left or right. You want to give complete separation of tracks to your audio engineer, ensuring that sync track audio is not mixed in with music or effects tracks.

When exporting split audio tracks, you should also make sure that any level adjustments you make in the Timeline are taken off before mastering to tape. Making the tracks flat is necessary because audio engineers prefer the tracks to come in flat, without any level adjustments or effects. If you don't want to lose your changes, duplicate your sequences and remove the adjustments from the sequence that you plan to master to tape. Keep the other copy of the sequence handy as a backup.

Often, you will have more audio tracks on your Timeline than channels available on your tape deck. Depending on your hardware setup, you will probably have access to just two channels of audio on your tape deck. As a workaround, you can lay down the program multiple times on the same tape. For example, if a Timeline has eight tracks, lay down the program four consecutive times on the tape, each time turning on just two of the audio tracks in the Timeline. The audio engineers can then recapture two tracks each from the laybacks and line them up in their workstations to make eight tracks.

Placing a minus 2 beep in the Timeline

A critical step in exporting audio to a professional sound facility is laying down a *minus 2 beep* on your tape. A minus 2 beep is a single frame of 1 kHz 0dB beep tone laid down in your Timeline exactly two seconds before the first frame of video appears. You should lay this single frame of beep on all audio tracks. Audio engineers use this beep as a reference marker to line up all the audio tracks.

Before you place the beep in your Timeline, make sure that you have duplicated your sequence and cleaned up the tracks by panning them hard left and hard right. If your first video clip begins at the start of the Timeline, as most do, you will need to create the space ahead of your first video clip in which to insert the minus 2 tone. The area before the first frame of picture and sound is usually black and soundless and can be filled with a generator clip of solid black, called a *slug*.

1. **Move the Timeline playhead to the beginning of the sequence.**

   In your Timeline, hold down the Up Arrow key (Previous Edit command) until the playhead is at the beginning of the Timeline, or press the Home key.

2. **Select the Viewer window and choose Slug from the Generator pop-up menu.**

   The Generator pop-up menu is located in the lower-right corner of the window. By default, Slugs have a duration of two minutes.

3. **Highlight the duration field in the upper-left corner of the Viewer window and type 1000 to specify a duration of 10 seconds, then press Enter on your keyboard to set this duration.**

4. **Insert the 10 second slug of video and audio into the beginning of your sequence by pressing F9 key.**

   You can also insert the slug by dragging the clip from the Viewer window to the Canvas "Insert" overlay. Either way, make sure there is no In or Out point set in the sequence, or these reference point will be used instead of the playhead position for inserting. Press Option+X to clear any In and Out points in the Timeline before performing Insert.

5. **While still in the Timeline, press Command+Shift+A to make sure that no items are selected in the Timeline, and then type –200.**

   This action jumps the playhead exactly two seconds back along the Timeline.

6. **Select the Viewer window and choose Bars and Tone from the Generator pop-up menu.**

   The Generator pop-up menu is located in the lower-right corner of the window. By default the Bars and Tone have a duration of two minutes.

7. **Highlight the duration field in the upper-left corner of the Viewer window and type 01 to specify a duration of one frame, then press Enter on your keyboard to set this duration.**

8. **Press the F10 key to make an overwrite edit into the Timeline.**

   The single frame of Bars and Tone are placed exactly two seconds before your first frame of edited material.

9. **Press Command++ (plus sign) to zoom in the Timeline, and then Option+click on the video portion of the bars and tone.**

   Just the video portion should be highlighted.

10. **Press the Delete key to delete the bar frame.**

    You should now have just a single frame of beep in the Timeline.

11. **Copy the beep by selecting it and choosing Edit ⇨ Copy.**

12. **Paste the beep into all audio tracks in the Timeline.**

    You must enable the target track controls on the appropriate audio tracks in order to paste the beep into each track.

Cross-Reference See Chapter 11 for more on working with target tracks.

Exporting AIFF files

Another common way to export audio tracks is to export them as AIFF audio files. AIFF is a widely used sound file format, and AIFF files can easily be imported into any digital audio workstation. You can take each audio track in your Timeline and export them as individual AIFF files. For a sequence with eight audio tracks, you would end up with eight AIFF files.

The major advantage to exporting audio tracks as AIFF files is that files remain digital and thus do not lose quality as they are laid down on tape. Unlike the EDL export method, you also do not have to worry about timecode information. Any CD tracks or sound effects you have used are included in the AIFF files.

Each track of audio should be exported as a separate AIFF file. The most affordable and easiest way to export AIFF files is to use recordable CDs, but check with your sound facility to coordinate a media format that you can both work with. Before you begin exporting, add the minus 2 beep as described in the previous section. Then you can export the files:

1. **Turn off the visibility of all tracks except the one you are about to export.**

   To do this, Option+click the Visibility button for the track you want to export. All other tracks are turned off as shown in Figure 14-29.

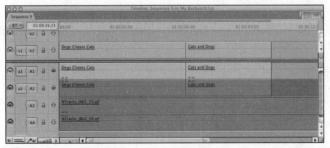

Figure 14-29: Option+click one of the Track Visibility buttons to turn off all other tracks.

2. **Choose File ➪ Export ➪ Using QuickTime Conversion.**

3. **Enter a name for your file and select a location to save it, as shown in Figure 14-30.**

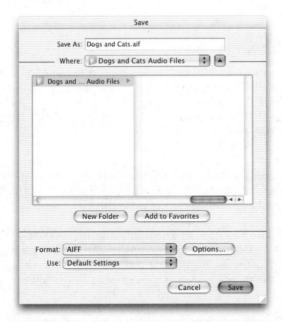

Figure 14-30: Name your file, pick a location to save it in, and choose AIFF from the Format pull-down menu.

4. **Choose AIFF from the Format pull-down menu.**

5. **Click the Options button to open the Sound Settings dialog box and set your export options.**

   You should keep the Rate setting the same as the sampling rate used by the files in your Timeline. Select 16 bit and Mono as shown in Figure 14-31. Each track is exported as a single mono file.

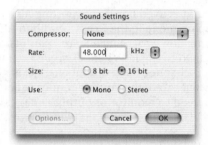

Figure 14-31: Select Mono because each track will be exported as a single mono file.

6. **Click Save to start the export.**

Exporting Audio to AIFF(s)

In addition to exporting individual audio tracks as AIFF with Export Using QuickTime Conversion, there is a new feature in Final Cut Pro 4—Export Audio to AIFF(s). Why are there two AIFF exporting options? Using Export Audio to AIFF(s) has many advantages, including:

✦ **Simultaneous exporting of every audio output channel as defined in the Audio Output tab in the current sequence's Settings as a separate AIFF file.**

✦ **The ability to downmix your sequence audio tracks to a single stereo-pair AIFF file.**

✦ **The ability to export AIFF files with a resolution higher than 16-bit.**

Exporting multiple AIFF files

One of the primary uses of Exporting Audio to AIFF(s) is exporting your sequence audio output channels separately, thus preserving the channels' mix and the track assignments you defined in the Audio Output sequence Settings. This is extremely useful when your project is output for foreign distribution, for which you need to provide separate AIFF files for dialogue, music, and sound effects.

Stereo audio output channels are exported as a stereo AIFF file, and mono audio output channels are exported to single, mono AIFF files.

Cross-Reference   For more detail about settings in the Audio Output tab in sequence Settings, see Chapter 6.

Downmixing an AIFF export

Look familiar? Yes, this option is similar to the function of the Downmix control in the Master pane of the Audio Mixer, but it is used here for exporting AIFF files only. Selecting Stereo Mix from the Files pop-up menu in the Export Audio to AIFF(s) dialog box forces all output channels to mix down to a single stereo pair of outputs. All odd-numbered audio outputs are assigned to the left channel, while even-numbered audio outputs are assigned tot the right channel. Each output channel is reduced by the dB amount set in the Audio Output tab of the current Sequence Settings. This option might be useful when you need to monitor or output audio as a single stereo pair, say for Web delivery or to VHS tape, even though your output is set up for multi-channel output.

Exporting AIFF Files with24-bit resolution

Final Cut Pro now processes all audio at an internal resolution of 32-bit. This is a quantum improvement of previous 16-bit resolution because many high-end, third-party capture cards and external audio interfaces are 24-bit capable. This higher audio resolution can only be preserved in exported files by using Export Audio to AIFF(s) or Export Audio to OMF options. But even if you are using only 16-bit audio files, you might want to export your audio files at 24-bit resolution to preserve the more precise calculations of effects applied to your audio and processed at Final Cut Pro's internal resolution of 32-bit.

Using exporting audio to AIFF(s)

To export audio to a single stereo (downmixed) or multiple AIFF files:

1. **Select a sequence in the Browser and open it in the Timeline, or it if it's already open, select the sequence tab in the Timeline to make it active.**

2. **Make sure there are no In or Out points set in the selected Sequence.**

   If any In or Out points are set in the selected sequence, exported files will use the selection as defined by In and Out points and not export your complete sequence tracks. To delete any In and Out point, open the sequence in the Timeline and choose Mark ➪ Clear In and Out, or press Option+X.

3. **Select File ➪ Export ➪ Audio to AIFF(s).**

   The Save dialog box opens, as shown in Figure 14-32.

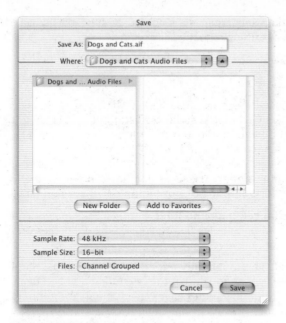

Figure 14-32: The Save dialog box opens when you select Export Audio to AIFF(s).

4. **Choose a location and enter a new name for the file if the sequence name does not suffice.**

You can create a new folder to save all exported audio files in. First, navigate to a desired directory, then, click the New Folder button and name it.

5. **Select file options of sample rate, sample size (resolution), and file type from the pop-up menus:**

   • **Sample Rate:** Choose from 32 kHz, 44.1 kHz, and 48 kHz.

   • **Sample Size:** Choose from 16-bit or 24-bit.

   • **Files:** Choose either Stereo Mix for a single, downmixed stereo AIFF file, or Channel Grouped for multiple mono or stereo AIFF files based on the sequence's audio output groupings.

6. **When your selections are done, click the Save button to export audio files.**

Note   All audio files needing rendering are rendered at high quality before being exported, regardless of existing render quality settings.

Exporting OMF files

Another format you can use for exporting audio is OMF (Open Media Format). The OMF file format is used by many digital audio workstations and is an industry-wide standard. You can export all your audio information as OMF files from Final Cut Pro. There are many advantages to using OMF files:

✦ **OMF files can contain as many tracks as you have in your Timeline.** This eliminates the need for multiple EDLs or multiple laybacks on tape.

✦ **OMF files ignore all level, pan, and filter settings.** This means you don't have to go in and make a lot of changes before you export. OMF files do maintain cross fade information, however.

✦ **You can have handles automatically added to all your clips.** Handles are the extra portions of audio that you add at the beginning and end of a clip to simplify audio edits. Automatic handles saves the manual labor of having to go in and add handles to each and every one of your clips.

Like AIFF files, OMF files are self-contained. They have the necessary timing information, as well as all the media needed for the audio. Timecode information is not necessary because OMF includes all the audio files regardless of how they were captured.

Exporting OMF files is like exporting any other file from Final Cut Pro. All options are located in the File ⇨ Export menu. Keep in mind that OMF export will ignore any disabled tracks. If you want to restrict a certain track from being included in the OMF export, turn off its visibility by clicking on the green visibility control button located to the left of the track in the Timeline. When that is done, you can start exporting your OMF file:

1. **Open a sequence whose audio files you want to export as OMF.**

2. **Choose File ⇨ Export ⇨ Audio to OMF.**

   The OMF Audio Export window appears as shown in Figure 14-33.

Figure 14-33: Select your options in the OMF Audio Export dialog box.

3. **Choose the appropriate sample rate from the Sample Rate pull-down menu.**

   Remember, the rate you choose here should be the same as the sample rate at which the audio was originally captured.

4. **Select Sample Size.**

   In addition to the standard resolution of 16-bit used by DV equipment and CDs, you now have the option to select 24-bit resolution used by many third-party, high-end capture boards. Selecting 24-bit sample size will preserve the highest degree of fidelity of audio source files, including any effects applied to lower resolution audio clips that is computed at Final Cut Pro improved 32-bit internal working resolution.

5. **Enter a number in the Handle Length field if you want your clips to have some extra frames or seconds added on either side.**

   Handles allow the audio engineer to make crossfades and smooth cuts.

6. **Enable the Include Crossfade Transitions option if you want to export crossfades as part of your audio OMF export.**

   Most of the time it's probably a good idea to turn this feature off because many OMF import modules do not handle crossfades well.

7. **Click OK in the OMF Audio Export dialog box when you are finished.**

8. **Select a Location and name your OMF file in the dialog box shown in Figure 14-34.**

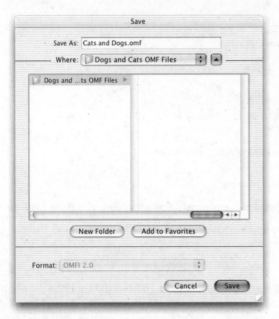

Figure 14-34: Select a location for your OMF file before saving.

9. **Click Save to save your OMF file.**

Caution

OMF files have a size limit of 2GB (gigabytes). Apple engineers state that 2GB represents over seven hours of audio material for a single mono audio file. This means that for a single stereo file it represents approximately three-and-a-half hours of material, and just over one-and-a-half hours of audio material for two pairs of stereo tracks. If you have a long program with eight tracks of audio, you will probably hit the file size limit at around 53 minutes. If you come up against this limit, an error message will appear. To get around this limit, break your sequence up into sections and export separate OMF files for each sequence.

✦   ✦   ✦

Using Soundtrack with Final Cut Pro

In case you haven't noticed, this version of Final Cut Pro comes with *four* additional applications! No longer content to merely deliver the world's most popular NLE, Apple now includes Soundtrack, LiveType, Compressor, and Cinema Tools as part of the whole package. Soundtrack is the first of these additional applications that we're going to look into.

Imagine this, if you will. Right around the time that you're beginning to feel reasonably happy with an edited sequence, your producer points out that no one has selected any music for it yet. Invariably, you go looking through the same royalty-free CDs, and if you're lucky, you end up with a track that serves the video well. Unfortunately, sometimes you end up trying to work with music that lacks the right punch to match the picture. When that happens, you either drop the track altogether or hire a composer/musician to come up with something original (if not expensive). Have you ever found yourself in this situation?

Well, now you have another trick up your sleeve. Soundtrack enables you to make your own music tracks quickly and easily, and you don't have to be a natural-born musician to use it well. With Soundtrack, you can compose your own royalty-free tracks to match your video edits. With this news, some editors might get nervous that they will soon be asked to compose music in addition to their other responsibilities. These days, practically all editors do titles and some other compositing, but that wasn't the case until fairly recently. Will we be regularly asked to mix original music before long? Only time will tell. In any event, Soundtrack is a sleek and nifty tool that's easy to use after a modest investment of your time.

Enhancing Your Video with Your Own Score

It's always frustrating to do a lot of work on a sequence only to find that your edit points don't line up well with the music that you end up using. With Soundtrack, you can change the tempo of your musical composition to match the length of your video sequence. Further still, you can change the tempo of various sections of your musical score if need be.

Figure 15-1 gives you an overview of the Soundtrack interface. One thing you might notice right away is the presence of a video track. In case you didn't know, the video plays in real-time as you mix your audio in real-time. I'll go into more detail shortly, but take comfort in knowing that the interface was designed with video editors in mind. For example, the spacebar works for stopping and starting playback, and units of time are measured in NTSC timecode.

Note   Soundtrack is a serious piece of sophisticated software. My plan is to get you up and running so that you can use it to effectively enhance your video editing capability. Bear in mind that I won't be giving you the whole picture, since Soundtrack and its many facets could easily fill the pages of a book solely dedicated to the subject.

Media Manager   Project Workspace

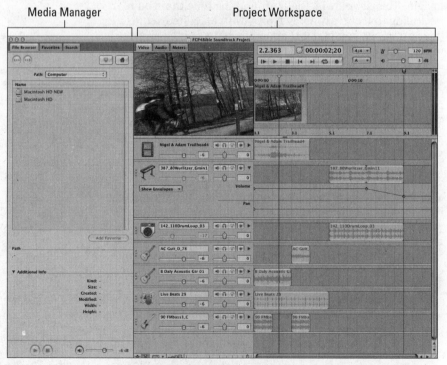

Figure 15-1: Soundtrack is an elegant addition to the suite of five (!) Final Cut Pro applications.

Navigating the Soundtrack Interface

The Soundtrack interface consists of two basic areas in which you'll be doing your work. The first of these is the Media Manager, and the second one is called the Project Workspace. The Media Manager works a lot like the Finder in that you use it to locate files, only in this case you'll be finding those files in order to create your sonic masterpiece. The Media Manager contains three tabs: File Browser, Favorites, and Search.

Using the Media Manager

The Media Manager enables you to organize your media files before adding them to the Timeline. With the Media Manager, you can also preview an audio or video file adding it to your Soundtrack project. I'll take a look at the preview controls after going over the three tabs in the Media Manager. Fortunately, Apple has designed Soundtrack in such a way that the interface is extremely intuitive and very pretty to look at, so mastering the Media Manager is a painless exercise.

File Browser

If you click on the File Browser tab (shown in Figure 15-2), you'll see that this part of the Media Manager is practically identical to viewing the contents of your system using a Finder window in list view. Once you've homed in on a file you want to use in your project, you can either preview it using the controls at the bottom of the Media Manager, or you can drag the file directly into a track in the Timeline of the Project Workspace. The following is a description of the buttons and their functions in this part of the interface:

✦ **Forward:** Operates like the Forward button in a web browser in that it takes you forward through places you've searched.

✦ **Back:** Operates like the Back button in a web browser in that it takes you backward through places you've searched.

✦ **Computer:** Shows you your hard drives as well as any other media connected to your computer.

✦ **Home:** Shows you the files in your home directory.

✦ **Path Menu:** Shows you the path to the current directory.

✦ **File List:** Shows you the contents of the current directory.

✦ **Add Favorite:** Adds any file that you've selected to the list of files in the Favorites tab. If the file already happens to be a favorite, then the button becomes the Remove Favorite button, which — you guessed it — removes the file from the Favorites tab. You should really take advantage of the Add Favorites button for those files that you'll be using again and again.

Note   The Add Favorite, Forward, and Back buttons are available in all three tabs of the Media Manager.

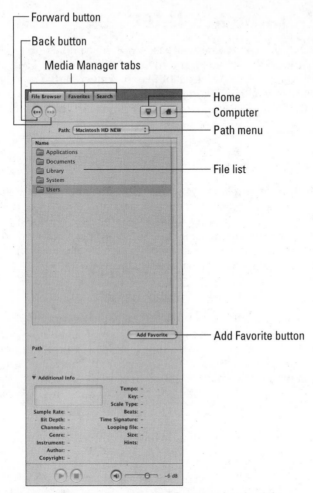

Figure 15-2: You can use the File Browser tab of the Media Manager to locate the files you'll be using to make your musical score. It works like a Finder window.

Favorites

The Favorites tab of the Media Manager (shown in Figure 15-3) works almost exactly like the File Browser, except that you use it to browse through those media files that you've selected as your favorites. Some projects can get pretty big before long, and you'll appreciate having your assets handy. It's especially annoying to always have to drill down into a complex directory structure to find that video clip you need to use, so use the Add Favorite button whenever you can. It's a handy timesaver.

Back button

Forward button

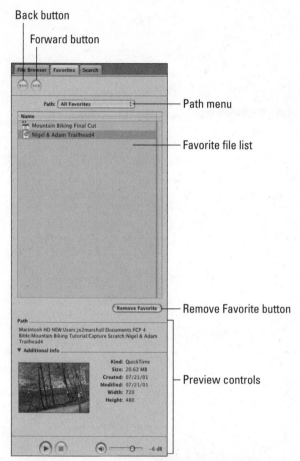

Path menu

Favorite file list

Remove Favorite button

Preview controls

Figure 15-3: Use the Favorites tab of the Media Manager to browse through your favorites.

Search

With the Search tab (shown in Figure 15-4), you can look through a detailed index of your audio files. There are a number of ways to take advantage of this index. For instance, you can look for an audio sample based on its mood, what instrument was used to create it, whether it's rock or classical, and so on. The Search tab of the Media Manager is the one that you'll be using most of the time. Once you've found a file you want to use in your project, you can either preview it or drag it directly into the Timeline.

Keyword pop-up menu

Columns View button

Buttons View button

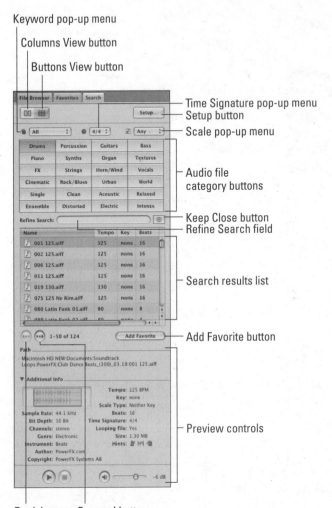

Time Signature pop-up menu
Setup button
Scale pop-up menu

Audio file
category buttons

Keep Close button
Refine Search field

Search results list

Add Favorite button

Preview controls

Back button Forward button

Figure 15-4: Use the Search tab of the Media Manager to look through a detailed index of audio files. Want acoustic? Or would you prefer electric? Find them here.

Caution   If you've just installed Soundtrack, the Search tab won't contain any files until you properly load your index of Soundtrack Loops. If there aren't any files listed in the Search tab, check out the nearby sidebar entitled "Indexing your Soundtrack Loops library."

Because of the way in which Soundtrack Loops are indexed, you can tell a lot about an audio file. If you take a look at Figure 15-5, you'll notice that an audio file can be tagged for a number of criteria (original tempo, the number of beats, as well as the key in which it was recorded). Depending on your preference, you can sort through your loops using either the Columns or Buttons view. The Buttons view is great, but Columns allows for a more detailed search. For example you can click on Cheerful in the left column, at which point you can perform a more meticulous search of the results returned by Cheerful (by Acoustic Guitar or Electric Guitar). The following is a description of the remaining buttons and their functions in this part of the interface:

✦ **Setup button:** This button enables you to add files to the index that Soundtrack keeps in its Search records. (See the "Indexing your Soundtrack Loops library" sidebar.)

✦ **Keyword pop-up menu:** In either the Columns or Buttons view, this menu changes the category of keywords.

✦ **Time Signature pop-up menu:** This menu limits your search to include only those audio files that have the time signature you select.

✦ **Scale Type pop-up menu:** This menu limits your search to include only those audio files that are defined by their musical key (that is, Major, Minor, either, and so on).

✦ **Keep Close button:** This menu limits your search to include only those audio files that are within two semitones of the key you've specified in your project.

✦ **Refine Search field:** If you type in the this field and hit Return, the Search Results list will only show you those files whose names include the text you've specified.

✦ **Search Results list:** This is where the files you're looking through are displayed, complete with their name, tempo, key, and the number of beats contained in the loop. The list is sorted alphabetically, but you can click on the individual column names to sort the list according to name, tempo, or key. When you click on a file, you can listen to it using the Preview controls.

Preview Controls

The Preview Controls enable you to listen to an audio file before putting it into your project, and they're available to you in any of the three Media Manager tabs. The controls are pretty self-explanatory: There are Play, Stop, and Mute buttons, as well as a volume slider (shown in Figure 15-6). If you click on the Additional Info twirler (or as Apple calls it, the disclosure triangle), you can learn a lot about any file you want to look at.

Note

When you listen to an audio file using the Preview Controls, it will play in the key and tempo of the project, both of which are set at the top of the Project workspace. If you preview a file while your project is playing, then Soundtrack will play your selected preview file on top of the tracks in your project, allowing you to see how the new track will fit into the overall scope of the score.

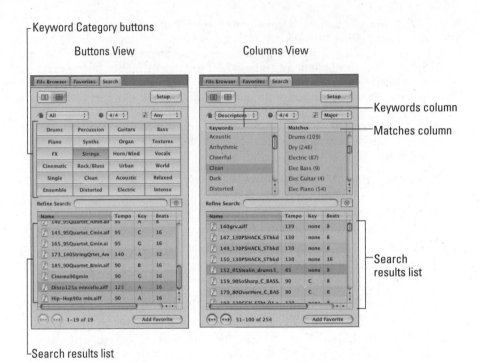

Figure 15-5: Within the Search tab, the Buttons and Columns Views offer two different ways to search through your Soundtrack Loops.

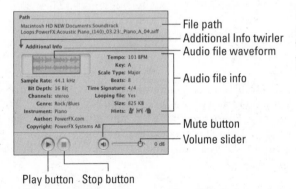

Figure 15-6: The Preview Controls enable you to listen to a track before adding it to your project.

Using the Project Workspace

The Project Workspace is where you start putting the pieces of the puzzle together. If you're a video editor, getting your head around this part of the interface should be relatively easy since most of the controls are similarly intuitive.

Indexing your Soundtrack Loops library

If you're starting up Soundtrack for the first time, your Search tab won't contain the Soundtrack Loops library. In order to have access to these files, you need to follow a couple of quick steps.

1. In the Media Manager, click the Search tab.

2. Click the Setup button.

The Search Setup window appears.

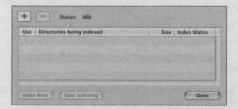

3. Click the Add button.

The Open window appears.

4. Navigate to the location of your Soundtrack Loops.

If you can't find them anywhere on your hard drive, you may need to copy them from the Final Cut Pro installation DVD-ROM.

5. Select the folder named Soundtrack Loops, and click on the Open button.

6. Now that the Soundtrack Loops directory has been added to the list, click the Index Now button in the Search Setup window.

The indexing should finish after a couple of seconds (your Search Setup window should look something like the figure shown here).

7. Click the Done button.

Voilà. Your Search tab should now be full of options when you go looking for audio files.

You can start to experiment with making music by following these quick steps:

1. **Click and drag an audio file from the Media Manager into the Timeline area of the Project Workspace.**

   You can drag it from either the list or the waveform thumbnail in the Preview controls.

2. **Release the mouse when the interface displays a green bar where your file will be placed in the Timeline (see Figure 15-7).**

   After you release the mouse, you'll see your audio file in its own track, complete with its name and icon in the Track Header. The file's waveform will be visible as a layer with a waveform in the central part of the Timeline.

3. **Press the spacebar.**

   As you can see, Soundtrack loops your project by default. Since you've only added the one file, that's all there is to loop at the moment.

4. **In the Master Controls, experiment with the tempo by moving the Tempo Slider forwards and backwards (see Figure 15-8).**

   By default, it's set to 120 bps (beats per minute). In case it isn't clear, by doing this you can speed up or slow down the project in real-time. Pretty nifty, huh?

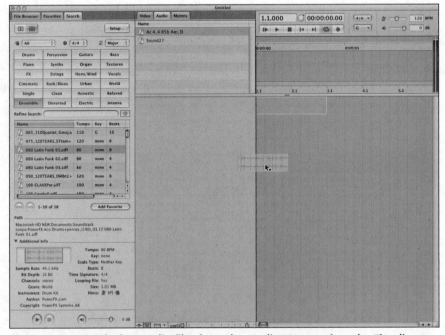

Figure 15-7: Simply drag audio files from the Media Manager into the Timeline to begin building your Soundtrack project.

Master Controls

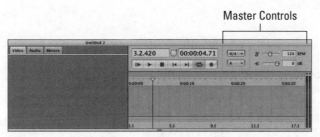

Figure 15-8: The Master Controls enable you to change the key, tempo, volume, and time signature of your project.

5. **Also in the Master Controls, use the Key pop-up menu to change the key of your project.**

   If you're using an audio file that was tagged for a specific key, you'll notice that the pitch changes. For example, a guitar's pitch will change, but a drumbeat's will not.

Note   The key info for a particular file is specified in the Search Results list of the Search tab of the Media Manager. You can also find it in the additional info for an audio file in the Preview Controls.

Just by playing with one audio file, you should be able to grasp Soundtrack's potential as a tool that can help along your video productions, and you're only getting started. The following sections explain in detail what all the buttons in the Project Workspace actually do.

Viewer

The Viewer is the small but useful window where your video plays. In it, you can also see the list of files that are currently in use in your project, and it also happens to be where you can monitor the levels of your project to see if they're too hot or distorted. You'll end up using the three tabs in this small part of the Project Workspace quite a bit. You'll find them located above the Track Headers.

Video

The power of the Soundtrack becomes apparent when you see how easily video fits into your project. Follow the next few steps to incorporate a video clip into your Soundtrack project:

1. **Click on the Video tab (shown in Figure 15-9) to make it active in the Viewer.**

2. **Use the Media Manager to locate a video file.**

3. **Click and drag the video file onto the Viewer.**

4. **Press the spacebar.**

   This will play the video on top of the audio tracks that you've already put into the Timeline.

Video tab Viewer

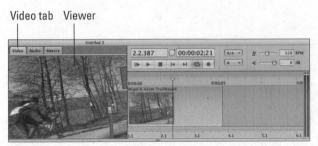

Figure 15-9: The Video tab of the Viewer is where you
drag your video clip to add it to your project.

You can probably see where this is going. Typically, a workflow involving Final Cut
Pro and Soundtrack plays out like this: First, you edit the scene of your sequence
that needs music as well as you can, paying attention to visual continuity and rhyth-
mic flow. Once you've finished, you export that scene of your sequence as a contiguous clip, which you then import into Soundtrack. Once you've brought the file
into Soundtrack, you can build a musical arrangement that is precisely as long as
your scene. Compare that with the not-so-old days. It certainly beats finding out
that the music you've been handed on a CD doesn't come close to working well
with the editing that you've already done.

Audio

The Audio tab of the Viewer (see Figure 15-10) is fairly straightforward. It offers you
a condensed view of your work, showing those files that are being used by your
Soundtrack project. It has one interesting feature: If you delete a file from your project, it will still appear in the Audio tab, making it easy to find if you ever change
your mind and decide you want to use it again. If that ever happens, just grab it
from the Audio tab and add it to the Timeline again.

Figure 15-10: The Audio tab of the Viewer shows
you which audio files are currently in use in your
Soundtrack project.

Audio files in use by the project

Meters

The Meters tab of the Viewer (see Figure 15-11) becomes critical when you're almost ready to export your work. You want to avoid any distortion, or clipping in your audio, and the Meters will point you toward the "hot" spots in your project. These audio meters are larger and more detailed than the small ones that are always in view on the far right side of the Project Workspace, and they also contain some useful controls.

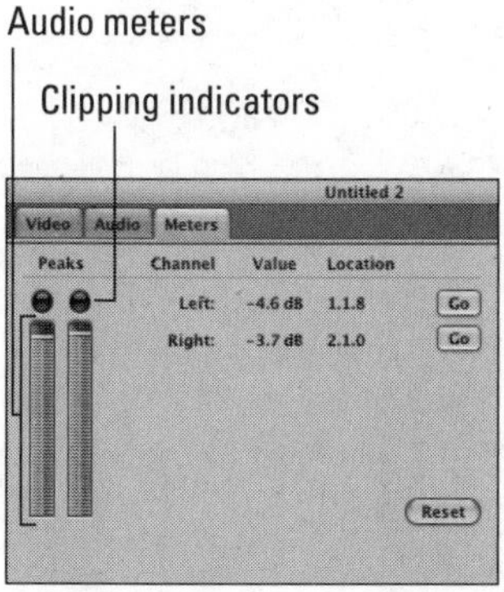

Audio meters

Clipping indicators

Figure 15-11: The Meters tab of the Viewer is a powerful tool that can point you to the areas where the audio is clipping in your project.

If your project ever clips in one of the stereo channels, its clipping indicator will light up (the clipping indicator is the red circle at the top of each channel's audio meter). Once it's lit up, it will stay that way until you reset it. You can reset it either by clicking the Reset button (which resets both meters), or you can click directly inside either channel's clipping indicator. Before you rush ahead and reset it, take a moment to see where the clipping is taking place in your project. That's where the rest of the information in the Meters tab comes in.

You'll notice that right next to the audio meters are three columns labeled Channel (left or right), Value (volume measured in dB, or decibels from –96 to 0), and Location (where it is in the Timeline). Press the spacebar to play your project, and you'll see that the Value returned shows the highest volume level reached in each channel from the time at which you started playing back your project. The Location column tells you the point in the Timeline when these levels occurred. If you stop playback and press Go, the Playhead will jump to the point in time indicated by the Location. Obviously, this is a handy tool if you're trying to pin down where the clipping in your project is happening. If it's occurring in multiple places, you can keep playing your project back and using the Go buttons until you've isolated all your problem areas.

Tip

Lowering the overall level of your project can solve a lot of clipping problems, but you can also lower the level of individual tracks, which I'll discuss a bit later.

Note Clicking the Reset button not only resets the clipping indicators, but it also resets the values returned in the Value and Location columns for each channel.

Timeline

The Timeline is a pretty easy thing for a video editor to grasp (see Figure 15-12). This is where you can see your audio clips laid out as visual objects spread out across a graphical representation of time.

Time Ruler

Playhead   Video Track

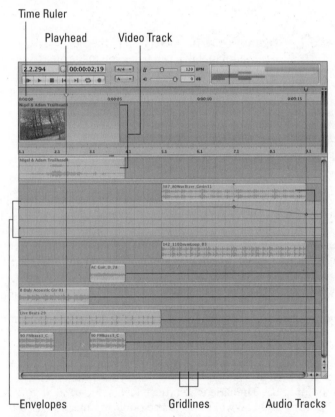

Envelopes   Gridlines   Audio Tracks

Figure 15-12: The Timeline gives you the big picture of your Soundtrack project.

The following list tells you what all the buttons and markings actually do:

✦ **Playhead:** The Playhead tells you where you are in your Soundtrack project. If you're playing your project, it moves forward in time. You can move it around your project at will. You can move the location of the Playhead by using keyboard shortcuts, some of which are identical to those in Final Cut Pro. For example, to place the Playhead at the beginning of your project, press the Home key (Return also works). To jump to the end, press End. Also, if you click anywhere in the Timeline, the Playhead will jump to that position. Finally, you can use the Transport Controls to navigate in time—I explain how those work just a bit later.

✦ **Time Ruler:** The Time Ruler displays the units in which time is measured in the Timeline. By default, it shows the standard measurement of minutes and seconds, but when you add a video clip to your project, you can change the units of measurement to Frames, Drop Frame, or Non-drop Frame. You can change them by selecting View ⇨ Time Ruler Units. Whichever units you select, their increments change as you zoom in and out of the Timeline.

✦ **Beat Ruler:** This ruler measures time in musical measures and beats. For example, for the first measure of 4/4 time, the Beat Ruler will show markings for, 1.1, 1.2, 1.3, 1.4, 2.1, 2.2, and so on.

✦ **Gridlines:** The gridlines correspond to the beat measurements. Depending on your level of magnification, they can be separated by multiple measures, single measures, beats, or fractions of beats.

✦ **Video Track:** This is where the video track goes in the Timeline. Unlike the rest of the tracks, this one can't be edited. Once you drag a video clip into the Viewer, the clip is locked in the video track. It starts at the very beginning of the project, and you can only have one.

✦ **Audio Tracks:** Apparently, you can have up to 127 audio tracks. Once you drop audio files into these tracks, you can begin working with them (that is, move, extend, and cut them, or add effects, automate level changes, and so on).

✦ **Envelopes:** You use envelopes to control parameters like volume or pan levels. Tracks have envelopes for volume, pan, and effects, and a Soundtrack project also has Master Envelopes for volume, transpose, tempo, and effects. You can automate changes in envelopes, making a track louder over time or changing the key of your project at a fixed point in time. Automating changes in an envelope is essentially like setting keyframes for a layer in Final Cut Pro.

Tip Control-clicking in the various parts of the Soundtrack Interface will often show you a number of useful options for an audio file or an audio track. If you're not big on learning keyboard shortcuts, build a simple project and start Control-clicking on the objects in the Media Manager and the Project Workspace to see what's possible.

Track Headers and Track Controls

The areas to the left of the individual tracks are called Track Headers, and they contain a number of important buttons, or Track controls, that will factor into your workflow as you begin to put projects together (see Figure 15-13).

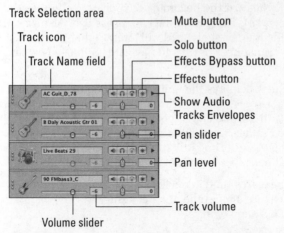

Figure 15-13: These are Track Headers and Track Controls.

✦ **Track icon:** This is the little picture that gives you a clue as to what kind of instrument was used to create your audio file, at least within the library of audio files that ships with Soundtrack. You have to set these yourself if you create your own index of audio files, or you could change the preset image simply by clicking on the icon. This opens a pop-up menu that will give you a wide range of choices. If that's not good enough and you want to create your own, drag a graphics file from the Finder directly onto the Track Icon to make your own.

✦ **Track Name field:** As its name indicates, this is the field that contains the Track Name. You can click in the field and enter your own if you need to change it for the sake of organizing a complicated project.

✦ **Track Selection area:** These three little beveled metallic bumps on the left side of the Track Header indicate the area you need to click on in order to select a track. If you click and drag on this area, you can rearrange the stacking order of your tracks.

✦ **Volume slider:** This slider sets the relative volume of a track. In this case, *relative* means relative to the range set by the master volume of the Soundtrack project. You can also type a volume value directly in the volume field. It also works in real-time.

✦ **Pan slider:** This slider sets the pan position of a track anywhere from 100% left to 100% right. This works in real-time as well.

✦ **Mute button:** As you might expect, this one mutes and unmutes the audio track.

✦ **Solo button:** This button solos and unsolos an audio track. You can solo multiple tracks if you like.

✦ **Effects Bypass button:** This button turns off all the effects that you've applied to an audio track. You may find this necessary if you need to hear the original audio track for reference.

✦ **Effects button:** This button pops open the Effects window, which I'll cover a bit later.

✦ **Track envelopes twirler:** Click on this to view or hide an audio track's envelopes. If a track's envelopes are in view, you can use the Show Envelopes pop-up menu to individually hide either the volume, pan, or, if applicable, effects envelopes.

Timeline Controls

Timeline Controls (see Figure 15-14) are the small buttons in the lower left-hand corner of the Project Workspace. They have similar cousins in the Final Cut Pro Timeline.

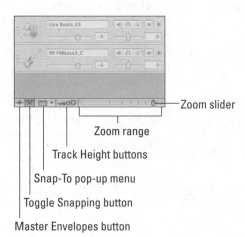

Zoom slider

Zoom range

Track Height buttons

Snap-To pop-up menu

Toggle Snapping button

Master Envelopes button

Figure 15-14: The Timeline Controls are similar to the controls in the same area of the Final Cut Pro Timeline window.

✦ **Master Envelopes button:** Click on this to view or hide the master envelopes. A Soundtrack project has envelopes for volume, transpose, tempo, and effects.

✦ **Snapping button:** This button toggles snapping on and off.

> **Tip** The G key also performs the same function.

✦ **Snap To pop-up menu:** This menu sets the increments at which snapping occurs, which, by the way, includes almost everything in the Timeline.

✦ **Track Height control:** These four buttons set the track height. The reduced track height all the way to the left does not allow for an audio waveform or a Track Icon.

✦ **Zoom control:** This slider sets the zoom level of the Timeline.

Tip   The Up and Down arrow keys also perform the same function. Just like in Final Cut Pro, pressing Shift+Z fits the whole project into view.

Beat Display and Time Display

The Beat and Time displays live in the upper left-hand corner of the Project Workspace.

✦ **Beat Display:** Displays the current time (where the playhead is at any given moment) in measures, beats, and beat divisions (as you can see, to three decimal places). You can move the location of the playhead by manually entering a value in the Beat Display field.

✦ **Time Display:** Displays the current time (where the playhead is at any given moment) in the standard measurement of hours, minutes, and seconds. This same display returns video timecode (hours, minutes, seconds, and frames) when you add a video clip to your project. You can move the location of the playhead by manually entering in a value in the Time Display field.

Note   One particularly cool feature worth noting is that the Time Display frame rate matches the frame rate of the video clip you import into your Soundtrack project.

Transport Controls

The Transport Controls (see Figure 15-15) enable you to play your Soundtrack Project as well as navigate around it. They're a lot like the buttons on a CD player, and while they look great, most of the time you'll prefer to use simple and, more importantly, quicker keyboard shortcuts, which are also explained below:

Figure 15-15: The Transport Controls look like the buttons on a CD player.

Record
Loop Playback
Go to End
Go to Beginning
Stop
Play
Play from Beginning

✦ **Play from Beginning:** This button is self-explanatory.

✦ **Play:** This button plays your project from wherever the playhead is parked. The spacebar also serves the same function.

✦ **Stop:** This button stops playback, as does the spacebar if your project is playing.

✦ **Go to Beginning:** This button brings the playhead to the beginning of your project, but bear in mind that it also returns the playhead to the start of the playback region if you've defined one. The Home key serves the same purpose, and it's a lot faster.

Tip
If you've set a playback region, the first time you press Home, the playhead will return to the In point of the playback region. The second time you press Home, the playhead will return to the beginning of your project.

✦ **Go to End:** This button brings the playhead to the end of your project unless you've defined a playback region, in which case it goes to the playback region's Out point. Still, the End key works more quickly.

Tip
If you've set a playback region, the first time you press End, the playhead will return to the Out point of the playback region. The second time you press End, the playhead will return to the end of your project.

✦ **Loop:** If this button is turned on (which it is by default), then your project will start playing again once the playhead reaches the end of the last audio file in your project; however, Soundtrack will only loop the playback region if you've defined one.

✦ **Record:** This button opens the Recording window.

Master Controls

The Master Controls (shown in Figure 15-16) dictate the overall parameters for the whole of your Soundtrack project. If you covered the Key pop-up menu and the Tempo slider in our earlier exercise, you'll recall that you can change the key and tempo of your project in real-time. Remember that these settings affect all the tracks in your Soundtrack project. Also, if your computer's volume is turned down low, then raising the Master Volume slider won't seem to have much of an audible effect. Apple recommends that you turn your computer's volume up all the way to offer the greatest dynamic range for your Soundtrack output. If you like, you can change any of the Master Control defaults in the Preferences by selecting Soundtrack ➪ Preferences.

✦ **Time Signature pop-up menu:** By default, the time signature is set to 4/4. In remembering gradeschool music class, 2/4 is a march, 3/4 is a waltz, and 4/4 covers just about every pop song you hear on the radio, which probably explains the default setting.

✦ **Key pop-up menu:** This is set to A by default. You can automate changes to the project key using the Master Envelopes, which I'll cover a bit later.

✦ **Tempo slider:** Moving this slider changes the *tempo,* or speed, of your project. You can also type a value directly into the Beats per Minute field, which is set to 120 by default. The Tempo slider has a range of 60 to 200 bpm.

✦ **Master Volume slider:** This is the volume control for your entire project, and it's set to 0 dB by default. You can also type a value directly into the dB field.

Time Signature pop-up menu

Tempo slider

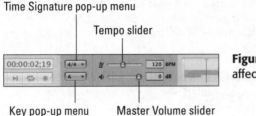

Figure 15-16: The Master Controls affect all the tracks in your project.

Key pop-up menu   Master Volume slider

Global Timeline view

The Global Timeline view (see Figure 15-17) is in the upper right-hand corner of the Project Workspace. This graphic tool helps you jump around the Timeline of your project with ease.

Playhead

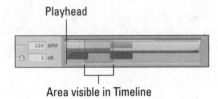

Figure 15-17: The Global Timeline view is like an interactive large-scale map of your project.

Area visible in Timeline

Caution   If you have a small monitor or if you've set your monitor to a really low resolution, you may not be able to see the Global Timeline view. If this is the case, fear not. You just need to select View ➪ Layouts ➪ Hide Media Manager. For that matter, there are a number of Soundtrack layouts you can experiment with in the Layouts menu.

Inside the box is a small graphic representation of your project's Timeline. The black line indicates the position of the playhead, and the shaded area tells you which part of the project is currently in view in the Timeline. If you place the mouse over the shaded area, it turns into a pointer that looks like a hand, at which point you can click and drag it to change the part of the Timeline that's currently in view. Think of it as a large-scale interactive map.

Effects window

The Effects window isn't really part of the Project Workspace, but it's definitely an integral part of the Soundtrack interface. You can open it either by clicking on the Effects button in an audio track, or by selecting View ➪ Show Master Effects.

Tip   You can also open the Effects window by pressing Command+E.

Follow the next few steps to apply an effect to an audio track, and you'll observe firsthand how simple it is:

1. **If you haven't already done so, drag an audio file from the Media Manager into the Timeline to create an audio track.**

2. **Click on the audio track's Effects button to open the Effects window (see Figure 15-18).**

   The pop-up menu will indicate that you'll be applying effects to the selected audio track, but if you wanted to, you could change it so that the effect would be applied to the entire project by selecting Master Effects.

3. **Click on Apple from the Category list on the left.**

   Soundtrack ships with effects from Apple as well as some from EMagic. Some of the EMagic filters have custom effect controls if you're curious. If you install other third-party effects, different vendors will appear in this list.

4. **Click on one of the effects in the Effects list to the right.**

   Pick any one you like.

5. **Click on the Add Effect button, which looks like a plus sign.**

   This will add the effect to the audio track, and now you'll be able to see it in the Effect Parameters list in the lower half of the window. If you ever need to add more than one effect to an audio track, you can select more effects from the effects list and add them to the list, creating an "effects chain." If you need to remove one, just select it and press Delete or click on the Remove key, which looks like a minus sign.

6. **In the Effect Parameters list, click the newly added effect's twirler to see its parameters.**

   The number of parameters can vary greatly between effects.

7. **Press the spacebar to play your project.**

   Listen to what the effect does to the audio track as it plays.

8. **Move some of the parameter sliders around to see how the effect changes the audio track in real-time.**

   If you check a parameter's Auto Checkbox, then that parameter's envelope will appear under the audio track in the Timeline. I'll cover envelopes a bit later, but enabling an effect parameter envelope gives you the option of changing that parameter over time. If you want to turn an audio track effect off, simply uncheck the checkbox for the effect to the left of the effect name.

Category list

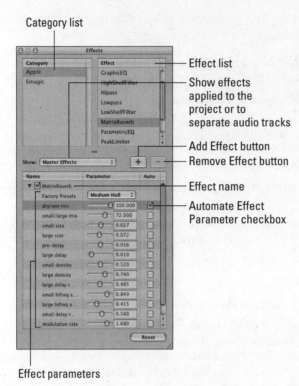

Effect list

Show effects
applied to the
project or to
separate audio tracks

Add Effect button
Remove Effect button

Effect name

Automate Effect
Parameter checkbox

Effect parameters

Figure 15-18: Use the
Effects window to apply
effects to a track or the
entire Soundtrack project.

As you can see, adding an effect doesn't require a Ph.D. in rocket science. The trick-
ier part is knowing when to use one and how to make it add just the right touch to
your overall mix. That takes patient experimentation and time spent with "sound
guys." We'll take another look at some effects a bit later on as we get into the more
complex aspects of creating a Soundtrack project based on an edit coming from
Final Cut Pro. The good news is, if you've read the chapter up to this point, you
know what most of the buttons do.

Building and Mixing a Soundtrack Project

As you may have already learned, the quickest way to start making a score with
Soundtrack is to simply begin dragging audio files into the Project Workspace. The
time has come to start using audio and video tracks together. When you're finished
with this section, you'll be ready to kick your output back to Final Cut Pro where
you can place your new music into your finished edit.

Working with audio tracks

There's obviously a lot more to building a Soundtrack project than merely dragging audio files into the Timeline. Things start to get interesting when you build a mix of multiple tracks.

Note Soundtrack projects are similar to Final Cut Pro sequences in that your edits are nondestructive. Put another way, nothing is ever done to the original files on your hard drive. All the audio clips in the Timeline are simply pointers to the original files.

Adding audio files

Just a quick reminder on adding audio files to the Timeline: You can bring them in via the Media Manager, from the Audio tab of the Viewer, and also directly from the Finder if you like. That said, in order to make multiple tracks in your project, drag an audio file into the project, and then drag another one into the Timeline beneath the newly created track (see Figure 15-19).

Note If you add an audio file to your project from the Preview Controls of the Media Manager, its volume will be set to the level at which you previewed it.

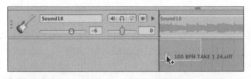

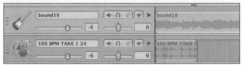

Figure 15-19: Create multiple tracks in the Timeline by dragging in additional audio files. You're limited to 127, which should keep you from hitting a wall for the moment.

If you like, you can add tracks before directly inserting audio files. Select Project ⇨ Add Track (or Command+T) to add one, or Project ⇨ Remove Track (Command+ Shift+T) to remove one. Following from there, you can put as many different audio files as you want on a single track. It only depends on how you want to structure your project. If you have the screen real estate or you don't mind using the scroll bar to view all your tracks, then you may prefer to keep different audio files on separate audio tracks.

When you add an audio file to your Timeline, you may have noticed that you don't need to position it at the beginning of your project. You can release it anywhere in the Timeline. Don't forget that when you add files to your project, they will all be in the same key, which is determined by whatever key is specified in the Master Controls Key pop-up menu.

Tip   The default key for a project is A. You can change the default settings for new Soundtrack projects in the Preferences, which you'll find by selecting Soundtrack ⇨ Preferences or by pressing Command+, (comma).

Editing audio files

So, now that you've created a number of audio tracks by dragging audio clips into the Timeline, what happens next? You've already learned that if you hit the space-bar, you can hear how all the pieces fit together, but how do you move around the clips? How do you cut them, or for that matter extend them? Easily. Press on.

Moving audio clips in the Timeline

First off, if you want to move a clip to an earlier or later time in your project, it's practically the same as moving a clip in Final Cut Pro. Click and drag it forward or backward. If you feel so inclined, you can also drag a clip up or down to place it in a different audio track.

If you experiment with moving a clip forward or backward in time, there's no doubt you'll notice that the clip moves in a kind of jerky fashion instead of sweeping smoothly across the screen. This is because snapping is turned on by default. If you like, you can turn off snapping by clicking on the Snapping button in the Timeline controls, but you may want to exercise caution here. Leaving snapping turned on ensures that your audio clips fall on the beats of your project. It's not quite as benign as moving video clips around. If your strumming guitar is out of time with your drums, then you won't be happy unless you're expressly going for an unusual sound (which you may well be). With snapping turned on, you can change the distance between snaps by selecting a different setting in the Snap To pop-up menu. You can select units as large as ¼ notes to increments as small as ¹⁄₆₄ notes (see Figure 15-20).

Note   By default, the Snap To pop-up menu is set to Ruler Ticks, which changes in relation to the zoom level of your project.

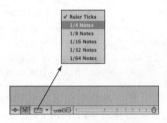

Figure 15-20: If snapping is turned on (which it is by default), the Snap To pop-up menu determines the amount of time by which a clip "hops" as you move it around the Timeline.

Resizing audio clips in the Timeline

Now that you've assembled some tracks and are starting to build a mix, you may want to know how to extend a certain clip. Suppose you wanted to run a drum loop under most, if not all, of your project. You've added the file to your Timeline, but it only lasts for one or two measures of your project. Should you copy and paste it? Well, that will work, but there's a much easier way that's better suited to a Final Cut Pro editor. Position your mouse pointer on the edge of a clip until its pointer changes to a bracket. Click and drag in either direction to shorten or lengthen the clip. If you lengthen it, what you're really doing is looping it, since your average Soundtrack file is typically going to last for 16 beats or less. The points at which a clip starts to loop are graphically represented in the Timeline, as shown in Figure 15-21.

Note   When you resize audio clips in the Timeline, they are lengthened and shortened in increments determined by the selected setting in the Snap To pop-up menu.

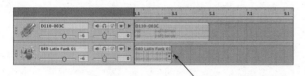

Pointer indicates that you can resize the audio clip

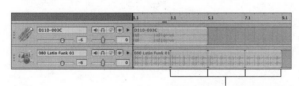

Track shows that the audio
clip has been looped an
additional three times

Figure 15-21: Resizing a clip is as simple as placing your pointer over the edge of an audio clip and then clicking and dragging it to your desired length.

Is it a loop or a one-shot?

In Soundtrack, an audio file is either a loop or a one-shot. What's the difference? You've just seen that an audio file can be resized in the Timeline so that it loops as often as you want, but resizing a one-shot produces a different result. Instead of looping, an extended one-shot merely becomes silent. Even more important, loops adapt to a project's key and tempo. Most one-shots sound the same whether or not you change the key or tempo, since they usually don't have tags for either (although they can).

Typically, one-shots consist of a sound that wouldn't loop well, such as a dramatic gong or a siren, for example. In Soundtrack, you can tell the difference between a loop and a one-shot by the way they look in the Timeline. A one-shot's corners are hard and angular, whereas a loop's edges have rounded corners (see the figure). If you feel you must turn a loop into a one-shot, simply Control+click on the clip and select Make One-Shot.

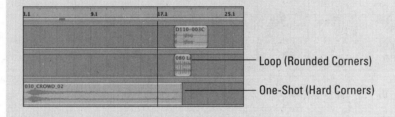

Loop (Rounded Corners)

One-Shot (Hard Corners)

Splitting audio clips in the Timeline

If you want to edit audio clips as though they were video clips, you can come pretty close. Follow the next few steps to see how:

1. **Select the clip or clips you want to cut.**

Tip

There are several ways to select multiple clips. If you're familiar with the concept of contiguous selections in Final Cut Pro, then you already know this. Command+ clicking numerous clips will select them one by one Command+clicking a selected clip deselects it. Shift+clicking clips will include the entire range of clips between clicks. To select multiple clips in the same track, you can click and drag across a range of them. Just make sure that you begin dragging before the start of the first clip in the range that you want to select.

2. **Position the Playhead where you want to make your cut.**

3. **Select Edit ⇨ Split, or even better, press S.**

   Your clip should resemble Figure 15-22.

Figure 15-22: To split an audio clip, select it, position the Playhead where you want to split it, and then press S.

And that's all folks, at least as far as splitting a clip is concerned. If you want to join split parts of the same clip back together, line up the split segments, select both of them, and then press J (or select Edit ⇨ Join).

Tip

Here's another clip selection method worth pointing out. If you Control+click on an audio file in the Audio tab of the Viewer, you have the option of selecting all occurrences of that file in the Timeline.

It's worth pointing out that good old copy and paste work in Soundtrack just like they do in Final Cut Pro. They apply to either single or multiple clips, the important factor being the position of the playhead when you paste the clips you've copied. To copy, select Edit ⇨ Copy, and to paste, select Edit ⇨ Paste. As you're probably well aware, you'll save more time if you use Command+C to copy and Command+V to paste.

There's a beefed up version of Paste called Paste Repeat (Edit ⇨ Paste Repeat, or Command+Option+V), which enables you to paste whatever audio clips you've copied as many times as you like (see Figure 15-23).

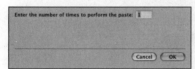

Figure 15-23: Press Command+ Option+V to invoke the Paste Repeat command, key in the number of times you want to paste the audio clips you've copied, and then click OK.

Editing audio clips goes beyond cutting, pasting, moving and resizing. You can offset an audio clip and transpose it as well. When you place an audio file in the Timeline, it plays from the beginning of its source. In other words, its offset is zero. If you want to change the offset for an audio clip, you can do so by holding down both the Command and Option keys and then clicking and dragging across it (see Figure 15-24).

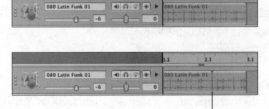

Figure 15-24: Changing the offset of an audio clip alters its appearance in the Timeline.

Offset

Transposing an audio clip changes that audio clip's pitch relative to the key specified in the Master Controls. If you Control+click on a clip in the Timeline, select Transpose, and then select the degree to which you want to transpose the clip (see Figure 15-25). You can go up to 12 semitones in either direction.

Note   Twelve semitones make up a full octave. If you're a musician, this isn't news, but if you aren't, 12 semitones refer to all the black and white keys on a piano that make up the distance between one pitch and the same pitch a full octave apart. Put another way, 12 semitones cover all the half steps of a complete scale.

Tip   At the risk of repeating myself, don't forget that Control+clicking on items in your project provides you with a number of options you may not have known were accessible this way.

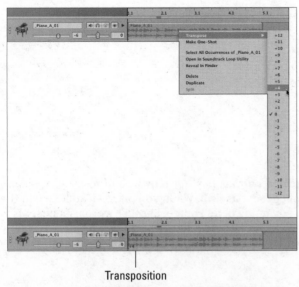

Transposition

Figure 15-25: Control+click on a clip in the Timeline to transpose its pitch relative to your project's key.

Scoring video with Soundtrack

As you might expect, Soundtrack fits very cleanly into a Final Cut Pro workflow. You can now add Scoring markers to a Final Cut Pro sequence, export the sequence specifically for Soundtrack, and then import the resulting video clip into Soundtrack with all your markers intact, complete with labels. It's extremely straightforward, and it's also particularly convenient to not have to mark the same sequence twice. The next set of steps will show you how this process unfolds:

1. **In Final Cut Pro, add markers to your sequence with only your score in mind. As your sequence plays down, you can add a marker in real-time by pressing M.**

   Of course, you want to place these in the inherently dramatic moments where you think the score should change in some way. Where would you start to increase the volume? Where would you change key? When is the visual payoff, and what do you want it to sound like?

2. **Go back to one of your new markers.**

   By holding down the Shift key and using the Up and Down arrow keys, you can jump from one to the next.

3. **With the Playhead parked on one of your markers, press M to bring up the Marker dialog box, shown in Figure 15-26.**

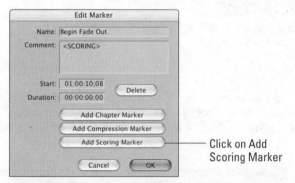

Figure 15-26: The Marker dialog box in Final Cut Pro 4.0 offers many new options. In this case, we're concerned with adding a Scoring marker. Click on the Add Scoring Marker button, and be sure to label the new marker with as much detail as necessary.

4. **Click the Add Scoring Marker button and be sure to label the new marker with as much detail as you will need later on in Soundtrack.**

5. **Repeat Step 4 for all your new markers.**

6. **Export your sequence for Soundtrack by selecting File ⇨ Export ⇨ For Soundtrack.**

   By default, the resulting dialog box will have pop-up menus for Setting, Include, and Markers. Accept the defaults, the most important of which is Audio Scoring Markers. Give the file a name and save it wherever you want.

7. **Leave Final Cut Pro and jump over to Soundtrack.**

8. **In Soundtrack, find your newly exported file using the Media Manager.**

9. **Select it and drag it over to the Video tab of the Viewer.**

That's it! If you look at Figure 15-27, you'll see that the video track now contains labeled markers. As part of a nice design touch, the video track also contains a new frame thumbnail wherever you placed a Scoring marker.

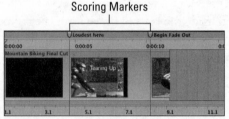

Figure 15-27: The video clip in the Timeline now contains Scoring markers that were imported from Final Cut Pro.

Caution   If for some reason your video clip goes offline, it will be replaced by a blue-colored placeholder in the video track. Control+click on the placeholder, and you will be offered two choices: either to delete it from your Soundtrack project or reconnect it if you inadvertently changed its location.

Note   If you make changes to your sequence in Final Cut Pro, you can export it for Soundtrack once again and replace the original. Soundtrack will incorporate the changes automatically.

Note   Since Soundtrack's video component is based on QuickTime, Soundtrack will work with any video that is QuickTime-compatible.

When you're finished creating your score and it's time to bring your final Soundtrack mix into Final Cut Pro, the process is even easier. I'll cover that at the end of this chapter.

Using markers

Here are a few more words about markers. Besides Final Cut Pro Scoring markers, Soundtrack also has Time markers, Beat markers, and an End-of-Project marker. There's not much difference between a Time marker and a Beat marker, except for the fact that a Time marker is green and a Beat marker is purple. Besides that, they're measured in different time standards — time and beats, accordingly. Final Cut Pro Scoring markers, which are orange, cannot be moved, but the others can. The End-of-Project marker, which is red, is self-explanatory. Wherever that one is placed is where the music stops, quite literally. It also marks the Out point of a project that you export from Soundtrack.

So what purpose do they serve? The answer isn't much different in Soundtrack as compared to Final Cut Pro. You use them to point things out to yourself. They don't affect the project in any audible way. You may place them at a point in time where you want to remind yourself to increase the volume or add an effect. You get the idea.

✦ **To add a Time Marker,** select Project ➪ Insert Time Marker, or press M.

✦ **To add a Beat Marker,** select Project ➪ Insert Beat Marker, or press B.

✦ **To move a marker (except a Final Cut Pro Scoring marker),** click and drag on its handle, which is located on top of it.

✦ **To rename a marker (except a Final Cut Pro Scoring marker),** Control+click on its handle, select Edit, and label it as you choose (see Figure 15-28). You can also manually enter a time in the Time field.

Note   For Beat markers, time is measured in beats. For Time markers, time is measured in the time standard used in the project.

Handle

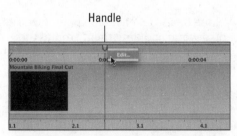

Figure 15-28: Put a label on a marker by Control+clicking its handle, selecting Edit, entering text, and clicking OK.

Using envelopes

An *envelope* is really just a level that you can control. There are master envelopes for Volume, Transpose, and Tempo, and there are track envelopes for Volume and

Pan. There are also envelopes for effect parameters, but these have to be enabled in the Effects window.

✦ **To see the envelopes for a track,** twirl them open using the Track Controls.

✦ **To see the envelopes for the project,** click the Master Envelopes button in Timeline Controls.

Note   You can also select View ⇨ Show Master Envelopes, or Control+click in the gray area of the Track Header and select Show Master Envelopes.

The Timeline in Figure 15-29 shows envelopes visible for both a track and its project.

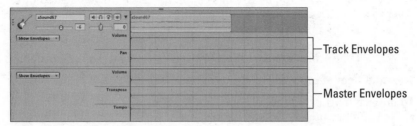

Figure 15-29: With envelopes shown, you now have a great deal of control over your project and its tracks.

At the beginning of the Timeline, you'll notice that each envelope has a drag handle, and you can manipulate these to change their levels. Going one step farther, you can add envelope points that then act as keyframes, automating changes to these levels at specific points in time.

Double click on the graph line of an envelope to add an envelope point (see Figure 15-30). Once you've got the hang of it, add several and drag them around the Timeline. You can change their position in time a well as their level. For more control, you can Control+click on them and enter precise values.

So go ahead, change key when you reach the climactic tear-jerking moment of your edit. Fade out the echo effect, and increase the volume perfectly, yet imperceptibly to a spellbound audience. You're in charge.

Tip   You may want to increase the size of your project's tracks in order to be more precise when setting the position of an envelope point.

Tip   Single or multiple Envelope points can be copied and pasted, but they have to stay within the same parameter.

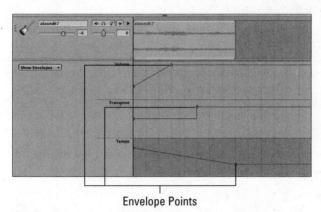

Envelope Points

Figure 15-30: Use envelope points to automate level changes. To video editors, they look and behave like keyframes.

Note   Transpose envelopes cannot be gradual. Wherever you set a transpose envelope point, the key changes immediately.

Exporting Your Soundtrack Project

So, in this whirlwind tour of Soundtrack pointed towards editors just getting started with this new tool, what are the important things to remember? Well, the first thing that comes to mind is to avoid clipping. Audio that's distorted can't be "undistorted" once it has been exported as an AIFF. So, in other words, be vigilant with your meters, find the trouble spots, and clean them up. If you're going to edit with this track, you'll thank yourself. If someone else is going to edit with it, they won't come looking for you.

So when you're ready, exporting your Soundtrack for Final Cut Pro is a breeze. Just select File ➪ Export Mix. This will bring up a dialog box asking you where you want to save your AIFF mix and whether you want to include the video's audio track. By default, any audio that's part of the video file will not be exported. In fact, you may want to mute the video's audio track before you begin the final stages of checking your mix, if only to ensure that it's not the source of any clipping.

And that's it. Bring your mix into Final Cut Pro and finish your edit. It shouldn't be too hard, because you've already scored the video in your Soundtrack project. And may there be many more happy mixes in your future.

✦   ✦   ✦

Transitions and Effects

Working with Transitions and Text

CHAPTER

16

Sequences in Final Cut Pro are built by arranging multiple shots in a Timeline, and the visual move, or cut, from one shot to the next is called a *transition*. Plain cuts between shots are the most common transition, but they may lack visual and editorial interest after a while. If some variety is needed, other types of transitions can be used. Sometimes the style of the piece calls for certain types of transitions, while other times it's a matter of the conventions that editors work with. Dissolves, for example, are often used to indicate passage of time. Transitions such as Page Peels and Diamond Iris are often seen on late-night cable channels during used-car commercials. And if this isn't gimmicky enough, you can even add thick and colored borders to some of these transitions! But don't let me prejudice you with my own opinions. All transitions and effects have a place on God's green Earth.

As you might know already, many different transitions are possible in Final Cut Pro. The selection is made even more diverse by the wide range of options you have to modify transitions. You can use the FXBuilder to view and modify the source code for transitions and effects, or make completely *new* transitions and effects of your own, but that is for a later chapter. For now, let's dive into the workings of the transitions bundled with Final Cut Pro.

Final Cut Pro has many features for viewing, modifying, and saving effects and transitions. These are important because they increase productivity and make editing easier. For example, you can modify a transition to suit your needs, rename it, and mark it as your favorite. You can then apply this "favorite" transition by using a simple keyboard shortcut.

Creating text for your edited programs is another common and important task you will need for your project. Final Cut Pro has numerous options for creating text. Later in this chapter, I will show you how to create and use text in Final Cut Pro.

Working with Transitions

A *transition* is the effect you use to change from one shot to another. Besides a simple straight cut from one shot to the next, the most common transition is a *dissolve*. In a dissolve, Clip A fades away while Clip B fades in. Another common transition is a *wipe,* where one image wipes off to the next. There are many other types of transitions, as you will see throughout this chapter. The transitions you use may depend on the venue for your edited programs. Learning to apply, control, and modify transitions is an important skill when editing in Final Cut Pro.

Adding transitions

For the next few sections you can work with the Mountain Biking.fcp project located in the Mountain Biking Tutorial folder on the DVD-ROM. Copy this folder to your hard drive, and then open the project by double-clicking on the Mountain Biking.fcp project file. You can use any two shots to create a transition.

Adding a simple transition between two shots is easy in Final Cut Pro. If you have used other editing applications, you may be familiar with the A/B model of tracks. In some other editing applications, you have to have one clip on Video Track A and another on Video Track B in order to make a transition between them. Final Cut Pro works differently. Both the clips must be on the same video track to make a transition between them. To make a transition between two clips:

1. **Make a new sequence and bring two clips into it.**

2. **To make sure these clips are trimmed a bit before inserting them into the sequence, place your pointer at either side of a clip so that the pointer turns into a Resize cursor.**

3. **Trim the In and Out points for both clips so that there are some extra frames available to create a dissolve.**

   Each clip should have at least half a second of extra material at each end for accommodating transitions.

See Chapter 9 for more on adding In and Out points to a clip.

4. **Click the Effects tab in the Browser window to bring it to the front.**

5. **Twirl down the small disclosure triangle to open the Video Transitions folder.**

6. **Twirl down the small disclosure triangle to open the Dissolve folder.**

7. **Select the Cross Dissolve transition and drag it from the Browser window directly into your Timeline onto the edit point between the two clips.**

   Note that you could also select any other type of transition. Figure 16-1 shows what the Cross Dissolve looks like when applied between two clips.

Transition between two clips

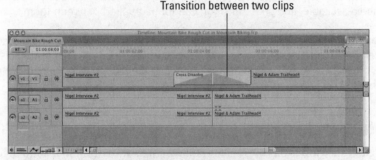

Figure 16-1: A Cross Dissolve transition is applied between two clips.

Note

You can also apply a transition to an edit point by first selecting the edit point, and then picking your transition by choosing Effects ➪ Video Transitions and selecting a transition from the submenus.

Cross-Reference

For a list of transitions available in Final Cut Pro, see Appendix C.

8. **If a red render indicator bar appears above the transition on the Timeline ruler, click on the transition to select it and choose Sequence ➪ Render Selection ➪ Video (or press Command+R).**

   Depending on your system speed and playback options selected in the Real Time (RT) pop-up window in the patch panel area of the Timeline, you might have to render this transition. If this is the case, a red render bar appearing above the transition in the Timeline Ruler indicates you must render this transition before you can play it through. If you attempt to play the unrendered transition, you will see an "Unrendered" notice in the Canvas window.

Cross-Reference

See Chapter 18 for more detail about rendering in Final Cut Pro.

After the transition has rendered, you can play it. By default, a transition has a duration of 1 second, but this can be modified at any time. See the section "Modifying Transitions in the Timeline" later in this chapter to learn how to modify the duration and other aspects of a transition.

Caution   You cannot add a transition between shots unless you have enough overlapping frames to cover the duration of the transition. If you have trimmed the clips before using them in the Timeline, then you have some "inactive source media" for these clips that is not seen in the Timeline. This inactive source media provides the overlapping frames for the transition. If two clips are placed side-by-side in a sequence in their entirety, without being trimmed, then they do not have any inactive source media available, and so a transition cannot be applied between them.

Cross-Reference   You can also add a transition between clips while making an edit. Insert with Transition and Overwrite with Transition are two types of edits that allow you to add a transition while editing clips into the Timeline. For more information, see Chapter 10.

Deleting transitions

Deleting a transition is simple. Select an unwanted transition in a sequence and press the Delete key on your keyboard. You can also Control+click on a transition and choose Cut from the contextual menu that appears.

Aligning transitions in the Timeline

By default, transitions will center on a cut between two clips. This means that the middle of the transition lies at the exact edit point between the two clips. But you can align a transition so that it starts or ends at the edit point rather than being centered on it. To align a transition in the Timeline:

1. **Select a transition in the Timeline and Control+click on it.**

2. **From the contextual menu that appears, choose Transition Alignment and make a selection from the submenu that appears.**

   Figure 16-2 shows the contextual menu and the choices it offers.

Tip   You can also align a transition in the Timeline as you are dragging it from the Browser and applying it to the edit point. Transitions snap to edit points at center, end, and start. You can drag a transition to an edit point and make it snap to the alignment of your choice.

Contextual menu for choosing transition alignment

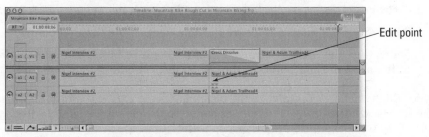

Transition centered on edit point

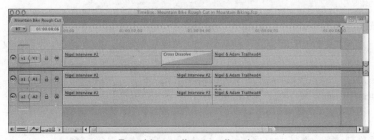

Transition starting on edit point

Transition ending on edit point

Figure 16-2: You can center transitions on an edit point, or align them to start or end at the edit point.

Fading to (or from) black

A common transition is a fade *from* black or a fade *to* black. A fade *from* black is often used to start off edited sequences and a fade *to* black is commonly used at the end of a sequence. To make a fade from black or a fade to black in Final Cut Pro:

1. **Drag a clip from the Browser to the Timeline.**

   The clip should not have any other adjacent clips.

2. **Click the Effects tab in the Browser window.**

3. **Twirl down the small disclosure triangle to open the Transitions folder.**

4. **Twirl down the small disclosure triangle to open the Dissolve folder.**

5. **Select the Cross Dissolve transition and drag it from the Browser window onto one of the end points of the clip in the Timeline.**

If you added the Cross Dissolve to the beginning of the clip, the transition will fade up from black. If the Cross Dissolve was added to the end of the clip, the transition will fade to back. Figure 16-3 shows a clip with both a fade in and a fade out.

A fade from black   A fade to black

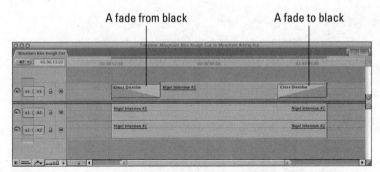

Figure 16-3: This clip fades in from black, and fades out to black again.

Tip   You can use any transition placed between the head or end of a clip and an empty area of the Timeline to make a transition from or to black.

Adding and modifying the Default Transition

Adding many transitions can be a tiring and tedious process. To save you from Carpal Tunnel Syndrome, Final Cut Pro designers created the Default Transition feature. The Default Transition can be applied with a keyboard shortcut. Also, the Default Transition will be used by the Canvas edit commands and buttons Insert with Transition and Overwrite with Transition. When you first install Final Cut Pro, the Default Transition is Cross Dissolve. You can change the Default Transition to any transition you choose.

Adding a Default Transition

There are many ways to add a Default Transition in Final Cut Pro. Here is one of the easiest methods:

1. **Select two clips and create an edit point between them in the Timeline.**

2. **To add the Default Transition, Control+click on the edit point and choose Add Transition from the contextual menu that appears.**

   The Default Transition is applied to the edit point. The menu choice shows you the name of the current Default Transition. For example, if you have not modified your Default Transition, the Add Transition choice will read "Add Transition 'Cross Dissolve'" as shown in Figure 16-4.

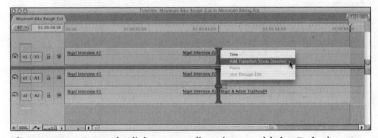

Figure 16-4: Control+click on an edit point to add the Default Transition.

Note

You can also use the keyboard shortcut Command+T to apply the Default Transition. To do so, first select an edit between two clips, and then press Command+T to apply the Default Transition. The keyboard shortcut for applying the default audio transition is Command+Option+T.

Setting the Default Transition

By default, the Default Transition is a Cross Dissolve because this is the most commonly used transition. However, you can select any other kind of transition as your default. To set a new Default Transition:

1. **In the Browser window click the Effects tab.**

2. **Twirl down the small disclosure triangle to open the Video Transitions folder.**

3. **Select a transition and choose from the menu bar Effects ⇨ Set Default.**

   You can also Control+click on any transition and choose Set Default Transition from the contextual menu that appears as shown in Figure 16-5.

The transition you chose will now be the Default Transition. The Default Transition is always underlined in the Browser. To apply the Default Transition, press Command+T. When you perform an insert or an overwrite edit with transition, the Default Transition will be used.

The default transition is always underlined

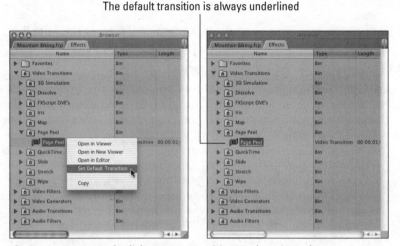

Figure 16-5: Control+click on any transition and set it as the new Default Transition.

Modifying Transitions in the Timeline

Transitions can be modified in a number of ways after they are applied to clips in the Timeline. You can modify the duration of the transition, you can replace it with another kind of transition, or you can drag the transition to a new location.

Changing the duration of a transition

By default, all transitions are applied with default duration of 1 second. However, you can modify the duration of any transition in a sequence. Two methods are available for changing a transition's duration. The first method involves resizing the transition with your mouse. The second method allows you to enter a numeric value using your keyboard.

Resizing transitions in the Timeline

Transitions in the Timeline can be resized in the same way as a clip. Here's how:

1. **Make sure the selection arrow tool is active.**

   If not, press the A key on your keyboard.

2. **Move the selection arrow tool to the edge of the transition that you want to resize.**

   The selection tool turns into a Resize cursor.

3. **Drag the edge of the transition to change its duration.**

   A small yellow box like the one shown in Figure 16-6 indicates the new duration and the amount of your change in number of frames.

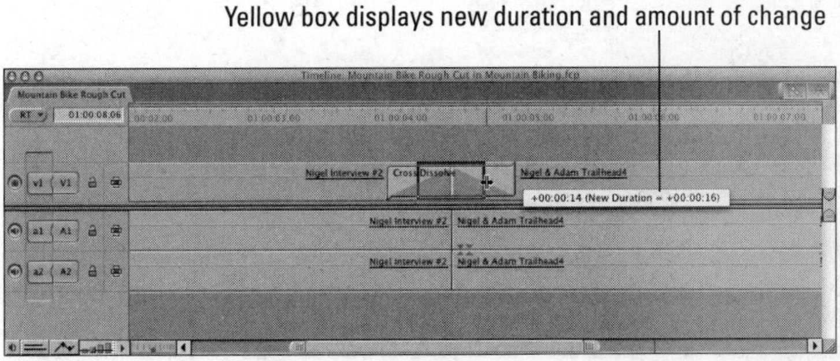

Yellow box displays new duration and amount of change

Figure 16-6: Click and drag a transition's edge to change its duration.

4. **Release the edge of the transition when you are satisfied with the new duration.**

Caution Modifying a transition's duration has different results depending on the alignment of the transition. When you modify the duration for a transition that is *centered* on a cut, the change in duration will extend in both directions. If the transition *ends* on the cut, the change affects the clip to the left. If the transition *begins* on a cut, the change in duration will affect the clip to the right of the transition. Bear in mind that you must have enough inactive source media for the clips for these modifications to work.

Modifying transition durations numerically

You can also modify the duration of a transition using numeric values typed in on the keyboard. I find this method quite fast and generally easier to use. Entering a numeric value allows you to enter an exact number in frames or seconds to obtain a new duration for a transition. Here's how:

1. **Select a transition in the Timeline and Control+click on it.**

   Be sure that the transition is selected and not the edit. Figure 16-7 shows the difference. Proper selection is especially important because the contextual menus will be different if you Control+click on an edit as opposed to a transition.

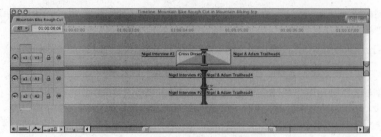

A selected edit in the Timeline

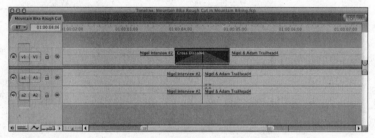

A selected transition in the Timeline

Figure 16-7: Make sure you select the transition, not the edit point.

2. **Choose Duration from the contextual menu that appears, as shown in Figure 16-8.**

   The current duration of the transition is displayed in the contextual menu. Selecting it will bring up the Duration dialog box, as shown in Figure 16-8.

3. **Enter a new duration using your keyboard and click OK or press Enter when you're done.**

Tip

If you enter a duration that is longer than the amount of overlapping frames (determined by the amount of inactive source media for the clips) between the two clips, you will hear an error beep. The Duration dialog box will display the maximum duration possible.

Replacing a transition in the Timeline

What if you hate the Cross Dissolve? Or the Page Peel you used elicits screams of pain from your viewers? Fortunately, you can easily replace a transition in Final Cut Pro. To do so, click and drag a transition from the Effects tab in the Browser and drag it over the transition that you want to replace in the Timeline. The new transition will maintain the duration and the alignment of the transition it replaced.

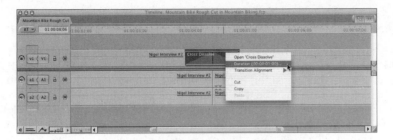

Figure 16-8: Control+click on a transition in the Timeline and select Duration to open the Duration dialog box. Enter a new value to change the duration of the selected transition.

Moving a transition in the Timeline

You can move a transition in the Timeline from one edit point to another. You can also replace a transition by dragging another one on top of it. To move a transition, select it and drag the transition from one edit point to another. The transition will move from the previous edit point to the new one. If there is already a transition at this new edit point, it will be replaced by the one you are dragging.

Copying and pasting a transition in a Timeline

If you move a transition from one edit point to another, it will be removed from its original location. Sometimes, this may not be what you want. You may simply want to copy a transition and paste it into another edit point. To copy and paste a transition in the Timeline, follow these steps:

1. **Select a transition in the Timeline and choose Edit ➪ Copy (or press Command+C).**

   You can also Control+click on a transition and choose Copy from the contextual menu.

2. **Select an edit point where you want to paste the copy of the transition.**

   Click on an edit point with the arrow selection tool to select it.

3. **Choose Edit ➪ Paste (or press Command+V) to paste your copied transition to the new edit point.**

   You can also Control+click on an edit point and choose Paste from the contextual menu.

Editing Transitions in the Transition Editor

The previous section described a number of ways to modify transitions in the Timeline. However, there are times when you need more control and precision when modifying transitions. The Transition Editor window is where you can make much more refined changes to a transition. For example, the Transition Editor allows you to reverse the direction of a transition such as a wipe, and you can adjust the percentage of completion of a transition. The Transition Editor also allows you to slip your outgoing or incoming clips, roll your edits, or resize the transition.

To open the Transition Editor window, select a transition in the Timeline and choose View ➪ Open Transition Editor. You can also double-click on a transition in the Timeline to open the Transition Editor window. Figure 16-9 shows the Transition Editor window and its controls. The appearance of the Transition Editor window and the effects controls available will vary depending on the transition that is loaded into the editor. Table 16-1 lists the controls and features that you will find in the Transition Editor window.

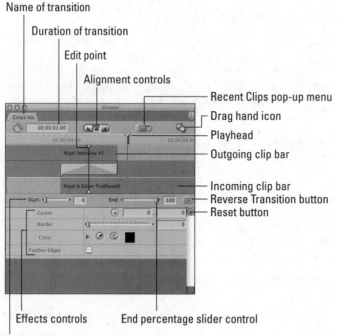

Name of transition

Duration of transition

Edit point

Alignment controls

Recent Clips pop-up menu

Drag hand icon

Playhead

Outgoing clip bar

Incoming clip bar

Reverse Transition button

Reset button

Effects controls

End percentage slider control

Start percentage slider control

Figure 16-9: Double-click on a transition in the Timeline to open it in the Transition Editor window.

Table 16-1
Details of the Transition Editor Window

Control	Name	Description
Cube Spin	Name of Transition	The name of the transition loaded into the Transition Editor.
00:00:01;00	Duration of Transition	The current duration of the transition. Highlight and enter a new amount to change the duration.
	Alignment controls	Click to change the alignment of the transition on the edit point. Selected button indicates the current alignment (centered, in this case).
	Recent Clips pop-Up menu	This menu allows you to select from a list of recently used clips in the View window. Selecting one will switch the current window from the Transition Editor to the Viewer view.
	Drag Hand icon	Use to drag this transition to another edit point in the Timeline, or into the Browser.
01:00:06;00	Ruler and playhead	The ruler displays an enlarged view of the frame count around the transition in the Timeline. The playhead is locked to the playhead in the Timeline. Use Command ++ (Plus) and Command+− (Minus) to change the scale.
	Outgoing and incoming clip bar	Displays the outgoing clip on top and the incoming clip at the bottom. The edit point is seen as the black line in the center, if the transition is aligned at the center. You can drag the edges of the clips to perform a slip, drag the center of the transition to perform a roll, or drag the edges of the transition to resize the transition.

Continued

Table 16-1 *(continued)*

Control	Name	Description
	Reverse Transition button	Reverses the transition's direction. For instance, a Clock Wipe, which moves clockwise, will move counterclockwise when reversed.
	Reset button	Resets all effect control settings. This button does not reset the duration, alignment, or percentage.
Start: ◄ [0] %	Start Percentage slider control	Allows you to set the starting percentage of a transition. For example, for a wipe, 0% represents no change, while 50% represents a point halfway through the wipe, and 100% represents a completed wipe.
End: ◄ [100] %	End Percentage slider control	Allows you to set the ending percentage of a transition.
	Effect controls	These controls vary for different transitions and allow custom changes to the particular transition.

Note You can view the thumbnail of your two clips in the Transition Editor window. This is similar to viewing the thumbnail for clips in the Timeline. Choose Sequence ➪ Settings and click the Timeline Options tab. Under the Thumbnail Display option, choose Name Plus Thumbnail.

Using the Transition Viewer to edit transitions

Before you start editing transitions with the Transitions Editor, you should understand the rules of working with this window. You already know that you can double-click on a transition to open it in the Transition Editor. But *where* that transition was located when you double-clicked on it produce have different results. If you open a transition that was located in the Timeline, any modifications you make will be reflected immediately in the Timeline. If you open a transition that was located in the Effects tab of the Browser, then what you will open is a *copy* of the actual transition. You can modify this copy of the transition and use the hand icon to drag it to any edit point in your sequence.

Resizing a transition in the Transition Editor window

Resizing is the act of modifying the duration of a transition. You can resize transitions in much the same way you resize clips. To resize a transition, follow these steps:

1. **Double-click the transition to open it in the Transition Editor.**

2. **Place your pointer at the either edge of the transition in the Transition Editor window.**

   The pointer will turn into a Resize cursor.

3. **Click and drag the edge of the transition to resize it as shown in Figure 16-10.**

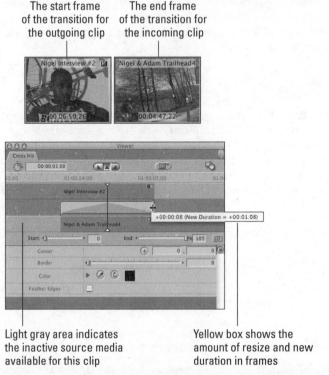

The start frame
of the transition for
the outgoing clip

The end frame
of the transition for
the incoming clip

Light gray area indicates
the inactive source media
available for this clip

Yellow box shows the
amount of resize and new
duration in frames

Figure 16-10: Place your cursor at the edge of a transition
in the Transition Editor window and drag with the Resize cursor.

Tip   You can also highlight the duration field in the upper-left corner of the Transition
Editor window and enter a new duration with your keyboard to resize the transition.

Note that while you drag at the edge of the transition, a yellow box will appear in
the Transition Editor window indicating the amount you have resized and the new
duration of the transition. While you are resizing the transition by dragging, the
Canvas window will show a two-up display with the first frame of the transition for
the outgoing clip on the left side, and the last frame of the transition for the incoming clip on the right side.

Rolling a transition in the Transition Editor window

By rolling a transition, you can move the entire transition to the left or to the right.
This process maintains the duration of the transition and the clips but moves the
transition to a different location between the two clips. To roll a transition, follow
these steps:

1. **Double-click the transition to open it in the Transition Editor.**

2. **Place your pointer in the middle of the transition in the Transition Editor window.**

   The pointer will turn into a Roll cursor.

3. **Click and drag to roll the transition, as shown in Figure 16-11.**

   A small yellow box indicates the progress of the roll amount in frames. The Canvas window provides a two-up display showing the new In and Out frames for your transition.

The start frame of the transition for the outgoing clip   The end frame of the transition for the incoming clip

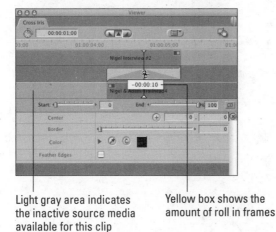

Light gray area indicates the inactive source media available for this clip

Yellow box shows the amount of roll in frames

Figure 16-11: Place your cursor in the middle of the transition icon in the Transition Editor window and drag with the Roll cursor to roll a transition.

Rippling in the Transition Editor window

By rippling a transition, you can change the In and Out points of the outgoing or the incoming clips that lie beneath a transition. This changes both the duration of the transition and the clip, but the duration of the sequence remains unchanged. You can ripple-drag either the Out point of the outgoing clip or the In point of the incoming clip. To ripple in the Transition Editor window, follow these steps:

1. **Double-click the transition to open it in the Transition Editor.**

2. **Place your pointer at the edge of the outgoing or incoming clip in the Transition Editor window.**

   The pointer turns into a Ripple tool. Be sure to check if you have additional inactive source media for the clip. A light gray area on the clip bar indicates inactive media frames.

3. **Drag the edge to the left or the right to ripple.**

   A small yellow box indicates the ripple amount, and the Canvas window displays the new frame for the outgoing or incoming clip as shown in Figure 16-12.

New start or end frame of the
transition in the clip being rippled

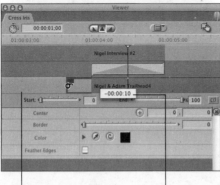

Light gray area indicates   Yellow box shows the
the inactive source media   amount of ripple in frames
available for this clip

Figure 16-12: Placing your cursor at the edge of a clip will turn the pointer into the Ripple cursor. Drag to perform a ripple.

Working with favorite transitions

All transitions found under the Effects tab of the Browser window have default durations and settings. You can modify these defaults whenever you want. You can also modify and save any transition as a Favorite Transition. Favorite transitions are saved in the Favorites bin in the Effects folder. All Browser windows have a default Favorites folder under the Effects tab. Any transitions saved in the Favorites folder are then available through menu choices and as transition icons in the Favorites folder that can be applied using the drag and drop method. Figure 16-13 shows the Favorites folder in the Browser and the Favorites submenu in the Effects menu.

Figure 16-13: When you place a transition in the Favorites folder in the Browser, that transition will also be available through the Effects ➪ Favorites menu.

By far the most common use of the Favorites folder is to create and store transitions of various lengths. Many editors find that the 1-second default duration is a bit too long for common transitions. Editors often create ten frame dissolves and then save them as favorites.

Creating a favorite transition

To create a favorite transition, you can select any transition on the Effects tab in the Browser menu, modify it as you see fit, and save the transition in the Favorites folder. Follow these steps to modify and save a transition as a favorite:

1. **Click the Effect tab in the Browser window.**

2. **Twirl down the small disclosure triangle to open the Transitions folder.**

3. **Select a transition and double-click it to load it into the Transitions Editor window.**

4. **In the Transition Editor window, make any changes to the transition that you want.**

   For example, you can highlight the Duration field and enter a new duration for your transition. The Transition Duration field is located in the upper-left corner of the Transition Editor window.

5. **Using the hand icon on the upper-right side of the Transition Editor window, drag the current transition into the Favorites folder in the Browser window.**

   You can also choose Effects ⇨ Make Favorite Effect (or press Option+F) to send the currently loaded transition into the Favorites folder.

6. **To rename this transition in the Favorites folder, click once on the name of the transition, wait a moment, and then click the name again.**

7. **Type a new name and press Return.**

   For example, you may want to call a transition "C Dissolve 10fr" to indicate that it is a ten-frame Cross Dissolve.

Tip You can drag any transition from the Video Transitions folder under the Effects tab to the Favorites folder. You will get a copy of the original transition, which you can highlight and rename if you like. You can also drag a transition from the Timeline to the Favorites folder.

Using a favorite transition

After you set a favorite transition, it will appear in the submenu that appears when you choose Effects ⇨ Favorites. To use a favorite transition, follow these steps:

1. **Select an edit point in the sequence where you want to insert a transition.**

   Edit points are locations between two clips.

2. **Choose Effects ⇨ Favorites and select your favorite transition from the submenu.**

Organizing your favorite transitions

As you create more and more favorite transitions, your Favorites menu can get pretty full. The most important step you can take to keep your favorite transitions organized is to name them descriptively. You can create new bins in which to organize your favorites, but you cannot create bins directly in the Effects tab window. Never fear, here is a workaround trick:

1. **Select the tab for your current project in the Browser window.**

2. **Choose File ⇨ New ⇨ Bin.**

3. **Rename the new bin by clicking once on its name, waiting a moment, and then clicking once again.**

4. **Type a new name for the bin.**

5. **Click the Effects tab in the Browser window and drag it away so that the Effects tab becomes a separate window.**

6. **Drag the new bin you created to the Favorites bin in the Effects tab window.**

   The new bin now appears as a submenu under Effects ⇨ Favorites. You can make different folders and store your commonly used transitions in them.

Tip   You are not limited to just storing transitions in the Favorites folder. You can store Video Filters, Audio Filters, and Audio Transitions in the Favorites folder.

Previewing and rendering your transitions

Applying a transition is just the first step in working with and viewing transitions. In order to play your transitions in real time, you might have to render them first. Huh? I know you're thinking the new Real Time Extreme architecture of Final Cut Pro 4 should all but eliminate rendering, but the reality of it is less idyllic than our fantasy for a render-free world. Real-time playback of transitions (and effects) depends on your media's codec, system speed, and playback options selected in the Real Time (RT) pop-up window in the Timeline. Also, the number of layers of transitions and effects, and their complexities will impact your system's ability to play back in real time without rendering. Unless your whole project is using straight cuts, or perhaps one or two effects, rendering your transitions and effects will probably be unavoidable. Of course, rendering takes time, and if you don't like what you see, you'll have to change your transition and re-render it. Fortunately, you can preview a transition before rendering it. A preview allows you to view a quick version of what your transition will look like after it is rendered.

Cross-Reference   See Chapter 18 for more details about Rendering in Final Cut Pro.

Previewing transitions

The simplest way to preview a transition is to drag the playhead across an unrendered transition in the Timeline or the Transition Editor window. A preview of the transition will appear in the Canvas window. Final Cut Pro will attempt to display each frame as quickly as it can on the Canvas window and out to the external NTSC monitor (if you have one). It might not be as clean as a rendered transition, but you can get a general idea of how the transition will look. You can also play a preview of the transition by following these steps:

1. **Place the playhead just before an unrendered transition in the Timeline.**

2. **Choose Mark ⇨ Play Every Frame (or press Option+\ [forward slash]).**

   Final Cut Pro plays each frame of your transition. The playback will *not* be in real time, however.

Rendering transitions

When you place a transition in the Timeline, a red line might appears above the transition in the Timeline ruler area indicating that the transition needs to be rendered before you can play it in real time. Because of Final Cut Pro's new RT Extreme architecture, many transitions can be played in real time without needing rendering, but this depends on your computer's system speed, the playback quality selected in the RT pop-up menu in the Timeline, and the complexity of the transition. Rendering is the process where Final Cut Pro combines your video files with the transition information and creates a render cache file. This render cache file is what plays during the playback of a transition in the Timeline.

Colors in the render bar above each item convey important information about their render status. For more information on these colors and what they mean, see Chapter 18.

To render a transition, follow these steps:

1. **Select one or more transitions in the Timeline.**

   To select more than one transition, hold down the Command key as you click on each transition.

2. **Choose Sequence ⇨ Render Selection ⇨ Video (or press Command+R) to render the selected transitions.**

3. **To cancel rendering at any time, click the Cancel button in the render status box or simply press the Escape key.**

To render all transitions in a sequence, open the sequence and choose Sequence ⇨ Render All ⇨ Both (or press Option+R).

Working with Text in Final Cut Pro

When the first version of Final Cut Pro came out, many editors and users rightfully derided the text tool. The options for making text in Final Cut Pro were, to put it mildly, lame. In some broadcast programs, text can play an enormous role. For example, in a show requiring subtitling for a foreign language, working with text can be a major chore. I've worked on two-hour foreign language documentaries that had barely a moment in them without any subtitles. Jobs like that mean a lot of text work.

Thankfully, tools for creating text are much improved in Final Cut Pro, providing some solid titling and text tools that should cover most titling needs.

Making text

The basic technique for making text in Final Cut Pro is the same no matter what you plan to use it. Text is made in Final Cut Pro using generators. *Generators* are media files created in Final Cut Pro. Commonly used generators are bars and tone, color mattes, and text. Final Cut Pro has a few different kinds of text generators. These include Crawl, Lower Third, Scrolling Text, Outline, Text, and Typewriter.

Making Lower Third text

On the DVD-ROM

If you don't have your own material to work on, you can follow along with the next few sections by using the Mountain Biking.fcp project located in the Mountain Biking Tutorial folder on the DVD-ROM. Copy this folder to your hard drive and then open the project by double-clicking on the Mountain Biking.fcp project file. The Nigel Interview #2 clip works especially well for adding Lower Third text. To view the final results of this exercise, open the Mountain Biking-Rough Cut sequence, located in the Exercises folder of the Mountain Biking.fcp project.

One of the most common uses for text is Lower Third text. Lower Third text appears in the lower third of the screen and is a common text tool used to identify speakers on a video show. The Lower Third text generator in Final Cut Pro creates two lines of text, placed in the lower third of the frame. In this generator, you can change the font, style, size, tracking, and color of each line. Lower Third text is often placed above a small line or a colored bar to make it stand out above the background video. The Background pull-down menu in the Lower Third text generator allows you to select between a Bar or a Solid background to place behind the text, and you can choose the color and opacity for the Bar or Solid. To add Lower Third text to a subject for an on-camera interview:

1. **Double-click the Nigel Interview #2 clip to load it into the View window.**

2. **Set an In point around 00:06:45:29, just before Nigel starts talking.**

3. **Set an Out point at around 00:06:54:06, when Nigel finishes his first sentence.**

4. **Edit the Nigel Interview #2 clip into a sequence by pressing the F10 key to perform an overwrite edit.**

5. **In the View window, open the Generator pull-down menu and choose Text ⇨ Lower 3rd as shown in Figure 16-14.**

   The text generator opens in the View window.

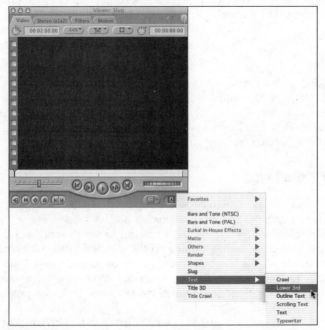

Figure 16-14: All text choices are located in the Generator's pull-down menu in the View window.

6. **Click the Controls tab in the View window.**

   The Control tab appears when the Generators are used. On the Control tab, you can see settings for the Lower 3rd text generator as shown in Figure 16-15.

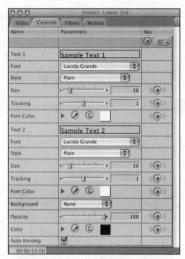

Figure 16-15: The Controls tab provides settings for the text generator you are currently using.

7. **In the Text 1 field, you'll see the text Sample Text 1. Highlight this text to delete it, and enter the name for the text.**

I called my text "Nigel Hall," which is the name of biker in the interview. Choose a different font, style, or size for the text as you see fit. You can click the Video tab in the View window to view how your choices affect the text.

> **Tip**
>
> While working on text, I often click on the Video tab in the View window and drag it away to form a separate window. That way I can make changes on the Controls tab and not have to click on the Video tab to see the changes. I can simply keep them side by side for quick feedback. The default font size of 36 points will work well in most situations. Also, I set my background color to Black if I am creating white type, and visa versa, allowing easier viewing of text than the checker background. The background selection is found in the overlays pop-up button on the Viewer's Video tab.

8. **In the Text 2 field you'll see the text "Sample Text 2." Highlight this text to delete it, and enter descriptive text for this sample.**

I renamed Sample Text 2 to Mountain Biker. Again, make any changes to the font, size, or style of the text that you want.

At the bottom part of the Controls tab, you can use the Background pull-down menu to select a background for your Lower Third text. The Bar options places a thin bar between the two lines of text. The Solid option places a solid background behind the two lines of text. You can set the color and the opacity of the background here. Semitransparent solids are often used to make white text stand out above the video background.

9. **In the sequence, park the playhead anywhere over the clip to which you want to add this text.**

10. **On the Video tab in the View window, drag the text image from the Viewer into the Canvas window and drop it over the superimpose edit overlay.**

   You can also press the F12 key to perform a superimpose edit.

   The Lower Third text you prepared is superimposed over the clip in the Timeline. The text is laid down in the video track above the current clip. The superimpose edit, when used without an In or Out point, uses the In and Out points of the clip in the target track where the playhead is located.

11. **In the Timeline, select the superimposed text clip.**

   A turquoise color border appears around the text layer borders in the Canvas window.

12. **In the Canvas window, choose Show Title Safe from the view choices pull-down menu as shown in Figure 16-16.**

   The Title Safe area appears on the video to help align the text.

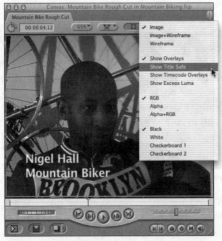

Figure 16-16: Choose Title Safe in the Canvas window's View pull-down menu.

13. **In the pull-down View menu in the Canvas window, choose Image+Wireframe.**

    A wireframe overlay is added to the text layer and a number appears in the center indicating the track number the clip is located on in the Timeline.

14. **Click anywhere in the wireframe and drag the text layer around in the Canvas window by clicking and dragging on it.**

    The pointer turns into a cross hair cursor as the text layer is moved as shown in Figure 16-17.

Action Safe border

Title Safe border   Crosshair cursor

Figure 16-17: Use the crosshair cursor to move the text layer around for placement.

15. **Select your text layer and choose Sequence ➪ Render Selection ➪ Video (Command+R) to render your text.**

    After the text is rendered, the sequence can be played with the superimposed text.

If you need to re-edit your text, double-click the text clip in the Timeline. The text clip will be loaded into the Viewer as a sequence clip. Click on the Controls tab to make any changes you like. You will have to re-render to be able to play your altered text again.

Caution

The default white that Final Cut Pro uses for text may be too "hot" or above the limit of brightness values for NTSC broadcast video. If you click on the color swatch in the text generator next to the Font Color setting, you will be presented with the HSV style color picker. To keep your brightness values within "legal" NTSC limits, be sure to avoid values below 6 percent and above 92 percent in the Value field of the HSV style color picker. To make an NTSC-safe white for your text, twirl down the Font Color settings by clicking on the disclosure triangle icon in the Controls tab of the Text generator. You will see the HSB (Hue, Saturation, Brightness) slider controls and fields for the font color. Enter 0° for Hue Angle, 0% for Saturation, and 92% for Value. Bear in mind that this is just a general rule. In a broadcast environment, professional-level Waveform Monitors are used to ensure that the brightness levels of your video program are not exceeding NTSC limits.

Cross-Reference

Any attribute of the text generators can be animated by setting *keyframes*. For more information on keyframing and animation, see Chapter 17.

Fading text in or out

If you play the text you just made in the previous section, it will just pop on and then pop off. There will be no smooth fade in or fade out of the text. Lower Third text generally fades In and Out, and that effect is easy to apply in Final Cut Pro. To fade text in and out:

1. **Turn on the clip overlays in the Timeline by clicking the Clip Overlays control button.**

   This button is located on the lower-left side of the Timeline window. You can also use my preferred way of turning on Clip Overlays: I use Option+W to toggle the clip overlays control on and off. A black line for the opacity overlay appears on all video clips, as well as the text clips.

2. **Drag this black line (the opacity overlay) up or down to change the opacity of the clips, as shown in Figure 16-18.**

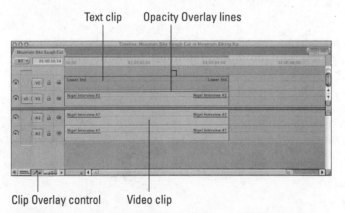

Figure 16-18: Use the opacity overlay line to fade text clips in and out.

3. **Select the Pen tool from the Tools palette.**

   Or you can simply press P on your keyboard.

4. **Click with the Pen tool and add two opacity keyframes to the beginning portion of the text clip's opacity overlay line.**

5. **Drag the first keyframe down to the bottom of the text clip area as shown in Figure 16-19.**

   The bottom of the clip area represents 0 percent opacity. A small yellow box shows the current opacity as you drag the keyframe up or down. Leave the next keyframe up at the top of the clip area. The top of the clip area represents 100 percent opacity.

First keyframe dragged down to 0%

Second keyframe at 100%

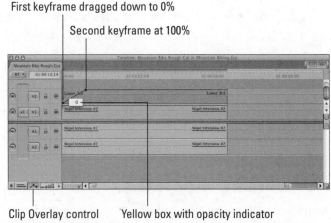

Clip Overlay control   Yellow box with opacity indicator

Figure 16-19: Drag the first keyframe down to 0%. The small yellow box indicates the opacity as you move the keyframe.

6. **Follow similar steps to create a fade out at the end of the text clip and create two keyframes near the end of the clip.**

7. **Drag the last keyframe down to 0 percent.**

   Now you have a fade-out from 100 percent to 0 percent opacity for the text clip. Figure 16-20 shows a fade in and a fade out on a text clip.

A fade in   A fade out

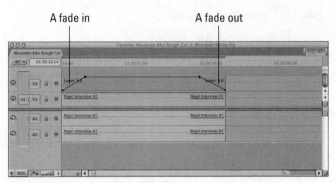

Figure 16-20: This text clip fades in and fades out.

8. **Select the text clip and choose Sequence ⇨ Render Selection ⇨ Video.**

   When the clip finishes rendering, you can play it by pressing the spacebar.

Tip

You can also make quick fade ins and fade outs on the text layer by adding a Fade In Fade Out Dissolve transition to the text layer. To create a fade in, add this transition at the beginning of the text layer. To create a fade out, add this transition at the end of the text layer. The Fade In Fade Out Dissolve can be found under the Dissolves folder, located in the Video Transitions folder, which is found under the Effects tab of the Browser.

A few tips for working with text

Text may seem simple enough, especially considering that you've been working with it since your earliest days in grade school. But when it comes to working with text in video programs and Final Cut Pro, there are some special considerations to keep in mind. The next few sections offer some tips to help make your text better and more effective.

Recognizing the limitations of making text with Final Cut Pro text generators

Despite improvements in the text features of Final Cut Pro text generators, you should be aware of some limitations when working with text. Text generators limit you to one font size and one style per title. The text features in Final Cut Pro do not allow you to change the spacing between individual characters manually. You will note that certain text generators in Final Cut Pro (such as the basic Text generator) have auto-kerning features. Selecting the Auto Kerning option in this generator tightens up the space between characters. I advise you to consider the use of this feature carefully. With certain fonts, the spacing may turn out to be too tight. And if your output format is DV or VHS, you may end up with titles that are hard to read if the Auto Kerning option is used.

Working with fonts

Like most applications on the Macintosh platform, Final Cut Pro uses the fonts available to it via the operating system. However, unlike previous versions of Macintosh Operating Systems, applications running natively in OS X, like Final Cut Pro 4.0, will find fonts kept in two separate locations. The default Fonts folder is located in the Library folder on the startup volume. It's very important that you know this is the Library folder on the *same* root level as the OS X System folder, and not the Library folder *inside* the System folder. If you want to add a font for use in Final Cut Pro, you should copy it into the Font folder located into this particular Library folder. If you want to install a font for use only by a User logged-in OS X's multiuser environment, then copy the font into the Fonts folder in the Library folder located in the individual's Users folder, also found at the root level of the startup volume directory.

Cross-Reference For more about working with Final Cut Pro under OS X, see Chapter 29.

The Mac OS can work with three types of fonts. These types are TrueType fonts (which were invented by Apple for the Macintosh), PostScript fonts, and bitmapped fonts. However, Final Cut Pro only works with TrueType fonts. Any TrueType fonts you place in the Fonts folder will appear in the text generators of Final Cut Pro. PostScript and other varieties of fonts *cannot* be used by Final Cut Pro and will not be available as choices.

You should also avoid serif fonts when working in Final Cut Pro. *Serifs* are the small curlies that some font styles have at their edges. For example, Times is a serif font. If you look closely, you will see thin curls at the edge of serif fonts. These curls, or strokes, are generally placed on the arms, stems, and tails of characters in serif fonts. These thin curls flicker when used in video that has interlaced fields. For video work, you should stick with *sans serif* fonts (meaning fonts that don't have serifs). Helvetica is a common example of a sans serif font. Thin fonts with serifs are especially ill advised. Use thicker sans serif fonts.

Prepare titles in other applications

You can use other applications, such as Adobe's Photoshop, to prepare text, and then import the text as files into Final Cut Pro. If you have an Alpha channel in these Photoshop files, you can superimpose them over a video track in Final Cut Pro. Alpha channels are used to describe the transparency values of a file and allow for keying and superimposition over other files.

The advantage to preparing text in third-party applications is that you are not limited to the font types available in Final Cut Pro. Also, many more fancy effects and choices for working with text are available in Photoshop as opposed to Final Cut Pro.

The disadvantage to making your text files in Photoshop is that if you want to make any changes to them, you have to go back into Photoshop, make your changes, and re-import the files back in Final Cut Pro.

For more information on preparing files in Adobe Photoshop for import into Final Cut Pro, see Chapter 24.

Use an NTSC monitor to preview text

If you have an NTSC monitor hooked up to your Final Cut Pro system, use it to view your final text over the video portions of your programs. Some fonts, especially serif fonts, will flicker badly on an NTSC monitor. This flicker will not always be visible on the RGB monitor of your computer. This flicker is the result of the thin font lines falling between the interlaced lines of NTSC video. The NTSC monitor shows your video with interlaced fields. Your computer's RGB monitor is not interlaced but instead uses progressive scan.

For more information on fields and interlacing, see Chapter 3.

Always check Title Safe

Televisions do not all scan equally and are frequently out of calibration when it comes to picture registration. If you place titles too close to the edge of your video, they may get cut off on some televisions because of a problem called *overscan*. Overscan occurs when the electron gun of a CRT projects some of the image off the edges of the screen. Some televisions overscan as much as 25 percent of the image, meaning that the viewer can be missing a good portion of video content.

Title Safe is an area determined to be safe for placing your titles on a video screen when preparing text for your programs. When working with text for broadcast video, always check against the Title Safe overlay. You can select the Title Safe overlay using the View Choices pull-down menu in both the Canvas and View windows. Selecting this option will give you two sets of borders in your window. The inner border represents the Title Safe area. No title should fall outside of this inner rectangle area. The outer border is the Action Safe area. No action of importance should fall outside of this outside rectangular area.

Using Apple text generators in Final Cut Pro

Besides the Lower Third text generator described earlier, there are other text generators created by Apple that you can use in Final Cut Pro. They can all be found in the Generators pull-down menu in the View window in the submenu under Text. These generators are Crawl, Outline Text, Scrolling Text, Text, and Typewriter. These generators are described briefly in the following sections. Note that the options that appear on the Controls tab of the Viewer will change depending on which text generator you are working with.

Crawl

The Crawl generator allows you to create a single line of text that moves horizontally across the screen. You can enter your text in the text entry field in the Controls tab of the Viewer. All returns are ignored, and the text you enter shows up as one long line of text. This generator is ideal for creating a stock ticker tape effect or a special weather bulletin that scrolls across the bottom of your viewer's screen.

The Crawl generator allows you to select the font size, style, spacing between the text, and the location of the text on the screen as it crawls across. At the bottom of the choices, you can choose the direction in which the text crawls.

If no location keyframes are set for the Crawl generator, it uses the length of the generator clip as the timing for the crawl. The longer the clip, the slower the crawl. For best results, set location keyframes to begin and end the text crawl.

To learn more about keyframing, see Chapter 17.

Outline Text

The Outline Text generator has more options on the Controls tab of the View window than any other text generator in Final Cut Pro. This generator is used to draw text with outlines and backgrounds. The main benefit of the Outline Text generator is that you can fill the text, the outline, and the background with still graphics of your choice. If you dislike the outline for the text (as I do), you can get rid of it by moving the Line Width slider to 0. You can modify the basic text size, style, color, tracking, leading, and numerous other settings.

If you drag and drop a still graphic in the Text Graphic area with the question mark icon on it, this graphic will be used to fill your text. (To get rid of the still, Control+click on the Text Graphic area and choose Clear.) Similarly, adding a still graphic to the Line Graphic area will result in the graphic filling in the outline part of the text. Drag and drop a still graphic into the Back Graphic area, and it will be used to fill the background. You'll have to set the controls for the Background Settings to view this still graphic as a background. Figure 16-21 shows the graphic settings and the area of the text they affect.

You can experiment with the Back settings by choosing different colors and setting the Horizontal and Vertical Size sliders to 100 each. Doing so will display a color background behind the text, and you can modify the background to your needs by changing the sliders for the Back settings.

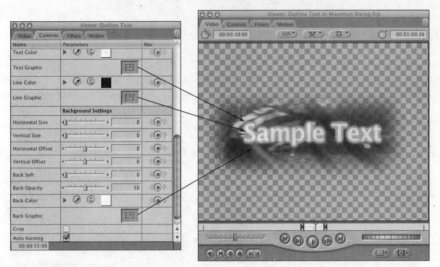

Figure 16-21: Drag and drop images into the small graphic windows to apply them to areas of the text.

Scrolling Text

The Scrolling Text generator is the one to use if you want rolling credits at the end of your show. This generator allows you to enter text (carriage returns are recognized) and move text from the bottom to the top of the screen. You can change the direction that text scrolls, if you wish.

The obvious settings you can change on the Controls tab of the Viewer are the font size, style, alignment, and color. Use the Spacing slider to control space between *all* letters of the text input (this is like a clip-wide tracking control, which does *not* allow you to adjust individual spacing between two characters — that adjustment is *kerning*) and use the Leading slider to adjust space between lines of text. The Fade Size slider does something interesting. It fades the scrolling text at both the top and the bottom. The text remains fully opaque in the center of the screen. Use the Direction menu to choose a direction for scrolling text.

An elegant and easy-to-use feature of Scrolling Text is the ability to set up two columns of text, usually used for listing names and job titles, as shown in Figure 16-22. The space between the columns is defined by typing an asterisk in the Text Input field in the generators Control tab. Use the Gap Width control to adjust the spacing between two group of words. The column layout and Gap Width setting work only with Center Alignment text.

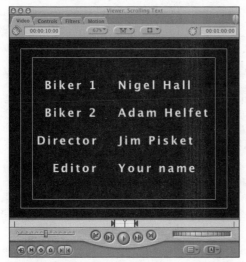

Figure 16-22: Setting up columns of text in the Scrolling Text generator is easy and quick.

The length of the scrolling text clip determines the speed of the scroll. The longer the scrolling text clip, the slower the resulting speed of the scroll. Note that when you first choose this generator you may not see any sample text on the Video tab of the View window. Drag the playhead around in the View window to see the sample text scroll up.

Text

The plain, old Text generator creates a still text element. You can modify the font size, style, alignment, and color of text. Tracking and leading controls help you adjust the space between text and lines of text. The Auto Kerning option automatically adjusts the spacing between text letters. Depending on the font (because different fonts have different default kerning values), you may want to try turning off this setting if the spacing between letters seems irregular.

The Use Subpixel setting forces Final Cut Pro to render the text at subpixel accuracy. Selecting this option makes the rendering process longer, but it provides smoother outlines and motion for the text.

Typewriter

The Typewriter text generator makes it possible for you to type your text on-screen one letter at a time. Like the other generators, you can modify many text attributes using the Controls tab of the View window. The Spacing slider alters the spacing between each letter. The Location slider moves the text up and down on the screen, while the Indent setting moves it from side to side. The Pause slider increases or decreases the time it takes for each letter to appear.

When you first choose the Typewriter generator, you may not see any sample text in the Video tab of the View window. Drag the playhead around in the Viewer to see the sample text type itself across the screen.

Working with Boris text generators

In addition to Apple text generators, Final Cut Pro also comes with a pair of text generators from Boris FX, software developers of compositing and vector graphic plug-ins. The two generators — Title 3D and Title Crawl — make up the Boris Calligraphy set and appear below the Apple text generators in the Generators pop-up menu, shown in Figure 16-23.

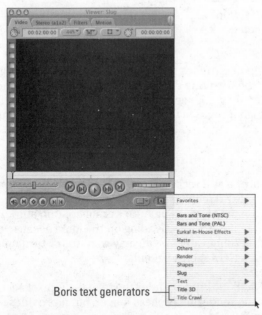

Figure 16-23: Two additional text generators from Boris are included with Final Cut Pro and appear at the bottom of the Generator pop-up button menu.

While working natively in Final Cut Pro, the Boris generators offer many features missing from Final Cut Pro text generators, primarily, the ability to select different type properties for individual letter characters, such as font family, style, size, color, skew angle, and even kerning. However, while you can set these properties, you cannot animate the settings of individual letters, only the properties that affect all text in the generator. Figure 16-24 shows the input interface of the Title Crawl generator.

Figure 16-24: Boris FX text generators, such as the Title Crawl shown here, allow you to set different property values for individual text characters.

The Boris text generator interface shows real-time previews of your selections and settings before creating the clip. After you create the text clip, you can animate available text properties in the Controls tab as you would with any Apple text generator. Many of the controls and settings of the input interface are similar to Final Cut Pro controls, but it still takes some time to learn and be proficient in. This being said, for many editors the learning curve of using plug-ins, such as Boris, is preferable to that of a stand-alone compositing application, like Adobe After Effects. For detailed instructions on using the Boris Calligraphy generators, go to the Boris FX Web site (www.borisfx.com) and download the free PDF User Manual for Boris Graffiti (Boris Calligraphy plug-ins are actually from the larger Boris Graffiti plug-in suite).

✦　　✦　　✦

Multilayering and Compositing with Final Cut Pro

CHAPTER

17

♦ ♦ ♦ ♦

In This Chapter

Layering clips
and stills

Working with
transparency

Using basic effects

Working with
keyframes

Using filters

Working with
keyframes in the
Timeline

Viewing the sequence
in the QuickView tab

♦ ♦ ♦ ♦

Layers in video editing today are inescapable. Turn on your television and you'll see layers almost everywhere: layers of text fly over images; stills layers are mixed in with video footage; layers of colored swatches fly across our screens untethered. Multilayering of video clips (also called *compositing*), stills, and other images is now a common technique in video and film editing.

Stacking, or layering clips atop one another, is a technique that was developed extensively by early animation artists for cartoons, and it was later used for special effects in motion pictures. Each element of an animation scene was drawn on its own sheet of clear cellulose, or *cels* as they were called, and then precisely stacked together (in registration) to create a finished scene. Viewed from the top of the stack, all elements not covered by another image on layers above it are visible and add to the illusion of a single scene. The advantage of having elements on separate layers is the ability to move or redraw an isolated element without affecting the others. A simple example of this method is the animation of a balloon floating across a ballroom. Although the balloon cel would need to be redrawn in incremental positions of its flight, it would not be necessary to move or redraw the background (on its own cel layer) for each frame of the balloon's movement.

This paradigm of compositing is still used by most compositing applications and nonlinear editors today, including Final Cut Pro. As a matter of fact, one of Final Cut Pro's strengths from its first release has been its extensive compositing and multilayering interface. These compositing capabilities are easy to overlook if you normally use Final Cut Pro for more "standard" editing. For instance, documentary makers who use Final Cut Pro may not have much need for layering and compositing. But for editors who want to create music videos with many different layers of video, Final Cut Pro's compositing capabilities will be invaluable because a sequence in Final Cut Pro can have up to 99 video layers.

Besides layering clips, Final Cut Pro also allows you to change and animate various motion attributes for each clip in the Timeline. Clips can be rotated, moved, cropped, and distorted. Final Cut Pro also has many video filters that you can apply to your clips. These filters extend the capabilities of the effects palette, as well as apply fancy effects such as a wave effect or zoom blur.

Layering Clips and Stills

Layering clips is the first step in the process of multilayering and compositing. By placing clips on top of one another and controlling the way they interact with each other, you can create a richly textured look for your programs. For any layer, you can control opacity, location, movement, and rotation. Each clip can also have any number of filters applied to it.

On the DVD-ROM

For the steps in this section, you can use your own footage, or you can use the Mountain Biking.fcp project from the Mountain Biking Tutorial folder on the DVD-ROM. Copy this folder to your hard drive and then open the project by double-clicking on the Mountain Biking.fcp project file.

Layering two or more shots in Final Cut Pro is easy. Just follow these steps:

1. **Create a new sequence and call it Layering.**

2. **Double-click the Nigel & Adam Pass clip to load it into the Viewer.**

   This clip is located in the At the Trail bin within the Mountain Biking.fcp project.

3. **Select about 5 seconds of the clip and mark an In point by pressing the I key at around 00:00:50:29 and an Out point at around 00:00:55:28 by pressing the O key.**

4. **Edit the clip into the Layering sequence by pressing the F10 key to perform an overwrite edit.**

5. **Double-click the Nigel & Adam Trailhead4 clip to load it into the Viewer.**

   This clip is located in the At the Trail bin within the Mountain Biking.fcp project.

6. **Select about five seconds of this second clip and mark an In point by pressing the I key at around 00:04:45:28 and an Out point at around 00:04:50:27 by pressing the O key.**

7. **Place your playhead anywhere over the first clip in the Layering sequence.**

8. **With the Nigel & Adam Trailhead4 clip still loaded into the Viewer, perform a superimpose edit by pressing the F12 key.**

The Nigel & Adam Trailhead4 clip superimposes over the Nigel & Adam Pass clip in the sequence. This superimposed clip is automatically placed in a new video track called V2. As you continue to add clips by performing superimpose edits, new tracks are automatically added. Figure 17-1 shows a sequence with two layered clips. Note that at this stage only the top layer is visible in the Canvas window. That is how the stacking order of layers works in Final Cut Pro. The topmost layer is the one that is visible unless you change the location, opacity, or scale of upper layers so that layers underneath can be seen.

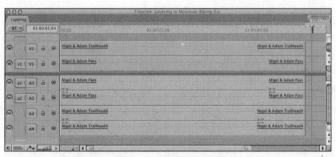

Figure 17-1: This sequence includes two layered video clips.

You can also layer stills over video clips. Follow these steps to add a couple of stills to the sequence you just created:

1. **In the Layering sequence you just created, place the playhead anywhere above the video clips.**

2. **Target track V2 by selecting it as the video Destination track.**

This is done by clicking on the track Destination control button, marked V1, in the patch panel area of the Timeline. The Source control button, marked V1 will jump to the V2 Destination control button. Make sure the Source and Destination control buttons are together (close) to insure track targeting is on. If the Source and Destination control buttons are apart, or open, click on either button to toggle it closed (on).

Cross-Reference

For more about track targeting with the Source and Destination control buttons, see Chapter 11.

3. **Drag the Blue Stripe still from the Stills folder in the Browser into the Canvas window.**

As you drag the still graphic into the Canvas window, the Edit Overlay automatically appears. Drag and drop the still to the Superimpose Edit Overlay.

The Blue Stripe still will be layered above the video clips into a new video track called V3, which will be automatically added to the sequence. Final Cut Pro automatically extends the length of the still to match those of the video clips over which the playhead is parked. Note that a red line will appear above the still in the sequence. This red line indicates that you have to render the still before you can play it.

4. **Target track V3 by clicking on the Destination control button for track V3.**

The source control button v1 will jump to the V3 Destination control button.

5. **Drag the Red Stripe still from the Stills folder in the Browser into the Superimpose Edit Overlay in the Canvas window.**

The Red Stripe still will be layered above the current video clips in the sequence into a new video track called V4. Final Cut Pro automatically extends the length of the still to match the length of the still below it as shown in Figure 17-2.

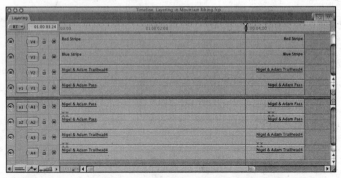

Figure 17-2: Two layers of stills have been layered above two layers of video in this sequence.

Tip   You can also superimpose clips by dragging them to an empty area of the Timeline. New tracks will be added automatically.

Note   To see more examples of layering, open the Nigel Pass – Title_V04.psd (For Exploring) sequence located in the Exercises bin of the Mountain Biking.fcp project. This sequence has 29 layers that are used to create the opening segment of a mountain biking tutorial. By placing your playhead at various points in the sequence and double-clicking on individual layers, you can see what each layer's image consists of.

Working with Transparency

Transparency refers to the level of visibility for each clip. You can choose to make clips and stills partially visible to create a more pleasing look or a special effect. In the previous section, you layered some stills above video clips. If you followed the instructions there or have layered some stills over video in your own project, the stills are now fully *opaque*. This means that they obscure any layers that are below them. If you want to be able to see through these upper layers to achieve a more layered look, you must reduce the *opacity* of the upper layers.

Another way to see through one layer to layers underneath is by using *alpha channels*. Alpha channels let you make certain parts of a layer transparent while leaving the rest of it opaque. The next few sections show you how to work with opacity and alpha channels.

On the DVD-ROM

To follow the steps in the next couple of sections, you can use your own footage or you can use the Mountain Biking.fcp project. This project is located in the Mountain Biking Tutorial folder on the DVD-ROM. Copy the folder to your hard drive and then open the project by double-clicking on the Mountain Biking.fcp project file. You can make your own layered sequence for this exercise or use the Layering sequence located in the Exercises bin in the Mountain Biking.fcp project.

Controlling the opacity of layers

A layer that is opaque is like a wall that you cannot see through—it completely obscures layers behind or underneath it. If you want other layers to show through, you can reduce the opacity of upper layers in Final Cut Pro. This can give a sequence a more layered and aesthetically pleasing look. To change the opacity for a layer:

1. **In the Layering sequence (or your own layered sequence) turn on the Clip Overlays control.**

   This control is located in the lower-left section of the Timeline window. You can also press Option+W to toggle the Clip Overlays control on or off. When you turn on the Clip Overlays control, the black opacity overlay line appears at the top of the video portion of each clip in the Timeline with video.

2. **Click and drag the black opacity overlay lines for each individual clip up or down to adjust that clip's opacity.**

   When you place your pointer near the black opacity line, the pointer will turn it into an Adjust Line Segment pointer.

3. **Click and drag on the black opacity line with the Adjust Line Segment pointer.**

   A small yellow box indicates the current opacity in percentage. A "0" indication, which appears when you drag the line to the bottom of the clip area, means the clip is completely transparent. A "100" indication, which appears when you drag the line to the top of the clip, means the clip is completely opaque, or solid. You can view the results of the opacity changes in the Canvas window. Note that you must first release the mouse button to view the results in the Canvas. It can be a bit awkward in that you must stop and start to get the right setting.

4. **Adjust the opacity for each clip in each layer in the sequence using this method.**

   Figure 17-3 shows how to adjust opacity for clips in a sequence.

Tip

You can make finer opacity adjustments by holding down the Command key as you move the black opacity line. This "gears down" your mouse movements, allowing you to make adjustments in smaller increments.

Adjust Line Segment pointer

Opacity Overlay line   Current opacity level indicator

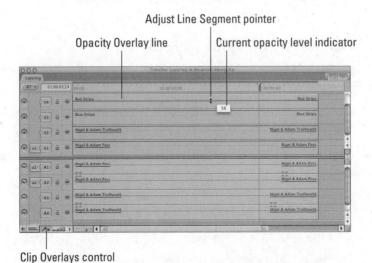

Clip Overlays control

Figure 17-3: Change the opacity of the layer with the Adjust Line Segment pointer.

Working with alpha channels

I wish I had a nickel for every time I've had to explain alpha channels to people in my career. A typical digital image consists of three channels: red, green, and blue. These color channels contain the color information for the image. However, a fourth channel, called the *alpha channel,* is included in some images for transparency information. The alpha channel of an image determines which part of an image will be opaque (solid) and which part of an image will be transparent (see-through). Many third-party applications such as Adobe Photoshop, After Effects, and some 3-D imaging programs can generate images files with alpha channels.

When image files containing alpha channels are imported into a project, Final Cut Pro recognizes the alpha channel and uses the transparency information contained therein for compositing. For example, if you create an image in Photoshop that contains text that you want to superimpose over a video clip in Final Cut Pro, you have to make sure that the image file has an alpha channel defining the area around the text as transparent. When you superimpose this text file over a video clip in Final Cut Pro, the text will appear and the area around the text will be transparent. The video will be visible in this transparent area around the text. The alpha channel is used to define that transparent area in Final Cut Pro.

Using alpha channels

Telling Final Cut Pro to use alpha channel information for a still or a clip is pretty easy. Follow these steps:

1. **Create a sequence and place any video clip into it.**

   You can use a clip from the Mountain Biking.fcp project if you want.

2. **Double-click a file that has an alpha channel from your bin that holds still files.**

   If you need a file to work with, double-click Frame Matte from the Stills Bin of the Mountain Biking.fcp project to load it into the Viewer. This still has an alpha channel.

3. **In the Viewer choose View ⇨ Alpha.**

   The image turns into a black-and-white graphic. In Alpha view, black represents transparency and white represents opacity. If you are using the sample Frame Matte file, you can see that the center part of the oval frame is transparent.

4. **Place your playhead anywhere over the first clip that you edited into the Timeline.**

5. **With your still loaded in the Viewer, perform a superimpose edit by pressing F12.**

Your still is placed over the video clip. Immediately you are able to see the video through the oval part of the image in the Viewer. This is because Final Cut Pro understands the alpha channel information in your still.

Tip   You can make QuickTime movies in Adobe's After Effects (or another 2-D or 3-D application) with alpha channels and superimpose these QuickTime movies above video tracks in Final Cut Pro. This can be used to combine video clips with 3-D models, as well as stills and graphics created in other applications.

Changing the alpha channel type for an image

There are different kinds of alpha channels, and occasionally you may have to change your alpha channel type to better suit Final Cut Pro. You can also use different alpha channel types to suppress or change an alpha channel. To change an alpha channel type:

1. **Select an image in the Browser whose alpha channel you want to change.**

2. **Choose Modify ⇨ Alpha Type and select the proper type in the submenu.**

See the sidebar "Curse of the alpha channels" for details on the different kinds of alpha channels.

Tip   You can view the type of alpha channel that an image has by bringing up the Alpha column in the Browser. You can also Control+click on an alpha type in this column and select another choice from the contextual menu to change the alpha channel type.

Curse of the alpha channels

Alpha channels are an often-misunderstood concept in digital imaging. The most confusing part for some users is that when an image has an alpha channel with it, it doesn't seem to look much different than when it does not—until you superimpose it over another image.

If you place two images side by side, one with an alpha channel and one without, they probably look similar; both have an image with a black area around it. However, only the image with the alpha channel will superimpose properly when placed in a Final Cut Pro video track. In this case, the black area of the image will become transparent and the image will remain. If the image actually has the color black around the image rather than an alpha channel, then the black will remain and be opaque when placed in a video track in Final Cut Pro.

Alpha channels come in a few different varieties. Final Cut Pro has several options for interpreting and changing alpha types. Final Cut Pro settings for working with alpha channels include:

✦ **Straight:** This is a common alpha channel type created in 3-D and 2-D applications. The areas around the image appear black, because only the pixels for the actual image are included. The black will disappear when placed in a Final Cut Pro video track above another clip.

✦ **Black:** Alpha channels created in Photoshop and some other graphics programs tend to be of this variety. In this case, the entire image is "pre-multiplied" or embedded, with the color black. If an image file with a Black alpha channel is interpreted as one having a Straight alpha channel, you will see an objectionable black fringe around the edges of the image. If you see this black fringe, change the alpha type in Final Cut Pro. Select the image and choose Modify ➪ Alpha Type ➪ Black.

✦ **White:** This type of alpha channel is just like a Black alpha channel, except that the color used for compositing is white.

✦ **None/Ignore:** If an image doesn't have an alpha channel or if you've turned it off intentionally, this is the alpha type that you'll see.

✦ **Reverse Alpha:** Many applications create alpha channels that use an opposite scheme of where the transparency information is kept as opposed to the information about the opaque parts. If you see an image where the alpha channel appears to be reversed (that is, the part that should be transparent is solid and the part that should be solid is transparent), then you need to reverse the alpha on that image. To do so, select a file in Final Cut Pro and choose Edit ➪ Item Properties. The Reverse Alpha option is a check box in the Item Properties dialog box. You can also press Command+9 on your keyboard to call up Item Properties.

Setting clip composite modes

Composite modes control how the color and brightness values of pixels in one layer interact and combine with the color and brightness values of pixels in underlying layers. Final Cut Pro has a variety of composite modes for you to choose from. You can change the composite mode for a layer by selecting it and choosing Modify ➪ Composite Mode. Then select a new composite mode from the submenu. Composite modes found in this submenu include:

✦ **Normal:** No composite mode is set for this clip.

✦ **Add:** Combines the color values of the layer with the underlying colors. The final image is lighter than the original. Pure black in a layer will not alter underlying colors. Pure white in the underlying layer is never changed in this mode.

✦ **Subtract:** Subtracts the color values of the clip from the color values of the clip below. The final image is darker than the original.

✦ **Difference:** Subtracts the color values of the clip from the underlying clip. Artistically, this is one of my favorite modes. Depending on the colors of the layers, you can get some pretty neat looking shifts in colors.

✦ **Multiply:** Multiplies the color values in the layers. For a dark image, there is little or no effect. For a lighter image, the Multiply mode darkens it. In certain cases if you have an image with a white background, applying the Multiply mode can drop out the white background. This can be useful for superimposing graphics, although it is much cleaner and simpler to use alpha channels to achieve the same results.

✦ **Screen:** Multiplies the inverse brightness values of the colors in the interacting layers. Although this may sound mathematically beautiful and practically useless, Screen is actually one of the more useful composite modes. For images that have pure black, using this mode will take out all the black present in an image. Many stock companies sell images that do not include alpha channels, but instead have pure black where you might expect an alpha channel to be. To get rid of this black, set the composite mode of the stock clip to Screen. This is often found in stock footage of explosions and fires.

✦ **Overlay:** Mixes colors between layers. This is done while preserving highlights and shadows to show the light and dark areas of the layer colors.

✦ **Hard Light:** Multiplies or screens the resulting color, depending on the original layer color. Apple says that this is like "shining a hard spotlight on the clip." I don't know if I agree with that description because I have yet to see a spotlight that creates this effect. The Hard composite mode, depending on the underlying color, creates either a screened or a multiplied look. If the underlying color is light, then the Hard Light mode creates a screening effect for the clip. If the underlying color is dark, then the multiply effect is created. Primarily this mode creates the appearance of shadows on a layer.

✦ **Soft Light:** This mode darkens or lightens the colors of the clip. This mode also depends on the lightness or the darkness of the colors of the underlying layer. If the underlying layer is dark, the clip darkens. If the underlying layer is light, the clip lightens.

✦ **Darken:** Groucho Marx once said, "Go and never darken my towel again." Instead of darkening your towel, this mode compares the color values of the layers and displays the darker color of the two layers.

✦ **Lighten:** Compares the color values of the layers and displays the lighter of the two layers.

✦ **Travel Matte-Alpha:** Travel mattes are created by combining three layers. You create a foreground layer on top, a matte in the middle, and a background layer on the bottom. This mode applies a matte to the selected layer using the color and brightness information from the layer just below the clip to which you applied the mode. If the information for the transparency is contained in an alpha channel, this mode needs to be applied to the clip.

✦ **Travel Matte-Luma:** Use this mode to make travel mattes using the luma information or the black and white values of a layer.

For more information on creating travel mattes with alpha or luma information, see "Creating Traveling Mattes," later in this chapter.

If you are familiar with the Adobe After Effects or Photoshop applications, the composite modes in Final Cut Pro are similar in name and operation to the layer modes in After Effects and Photoshop.

Using Basic Effects

Final Cut Pro allows you to create and apply a variety of effects to your projects. This section describes a few basic effects for you. It starts by showing you how to create travel mattes and change the speed, as well as modify a clip's opacity, scale, and other geometric properties.

Creating traveling mattes

Traveling mattes are used for creating various effects with clips. You can use a travel matte to create a frame around a video clip or to create a soft spotlight effect. To create a travel matte, you usually work with three layers: The foreground layer is placed on the top, the matte layer is in the middle, and the background layer is placed at the bottom. The matte layer is not seen in the final layering; it is simply used to control the interaction of the foreground and background layers. Travel mattes use the information contained in the middle layer to affect the top layer and reveal the bottom layer.

Like many of the concepts of compositing, the name *traveling matte* originated from an earlier era. *Matte* is simply an old term from the days of optical compositing with film negatives where soft back frame cutouts and other "mattes" were used to screen off portions of the image. They are called *traveling mattes* because they often track along with a moving image.

Okay, enough inaccurate history lessons. Let's make a traveling matte.

Making a traveling matte

To create a traveling matte, you need three layers. You should select any two video layers, one to serve as the foreground and one for the background. For the matte layer use the Frame Matte located in the Stills bin of the Mountain Biking.fcp project. To see the final matte, you can open the Traveling Matte sequence located in the Exercises folder in the Mountain Biking.fcp project.

To create a traveling matte:

1. **Create a composite of three layers in a sequence.**

   The only requirement here is that the middle layer be the Frame Matte still. This still is located in the Stills folder in the Mountain Biking.fcp project. The top and the bottom layers can be any video clips of your choice. You can look at the Frame Matte still by double-clicking it to load it into the Viewer. The still was created in Adobe Photoshop and has an alpha channel for transparency control. You can use this as a model for creating your own matte layer stills. Your three-layer composite should resemble Figure 17-4.

Cross-Reference See Chapter 26 for more on creating mattes with alpha channel.

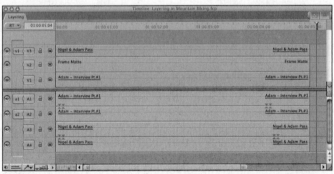

Figure 17-4: A three-layer composite is needed to create a traveling matte. The three layers above are laid out in V1, V2, and V3 tracks.

2. **Select the top clip in the layering and choose Modify ➪ Composite Mode ➪ Travel Matte-Alpha.**

   A soft-bordered frame will surround Adam if you've used the same clips shown in Figure 17-4. The outside of the border will be filled by the topmost clip, while the inside of the frame will be filled by the bottom clip.

3. **Select any clip and choose Sequence ➪ Render Selection.**

   After it finishes rendering, you can play your traveling matte. Figure 17-5 illustrates how the traveling matte works.

Background Layer

Traveling Matte Layer

Foreground Layer

Traveling Matte Composite

Figure 17-5: Traveling mattes are created by placing the matte layer in between two clips. The top clip has the Traveling Matte-Alpha composite mode applied to it.

Tip

To use the Travel Matte-Alpha option in the Modify ➪ Composite Mode submenu, you must have a proper alpha channel prepared for your matte image. Alternatively, you can also create a fully black-and-white image and choose the Travel Matte-Luma option from the Modify ➪ Composite Mode submenu. Use the Matte-Luma option if you do not have an alpha channel on your image but you want to use the black and white portions of your image to define the matte.

Modifying the speed of a clip

You can change the speed of a clip by slowing it down or speeding it up. Of course, the duration of the clip will change when you modify its speed. A common use of this effect is to create a slow-motion look. If you slow down a 5-second clip to 50 percent of normal speed, the duration of the clip will extend to 10 seconds. Slow-motion effects, by the way, are commonly seen in Hollywood movies as the protagonist is in the throes of death while being fired upon by enemy forces. Some sad and loud violin music completes the effect.

To modify the speed of a clip in Final Cut Pro:

1. **Select a clip in the Timeline and choose Modify ➪ Speed, or press Command+J.**

   The Speed dialog box will appear as shown in Figure 17-6.

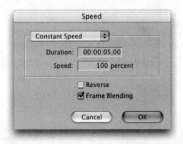

Figure 17-6: The Speed dialog box is used to change the speed of a clip.

2. **Enter a new percentage in the Speed field.**

3. **Click OK.**

   Your clip speed will be modified.

4. **Select the clip in the Timeline again and choose Sequence ➪ Render Selection.**

   Once rendered, you can play the clip at the new speed.

You have several options that can be set in the Speed dialog box. These options include:

✦ **Constant Speed/Variable Speed:** This pop-up menu allows you to select a constant speed rate or a variable speed rate for the clip. Leave this set to Constant Speed. For variable speed changes, see the Applying Time Remap section later in this chapter.

✦ **Duration:** You can also enter a duration to change your clip's speed to fill a gap. Keep in mind that this may change your speed to odd-looking numbers such as "210.83%." I strongly discourage you from using odd speed percentages like this. Try to stick with whole number changes such as 25%, 50%, and so on. Final Cut Pro often creates jittery playback and unsatisfying speed changes when odd and fractional speed changes are used.

✦ **Speed:** Unmodified clips have a speed of 100 percent. Entering 50 percent for a 5-second clip will slow the clip down to half of its original speed, and the duration will increase 10 seconds. Entering 200 percent for a 5-second clip will speed the clip up to twice its original speed, and the clip's new duration will be 2.5 seconds.

✦ **Reverse:** Check this box to make your clip play in reverse. You can achieve similar results by entering negative percentages, such as –100%, to make the clip play backward at normal speed.

✦ **Frame Blending:** Radically slow-motion speed changes can sometimes result in strobing artifacts. The playback seems jumpy and skips from frame to frame. This is commonly seen when you try to slow down a clip to 10 percent of its original speed. There simply aren't enough frames in most clips to spread out that much. Supposedly, you can use frame blending to rectify this problem. According to Apple, "Frame blending takes all of the adjacent frames that have been slowed down and interpolates them to create new intermediate frames that play in between the original frames." Take this glorious claim with a grain of salt. Frame blending is not a magic cure, and the intermediate frames it creates can be objectionable at times. There will be times when frame blending will work, and other times where you might prefer to live with the strobing artifacts. Experiment with the frame blending setting on your clips to achieve a favorable result.

Be aware changing the speed of a clip works very much like a ripple edit. The best thing to do is to put any elements on a new track and to lock all other tracks prior to changing the speed. This will avoid putting other clips out of sync.

Tip

I had a difficult time remembering what the speed percentage of clip meant until I figured out this visual mnemonic: I think of the percentage of a clip's speed as miles per hour and then only need to remember that the normal speed of a clip is 100 percent — or 100 *MPH*, rather. So if a clip is set to a lower percentage, say 30 percent, I think of it as 30 MPH, which is slower than 100 MPH, or normal speed, and therefore its playback is slower than normal. Conversely, a clip set at a speed rate of 300 percent is much faster than normal and will play back at a turbo-charged speed.

Working with the Motions tab

Each video clip has many parameters that are shown in the clip's Motions tab (because motion properties in Final Cut Pro describe only visual motion, audio-only clips do not have a Motion tab). If you double-click a clip into the Viewer, the Motions tab will also appear in the Viewer and you can click on it to view the motion parameters. Figure 17-7 shows the motion parameters that can be found on the Motion tab for a clip.

Figure 17-7: Double-click a clip to load it into the Viewer, and click the Motion tab to view the motion properties of the clip.

The sets of motion parameters are Basic Motion, Crop, Distort, Opacity, Drop Shadow, Motion Blur, and Time Remap. Of course, not all of these are "motion" properties, but that's how they're categorized in Final Cut Pro. Each set of motion parameters has a small disclosure triangle, which you can click to reveal the properties for that set. The motion parameters include:

✦ **Scale:** Changes the size of the image proportionally.

✦ **Rotation:** Rotates a clip on its axis. You can rotate a clip for up to 90 rotations, but for the love of Gumby don't actually do it. Someone is bound to get nauseated looking at a clip that rotates 90 times.

✦ **Center:** Determines the center point of a clip on the Canvas window. Center coordinates are for X-axis (running left to right on the screen) and Y-axis (running up and down on the screen).

✦ **Anchor Point:** Sets the point that is used to center a clip's position and rotation. A clip's anchor point is normally the center of the clip, but this does not have to be so. You can specify any other point on the clip as its anchor point. Changing the anchor point on a clip will change the point from which the clip will rotate and how it will center itself.

✦ **Crop:** Crops the clip from the side you choose. You can crop all four sides independently of one another. You also have the choice of feathering the cropping. The Feathering option is ideal for the video you plan to shoot for Cousin Bobby's wedding day.

✦ **Distort:** Allows you to distort your clip beyond recognition. The Corners controls allow you to move each corner independently. The Aspect Ratio control allows you to squeeze your clip vertically or horizontally.

✦ **Opacity:** Changes the transparency of the clip. A setting of 0 percent indicates a completely transparent (invisible) clip. A setting of 100 percent makes the clip completely opaque, or solid.

✦ **Drop Shadow:** This allows you to place a drop shadow behind a clip. You can change the offset, angle, color, softness, and opacity of a drop shadow with this parameter.

✦ **Motion Blur:** This effect blurs any clip that is in motion. The Samples setting controls the detail level of the blur, depending on the speed of the clip. The Percent of Blur setting affects how smooth your blur will be. Note that the blur is applied to clips that are moving within the frame, and *not* to items moving within the video such as a basketball player running across the court.

✦ **Time Remap:** Allows you to change the playback speed of a clip using either a constant or a variable rate. If you use a constant rate speed change, all frames of the clip play back faster or slower at the same percentage. If you apply variable speed to a clip, frames will play back at different rates within the same clip. This is a very dramatic effect in which the clip speeds up and slows down seamlessly within the same shot.

Note

Time Remap is covered in detail later in this chapter, including a list of all its parameters in the Motion tab as well as a description of each of its functions.

Using basic motion effects

Final Cut Pro allows you to create special motion effects with your clips as well. You can actually move a clip around on the screen. You do this by adjusting the motion properties for a clip in the Timeline. In a multilayered sequence, each layer has its own set of motion properties, and these can all be modified and animated independently. To adjust the motion properties of a clip:

1. **Double-click a clip in a sequence to load it into the Viewer.**

2. **Click the Motion tab in the View window to bring the motion properties forward as shown in Figure 17-8.**

3. **Highlight the Scale field and enter** 50%.

   This reduces the clip down to 50 percent of its original size. You can also drag the Scale slider to achieve the same results. The results of your changes appear in the Canvas window.

4. **Highlight the Rotation field and enter** 120.

   This rotates the clip 120 degrees clockwise. You can also drag the black line in the Angle control dial to change this setting. You can switch back and forth between the Motion and the Video tab in the View window to see the effects of your changes.

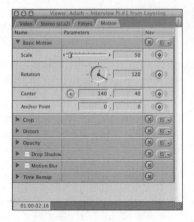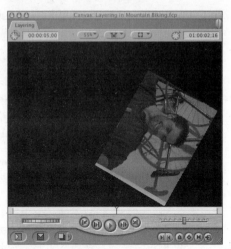

Figure 17-8: Changes made in the Motion tab for a clip in the Timeline are immediately visible in the Canvas window.

Tip

When adjusting Angle control you can hold down the Shift key to constrain the dial to 45-degree increments. For a slider, holding down the Shift key changes with two decimal places of accuracy. When the Command key is held down while adjusting a slider, you get more refined control of the values.

5. **Click the first Center field (the X coordinate) and enter** 140, **and click the second Center field (the Y coordinate) and enter** 40.

   This sets the center point of the clip to 140 on the X-axis and 40 on the Y-axis. Your results in the Viewer should resemble Figure 17-8. Note that like most Macintosh fields, you can move between fields by pressing the Tab key on your keyboard. (Shift+Tab moves you backward.) Also, pressing the Enter key initiates the action for each field. That way, you can see the action before having to leave the field.

Tip

Another way to set the center for your clip is to click the small crosshair icon next to the Center property and then click with it anywhere in the Canvas to move the center of the image to that location.

6. **Select the clip in the sequence and choose Sequence ➪ Render Selection.**

   After the clip has finished rendering, you can play it and view the results.

If you are dissatisfied with the results, you can click the appropriate X in the Nav (or Navigation) column, and the default values are restored.

Know your coordinates

When working with motion properties, a basic understanding of the coordinates used by Final Cut Pro is important. The coordinates are laid out along the X- and Y-axis of the Canvas for any image. The X-axis runs horizontally (left to right) across an image, and the Y-axis runs vertically (top to bottom) along an image.

Final Cut Pro assigns the values X=0 and Y=0 to the center of the image. For a 720 × 480 image (for the size of DV video) the image is divided into equal parts as shown here. The frame is divided into equal portions across the X- and the Y-axis no matter what the size or shape of the image.

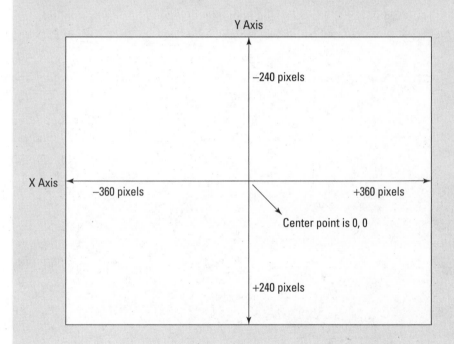

Continued

Continued

To change the location of an image on-screen, you specify a new value for the center. The numeric values are expressed in pixels. Note that in the preceding figure, positive values move the image right of center along the X-axis and down from center along the Y-axis. This means that if you set the X coordinate to 140 and the Y coordinate to 40, the result will look like the following figure. If you want to move the image up on the screen rather than down, enter a negative value for the Y coordinate, such as –40.

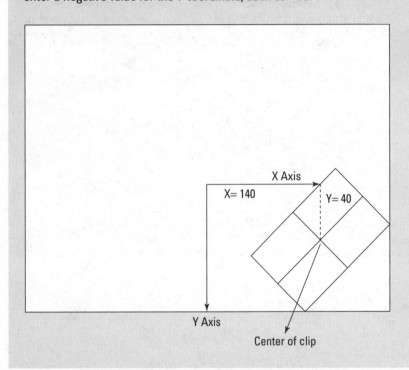

Copying and pasting clip attributes

Sometimes after you are done changing motion attributes for one clip, you may want to apply the same attributes to another clip. Instead of changing the motion attributes for all clips individually, you can copy and paste attributes from one clip to another. This is a major timesaving feature and provides greater accuracy when attempting to duplicate the attributes from one clip to another. To copy and paste attributes from one clip to another:

1. **Select a clip in the Timeline and double-click it to load it into the Viewer.**

2. **Click the Motions tab to bring it to the front, and change the motion properties to suit your needs.**

3. **Select this clip in the Timeline and choose Edit ➪ Copy.**

4. **Select the clip to which you want to apply the attributes and choose Edit ➪ Paste Attributes.**

   You can also press Option+V to paste the attributes. The Paste Attributes dialog box appears, as shown in Figure 17-9.

Figure 17-9: The Paste Attributes dialog box allows you to paste attributes from one clip to another.

5. **Check the attributes you want to paste and click OK.**

   The selected attributes will be pasted into the second clip. Selecting the *Scale Attributes Times* will shrink or stretch the keyframes, if your clip has any, of your copied clip attributes to fit the duration of longer or shorter clips that you paste them into.

Keyframes are explained later in this chapter.

Using the Paste Attributes feature

The ability to paste attributes from one clip to another is a powerful feature that can save a lot of labor. However, as with any powerful application feature there are caveats. Some of the issues and idiosyncrasies you should be aware of when using the Paste Attribute command are:

✦ Choosing the Content setting under Video Attributes in the Paste Attributes dialog box will paste only the video frames from one clip to another. You must have enough material in the copied content to match the clip you are copying into.

✦ Similarly, selecting the Content setting under Audio Attributes in the Paste Attributes dialog box will paste only the audio frames from one clip to another. You must have enough material in the copied content to match the clip you are copying into.

✦ Options that do not apply to the attributes you are copying will be grayed out. For example, if you do not have any filters in the clip you are copying from, the Filters setting will be grayed out.

✦ All settings in the Motion tab of the clip you are pasting the attributes into will be replaced.

✦ Filters will be added in addition to the ones already applied to a clip.

✦ Pasting attributes between clips with different frame rates will produce unreliable results.

Working with Keyframes

In the previous section, you learned how to adjust the motion properties for a layer in a sequence. For instance, in one series of steps you shrunk a clip down, rotated it, and moved it to the lower-right corner of the screen. If you followed the steps exactly, the motion properties won't really provide the sensation of motion because the properties will apply to the whole clip. When it's played, the whole video clip will be displayed as small, crooked, and in the corner for the duration of the clip. To animate the clip and actually see it in motion, you must use keyframes. Keyframes are icons that you use to lock a property's value to a particular point in time along the clip. You can set another keyframe later in the clip with a different value. Final Cut Pro will automatically *interpolate,* or calculate the values, between the two values represented by the keyframes and animate the clip.

Using the keyframe graph area in the Viewer

The keyframe graph area can be found on both the Motion tab and the Filter tab of the Viewer. Double-click any clip into the Viewer and click the Motion tab to view the motion attributes. Drag at the lower-right corner of the window to extend out the border to view the keyframe graph area as shown in Figure 17-10.

Next Keyframe button ⎯⎯⎯

Add Keyframe button ⎯⎯⎯

Previous Keyframe button

Light gray indicates clip duration

Keyframes

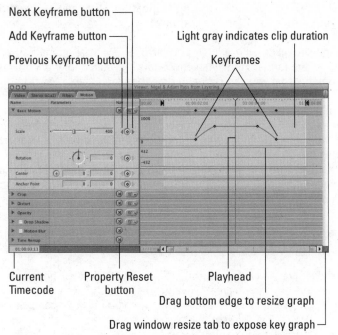

Current Timecode

Property Reset button

Playhead

Drag bottom edge to resize graph

Drag window resize tab to expose key graph ⎯

Figure 17-10: The keyframe graph area is made visible by extending out the window under the Motion or Filter tabs.

Note

When working with sequence clips opened from the Timeline into the Viewer, the timecode ruler that appears above the keyframe graph area displays sequence time, not clip time. The playhead in this ruler area is locked to the playhead in the Timeline, and any markers placed in the Timeline also appear in this timecode ruler area. While working in the keyframe graph area, you can navigate and snap to items just as if you are working in the Timeline.

When working with keyframe graphs, you can zoom in using the Zoom tool (press the Z key) and clicking in the keyframe graph area. You can also increase the vertical work area of any keyframe graph by dragging the bottom edge between the graphs to increase the size. Double-clicking on this edge between graphs will then toggle between the default size and the "dragged out" customized size. The common navigation keyboard shortcuts also work in the keyframe graphs. You can press Shift+Z to fit all the keyframes for an item in the current view. You can also use the Home and End keys to jump to the beginning or end of a graph, and use other shortcuts to jump to In or Out points and navigate to markers.

You may find that, often times, you may need to magnify your work area. You can press the Z key on your keyboard to select the Zoom tool and click with it in the work area to enlarge it. Holding down the Option key while the Zoom tool is selected will turn it into a Zoom down tool. Alternatively, you can also use the zoom slider located at the bottom of the window. Drag at the thumb areas at either end of the slider to increase or decrease your magnification. Dragging at the middle of the slider moves your view around in the window.

Tip   If you find yourself struggling with a large portion of a keyframe animation, you may find that the square format of the Viewer window is ill-suited for work on long animations. Remember that you can click and drag the Motion tab away from the View window and add the tab to the Timeline window. This provides two benefits. First, your Motion window will lay itself out in an elongated manner, which is better-suited for animations. Second, you won't have to click back and forth between the Motion and the Video tabs in the View window to see the results of your animation. By placing the Motions tab in the Timeline, you can switch the Viewer to the Video tab. That way, you can view your changes instantly in the View window as you modify your keyframes. When you are done, you can click and drag the Motion tab back from the Timeline to the View window.

The four types of keyframe graphs

If you are going to utilize the Motion and Filter controls in Final Cut Pro, you will find yourself spending a lot of time in the keyframe graph area. Like any other aspect of Final Cut Pro, the keyframe graphs are sophisticated and can display behavior that you may find confusing at first. Some keyframe graphs may appear to resize themselves as you drag a keyframe up or down. Others may not. Control+clicking on some keyframes may show a Smooth option in the context menu, while this choice may be absent for some other keyframes.

Some of the strange behaviors of the keyframe graphs depend on the type of graph you are looking at. There are essentially four kinds of keyframe graphs in Final Cut Pro:

✦ **1-D graphs:** This is a simple one-dimensional graph where the interpolation between keyframes is limited or not applied in the graph. The color swatch in some of the filters and under the drop-shadow section of the Motion tab is a good example of a 1-D type of graph. You can set keyframes for a color swatch, but you cannot smooth the keyframes. Control+clicking on any 1-D keyframe will only provide a Clear option and not a Smooth one, as for some other types of graphs.

✦ **2-D graphs:** You will encounter these standard graphs most often. The Opacity parameter is an example of a 2-D graph. Interpolation between keyframes on a 2-D graph defaults to linear. But you can Control+click on any keyframe to change this linear interpolation to Smooth. Changing the interpolation to smooth will provide a Bezier handle that can be used to smooth the incoming and the outgoing velocity to the keyframe. (Bezier handles are used to change the control points of parametric curves.)

✦ **Logarithmic graphs:** Scale is an example of a logarithmic graph. Certain parameters, such as Scale, have a wide range of values, even though the range of values that are actually useful is usually limited. In the case of Scale, you can set a value as high as 1000 percent, although the most useful range is between 0 and 100 percent. Because of this, the logarithmic graph for the Scale attribute allows a wider space for setting keyframes from 0 to 100 percent and less room as your values approach 1000 percent. The sliders for logarithmic values are also marked with uneven indentations. In a standard 2-D slider, the rate of change is even across the range. The figure here compares the slider for Scale (a logarithmic value), the Offset slider for Drop Shadow (a double-sided logarithmic slider), and the Opacity slider (a simple 2-D value).

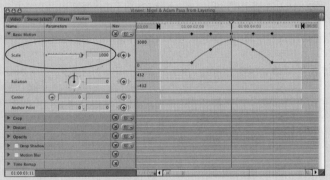

A logarithmic slider with nonlinear markings

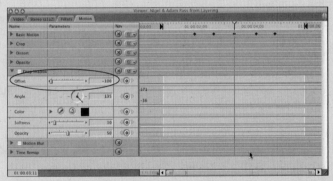

A double-sided logarithmic slider with nonlinear markings on both ends

A standard 2-D slider with evenly spaced markings

Continued

Continued

> When audio level keyframes are applied in the Viewer or the Timeline, they are also logarithmic in behavior. When you drag the level line for an audio clip in the Viewer or the Timeline, you will notice that there is more room for changing from 0db to +10db (the most common range) than for 0db to –60dB. When you use keyframes in a logarithmic graph, Final Cut Pro applies a preset nonlinear response curve for the effect.
>
> ✦ **Boundless graphs:** Some values can be set without limits. Rotation is a good example of a parameter with a boundless graph. If you click and drag a keyframe for Rotation in the keyframe graph, Final Cut Pro will indicate the change you are making with a small yellow box. The graph itself will not change to accommodate the new change no matter how vast it is.

Animating a motion property with keyframes

On the DVD-ROM

For the next few sections, you can use your own footage or you can use the Mountain Biking.fcp project. This project is located in the Mountain Biking Tutorial folder on the DVD-ROM. Copy this folder to your hard drive and then open the project by double-clicking on the Mountain Biking.fcp project file. For the following exercise, you can take a look at the Keyframes sequence located in the Exercises folder of the Mountain Biking.fcp project. The Keyframes sequence contains the finished version of this exercise.

Keyframes provide reference points for use when animating a clip. In the following steps, you will animate the scale and center of a clip, but the basic concept works the same for any motion property. To animate with keyframes:

1. **Layer two clips in a sequence.**

   You can do this by editing the first clip into the sequence with an overwrite edit, and then performing a superimpose edit with the second clip. For the example shown here, I am placing the Adam - Rear Algn clip (In point: 00:23:01;00, Out point: 00:23:05;00) on the first video track and the Adam – Interview Pt.# 1-2 (In point: 00:13:21;00, Out point: 00:13:25;00) above it in track V2.

2. **Double-click the top clip to load it into the Viewer.**

3. **Click the Motion tab to view the motion attributes.**

4. **Drag at the lower-right corner of the Motion tab to extend the window to the right.**

   The keyframe graph area appears.

5. **Press the Home key to take the playhead back to the first frame of your clip.**

6. **Type +20 to jump the playhead 20 frames forward.**

7. **Add a keyframe for the Scale and Center attributes.**

   You can do so by clicking on the center round buttons in the column marked Nav for both Scale and Center attributes. The buttons turns green. This indicates that the playhead is located above a keyframe.

8. **Type +20 and press the Enter key to jump the playhead 20 frames forward.**

9. **Highlight the Scale field, type 40, and press the Enter key on your keyboard.**

   The clip is scaled down to 40 percent of its original size. Notice a keyframe is automatically created at this position. Final Cut Pro will set a new keyframe for any property that already has at least one keyframe, whenever that property value is changed.

10. **In the X-axis field of the Center property, enter –204 (this is the first field in the Center attribute) and enter –127.27 in the Y-axis field of the Center attribute.**

    Be sure to press the Enter key to register your change. Your clip should now be 40 percent in size and in the upper-left corner of the Canvas.

11. **Jump forward in the Timeline by about 2 seconds.**

    You can do so by typing +200 and pressing the Enter key while in the Motion tab or the Timeline.

12. **Set additional keyframes for Scale and Center.**

    You are setting these keyframes manually, because you are not changing the values of the scale or position. By setting another keyframe with the same values as previously, the animation of these properties is frozen for the duration between these keyframes.

13. **Type +20 to jump forward by 20 frames and press the Enter key.**

14. **Change the Scale value back to 100 percent and enter 0 and 0 for the Center X- and Y-axis.**

    This action brings the image back to 100 percent and into the center of the Canvas.

You have just created a picture-in-picture effect. Adam's interview clip starts out at 100 percent and in the center of the Canvas. As he begins to speak, the clip scales down and moves up into a corner as he continues to talk about checking his bicycle, while underneath you see him working on his bike. At the end, the clip scales back to 100 percent and re-centers. The keyframe graph for this simple animation should look similar to Figure 17-11.

15. **Select the clip in the sequence and choose Sequence ➪ Render Selection ➪ Video.**

When the rendering is finished you can play the Timeline.

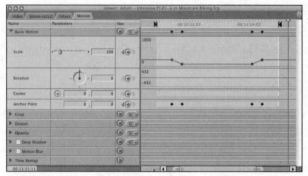

Figure 17-11: Keyframes are used to animate, scale, and move layers in a sequence.

Tip   You can move keyframes by clicking and dragging on them. Your pointer will turn into a crosshair, allowing you to drag the keyframe. To delete a keyframe, drag the keyframe off the graph using this crosshair. A small trashcan will appear next to the crosshair when you drag a keyframe away to delete it.

Working with keyframes

Keyframes are handy for a variety of reasons. With keyframes, you can animate any attribute, and the properties within that attribute. For example, for a Drop Shadow effect in the Motions tab you can animate the Offset, Angle, Color, Softness, and Opacity. When you consider that almost any of the properties under the Motion tab can be animated independently of any other property, and that each clip has its own Motion tab, you get some idea of just how powerful keyframing can be. When you add filters to your clips, the properties for the filters can also be animated using keyframes.

When working with keyframes, keep these tips in mind:

✦ You can adjust a line between two keyframes by placing your pointer on the line. Your pointer will turn into an Adjust Line Segment pointer as shown here.

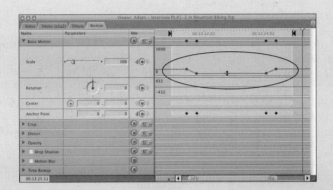

✦ You can delete all the keyframes for a parameter by clicking on the Reset button (shown here) for the corresponding property.

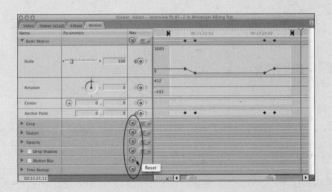

✦ You can Smooth a keyframe by Control+clicking on it and choosing Smooth from the contextual menu shown here. Click the Clear option to delete the keyframe.

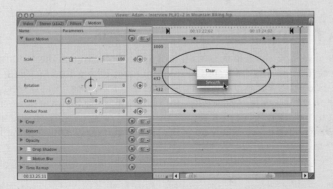

Continued

Continued

✦ When you Smooth a keyframe, the way values are interpolated from one keyframe to another changes. By default, all keyframes are added with a Linear interpolation, which causes sudden changes from keyframe to keyframe. Smoothing keyframes in the keyframe graph eases the rate at which values change going into and out of a keyframe. Bezier handles are added to smoothed keyframes. These handles, shown here, can be manipulated to control the velocity of the keyframes. Smoothing keyframes does not change the timing of the keyframes, but it does change the way items speed up and slow down when going from keyframe to keyframe.

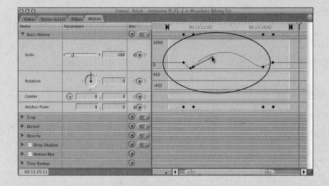

✦ If you hold down the Option key and move your pointer close to the overlay line of the parameter you want to adjust, the pointer will turn into a Pen tool. Click with this Pen Tool to add a keyframe.

✦ After a keyframe is added, the pointer over a keyframe turns to a crosshair that can be used to drag the keyframe up or down, move it along the animation line, adjust its value, or even drag it out of the keyframe graph area to delete the keyframe.

Editing motion properties in the Canvas

On the DVD-ROM

For the next exercise, you can use your own footage or you can use the Mountain Biking.fcp project. This project is located in the Mountain Biking Tutorial folder on the DVD-ROM. Copy this folder to your hard drive and then open the project by double-clicking on the Mountain Biking.fcp project file. For the following exercise, you can look at the Motion Properties sequence located in the Exercises folder of the Mountain Biking.fcp project. The Motion Properties sequence contains the finished version of this exercise.

In the previous section, you edited the motion properties of a clip by entering values in the Motion tab of the View window. You can also perform this type of manipulation and editing directly in the Canvas window. Note that in the next exercise, you are going to re-create exactly what you just did in the last exercise, except you're going to do it via an entirely different method. Arranging motion attributes in the Canvas window can be more intuitive and provides faster feedback for your layout. The following steps create a similar effect to the one produced in the last section, except this time you're using the Canvas. Follow these steps:

1. **Layer two clips in a sequence.**

   You can do this by editing the first clip into the sequence with an overwrite edit and then performing a superimpose edit with the second clip. For the example shown here, I am placing the Adam – Rear Algn clip (In point: 00:23:01;00, Out point: 00:23:05;00) on the first video track and the Adam – Interview Pt.# 1-2 (In point: 00:13:21;00 Out point: 00:13:25;00) above it in track V2.

2. **Press the Home key to return to the beginning of your sequence.**

3. **Type** +20 **and press the Enter key to jump the playhead 20 frames forward.**

4. **Select your top clip in the Timeline.**

   A turquoise border appears around your clip in the Canvas window. It is very important that this clip remain selected while you animate your settings in the Canvas window.

5. **Control+click the Add Keyframe button at the bottom right of the Canvas and choose Scale from the context menu shown in Figure 17-12.**

   This will add a keyframe for the Scale property to the Adam – Interview Pt.# 1-2 clip.

6. **Control+click the Add Keyframe button at the bottom right of the Canvas window and choose Center from it.**

   This action adds a keyframe for the Center (position) property to the Adam – Interview Pt.# 1-2 clip.

7. **Press Command+Shift+A in the Timeline window to deselect your clip. Type** +20 **and press the Enter key to jump the playhead 20 frames forward.**

   You deselected the clip because otherwise your clip (and not the playhead) will move by 20 frames.

8. **Now you are ready to scale your clip down.**

   Make sure that the clip is selected in the Timeline and choose Image+Wireframe from the View menu at the top of the Canvas window, as shown in Figure 17-13.

Figure 17-12: Control+click on the Add Keyframe button to bring up the choices of attributes shown here.

Figure 17-13: Select Image+Wireframe from the View Choices menu.

9. **Click on any corner of the Wireframe around the image and drag inward.**

   This action scales the image to your needs.

    Tip If you want to get precise feedback in numbers for values and changes, double-click the Adam – Interview Pt.# 1-2 clip from the Timeline into the View window and click the Motions tab to view the motions attributes. While you edit items in the Canvas window, you can see the properties and the numbers change in the Motions tab.

10. **Move the your clip to the upper-left side of the frame by simply dragging at the center of the clip in the Canvas.**

    During any of these operations, you should make sure that the Adam – Interview Pt.# 1-2 clip is selected in the Timeline. Otherwise, you will not see the Wireframe for the clip.

11. **Jump forward in the Timeline by about 2 seconds. You can do so by typing +200 and pressing the Enter key while in the Timeline.**

    Again, be sure that the clip is deselected in the Timeline before entering the timecode value. Otherwise, the clip (and not the playhead) will move by 2:00.

12. **Use the Control+click method you used in Steps 5 and 6 to add keyframes for both Scale and Center attributes.**

13. **Type +20, and press the Enter key to jump 20 frames forward.**

14. **Change the Scale value back to 100 percent by dragging at the corner of the image for your clip.**

    A keyframe for the Scale attribute is automatically added.

15. **Move the clip back to the center of the Canvas window by dragging it.**

    A keyframe for the Center attribute is automatically added.

    Tip To rotate a clip in the Canvas, place your pointer near a corner until you see the rotate cursor. Drag with this cursor to rotate a clip. To distort a clip, you can select the Distort tool in the Tools Palette and drag any corner to distort the shape of the image.

16. **Select the clip and choose Sequence ➪ Render Selection.**

    When the rendering is finished, you can play your Timeline.

You've just animated a clip entirely within the Canvas window. As you can see, this method is a bit less precise when it comes to setting values, but it works best if you do not care about the numbers and simply want to animate clips visually.

Tip   While using the Canvas to set motion keyframes, keep an eye on the colors of the wireframe outline in the Canvas window. When parked on a Scale keyframe, the crosshairs of the wireframe turn bright green. If you are parked on a Center keyframe, the center point for the wireframe will turn green. If you are parked on a rotation keyframe, the outer boundary of the wireframe will turn green. (The layer must not be selected to view this green frame.)

Working with Filters

Besides the basic motion settings described earlier in this chapter, Final Cut Pro also provides a variety of filters. Filters can be used to enhance clips, correct color and contrast, and apply special effects such as keying and blue-screening. Other filters add such diverse effects as Cylinder, Wave, and Blurs. Still other filters are designed to help you work with clip transparency. These transparency filters work with alpha channels, as well as color-based keying and effects.

You can add as many filters as you like to a clip. All filters have their own parameters, which you can animate using keyframes. The techniques for animating filters are very similar to the techniques used to animate motion attributes.

Filters are controlled using the Filters tab in the Viewer. Just like the Motion tab, you can drag the lower-right corner of the window to expose the keyframe graph area. Figure 17-14 shows the details of the Filters tab for a clip that has a few filters applied to it.

Cross-Reference   For a list of Filters available in Final Cut Pro, see Appendix C.

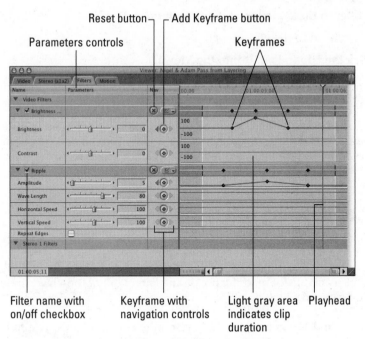

Figure 17-14: The Filters tab in the View window is where you control filters that are applied to clips.

Applying filters to a clip

Before you can adjust settings for a filter or animate it, you must apply a filter to a clip in a sequence. To apply a filter to a single clip:

1. **Drag any clip into a sequence.**
2. **Click the Effects tab in the Browser window.**
3. **Twirl down the small disclosure triangle next to the Video Filters bin.**

   This action displays all the subcategories of filters.

4. **Click open a triangle next to a subcategory bin and select a filter such as the Brightness and Contrast filter under the Image Control subcategory.**

5. **Drag this filter to the Timeline and a drop it on a clip.**

   The filter is applied to the clip.

6. **Double-click the clip to load it into the Viewer.**

7. **Click the Filters tab to view and change the filter settings.**

Tip

You can select multiple clips by holding down the Command key and clicking on multiple clips. To apply a filter to all the selected clips, choose Effects ➪ Video Filters and select a filter from the submenus that appear. You can also drag a filter into the View window with the Filters tab selected, and it will apply to the current clip in the Viewer.

Modifying or deleting filters

Filters can be modified in a variety of ways. You can turn individual filters on or off, delete them, and copy and paste them from one clip to another. To modify a filter, double-click on a clip to load it into the Viewer. If the clip has filters applied to it, these filters will be available for modification in the Filters tab of the View window. Modifications you can make include the following:

✦ **To turn individual filters on and off:** Click on the check box next to a filter's name (see Figure 17-15) in the Filters tab of the View window. This is handy because you can disable filters temporarily with this check box.

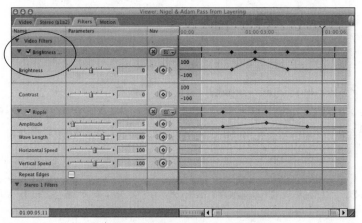

Figure 17-15: This check box disables individual filters.

✦ **To remove a filter from the Filters tab of the clip:** Select the filter in the Filters tab, by clicking on its name, under the Name column, and press Delete. You can also select the filter in the Filters tab and choose Edit ➪ Clear.

✦ **To cut or copy a filter:** Control+click on the name of a filter in the Filters tab and choose Cut or Copy from the contextual menu.

✦ **To paste a filter you have copied:** Double-click a clip to load it into the Viewer. Switch to the Filters tab and choose Edit ➪ Paste. The filter you copied earlier will be pasted into the new clip.

Creating a favorite filter

Saving a Filter as a favorite saves time and effort. You can modify and rename any filter and place it in the Favorites folder. This favorite filter will then be available to you through various means. To create and use a favorite filter:

✦ **To make any filter a favorite:** Drag the filter from the Filters tab of the Viewer to the Favorites bin in the Browser. You can also select a clip that has filters applied to it and choose Effects ➪ Make Favorite Effect.

✦ **To apply a favorite filter:** Drag your favorite filter from the Favorites bin in the Browser to any clip in the Timeline or the Viewer. You can also select a clip and choose Effects ➪ Favorites.

✦ **To delete a favorite filter:** Select it in the Favorites bin and press the Delete key.

Using third-party After Effects filters

Adobe After Effects is the premiere compositing application of our times. Period. After Effects has set the standard for 2-D (and since version 5.0, 3-D) compositing. This application has revolutionized the process of adding effects and, compositing and animating moving images for video production. Because After Effects is an industry standard for 2-D compositing, there is a large industry writing third-party plug-ins for After Effects. Many of these plug-ins are valuable and fun to use.

Final Cut Pro designers knew that it was going to be hard to ask users to choose Final Cut Pro over After Effects for compositing and multilayering. Rather than forcing people to make that choice, they designed Final Cut Pro to accommodate After Effects–style plug-ins. This is an impressive feature because After Effects plug-ins are by far the most popular in the effects and compositing industry. There are literally thousands of third-party plug-ins designed for After Effects. As more plug-ins are rewritten for After Effects running natively on OS X, many, if not most of these filters can be used with Final Cut Pro, too. To do so, simply copy the third-party After Effects filters into Final Cut Pro's Plugins folder. The Plugins folder is located in Library/Application Support/Final Cut Pro/Plugins. These plug-ins will become available in the Effects ⇨ Video Filters menu under a new submenu called AE Effects.

Tip

You can also make aliases of third-party After Effects filters and drop them into the Final Cut Pro Plugins folder.

There are a few precautions you should observe when working with After Effects filters in Final Cut Pro:

✦ **Increase your RAM allocation for Final Cut Pro.** Some After Effects filters can be memory hogs. Increase the RAM allocation for Final Cut Pro if you are using After Effects filters, and always close any applications that you don't absolutely need to keep Final Cut from activating virtual memory. The Golden Rule of buying as much RAM as you can afford is never more relevant than when you're working with effects filters.

Cross-Reference

See Chapter 4 for information on how to change RAM allocation for Final Cut Pro.

✦ **Not every After Effects plug-in will work in Final Cut Pro.** Some After Effects filters won't work with Final Cut Pro. (I know, I know. Nothing is perfect. But it's a start, right?) Oddly enough, you may have more issues with the standard After Effects plug-ins from Adobe than with some third-party plug-ins for After Effects. Some third-party After Effects filters are entire applications on their own with deep interfaces and a dizzying array of sliders and settings. Some of these third-party plug-ins cost more than After Effects itself. Don't expect all these third-party plug-ins to work in Final Cut Pro, especially the larger, more complicated ones. Test plug-ins first and if they give you problems, take them out of Final Cut Pro's Plugins folder.

✦ **Be aware of the difference in origin points.** In Final Cut Pro, the origin (X and Y coordinates) is assigned to the center of a clip. In After Effects all filters use the upper-left corner of the frame as the origin point. Take this into account when adjusting values for third-party After Effects filters in Final Cut Pro.

✦ **Watch out for color shifts.** Most After Effects filters work in the RGB color space. Final Cut Pro usually works in the YcrCb color space. You may see a shift in your color values.

Control settings: Tips for using filters

When working with filters you will encounter many different types of control settings. Some of these settings include:

✦ **Slider control:** Sliders are used to change the values of parameters. Drag the slider handle to change the value. By default, sliders show whole integer values. Press and hold down the Shift key while dragging a slider to change the values to within two decimal points of accuracy. You can also use the Command key while moving a slider to gear down the changes. A slider control is shown here.

Slider control

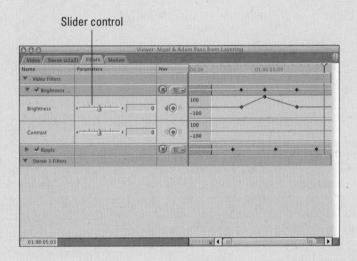

✦ **Point control:** Point controls are used to specify precise locations on a Canvas. Click the point control, which looks like a crosshair, and set a new point by clicking anywhere on the Canvas. A new point based on the X and the Y coordinates on the Canvas will be chosen. A point control is shown here.

Continued

Continued

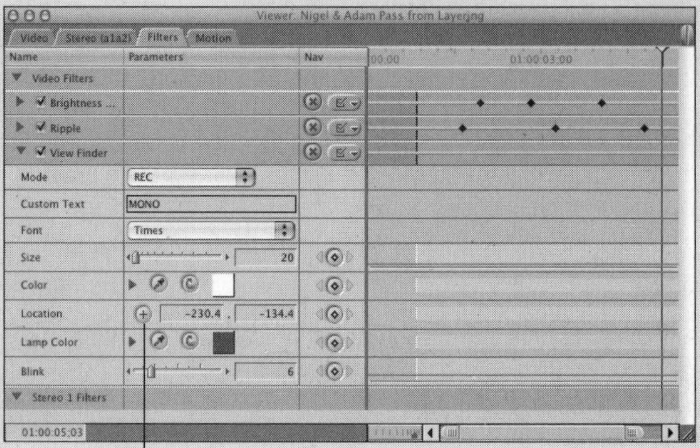

Point control

✦ **Angle control:** This control is used to change the angles and rotation of items. The longer black line in an angle control indicates the angle. The smaller red line indicates the total number of rotations. Holding down the Shift key while changing the angle control will result in constraining changes to 45-degree increments. Holding down the Command key while changing the angle control will gear down your mouse movements. An angle control is shown here.

Long black hand

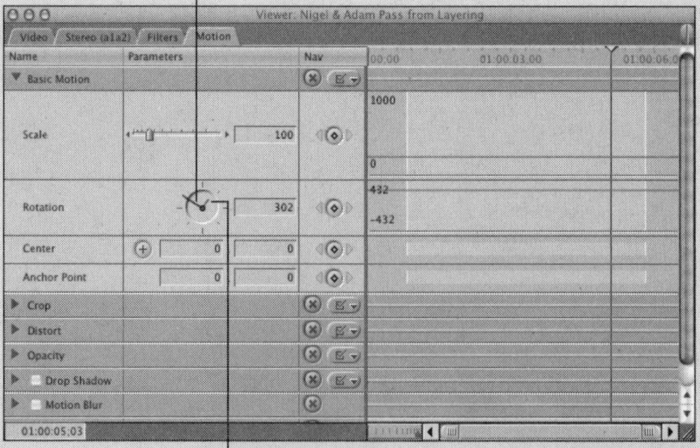

Short red hand

✦ **Color control:** Use this control to make color selections. A small disclosure triangle next to the color control opens up sliders and fields, allowing you to change the Hue, Saturation, and Brightness of a color. Hue determines the color. The Saturation slider determines how deep the color will be, and the Brightness slider changes the color to a lighter or darker shade. You can click the Eye Dropper button and click anywhere on the Canvas or the Viewer to select a color. You can also click on the small color swatch to get a standard color picker. A color control area is shown here.

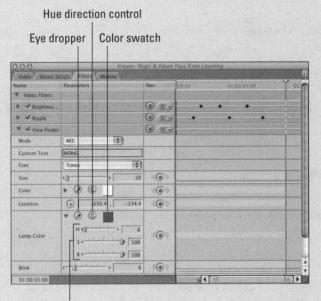

Hue direction control

Eye dropper   Color swatch

Hue, Brightness, and Saturation sliders

Continued

Continued

✦ **Clip control:** You can drag any clip or a still graphic into this area to affect the relevant attribute. The still graphic will be used for the filter property it is applied to. To clear the graphic, Control+click on the clip control area and choose Clear from the contextual menu. A clip control is shown here.

Clip control

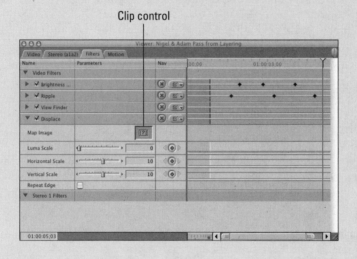

Working with Keyframes in the Timeline

Previous sections in this chapter have covered how to work with motion attributes and filters and how to adjust them in the View window. You have also learned how to work with motion attributes in the Canvas window. However, as always, the more you can accomplish right in the Timeline, the faster your work will be. Thankfully, Final Cut Pro allows you to adjust motion attributes and filters directly in the Timeline.

Viewing the Clips Keyframe area in the Timeline

In order to work with motion attributes and filters in the Timeline, you must first enable the option that lets you view the respective bars in the Timeline. To display the keyframe area in the Timeline, click the Clip Keyframes control in the bottom-left corner of the Timeline window, as shown in Figure 17-16.

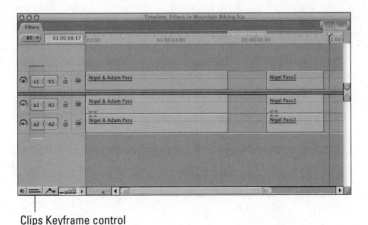

Clips Keyframe control

Figure 17-16: Click the Clip Keyframes control to turn on the Clip Keyframes area.

If a motion setting has been changed for a clip, a blue bar appears under that clip. If a filter has been added to a clip, a green bar will appear under that clip. If any keyframes have been added for motion or filters, these will be represented by small, diamond-shaped icons, which can be moved and modified directly in the Timeline. The Motion and Filter bars in the Clip Keyframes area are shown in Figure 17-17.

Video Filter Keyframe   Video Filter bar - green   Audio Filter Keyframe

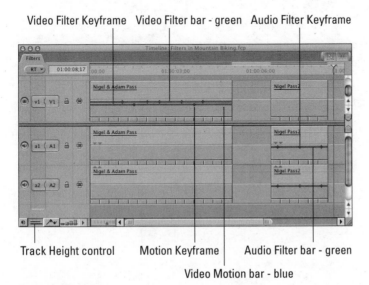

Track Height control   Motion Keyframe   Audio Filter bar - green

Video Motion bar - blue

Figure 17-17: With the Clip Keyframes control on, additional space is added under each audio and video track in the Timeline window.

In addition to the motion and filter bars, two more graphical indicators appear in the Clip Keyframes area. If you look just below the motion and filter bars, you'll see the Keyframe editor. This graph is identical to the keyframe graph found in the Viewer, with the exception of its ability to display only one keyframe property at a time. Although you can select from all parameters of the clip that are available for keyframing, this interface is best suited when only one or two parameter needs to be adjusted. You can add, subtract and modify keyframes as you would in the Motion or Filters tab keyframe graph. Working with the Keyframe editor is extremely useful if you need to reference your animation to other events in the Timeline, such as other clips in the sequence, or Timeline markers. To select which property of a clip to display in the Keyframe editor, Control+click anywhere in the Keyframe area to view the contextual menu of Filters or Motion properties available for this clip, as shown in Figure 17-18.

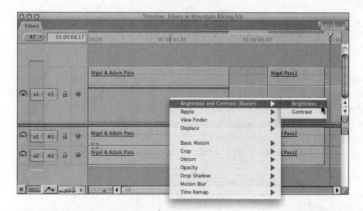

Figure 17-18: Selecting a property to view in the Keyframe editor by Contol+clicking anywhere in the Keyframe Editor space.

When you edit keyframes in the Keyframe editor, you will probably need more vertical size and resolution than the default size. You can resize the Keyframe editor graph height by clicking and dragging in the resize column in the header section of the Keyframe editor track, as shown in Figure 17-19.

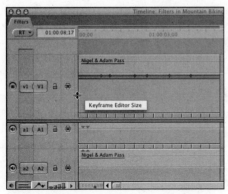

Figure 17-19: Resize the height of the Keyframe editor by dragging up or down in the Resize column in the header area of the track.

The last item that appears in the Clip Keyframes area is the Speed Indicator. The Speed Indicator is a series of vertical tic marks that represent the playback speed of a clip and is used for a quick and general assessment of the speed changes that have been applied to the clip. If the speed of a clip has been increased, the tic marks will appear closer to each other. If the clip speed has been slowed, then the tic marks will appear farther apart from one another. Normal, forward play of a clip shows black tic marks, while reverse play of the clip will display red tic marks in the Speed Indicator. You cannot modify any speed properties in the Speed Indicator.

If all four graphic indicators provided by the Clip Keyframes area are more than you need, Final Cut Pro enables you to select which display in the Clip Keyframes area you wish to view. Control+clicking on the Clip Keyframes toggle button will show you a contextual menu that allows you to toggle on or off each of the Clip Keyframes displays for both Video and Audio tracks. For example, you may want to see only the Motion bar and the Keyframe editor but neither the Filter bar nor the Speed Indicator. You also have the option to choose Select All (views), or Select None to show none of them when the Clip Keyframes area is toggled on. Figure 17-20 shows the contextual menu of the Clip Keyframes control button.

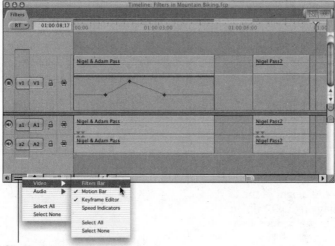

Clip Keyframes control

Figure 17-20: Control+click on Clip Keyframes control button to display a contextual menu for you to select the displays of the Clip Keyframes area that will appear below each track in the Timeline when Clip Keyframes is toggled on.

Viewing keyframes selectively for Motion and Filter bars

Though you can have more than one filter applied to a single clip, and have animated motion properties such as scale, opacity, position, and rotation, you can only view keyframes from a single property at a time on the Motion and Filter bars, and Keyframe editor. In order to modify any keyframes in the Clip Keyframes area, you must first select the property for which you want to view and modify the keyframes.

To selectively choose the property to view keyframes, Control+click on a Motion or Filter bar, or in any empty area in the Keyframe Editor area in the Timeline. From the contextual menu, choose the parameter you want to view. You can also choose Show All (keyframes), or select Hide All to hide all Motion or Filter keyframes. Equivalent controls for these contextual menus are also available in the Motion and Filters tabs. These equivalent controls are pop-up menus located next to the Reset button, and they work just like the contextual menus. Setting the control in one location will update the other. Figure 17-21 shows how the contextual menus appear for Motion and Filter bars, as well as the related pop-up menus.

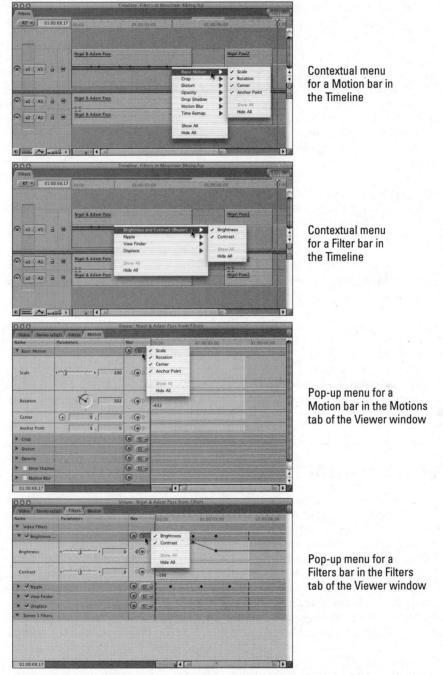

Contextual menu
for a Motion bar in
the Timeline

Contextual menu
for a Filter bar in
the Timeline

Pop-up menu for a
Motion bar in the Motions
tab of the Viewer window

Pop-up menu for a
Filters bar in the Filters
tab of the Viewer window

Figure 17-21: Control+click on a Motion or Filter bar to choose which parameter's keyframes you want to view in the Timeline. A pop-up menu, which performs the same function, is also found under the Motion or the Filter tab.

Tip   You can double-click a Filter or Motion bar to open a clip in the Viewer with the appropriate tab open. You can also double-click on individual keyframes to get the same results.

Modifying keyframes in the Timeline

Because you can only move the position of keyframes in the Motion and Filter bars, making changes to the keyframes is relatively easy to do. To move a keyframe in a Motion or Filter bar, place your pointer above a keyframe. The pointer will turn into a crosshair cursor. Drag the keyframe with the crosshair cursor to relocate it earlier or later in the Timeline.

Working with keyframes in the Keyframe Editor is the same as working in the keyframe graph of the Motion or Filters tab in the Viewer window. You can use the Pen and Arrow selection tool to make, delete, move, and change the values of either the motion or filter parameters of a clip.

Tip   When working with keyframes and levels in the Keyframe Editor, for finer control, press the Command key while you drag to "gear down" the increments of the value you are adjusting.

My only problem with this interface is not being able to see *which* property is currently displayed in the Keyframe Editor. In order to find out which property is showing in the Timeline, you have to Control+click in the Keyframe Editor and scroll through each property listed in the contextual menu to see which property is selected, indicated by a check mark in front of its name. Still, for simple and quick adjustments, this feature works extremely well. Any tool that can help you work faster, even in limited applications, is always an added advantage for editors.

Using Time Remapping

Time remapping is the application of variable speed change to a clip. To do this, a frame in a clip—called the *source frame*—is moved earlier or later within itself, while holding the frames at the In and Out point. Because the duration of a clip is not changed with time remapping, the frames before the relocated source frame will play faster, while those frames after the source frame will conversely play slower (or vice versa, depending on the direction in which you moved the source frame). This "rubber band effect" gives the illusion of time speeding up or slowing down seamlessly within the same clip. Although applying time remapping is not difficult, understanding and predicting the end results of this powerful and complex effect can be as abstract as the concept of time itself and is best explained by example.

Using the Time Remap tool

The Time Remap tool can be used only in the Timeline on sequence clips. It can be selected in the Tool palette, located with the Slip and Slide tool, shown in Figure 17-22. Alternatively, you can use the keyboard shortcut of pressing the S key three times (SSS).

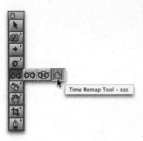

Figure 17-22: The Time Remap tool is located in the Tool palette with the Slip and Slide tools.

There are two ways to use the Time Remap tool.

✦ Move the source frame from another time location in the clip to the playhead position.

✦ Drag a selected source frame to a new position in the clip.

On the DVD-ROM

For the following exercise, I use the Mountain Biking.fcp project. This project is located in the Mountain Biking Tutorial folder on the DVD-ROM. Copy this folder to your hard drive and then open the project by double-clicking on the Mountain Biking.fcp project file. In the Browser, open the folder named Exercise, and double-click on the Sequence named Time Remap. The sequence contains one clip that is a simple animation of a circle moving across the frame from left to right. Also on this clip is a timecode burn-in that runs for the duration of the clip, from 00:00:00:00 to 00:00:04:29, totaling a time of 5 seconds. Play it through to see the normal speed of the clip and rolling timecode.

Moving the source frame from another time

This is the default behavior of the Time Remap tool. The main aspect to remember about this method is that you will select *another frame* in the clip as the source frame and move it to the current playhead position. The speed of all frames before and after the new source frame will be varied accordingly, or "remapped," in order to keep the same In and Out frames of the clip.

1. **Open the Time Remap sequence located in the Exercise folder in the Mountain Biking.fcp project, if you haven't already.**

   You will see a sequence with a video clip — TimeRemapTC.mov — already in the Timeline, as shown in Figure 17-23. You will see the Motion bar, a time graph in the Keyframe Editor, and the Speed indicator all displayed to help better see the effects of Time Remapping.

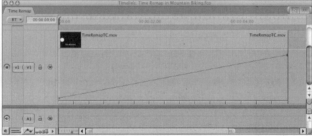

Figure 17-23: The clip in the Time Remap sequence shows a simple animation of a circle moving across the frame with timecode burn-in.

2. **Move the Timeline playhead to 2:00.**

   Although you can simply scrub on the Timeline ruler to get to 2:00, another way is to enter 200 in the Current Timecode field in either the Timeline or Canvas and press Enter.

3. **With the Time Remap tool selected, click on the sequence clip at the playhead's position and drag right or left to locate the new source frame.**

   As you scrub with the Time Remap tool, the canvas will display the frames that you can select as the source frame. Also, a Tool Tip information box appears over the Time Remap tool, displaying dynamic timecode data about the current position of the Timeline playhead, the position of the original source frame, the current position of the new source frame, and the speed changes of the frames before the current source frame ("Speed Left") and after ("Speed Right"). Figure 17-24 shows the information box that appears over the Time Remap tool.

Tip

As you drag with the Time Remap tool, a dark outline representing the total number of frames of the clip will appear, showing you where the current source frame is located in the original clip.

Figure 17-24: As you drag with the Time Remap tool, a tool tip information box is displayed with real-time information.

4. **While still holding down the mouse, drag the Time Remap tool to the right, until you see the frame mark with Timecode 4:00 in the Canvas window.**

5. **Release the mouse to select this as the new source frame.**

Note that the source frame originally at 4:00 is now located at the Timeline playhead position at 2:00. Note the difference between the timecode of the source frame burn-in with the timecode location of the clip in the Timeline. Figure 17-25 shows the Canvas and Timeline after a new source frame is selected.

Figure 17-25: These are the results of Time Remapping.

Tip

For more precise control when dragging, press down and hold the Command key while dragging to "gear down" movement to smaller increments. To constrain time adjustments to 10 percent increments when using the Time Remap tool, hold down the Shift key *after* you begin dragging.

Now, play the clip from the beginning and you will see the circle image travel across the screen faster than normal for the first 2 seconds, then play slower than normal speed for the remainder of the clip. This is the result of remapping the source frame originally at 4:00 to the Timeline position at 2:00. Time remapping has forced all the frames before the source frame to play quicker, in order to get to the 4:00 frame in just 2 seconds, and then play the rest of the frames (one second's worth) over the remaining 3 seconds of the clip. Pretty cool, no? You will also notice changes to the Keyframe Editor graph after time remapping in the preceding exercise. The graph in the Keyframe Editor will now display a fairly quick rise in the Time Graph up to the keyframe at 2:00 in the Timeline, and then a slower rise from the source frame keyframe to the end of the clip. (If you don't see the time graph, enable it by Control+clicking anywhere in the Keyframe Editor and selecting Time Remap ⇨ Time Graph from the contextual menu.) Interpreting time graphs is covered in more detail later, but for now, you should know that the steeper the rise of a time graph section, the faster the speed of the frames between the keyframes. Conversely, the flatter the rise of a time graph section, the slower the frames will play.

Tip   You can resize the height of the Keyframe Editor area by dragging in the Resize column on the left edge of track.

The Speed Indicator tics show a correspondence between the speed of the frames and spacing of the tic marks. Frames with faster speeds display tic marks closer to one another, while a slower speed of frames will display tic marks farther apart.

Dragging the source frame to another position

This method of time remapping requires the use of the Option modifier key with the Time Remap tool. Unlike the previous method of time remapping in which you scrubbed through the clip to find a new source frame, with this method you select the source frame first, and then drag it to a different point of time in the sequence clip. Of course, the speed of all frames before and after the new source frame will be remapped in order to keep the same In and Out frames of the clip.

In this next exercise, you will use the same setup and source frame as in the previous exercise to contrast the different results by using this method.

1. **Open the Time Remap sequence located in the Exercise folder in the Mountain Biking.fcp project.**

   If you have the sequence opened from the previous exercise, simply undo all modifications by pressing Command+Z repeatedly until there are no keyframes on the time graph in the Keyframe Editor.

2. **Move the Timeline playhead to 2:00.**

   You can scrub on the Timeline ruler to get to 2:00, or simply enter 200 in the Current Timecode field in either the Timeline or Canvas and press Enter.

3. **With the Time Remap tool selected, Option+click on the sequence clip and drag right or left to relocate the source frame.**

   As you drag with the Time Remap tool, a dark outline representing the total amount of frames in the clip will move left or right, showing you where the source frame located in the original clip will be mapped to in the sequence clip. Also, the Tool Tip information box appears over the Time Remap tool, displaying dynamic timecode data about the current position of the Timeline playhead, the position of the original source frame, the current position of the new source frame, and the speed changes of the frames before the current source frame ("Speed Left") and after the current source frame ("Speed Right"). Figure 17-26 shows the Time Remap tool used with the Option key to drag the source frame to a new position.

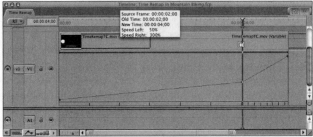

Figure 17-26: Use the Time Remap tool with the Option key to drag a source frame to a new position.

4. **While still holding down the mouse, you don't need to keep the Option key pressed after you start dragging, so just drag the Time Remap tool right until the playhead is located at 4:00 in the Timeline.**

5. **Release the mouse to relocate the source frame to this Timeline position.**

Note that the source frame originally at 2:00 is now located in the Timeline at the playhead position at 4:00. This is evident from the source frame now displayed in the Canvas window. Figure 17-27 shows the Canvas and Timeline after a source frame has been moved.

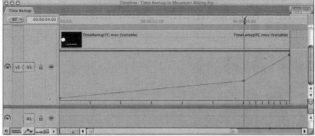

Figure 17-27: Results of Time Remap with Option key to drag a source frame to another position.

Tip

For more precise control of movement when dragging, press down and hold the Command key while dragging to "gear down" movement to smaller increments. To constrain time adjustments to 10 percent increments when using the Time Remap tool, hold down the Shift key *after* you begin dragging.

Now when you play the clip from the beginning, you will see the circle move *slower* than normal for the first 4 seconds, then play faster than normal speed for the remainder of the clip. The reason for this is the result of remapping the source frame of 2:00 to the new Timeline position at 4:00. Time remapping has forced all the frames before the source frame to play slower in order spread 2 seconds of frames (30 of them) over 4 seconds of time, and then play the rest of the frames after the source frame, 3 seconds' worth, faster over the remaining 1 second of the clip. You can see the result is the opposite of the first method used in the previous exercise.

Understanding time graphs

Although using the Time Remap tool is a quick and easy way to apply variable time speed, you can also time remap on the time graph of the Keyframe Editor in the Timeline, or on the Motion tab of the Viewer window. More importantly, working on a time graph is the only way to modify keyframe velocity, easing the speed of change from one keyframe to the next. This is accomplished using smoothed keyframes with Bezier handles.

Before we can modify time graphs, lets take a quick look at interpreting them. The following examples are time graphs as seen in the Motion tab of the Viewer window taken of clips with speed adjustments, In the time graphs, the vertical axis of the graph represents the frames of a source clip, while the horizontal axis represents the playback frames in a Timeline.

  ✦ **Linear:** A straight diagonal line means one frame of the source clip is played for one frame in the Timeline. This is real-time playback. The time graph for this is shown in Figure 17-28.

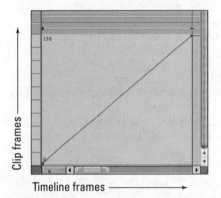

Figure 17-28: Time graph of linear speed of a clip that will play back normal speed in real time.

  ✦ **Slow motion:** A flatter line means one frame of the source clip is played for the duration of more than one frame in the Timeline. A time graph for this is shown in Figure 17-29.

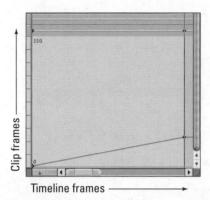

Figure 17-29: Time graph of slow motion speed of a clip that will playback slower than normal.

✦ **Fast motion:** A steeper line means more than one frame of the source clip is played for one frame in the Timeline. A time graph for this is shown in Figure 17-30.

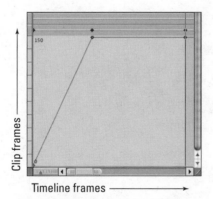

Figure 17-30: Time graph of fast motion speed of a clip that will play back faster than normal.

✦ **Freeze frame:** A flat line indicates no motion forward or backward. This is a freeze-frame time graph, shown in Figure 17-31.

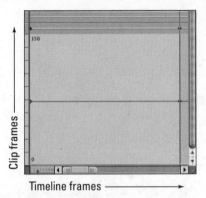

Figure 17-31: Time graph of a freeze frame clip that will play back a single frame.

✦ **Reverse speed:** A time graph line that angles downward represents frames of the source clip played in reverse order in the Timeline, at a rate represented by the slope of the line. A time graph for this is shown in Figure 17-32.

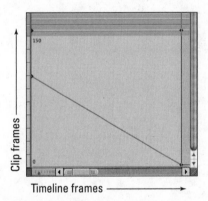

Figure 17-32: Time graph of reverse motion speed of a clip that will play backward at a speed indicated by the slope of the line.

✦ **Acceleration/deceleration:** The ability to accelerate or decelerate the velocity of a speed change of a clip is represented as curved lines in a time graph. A time graph for this is shown in Figure 17-33.

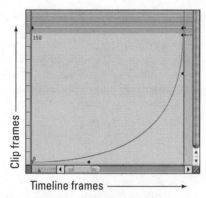

Clip frames

Timeline frames ⟶

Figure 17-33: Time graph of an accelerated or decelerated speed that will play back faster or slower as it approaches another speed change.

From this we can begin to read the time graph of a clip with variable speed changes. In Figure 17-34, you can see from the time graph in the Keyframe Editor that the clip starts in slow motion, accelerates quickly, then freezes on screen before ending in reverse play.

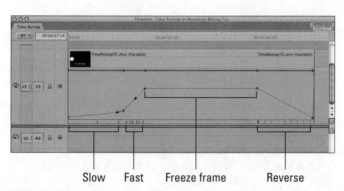

Slow   Fast   Freeze frame   Reverse

Figure 17-34: The time graph of this clip, shown in the Timeline Keyframes Editor, indicates multiple speed changes have been applied.

You can modify keyframes in a time graph of the Keyframe Editor and Motion bar just as you would any other motion or effect. However, there is a big caveat: Moving the position of a time remap keyframe actually moves the position of the *source frame.* In order to change the source frame once it has been selected, you will need to delete it from the time graph (Control+click on the keyframe and select Clear from the contextual menu) before reselecting a new one with the Time Remap tool (or by adding new keyframes in the time graph).

Working with Time Remapping in the Motion tab

For more control, you can also edit Time Remapping in the Motion tab of the Viewer. In addition to the large time graph where you can add, delete, move, and smooth keyframes as you would with any motion or effect keyframe graph, the Motion tab also provides Time Remap input controls and many useful indicators that are always at hand, displaying real-time data as you work in the time graph. The Time Remap properties and time graph in the Motion tab are shown in Figure 17-35.

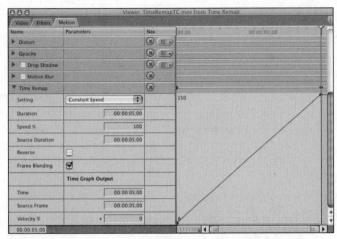

Figure 17-35: Time Remap properties and time graph in the Motion tab of the Viewer are a good workspace for fine-tuning the time graph.

Working with the Time Remap parameters in the Motion tab can be perplexing at first because many of the properties are not modifiable—although they appear as entry data fields, most of the timecode fields are merely indicators that provide real-time data about the current source frame under the playhead. You can click into any of these fields, which will highlight the timecode data, but nothing will happen except a system beep when you try to enter a different timecode. Of the timecode fields, only Duration (this is the sequence clip duration, not the Source Duration) will accept modification. The parameters of Time Remap in the Motion tab are:

✦ **Setting:** This pop-up menu enables you to select between constant and variable speed. This option is dimmed and unavailable for all but sequence clips.

✦ **Duration:** This is the total time of the sequence clip between In and Out points, accounting for any constant speed changes. This is the only timecode field in Time Remap that you can modify.

✦ **Speed %:** The speed percentage at which the clip will play back if a constant speed change is applied. If the clip has variable speed changes, the word *Variable* is displayed in this field.

✦ **Source Duration:** This is the total duration of the clip including unused media before and after the In and Out points.

✦ **Reverse:** If selected, the clip will play backward.

✦ **Frame Blending:** When selected, frame blending is enabled to create interpolation frames for slow motion.

✦ **Time:** Timecode of the current playhead position.

✦ **Source Frame:** This is the original timecode of the clip mapped to the current position.

✦ **Velocity %:** This field indicates the rate of speed change from one keyframe to the next when Bezier smoothing is applied to variable speed clips.

Tip

You can save Time Remap effects by highlighting the clip with your modifications, then choose Effect ➪ Make Favorite Motion, or press Control+F. The motion effect will be added to the Motion Favorites in the Effects menu, but I've found it more reliable to drag my favorite motion effects on to a clip directly from the Favorites bin in the Browser.

Viewing the Sequence in the QuickView Tab

Often you will want to preview your hard-earned motion compositing and effects work before you render the entire effect. For this you can use the QuickView tab in the Tool Bench window. The QuickView uses frames cached in memory, making it a very fast way to preview complex compositing and effects without the need to render to your hard disk drive first. Another advantage of previewing with the QuickView tab is that you don't have to resize the Canvas window to preview the complete frame size of the composition when you are zoomed in to work on a motion path. Figure 17-36 shows the QuickView tab.

Note

The QuickView tab is only for previewing a part of your sequence and does not affect rendering or final output. You cannot drop clips on it, nor can you edit with this window.

Resolution pop-up menu   View pop-up menu

Play button   Range slider   Playhead in
                             Scrubber bar

Figure 17-36: The QuickView tab in the Tool Bench
window is a fast way to preview compositing and effects
of our Sequence.

The parts and controls of the QuickView tab are:

✦ **Resolution pop-up menu:** This setting is for selecting the display resolution of
the QuickView preview only — it does not affect rendering or output of the
Sequence. Choosing lower resolutions will enable faster playback and allow a
greater number of frames in the Timeline to be cached into RAM.

✦ **View pop-up menu:** This pop-up menu lets you choose the window to cache
video from.

• **Auto:** With this option selected, QuickView caches video from the
Viewer or the Canvas, whichever window is currently active.

• **Viewer or Canvas:** QuickView caches video from the window selected
here.

• **None:** This disables the QuickView window. No playback if viewed.

✦ **Play button:** Click to start playback in the QuickView window. You can also press the spacebar to start and stop.

✦ **Range slider:** Set this slider to define the duration of your sequence that will be cached by QuickView, from 2 to 10 seconds.

Note

If both In and Out points are set in the Timeline, the range slider doesn't appear.

✦ **Scrubber bar area:** The scrubber bar and playhead operate the same as in the Viewer and Canvas. In the QuickView window, the width of the scrubber bar represents the total duration of video that is to be cached. You can drag the playback indicator to navigate within this cached duration.

Because QuickView is based on frames cached to RAM, the amount of RAM allocated to Final Cut Pro can impact the amount of frames QuickView can play back. The desired amount of QuickView playback time is settable with the Range Slider, but the selection of the frames that will be cached is determined by the Timeline In and Out points.

✦ **If In and Out points are set in the Timeline,** Final Cut Pro will use frames in this selection for QuickView playback.

✦ **If an In point is set in the Timeline, but no Out point is set,** Final Cut Pro caches frames from the In point through the duration set in the Range Slider for playback in the QuickView tab.

✦ **If neither an In nor an Out point is set in the Timeline,** Final Cut Pro will use the position of the playhead and cache half the duration set in the Range Slider before the playhead and the other half from after the playhead position for QuickView playback.

As the frames are being cached into RAM, you will see them play back in the QuickView tab. However, when the duration set in the QuickView tab has been reached, the playback will loop back and play again, this time much faster as it is already cached.

✦   ✦   ✦

Rendering in Final Cut Pro

Users of nonlinear editing applications like Final Cut Pro can be divided into two basic groups. The first group consists of users who just want to edit and couldn't care less about what goes on "behind the scenes" of the editing application. These users are perfectly content to work in Final Cut Pro's many editing windows, rarely venturing to the Macintosh Finder to poke around and find out what's going on "behind" the application. There is nothing wrong with that. The application serves their needs and they are happy.

The second group of users wants to know *everything* about the operations of the application. I place myself in this second group.

I believe that it never hurts to know how an application manages itself behind the scenes. This knowledge is useful for two reasons. First, knowledge can bring insight to problem solving when trouble strikes. It may be that you never venture behind the scenes of Final Cut Pro to investigate how media and render cache files are managed. Similarly, if you've followed the Final Cut Pro manual's advice but found yourself in trouble, then you will have a difficult time troubleshooting problems you encounter. Final Cut Pro is not a magic application. Depending on the complexity of your projects and your daily editing needs, you might find that understanding the details of Final Cut Pro's behavior will one day save you from massive headaches.

Rendering is one of the most important topics to understand when working with digital nonlinear editing in general, and Final Cut Pro in particular. Managing render files is done using the Render Manager in Final Cut Pro. Final Cut Pro also has many rendering options that are often misunderstood by users. This chapter explains rendering and clears up some of the myths surrounding this subject. It also takes you behind the scenes of how Final Cut Pro manages and organizes its render files.

Rendering Content

Anything that Final Cut Pro cannot play in real time needs to be rendered. Rendering is the process whereby Final Cut Pro combines the video or audio portion of your clips with any transitions and effects applied to them to generate a *render cache file*. Final Cut Pro plays this render cache file back during the transition or effect that is applied to a sequence.

For example, suppose you have a Dissolve transition applied between Clip A and Clip B. The render cache file contains only the dissolve frames between Clip A and Clip B. While playing Clip A, the source media file for Clip A is played. However, when the playhead reaches the rendered transition, the render cache file for the transition is played. When the playhead gets to the end of the dissolve, the source media file for Clip B starts to play.

Final Cut Pro 4's new RT Extreme is a software-based architecture that can play and output many effects and transitions *without* rendering, at various quality levels that you select. The number of simultaneous effects that can be played in real time is determined by many factors, primarily your system's speed, the settings you've selected in a Timeline's Render Control tab, the quality of playback selected in the RT pop-up menu in the Timeline patch panel, and the complexity of each effect. In addition, there are third-party capture cards that provide hardware-based, real-time effects of some, but not all, effects. The reality of rendering at least some effects is as inevitable as taxes and growing old.

Managing render cache files

When you capture clips from tape into Final Cut Pro, the clips in the Browser are actually just links to the source media files that are stored on the scratch disk. Without these source media files, the clips become offline and cannot be played.

Render cache files created during the rendering process are another kind of source media file. Transitions and effects indicators in the Timeline are links to the render cache files, just as clips are links to source media files. Without these render cache files, you cannot play back your effects, transitions, or motion animations that you have created. Render cache files take a long time to produce—a complex sequence and its effects can take many hours to render. Losing your render cache files can mean many hours of lost work. You must carefully manage render cache files to ensure you don't lose valuable time and work.

Setting a storage location for render cache files

You can specify the disk location for your render cache files on the Scratch Disk tab of the Preferences dialog box. Choose Edit ➪ Preferences and click on the Scratch Disk tab to set your render scratch location.

Cross-Reference For more information on setting scratch disk preferences, see Chapter 6.

If you run out of disk space while rendering, a dialog box appears that allows you to delete unneeded render files. This helps you clear space for new render cache files, but use caution when deleting other render files to ensure you don't create more work for yourself later on.

Locating render files for a project

When you specify a disk as a scratch disk, Final Cut Pro creates scratch folders on that disk. These scratch folders are named Audio Render Files, Capture Scratch, Render Files, Thumbnail Cache, and Waveform Cache. Inside the Capture Scratch and Render Files folders, Final Cut Pro creates a folder for each one of your projects. This is where relevant files are stored. Final Cut Pro automatically generates names for render cache files and targets them to the proper folder as you switch between projects. The sequence's name is used as the first part of the render cache folder's name. Figure 18-1 shows the Render Files folder for the My Backyard.fcp project. Render files can multiply very quickly, and tracking them can be important for storage reasons and for troubleshooting.

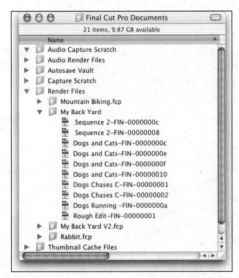

Figure 18-1: Final Cut Pro creates folders for each project within the Render Files folder.

Cross-Reference For more information on scratch disk behavior, see Chapter 12.

Understanding render-file behavior

As you work and make changes to rendered effects, transitions, layers, and animations, the render files for those items are no longer valid. For example, if you render a dissolve and then change its duration, the render cache file for the dissolve is no longer valid. The dissolve must be re-rendered because of your change. When you do render it again, the old invalid render file is deleted when the project is saved again, or when the change (back to the first render file being valid) falls off the undo queue, whichever comes later.

Given the relatively automated behavior of render cache files, it may seem like there's no reason to know more details about the render cache files themselves. However, keeping track of your render files makes media management easier, and you learn much more about what goes on behind the scenes with Final Cut Pro. This knowledge is especially useful as you troubleshoot projects in Final Cut Pro.

One of the most confusing aspects of render-file management is the file-naming scheme. The filenames can look cryptic, but they can tell you a lot about the render file. You can also learn a lot about your render files by viewing them a certain way. Here are a few tips to help you better manage your render files:

✦ **View render files by date.** A common technique for tracking render cache files is to view the Render Files folder in the Finder by the List view (View ➪ As List) and then by date. Open the Render Files folder for a project in the Macintosh Finder (the Render Files folder can be found on your Final Cut Pro scratch disk). Now, sort the folder by date by clicking on the Date Modified column (or choose View ➪ Sort List ➪ By Date Modified in the Finder). The most recent render files appear at the top, as shown in Figure 18-2.

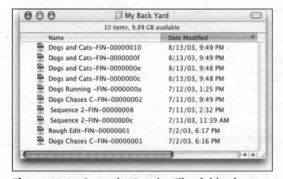

Figure 18-2: Open the Render Files folder for a project and view it by date in the Finder to see which render files are newer.

✦ **Use QuickTime Player to view render files.** Render files can be hard to identify in a Finder list. You can drag and drop any render cache file onto the QuickTime Player, as shown in Figure 18-3. The QuickTime Player opens the file and plays it just like any movie file. By viewing this file, you may be able to determine whether it is a file you want to save.

Tip

To make QuickTime Player easier to reach, keep an alias for the QuickTime Player on your Desktop. The QuickTime Player is usually found on your main system's drive in the Applications folder. To create an alias, select it and choose File ➪ Make Alias or press Command+L. Don't forget to drag the new alias to your desktop! Or using the Dock, simply drag the QuickTime player onto the dock and it will be there whenever you need it.

Figure 18-3: Drag and drop a render cache file on the QuickTime Player to view it.

Rendering indicators

Final Cut Pro has a few ways to warn you when an item in the Timeline needs to be rendered. Some of the indications are quite subtle, while others bring your work to a screeching halt. Rendering indicators in Final Cut Pro include the following:

✦ **Render Status Bar:** The Render Status Bar is the area just above the timecode ruler in the Timeline and it uses color-coded bars to indicate the render status of clips directly below in the Timeline. For example, when you apply a non-real-time transition to an edit in the Timeline, you see a red line in the Render Status Bar. This indicates that the transition needs to be rendered before it can be played back. The top part of the bar indicates the render status for the video portions of a clip, while the bottom portion shows the render status for the audio tracks of a clip. This is shown in Figure 18-4.

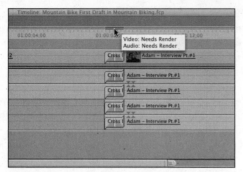

Figure 18-4: Hovering your cursor over the
Render Status Bar in the Timeline will display
a tool tip info box for the upper video render
bar and the lower audio render bar.

Most of the color indications of the Render Status Bar are also used in the
Render commands submenus to select corresponding render states in the
Timeline to render, and include the following:

- **Light gray:** There is no clip under the Render Bar.

- **Dark gray:** The clip does not need to be rendered.

- **Steel or purplish gray:** Effects or transitions that needed to be rendered
  have been rendered.

- **Dark Green:** This indicates a transition or an effect that can be played
  and output to video at high quality in real time without being rendered.

- **Medium Green:** This indicates a transition or an effect that can be
  played in real time on the computer. When played back on a third-party
  real-time card or output over FireWire on a fast enough computer, a
  lower quality playback of motion effects and scaling is displayed.

- **Yellow:** This indicates an effect or transition that will display an approximation of the effect during real-time playback. Some filter controls might
  be ignored in order to play this effect or transition in real-time. You can
  preview the effect, but it must be rendered before you output it to tape
  at full resolution. The final effect is visible when play is stopped or when
  scrubbing.

- **Dark Yellow:** This indicates an effect or transition has been rendered at a lower quality than the settings in the Render Control tab of the Sequence settings. These render files are preserved even if Render Controls are changed back to 100%.

- **Orange:** This indicates an effect or transition that exceeds the real-time playback capabilities of your computer system, but is enabled to play anyway because Unlimited RT is selected in the Real-Time Effects (RT) pop-up menu in the Timeline. Unlimited RT allows you to play more effects and transitions than your computer is capable of at the expense of possible dropped frames during playback.

- **Blue:** This indicates an effect or transition that is an unsupported real-time-enabled filter that might drop frames during playback.

- **Red:** An effect or transition needs to be rendered before playback is possible at selected quality.

Caution

If a clip is simply edited into a sequence without any transitions or effects and the red line appears in the Render Status Bar for the duration of the clip, it generally means that there's a conflict between the clip's capture settings and the sequence settings. This conflict must be resolved. For more on resolving conflicts between a clip's capture settings and a sequence's settings, see Chapter 10.

✦ **"Unrendered" message in the Viewer or the Canvas window:** When you attempt to play an unrendered item in the Timeline, you will see in the Canvas window a blue background with the word *Unrendered.* This indicates that the item needs rendering and cannot be played back in real time. If you have the Play Base Layer When Needs Rendering option enabled in the Real-Time Effect (RT) pop-up menu in the Timeline, the base video layer will play without any transitions or effects and this warning does not appear.

✦ **Audible beep while playing in the Viewer or Canvas:** Audio needs rendering before real-time playback can be achieved.

Setting Render controls

Final Cut Pro allows you to customize and save render options using the Render Control window, shown in Figure 18-5. Here you can select or deselect processor-intensive effects, thus speeding up your workflow. The options selected in the Render Control tab affect real-time playback, rendering, video and QuickTime output.

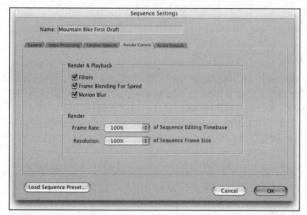

Figure 18-5: The Render Control tab window is identical in both the Sequence Settings and User Preferences windows but affects different sequences.

You can set render options for all new sequences or just the currently selected sequence:

✦ To set Render Control options for all new sequences:

   1. Choose Final Cut Pro ⇨ User Preferences.

   2. Click on the Render Control tab.

   3. Make your selections and then click OK.

✦ To set Render Control options to an existing sequence only:

   1. Select the sequence in the Browser or the Timeline.

   2. Select Sequence ⇨ Settings, or press Command+0 (zero).

   3. Click on the Render Control tab.

   4. Make your selections and then click OK.

The Render Control window is identical in both the User Preferences and the Sequence Settings windows, so be sure you are making selections with regard to the correct settings. The settings in the Render Control window are:

✦ **Filters:** Check this box to allow filters to be processed when rendering or during playback. If this option is not selected, all unrendered filters are ignored.

✦ **Frame Blending for Speed:** Check this box to enable frame blending for rendering or playback. This setting works with clips that have speed modifications applied to them.

✦ **Motion Blur:** Check this option to enable motion blur for rendering or playback.

✦ **Frame Rate:** Use this pop-up menu to select a lower frame rate of rendered effects. Lower frame rates can greatly reduce rendering time, the trade-off being lower playback quality. The setting for this control is a percentage of the Timeline frame rate. For example, setting 50% in a DV NTSC Timeline will play back effects rendered at 15 frames per second.

✦ **Resolution:** Use this pop-up menu to select a lower resolution of rendered effects. Lower resolution can greatly reduce rendering time, the trade-off being lower playback quality. The setting for this control is a percentage of the Sequence frame size. For example, setting 50% in a DV NTSC Sequence of 720 × 480 will play back effects rendered at 360 × 240, interlaced. When the rendered effect is played back, they are still displayed full frame, but at the reduced resolution that will appear less sharp and non-interlaced. At a lower-resolution percentage, Final Cut Pro has to process fewer pixels and thus rendering is faster. The resolution is set as a percentage of the current frame size of the sequence.

Caution

I strongly recommend that the two settings in the Render Control tab never be changed from their default values of 100 percent as these settings affect the final video output of *all* rendered items *including real-time effects.*

Understanding sequence render commands

Working with Final Cut Pro's rendering commands and options can be daunting, if not outright confusing at times. To be fair, the many render options do afford you more control over one of the most time-consuming, processor-intensive operations you'll perform in Final Cut Pro, so unraveling the mysteries of rendering can ultimately translate into real workflow savings.

Rendering with the Render command

When you need to render effects in your Timeline, you'll need to decipher the three Render menus and their submenu commands and selections, available under the Sequence menu. The first command you can select is the Render command, shown in Figure 18-6. If you have selected individual clips, or defined a region of the Timeline using In and Out points, the render commands will operate only on these clips. If no selection is made, the entire Timeline is rendered.

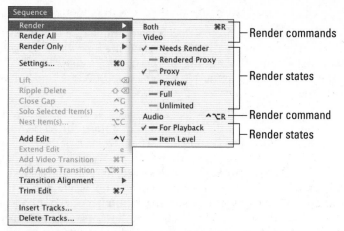

Figure 18-6: The Render command and its submenu offer many option combinations.

The first thing to clarify in the Render submenu is the difference between the render commands and the selectable render states. The menu choices of Both, Video, and Audio are actual render commands that will render the items with the selected render states in your Timeline when selected. The render states listed below Video and Audio render commands can be selected or deselected, but *do not* invoke any rendering in your Timeline. Selecting a render state in the submenu only toggles between selected and not selected, indicated with checkmarks, or no checkmarks, respectively.

You can select one or more render states to render when render commands are invoked. This might be efficient if you want to render only clips with Needs Render (red render bar) and Unlimited render status when editing. Later, when you are ready to output to tape, you can select more render states to be rendered for the highest quality possible.

Note   Although rarely the case, it is possible to have no render states selected. If all render states are deselected, nothing renders in your Timeline when render commands are selected. To resolve this, simply choose a render state first, then render just Video, or Audio, or Both.

The render states in the Render submenu correspond to the render bar indicators in the Timeline. A Timeline's render states are affected by the Render Control settings of your sequence, as well as the real-time options and Playback Video Quality settings selected in the Real-Time (RT) pop-up menu in the Timeline.

Note

Proxy render cache files are created when rendering effects with Frame Rate or Resolution settings lower than 100 percent, or with Filter, Frame Blending, and Motion Blur deselected Proxy files are suitable for fast previews of effects, but not for final output of your project. However, Final Cut Pro automatically renders all proxy effects when using Print to Video or Edit to Tape, but only if Full Quality is selected in the Real-Time (RT) Effects pop-up menu in the Timeline. If Use Playback Settings is selected instead, Final Cut Pro does not automatically render proxy effects before outputting.

The three render commands are:

✦ **Both:** This command renders both the video and audio of the selected clips or clips in a selected region of the Timeline. Only effects with the render status selected (indicated with checkmarks) in the Render submenu are rendered.

✦ **Video:** Renders only the video effects of selected clips or clips in a selected region of the Timeline. Only effects with the render status selected (which are indicated with checkmarks) below the Video render command are rendered.

✦ **Audio:** Renders only the audio effects of selected clips or clips in a selected region of the Timeline. Only effects with the options selected (which are indicated with checkmarks) below the Audio render command are rendered. For Playback Selection are audio clips that appear with red render bars; Item Level are clips that need to be resampled or have filters applied.

Rendering with the Render All command

The second render command you can select is the Render All command, shown in Figure 18-7. Like the command's name, selecting this command renders all clips in the Timeline with corresponding render states selected in the submenu, regardless of any items selected or regions defined with In and Out points in the Timeline.

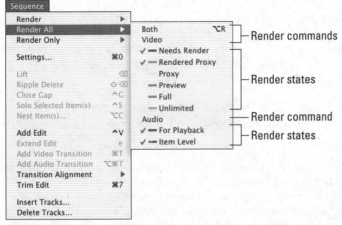

Figure 18-7: Use the Render All command and its submenu to render all clips in your Timeline with matching render status.

Selecting render commands and choosing the render status of clips to be operated on is the same for the Render All command as it is for the Render command (detailed earlier). The only difference is the Render All command's unalterable selection of the entire Timeline instead of selected clips or regions when rendering selected render states.

Rendering with the Render Only command

Using the Render Only command will operate on selected clips or clips in a region of the Timeline defined by In and Out points, or the entire Timeline if no selection is made. The Render Only submenu, shown in Figure 18-8, looks and operates differently than the other two render submenus.

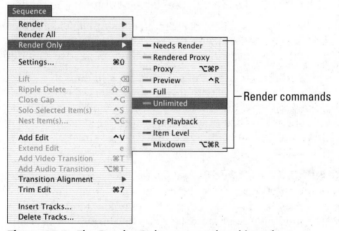

Figure 18-8: The Render Only command and its submenu operate on render states one at a time.

Unlike the previous two render commands, the Render Only command is a one-step operation that renders the clips with the matching render state when you select it. In other words, selecting the render state in the Render Only submenu is a render command for that render state of clips selected in the Timeline, or the whole Timeline if no selection is made.

Note   The Unlimited render state (indicated with an orange render bar) is available in the Render Only menu if Unlimited is selected in the Real-Time Effects (RT) pop-up menu in the Timeline.

In addition to the mysteriously missing Video and Audio subgroup headings, you will also notice another render option has been added to the audio section—Mixdown. Depending on the number and complexity of your audio tracks, even items rendered For Playback and Item Level do not guarantee real-time playback. Using the Mixdown audio command renders all audio in a sequence to a single group of render cache files, one for each audio output channel assigned to the selected sequence. This can greatly improve playback by freeing up processor overhead used for real-time audio mixing.

Note

> When using either the Item Level option in the Render or Render All submenus, or the Mixdown command in the Render Only submenu, audio is rendered at the highest possible quality regardless of the setting selected in the Audio Playback Quality pop-up menu in the General tab of the User Preferences.

Rendering one item

Often you need to render a single item in a sequence. This may be a single transition that you have just added between two shots or a clip to which you have applied some filters. To render a single item with the Render Selection command:

1. **Select the item in the Timeline.**

   Figure 18-9 shows one clip selected for render in a Timeline.

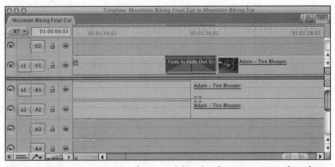

Figure 18-9: Here, a single transition in the sequence has been selected to be rendered.

2. **Select the render states your wish to render in the Render Selection submenu.**

   This should match the render status of the selected item.

3. **Choose a render command:**

   - **Sequence ⇨ Render Selection ⇨ Both:** Choose this to render both audio and video effects of your selected item. Alternatively, you can press Command+R on your keyboard.

   - **Sequence ⇨ Render Selection ⇨ Video:** Choose this to render just the video portion of the selected item.

   - **Sequence ⇨ Render Selection ⇨ Audio:** Choose this to render just the audio portion of the selected item.

At this point, if your project has not been saved, you will be prompted to do so by Final Cut Pro. A render status window appears showing you the progress of rendering. If you cancel rendering before it finishes your selection, all render cache files up to that point are saved and will be played in the sequence. When rendering is resumed, rendering will continue from that point on.

Tip   One or more clips must be selected in the Timeline for Render Selection to appear. Otherwise, only Render appears in the Sequence menu.

Selecting any Render commands will not render your selected clip if the render state of your clip is not currently selected in the Render Selection submenu! The surest way to avoid this is to use the Render Only command. To do this:

1. **Select the item in the Timeline you wish to render.**

2. **Note the color of the render bar indicator above the selected clip.**

3. **Choose Sequence ⇨ Render Only, and then the corresponding render state of the selected clip.**

   Note that the last three selections in the Render Only submenu are audio render states.

If your project has not been saved, you will be prompted to do so. A render status window appears showing you the progress of rendering. If you cancel rendering before it finishes your selection, all whole and partial render cache files are saved and will then be played in the sequence.

Tip   If you find yourself visiting the Render Only submenu often, you might consider creating your own keyboard shortcuts or custom buttons—two new features implemented in version 4 of Final Cut Pro.

Rendering multiple items in a sequence

Although you'll probably render individual items most often, there may be times when you wish to render several items at once. To render multiple items in a sequence:

1. **Select multiple clips with the Arrow Selection, Group Selection, or Range Selection tool.**

   Figure 18-10 shows multiple clips selected for rendering.

Figure 18-10: Render multiple items in a sequence by first selecting them in the Timeline.

2. **Select the render states you wish to render in the Render Selection submenu.**

3. **Choose a render command:**

   • **Sequence ➪ Render Selection ➪ Both:** This will render both audio and video effects of your selected clips. Alternatively, you can press Command+R on your keyboard.

   • **Sequence ➪ Render Selection ➪ Video:** This will render just the video portion of the selected items.

   • **Sequence ➪ Render Selection ➪ Audio:** This will render just the audio portion of the selected items.

If you have not saved your project, you will be prompted to do so. A render status window appears showing you the progress of rendering. If you cancel rendering before it finishes your selection, all whole and partial render cache files are saved and will be played in the sequence.

Tip
One or more clips must be selected in the Timeline in order for Render Selection to appear. Otherwise, only Render appears in the Sequence menu.

As you work, you may find you have many transitions and filters spread over a Timeline that all need to be rendered. Rather than spend a lot of time trying to select each item to render, you can render an entire portion of a sequence. To render a portion of a sequence:

1. **Select a portion of the sequence by setting In and Out points in the Timeline.**

   Figure 18-11 shows a region of the sequence selected for rendering using In and Out points.

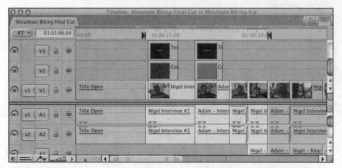

Figure 18-11: In the Timeline shown here, using In and Out points in the Timeline to define a portion of the sequence to render includes two superimposed graphics and mattes (clips on V2 and V3), but not the Title Open clip before the In point.

2. **Select the render states your wish to render in the Render Selection submenu.**

3. **Choose a render command:**

   • **Sequence ➪ Render In to Out ➪ Both:** This will render both audio and video effects of your selected clips. Alternatively, you can press Command+R on your keyboard.

   • **Sequence ➪ Render In to Out ➪ Video:** This will render just the video portion of the selected items.

   • **Sequence ➪ Render In to Out ➪ Audio:** This will render just the audio portion of the selected items.

If you have not saved your project, you will be prompted to do so. A render status window appears showing you the progress of rendering. If you cancel rendering before it finishes your selection, all whole and partial render cache files are saved and will then be played in the sequence.

Tip
    You must have an In and Out point set in the Timeline in order for Render In to Out to appear in the Sequence menu.

Tip
    If you are working on a procedure that requires a great deal of processor resources such as motion animation, you may want to temporarily disable rendering. Press the Caps Lock key to disable rendering. A warning appears in the Viewer or Canvas that says, "The Caps Lock key is on; rendering is disabled."

Rendering one or more sequences

If you have a sequence to which you have applied numerous transitions, effects, and filters, you may want to render your entire sequence all at once. Or you might have more than one sequence you want to render at the same time. With Final Cut Pro, you can render a single sequence or batch-render many. Because rendering one or more sequences can take a long time, it is an ideal, if not forced, time to take a break from staring at your computer monitor and stretch your legs. But before you take that well-deserved break, check your Scratch Disk settings to make sure you have enough space available on your scratch disk for the rendered files. To render one or more sequence:

1. **Select a sequence or multiple sequences in the Browser to render.**

   Alternatively, if you are rendering only one sequence, you can select it by double-clicking it, opening it in the Timeline. If the sequence is already open, click its tab in the Timeline, to bring it to the front and making it active.

2. **Select the render states your wish to render in the Render Selection submenu.**

3. **Choose a render command:**

   - **Sequence ⇨ Render All ⇨ Both:** This will render both audio and video effects of the selected sequences. Alternatively, you can press Option+R on your keyboard.

   - **Sequence ⇨ Render All ⇨ Video:** This will render just the video portion of the selected sequences.

   - **Sequence ⇨ Render In to Out ⇨ Audio:** This will render just the audio portion of the selected sequences.

If you have not saved your project, you will be prompted to do so. A render status window appears showing you the progress of rendering. If you cancel rendering before it finishes your selection, all whole and partial render cache files are saved and will then be played in the sequence.

Tip

There is a wonderful new feature in Final Cut Pro called Auto Render. At a time interval you select, Final Cut Pro will automatically render your sequence when you are not working. For more details on the options for Auto Render, see Chapter 6 on Presets and Preferences. Be aware if you have lots of footage that is offline in a sequence, Final Cut Pro will render offline clips with media clips that say "media off line," which will use up valuable drive space.

Rendering all audio in a sequence

Final Cut Pro is capable of playing up to eight tracks of audio in a sequence in real time. However, if you have audio transitions and effects applied to audio clips, they reduce your capacity to play the audio tracks in real time.

Cross-Reference   For more information on Final Cut Pro's real-time audio capabilities, see Chapter 14.

Using the Mixdown command, you can render all audio in a sequence to a single render cache file. This greatly improves performance and allows you to play your audio tracks with transitions and effects in real time. To render all audio in a sequence with the Mixdown command:

1. **Double-click to open the sequence you want to render.**

   If the sequence is already open, click its tab to make sure it is the frontmost sequence in the Timeline window.

2. **Choose Sequence ⇨ Render Only ⇨ Mixdown.**

   You can alternatively use the keyboard shortcut by pressing Command+Option+R.

Tip   I almost never master a long, complex sequence to tape without first using the Sequence ⇨ Mixdown Audio command. This consolidates all my audio tracks for that sequence. On a complex sequence the Mixdown Audio command may take a while, but it is well worth the time because it avoids audio dropouts and prevents dropped video frames on the final master tape.

Caution   If you modify or move any audio files, the render file created by the Mixdown Audio command is lost. You must use the Mixdown Audio command again to create another render file.

Understanding the rendering hierarchy and speed

Final Cut Pro has a rendering hierarchy. For a video layer, rendering occurs in the following order: The top layer of the video track, or the highest numbered track, is rendered first. This track is then layered on the track below, and so on. Note that basic video and audio clips do not need to be rendered. The items that need rendering are transitions or effects of any kind applied to these clips.

Different kinds of effects also have a rendering hierarchy. Within each video track, effects are rendered in the following order:

1. Speed

2. Filters

3. Motion

4. Motion Blur

5. Opacity

6. Transitions

During rendering, a progress bar shows the percentage of rendering that has been completed and an estimated time remaining to finish rendering the selection. One of the more common questions editors have about rendering is, "How long does it take to render an effect in Final Cut Pro?" There is no simple answer to that question. Rendering is a complex process and it depends on many factors. One factor that complicates the rendering process is the image in the video frame itself. If the video frames consist of a simple image, such as large portions of solid colors, the rendering happens faster. If the image in the frames is a complex one with many colors, brightness values, objects, and intricate shapes, the rendering takes longer.

Of course, another factor that affects rendering speed is the speed of the computer's processor. If you have a 2.0 gHz Dual Processor G5, you can expect faster rendering times than if you are working on a 400 MHz Single Processor G4. However, don't look at processor speed alone when it comes to rendering. The rendering process has three phases:

✦ Phase 1: Read from disk

✦ Phase 2: Render calculations

✦ Phase 3: Write to disk

In Phase 1, Final Cut Pro reads the required video frames from the disk. In Phase 2 of the render process, Final Cut Pro performs rendering calculations on the frames. And in Phase 3, the video frames are written back to the disk again. Before you decide that a faster processor will give you considerably faster rendering, keep in mind that the majority of rendering time is taken up by Phase 1 and Phase 3. *Only Phase 2 of the rendering process relies solely on processor speed.* This means that a 50-percent jump in processor speed *does not* necessarily provide a 50-percent decrease in rendering time. In fact, a 50-percent increase in processor speed may only cut rendering time by 8 to10 percent. Consider this before you go out and spend lots of money on a faster processor just to cut render times.

Working with the Render Manager

The Render Manager in Final Cut Pro is a tool that allows you to manage render files by deleting those that are no longer needed. This can free up precious disk space. You will soon realize that you can always use more disk space when working with digital media. You can use the Render Manager to delete files from previous projects, or delete render cache files that are no longer needed in existing projects. For example, if you employ low-resolution renders for previews, you want to delete those render files when they are no longer needed.

The Render Manager locates files from the current project as well as any unopened projects. However, the Render Manager does not search any drive that is not specified as a scratch disk. While looking through the Render Manager, you can locate unwanted render files by looking at their names, modification dates, or render file type. To view and delete render cache files with the Render Manager:

1. **Choose Tools ⇨ Render Manager.**

   The Render Manager window opens, as shown in Figure 18-12.

2. **Click in the Remove column to place a check mark next to each render cache file you want to delete.**

3. **Click OK when you're done.**

   All files that are marked with the small check mark are deleted from the scratch disk.

Caution   If you delete files using the Render Manager, you cannot restore them using the Undo command.

Open project

Unopened projects are shown under   Select files to be deleted by
Additional Render File folder   selecting it with a checkmark

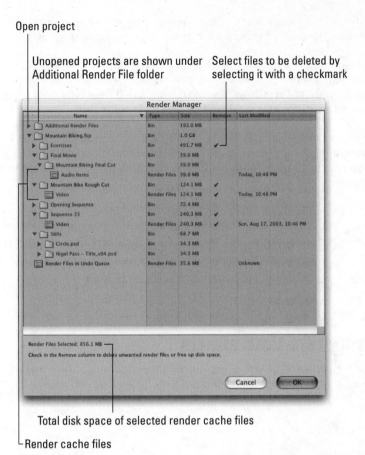

Total disk space of selected render cache files

Render cache files

Figure 18-12: Choose Tools ➪ Render Manager to bring up the
Render Manager window.

Rendering Real-Time Effects in Final Cut Pro

Wait a minute. Doesn't real-time effect mean you don't have to render an effect to
see it? The answer is yes, and no. All real-time effects are not created equal in Final
Cut Pro; in fact, many real-time effects may need to be rendered before your project
can be output. This is because a real-time effect needn't playback at full resolution
nor smoothly and free of dropped frames, as long as the effect *plays back* in real
time. Final Cut Pro's software-based, real-time architecture, named RT Extreme,
uses this fact to enable you to play back more real-time effects than your system is
actually capable of by allowing effects to play at less-than-full resolution, or with an
occasional dropped frame. Most editors welcome this time-saving feature for the

instant feedback it provides when editing, while accepting the tradeoff of having to still render some "real-time" effects for the best quality video output.

RT Extreme works only with specific codecs that include DV/DVPRO, Final Cut Pro's Offline RT as well as uncompressed 8-bit and uncompressed 10-bit. Using any of these codecs, Final Cut Pro allows you to playback real-time effects of superimposed video, filters, transitions, motion effects and still frames.

Note   The number of real-time effects you can play simultaneously depends on your system's throughput capabilities and your project's codec. Some codecs, like uncompressed 8-bit or 10-bit for example, have higher system requirements than others, like DV.

Final Cut Pro also supports hardware-based real-time effects of third-party capture cards. You can select to use Final Cut Pro's RT Extreme or an installed third-party capture card for each real-time capable codec in the Effects Handling tab in the System Settings.

Cross-Reference   For more details about the Effects Handling tab and other options in System Settings, see Chapter 6.

Identifying real-time effects

Whether you're using RT Extreme, or a third-party capture card with real-time effects, Final Cut Pro displays all filters and transitions that are real-time capable in bold type in the Effects tab bins and Effects menu, as shown in Figure 18-13.

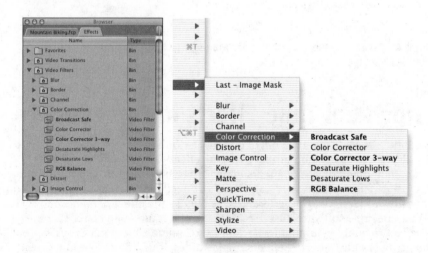

Figure 18-13: Filters and transitions that are displayed in bold type in the Effects bins in the Browser and Effects submenus indicate they are real-time capable.

The number of effects that appear in bold is determined by the video codec of the current sequence. A sequence using a codec that has higher system requirements for real-time playback will show fewer effects in bold.

It's important to note that an effect appearing in bold may need rendering before you can preview it. An effect displayed in bold type indicates only that it's real-time *capable* with the current codec, but doesn't account for any pre-existing demands on your systems throughput, such as the number of effects already applied to your clip, or the display quality set in the Real-Time Effects (RT) pop-up menu in the Timeline. When your system's throughput capability is exceeded, you'll have to render even real-time capable effects before you can preview them.

Using the Real-Time Effects (RT) pop-up menu to control rendering

Using, you can choose the playback quality of real-time effects in Final Cut Pro. Selecting various options from the pop-up menu, shown in Figure 18-14, allows you to choose between high image quality playback and the number of real-time effects that can be played simultaneously.

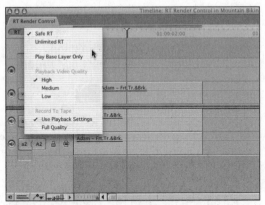

Figure 18-14: Use the options in the Real-Time Effects (RT) pop-up menu in the Timeline to control playback quality and real-time effects.

Cross-Reference

The options in the Real-Time Effects (RT) pop-up menu are the same options available in the Playback Control tab in System Settings. Changing any selection in one will change the corresponding selection in the other. For a detail explanation of the Playback Control options, see Chapter 6.

For example, selecting the Safe RT and High Playback Video Quality options in the Real-Time Effects (RT) pop-up menu will ensure the highest playback quality with no dropped frames, but also limits the number of real-time effects that can be played at the same time. If, on the other hand, you want to be able to playback more real-time effects at the expense of lower preview video quality, you may instead choose Unlimited RT and Low Playback Video Quality options in the Real-Time Effects (RT) pop-up menu.

Put another way, look at the Real-Time Effects (RT) pop-up menu in the Timeline as a way to control if and when real-time effects must be rendered, instead of controlling just playback quality. This means selecting either Unlimited RT or a lower Playback Video Quality setting may lower the demand on your system's throughput capability enough to enable a real-time effect that requires rendering at a higher video playback setting, to now play back without rendering.

Note   Lowering the Playback Video Quality setting in the Real-Time Effects (RT) pop-up menu affects only the video quality of playback for previewing, not necessarily video output quality. Final output quality is determined by the Record to Tape options in the Real-Time Effects (RT) pop-up menu, and the Resolution and Frame Rate settings in the Render Control tab in the Sequence Settings. For details on options available in either of these windows, see Chapter 6.

Forcing render of real-time effects

When you're ready to output your project you'll need to render all non real-time effects if you haven't already. To ensure the highest video quality and dropped-frame free playback during output, you can also render all real-time effects in your final sequence. This can be accomplished in a few ways:

✦ **Render an open sequence using Auto Render with the Render RT Segments option selected in the General Tab of User Preferences.** If your sequence is Auto Rendered with the Render RT Segments option selected, then all effects, including real-time effects, in the sequence are rendered at full quality.

✦ **Render a sequence using Print to Video or Edit to Tape with the Full Quality option selected in the RT pop-up menu in the Timeline.** When you use the Print to Video or Edit to Tape command for output, the selected sequence is rendered automatically before any output to your video and audio output interface. If you have Full Quality selected in the Real-Time Effects (RT) pop-up menu in the Timeline, as it is in Figure 18-15, all effects, including real-time effects, in the sequence are rendered at full quality.

If, instead, the option Use Playback Settings is selected, only non real-time effects (indicated with red render bars in the Timeline) are rendered. All real-time effects will output at their current playback quality, which is usually less than full quality. Final Cut Pro does warn you, however, with a final dialog box stating less than full quality effects are being output to tape. You can choose to continue or abort the output by clicking either the OK or Cancel button.

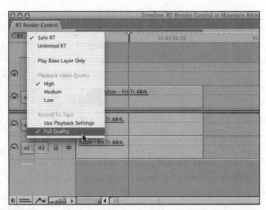

Figure 18-15: Select Full Quality in the Real-Time Effects (RT) pop-up menu to force render all effects, including real-time effects when the Print to Video or Edit to Tape command is used.

✦ **Render manually a sequence by selecting _all_ render states in the Render All submenu.** Select all render states in the Render All submenu, as shown in Figure 18-16, before choosing Render All command.

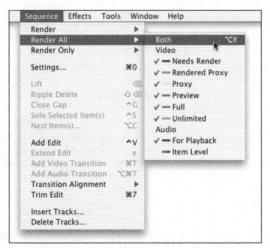

Figure 18-16: Select all render states in the Render All submenu before using the Render All command to force render all effects, including the selected real-time effects.

After real-time effects are rendered, their render bars in the Timeline will change from their various colors to the same purplish gray that appears above all non real-time effects that have been rendered. Now that render cache files have been created for the real-time effects and will be used for their playback and output, the demand on your system's throughput capacity to process real-time effects on the fly is greatly reduced, if not eliminated. This reduced load on your processor and drives is one of the best ways to maximize your system's performance for the final output of your project. Of course, rendering does require time, often *a lot* of time, but rendering all effects, including real-time ones, only helps to show the labor of your hard work in its best light.

✦   ✦   ✦

Animating Text with LiveType

As its name suggests, LiveType is all about creating dynamic text treatments for your editing projects. Much like Soundtrack, Apple has designed LiveType so that it's a tightly integrated part of your Final Cut Pro workflow. For a very small investment of your time, you can generate vibrant looking typography to lay into your edit.

LiveType and Soundtrack have a good deal in common. Both usually rely on royalty-free art as the basis for a project. With Soundtrack, you use royalty-free sound loops to generate an original score. With LiveType, you employ royalty-free animated textures and pre-designed effects in order to create titles. Granted, these are generalizations, because you can record your own original audio directly into Soundtrack, and you can also create your own custom effects and textures for use in LiveType, but you get the quickest turnaround from these applications when taking advantage of their intrinsic strengths.

As you're probably already aware, most editing projects need text overlays in some form, and more often than not, these text treatments need visual punch. LiveType can create simple and elegant treatments, or if you prefer, you can use it to generate elaborate, colorful, and motion-intensive titles. If you or your producer needs lower-thirds in a hurry, LiveType can help you make some useful ones in a flash. Simply export a portion of your Final Cut Pro sequence, complete with timing markers, and import it into LiveType. I'll cover what you do from there as the chapter progresses.

What Is LiveType?

As a standalone application, LiveType is a sophisticated piece of software. As was the case with Soundtrack, we will provide you with a guided tour fit for a video editor. There is more to say than can be included in a single chapter, but once you get your feet wet, you shouldn't have any problems raising the bar on your own.

LiveType is a compositing application. Well, what's compositing then? The answer is simple: Compositing is the name given to video that is comprised of more than one element. A lower third over a video track is a simple example. An eye-popping sequence in *Star Wars* is a complex one. For our purposes, LiveType is concerned with adding good-looking text to your video edit in rapid time.

When you open up the application, you'll see that its design is cut from the same mold as Final Cut Pro and Soundtrack. If you come to LiveType by way of After Effects, you'll probably find the LiveType interface to be a bit challenging at first. I'll cover the contents of LiveType's four main windows in the following section.

Navigating the LiveType Interface

Folks who are familiar with Final Cut Pro will no doubt be happy to see the Canvas and the Timeline. These are essentially no different from their editing counterpart. The Timeline is where you build tracks, and the Canvas is where you see how these tracks fit together as a composite (see Figure 19-1).

Understanding the Canvas

The Canvas is where the layers of your project come to life. This is where you pre-flight your composite before firing off a render. Here, you can drag your text tracks into position, define their motion paths, and shape the feel of the finished product. Take a look at Figure 19-2 to see the various features it contains.

Canvas   Inspector   Media Browser

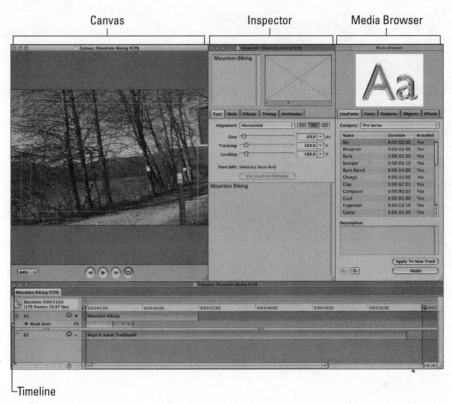

Timeline

Figure 19-1: The Canvas and the Timeline are about the same as they are in Final Cut Pro, but the Inspector and Media Browser won't be immediately familiar.

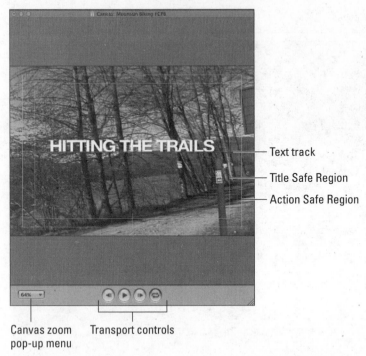

Text track

Title Safe Region

Action Safe Region

Canvas zoom pop-up menu

Transport controls

Figure 19-2: The Canvas is where the layers of your LiveType project come to life.

✦ **Transport Controls:** These are fairly straightforward. Click on the Play button (or press the spacebar) to load up a real-time RAM Preview of your project. Once it's loaded up, it will loop until you click the button again (at this point, it's a Pause button). Use the buttons on either side of the Play/Pause button to advance the playhead in either direction by one frame. The button on the far right turns looping on and off.

✦ **Canvas Zoom menu:** This menu enables you to zoom in and out of your project for tighter control over individual elements.

✦ **Action and Title Safe:** The Action and Title Safe boundaries are there to remind you how far you can go with your text elements. All typography should land inside the Title Safe line (this is the one on the inside). The Action Safe boundary is there to show you where older television sets stop scanning.

✦ **Tracks:** The lowest common denominator of LiveType is a track. All elements exist as a track in both the Timeline and the Canvas, although the Background Video track offers fewer options for control. LiveType is all about getting the most from text tracks, and that's what the rest of the chapter will focus on.

There's actually quite a bit more to say about the Canvas, but as you begin to follow some of the step exercises later in this chapter, you'll see where some of its additional functionality comes into play.

Note The appearance of the Canvas depends on your Project Property settings, which I cover just a bit later in the chapter.

Understanding the Inspector

The Inspector (sounds Soviet, doesn't it?) is the part of the interface that you use to transform your graphic elements. In most cases these elements will consist of text but can include other objects. To better understand how it works, take a look at Figure 19-3 and read the description that follows.

Text tab

Text entry boxes

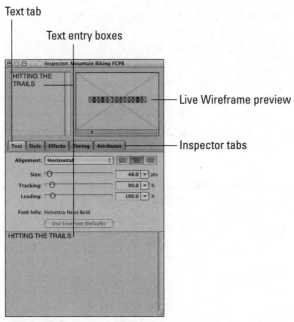

Live Wireframe preview

Inspector tabs

Figure 19-3: The Inspector (with the Text tab displayed) contains the controls for all the elements in your LiveType project.

The top of the Inspector contains both a text-entry box as well as a live Wireframe Preview at the top of the window. This Wireframe Preview loops in real-time to give you a clear idea of what your animation will look like before you render a RAM Preview. There are also five tabs worth of parameters, and the settings in these apply to the element that is currently selected in the Canvas or Timeline. Most of the time, the elements you'll be working with will be text tracks, but in some cases they'll be individual characters or effects.

✦ **Text-Entry boxes:** Text-Entry boxes would seem somewhat self-explanatory, but actually, they provide you with a way to figure out which track or element has been selected. The Text-Entry box in the upper-left corner of the Inspector is always visible, and either one highlights any selected characters or elements.

Note   The larger Text-Entry box that makes up most of the Text tab is only visible if the Text tab is selected.

✦ **Live Wireframe Preview:** The Live Wireframe Preview goes and goes unless you click directly inside of it, at which point it will stop looping your animation. Click inside the box to make it start looping again. The beauty of this little part of the interface lies in the fact that it dynamically incorporates any changes you make to your LiveType project. This enables you to see the results of your changes immediately, which is a great timesaver when compared to grinding through a complete RAM Preview.

✦ **Inspector Tabs:** The five Inspector tabs contain many controls. Take a look at the following figures and descriptions to see what you can accomplish with each one.

• **Text:** The Text tab enables you to enter whatever text you want as well as control its size, alignment, and spacing. Remember that each track has its own individual Text tab settings.

• **Style:** The Style tab (shown in Figure 19-4) contains controls that enable you to add Shadow, Glow, Outline, or Extrude treatments to the selected track. Each of these has its own individual controls that create somewhat predictable looks for text tracks. For elements besides typography, these controls occasionally produce unusual results.

Style tab   Text entry box

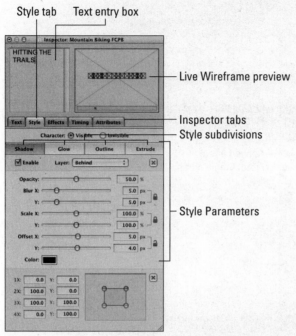

Live Wireframe preview

Inspector tabs

Style subdivisions

Style Parameters

Figure 19-4: Use the Style tab of the Inspector to apply changes to a track's Shadow, Glow, Outline, or Extrude settings.

- **Effects:** The Effects tab (shown in Figure 19-5) lists whatever effects, if any, have been applied to the active track. You use this tab to change effect parameters once an effect has been applied. The On column of the effects stack enables you to turn an effect on or off for individual characters within a text track.

Text entry box

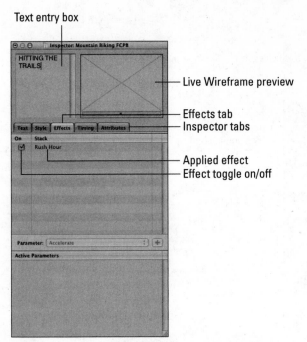

Live Wireframe preview

Effects tab
Inspector tabs

Applied effect
Effect toggle on/off

Figure 19-5: The Effects tab of the Inspector lists the effects that have been applied to the selected track.

Note

Effects are combinations of movement and transformation that can be applied to any track. Effects are covered in greater detail in the description of the Media Browser a bit later in the chapter.

- **Timing:** As its name suggests, the Timing tab (shown in Figure 19-6) enables you to tightly control distinct aspects of the graphic elements that you're animating. There are keyframes in the Timeline for any elements that you animate, and these will usually offer enough control, but the distinct numerical values of the properties of the selected track can be changed here.

Text entry box

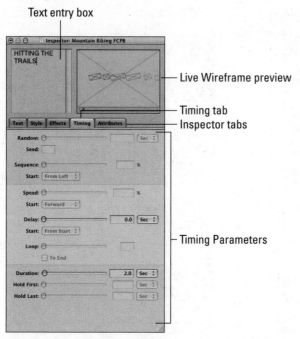

Live Wireframe preview

Timing tab

Inspector tabs

Timing Parameters

Figure 19-6: The Timing tab of the Inspector contains controls that enable you to tightly choreograph the motion of your elements.

- **Attributes:** The Attributes tab (shown in Figure 19-7) is where you go to change an element's opacity, blur, scale, offset, rotation, and color. Again, these attributes can be applied to an entire track, or only those parts of it that have been selected, which could include only a single character. The second half of the Attributes tab deals with the Matte options for a selected element. A Matte acts as a window onto another element. By turning your text into a matte, you can make it a window on to a different background or texture.

Glyph Parameters ¬   Matte to pop-up menu

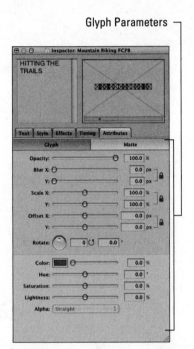 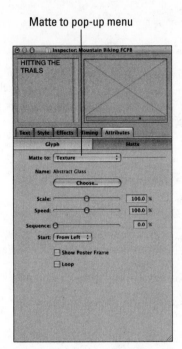

Figure 19-7: The Attributes tab of the Inspector includes two subdivisions, one that deals with basic graphic concerns such as color and opacity, and another one that deals with Matting options.

Once you get a handle on how the Inspector tabs work, you're on your way to becoming a LiveType aficionado. When it comes to the Inspector, the important thing to remember is this: whatever you do here, you only affect whatever is selected in the Text entry box.

Understanding the Media Browser

The Media Browser is another window that contains numerous tabs, but it's quite different from the Inspector. You'll most likely be working with video clips that originate from the Final Cut Pro project that you're building a title sequence for. You'll need to import those clips yourself, but you'll find most of the media, fonts, and effects that you can add to your project right here in the Media Browser, shown in Figure 19-8.

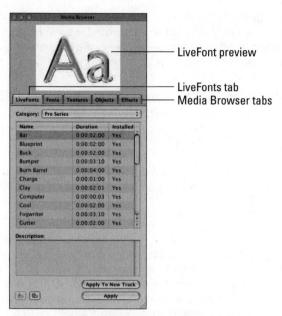

Figure 19-8: The Media Browser contains fonts, effects, and textures that you can add to your LiveType projects.

The Media Browser contains tabs for LiveFonts, Fonts, Textures, Objects, and Effects.

✦ **LiveFonts:** These are animated fonts. That is to say, they already contain not only a look in terms of shape and style, but they also contain motion. Typically, fonts are a collection of vector-based characters that can scale up or down and always retain clean edges on account of their vector origins. LiveFonts are unusual in this respect, since they are actually a collection of rasterized QuickTime movies that contain alpha channels for transparency. The animations in LiveFonts cannot be changed. Either you like them or you don't.

Note   Since a LiveFont is a flattened QuickTime movie, if you scale any LiveFont up beyond a certain size, it will begin to fall apart.

✦ **Fonts:** Compared to LiveFonts, Fonts behave more like you'd expect.

✦ **Textures:** Similar to LiveFonts, Textures are predesigned QuickTime movies that you can use as background movies in your LiveType projects. These are listed by category, and double-clicking on one will place it as the background layer in the open project.

✦ **Objects:** Objects are very similar to LiveFonts. These are also QuickTime movies with alpha channels. A LiveFont contains a movie for each character in a given font, but an Object only contains one. These can be superimposed over your video to create a frame for your type, or they could be used on their own as design elements in a composite.

✦ **Effects:** These are effects that can be applied to any layer, although you'll probably apply them to text most of the time. These are scripted motions, but after you've applied one to a layer, you can change that effect's properties by using the Inspector to alter the effect's property values.

Later in the chapter, I'll work with a number of elements from the Media Browser, and at that point, your understanding of these elements will be a little less abstract.

Understanding the Timeline

You may have noticed that the Timeline contains one noticeable feature that looks different from your work in Final Cut Pro. The gray bar that separates the two blank tracks is not the dividing line between audio and video. In LiveType, the bottom track is for the background video (and there's no audio to be found anywhere in the app). The track(s) above that divider are for all remaining graphics. These can be video, textures, objects, or text. Look at the Timeline in Figure 19-9.

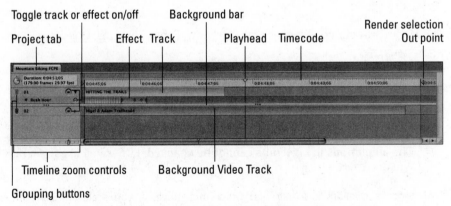

Figure 19-9: The Timeline contains some new controls worth learning.

✦ **Project Tabs, Playhead, and Timeline zoom control:** These work in exactly the same manner as their counterparts in Final Cut Pro. The active project is the one whose tab is visible in the foreground. The playhead can be dragged to a new location, or you can click on the timecode ruler to make the playhead jump directly to that point in time. To zoom in or out on a particular area of the Timeline, use the sliding zoom control.

Note

Unlike Final Cut Pro, when you press the spacebar (or click Play) in LiveType, the application begins to load all the frames between the Render selection In and Out points that are specified in the Timeline. Once they're loaded, the selection plays in real-time.

✦ **Tracks and effects:** Tracks are numbered starting from the top down. If an effect is applied to a track, it will appear beneath it. You can hide a track's effect(s) by clicking on the track's disclosure triangle. You can turn either a track or an effect on or off by clicking on its Enable/Disable switch.

Note

The Background Video track is a different color from either text tracks or their effects, reminding you that this is a different beast from its neighbors. You cannot apply effects to a Background Video track in LiveType. It pretty much just sits there.

✦ **Keyframes:** When you render a movie in LiveType, the software interpolates the movement of your project's elements in between the values specified by the keyframes that have been set within any applied effects. The end result is continuous motion, alleviating the need for an animator to specify a discrete value for every frame of an animation. Keyframes appear as small diamond shapes within an effect in the Timeline.

✦ **Render selection In and Out points:** You set the In and Out points in LiveType to control which part of your project you want to render. You may only want to focus in on a part of it, or you may want to render all of it to import back into Final Cut Pro. The more frames that are included between these markers, the longer it takes for you to view a real-time RAM preview.

✦ **Grouping buttons:** These work like their counterparts in Adobe Photoshop. The active project is the one whose tab is visible in the foreground. The play-head can be dragged to a new location, or you can click in the Timecode ruler to make the playhead jump directly to a chosen location in time.

✦ **Toggle Track/Effect On/Off switch:** These switched disable tracks or effects. If a track or an effect has been turned off, it will not be included in your render.

Creating a LiveType Project

There are two ways to create a new project in LiveType. One way is to begin working from scratch. Another way is to use a pre-existing template. I'll take a look at both approaches in the next few sections. Truth be told, setting up a new LiveType project is about as easy as starting up the application, selecting File ➪ Save As, giving the project a name, and clicking OK. Moving forward from there, let's look at the Project Property settings.

Setting your project's properties

First things first. Start up LiveType, and make sure your project contains the right settings for the video configuration you are using. For example, if you are working with regular DV video, you need to design your titles at NTSC DV 3:2, 720 × 480, Lower Field first, and so on. Whatever your specs happen to be, make sure you set them correctly in the Project Properties dialog box, shown in Figure 19-10. Invoke the Project Properties dialog box by selecting Edit ⇨ Project Properties.

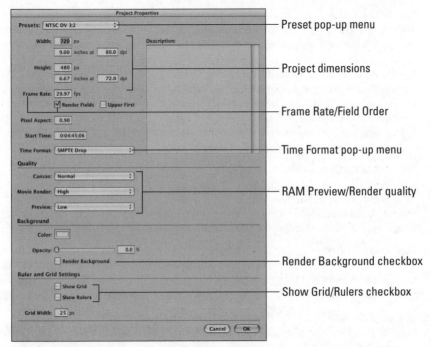

Figure 19-10: Make sure your project properties match the video specs of your delivery format.

There are a number of useful presets here, and most video configurations are covered in these. The Project Properties dialog box also gives you control over the quality settings of your RAM previews. Depending on the complexity of your project, you may wish to downgrade the quality of your RAM preview in order to speed up your creative process. For example, if your project has many layers, choosing a high-quality setting for a RAM preview will result in lengthy render times. In a case like this, you may opt for a lower quality setting — and don't forget that you always have a looping wire frame preview for reference in the Inspector.

Last but not least, you can control the appearance of the canvas in the project Properties settings. The presence of a background color, rulers, as well as any grid and its settings are all controlled here.

Tip   Be sure to select the Render Background checkbox if you want your background to appear in your final render. This applies to your own imported background video layer.

Setting up a new LiveType project

LiveType is built around the idea that you layer text and graphics on top of a base layer of video. After all, that's what title sequences are all about. So let's start at the beginning with the background, or bottom layer. You have three choices here. You can use your own video that you exported directly from Final Cut Pro. You can use a background texture, many of which are stored in the Media Browser. Or you can use a background color, which you specify in the Project Properties settings.

To use a background texture, simply browse through the offerings in the Textures tab of the Media Browser. The popup menu contains the categories of textures, and the list contains each texture within a given category. As you click on each individual texture, its preview will loop in this small window at the top of the Media Browser. Once you find one you like, double-click on it and it will become the background video track.

Note   In the Project Properties settings, make sure the Render background check box is selected if you want your background video to appear in your final rendered movie. It doesn't matter whether it's a video or a background color; if it's beneath the background bar in the Timeline, it will only be rendered if you check this box.

Importing your own video into your LiveType project

More often than not, you're going to import a background movie that comes from your editing project in Final Cut Pro. This could be a still, or it could be a movie. If you want to place a background movie into your project, select File ⇨ Place Background Movie, find your background movie in the next dialog box, and then click OK. The Timeline will reflect the addition of the background movie layer underneath the background bar, and you're on your way toward building a LiveType project.

Note   Whatever you choose as your background movie will stretch to fit the dimensions of the project. In other words, if your project is set to 720 × 480, and the movie you import was created to 320 × 240, it will stretch to fit the larger dimensions of your project. It may sound like common sense, but you must be sure to standardize your settings across applications for a given project.

Using a template to create a LiveType project

Now that you know how to set your project's properties correctly, your next choice is whether you're going to create a LiveType project with or without the benefit of a template. A LiveType project template contains a number of preselected animated graphic elements. Using a template, you can enter your own text into the preset animations, or going further, you can tweak and change the existing animations to suit your taste. To open a template, select File ⇨ Open Template. The resulting Template browser dialog box is shown in Figure 19-11.

Figure 19-11: The Template Browser dialog box lets you preview any template in the list.

Select any one of these and click OK, and the project will fill up with all the layers that make up the animation you've just selected. Customizing it is as easy as changing the text within the various text tracks to fit your program. Going further, you may want to change the shape or color of objects that happen to be in the mix. The aesthetics are up to you, and I'll be covering how to create and edit tracks for the remainder of the chapter.

Setting Up Tracks

The next few sections are going to assume that you're working from scratch rather than work with a template. Editing a template will be a lot more intuitive once you understand the basic mechanics of a LiveType project.

Once you import a background movie, you want to create an animation that works well with the timing of your clip. The first thing to do is to set the RAM preview work area to the length of your imported clip. By default, the In point is set to the first frame of your project, but to set the Out point, drag the Playhead to the last frame of your imported clip, and then press the O key to set the Render Selection Out point. You may want to use the Timeline zoom slider to narrow the focus of your project down to the length of your background movie. Figure 19-12 shows a LiveType project's Canvas and Timeline with a background video layer.

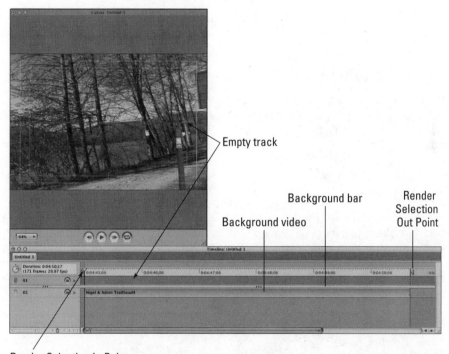

Figure 19-12: The Render Selection In and Out points should be set to the length of your imported background video.

You'll notice that the canvas has a blue line showing. This blue line is an empty track. To add some text to this empty Track, complete the following short list of steps:

1. **To select the track, either click on the blue line or click in the empty track in the Timeline.**

2. **Using the Media Browser, select a font from the Fonts tab.**

   If you want to get wild and crazy, you could even select a LiveFont.

3. **In the Inspector, type some text into the Text tab.**

   Notice that, as you type, there is now a blue track in the Timeline. This is your type layer, and its name in the Timeline will reflect whatever you just typed.

Note Selecting a LiveFont may result in a change to the length of your text track. There is no cause for alarm here. As discussed earlier, LiveFonts are comprised of QuickTime movies, not vector-based Fonts, and because of this peculiarity, they have discrete timings. If you want to get a LiveFont to fit within a specific time-frame, you can stretch the track by dragging its handles out from its sides. You can also extend its first and last frames by using the Timing tab in the Inspector.

Just so you know, if you want to add another track to your project, select Track ⇨ New Text Track, or Command+T.

Working with text

Do you like where your text is positioned in the frame? You can move the entire track around by dragging the blue track line in the canvas. You can also drag individual letters directly, but for the moment stick with moving the entire track around.

Caution If you drag it by one of its endpoints, you'll see that this only changes the angle of your text.

With the text track selected (in which case the text track in the Timeline will appear a darker blue), you can use the Text tab in the Inspector to change the text's alignment, size, tracking, and leading. Pick these to suit to your taste. Figure 19-13 shows a text track on the Canvas next to all these various settings on the Text tab of the Inspector.

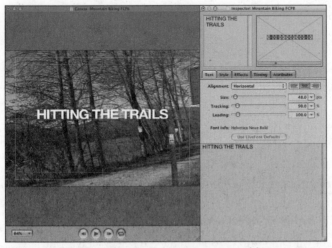

Figure 19-13: The Text tab of the Inspector enables you to change the text track's alignment, size, tracking, and leading.

With the text track still selected, go through the remaining tabs in the Inspector to see what other parameters you can change. In Attributes (shown in Figure 19-14), you can change the text track's color. In the Style tab, you can give your type a drop-shadow. Browse through your options to see all that's available.

Note   You may be wondering how to set keyframes for all these parameters. In order to animate them, you have to work with Effects. I'll cover Effects as well as how to customize them a little later in the chapter.

Figure 19-14: The Attributes tab of the Inspector enables you to change the text track's color, among other things you can see here.

If you need help positioning your text, simply turn on either the grids or rulers, or both if you prefer. Select View ➪ Rulers, or View ➪ Grid (Command+/ and Command+G, respectively). Turning on rulers enables you to use guides. Just click inside a ruler and drag it out into the middle of the canvas to create a guide. Guides will help you lay elements into the Canvas with precise control (see Figure 19-15).

Note   When moving a track around the Canvas, you can also use the arrow keys on the keyboard to nudge the track by one pixel at a time.

Note   If you like, you can go back to the Project Properties dialog box and change the default distance between the Grid lines.

Caution   Remember to position your text within the Title Safe boundary.

Rulers

Guides

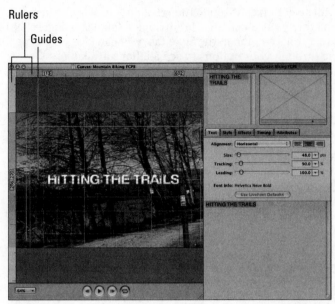

Figure 19-15: Use Rulers, Guides, and the Grid to position your graphic elements on the Canvas.

Using a LiveFont

Earlier, I mentioned that LiveFonts behave differently from regular fonts since they are groupings of QuickTime movies as opposed to vector shapes like regular fonts.

If you want to do a quick study of how a LiveFont compares to its old-fashioned counterpart, follow these quick steps:

1. **Create a new track and enter some text into it.**

2. **Select a LiveFont from the Media Browser.**

    As you can see, you can preview quite a few.

Note   LiveFont timings are listed in the Media Browser. These tell you how long the LiveFont takes for its letters to animate all the way on-screen.

3. **Click Apply at the bottom part of the LiveFont tab of the Media Browser.**

Caution   Make sure the new text track is selected before you click Apply, which you can do by clicking the new text track in the Timeline.

4. **Press the spacebar to load up a RAM preview of your LiveFont animation.**

There are a couple of things you'll want to know how to do as far as fine-tuning is concerned:

✦ **Dragging a LiveFont's track handles resizes them in the Timeline, but more importantly changes the duration of their animation.** You can also accomplish the same thing by selecting your LiveFont track and changing the speed setting in the Timing tab of the Inspector.

✦ **Once a LiveFont's animation has finished, you probably don't want it to just disappear. To hold the last frame of the animation, use the Timing tab of the Inspector to add this critical element to your LiveFont track.** You'll notice the extended last frame in the Timeline because it's a different color from the rest of the track, as shown in Figure 19-16.

Figure 19-16: LiveFonts usually benefit from an extended last frame.

Using LiveType Effects

What would compositing be without some effects? You can add effects to anything in LiveType except for the background Video track. You'll need to use effects to achieve some very basic motion graphic designs for a title sequence. For instance, if you want to fade your text in and then fade it out, you'll need to employ the Fade

In and Fade Out Effects. If you're used to working with After Effects, there is no easy way to set opacity keyframes for a layer. Working backward from preset effects is easiest.

Follow this quick set of steps to apply an effect to a text track:

1. **Select a text track in your Timeline.**

2. **In the Media Browser, click the Effects tab.**

3. **In the Categories pop-up menu, select the Fade Effects.**

   If you preview them, you'll see that some are fancy while others are simple.

4. **For the time being, select a simple one such as Fade In, and then click Apply.**

   Right away, you'll notice the addition of an effect track underneath your text track in the Timeline. There are keyframes in it, with a set of striations for each letter in your text track. Each letter has its own Fade In animation timed one after the other, and that's why the keyframes appear this way in the Timeline.

 Note   In much the same way as extending text tracks, you can change the timing of effects by grabbing their handles and stretching them in the Timeline. You can lengthen or shorten an effect, or you can change its position in the Timeline by simply dragging it to a different location.

5. **Press the spacebar to load and view a RAM preview of your titles.**

You can see that applying effects is no big deal. Know that you can also apply more than one effect to a track. Like anything else in LiveType that's prefabricated, bringing it into your project is easy, but your strength lies in your ability to customize an effect. That said, the flashier effects are just as easily applied as a simple Fade In but are a bit more difficult to customize and control. Figure 19-17 looks at a more complicated effect.

You can see from the interface that it's fairly self-explanatory. You can double-click on any parameter at the bottom of the Effects tab in the Inspector if you want to directly enter in a value of your own choosing. For that matter, you can add more parameters to an effect, or you can take some existing ones away. Since this is an overview, I won't go too far into the details. If you get good enough at this part of LiveType, you can start saving your own effects (select Track ➪ Save Effect).

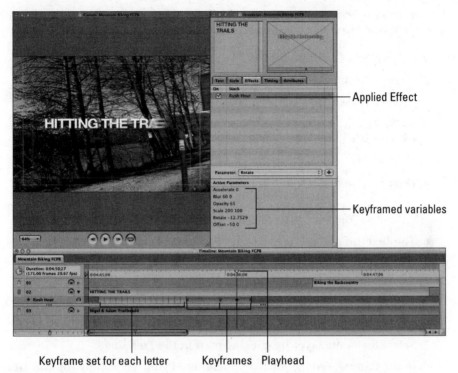

Keyframe set for each letter   Keyframes   Playhead

Figure 19-17: The playhead is parked on a keyframe in the effect track, and the Effects tab of the Inspector shows you what variables are being keyframed.

Using Objects

Even though you've only been working with text so far, it's important to point out that LiveType really doesn't discriminate between type and other kinds of graphics, and that includes movies and graphic objects. Actually, it looks at those as individual characters, thereby making all the various ways in which you can manipulate text completely applicable to anything else you import into LiveType.

As far as objects go, you can use one of the many supplied with LiveType, or you can create your own in an application like Adobe Photoshop. LiveType works with most graphic formats, so if you export a TIFF or a JPEG, you're in business. To keep things relatively simple though, let's stay in LiveType for the moment.

Follow the next few steps to see how LiveType handles graphic objects, and then you might begin to get a sense of what it can do for you.

1. **Open a new LiveType project.**

2. **Insert a background of your own choosing.**

3. **Insert a text track, built in whatever style you prefer.**

4. **In the Media Browser, select a graphic from the Mattes category of the Objects tab.**

   Your goal is to create an animated backdrop for your text.

5. **Once you've found one you like, click Apply to New Track.**

   In the Canvas, you'll notice that you have a rather ugly shape blocking most of your view. That's the new matte.

6. **The first thing to do is to change the stacking order of the layers in the Timeline: Swap the Text and the Object layer by dragging one above the other.**

Tip   You can do this by clicking in the left-hand margin of the Timeline and then dragging one track above another.

7. **Select the matte layer by clicking on it in the Timeline.**

8. **In the Canvas, reduce the magnification of your view until you can clearly see the bounding box of your matte object.**

9. **By dragging directly on the corner of the bounding box in the Canvas, resize the matte until it neatly frames the text layer above it.**

10. **Now, click the Attributes tab of the Inspector, then click the Matte button.**

11. **Select Matte to: Texture from the popup menu, and then select a texture from the Media Browser. When you've found one you like, click the Choose button.**

12. **For extra credit, you might want to change the color of your matte to reflect the background movie. If so, simply click the Glyph button of the Attributes tab of the Inspector, choose a color, and ramp up its opacity slider.**

That might have seemed like a long road, but it all goes pretty quickly. What you should have is an animated backdrop for your text that's comprised of a texture of your choice. The matte you initially chose is exactly that: a matte for another element to cut through. And as a graphic element, LiveType "thinks" of it in the same manner as type. Figure 19-18 shows a possible end result from the preceding steps.

Figure 19-18: Here's a matte object, resized and matted to a texture to serve as a backdrop for text.

If you want to get fancy in a hurry, there's no better way to learn LiveType than to reverse-engineer a complicated template. A quick look at the Timeline in Figure 19-19 will give you a clue as to how much you can push this application to get a really sophisticated composite.

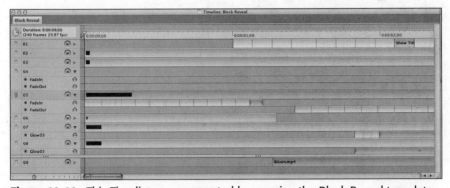

Figure 19-19: This Timeline was generated by opening the Block Reveal template.

Rendering Your LiveType Text Treatment

If you haven't already tried it, press the spacebar to load a RAM preview of your animation. When it's finished loading, your animation will play in real-time, or as close to real-time as your system will allow. ***Remember:*** It's whatever is between the render selection In and Out points that gets rendered (see Figure 19-20).

If you've made all the adjustments you're going to make to your title sequence, it's time to bring it back into Final Cut Pro.

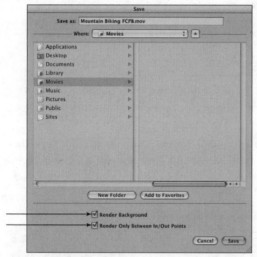

Figure 19-20: The Render Movie dialog box gives you another chance to incorporate the Background movie.

Now, all you need to do is bring your newly rendered clip back in to Final Cut Pro, lay it exactly over the clip you exported for LiveType in the first place, and you're done. Congrats — and welcome to the world of speedy compositing, courtesy of LiveType!

✦　　✦　　✦

Color Correcting in Final Cut Pro

Learning the Basics of Color Correction

Not too long ago, in a galaxy not so far away, color correction for video was available only to those who could afford the price tag of a master colorist and his proprietary color correcting machine. Although the art of color correction and a professional colorist should not be undervalued, many of the tools for precise fine-tuning of digital video's colors are now available to all who wield a mouse in Final Cut Pro.

There are many reasons you might need to color correct shots in your project. Incorrect exposure or white balance settings during a production shoot can be color corrected surprisingly well if the problems are not too extreme. But even well shot footage might need color correction — different shots of the same scene can have unmatched color balance caused by differences between multiple cameras, or scene lighting shifts that can happen for myriad reasons. You can even use Final Cut Pro's color correction tools to create a color imbalance for a desired color effect, such as changing only a selected range of colors in a scene. A good example of this last effect is in the movie *Pleasantville,* in which some of the characters are selectively colorized against a decolorized black-and-white background.

Using Final Cut Pro's analyzing tools — Video Scopes, the Frame Viewer, and range check overlays — along with its many color correct filters, you can correct, match, or otherwise alter a clip's color to create a stylistic "look."

In this chapter, I cover the fundamental components of color, show you how to analyze color with the Final Cut Pro toolset, as well as introduce you to the basic yet powerful Color Corrector filter.

Understanding Basic Color Theory

In order to make color correction decisions, you will need an understanding of basic color theory. Luckily, for the purpose of color correction, *basic* is the operative word here. When dealing with video clips, two components constitute a video image — luminance and chrominance.

Understanding luminance

Luminance, commonly referred to as *luma,* is the lightness and darkness of a video image, from pure black to pure white, and all the grays in between. If you were to remove all color from a video image, the grayscale image that would be left would reflect the luminance of the image, as illustrated in Figure 20-1.

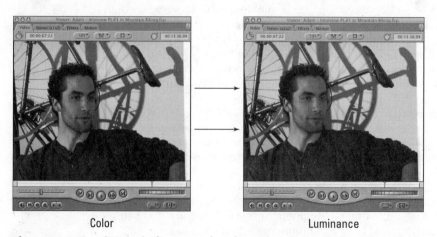

Color   Luminance

Figure 20-1: Luminance is the grayscale values of an image without the color information.

A video image's luminance is measured by Final Cut Pro on a digital scale from 0 to 100 percent, where 0 is pure black and 100 is pure white. Final Cut Pro is also capable of showing and controlling levels above 100 percent white, from 101 to 109 percent, known as *super-whites.* Super-whites are not within the NTSC broadcast range of "legal" broadcast levels; however, many consumer camcorders record these levels and Final Cut Pro does have options for processing super-whites. Figure 20-2 shows a gradient scale representing the full luminance range of a video image.

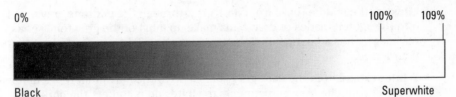

Figure 20-2: Final Cut Pro can see the luminance range from 0 to 100 percent, and even beyond to super-whites.

Cross-Reference

For more on super-white processing options in the Video Processor tab, see Chapter 24.

Luminance in analog video is measured on a different scale in IRE units. In NTSC, black is 7.5 IRE, while black in PAL or NTSC in Japan is set up at 0 IRE. Because Final Cut Pro works only with digital signals of 0 to 100 percent luminance levels, IRE measurements are not relevant within Final Cut Pro. This issue of IRE versus digital black levels has caused much confusion but can be put to rest if you remember a simple rule: *Always set blacks at 0 percent when working in Final Cut Pro.*

Cross-Reference

See Chapter 2 for more detail about luminance issues with the DV codec.

When working with Final Cut Pro's color correction filters, most of the controls and settings are applied to a specific range of an image's luminance scale. These areas can be broken down into three overlapping ranges of blacks, midtones — called *mids* — and whites, shown in Figure 20-3.

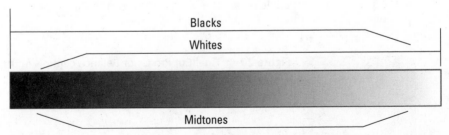

Figure 20-3: Final Cut Pro Color Corrector filters can operate on three ranges of a clip's luminance scale: Blacks, Mids, and Whites.

✦ **Blacks** are the darker tones through the mid grays of the image — from pure black and into the lighter grays. Adjustments to black do not affect the brightest whites of the image.

✦ **Mids** are the middle tones from dark gray, through the midtone grays, and into the lighter shades of gray. Mids make up most of the gray tones of a typical image. Mids adjustments do not include the brightest and darkest parts of your image.

✦ **Whites** extend from the dark gray shades up to the maximum range of luminance in your clip. Any adjustments to whites do not affect the darkest parts of your image.

These defined ranges of luminance are extremely important because most Final Cut Pro color correction controls can be selectively applied to one of these ranges when making adjustments to luma, hue, or saturation. The control over selected luminance areas of your image allows you to modify targeted areas. An example of this could be the need to remove excessive blue from a scene's shadow without affecting the highlights.

Note   See Chapter 2 for more detail about luminance issues with the DV codec.

Because the three luminance ranges share considerable overlapping values, manipulation to one luminance range will have some impact on other parts of the image.

Understanding Chrominance

Chrominance is the color aspect of your video image. Although most people might think of color as just its name, like red, blue, or green, chrominance has two properties: hue and saturation.

✦ **Hue** is the name of the color, such as red, yellow, and blue. In Final Cut Pro, hue is measured as an angle on a color wheel, as shown in the color wheel of the Color Corrector filter in Figure 20-4.

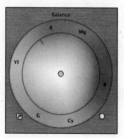

Figure 20-4: Final Cut Pro Color Balance controls in the Color Corrector filters use color wheels to represent color hues and saturations.

✦ **Saturation** is the amount of pure hue present. Saturation can also be thought of as the intensity of a color. The more saturated a color is, the more of its pure color is present, and the more intense it will appear. Conversely, if a color is desaturated, there is less pure color and more grayscale present, and can be described as low intensity, or weak, in color. Saturation is measured on a color wheel by the distance from the center of the wheel to the outer edge. The farther away from the pure white of the wheel's center, which represents the absence of color, the higher the saturation of a color.

You will notice that the color wheel is made up of the primary colors of red, green, and blue and their combined colors. The secondary colors are the combination of two of the three primary colors, and are yellow, cyan, and magenta.

Wait a minute! Weren't we taught in elementary school the primary colors are red, *yellow*, and blue? That's right — red, yellow, and blue are the primary colors when dealing with pigments that *reflect* light falling on them, but when you are working with *transmitted* light, as you do in video, red, green, and blue are the primary colors (whence the name *RGB* monitors is derived).

Illegal broadcast levels

All broadcast facilities have established technical guidelines of maximum luma and chroma levels of their broadcast signal. If these limits are exceeded, distortion of a video's image and audio can be severely degraded, resulting in unacceptable transmission quality. At some time, you've seen these symptoms before: colors "blooming" or bleeding into each other, washed out image quality, and distorted audio that can result from excessive video levels that bleed into the audio signal.

If your project's final destination is for broadcast, making and keeping your final project broadcast legal must be carefully monitored when color correcting. It is extremely easy to exceed broadcast safe levels while trying to add some visual punch to the colors of your project. Keeping your project within a broadcast safe range can be achieved using Final Cut Pro's scopes, range-checking overlays, and an assortment of many powerful tools found the Color Correction bin in the Effects tab.

Although many broadcast companies publish their own broadcast guidelines and standards, a good set to follow for broadcast legal limits are those established by the Corporation for Public Broadcasting. Because these levels of acceptable video luma and chroma are conservative by most standards, it is well regarded as a very safe standard accepted by most broadcasters.

Using Final Cut Pro Tools to Analyze Clips

Color correction can be broken down into a two-step process: First, analyze the shots that need to be color corrected, and then, apply and adjust the appropriate color correction filters. In order to correctly assess your clips, Final Cut Pro offers many tools to analyze the luminance and chrominance of a video clip.

Working with scopes

Video scopes have long been the standard by which video signals are measured. Used at nearly every stage of professional production — from video camera setup, to editing, to broadcast delivery — video scopes can help ensure accurate and reliable results. Final Cut Pro provides three video scopes — the Waveform Monitor, Vectorscope, and Parade scope — that work similarly to their hardware equivalents used with most color correction workstations. A fourth analyzing tool, the Histogram, which you may already be familiar with if you use Photoshop, shows you the clip's distribution of luminance values.

Because of the inherent differences between digital video clips and their final analog video signals that are output at the end of a project, Final Cut Pro's video scopes are the most important, if not most accurate, tools you have for analyzing a clip's color and contrast when working inside Final Cut Pro. Learning to read the video scopes can be challenging if you are not familiar with them; however, once you learn to read the different video scopes, you will be able to quickly and easily access a clip's luma and chroma levels. The graphical interface of all scopes makes comparing the luma and chroma differences of clips you are matching quick and accurate when using Final Cut Pro scopes.

Cross-Reference   Working with professional, standalone analog Waveform monitors and Vectorscopes is detailed in Chapter 3.

Opening Video Scopes in the Tool Bench

Final Cut Pro Video Scopes open in the Tool Bench window. To open the Video Scopes, you can do one of the following:

✦ **Choose Window ➪ Arrange ➪ Color Correction.**

✦ **Choose Tools ➪ Video Scopes.**

✦ **Press Option+9.**

The Video Scopes tab appears in the Tool Bench window, shown in Figure 20-5, and contains two pop-up menus, as well as some hidden options accessible by Control+clicking anywhere within a scope's window.

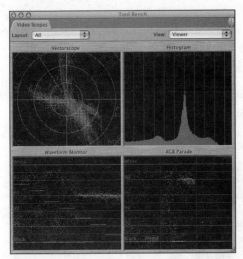

Figure 20-5: The four types of video scopes in Final Cut Pro open on a Video Scopes tab in the Tool Bench window.

The controls for the Video Scopes tab are:

✦ **Layout:** Click on this pop-up menu to display different combinations of single or multiple scopes for display in the Video Scopes tab. Choosing a single scope from the list will display that scope enlarged fully to fill the Video Scopes tab, making it easier to see. Choosing any of the multiple scope layouts will display the selected scopes at the appropriate reduced size needed to fit all into the Video Scopes tab.

✦ **View:** Use this pop-up menu to choose which frame is being analyzed by the Video Scopes in the Tool Bench. Choosing Current Frame will analyze the current frame at the position of the playhead in the Canvas. The other options available allow you to select various edit points in the currently selected sequence. You can also select Viewer to analyze the frame at the position of the playhead in the Viewer. Choosing None will disable all the scopes.

Tip

For maximum viewing ease and scope resolution, you can view multiple Video Scopes, each full-size in its own window. Simply select a single video scope from the Layout pop-up menu, then select Video Scopes again from the Tools menu to open a second Video Scope tab in the Tool Bench. Now "tear off" either of the Video Scope tabs by clicking on and dragging its tab away from the Tool Bench window. You will now have two Video Scope windows that can be set up separately.

✦ **Display Options for Video Scopes:** Control+click anywhere within a scope's window to display a contextual menu of display options for that specific video scope. Figure 20-6 shows the contextual menu for the Vectorscope.

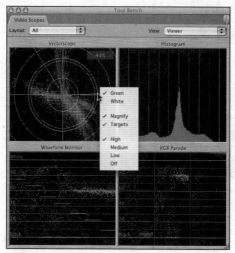

Figure 20-6: Contextual menus offer different options depending on which video scope you Control+click.

- **Green or White:** The waveforms, or traces, displayed in all the scopes can be green or white. I find the green easier to look at because almost any color is less fatiguing on the eyes than white, but Final Cut Pro's default color is set to white to minimize any color biasing it might have on your eyes when viewing video clips. These same options in the Parade scope are called Pale and Bright.

- **Pale or Bright:** Because the waveforms are displayed in red green, and blue, there is not an option for Green or White. Instead the scope's waveforms can be pale or bright.

- **Saturation:** This option applies to the Waveform Monitor only and toggles on or off the display of saturation. With saturation disabled, the waveforms on the Waveform Monitor appear as horizontal lines or dots and indicate only the luminance values of the selected clip. When you want a quick read of just the luminance values of your clip, this is the display option to use. With saturation *enabled,* you will see these lines extend vertically if color bars are being displayed, or more commonly with a video clip selected, a thicker series of waveforms. The thickness of the waveform represents the amount of saturation in the chroma of your video clip.

- **Include Black:** This applies to the Histogram only. If this option is selected, the Histogram's height will include the blacks in the picture. When this option is deselected, the height scales, excluding any reading of the blacks. You should leave this option on in order to accurately access the full luma range of your video clip. You might select this option if there is an excess amount of black that you don't need to see, such as a video clip composited against a matte of black.

- **Magnify:** This applies to the Vectorscope only. Selecting this option zooms in on the inner 55 percent of the Vectorscope's display, useful for seeing more detail in images with low saturation and a smaller waveform.

- **Targets:** Selecting this option toggles on or off the display of ideal targets you use to calibrate a video signal of color bars. These targets can be toggled off as well.

- **High, Medium, Low, or Off:** This option refers to the reference scale brightness. Select High, Medium, or Low to set the scale brightness of the video scopes that is the best contrast for you. You can also choose Off to turn display of the scales off completely.

Learning to read the Waveform Monitor

The Waveform Monitor shows you the levels of luminance and saturation of the current video clip. Waveform levels are displayed from left to right, mirroring the levels from left to the right of the frame you are analyzing. In other words, spikes or drops in the displayed waveforms correspond to the horizontal position of the hot spots or dark areas in your picture. Figure 20-7 shows the Waveform Monitor read-out of the video clip to the right. Notice how the waveform levels correspond to the position of the boy in the frame.

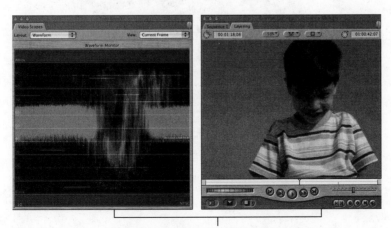

Waveform matches position of child in frame

Figure 20-7: The Waveform Monitor luminance and saturation levels of video clips.

The Waveform Monitor is an excellent tool for spotting clipped highlights (indicated by waveforms bunched up and flattening into a single line at the top of the scale), "crushed" blacks (like the clipping of the whites, but at the bottom of the scale), and distribution of the midtones, displayed in the middle portion of the scale.

Viewing the Waveform Monitor with saturation enabled, you can also compare the relative saturation levels of two clips by comparing the thickness of their displayed waveforms. You can then match the saturation of one clip to that of another by adjusting the Saturation control of the color correction filters in one of the clips until the waveforms closely match.

Learning to read the Vectorscope

The Vectorscope shows you the overall hue and chroma levels of your image. The chrominance of the video image is represented by a series of connected points around the Vectorscope's circular scale. The position (or *angle*) around the scale represents the hue, with target boxes for the primary hues of red, green, and blue and the secondary hues of yellow, cyan, and magenta. The saturation of a color is measured as the distance from the center of the scale to the outer ring. At the center of the scale is zero saturation, while the outer ring represents maximum saturation. The Vectorscope's scale corresponds to the color wheel controls found in the Color Corrector filters, shown in Figure 20-8.

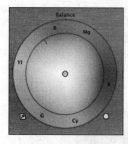
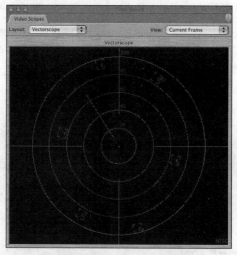

Figure 20-8: The Vectorscope's targets and circular readout matches the Color Balance control, making adjustments easier.

Analyzing video with the Vectorscope makes it easy to graphically see any color difference between clips because their color readings will fall on different spots within the Vectorscope's scale. To this end, there is even a reference line for human flesh tone. Although flesh tone varies greatly from person to person, most human flesh tone falls within a very narrow color range. The flesh tone target line gives you a general reference when color balancing for proper skin color in your clips. Because of the vast variations of skin tones, the final assessment of the proper reference line is usually done by viewing the image on a calibrated monitor. Figure 20-9 shows you a Vectorscope reading of the video clip to the right. Notice the cluster of color around the flesh tone target line.

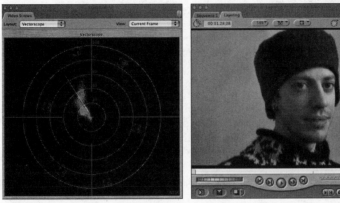

Figure 20-9: Flesh tone readings and adjustments are relatively easy to ballpark using the Flesh Tone target line on the Vectorscope.

Learning to read the Histogram

The Histogram is a graph showing the relative distribution of pixels at each luminance level in the video frame. The horizontal axis of the Histogram scale, from left to right, represents the luminance levels from 0 to 110. The vertical height of a waveform spike represents the relative number of pixels at that luminance value in the video frame. At a glance, you are able to see where the majority of the pixels in the frame are located on the luminance scale. For example, the Histogram in Figure 20-10 represents a frame that has most of its pixels in the lower luminance range. Notice also the absence of pixels in the upper luminance portion of the Histogram scale; this would indicate an image that is not only predominantly dark, but also lacks *contrast* (the amount of difference between the darkest and brightest luminance values).

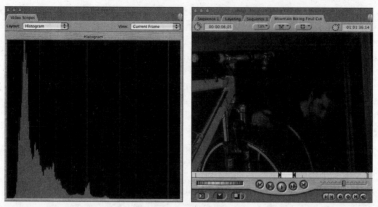

Figure 20-10: This Histogram is of the video clip on the right and indicates a predominance of dark tones and very little to no highlight values.

The Histogram in Figure 20-11 represents the luminance distribution of a video frame that has most of its pixels in the midtone luminance range, with some pixels in the black and highlight ranges, and even some pixels with super-white values (and out of broadcast legal limit). With only these two examples, you can begin to see how quickly and easily you can judge the overall luminance range of a video clip using the Histogram.

Figure 20-11: This Histogram of the frame on the right, indicates an image with plenty of Mids tonal values.

Learning to read the Parade scope

The Parade scope is a relatively new type of scope used in analyzing video. Not *completely* new in concept, the Parade scope is actually three Waveform Monitors in one. The difference is the Parade scope measures the image's three primary color components of red, green, and blue, and displays each waveform separately, side-by-side. Each waveform is tinted red, green, or blue, corresponding to the signal component it represents, as shown in Figure 20-12.

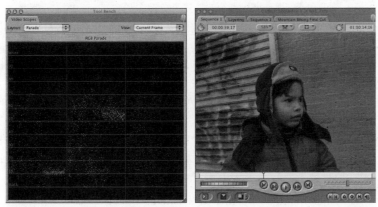

Figure 20-12: The Parade scope read-out of the video clip on the right shows a preponderance of blue.

Because the image is broken into three discrete components, it is very easy to compare the red, green, and blue levels and saturation of two clips. If one clip has more red in it than the other, this will immediately be apparent in the different waveform levels.

Using scopes and your eye

Although video scopes are invaluable tools for precise measuring and comparing of video levels, don't forget an equally important tool — *your eye.* **Remember:** Video is primarily a *visual* medium, and as such, is not something that can be simply quantified and adjusted without also viewing the results on a calibrated broadcast monitor.

To help you visually compare clips in your Timeline, Final Cut Pro provides keyboard commands that temporarily move the Timeline playhead forward or backward to instantly preview another clip for color matching. The playhead remains at the preview position as long as the keyboard keys are held down; and returns to its former position when the keys are released. This allows you to quickly flip back and forth between clips you are color matching. The keyboard commands for temporarily moving the Timeline playhead are shown in Table 20-1.

Table 20-1
Temporary Move Commands

Command	Description
Control+Shift+Up Arrow	Temporarily move the playhead to the Out point two edits back
Control+Up Arrow	Temporarily move the playhead to the Out point one edit back
Control+Down Arrow	Temporarily move the playhead to the In point one edit forward
Control+Shift+Down Arrow	Temporarily move the playhead to the In point two edits forward
Control+Left Arrow	Temporarily move the playhead to the In point set in the Timeline
Control+Right Arrow	Temporarily move the playhead to the Out point set in the Timeline

Note Because computer monitors operate in a different color spectrum (RGB) than NTSC broadcast monitors and televisions (YUV), you should not use your computer monitor for viewing when color correcting video that is intended for television. Use a *calibrated* NTSC monitor for the most accurate colors of your video. See Chapter 3 for details on how to calibrate a broadcast monitor, and Chapter 24 for more about RGB and YUV handling by Final Cut Pro.

Using range-checking overlays

Final Cut Pro offers you range-checking overlays that give you immediate feedback on any areas of your clip that exceed the broadcast legal range. With the range-checking options enabled, any areas exceeding legal levels are indicated with zebra stripes. Zebra stripes look a bit like the "marching ants" of a selection you make in Photoshop. You can see them in Figure 20-13.

Green zebra stripes
indicate luma
between 90 and 100%   Warning icon

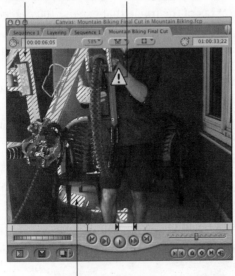

Red zebra stripes indicate
luma above 100%

Figure 20-13: With Range Check enabled,
zebra stripes in your frame indicate levels
near or exceeding broadcast safe levels.

Range checking can be enabled in both the Viewer and Canvas windows. To enable
range checking:

1. **Click on the window for which you want to enable the range checking
   option.**

2. **Select View ⇨ Range Check, and then select an option from the submenu.**

   The Viewer or Canvas now displays zebra stripes over any illegal areas in
   your clips.

In the Range Check Submenu, you have the following options:

✦ **Excess Luma:** Selecting this option displays several indicators:

- **Red Zebra Stripes** indicate areas of the frame that exceed 100 percent luminance levels.

- **Green Zebra Stripes** indicate areas of the frame with luminance that fall between 90 and 100 percent.

- **Yellow Exclamation Point Indicator** warns you that there are areas of the frame that exceed legal luma limits.

- **Green Checkmark** means you're a-okay, or in other words, all the luma levels in your picture are within legal limits.

- **Green Checkmark with Arrow** pointed upward indicates areas of your frame with luma ranging from 90 to 100 percent but with none that exceed 100 percent legal limit. This indicator is helpful because it tells you there are areas in your frame that are approaching the legal limits.

✦ **Excess Chroma:** Selecting this option can display two indicators:

- **Red Zebra Stripes** indicate areas of the frame that exceed legal chroma levels.

- **Yellow Exclamation Point** icon indicates the presence of areas within the frame that exceed legal chroma limits.

✦ **Both:** Selecting this option enables both the excess luma and excess chroma indicators. Red zebra stripes indicate areas of the frame that exceed legal luma levels *or* with illegal chroma values. If any zebra stripes appear, a yellow exclamation point indicator also appears.

Using the Frame Viewer

The Frame Viewer is a new Final Cut Pro 4 tool that allows you to view multiple video frames from the current Timeline. The Frame Viewer can display two different frames side by side in a split screen view; however, you can open as many Frame Viewer windows as you want to compare multiple frames. The Frame Viewer allows you to choose which frames to display: Select the frame: at the Timeline playhead, the frame from an edit point before or after the playhead position, or the frame at the Timeline's In or Out point. You can even choose to compare the current frame with and without applied filters — this before-and-after view is ideal when applying color correcting filters. To open a Frame Viewer window, choose Tools ⇨ Frame Viewer, or press Option+7. The Frame Viewer window opens on its own tab in the Tool Bench window, shown in Figure 20-14.

Frame boundary indicators

Timeline timecode of frames

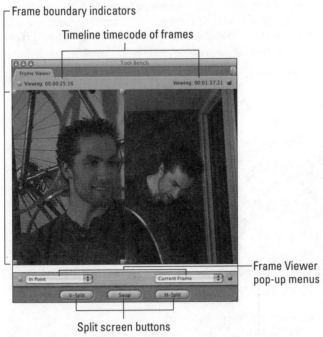

Frame Viewer pop-up menus

Split screen buttons

Figure 20-14: The Frame Viewer window allows you to compare two different frames from your Timeline in a split screen display.

The Frame Viewer is designed to compare *single* video frames from your sequence and therefore does not update while the Timeline is playing. Once play is stopped, the Frame Viewer then updates and displays the designated frames based on the current position of Timeline playhead.

Setting up the Frame Viewer

When the Frame Viewer first opens, its default settings are set to display a vertically split screen showing the frame currently beneath the Timeline playhead and the last frame of the outgoing clip from the previous edit point. These settings can be easily modified using the Frame Viewer controls:

✦ **Viewing fields:** These two fields indicate the Timeline timecode of each of the selected clips. Unlike timecode fields in most other Final Cut Pro windows, the timecode fields of the Frame Viewer are not user definable.

✦ **Green and blue square indicators:** These color square indicators show the corresponding timecode, frame boundary and Frame Viewer pop-up menu and its selection for the two frames displayed in the Frame Viewer.

✦ **Frame boundary indicators:** A frame's boundary is defined by a color square indicator in each corner of the selected frame. You can show more or less of a frame by dragging any of the frame boundary squares. Drag inside a frame's boundaries to reposition the frame within the Frame Viewer.

✦ **Frame Viewer pop-up menu:** These two pop-up menus allow you to select which two frames from the Timeline are displayed in the Frame Viewer. The options for the frames displayed, shown in Figure 20-15, are:

Figure 20-15: Use the Frame Viewer pop-up menus to select the two frames in the Timeline you want to see in the Frame Viewer.

- **None:** Select this setting if you want to use the entire Frame Viewer to display a single frame and not use the split-screen feature. This option only appears in the right (blue square indicator) Frame Viewer pop-up menu; when selected, only the frame selected in the other Frame Viewer pop-up menu, indicated with green square indicators, is displayed.

- **2nd Edit Back:** Displays the last frame of the outgoing clip two edits back.

- **Previous Edit:** Displays the last frame of the outgoing clip one edit back.

- **Current Frame:** Displays the frame currently beneath the playhead in the Timeline.

- **Current w/o FX:** Same as Current Frame, but without any effects applied to the clip.

- **Next Edit:** Displays the first frame of the incoming clip one edit forward.

- **2nd Edit Forward:** Displays the first frame of the incoming clip two edits forward.

- **In Point:** Displays the frame at the In point set in the Timeline. If no In is set in the current Timeline, the first frame of the sequence is used.

- **Out Point:** Displays the frame at the Out point set in the Timeline. If no Out is set in the current Timeline, the last frame of the sequence is used.

✦ **Split screen buttons:** Use these buttons to quickly switch between a vertically and horizontally split screen. A split screen displays both selected frames in a divided Frame Viewer window.

- **V-Split:** Click this button to display a vertically split screen divided exactly in half. Click this button twice to swap the viewing position of the two displayed frames.

- **Swap:** Click this button to swap *both* the position of the two displayed frames and the Frame Viewer pop-up menu selections. Use this control to swap displayed clips if you have set up a custom split screen.

- **H-Split:** Click this button to display a horizontally split screen divided exactly in half. Click this button twice to swap the viewing position of the two displayed frames.

Using the Color Corrector Filter

The Color Corrector filter, sometimes referred to as the "one-up" or "one-way" color correction filter, can be found in the Color Correction bin in the Effects tab of the Browser. To open the filter, double-click on its icon. If you it open in the Filters tab of the Viewer window, click on the Visual button next to the Color Corrector's name, or simply click on the Color Corrector tab in the Viewer to select the filter's visual interface, as shown in Figure 20-16.

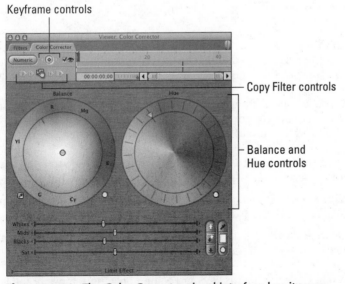

Figure 20-16: The Color Corrector visual interface has its own tab in the Viewer window.

Adjusting the general controls

This graphical user interface is based on the same controls used by professional colorists with online color correction equipment. The general controls of the color corrector filter are:

✦ **Numeric button:** Click this button to view the numeric controls in the Filters tab. This is the same thing as clicking on the Filters tab.

✦ **Visual button:** This button appears only when viewing the Color Corrector in the Viewer tab. Click this button to view the graphical interface controls in the separate Color Corrector tab.

✦ **Keyframe controls:** Use these three keyframe controls to set *all* keyframe parameters in the Color Corrector filter at the same time. To set keyframes for individual color corrector parameters, you need to use the numeric controls in the Color Corrector's filters tab.

For more information about setting keyframes, see Chapter 17.

✦ **Enable Filter check box:** Select this check box to turn on or off the entire filter. Use this option to view your clip with and without the Color Corrector filter *without* losing any render files associated with this clip. You can toggle this filter on and off by pressing Control+1.

✦ **Copy from 2nd Clip Back:** Clicking on this button copies the settings from the Color Corrector filter from two clips before the current clip. These new settings replace any existing settings and keyframes that were set in the current filter.

✦ **Copy from 1st Clip Back:** Clicking on this button copies the settings from the Color Corrector filter from one clip before the current clip. These new settings replace any existing settings and keyframes that were set in the current filter.

Note If the filter that you're copying from is keyframed, then only the settings of the last keyframe are copied to the current filter. This control is dimmed and unavailable if the second clip behind the current clip has no color correction filter.

✦ **Drag Filter:** Drag this icon on to another clip in your sequence to copy the current Color Corrector filter with all its current settings into that clip.

✦ **Copy to 1st Clip Forward:** Clicking on this button copies the settings from the current Color Corrector filter to the first clip following the current clip.

✦ **Copy to 2nd Clip Forward:** Clicking on this button copies the settings from the current Color Corrector filter to the second clip following the current clip.

Note If the current Color Corrector filter is keyframed, then only the settings of the last keyframe are copied to the clips forward. If there are no color correction filters in the clips following the current clip, one is applied automatically.

Rules to copy by

Yes, more rules! Because the Copy filter controls are powerful tools that allow you to copy and paste to and from other clips in the Timeline, it seems appropriate that there should be some ground rules established before operating on or from other clips.

Copy From

The Copy From control buttons use the following rules when applied:

✦ If both the current clip and the clip you are copying from have multiple filters, Final Cut Pro copies from the filter with the same index number as the current filter selected, if possible. For example, if the previous clip has four filters, and the current clip you've selected has four filters, then selecting Copy from 1st Clip Back button in the Color Corrector-4 tab copies the settings from the fourth Color Corrector filter in the previous clip.

✦ If the clip you are copying from does not have the same number of filters as the currently selected clip, selecting either of the Copy From buttons copies settings from the first matching type of color correction filter as the current one.

✦ If there are no color correction filters applied to the previous clips, the Copy From buttons are dimmed and inactive.

Copy To

The Copy To control buttons use the following rules when applied:

✦ If both the current clip and the clip you are *copying to* have multiple filters, Final Cut Pro copies the settings of the current filter to filter with the same index number as the current filter selected. For example, if the current clip has four filters, and the next clip has four filters, then selecting Copy to 1st Clip Back button in the Color Corrector-2 tab copies the settings into the second Color Corrector filter in the next clip.

✦ If the clip you are copying to does not have any color correction filters, the Copy To buttons add a newly created filter with the settings of the current filter.

✦ If there are no clips after the current clip in the Timeline, the Copy To buttons are dimmed and inactive.

✦ **Color Balance control:** The color wheel in the top left of the Color Corrector filter is the Color Balance control. To make a color adjustment, simply drag anywhere in the color wheel toward the desired hue position to move the color balance indicator in that direction; drag away from the center of the wheel for more color saturation, and toward the center for less color saturation. Add the Shift key when dragging to limit the movement to affect saturation only, constraining any change made to the hue angle. In Figure 20-17, the Color Balance control is shown with the color balance indicator adjusted toward Magenta.

Color Balance indicator

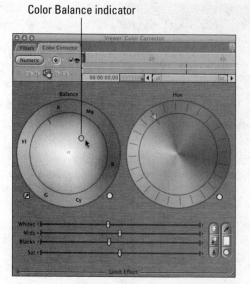

Figure 20-17: The Color Balance indicator shows the color mix added to the clip.

Note

The Color Balance control in the Color Corrector filter affects primarily the whites of the clip it is applied to.

The first time you try to adjust the Color Balance control, it might seem to have no effect. But there is color balance change, it's just too small and refined an adjustment to readily seen. To make larger incremental changes, press the Command key when you drag in the color wheel. This has the effect of "gearing up" the control adjustment, instead of its usual "gearing down" property.

✦ **Whites Select Auto-Balance Color button (eyedropper):** Clicking on the Whites Auto-Balance button causes the cursor to change into an eyedropper when moved over the Viewer or Canvas window. Click the eyedropper on an area of the image that *should be* neutral white (it will probably be tinted with color, or you probably wouldn't be color correcting it) such as a white shirt or white wall, and the Color Balance control is automatically adjusted to make the selected sampled pixel neutral white.

Note

When making a selection with the Whites Auto-Balance eyedropper, don't select an area that's overexposed, like a light source or a shiny highlight. The lack of any color in these areas can cause incorrect results. Select instead a well-lit white object, like a shirt or white wall.

When color correcting, adjusting color balance is usually done *after* adjusting luma levels for proper contrast.

✦ **Color Balance Reset button:** Click this inconspicuous little button to reset the Balance control to its default settings and restore your clip to its original color balance. Pressing the Shift key while clicking this button resets all controls in the Color Corrector filter, including the Hue control, Whites, Mids, Blacks, and Sat slider controls.

✦ **Hue control:** Click and drag the outer ring of this control to change the overall hue of the entire clip.

✦ **Hue Reset button:** Click this little button to reset the Hue control to its default settings and restore your clip to its original hue. Pressing the Shift key while clicking this button resets *all* controls in the Color Corrector filter, including the Color Balance control, Whites, Mids, Blacks, and Sat slider controls.

✦ **Auto White Level button:** Clicking this button automatically set the whitest level in the frame to 100 percent, as seen on the Histogram. The Whites slider control is adjusted to reflect this change. The Auto White Level button and other controls are shown in Figure 20-18.

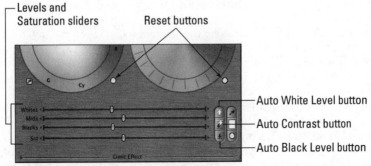

Figure 20-18: The levels and Sat slider controls are located with the auto-levels and Match Color buttons.

✦ **Auto Black Level button:** Clicking this button automatically set the blackest level in the frame to 0 percent, as shown on the Histogram. The Blacks slider control is adjusted to reflect this change.

✦ **Auto Contrast button:** Click this button to perform both the Auto White Level and Auto Black Level at the same time.

✦ **Whites slider:** Use this control to adjust the maximum white level in the clip the filter is applied to. Moving the slider to the left lowers the maximum white level. This is how you might manually bring down super-white levels (those between 100 and 109 percent on a Waveform Monitor) in your clip to broad-cast legal limits (100 percent or less, as measured on a Waveform Monitor). Move this slider to the right to raise the level of whites. Although difficult to see, the small arrows to the right and left of the slider control will move the slider incrementally when clicked on.

✦ **Mids slider:** Use this control to adjust the midtone values in the clip the filter is applied to. Adjusting the midtones of your clip increases or decreases the apparent contrast of your image without much effect to the whites or blacks. A good application of this control might be to raise the (midtone) detail in shadowed areas of a clip. Click the small arrows to the right and left of the slider control to adjust the slider incrementally.

✦ **Blacks slider:** Use this control to adjust the minimum level of black in the clip the filter is applied to. Adjust this control to lighten or deepened the blacks of your image. Click the small arrows to the right and left of the slider control to adjust the slider incrementally.

✦ **Sat slider:** Short for *saturation,* this slider control raises or lowers the overall saturation of the clip the filter is applied to. If you drag the slider all the way to the left, all colors are completely desaturated, leaving you with a grayscale (black-and-white) image. Dragging the slider to the right increases the satura-tion of all colors in the clip the filter is applied to. Click the small arrows to the right and left of the slider control to adjust the slider incrementally.

Caution   Be extremely careful when raising the saturation of a clip. It is dangerously easy to exceed broadcast legal chroma levels unintentionally while trying to add more color intensity to your video. For this reason, it is advisable to enable the Excess Chroma option in the Range Check overlays when you are color correcting.

✦ **Hue Matching Controls:** These three controls allow you to match the overall hue of your clip to the hue of another. Deceivingly small, these controls con-stitute Final Cut Pro's powerful ability to sample and match hues from another clip — no small feat. The Hue Matching controls are available in both the Color Corrector and Color Corrector 3-way filter. These controls are detailed in the next chapter, along with other advanced color correction features and techniques.

Note   The Hue Matching feature is intended for matching similar colors to one another, not for matching completely different colors.

Using the Color Corrector filter

Let's use all this information and finally do some real-life color correcting. In the fol-lowing example we'll use the Color Corrector filter to adjust a clip that's incorrectly color balanced and underexposed. The video clip that will be color corrected of a little boy on a city street is shown in Figure 20-19.

Figure 20-19: The video clip to the left is underexposed and is tinted with excessive blue.

The camera was incorrectly white balanced for the excessive blue in the open shadows, and the shot is underexposed. Using the Color Corrector filter, you can easily correct both of these problems.

1. **Move the playhead over the clip you want to color correct to preview in the Canvas window changes as you work.**

2. **Apply the Color Corrector filter to the clip in the Timeline you want to correct.**

   Drag the Color Corrector filter out of the Color Correction bin in the Effects tab, and drop it onto the desired clip, or select the clip in the Timeline by clicking on it once, then choose Effects ➪ Video Filters ➪ Color Correction ➪ Color Corrector.

3. **Open in the Viewer window the clip with the Color Corrector filter by double-clicking on it in the Timeline.**

4. **Click on the Color Corrector tab in the Viewer to bring it to the front.**

5. **Choose Window ➪ Arrange ➪ Color Correction.**

   This layout displays the Video Scopes tab opened in the Tool Bench window. It's a good idea to have the Video Scopes open when you're color correcting for analyzing and monitoring your changes.

6. **Enable Range Check overlay in the Canvas window by clicking on the Canvas window, then selecting View ➪ Range Check ➪ Both.**

   This turns on both the Excess Luma and Excess Chroma Range Check overlays in the Canvas.

Note

When color correcting, it is standard procedure to first adjust an image's lumi-nance range, and then make any necessary color-balance adjustments. Further adjustments to both may be necessary for the final desired affect.

7. **Click the Auto Contrast button to automatically maximize the tonal range of the clip's image.**

The Auto Contrast button is shown in Figure 20-20. The sliders for the Whites, Mids, and Blacks will move to the position that reflects the best distribution of the video's pixels, as shown in the Histogram. This is a good starting point.

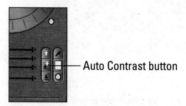
— Auto Contrast button

Figure 20-20: Click on the Auto Contrast button to automatically optimize contrast.

8. **Adjust the Mids slider to bring out more detail in the image, without exceeding broadcast legal limits.**

Because the shot was underexposed, the midtones still looked slightly heavy and muddy. Using the Mids control allows you to raise the midtone levels without immediately pushing the whites over the broadcast legal limits. However, it is still possible to exceed safe limits when adjusting Mids, so keep an eye on the Canvas for any Excess Luma zebra indicators telling you levels are too high. For more detailed information, watch the Waveform and Parade scope levels.

9. **Click on the Select Auto-Balance Color button.**

To correct the blue cast of the open shade daylight, we will use the auto-balance control. Selecting this control changes the cursor to an eyedropper when it is moved into the Viewer or Canvas window. The Select Auto-Balance Color button is shown in Figure 20-21.

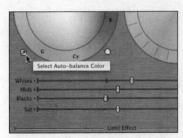

Figure 20-21: The Select Auto-Balance Color button is the small eyedropper on the lower-left side of the Color Balance control.

10. Click the eyedropper in an area of the image that should be pure white.

The Color Balance control is automatically adjusted to compensate for the blue cast. Notice the Color Balance indicator has moved toward the reds and yellows, directly opposite the blues on the color wheel, in order to neutralize the blue that was sampled. *Remember:* In order for this auto-balancing to work properly, select an area that is bright white, and not an overexposed highlight or light source. In this example, I selected a section of white paint on the metal roll door behind the boy.

Note

If you have a scene with multiple color temperature sources, such as an interior scene lit by florescent lighting *and* daylight from an open window, keep in mind that color correcting for one source often exacerbates the imbalance of the other. The best you might be able to accomplish is to select a white object that has a good mixture of both light sources, effectively splitting the color balance compensation between the two.

11. To fine-tune the color balance of your clip, click in the Color Balance Control and drag in the desired direction.

Using the auto-balance control should get you into the general area of neutral color balance quickly and easily. However, you might still need to tweak your settings by hand using the Video scopes and a calibrated broadcast monitor.

12. After you have the desired color balance, carefully adjust the Saturation of the clip by moving the Sat slider control.

This should be the last step when color correcting. Drag the Sat slider right to increase overall color saturation; drag the Sat slider left to desaturate overall colors.

Caution

Be extremely careful when raising the saturation of a clip. It is dangerously easy to exceed broadcast legal chroma levels unintentionally while trying to add more color intensity to your video. For this reason, it is advisable to enable the Excess Chroma option in the Range Check overlays when you are color correcting.

Figure 20-22 shows a before-and-after comparison the application of the Color Correct 3-way.

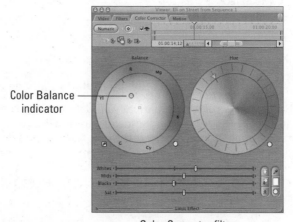

Color Balance indicator

Color Corrector filter
with final adjustments

Before color correction

After color correction

Figure 20-22: On the top are the final Color Corrector settings for the corrected clip on the bottom right.

✦   ✦   ✦

Mastering Advanced Color Correction

Color correction has much in common with editing, and I'm not just talking about the obvious fact that they're both post-production processes. The common ground these two crafts share goes beyond their production proximity. Like editing, good color correcting should be transparent to the viewer and yet contribute information and aesthetic value to the medium's power of communication. Like editing, color correcting is both a science and a craft that can seem deceptively easy to apply, and still take a lifetime to master. And the only way to master anything is to practice, practice, and then practice some more.

With Final Cut Pro's small, yet powerful toolset for color correcting, practice and application is just a click away. And not just elementary color correction, but advanced capabilities like separate control of color balance and luminance levels of the Blacks, Mids, and Whites of a video image; color correct using color-keyed selections; and automatic color matching from one clip to another. Add to this a couple of broadcast legal filters and you have a veritable color-correction system built into the world's most professional, affordable, and fun nonlinear editor (NLE). I'll start the tour of advanced color correction with the powerful and mighty Color Corrector 3-way filter.

Understanding the Color Corrector 3-Way

The Color Corrector 3-way filter is such a powerful tools, for many Final Cut Pro users, it's *the* color corrector filter to use. By allowing you separate control over the blacks, mids, and whites of your clip, the Color Corrector 3-way gives you selective and precise adjustment over the full color range of your clip. Similar in most ways to the Color Corrector filter, there are a few more controls added for its extended capabilities, shown in Figure 21-1.

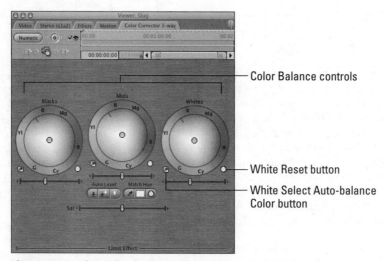

Color Balance controls

White Reset button

White Select Auto-balance Color button

Figure 21-1: The Color Corrector 3-way filter uses three color balance controls for more precise adjustments of a clip's highlights, midtones, and shadows.

Using the Color Corrector 3-way controls

The controls in the visual interface of the Color Corrector 3-way are identical to those in the Color Corrector filter, with the exception of two Color Balance control wheels that replace the Hue control. The slider controls for the Blacks, Mids, and Whites have been repositioned beneath their corresponding Color Balance controls but operate exactly as they do in the Color Corrector filter.

✦ **Blacks Balance control:** Click and drag anywhere in the color wheel to move the color balance indicator toward the desired color. Use this control to change the color mix of just the blacks of your image. Drag away from the center of the wheel for more color saturation, and toward the center for less color saturation. Add the Shift key when dragging to limit the movement to affect saturation only, constraining any change made to the hue angle.

Tip

To make larger incremental changes, press the Command key when you drag in the color wheel. This has the effect of "gearing up" the control adjustment, instead of its usual "gearing down" property.

✦ **Blacks Select Auto-Balance Color button (the eyedropper):** Clicking on the Blacks Select Auto-Balance Color button causes the cursor to change into an eyedropper when moved over the Viewer or Canvas window. Click the eyedropper on an area of the image that *should be* the blackest part of your image such as black clothing or deep, black shadow, and the Blacks Color Balance control is automatically adjusted to make the selected sampled pixel pure black.

Tip

When color correcting, adjusting color balance is usually done *after* adjusting luma levels for proper contrast.

✦ **Blacks Reset button:** Click this button to reset the Blacks Balance control to its default settings and restore your clip to its original color mix. Pressing the Shift key while clicking this button resets *all* controls in the Color Corrector 3-way filter, including the Blacks, Mids, and Whites Color Balance controls *and* Whites, Mids, Blacks, and Sat slider controls.

✦ **Mids Balance control:** Click and drag anywhere in the color wheel to move the color balance indicator toward the desired color. Use this to control to change the color mix of the midtone areas of your image.

Note

Because the midtone range overlaps both the Blacks and the Whites range of the image, adjustments to the midtones affect these overlapping regions. Further control of the Blacks and Whites can be made using their Color Balance control.

✦ **Mids Select Auto-Balance Color button (the eyedropper):** Clicking on the Mids Select Auto-Balance Color button causes the cursor to change into an eyedropper when moved over the Viewer or Canvas window. Click the eyedropper on an area of the image that should be neutral gray, and the Mids Color Balance control is automatically adjusted to make the selected sampled pixel neutral gray.

Note

Neutral gray, as defined here, corresponds to a Kodak 18-percent gray card, or the neutral gray chip on a production color shot. Lacking either of these references in your shot, try to locate an area in your clip that should be middle gray in value and without any color tint. I find slightly dark cement sidewalks to be a good neutral starting point.

✦ **Mids Reset button:** Click this button to reset the Mids Balance control to its default settings and restore your clip to its original color mix. Pressing the Shift key while clicking this button resets *all* controls in the Color Corrector 3-way filter, including the Blacks, Mids, and Whites Color Balance controls *and* Whites, Mids, Blacks, and Sat slider controls.

✦ **Whites Balance control:** Click and drag anywhere in the color wheel to move the color balance indicator toward the desired color. Use this to control to change the color mix of the Whites of your image.

✦ **Whites Select Auto-Balance Color button (the eyedropper):** Clicking on the Whites Select Auto-Balance Color button causes the cursor to change into an eyedropper when moved over the Viewer or Canvas window. Click the eyedropper on an area of the image that should be neutral white (it will probably be tinted with color, or you probably wouldn't be color correcting it) such as a white shirt or white wall, and the Color Balance control is automatically adjusted to make the selected sampled pixel neutral white.

Note

When making a selection with the Whites Auto-Balance eyedropper, don't select an area that's overexposed, like a light source or a shiny highlight. The lack of any color in these areas can cause incorrect results. Select instead a well-lit white object, like a shirt or white wall.

✦ **Whites Reset button:** Click this button to reset the Whites Balance control to its default settings and restore your clip to its original color mix. Pressing the Shift key while clicking this button resets *all* controls in the Color Corrector 3-way filter, including the Blacks, Mids, and Whites Color Balance controls *and* Whites, Mids, Blacks, and Sat slider controls.

Note

Using the Auto Contrast controls and the Whites, Mids, and Blacks sliders to maximize the contrast of your image is usually the first step you take when color correcting a clip.

✦ **Auto White Level button:** Clicking this button automatically sets the whitest level in the frame to 100 percent, as seen on the Histogram. The Whites slider control is adjusted to reflect this change.

✦ **Auto Black Level button:** Clicking this button automatically sets the blackest level in the frame to 0 percent, as seen on the Histogram. The Blacks slider control is adjusted to reflect this change.

✦ **Auto Contrast button:** Click this button to perform both the Auto White Level and Auto Black Level at the same time. The Auto Level controls are shown in Figure 21-2.

✦ **Whites slider:** Use this control to adjust the maximum white level in the clip the filter is applied to. Moving the slider to the left lowers the maximum white level. This is how you might manually bring down super-white levels (those between 100 and 109 percent on a waveform monitor) in your clip to broadcast legal limits (100 percent or less, as measured on a waveform monitor). Move this slider to the right to raise the level of whites. Although difficult to see, the small arrows to the right and left of the slider control will move the slider incrementally when clicked on.

Auto Black Level button

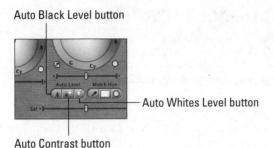

Auto Whites Level button

Auto Contrast button

Figure 21-2: The Auto Level controls are used for quick, ballpark adjustments from which you can start to color correct.

✦ **Mids slider:** Use this control to adjust the midtone values in the clip the filter is applied to. Adjusting the midtones of your clip increases or decreases the apparent contrast of your image without much affect to the whites or blacks. A good application of this control might be to raise the (midtone) detail in shadowed areas of a clip. Clicking the small arrows to the right and left of the slider control will adjust the slider incrementally.

✦ **Blacks slider:** Use this control to adjust the minimum level of black in the clip the filter is applied to. Adjust this control to lighten or deepen the blacks of your image. Clicking the small arrows to the right and left of the slider control will adjust the slider incrementally.

✦ **Sat slider:** Short for *saturation,* this slider control raises or lowers the overall saturation of the clip the filter is applied to. If you drag the slider all the way to the left, all colors are completely desaturated, leaving you with a grayscale (black-and-white) image. Dragging the slider to the right increases the saturation of all colors in the clip the filter is applied to. Clicking the small arrows to the right and left of the slider control will adjust the slider incrementally.

Caution

Be extremely careful when raising the saturation of a clip. It is dangerously easy to exceed broadcast legal chroma levels unintentionally while trying to add more color intensity to your video. For this reason, it is advisable to enable the Excess Chroma option in the Range Check overlays when you are color correcting.

✦ **Hue Matching Controls:** These three controls allow you to match the overall hue of your clip to the hue of another. Deceivingly small, these controls constitute Final Cut Pro's powerful ability to sample and match hues from another clip — no small feat. The Hue Matching controls are available in both the Color Corrector and Color Corrector 3-way filter. These controls are detailed in their own section, later in this chapter.

Note

The Hue Matching feature is intended for matching similar colors to one another; it is not intended for matching completely different colors.

Using the Color Corrector 3-way filter

The power of the Color Correct 3-way lies in its ability to selectively affect and control the luminance and chroma of the Blacks, Mids, and Whites. Because the midtone range overlaps both the Blacks and the Whites of the image, adjustment to any one of these areas can affect another. Back and forth adjustments, or *tweaking,* are usually necessary to obtain a specific color balance.

In the following example, I'll use the Color Corrector 3-way filter to correct a clip, shown in Figure 21-3, that was underexposed and shot with an incorrect white balance, giving it an orange cast.

1. **Set up your programs screens to show the clip you will be working on. Move the playhead over the clip you want to color correct to preview in the Canvas window changes as you work.**

   If you have an external broadcast monitor connected to your computer, make sure it is selected in the A/V Devices tab of the Audio Video Settings, and View ➪ External Video is set to All Frames, in order to see your modifications on the external monitor as you work.

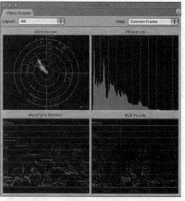

Figure 21-3: This clip was underexposed and shot at the wrong white balance settings.

2. **Apply the Color Corrector filter to the clip in the Timeline you want to correct.**

   Drag the Color Corrector 3-way filter out of the Color Correction bin in the Effects tab, and drop it onto the desired clip, or select the clip in the Timeline by clicking on it once, then choose Effects ➪ Video Filters ➪ Color Correction ➪ Color Corrector 3-way.

3. **Open the clip with the Color Corrector 3-way filter in the Viewer window by double clicking on it in the Timeline.**

4. Click the Color Corrector 3-way tab in the Viewer.

The Color Corrector 3-way visual controls will come forward, as shown in Figure 21-4.

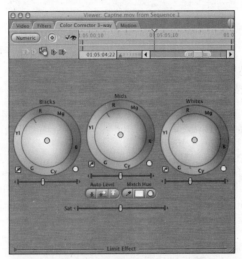

Figure 21-4: The Color Corrector 3-way filter has both a visual interface and numeric settings in the Filters tab of the Viewer.

5. Choose Window ➪ Arrange ➪ Color Correction.

This layout displays the Video Scopes tab opened in the Tool Bench window. It's a good idea to have the Video Scopes open when you're color correcting for analyzing and monitoring your changes.

6. Enable Range Check overlay in the Canvas window by clicking on the Canvas window, then selecting View ➪ Range Check ➪ Both.

This turns on both the Excess Luma and Excess Chroma Range Check overlays in the Canvas.

Note

When color correcting, it is standard procedure to first adjust an image's luminance range, and then make any necessary color balance adjustments. Further adjustments to both may be necessary for the final desired affect.

7. Click the Auto Contrast button, shown in Figure 21-5 to automatically maximize the tonal range of the clip's image.

The sliders for the Whites, Mids, and Blacks will move to the position that reflects the best distribution of the video's pixels, as shown in the Histogram. This is a good starting point.

Figure 21-5: The Auto Contrast control sets both your black and white levels for maximum distribution of your clips luminance values.

8. **Adjust the Mids slider to bring out more detail in the image, without exceeding broadcast legal limits.**

   After using the auto-contrast to get you in the ballpark, you will probably need to make further adjustments. In the example, because the shot was underexposed, the midtones still looked slightly heavy and muddy. Using the Mids control allows you to raise the midtone levels without immediately pushing the whites over the broadcast legal limits. However, it is still possible to exceed safe limits when adjusting Mids, so keep an eye on the Canvas for any Excess Luma zebra indicators telling you levels are too high. For more detailed information, watch the Waveform and Parade scope levels in the Video Scope tab, as shown in Figure 21-6.

Figure 21-6: It's a good practice to keep Final Cut Pro Video Scopes visible when color correcting.

At this point, you can also adjust the Blacks and Whites sliders to refine those levels, if needed. Once the contrast range of your clip is set to your liking (and within broadcast limits, of course), you can now address the color balance of the clip.

9. **Click on the Whites Select Auto-Balance Color button.**

   In this example, there is an orange cast caused by the improper color-balance setting on the video camera. Although this seems obvious by simply looking at it, you can also see a predominant cluster in the red/yellow (orange) sector of the Vector scope, and an elevated level of reds in the Parade scope. You will use the White Select Auto-Balance control to begin correcting for this color imbalance. Selecting this control will change the cursor to an eyedropper when it is move into the Viewer or Canvas window.

10. **Click the eyedropper in an area of the image that should be pure white.**

    The Whites Color Balance control is automatically adjusted to compensate for the blue cast. Notice the Whites Color Balance indicator has moved toward the blue and cyan, directly opposite the reds and yellows on the color wheel, in order to neutralize the orange that was sampled.

Remember: In order for this auto-balancing to work properly, select an area that is bright white with a hint of color or texture in it, and not an over-exposed highlight or light source. In this example, I selected a second bright-est white highlight on the hat, as you can see in Figure 21-7.

Click eyedropper
on bright white area

Figure 21-7: When using the Whites Auto-Balance control, click on the whitest part of your frame that is not a direct light source; also avoid whites that are washed out.

Note

Be aware if you have a scene with multiple color temperature sources, such as an interior scene lit by florescent lighting *and* daylight from an open window. Color correcting for one source often worsen the imbalance of the other. The best you might be able to accomplish is to select a white object that has a good mixture of both light sources, effectively splitting the color balance compensation between the two.

11. **Focus on the blacks in your image, making further adjustments for more accurate colors: Click the Blacks Select Auto-Balance Color button.**

12. **Click the eyedropper in an area of the image that should be neutral black.**

The Blacks Color Balance control is automatically adjusted to compensate for remnant red cast. Notice the Blacks Color Balance indicator has moved toward the blue and cyan, directly opposite the reds and yellows on the color wheel, in order to neutralize the orange that was still in the shadows. Figure 21-8 shows you this control.

Figure 21-8: Move the color balance indicators in the opposite direction from the color you want to neutralize.

Like the Whites Auto-Balance selection, in order for this auto-balancing to work properly, select an area that is not absolute black; choose instead a value just above pure black that might have a hint of color in it. In this example, I selected the textured bib of the overalls, shown in Figure 21-9.

Click eyedropper on black
area with some texture

Figure 21-9: When using the Blacks
Auto-Balancing controls, choose a black
that still has some detail or texture.

13. **At this point, you could further neutralize the Midtones using the Mids Select Auto-Balance Color button.**

    This step is optional, and relies on having a good neutral-gray reference area in your clip. Usually, the adjustments to the Whites and Blacks will produce decent color correction without further modification to the Mids.

    If you want to correct the mids, click on the Mids Select Auto-Balance Color button, then click an area in of the clip that should be neutral gray. The Mids Color Balance indicator will be adjusted to compensate for any color tint in the sampled selection.

14. **To fine-tune the color balance of your clip, click in one of the Color Balance Controls and drag in the desired direction.**

Note   When adjusting color balance, you should correct the Whites first, the Blacks secondly, and only then the Mids.

15. **Now that you have made general color corrections to your clip's color balance using the Auto-Balance controls, you might need to fine-tune the result by manually adjusting the settings while watching the Video scopes and previewing the clip on a calibrated broadcast monitor.**

    Figure 21-10 shows a before-and-after comparison using the Color Corrector 3-way.

16. **After you have the desired color balance, *carefully* adjust the Saturation of the clip by moving the Sat slider control.**

    This should be the last step when color correcting. Drag the Sat slider right to increase overall color saturation; drag the Sat slider left to desaturate overall colors.

Before using Color Correct 3-way

After using Color Correct 3-way

Figure 21-10: The Color Corrector 3-way offers separate control of shadows, highlights and midtones.

Caution

Be extremely careful when raising the saturation of a clip. It is dangerously easy to exceed broadcast legal chroma levels unintentionally while trying to add more color intensity to your video. For this reason, it is advisable to enable the Excess Chroma option in the Range Check overlays when you are color correcting.

Using Limit Effect Controls in the Color Corrector Filters

You might be wondering about the controls at the bottom of the Color Corrector and Color Corrector 3-way filter, under the section labeled Limit Effect (or wondering when I was going to explain them). If you've not seen them yet, it's probably because the Limit Effect panel was hidden, which is the default setting whenever this filter is first applied. To see the controls of Limit Effect, click on the disclosure triangle button in the bottom-left corner of either Color Corrector filter's tab in the Viewer. The Limit Effect panel and controls will be displayed at the bottom Color Corrector tab, as shown in Figure 21-11.

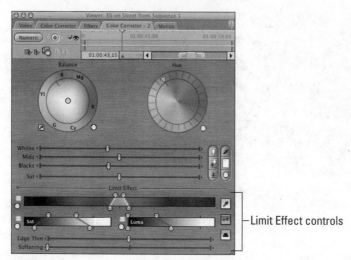

Limit Effect controls

Figure 21-11: The Limit Effects controls are located in a panel at the bottom of both Color Corrector filters.

The controls of the Limit Effect allow you to apply color correction to areas of your frame that contains a specific color you select. Put another way, with this powerful feature, you can apply color changes, either big or small, to a single object or area in your video frame based on its original color. For example, if it is determined that an actor's shirt needs to be a different color *after* shooting is completed, the Limit Effect can change just the shirt's color, as long as there is nothing else in the frame with the same color values as the original shirt color.

If you're familiar with Photoshop, this feature resembles the Magic Wand tool and Color Range command; however, the Limit Effect feature goes even deeper in allowing you to make selections based on just hue, saturation, or luminance within your video frame. For example, you could modify a defined range of shadows in your image by disabling the color and saturation controls — in essence, creating a luma key. (A *key,* short for keyhole, is a matte that allows modifications only to the selection represented by white areas in the matte.)

Tip   You can use multiple Color Corrector filters with Limit Effect on a single clip to selectively color balance different areas of the image. This can be labor intensive but offers you a huge range of control from the smallest area to the entire frame, and everything in between.

Note   Like any other filter, color correction filters work serially, or additively; multiple filters work on the modified image from the preceding filter, not on the original image.

Understanding the Limit Effect controls

Like many of Final Cut Pro features, the Limit Effect has controls that are deceivingly small in number, yet big in their abilities to help you accomplish this sophisticated and complex effect. Understanding the Limit Effect controls, shown in Figure 21-12, is crucial to using this feature to its fullest capacity.

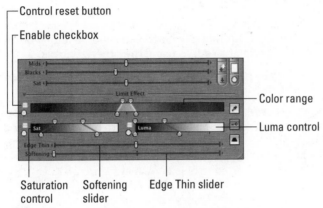

Figure 21-12: The Limit Effect controls offer you a great amount of control over a clip's selected key.

✦ **Enable/Disable check boxes:** In font of each of the three controls — Color, Saturation, and Luminance — is a check box to add (enabled) or subtract (disabled) the color component from the selection key.

✦ **Reset button:** Click these buttons to restore the Color Range, Saturation, and Luminance controls to their default settings. Shift-click any of the reset buttons to reset all three controls at once.

✦ **Color Range control:** This color gradient and its knobs, or handles, are used to fine-tune the range of hues to key on after making your initial selection with the Select Color eyedropper.

   • **Top handles:** Drag these handles farther apart or closer together to select a larger or smaller range of colors that are keyed. Handle controls correspond to the Chroma Width control in the numeric filter controls.

   • **Color gradient:** Click and drag left or right within the color gradient to shift the overall hue of the color range set between the top set of handles. The hue located at the center tic mark corresponds to the Chroma Center control in the numeric filter controls.

   • **Bottom handles:** Open or narrow the bottom handles to define the tolerance of your key. These handles correspond to the Chroma Softness control in the numeric filter controls.

✦ **Sat control:** Use this control to adjust the amount and range of saturation used to define your key. The top and bottom handles work the same as those in the Color Range control. However, dragging left or right within the gradient moves all four handles simultaneously instead of the gradient strip.

✦ **Luma control:** Use this control to adjust the amount and range of luminance used to define your key. The top and bottom handles work the same as those in the Color Range control. Drag left or right within the gradient to move all four handles simultaneously.

✦ **Edge Thin slider:** Use this control to shrink or expand the keyed selection. The Edge Thin control is great for filling in small gaps and including border-line values that would be difficult to get at using the other controls.

✦ **Softening slider:** Allows you to feather the edges of the key, creating gradual transitions between selected and unselected parts of the image.

✦ **Select Color button (the eyedropper):** Clicking on this button turns the cursor into an eyedropper you can use to select a color from a clip displayed in the Viewer or Canvas. Shift+clicking this button allows you to add another color to the key. This can be done repeatedly to broaden the selection of colors to be keyed. The Select color control is shown in Figure 21-13.

—Select Color button
—View Final/Matte/Source button
—Invert Selection button

Figure 21-13: Use the Select color eyedropper found in the upper right of the Color Corrector filters.

✦ **View Final/Matte/Source button (the key):** This button has three states you toggle through by clicking on it:

- **End result** (gold key against a gray background): This is the default state that will display the end result of any color correcting of the keyed area.

- **Matte** (a black key against a white background): The second state displays the key as a grayscale image. This black-and-white matte makes it very easy to immediately see areas that are keyed.

- **Source** (a gold key against a blue background): The third state shows only the original video image and is the same as disabling the entire filter.

✦ **Invert Selection button:** Click this button to invert the key you've defined. This is useful if you want to affect everything in the frame *except areas with your selected key color.* You can then apply an effect, such as desaturation, or *draining,* all color leaving you a black-and-white scene with only your selected object in color — á la the movie *Pleasantville.*

Using the Limit Effect controls to change a specific color

Let's see how to use the Limit Effect controls to selectively change the color of a skier's jacket from blue to red, without altering the colors of anything else in the scene. Figure 21-14 shows the original clip without any filter applied.

Figure 21-14: This is the original clip before I applied selective color manipulation using the Limit Effect controls.

Tip   For large color changes, I find it easier to use the Color Corrector filter because the Hue control allows for quick and large color modification.

1. **Starting with the Color Corrector filter already applied to a clip, click the Select Color button (the eyedropper) to activate the Select Color tool.**

2. **In the Canvas, click the eyedropper on the skier's blue jacket to select a primary key color.**

   In Figure 21-15, you can see where I selected in the clip using the Select Color eyedropper.

Figure 21-15: Try to select a middle tone for your key color.

For a good, average starting point, try to choose a color value between the brightest and darkest areas of your sample color. Although you've made a key selection, you won't see it because you've made no color adjustments.

3. **To see the keyed areas, change the Hue control by dragging the Hue control's out ring toward the red color values.**

   You can also view just the key as a grayscale image while you make your adjustments by clicking on the View/Final/Matte/Source button. If you use this view, it's sometimes easier to spot stray keyed colors in larger unkeyed areas.

4. **Enlarge the key selection by moving the top two handles of the Color Range control outward to include more of the blue area of the picture.**

   Widening the bottom handles increases the tolerance of the selected color range including a greater range of key color. Figure 21-16 shows an adjustment to these controls.

Widen selection range from this

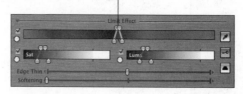

to this selection range.

Figure 21-16: Adjusting the handles over a range control allows you to define a key's values.

To readjust the whole range of hues between these handles, drag anywhere in the color gradient to move the range of hues left or right in relation to the Color Range handles. Figure 21-17 shows a limited range of blues that are being affected and colored red.

Figure 21-17: Some, but not all, of the ski jacket's blue is within the current range of selection.

5. **When you're finished selecting the main key color range, adjust the luminance control to increase the amount of the picture that is affected by the key.**

   Move the top handles in the Luma control to select a primary luminance range to affect, then adjust the bottom handles to affect the tolerance. As you can see in Figure 21-18, the increased luma range resulted in more of the ski jacket affected.

6. **Adjust the Sat control to further increase the range.**

   The saturation adjustment selects the last bit of the ski jacket, shown in Figure 21-19.

Figure 21-18: Increasing the luma range broadens the accepted tonal range of the key color.

Figure 21-19: Using the Limit Effect has selectively altered the color of the skier's jacket without affecting other areas of the image.

Tip   It's a good practice to periodically check the Matte view of the key to see if your selection is too wide. Although the key selection is grayscale, the majority of the unselected area will be solid black, making it easy to see exactly how much and where your key might be spilling out.

Here is a quick example of using a key to *not* affect color change. Instead, the unkeyed area of the frame will be targeted for chroma desaturation, resulting in a grayscale image except for the keyed areas. I'll use the Limit Effect controls of the Color Corrector filter to create this effect with the sunflower clip, shown in Figure 21-20, against a grayscale background.

Figure 21-20: I'll use the Limit Effect controls to isolate this sunflower against a grayscale background.

1. **With the Color Corrector filter already applied, use the Limit Effect controls to select the yellows of the flower petals, then move the Sat slider all the way to the left.**

   The settings and sunflower image at the end of this stage as shown in Figure 21-21.

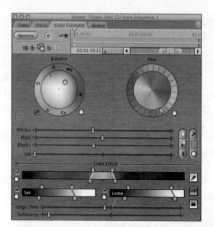

Figure 21-21: With the Color Corrector filter applied, use the Limit Effect controls to select the yellows of the sunflower, and then desaturate the selection.

2. **Click the Invert Selection button to reverse the key created by the Limit Effect controls.**

   The final effect is shown in Figure 21-22.

Figure 21-22: When the key selection is inverted, the sunflower is left unaffected while the surrounding background is desaturated.

Note that some center portions of the flower are not keyed and have been desaturated along with the background. This is because the color of this area is too close in color to some yellow-green leaves in the background. In order to not key the background leaves, I decide to leave well enough alone and compromised by getting all the flower petals keyed. This points out the requirement for unique color values in the video frame for the best keying.

Understanding Hue Matching

Hue Matching is the process of making automatic adjustments to the color balance of a clip by matching the color from another clip. A common application using Hue Matching is to match flesh tones, or other common color references, of two identical, or near-identical, scenes that were shot under different lighting conditions.

 Note Hue Matching is a color balance tool and does not affect the luminance of your image. You will still need to adjust the Whites, Blacks, and Mids levels controls to maximize the contrast in your image before using Hue Matching.

After using the Hue Matching controls, you will still need to fine-tune your clip's color balance using other color correction settings. Although the Hue Matching controls are positioned differently in the Color Corrector and Color Corrector 3-way filters, as shown in Figure 21-23, they work identically.

Hue Matching controls

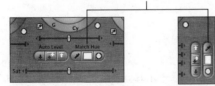

Hue Matching controls in
Color Corrector 3-way filter

Hue Matching controls in
Color Corrector filter

Figure 21-23: The Hue Matching controls in Color
Corrector filters work exactly the same in both.

 Note The Hue Matching feature is intended for matching similar colors to one another; it is not intended for matching completely different colors.

Understanding the Hue Matching controls

There are only three Hue Matching controls that you use along with the Color Corrector's Auto Balance buttons for automatic hue matching. The three Hue Matching controls are:

✦ **Select Auto-Balance Color button (the eyedropper):** Choosing the Select Auto-balance Color button causes the pointer to change into an eyedropper when it's moved into Canvas window, or a Frame Viewer.

✦ **Match Color indicator:** Shows the currently selected match color. The color displayed in the match color indicator affects how the Whites, Blacks, and Mids Auto-Balance controls make their correction.

✦ **Reset Match Color button:** Resets the Match Color to white; this is the default behavior of the Whites color-balance control.

Selecting a match color using the Select Auto-Balance Color eyedropper, the match color becomes the new reference for the Whites, Mids, or Blacks Auto-Balance buttons. Select one of the auto-balance buttons and click the eyedropper in an area of the current clip that's supposed to be the same as the match color. The color-balance control corresponding to the eyedropper you selected will automatically adjusts the Whites, Mids, or Blacks Balance control in an attempt to rebalance the clip to match the color you selected with the match color.

Note   With a Match Color selected, the Whites, Blacks, and Mids balance controls are unaffected. Only the operation of the auto-balance controls is affected by the Hue Matching controls.

Using the Hue Matching controls

In the following example, you'll see how to use the Hue Matching controls in the Color Corrector 3-way filter. You'll match the flesh tones of an actor in two shots made in the same location, but who was actually filmed on different days. The difference in light quality between the two days of shooting resulted in a color-balance difference (shown in Figure 21-24) that would be too noticeable when the shots were cut together, if not corrected.

Clip1   Clip 2

Figure 21-24: The different color temperature of these two clips can be closely matched using the Hue Matching controls.

1. **Choose Window ⇨ Arrange ⇨ Color Correction to select the Color Correction layout.**

   This layout makes it easiest to use the Hue Matching controls. Click on the Frame Viewer tab to bring it forward, or choose Tools ⇨ Frame Viewer to display it in the Tool Bench window.

2. **Apply the Color Corrector 3-way filter to clip 2.**

   This is the cooler image we want to eventually match the warmer shot to.

3. **Double click clip 2 to open it in the Viewer, then click the Color Corrector 3-way tab.**

4. **Adjust the contrast of clip 2 to match that of clip 1 as best as possible.**

   In this case, bumping up the Blacks level keeps the shot from looking too contrasty, which is an optical property of cooler light.

5. **Click the Select Auto-Balance Color button (the eyedropper), shown in Figure 21-25.**

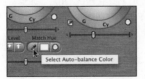

Figure 21-25: Use the Select Auto-Balance Color button to choose a reference Match color.

6. **Move the pointer into the Frame Viewer tab where clip 1 is displayed.**

When the cursor becomes an eyedropper, click a highlight in the actor's face in clip 1. For this shot, I clicked on the actor's forehead (see Figure 21-26).

Figure 21-26: Select an evenly lit tone with which to color match another clip.

As shown in Figure 21-27, the Match Color indicator fills with the color you just selected. Also, the color-balance auto-select control (the eyedropper) closest in value to the match color will automatically highlight green, indicating the best luminance range tool to match the selected hue.

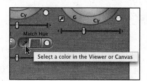

Figure 21-27: The Match Color indicator shows the color currently selected to be matched when any of the auto-balance controls are used.

Note Like the selecting of any highlights, don't select a shiny or too bright highlight on a face. Instead, choose an evenly lit, lighter part of the face.

7. **In the Color Corrector 3-way tab in the Viewer, click the highlighted Whites Auto-Balance button.**

8. **With the Whites Auto-Balance button selected, move the pointer into the Canvas where clip 2 is showing. When it becomes an eyedropper, click a highlight on the actor's face in clip 2 that matches, as closely as possible, the highlight you selected in clip 1, as shown in Figure 21-28.**

Figure 21-28: Click in the target clip the color you wish to match.

9. You will notice the automatic Color Balance control changes.

The Whites Balance indicator has moved toward the reds to compensate for the overly cool lighting. The color balance of clip 2, as shown in Figure 21-29, now approximates that of clip 1 much more closely.

Figure 21-29: Although there are still color differences between these two clips, the Hue Matching controls have brought them much closer than where they were before color correction.

10. When you've achieved the results you wanted, you can stop.

Usually, additional manual adjustments are made before the desire effect is reached.

And that is the very powerful Hue Matching controls. Used with the Limit Effect controls of the Color Corrector filters, you have yourself a veritable arsenal of color correcting tools that were unmatched a few years ago, right in your own Mac. But wait, there are a couple more handy and useful filters that can help you keep your project within broadcast legal limits.

Using the Desaturate Highlights and Desaturate Lows Filters

When using one of Final Cut Pro's Color Corrector filters, it is not uncommon that color will also be added to the highlights or shadows of your shot. Coloration of the highlights or shadows has a perceived effect of the image having lower contrast than if the shadows and highlights were neutral, or *clean*. A good way to remove unwanted color from these areas of your video image is to use the Desaturate

Highlights or Desaturate Lows filter. The Desaturate Highlights and Desaturate Lows filters allow you to set a specific target range for the brightest and the darkest areas of your image to be desaturated of color. **Remember:** The absence of all color from full desaturation results in a grayscale image. For the best looking, *cleanest* image, this is exactly the effect you want for your video's highlights and shadows.

Strangely enough, the Desaturate Highlights and Desaturate Lows filters are actually the same filter, but with different default settings enabled. You can apply either filter to desaturate the highlights or shadows of your clip by simply enabling the Highlights or Lows Desaturation controls in the filter tab. If you need to desaturate the highlights and the lows, apply either filter once, then select both options. Figure 21-30 shows the controls of the Desaturate Highlights filter in the Filters tab in the Viewer.

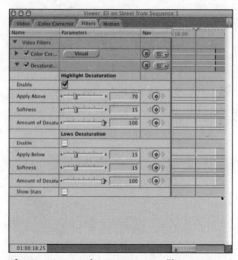

Figure 21-30: The Desaturate filters are really one and the same, just with different default settings enabled.

Highlight Desaturation controls

The controls under this section of the filter are used to select the range and amount of desaturation of the Highlights of your clip:

✦ **Enable:** Click this checkbox to enable or disable the Highlight Desaturation controls.

✦ **Apply Above:** Use this slider, or enter a numeric value, to set the percentage of luminance and above this filter will desaturate.

✦ **Softness:** Use this slider, or enter a numeric value, to adjust the transition amount between the affected and unaffected areas of the picture. This is also known as *feathering*.

✦ **Amount of Desaturation:** Use this slider, or enter a numeric value, to set the percentage to desaturate the selected highlights.

Lows Desaturation controls

The controls under this section of the filter are used to select the range and amount of desaturation of the shadows and blacks of your clip:

✦ **Enable:** Click this checkbox to enable or disable the Lows Desaturation controls.

✦ **Apply Below:** Use this slider, or enter a numeric value, to set the percentage of luminance and all values below that value which this filter will desaturate.

✦ **Softness:** Use this slider, or enter a numeric value, to adjust the transition amount between the affected and unaffected areas of the picture. This is also known as *feathering*.

✦ **Amount of Desaturation:** Use this slider, or enter a numeric value, to set the percentage to desaturate the selected lows. If you set this amount to 100 percent desaturation, the targeted lows will be become grayscale tones.

The application of a Desaturate filter is the same except for the range you select to remove color. Here is a typical procedure for using the Desaturate Highlights filter:

1. **Apply the Desaturate Highlights to the desired clip in your sequence.**

   This is the same as it is for any filter. I like to drag the filter from the Effects tab in the Browser onto the clip in the Timeline.

2. **Double-click the clip with the Desaturate Highlight filter in the Timeline to open it in the Viewer window.**

3. **Click on the Filters tab in the Viewer to bring it to the front.**

   You will see the Desaturate Highlights filter under the top Video Filters section.

4. **Click the disclosure triangle next to the filter's name to twirl down the controls for this filter.**

5. **While watching your calibrated broadcast monitor that is displaying the clip you are adjusting, gradually move the Apply Above slider to the left to select more highlight areas of your image that will be desaturated.**

6. **Adjust the Softness slider to feather the transition between the select areas being affected and the areas that are not.**

By tweaking these settings, you should be able to find settings that remove undesired color from the whites of the clip without it being noticeable. Applying sufficient softness will help keep the effect of this filter from looking conspicuous.

Learning the Broadcast Safe Filter

The Broadcast Safe filter is a fast and easy way to limit a clip's luminance and chrominance levels from exceeding broadcast legal limits. When applied, this filter automatically uses the proper settings for NTSC or PAL broadcast safe levels using the sequence settings of the clip it is applied to.

Because the Broadcast Safe filter simply clamps any luma and chroma levels above a set limit, care must be taken when using it. By arbitrarily applying this filter to clips that have large amounts of white exceeding broadcast legal limits (like DV footage with super-whites), many of the whites will be clamped, or limited, to broadcast safe levels at the expense of washed out details in the highlights. It is better to use this filter as a secondary levels control after most of the highlights have been brought within legal limits (100 percent for DV) using the Whites level control in the Color Correct 3-way. The Broadcast Safe filter can then clamp any remaining spikes of luma or chroma levels, thus preserving as much detail in the highlights as possible.

The default settings, available in the Mode pop-up menu, work for most applications. The available options in the Mode pop-up menu, shown in Figure 21-31, are:

✦ Custom-Use Controls Below (May be unsafe)

✦ In house (133-Unsafe)

✦ Normal (120)

✦ Conservative (115)

✦ Very Conservative (110)

✦ Extremely Conservative (100)

Note   Although the Normal setting of 120 will work in most situations, always consult with the broadcast facility airing your video for their requirements and limits.

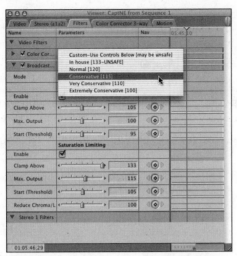

Figure 21-31: When using the Broadcast Safe filter, you can use the default settings available in the pop-up menu, or use the controls below it to customize your own.

If you select one of the default settings in the Mode pop-up, the slider controls below have no effect. If you need to make custom settings, select Custom-Use from the Mode pop-up and adjust any of the following controls:

✦ **Enable (under Luminance Limiting):** Click this checkbox to enable or disable the Luminance Limiting controls.

✦ **Clamp Above:** Use this control to set the maximum allowable percentage of luminance; any luminance values higher than this setting will be clamped. The default setting is 109.

✦ **Max Output:** The values between Start (Threshold) and Clamp Above will be compressed so that no values are clipped.

✦ **Start (Threshold):** Use this control to set a value where luminance will begin to be compressed, up to the value set in Clamp Above.

✦ **Enable (Under Saturation Limiting):** Click this checkbox to enable or disable the Saturation Limiting controls.

✦ **Clamp Above:** Use this control to set the maximum allowable percentage of saturation; any saturation values higher than this setting will be clamped. The default setting is 133, which should be acceptable for most broadcasters.

✦ **Max Output:** The values between Start (Threshold) and Clamp Above will be compressed so that no values are clipped.

✦ **Start (Threshold):** Use this control to set a value where the saturation of your clip will begin to be compressed, up to the value set in Clamp Above.

✦ **Reduce Chroma/Luma:** Use this control to set the amount the chroma will be reduced, when needed.

✦   ✦   ✦

Creating Final Output with Final Cut Pro

◆ ◆ ◆ ◆

◆ ◆ ◆ ◆

Generating Output from Final Cut Pro

◆ ◆ ◆ ◆

In This Chapter

Understanding
output options

Outputting
content to tape

Working with EDLs

◆ ◆ ◆ ◆

In the previous chapters of this book, you learned all about editing with Final Cut Pro. You learned how to capture media, import files, and edit them together to create your final program; you learned how to add text and effects; and you saw how to render your effects and create a seamless playback of the Timeline.

When the editing is finished, it is time to output. Part of the joy of working with digital media is the many options you have for outputting your content. As you know, the backbone of Final Cut Pro is QuickTime. QuickTime is a multimedia technology created and developed by Apple Computer. It is a versatile architecture that merges many different kinds of digital media seamlessly. Because Final Cut Pro is built on this versatility, you have many options for distributing your media. This chapter mainly covers creating output for videotape, be it analog or digital. However, it also covers the many other ways in which you can output your final program from Final Cut Pro. So saddle up, because it's time to show the world what you have created.

Understanding Output Options

Final Cut Pro provides numerous ways to output and distribute your final video program. Your choice on how to output depends on your venue or avenue of distribution. Each option has some pros and some cons. Some options are limited simply by the initial digital resolution of your files. Output options in Final Cut Pro are described in the following sections.

Outputting to videotape

The simplest output path you can take in Final Cut Pro is to send your output to tape. If you have a FireWire and DV-based editing system, outputting your video program to tape is quite simple. With a system equipped with a FireWire port you can simply send your program from the Timeline to your DV device and record it on a DV tape.

If you want to send the output to a VHS tape, you need either an analog video card, or a FireWire-to-analog converter device. There are many such devices on the market. FireWire-to-analog converters allow you to convert a DV stream to analog and vice versa. The Canopus ADVC-100 is one such device. If you plan to generate output for high-end professional formats such as Betacam SP, Digital Betacam, and others, you should consider a higher-end video card, such as an Aurora Igniter X or Kona card. The Sony Media Converter and other converters of its type are not suited for professional formats.

Other companies manufacturing similar DV converters (often known as a *DV bridge*) are TVOne, Datavideo-tek, Dazzle Hollywood, Leitch, FastWare, Formac Studio, Laird Telemedia, Miranda, and Pro Max.

Note   If you own a DV deck (even a simple one like the Sony DSR-11), you can also output directly from the DV deck into your VHS deck. In other words, the DV deck can also act as a FireWire-to-analog converter. Using the setup just described, simply play down your DV timeline in Final Cut Pro while recording on the VHS deck. This comes in handy for sending your rough cuts to clients. Many DV Camcorders can manage this task as well; consult your manual to see if your camera has analog output capabilities.

Outputting high-resolution digital files

In today's post-production environment, exchanging high-resolution digital files of your video is a common practice. For example, it is quite common for video editors to exchange digital movie files with After Effects artists. In large production facilities, editors take care of editing and After Effects artists create graphics, layered openers for programs, and other material for the final edits. QuickTime movies exported from Final Cut Pro may be given to After Effects artists on a FireWire drive or across a network, for example. The After Effects artists then create a new, layered movie and render it back to a QuickTime movie compatible with Final Cut Pro.

There are many factors to consider when outputting high-resolution digital files. You must consider the size of the file, the resolution of the image, and file compatibility. For example, you must know the frame size of your video in Final Cut Pro when preparing a short layered opener for a program when using Adobe After Effects.

When exchanging files, you can choose from many different types of codecs for your QuickTime movie. Codecs are specified in the QuickTime dialog box for exporting movies from Final Cut Pro. Codec choices include:

✦ **None/Uncompressed:** When exporting a QuickTime movie from Final Cut Pro, Uncompressed is one of the options you can use. It is often listed as None because it has no compression. This codec creates very-high-resolution files. However, the sizes of files created with this codec can be prohibitively large — as much as 32MB/sec. Uncompressed movies can have Alpha channels.

In Final Cut Pro 4, there are two "flavors" of Uncompressed. One is the old Uncompressed, now called Uncompressed 8-bit 4:2:2, and the other is the new Apple FCP Uncompressed 10-bit 4. You may have noticed that None is also listed as a choice.

Alpha channels might be important for After Effects artists and other editors who may work on the content that you are outputting. For more information on Alpha channels, see Chapter 17.

✦ **Animation:** This codec is generally misunderstood and underutilized. Most people assume that, because of its name, this codec is only for animated clips. In fact, this is an extremely versatile and useful codec that offers the greatest varieties of color depths and choices. At the Best setting, this codec is lossless and creates high-resolution files. Animation is an all purpose codec that is an excellent choice for exchanging digital media between applications.

✦ **M-JPEG:** There are two types of M-JPEG (Motion-JPEG) codecs. These types are MJPEG-A and MJPEG-B. Many third-party video cards for Final Cut Pro employ one or the other of these M-JPEG codecs. For example, Aurora Video Systems' Igniter X card uses the MJPEG-A codec. Other cards may use MJPEG-B. You can use variable data rates on these codecs, and they can create very-high-quality images for video files. M-JPEG codecs are *lossy*, which means that there is always some loss in the image quality, but even at data rates as low as 3 to 8MB/sec, they still provide a surprisingly good image resolution.

Part of the benefit of using the M-JPEG codecs is that some hardware manufacturers, like Aurora Video Systems, use it as their default codec. Also, most Macintosh computers with QuickTime have both M-JPEG codecs available on them. Anyone with a Macintosh, and Adobe's After Effects application for example, can render a QuickTime file in the MJPEG-A codec. If this QuickTime movie is imported into Final Cut Pro and placed in a sequence based on Aurora's Igniter MJPEG-A codec, the movie plays seamlessly. This is important if you do extensive work in After Effects and combine the resulting QuickTime files with shots in a Final Cut Pro Timeline. You can use many other video cards with Final Cut Pro that do not offer this benefit, and thus every time you import a rendered file from After Effects, it has to be rendered all over again in Final Cut Pro.

Caution   When rendering QuickTime files in After Effects for use in Final Cut Pro sequences, you must double-check some items in the After Effects program. Make sure that the final movie's frame rate, frame size, field order, codec, and data rates match your sequence settings in Final Cut Pro.

✦ **DV-NTSC and DV-PAL:** These are the basic codecs used for the DV format and compression. These codecs are used for DV capture and are also available in the QuickTime dialog box as choices for export and rendering. Movies rendered in After Effects or other third-party applications with the DV codec can be played back in a Final Cut Pro DV-based sequence.

✦ **DVCPRO50:** The DVCPRO50 codec has a data rate of 7MB/sec, which is twice that of ordinary DV. This codec works with FireWire-enabled DVCPRO50-compatible camcorders and decks. It has half the compression of the DV codec and uses better color sampling than its DV counterpart.

Cross-Reference   For more information on codecs and creating QuickTime movies, see Chapter 23.

Alphas or no Alphas

Alpha channels are used to define transparency for a digital image. Besides the three color channels of RGB colors, a fourth Alpha channel is included in digital images. This Alpha channel creates transparency and is used to superimpose items over layers and other effects.

For example, a digital file rendered with a logo in the center must have an alpha channel around the logo. This logo file, when superimposed over a video layer in Final Cut Pro makes everything around the logo transparent (or invisible). Only the logo is visible over the video track.

Editors and graphic artists often create movie files in Adobe After Effects and many other applications that are meant for superimposition over video files in Final Cut Pro. These files need an alpha channel for defining areas of transparency.

It is important to point out during any discussion of codecs that some codecs do not allow the option of including an Alpha channel. For example, the MJPEG type codecs that are commonly used for digital video do not allow the option of including an Alpha channel.

Alternatively, the Animation codec is a versatile one and allows for an Alpha channel, as does the Uncompressed codec.

Outputting to film

Many filmmakers now make their films in DV or other video formats before transferring the final output to film. There was a time when most film festivals scoffed at entries that were "films" originally shot on tape, but those days are long gone. Some recent success stories in independent filmmaking involve films that were created in this fashion. In fact, certain film companies exclusively create their movies this way, and the trend is likely to keep moving in that direction, especially as the DV gear continues to improve. Most film festivals now accept films that were originally shot on tape, and the trickle of movies shot on video and later transferred to film has recently increased to a flood. At the high-end of the video spectrum, there are artists shooting HD at 24P before transferring to film. Chief among these is George Lucas and his *Star Wars* prequels — and those were only the beginning.

Transferring video material to film is a complex and sophisticated process. If you are planning to shoot a video for transfer to film, you should first research the transfer facilities that provide such services and ask them detailed questions about their process. Some of these facilities even have handbooks that they provide to aspiring video-filmmakers. These booklets contain tips and information about shooting in video when the final print is on film. Here are a few basic tips:

✦ **Work in PAL, or with a 24P-enabled camera.** PAL is the European and Asian standard for video (the American standard is NTSC). Experts advise that you shoot your movie on PAL rather than NTSC equipment. The reason for this is that the 25 fps (frames per second) frame rate of PAL is much easier to transfer to film's 24 fps than that of NTSC's complicated 29.97 fps. When transferred to film, NTSC's 29.97 frame rate can produce motion artifacts, called *ghosting* or *strobing*. PAL also has a slightly higher resolution than NTSC, and every bit counts when you want to get the most out of your video's resolution. Final Cut Pro, being the versatile application that it is, works seamlessly with PAL video. Better still is the new generation of 24P DV cameras (the *P* stands for progressive scan) currently made by Panasonic, such as the DVX100. Not only do these cameras shoot at the native frame rate of film, but Final Cut Pro 4 can digitize the footage and natively edit it in a 24 fps Timeline. The future has arrived.

✦ **Work with the limitations of the DV format.** When shooting on DV for eventual transfer to film, you need to observe many precautions with contrast and brightness ranges. The contrast range for DV video is quite limited compared to film's contrast ratios. Overexposures and underexposures that may pass without comment in the DV world can wreck your shots when they are transferred to film. Pay extra attention to your lighting. Also, avoid quick pans and zooms, and avoid any in-camera digital effects.

✦ **Shoot in progressive scan mode.** Most broadcast video is shot in interlaced mode. This produces two *interlaced* fields, which are combined to form one frame of video. Hence, for NTSC there are actually 60 fields per second making up about 30 frames per second. Some video cameras offer a non-interlaced *progressive* scan mode, which produces single frames instead of fields. Transfer facilities usually prefer that filmmakers use progressive mode *only* when working in PAL. The rule is: When shooting PAL, shoot in progressive mode; when shooting in NTSC, use the interlaced mode.

✦ **Shoot in 16:9 widescreen mode.** When shooting in DV, I highly recommend that you work in the 16:9 widescreen mode. Many new DV cameras offer a 16:9 mode. Working in widescreen creates an aspect ratio that is very close to the Academy standard aspect ratio for 35mm film. There are several versions of the 16:9 mode, and not all widescreen modes are created equal. The first and best method for shooting 16:9 is to get a camera with a CCD that is actually 16:9. These are found in higher end (more expensive) professional video cameras. The second is to get an anamorphic lens for a standard camera. This will distort the footage as it is recorded to tape so that FCP can then "un-distort" during editing. The last method is to use the built in 16:9 feature of the electronics of the camera, but this is a very poor idea and should be treated as a camera effect. In this scenario, the camera is lopping off the top and bottom of the material coming through the lens and effectively giving you significantly less resolution. Like all in-camera effects, it should not be used.

When shooting in the 16:9 widescreen mode, your video may appear slightly soft in the viewfinder. This is simply a function of the viewfinder electronics and does not soften your final image. When viewed on a proper 16:9-capable monitor, the 16:9 video appears normal.

Final Cut Pro can work with 16:9 widescreen media. For more information on working with 16:9 media, see Chapter 24.

✦ **Research the transfer options.** You should be aware that not all tape-to-film transfer methods are created equal. Four basic methods are used:

• **Kinescope:** This is the simplest way to transfer video to film and basically consists of pointing a video projector at a film camera and recording to film while you play the video. This type of transfer is quite inexpensive and may run around $50 to $100 per minute (you'll soon learn that *inexpensive* is a relative term when it comes to transferring video to film).

• **Electronic Beam Recording:** This is another basic and inexpensive way to transfer video to film, and the quality of this transfer method is quite high. Electronic Beam Recording has been around for about two decades and is relatively reliable and affordable.

- **Digital CRT Transfer:** This is a more expensive method of transferring video to film, but it also provides much higher quality. Transfers using this method run about $300 per minute.

- **Digital Laser Transfer:** This is the most expensive type of transfer. Laser transfers can easily run upwards of $500 per minute.

Many transfer facilities offer demo tapes that you can review to evaluate the quality of their work. Some transfer facilities also have very specific delivery requirements, such as splitting your program onto 20-minute reels to conform to lengths of 35mm print rolls. Research these issues well in advance.

Another method of working with film in Final Cut Pro involves films that were originally shot on film stock and were transferred to videotape for the editing phase. After editing is complete, the edit lists from the video edits are matched back to the original negative stock for the film using Cinema Tools, which is bundled with Final Cut Pro. This ever more popular workflow is covered in detail in Chapter 27.

Outputting to DVD

DVD (Digital Versatile Disc) is the latest and greatest craze in video exchange formats. For years, the standard for home movie rentals was the VHS tape format, but DVDs seem to have become the new standard. The DVD format generally consists of MPEG-2 video files, AC-3 audio files, and bits of code that dictate how the menus of a given DVD will function.

DVDs are discs that are exactly the same physical size as Compact Discs (CDs) but can hold up to 17GB worth of material. Currently this capacity is achievable only through a complex layering process during manufacturing, but you can still record your own DVDs that hold approximately 4.7GB of material. To create a DVD, you need a drive that is capable of recording DVDs. Apple's SuperDrive, which is included on most G4s and G5s, is able to record DVDs for you. These DVDs can then be played in almost any consumer DVD player.

To create a DVD, you must first export a high-quality QuickTime movie from your Final Cut Pro Timeline. This QuickTime movie can then be brought into a DVD authoring application such as Apple's iDVD2. You then use the authoring application for laying out your DVD's interactive features and other options. DVDs also use the Dolby AC-3 surround-sound audio format.

In order to integrate the best of both worlds, you can export a sequence directly from Final Cut Pro 4 into DVD Studio Pro 2. Using Final Cut Pro, you can set chapter and compression markers in your program, all of which will appear in their right places in your DVD Studio Pro Timeline.

Outputting to CD-ROM

Another output option is CD-ROM (Compact Disc Read-Only Memory). Most CD-ROMs can only hold 650MB of material. CD-ROMs are also slow and the format itself was not designed to play high-resolution 29.97 fps video. Movies for CD-ROMs are highly compressed, but due to the growth of Web streaming, the science of codecs has gone through a revolution in the last few years. There are many high-quality codecs that can be used to compress movies for CD-ROM.

To create CD-ROMs, you need a CD-ROM recorder, called a CD-R (Compact Disc-Recordable) or CD-RW (Compact Disc-Recordable/Rewritable) drive. Many brands and types of CD-R/RW drives are available, and they are very affordable.

As with DVDs, to record a movie on CD-ROM you must first export a QuickTime file from your Final Cut Pro Timeline. While exporting, you can choose QuickTime settings appropriate for CD-ROM playback. Some of the preferred codecs for CD-ROM playback are MPEG-1, Cinepak, and Sorensen. Cinepak used to be Apple's default codec for CD-ROMs, and then Sorenson replaced Cinepak as the "flagship" Apple codec, but these days the title goes to MPEG-4, the latest and greatest compression offering based on the standards of the Motion Picture Experts Group.

Cross-Reference   For more information on creating movies for CD-ROM using Compressor, see Chapter 23.

Outputting for the Web

Some movies for the Web require a very high level of compression because of the bandwidth limitations that are defined by the lowest common denominator of a wide audience, meaning 56Kbps. Even users with broadband connections to the Web simply don't have enough bandwidth to view high-quality, full-screen 29.97 fps video. For this reason, you must choose a codec carefully when exporting a movie for the Web. MPEG-4 or Sorensen are the best codecs for creating high-quality, low-bandwidth movies for the Web.

Final Cut Pro 4.0 now ships with Compressor, a standalone application that enables you to take your finished QuickTime movies and transcode them into any and all codecs and sizes you desire. You can encode the video in batch jobs, or you can transcode them one at a time as needed. In every version of Final Cut Pro up until the present, you needed to use an independent third-party compression utility to accomplish this task, but those days are gone. Compressor is part of the impressive group of applications that have been bundled with Final Cut Pro 4.0.

Cross-Reference   For more information on creating movies for the Web using Compressor, see Chapter 23.

Outputting audio

Final Cut Pro provides you with a number of audio mixing and control features. However, many editors and producers choose to mix audio for the final program on digital audio workstations at high-end audio-mix facilities. One of the export options available in Final Cut Pro is the ability to export the audio tracks of your Timeline as digital audio AIFF files. These AIFF files can be transported on a CD-ROM or other removable media to a digital audio mix station such as one based on Digidesign's ProTools system.

For more information on preparing and exporting audio AIFF files, see Chapter 14.

For more information on composing a score and mixing it into your sequence using Soundtrack, see Chapter 15.

Outputting for other editing facilities

Depending on the type of work you do, there may be times when you need to export your work in Final Cut Pro for use in another editing facility. If so, you may be required to produce Edit Decision Lists (EDLs). EDLs are tab-delimited text files that describe both the audio and the video edits within your Timeline. EDLs include reel, shot, and timecode information for source clips and identify their location in the Timeline. Many online and high-end editing facilities are set up to exchange EDLs. After finishing your work in Final Cut Pro, you can export an EDL. This EDL can then be imported into an online editing system and your program can be re-created by recapturing the shots and the transitions. With proper care, the re-creation of the program should be frame accurate and 100-percent true to the original. Final Cut Pro has the ability to both import and export EDLs.

EDLs are described in greater detail later in this chapter.

Depending on the editing facilities you are working with, you may also be asked to export audio information from your Timeline in Open Media Format (OMF). Digidesign and other systems in the field of audio and video post-production use the OMF format extensively. Final Cut Pro allows you to export OMF files of your audio tracks in a Timeline.

For more information on preparing and exporting OMF files from Final Cut Pro, see Chapter 13.

Creating Final Output for Tape

When you are done editing and refining your Timeline, it is time to layback your material to videotape. In Final Cut Pro, there are three basic ways to master a video program to tape:

✦ Record by playing the Timeline

✦ Print to video

✦ Edit to tape

The following sections describe each of these methods.

Recording tapes by playing the Timeline

The simplest method for recording your program back to tape from a Final Cut Pro Timeline is simply to record the Timeline as it is played. All you have to do is play the Timeline after you press the Play and Record buttons on your video deck. Items such as a black screen, color bars, or tone must be added to the Timeline before you begin recording. Many editors create a standard output movie, with their slate, color bars, and tone and save it for later placing in a Timeline, which is going to be output in the manner described here.

Before you record the Timeline to tape, you must check a few items and prepare your hardware. If you are using a FireWire-based DV setup, you have little to worry about. FireWire handles both the in and out paths for audio and video signals. For an analog setup, you may have to double-check that your hardware and signal paths are hooked up correctly.

To record your Timeline to tape, follow these steps:

1. **Before you master a sequence to tape, make sure that your sequence has all items rendered at the highest resolution.**

   You can press Option+R to render any item in your sequence that is unrendered. Check the Render Quality menu at the top-left side of the Timeline window to make sure that you have rendered items at the best resolution.

2. **Connect your hardware properly. If you are recording to a camcorder or deck, check to see if the device needs to be set to the VCR setting.**

   With a DV-based system, Final Cut Pro does not record to a camera that is in camera mode. The VCR setting may be labeled VTR on some cameras. If you are using a deck or camera with multiple inputs, make sure that the correct inputs are used.

3. **Choose Final Cut Pro ⇨ Easy Setup and review the settings in the Easy Setup, as shown in Figure 22-1.**

   Make sure that the External Video settings match the hardware you are using. If not, choose a different option from the Setup For pull-down menu. Click Setup to close the Easy Setup box.

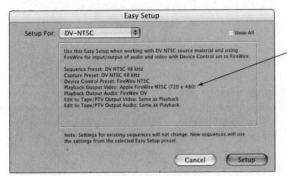

Figure 22-1: Check your settings in the Easy Setup dialog box.

4. **Choose Final Cut Pro ⇨ Audio/Video Settings and click the External Video tab.**

   The A/V Devices settings (see Figure 22-2) allow you to send video out via the FireWire port or through a third-party video card if you have one installed. If you are using a customized Easy Setup, make sure that you have selected the proper settings in the A/V Devices tab. The Playback Output choice allows you to choose how you want to view your video while playing your Timeline. The Different Output for Edit to Tape/Print to Video menu allows you to choose a different video capture interface from the one you are using to view your video during normal playback. Leave the box unchecked if you want to use the same interface as the Playback Output menu choice.

5. **Prepare your video deck by cueing the tape to the spot where you want to start the recording.**

Note   If you need black space or bars and tone on the tape, you must place these items in the Timeline before you start recording it to tape.

6. **Press Record on your tape deck and press the spacebar to start playback in the Final Cut Pro Timeline.**

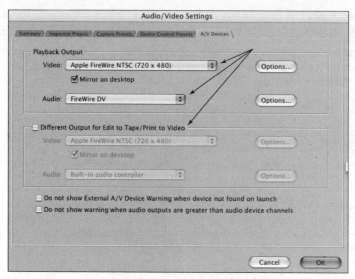

Figure 22-2: Review your A/V Devices options carefully.

7. **Press the Stop button on your deck when you are done recording.**

Final Cut Pro stops at the end of a sequence and holds the last frame. If this frame is an image from your video, you may get a long freeze frame at the end of the video. To avoid this, place a black clip at the end of the edited sequence.

Whenever you prepare to layback your video from the Timeline to a videotape, choose the Report Dropped Frames during Playback option in the General tab of the User Preferences window. Choose Final Cut Pro ⇨ User Preferences to view this option in the General tab. With this option enabled, you are warned any time a frame is dropped during layback to tape. Troubleshoot the cause of the dropped frames before continuing to lay the program to tape.

Printing to video

Using the Print to Video command, you can master a whole sequence or a clip to tape. This option gives you control over the items you choose to record to tape. You can, for instance, print just a portion of a clip to tape by marking in and out points. You can also include precise lengths for bars, black screen, slate, and a countdown for your program. And contrary to popular misconception, device control is *not* required for using the Print to Video command.

Using the Print to Video option

When preparing to use the Print to Video command, you must first follow Steps 1 through 5 in the previous section. These steps help you make sure all items in the Timeline are rendered, and that you check your hardware settings and the external video settings in Final Cut Pro. After you have followed Steps 1 through 5 in the previous section, proceed with the following steps to print your Timeline to tape:

1. **Open the sequence that you want to Print to Video.**

   If you like, you can set an In point in the sequence by pressing the I key and an Out point by pressing the O key. During the Print to Video process, only the portion marked by the In and Out points is printed to tape.

2. **Choose File ➪ Print to Video.**

   The Print to Video window appears as shown in Figure 22-3. Select the desired options. Elements in this window are listed in the order that they are seen on tape.

Select options for Leader elements

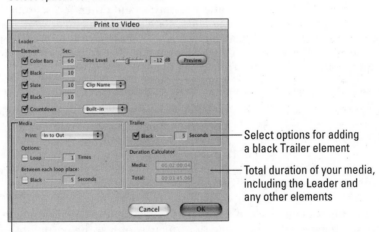

Select options for adding a black Trailer element

Total duration of your media, including the Leader and any other elements

Select options for Media and Looping elements

Figure 22-3: Choose options in the Print to Video window.

3. **Click OK when you are done choosing Print to Video settings.**

   A message appears advising you to start recording.

4. **Start recording on your deck and wait a few seconds for the tape to get rolling.**

   Then click OK in the message window to start printing your media to tape.

5. **Press the Stop button on your deck or camera when you are done.**

Understanding options in the Print to Video window

The Print to Video window has many options for adding elements to your programs. It is important to understand these options and their behavior before choosing what you want to add to your tape.

The first group of options is Leader Elements. These elements include:

✦ **Color Bars:** Adds color bars and a reference tone. This reference tone is a 1 kHz tone set to –12dBs. The bars and tone are used by engineers and editors to calibrate broadcast, playback, or capture equipment to your tape. You can change the time that the bars display and use the slider to modify the reference level of the tone.

Cross-Reference   For a detailed discussion of reference tone, see Chapter 14.

✦ **Black:** Adds a black clip of the specified length after the bars.

✦ **Slate:** Adds a slate after the black clip. It is common to add a slate for your program to tape. This slate includes information about the name of the program, date, timecode information, duration, and other notes. From the pull-down menu you can choose to add a slate that has a clip or sequence name, some text you type in a field, a PICT, or a QuickTime file. Some editors and edit facilities have a short QuickTime file they like to use as a slate for their tapes. You may select the QuickTime file with this menu.

✦ **Black:** Adds another black clip of your specified length after the slate.

✦ **Countdown:** Adds a countdown before your sequence starts. You can choose between a standard SMPTE countdown that Final Cut Pro offers as a default, or choose a QuickTime movie to use as your countdown.

The next group of settings in the Print to Video window is the Media options and loop settings:

✦ **Print:** Allows you to select which media you want to layback to tape. You can choose between the entire clip or sequence, or just the portion of either as specified by In and Out points.

✦ **Loop:** Loops the sequence or the clip. Enter the number of times you want to loop your material onto tape.

✦ **Black:** Adds a black clip of a specified length.

Finally, you also have the option of adding a trailer to the end of your sequence. It is common to add a length of black after the edited sequence finishes on tape.

Editing to Tape

The third and most sophisticated option for laying clips and sequences to tape is the Edit to Tape option. To perform this operation, you use the Edit to Tape window. Be aware that the Edit to Tape window looks a lot like the Canvas window and even behaves like it in some ways. This can be somewhat confusing. A good way to sort out this functionality overlap is to think of the Edit to Tape window as being just like the Canvas window — except that instead of making edits to the sequence, it makes edits to tape.

The Editing to Tape option gives you the most control in terms of where and how you want to edit your program onto a tape. When working with third-party video cards and using serial device control, such as the RS-422 type, you should use the Edit to Tape feature to lay off your edited program to tape.

Understanding different types of edits

You can perform two types of edits when editing to tape. These types are *assemble* and *insert* edits. To fully understand these two types of edits you have to know a little bit about the tracks on your videotape. Videotapes have video and audio tracks on them. Tapes can also have a control track and a timecode track. A control track is a simple track of "ticks" on your tape that is used by the deck for speed control. A device on the deck measures the passing of these ticks and adjusts the tape speed accordingly. If you use the Print to Video command to record to a videotape, this control track is also recorded on the tape on its own track. Breaks occur in the control track when you stop recording. Usually this is highly undesirable. Broadcast facilities do not like tapes with broken control tracks because they cause slight glitches when played through.

When you make an assemble edit to tape, *all* tracks are recorded, including the audio, video, control, and timecode tracks. Assemble edits are the only types of edits possible on DV tapes. To avoid breaks in the control track, let your assemble edits run a few seconds long. There should also be at least six seconds of tape before the In point of your content.

When you make an insert edit, you can choose between audio and video tracks or make edits with both audio and video. An insert edit does *not* record control or timecode tracks, but these tracks must be present on the tape for the insert edit to be successful. For this reason editors often use *blacked* tapes. These are tapes that have had black recorded on them to place both a control track and a timecode track on the tape. Insert edits cannot be performed on DV tapes.

Cross-Reference   For more on how to black tapes, see the section on Black and Code operation later in this chapter.

Caution

Do not perform assemble edits on a blacked tape, because where the assemble edit ends there is a break in both the control track and the timecode track.

Using the Edit to Tape window

The Edit to Tape window can be accessed from the Tools menu. Often this window appears over the Canvas window. The Edit to Tape window, shown in Figure 22-4, is the place where you control all your edit operations from Final Cut Pro to the video deck of your choice.

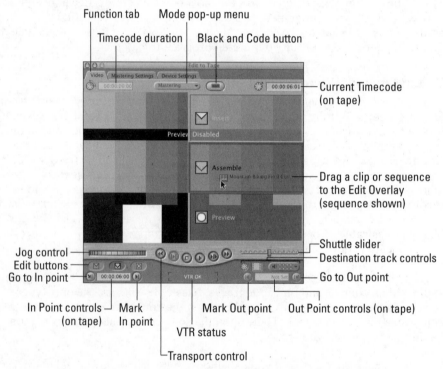

Figure 22-4: The Edit to Tape window is accessed from the File menu.

The Edit to Tape window contains a number of important tools. These include:

✦ **Mode pop-up menu:** This menu defaults to the Mastering setting. In Mastering mode, you output the entire video program along with leader, media, and trailer elements. Using the Mastering mode, you can only set an In point on your tape. The Out point is automatically calculated. This Out point is based on the choices you make on the Mastering tab and the length of your program. The other choice in this menu is the Editing setting. When using the Editing setting, you cannot add any of the Mastering options. You can set In and Out points on tape and only edit a clip or a sequence of your choice to the tape. Choose the Editing setting when you want to add a shot to an edited sequence that already exists on tape.

✦ **Black and Code button:** Allows you to black a tape. This button records black to your tape along with continuous timecode and control tracks.

✦ **Timecode Duration:** Indicates the total duration selected. If you have In and Out points marked on your clip or sequence, this field indicates the duration of the selection. If there are no In or Out points set, the Timecode Duration field shows the total length of the clip or the sequence you are editing to tape.

✦ **Current Timecode:** Indicates the current timecode on tape. Entering a new timecode moves the tape to that location.

✦ **Edit Overlay:** Dragging a clip or a sequence to the Edit to Tape window makes the Edit Overlay visible. Note the *Preview* choice available to you in this overlay. You can assemble, insert, or merely preview your edit using this Edit Overlay. The Preview choice is handy when you want to insert one shot in the middle of an edited sequence on tape. Doing a preview of such an insert edit shows you if there are any frame flashes or other issues with the edit you are about to perform.

✦ **Edit buttons:** Instead of dragging clips or sequences to the Edit Overlay, you can click one of these buttons to perform an assemble, insert, or preview edit.

✦ **VTR Status:** Indicates the status of the device connected to the Final Cut Pro workstation. Messages in this area provide clues to hardware issues you may have.

✦ **Shuttle slider:** Drag the slider left or right to move around on the tape. The shuttling speed depends on how far you drag the slider. The slider turns green when the speed is normal.

✦ **Jog control:** This control allows you to move forward or backward in increments of a few frames at a time. Use this to precisely locate specific frames on tape.

✦ **Destination track controls:** If you're using Serial Device control (such as RS-422), these buttons, as well as the pop-up menu, control the insert edit selection for tracks on your video deck. For example, if you only want to edit to the video track of tape in your video deck, uncheck the audio indicators from the pop-up menu. If you want to edit only to the audio tracks of your tape, uncheck the video indicator and specify which audio tracks you want to record to. You can also toggle the timecode indicator on and off. For example, if you're performing an insert edit, you'll probably want to turn the timecode switch off since you're using the *tape's* timecode as reference for your edit.

✦ **In Point controls:** Enter a timecode in the field to set an In point on your tape. The button on the right sets an In point at the current spot on tape. The button on the left shuttles the tape to the marked In point.

✦ **Out Point controls:** Enter a timecode in the field to set an out point on your tape. The button on the left sets an Out point at the current spot on tape. The button on the right shuttles the tape to the marked Out point.

✦ **Transport controls:** These controls allow you to navigate on tape. You can Rewind, Play In to Out, Stop, Play, Play Around Current, and Fast Forward using these controls.

Using the function tabs of the Edit to Tape window

The Edit to Tape window has several function tabs that you should review. The tabs contain Mastering Settings and Device Settings. Both tabs are shown in Figure 22-5.

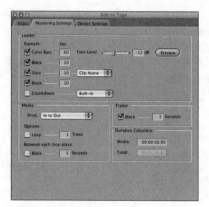

Figure 22-5: The Mastering Settings and Device Settings tabs are part of the Edit to Tape window.

The Mastering Settings tab allows you to select leader and trailer elements as well as looping options for your final layback to tape. These options are similar to options in the Print to Video window, described in a previous section of this chapter. The Device Settings tab has two menus:

✦ **Device Control:** Choose the type of device control you are using. For DV and FireWire-based setups, you may have to choose FireWire NTSC. Some third-party cards may require RS-422 or another type of serial device control.

For more information on Device Control, see Chapter 4.

✦ **Capture/Input:** This menu allows you to select how you want Final Cut Pro to play video in the Edit to Tape window. If it is set to a DV choice, you use the FireWire path to view the video. When using third-party analog cards, menu choices may include Composite, S-Video, or Component. The options in this menu are based on the Capture Presets tab of the Audio/Video Settings window, which is located under the Edit menu.

For more information on Capture Presets, see Chapter 6.

Preparing for an Edit to Tape operation

Before you edit a clip or sequence to tape, there are a few items you should check. Follow these steps before editing to tape:

1. **Render your sequence.**

   Before you edit to tape, make sure that all the items in your sequence have been rendered at the highest resolution. You can press Option+R to render any unrendered items in your sequence. Check the Render Quality menu on the top-left side of the Timeline window to make sure that you have rendered items at the best resolution.

2. **Check your hardware setup.**

   Make sure that your hardware is connected properly. If you are recording to a camcorder or deck, set the device to the VCR setting if necessary. Select the correct input if your device has multiple inputs.

3. **Calibrate your timecode.**

   You must calibrate the timecode for your editing setup before performing an Edit to Tape operation. This ensures proper placement of shots on tape. If there is a timecode offset between your deck and Final Cut Pro, your shots could be edited to the wrong frame. Frame accuracy while editing to tape is critical.

To learn more about calibrating the timecode for your Final Cut Pro setup, see Chapter 24.

4. **Check your Easy Setup.**

   Choose Final Cut Pro ➪ Easy Setup and make sure you have specified a way for the Easy Setup to send out external video to your hardware setup.

5. **Check your external video settings.**

   Choose Final Cut Pro ➪ Audio/Video Settings and click the External Video tab. The external video settings allow you to send video out via the FireWire port, or through a third-party video card if you have one installed.

6. **Cue up the tape.**

   Prepare your video deck by cueing up the tape to the spot where you want to start recording.

Blacking and coding tapes

Many years ago, my first job at an editing facility was to black tapes for editors. I used to use a video deck that had the ability to set a starting timecode. I'd feed a black signal from a black generator into the deck, set a starting timecode, and start recording on tape. Many large editing facilities keep blacked tapes for editors.

If there is no material on your tape, you should black and code the tape before you edit to it. During a blacking operation, Final Cut Pro records black along with time-code and control tracks on the tape. No audio is recorded during this operation.

In non-DV/FireWire setups you can specify the starting timecode of a blacked tape if you have a timecode generator in your video deck. It is common practice in editing facilities to start a blacked tape at 00:58:00:00. The first minute of black is usually left unused. The second minute is used for leader elements. This allows the program to start at 1:00:00:00 on a blacked tape.

During a black and code operation in Final Cut Pro, you get the Initialize Tape dialog box — if Final Cut Pro detects a timecode generator in your video deck. You can use the Initialize Tape dialog box to specify a starting timecode on the tape you are about to black. If you do not have a timecode generator in your deck, you cannot specify the starting timecode when blacking a tape.

Note   If you want to black and code a DV tape starting at 00:58:00:00 or whatever time you like, use a deck lie the DSR-40 or the DSR-1500 and send timecode to the deck via RS-422 while still sending the video out via Firewire.

Note   If you are planning to assemble edit a long video program to tape, you do not have to black and code the tape. However, if you are making this assemble edit to a brand-new tape, you should at least black and code the first minute or so of the tape. This allows you to set an In point to start the assemble edit. If you plan to perform a series of insert edits, you should take the time to black and code the entire tape.

To black and code a tape, follow these steps:

1. **Insert a tape in the video deck.**

2. **Choose File ⇨ Edit to Tape.**

3. **Click the Black and Code button in the Edit to Tape window.**

    Figure 22-6 shows this button. If the deck has a timecode generator, Final Cut Pro detects the generator and brings up the Initialize Tape dialog box.

Black and Code button

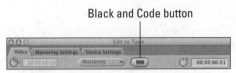

Figure 22-6: Click the Black and Code button to start blacking your tape.

4. **Enter a starting timecode in the Initialize Tape dialog box and click OK.**

Caution

If the video deck has a timecode generator, make sure that it is set to Preset. On many professional decks there is a button that allows you to choose between Preset and Regen for regenerate. Set this switch to Preset; otherwise, the deck is not going to use the timecode specified by Final Cut Pro.

5. **In the Black and Code dialog box, select an option in the Settings menu.**

Selecting Custom in this menu brings up the Sequence Preset Editor, and you can edit the settings that appear there. The other settings in the Settings menu, shown in Figure 22-7, are based on the sequence presets in your current Easy Setup. A message like the one shown in Figure 22-8 appears, warning you that your tape will be erased and written over with black.

Figure 22-7: Choose a setting to match your hardware in the Black and Code dialog box.

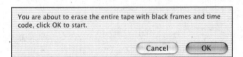

Figure 22-8: A warning indicates that you are about to erase and black your tape.

6. **Click OK.**

Your tape rewinds to the beginning and then is blacked. To cancel the Black and Code operation, press the Esc key on your keyboard.

Performing an assemble edit

After you have reviewed all your Edit to Tape settings and have some tapes blacked and ready, it is time to lay your video program back to tape. If you want to lay all tracks to tape simultaneously, you perform an assemble edit. To perform an assemble edit:

1. **Choose File ⇨ Edit to Tape.**

   The Edit to Tape window appears. In most cases, the Edit to Tape window appears on top of the Canvas window. The Preview option is disabled if you are using a DV device, and you see a Preview Disabled message over a set of color bars.

2. **Select Mastering or Editing from the pop-up menu in the top center of the Edit to Tape window.**

3. **Double-click the sequence you want to edit to tape to open it.**

   If you just want to edit a clip to tape, load it into the Viewer. If you want, you can set In and Out points in the sequence or the clip. Only the section between the In and Out points is edited to tape.

4. **Set In and Out points on tape.**

   If you are in Mastering mode, you can only set an In point. If you are in Editing mode, you can set both In and Out points on tape. To set In or Out points, cue the tape to the desired spot and press the Mark In or Mark Out buttons as appropriate. You can also manually enter timecodes in the In and Out timecode fields.

   Tip   Pressing I for In and O for Out also works here.

5. **If you are in Mastering mode, click the Mastering Settings tab.**

   Add leader and trailer elements as you see fit.

6. **Drag your sequence from the Browser to the Assemble Overlay in the Edit to Tape window.**

   If you are editing a clip to tape, load that clip in the Viewer and click the Assemble Edit button in the lower-left portion of the Edit to Tape window. You can also just drag a clip from the Browser or the Viewer to the Edit to Tape window and then release it when it's positioned over the Assemble Overlay.

   A dialog box shows you the rendering progress if any rendering is required. The Edit to Tape operation begins automatically. You can press the Esc key to cancel an Edit to Tape operation at any time.

Performing an insert edit

An insert edit is a bit more complicated than an assemble edit because you choose the tracks you want to edit to tape. For example, you can choose to edit just the video portion of a clip or sequence, and choose between Audio Channels 1 and 2. Insert edits are not possible with DV format. To perform an insert edit:

1. **Choose File ➪ Edit to Tape.**

2. **Select Mastering or Editing from the pop-up menu in the top center of the Edit to Tape window.**

3. **Double-click the sequence you want to edit to tape to open it.**

   If you just want to edit a clip to tape, load it into the Viewer. If you want, you can set In and Out points in the sequence or the clip. Only the section between the In and Out points is edited to tape.

4. **Set In and Out points on tape.**

   If you are in Mastering mode, you can only set an In point. If you are in Editing mode, you can set both In and Out points on tape. To set In and Out points, cue the tape to the appropriate spots and press the Mark In or Mark Out buttons as appropriate.

   You can also manually enter timecodes in the In and Out timecode fields. Timecode entries are critical if you plan to insert a single shot in between other shots on tape. Insert edits are often used to replace a single shot on a tape. *Note:* Be sure to check your timecodes to confirm you are inserting your shot at the correct location.

5. **Select the tracks in your sequence you want to insert to tape by disabling any tracks in the sequence that you do *not* want to record during the insert edit.**

   To disable a track, click the green track visibility button to the left of any track in the Timeline. The disabled track is grayed out and will not be used during the insert edit mode.

6. **Select the tracks you want to insert to on your video deck.**

   By checking on or off the destination track controls in the Edit to Tape window, you can determine which tracks of the tape in your video deck you want to make the insert edit to. If you only want to edit to the video track of tape in your video deck, uncheck the audio indicators from their pop-up menu. If you want to edit only to the audio tracks of your tape, uncheck the video indicator.

7. **If you are in Mastering mode, click the Mastering Settings tab.**

   Under this tab you can add leader and trailer elements to your edit.

8. **If you plan to perform a frame-accurate insert edit, you should perform a preview edit first.**

   When inserting a single shot to a master tape or a tape with a program on it, you could get a glitch or a flash frame if your insert edit settings are not correct. To prevent such incidents, perform a preview edit. Drag your sequence or clip to the Preview Overlay in the Edit to Tape window. A preview edit shows you what your final edit looks like, except that it does not do the edit. It only provides a preview.

9. **Drag the sequence from the Browser to the Insert Overlay in the Edit to Tape window.**

   If you are editing in a clip, load that clip in the Viewer and click the Insert Edit button in the lower-left portion of the Edit to Tape window. Alternatively, drag a clip from the Browser or the Viewer to the Insert Overlay in the Edit to Tape window.

10. **Click OK in the next dialog box to start recording.**

    If there are any Mastering Settings elements that require rendering, these are rendered first. Press the Esc key to stop the insert edit at any time.

Working with EDLs in Final Cut Pro

Edit Decision Lists (EDLs) are tab-delimited lists that detail the edits in a program. EDLs originated in the world of tape-to-tape editing and are used extensively to record and store the editing details of a program. EDLs also provide a way to exchange information about edited programs from otherwise incompatible systems. For example, if I edit a show on a Sony tape-to-tape editing system, I could export the EDL to a CMX-type editing system and re-create the edited show from the details in the EDL. High-end tape-to-tape editing systems can re-create edited shows by re-creating the edits in an EDL. Final Cut Pro allows you to export and import EDLs. Figure 22-9 shows a simple EDL.

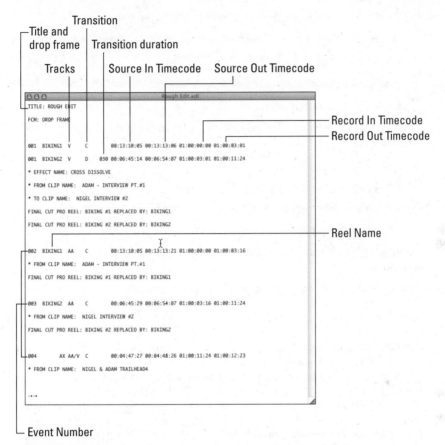

Transition

Title and
drop frame   Transition duration

Tracks   Source In Timecode   Source Out Timecode

Record In Timecode

Record Out Timecode

Reel Name

Event Number

Figure 22-9: An EDL provides information about edits in a sequence.

Reading an EDL

An EDL is a basic text document that uses simple codes and indications to describe edits. Editors should know how to read an EDL. There may be times when you have to edit an EDL directly. An EDL can be edited like any other text document. EDLs can vary dramatically depending on the options chosen, but some of the most common indications in an EDL are described here:

✦ **Title and Drop Frame:** The header of an EDL indicates the name of the sequence and the type of timecode used.

✦ **Event Number:** Every edit is represented by an event number.

✦ **Reel Name:** The reel used for each edit is indicated by name.

✦ **Tracks:** Indicates the tracks used on the record side. Track indicators include:

- **V:** Video track

- **A1 or A2:** Audio channel 1 or 2

- **AA:** Both channels of audio

✦ **Transition:** One letter indicates the type of transition used. Letters used include:

- **C:** Cut

- **D:** Dissolve

- **W:** Wipe (This is followed by a standard SMPTE Wipe code.)

- **K:** Key edit to represent video on Track 2

✦ **Transition Duration:** This number indicates the length (in frames) of the transition.

✦ **Timecodes:** Timecode information from the edit is shown in four columns. The columns indicate Source In, Source Out, Record In, and Record Out, respectively. In Final Cut Pro the Record columns list the sequence timecode.

Note   Events that represent a transition in an EDL occupy two lines. If the two shots needed for a transition are on the same reel, Final Cut Pro generates a B Reel EDL. This is because, in a tape-based editing system, transitions are created by playing the source tapes in two decks labeled A and B. The tape-based system transitions from Deck A to Deck B. The B Reel EDL helps in creating a B Reel that holds the shots necessary for creating transitions in tape-based systems. *Split edits* in EDLs (edits that have offset edit points between audio and video) take up three lines in an EDL.

Using EDLs

EDLs contain a lot of information about the edits in a program. They indicate the source reel name for each shot or event. EDLs also indicate the type of edit performed, the In and Out points for the edit on the source tape, and the In and Out points on the record tape.

Producers often perform basic offline cuts on a Final Cut Pro system, and then export an EDL to an online production house for a final refined edit. The edit facility imports the EDL into its system and re-creates the edits by placing the appropriate reels in the source-side decks.

Cross-
Reference   For more information on online and offline workflow, see Chapter 1.

There are many different EDL formats. The most common EDL formats are CMX, Sony, and GVG. EDLs are not only meant for going between a nonlinear editing system (such as Final Cut Pro) and a tape-based edit system (such as CMX), EDLs can also be exchanged between two different nonlinear editing systems. For example, you cannot open a sequence created in Final Cut Pro on an Avid nonlinear editing system. However, you can export an EDL from Final Cut Pro and import it into an Avid system to re-create and recapture your edited program.

Generating an EDL from Final Cut Pro

After you finish editing a sequence, you can export an EDL from Final Cut Pro. This EDL can be imported into other linear and nonlinear editing systems. To export an EDL from Final Cut Pro:

1. **Double-click a sequence to open it.**

2. **Choose File ⇨ Export ⇨ EDL.**

   The EDL Export Options dialog box appears, as shown in Figure 22-10.

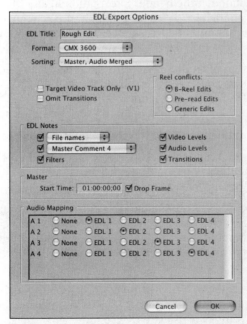

Figure 22-10: The EDL Export Options dialog box is where you select EDL options and formats.

3. **Choose the options you want and click OK.**

   Options in this dialog box are explained in the next section.

4. **Choose a location in which to save the EDL and click Save.**

5. **If you did not select the Pre-Read Edits option, another dialog box appears for you to save a B-Reel EDL. Choose a name and location for this B-Reel EDL.**

   Final Cut Pro exports the EDLs. If your sequence exceeds the maximum number of events for the EDL format you have chosen, Final Cut Pro automatically creates multiple EDLs.

Adjusting EDL export settings

The EDL Export Options dialog box is filled with many settings and choices. You should understand these settings before you export an EDL. Some EDL import modules can be quite fussy and reject an EDL if it doesn't have exactly the correct information in the correct format.

✦ **EDL Title:** This title is included in the header information of an EDL. Limit the length of this name to 60 characters or less. By default, the sequence name is used here. The EDL title is just the title that appears in the actual EDL text. It does not affect the name of the EDL file that is exported by Final Cut Pro.

✦ **Format:** Select a format from the pull-down menu. You should find out in advance what type of EDL formats are accepted by the edit location for which you are generating this EDL. The most common EDL format is CMX 3600, but you may very well be required to produce an EDL in a different format.

✦ **Sorting:** Select a Sorting option for your clips. Sorting options include:

   • **Master, Audio Merged:** Using this choice shows the clips in the order in which they appear in the sequence. Audio clips that start and end with the video portions are shown as a single edit event.

   • **Source, Audio Merged:** Clips are indicated in the order in which they appear on the source tapes. The first event is the earliest timecode starting with the lowest numbered reel. This saves a lot of tape shuttling on the source side. Again, audio clips that start and end with the video portions are shown as a single edit event.

✦ **Target Video Track Only:** Selecting this option only exports the main target video track and ignores any superimposed tracks. Audio tracks are not affected by this setting.

✦ **Omit Transitions:** Allows you to exclude transitions and create a simple EDL. You may want to do this to avoid creating issues for the editing system that is importing your EDL. If the transition codes are not understood by the destination system, you may have problems re-creating them. In this case, the transitions can be added in the online session.

✦ **Reel Conflicts:** This setting has three choices for dealing with reel conflicts:

- **B-Reel Edits:** If two shots needed for a transition are on the same reel, selecting this option causes Final Cut Pro to create a B-Reel EDL. This EDL is a short EDL that allows the editor to create a B-Reel with all the shots needed for the transitions onto a separate reel. Only use this option if you are exporting for an online session at a tape-based editing facility.

- **Pre-Read Edits:** Some high-end digital decks, such as the Sony Digital Betacam A-500, are able to perform dissolve transitions from a single tape using the Pre-Read function. Select this option only if you have full knowledge of the decks being used in the tape-based editing facility and you have discussed this option with the engineer or editor at that facility.

- **Generic Edits:** Use this option if you are taking an EDL from one nonlinear editing system to another. In this case, neither the B-Reel edits nor the Pre-Read options should apply.

✦ **EDL Notes:** This option allows you to include notes in your EDL. Notes include:

- **Clip Names:** Clip names are added to the Event lines.

- **Filters:** Describes the filters used on a clip.

- **Comments 4:** This option includes the notes from the Comments 4 column of the Browser window.

- **Video Levels:** Includes information on video opacity levels for Track V2 of your sequence. It also includes the timing information for any keyframes that may have been applied.

- **Audio Levels:** Audio level changes are indicated, along with the timing of any keyframes where changes occur.

✦ **Master:** Allows you to set a starting timecode for the master edit tape. Check these settings:

- **Start Time:** Use to set the starting timecode on the edit master tape. By default, the starting timecode of the sequence is used.

- **Drop Frame:** Allows you to choose Drop or Non-Drop frame type timecodes. This is indicated in the header information of the EDL as well.

✦ **Audio Mapping:** EDL formats, such as CMX and Sony, have limits on the number of audio tracks they allow. The Audio Mapping window allows you to map any audio tracks in the sequence to the number of tracks allowed by the EDL format. Table 22-1 lists EDL format limits.

Table 22-1
EDL Format Limits

System Limits	Reel Name Length	Reel Name Limits	Maximum # of Edits Allowed	Audio Track
CMX 340	1 to 3 characters	Numbers only, up to 253	999	2
CMX 3600	8 characters	Uppercase letters, numbers 0 through 9	999	4
GVG 4 Plus	6 characters	Uppercase letters, numbers 0 through 9	9999	4
Sony 5000	1 to 3 characters	Numbers only, up to 998	999	2
Sony 9100	6 characters	Uppercase letters, numbers 0 through 9	9999	4

Creating EDLs that work

Making the actual EDL is very easy. Making an EDL that is accurate and works properly in the destination editing system can be very, very hard. Whether EDLs are accurate or not is often determined before you even start the export process. Before you try to generate an EDL, heed the following tips and precautions:

✦ **Calibrate your timecode.** EDLs rely entirely on timecode for creating accurate edits. If your timecode has an offset, your EDL is inaccurate. Of course, you can edit the EDL and enter the proper timecodes by hand. But this takes time and may not always work if you add spaces and other characters into your EDL by mistake. Calibrate your Final Cut Pro workstation with your video deck to make sure your timecode is accurate before you capture any shots for editing.

Cross-Reference

To learn more about calibrating the timecode in Final Cut Pro, see Chapter 24.

✦ **Organize your reels.** An EDL assumes that your reel names are accurate and true. When you are logging and capturing shots in Final Cut Pro, it is easy to overlook reel name changes in the Log and Capture window. If you missed a reel name or entered the name incorrectly during log and capture, your EDL is going to reflect inaccurate reel names. For a complex project, this can turn into a nightmare in the online room. Online rooms are expensive and you don't want to waste time there sorting through inaccurate reel names. Within Final Cut Pro's Browser window, there are many ways to change the reel names of the clips you have captured. This ensures a reliable and accurate EDL.

Another way you can keep your reels organized is by setting unique time-codes on them. On professional-level decks, it is common to change the starting timecode for each reel being recorded in the field. For example, Reel #1 may have a starting timecode of 01:00:00:00, Reel #2 starts at 02:00:00:00, and so on. This ensures that the reels cannot be confused when working with an EDL. Even if the reel names or numbers were not accurately tracked at the log and capture stage, a look at the hour field of the reel indicates which reel it is.

Finally, label all your reels carefully. While you name them, observe the limitations that EDL formats have for reel names. Some EDL formats allow only three characters for reel names, while others allow six or eight characters (see Table 22-1 for more on reel name limits).

✦ **Label clips carefully.** Keep all clip names under 25 characters. This avoids confusion between clips with long, overlapping names.

✦ **Limit the number of edits in a sequence.** Some EDL formats have limitations on the number of events they can contain. Find out the limit of the format you are using and observe it in your sequences, if possible. Final Cut Pro also automatically creates multiple EDLs when the number of events exceeds the limit of the EDL format.

✦ **Locate transitions in track V1 only.** Keep your transitions in the V1 track of all sequences. V2 and other superimposed tracks are called Key tracks in EDLs and are used for superimposing shots. You generally cannot rely on being able to create accurate EDLs for sequences that have numerous video tracks with superimposed edits.

✦ **Limit the number of audio tracks.** EDL formats were developed for videotape-based systems. Tapes generally do not have more than four tracks of audio. Final Cut Pro can have up to 99 tracks of audio in a sequence. If you have more audio tracks than are allowed by your EDL format, you can make multiple copies of the sequence and delete tracks from some of them to make separate EDLs for all audio tracks.

✦ **Practice caution for audio levels.** Very few online rooms can translate audio level notes into an automatic level adjustment during EDL import. These notes are mostly used as references for editors.

✦ **Avoid nested sequences.** In Final Cut Pro, you can nest sequences by placing one sequence into another. EDLs have no way to accommodate this feature. You may have to generate separate EDLs for nested sequences, and keep notes on how to combine nested sequences in an online room.

✦ **Avoid fancy transitions.** Most EDLs can only work with certain standard SMPTE transitions. These are mostly dissolves and basic wipes. Final Cut Pro has many more transition choices. Avoid anything beyond a basic dissolve or wipe if you are exporting an EDL.

✦ **Observe caution when using stills and speed changes.** If you are using still graphics, you may have to plan carefully to accommodate them. One way to accommodate stills is to give all stills separate reel names and edit the stills to separate reels for use in the online room. Also, avoid strange numbers for speed changes. I recommend avoiding speed changes altogether, but if you are going to change clip speeds, use simple numbers like 25 percent or 50 percent. Professional decks have DMC (Dynamic Motion Control) that allows them to make speed changes for shots, but they generally work only with basic changes. Avoid Fit to Fill edits in a sequence at all costs if you plan to export an EDL. Fit to Fill edits create oddly numbered speed changes, such as 101.4 percent.

Importing and recapturing EDLs into a Final Cut Pro project

Just as you can export an EDL from Final Cut Pro, you can also import EDLs into a Final Cut Pro project. An EDL, when imported, will become an offline sequence in your project. At that point, all you have to do is to recapture your offline sequence, and you will be able to re-create the edited program represented by the imported EDL.

This feature is useful when you have to exchange information about an edited program from another nonlinear editing system into Final Cut Pro. For example, if you cut a program on an Avid or Adobe Premiere editing system, you can generate an EDL from those systems and import the EDL into Final Cut Pro for recapture. You can also do the same with a tape-to-tape-based editing system that can generate EDLs.

To import and recapture an EDL into Final Cut Pro:

1. **Select File ⇨ Import and choose EDL from the submenu.**

    The Import Options dialog box appears.

2. **Select your settings and click OK.**

    Figure 22-11 shows the Import Options dialog box for EDL imports.

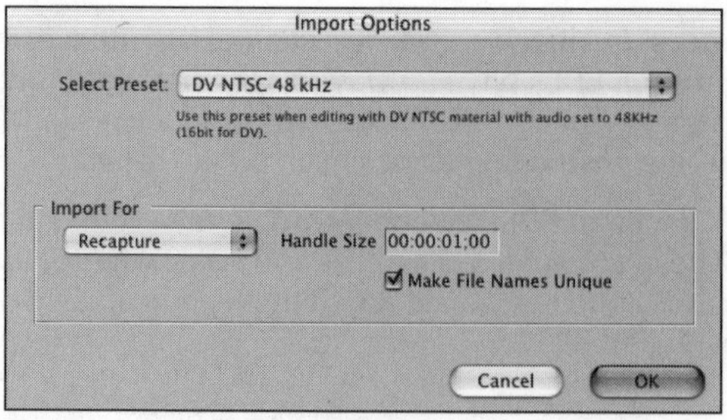

Figure 22-11: The Import Options dialog box for the EDL import option allows you to specify settings for the import.

Clips in an imported EDL

Clips in an imported EDL are named two ways.

✦ Clips imported from an EDL that was exported from a nonlinear editing system, such as Final Cut Pro, Media 100, or Avid system are named like this:

FROM CLIP NAME: CLIP NAME HERE

CLIP NAME HERE is the name of your clip. Final Cut Pro recognizes clips names from Media 100, Avid, and of course, Final Cut Pro EDLs.

✦ In all other circumstances of imported EDLs, Final Cut Pro uses the reel number and the starting timecode as the clip name. For example:

0002 01:15:20:15

Final Cut Pro uses SMPTE dissolve and wipe codes where appropriate and places markers in the created sequences when EDL import errors occur.

3. **Locate and select the EDL file you wish to import.**

Note that this imported EDL will become a sequence in your project.

4. **Select the sequence in the browser and select File ⇨ Batch Capture to begin batch capture of your offline sequence created by the imported EDL.**

Cross-Reference

For more information on the Batch Capture process see Chapter 7.

Understanding the settings of the Import Options dialog box

The Import Options dialog box has various settings that affect the import process of the incoming EDL. These are explained here:

✦ **Select Preset:** Using the drop-down menu, select the sequence preset you want to use for the incoming EDL, which will convert into a sequence.

✦ **Import For:** Select an option from the Timeline.

✦ **Recapture:** Use this option if you are importing an EDL from a tape-tape-edit system, such as a CMX or a Grass Valley edit system. Using this option makes the clip names unique and adds a one-second handle before and after the clip. (You can modify the size of the handles.)

✦ **Reconnect:** Select this option if you have the media files on disk. You can relink to these files from the clips in the sequence. You can use this option when you are importing an EDL and source media files from a QuickTime-based nonlinear editing system. Selecting this option maintains the original names for clips to make relinking easier. No handles are added for this option.

✦ **Custom:** Select this option to be able to specify handle size or drop frame timecode.

✦ **Handle Size:** This option is not available when selecting the Reconnect option because that assumes the source media files to be on disk. In other cases, the Handle Size setting is used to add extra media on either side of the clip. Adding handles allows you to have flexibility for trimming edits.

> **Caution**
>
> If you are using non-DV device control (such as RS-422 or RS-232) and plan to recapture an offline sequence that was created by an imported EDL, you *must* add at least ten frames of handles. Otherwise, you may end up having stuttering frames at the top of each clip in the Timeline.

✦ **Drop Frame:** Check the box if you want to use Drop Frame timecode mode for the clips.

✦ **Make File Name Unique:** Select this box if you are recapturing clips, so that all clips are uniquely named. Leave this box unchecked if you plan to relink clips to source media files already on disk.

✦   ✦   ✦

Making Movies with Compressor

Whoa! What's this? A standalone video compression utility that ships with Final Cut Pro at no extra charge? Am I dreaming?

Nope. Absolutely not. Sure as you're reading this, Compressor, Apple's new media transcoding application, is part of the application suite that comprises Final Cut Pro 4.0. It wasn't too long ago that you had to purchase expensive third-party software and in some high-end cases, proprietary hardware to handle your compression needs. The price and complexity factor always went up if you needed good MPEG-2 compression. In a fairly stunning development, those days seem to be over.

Compressor exports to any QuickTime format, most notably MPEG-2 and MPEG-4. MPEG-2 is the core of the ever more popular DVD format, and MPEG-4 is rapidly becoming the industry standard for streaming video online. MPEG-4's audio component, the AAC format, is now the foundation of iTunes, Apple's big moneymaker in the consumer digital audio market. All of these media formats are at your fingertips in Compressor. Basically, you can use it to convert your output from Final Cut Pro into almost any variation of QuickTime you can imagine.

So what does this mean exactly? The answer is simple. If you need your edit to be output for DVD, streamed online, or simply burned onto a CD, Compressor can do it all. This chapter will show you how.

Why Compress?

Final Cut Pro is based on Apple's QuickTime architecture, one of the leading multi-media enabling technologies in the world. The flexible QuickTime architecture is what enables Final Cut Pro to work so well with digital video formats, including online video. When compressing for other media, you need to get to know QuickTime a bit more closely. Fear not — Apple has made it fairly easy.

As an editor, there's one problem that you encounter again and again: Video files are just too big. Without compression, a single second of video can fill well over 20MB of disk space. Not only is that too big, but most computers and hardware are unable to provide enough throughput for data that comes in 20MB chunks *every second.* Compression is the solution to the problem of huge video file sizes. Compression is the science of reducing file sizes while keeping the image quality as high as possible. Compression technology is a sophisticated science that is based on the principles of human vision. The principles of human vision allow a lot of information to be removed from the video without being noticed. Compression is accomplished by using *codecs.*

Cross-Reference

For more information on video compression, see Chapter 1.

Working with codecs

The word *codec* is short for "compressor/decompressor," just as the word *modem* is short for "modulation/demodulation." Codecs are software components that fit within an architecture, such as QuickTime. The purpose of a codec is to make a movie small enough to play on a computer or over a network. MPEG-4, MPEG-2, and Sorenson are common codecs. Some codecs work on many different architectures.

Cross-Reference

Codecs are described in this chapter in the context of video for online use. If you plan to output your video to tape or another format, see Chapter 22 for more information on the codecs you should use in those situations.

The science of codecs has taken a massive leap forward in the last few years due to the interest in Web delivery. The technology behind codecs is complex, but they work on a few basic principles that all video professionals should understand. Codecs generally work by using one or both of the following types of compression:

✦ **Spatial compression:** Spatial compression occurs across space. The principle behind spatial compression is to remove redundant data in a given image. In spatial compression, areas of flat color with identical pixels are stored as numbers and coordinates. To provide a simple example, suppose you have a large area of blue sky in a shot. Instead of saving hundreds of pixels that are of the same blue color, the codec stores a number that says "Six-hundred blue pixels at coordinate XY." This number is then converted back to an image on the fly during playback. For this reason, images with lots of detail are ill-suited to spatial compression, but images with large areas of identical colors are ideal. Figure 23-1 shows an example of how spatial compression works.

Movie frame as it plays decompressed   Movie frame as it is stored

Figure 23-1: In spatial compression, the white areas in the image at right are stored as numbers instead of pixels because they represent areas of repeated color.

✦ **Temporal encoding:** Temporal compression occurs across time. During temporal encoding, only changes between frames are saved. Periodically (and you can sometimes control this timing), a full reference frame is saved. The original reference frames are called *keyframes*. The remaining frames are called delta or *difference* frames. Figure 23-2 shows the principle of temporal compression at work. While playing back an encoded file that has temporal compression applied to it, you never notice any keyframes or delta frames. The codec re-creates every frame on the fly, and all the viewer sees is one smooth movie.

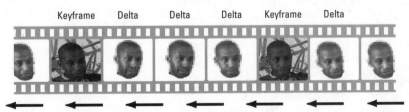

Figure 23-2: In temporal compression, keyframes are saved occasionally. Delta frames store just the changes between each frame.

Note The keyframes in compression are full-reference frames that are saved for filling in the difference frames to create a full image on the fly. These keyframes are not the same as the keyframes used for animation and effects in Final Cut Pro.

Now that you know the basics of how codecs work, you must determine how to shoot your video so that it is best suited for compression with the kind of codec you'll be choosing for delivery.

For example, you may be delivering your output for DVD delivery or for broadband Web streaming, in which case you'll have plenty of latitude in your production choices. The higher throughput of these formats is a lot more forgiving when it comes to dynamic changes in the picture.

On the other hand, if you're going to be delivering highly compressed output for narrowband Web streaming, your production will need to follow a few basic principles, which, in turn, will enable you to produce video that maximizes the compression capabilities of your chosen codec. If this happens to be your production scenario, these principles would include:

✦ **Keep it simple.** Videos with large areas of a single color are prime candidates for efficient compression. Try to design your backgrounds and sets with large areas of simple colors. The less detail in the image the better. Avoid intricate patterns and shapes whenever possible. Talking head interviews in front of simple backgrounds are ideal.

✦ **Work with the best quality.** Start with the best image quality possible. Compression relies on being able to throw away a lot of information. Thus, the more information you have to start with, the better off you are. Never presume that just because the final output is for the Web, you can use low-end cameras and bad lighting. Work with the best format, cameras, and lighting your budget allows.

✦ **Use a tripod.** Video content that changes very little from frame to frame compresses well. Don't use a handheld camera unless you absolutely have to. For any codec, a shot that has a lot of framing and image changes in each frame is more work to compress and may create larger file sizes and higher data rates. Rapid motion, frequent cuts, and fast zooms are also hard on temporal compression. Avoid them where possible.

Whatever your needs may be, Compressor contains the necessary tools for the job.

Introducing Compressor

So, here's the picture. You've just finished a draft of an edit for some producers, and now you'd like to deliver your latest cut to them on DVD or put it up on the Web. This is when you turn to Compressor. Compressor's ease of use is remarkable. In some ways, it's more like a print queue than a detailed application. If your transcoding needs are simple and straightforward, then all you have to do is load up the job and fire it off.

Follow this short list of steps to see just how simple this process can be:

1. **Using the Finder, find and select the source media that you want to transcode.**

2. **Drag and drop the selected media on to the Compressor icon (in either the Dock or the Desktop).**

   As you can see from Figure 23-3, multiple clips are no problem.

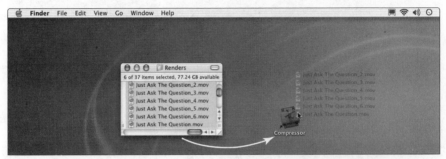

Figure 23-3: Take some source media clips that you want to compress and drag them on top of the Compressor icon or alias (in either the Dock or the Desktop). When you release the mouse, Compressor loads up your transcoding batch.

Once you release the mouse, Compressor starts up. After the Compressor splash screen, you'll see your media clips in the Batch window of the Compressor interface, as shown in Figure 23-4.

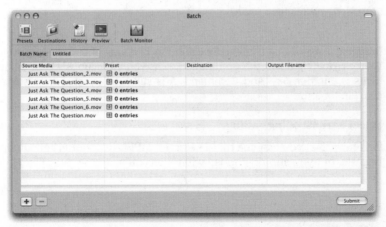

Figure 23-4: Your media clips are now listed in the Batch window of the Compressor interface.

3. **Give your batch a name by typing one into the Batch Name field in the Batch window.**

4. **Click and drag the pointer across the items in the source media column and then over to the Preset column, as shown in Figure 23-5.**

   You'll be offered a menu of transcoding presets for your source media.

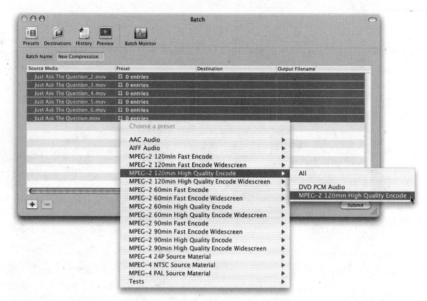

Figure 23-5: Click and drag the pointer across the source media and then over to the Preset column as shown here, where you'll be offered a menu of transcoding presets for your source media.

Note   Dragging across the source media column is one way of selecting multiple media sources. Holding down the Command key as you contiguously click on individual items is another way. And Command+A is still the fastest way to select all the items in the list.

5. **Select a transcoding setting.**

   In Figure 23-5, you can see that I selected MPEG-2 120min High Quality Encode, but you should choose whatever you need.

Tip

Also, you should know that your media source files can be encoded more than once without you having to add them to the Batch window again. In other words, if you need your source file to be transcoded into both an MPEG-2 and an MPEG-4, you can assign multiple encoding settings to the same source media.

6. **Be sure all your items are still selected by pressing Command+A, and then choose a destination for your encoded media from the Destination menu.**

If you want to, you can add your own destination to the list here by choosing Other from the menu. Figure 23-6 shows the state of my Batch window before submitting the job.

Figure 23-6: The source media has been assigned multiple presets and a common destination.

Tip

Just as the source media items in your batch can have their own encoding setting(s), they can also have their own separate destinations.

7. **Click Submit, and it's off to the races.**

The Batch Monitor window will pop up and tell you the status of the job as it transcodes your source media (see Figure 23-7).

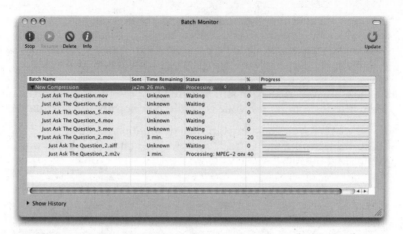

Figure 23-7: The Batch Monitor gives you an up-to-the-minute report on the status of your batch as it transcodes.

Pretty easy, isn't it? That's the overall gist of using Compressor. There are only a few more things really left to talk about concerning this application, at least as far as how it relates to your Final Cut Pro workflow.

The first of these is how you can create your own presets and add them to the list that's already there. The second involves previewing your compression results prior to submitting a batch. If you want better results, you can tweak the compression settings until the preview looks good. The last of these is a discussion on the various choices you have for compressing your video (and audio). What are the various formats? What purpose do they serve? We'll look at these questions at the end of the chapter.

It's worth pointing out that this chapter is meant to serve as an overview of a fairly sophisticated piece of software. Like the other chapters that deal with the additional applications that ship with Final Cut Pro 4, such as Soundtrack and LiveType, a single chapter can only offer so much detail.

Creating and Modifying Presets in Compressor

If you click the Presets button of the Batch window, you'll open up the Presets window, shown in Figure 23-8.

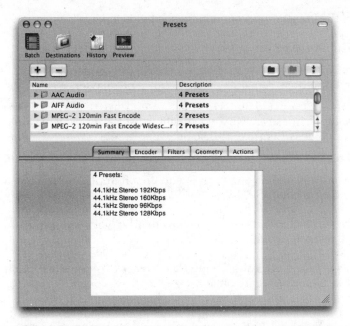

Figure 23-8: The Presets window contains the transcoding preset settings that you can select when placing source media into the Batch window.

The Presets window enables you to centrally administer your list of presets. You can change or fine-tune the transcoding settings of each preset here, as well as create new ones, or even groups of them subdivided by folder. Whether making a new one or modifying an existing one, you can change a preset's codec, its frame size, as well as the degree to which you want to crop the final output (referred to as *geometrics*). Since we're dealing with a workflow that deals exclusively with Apple's QuickTime, you can also add video filters to a preset.

The top half of the Presets window contains the Presets table, which displays the existing list of presets, as well as buttons on the left that enable you to add, remove, or duplicate a preset. The buttons on the right side let you create groups and Droplets.

Tip Droplets are nifty little script-driven commands that look like icons in the Finder. Once you make a Droplet, you can drop a media file directly onto it, at which point Compressor will launch and transcode the media using the preset specified when you created the droplet.

The bottom half of the Presets window contains the following five tabs:

✦ **Summary:** This tab gives you a detailed summary of the selected preset.

✦ **Encoder:** This tab enables you to choose a codec, or encoder, as well as other video and audio settings depending on the choice of encoder.

✦ **Filters:** This tab lets you add filters to your preset. Since this is an end-to-end QuickTime solution, these are what you might expect — for example, Color Correction, Brightness/Contrast, and so on.

✦ **Geometry:** This tab lets you precisely control the frame size of your output.

✦ **Actions:** This last tab offers you the choice to fire off AppleScripts and e-mails when transcoding is complete.

So try it out. The next few steps will show you how to make your own preset. After that, you should be off and running.

1. **In the Presets window, click the Create New Preset Group button that looks like a folder in the upper-right corner.**

   This creates a new group called Untitled in the list.

2. **Double-click on the word *Untitled,* and rename your new group anything you like (for example, My Compressor Settings).**

   Hit Return when you've finished

3. **Click on the New Preset button in the upper-left corner of the Presets window.**

   Notice that you have a choice here between MPEG-2, AIFF, QuickTime, TIFF, and MPEG-4.

4. **For the moment, select MPEG-2.**

   If you want, you can always modify this later.

5. **In the same way you renamed your group, double-click on your new preset and name it anything you like.**

6. **Drag and drop it into your Preset group, which you created in Steps 1 and 2.**

7. **Twirl open you preset group to reveal your preset, and then select your preset by clicking on it.**

8. **Look at the Summary tab to see what your new preset's default settings are.**

So as you can see, creating a new preset couldn't be any easier. The next few steps will show you that modifying that preset is equally straightforward.

1. **Select your new preset in the Presets window.**

2. **Using the various tabs, make changes to the preset.**

   For example, you could crop it, or you could change the encoder's bit rate.

3. **Click away from your preset.**

   This will bring up the dialog box shown in Figure 23-9.

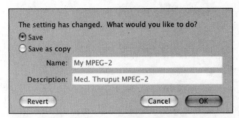

Figure 23-9: The save preset dialog pops up whenever you make changes to a preset.

4. **Click OK.**

   As you can see, you could have saved a copy in order to make a new one.

And that's it. If only the rest of digital video were this easy. The next couple of sections will deal with how to tweak these settings effectively *before* firing off a batch, as well as the specifics of the different encoders.

Tip   In the Presets window, you can also enter information into a preset's description field, and in fact, this is highly recommended. It's the only way to keep your settings straight. Good housekeeping reveals its merits when you find five listings for "Tony's MPEG."

Adjusting Compression with the Preview Window

"Okay," you might say. "So what do these presets do? What is my video going to look like as a result of these adjustments? Is it possible to know before I submit the batch?"

Glad you asked, because the answer is absolutely yes. You can see what your media looks like before and after transcoding, thanks to the Preview window, shown in Figure 23-10.

Figure 23-10: The Preview window gives you a look at your media before Compressor transcodes it (on the left) as well as a look at how it will turn out after transcoding it with the selected preset (on the right).

The Preview window is where you can see the effects of the preset you choose for the media in your batch. Any filters or resizing is updated in the Preview window, and what's more, you can play down the media and look at the effect of your adjustments in real-time (at a frame rate that's as high as your own particular Mac will allow).

To learn how the Preview window works, complete the short list of steps that follows:

1. **Make sure you have source media in the Batch window.**

2. **Make sure that your media has been assigned a preset.**

3. **In the Batch window, double-click the preset for the particular job that you want to preview.**

Tip Alternatively, you can select the media and then click the Preview button.

The selected source media file opens up in the Preview window (parked on the opening frame) and the title of the selected preset appears in the Clip Selection pop-up menu. The left half of the screen, called the Source view, displays the source media file in its original unchanged state, and the right half of the screen, called the Destination view, displays what the output image will look like with whatever filters and other settings you apply.

4. With the source media's preset selected in the Preset window, click on the Effects tab and add effects to your source media clip by clicking the checkboxes of the effects you want to apply.

The effect controls are to the right of the effect list. Notice that for every change you make, the effect on the source media is reflected in the Destination view of the Preview window.

Caution When applying effects, make sure their checkboxes have been checked, otherwise you won't see any changes in the Destination view of the preview window.

5. In the Preview window, view your media in real time by clicking on Play.

You can also go through the media using the Fast Forward and Fast Backward buttons. Notice that the clip plays in both the Source and Destination views in real-time.

Note Although the Preview window will play in real-time, the frame rate will depend on the speed of your system.

Creating Media Destinations

In the opening exercise, you selected a destination for your media in the Batch list. Most of the time, that's about as much thought as you'll put into your transcoding destination, but you can also customize this part of Compressor to suit your needs. The last of the Compressor windows is the Destination window, shown in Figure 23-11.

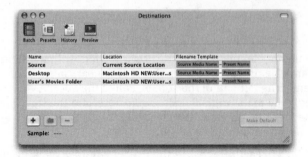

Figure 23-11: The Destination window lets you select
where your media will be stored when it's encoded.

This part of the interface is pretty intuitive, and you shouldn't have any problems
working it out. Carry out the following steps to add a new location to your
destinations.

1. **Open the Destination window either by clicking on its icon in the Batch
   window toolbar, or by selecting Window ⇨ Destination.**

2. **Click on the Create a New Destination button, which looks like a plus sign.**

3. **Choose Local instead of Remote.**

Note   If you were to choose Remote, you would see that it would be entirely possible to
have your batches encoded and sent elsewhere using the FTP protocol. All you
would need is a valid URL or IP address, a file path, and an FTP user account name
plus its password.

4. **Find a location on your system where you'd like your compressed media to
   go, and then click Open.**

5. **Double-click on your new destination's default name, Untitled, and rename
   it whatever you want.**

6. **If you like, click on the Make Default button to make this destination the
   default location for any media you add to a Batch.**

   Notice the symbol in the list of destinations for which one is the default.

There are settings you can tweak with regard to file naming conventions, and if you
plan on encoding tons of media, you should probably hatch a scheme that will help
keep your organization's output as orderly as possible. And that's about it, as far as
the Destinations window is concerned.

Exporting from Final Cut Pro into Compressor

As you might expect, Apple has integrated these two applications rather nicely. For example, imagine that you've edited a sequence in Final Cut Pro that you want to send to a producer on DVD. You need the compression to look as good as possible, but you're low on time. What do you do?

Well, the first thing you need to do is convert your sequence into an MPEG-2 file. But how do you ensure that that the compression will be smooth, especially seeing that your edit contains a lot of cuts, and among those, many that involve jarring changes in scenery and backdrops?

Easy. Here's how: In Final Cut Pro, select File ➪ Export ➪ Using Compressor. When the export is finished, Compressor will start up if it hasn't already, and your sequence will be sitting there in the Batch list. Double-click on the source media in the Batch window to see your sequence in the Preview window. You may notice that your sequence now has quite a few markers (see Figure 23-12).

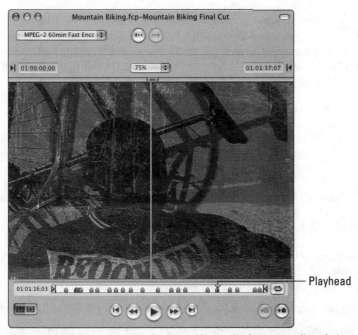

Figure 23-12: Exporting a sequence from Final Cut Pro directly into Compressor inserts Compression markers at every edit point in the original. To illustrate the point, you can see the marker that corresponds to the dissolve shown here in the Preview window.

These are compression markers, and whatever MPEG-2 preset you use to prepare this sequence for DVD, Compressor inserts compression markers at every edit point in the original sequence. Beats having to insert them manually, doesn't it? During transcoding, this ultimately results in Compressor inserting an I-frame wherever there's a marker. An I-frame is a reference frame not unlike the idea of a keyframe we discussed earlier in the chapter. Compressor builds output by creating the keyframes wherever the compression markers have been set, generating the frames in between these keyframes through interpolation.

Understanding Video and Audio Formats

Compressor can import and export many different flavors of video and audio, and this is an extension of the underlying QuickTime architecture that it shares with Final Cut Pro (see the sidebar "The magic of QuickTime"). On the downside, this does prevent it from working with RealMedia and Windows Media, but on the upside, this does make your workflow an end-to-end Apple solution, all at no added charge beyond your initial investment in Final Cut Pro.

When considering your compression options, remember your target audience. Is your media for DVD? Are you streaming it? Do you need to give your output to a specialized motion graphic artist who happens to work on a Windows platform? Are you going to need to deliver a CD-ROM that can play back on older systems? All of your encoding choices hinge on the answers to these questions.

If you look at Compressor's Encoder options in the Preset window, your choices from the pop-up menu are MPEG-2, AIFF, QuickTime, TIFF, and MPEG-4. The most immediately useful of these video formats are the ones that feature prominently in Compressor's presets, namely MPEG-2 and MPEG-4, but here's a brief description of all five.

 Note   MPEG stands for the *Moving Picture Experts Group,* which is an international consortium of engineers who work out the industry standards for video delivery so that markets like the one for DVDs and DVD players can exist.

✦ **MPEG-2** was designed to support high-resolution, high bit-rate video and is the video codec of choice for satellite television, Digital Television set top boxes, and perhaps most importantly, DVD video.

- All DVD players include the hardware necessary for MPEG-2 playback.

- MPEG-2 is not compromised in either its frame rate (23.98 to 29.97 fps) or its resolution, which is 720×480 for NTSC and 720×576 for PAL.

- MPEG-2 works with either interlaced or progressive scan video.

Note Unlike MPEG-1 or low-bit-rate compressions using MPEG-4, when you're playing back MPEG-2, the video frame rate remains steady and the picture looks gorgeous. This is because MPEG-2 streams are usually decoded locally on a DVD player rather than streamed over a congested public network like the Web. MPEG-2 is simply not suitable for streaming video files over the Internet because it requires a high bit rate to maintain acceptable image quality (2 to 9 Mbps). I wouldn't be surprised if that changes someday, but for the time being, it's not an option.

✦ **MPEG-4** is the latest and greatest standard for multimedia on the fixed and mobile Web. Since it's the most current offering, MPEG-4 offers higher quality video at lower data rates.

 • It has no constraints in terms of frame size and frame rate, and you control the data rate (constant or variable).

 • The audio half of MPEG-4 is the new Advanced Audio Coding codec (AAC), which delivers very-high-quality sound at low data rates. Its compression is more efficient than the wildly popular MP3 format, and some go so far as to say that it rivals uncompressed CD audio.

 • You can add hinting for better streaming.

✦ **QuickTime** is the label given to everything besides the options mentioned in the Encoding pop-up menu choices. This can get sort of confusing since everything in this chapter is QuickTime-compatible. More than anything, it seems to refer to QuickTime's legacy codecs. Look at the Table 23-1 to see all the video formats supported by Compressor. Following the table is an individual breakdown of these codecs.

✦ **AIFF,** otherwise known as the Audio Interchange File Format, is a file format for storing digital audio data. It supports a variety of bit resolutions, sample rates, and channels of audio. On standard audio CDs, this is 44.1 Khz, 16-bit, 2-channel resolution.

✦ **TIFF,** or Tagged Image File Format, is still one of the more common and reliable still-image output formats. It is widely compatible with hardware and software that's popular in the editing and motion graphics world. Essentially, this option exists if you have to send your video "out of house" in a non-Apple environment.

Note The previous descriptions of the Encoder pop-up menu options in the Preview window are merely topical. For example, tweaking MPEG-4 is a rather large subject unto itself, but remember, this is an overview of Compressor.

Table 23-1 tells you what video formats Compressor can import and which ones it can export. So what are you to make of all these different video formats? We'll take a look at some of these a bit later in the chapter.

Table 23-1
Compressor Video/Audio Formats: In versus Out

Video format	Input video format	Output video format
Animation	√	√
BMP	√	√
Video	√	√
Cinepak	√	√
DV	√	√
DVC Pro	√	√
DV PAL	√	√
DVC Pro PAL	√	√
H.261	√	√
H.263	√	√
JPEG 2000	√	√
M-JPEG A	√	√
M-JPEG B	√	√
Photo JPEG	√	√
Planar RGB	√	√
PNG	√	√
Sorenson2	√	√
Sorenson3	√	√
TGA	√	√
Video	√	√
MPEG2		√
MPEG4		√
TIFF Sequence		√

Audio format	Input Audio Format	Output Audio Format
AIFF	√	√
AAC		√
Alaw 2:1		√
IMA 4:1		√
MACE 3:1		√
MACE 6:1		√
Qdesign Music 2		√
Qualcomm PureVoice		√
uLAW 2:1		√

The magic of QuickTime

Most people experience QuickTime through the basic QuickTime Player. You click on a movie, and a small Movie Player window opens. That's QuickTime. Because of this, when most people think of QuickTime, they envision small, jittery 15 fps movies on a computer screen. But QuickTime is far more. QuickTime is an entire multimedia *architecture*. This architecture provides a structure and synchronization scheme for media delivery. Don't confuse architectures with file formats; a QuickTime movie is a file format, but QuickTime itself is an architecture.

QuickTime's architecture consists of over 200 separate components, each of which performs a specific job. QuickTime is a file format, a set of applications and plug-ins, and an entire software library with an API (Application Programmers Interface) that allows others to add components and plug-ins to it. QuickTime supports over 70 different types of digital media.

The QuickTime Player is just one facet of this extensive architecture. QuickTime's movie container is considered one of the more flexible ever created. A QuickTime movie is not dependent on specific frame rates, resolution, frame size, or codec. This means that a QuickTime file can have practically *any* frame rate, can be *any* resolution and frame size, and be compressed with almost *any* known codec. Thus, a QuickTime movie can be a tiny 320 × 240 25 fps movie playing on your computer, or a high-resolution 720 × 486 29.97 fps video file compressed in MJPEG-A. If you have ever wondered how Final Cut Pro is able to accommodate any frame size and so many different frame rates, it is because Final Cut Pro uses QuickTime as its backbone.

Beyond MPEG-2 and MPEG-4: Meeting QuickTime's extended family

Countless codecs exist in the world. However, some codecs are more common than others. Below is a brief tour of some of the more common video codecs that are available in the QuickTime portion of the Encoder options in the Preview window. In the not-so-old days, a lot of these codecs were popular for delivery on CD-ROM and the Web. Even if MPEG-4 is the ultimate panacea for delivery in those media nowadays, there are still a few good choices here. Audio-only codecs are described in the next section. Common video codecs include:

✦ **Sorenson video:** Before MPEG-4, Sorenson used to be considered the best choice for high-quality, low-data-rate movies. It still produces beautiful results. This codec has very high image quality at very low data rates. This codec works best if the height and width of your movie are divisible by four. There are a few versions of the Sorenson codec available. The Developer Edition of Sorenson comes with a two-pass variable bit rate (VBR) compression. This type of compression is slow to compress but offers extremely high quality.

A common mistake that users make with this codec is to set the keyframe rate too high. With most other codecs, you can expect to set one keyframe per second. However, with Sorenson you can set them as far as ten seconds apart. Sorenson is a modern and extremely well designed codec.

Note The latest iteration of the Sorenson codec is Sorenson 3. While it's obviously an improvement over its predecessor, be careful to ensure that your potential audience can play back a QuickTime movie encoded with it. In other words, if they don't have the latest codecs installed on their system, they won't be able to see the movie.

✦ **Cinepak:** Cinepak used to be the codec of choice for Apple, until it was displaced by Sorenson, which we know was displaced by MPEG-4. Cinepak is an older codec standard for CD-ROMs and Web use. A nice feature of Cinepak is that it plays in Windows Media Player, which is the flagship media player from Microsoft. Keyframes for Cinepak should be set to about one for every second.

✦ **H.261:** In my opinion, this is a highly underrated and underused codec. This is a standard video-conferencing codec, but it can produce fabulous results for Web-delivered movies. This codec was developed for the very low bit rates typical of modems and was used as a starting point for the development of MPEG compression. H.261 has a strong temporal compression component and works best on movies in which there is little change between frames.

✦ **H.263:** This is a later, better-quality version of the H.261 codec. H.263 was designed for real-time streaming and video-conferencing. For this reason the H.263 tolerates lost packets well. That's a valuable feature because video on the Web is sent in packets, and net-clog often results in lost packets. For best results when working with H.263, your image size measurements should be multiples of 16. H.263 is good for high-motion video and is available for many platforms.

AIFF and other audio files

For many visually oriented people, audio is the poor second cousin to video. Audio codecs always seem to get a short shrift. Having good audio quality is something that makes your streaming media stand out in the crowd. And audio on the Web is quite easy to stream because of its small size and tiny data rates (relative to video, that is). Lately there has been a boom in audio codec development. Some popular audio codecs include:

✦ **QDesign Music Codec:** This codec is optimized for instrumental music. The codec's name refers to music, but it can reproduce any type of audio material. The QDesign Music Codec produces very-high-quality sound even when streaming over a 14.4K or 28.8K modem! This codec was designed to handle data loss well in Web-based conditions. This codec places high demands on the CPU, and it may drop frames with high-bit-rate media tracks.

✦ **Qualcomm PureVoice Codec (Half and Full):** This codec is best suited to voice data, and provides telephone land-line quality at insanely low bit rates. This codec compresses in near real-time (the encoding delay is 160 milliseconds) and allows speech to stream live over even a 14.4K modem. This codec is not well-suited for sounds other than voice, such as music or sound effects. The Qualcomm PureVoice Codec comes in two versions. PureVoice Half is best for movies that also include video at low data rates. PureVoice Full is better if you're making an audio-only file.

✦ **IMA:** This is an early audio codec for QuickTime and Video for Windows. This codec is not ideal Web usage, due to relatively low compression ratio, which results in big file sizes. However, this codec asks very little of the CPU to decode. IMA's audio quality is lower than most newer codecs. Note that Apple and Microsoft use slightly different versions of IMA that are incompatible.

✦   ✦   ✦

Using Final Cut Pro in Advanced Settings

Advanced Issues

As you work with Final Cut Pro and grow more comfortable with it, you're likely to grow more ambitious and curious. The world of digital video is a curious place, and it is virtually impossible to anticipate the issues that you might come across from project to project. Despite years of working in and consulting on digital video, I still find that every new project has issues that I have not encountered before.

This chapter contains some advanced topics relating to digital video and editing in Final Cut Pro. It shows you the ins and outs of timecode, and it covers the YUV color space and Anamorphic 16:9 media.

Understanding Timecode

Legend has it that the idea of timecode came from NASA, the National Space and Aeronautics Administration. NASA, as you know, loves to fly rockets, and rockets send reams and reams of data back to the NASA engineers. Direction, speed, angle of flight, fuel status, and many other pieces of information stream down to ground-control stations. In the 1950s, NASA had developed a way of time-stamping all data (or *telemetry* as rocket scientists call it) that returns from the spacecraft to the ground control. This data was recorded on multitrack recorders and used for analysis and synchronization checks.

Some video engineers came across this time-stamping at NASA and decided it would be a great idea to adopt for video. Later in 1969, a consortium consisting of SMPTE (Society for Motion Picture and Television Engineers) and EBU (European Broadcast Union) standardized the timecode format and specifications. This format came to be known as the SMPTE timecode.

As you can see in Figure 24-1, SMPTE timecode displays use an 8-digit, 24-hour clock. The digits in the timecode format represent hours, minutes, seconds, and frames. SMPTE timecode is not just a format for displaying timecode. The technical specifications for timecode are very precise and standardized. To adhere to the SMPTE specifications, timecode has to do more than simply provide a unique marker for every frame of video on tape. Timecode can be used for logging, editing, and synchronizing. On most professional decks that conform to the SMPTE timecode specifications, it is possible to set a starting timecode by incrementing any of the time fields. SMPTE timecode also contains User Bits fields that can be used to store additional information that you can set, such as tape numbers, date, or time.

There are other timecode formats, but SMPTE is the most common standard and is the yardstick for working with timecode in professional environments.

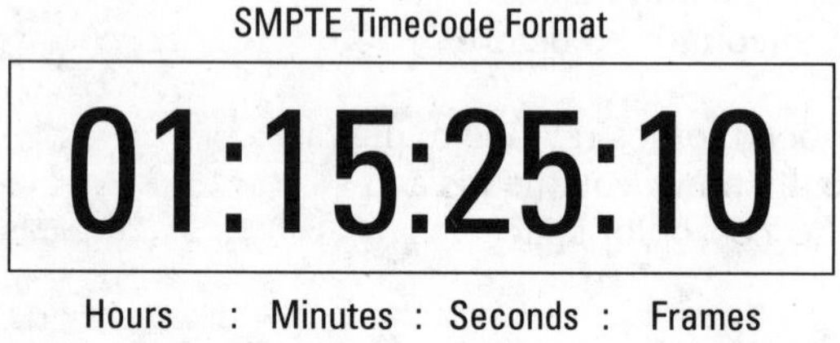

SMPTE Timecode Format

01:15:25:10

Hours : Minutes : Seconds : Frames

Figure 24-1: The SMPTE timecode format uses eight digits to show hours, minutes, seconds, and frames.

Methods of recording timecode

SMPTE timecode is recorded on videotape in two common ways. LTC (Longitudinal Timecode, often pronounced *lit-see*) is recorded lengthwise along a special address track on the tape. On many formats, LTC can also be recorded on audio tracks. VITC (Vertical Interval Timecode, often pronounced *vit-see*) is recorded on the vertical interval of the video signal itself.

Most professional-level decks can read and record LTC and VITC timecode. Such decks also have settings for recording and reading from LTC, VITC, or both. Always keep these selectors on the Both setting. This helps record and read from both locations. And as you see, each type of timecode has advantages and disadvantages. Reading and writing both types of timecode uses the best of both worlds.

Working with LTC

LTC timecode is recorded along dedicated horizontal address tracks, as shown in Figure 24-2. LTC timecode is simply a modulated audio signal that can also be recorded on audio tracks of a tape. If you like, you can actually hear this type of timecode. Connect the LTC timecode output into a speaker or a stereo and you hear whirring, digital-sounding squeaks. That's your LTC timecode talking to you. The benefits of LTC are:

✦ **LTC can be recorded on a separate address track or on an audio track.** On some tape formats LTC occupies a separate track. However, it can also be recorded on a single regular audio track, usually Channel 2.

✦ **LTC can be recorded after the video has been recorded.** Because the track for LTC is a separate track, it is possible to "restripe" LTC on a tape after the original video has been recorded. On some analog formats, such as VHS, S-VHS, Hi-8, or ¾-inch U-Matic, LTC can be recorded on Channel 1 or 2 of the audio track. This way the video information remains untouched, one audio channel is still free for sound, and the LTC timecode can run along a separate audio track.

✦ **LTC can be recorded from tape to tape.** Because LTC is a separate linear track (often an audio track), it can be recorded from tape to tape, just like copying an audio track.

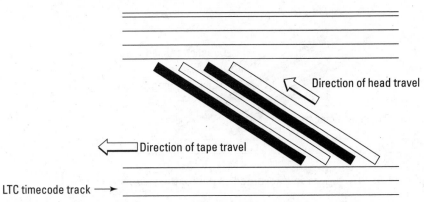

Figure 24-2: LTC timecode is recorded on a separate address track on some videotape. LTC can also be recorded on audio tracks.

LTC does have some disadvantages as well. Disadvantages include:

✦ **The "sound" of LTC may bleed.** When recording LTC timecode on an audio track, be sure that the audio level is kept low. LTC timecode sounds can leak into the nearby audio channels if the level is too high.

✦ **LTC takes up an audio track.** On some tape formats LTC takes up one audio track, limiting the ability to record multiple channels of sound.

✦ **There are reading limitations.** LTC timecode cannot be read when the tape is paused or being jogged at a slow speed.

✦ **The tape deteriorates.** Like any other analog audio track, each dub of the tape deteriorates the quality of the LTC timecode track.

Working with VITC

VITC timecode is actually recorded as part of the video signal itself. As you can see in Figure 24-3, VITC is recorded above the active picture and below the vertical sync, in an unused portion of the video image. Benefits of VITC timecode are:

✦ **VITC leaves an audio track free.** VITC does not take up an audio track, and thus you gain one audio track.

✦ **VITC is readable at many speeds.** VITC is readable forward or backward at speeds ranging from a still frame to over 10X normal speed.

✦ **Dubbing has no effect.** VITC can handle generational loss better than LTC.

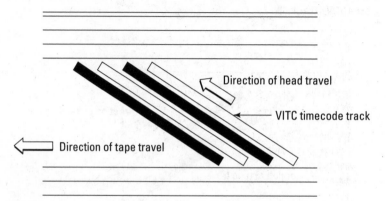

Figure 24-3: VITC timecode is recorded as part of the video signal.

Not surprisingly, there are some disadvantages to VITC as well:

✦ **VITC must be recorded with the original video.** VITC has to be recorded with the original video signal. There are some methods for adding VITC to a prerecorded tape, but they are expensive.

✦ **VITC cannot easily be recorded from tape to tape.** VITC requires dedicated timecode regenerators for it to be copied from tape to tape.

Using timecode on DV tapes

In the DV format (including DV, DVCAM, and DVCPRO systems), timecode is recorded into a separate portion of the video signal, which is then digitally recorded on tape, as shown in Figure 24-4. The timecode is encoded into the "sub-code" sectors of the helical tracks that are used to lay down video information.

What is RC and Hi-8 timecode?

SMPTE timecode isn't the only timecode format that exists in the world; it's just the most common. You may encounter two other formats, however. They are:

✦ **RC Timecode:** When SMPTE timecode originally came out, the decks and units that had SMPTE timecode were very expensive. Most prosumer- and consumer-level equipment did not have SMPTE timecode features. A few companies, such as Sony and NEC, banded together and put out something called RC (Rewritable Consumer) timecode. RC timecode was meant for consumer-level equipment, and it has the same display format as the SMPTE timecode. However, RC and SMPTE timecodes are entirely incompatible. Sony was able to offer RC timecode on many consumer and prosumer video devices, which put it into the reach of many mid-level users. RC timecode can be striped after the video has been recorded.

✦ **Hi-8 Timecode:** Hi-8 is another timecode format that Sony came up with. Hi-8 timecode is considered slightly more industrial than RC. Hi-8 timecode is an odd bird. This type of timecode is recorded in an area on tape that is used neither for sound nor picture. Hi-8 timecode (unlike LTC) saves an audio channel and (unlike VITC) can be recorded on tape after the video has been recorded.

Both RC and Hi-8 timecode follow the SMPTE *format* for timecode display, but they are not compatible with SMPTE and do not conform to its specifications. Hence, you cannot dub RC timecode to SMPTE or vice versa. Furthermore, RC and Hi-8 timecode are not compatible with one another.

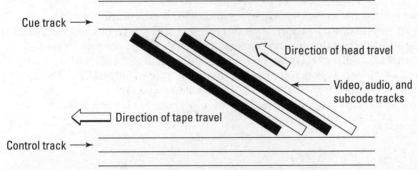

Figure 24-4: Timecode information in DV formats is encoded into the "subcode" sectors of the helical tracks created by the heads to lay down video information.

DV Timecode is generally known as DV Time. On basic DV tapes, the timecode is always drop frame. On DVCAM and DVCPro, you get a choice of setting non-drop or drop frame timecode. DV equipment with FireWire transmits timecode along the FireWire signal. Some DV decks have the ability to output timecode using RS-422 type controllers.

The most common problem with DV Time is that it automatically resets itself to zero if there is no overlap between shots. To get around this, let your shots run long and start recording without a break between shots to maintain a continuous time-code track.

Is DV Time the same as SMPTE timecode? Technically, no. DV Time does not conform to all the protocol requirements of SMPTE timecode. However, from a user's point of view, for all practical purposes, DV Time is close enough to SMPTE. When it comes to using either timecode format in Final Cut Pro, there is no difference. Final Cut Pro does not treat SMPTE timecode any differently from DV Time. Each follows the same format and each can be used to enter and locate shots in Final Cut Pro. Most current device controllers and different protocols have further eroded the differences between SMPTE timecode and DV Time.

Cross-Reference For more on using timecode in Final Cut Pro, see Chapter 9.

Understanding drop frame versus non-drop frame timecode

Before getting into a comparison of drop frame and non-drop frame timecode, take a look at where NTSC video's frame rate of 29.97 frames per second came from.

A long time ago, in a galaxy very nearby, the United States only had black-and-white televisions. These black-and-white televisions (and thus all video technology at the time) worked at an even rate of 30 frames per second, and an even 60Hz vertical sync. With the advent of color television, the developers and engineers wanted to make sure that the new color video technologies were compatible with the old black-and-white ones. In short, they did not want people to have to throw out their black-and-white televisions and buy new color TVs. The National Television Standards Committee (NTSC) adjusted the 60Hz vertical sync by an amount of 0.1 percent or 0.06Hz. This resulted in the final sync rate of 59.94Hz and the new frame rate of 29.97 frames per second. This change allowed space for the color burst signal. The color burst signal carries the color information for the video image.

Everyone was happy. People who had black-and-white televisions could keep them, and the people with the new color TVs could still watch the old black-and-white programs.

Timecode was standardized by SMPTE and EBU in 1969. Timecode standards were developed, and the most common type of timecode ran at an even 30 frames per second.

Keep in mind here that video is measured in frames, while timecode is measured in hours, minutes, and seconds. There is no way to evenly divide a second by 29.97. If you place a 30 fps timecode on video with a 29.97 fps frame rate, the difference is 0.1 percent. The timecode is 0.1 percent longer than the actual program running time, and after an hour this 0.1 percent offset equals 108 frames. This difference amounts to 3.6 seconds for every hour. Broadcast programs must be timed precisely, so this much differential is not allowed. This may not sound like a lot, but when you start selling commercial time, 3.6 seconds can equal many thousands of dollars.

To combat this problem, SMPTE and EBU came up with 29.97 drop frame timecode mode. In drop frame timecode, the first two frames of every minute are eliminated, except for every tenth minute. The final result cuts 108 frames from each hour of timecode, and the numbering sequence and timing is perfectly even. There is never an issue of audio or video being out of sync, or speeding up or slowing down, even if video with non-drop frame timecode is used in a drop frame sequence. All drop frame timecode does is synchronize the numbering sequence with the real clock time.

Tip   Most broadcast facilities require you to deliver air masters with drop frame timecode. Tapes that are not meant for on-air broadcast, such as industrial programs, corporate work, and other in-house presentations are often created with non-drop frame timecode.

Figure 24-5 illustrates the difference between drop frame and non-drop frame timecode.

Non-Drop Frame Timecode

01:00:59:29

01:00:59:28   01:00:00:00

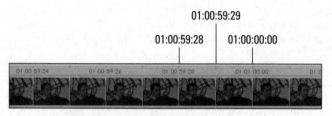

Non-Drop Frame Timecode uses a colon (:)
between the seconds and the frames fields

Drop Frame Timecode

01:00:59;29

01:00:59;28   01:00:00;02

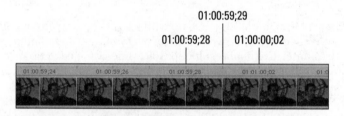

Drop Frame Timecode uses a semicolon (;)
between the seconds and the frames fields

Figure 24-5: Drop frame timecode changes the numbering
of frames at the beginning of each minute, except every
tenth minute.

Distinguishing drop frame from non-drop frame timecode

It is relatively easy to distinguish the drop frame timecode from non-drop frame
timecode. There are a few ways to distinguish the two types of timecode:

✦ **Colons versus semicolons:** Non-drop frame timecode uses colons (:) for sepa-
rators between the seconds and frames fields. Drop frame uses semicolons (;)
between the seconds and frames fields.

Tip

I use the perception that the comma symbol in the semicolon is "dropping down"
compared to a regular colon to help remember that drop frame uses semicolons.

✦ **Check minute marks on videotape:** You can also very easily tell drop frame versus non-drop frame timecode on videotapes. Shuttle your tapes to any minute mark and you notice that the timecode goes from 01:00:59:29 to 01:01:00:00 in a non-drop frame timecode. In a drop frame timecode tape there is no "straight up" minute (except every tenth minute.) So, for example, on a drop frame timecoded tape, the timecode goes from 01:00:59;29 to 01:01:00;02.

✦ **Timecode window burn indicators:** Many professional decks, such as Sony's Digital Betacam decks, use another subtle indicator on their timecode outputs that are used to create "window dub" tapes. The timecode displays on these decks show a single dot between number fields for drop frame timecode (think of it as a dropped-out dot), as shown in Figure 24-6. For tapes with non-drop frame timecode, these same fields show colons, or double-dots. The dot or colon between the minutes and seconds fields indicates the mode of the timecode *reader* on the deck, while the dot or colon between the seconds and frames fields indicates the mode of the timecode *generator* on the deck. The distinction is that the reader simply reads the timecode while the generator creates the timecode and stripes the tape with it.

Caution   Timecode displays vary in some professional decks. Check the user's manual for your decks for precise information.

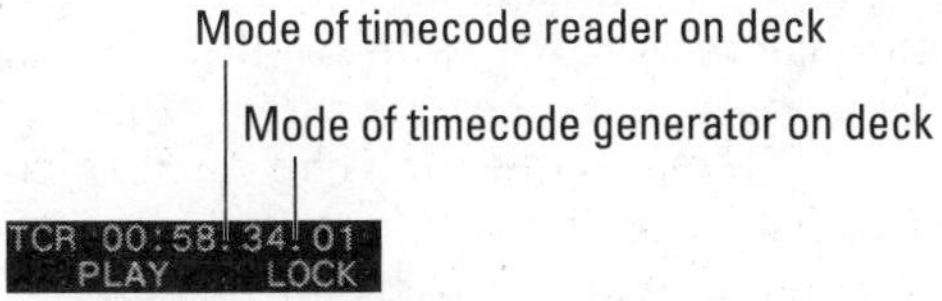

Mode of timecode reader on deck

Mode of timecode generator on deck

TCR 00:58·34·01
PLAY   LOCK

Figure 24-6: Professional video decks display drop frame timecode with single dots between number fields. For non-drop frame timecode, the display shows colons.

You can mix and match drop frame and non-drop frame timecode without any ill effects. You may drop a clip with a non-drop frame timecode base into a sequence that is drop frame. You may mix other clips into the sequence that also have drop frame timecode. Then you can master the sequence to a tape using either non-drop or drop frame timecode. Choose an output format based on the venue for which you are outputting. All tapes meant for on-air broadcast should be prepared with drop frame timecode. This is because broadcast facilities care greatly that your timecode matches the "real" clock time. However, if you are preparing a corporate presentation or other not-for-air material, you are free to use non-drop frame time-code for your final output. Also, always try to match the timecode mode of your Final Cut Pro sequences to the output mode that you plan to use when mastering to tape.

Following the three key rules of timecode

For your everlasting happiness and video editing bliss, remember these three key rules of timecode modes:

✦ **Key Rule#1:** Video in NTSC standard always runs at 29.97 frames per second. *Always.*

✦ **Key Rule #2:** The 29.97 fps rate for NTSC video can be represented either as drop frame or non-drop frame timecode. The frame rate is *never* affected by the timecode mode that is used. It is *never* 30 fps in NTSC video.

✦ **Key Rule #3:** Drop frame timecode drops the numbering order of timecode, *not actual video frames.*

Calibrating for timecode

When you capture video in Final Cut Pro, the timecode and the video signal usually arrive separately from your video deck into the computer. For example, if you are using a high-end third-party video card and a professional Betacam SP deck, your video arrives into the computer through the video card, whereas the timecode is sent through the device control cable. In the case of a Betacam SP deck, this device control is RS-422 device control, which uses a separate path from a 9-pin control plug in the back of the deck to the serial port of your computer. Even when using a DV deck, your video may be arriving through the FireWire port, while the timecode arrives via the device control cable. When video and timecode arrive separately into your computer, there can be a latency. The timecode for a clip can be incorrect. You need to calibrate your Final Cut Pro–based system for timecode. You do so by entering the amount of offset you observe in the Device Control tab.

Calibrating timecode for your system

To calibrate your system to the timecode output by your video deck, you'll need to locate a videotape with a video "burn-in" of LTC or VITC timecode on it. This timecode burn is also known as a "window burn." Some Betacam SP and DV decks have settings that allow you to display timecode. You can use such a deck and enable the option to display timecode. To calibrate timecode for your system:

1. **Capture a short clip of video from a tape that has VITC or LTC timecode window burn.**

2. **Double-click this clip in the Browser window to load it into the Viewer.**

3. **Play the clip and pause it somewhere in the middle of the clip.**

   Pause the clip by pressing the spacebar.

4. Check the timecode in the Current Timecode field of the View window.

Compare this value against the timecode you see in the window burn in the video clip at the current time, as shown in Figure 24-7. If both the timecodes match, there is no offset and no calibration is required. However, if there is any offset, make a note of it.

Current Timecode field

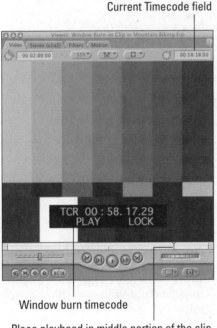

Figure 24-7: After capturing a shot with a timecode window burn, compare the Current Timecode field with the current timecode seen in the window burn. Here we see an offset of one frame.

Window burn timecode

Place playhead in middle portion of the clip

5. Choose Final Cut Pro ⇨ Audio/Video Settings.

6. Click the Device Control Presets tab to bring it to the front.

7. Select your current Device Control preset in the menu on the left and click Edit.

If you are using a locked preset, a new copy of the preset opens up.

8. Enter a new name and description for this device control preset.

Label it using the information about the deck you are calibrating for.

9. In the Capture Offset field, enter an offset value in frames.

If the timecode value in the Current Timecode field is greater than the burned-in timecode, you should enter an offset as a negative number as shown in Figure 24-8. If the value is less, enter the offset as a positive number.

Enter a description for Device Control Preset here

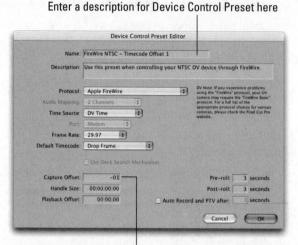

Enter the Capture Offset here

Figure 24-8: If the value of the Current Timecode field is greater than the burned-in timecode, enter a negative value in the Timecode Offset field. If the value is less, enter a positive value.

10. Click OK to close the Device Control Preset Editor and save your changes.

After entering the timecode offset, capture a few more clips and confirm that the timecode values in the Current Timecode field of the View window match the timecode seen in the window burn on the video image.

Note   You need to calibrate timecode each time you change the deck (or cable). Each deck has its own offset that you need to calibrate for. If you use more than one deck on a regular basis, you should create pre-calibrated presets for each deck in the Device Control panel and switch between them.

Calibrating timecode for playback offset

When you master your edited Timeline on tape, Final Cut Pro treats the entire Timeline as one big QuickTime movie. It takes the Timeline and lays it down on the tape at a spot that you specify.

However, there can be slight offset in the timing of the playback of the QuickTime movie of the Timeline. When laid back to tape, the first frame of your Timeline can end up being a black frame or a frame later than you wanted it to be. This is called a *Playback Offset*. When performing Assemble edits or laying programs to DV tape, this offset may not be critical. However, if you are using a high-end setup with

Betacam SP, for example, and plan to make insert edits that require frame accuracy, you should be concerned about any playback offset. Otherwise, you may get a black or incorrect frame as the first frame of layback during an insert edit.

To make sure that the first frame Final Cut Pro lays down on tape is the first frame of your Timeline, you need to calibrate your playback offset. To perform this calibration you first create a playback-offset test Timeline, then you lay down the test Timeline to tape and determine the offset of your playback. Later, you can use this setting to adjust the Playback Offset setting in Final Cut Pro. To calibrate your playback offset, follow these steps:

1. **Open any Final Cut Pro project.**

2. **Choose File ➪ New ➪ Sequence.**

3. **Select the View window.**

   If the View window is not visible, press Command+1 to bring up the View window.

4. **In the Generator pull-down menu of the View window (see Figure 24-9), choose Matte ➪ Color.**

Figure 24-9: Choose Matte ➪ Color in the Generator pull-down menu of the View window.

5. **Click the Controls tab in the View window.**

   The color matte is frontmost. The default color for any matte is gray.

6. **Click on the gray color swatch in the Controls tab of the View window.**

   Select a white color by moving the slider in the HSV color picker up to 100%.

7. **Click the Video tab of the View window.**

   The window is filled with a white color matte.

8. **Park your playhead at the beginning of the Timeline if it isn't there already, and press the F10 key to perform an Overwrite edit.**

   The default length of any color matte is ten seconds. If the starting timecode of your Timeline is 1:00:00;00, your white color matte should extend itself from 1:00:00;00 to 1:00:10;00 in the Timeline.

9. **Move the playhead to the end of the white color matte (the timecode at that point probably is 1:00:10;00) and press the I key to mark an in point in the Timeline.**

10. **Choose Bars and Tone (NTSC) from the Generator pull-down menu in the View window.**

    Bars and Tone are created by Final Cut Pro at a default duration of two minutes.

11. **Highlight the Duration field, located in the upper-left side of the View window, and enter** 01 **to create a bar and tone with a duration of just one frame.**

12. **Again, press F10 to perform an overwrite edit.**

    The single frame of bars and tone should now be placed in the Timeline after the ten seconds of white color matte.

13. **Repeat Steps 10 through 12 four more times, except for one crucial difference: Choose Matte ⇨ Color each time, instead of Bars and Tone.**

    Create a color matte of red, blue, green, and yellow, respectively, and edit each into the Timeline. (The precise colors are irrelevant, as long as each frame has a distinctive color.) When you are done, your Timeline should resemble Figure 24-10 and have ten seconds of white, one frame of color bars, one frame of red, one frame of blue, one frame of green, and one frame of yellow. The timecode for the last frame should be 1:00:10;04. Use the left and right arrow keys to move the playhead one frame at a time to confirm this timecode.

To get a reliable playback offset test, it is crucial that you have the elements lined up precisely to the timecodes in the Timeline as specified in these steps.

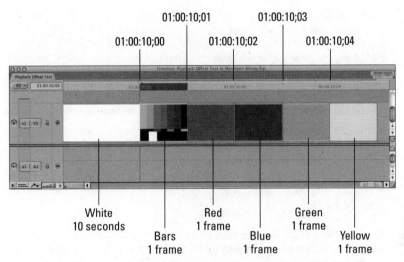

01:00:10;01   01:00:10;03

01:00:10;00   01:00:10;02   01:00:10;04

White
10 seconds

Bars
1 frame

Red
1 frame

Blue
1 frame

Green
1 frame

Yellow
1 frame

Figure 24-10: The final lineup of color mattes in the Timeline.

14. Select all elements in the Timeline by pressing Command+A.

Render all mattes by pressing Option+R.

15. Black and Code your tape using the Tools ⇨ Edit to Tape window.

The Black and Code button is located in the top center part of the Edit to Tape window and consists of a small black filmstrip icon.

If there is no material on your tape, you need to Black and Code your tape before you can edit to it. During a "blacking" operation, Final Cut Pro records black, no audio, and a timecode track and control track on your tape. In non-DV setups, you can specify the starting timecode of your blacked tape if you have a timecode generator in your video deck. It is common practice in editing facilities to start a blacked tape at 00:58:00;00. The first minute of black is generally left unused. The second minute is used for leader elements with allowance for starting your program at the 1:00:00;00 mark on a blacked tape. In your case however, you are laying down your Timeline starting at 1:00:10;00 on tape.

Cross-
Reference

For more information on the precise steps to Black and Code a tape, as well as edit to tape operations, see Chapter 22.

16. After you are done with the Black and Code process, edit your playback offset test Timeline to tape using the File ⇨ Edit to Tape window.

Drag the Timeline to the Insert edit overlay in the Edit to Tape window. Make sure that you specify in the Edit to Tape window for Final Cut Pro to edit the Timeline at precisely 1:00:10;00 on the tape. You can enter this starting timecode in the lower-left timecode field of the Edit to Tape window.

Final Cut Pro edits the test Timeline you just created to tape. In doing so, your one frame bars and tone should line up precisely at 1:00:10;00 on the video tape because you marked an in point at 1:00:10;00 in the Timeline. If there is no playback offset, the white matte that appears before the 1:00:10;00 mark should not be edited to the tape.

17. After the edit to tape process is finished, roll back your video deck and check the frame of video at 1:00:10;00 on your tape.

If it is one frame of bars, then you have no playback offset. If it is one frame of a colored frame, you can determine how many frames late Final Cut Pro was by looking at the color of the frame that is located at the 1:00:10;00 mark on tape. If the frame is red, for example, Final Cut Pro is one frame late, and if it is blue, it is two frames late. If the frame at 1:00:10;00 is white, Final Cut Pro is early.

Tip

If you want to know how many frames early Final Cut Pro is, you can replace your white-colored portion of the Timeline with multicolored single frames and do another test to see exactly how early Final Cut Pro is.

18. If there is no offset, you're done.

But if there is an offset, choose Final Cut Pro ⇨ Audio/Video Settings.

19. Click the Device Control Presets tab.

20. Select your current preset for Device Control in the menu on the left and click Edit.

The Device Control Preset Editor opens as shown in Figure 24-11. If you are using a locked preset, a new copy of the preset opens.

21. Enter a new name and description for the device control preset.

Label it using information about the deck for which you are calibrating offset.

22. Enter an offset in frames in the Playback Offset field.

If Final Cut Pro is playing the Timeline early (if the frame at 1:00:10;00 is white), you should enter an offset as a positive number. If Final Cut Pro is playing the Timeline late (if the frame at 1:00:10;00 is colored), enter the offset as a negative number.

23. Click OK to close the Device Control Preset Editor and save your changes.

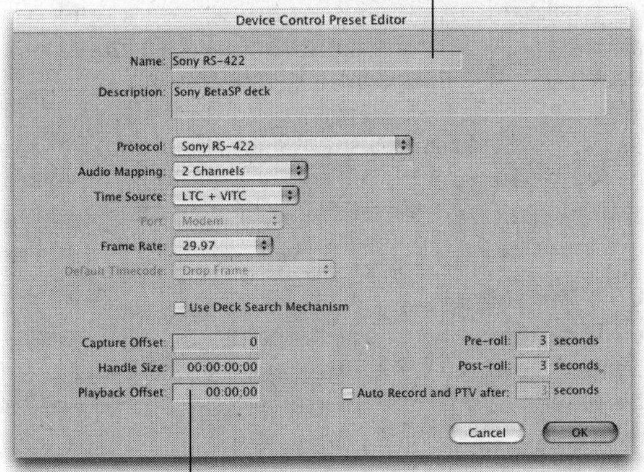

Enter a description for Device Control Preset here

Enter the Playback Offset in frames here

Figure 24-11: Enter a value in the Playback Offset field to fix any offset that Final Cut Pro may have when laying back a Timeline to tape.

After adjusting the Playback Offset, perform the edit to tape test a few more times to make sure that the frame laid down by Final Cut Pro at 1:00:10;00 on tape is a frame of color bars.

Working with discontinuous timecode

Throughout this chapter you have learned that the timecode signal is "stamped" onto each frame of video. When you capture clips into Final Cut Pro, you can navigate through them in the Viewer and see that each frame of the video clip has a timecode. This timecode, in theory, should be the same as it was on the videotape. It is simple to deduce then that Final Cut Pro has captured the timecode stamp for each frame along with the actual video and audio.

That simple deduction is actually incorrect.

The key to understanding timecode issues in Final Cut Pro is to remember that the program does not scan timecode throughout the capture of a clip. While capturing a clip, Final Cut Pro is not reading the timecode stamp from each frame. It actually reads the starting timecode for the capture and then it reads the ending timecode of the capture. Then Final Cut Pro quickly counts the number of frames (or *samples*, in the QuickTime language) in between and divides the timecode for those frames. Generally, of course, this works fine. All is well—until you hit a timecode break. If you encounter a timecode break, where the clip's timecode in Final Cut Pro does *not* match the timecode on tape, you suffer from discontinuous timecode.

Note   The discussion here is more relevant to situations where you are using analog video cards and RS-422 device control. During DV capture via FireWire, Final Cut Pro actually does scan the timecode for each and every frame.

Dealing with timecode breaks

A timecode break is simply a jump in timecode along its track. Often when DV cameras reset themselves, they revert to a timecode of 00:00:00:00. As a result, during capture you may see the timecode go from 1:20:14:10 to 00:00:00:00 in between shots. That's a timecode break.

When working with professional decks, such as a Betacam SP deck with RS-422 device control, you may come across videotapes that have timecode breaks, such as the one shown in Figure 24-12. Betacam SP tapes recorded in the field can have timecode breaks, which can cause the timecode to jump between shots to completely different and discontinuous values. These gaps or breaks can represent minutes or even hours of difference in timecode values. All timecode after the break is incorrect in Final Cut Pro.

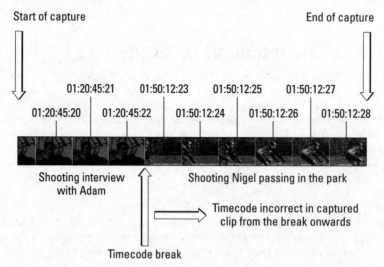

Figure 24-12: When capturing a clip, all timecode after the break is inaccurate in the captured clip.

In the example shown in Figure 24-12, an interview with Adam and a shot of Nigel riding in a park were both shot on the same tape. For some reason — say, the camera operator moved the tape from one camera to another between shots — a timecode break exists between these two shots. Because all of the timecode for the material after the break is incorrect in Final Cut Pro, you cannot use that material for any function that requires timecode accuracy. Such functions include batch captures and EDL exports.

Solving timecode breaks

Because timecode breaks are such a common occurrence, the Final Cut Pro team at Apple has come up with an ingenious feature to deal with this vexing problem. By selecting the option of On timecode break: Make New Clip, found on the General tab of User Preferences, Final Cut Pro will create new clips between timecode breaks, and then continue on its merry way with the rest of the batch capture. This option will allow you to successfully capture from large portions of tapes with timecode breaks; however, because of the possibility of clips from the same reel having identical timecode (that is, if the timecode was reset on the camera), this nifty feature does not remedy the insurmountable obstacle of recapturing or exporting an accurate EDL from tapes with timecode breaks.

 For more details about Capturing with timecode breaks, see Chapter 7.

If you choose not to select Make New Clip on timecode break, you can instruct Final Cut Pro to abort capture completely when it encounters a timecode break, or it can continue capturing *through* the timecode break and alert you after Capture is done. If you are capturing at low resolution, with the plan that you later recapture at high resolution, or if you are planning any timecode-sensitive functions, you should *never* casually bypass this error message. This warning message also appears after batch captures and provides a list of clips that have timecode breaks.

If you choose or need to manually capture from a tape with timecode break, a common work-around solution is to relog your clips and capture the sections between timecode breaks one at a time. The goal is to make sure that no timecode break itself is part of any capture.

Another possible solution to dealing with timecode breaks is to have your source tapes copied or cloned. The idea here is to transfer the whole tape to another tape while recording a new, unbroken timecode track. Be aware that the quality of analog video might suffer from generational loss inherent in duplication, but this can be minimized if done by a professional video house. Cloning is the digital equivalent of duplicating in the analog realm, but because the clone is an exact copy of discrete information of ones and zeros, there is no generational loss with digital clones.

Editors often use a labeling system to indicate timecode breaks on a tape. If you are capturing from Reel#004 and there is a timecode break, you should label the portion after the break as Reel#004a during the log and capture phase in Final Cut Pro. If you encounter another break, all captures from that portion should be labeled as Reel#004b, Reel#004c, and so on. Using this method, each portion between breaks is treated as a "sub reel."

Tip   Another way to head-off timecode breaks is to pre-code your tapes before shooting with them. To do this, simply record anything — some people put the lens cap on while recording — from start to end of a blank tape you will use for your production shoot. Now, even if you remove the tape during your shoot, when you reinsert it into the camera, the pre-coded timecode will be use as a reference for further recording and will not reset to 0:00:00:00.

Working with the YCrCb Color Space

Computer graphics usually use the RGB color space. Each pixel in an image is made up of red (R), green (G), and blue (B) components. However, the RGB format isn't ideal for video because there is no facility for separate encoding of the brightness or luminance values. The brightness information is derived from the interplay of the three RGB channels. This is a drawback because it means you cannot control the brightness values separate from the color values. In any processing circuitry that is designed to adjust the contrast for an RGB image, you need to change the value for each RGB channel. To calculate a hue change, you have to decode and re-encode each of the three separate channels.

Most digital video formats, on the other hand, use a color space known as YCrCb (sometimes also called YUV). The YCrCb color space is ideal for video because it keeps the brightness value separate from the color values. In the YCrCb color space, three elements are stored for each pixel. One element is for luminance (Y), and the other two (Cr and Cb) are for color (also called *chrominance*).

Image information is often converted from RGB to YCrCb and then back again during the process of manipulating digital video on computers. However, two issues occur when converting imagery between RGB and YCrCb color space. These issues are *chroma clamping* and *luma clamping*.

Chroma clamping occurs when certain colors cannot be described accurately in the new color space during conversion. These colors are then "clamped" or "clipped" and look less saturated after the color space conversion.

Luma clamping affects brightness values. The RGB color space uses a brightness range from 0 to 255. The YCrCb color space, however, uses a scale of 16 to 235 for brightness values. Some DV cameras and other high-end units can produce "super-white" areas that are brighter than the 235 range for YCrCb. During conversion from YCrCb video to RGB, the superwhites cannot be mapped higher than 255, meaning they lose their "superwhite" characteristic. When the same clip is converted from RGB back to YCrCb, the superwhites are now lower than 235 and are said to be "clamped" or "clipped."

Final Cut Pro can render in the YCrCb color space. By using this option, you choose to stay in the video's native color space of YCrCb at all times, thus avoiding the clamping that occurs during conversion.

For more information on luma clamping, see Chapter 2.

Some compositing operations in Final Cut Pro can give drastically different color values when you choose the RGB or YCrCb color space for rendering. If you are unsure about the results, do a test render and review the results before you proceed with a large layering or filtering operation.

Setting up sequences for YCrCb rendering

You can set up your sequences and presets to take advantage of the YCrCb color space. To set up a sequence preset for YCrCb rendering, follow these steps:

1. **Choose Final Cut Pro ➪ Audio/Video Settings.**

2. **Click the Sequence Presets tab.**

3. **Select a preset in the menu on the left and click Edit.**

   If the preset is locked, you are given a copy of the preset to edit. Otherwise, the preset opens in the Sequence Preset Editor for editing.

4. **Click the Video Processing tab to bring it to the front as shown in Figure 24-13.**

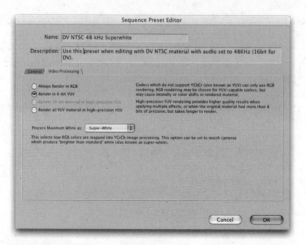

Figure 24-13: You can choose to render in YCrCb color space in the Video Processing tab of the Sequence Preset Editor window.

5. **Select the desired options on the Video Processing tab.**

   The settings on this tab are described in the next section. Keep in mind that not all codecs support YCrCb rendering. Apple's Final Cut Pro Web site has a listing of codecs that support YCrCb processing.

6. **Click OK when you are done to close the Sequence Preset Editor and save your changes.**

> **Note**   To change the color space choice for rendering in a current sequence, select the sequence and choose Sequence ➪ Settings. Click on the Video Processing tab and make your selections.

The Video Processing tab of the Sequence Preset Editor window allows you to determine whether you want to render in the RGB or YCrCb color space. Options on this tab include:

✦ **Always Render in RGB:** This option forces the codec to render in RGB instead of YCrCb. Using this option may cause occasional shifts in color intensity. The reason for this shift is that some codecs that normally process color in YCrCb color space will be forced to process in the RGB color space. However, in some cases, you may use this setting to achieve consistent colors. For example, if you are using filters for Adobe After Effects (some of which process in RGB) in combination with Final Cut Pro's filters (which work in the YCrCb color space) selecting this option will give you consistent colors.

✦ **Render in 8-bit YUV:** This option will render media in 8-bit YUV color space. This is the most common option that is appropriate for DV footage and third-party capture cards that capture in 8-bit video in YUV using a YUV-compatible codec.

✦ **Render 10-bit material in high-precision YUV:** Enables 10-bit rendering in YUV color space of 10-bit media files using a YUV compatible codec. Final Cut Pro can process 10-bit video with much more precision and latitude than 8-bit video.

✦ **Render all YUV material in high-precision YUV:** This option enables 10-bit rendering in YUV, even using 8-bit source clips. Although this will not improve or alter the original color space of an 8-bit YUV media clip, it does allow for improved quality of the render file of an 8-bit source clip that has multiple filters applied it. The trade-off to this option is longer render times than with 8-bit YUV rendering.

Caution

You must use a G4 computer to render with 10-bit precision. If you try to render effects at 10-bit precision, you will see an error message.

Cross-Reference

For more detail about 8-bit and 10-bit systems, see Chapter 3.

✦ **Process maximum white as:** This option is only available if the Always Render in RGB option is not selected. Selections in this menu affect how the colors from the RGB color space are converted to the YCrCb color space. This applies specifically to imported graphics files (such as those from Photoshop), and Final Cut Pro generators (such as the text generators). These settings also affect footage from certain cameras that capture *superwhites*. Superwhites are whites that are brighter than standard whites that are normally allowed in video. Choices in this menu are:

- **White:** Selecting this setting causes the whites of an RGB graphic to be mapped to the standard YCrCb video white at a luminance value of 235.

- **Super-White:** Selecting this setting causes the RGB whites in graphics to be mapped to the video superwhite value, which is a luminance value of 254.

Tip

In the NTSC standard, luminance values brighter than 235 are "illegal." If you are processing your video for on-air broadcast, select White in the Process Maximum White As setting. Many consumer-level cameras contain images that have superwhite signals of whites which are brighter than 235. You should choose Super-White in the Process Maximum White As setting if you want to match the whites of your imported graphics to the superwhites of these DV cameras. When you use the Super-White setting, your video signal no longer is broadcast legal.

Cross-Reference

For more information on luminance values and mapping see Chapter 2.

Updating older Final Cut Pro projects to YCrCb rendering

The ability to render in the YCrCb color space was a new feature of Final Cut Pro 2.0. Previous versions could only render in RGB. Thankfully, you can open projects created with earlier versions of Final Cut Pro and update them to take advantage of the new color space rendering options. To update earlier projects, follow these steps:

1. **Open a project that was created using an earlier version of Final Cut Pro.**

   You are presented with a message like the one in Figure 24-14 saying that the file's format is outdated and asking if you want to update it.

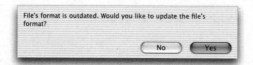

Figure 24-14: A message asks you to update your older project for the new version of Final Cut Pro.

2. **Click Yes.**

   If the project was created with a version of Final Cut Pro prior to version 2.0, an Update Project dialog box like the one shown in Figure 24-15 appears.

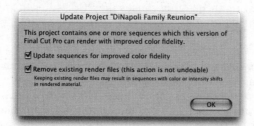

Figure 24-15: Use this dialog box to select options for updating your project to the new version of Final Cut Pro.

3. **Select the options you want (see below) and click OK.**

4. **Click OK when you are ready to update the project.**

The settings in the Update Project dialog are:

✦ **Update sequences for improved color fidelity:** Selecting this option sets the choices to YCrCb rendering and also sets the maximum white value to super-white in the Video Processing tab of the Sequence Preset Editor or the Sequence Settings window. Any further renderings in this sequence are done in the YCrCb color space.

✦ **Remove existing render files:** This option removes all render files that may be on the scratch disk for the sequences in the project. You may want to delete all existing render files if you plan to rerender all sequences in the new color space. This action cannot be undone.

You have updated your project, though you still have not rendered anything. To render, select the sequences in the project and choose Sequence ⇨ Render All.

Working with Anamorphic 16:9 Media

The term *aspect ratio* is used to describe the relationship of a frame's height and width. For example, the aspect ratio of a common television (and this is changing fast) is 4:3. This means for every 4 units in length, the frame is 3 units high. Virtually all televisions, no matter if they measure 9 inches diagonally or 36 inches, follow this aspect ratio.

However, there is a new standard emerging for video aspect rations. The new standard is the 16:9 aspect ratio. As you can see in Figure 24-16, this frame size is much more rectangular, because for every 9 units of height you have 16 units of length. The 16:9 aspect ratio, also called *widescreen* or *Anamorphic,* is important because it has been chosen as the new standard for DTV (Digital Television) in the United States. The new HDTV (High-Definition Television) standard employs the 16:9 aspect ratio as well. (The HDTV specification actually has numerous formats. But most HDTV units use an aspect ratio of 16:9.) More and more televisions and video screens are being manufactured with the 16:9 aspect ratio, and you can expect one day the 4:3 standard will become a thing of the past.

Note   The 4:3 and 16:9 ratios are sometimes also referred to by the harder to remember but mathematically correct 1.33:1 and 1.78:1 ratios, respectively.

Because 16:9 is the emerging aspect ratio, there is a slow transition in progress. Many videomakers are shooting in the 16:9 aspect ratio as more and more viewers acquire televisions that display a 16:9 image. When 16:9 image is seen on a 4:3 television, black bars appear at the top and bottom portion of the screen to accommodate the widescreen aspect ratio. This is sometimes called *letterboxing.*

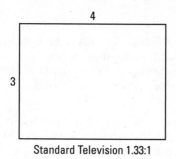

Standard Television 1.33:1

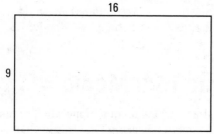

Widescreen Television 1.78:1

Figure 24-16: The 16:9 widescreen aspect ratio is much wider than the traditional 4:3 aspect ratio of televisions.

Most viewers have also come to associate the widescreen format with films, and it is common to use the widescreen aspect ratio to create a more cinematic experience for viewers. The 16:9 Anamorphic aspect ratio is a lot closer to the 35mm film aspect ratio of 1.85:1 But as you can see in Figure 24-17, the 16:9 ratio, which works out to about 1.78:1, is actually slightly narrower than 35mm film's 1.85:1 ratio. Still, it's close enough that many content creators choose the 16:9 format if they plan to eventually transfer their video to 35mm film.

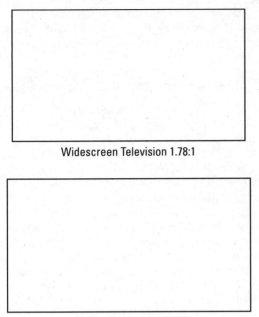

Widescreen Television 1.78:1

35 mm Film 1.85:1

Figure 24-17: The 16:9 aspect ratio is almost
(but not quite) as wide as 35mm film's 1.85:1 ratio.

Using cameras to capture 16:9 images

Before you can work with 16:9 media in Final Cut Pro, you must record a 16:9 image
with a camera. Video cameras normally record video images with a 4:3 aspect ratio,
but there are two common ways to acquire a 16:9 image instead:

✦ **The optical method:** In this method, an Anamorphic lens is fitted to the front
of the video camera. This special lens optically fits the 16:9 image into the 4:3
format before your camera's circuitry receives the image. Many companies
manufacture such lenses for some common brands and models of DV cameras.

✦ **The electronic method:** Many DV and professional cameras have an electronic switch that allows you to choose between a regular 4:3 and widescreen 16:9 aspect ratio. However, not all electronic methods are the same. There are two electronic methods:

- **The preferred method:** The preferred, or as some would say, the "correct" method, is to use a 16:9 chip in the camera. This chip, called a CCD (Charged Coupled Device) uses the entire 16:9 chip when shooting widescreen. When in 4:3 mode, only the center 4:3 portion of the CCD is used and the sides are ignored. You can always tell which cameras are using this preferred method. In a camera that uses the 16:9 chip correctly, when you switch to the 16:9 mode the image in the viewfinder has black borders on top or bottom or the image is squashed. But look closely and you see that even though the wider view is squashed, the same vertical view as with the 4:3 mode is visible. This is the correct way of making a 16:9 image electronically. When a camera uses this method, the horizontal view should show you *more* image (compared to the 4:3 view) on the left and right and the same image area in the top to bottom view. Cameras that use this method, such as Sony's line of DSR cameras, are expensive. The Sony DSR-570WSL is one such camera that handles 16:9 in the preferred manner.

- **The less preferred method:** The less preferred method, or as some would say, the "wrong" method, is to simply cut off the top and bottom portions of the image to make it widescreen. In cameras that employ this method, when you switch to 16:9 you notice that the horizontal view does not change, but the vertical image size is cropped by adding black bars above and below the image. You can switch back and forth between 4:3 and 16:9 to check this. If, when switching to 16:9, the vertical portion of the image is cropped relative to the 4:3 image, then the camera is using this less preferred method. Some cameras go further in this method and digitally stretch the image to fit without the black bars, but only 75 percent of the actual image from the 4:3 view is being used in the 16:9 view. Popular DV cameras such as the Sony VX 2000 and the Canon XL-1S use this method of creating a 16:9 image.

Caution   When working in 16:9 mode, images in the viewfinder and monitors tend to appear squashed. You need a proper 16:9 capable monitor to correctly display the widescreen image without this distortion.

Working with 16:9 media in Final Cut Pro

Final Cut Pro is fully equipped to capture, process, and master 16:9 media. In fact, I would say that working with 16:9 media in Final Cut Pro is a pleasure. You can create and use capture presets for accommodating 16:9 Anamorphic media, and use sequence and screen display settings that make working with 16:9 media a breeze. The next few sections describe the basic phases of working with 16:9 media in Final Cut Pro.

When capturing material into a project, Final Cut Pro uses the settings in the currently active capture preset. There is an Anamorphic 16:9 setting in the Capture Preset Editor window that needs to be checked when capturing 16:9 media. To create a new capture preset for Anamorphic 16:9 media, follow these steps:

1. **Choose Final Cut Pro ⇨ Audio/Video Settings.**

2. **Click the Capture Presets tab.**

3. **Select a preset in the menu on the left and click Edit.**

   The Capture Preset Editor window appears. Note that if the preset is locked, you are presented with a copy of this preset. If you do not find an Anamorphic preset that matches your needs, you can create a custom capture preset for your 16:9 media and label this preset as such.

4. **Make sure the Anamorphic 16:9 box is checked, as shown in Figure 24-18.**

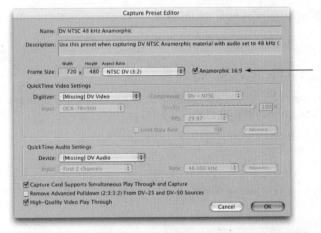

Figure 24-18: Create and label a new Capture Preset with the Anamorphic 16:9 option enabled.

5. **Click OK to close the Capture Preset Editor and save your changes.**

Caution   If you are about to capture 16:9 media that was recorded on a camera with the 16:9 electronic selection enabled, you generally do not need to worry about turning on the Anamorphic 16:9 option in the Capture Presets Editor window. Cameras with the 16:9 electronic option encode the tapes with information about the 16:9 aspect ratio. This code is detected by Final Cut Pro and such footage is automatically recorded in the Anamorphic 16:9 mode. However, if you used the optical method to shoot your 16:9 footage, Final Cut Pro has no way of knowing this, and so you must enable the Anamorphic 16:9 option in the Capture Presets Editor window.

Editing 16:9 material in Final Cut Pro

When you edit Anamorphic media in a sequence, the Anamorphic 16:9 option must be enabled in the Sequence settings so that the clips appear correctly. There are two ways you can do this:

✦ **Use a sequence preset.** Select as default a sequence preset that has the Anamorphic 16:9 option turned on, and then create a new sequence.

✦ **Change the individual sequence's settings.** Create a sequence and then enable the Anamorphic 16:9 option for that sequence.

Both of these methods are outline in the following sections.

Caution   You should follow one of the steps described above before you add any 16:9 clip to a sequence.

Selecting an Anamorphic capture preset

Before you begin a batch capture to acquire Anamorphic 16:9 media from a tape, be sure to select the new Anamorphic capture preset. To select a sequence preset:

1. **Choose Final Cut Pro ⇨ Audio/Video Settings.**

2. **On the Summary tab, select an Anamorphic preset in the Capture Preset pull-down menu as shown in Figure 24-19.**

   You can now proceed to capture 16:9 media.

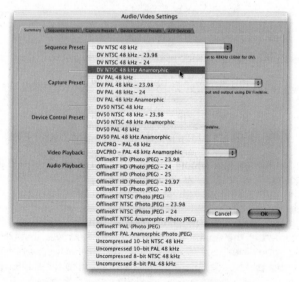

Figure 24-19: Select an Anamorphic capture preset before capturing Anamorphic 16:9 media.

Caution Be sure to deselect the Anamorphic capture preset before selecting regular 4:3 media.

Changing sequence settings for 16:9 media

You can also enable 16:9 media in a sequence after the sequence has been created. To change the sequence settings to accommodate 16:9 media, follow these steps:

1. **Double-click the sequence in the Browser to open it in the Timeline window.**

2. **Choose Sequence ⇨ Sequence Settings.**

3. **Check the small box next to the Anamorphic 16:9 option to enable it as shown in Figure 24-20.**

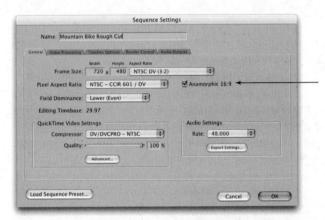

Figure 24-20: Enable the Anamorphic 16:9 setting in the Sequence Settings window to work with Anamorphic media.

4. **Click OK to close the Sequence Settings dialog box.**

You can now edit 16:9 media in the sequence.

Rules for working with Anamorphic media

If you've got your capture and sequence settings adjusted correctly, Final Cut Pro handles Anamorphic 16:9 media easily and without much fuss. You can view the 16:9 media on your computer screen without any distortion or any rendering required. However, there are a few rules to keep in mind when editing 16:9 Anamorphic media:

✦ Any non-16:9 media that is added to a 16:9 sequence is automatically adjusted to match the aspect ratio.

✦ In both the Viewer and Canvas windows, the default setting is Show as Sq. Pixels in the Zoom pop-up menu as shown here. This setting correctly adjusts the Anamorphic 16:9 media for proper viewing on your computer monitor.

There are also some rules to follow when you render items that contain 16:9 Anamorphic media:

✦ When you add 16:9 clips to a 16:9 sequence, no rendering is required.

✦ Tricky transitions such as an oval wipe or star iris are correctly shaped to the widescreen aspect ratio, and any motion effects you apply adjust automatically to the Anamorphic shape.

✦ Any clip with the Anamorphic setting turned on in the Item Properties window is correctly rendered.

✦ If you are editing in a sequence preset that has the 16:9 Anamorphic setting turned on, all clips in the sequence are rendered in Anamorphic 16:9 format.

✦ If you add non-16:9 media to a 16:9 sequence (or vice versa), the new media is adjusted for the proper aspect ratio and must be rendered.

Altering clip properties for 16:9 media

Occasionally, you may capture 16:9 media without first selecting a proper Anamorphic capture preset. Or, you may have accidentally captured a regular 4:3 media while using a 16:9 capture preset. You need not recapture the material in either case. The 16:9 setting is an encoded software bit on the DV clips, and Final Cut Pro can turn it on or off. To adjust the Anamorphic setting for a clip:

1. **Control+Click on any of the Browser window's column headings and select Show Anamorphic from the contextual menu that appears.**

   A new column with the Anamorphic heading is added.

2. **Locate the clip for which you want to alter the Anamorphic setting.**

   Control+click in the Anamorphic column for the clip and choose Yes or No from the contextual menu that appears, as shown in Figure 24-21. You can also select multiple clips and adjust this setting for all of them simultaneously. Choose Yes if you want the clip to be 16:9 Anamorphic, and No if you want the clip to have the standard 4:3 aspect ratio.

Figure 24-21: Control+click in the Anamorphic column for any clip and choose Yes or No to control the clip's aspect ratio.

Mastering 16:9 sequences to tape

Before you master a 16:9 sequence to tape, you should consider your options carefully. You can simply take your 16:9 sequence and edit it to tape like any other sequence. In this case, when your 16:9 sequence is played from the tape on a regular 4:3 monitor, it appears squashed. Your viewers require a 16:9-enabled monitor. Many broadcast-quality monitors have a 16:9 setting. When you enable this setting, the sequence plays properly in the 16:9 format. My suggestion is to only use this option when you are sure that your intended viewers have such a monitor.

If your 16:9 sequence is intended for playback on a regular 4:3 television, you should *letterbox* your sequence. Letterboxing is the process of creating black bars above and below the picture. This process requires significant rendering, but it ensures that your 16:9 image appears as a widescreen program on any old 4:3 monitor. To letterbox your edited 16:9 sequence, follow these steps:

1. **Double-click your 16:9 sequence to open it in the Timeline window.**

2. **Create a new sequence that is *not* 16:9 Anamorphic.**

   The settings for this sequence should, of course, conform to your output method.

3. **Drag the non-16:9 sequence's icon from the Browser to the overwrite area of the Edit Overlay in the Canvas window.**

4. **In the Timeline, open a clip from your 16:9 sequence in the viewer.**

5. **Click the Motion tab to bring up the motion properties.**

6. **Click the disclosure triangle next to the Distort property in the Motion tab.**

7. **Click the Reset button in the Distort property.**

   The Reset button is the red X inside a circle next to the Distort property label. Your sequence is rescaled to –33.33 in the Distort property.

8. **Render the new sequence and master it to tape.**

Caution   It took a lot less time for me to write the "Render the new sequence . . ." sentence than it actually takes for Final Cut Pro to render the sequence. Depending on the length of your program though, you may be in for a long wait. But that's okay. Sit back and relax for once.

Cross-Reference   To learn how to edit sequences to tape see Chapter 18.

Exporting 16:9 QuickTime movies

If you simply export a QuickTime movie from a 16:9 sequence like any old QuickTime export, you may be in for a surprise. Your final export looks squashed. You need to make a few adjustments before you can export a proper widescreen

QuickTime movie. To properly export a QuickTime movie from a 16:9 sequence, follow these steps:

1. **Select your 16:9 sequence in the Browser.**

2. **Choose File ⇨ Export ⇨ QuickTime Movie.**

3. **Click the Setting pull-down menu and select Custom at the very bottom of the list of Presets.**

   The Sequence Preset Editor dialog box appears.

4. **Click on the Aspect Ratio pull-down menu located next to the Frame Size fields at the top of the General tab, and select Custom.**

5. **Enter values for the width and height so that the desired height is ⁹⁄₁₆ of the desired width.**

   To determine this value, multiply the width by 0.5625. For example, if you are exporting from the native DV-NTSC frame size of 720×480, set the output frame size at 720×405. Another example of a smaller 16:9 frame size would be 400×225.

6. **Click OK when you are done.**

7. **If you want, select further video, audio, and compression settings for your QuickTime export, and click OK.**

8. **Select a location to save the movie file in and give your movie a name, then click Save to start the export.**

What is letterboxing?

Films are shot in aspect ratios that range from 1.33:1 to 2.35:1 and higher. There are two methods for projecting these films on a 4:3 (or 1.33:1) shaped television. *Pan and scan* is the process by which a widescreen movie is panned and scanned by the telecine transfer technician during the transfer of film to a 4:3 aspect ratio format. If you go to a video store and pick up a movie, you may see a notice on the back that reads, "This film has been modified from its original version. It has been formatted to fit your TV." That notice means you are about to watch a panned and scanned movie. During the pan and scan process, the technician moves the 4:3 area of transfer around the widescreen of the film to capture the action and details. Many people are offended by this process because they say that it violates the integrity of the original film. Indeed, watching a panned and scanned version of *Lawrence of Arabia* is a dramatically different experience from watching the widescreen original. Another Hollywood epic, *Ben Hur,* was originally shot on a 2.66:1 aspect ratio. You can do simple math to see that the 1.33:1 aspect ratio of television is half as wide as 2.66:1. This means that half of the screen is missing when you watch the panned and scanned version of *Ben Hur.* (Chariots? What chariots?)

Continued

Continued

The alternative to pan and scan is to *letterbox* the movie. Letterboxing is the set of black bars you see on the top and bottom of your screen as you watch a widescreen movie on your 4:3 television. The black bars are added so that widescreen movie can display on a 4:3 TV screen in its original aspect ratio. The wider the original film, the thicker the area of the black bars is. In a 2.35:1 movie, the bars are going to be considerably thicker than in a 1.66:1 movie. The following figure shows you an example of a letterboxed clip, created with the Widescreen video filter in the Effects bin.

Letterboxing has spawned a whole revolution of viewers who demand that movies be seen in their original aspect ratio. There are numerous clubs and Web sites devoted to tracking which movies have been released in the widescreen or letterboxed format. There are even some Web sites that track the schedule of letterboxed movies on cable TV. There is also a faction of people who just cannot stand letterboxed movies. A dear old friend of mine, when she first saw a letterboxed movie years ago, referred to it as the "stupid, squished format." There are many Web sites and advocacy groups devoted to discouraging letterboxing.

✦   ✦   ✦

Understanding the FXBuilder

One of Final Cut Pro's most powerful features is FXBuilder, the video effects creation tool. You can use FXBuilder to create new transitions, filters, and generators, or you can modify the ones that come with Final Cut Pro. FXBuilder is actually a small programming environment, and all Final Cut Pro filters and transitions were created by using FXBuilder. You can open the Final Cut Pro effects and transitions, modify them, and resave them for your needs. You can also create new effects and transitions from scratch to have a set of effects that is truly unique to you.

As an added bonus, FXBuilder in Final Cut Pro brings the ability to program new and cutting-edge effects to the user level. Unlike programming plug-ins for other applications — say, for example, Adobe's After Effects, which requires a full understanding of programming languages and principals (not to mention a compiler like Code Warrior) — FXBuilder is much easier to understand. Regular users can use FXBuilder to make tedious tasks easy or to make new and exciting filters and transitions.

The implications of FXBuilder's flexibility are important — not only does it provide you with a variety of effects limited only by your imagination, but it also enables you to examine the inner workings of both simple and complex tasks, such as masking or keying. Armed with this understanding, you can use FXBuilder's simple syntax to chain tasks together in any way that you choose. The inclusion of FXBuilder in Final Cut Pro may bring forth a new generation of effects and manipulation techniques unlike any seen before. Numerous third-party coders have already begun to spin off transitions, filters, and other effects based on the FXBuilder.

Understanding the FXBuilder

FXBuilder is, among other things, a programming environment for creating and modifying effects in Final Cut Pro. You may be thinking, "Wait, I am not a programmer!" Don't panic — FXBuilder is what computer scientists call a *high-level language* (meaning that it presents the user with a set of commands, or *functions,* and performs most of the complexities of the language behind the scenes).

This sort of programming language is also called a scripting language. The functions are assembled in order, one after the other, to carry out the steps required to process the video elements as desired. Each function accepts one or more pieces of information, or *parameters,* that tell it what media elements to act on and what to do to them.

For example, the Blur function accepts four parameters. The first parameter specifies which image to blur. The second parameter identifies another image, whose contents will be replaced by the blurred image data. The third parameter is the radius or amount to blur, and the fourth parameter sets an aspect ratio. Each bit of information belongs to a small set of *basic data types* — in the previous example, the first two are image buffers (or single video frames), and the last two are real numbers. The beauty of scripting in FXBuilder is that the programming language used has a simple structure and follows a fairly linear and orderly progression. Some words used in the scripting are quite similar to English.

Understanding FXScript Commands

The FXScript commands perform many functions. Statements, Variables, Constants, and others can be strung together to form complex and sophisticated effects for Final Cut Pro. The next sections provide a basic overview of the commands used in the FXScripting language.

Statements

A statement in the FXScript language is a command that performs a single action. Types of statements in the FXScripting language include:

✦ **Definition statement:** The first statement of every script needs to be a definition statement. The definition statement tells Final Cut Pro whether the script is for a transition, an effect, or a generator. The definition statement also helps locate the script in the proper group. For example, the statement:

```
filter "Gaussian Blur";
group "Blur";
```

is a definition statement that tells Final Cut Pro that the script is for a filter named Gaussian Blur and that it should be located in the folder or group called Blur.

✦ **Conditional statement:** A conditional statement lays down a condition for an action to take place. Conditional statements always begin with if and end with end if. Consider this statement:

```
if centerofblur == origin
    offset(centerofblur, 0.00001, 0.00001);
end if;
```

This statement tells Final Cut Pro, if the centerofblur is equal to the origin, then create an offset. The end if ends the conditional statement.

Adding more conditions to a conditional statement is possible by using the else if clause. Each else if clause allows you to add one more condition to the statement. The else clause essentially says: in all cases not covered by a previous set of conditions. For example, in the code:

```
if fontalign == 1               //     left
        setTextjustify(kleftjustify);
else if fontalign == 3          //     right
        setTextjustify(krightjustify);
else                            //       center
        setTextjustify(kcenterjustify);
end if;
```

Final Cut Pro is told in the previous code to first check if the value of font align is equal to 1. If it is, then the setTextjustify action is performed. Two more else if clauses set more conditions. The end if statement ends the conditional statement.

✦ **Input statement:** Input statements enable you to create controls in a script. You can create one control or many sets of controls that include sliders, color selection swatches, and dials to maintain control over the inputs to your script. For example, the input statement:

```
input fontsize, "Font Size", Slider, 56, 1, 150;
```

tells Final Cut Pro to create an input slider for font size. The default value of this slider is 56, while the minimum is 1 and the maximum is 150.

Loops

A *loop* is a piece of code that repeats until a condition is met. Different types of loops are found in an FXScript:

✦ **For...Next loop:** This kind of loop runs the script lines between the For and Next statements for the number of times specified.

✦ `Repeat...End Repeat loop`: This type of loop has a few forms:

  • `Repeat While` **or** `Conditional` **loop:** This loop repeats the lines between the `Repeat` and `End Repeat` statements until a specified condition is met.

  • `Repeat With Counter` **(similar to the** `For...Next` **loop):** This loop repeats the lines between the `Repeat` and `End Repeat` statements for the number of times specified.

  • `Repeat With List`: This type of loop repeats the script lines between the `Repeat` and `End Repeat` one time for each element of a *list* parameter. It assigns each element from the list in turn to the variable.

Subroutines

A subroutine is a very handy piece of code. A *subroutine* is a portion of a code that can be called upon from any other portion of the script. If your script is working its way down through the code, it may encounter a call to a subroutine. In that case, the script jumps to the subroutine, executes it, and then returns to the main script where it was before the detour. Subroutines are useful because they can be called upon many times in different portions of a script. This saves a lot of repetition in the code. You can write a subroutine one time and call it repeatedly in the code.

When you use subroutines, keep these things in mind:

✦ All subroutines begin in a script with the `on` command. For example, in the line:

`on newsub (parameter 1, parameter 2...)`

The subroutine `newsub` is being called.

✦ A subroutine ends with the word `end` on a line by itself.

✦ All code between the words `on` and `end` is part of a subroutine.

Variables

A variable is used as a holder or container for information that is unknown. You can create your own variables by first declaring them or by using one that is predefined in the FXScript language in Final Cut Pro. Variables can hold numbers or text. The code for the script can then make calls to check the value of these variables at different times. The FXScript language has three types of variables:

✦ **Predefined variables:** These variables are provided to you as part of the scripting language. For example, the predefined variable `kRed` is used to define the color red in drawing routines. Similarly, the predefined variable `kleftjustify` is used to justify text to the left. A helpful listing of the predefined variables is provided for you in Appendix E.

✦ **Global variables:** These are variables that are defined by you in the code. The global variables are reset to zero after each frame of video to which the effect may be applied. Global variables must be declared before they can be used. In a declaration for a global variable, you have to define the data type of the variable as well as the name for it. After a variable is declared, you can use these variables anywhere in the script.

✦ **Static variables:** Static variables are always declared before the code section of the script begins. These variables maintain their values unless changed by the code.

Constants

A *constant* is a number whose value never changes. Colors such as kRed and kGreen are constants.

Data

Data is any type of information that the script is called upon to process. FXScripts can have many types of data. Some data types are:

✦ **Strings:** Strings are a sequence of characters. Strings are never processed as mathematical operations, whether the characters are text or numbers. Strings are simply characters to be displayed.

✦ **Numbers:** With FXScripts you can work with several different types of numbers. You can use floating-point numbers, numeric coordinates, and numbers that correspond to colors.

✦ **Images:** This data type is a buffer used to hold frames of video.

✦ **Regions:** Regions are used to define areas of a video frame.

✦ **Clips:** These type of data type are larger buffers than can hold entire clips of video.

Arrays

An *array* is a grid of one or more dimensions. A video frame can be thought of as an array of two-dimensional colored pixels. Arrays are used in scripts that are designed for pixel modification.

Operators and expressions

An *expression* is a statement about the value of a number or a set of numbers. An expression consists of numbers, or variables, and relational operators. *Relational operators* are mathematical functions, such as subtraction, addition, or a state of being, such as greater than or less than.

Expressions are phrases or sentences made up from scripting words, numbers, and operators, along with parentheses. The operators determine what sort of calculation is to be performed. The parentheses determine the order in which the calculations are performed.

Here are a few rules for using expressions:

✦ Expressions are read from left to right.

✦ Multiplication and division operations take priority over addition and subtraction.

✦ Portions of expressions that are contained within parentheses are given priority over those that are not. Within layers of parentheses, calculations are performed from the innermost set of parentheses to the outermost.

Note   You may notice that the rules for using expressions in FXScript are the same rules you learned in grade school when using expressions in arithmetic.

Functions

A *function* is a predefined calculation. Cosine and arctangents are types of predefined mathematical calculations.

Comments

Coding would be very hard to figure out without comments. Programmers frequently add comments to describe what a script is doing at any given point. Any line of code that begins with two forward slashes (//) is a comment and is not processed as part of the script.

Using the FXBuilder

Take the time to learn the FXBuilder interface and scripting functions. The interface is relatively simple and well laid out. The scripting ability of FXBuilder takes time to learn; however, the power to manipulate and create your own effects makes this tool well worth your time.

Mastering the FXBuilder interface

The FXBuilder interface has four main components:

✦ **FXBuilder window:** Write, edit, modify, and test scripts in this window. The FXBuilder window has two tabs:

- **FXBuilder Text Entry tab:** Enter text in this tab for a script (see Figure 25-1).

- **FXBuilder Input Controls tab:** Control the inputs to test the script (see Figure 25-2). The Input Controls tab is for dynamic testing of the input controls only and will not change any settings of the script.

✦ **FXScript language:** Use this scripting language to create the scripts, similar to the script shown in Figure 25-1.

✦ **FXBuilder menu:** Appears next to the tools menu when the FXBuilder window is active (see Figure 25-3). Commands in the menu enable you to add script text, modify scripts, save scripts, and run scripts.

✦ **FXBuilder playback window:** One important tool in FXBuilder is the playback window, because it enables you to see the results of your script as you run the script in debug mode by using FXBuilder (see Figure 25-4). You can even change parameters (or input controls) of your script and see the result window update in real time.

Figure 25-1: The text for the script is entered in the FXBuilder Text Entry tab of the FXBuilder window.

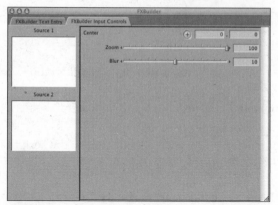

Figure 25-2: The FXBuilder Input Controls tab enables you to test your script and modify the input controls.

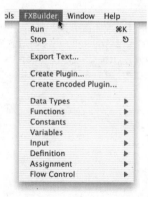

Figure 25-3: The FXBuilder menu appears next to the Tools menu when the FXBuilder window is active.

Figure 25-4: The playback window plays back the final results of your script.

The FXBuilder is a powerful and flexible tool. You can create scripts for sophisticated effects and save them as plug-ins for later use, just like any of the other effects that came with Final Cut Pro. Furthermore, all transitions, effects, generators, and filters that came with Final Cut Pro can be opened and modified in the FXBuilder. Simply being able to review the script for existing effects can be helpful when you set about the task of creating a new script.

Understanding the structure of FXScript

The easiest way to understand FXBuilder's scripting language is to look at an example of it. This section guides you through the process of viewing a script and walking through it line by line. To open a script, follow these steps:

1. **Click the Effects tab in the Browser window to bring it to the front.**

2. **Click the disclosure triangle next to the Video Generators folder.**

3. **Click the disclosure triangle next to the Text folder.**

4. **Select the Text generator in the Text folder.**

5. **Choose View ➪ Effect in Editor.**

   The FXBuilder window opens and displays the script for the Text generator. Figure 25-5 shows the text generator script in the FXBuilder window.

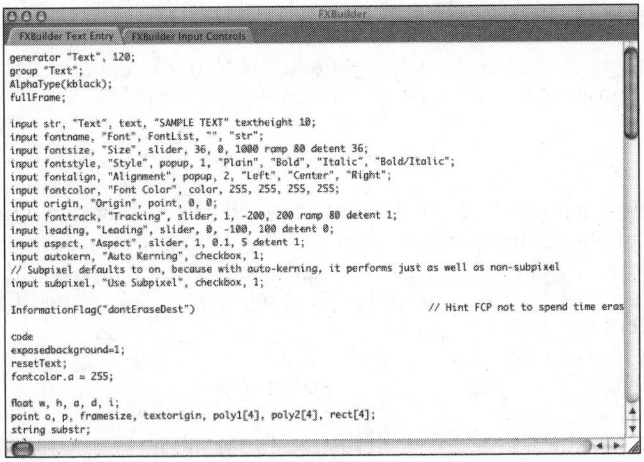

Figure 25-5: The text generator script as viewed from the FXBuilder window.

Understanding the basic structure of an FXScript is fairly straightforward. Each script has three main portions. The main portions of a script are as follows:

✦ The first portion specifies the name and category for the script.

✦ The second portion is dedicated to creating the input controls, such as sliders and pull-down menus.

✦ The last portion is devoted to the actual code that runs the script.

The next few sections provide a line-by-line breakdown of the Text generator script you just opened in the preceding steps.

Naming the script and defining the script category: Lines 1 through 4

The first four lines identify the plug-in being created. In lines 1 through 4, the name is provided for the script as well as for the category or group the script belongs to under the Effects tab in the Browser.

This first line is a `generator` declaration. This line states that this script is a generator of the name `Text` and that the default duration value will be 120 seconds.

```
generator "Text", 120;
```

Tip   The name of your custom effect or transition as it will appear in the Effects bin and Effects menu is determined by the name you give it in line 1, and not the name you save with your final custom plug-in.

The next line states that this script will reside in the folder called `Text` in the Effects tab of the Browser:

```
group "Text";
```

The next line states that the Alpha Type for the result created by this filter will be of an alpha type black. Alpha types are very important to know, because transparency is generated by Final Cut Pro using Alpha and RGB channels and Final Cut Pro needs to know if the image is matted against white or black in the RGB to know how to properly key the image.

```
AlphaType(kBlack);
```

The next declaration states that the script is to render full frame, rather than in fields. If you rendered in fields, you could have oddities when Final Cut Pro goes to render its own motions in fields.

```
fullFrame;
```

Specifying input controls for your script: Lines 5 through 16

Lines 5 through 16 specify the input controls that are needed for this script to run. For example, in this script, a total of 12 inputs are needed. Some inputs are sliders, while others are color selection swatches.

The first input control should be obvious; it's the text that you want the text generator to write. Note that all input controls have basically the same setup:

✦ First, the word `input` lets FXBuilder know that this text is an input control.

✦ The declaration of the variable that is a part of the input line follows. Normally, you have to declare a variable. But in the input case, it's done for you automatically (that's the beauty of a scripting language). This variable is called `str` (short for *string*, which is a fancy programmer's term for text to be displayed).

✦ Then the Text in quotes is the User interface name that appears to the user in the generator controls.

✦ The next `text` indicates that the control should be a text input box.

✦ The next `SAMPLE TEXT` in quotes indicates the initial value of the variable, and the default text that appears in the text box when you first start it up.

✦ The next line states that the text-input box's height should be 10 lines.

Thus the final line created is

```
input str, "Text", text, "SAMPLE TEXT" textheight 10;
```

The following input control determines the font that you want to use. Note that the variable `fontname` is a simple, plain-English variable that can be easily understood anywhere in the script. Always create easy-to-understand names for yourself.

```
input fontname, "Font", FontList, "", "str";
```

The next input control is for the size of the font. The input has a variable called `fontsize` that requires a slider with the value set to 36 by default. The minimum value of this slider is 0 and the maximum is 1000. This slider is ramped by increments of 80-point size. If this value is set to 10 or 20, the increments are smaller, and the slider-handle default position is on one side. If the value is set to 80 (or 1000, which is the max) the slider-handle default is more toward the center. At a value of 1000, the slider handle is all the way to the right, with no more sliding possible. The detent value of this slider currently is at 36, as well.

```
input fontsize, "Size", slider, 36, 0, 1000 ramp 80 detent 36;
```

The next input control is for font styles, and you enter your data in a pop-up type input. The variable created for this input is called fontstyle, and the value of this variable is set to 1, which represents Plain style. (This is clear in the code that follows.) This value can be 1, 2, 3, or 4, which represents each of the four possible style types. The four styles are labeled Plain, Bold, Italic, and Bold/Italic. These inputs create the sliders and the buttons, and they give labels to items. The real work of defining what the string Bold means to the FXBuilder is done in the code.

```
input fontstyle, "Style", popup, 1, "Plain", "Bold", "Italic",
"Bold/Italic";
```

Yet another input. This input is for font alignment, and this is also a pop-up type input. The variable is called fontalign, and the value of this variable is set to 2, which represents the Center style. This value can be 1, 2, and 3, which represents each of the three types of alignments possible. The three alignments are labeled Left, Center, and Right. This input control is the input control for the alignment of the text, or the justification, just like in a word processor.

```
input fontalign, "Alignment", popup, 2, "Left", "Center",
"Right";
```

The fontcolor input allows the user to set the font color. The default color is set to white by using the RGB+A (A is for alpha) color palette. Of course, it figures that we call it RGB+A, but the number positions in the input control line are ARGB. (The first 255 is Alpha.) Fontcolor yields a color input control that works in RGB. The first 255 value is for the Alpha channel. All color values and functions in FXBuilder also carry alpha. The next three 255s are for Red, Green, and Blue, respectively. This line sets up the input control for a color picker. This color picker gives you an eyedropper and access to the Macintosh color picker. The numbers at the end tell you the default color combination, which equals white (all 255s).

```
input fontcolor, "Font Color", color, 255, 255, 255, 255;
```

The following line is used to set up the input for the origin of the text. You can have the text originate from the middle of the image or from some other part of the image. This input control is a crosshair point shooter with which you can select a point in the canvas, much like the eyedropper. The origin point of this text is X=0 and Y=0. In short, this text originates at the very center of the screen. You can modify these values to start your text out in another portion of the screen by default.

```
input origin, "Origin", point, 0, 0;
```

The next input is a variable called *fonttrack*. It uses a slider to set up the text tracking, which is manipulating the spacing between characters. This control for tracking is very much like what you may have used in word processing utilities. You have to build these tracking controls in the FXBuilder. The value of this variable is set to 1 by default. However, the value of this slider can vary between –200 and 200. This slider moves in values of 80, and the current detent is at 1.

```
input fonttrack, "Tracking", slider, 1, -200, 200 ramp 80
detent 1;
```

The following input control is for the leading of the text, also known as changing the space between a single set of characters. The word slider indicates that this input control is to be a slider. The first 0 is the starting value, the second -100 is the min value, the 100 is the max value, and the detent call means that 0 will be sticky, so you can set this control back to 0 if you want.

```
input leading, "Leading", slider, 0, -100, 100 detent 0;
```

The next input control enables you to adjust the aspect of the text that is generated. The reason we may put this control in here is really just to give you more flexibility in altering the text to make it look good for the video. By now, you should be familiar with what the rest of the items in this line mean.

```
input aspect, "Aspect", slider, 1, 0.1, 5 detent 1;
```

The following line of script creates a simple on/off control to turn auto kerning on or off. The default value for this check box is 1, which means it is on. You can change it to 0 so that it turns off by default.

```
input autokern, "Auto Kerning", checkbox, 1;
```

The next input is in there so that you may turn sub-pixel calculations in this generator on or off. If you're doing some motions with the origin control (remember, everything in Final Cut Pro is keyframeable) then you would be performing a move in the generator, not with the motion tab of Final Cut Pro. If you did that, you'd have to do sub-pixel calculations to make the move look good. Because you use FXBuilder, it is slow to do these calculations, so there is a switch to turn the calculation function on or off depending on your needs. You really only need sub-pixel during slow moves of items in Final Cut Pro. During fast moves of items across screen, you usually don't notice if there is no sub-pixel math.

```
input subpixel, "Use Subpixel", checkbox, 0;
```

Specifying code to run your script: Line 17 to the end

The following script beginning with the code indicator contains all the relevant source code needed to run. The next line of script is the marker or flag for the beginning of the code portion of the script. Anything after the code flag is considered code.

```
code
```

The following line determines whether the background is visible behind what is generated. In the case of text, you generally want the background to be visible. So set this to 1 or, true.

```
exposedbackground=1;
```

The next line resets the text parameters of the Final Cut Pro render engine. Resetting memory in programming is always a good idea. If you do not, stray values may be in memory, and you may end up with weird results. So, this line resets text values (font, size, color, and so on) before you even get started.

```
resetText;
```

After the text parameters are reset, set the font color parameter to 255, or white. In Final Cut Pro, a reset of text parameters sets the text to black. As a general rule, you do not want to use a lot of black text in video, so set the font color parameter to white for an initial value.

```
fontcolor.a = 255;
```

In the next line of code, you have a variable declaration area for the variables that you use in this script that were not declared as a part of the input controls. These particular variables are simple numbers. They are floating-point numbers (decimals) but simple nonetheless. The reason you predefine these variables is that Final Cut Pro needs to know how much memory to allocate to this script before Final Cut Pro executes it. This is the location where the memory is tallied and assigned names.

```
float w, h, a, d, i;
```

This line contains more variable declarations. FXBuilder has variables that are points based on an X- and Y-coordinate system. Final Cut Pro does not operate with a Z-axis. In short, no 3-D.

```
point o, p, framesize, textorigin, poly1[4], poly2[4], rect[4];
```

This is another declaration but for another special FXBuilder variable, string. This is a variable that will hold text. In this text script, you need a buffer to hold a text variable while you perform some manipulations onto it. So, you must predefine the variable here.

```
string substr;
```

This special variable is called color. The color variable has a three number values — an R, G, and B value. Sound familiar?

```
color opacity;
```

This line is sort of like the resettext line. The idea here is resetting the dest image buffer. The dest is the image buffer that is the resulting final frame. You put all your work into the dest buffer. You can use dest as a buffer while you are working, too. You don't have to fill it with the final numbers until the end. It's good to reuse buffers, especially image buffers, to economize on RAM usage and keep your script from becoming a RAM hog.

The channelfill function is used a lot, and it fills all the numbers in the image array with the specified variables. In this particular case, the image array is filled with simple 0s. Note that the breakdown is (dest, A, R, G, B). A is Alpha. R is red, G is green, and B is Blue. After this function, if you were to look at dest, you would see a totally black and opaque frame.

```
channelFill(dest, 0, 0, 0, 0);
```

The following line is designed to gather the image dimensions of the destination image buffer. Because Final Cut Pro is resolution independent, you must write scripts in a similar manner as well. You cannot count on the image buffer being 720 × 486 pixels. You have to keep in mind that the buffer could be 720 × 480 pixels, 640 × 480 pixels (or even 320 × 240 pixels). When you declare image buffers, you have to know how much RAM to allocate. As a result, you have to know how big the frame is going to be before you can declare an image buffer. Note that the framesize point variable that you declared earlier is used. Instead of using the framesize point variable as a point, this time the variable is used in terms of width/height. You can also use w and h as variables here. You would have just needed to declare w and h as a part of the float-point declare process.

```
dimensionsof(dest, framesize.x, framesize.y);
```

Because you found out how big the image buffers need to be for this script, you can now declare image buffers that you want to use in this script. Note that you have to set up how big these image buffers are; there is no choice about not doing it.

```
image buf0[framesize.x][framesize.y],
buf1[framesize.x][framesize.y];
```

The following line is an important moment in this script. This line is the first big function in the script. A poly is a four-point array that has four XY coordinates in it. The script is meant to determine the bounds of the image buffer buf0 and then take those values and place them into the poly called poly1.

```
boundsof(buf0, poly1);
```

The following line is meant to zero out (remember the whole thing about clearing memory?) the variable o. The variable, o, is being set to 0,0 or the origin. The origin point in the Final Cut Pro render world is the middle of the image, not the upper left as in other applications and the computer world in general. Moving the origin to the middle of the image is intended to make calculating the XY coordinates that you would want to use easier.

```
o = {0, 0}                    //      origin
```

The next line of script sets the `fontsize` that was chosen by the user to be a function of the frame size. This way, when you set up size-specific text in an offline mode by using 320 × 240 pixels media and then go to online your material, you still get text that is the right proportion to the new frame size (which is probably 720 × 486 pixels). If you didn't make the font size a function of framesize in this way, then if you prepare offline (low-resolution) text, which you then later use online at high resolution, the resulting text would be too small. It would look good in the offline but not in the online. The text needs to look the same, and this next line of code is how you do that:

```
fontsize *= (framesize.x / 640)
```

The next line of script is the general font parameter setting that needs to be set. FXBuilder maintains a set of variables for fonts in the render engine, and these variables need to be set. By setting up the input controls, you only set the variables that you are going to use. Here you use the `fontname` variable to set the font that is used by Final Cut Pro when rendering the text.

```
setTextFont(fontname);
```

Same as the preceding line of script, the next line sets the final rendered size of the text. Note that you already adjusted for the frame size two lines earlier.

```
setTextSize(fontsize);
```

This next big block of code is an `if...else` flow-control setup. It's what you use when you have a whole bunch of parameters to choose from, and you need to do this for one and that for the other. In this case, the code addresses a pretty common situation — adjusting the text's justification.

The FXBuilder will justify text, but you have to tell it what kind justification you want. So, you go through the code and say in essence:

✦ If the `fontalign` variable is equal to 1, then the script needs to be set to `text justify` in FXBuilder to the left. (The input control for Alignment was a pop-up menu. The result of the pop-up menu is a numerical 1 for the first position, 2 for the second, and so on.)

✦ If the `fontalign` variable is not equal to 1, then you move to the next option. You say, using the code line `else`, if the `fontalign` variable is equal to 2, then set it to be right-justified. Or (`else`) if it's 3, then set it to `center`. If you go back and look at the align input control, you'll see that these match up: 1 is `left` justify, 2 is `right` justify, and 3 is `center` justify.

Note that the writer of the script left in comments that 1 is left justification and 2 is right justification. Adding simple reminders makes it easier to come back later and know what's going on and not have to scroll up to look at the input control. This type of thinking is counter to the other type of coder who makes everything Greek so that he or she has better job security. If nobody can figure it out, then nobody else can do it. Good thing that Apple isn't that kind of company!

The resulting block of code goes like this:

```
if fontalign == 1                 //        left
    setTextjustify(kleftjustify);
else if fontalign == 3            //        right
    setTextjustify(krightjustify);
else                              //        center
    setTextjustify(kcenterjustify);
```

Tip A line preceded by two forward slashes (//) indicates a comment that is not part of the actual code in the script. The two forward slashes (//) can also appear in the same line as the code. Programmers often write comments in scripts to help themselves and others read and decipher the scripts later. Leaving remarks is important because, though a line of script may make sense at the time, when you look at that line again a few months from now, you may have a hard time recalling what the purpose of that line was. To save yourself headaches later on, add comments to your scripts as often as possible.

The end if line basically signals that this is the end of the conditional section. Remember, in a condition, the line is only executed if the condition is met. Like X=1, if not, then FXBuilder skips the line and moves on to the next. Skipping a line indicates that FXBuilder is out of conditions and executes every line following. Until another if that is:

```
end if;
```

Speaking of another if, here is another one. (Most programming, by the way, is nothing but a huge series of if...else statements.) In this if...else block, FXBuilder assigns the text style based on the Style input control that you set up in the beginning of the script.

The code segment for creating fontstyle goes like this:

```
if fontstyle == 4            //        bold & italic
    setTextstyle(kbolditalic);
else if fontstyle == 3       //        italic
    setTextstyle(kitalic);
else if fontstyle == 2       //        bold
    setTextstyle(kbold);
else                         //        plain
    setTextstyle(kplain);
end if;
```

You may not know some of the standard conventions, such as a double equals sign checks if something is equal. An = sets an assignment, and an = = is a comparison. If the variable fontstyle = = (equals) 4, then settextstyle to be the predefined constant kbolditalic and so forth. kbolditalic is one of the Final Cut Pro's predefined constants that are included in the FXBuilder.

Note   Many predefined commands in Final Cut Pro's FXBuilder start with a K because the original codename for Final Cut Pro was Keygrip. In the past, many of the variables were called kgthis and kgthat. Distinguishing an FXBuilder command from a regular programming command was easy.

The following line of script contains a simple assignment (not a comparison) (note the single = rather than the double == like in an if statement), followed by a function. This assignment alters the numbers for the origin calculations based on the frame size of the destination frame. Again, remember that you must program with flexibility in mind. You never know what the frame size of the dest (or destination frame) may be. It could be 320 × 240 pixels, 720 × 486 pixels, or even 1920 × 1080 pixels. The first line uses the point variables framesize and textorigin to begin the framesize offset function. You set the variable textorigin to equal framesize.

```
textorigin = framesize;
```

Then in this next line, you multiply the textorigin variable by origin and then set it to the result. That's what the *= does. Now the variable textorigin is scaled for the framesize that's in use when the generator is rendered.

```
textorigin *= origin;
```

Adding conditionals

Here you enter the valley of the big tamale. Conditionals stir the pot some more and add some complexity. Conditionals are statements that take more than one variable into consideration. The next if block is the meat of the generator.

The following line of code is a double condition. If the length of the string is greater than 0 and if the fontsize is greater than 0, then continue. Otherwise the generator would basically stop right here, because no commands or conditions are after the endif that is matched to this if. Notice the structure of the if and end ifs: The conditions are lined up with tabs so that you know which endif goes with which if. Keeping your conditional statements organized is a good practice and you won't regret this decision — especially if you have to troubleshoot your code at a later date.

```
if length(str) > 0 && fontsize > 0
```

The next line of script is a simpler `if` — is autokern true or false? If the line is true (or equal to 1), then the FXBuilder executes the next line, if the condition is false (or equal to 0), FXBuilder skips to the next line.

```
if autokern
```

If `autokern` was true, then you measure the string with the `measurestring` function rather than the `measurestringplain`. The `measurestring` function takes the specified string and returns numbers based in its dimensions. What's special about the `measurestring` function is that it includes spacing considerations. Estimation of the spacing is an added parameter in the function that `measurestringplain` doesn't have.

Note that the `fonttrack*fontsize/18` is a function that determines the spacing to be input into the measure string function.

Note that the code calls for multiplication of the `fonttrack` and `fontsize` and then division by 18 to yield spacing. Why 18? We get that number by a lot of testing of the generator. The idea is to get a result that the user would expect. So, by using trial and error, I could see the `fonttrack` value fluctuating from –200 to 200. The result you would expect to be a divisor of 18. Coming up with the right number is a kind of trial and error situation.

```
measurestring("M", fonttrack*fontsize/18, w, h, a, d,
aspectof(dest)*aspect);
```

The next line of code is the `else` statement that says if you didn't execute the earlier line, then do this one.

```
else
```

The next bit of code utilizes `measureStringPlain`. `measureStringPlain` executes if the autokerning is not on. The `measureStringPlain` function actually measures the size of the string for calculations later on. All `measureStringPlain` does is to tell you how big the string is in terms of size. You may want to know the space taken up in the string with four 1s (1111) is much smaller than the space taken up by four Ws (WWWW).

```
measureStringPlain("M", w, h, a, d,
aspectof(dest)*aspect)
```

This is the `end if` from the `if...autokern` statement. Notice how the `end if` is lined up with the `if...autokern` statement four lines above. That's important in keeping the code formatting in order when you're debugging your script.

```
end if;
```

This line of code addresses the subpixel mentioned earlier while creating inputs. If the if pixel is on, then the generator executes the subpixel path of the code.

```
if subpixel
```

The following code prepares a loop situation. The loop repeats the command over and over until it meets the number of times specified. In this case, the number of times is set by a counttextlines function. The counttextlines function counts the number of lines of text and provides the results.

```
for i = 0 to counttextlines(str)-1
```

In the next line, a single line of text from the string variable str is stuffed into the string variable substr .You are getting line I, which will be 0, 1, or 2, depending on how many lines there are and where the code appears in the for...next loop.

```
getTextLine(str, i, substr);
```

The next line is another conditional set to only execute if the length of the substr is longer than 0. Use these kinds of traps to stop executing code if the code has no purpose to continue. Allowing code to continue to run slows the script down. This part of making a script efficient is very important in an emulator environment, such as FXBuilder.

```
if length(substr) > 0
```

If the string is big enough, fill two buffers with 0s, basically zeroing out the buffers like I mentioned earlier. It's good practice to zero out buffers and memory before you use them. These two lines zero out the two buffers buf0 and buf1.

```
channelfill(buf0, 0, 0, 0, 0);
channelfill(buf1, 0, 0, 0, 0);
```

The next line sets the point variable p to the textorigin. However, textorigin strips any decimals off the number and leaves an integer. If you had a *p* variable of 2.38, textorigin changes the variable to an integer of 2. This sets the position of the text to a clean starting place so that you can move it a precise amount to get subpixel accuracy.

```
p = {integer(textorigin.x),
integer(textorigin.y)};
```

This is the autokern if. Everything you do sort of starts out with an "if auto kerning is on then . . . " so here it is. Again.

```
if autokern
```

If the autokern is in fact on, then when you draw the text you can use the `draw string` routine rather than the `drawstringplain` routine because you need the ability to control the spacing. (`drawstringplain` is a faster string routine that does not perform auto-kerning.) Also notice that because you're still in the subpixel portion of the code, you're using the `p.x` and `p.y` stripped of decimals. The `font track*fontsize/18` that was used in the last autokern function to set the spacing in `measurestring` is used here, too.

```
                  drawstring(substr, p.x, p.y,
   fonttrack*fontsize/18, buf0, fontcolor, aspectof(dest)*aspect);
```

If `autokern` is not used, then the generator executes the following command, `Else`, and executes the next few lines instead of the previous line.

```
          Else
```

`Rect` is a four-point variable that was set up earlier in the point declarations. It's going to be a rectangular region. Set `rect` to 0, just to make sure you have a clean slate.

```
          rect *= o;                    //    clear
```

With the following code, set the size of the `rect` to be the size of the text's offset from the origin, or the `textorigin`.

```
          rect += p;
```

You now need to `offset` the `rect` by a small amount. That amount is XY and it's going to be 0 horizontal and a `-a` ascent. You got the ascent from the `measure string` functions that you performed earlier. The data from the `measurestring` command is used here.

```
          offset(rect, 0, -a);
```

Now that the poly is set up properly, you can draw text into it. This is the drawing routine that actually draws the text.

```
                  drawStringPlain(substr, rect, buf0,
   fontcolor, aspectof(dest)*aspect);
```

Here you're going to measure the `dest` poly and take those numbers and put them into the `poly2` poly declared in the beginning of the script. (I declared the `poly2` poly in the variable declaration section earlier titled "Specifying code to run your script." You can check line 22 of the script to see this declaration.)

```
          boundsof(dest, poly2);
```

Now you're going to offset the `poly` a tiny bit. The decimal amount shaved off P is what you use. The reason you offset the `poly` is because the drawstring routine in FXBuilder is not subpixel accurate; it will round the number off to the nearest whole number. But the *bliting* (redrawing) routines are accurate so that is how you can do subpixel drawing. You simply draw and then blit (redraw) in another place. This line offsets the `poly2` by the `1.38-1` amount, which would be `.38` for example.

```
                        offset(poly2, textorigin.x-p.x,
    textorigin.y-p.y);
```

Next, you do a *blit*. The next line of script takes the source `bof0` and the source `poly1` (which is the size of the `buf0` — you did this much earlier) and stuffs them into the `buf1` and the `poly2` made here. The source is offset by the tiny little bit that will be subpixel.

```
                    blitrect(buf0, poly1, buf1, poly2);
```

The next line adds the new buffer to the `dest` buffer (`dest` is the end result) just in case there is more than one line of text. The text draw routine only draws one line at a time. You have to draw lines yourself here.

```
                    dest += buf1;
```

This line is the end of the line that checked if the `substr` was bigger than 0. If the text had been smaller than 0, you could have skipped the code to this point.

```
                end if;
```

Remember the part about drawing lines yourself? Here is the next `offset` to draw the next line. `Offset` the `textorigin` by the h value of the frame and a function of amount of leading in the text.

```
            offset(textorigin, 0, h*(1+leading/100));
```

The following line of code is for the loop that makes up the lines. If there is another line, the preceding code runs through again with the new offset as set by the preceding line to draw the next line of text.

```
            next;
```

The following piece of script is the `else` for the very first `if` — the subpixel if. If the subpixel is not on, then the following lines are the ones that will run and all the preceding lines in the meat of this generator script would not run.

```
        Else
```

Even with no subpixel, you still have the same problem in having to draw your own lines. So, count the lines (just like before) and then go through the drawing one line at a time. Note the big difference in this section is only that you never strip the textorigin to an integer. Note too that the first drawstring uses the text origin.x and textorigin.y variables just the way they are. FXBuilder then rounds the decimals off and draws straight integer line values. Everything else is the same as the previous lines of code. In fact, the code was probably copied, pasted, and then massaged — the standard thing to do. It's considered bad practice, but hey, I copy and paste code all the time.

```
        for i = 0 to counttextlines(str)-1
            getTextLine(str, i, substr);
            if length(substr) > 0
                if autokern
                    drawstring(substr, textorigin.x,
textorigin.y, fonttrack*fontsize/18, dest, fontcolor,
aspectof(dest)*aspect);
                else
                    rect *= o;                  //      clear
                    rect += textorigin;
                    offset(rect, 0, -a);
                    drawStringPlain(substr, rect, dest,
fontcolor, aspectof(dest)*aspect);
                end if;
            end if;
            offset(textorigin, 0, h*(1+leading/100));
        next;
    end if;
```

Also note that the same offset stuff wasn't re-created with the buffers 0 and 1. That's because you are not doing the subpixel in this second condition of the subpixel if.

```
    end if;
```

And there you have it, you aspiring code warrior. Go forth and produce with FXBuilder.

Modifying an existing effect in the FXBuilder

Imagine this scenario: You are the supervising editor for a big production house where many editors come to work on Final Cut Pro–based workstations. Your edit house, which I'll call Eureka! Digital Video Productions, has a standard set of text guidelines. These guidelines call for the text to be green and 46 points tall, among other things. However, you find that the editors cannot keep these standards straight. For the sake of consistency, you decide to make a Eureka! Text effect that has these values preset and ready to use.

The easiest way to create a new effect with FXBuilder is to open and modify an existing script. To open a script, follow these steps:

1. **Click the Effects tab of the Browser window.**

2. **Click the disclosure triangle next to the Video Generators folder.**

3. **Click the disclosure triangle next to the Text folder.**

4. **Select the text generator in the Text folder.**

5. **Choose View ➪ Effect in Editor.**

   The FXBuilder window opens and displays the source code for the text generator.

6. **To make a quick and basic modification in this generator, give the generator a new name first, so that it is easy to recognize.**

   Change the first line to the following:

   ```
   generator "Eureka!Text", 120;
   ```

Tip   The name of your custom effect or transition as it will appear in the Effects bin and Effects menu is determined by the name you give it in line 1, and not the name you save with your final custom plug-in.

7. **Next, create a new group for the effect by changing the second line to the following:**

   ```
   group "Eureka!In-House Effects";
   ```

   With this change your effect appears in its own folder, called Eureka! In-House Effects under the Generators folder in the Effects tab. Making this change also provides a Eureka! In-House Effects submenu in the Generators pull-down menu of the View window, as shown in Figure 25-6.

8. **Next, change the plug-in's default text that shows when the plug-in is first applied.**

   In the fifth line from the top, change the line:

   ```
   input str, "Text", text, "SAMPLE TEXT" textheight 10;
   ```

   to the following:

   ```
   input str, "Text", text, "Final Text" textheight 10;
   ```

   The notation `str` is short for *string,* which is a programmers term for plain old text. All you've done here is change the text input string from `SAMPLE TEXT` to `Final Text`.

9. **Change the default font size of this script from 36 to 46.**

   In line 7, change:

   ```
   input fontsize, "Size", slider, 36, 0, 1000 ramp 80 detent 36;
   ```

   to:

   ```
   input fontsize, "Size", slider, 46, 0, 1000 ramp 80 detent 46;
   ```

Figure 25-6: Making a new group will add another submenu in the Generator pull-down menu at the bottom right of the View window.

10. Change the default color of this text plug-in to green.

The original color of the text is white. You change the text color to green by changing line 10 from the following:

```
input fontcolor, "Font Color", color, 255, 255, 255, 255;
```

to

```
input fontcolor, "Font Color", color, 255, 0, 191, 0;
```

Make additional changes to the script if you like. Make sure that you don't modify any of the syntax of the script. For example, do not delete any semi-colons or quotation marks around the text.

Caution

If you accidentally modify the syntax of the script, a syntax error message appears when you try to run the script.

11. To run this script, choose FXBuilder ⇨ Run.

The FXBuilder window automatically switches to the FXBuilder Input Controls tab, as shown in Figure 25-7, and you can see your changes reflected in the sliders and fields that appear in this window. A separate FXBuilder window also opens and continues to run the script over and over again. The controls of the Input Controls tab are for dynamic testing of the input controls only and will not change any settings of the script.

Now that you have modified this script, you should save it. But rather than just save it, save it so that this script cannot be opened and modified.

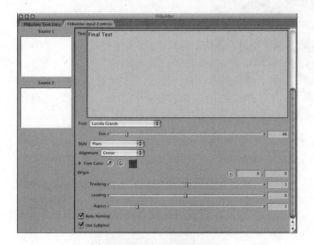

Figure 25-7: The FXBuilder Input Controls are seen, in the top figure, after the modified script is run. The small FXBuilder window, on the bottom, shows the running script.

12. **Choose FXBuilder ➪ Create Encoded Plug-in.**

   This feature allows you to create a locked plug-in.

13. **Enter a name and select a location to save it for now.**

   After you have saved the plug-in, the plug-in's icon should look like Figure 25-8.

Caution The FXBuilder window must be active in order for the FXBuilder menu to be available to you.

Figure 25-8: The new text plug-in you've created should look similar to the one shown here.

14. **To use this plug-in, drag it into the Plugins folder, located at** Home/
    Library/Preferences/Final cut Pro Data/Plugins.

    This new plug-in is now available to you in the Generators subcategory, as shown in Figure 25-9.

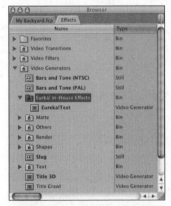

Figure 25-9: Your final creation is available to you under the Generators category, under your very own subfolder labeled Eureka! In-House Effects.

Now, you can issue orders to your legions of editors to use the Eureka!Text plug-in because it is set to the right color, size, and any other attributes you chose.

Testing and running scripts

When you are working on a script in the FXBuilder, it is critical that you test the script before you try to use it. Any script can be tested and checked in the FXBuilder window.

Follow these steps to run or test a script:

1. **Click the Effects tab of the Browser window.**

2. **Click the disclosure triangle next to the Video Transitions folder.**

3. **Click the disclosure triangle next to the Iris folder.**

4. **Select the Cross Iris transition.**

5. **Choose View ➭ Effect in Editor.**

6. **The FXBuilder window opens and shows you the source code for the Cross Iris transition.**

7. **Click the FXBuilder Input Controls tab.**

   You'll see two windows on the left side of the Input Controls tab.

8. **Drag any clip from the Browser, Timeline, or Viewer into the Source 1 clip area.**

9. **Drag another clip from the Browser, Timeline, or Viewer into the Source 2 clip area.**

10. **Click the FXBuilder Text Entry tab.**

    The FXBuilder Text tab must be active before a script can be run.

11. **Choose FXBuilder ➭ Run.**

    A separate playback window appears, as shown in Figure 25-10, and the scripted effect will play back in a loop.

    During playback you can click back on the FXBuilder Input Controls tab and make changes to the controls while the script is running. If you click to stop playback of the effect, the controls will revert to the default settings. The controls of the Input Controls tab are for dynamic testing of the input controls only and will not change any settings of the script.

Figure 25-10: The playback window of the FXBuilder.

Exporting and using FXBuilder scripts as text

Earlier in this chapter, I described how to export an FXBuilder script as an encoded plug-in that cannot be modified by anyone. However, if you choose to save your script as text, you make it possible for yourself or others to modify the script again later. You can still use this script like any other plug-in and apply it to your clips, or you can use the text from the script to create new scripts. To save an FXBuilder script as text, follow these steps:

1. **Open and modify a script as described earlier in this chapter.**

2. **When you get to the stage where you want to save the script, choose FXBuilder ⇨ Export Text.**

3. **Enter a name and destination; then click Save.**

   Use the .txt suffix on your filename to identify the script as a text file.

You have just saved your script as a text file. Note that you can always copy your code and paste it in a word processing utility.

Follow these steps to use this script:

1. **Quit Final Cut Pro.**

2. **Drag the exported text script to the FXScripts folder into the Plug-ins folder.**

   The location of the Plug-ins folder is Home/Library/Preferences/ Final Cut Pro Data/Plugins.

3. **Start up the Final Cut Pro application again.**

   Your new script appears in the appropriate category of effects.

   The icon for the script will be different when you save it as a text file. Figure 25-11 compares the icon for a script saved as a text file with a locked and encoded plug-in.

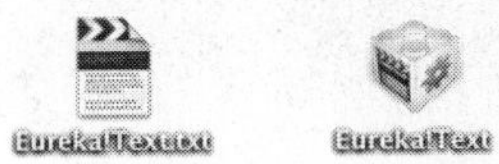

Figure 25-11: On the left is the Eureka!Text plug-in saved as a text file. On the right is the icon for an encoded and locked Eureka!Text plug-in.

✦   ✦   ✦

Using Final Cut Pro with Photoshop and After Effects

✦ ✦ ✦ ✦

In This Chapter

Working with
Adobe Photoshop

Working with
Adobe After Effects

✦ ✦ ✦ ✦

If you are working with digital video in any capacity, chances are good that you are using a few other applications along with Final Cut Pro. Many users work with Adobe Photoshop or After Effects to create content for use in their edited programs. Final Cut Pro is a great application, but it cannot do everything. Many people prefer the familiarity and ease of use of Adobe After Effects to create their layered and animated movies. In turn, these products can then be imported into Final Cut Pro for use as a video clip in a Timeline. Stills and titles can also be prepared in Photoshop and used in Final Cut Pro.

I should warn you that this chapter provides an overview on how to use Adobe Photoshop and After Effects, but I couldn't possibly cover every detail of these two very advanced programs. If you really want to master these programs, you should purchase a book that covers Photoshop or After Effects specifically. I would suggest Deke McClelland's *Photoshop 7.0 Bible,* Professional Edition, and my own book, *Adobe After Effects 5 Bible* (both published by Wiley). In this chapter, I assume that you have some working knowledge of both Photoshop and After Effects. I cover the main stumbling blocks that Final Cut Pro users face when going back and forth among Photoshop, After Effects, and Final Cut Pro. If I can help you avoid some common problems, the goal of this chapter will be met.

Note   The instructions in this chapter work best with Photoshop 7.0 and After Effects 5.5 and newer versions of these two programs. Older versions follow a similar logic, if not the precise steps and locations for commands.

Working with Adobe Photoshop

What can I possibly say about Adobe's Photoshop that has not previously been said? Photoshop is by far the world's most popular program for image editing. By some estimates, Photoshop owns 80 percent of the huge image-editing software market. You can find many excellent books on Photoshop as well as training tapes, seminars, classes, and Web sites full of tips and tricks. Large conventions devoted entirely to Adobe Photoshop are held across North America. Chances are that if you create or edit still images on your computer, you are using Adobe's Photoshop.

Final Cut Pro's video editing capabilities are unbeatable. But when it comes to creating and editing text and still graphics, the capabilities are quite limited. Final Cut Pro is not, after all, an image-editing application. If you want greater image-editing and creation capabilities, you should use a dedicated image-editing program, such as Adobe Photoshop. The next few sections take you through some basic procedures in Photoshop that you are likely to encounter when preparing material for Final Cut Pro.

Note   This section assumes that you have a working knowledge of Adobe Photoshop. To cover all the details of this application is beyond the scope of this book.

Creating images in Photoshop

While computer graphics applications generally use square pixels, most video formats (such as DV) use rectangular pixels. If you simply created an image in Photoshop and then imported it into Final Cut Pro, your image would appear slightly distorted or squished because of this difference in pixel shapes. To prevent this distortion, you should alter the graphics file's pixel aspect ratio *before* importing it into Final Cut Pro. Figure 26-1 shows a simple circle graphic created in Photoshop as well as how the same file appears in a Final Cut Pro D1/DV sequence *without* its aspect ratio adjusted for square pixels.

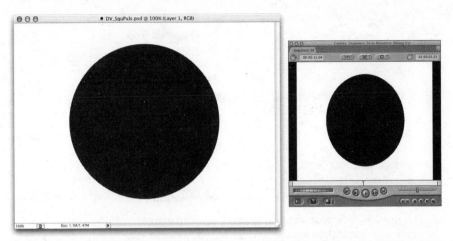

Figure 26-1: On the left is a simple graphics file created in Photoshop. On the right is this same file imported into a Final Cut Pro D1/DV sequence without pixel aspect ration compensation.

As you can see from the preceding example, care must be taken when preparing material in Photoshop for Final Cut Pro projects. To prepare images in Adobe Photoshop that will not be distorted when used in a DV-based project in Final Cut Pro:

The image sizes used in the following steps assume that you are working on a DV-based NTSC project. If you are working with a different video format, see the next section for more on choosing appropriate image sizes.

1. **Start Adobe Photoshop.**

2. **Choose File ⇨ New.**

   The New dialog box, shown in Figure 26-2, appears.

3. **In the New dialog box, set the following settings:**

   • **Width:** 720 Pixels

   • **Height:** 534 Pixels

   • **Resolution:** 72 pixels/inch (300 pixels/inch if you plan to zoom or pan in Final Cut Pro)

   • **Color Mode:** RGB Color

   • **Contents:** Choose Background Color if you want color. (Select Transparent if you want this image to superimpose in Final Cut Pro.)

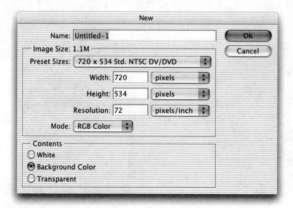

Figure 26-2: Choose these settings to prepare images in Adobe Photoshop for use in a DV-based Final Cut Pro project.

4. **Click OK to close the New dialog box and start creating your image.**

5. **Lay out the artwork, text, or images that you plan to use.**

6. **Save a backup copy of the image.**

   To save a backup, choose File ➪ Save As and name and save the file. Save the files as a .psd (Photoshop) file. Note that this is a backup file and is not the one you import into Final Cut Pro.

7. **Back in Photoshop, choose Image ➪ Image Size.**

   The Image Size dialog box, shown in Figure 26-3, appears.

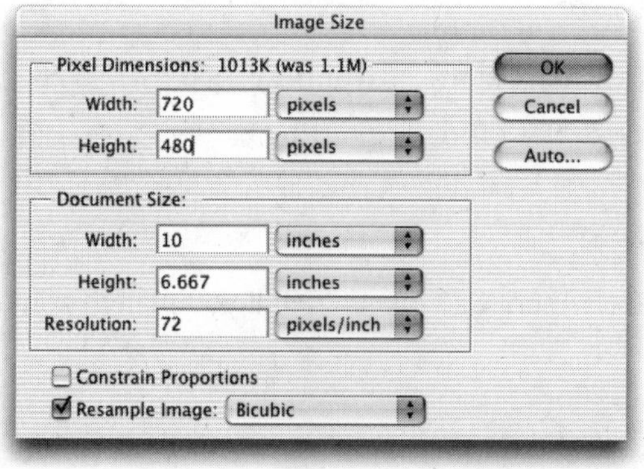

Figure 26-3: Uncheck the Constrain Proportions check box and enter 480 in the Height field to prepare this file for import into Final Cut Pro.

8. Turn off the Constrain Proportions check box.

This is key to modifying the file's pixel aspect ratio.

9. Change the number in the Height field from 534 pixels to 480 and click OK.

This change is made to accommodate for the change in pixel aspect ratio.

Be sure the Resample Image check box is always enabled. This option allows Photoshop to adjust the number of pixels according to the new size.

When you look at your image after the preceding step, it appears slightly squashed. Don't worry; this is how it is supposed to look. Figure 26-4 illustrates how a simple circle appears before and after image size conversion. When imported into Final Cut Pro, this image is stretched because the pixels convert from square to rectangular, and the proportions are correct.

A circle as it appears when working in 720X534

A circle as it appears after conversion to 720X480

Figure 26-4: Image size conversion makes your graphics appear squashed in Photoshop, but when imported into Final Cut Pro they will appear correctly.

10. Save the file as a .psd file and give it a unique name.

11. Import this image into Final Cut Pro.

Be sure that the Show As Sq. Pixels setting is selected in the Canvas or the View window's View selector pop-up menu. Doing so ensures a correctly proportioned view of your graphics.

Colors that may look great on your computer screen in Photoshop may be too bright for video. To prevent this when working in Photoshop, choose Filters ⇨ Video ⇨ NTSC Colors to convert the image to NTSC-safe colors.

Mixing square pixels of computer-generated imagery with the non-square pixels of most video formats has always been a headache for video and graphic artists. The purpose of working with odd, larger image sizes, such as 720 × 534 pixels in Photoshop, is so the graphic image will still fill the entire video frame after its pixel aspect ratio has been adjusted (image size is usually smaller after aspect ratio compensation). Altering the file's pixel aspect ratio as the last step before importing the file into Final Cut Pro allows artists to view and work in correct proportions with square pixels. Later, this image can be distorted in Photoshop in anticipation of the stretching that will occur when this file is imported into Final Cut Pro. The final image, though distorted in Photoshop, appears correctly proportioned in video.

If you are working with NTSC DV video, the video frame size of your final output is 720 × 480 pixels. The proper pre-conversion image size to work with in Photoshop is usually 720 × 534 pixels. However, other formats demand different measurements to ensure they fit properly in your video image. For example, if you are working with a CCIR 601-compliant NTSC video card, such as the Aurora Video System's Igniter card, the final video frame size is 720 × 486 pixels. Hence, the image size to start out with in Adobe Photoshop should be 720 × 540 pixels. Table 26-1 lists the frame and image sizes you use when working with various video formats.

Table 26-1
Photoshop-to-Video Conversion Sizes

Video Format	Starting Size	Convert to
DV-NTSC	720 × 534	720 × 480
CCIR 601-NTSC	720 × 540	720 × 486
Anamorphic 16:9 DV-NTSC	864 × 534	720 × 480
Anamoprhic 16:9 CCIR 601-NTSC	864 × 540	720 × 486
CCIR-601/DV PAL	768 × 576	720 × 576

Tip

If you are using Photoshop 7.0 or later, the New file-setup dialog box has an added pop-up menu called Preset Sizes. These presets include many of the file sizes for NTSC and PAL DV, D1, wide screen and High Definition, all of which appropriately incorporate the correct pixel aspect ratio adjustment.

The pixel conundrum

Standard Definition video (or SD) is different from computer displays in two significant ways. Video is interlaced, and it uses non-square pixels. These pixels are slightly taller than they are wide. Computer monitors, on the other hand, use progressive scanning and square pixels.

When working with video, always remember that pixels for NTSC video are taller than computer pixels, whereas in PAL video the pixels are wider than those on a computer display. An NTSC video image captured at 720 × 486, which has non-square pixels, appears distorted when viewed on a square pixel computer monitor. Circles appear squashed top to bottom and elongated on the sides. Both the Viewer and the Canvas windows in Final Cut Pro have settings that let you view non-square pixels correctly on a square pixel monitor. Open the View pop-up menu located in the top center of the Viewer or Canvas window and select the Show As Sq. Pixel choice. Note that high-definition television (HDTV) uses square pixels only, so you do not see this behavior when working with it.

Creating layers in Photoshop

Files created in Photoshop with multiple layers are imported into Final Cut Pro with each layer corresponding to a track of video. When a three-layer Photoshop file is imported into Final Cut Pro, it turns into a sequence, and the layers are placed on tracks V1, V2, and V3, respectively. This can be very helpful when creating animations in Final Cut Pro. You can prepare your layers in Photoshop and then animate them in Final Cut Pro by using motion effects, filters, and keyframes. To create a layered file in Photoshop, use these steps:

Cross-Reference

The following steps assume that you are working with DV video in Final Cut Pro. If you are working with a different video format, you need to modify the image size as described earlier in this chapter.

1. **Start Adobe Photoshop.**

2. **Choose File ➪ New.**

   The New dialog box appears.

3. **In the New dialog box, set the following settings:**

   - **Width:** 720 pixels

   - **Height:** 534 pixels

   - **Resolution:** 72 pixels/inch (300 pixels/inch if you plan to zoom or pan in Final Cut Pro)

- **Color Mode:** RGB Color
- **Contents:** Choose Transparent if you want this image to superimpose in Final Cut Pro.

4. Click OK to close the New dialog box and create the new image.

5. Make the Layers Palette visible by choosing Window ⇨ Layers.

Figure 26-5 shows the Layers palette as it appears for your new file.

Figure 26-5: Do not add any items to the first layer if you plan to superimpose this layered file in Final Cut Pro.

6. To create a new layer, choose Layer ⇨ New ⇨ Layer.

You can also press Command+Shift+N to create a new layer, or click the small arrow in the upper-right corner of the Layers palette and choose New Layer from the menu. Remember that each new layer equals another video track in Final Cut Pro, so plan accordingly. Figure 26-6 shows the Layers palette for an image with four separate layers.

Figure 26-6: Each layer in your image can contain artwork you want to animate or control as a separate video track in Final Cut Pro.

7. Save a backup copy of your image before you resize it for video.

To save a backup, choose File ⇨ Save As and name the file. Save the file as a .psd (Photoshop) file.

8. **Choose Image ⇨ Image Size.**

   The Image size dialog box appears.

9. **Turn off the Constrain Proportions check box.**

10. **Change the number in the Height field from 534 pixels to 480 and click OK.**

    This change is made to accommodate for the shift in pixel aspect ratio.

    Your image now appears slightly squashed. When imported into Final Cut Pro, this image is stretched again and the proportions are correct.

11. **Save the file as a** `.psd` **(Photoshop) file and import the image into Final Cut Pro.**

Working with layers in Photoshop

Layers are a very powerful feature of Adobe Photoshop. You can freely composite images while keeping each layer entirely independent of the others. When I am working in Photoshop to prepare files for Final Cut Pro, I make sure that each word or element that I plan to animate goes on a separate layer. Doing so gives me maximum flexibility within Photoshop and Final Cut Pro. The Photoshop Layers palette is shown here.

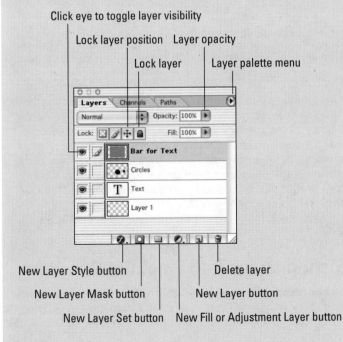

Click eye to toggle layer visibility

Lock layer position   Layer opacity

Lock layer   Layer palette menu

New Layer Style button   Delete layer

New Layer Mask button   New Layer button

New Layer Set button   New Fill or Adjustment Layer button

Continued

Continued

Here are a few handy rules and shortcuts for working with layers:

✦ You can select a layer by clicking it in the Layers palette.

✦ You *cannot* select more than one layer at a time.

✦ You can reorder layers by selecting one layer and dragging it up or down in the Layers palette.

✦ You can delete a layer by selecting it and dragging it to the Delete Layer icon, which looks like a little trash can.

✦ Command+Shift+N presents the dialog box for creating a new layer.

✦ Command+Shift+Option+N creates a new layer and bypasses the New Layer dialog box.

✦ Option+[selects the next layer up.

✦ Option+] selects the next layer down.

✦ Option+Shift+[selects the top layer.

✦ Option+Shift+] selects the bottom layer.

✦ Command+[moves the selected layer up one level.

✦ Command+] moves the selected layer down one level.

✦ Command+Shift+[moves the selected layer to the top.

✦ Command+Shift+] moves the selected layer to the bottom.

While we're on the topic of layers, I must warn you about an unforeseen problem you may encounter. Early versions of Photoshop were entirely bitmap- (or pixel-) based. The newer versions of this application employ vector graphics that are actually mathematical descriptions of images. You may find that some effects you have applied to your layers, such as bevel and drop shadow, may disappear when imported into Final Cut Pro. To fix this problem, select your image and choose Layer ⇨ Rasterize ⇨ All Layers. Rasterization is the process of converting vector-based images into bitmapped graphics. Your image should now import into Final Cut Pro with all effects intact.

Importing Photoshop layers into Final Cut Pro

You can import a layered Photoshop file into Final Cut Pro. Your layered file automatically turns into a sequence, with each layer created in Photoshop occupying its own video track in Final Cut Pro. To import a layered Photoshop file into Final Cut Pro, follow these steps:

1. **Start a project in Final Cut Pro.**

2. **Choose File ➪ Import ➪ File.**

3. **Locate your layered Photoshop file, select it, and click Open.**

   Your layered Photoshop file is imported as a sequence. Each layer occupies a separate video track as shown in Figure 26-7.

A layered Photoshop file imports as a Sequence into Final Cut Pro

Each Photoshop layer occupies a separate video track

Figure 26-7: A layered Photoshop file will be imported as a sequence into Final Cut Pro. Each layer will occupy a separate video track.

The frame size of the sequence is matched to the file dimensions of the Photoshop file, and the duration of the sequence will be the same as any imported still, set in the Still/Freeze Duration setting in the General Preferences tab of User Preferences. Layer order, opacity, modes and visibility are preserved, but layer masks as well as most vector base effects are not.

At this point, you can simply superimpose this multilayered sequence on top of a video track, or you can copy and paste all the layers of this file into a folder to create separate stills from each layer.

Tip

You can drag and drop layered Photoshop files from your desktop directly into Final Cut Pro.

Caution

Although you can modify a Photoshop file once it is imported into Final Cut Pro, you should never add or delete layers in the original file. Doing so almost always causes unpredictable results rendering your Photoshop sequence unusable. As a rule of thumb, don't move or change *any* media files unless absolutely necessary once they are in use in Final Cut Pro. If you have to add or delete layers from a Photoshop file after it is in your project, save another modified version of it and re-import it into your project.

Importing other file formats into Final Cut Pro

When you import supported graphic file formats other than layered Photoshop files like JPEG, PICT, Targa (TGA), or TIFF, to name the more popular ones, Final Cut Pro will recognize the file's pixel aspect ratio and *automatically* compensate for the difference. Once an imported graphics clip is placed in a sequence, its sequence clip's aspect ratio is automatically calculated and adjusted to best match the pixel aspect ratio of the Timeline. Figure 26-8 shows the Aspect Ratio of a circle graphic, saved as a TIFF, after its sequence clip is adjusted by Final Cut Pro to compensate for the file's square pixels when used in a D1/DV sequence.

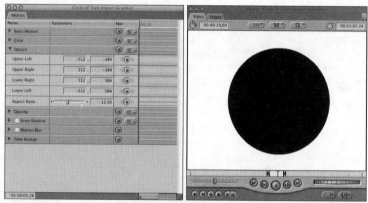

Figure 26-8: When importing most graphic file formats, Final Cut Pro will automatically compensate for a different pixel aspect ratio by modifying its sequence clip's Aspect Ratio, left, to keep the image free of distortion, shown right.

The reason the Aspect Ratio is adjusted in a sequence clip, and not a master clip, is because Final Cut Pro first needs to know the Aspect Ratio of a sequence that the clip will be used in order to make any necessary compensation. When a master clip is first imported into the Browser, it has not yet been placed into any sequence and therefore needs no correction.

As if this weren't enough automated sophistication, when you insert a file with dimensions larger than the frame size of your sequence, Final Cut Pro automatically scales the clip proportionally to fit within the frame size of the sequence. This is the same as using the Modify ⇨ Scale to Sequence command, only automatically.

Note   Sadly, these two great automatic import features do *not* work with files saved in Photoshop's native format (PSD). Even when you cut and paste layers from an imported Photoshop sequence, the clips appear in the Timeline with no aspect ratio compensation, nor do they scale to fit the composition's frame size. However, you can manually modify the clip's aspect ratio and scale in the Motion tab of the Viewer.

Preparing graphics for Final Cut Pro

When preparing still images and graphics for use in Final Cut Pro, you must consider a few common issues. Use of proper fonts and lines, video legal colors, and the proper resolution are some of the items to keep in mind. The next few sections describe these issues and show you what to look for when preparing graphics for Final Cut Pro.

Using fonts

When choosing graphics for use in Final Cut Pro, avoid using lines whose thickness is a single pixel. Such lines are often used for print images, but these lines are not appropriate for video. Single-pixel lines appear on a single field and flicker as the field turns on and off. You'll notice this flickering around some graphics that contain very thin lines. Likewise, avoid using fonts that are thin or of the serif family. Serifs are the curlies or extra finishing strokes that some fonts (such as the font you are reading right now) have at the arms, stems, and tails of characters. Serifs can flicker between fields in video as well. For best results, use a sans serif font such as Arial or Helvetica.

 For more information on use of fonts in Final Cut Pro, see Chapter 16.

Choosing colors for video

The range of colors that video can display is far smaller than the range that a computer can display. Most graphics applications, such as Adobe Photoshop, are capable of displaying bright and saturated colors that would be considered illegal in video because they fall out of the range of NTSC's color gamut or range. You can fix this problem. Many graphics applications have filters and settings to tone down colors to the NTSC range. For example, in Adobe Photoshop you can select Filters ⇨ Video ⇨ NTSC colors to make your colors NTSC safe. If you have a Vectorscope, you can also use it to make sure that your colors are not falling out of the NTSC safe range.

In general, when making text in Adobe Photoshop for use in NTSC video, use RGB values of 16 for black and 235 for white. (By default, black has an RGB value of 0 and white of 255 in Photoshop.) This will keep your text within "legal" NTSC brightness levels.

 For more information on using a Vectorscope, see Chapter 3.

Setting resolution for video

When working with graphics and still images you should always keep in mind that video (at least standard definition, as opposed to high definition) always works at a resolution equivalent to about 72 dpi. When scanning photographs or preparing stills, a 300 dpi setting may look better than 72 dpi if the final output medium is print. In video, this may not necessarily be the case.

Importing an image with a resolution of 300 dpi (or, as Photoshop calls it, pixels/inch) into Final Cut Pro, which displays all files at 72 dpi, makes the image very large, and the image will spread itself beyond the confines of a simple Viewer or Canvas window view. This "overflow" effect is ideal of course, if you plan to pan and scan around the image to create a sort of motion control camera effect. In Final Cut Pro, you can use the Center, Position, and Anchor Point parameters to move around on the image. Many contemporary documentaries, such as Ken Burns's *Civil War* documentary series, have used this motion control effect over photographs to great effect.

For more information on animating motion properties, see Chapter 17.

Keep in mind that if you plan to zoom and scan around on an image, you should make it a high-resolution image, such as 300 dpi. As a rule, you should never scale an image more than 100 percent during the zoom and scan process. Otherwise you will see artifacts and pixel break up. You can usually scale a high-resolution image down to fit in the View or Canvas windows, however. Here's how:

1. **Select a graphic in your sequence that you want to scale.**

2. **Choose Modify ➪ Scale to Sequence.**

   Your image is scaled to fit inside the frame size of your sequence.

If the aspect ratio of your image is different from that of the sequence, you will see black bars of empty space around your image. If your still image is wider than it is tall, black space appears on the top and on the bottom. If your image is taller than it is wide, the black appears on the left and right sides.

Opening items in their original application

While working in Final Cut Pro, you can open the application with which your clip was originally created. For example, while working on a still image created in Photoshop, you can reopen the still image file in Adobe Photoshop from within Final Cut Pro. Of course, you must have Photoshop installed on your computer and enough memory to be able to open both applications simultaneously. To open a clip in its native application:

1. **Double-click the clip to open it in the View window.**

2. **Choose View ➪ Clip in Editor.**

   The application originally used to create the still or clip opens.

You should note that this is the default operation if *no* external editor has been assigned to handle that type of media file in the External Editors tab under System Settings. If an application is defined for Still Image Files, then *all* still graphic files imported into Final Cut Pro will open with the assigned application when Clip in Editor is selected, regardless of which program the file originated in.

Cross-Reference External Editors are selected in the System Settings, covered in Chapter 6.

Working with Adobe After Effects

Adobe After Effects rocks — that's all there is to it. I've had more fun working with After Effects than anything else I can think of. After Effects is hands down the industry standard for creating 2-D (and now, 3-D) motion graphics for any and all venues and formats. With its phenomenal control, sub-pixel rendering, and unlimited palette of effects, After Effects has set the standard for creating animation and graphics for video.

Users who have worked with both Final Cut Pro and After Effects don't need to be told that overlaps occur in terms of animation and multilayering interfaces. Final Cut Pro's animation Timeline and keyframing principles have quite a lot in common with After Effects. This comment is not meant to take anything away from the talented programmers at Apple who created Final Cut Pro. It's just that the animation channel, keyframing, and filter settings interface is the common standard when it comes to creating multilayering and special-effects animations.

Many users who edit in Final Cut Pro may already know After Effects. Others may want to learn what they could gain from using After Effects. The object of this section is not to teach you After Effects from the ground up. As with the Photoshop section, I am going to assume that you have some working knowledge of After Effects. Many resources are available for learning After Effects, including books, training tapes, and Web sites. In this section, I am going to show you the rules and issues you need to know when working between Final Cut Pro and After Effects.

Exporting from Final Cut Pro for After Effects

The first step in working between Final Cut Pro and Adobe After Effects is to export footage from Final Cut Pro to After Effects. Note that After Effects, when importing files, creates a link to these files *only*. For this reason, you should organize all your exported footage, and other items you plan to use in an After Effects project *before* you start working in After Effects. Moving items between folders and disks after they've been used in an After Effects project will cause After Effects to lose the link to that item. However, you can relink the items in After Effects.

Here's what to do to export footage from Final Cut Pro in preparation for working in After Effects:

1. **Make a selection for export.**

   You can do so by selecting a clip or a sequence in the Browser, or by double-clicking a clip into the Viewer. You can also set In and Out points in the Timeline to mark the section that will be exported.

2. **Choose File ⇨ Export ⇨ QuickTime Movie.**

   The export dialog box appears, as shown in Figure 26-9.

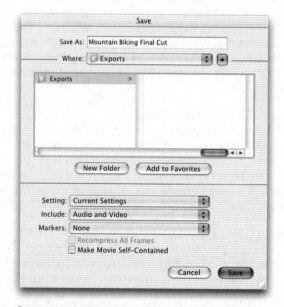

Figure 26-9: Choose your settings in the export dialog box.

3. **In the export dialog box, choose a location where you want to store the exported movie and name your movie.**

4. **In the Settings selections menu, choose Current Settings.**

   Making this selection will use the current compression settings for your selection. These current settings are found in the Item Properties window (if your selection is a clip) or in the Sequence Settings window (if your selection is a sequence).

5. **In the Include menu, choose Audio and Video.**

Of course, if your selection only contains video, you should choose the setting for Video Only. Audio tracks with nothing in them still take up precious disk space. If your selection does not include audio, select Video Only to save space.

6. **In the Markers menu, choose None.**

This setting is for selecting marker types when exporting a movie to be used in other applications.

7. **Uncheck the Make Movie Self-Contained check box.**

This step ensures the making of a reference movie. (See the sidebar "Making reference movies for After Effects.")

8. **Click Save to save your exported movie.**

Caution

Keep your files very organized when preparing to work between Final Cut Pro and After Effects. Create carefully labeled folders for storing movies and elements. Place them on a disk where you can store them for the duration of the project. Storing files in an unorganized manner is detrimental to working in After Effects because that program creates links to all imported files. If these files are later moved, After Effects loses the link, and the files must be relinked.

Making reference movies for After Effects

Reference movies were put on this Earth by the gods of digital video to ease the burden and suffering of editors. When the Make Movie Self-Contained box is left unchecked in the export settings window, Final Cut Pro creates a reference movie. A *reference movie* is a movie that only creates pointers to the original source media or render files. This reference movie can be used in After Effects or other QuickTime-compliant applications. The reference movie has two major advantages that make it a good choice. First, a reference movie is tiny in size compared to a self-contained movie. Second, a reference movie exports much faster than a self-contained one. These two advantages save both disk space and an enormous amount of export time.

When exporting media for After Effects, you can choose Video Only in the Include pop-up menu in the Export dialog box if you plan to work with video only in After Effects. In this case, you really don't need the audio, so exporting only the video will save additional disk space and export time.

However, using reference movies is a disadvantage, too. Because the reference movies are pointers to the original media, this media must be located on the same computer where they are going to be used. If you delete the original media, the reference movies will not work. Also, if you export a reference movie and copy it to a Zip, Jaz, or other removable media and take it over to another workstation, the movie will not work because the required media is on another computer. Consider your options carefully when you are choosing export options in Final Cut Pro. Also, get in the habit of naming your reference files with a "ref" post-fix for easy identification.

Working with Final Cut Pro footage in After Effects

After exporting footage from Final Cut Pro, you can start working with it in After Effects. As a general overview the steps a project goes through in After Effects are the following:

1. Import the footage into After Effects.

2. Prepare your animation and effects within After Effects.

3. Render movies from After Effects for use in Final Cut Pro.

The next few sections take you through these steps.

Importing and preparing footage in After Effects

The first stage in the process of working in After Effects is to import some footage and then to set its interpretations correctly. After Effects can autodetect a lot of information about an imported item. However, by setting interpretations, you tell After Effects more of what it needs to know about the type of footage it is taking in. To import Final Cut Pro footage into After Effects and set its interpretations, follow these steps:

1. **Start Adobe After Effects.**

   You can do so by double-clicking the After Effects application icon or an After Effects project file you have created. If you start from the Application icon, an empty After Effects project window appears.

2. **Choose File ⇨ Save As and save the After Effects project file with a name and location of your choice.**

3. **Choose File ⇨ Import ⇨ File.**

   You are presented with the Import File dialog box.

4. **Locate your exported Final Cut Pro movie, select it, and click Import.**

   The footage is imported and appears in the After Effects project window. In later versions of After Effects, the application recognizes the type of footage and assigns the footage the correct field order. In Figure 26-10, you can see that After Effects has recognized this exported movie as DV format and has interpreted it as being Lower field ordered.

Tip   You can also drag and drop footage items directly from your desktop into the After Effects project window.

Selecting an item in the project
window provides information
about the project in this area

Imported file

Figure 26-10: A new project
window shows information about
an imported file in After Effects.

5. **If you are using an earlier version of After Effects, and your footage is not recognized correctly, manually set the field order of the incoming footage by choosing File ⇨ Interpret Footage ⇨ Main (or press Command+F).**

   The Interpret Footage dialog box appears. Note that in some early versions of After Effects, the correct pixel aspect ratio choice may be labeled "D1-NTSC."

6. **In the Fields and Pulldown section, select Lower Field First from the Separate Fields pull-down menu.**

   You can also select the Pixel Aspect Ratio under the Other Options section. The settings shown in Figure 26-11 are set to D1/DV NTSC because this media is DV-NTSC video.

7. **Click OK to close the Intepret Footage dialog box.**

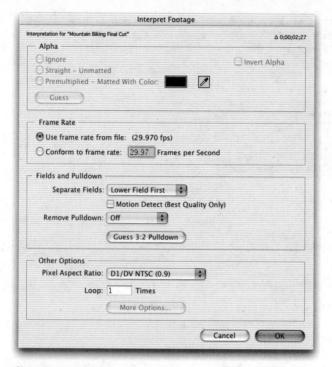

Figure 26-11: The Interpret Footage dialog box is used to set numerous interpretations for imported items.

Creating compositions in After Effects

The second phase of your work with After Effects entails creating compositions in After Effects. Follow these steps to create a composition for use with Final Cut Pro footage:

1. **Choose Composition ⇨ New Composition.**

   You can also press Command+N to create a new composition. A Composition Settings dialog box for your new composition appears, as shown in Figure 26-12.

Figure 26-12: The correct settings for an After Effects composition for DV-based footage are shown here.

2. **In the Composition Settings dialog box, choose the following settings:**

   • **Enter a name for the composition.**

   • **In the Preset pull-down menu, choose NTSC DV or 720X480, or simply enter 720 in the Width field and 480 in the Height field.** This selection represents the frame size of DV NTSC video.

   • **In the Pixel Aspect Ratio pull-down choose D1/DV NTSC, if that is the video format you are working with.**

   • **Set the Frame rate to 29.97.** Bear in mind that *all* video in NTSC standard runs at 29.97 frames per second and not 30 frames per second. This slight difference is critical. Remember also that drop-frame versus non-drop-frame timecodes have absolutely no bearing on frame rates.

   • **Set the Resolution to full.** After Effects allows you to create compositions and renders at less than the full resolution for speedy checks and rough comps. For final playback and use, always select the full resolution setting.

   • **Select the proper timecode mode and the duration.** You can choose to select a different starting timecode if you need a reference to some other material. The duration can also be set to whatever you like. However, it is best to set the duration to the precise length of your material. This will avoid any black or empty space at the end of your final render.

3. **Click OK when you are done.**

You now have an After Effects composition ready into which you can import the Final Cut Pro exported movie and arrange any animation or effects for it in After Effects.

Tip
If you drag a footage item in the After Effects project window and drop it on the New Composition button at the bottom of the Composition window, After Effects automatically creates a new composition based on the name, duration, frame size, frame rate, and pixel aspect ratio of the footage.

Mixing square-pixel stills with Final Cut Pro footage

Earlier in this chapter, I describe how computer graphics applications, such as Adobe Photoshop, use square pixels whereas video applications tend to use rectangular pixels. Mixing these two pixel aspect ratios causes unacceptable distortions. Bringing square-pixel stills and graphics into a DV- (or rectangular-pixel-) based After Effects composition requires a few precautions and some extra steps. Here's the step-by-step process for working with square-pixel images in a DV-based composition:

1. **Prepare your stills and graphics in Photoshop.**

   If you're working with DV NTSC video, the graphics should have a starting image size of 720 × 534 pixels. This size is chosen to accommodate for the pixel aspect ratio difference between Photoshop and DV NTSC video. Photoshop uses square pixels, whereas DV NTSC uses non-square pixels. Later this 720 × 534 pixel image will be squeezed down to 720 × 480 pixel frame size of DV NTSC video.

2. **Import the still footage into the After Effects project.**

3. **Choose Composition ⇨ New Composition.**

   The Composition Settings dialog box appears.

4. **For DV video, select NTSC DV, 720 × 480 for the Frame Size and D1/DV NTSC for the Pixel Aspect Ratio.**

   The 720 × 480 pixel size represents the frame size of DV NTSC video. The D1/DV NTSC pixel aspect ratio is the aspect ratio of all pixels in a DV video image.

5. **Select other composition settings, such as frame rate and duration, as needed.**

6. **Add the square-pixel still footage to your new composition.**

7. **Select the still image layer in the composition's Time Layout window and press Command+Option+F to apply the Shrink to Fit command.**

   Your square-pixel-based still image can now fit within the composition with the proper adjustments necessary for final rendering.

   Your stills may have some distortion on your computer screen after you have correctly followed the above steps. This is normal.

8. **To view the footage without distortion, click the arrow above the vertical scroll bar in the Composition window and choose Pixel Aspect Correction, as shown in Figure 26-13.**

Keep in mind that this option is for viewing only and has no effect on the final render.

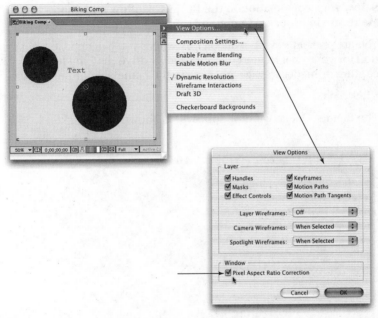

Figure 26-13: Selecting Pixel Aspect Correction fixes any distortion in your composition window for viewing purposes.

Caution

If you've prepared your square-pixel still in Photoshop at an image size of 720 × 480 pixels or 720 × 486 pixels, you should select the still in the After Effects project window and choose File ➪ Interpret Footage ➪ Main. Then choose Square Pixels from the Pixel Aspect Ratio pop-up menu and click OK. This step is critical because After Effects automatically assigns the D1 or rectangular-pixel aspect ratio to any item that conforms to the 720 × 480 pixels or 720 × 486 pixels sizes. For still images that are prepared in Photoshop or other such applications, you need to set the correct interpretation and tell After Effects that these stills are composed of square pixels. From here you can proceed to use these stills in your compositions without using the Shrink to Fit command.

Rendering in After Effects for Final Cut Pro

After you finish laying out your composition and preparing your effects in After Effects, you are ready to render. Rendering is the process of combining the footage with the effects and changes and creating a final output movie. In most cases, you will make a QuickTime movie for playback in your Final Cut Pro Timeline. Follow these steps to render a composition for DV video in After Effects:

1. **Select your composition in the Project window and choose Composition ➪ Make Movie (or press Command+M).**

   You are presented with a dialog box where you can choose a name and a location for your final rendered movie. Pick a drive that you normally use for your capture or media storage and type in the name of your final movie.

2. **Click Save.**

   The Render Queue window appears, as shown in Figure 26-14.

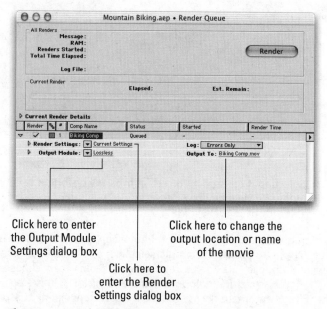

Click here to enter the Output Module Settings dialog box

Click here to change the output location or name of the movie

Click here to enter the Render Settings dialog box

Figure 26-14: The Render Queue window allows you to make rendering choices.

3. **Make your rendering choices and view the rendering process.**

4. **Click Current Settings in front of Render Settings.**

The Render Settings dialog box appears, as shown in Figure 26-15.

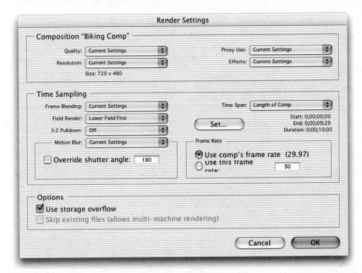

Figure 26-15: Choose settings in preparation for rendering DV video.

5. **Set the following settings in this box:**

   - Set Quality to Best
   - Set Resolution to Full
   - Set Field Render to Lower Field First (for DV video)
   - Select Length of Comp in the Time Span menu

6. **Click OK to close the Render Settings dialog box.**

7. **Back in the Render Queue, click the setting name next to the Output Module choice.**

The Output Module Settings dialog box appears, as shown in Figure 26-16.

8. **Click the Format Options button in the Output Module Settings dialog box.**

The QuickTime Compression Settings dialog box appears, as shown in Figure 26-17.

Figure 26-16: The Output Module Settings dialog box.

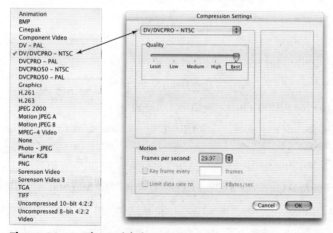

Figure 26-17: The QuickTime Compression Settings dialog box lets you choose a codec as shown here.

9. **Choose DV-NTSC from the Compressor pull-down menu.**

The list of codecs in the Compressor menu varies depending on what codecs are installed on your machine.

10. **Click OK when you are done.**

Note The Quality slider in the QuickTime Compression Settings dialog box does not have any effect when using the DV codec. DV compression works at a consistently high quality and data rate.

11. **Back in the Output Module Settings dialog box you can choose to include audio by checking the Audio Output check box at the bottom of the dialog box.**

Be sure to select the correct sampling rate.

Caution After Effects settings always default to the 44.1 kHz setting in the Output Module Settings dialog box, but most DV audio is captured either at 32 kHz or 48 kHz. Be sure to keep the original sampling rate.

12. **Click OK when you are done.**

13. **Back in the Render Queue window, click the Render button to begin rendering.**

When rendering is complete, you can import this QuickTime movie back into the Final Cut Pro project and use it just like any other clip you may have captured.

Tip After you select the correct settings for both the Render Settings and the Output Module, you may want to save these settings as templates to be used over and over again. Select the small downward-pointing arrow located to the right of the Render Settings label and choose Make Template from the drop-down menu. Give your Render Settings template a name and save it. Your new template now appears in the drop-down menu choices.

Using footage captured from third-party video cards

Throughout this chapter, the focus has been on working with DV-based footage. All settings and options I have discussed are geared toward exporting, importing, creating, and rendering DV video. But what if you are using a third-party video card to capture footage for use in a Final Cut Pro project? When you bring such material into After Effects, a few more options and workflow considerations become important. The following sections describe issues that you must consider when bringing material from Final Cut Pro into After Effects, if that material was captured using a third-party video card.

Selecting a frame size

When you export third-party video card footage from Final Cut Pro into After Effects, you need to know the frame size of this footage so that you can enter this frame size in the Composition Settings dialog box.

The process of determining the frame size for any footage in After Effects is very simple. Import the footage into the After Effects project window and click on the footage to select it. As you can see in Figure 26-18, you will see a thumbnail of the footage in the upper-left corner with the name of the file and information about it to its immediate right. The line just below the filename contains the frame size of the footage. Use this size when entering the Height and Width setting in the Compositions Settings dialog box.

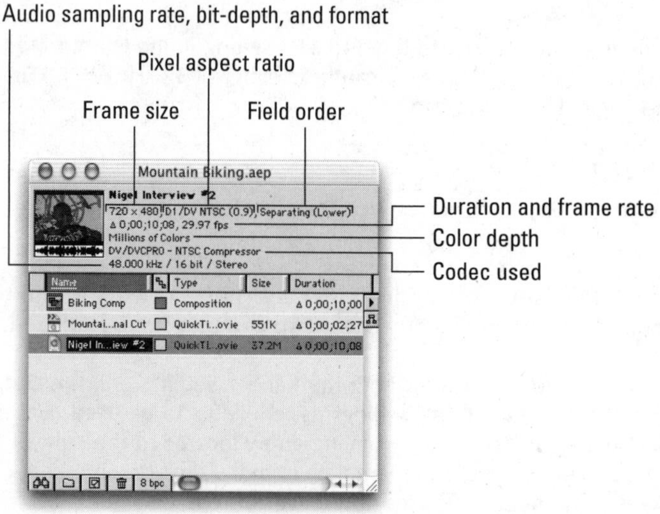

Figure 26-18: Select any file to see its frame size and other information about the file.

Selecting a frame rate

The frame rate for NTSC video is always 29.97 frames per second. This rate has no exceptions. Keep in mind that drop-frame versus non-drop-frame timecodes have absolutely no bearing on frame rates. The frame rate for PAL video is 25 fps. Enter this frame rate in the Composition Settings' Frame Rate field.

Choosing a pixel aspect ratio

Next, you need to know about the pixel aspect ratio in relation to the media clip. In many cases, After Effects automatically recognizes the pixel aspect ratio of imported footage. However, depending on the card you are using, this process may not work properly or at all. You need to know the pixel aspect ratio so that you can make the proper selection for the incoming footage in the File ⇨ Interpret Footage ⇨ Main dialog box as well as the Pixel Aspect Ratio pull-down menu in the Composition Settings dialog box.

Pixel aspect ratios are not random and are related to standard frame sizes. For example, square pixels are mostly used with video that has a frame size of 640 × 480 pixels, and the D1 pixel aspect ratio is used for 720 × 480 pixels and 720 × 486 pixels frame sizes.

Below is a list of pixel aspect ratios available to you in After Effects. The list includes the precise numbers for the aspect ratios as well as the common frame sizes that use these pixel aspect ratios:

- ✦ **Square Pixels:** This setting uses a 1.0 pixel aspect ratio. This setting is commonly used for a 640 × 480 pixels or 648 × 486 pixels frame size video.

- ✦ **D1/DV-NTSC:** This setting uses a 0.9 pixel aspect ratio. Use this setting if you are working with 720 × 480 pixels or 720 × 486 pixels frame-size video and your final output is meant for a 4:3 aspect ratio (as opposed to 16:9 widescreen).

- ✦ **D1/DV-NTSC Widescreen:** This setting uses a 1.2 pixel aspect ratio. Use this setting if you are working with 720 × 480 pixels or 720 × 486 pixels frame-size video and your final output is meant for the 16:9 widescreen aspect ratio.

- ✦ **D1/DV-PAL:** This setting uses a 1.0666 pixel aspect ratio. This is the setting to use if you are working in PAL (Frame Size 720 × 576 pixels) and the final output is meant for a 4:3 aspect ratio (as opposed to 16:9 widescreen).

- ✦ **D1/DV-PAL Widescreen:** This setting uses a 1.422 pixel aspect ratio. Use this setting if you are working with 720 × 576 pixels PAL video and your final output is meant for the 16:9 widescreen aspect ratio.

- ✦ **Anamorphic 2:1:** This setting uses a 2.0 pixel aspect ratio. This setting should be used with film footage shot with an anamorphic lens.

- ✦ **D4/D16 Standard:** This setting uses a 0.948 pixel aspect ratio. Use this setting if your frame size is 1440 × 1024 pixels or 2880 × 2048 pixels and your final output is for a 4:3 aspect ratio.

- ✦ **D4/D16 Anamorphic:** This setting uses a 1.896 pixel aspect ratio. Use this setting if your frame size is 1440 × 1024 pixels or 288 × 2048 pixels and your final output is for a 16:9 widescreen aspect ratio.

Selecting a codec for rendering

When rendering in After Effects for a third-party video card, you should use the codec that the card employs. In many cases, the card makers use proprietary codecs. When you install a card and its accompanying software driver, it also installs the codec for that card. You will see this codec in the QuickTime list of codecs as you prepare to render. Often this codec includes the name of the card maker, such as Aurora MJPEG-A, for easy identification. Aurora MJPEG-A is the name of the codec used by the Aurora Video System's Igniter card.

Occasionally, third-party codecs *require* that a hardware card be present in the machine where you render. For example, if your After Effects workstation happens to be on a different computer than your Final Cut Pro workstation, you may be out of luck. You cannot render with the proper codec for your card. You'll have to use a generic codec, such as Animation. The disadvantage to using Animation is that you have to re-render your QuickTime movie when you bring it back into a Final Cut Pro Timeline.

Other third-party card makers are smarter and more generous. Aurora Video Systems, for example, uses a generic version of the Apple MJPEG-A codec. Any Macintosh that has QuickTime installed on it (and most come with QuickTime pre-installed) has the MJPEG-A codec. Simply select this codec and render away. You can later drop this QuickTime movie into an Aurora Igniter–based Timeline and play it without having to render. Some third-party manufacturers also offer software-only codecs that can be installed on your After Effects workstation.

Note   For situations in which you require transparency or an alpha channel for layering purposes, you need to select a codec that allows for an alpha channel.

Determining data rates for your renders

When rendering from After Effects using a DV codec, determining the data rate is not an issue. The Quality slider in the QuickTime compression dialog box has no effect when using the DV codec. The DV compression is always at a high quality and never varies from the data rate of 3.6MB/second. Other codecs, however, employ this slider to change their data rate. For example, when using the Animation codec, if the Quality slider is set to the Best setting, the resulting data rates are somewhere around 20MB/second. That is a huge data rate and may cause problems with playback in your Timeline. The best way to determine your data rate is to check the documentation that came with your card. Card makers often provide information on the use of the QuickTime Compression Quality slider when using their codec.

You can also do a test to determine the proper data rate for your After Effects render. Check the Vid Rate column in the Browser window of your Final Cut Pro project. Try to get an idea of the average data rate at which your clips are being captured with your video card. Go back to After Effects and do test renders at various quality slider settings. Import these test clips (and label them Best, Medium, Low, and so on) into the Browser of your Final Cut Pro project and check the Vid Rate column for each clip. Choose the setting that falls nearest to the Vid Rate of the rest of your media.

Finding the field order of your clips

Knowing the field order of your incoming video footage is very important. You should set interpretations for your video footage and choose the right field order when doing so. At the rendering stage you also need to tell After Effects which field order you want to use. Of course, field orders for some video formats are well known. DV is lower field ordered, for example. If you are using a third-party video card, more than likely the manufacturers list the field order for the card in the accompanying documentation. However, situations occur where you don't know the field order of some footage and must determine it on your own.

But first, a story: New York is an unpredictable town. Any oddball thing can happen to you there. This was proven many years ago when the famous CBS news anchor Dan Rather was out for an early morning walk. On his way back home, Rather was accosted by two fairly respectable looking men. According to Rather, they asked him, "What's the frequency, Kenneth?" and when he was unable to reply, they punched him in the kisser. This mystery was never cleared up. But for a long time the Kenneth character loomed large in video technology. Whenever the field order or voltage was in question, Kenneth became sort of a warning of an impending punch to some annoying video editor or engineer.

Alphas or no alphas?

If you are rendering for DV, your codec choice is fairly simple. You should choose the DV-NTSC codec from the QuickTime selection dialog box. When rendering for a third-party video card, you should use the codec that the card maker provides. However, an issue to keep in mind is that many codecs do not allow for alpha channels. If you want to use transparency and superimpose your final render over a video track in Final Cut Pro, you must use a codec that allows alpha channels.

You can easily find out which codecs allow alpha channels. In the Format Options dialog box of After Effects' Output Module Settings, select any codec using the top pull-down menu under the Compression Settings, then click OK. Back out in the Video Output section, check the pull-down menu for Channels, located to the right of the codec menu. If the choices in the color depth menu include RGB + Alph, as shown in the illustration here, then your codec allows an alpha channel in addition to the RGB channels. If the selection in the Channels pop-up is limited to RGB *or* Alpha, then the codec does not allow for an alpha channel to be generated along with the image. You can select one or the other, but you won't be able to create both together in a single file Note in the illustration that the Animation codec allows for an alpha channel, whereas the DV and the Motion JPEG-A codecs do not.

To use an alpha channel, you should select the Animation codec because it allows you to have an alpha channel. Be sure to turn the Quality slider for the Animation codec down to Low because at higher settings the data rate of the Animation codec may far exceed that of your Timeline and your hardware.

Continued

Continued

DV/DVCPRO NTSC codec

Animation codec

Output Module Settings

Composition "Biking Comp"

Format: QuickTime Movie
Embed: None
Post-Render Action: None

☑ Video Output

Format Options...

Animation Compressor
Spatial Quality = High (100)

Channels: √ RGB
                Alpha
                RGB + Alpha

Depth:
Color:

☐ Stretch

Width   Height
Rendering at: 720   x   480

Stretch to: 720   x   480   Custom
Stretch %:   x   Stretch Quality: High

Output Module Settings

Composition "Biking Comp"

Format: QuickTime Movie
Embed: None
Post-Render Action: None

☑ Video Output

Format Options...

DV/DVCPRO - NTSC Compressor
Spatial Quality = High (100)

Channels: √ RGB
                Alpha
                RGB + Alpha

Depth:
Color:

☐ Stretch

Width   Height
Rendering at: 720   x   480

Stretch to: 720   x   480   Custom
Stretch %:   x   Stretch Quality: High

Output Module Settings

Composition "Biking Comp"

Format: QuickTime Movie
Embed: None
Post-Render Action: None

☑ Video Output

Format Options...

Motion JPEG A Compressor
Spatial Quality = High (100)

Channels: √ RGB
                Alpha
                RGB + Alpha

Depth:
Color:

☐ Stretch

Width   Height
Rendering at: 720   x   480

Stretch to: 720   x   480   Custom
Stretch %:   x   Stretch Quality: High

Motion JPEG-A codec

I tell that story to give you a warning of sorts to make sure you know your field order. If you don't know the field order, the results can be unpredictable and perhaps even painful.

Oddly enough, there is no surefire way to determine field order in After Effects or Final Cut Pro. After Effects does auto-recognize certain video frame sizes and tags them with a field order. This is usually accurate but in some cases it may fail you. In order to find out the field order, you can use one of two methods. These methods are the interpretation playback test, and the render test.

Imagine this common scenario. You are an After Effects artist working with a Final Cut Pro editor. The Final Cut Pro system is using some high-end third-party card that has a field order — but no one can figure out what that field order is. Ask your editor friend to give you a few seconds of footage captured via that card. Ideally, this footage should contain images of fast action, such as someone running or riding a bicycle. Now use this footage to perform an interpretation playback test by following these steps:

1. **Bring the high-motion footage into After Effects.**

2. **Select the footage in the After Effects project window and choose File ⇨ Interpret Footage ⇨ Main.**

   Choose Upper field or Lower field in the Field Order pull-down menu.

3. **Click OK.**

4. **Option+double-click on the footage in the After Effects project window.**

   It opens in an After Effects playback window.

5. **Play the footage in the After Effects playback window.**

   If you see a back-and-forth movement in sections of fast action, the field order you selected is incorrect. If you see no back-and-forth movement, you chose the field order.

The other test you can use to determine field order is the render test. Unlike the interpretation playback test, you do not actually need any footage from the capture card in question. Simply render a QuickTime movie in After Effects by using the capture card's settings for frame size, frame rate, and codec. In this movie, take any object — such as some text — and move it across the screen from one direction to another in a duration of about half a second or so.

Next, render this QuickTime movie as Upper field ordered and then again as Lower field ordered. Take both of these movies to the Final Cut Pro editing system with the video card and play the movies. The QuickTime movie that has the correct field order should play fine, while the one with the incorrect field order should have a stuttering glitch in the moving item.

By the way, over the years many people have speculated about what happened between Dan Rather and the mystery frequency-seeking men. Newspapers even held write-in competitions, asking readers to send in possible explanations. By far, the best explanation provided was that Rather had misheard what one of the men had said. Readers suggested that the men had not asked Rather, "What's the frequency, Kenneth?" but instead were talking to one another when they said, "Watch the freak wince, see Kenneth," or, "What freaks in this city, Kenneth," before they punched poor Dan Rather. The real truth shall never be known.

✦   ✦   ✦

Editing Film with Final Cut Pro and Cinema Tools

As I have mentioned throughout this book, Final Cut Pro is a scalable editing application. This concept is relatively new in digital nonlinear editing (NLE) applications. Final Cut Pro relies on QuickTime as its base architecture and, thus, can accommodate various codecs, formats, and even frame rates. The ability to play media at 24 frames per second (the frame rate for film) has always been a part of Final Cut Pro's impressive scalability. Apple engineers shrewdly designed this feature in Final Cut Pro with an eye toward attracting film editors to this application.

Most people still don't realize that it is possible to edit film in Final Cut Pro. But in fact, a number of recent high-profile Hollywood releases were edited almost entirely in Final Cut Pro. And many more are now in the post-production phase. I may sound casual here, but this really is revolutionary. To edit films on nonlinear editing systems used to require systems that cost hundreds of thousands of dollars. But using a combination of Final Cut Pro and a few other third-party items, you can set up your own Hollywood factory at home. Not too shabby, eh?

In this chapter, I provide an overview of the film editing process using Final Cut Pro and Cinema Tools. And let it be said that Cinema Tools, formerly known as the third-party tool called Cinema Tools, is yet another member of the impressive suite of applications that Apple includes with Final Cut Pro 4.0. Clearly, they see a big market here. So get to it, and start cutting your movie!

Understanding Film Editing Basics

Final Cut Pro and other nonlinear editing systems represent a vast change from the traditional methods of video editing. The concept of nondestructively rearranging digital representations of shots is a recent one. This has only been possible in the last decade or so with the advent of reliable digitizing systems, access to affordable storage, and the creation of software to allow digital editing on computers.

Computer technology and a common interface have opened up the film world to a lot of people that never would have so much as seen a film editing lab, much less used one. The fast and very powerful desktop computer has provided a universal working environment for film, sound, lighting, and so on. This environment has vastly broadened the bandwidth of the multitudes. Good-bye proprietary (read, *expensive*) environments, hello movie production for the common man (or woman)!

Nonlinear editing systems for film are even more sophisticated and expensive. Editing video on a computer-based nonlinear editing system is one thing, but it's quite another to edit film reliably on a computer-based nonlinear editing system.

Knowing what constitutes a *film* these days can be confusing. Making a film used to mean a production that was shot on celluloid material with a traditional film camera. However, the changing nature of production has produced many format hybrids. You can make a film in a number of ways these days. These include:

✦ **Shoot on video, end on film:** Some people choose to shoot and edit their production on videotape and then have the final edit transferred to film. Film festivals haven't always accepted films that were made in this manner, but this really has changed for the most part. The most conspicuous example of films that follow this workflow are the *Star Wars* prequels. These are shot on video and later transferred to film for final release.

For more information on transferring video to film, see Chapter 22.

✦ **Shoot on film, edit on video, end on video:** Another film option is to shoot on film and then transfer the film to tape. These films are edited and often released on tape. Some film productions that follow this workflow are never intended to make it back to film. This method, on the surface, may make no sense. However, consider the savings in expenses and also the fact that many hundreds of independent and other films made never find a distributor and end up gathering dust on the shelves. Releasing a film on tape only allows the producers of the film to find an audience where there previously was none.

✦ **Shoot on film, edit on tape, end on film:** In this process, producers shoot on film and transfer the film to tape for editing. Usually, features are shot on 35mm or 16mm film and then transferred to video tape by using a telecine process. The telecine process is where the 3:2 pulldown is added to make the film frame rate compatible with the video frame rate. (The 3:2 pulldown is explained later in this chapter.) During the telecine transfer, the edge codes on the film negative are burned in on the tape along with the video timecode. These videotapes are then digitized into Final Cut Pro and edited. After an acceptable cut is reached, a film Cut List is generated. This Cut List is much like an Edit Decision List intended for film. The Cut List is sent back to the negative cut house for matchback to the negative, which results in the final release of the film print. The matchback process is also known as *conforming* the negative. This film-tape-film process, illustrated in Figure 27-1, is the focus of this chapter. Note that almost all films are being edited this way. Sure there are directors, editors, and producers who still prefer the old moviola and flatbed-style editing for film. But by and large the balance has shifted for films to be edited in the manner described here.

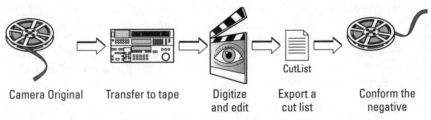

Camera Original   Transfer to tape   Digitize and edit   Export a cut list   Conform the negative

Figure 27-1: A combination of Final Cut Pro and Cinema Tools is used to create films using this type of workflow.

Editing Film with Final Cut Pro

Editing film in any nonlinear editing system can be tricky. Final Cut Pro, though amazing, is no exception. With the combination of Cinema Tools and the film-editing capabilities of Final Cut Pro, you can successfully edit and finish a film. You should be concerned about two issues when editing film in Final Cut Pro:

✦ Reliable tracking of the film edgecode with the tape timecode

✦ Working around the 3:2 pulldown to generate a frame-accurate Cut List

Both of these topics are discussed in subsequent sections. But first, let's look at what you need to edit film with your Final Cut Pro system.

What you need to edit film in Final Cut Pro

To edit film in Final Cut Pro, in addition to Cinema Tools, you'll find it very helpful having the Aurora IgniterX card with the film option enabled. You do not *need* the Aurora IgniterX card and its film playback capability for film editing; however, having this card makes your film editing life a whole lot easier.

Note   All the upgrades to the IgniterX base card include the film option. The three upgrades are the Pro or Component option, the SDI option, or the Studio option. If you have a DV-based setup and you are receiving your film-to-tape transfers on DV tapes, and if you intend to edit your film at 29.97 fps, you can skip trying to acquire the Aurora Igniter Film Option. (The Aurora IgniterX's film playback is best used when you want to edit your film at 24 fps.)

Tracking film edgecode and tape timecode

Just as video has timecode that marks every frame of tape, film negatives have *edgecodes* that mark every frame of film. The edgecode (or keycode) is said to be *latent,* because it is exposed on the film and appears when the film is developed.

When film is transferred to tape for editing, the edge codes on the film negative are burned in along with the video timecode on the tape. This process is called a *burn-in* because the numbers are a permanent part of the image. This process is crucial for your purposes because you need to be able to match any frame on tape back to the frame of film sitting at the film lab at any time. Figure 27-2 shows the edgecode and timecode on a telecined video file.

Figure 27-2: Telecine transfer to tape shows the timecode and edgecode in the Final Cut Pro View window.
Month of August still courtesy of Angelic Entertainment, Inc.

Final Cut Pro must be able to keep track of the film edgecodes along with the video timecode throughout the digitizing, editing, and Cut List generation process. This process is complicated, and it must be transparent to the editors so that they can concentrate on being creative instead of trying to keep track of a lot of numbers.

When transfer houses convert film to tape, they use telecine log files to keep track of this relationship between tape timecode and film edgecode. In Final Cut Pro, you need a reliable way to interpret these log files and convert them for editing use.

Explaining the 3:2 pulldown

Film runs at 24 fps, and NTSC video runs at 29.97 fps. The process of achieving a transfer from 24 fps film to 29.97 video is known as a *3:2 pulldown*. In this process, five frames of video are created from four film frames. One film frame is converted to three video fields (remember, a video frame has two fields), and the next film frame is converted to just two video fields. The sequence of three fields and then two fields alternates, hence the 3:2 in the name of this process. Some video frames consist of two fields that are actually from two different film frames. The 3:2 pulldown process is shown in Figure 27-3.

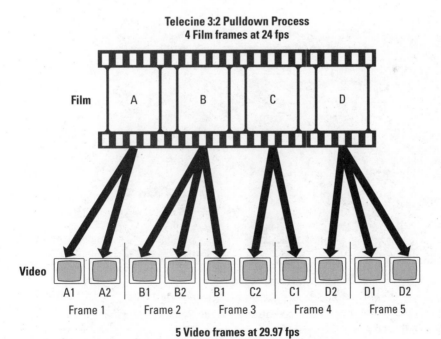

Figure 27-3: The 3:2 pulldown process creates five video frames from four frames of film.

If your head isn't spinning yet, consider this: For the 3:2 pulldown to work correctly, film is also slowed by 0.1 percent (to 23.976 fps) before this process is achieved. Therefore, the audio has to be slowed down by 0.1 percent, as well. In other words, sound is *pulled down*. When the time comes to convert the video from 29.97 back to 24 fps, you must find a method for removing this pulldown. As you can see in Figure 27-3, some video frames consist of two fields that are from two different film frames. Working with a 3:2 pulldown introduces an unreliability factor of +/– 1 frame when the negative is conformed to the video. This 1 frame error is acceptable, but not to everyone.

You can see what a 3:2 pulldown looks like by playing the Pulldown Movie included in the Media folder in the Film Tutorial folder on the DVD-ROM provided with this book. Double-click the Pulldown Movie on the Finder level of your Mac so that it opens in the QuickTime Player. At frame 06:00:28:07, you'll see one frame that seems to break up around the woman's moving hand. That "breakup" is the 3:2 pulldown being added. Figure 27-4 shows the pulldown on a clip. You can also find the same pulldown in this clip at 06:00:28:12, 06:00:28:17, and so on. The 3:2 pulldown is easier to see in areas of motion. Note that you can even count down the 3:2 pulldown. You get three clean frames of video before you get to the two frames with field breakup.

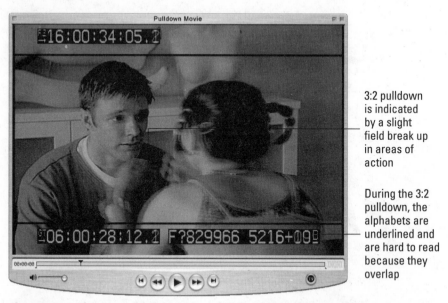

3:2 pulldown is indicated by a slight field break up in areas of action

During the 3:2 pulldown, the alphabets are underlined and are hard to read because they overlap

Figure 27-4: The 3:2 pulldown can be seen in the Pulldown Movie included on the DVD-ROM.

Month of August still courtesy of Angelic Entertainment, Inc.

Caution Be sure to view the Pulldown Movie in the QuickTime player to view the 3:2 pull-down clearly. Playing this clip in Final Cut Pro produces less-than-ideal results for viewing the pulldown.

Understanding Film Transfer Methods

Film-to-tape transfer is a technically complex process. Beyond the 3:2 pulldown added to transfer 24 fps film to 29.97 fps video, numerous other factors have to be considered. There are two possible methods for transferring film to tape. These methods are called Camera Roll Transfer and Scene and Take Transfer. Each method has different implications to your editing workflow in Final Cut Pro.

Camera Roll transfer

In a Camera Roll transfer, one camera roll of film is transferred to tape at a time. This method is for transferring film to tape. However, no telecine log file is generated in this method. This lack of a telecine log file is not a problem because Cinema Tools allows you to manually create a database. Manually creating a database in Cinema Tools takes a while, but if you're a poor filmmaker like me, you probably have more time than money. Of course, if you have more money than time, then you should have the film transferred via a Scene and Take transfer so that you *do* get a telecine log file.

Scene and Take transfer

The preferred method for a film-to-tape transfer is the Scene and Take method. In this method, film is transferred to tape on a scene-by-scene or take-by-take basis. This process takes longer and is more expensive, but it is helpful for the editing process because it also generates a telecine log file. The telecine technician making the transfers creates this file. The telecine log file is a batch list that tracks the relationship between the edgecodes on the film negative and the timecode on the telecined tape. The telecine log file makes the entire editing process in Cinema Tools and Final Cut Pro a breeze.

Note Another advantage of doing a Scene and Take Transfer is that it allows for color correction on a take-by-take basis.

What is a telecine log file?

A telecine log file is a basic plain-text document that describes the relationship of the film edgecode to the timecode on the tape. The telecine transfer technician overseeing the transfer of film to tape generates this file. Figure 27-5 shows a telecine log file.

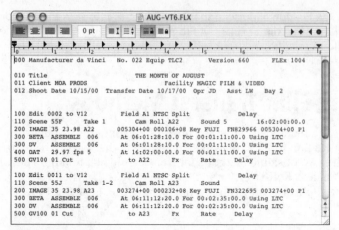

Figure 27-5: This is an example of an .flx format telecine log file.

Month of August FLX file courtesy of Angelic Entertainment

Telecine log files often have a suffix, such as .flx, that denotes their format. Besides matching film edgecodes with tape timecodes, a telecine log file also often contains information about slates and sound timecodes. A telecine log file may contain comments added by the telecine technician.

The most common telecine log file formats are .flx files from TLC, .ftl files from Evertz, and .atn files from Aaton. Another log file format is the Avid Log Exchange file (.ale) from Avid. An Avid Log Exchange file usually contains much more information, but for our purposes you can ignore that information for now.

A telecine log file contains all the information needed for creating a capture log for Final Cut Pro. However, Final Cut Pro cannot directly import a telecine log file and make use of it. This is where Cinema Tools comes in.

Working with Cinema Tools

Cinema Tools began life as the brainchild of a man named Loran Kary. Loran is the lead developer at Focal Point Systems, and he has single-handedly made film editing possible on a low budget with his Cinema Tools software (see Figure 27-6). Loran is also a pretty smart guy. He really listened to his users and over the years made Cinema Tools a first-rate application by adding numerous features and suggestions offered by his users. Cinema Tools was a great example of one man's dedication and hard work, and an open and willing attitude to listen to his users.

For years Cinema Tools was available only for users of Adobe Premiere, Avid, Edit DV, and Media 100. When Final Cut Pro was released, Loran immediately saw the potential and quickly upgraded Cinema Tools so that it worked seamlessly with

Final Cut Pro. Shortly thereafter, Apple Computer acquired Focal Point Systems, maker of the Cinema Tools software. The next version of the product was named Cinema Tools, and as you can see, it ships with Final Cut Pro 4.0 at no extra charge. The future of filmmaking is now the present — and it's all happening on a Mac.

Keep in mind that Cinema Tools is not an editing application. The software works in conjunction with Final Cut Pro to add film editing capabilities to your editing toolset. Cinema Tools works with Final Cut Pro to translate the edited Timelines or edit decision lists into the negative cut lists needed to conform the negative or the workprint for a final release print. If some parts of that last paragraph didn't make sense to you, read on. More will be revealed.

Cinema Tools can import most formats of telecine log files and generate a batch list for Final Cut Pro. Cinema Tools can do so much more than that, but for your purposes here, being able to generate a batch list for Final Cut Pro and create a basic data base for the film clips is the main advantage of Cinema Tools. Cinema Tools enables you to work within Final Cut Pro and manage your database of edgecodes and timecodes. This process remains generally invisible to the editor, but as mentioned earlier, it is critical to your success with film editing. Cinema Tools is a versatile program and can accommodate a variety of workflows. This chapter covers a few of the possibilities, but a full accounting of Cinema Tools' capabilities is beyond the scope of this book.

Considering frame rates and the reverse telecine process

The first and most important decision you need to make is what frame rate you want to work with as you edit your film in Final Cut Pro. Choosing a frame rate to work with can have serious implications on your workflow, and changing your mind in the middle of a film edit can require nightmarish acrobatics. Recall how the telecine 3:2 pulldown process creates 29.97 frames of video for every 24 frames of film. There is no one-to-one relationship between the video frames and film frames. The lack of a one-to-one ratio between the film and video frames creates a conundrum when matching back video to film, because it is not easy to figure out which film frame matches to which video frame. If you look back at Figure 27-3, you can see that some video frames consist of equal parts of two different film frames.

In a perfect world, there would be a perfect one-to-one correspondence between film and video frames. This would erase any confusion or inaccuracy when matching video back to film. Well, guess what? This one-to-one correspondence is available through a process called *reverse telecine*. This term comes from the fact that the extra video frames added during the telecine process are removed in the reverse telecine process. A 29.97 fps clip put through the reverse telecine process ends up as true 24 fps video with all the extra repeating frames removed. Figure 27-6 illustrates the reverse telecine process.

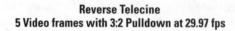

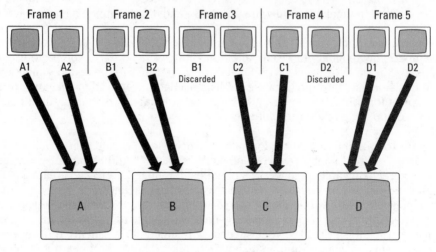

Reverse Telecine
5 Video frames with 3:2 Pulldown at 29.97 fps

Frame 1   Frame 2   Frame 3   Frame 4   Frame 5

A1   A2   B1   B2   B1   C2   C1   D2   D1   D2
                      Discarded   Discarded

A   B   C   D

4 Video frames at 24 fps

Figure 27-6: The reverse telecine process is shown here.

Cinema Tools allows you to take any clip that was digitized at 29.97 fps and put it through the reverse telecine process to obtain a 24 fps video clip. Cinema Tools's reverse telecine window is shown in Figure 27-7.

Reverse Telecine

Remove the telecine 3:2 pulldown

Capture Mode: File:
S5F-1 was captured   ⦿ New (smaller)
as: ○ Same (faster)

○ Field 1 Only
○ Field 2 Only   Conform to:
⦿ F1 – F2   [24.0   ⇕]
○ F2 – F1   ☑ Standard upper/lower

Fields:
⦿ AA   ○ BB   ○ _BC_   ○ _CD_   ○ DD
[Style 1   ⇕]

(Cancel)   (OK)

Figure 27-7: The reverse telecine window in Cinema Tools.

Note When doing reverse telecine in Cinema Tools, the process takes time, especially if you are working on a feature film with hours of material. Another solution is to use Aurora Video Systems's film playback for the IgniterX card. This option reverses telecine in real time during capture and thus saves a great deal of time.

Cross-Reference You can find more on the Aurora Video Systems's Film playback capability later in this chapter in the section entitled "Capturing clips using the Aurora IgniterX Film Option."

Selecting a frame rate

When editing film with Cinema Tools and Final Cut Pro, you can choose to work with 29.97 fps (for NTSC) or 24 fps. Final Cut Pro is flexible enough to enable you to create 24 fps Timelines and work with 24 fps media. Each frame rate has advantages and disadvantages. The next few sections evaluate each choice.

Working at 29.97 fps

When working at 29.97 fps, you simply digitize the telecined video into your Final Cut Pro editing system and cut at 29.97 fps just like regular video. With Cinema Tools, you can easily get a cut list at the end of the process.

Advantages to working at 29.97 fps are:

✦ **No special hardware is required.** If you choose to work at 29.97 fps, you need nothing more than what you already have for a basic Final Cut Pro editing system.

✦ **No post-processing is required.** When working with 29.97 fps, you need not put every clip through the reverse telecine process in Cinema Tools. The reverse telecine process can be quite time-consuming.

✦ **Going to video tape is easy.** The process of film editing is long and compli-cated. Producers, directors, editors, and many other people may be involved in the viewing and critiquing of the rough-cut process. If you choose to remain at 29.97 fps, you can easily make video copies of the rough cut during the edit-ing process. No frame-rate conversion is necessary when outputting to tape.

Working at 29.97 fps has some disadvantages, as well. They are the following:

✦ **Frame accuracy is not guaranteed.** The main disadvantage of working at 29.97 fps is that, because of the mathematical calculations and the uneven frame rates, you cannot guarantee accuracy of better than plus-or-minus one frame. Film editors use various methods to work around this problem. For example, editors make sure that they never use the very first good frame of a shot they are planning to edit, and they never use the very last good frame of a shot. When working at 29.97 fps, you should set an In point one frame past where your shot starts. A similar precaution is necessary when setting the Out points; editors set it one frame earlier than the last good frame. Doing so prevents the last frame of the previous shot, or the *slate,* from appearing in the final match back on film.

✦ **29.97 fps presents some sound sync issues.** When film at 24 fps is transferred to video at 29.97 fps, it is slowed down by 0.1 percent before the 3:2 pulldown is applied to it. In NTSC video at 29.97 fps, the film is considered to be in the *pulled down* state. If the audio for the film was captured separately from the original sound rolls, then it needs to be pulled down by 0.1 percent as well, otherwise you will lose one frame of sync for every 33 seconds. This adjustment is easily done in Final Cut Pro by selecting the audio clips that were captured separately and using the Modify ⇨ Speed command. Double-click the clip to load it into the Viewer (or select it in the Timeline), and choose Modify ⇨ Speed. By default the speed will be 100%. Enter a value of 99.9% to pull down the clip to match the video. Again, this can add time to your workflow as well.

Working at 24 fps

When working at 24 fps, you digitize the telecined video (which is at 29.97 fps) into your Final Cut Pro editing system and use the reverse telecine process to convert these files down to 24 fps by removing the extra frames. This reverse telecine process in Cinema Tools takes time and can be avoided by using the film playback capability of the Aurora Video Systems's IgniterX card. With this film option installed, this card performs reverse telecine in real time during the capture phase. Advantages to working at 24 fps include:

✦ **Frame accuracy is guaranteed.** Most high-end film editing systems, such as Lightworks and Avid, work at 24 fps on clips that have been reverse telecined. Final Cut Pro enables you to work with 24 fps clips in a 24 fps–based Timeline. Because of this feature, Final Cut Pro is becoming popular as an affordable alternative to expensive film editing systems. Frame accuracy is guaranteed when working with 24 fps clips because all the extra frames associated with NTSC video have been removed.

✦ **There are no sound sync issues.** If you have captured the video from a telecined tape and applied the reverse telecine process to it, the clip is no longer pulled down. It is said to be *pulled up.* In this case, the sound can then be digitized separately from the original production sound rolls without being pulled down. This audio will maintain proper sync at all times with the pulled-up picture.

Note   There is yet another scenario in which sound has been captured separately from the telecined videotapes, and the picture has been pulled up with reverse telecine. In this case, the sound must be pulled up to maintain sync. Double-click the clip to load it into the Viewer, or select it in the Timeline and choose Modify ⇨ Speed. Enter a speed of 100.1% to pull up the sound clip.

✦ **24 fps delivers a lower data rate.** When working with files that have been reverse-telecined down to 24 fps, you have a lower data rate for your clips because the extra frames have been removed. This reduces the workload on your processor and the files play smoother. Your file sizes for 24 fps clips are smaller than for 29.97 fps clips, which enables you to store more media on your disk drives.

Alas, the disadvantage to working at 24 fps is that your Video Output may be unacceptable to some producers and editors. If you have converted your clips to 24 fps by applying the reverse telecine process, you face a quandary when you need to output rough-cut screening copies on videotape.

If you are editing DV and outputting to FireWire, you can view your 24 fps project on an NTSC monitor, and you can output to tape. You just don't get real 3:2 pulldown. Frames are duplicated as necessary to convert 24 to 30, and some people say that it looks jerky (but it looks okay to me). I find that it's acceptable just for viewing.

Many editors use Adobe After Effects to import 24 fps video and apply a 3:2 pulldown in After Effects for a final rendered file at 29.97 fps. This file can then be laid back to tape. This cumbersome process requires additional rendering time.

Another (and very ideal) solution is to use the film option of the Aurora IgniterX card. When playing a 24 fps clip in the Timeline, you can use this option to add back the 3:2 pulldown and adjust the timing for accurate 29.97 playback to the video monitor or videotape. This real-time process is an excellent choice for editors working at 24 fps.

Editing a short film scene with Cinema Tools and Final Cut Pro

I'll walk you through a sample film editing project. Assume that you're in Hollywood, and you're about to edit a short scene from a film. Your project is called *Month of August,* which is the name of the film made by Angelic Entertainment in San Diego, California. (See the sidebar *Month of August.*) The workflow for your editing process consists of the following steps:

1. Import a telecine log file into Cinema Tools.

2. Export a Final Cut Pro batch list from Cinema Tools.

3. Import the batch list into Final Cut Pro.

4. Capture clips using batch capture in Final Cut Pro.

5. Check your captured clips in Final Cut Pro.

6. Edit in Final Cut Pro.

7. Export a cut list from Cinema Tools.

8. Check your final cut list.

The following events should have already occurred, if this were a real-world film editing situation:

✦ **The telecine house has transferred the film dailies to tape by using a Scene and Take Transfer and generated a telecine log file.** If you need material to use, I've provided the AUG-VT6.FLX file that is located on the DVD-ROM in the Film Tutorial folder.

✦ **You received the tape with the transfer, and the disk containing your file, or in my case, the AUG-VT6.FLX file.**

On the DVD-ROM

If you don't have material of your own, you can follow along with the next few sections by locating the Film Tutorial folder on the DVD-ROM accompanying this book.

Month of August

Month of August is a romantic comedy by San Diego's Angelic Entertainment, Inc. The actors you see in this scene are Mackenzie Astin and Ali Hillis. The film was written by Scott Benefiel, directed by Rex Piano, and produced by Mark Maine and Charlie Jackson. The director of photography on *Month of August* was Daniel Yarussi, A.S.C. Shawn Paper edited this film all on Final Cut Pro.

Shot in 35mm late in 2000, *Month of August* was completed in post-production early in 2001 and was edited entirely with Final Cut Pro. Then an edit list was created, and the original 35mm exposed negative was cut, assembled, and projected. Angelic Entertainment's decision to edit *Month of August* in Final Cut Pro gave the film the quality look of similar films edited by more traditional methods, at a tremendous savings.

Angelic Entertainment is a rare company in that it produces only content-responsible entertainment within the G to PG-13 range without gratuitous language and sexual and violent scenes. Another unique feature about Angelic is that they like to involve the writer throughout as much of the process as possible so as to maintain integrity to the writer's original vision. You can learn more about Angelic and *Month of August* on its Web site at www.AngelicEntertainment.com/august.

Importing a telecine log into Cinema Tools

On the DVD-ROM For the next few sections you need to work with the files included in the Film Tutorial folder on the DVD-ROM. Drag the Film Tutorial folder to your hard drive and use the files contained in that folder to work though these film editing exercises.

The first step is to create a Final Cut Pro batch list by using Cinema Tools. First, import the telecine log file that was delivered to you and import that into Cinema Tools. Then export a Final Cut Pro batch list from Cinema Tools. Follow these steps:

1. **Start Cinema Tools.**

2. **Cinema Tools starts by asking you to locate an existing database, if there is one already. Cancel this request because you're about to create a new one.**

3. **Choose Database ➪ New Database.**

   A dialog box appears like the one shown in Figure 27-8.

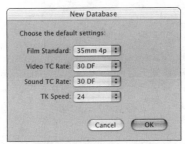

Figure 27-8: Select the proper settings for your film database.

4. **Select the type of film and video settings to be used for your database.**

   These settings are not critical because Cinema Tools automatically overrides any default settings with those specified in the telecine film log.

5. **Check your timecode on the tape carefully.**

   Remember that colons (:) mean non-drop-frame timecode, and semicolons (;) mean drop-frame timecode. Enter the proper timecode mode here in the New Database window. Otherwise there may be some discrepancies in time-code values as you attempt to capture your material.

6. **Cinema Tools asks you to name your database and save it.**

   I named mine MOACTDB (an acronym for Month of August Cinema Tools Database). Next, you see a List View and Detail View box. You can ignore these options for the moment.

7. Choose File ⇨ Import ⇨ Telecine Log.

8. Locate and select your telecine log and click Open.

I located my AUG-VT6.FLX file. The AUG-VT6.FLX file is located in the Film Tutorial folder on the DVD-ROM. The events will be imported in both the List View and Detail View boxes, shown in Figure 27-9.

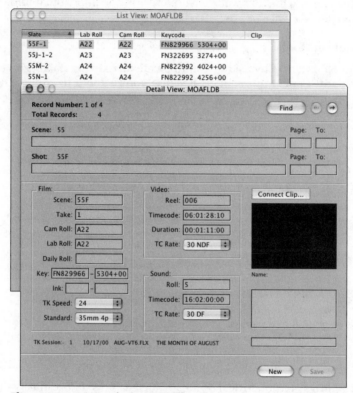

Figure 27-9: Your Telecine Log file will be imported into the List and the Detail view in Cinema Tools.

Cinema Tools also gives you a warning telling you that four of four total events were imported. Keeping an eye on this dialog box is crucial because it tells you the number of records from the total that were imported. Occasionally, Cinema Tools may not import an event due to formatting or other problems with the telecine log file. Click OK on this notice.

Exporting a Final Cut Pro batch list from Cinema Tools

Your next step is to export a batch list from Cinema Tools for Final Cut Pro. When this batch list is imported into Final Cut Pro, you can batch capture from telecined tapes. To generate a batch list for Final Cut Pro, follow these steps:

1. **Choose File ➪ Export ➪ Batch Capture.**

2. **Select Final Cut Pro Video from the Export batch capture window as shown in Figure 27-10.**

   A Final Cut Pro batch list is generated.

Figure 27-10: Select Final Cut Pro in the Export batch capture window.

3. **Name the batch list and save it.**

   I named my list MOABatch.

4. **Quit Cinema Tools.**

Importing a batch list into Final Cut Pro

After you have exported a batch list from Cinema Tools, you are ready to import that list into Final Cut Pro. Here's how:

1. **Start Final Cut Pro.**

2. **Open a new or preexisting project in Final Cut Pro.**

3. **Choose File ➪ Import ➪ Batch List at 29.97 fps.**

4. **Locate and import the batch list created by Cinema Tools.**

   This batch list creates a log within the Final Cut Pro Browser. Figure 27-11 shows the log created in the Final Cut Pro Browser window after importing a batch list.

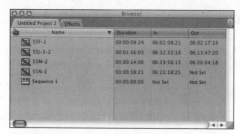

Figure 27-11: Importing the batch list will create a log in Final Cut Pro.

You can now highlight the clips and capture by using the batch-capture feature, as described next.

 Caution   There's a gotcha here that you should know about, especially if you are working at 24 fps. Final Cut Pro uses the default setting for sequences to determine what the frame rate of a batch log should be. The default setting has to be something with a 29.97 timebase to import batch capture logs with 29.97 timecode. If the default setting is 24, Final Cut Pro will not import the batch log correctly, and there will be no indication that there is a problem.

Capturing clips with batch capture

The next stage is to digitize the tape into the computer for editing in Final Cut Pro. Using Final Cut Pro's batch capture feature, capturing the shots is a relatively easy process. Final Cut Pro requires a batch list or a log for batch capture. This list is a list of reels and in and out timecodes. (Refer to Chapter 4 for more details on the batch-capture process.)

 Cross-Reference   To learn more about the batch-capture process in Final Cut Pro, see Chapter 7.

Capturing clips using the Aurora IgniterX Film Option

You will capture your media from video tapes that were provided to you by the transfer house. These tapes contain the film-to-tape transfers. If you are using the IgniterX Film Option follow these steps to set up for film capture:

 Caution   The process of film editing and accurate cut list generation depends heavily on accurate timecodes throughout the capture, editing, and cut list generation process. Before you actually capture these clips, you *must* make sure that your Final Cut Pro editing setup is correctly calibrated for timecode. To learn how to perform this calibration, see Chapter 24.

If you are using the IgniterX Film Option, perform the following:

1. Choose Apple Menu ⇨ System Preferences, then click the Ignition pane.

The Ignition control panel appears as shown in Figure 27-12.

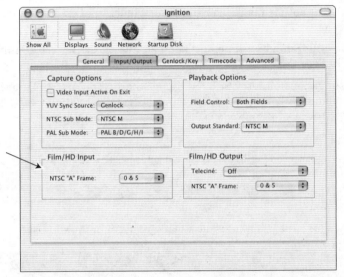

Figure 27-12: Set your NTSC "A" Frame Offset correctly in the Ignition System Preference Pane. The default settings of 0 and 5 are usually correct.

2. Click the Input/Output tab.

3. Set your NTSC "A" Frame Offset correctly.

You must have the Film Option installed to have this option available to you. The default settings of 0 and 5 are usually correct.

Checking captured clips in Final Cut Pro

After capturing your clips, you should carefully check them before editing them. If you used the IgniterX Film Option, or if you performed the reverse telecine process by using Cinema Tools, you should check your resulting 24 fps clips to make sure the frame rate is accurate. To check the frame rate of a 24 fps clip, select the clip in the Browser and choose Tools ⇨ Analyze Movie ⇨ Clip. Make sure that the clips are 24 fps.

Checking clips for proper telecine removal

If you captured your clips with the Aurora Film Option, or if you performed the reverse telecine process in Cinema Tools, you should check your resulting 24 fps clips to make sure that the 3:2 pulldown was removed correctly. To check for telecine removal:

1. **Double-click any 24 fps clip on the Finder level to open it in QuickTime player.**

2. **Play the clip frame by frame and keep an eye on the letters and numbers as shown in Figure 27-13.**

   There should be no blurry or overlapping characters. A, B, C, D, and E should turn around clearly and without blurring. This tells you that the 3:2 pulldown removal process was successful.

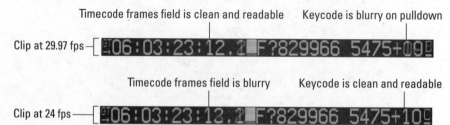

Figure 27-13: Proper removal of the 3:2 pulldown is shown in the bottom image. The clip on the top has blurry keycode alphabets, which indicates a clip at 29.97 fps or an incorrect 3:2 pulldown removal.
Month of August still courtesy of Angelic Entertainment, Inc.

If you see blurry or overlapping characters, then there was some problem with the 3:2 pulldown removal. To fix this problem, check the IgniterX Card settings first. Then check the tape transfer. On your tape, the letter *A* of the keycode should fall on the timecode frame 00 or 05s on the videotape. Otherwise, this was not a proper SMPTE A transfer and should be sent back to the transfer house. Looking for the SPMTE A transfer is how the Aurora IgniterX Film Option works. It assumes the A falls on 00 or 05s. You can also change the location of the A frame in the Capture panel of the Ignition Control panel, under the NTSC A Frame Offset setting.

Linking and verifying the clips

Remember that at the end of the editing process in Final Cut Pro, you generate a cut list to be sent back to the negative cut house. Again, you utilize Cinema Tools to do that. Cinema Tools uses the database you created earlier to create this cut list. In my situation, the MOAFLDB file was created with nothing more than a telecine log file. Now that you have digitized these clips, Cinema Tools needs to link these digitized clips to its database. Cinema Tools uses this link to maintain the relationship between clips and the edgecodes.

Ideally, you should do linking and verifying *after* clips have been captured, but *before* editing has begun. Linking and verifying *must* be done before you generate a cut list. To link and verify:

1. **In the List View window (see Figure 27-14) double-click the first record.**

   In the MOAFLDB file, the first record is located at Scene 55F Take 1 and Roll A22. The record you double-clicked is loaded in the Detail View window, as shown in Figure 27-15.

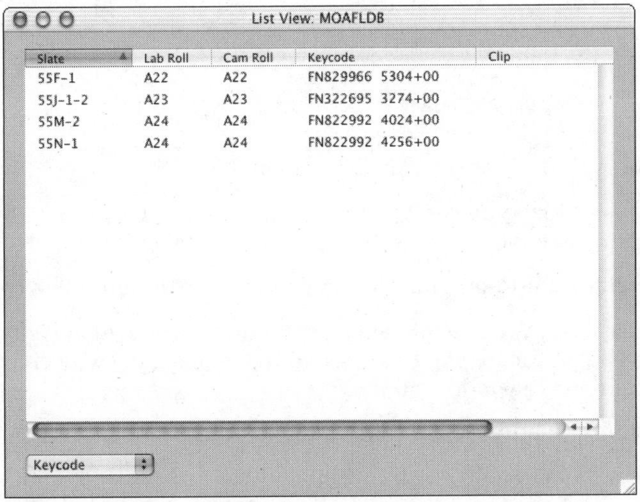

Figure 27-14: The List View window for the Cinema Tools database is shown here.

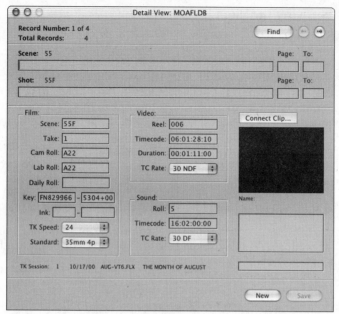

Figure 27-15: The Detail View window shows the details for each record.

2. **Click Connect Clip.**

   A dialog box in which you can locate the clip appears. Of course, this is the clip for which you have clicked the record.

3. **Locate the clip "55F-1" on your media drive, select it, and click Open.**

   Cinema Tools loads the clip into another window, as shown in Figure 27-16. The idea here is to locate and link the clip that goes along with the record you double-clicked in the window above.

4. **Click Snap Shot to add the current image to your database.**

   Note that you can move to any frame and add this as the Snapshot to your clip.

5. **This is a good place to check your timecode match. Click the Identify button in the window shown in Figure 27-17.**

   Compare the timecodes and the keycodes between the Identify window and the burn in on the clip. Figure 27-17 shows this comparison process. Note that you can locate your playhead anywhere on the clip and click the Identify button.

Figure 27-16: Click Poster Frame to add an image of the shot.
Month of August still courtesy of Angelic Entertainment, Inc.

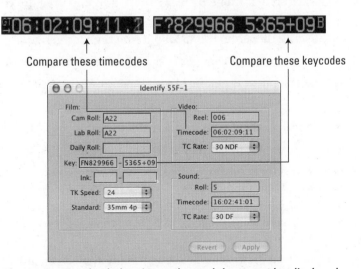

Figure 27-17: Check the Timecodes and the Keycodes displayed in the Identify window against the burn in on your clip.
Month of August still courtesy of Angelic Entertainment, Inc.

Synching sound clips in Final Cut Pro

When shooting a film in the field, the sound is often recorded on a DAT (Digital Audio Tape) or other separate audio recording device. A clapper is used on the set to create a sync mark between the picture and sound. During the telecine process, audio is synchronized to video by matching the visual of the clapper to its sound. The audio is then transferred to videotape along with the video during the telecine process. You can simply capture your sound along with the picture into Final Cut Pro.

However, you may have times when editors and producers choose not to sync sound during the telecine phase, or they choose to digitize the audio separately from the audio tapes for better quality. In a case where the audio was recorded and digitized from separate sources, you need to capture this audio into Final Cut Pro and sync it to the picture before editing with it. Follow these steps to synchronize audio with video:

1. **Open your Final Cut Pro project and double-click the video portion of the clip to load it into the Viewer and to locate the frame where the clapper on the slate just closes.**

2. **Place a marker on that frame by using the M key, and drag the clip to a video track into a sequence.**

3. **Now double-click the audio file to load it into the Viewer.**

4. **Add any necessary speed changes to pull up or pull down the audio.**

   This critical component is helpful in maintaining sync between picture and sound.

For more information about pulling up or pulling down sound, see earlier in this chapter.

5. **Viewing the waveform for the audio clip in the View window, move your playhead to the location where you can see the waveform of the clapper just closing.**

   You can turn on scrubbing (Shift+S) to hear your audio as you scrub through to locate the clapper sound.

6. **Place the playhead on the clapper sound in the waveform, and set a marker by pressing the M key.**

7. **Drag this audio clip into the sequence under the video clip.**

8. **Drag the audio clip sideways until you can see the markers of the video and the audio clip snap together.**

9. **Select the two clips by holding down the Shift key and choosing Modify ➪ Link (or press Command+L).**

   Now link the two clips.

10. **Select this new synchronized clip and drag it from the Timeline into the Browser window.**

Make sure that you create a separate bin in which you place the newly synchronized clips to keep organized. Later, you can delete the original separate audio and
video clips from their bins, because you only need the new synchronized clip.

Editing in Final Cut Pro

You are finally ready to edit your 24 fps clips in Final Cut Pro. An important point to
remember if you are working at 24 fps is that you must set your sequence's frame
rate to 24 fps. If you have chosen not to reverse telecine and are working at 29.97
fps, you can simply edit in a normal 29.97 fps sequence in Final Cut Pro.

You can work with the Month of August.fcp project that is included in Film Tutorial
folder on the DVD-ROM. It is best that you copy the Film Tutorial folder to your
hard drive and start up the Month of August.fcp project. I have included my own
version of a basic edit of this scene in the Scene 55 sequence. You are free to edit
this scene any way you prefer and generate a cut list.

For more information about changing sequence presets and creating new
sequence presets, see Chapter 6.

Besides setting the correct frame rate for your sequence, there are a few more
items you should think about when editing film in Final Cut Pro:

✦ **Don't cut on the missing frame.** I use the term *missing frame* here to clarify an
   important point. Some editors believe that when editing film-based clips at
   video frame rates (that is, 29.97 fps), they must be careful not to make edits
   on certain frames that "may not exist." This misunderstanding is common.
   There are no "nonexisting" frames. Editors just need to keep in mind that,
   when they are editing at video rates, the film frame that may be matched back
   may be the one frame before or the one after. For this reason, the only strong
   caution you need to observe is to not edit in on the first good frame and not
   edit out on the last good frame. This caution only applies if you have chosen
   to work at 29.97 fps and not remove pulldown. If you are working at 24 fps
   after performing the reverse telecine process, you can place your cuts wherever you want.

✦ **Keep your edits on the first video track.** When working in a Final Cut Pro
   sequence, keep all your video edits on the V1 (or main) video track. Any items
   that you place in V2, or video track 2, are assumed to be a superimpose or
   title effect and can come out in the foreground layer when you export a
   Cinema Tools cut list. Anything you place above the V2 track in Final Cut Pro
   is ignored by Cinema Tools altogether.

✦ **Observe cautions for audio tracks.** If you plan to export an audio EDL, keep
   in mind that one EDL from Final Cut Pro can only describe four audio tracks.
   Cinema Tools is a bit more versatile and enables you to export the first eight
   tracks of audio for an audio EDL. Any audio tracks after that cannot be read
   by Cinema Tools's EDL capabilities.

Generating a cut list from Cinema Tools

After you finish editing, you can export a cut list from Cinema Tools. This cut list is sent to the negative cut house to create a matchback for your final film print. The matchback, or conform process, consists of the negative cutter physically matching the negatives of the film to the numbers shown in the cut list.

To export a cut list, follow these steps:

1. **Select your sequence and choose File ⇨ Export ⇨ Cinema Tools Film Lists.**

2. **In the Cinema Tools Film List dialog box (see Figure 27-18), select the appropriate options and click OK.**

Cross-Reference

The options in the Cinema Tools Film List dialog box are described in the next two sections.

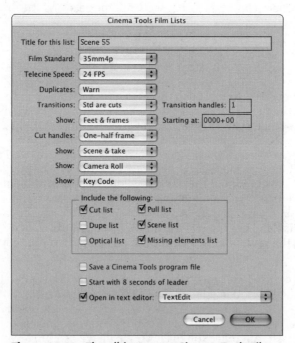

Figure 27-18: The all-important Cinema Tools Film Lists dialog box is shown here.

3. **Cinema Tools asks you to locate the database that this list is based on. Navigate the directories and locate the file you created earlier.**

   If all goes well you'll see a cut list similar to the one shown in Figure 27-19.

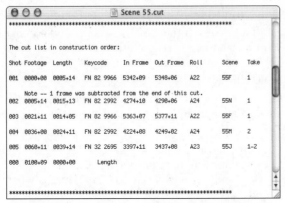

Figure 27-19: A portion of a final Cut List exported from Cinema Tools.

 The first time you choose to export from Final Cut Pro, Cinema Tools asks you to locate the Cinema Tools application. After you've done that, Cinema Tools remembers this location and you are not be asked this again in the future. However, if the Cinema Tools application is *open,* the plug-in will find it and not ask.

Understanding Cinema Tools lists

Cinema Tools can export a few different kinds of lists. These choices are seen in the Cinema Tools Cut List dialog box. Cinema Tools's cut list choices are explained here:

✦ **Include a cut list:** The cut list is the main list that contains the data for conforming the negative to the digitally edited program.

✦ **Include a dupe list:** In a nonlinear editor, such as Final Cut Pro, using the same shot twice or even many times is not a problem. However, when dealing with film you have to keep in mind that the shot exists only once on the original film negative. The dupe list provides information on the use of duplicate shots in the final edit.

✦ **Include an optical list:** Cinema Tools generates a list for three kinds of opticals — titles, motion effects, and transitions.

✦ **Include a pull list:** This list is optional. The pull list is the same as the cut list but with one big difference: The shots appear in the order in which they are found on the negative rolls. The negative cut lab uses the pull list to first locate shots from the rolls. Each listing in the pull list shows the shot number from the cut list.

✦ **Include a scene list:** The scene list is optional as well. A scene list is a list of the shots that are used in the cut list. Each shot is listed only once in the scene list. The scene list is used to order prints of the shots used in the edit to conform a work print before cutting the negative.

Cinema Tools Cut List dialog box options

The Cinema Tools Cut List dialog box contains many options and settings for configuring your lists. These options and settings include:

✦ **Timebase:** Making a distinction between timebase and frame rate is important.

- Timebase establishes how many frames are in every second, and any cut list for a film always ends up at 24 fps when Cinema Tools generates the cut list.

- Frame rate is the rate of frames in every second for the media in that sequence. However, your timebase setting here should be set to what the timebase of your sequence is. If it is 29.97 fps, that is what the timebase should be set to.

✦ **Film Standard:** This setting should be the same as the Default settings that you created in your database settings. Also, this should be the standard in which your final cut on film is going to be made.

✦ **Duplicates:** Setting this to Warn generates warnings about duplicates in the cut list. The Ignore setting simply ignores any duplicates.

✦ **Transitions (All are cuts, Std are cuts, All are opticals):** Set this to All Are Cuts if this cut list is for a work print. Cinema Tools places a cut in the middle of the transition. For a final negative matchback, set this setting to All Are Opticals. This results in complete information and an optical.

✦ **Starting footage or time:** This enables you to set the starting count for the cut list. You can also zero, or reset it by clicking the zero button.

✦ **Cut handles:** This setting adds handles to the cuts. These handles don't show up in the cut list, but are used by Cinema Tools to ensure all frames are available. This is because Cinema Tools knows that for each cut, half a frame is lost on either side.

✦ **Transition handles:** Some negative cutters prefer extra handles around transitions. This setting generates those extra frames.

✦ **Include (entire project or work area only):** This setting helps you create a cut list from a work area in a sequence or the full Timeline. This option works for Premiere projects only. For Final Cut Pro leave this set to entire project.

✦ **Show (feet & frames or time or count):** *Feet & frame* shows the count in the film standard you have selected. *Time* results in a list showing timecode and is useful for keeping track of running time. *Count* shows simple frame counts. Often this setting is helpful for gauging frames for timing transitions and other such operations.

✦ **Show (scene and take or clip name):** Selecting *Clip name* makes it easier to relate the cut list back to the Timeline. Selecting *Scene and Take* is useful if you need to compare the cut list back to the Cinema Tools database.

✦ **Show (camera roll or lab roll):** Some negative cutters prefer to store their negatives as lab rolls, but camera rolls are how most rolls are stored and labeled. Select the option appropriate for your needs.

✦ **Save a Cinema Tools program file:** This setting allows you to label and save a Cinema Tools program file. At the moment Cinema Tools makes no use of this file, but in the future there may be added functionality that this option will take advantage of.

✦ **Start with 8 seconds of leader:** Eight seconds is the standard length for an Academy or SMPTE leader. This option adds an 8-second leader to the cut list.

✦ **Open in text editor:** This option enables you to open the document with a word processing utility. The default for this entry is SimpleText, a common text editor. However, you can choose another word processing or text utility in the menu.

Checking your exported cut list

Negative matchbacks are expensive. Before you send the cut list for your master-piece to the negative cutters, spot-check your cut list for errors. This avoids further time, expense, and phone calls from angry lab technicians. Here are the steps to check one of your edits:

1. **Open the cut list you just generated from Cinema Tools.**

2. **Locate the same edit in your Final Cut Pro sequence.**

3. **Double-click the edit to open the Trim window.**

4. **Check the edgecodes on the cut.**

   The edgecodes should match the codes in the cut list as shown in Figure 27-20. You may want to check numerous edit points in this fashion.

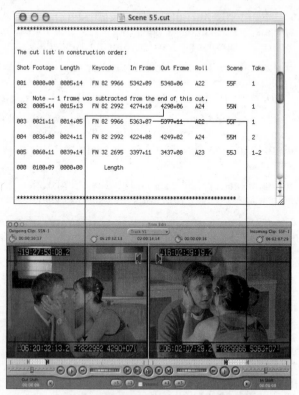

Figure 27-20: Compare the edit point codes between the Trim window and the final cut list. If you are working at the 29.97 fps rate, your cuts can be plus or minus one frame off.

Month of August still courtesy of Angelic Entertainment, Inc.

After spot-checking your cut list against the edit in the sequence, you can send this cut list to the negative house for matchback to your camera negatives. Hollywood awaits.

Troubleshooting film editing in Final Cut Pro

As you may have gathered by now, film editing in nonlinear editing systems is an intricate and complex process. Mistakes can be made in many places. Most problems manifest themselves in frame inaccuracies. If you have problems, here are a few places to start troubleshooting:

✦ **Calibrate your timecode to your deck.** You must do this before any captures occur.

Cross-Reference

I explain the timecode calibration process in Chapter 24.

✦ **After the Verifying and Linking process, spot-check some of your clips.** Check the burned-in timecode against the database entries in Cinema Tools.

✦ **After generating the cut list, spot-check your edits in the cut list against the actual edits in the Final Cut Pro sequence.** There is no limit to the number of edit points you may want to check. I know editors who check 30 or 40 edit points throughout the film.

Editing film in Final Cut Pro is a fascinating and extremely rewarding process. Accurate film editing is the gold standard of any nonlinear editing system. Just a few years ago, the idea that you or I could sit at home and edit a feature film was insane. These days, thanks to Final Cut Pro and Cinema Tools, the process of film editing is accessible to many.

The film-editing market is still dominated by expensive and high-end systems such as Avid and Lightworks. This situation is changing day by day as more and more feature-film producers are choosing Final Cut Pro. There is a great deal of hesitation in doing so. Despite the expense of an Avid film-editing system, producers derive comfort from the fact that it's a known quantity. Final Cut Pro represents something new as well as something that producers lack experience with. Nonetheless, the changes can be felt throughout the industry.

✦   ✦   ✦

Troubleshooting

Troubleshooting Final Cut Pro

◆ ◆ ◆ ◆

In This Chapter

Troubleshooting in
Final Cut Pro

Fixing dropped
frames and sync
issues

Troubleshooting audio
distortion issues

Troubleshooting
timecode problems

Deleting Final Cut Pro
preferences

◆ ◆ ◆ ◆

Troubleshooting is a big part of any editor's life. If you work with a full-featured editing application such as Final Cut Pro, some amount of your time will almost certainly be devoted to troubleshooting. This doesn't necessarily mean that something is wrong with Final Cut Pro—the need for troubleshooting is a constant issue in any editing setup.

Of course, most editors face some common issues when working with Final Cut Pro. Some problems are caused by not choosing the correct settings. Final Cut Pro has many options and settings that must be carefully manipulated to get the desired results. Set one or two items incorrectly, and you may find yourself throwing up your hands or pulling out your hair because of problems that hinder capture, editing, or layback to tape performance.

The art of troubleshooting requires a mixture of basic knowledge, logic, a little patience, and a process of elimination. This chapter looks at some basic troubleshooting techniques as well as addresses some specific issues you may encounter when working with Final Cut Pro.

Troubleshooting in Final Cut Pro

When everything goes your way, Final Cut Pro is an amazing program. However, when things don't go as planned, the editing experience can get truly frustrating. A few basic troubleshooting techniques have served me well over the last few years when working with Final Cut Pro. These techniques are described in the next few sections and serve as a good place to start when troubleshooting your projects. The first two sections cover basic troubleshooting techniques, and the third section contains troubleshooting steps for specific problems that you may encounter in Final Cut Pro.

Isolating the problem

As you approach a problem, remember that Final Cut Pro works in tandem with QuickTime, the Macintosh operating system, and the hardware you are using. Not every problem you have while working in Final Cut Pro is necessarily a Final Cut Pro issue. Learning to isolate your problem's source is the first step toward solving your problem.

The key to isolating the source of a problem is to use the QuickTime Player. Imagine a scenario where you hear loud clicks in the audio clip when you play it in Final Cut Pro. Before you start changing settings in Final Cut Pro, take a minute to locate the source media file for that clip by using the Finder, and then use the QuickTime Player to play the file. If you hear the audio clicks in QuickTime, then the issue is not necessarily Final Cut Pro's. You may want to review your source tape to determine whether the audio clicks exist on the original recording. If the audio distortion does not exist on the tape, then clearly the capture settings are an issue.

You can use this technique to isolate video problems, as well. For example, if you use a third-party video capture card and a clip in the Final Cut Pro Timeline shows some video distortion, find and play the clip by using the QuickTime Player. Observe the clip carefully as it plays in the QuickTime Player and on your external video monitor (if you're using one). Is the distortion present just in the QuickTime Player window on the computer monitor? Or is it *also* visible on the external video monitor connected to the video card? If the distortion only appears on the external monitor, then most likely the clip is fine. This may, however, indicate a problem with the video card.

Playing "find the delta" in the Browser

Even though the purpose of the Browser is to help you organize your project and material, it is by far one of the best troubleshooting tools in Final Cut Pro. My favorite troubleshooting technique in the Browser is what I call the "find the delta" game. *Delta* is a term often used in programming to indicate the difference between two values. In video editing, *delta* refers to finding the difference between one troublesome item and another item that is not troublesome.

Editors often come across clips that have stuttering, video distortion, or audio distortion during playback. If you come across such a clip in a sequence, drag it back into the Browser and compare its settings with other items in the Browser. Check the columns listing Data Rate, Vid Rate, and Pixel-Aspect ratio and see if the troublesome clip differs in any way from other clips in the current project. The Vid Rate column, for example, may show you if a clip was captured at a data rate that doesn't match your sequence or exceeds the capabilities of your machine. Also, check the Frame Size column to see if the clip was captured at an incorrect frame size.

The Browser can also be used to troubleshoot problems with the Batch Capture process. If you are having problems batch-capturing a particular clip, compare the clip's settings in the Browser with others in the project. Check the In and Out point columns as well as the Duration column of your logged clips. I was once called by an editor who said that Final Cut Pro started batch-capturing a clip but never stopped. I asked her to check the duration of her logged clip. She had inadvertently entered a duration of over 10 hours (which is easy to do with a single incorrect keystroke) and Final Cut Pro was merrily attempting to capture over 10 hours of material.

Playing "find the delta" can also be used for troubleshooting in many other areas for Final Cut Pro. For example, if a problem manifests constantly on one Final Cut Pro workstation versus another, try to locate the delta between the two computers.

 For more information on working with the Browser, see Chapter 8.

Troubleshooting common issues

Some common issues can plague most Final Cut Pro users at one time or another. Due to the Final Cut Pro scalable architecture, Final Cut Pro can work with many types of video and audio. This scalability is facilitated by many settings and options that, if not set correctly, can cause a variety of problems. This chapter cannot possibly cover every conceivable issue you may have with Final Cut Pro. However, I have attempted to list the most common trouble spots in the following sections.

Video deck or camera issues

Video devices are a common source of problems when you are working with video in Final Cut Pro. This is especially true if you are using device control to control the camera or deck from within Final Cut Pro. Below are two common problems you may have with your video deck or camera.

Problem:

An Unable to Locate the Capture Device error appears when starting up Final Cut Pro or the DV device is not recognized by Final Cut Pro.

Solutions:

✦ Make sure that the DV device is properly connected to the computer.

✦ Make sure that the DV device (probably a deck or camera) is turned on and set to VCR/VTR. Also, check its power supply to make sure it is properly connected and working.

✦ Confirm that the proper protocol is selected in the Device Control preset.

✦ Quit Final Cut Pro, shut down your computer, and turn your DV device off and then back on. Then restart your computer and Final Cut Pro.

Problem:

Control is limited on certain video device functions.

Solutions:

✦ Make sure that the device control cable is properly connected.

✦ Make sure that the video device is in Remote mode, as opposed to Local. Many professional decks have a Remote/Local switch. The Local setting is used to control the deck from its on-board buttons and controls. The Remote setting allows the control of deck via remote options, such as a computer.

✦ Select the proper protocol in the Device Control preset. If you are using FireWire device control, try switching between the Apple FireWire and Apple FireWire Basic protocols.

✦ Sometimes just simply removing the cable from the FireWire port and reattaching it will solve the problem. (It reinitializes the port, and sometimes that restores the lost or scrambled connection.)

✦ Visit the Apple Final Cut Pro Web site and make sure that your device is approved for use with Final Cut Pro. Often, Apple lists caveats on this site, such as special scripts and extensions that must be used with specific video devices.

Capture issues

Most problems that occur while capturing audio or video pertain to device control and an inability to capture logged clips. When you open the Log and Capture window, you may get some error messages, and the deck status may indicate No Communication or Not Threaded messages. Below are common issues that occur during capture.

Problem:

The Unable to Initialize error message appears when you try to open the Log and Capture window.

Solutions:

✦ Ensure that the DV device control cable or camera control cable is properly connected.

✦ Make sure that the DV device is turned on and set to VCR/VTR (rather than "Camera" setting found on most camcorders).

✦ Close and reopen the Log and Capture window. If the message appears again, restart Final Cut Pro. You might also try to restart the computer.

Problem:

A No Communication indication appears in the deck status window in the Log and Capture window.

Solutions:

✦ Ensure that the DV device control cable or camera control cable is properly connected.

✦ Make sure that the DV device is turned on and set to VCR/VTR (as opposed to the Camera setting found on most camcorders).

✦ If the deck was not powered up when the computer started up, the video deck may not be recognized by Final Cut Pro. Turn on the deck and then restart the computer.

✦ In addition, if you are using a serial cable, it may not be recognized if you plug it in after the computer starts up. Connect the serial cable and then restart the computer.

Cross-
Reference   For more information on device control, see Chapter 4.

Problem:

A Not Threaded indication appears in the deck status window in the Log and Capture window.

Solution:

This message indicates that there is no tape inserted into the video device. Insert a tape, and the message goes away.

Problem:

A Break in Timecode error message appears during capture.

Solutions:

✦ Relog the clips, taking care to avoid timecode breaks.

✦ Recapture the clips that are reported to have timecode breaks.

✦ If you wish to use Final Cut Pro 4's new feature of capturing through timecode breaks, enable this option in the General tab of the User Preferences. Select Final Cut Pro ⇨ User Preferences and select Make New Clip in the pop-up menu after On Timecode Break. Final Cut Pro will complete the capture of the clip up to the timecode break, then capture a new clip starting after the timecode break. For more details about this feature, see Chapter 6.

For more information on timecode breaks, see Chapter 24.

Problem:

The Servo Can't Lock error message appears.

Solutions:

+ This error indicates that the mechanism of the video device was unable to reach proper capture speed quickly enough. Increase the Pre-Roll time in your Device Control preset.

+ For a DV device using FireWire, switch between the Apple FireWire and Apple FireWire Basic protocols under the Device Control settings.

Problem:

Final Cut Pro aborts a batch-capture before the capture is finished.

Solutions:

+ Try batch-capturing again, and during the batch-capture process pay close attention to the text field under the large capture screen that appears on your computer monitor. Here you can see information about each clip as it is captured, and the timecode that Final Cut Pro is looking for when the process is aborted. Use this information to help identify the problem clip. Make sure that the referenced timecode is present on this tape, and look to see if a timecode break is impeding Final Cut Pro's search.

+ If one or more of the clips cannot be captured, sort the clips in the Browser by using the Duration, Media Start, and Media End columns to see where a timecode error may be located. During the logging process, entering an incorrect timecode or an incorrect duration for a capture can easily happen.

Problem:

Final Cut Pro searches for an incorrect timecode.

Solutions:

+ Make sure that your timecode mode for the logged clips is the same as the mode on tape. For example, if the tape is recorded in drop-frame timecode, but you logged your clips in non-drop mode, Final Cut Pro may have problems locating the correct timecode. This problem is common when you manually enter timecodes in the Log and Capture window to create a log for batch capture. To initialize the timecode when logging in Final Cut Pro, simply play any portion of your source video tape and in the Log and Capture window mark an In point. Marking the In point allows Final Cut Pro to read the timecode mode on the tape. Now when you can manually enter the timecodes for your In and Out points, this timecode mode is used.

✦ If you have a timecode break, on your videotape, there is a high probability of duplicate timecodes if the break was caused by the camera resetting its internal timecode clock. Back in your edit suite, when the camera or recorder starts to search for a timecode on your tape, it has no way of knowing *which* repeated timecode you want. The simplest solution to this problem is to make sure the camera or recorder deck is in the same segment of timecode that you want Final Cut Pro to search in. Do this by simply playing the tape and stopping it anywhere around the desired timecode. The Log and Capture function of Final Cut Pro should easily find it at this point.

Cross-Reference

For more information on timecode, see Chapter 24.

Playback issues

Potential problems when working in Final Cut Pro are certainly not limited to the capture process. They are also common when playing back your video. Common playback problems are listed here.

Problem:

When you drop a clip into the Timeline, a red line appears above it, indicating that the clip needs to be rendered.

Solution:

✦ Make sure the Capture Preset settings match those for the Sequence Presets. Select the clip in the Browser and choose Tools ➪ Analyze Movie ➪ Clip to view the properties of the captured clip. Then select the sequence in question and choose Sequence ➪ Settings. Make sure there are no discrepancies between the clip properties and the sequence settings.

Problem:

Video is not visible on the external video monitor.

Solutions:

✦ Check the cable between the computer and the video monitor. If you are using a DV device with FireWire, make sure that the video output of the DV device is feeding the video monitor.

For more information on proper hardware setup, see Chapter 4.

✦ If you are using a FireWire-based setup, make sure the camcorder is set to VCR or VTR mode (as opposed to Camera).

✦ Make sure the Log and Capture window is closed.

✦ If you are using a FireWire-based setup, make sure that the clip is DV compressed. For example, you cannot view MPEG-A compressed clips on an external video monitor using a FireWire-based setup.

✦ Make sure you have selected All Frames or Single Frames in the View ➪ External Video menu.

✦ Check your settings in the A/V Devices tab. Choose Final Cut Pro ➪ Audio/Video Settings and use the A/V Devices tab to change your settings.

Problem:

Playback stutters and skips when you are editing.

Solution:

✦ Check the media codec and make sure it does not use temporal compression built on keyframes. Sorenson and Cinepak are two such codecs.

Problem:

DV clips look soft and of low quality on the computer monitor.

Solutions:

✦ Slower Macintosh G4s drop the quality of DV clips to low resolution in order to maintain full frame rate playback. When this happens, only one-fourth of the DV data is shown on the computer screen. However, this does not affect the final output quality of the clips. It is merely a viewing issue. Video output to an external video monitor will always be high quality. Note that when you pause playback, the quality switches to high resolution on your computer monitor. To see your DV footage play back at full resolution, connect your computer to a camcorder or deck via FireWire. Any preview through the external FireWire devices are decompressed and displayed at their full resolution and frame rate. This is the real image quality of your DV footage, not the footage on your computer monitor.

✦ To force high-quality playback at all times, you need the Final Cut Pro–enabled version of the QuickTime Player. Open the source media file of the clip with QuickTime Player, and choose Get Info from the Movie menu. In the Movie Info window, choose Video Track from the left pop-up menu. Choose High Quality in the right pop-up menu. Check the High Quality Enabled check box to view the movie at full quality. Note that by doing so the frame rate of the movie will decrease substantially. After you save a movie with high quality enabled, it will play at best quality in Final Cut Pro.

Problem:

The external monitor is showing an orange frame with the message "Video card not supported for RT Effects, it may have insufficient video memory or be an unsupported type."

Solution:

✦ Make sure the monitor is connected to a video display card that is compatible with Final Cut Pro.

Other issues

A variety of other common problems may occur as you work with Final Cut Pro. Listing every conceivable issue is impossible; however, I've described the more-common problems here.

Problem:

Final Cut Pro runs sluggishly.

Solutions:

Final Cut Pro does not operate smoothly when OS Virtual Memory is used. Because OS X dynamically employs Virtual Memory when applications require more RAM than is physically available, there is no setting to disable it. There are, however, a few preventative measures you can use to avoid the use of Virtual Memory when you are editing with Final Cut Pro.

✦ Final Cut Pro is a memory intensive program. This means it needs as much RAM as possible to run efficiently and smoothly. Although the minimum amount of RAM recommended by Apple to operate Final Cut Pro 4 is 384 to 512MB, 1GB (or more) is more realistic if you plan to work on any long-form or complex projects.

✦ Under OS X, you can no longer set memory allocation for applications. However, there is a derivation of this in Final Cut Pro that allows you to set the percentage of available RAM Final Cut Pro will use when booting up. By limiting the amount of RAM Final Cut Pro uses, you can avoid, if not minimize, the use of Virtual Memory. Memory usage is set in the Memory & Cache tab in the System Settings.

Cross-Reference   See Chapter 4 for more information on Memory Usage settings in Final Cut Pro.

Problem:

No audio plays through the DV deck, camcorder, or computer speakers.

Solutions:

+ Check your audio cable connections.

+ If you have an external sound system (anything from mere amplified speakers to a high-end system), make sure the power supply is turned on, the volume control is adjusted to the proper level, and that the system is working independent of the computer.

+ Check the waveform on your clip to make sure that it has proper audio.

+ Increase the volume of your computer's audio output. Choose Apple Menu ⇨ System Preferences ⇨ Sound. Adjust the volume on the Output tab. If selected in the Sound pane, a speaker icon in the menu bar allows you to adjust the audio volume of your computer without needing to open System Preferences. Make sure the Mute option is not checked.

+ Check the settings under View ⇨ External Video. If you have selected All Frames, which is used to monitor video using a camcorder or third-party video card, both the video and the audio should play through the external monitor or speakers. The audio is *not* sent to the computer's speakers in this case.

Problem:

The tape deck will not locate the correct timecode for an edit-to-tape operation.

Solutions:

+ Check the timecode mode for the tape you are laying back to. Make sure that the timecode mode matches your entry in the Edit to Tape window.

+ Confirm that the timecode you are asking for in the Edit to Tape window actually exists on tape.

Problem:

You are unable to set an In point when editing to tape.

Solutions:

+ If you are using a brand-new tape, you must first Black and Code the tape to format it with timecode. Rewind the tape to the beginning and Black and Code the tape for at least 30 seconds before attempting to set an In point.

To learn how to Black and Code a tape, turn to Chapter 22.

✦ If you are using a tape that has existing video with blank sections between the video clips, you need to begin the edit-to-tape process on a part of the tape with valid timecode. Otherwise, you must Black and Code the blank section of the tape.

The Tape Deck status area at the bottom center of Edit to Tape window reports any issues or malfunctions you may have during the Edit to Tape process. Keep an eye on that area for indications of trouble.

Problem:

Edit to Tape seems to be functioning properly, but there is no output recorded to the tape.

Solution:

✦ Edit to Tape requires the sequence or clip you are outputting opened in the Viewer *before* Edit to Tape is executed. For more detail on outputting, see Chapter 22.

Problem:

You cannot import an EDL or Batch Capture list.

Solution:

✦ Final Cut Pro cannot import RTF files. *Rich Text Format* is the default format of Apple's TextEdit application. In order to import data in an RTF file, first open it in another text editing program, such as simple text, then save the file as a plain-text document. Final Cut Pro can then import this file format.

Fixing Dropped Frames and Sync Issues

Dropping frames is one of the more common problems you are likely to encounter when working with Final Cut Pro. If you have experience with the Avid or Media 100 editing systems, you are likely to be completely baffled by this dropped frame issue in Final Cut Pro. "I don't remember dropping frames with Avid or Media 100," you might say. If you're new to the video editing process, you might say, "I have no idea what you're talking about. What are dropped frames?" Before you actually fix a dropped-frame issue, you must first know how to spot dropped frames.

Ensuring proper reference

If you are using a third-party video card (such as the Aurora Igniter) and a professional deck, you should make sure that you have the proper reference signal set up for your hardware before conducting any sync tests. *Reference*, also known as *black and sync*, is a signal that is used by production facilities to lock the timing of video equipment. A black burst generator can be used to generate and send a black reference signal to the equipment. The following figure illustrates one such wiring setup using a Horita CSG-50 Sync Generator, a standard Sony broadcast monitor, and a Sony Digital Betacam deck. This setup uses the Aurora Igniter card's component option that has a Genlock input on its breakout box. Of course, a similar setup can be created with any professional-level equipment that has facility for a black reference interface.

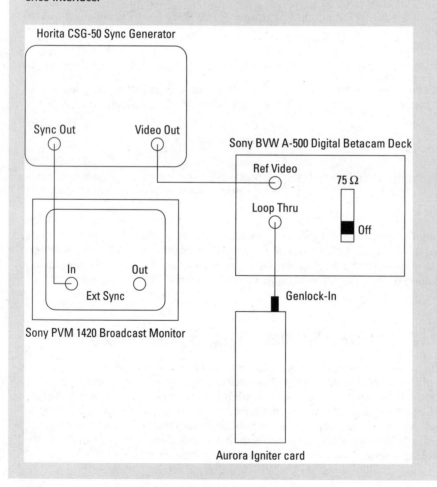

Confirming dropped frames on capture

Final Cut Pro warns you about dropped frames and helps you identify them in a few ways. However, you must have Final Cut Pro configured to warn you when this problem occurs. To ensure that Final Cut Pro warns you about dropped frames, perform the following:

1. **Choose Final Cut Pro ⇨ User Preferences.**

2. **On the General tab, place a check mark next to the following two items:**

   - **Report dropped frames during playback.** This setting causes Final Cut Pro to warn you about dropped frames during playback.

   - **Abort capture on dropped frames options.** Capture is aborted when frames are dropped. This setting must always be enabled during capture if you hope to capture and edit quality material.

Final Cut Pro provides various methods for detecting and confirming dropped frames. These methods include:

   ✦ **A big warning during playback:** Final Cut Pro displays a large warning when your system drops frames during playback. The warning includes a checklist of items that may be causing the problem.

   ✦ **The Capture column in the Browser:** If you select the Abort Capture on Dropped Frames option on the General tab of the Preferences window, Final Cut Pro automatically aborts any captures that drop frames. However, even after capture you can confirm whether or not you have dropped frames by using the Capture column in the Browser. If the Capture column is not visible, Control+click any column heading in the Browser window and choose Show Capture from the contextual menu. The Capture column for clips generally indicates Not Yet, OK, or Queued, depending on the capture status of the clip. However, for a clip with dropped frames, this column will indicate Error in red.

Tip

You can sort the Capture column by clicking its heading. This action places all the clips with the Error indication next to one another. From here, it is simply a matter of selecting and recapturing the frames.

   ✦ **The Analyze window:** Yet another method for confirming dropped frames is to select a suspect clip in the Browser and choose Tools ⇨ Analyze Movie ⇨ Clip. The Movie Analysis window for the selected clip appears. For a clip that doesn't have any dropped frames, the video analysis section ends in the Average Data Rate category. However, if dropped frames are present, the video track section of the report contains an analysis such as:

```
"This track appears to have dropped frames.
      This track contains:
            3021 frames of a duration of 1.0000 frames
            1 frame of a duration of 7.0000 frames
            641 frames of a duration of 2.0000 frames"
```

The exact number of frames and the duration may vary, but a message like this is a sure sign of dropped frames in a clip.

But consider this: When working with Final Cut Pro in a DV and FireWire-based setup, almost every single calculation is being performed on the main processor of the computer. Applications such as Avid and Media 100, on the other hand, use their own high-performance cards to do much of these processor-intensive calculations. Processing digital video the way Final Cut Pro does involves many millions of calculations. Simultaneously capturing DV while displaying it on both the computer and NTSC monitor and handling multiple layers of video and audio tracks is a bit too much even for the vaunted G4 processor. Final Cut Pro walks a delicate balance with the software and the hardware on a computer to perform its work. If all the settings are set correctly, you should never encounter a single dropped frame. But if a setting or two is awry, frames may drop. Dropped frame issues are usually closely related to sync issues. You may find that your audio seems to drift out of sync with the video.

When working with Final Cut Pro, you are likely to drop frames in three places:

✦ **Dropped frames during capture:** Dropping frames during capture is the most serious version of this problem. If you drop frames during capture, the clip stutters and seems to skip when you play it. If you drop frames during capture, you *must* recapture the clips before proceeding. This is the *only* way to fix dropped frames during the capture phase.

✦ **Dropped frames during playback:** Dropping frames during playback is the least serious issue because it may simply represent a performance issue. If you get a large warning about dropped frames during playback, you need to check and adjust all settings that affect playback performance.

✦ **Dropped frames during layback to tape:** Dropped frames during layback or editing to tape is also a serious problem because it means that your final output on tape may be out of sync or may have stutters and skips during layback. You can remedy this performance issue by following the suggestions outlined below.

Solving dropped frames and sync issues

Almost all dropped frame and sync issues are caused by improperly configured hardware or incorrect preference settings. With careful attention to your hardware and settings, you can resolve most dropped frame and sync issues. When you run into dropped frames or sync problems, check the following:

✦ **RAM for Final Cut Pro:** Remember the rule of thumb: Buy as much RAM as you can afford. Think of 1GB as your minimum requirement.

✦ **Virtual Memory:** Make sure that Virtual Memory is not being used by setting the RAM usage in Final Cut Pro, and closing any unnecessary applications. Choose Apple Menu ➪ Control Panels ➪ Memory to check the Virtual Memory status.

Cross-Reference

For more information on Memory control panel settings, see Chapter 4.

✦ **External video settings:** If you're using external speakers connected to a camcorder, deck, or a third-party video card and the External Video setting is set to All Frames, the video shown on your computer monitor in the Viewer or the Canvas window will not be in sync with the audio from your speakers. Instead, the audio will be in sync with the video seen on the external NTSC or PAL monitor. Choose View ➪ External Video to see the current settings.

✦ **Zoomed video in windows:** If you are zoomed in on your video in the Viewer or the Canvas window, dropped frames can result. Choose Fit to Window or Fit All from the View menu in the Viewer or Canvas windows.

✦ **Incorrect window size:** When using a third-party video card such as the Aurora Igniter, the Viewer and Canvas windows must be set to 100% or 50%. Check the user's manual provided with the cards to determine the optimum setting for your windows.

✦ **Overlapping windows:** Make sure that the Viewer and Canvas windows are not overlapping. Overlapping windows places an overhead on screen redraw operations and causes you to drop frames.

✦ **Monitor refresh rate:** You may drop frames if the resolution of your computer monitor is set to 60Hz. The refresh rate of your monitors should always be set to 75Hz or higher to avoid dropped frames. Choose AppleMenu ➪ System Preferences ➪ Displays to select the proper refresh rate. A refresh rate of 75Hz is acceptable, although you get the best performance at 85Hz. For flat-panel LCD monitors, there is no refresh rate setting.

✦ **Incorrect software:** Make sure you have the correct versions of the Mac OS and QuickTime. To check and update the version of all Apple system software:

1. **Choose Apple menu ➪ System Preferences.**

2. **Click on the Software Update pane.**

3. **In the Update Software tab, click the Check Now button.**

   Software Update will scan your installed software and compare it to the latest version available on the Apple Website. If there are newer versions available, they are displayed in a new Software Update dialog box, which allows you to select the updates you want.

4. Select or deselect the items that need updating.

Click on the checkbox in front of each update to select or deselect software updates.

5. When you're done selecting, click on the Install button at the bottom.

The system updates are downloaded *and* installed at this time. In order to use the updated software, you might be required to restart your Mac after installation is finished. If this is the case, you will be prompted by a dialog box. Also, to use the Software Update, your computer must be connected to the Internet.

✦ **A large number of real-time audio tracks:** Choose Apple menu ⇨ System Preferences and check the Real-Time Audio Mixing field on the General tab. If you have set a higher number of tracks than your computer can handle, you are bound to drop frames. When you reduce the number of real-time audio tracks, you render the audio in your sequence, your playback performance improves.

✦ **Slow disk drives:** You will get dropped frames if you capture to drives that are not rated for audio/video capture. For example, most internal drives that come with new Apple computers are capable of handling DV video capture and playback. However, by adding numerous audio tracks and video layers, it is easy to exceed the capacity of these drives during playback and layback to tape. It is highly recommended that you use a drive other than your main system drive as your capture drive for audio and video media.

For more information on selecting proper drives for media capture and storage, see Chapter 4.

✦ **Fragmented disks:** Fragmentation on disk drives occurs when numerous files are captured, stored, or deleted, and then the space on the drives is reused again for more captures, storage, and deletions. The disk is said to be *fragmented* because empty spaces are scattered all over the physical disk surface and new files must be broken up into smaller fragments by the operating system to fit on the disk. To avoid this, try to maintain separate drives specifically reserved for video and audio capture. Avoid installing applications and utilities on these drives. Three common solutions for fragmented drives are:

- **Recapture the files:** Apple recommends that you quit Final Cut Pro and delete all media files from the fragmented drive. Be sure to only delete material that can be recaptured; don't delete project files or graphics that are not backed up. When you restart your project, all your files will be offline. Select them all and recapture them by using batch capture. You should only use this method on smaller projects; on larger projects, deleting all your files can be risky.

- **Move the files:** You can move all your files from the fragmented disk to another disk with sufficient space. The process of moving files defragments them on the volume to which they are copied. Restarting Final Cut Pro automatically starts the process of relinking to the files on the new drive. You can then capture more material to the old fragmented drive.

- **Use defragmentation software:** Many third-party applications such as Norton Speed Disk, Alsoft DiskExpress Pro, and TechTool Pro allow you to check and repair the fragmentation on your drives. Use these applications between large projects. If you need to defragment during a project, back up your Final Cut Pro project file before defragmenting your drive.

✦ **Too many open sequences:** If you have dropped-frame issues during playback or layback to tape, make sure that only the current and relevant sequence is open. Keeping numerous sequences open, especially ones with many clips and edits, seriously erodes your playback performance. Control+click each sequence's tab and choose Close Tab from the contextual menu.

✦ **The Mirror on Desktop setting:** Choose Final Cut Pro ⇨ Audio/Video Settings and click the A/V Devices tab. You will see settings labeled Mirror on desktop under the Playback Output section and Different Output for Edit to Tape/Print to Video. If you are dropping frames during layback to tape, try turning off the Mirror on desktop in the Different Output for Edit to Tape/Print to Video section. Doing so disables the recording preview on your computer monitor, thus giving better performance due to a lack of overhead for screen redraw on the computer monitor. This technique is especially useful on older, slower computers.

✦ **Mixed sample rates:** One frequent cause of a loss of audio and video sync is the mixing of audio sample rates when working with DV-based footage. For example, if you shoot in the field with your camera set to record 16-bit (48kHz) audio, and then you capture that same audio into Final Cut Pro at 12-bit (32kHz), you are quite likely to create sync issues. You may further create an offset by mixing these clips into a sequence that is set to yet another sampling rate, such as 44.1kHz. Pay close attention to your audio sampling rates at all times. Keep the rates consistent from the tape through capture, editing, and output back to tape.

Testing hard drives

Ideally, you should be using hard drives that are rated for audio and video capture and playback. If you are working with DV-based video and a FireWire signal path, you have little to worry about. The data rate for DV video is a consistent 3.6MB/sec. Most Apple computers these days have internal drives that are fully capable of handling the capture and playback of DV video.

Cross-Reference Chapter 4 covers details about recommended hard drives and their specifications.

Working with analog video can present some additional storage challenges, however. Analog data rates can vary dramatically. Rates of 8 to 10MB/sec are common. If you are working with high-data-rate analog video, you will need drives that are rated for high-data-rate capture and playback. However, if you are unsure about the data rates that your current drives can handle, you can perform checks on your drives to determine their throughput rate.

Determining disk-drive throughput

As helpful as a disk benchmark utility is in determining the data rate of disk drives, it still does not represent the real *throughput* of your system. *Throughput* is a general term used to describe the final working data-rate capacity of your system after all the overheads have been taken into account. For example, a benchmark utility cannot address the processor speed or the performance of Final Cut Pro. Hence, you need to determine the real-world data rate, or throughput, of your system. With analog video, you can determine throughput by performing a simple test. In this test, you simply raise the data rate of your capture until dropped frames are reported.

Caution This test only works with analog video. When working with DV video, this test is not necessary.

In the following steps, I will assume that you are working with the Aurora Igniter capture card. Most other cards should follow a similar logic and steps, however. To determine the throughput of your drives:

1. **Start Final Cut Pro.**

2. **Choose Edit ⇨ Preferences.**

3. **On the General tab of the User Preferences window, turn on the Abort capture on dropped frames option. Click OK to close the window.**

4. **Choose Final Cut Pro ⇨ System Settings,**

5. **In the Scratch Disks tab, select a Scratch Disk for your video and audio capture.**

   This drive should be the one you are attempting to check.

6. **Click OK when you are done.**

7. **Choose Final Cut Pro ⇨ Audio/Video Settings.**

8. **Click the Capture Presets tab in the Audio/Video Settings window.**

9. **Select an Aurora preset (or the analog preset for the card you are using) and click Edit.**

The Capture Preset Editor window appears as shown in Figure 28-1.

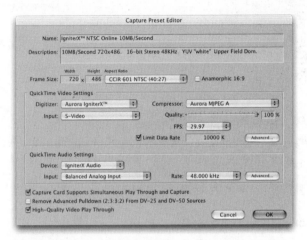

Figure 28-1: Use settings in the Capture Preset Editor window to test the throughput of your system.

10. **In the Limit Data Rate field, enter 3000K (for 3MB/sec).**

11. **Click OK to close the window.**

12. **Capture a video clip from tape.**

Select a length of approximately one to three minutes. This guarantees a length that would test your drive for a sufficient time period.

13. **If no dropped frames are reported and Final Cut Pro does not abort capture due to dropped frames, repeat Steps 6 through 10 and increase the data rate by 0.5MB/sec to 3500K.**

If you do drop frames, check this chapter for eliminating the dropped-frame issues.

14. **Now you must recapture the same clip. Select the clip you captured in Step 11 and Control+click it.**

A contextual menu appears.

15. **Choose Make Offline.**

The Make Offline dialog box appears as shown in Figure 28-2.

Figure 28-2: Delete the media for your previously captured clip in preparation for recapture at the new data rate.

16. **Select the Delete Them from the Disk option and click OK.**

    A warning appears indicating that this step is not undoable.

17. **Click OK to approve this step.**

    The media for the clip is deleted, and the clip becomes offline with a red line across it.

18. **Select the offline clip and choose File ➪ Batch Capture.**

    Recapture the clip at the new data rate of 3500K.

19. **Repeat Steps 6 through 15, increasing the data rate of your captures by 0.5MB (or 500K) each time, until Final Cut Pro aborts capture and reports dropped frames.**

This process helps you determine the throughput of your editing system. From the final figure deduct 1MB (or 1000K) and set that as the maximum data rate at which you should capture clips.

Troubleshooting Sound Distortion Issues

Another common problem you may encounter in Final Cut Pro is sound distortion. Noises such as popping, crackling, or static may occur when working with audio in Final Cut Pro. Most audio distortions heard in Final Cut Pro have two main causes:

✦ **Mixed sample rates during capture:** A common reason for sound distortion in Final Cut Pro is when users capture audio from a DV tape at a sampling rate that is different from the one used on the tape during the original recording. For example, if a sampling rate of 32kHz was used when recording in the field, but this audio is then captured into Final Cut Pro at 48kHz, sound distortion (as well as sync problems) may occur.

    ✦ **Mixed sample rates during playback:** Mixing clips with different sampling rates in a sequence may also create distortion and static.

Caution

Before you start changing settings within Final Cut Pro to fix audio distortion issues, first *confirm* that the issue originates in Final Cut Pro. An easy way to do this is to locate the source media file for the clip with the distorted sound. Play the source media file using the QuickTime Player. If the sound distortion is present in the audio track even when playing with the QuickTime Player, then clearly the settings within Final Cut Pro are not the problem. If, however, the clip sounds clean and distortion-free in the QuickTime Player, then clearly something is wrong with the settings in Final Cut Pro.

Fixing audio distortion during capture

Most audio distortion is caused by an error in the capture process. If you capture a clip into Final Cut Pro at the wrong sampling rate, you may get static and audio pops. DV tapes are recorded at two different sampling rates:

    ✦ 32kHz or 12 bit

    ✦ 48kHz or 16 bit

Many DV cameras and decks display the audio sampling rate during playback. You should always try to ascertain the original sampling rate before you create a Capture Preset in Final Cut Pro for the audio. Generally, you should try to record DV tapes at the 48kHz or 16-bit setting.

When creating a capture preset, make sure that the sampling rate of the Capture Preset is set to the same rate as the original audio on the DV tape.

Cross-Reference

For more information on creating Capture Presets, see Chapter 6.

Fixing audio distortion during playback

You are also likely to encounter audio distortion during playback. Again, a combination of too many different sampling rates being mixed together is usually the distortion culprit during the playback stage. You may even get some skips in the audio playback if too many sample rates are mixed together in one sequence.

Tip

Final Cut Pro and most digital audio workstations are better at up-sampling than down-sampling. For this reason, if you do have clips with both 44.1kHz and 48kHz sampling rates in a sequence, set the sequence's sampling rate to 48kHz, and not 44.1kHz.

Playback distortion is common when you use CD audio tracks in a sequence. CD audio usually has a sampling rate of 44.1kHz. Although Apple engineers claim that this won't cause a problem when used in a 48kHz sequence, you should still try to maintain a uniform sampling rate throughout the sequence. To prevent distortion, export all your CD tracks at 48kHz (if that is the sampling rate used by your sequence) and then re-import them back into the sequence.

Cross-Reference   To learn more about exporting CD audio and re-importing it, see Chapter 14.

Occasionally, your final audio mix may be distorted due to a high, unwanted dynamic range. In that case, you can apply the Compressor/Limiter audio filter located in the Audio Filters folder of the Effects tab in the Browser. Apply this effect to clips with unwanted dynamic range and adjust the settings to eliminate the distortion. The only caution I offer is not to overdo the Ratio parameter on this filter. Adjust the Threshold (which defines how loud the loudest portion of the clip can be before compression is applied), Attack Time (how quickly the filter reacts), and Release Time (which defines how slowly the filter lets go). The default settings on this filter are usually fine, and a lot of tweaking often provides unsatisfactory results.

Troubleshooting Timecode Errors

Final Cut Pro is designed to capture frame-accurate timecode from a variety of sources. You can use timecode from DV, as well as SMPTE timecode used in professional decks and videotape formats. Timecode is the yardstick for everyone who works with video. Timecode allows you to identify any frame on your tape.

Final Cut Pro uses timecode for a variety of very critical functions. For example, functions such as recapturing and using the Media Mover rely heavily on accurate and reliable timecode. Any EDL (Edit Decision List) that is exported is only as accurate and reliable as the timecode that came with the original clips.

Keep your eye on three issues when trying to create reliable timecode in Final Cut Pro:

✦ Maintain correct reel numbers.

✦ Avoid timecode breaks.

✦ Calibrate timecode offset.

How you approach timecode issues depends on the type of timecode you are working with in Final Cut Pro. Final Cut Pro can capture timecode in one of two different ways. The first is using a FireWire cable, which is used as a standard interface with DV devices. The other method of obtaining timecode is with a serial device control, such as the RS-232 or RS-422 machine control found on most professional-level video tape recorders.

Issues with FireWire device control

The main issue to watch out for when using FireWire-based device control is that each mini-DV tape switches to a starting timecode of 00:00:00:00 when you start recording. Unlike DVCAM and other professional level formats, mini-DV does not have the ability to set a user selectable timecode. In professional environments, production personnel set the starting timecode for each tape to represent the tape number. The first tape starts at 1:00:00:00, the second one at 2:00:00:00, the third one at 3:00:00:00, and so on. You cannot do this with mini-DV-based camcorders. Before capturing from these tapes, you must physically label each individual tape and be diligent about changing reel numbers in the Log and Capture window as you switch reels.

Any timecode break on a mini-DV tape resets the timecode back to 00:00:00:00. To avoid confusion, label sections of mini-DV tape separated by timecode breaks with letters. For example, if a tape were labeled Tape 1, the same tape would be labeled Tape 1a after the first timecode break. If another timecode break occurs, the tape is labeled Tape 1b. This labeling system is crucial for the logging and capturing process. During log and capture, you should be sure to change the reel number to Tape 1a or Tape 1b when capturing from the appropriate section from the tape *even though it is still physically the same tape.* If you are recapturing from such a tape, shuttle forward past the timecode break before you start recapturing from the Tape 1a or Tape 1b sections.

Issues with serial device control

If you are using serial device control (such as RS-232 or RS-422 device control), you experience two common sources of timecode problems — timecode breaks and timecode offset calibration. Timecode breaks most often occur when a videotape is started or stopped while it is being recorded, and a gap appears in the timecode track of the tape. This gap can occur if the camera or the deck is powered off while being used, as well as for other reasons. Timecode breaks do not necessarily occur after every shot, but they are not hard to come by on source material that was shot in the field. During the log and capture phase it is all too easy out of sheer laziness to log and capture long sections of the tape. (I know, I've been an editor for a long time.) However, in doing so, you are likely to capture a timecode break somewhere within that long section.

If you capture a long clip across a timecode break, you need to remember that all timecode past the point of the break will be incorrect. This can cause major problems because you will be unable to recapture portions of the tape that lie after the timecode break. This is true even if you are using Final Cut Pro's new option to Create a New Clip on timecode break. Although the capture was successfully batch-captured, if you try to recapture it later, there is no way for Final Cut Pro to know which side of the timecode break to recapture from.

The other timecode problem common when using serial device control is trouble with timecode offset calibration. This can be calibrated using the Timecode Offset field on the Device Control Presets tab under Final Cut Pro ➪ Audio/Video Settings. You have to select a Device Control preset and click Edit to edit the timecode offset. This timecode offset allows you to account for any offset that may exist between a deck and Final Cut Pro. Often the timecode that Final Cut Pro captures is off by a few frames from the true timecode on the tape. This setting must be calibrated before capturing media. In an editing house with many edit workstations, this timecode-offset calibration is critical because it allows projects to be edited at a variety of workstations.

 Cross-Reference To learn how to calibrate the Timecode Offset, see Chapter 24.

Deleting Final Cut Pro Preferences

When troubleshooting in Final Cut Pro, a possible remedy for some problems is to delete the Final Cut Pro preferences file. In Final Cut Pro 4.0, this file is called Final Cut Pro 4.0 Preferences. However, there is a very good reason why I have placed this section at the very end of a troubleshooting chapter: Deleting the Final Cut Pro Preferences file should be done as a last resort, after all other troubleshooting avenues have been exhausted.

 Caution The Final Cut Pro preferences file contains user preferences for scratch disk settings, some window layouts, capture presets, sequence presets, and more. Deleting the preferences file restores Final Cut Pro to the default settings.

To prevent the loss of all your settings when you delete your preferences file, you should make a backup of the file. Copy and store the Preferences file in a safe place. Making a backup of the Preferences makes it easy to delete the preferences file as part of a troubleshooting operation, because you know that you can restore the backed up Preferences file to get your settings and preferences back.

Follow these steps to delete the Final Cut Pro Preferences file:

1. **Quit Final Cut Pro.**

2. **Delete the Final Cut Pro Preferences file.**

    The directory path of the Final Cut Pro preferences file is:

    ```
    Boot Volume/User/User name/Library/Preferences/Final Cut Pro
    User Data
    ```

    Do not delete any other file in the Preferences folder. Figure 28-3 shows the Final Cut Pro Preferences file in the Final Cut Pro Data folder.

Figure 28-3: Deleting the Final Cut Pro Preferences file can serve as a last-resort troubleshooting technique.

3. **Restart Final Cut Pro.**

✦   ✦   ✦

Working with Mac OS X

The Macintosh, in my opinion, is a magical computer. I've never had so much fun as when I am playing with a Mac. Oops! I meant *working* with a Mac. But that's the joy of owning one. Working with a Mac is just plain fun. As the battle for platform superiority continues to rage between the Mac-heads and the Windows proponents, there is one point that is obvious: Macintosh owners really *love* their computers. I've heard users of other platforms tout their superiority, but I've never heard them say that they love their boxy, beige computers. A key ingredient of the Macintosh's appeal has always been its graphic-based operating system. Macintosh Operating System (Mac OS) is one of the many operating systems available for personal computers. However, Final Cut Pro is an Apple product that was designed to work solely with the Macintosh computer.

Two years ago, Apple bravely revamped the Macintosh Operating System with the release of OS X. (The Operating System prior to OS X was OS 9, so OS X is also referred to correctly as OS 10.*x.*) Rewritten from the ground up, OS X jettisoned the proprietary code used in all the earlier Mac Operating Systems. Instead, OS X is Unix-based code that is extremely stable and capable of true multitasking. Its proven architecture is used by many mainframe systems and dedicated graphic workstations. The OS X interface not only retains the Mac's graphic user interface (GUI), its enhanced graphics and operating functions have once again captured the hearts of Mac owners and users. Perhaps it's a good time to point out that Final Cut Pro 4 will only operate properly on Mac OS X, or more specifically, OS 10.2.5 or later.

History lessons aside, the Mac OS is full of hidden features designed to make your life easier. In this chapter, you tour the Macintosh operating system and explore the many hidden features and options that may come in handy as you work with Final Cut Pro.

Understanding the Mac Operating System

If you're reading this book, chances are you're at least familiar with Mac OS X. There are entire books written about Mac OS X, but if you're new to Macs or OS X, a brief overview is useful. The next few sections introduce you to some of the basic concepts of Mac OS 10.2, also known as Jaguar, including some key differences from the previous version of the Mac OS. To that end, the focus of this chapter will be on the features and controls that most impact you when working with Final Cut Pro.

Understanding the System Folder and the Finder

Unlike previous versions of the Mac OS, OS X does not have a System Folder, per se, but it now has a folder called System, which is located on the main level of your Startup hard drive. The System folder contains the operating system (OS) software that makes your Mac run and cannot (and should not) be changed. When the computer powers up (generally known as the *boot-up process*), the OS loads into the Random Access Memory (RAM), where it manages all tasks running on your computer. The OS remains loaded in the RAM until the machine is powered down.

The System contains most of the code and functions to run your computer. It communicates with hardware devices and between applications to perform all kinds of nifty functions: Windows are drawn, functions are called, calculations are performed, dialog boxes are opened, and various files perform other work. The System folder Icon is shown in Figure 29-1.

 Caution   It is critical to the proper operation of your Macintosh that the System folder and its content not be moved or renamed. This applies to any OS X installed folders and files, including the Library folder where system preferences are stored.

    Figure 29-1: The System folder is located on your main hard drive.

System

The Finder is the main screen that appears when you start your Macintosh and will look something like Figure 29-2. The main window is also called the *desktop*. This desktop provides the graphical interface to help you interact with your computer. You can work in the Finder to make new folders, open files, launch applications, and perform other tasks on your Mac.

Desktop

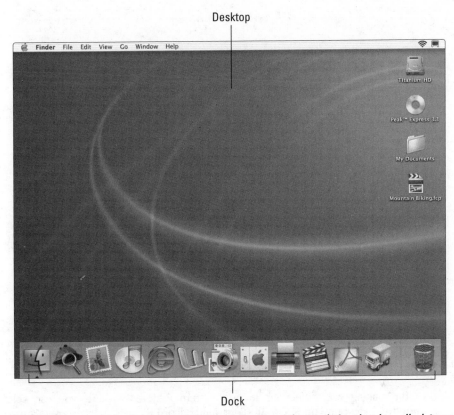

Dock

Figure 29-2: With the addition of the Dock and its enhanced visual style, called Aqua, the Finder in OS X is much like the Finder of the previous Mac OS.

Understanding the System Preferences panel

Under OS X, separate Control Panels and Extensions are a thing of past. Actually, many of these useful mini-applications and system enhancers are not truly extinct, but rather have been folded into the Mac OS and consolidated into one centralized window called the System Preferences panel. Access the System Preferences panel by choosing System Preferences under the Apple icon. The System Preferences panel, shown in Figure 29-3 is divided up into separate panes that represent the different OS parameters you can modify.

To make changes to any settings, click on the System Preference pane you wish to modify. All available controls for that parameter will appear. Most Preferences will update in real time as you choose them. Selecting another pane to modify or closing the System Preferences panel altogether will accept and save all settings selections.

Figure 29-3: The System Preferences panel is where you set various OS options.

Tip After making your selections in one System Preference pane, you can select another by clicking on Show All (light switch icon) in the top-left corner. You will once again see all the Systems Preferences available for modification.

If you install any third-party utilities, drivers, or OS X "helper" applications, any controls for these will appear in an additional pane, called Others at the bottom of System Preferences panel.

Logging In on OS X

Under OS X, multiple users of one computer can set up their own User account that creates dedicated files and folders with user access privileges. The boon of this function for Final Cut Pro users is that application preferences are saved to the User's preference folders, thus preserving all your project and system settings, especially your scratch disk selection, no matter how many others are sharing your computer. Just remember to Log In before you begin working, and don't let others work under your User account (Log Out when you're finished working on your project).

Creating a User Account

You'll need to create your User Account to Log In and Out. You can have this done by a user with Administer access privileges, or do it yourself when you're logged in as an Administer:

1. **Select System Preferences from the Apple menu icon.**

2. **Click on the Accounts pane in the System section at the bottom of the System Preferences Panel.**

3. **In the Users tab of the Accounts window, click on New User.**

   A new window appears with fields and options to set up your User account. This window is shown in Figure 29-4.

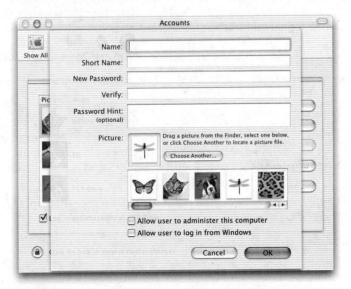

Figure 29-4: Fill out this form to set up your User Account.

4. **Fill in the Name field.**

   This User name will appear in the Log In dialog box. You can modify it at any time.

5. **Fill in Short Name carefully.**

   The name you enter here will be used for all access privileges. The name you enter is case-sensitive and cannot be modified, even if you change the User name. It is best to choose an easily remembered name, but for security reasons, preferably not exactly the same as the User name.

6. **Enter a Password, and then enter it again in the Verify field to confirm it.**

   A password hint is optional and is displayed after a number of failed attempts of incorrectly entered passwords.

7. **Select a picture for your User account display in the Log In dialog box.**

8. **Check additional options.**

   Check the appropriate options if you want administrator status or will need to log in remotely from a Windows computer.

9. **Click OK to create a new User account.**

Logging In and Out of your User account

Logging In and Logging Out is easy once your account is set up. If you are booting up your computer, the Log In dialog box will automatically display after the startup cycle is completed. If the Macintosh is already booted, you will have to log out first:

1. **Select Log Out from the Apple menu icon, or press Command+Shift+Q.**

   A dialog box will appear to confirm your intentions to Log Out. You can cancel the Log Out procedure if you need to.

2. **Click Log Out.**

   If there are any open files that need to be saved, you will be presented with a dialog box for each to Save, Don't Save, or Cancel. When in doubt, always choose Save. Choosing Cancel will stop the quitting of the application and the Log Out.

   When all applications are finished closing, the Desktop will display only the Log In dialog box.

To Log In using your User account:

1. **Click on your User name or icon in the Log In dialog list.**

2. **Enter your password in the next dialog box.**

3. **Click the Log In button in the bottom-right corner, or press Enter.**

Your Desktop and files appear as you last left them. More importantly, your Final Cut Pro settings are sure to be yours (if no one has worked with Final Cut Pro in your User account) and *not* the settings of the last user of Final Cut Pro.

After the first time you Open and save a Final Cut Pro project, a Final Cut Pro Preference folder and file is created in the directory Startup Volume/Users/*User Account*/Library/Preferences/Final Cut Pro User Data, shown in Figure 29-5.

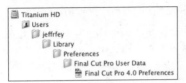

Figure 29-5: By default, Final Cut Pro saves a Preference file in the Final Cut Pro User Data folder, which is located in the User's Preferences folder as shown here.

Setting access privilege

Whenever a new file is created by saving a project, capturing media, or creating computer graphics, its access privilege is set to the system default of Read & Write for the file's Owner and Read Only for all others. If you need to change the access privilege of a file, say to let another user work on your project, do the following:

1. **Select the file in the Finder that you want to modify, by clicking on it once to highlight it.**

   Don't double-click on it. You don't want to open it, just select it.

2. **Choose File ➪ Get Info, or press Command+I.**

3. **In the item's Info window, click on the disclosure button in front of Ownership and Permissions.**

   This will reveal the three classes of Users and their access privileges, shown in Figure 29-6.

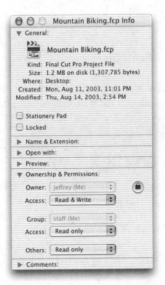

Figure 29-6: Access privileges are modified in the Info window of a file.

4. Select a User and set his access privilege in the Access pop-up menu.

The easiest and quickest way to allow anyone access to a file is set Others (meaning other users) to Read & Write, as shown in Figure 29-7.

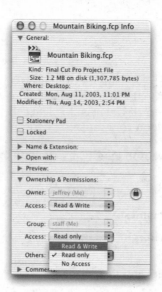

Figure 29-7: Changing the Access privilege of Others to Read & Write allows anyone to access your file.

Note   You must be the Owner of the file or have administrative privilege in order to change the access privilege of a file.

5. Close the Info window to save the modifications.

Tip   Because FireWire drives are hot swappable, Mac OS X sees them as removable media and sets the default Read & Write privileges for all Users for all contents of the drive.

Installing Fonts and Plug-ins on OS X

The fonts available for use by Final Cut Pro can be installed into two different folders. The default Fonts folder is located in the Library folder on startup volume. It's very important that you know this is the Library folder on the *same* root level as the OS X System folder, and not the Library folder *inside* the System folder. If you want to add a font that will be available to all users of Final Cut Pro, copy it into the Font folder located in the root-level Library folder. This is shown in Figure 29-8.

If you want to install a font accessible to only a single User logged in OS X's multiuser environment (like yourself), then copy the font into the Fonts folder in the Library folder located *in the individual's Users folder,* also found in the root level of the startup volume directory, as shown in Figure 29-9.

Figure 29-8: Fonts installed into the root-level Library Fonts folder will be available to all Final Cut Pro Users logged onto your computer.

CORRECT
Library/Font
folder

WRONG
Library/Font
folder

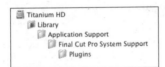

Figure 29-9: Fonts installed into a User's Library Fonts folder will available only to that User when logged on to the computer.

Third-party plug-ins, including any you might create yourself using the FXBuilder, are like fonts in that they can be installed in two different locations, depending on how you limit access to them. To make a plug-in available to all Final Cut Pro Users, copy it into: Startup Volume/Library/Application Support/Final Cut Pro System Support/Plugins. Figure 29-10 shows a hierarchal directory path to this folder.

Figure 29-10: Install plug-ins into this Plugins folder so that they'll show up in the Effects tab of all Final Cut Pro Users logged onto your computer.

To limit the access of the plug-in to a selected User, install the plug-in into Home/Library/Preferences/Final Cut Pro User Data/Plugins, shown in Figure 29-11.

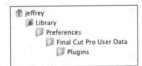

Figure 29-11: Install a plug-in into this Plugins folder to limit the access of it to the selected User.

Allocating memory to Final Cut Pro

Computers ship with different amounts of RAM preinstalled, although you can purchase and install additional RAM. When you open a file on a Mac, it is loaded into the computer memory, called RAM (Random Access Memory). In addition to the data of the file being opened, it should be pointed out that the application running the file, the operating system, extensions, and other utilities all take their own bite out of the computer's total RAM as well.

To use Final Cut Pro, Apple recommends that you have a minimum of 384MB of RAM installed in your computer; 512MB is recommended to add Soundtrack and RT Extreme. However, for real-world use, 1GB or more is preferable.

"Why so much memory?" you might ask. In order for Final Cut Pro to perform its feats of editing magic, it requires a fast CPU, hence the G4 minimum processor requirement, and *tons* of RAM. But there is another very important reason to install as much RAM as you can mortgage: Final Cut Pro has never run smoothly when virtual memory was enabled in the OS System Preferences — it still doesn't. But in OS X, there is no longer an option to turn off virtual memory or allocate RAM for most native OS X applications. In Final Cut Pro, however, you can set a *percentage* of unused RAM allocated to Final Cut Pro at startup, which can prevent the Mac OS from using virtual memory unnecessarily. To set this RAM allocation for Final Cut Pro:

1. **Start Final Cut Pro application.**

2. **Go to System Settings under the menu heading Final Cut Pro or press Shift+Q.**

3. **Click on the Memory & Cache tab.**

   Figure 29-12 shows this preference tab.

4. **If the Application slider is not at 100 percent (all the way to the right), set it there.**

   Or you can click in the Application percentage field, type 100, and press Enter.

5. **Note the amount of unused RAM currently available in parenthesis to the right of the slider.**

   This tells you how much RAM you currently have allocated to Final Cut Pro less the RAM used by the OS.

6. **Move the Application slider to the left to allocate less RAM to Final Cut Pro when it starts up.**

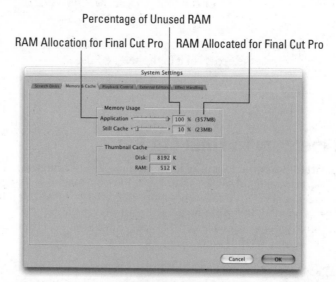

Percentage of Unused RAM

RAM Allocation for Final Cut Pro   RAM Allocated for Final Cut Pro

Figure 29-12: The Memory & Cache preference setting allows you to allocate RAM for Final Cut Pro.

Allow for some unexpected RAM overhead and one or two smaller applications to run concurrently with Final Cut Pro. If the total of RAM used by Final Cut Pro and the other applications does not exceed the total amount of unused RAM available as noted in Step 5, then virtual memory will not be used, or at worst, used minimally.

Note

The minimum RAM needed to run Final Cut Pro is 125MB. If you have less than this available, the slider will be dimmed.

7. **Click OK to accept changes.**

8. **Save your project by pressing Command+S.**

9. **Quit Final Cut Pro.**

Your RAM allocation changes will be used at the next restart of Final Cut Pro.

Startup key combinations

By holding down certain keys while booting up your Mac, you can perform many critical functions. Some functions allow you to disable certain items that may be causing a problem, and others can force your Mac to behave in one way or another. Table 29-1 lists the available keyboard combinations and the functions that they perform when starting up your Macintosh.

Table 29-1
Macintosh Startup Key Combinations

Key Combination	Action
C	Start up from CD/DVD.
Option	Select a startup disk (only works on some models). Allows you to select from all bootable Systems, include any pre–OS X systems, and volumes.
Shift	Prevents startup items from opening. Also, closes any Finder windows that were open at the last shutdown or restart.
Shift+Mouse down	Holding down the *left* shift key and the mouse button when you see the progress bar loading will prevent any automatic Log In.
Command+ Option+P+R	Reset PRAM (see sidebar "What's in a PRAM?" for more information).
Command+V	Show console messages (verbose mode).
Command+S	Start up in single user mode.
Command+X	Start up using Mac OS X instead of Mac OS 9.
N	During the startup process, pressing and holding down the N key forces the Mac to start up from the network. This combination was originally designed for iMac computers.

What's in a PRAM?

"Zapping the PRAM" is a common step taken during troubleshooting a Mac. By the way, clearing the PRAM (Parameter RAM) also clears the NVRAM (Non-volatile RAM) if your Mac happens to have it. Starting up the Mac while holding down Command+Option+P+R will give a second startup chime, which indicates the PRAM and NVRAM have been "zapped," or cleared. Simply stated, Parameter RAM (PRAM) is a small bit of memory where settings are saved when the computer is powered off. But have you ever wondered what exactly is in the PRAM?

Following is a list of the contents of the PRAM. Take a close look at this list because items such as status of AppleTalk, monitor depth, and memory panel settings affect the performance of Final Cut Pro. If you plan to clear the PRAM, be sure to go back and check these items before working with Final Cut Pro. Note that not all Macs may have all these items present in the PRAM.

PRAM or parameter RAM contains the following settings (settings that affect Final Cut Pro are indicated by an asterisk):

✦ Status of AppleTalk*

✦ Serial Port Configuration and Port definition*

✦ Application font

✦ Printer location

✦ Autokey rate

✦ Autokey delay

✦ Speaker Volume*

✦ Attention or beep sound

✦ Double-click time

✦ Caret blinking rate (insertion point rate)

✦ Mouse scaling (mouse speed)

✦ Startup disk

✦ Menu blink count

✦ Monitor depth*

✦ 32-bit addressing

✦ RAM Disk*

✦ Disk Cache*

Now when you hear people talk about zapping the PRAM, you'll actually know what you're zapping!

Navigating the Mac OS X Interface

In Mac OS X, the most conspicuous changes are to the Finder. The new, elegant look of the Finder desktop, as seen in icons that have three-dimensional modeling and highlights, Finder windows with rounded corners, drop shadows and semi-transparent title bars, only reveals some aspects of OS X's interface, dubbed Aqua. Of the dozens of new operational features in OS X, two in particular, the Dock and the Column view, will help you navigate in the Finder more efficiently when working with Final Cut Pro.

Understanding the Dock

The Dock is a new feature of the OS X Finder that replaces the Applications menu from previous versions of the Mac OS. The Dock, shown in Figure 29-13, is a floating bar area from where you can launch or select applications, documents, and other frequently used items.

Figure 29-13: The Dock is a main component of the OS X Finder.

Any application currently open will be shown in the Dock with a small black triangle below it and can be activated by simply clicking on its icon. When you want to add a frequently used file, folder, application, or even a disk volume to the Dock, there are many ways to do this:

✦ From the Desktop, just drag the icon from the Finder onto the Dock. Applications can only be docked to the left of the thin separator line, while all other documents and files will only be accepted to the right.

✦ If the application is currently open and running, click and hold down on its icon in the Dock, and select Keep in Dock from the pop-up menu. When you close the application, the icon for the application will remain in the Dock and can be launched from there by simply clicking on it.

✦ To dock an open window, click on the middle, *minimize* button in the upper-left corner of the window, or double-click on the window's title bar. As shown in Figure 29-14, the minimize button will display a minus sign when the cursor is near or above it.

When you want to work with a docked window or document, or application, simply click on its Dock icon and it will open out onto the Desktop, selected and ready to be worked on. This works for launching a closed document or application stored in the Dock.

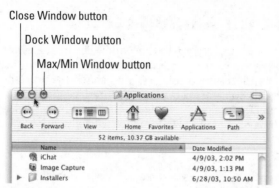

Close Window button

Dock Window button

Max/Min Window button

Figure 29-14: Use the window control buttons in the top-left corner of Finder windows to close, dock, or resize the window.

The last option of docking open windows can be very useful when working with Final Cut Pro and limited monitor real estate. As an option to rearranging or closing inactive Final Cut Pro windows, I often dock program windows in the Dock until I need them. The great thing about this is when you activate a window that is docked, it appears *exactly* where it was positioned before it was docked so you don't need to rearrange your window layout.

Viewing Windows in Column View

In previous versions of the Mac OS, there were two ways to view the contents of a Finder window—View as Icons and View as List. Both of these viewing options are still available in OS X, with the addition of View as Columns. Figure 29-15 shows the same Finder Window viewed in the three different ways.

The best keyboard shortcut ever

When working with Final Cut Pro, the handiest keyboard shortcut I have ever come across is simply holding down the Option key and clicking on the desktop. If you are working in Final Cut Pro and you invoke this shortcut, Final Cut Pro hides from view, and you switch to the Finder level. You may find this shortcut useful because Final Cut Pro takes up all of the screen space, and occasionally you may need to go to the Finder to look at some other items. Of course, you can also return to the Finder by using the application icons in the upper-right corner of the computer screen, but the shortcut is a much faster way.

When you are done working in the Finder, you can quickly return to Final Cut Pro by pressing Command+Tab. This shortcut toggles you through the hidden applications. By using a combination of these two easy shortcuts, you can hide Final Cut Pro and bring it back to view in the fastest manner possible.

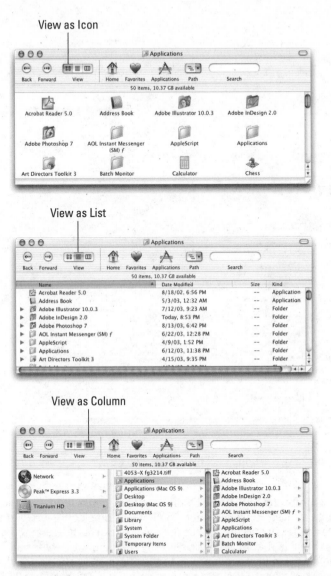

Figure 29-15: You can view the contents of a Finder window three different ways.

You can select the viewing option of a Finder window when it is active by choosing it from the View menu, or by clicking on the View button in the toolbar of the Finder window, detailed in Figure 29-16. The column view is a horizontal hierarchal display showing each directory level *down* in the column to the *right*. Figure 29-16 shows the correlation between the List and Column views.

View as List

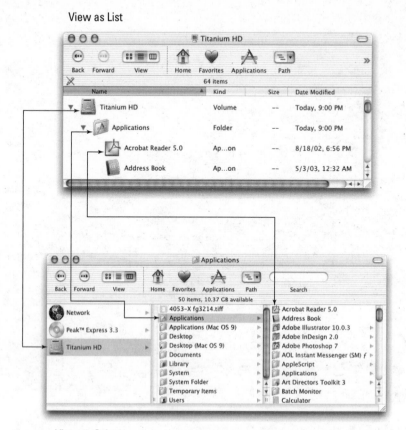

View as Column

Figure 29-16: The column view is a horizontal hierarchal directory.

After using the vertical hierarchy of View as List for so many years, you might find the column view strange at first. However, once you get the knack of it, navigating in the columns view can be easy and quick. But the most important reason to learn how to work in column view is that Mac OS X uses only the column view for all file-management dialog boxes. This protocol applies to file commands such as Save, Open, Import, and Export of all applications running natively in OS X. Figure 29-17 shows an Import File dialog box in Final Cut Pro.

There is a fantastic feature of the column view that displays a thumbnail preview of most types of graphics files, without having to open them. Simply click on the file and the preview will display in the column to the right. In Finder windows only, this includes the ability to play QuickTime movies of captured video and audio clips. Figure 29-18 shows a video clip preview in the column view of a Finder window. This is a great help when you're looking for a specific media file.

Figure 29-17: All file-management dialog boxes in OS X use the column view, like the Final Cut Pro Import File command shown here.

Figure 29-18: In the column view, you can preview most graphics files, including videos and audio with the built-in QuickTime player.

Making screenshots

A *screenshot*, as the name suggests, is a picture or snapshot of the screen on your Macintosh. Taking screenshots on your Mac has many uses. For example, you may be one of those Final Cut Pro editors who keeps telling people you are seeing some strange behavior on your Mac, but when the tech support staff arrives, the gremlins disappear. In other instances, if you are trying to capture the state of your Browser or Filter settings, a simple screenshot of your Macintosh screen may be just the answer. Most graphics in this book are screenshots from my Macintosh screen.

OS X comes bundled with a stand-alone screenshot utility, called Grab. Grab is located in the Utilities folder; however, you can still make Preview PDF screenshot using the OS built-in capability and keyboard shortcuts:

✦ **Command+Shift+3:** Press this shortcut, and you'll hear the sound of a camera click. Your screen freezes for just a moment and a screenshot labeled Picture 1 is dropped into your hard drive. Subsequent pictures are labeled Picture 2, Picture 3, and so on. This takes a screenshot of your *whole* screen.

✦ **Command+Shift+4:** This shortcut turns your pointer cursor into a crosshair. Drag a marquee on a portion of the screen by using this crosshair and you take a screenshot of just that selection of your screen.

✦ **Command+Shift+4, then press the spacebar:** This shortcut turns your pointer into a camera icon. As you hover the camera icon cursor over an individual screen item, like a window, a toolbar, the dock, or a dialog box, the selected item will highlight, indicating it is currently selected for a screen shot. Click the mouse when you want to make a screenshot of just the selected item. Using this shortcut is a great way to avoid having to crop your screenshots. If you wish to cancel this option at any time, simple press the Escape key.

✦ **Add the Control key:** If you want to save the screenshot to the Clipboard instead, hold down the Control key with any of the preceding keyboard shortcuts. You can then paste the screenshot into a document.

To view a screenshot, just double-click the PICT file. It opens in Preview. Now you can provide evidence to your tech support staff of any odd behavior that you can capture on your screen.

Navigating with Keystrokes

Keyboard shortcuts are a lifesaver for any video editor working on a computer. With the amount of time editors spend on their machines and the high number of keystrokes and mouse movements made, getting a sore wrist is not all that uncommon. The Mac OS is full of hidden features and keyboard modifiers that make your work a whole lot easier. The following sections provide a handy guide to making your workload easier.

Using Command+Option to close all windows

Looking for items buried deep in a Mac folder hierarchy can be a messy and painful affair. You open folders upon folders to find something, and then you have to close everything to get your clean desktop back. Many Mac users know that Command+W closes the currently active window. However, if you press Command+Option+W, all the open windows close.

Using the Option key to clean the desktop

Here is a little trick using the Option key that will keep your desktop clear of folder clutter: If you launch an application while holding down the Option key, the folder that contains it closes as the application launches.

Walking backward with the Command key

When a Finder window is selected as View as Icon or List, navigating back a level or two is easily done by clicking on the back button in the window's toolbar. Of course, there is another way to do this that is not limited to the window's previous location: If you hold down the Command key and click the title of the currently open window, you get a pull-down menu (see Figure 29-19) showing the path you took within your folders to get to the current window. Select any of the folders from the pull-down menu, and you jump back to that folder.

Making aliases

Aliases are pointers to original files. You can make aliases for files, applications, folders, and just about anything else in the Mac OS. You can make aliases to your original Final Cut Pro project files and place those aliases on the desktop where they are easy to find and use. You can drop an alias into the Dock where it will be easily available.

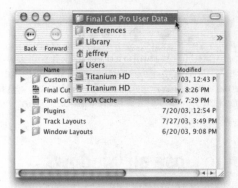

Figure 29-19: Command+click a window's title bar to display the file's folder path. Select a folder from the list to return to that folder.

To make an alias of an item, select the item and drag it while holding down Command+ Option. This keyboard shortcut creates an alias of the original file. You can also press Command+L or choose File ➪ Make Alias in the Finder menus. Figure 29-20 shows a Final Cut Pro project file and its alias.

Figure 29-20: The alias on the right serves as a pointer to the original file on the left.

Finding originals from aliases

Sometimes you need to locate an original item from its alias. To find an original from its alias, select the alias and press Command+R. This keyboard shortcut opens the appropriate folder and highlights the original item. You can also select an alias and choose File ➪ Show Original.

Other useful Mac keyboard shortcuts

There isn't room in this chapter to list all the keyboard shortcuts available to you when you work on a Mac. However, here are a few nifty shortcuts you may find useful, as well. These include:

✦ **Command+Option+Escape:** This shortcut calls up the Force Quit dialog box, which allows you to select which open application you wish to force to quit. Note that any open documents of an application that is forced to quit will not be saved with changes made since they were last saved. The good news is that OS X's protective memory feature prevents a force quit from affecting any other open application, including the OS.

✦ **Command+E:** This shortcut ejects a floppy or CD and is the best way to eject disks. Most users select the disk's icon on the desktop and drag it to trash. I select the CD-ROM by typing the first few letters of its name and pressing Command+E.

✦ **Command+Delete:** This shortcut moves selected item(s) to the trash.

✦ **Command+Shift+Delete:** This shortcut empties the trash.

✦ **Command+Control+Power:** This shortcut forces a Power Mac to reboot without the option of saving any open documents.

✦ **Power Button:** Pressing this button brings up the Shutdown/Sleep/Restart dialog box. In this dialog box, you can press Return to shut down, press R to restart, press S to sleep, or press Command+. (period) to cancel the box.

✦   ✦   ✦

Appendixes

Installing Final Cut Pro

Installing Final Cut Pro 4 is similar to installing most any application on OS X, with the only exception being that it has stringent hardware system requirements. Unlike most applications past and present, the installer for Final Cut Pro will *not* install the program if it does not detect the minimum system requirements.

Identifying the Hardware Requirements

Before you begin installing Final Cut Pro, you should know what hardware this application requires. To install and use Final Cut Pro you need:

+ Macintosh computer with a 350 MHz or faster G4 processor (Sorry, G3 users!)

+ Accelerated Graphics Port (AGP) card

+ Mac OS 10.2.5 or later

+ QuickTime 6.1 or later

+ 384MB RAM (512MB RAM is suggested for Soundtrack or RT Extreme capabilities.)

+ DVD-ROM drive

+ 6GB available on an audio/video-rated disk for installation (20GB or more is recommended.)

+ A DV source, such as a camera or deck, connected to your system via FireWire

+ One or more high-performance media drives (This is recommended but not required.)

Note   When Final Cut Pro is configured properly on a G4 PowerBook, you have a first-rate mobile editing workstation. All importing, editing, and exporting features of Final Cut Pro work with recent PowerBook G4 Series computers.

Preparing Mac OS and QuickTime Pro

Before you install your copy of Final Cut Pro, you must first upgrade to the latest version of Mac OS X and QuickTime. Apple's recommended way to do this requires you to have access to an Internet connection.

Upgrading Mac OS X and QuickTime

Follow these steps to upgrade to the latest version of OS X and QuickTime. You must do this *before* you install Final Cut Pro:

1. **From the Apple menu, choose Apple ➪ System Preferences.**

2. **In the System Preferences window, click on Software Update.**

3. **Click the Software Update tab if it isn't selected already, then click the Check Now button.**

   The Software Update will download and install the latest version of OS X and QuickTime, along with any other Apple programs it finds later versions for.

4. **Restart your computer after any new OS system upgrades are found and installed.**

Unlocking the Pro version of QuickTime

Once you have installed QuickTime, you should unlock the QuickTime Pro version. To do so, you need the registration name and number that comes on the small label attached to the installation documentation. To unlock the Pro version of QuickTime, follow these steps:

1. **Choose Apple ➪ System Preferences.**

2. **In the System Preferences window, click on QuickTime.**

3. **In the Update tab, click on the Registration button.**

4. **In the Registration To field, enter QuickTime Pro.**

5. **Enter your registration information.**

   It is extremely important that you enter this information exactly as listed on your installation documentation.

6. **Click OK to finish.**

If you have trouble with the registration process for QuickTime Pro, check the following common problems:

✦ If the OK button remains unavailable or an error message tells you that the registration information is not valid, follow the preceding steps again. Take great care when entering the Registered To and Registration Number — it must be entered precisely as shown on your documentation. Be sure to enter 0 for the number zero and O for the letter O. Check your capitalization. And remember, kicking your desk does not help.

✦ The Final Cut Pro installation documentation comes with two small stickers. Each sticker has registration information for QuickTime and Final Cut Pro. Do not use these names and numbers interchangeably. Entering the number for Final Cut Pro is not going to work in the QuickTime Settings panel, and vice versa.

✦ Early QuickTime registration numbers from QuickTime 4 do not work. You need a new and valid registration number for QuickTime 6.

Installing Final Cut Pro software

After you've installed the latest version of OS X and QuickTime, and unlocked the Pro features of QuickTime, install your Final Cut Pro software. Follow these steps to install Final Cut Pro:

1. **Insert the Final Cut Pro 4 Install DVD into your DVD-ROM drive.**

2. **Double-click the Install Final Cut Pro icon, and follow the on-screen instructions.**

3. **When prompted, enter your administrator name and password, then click OK.**

4. **Read the Welcome screen and then click Continue in the Installer window.**

   You will be greeted, again, by a dialog box of System and software required prior to the installation of Final Cut Pro.

5. **If you are in doubt about your current system specifications, read the information provided in the dialog box, then click Continue.**

6. **Read the software license agreement, click Continue, and in the next dialog box, click Agree.**

Note   I strongly encourage you to actually *read* this licensing agreement. You can learn a lot of useful information. For example, you should not use Final Cut Pro in the operation of a nuclear facility. (So much for your dreams of a Final Cut Pro–based nuclear reactor!) You should also not pass on a copy of Final Cut Pro to anyone in the Taliban-controlled areas of Afghanistan. (If they only knew what they were missing.) You also learn that Apple's liability for any damages suffered by you during the use of Final Cut Pro comes to a grand total of $50. That should keep you from kicking your machine or punching holes in the wall when trouble strikes.

7. **In the Licensing dialog box, you must enter your first and last name; entering an organization is optional.**

8. **In the Serial Number field, enter the Final Cut Pro serial number.**

   The serial number can be found on small stickers included with your disks.

9. **Select an installation location from the pop-up menu at the bottom of the screen, and click Continue.**

10. **To perform an easy installation, click Install. To perform a Custom installation, select the applications you want to install, then click Continue Installation.**

After installation is finished, a dialog box appears indicating a successful installation. You will then be prompted to install additional media for LiveType and Soundtrack. This additional media is located on separate DVD disks that came with your Final Cut Pro Installer DVD, and is optional and not required to run LiveType and Soundtrack. If Compressor was selected to install, you will have to restart your computer after installation is complete.

You are now ready to use Final Cut Pro. For initial setup of System and Project presets, see Chapter 6.

✦   ✦   ✦

Keyboard Shortcuts

When you need to edit quickly and efficiently, keyboard shortcuts are invaluable assets. This fact is evident from Final Cut Pro's new feature that allows you to remap keyboard shortcuts using the Keyboard Layout tool. Whether you customize any keystroke commands or not, the number of keyboard shortcuts provided in Final Cut Pro is both staggering and a testament to Final Cut Pro's professional toolset. The following is a breakdown of the default keyboard shortcuts.

Note: Any keystroke command assignment that has been changed from the previous version of Final Cut Pro is in bold type. Where new keystroke shortcuts are in place for new functions, both the command name and its description appear in bold type.

General Control Commands

Command	Description
Command+Shift+N	New project
Command+N	New sequence
Command+Option+N	New sequence with presets
Command+O	Open file
Command+I	Import file
Return	Open selected item
Shift+Return	Open in new window
Option+Return	Open item editor
Control+X	Open text generator
Command+W	Close window
Control+W	Close tab
Command+Q	Quit
Command+S	Save
Command+Shift+S	Save project as
Command+Option+S	Save all
Command+Z	Undo
Command+Shift+Z	Redo
Shift+S	Audio scrub on or off
Control+L	Loop playback
N	Snapping on or off

Window Control Commands

Command	Description
Command+1	View
Command+2	Canvas
Option+5	Tool Bench
Command+3	Timeline
Option+4	Audio Meters
Command+4	Browser
Command+5	Effects

Command	Description
Command+6	Favorites bin
Command+7	Trim edit
Command+8	Log and capture
Command+9	Format (Item properties)
Command+0	Sequence settings
Option+Q	**User Preferences**
Command+Option+Q	Audio/Video Settings
Control+Q	Easy Setup
Shift+Q	**System Settings**
Command+H	Hide Final Cut Pro
Command+Option+H	Hide others

Log and Capture Commands

Command	Description
I	Mark In point
O	Mark Out point
Shift+I	Got to In point
Shift+O	Go to Out point
F2	Log clip
Control+C	Batch capture
Shift+C	Capture now

Browser Commands

Command	Description
Shift+H	Change list (icon view)
Command+B	New bin
Right Arrow	Open bins (works in List view)
Left Arrow	Close bins (works in List view)
Option+B	Set logging column layout
Shift+B	Set standard column layout

Select, Cut, Copy, and Paste Commands

Command	Description
Command+C	Copy
Command+X	Cut (lift to Clipboard)
Option+D	Duplicate
Option+A	Make In/Out a selection
Command+V	Paste or overwrite
Option+V	Paste attributes
Command+Option+V	Remove Attributes
Shift+V	Paste insert
Command+A	Select all
Command+Shift+A	Deselect all

Navigation Commands

Command	Description
Right Arrow	Forward one frame
Left Arrow	Back one frame
Shift+Right Arrow	Forward one second
Shift+Left Arrow	Back one second
Shift+Space or J	Play reverse
Spacebar or K	Stop/Pause
Spacebar of L	Play forward
F	Match frame
Shift+ F	Reveal master clip
Command+Option+F	**Match frame/Source file**
V	Select an edit
Control+V	Add edit
Down Arrow	Next edit
Up Arrow	Previous edit
Shift+G	Next gap

Command	Description
Option+G	Previous gap
Control+G	Close Gap
Home	Go to beginning of media
End or Shift+Home	Go to end of media
Shift+Down Arrow	Go to next marker
Shift+Up Arrow	Go to previous marker

Find Commands

Command	Description
Command+F	Find
Command+G, **or F3**	Find next
Shift+F3	Find previous

Scrolling Commands

Command	Description
Shift+Page Up	Horizontal scroll left
Shift+Page Down	Horizontal scroll right
Page Up	Vertical scroll up
Page Down	Vertical scroll down

Screen Layout Commands

Command	Description
Shift+U	Custom layout 1
Option+U	Custom layout 2
Control+U	Standard layout
Shift+Option+U	**Restore Window Layout**

Timeline Commands

Command	Description
Command+L	Create or break video and audio link
Shift+L	Linked selection on or off
Option+L	Create or break stereo pair
Shift+T	Change track size
Option+T	Clip keyframes on or off
Option+W	Clip overlays on or off
Command+Option+W	Turn on waveforms
Option+Z	Show timecode overlays
Delete	Delete and leave gap
Shift+Delete	Ripple delete (delete and close gap)
Shift+Z	Fit media in window
F4+Track Number	Lock video track (press F4 and then a number for the track)
Shift+F4	Lock all video tracks
F5+Track Number	Lock audio track (press F5 and then a number for the track)
Shift+F5	Lock all audio tracks
Command+0 (zero)	Sequence settings

Playback Commands

Command	Description
Shift+Spacebar or J key	Play in reverse
Spacebar or K key	Stop/pause
Spacebar or L key	Play forward
Backslash (\)	Play around current
Option+P	Play every frame
Shift+P	Play here to out
Shift+Backslash (\)	Play in to out

In and Out Point Commands

Command	Description
I	Set in point
O	Set out point
Control+I	Set video in only
Command+Option+I	Set audio in only
Control+O	Set video out only
Command+Option+O	Set audio out only
Command+Option+K	Audio level keyframe
Option+I	Clear in
Option+O	Clear out
Option+X	Clear in and out
X	Mark clip
Shift+A	Make selection
Option+A	Select In to Out
Control+A	Mark to Marker
Control+P	Set Poster frame
Shift+I	Go to In point
Shift+O	Go to Out point

Marker Commands

Command	Description
M	Add marker
M+M	Add and name marker
Command+Tilde (~)	Delete marker
Control+Tilde (~)	Delete all markers
Option+Tilde (~)	Extend marker
Shift+Tilde (~)	Reposition marker
Shift+Down Arrow	Next marker
Shift+Up Arrow	Previous marker

Editing Commands

Command	Description
Delete	Delete (lift and leave gap)
Shift+Delete	Ripple delete (delete and no gap)
E	Extend edit
F9	Insert edit
Shift+F9	Insert with transition
F10	Overwrite
Shift+F10	Overwrite with transition
F11	Replace
Shift+F11	Fit to fill
F12	Superimpose
Command+U	Make subclip
Control+B	Toggle clip visibility
Control+D	Modify duration
Command+J	Change clip speed
Command+Option+L	Gain adjustment
Shift+D	Make offline
Shift+R	Toggle between ripple/roll type edits
Shift+X	Ripple cut to Clipboard
Shift+Click In or Out	Slip edit
Option+Click In or Out	Clear edit
F6+Track Number (1-9)	Set target video
Shift+F6r	Disconnect current video target track
F7+Track Number	Set target Audio 1
Shift+F7	Disconnect current Audio 1
F8+Track Number	Set target Audio 2
Shift+F8	Audio 2 Disconnect current target track
[	Trim backward one frame
Shift+[	Trim backward x frames
]	Trim forward one frame
Shift+]	Trim forward x frames

Output Commands

Command	Description
Command+F12	External Video/All frames
Shift+F12	Display current frame on External Video
Control+M	Print to video

Compositing Commands

Command	Description
Option+C	Nest item(s)
Control+K	Add motion keyframe
Command+Option+K	Add Level keyframe
Shift+K	Next keyframe
Option+K	Previous keyframe
Shift+N	Make still frame
Command+K	Run (in FXBuilder)
Command+R	Render both
Option+R	**Render All/ both**
Command+Option+R	Render only/ Audio mixdown
Control+Option+R	**Render Audio**
Control+R	**Render Only/ Preview**
Comand+Option+P	**Render Only/ Proxy**
Caps Lock	Rendering on or off
Command+J	Speed
W	Change Image/Wireframe view
Shift+W	Change RGB/RGB+A/Alpha
Shift+Z	Fit in window
Option+Down Arrow	Nudge position down
Option+Back Arrow	Nudge position left
Option+Right Arrow	Nudge position right
Option+Up Arrow	Nudge position up

Continued

Compositing Commands *(continued)*

Command	Description
Command+Down Arrow	Sub pixel down
Command+Back Arrow	Sub pixel left
Command+Right Arrow	Sub pixel right
Command+Up Arrow	Sub pixel up
Command+=	Zoom in (current window)
Command+-	Zoom out (current window)
Option+ -	Zooms out Timeline window only
Option +=	Zooms in Timeline window only

Effects Commands

Command	Description
Option+F	Make favorite
Control+F	Make favorite Motion
Command+T	Default video transition
Command+Option+T	Default audio transition

Keys and Modifier Scheme

Key	No Modifier	Shift+Key	Option+Key
I	Set in	Go to in	Clear in
O	Set out	Go to out	Clear out
M	Set marker	Next marker	Previous marker
E	Extend edit	Next Edit	Previous edit
G	•	Next gap	Previous gap
K	•	Next keyframe	Previous keyframe

Tools

Command	Description
Option+6	**Audio Mixer**
Option+7	**Frame Viewer**
Option+8	QuickView
Option+9	Video Scopes
Option+0	Voice Over
Option+J	**Button List**

Tools and Modifier Commands

Tools	Press	Tool+Command	Tool+Shift	Tool+Option
Arrow	A	Select additional	Select range	Link on/off
Edit selection	G	Select additional	To Ripple Tool	link on/off
Group selection	G+G	Select additional	Select addtional	link on/off
Range selection	G+G+G	•	•	Link on/off
Track forward select	T	•	All forward	Link on/off
Track backward select	T+T	•	All backward	Link on/off
Track selection	T+T+T	•	•	Link on/off

Continued

Tools and Modifier Commands (continued)

Tools	Press	Tool+Command	Tool+Shift	Tool+Option
All tracks forward select	T+T+T+T	•	Track forward	Link on/off
All tracks backward select	T+T+T+T+T	•	Track backward	Link on/off
Roll edit	R	Select additional	To Ripple Tool	Link on/off
Ripple edit	R+R	Select additional	To Roll Tool	Link on/off
Slip	S	Select additional	Select clip	Link on/off
Slide	S+S	Select additional	Select clip	Link on/off
Time Remap tool	S+S+S	Gear down movements	Scrub tool	Reposition Source frame
Razor blade	B	•	To blade all	Link on/off
Blade all	B+B	•	To blade	•
Hand	H	Zoom in	•	Zoom out
Scrub Tool	H+H	Selection tool	Selection tool	•

Tools	Press	Tool+Command	Tool+Shift	Tool+Option
Zoom in	Z	To Hand tool	Zoom out maximum	Zoom out
Zoom out	Z+Z	To Hand tool	Zoom out maximum	Zoom in
Crop	C	All Sides	Two Sides	•
Distort	D	•	Perspective	Resize
Pen	P	Smooth on/off	Adjust Line	Pen delete
Pen delete	P+P	•	•	Pen
Pen smooth	P+P+P	•	•	•

Customizing Your Keyboard with the Keyboard Layout Tool

A feature sorely missed in earlier versions, keyboard remapping is now possible in Final Cut Pro 4. This means you can create a keyboard shortcut for every command, and even reassign most default keystrokes. Because using keystroke shortcuts can greatly help your editing workflow, the ability to customize your keyboard commands is a feature most editors have come to expect from a professional NLE. Better late than never, Final Cut Pro's Keyboard Layout tool rises to the occasion.

Using the Keyboard Layout interface

To customize your keyboard layout, you'll use the Keyboard Layout tool, which you can open by selecting Tools ⇨ Keyboard Layout ⇨ Customize, or press its keyboard shortcut Option+H. The Keybaord Layout window opens, as shown in Figure B-1.

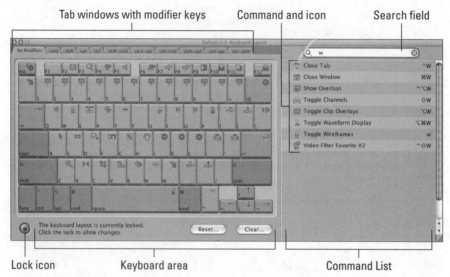

Tab windows with modifier keys　　Command and icon　　Search field

Lock icon　　　　Keyboard area　　　　　Command List

Figure B-1: The Keyboard Layout window is where customize your keyboard commands by creating new keyboard shortcuts, or reassigning old ones.

There are two main areas of the Keyboard Layout window: the Keyboard area is on the left and the Command List is on the right side, with the following controls:

✦ **Keyboard tabs:** Each tab in this window is labeled with a modifier key, or a combination of two modifier keys, and shows all keyboard keys and currently assign commands to their corresponding key.

Note

Any keys that appear in red cannot be assigned using the modifier key or keys named in the current tab.

✦ **Lock button:** Click this lock icon to the open position (unlocked) to make any modifications to the keyset; click the lock icon to the closed position (locked) to lock the keyboard layout and prevent any changes.

✦ **Reset button:** Click this button to reassign *all* keyboard shortcuts to their original default key combinations.

✦ **Clear button:** Click this button to remove *all* keyboard shortcuts. All the keys will then be blank. A few commands cannot be cleared, such as Copy and Paste.

✦ **Search field:** Enter a command or key to perform a search for.

✦ **Disclosure triangle:** Click the black triangle to display all commands and their corresponding keyboard shortcuts for a menus or command group.

✦ **Magnifying glass icon:** Click this icon to display alphabetically all commands in the command list, along with their keyboard shortcut.

✦ **X icon:** This icon appears in the right side of the search field once commands are displayed alphabetically. Click this icon to toggle the command list to display by menu and command group.

Assigning new keyboard shortcuts

So, here's how to assign new keyboard shortcuts for Final Cut Pro using the Keyboard Layout tool:

1. **Select Tools ➪ Keyboard Layout ➪ Customize**

2. **Click the Lock in the lower left corner of the window to unlock the keyboard layout, otherwise you won't be allowed to make any changes.**

Note You can delete all the keyboard shortcuts by clicking on Clear. You can restore them all to their original default settings by clicking on Reset.

3. **Click one of the tabs to choose a modifier key.**

Notice that there are 11 to choose from. One tab represents the keyboard without a modifier key, but the others all contain some variant involving Command, Option, Control, and Shift.

4. **In the Command List Area in the right part of the window, select the command you wish to map to a new shortcut by clicking on it.**

You can view all the commands by opening the twirlers, or disclosure triangles, or you can narrow your search of the commands listed here by using the text entry field, which dynamically narrows your search as you type (see Figure B-2).

Note When you type into the text entry field in the Command List Area, you may notice some cool features. Type a word contained in a command such as 'play,' and you'll see all the commands that include the word play. Type in a single letter, say 'w,' and you'll see all the commands that use w as part of their keystroke. Pretty intelligent, eh?

5. **With the command selected, either press the key that you want to map the command to, or drag the command from the Command List Area over to the desired key and then release the mouse button.**

Note If the keyboard shortcut is going to replace a preexisting one, then you'll be asked if you want to reassign it. Click Yes, and the command in the Command List will reflect the command's new shortcut, as well as any other it might have had. All the shortcuts listed for a command are valid and will work.

Drag any command to a key in the keyboard

Search field

Q play ⊗	
🔊 Audio Playback Quality: High	
🔊 Audio Playback Quality: Low (faster)	
🔊 Audio Playback Quality: Medium	
🔁 Loop Playback	^L
▶ Play	space
▶▶ Play Around Current Frame	\
▦ Play Base Layer Only	
▶◆ Play Current Marker	^⌥6
▣ Play Every Frame	⌥\, ⌥P
▶▌ Play In to Out	⇧\
◀ Play Reverse	⇧space
▶◆ Play To Next Marker	^⌥1
▶▌ Play to Out	⇧P
▶ Play: Rate −1	^F6
▶ Play: Rate −2	^F5
▶ Play: Rate −3	^F4
▶ Play: Rate −4	^F3
▶ Play: Rate −5	^F2

Current keystroke commands

Figure B-2: The text entry field of the Command List Area yields intelligent search results.

Tip

To get rid of a single existing shortcut, click on the key and drag it out of the Keyboard Layout window. Do *not* click on Clear, as this will wipe out your entire layout.

Exporting and importing your own sets of keyboard shortcuts

If you're a freelance editor who travels a lot, you might find this feature particularly helpful. You can export your own keyboard layout, take it on the road with you and then import it on site at a freelance job. Here's how:

1. **Select Tools ➪ Keyboard Layout ➪ Export, and save your layout with your own specified location and name.**

2. **To bring your layout into another system, select Tools ➪ Keyboard Layout ➪ Import, navigate your way to your own layout file, and then click Choose.**

Creating Shortcut Buttons

In addition to keyboard shortcuts, you can create shortcut buttons for any command and place them in the button bars on Final Cut Pro windows. This can be a fast an easy method to access often-performed commands if you prefer to work with your mouse.

To create a shortcut button requires only two steps:

1. **Open the Button List window by choosing Tools ⇨ Button List, pressing Option+J, or Control+clicking on any button bar on a Final Cut Pro window and select Show Button List from the contextual menu.**

   The Button List window opens. Commands are grouped first by menu order, and then alphabetically by operation name. Click on the disclosure (triangular) button to see all available commands you can assign a shortcut button to. Figure B-3 shows the commands for Capture.

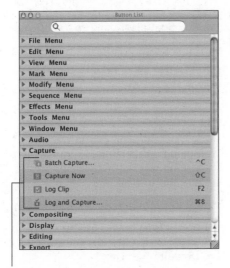

Drag any command to a button bar

Figure B-3: The Button List window contains all Final Cut Pro commands that you can assign to a shortcut button.

2. **Select and drag a command to the button bar on a Final Cut Pro window.**

   A shortcut button with a corresponding icon appears in the button bar. Hovering your cursor over the button will display a tooltip with the command name and keyboard shortcut.

Tip   You can add as many buttons to a button bar as you want, however, depending on the current size of your window, not all of them may show.

Modifying a shortcut button

After you create a shortcut button, you can move or copy it to another button bar, reorder its position on the button bar, and even assign it a color:

✦ **To move a shortcut button to another button bar,** drag a shortcut button from its current location and drop it in the button bar of another Final Cut Pro window.

✦ **To copy a shortcut button to another button bar,** press and hold the Option key as you drag the shortcut button to another button bar.

✦ **To rearrange a shortcut button's position on the button bar,** drag it forward or backward on the button bar; all other buttons will slide left or right to accommodate the selected button. Release the mouse to drop the button into its new position.

Tip   You can add spacer between buttons by Control+clicking on a shortcut button and selecting Add Spacer from the contextual menu.

✦ **To color-code a shortcut button,** Control+click on any shortcut button and choose Color, and then a color from the submenu.

Deleting a shortcut button

You can easily delete a shortcut button using either of the following methods:

✦ **Simply drag a shortcut button from the button bar.**

✦ **Control+click on a shortcut button and choose Remove ⇨ Button.**

You can also delete all of your shortcut buttons and restore any default shortcut buttons in the button bar if you Control+click anywhere in the button bar, and select Remove ⇨ All/Restore Default.

Note   Shortcut buttons are automatically saved whenever you quit Final Cut Pro and are loaded when Final Cut Pro is opened. You can also save and reload your shortcut buttons by using the Save Main Button Bars and Load Main Buttons Bars options in the contextual menu that appears when you Control+click on a button bar. Loading your custom buttons can save you time when you need to recreate your shortcut buttons on another Final Cut Pro 4 edit station.

✦   ✦   ✦

Effects and Transitions

A major asset of Final Cut Pro since its first release is its effects, filters and transitions. No, it's not just the sheer number of the more than 200 transitions, effects and filters that come bundled with Final Cut Pro 4, but the ease by which you can apply and modify them. Unlike many other high-end non-linear editors, Final Cut Pro's filters, generators, and transitions are always available to you without having to switch to another operational mode or tool. The following tables of filters, generators and transitions are grouped as they are in the Effects bins and menu.

Video Transitions

Final Cut Pro ships with many built-in video transitions. The following tables are a listing of the transitions that come with Final Cut Pro, along with explanations detailing each one. The transitions are organized by folders located in the Effects tab of the Browser window.

3-D Simulation

Name	Description
Cross Zoom	Zooms in on the first clip, switches to the second clip at maximum zoom, and then zooms out. You can control the center point, the amount of magnification in the zoom, and the degree of blur applied to the zoom.
Cube Spin	Makes a three-dimensional cube from each of the clips and spins it in a direction you choose. You can also elect to view the cube from the inside or the outside.
Spin 3D	Spins the first clip on its center point and reveals the second clip. You can specify the angle of the spin axis.
Spinback 3D	Much like the Spin 3D transition, this effect spins the first clip on its center point until the clip is seen from the edge. Then the transition switches to the second clip, which spins into full view. You are able to specify the angle of the spin axis in this transition.
Swing	This transition swings the first clip in toward the screen or out toward the second clip. The second clip is then revealed as the swing widens out. You can control the angle of the swing axis.
Zoom	Zooms the second clip in from a center point to a full screen and over the top of the first clip. You are able to select the center point of where the zoom begins.

Dissolve

Name	Description
Additive Dissolve	Adds the luminance values of the two clips together while cross-fading between them.
Cross Dissolve	Creates a smooth blend from the first clip into the second. This transition is the most common type of dissolve transition used.
Dip to Color	Fades the first clip to the color of your choice and then fades up from the color to the second clip. You can control the speed of the fade.
Dither Dissolve	In this dissolve, random pixels are removed from the first clip in the process of revealing the second clip.
Fade In, Fade Out	Fades in the second clip as the first clip fades out. This reveals the track below the current track in a transition.

Name	Description
Non-Additive Dissolve	This transition compares the pixels in the two clips and shows the lighter of the two as the first clip is faded out and the second clip is faded in.
Ripple Dissolve	Creates a water ripple effect on the first clip while blending into the second. In this transition, you can choose the number of ripples, the center point of the ripples, and the amplitude and acceleration of the ripples. This effect is perfect for that "I remember when . . ." shot where your video subjects recall an event from the past. You can also apply a circle highlight to the ripples.

Iris

Name	Description
Cross Iris	An iris transition starts out with the first clip and creates the appearance of an iris that opens to reveal the second clip. In this case the shape of the iris is a cross. You can change the center point around which the iris opening is created and feather the edges, creating a soft edge.
Diamond Iris	Same transition as the Cross Iris except the shape of the iris is a four-point diamond shape.
Oval Iris	Same transition as the Cross Iris except the shape of the iris is an oval.
Point Iris	Same transition as the Cross Iris except the shape of the iris originates from a center point of four triangles.
Rectangle Iris	Same transition as the Cross Iris except the shape of the iris is a rectangle.
Star Iris	Same transition as the Cross Iris except the shape of the iris is a five-point star.

Map

Name	Description
Channel Map	This transition maps the channels from the first and second clips. It can also fill the channels with black. You can choose to invert the individual channels.
Luminance Map	Same transition as the Channel Map except the mapped colors use the luminance or brightness values of the clip.

Page Peel

Name	Description
Page Peel	Peels away the first clip to reveal the second clip beneath. The appearance of the peel is adjustable.

QuickTime

Name	Description
Channel Compositor	Merges two images by using a selection of R, G, B, and Alpha channels of those images to control the final blending.
Chroma Key	Layers two sources by replacing the pixels of the first source that are of the specified color with the pixels of the second source. This allows the second source to show through the first. The selected color is made transparent. This effect is often seen on television during the weather reports.
Explode	The second clip grows out from the center point and covers the first one. You can alter the point of explosion.
Gradient Wipe	Uses a matte image to create a transition between two sources. This transition is controlled by a gradient matte, and the first clip fades first where the matte source is darkest and last where it is brightest.
Implode	Opposite of the Explode effect. The first clip shrinks down to a single point, revealing the second clip. You can change the center point of the implosion.
Iris	The first clip opens like an iris to reveal the second one.
Matrix Wipe	This effect allows a series of matrix reveal effects between two sources.
Push	One clip replaces the other by pushing it off the screen. Both of the clips move.
Radial	The first source clip sweeps in a radial pattern to reveal the second source clip.
Slide	The second clip slides onto the screen and covers the first clip. The angle from which the slide occurs can be specified.
Wipe	The second clip is revealed by a wipe away.
Zoom	One clip zooms out of the other.

Slide

Name	Description
Band Slide	Bands of the first clip slide in parallel and reveal the second clip. You can change the number of bands and the direction of the slide.
Box Slide	Bands of the first clip slide one at a time perpendicularly to reveal the second clip. You can change the number of bands and the direction of the slide.
Center Split Slide	The second clip is revealed by splitting the first clip down the center and horizontally sliding the two halves away from each other.
Multi Spin Slide	The first clip spins and zooms in the shape of boxes to reveal the second clip. You can change the number of boxes and the center of the spin for the first clip and the center of spin for the boxes.
Push Slide	The second clip pushes the first clip off the screen. You can control the direction of the push.
Spin Slide	Spinning boxes of the first clip zoom to reveal the second clip. You can control the center of the spin as well as the number of boxes.
Split Slide	The first clip splits and slides to reveal the second clip. You can control the orientation of the split.
Swap Slide	The first and second clips slide in opposite directions, swapping places and sliding back, revealing the second clip. You can change the slide direction.

Stretch

Name	Description
Cross Stretch	The first clip is squeezed as the second clip stretches out from a specified edge in the opposite direction.
Squeeze	The first clip is squeezed from the opposite edges toward the center and reveals the second clip. You can change the direction of the squeeze.
Squeeze and Stretch	The first clip is squeezed from opposite edges toward the center and stretched in a perpendicular direction to reveal the second clip. You can change the squeeze orientation.
Stretch	The second clip stretches from a specific edge over the first clip.

Wipe

Name	Description
Band Wipe	Wipes a band across the first clip to reveal the second clip. You can change the number of bands and the direction of the wipe.
Center Wipe	A linear wipe that starts from a point of your choice on the first clip to reveal the second clip. You can alter the wipe direction.
Checker Wipe	Checkered boxes on the first clip reveal the second clip. You can change the number of boxes and the direction of the wipe.
Checkerboard Wipe	Checkered boxes wipe individually on the first clip to reveal the second clip. You can change the number of boxes and the direction of the wipe.
Clock Wipe	A circular wipe over the first clip reveals the second clip. You can change the start and direction of the wipe and the center of the rotation.
Edge Wipe	A linear wipe that starts from the edge of the first clip to reveal the second clip. You can change the direction of the wipe.
Gradient Wipe	This wipe uses a gradient wipe image to wipe across the first clip, revealing the second clip. You can change the softness of the wipe and invert the gradient wipe image. You can use any image as the gradient by dragging it to the gradient clip control window.
Inset Wipe	A rectangular wipe from the edge or the corner of the first clip reveals the second clip.
Jaws Wipe	Just when you thought it was safe to go back into the editing room. This is a jagged-edge wipe from the center of the first clip that reveals the second clip. You can change the direction of the wipe and the shape of the jagged edge.
Random Edge Wipe	A linear wipe with a random edge from the edge of the first clip reveals the second clip. You can change the direction of the wipe and the width of the random edge.
V Wipe	A V-shaped wipe that starts from a selected edge of the first clip and reveals the second clip.
Venetian Blind Wipe	Venetian blind–type bands wipe across the first clip to reveal the second. You can change the angle and the number of bands.
Wrap Wipe	Bands wipe in the chosen direction across the first clip to reveal the second. You can change the start and the orientation of the wipe and the number of bands.
Zigzag Wipe	Bands wipe in a zigzag pattern over the first clip to reveal the second clip. You can alter the start and the orientation of the wipe and the number of bands.

Video Filters

Final Cut Pro's filters are numerous, and their variety is impressive for any editing application. Filters require a light hand when styling your footage. For example, according to Apple, "With enough blur applied, you can turn almost any video image into a stylized blend of colors and shapes." But that's like saying if you throw enough color at a canvas, you'll end up with a painting. Use these filters with restraint. In the following tables, I describe these filters by the folders in which they are stored in the Effects tab of the Browser window.

Blur	
Name	**Description**
Gaussian Blur	By default, applying this filter changes the entire image in a frame by blurring all channels; however, you can blur individual channels by using a pop-up menu. The slider allows you to control exactly how much blur you'd like to apply.
Radial Blur	When applied, this blur filter makes an image appear as though it is revolving around a center point. You get to define the center point, and you also control just how heavily the image appears to spin.
Wind Blur	This filter makes an image appear as though wind is blowing in from off-screen, creating a blur in the image relative to the strength of the wind. You can control wind speed (blur radius and steps) and direction.
Zoom Blur	This filter creates the illusion that the image is moving either toward or away from the viewer depending on which option you select. You also control the smoothness of the move's appearance.

Border	
Name	**Description**
Basic Border	This filter enables you to frame an image around its edges. Two sliders give control over both the width and color of the frame.
Bevel	This filter also frames your image but adds depth to the frame with a bevel. Again, you determine the width and color of the frame, but you also control the angle of light that falls on the raised edge as well as its transparency.

Channel

Name	Description
Arithmetic	Applies a mathematical function or operator to a channel you specify with the use of a pop-up menu. The operator applies to the chosen channel by blending with a color you select with the color picker.
Channel Blur	Blurs channels individually with slider controls. The channels include the Alpha channel.
Channel Offset	You select a channel and determine how much it is offset from the rest of the image by using x and y values. You also choose how the filter handles the edges created by the offset.
Color Offset	Enables you to alter the color values in the red, green, and blue channels with sliders.
Compound Arithmetic	This filter works on the clip to which it is applied by blending data from a second clip that you specify by dragging it to the clip control icon. After the second clip is chosen, you determine an operator for blending the two clips by choosing an operator from a pop-up menu. The data in the first clip is compounded by the data from the second clip in a manner determined by the operator of your choice.
Invert	Inverts the channel(s) you specify in a pop-up menu. You control the amount by which the image is inverted by manipulating a slider.

Distort

Name	Description
Bumpmap	After you select a second clip using the clip control function, this filter offsets the pixels of the clip to which it has been applied using the luminance values of the second clip as the basis for the offset. You can influence the amount of the offset by using the direction control and the outset slider. Experiment with the luma scale slider and the repeat edges switch to alter the appearance of the offset.
Cylinder	Visually distorts a clip so that it appears wrapped around a cylinder whose dimensions you control with the radius, center, and amount sliders. You also control whether the cylinder is horizontal or vertical.
Displace	Like the bumpmap filter, this filter offsets pixels of the clip to which it has been applied, but it uses the red and green channel information from a second clip rather than its luminance.

Name	Description
Fisheye	Enlarges or shrinks a clip from a point on the image to the edges of a given radius, both of which you define with an x and y coordinate as well as a radius value determined by a slider. You also determine the severity of the fisheye by specifying an amount that the image will distort.
Pond Ripple	Makes a clip appear as though it were laid over a ripple created by throwing a stone on the surface of still water. You choose the origin of the ripple, the radius of the waves as they move outward, the height of the waves, the speed at which they move, whether they reflect ambient light, and how quickly the waves deteriorate.
Ripple	This filter differs from the pond ripple filter considerably because no concentric circles emanate from any central point. Instead, you control simulated wave action that is both horizontal and vertical. With sliders, you determine the speed, length, and amplitude of waves as they move across the image. You can also repeat the edges of an image to limit the amount of black that may appear as a result of heavy wave action.
Wave	Similar to the ripple filter but different in that its waves are only horizontal or only vertical depending on which direction you choose.
Whirlpool	Makes an image appear as if it's going down a drain. You can choose where the drain goes as well as the intensity of the "whirl" and whether or not to repeat the edges created by the distortion.

Image Control

Name	Description
Brightness and Contrast	Use the two sliders in this filter to alter the brightness and contrast by −100 to 100 percent. Because this filter's reach extends through all of a clip's channels, most videographers prefer the levels and proc amp filters over the brightness and contrast filter when making adjustments to overexposed or underexposed video.
Color Balance	This filter gives you direct control of the color in a given channel as well as enables you to exert influence on that color as it appears in the highlights, midtones, and shadows of an image.
Desaturate	Takes all color out of an image by a percentage you specify.
Gamma Correction	Through a single slider, this filter gives you control of the gamma, or midtones, of an image.
Levels	This filter gives you very specific control of each color channel as well as the Alpha channel. Within each channel, you can specify a gamma value, as well as input and output thresholds.

Continued

Image Control *(continued)*

Name	Description
Proc Amp	This single filter enables you to control the black and white levels of a clip, as well as the saturation and hue of its color. The setup slider corresponds to the black level, the video slider corresponds to the white level, the chroma slider controls the color saturation, and the phase angle control determines the hue of the color distribution.
Sepia	Tints a clip with a sepia-tone color by default, but you can change the color of the tint with a color picker or use two separate sliders (amount and highlight) to control the amount and the brightness of the tint.
Tint	Less useful than the sepia filter, you can only select the color and the amount.

Good video keying is an art and very difficult to pull off without footage shot in professionally controlled blue/green-screen environments. DV footage shot on a poorly lit green background produces very disappointing results if used in conjunction with the set of keying filters listed here. For best results, shoot with Betacam SP or Digital Betacam in a green-screen studio with professional lighting. You'll be glad you did, because these filters are hard enough to use with properly prepared footage. Throw in variables such as poor lighting or low recording quality, and usable keys become virtually impossible.

Key

Name	Description
Blue and Green Screen	This filter gives you control over how much of a clip shot against a green or blue screen should be knocked out, or made transparent. A very useful pop-up menu enables you to see the matte (transparent area) created by your key, or if you prefer, the source footage, the final output, or a miniaturized composite of all three. First, you must choose either blue or green from the first pop-up menu, then you need to set the color level slider to determine how much background to knock out, and finally, you should experiment with the color tolerance slider to allow for a variance in the blue/green color. Doing so helps the filter account for slight shadows and other subtle color shifts. Also, edge thin and edge feather sliders help you hone the edges of your matte, but for best results these sliders should be set to zero and complemented by the additional use of the matte choker filter which makes for much better edges in your key. Last, but not least, you can invert your matte with the invert check box.

Name	Description
Chroma Key	This is similar to Blue and Green Screen keying filter, but with the additional options to base the selection on a user selected color, or range of colors, as well as its saturation and luminance. Also, the option to control this filter using a visual interface like that of the Color Correction tool makes this difficult task much easier.
Color Key	Like the blue and green screen filter, the color key also creates a matte, but this filter enables you to determine the color that is to be keyed. Other than that, the sliders are the same.
Color Smoothing −4:1:1 Color Smoothing −4:2:2	These filters improve Chroma keying of DV25 and DVPRO50 clips, respectively. There are no controls or settings for these filters except the enabling checkbox. Simply apply a filter to a clip with a chroma key filter, but make sure the smoothing filter always remain on the top level of applied filters in the Filters tab of the Viewer.
Difference Matte	This filter is another one that is contingent upon a second clip that you must drag and drop on to the clip control part of the filter in the Viewer. The filter compares the two clips and creates a matte based upon those areas that are the same between both clips. Use this filter if you are in possession of footage that contains a backdrop both prior to and during any action occurring in it. A good example of this is when you lock down a camera and get footage of an environment before actors play out a scene in front of it. With the camera still locked down, you shoot your various takes of actors playing their scene, and then in post production use the difference matte filter to create a difference matte between the shots with and without actors. In so doing, you can then superimpose your keyed out talent over any other footage you choose.
Luma Key	With this key, the matte is created from the luminance values of a clip. Therefore, clips with a high degree of contrast work well with this filter. You control whether the matte is created from light, dark, similar, or dissimilar areas in the composite of the two clips.
Spill Suppressor, Blue	The spill suppressor is applied after using the blue and green screen filter to further key out any blue fringes still left behind. Make certain that, when you apply these filters in tandem, the spill suppressor comes after the blue and green screen filter in the list of filters applied to a clip.
Spill Suppressor, Green	This filter works with green-screen footage in exactly the same manner as its blue counterpart does with blue-screen footage.

Matte

Name	Description
8-Point Garbage Matte	This filter allows you to set the coordinates of eight points that combine to create the shape of a matte. By default, the area inside the polygon is visible; the area outside of it is transparent. Additionally, you can opt to smooth the corners, soften the edges, and invert the matte.
Extract	Performs a function very similar to the Luma key. This filter creates a matte based on the luminance of the clip to which it is applied. You can apply the results to either the Alpha channel or the combination of the RGB channels. You can also invert it. Sliders control threshold, tolerance, and softness.
4-Point Garbage Matte	Works in exactly the same way as its eight-point cousin, except that there are only four points to manipulate.
Image Mask	This filter takes the luminance or Alpha channel values from a second clip that you select and uses that information to create a matte.
Mask Feather	This filter blurs the Alpha channel of the clip to which it is applied by the amount you specify with the soft slider.
Mask Shape	Creates a mask or matte with a preset shape that you select from a pop-up menu. You also control the dimensions of those predefined shapes.
Matte Choker	Apply this filter to a clip that you've already keyed. This provides you with the most control over the edges of your matte.
Soft Edges	This is similar to a blur filter except that it's only applied to the edges of a selected clip.
Widescreen	Places a letterbox with the aspect ratio of your choice over the selected clip. You can also control the clip's offset as well as a border within the letterbox you've defined.

Perspective

Name	Description
Basic 3D	Enables you to take a selected clip and make it appear as though it is moving in three dimensions. Controls let you define the x-, y-, and z-axis rotation as well as the center and scale.
Curl	Similar to the page peel transition, this filter curls a clip back on itself as though it were a piece of paper. You control the direction, radius, and amount of the curl as well as whether you want another clip to appear on the other side of the curl.

Name	Description
Flop	This very useful filter enables you to flip-flop a clip either horizontally or vertically.
Mirror	Creates a mirror image of the clip by using a point that you define as its basis for the reflection axis. You can also change the angle of the reflection.
Rotate	Enables you to rotate an image in 90-degree increments while scaling the clip to fit the dimensions of the frame.

Final Cut Pro is built on top of QuickTime's architecture, so it only follows that the filters available in QuickTime as a standalone product would be available for use in Final Cut Pro. This can make your choices appear confusing because a number of these filters go by the same or similar names as those in the other video filter bins. In those cases, opt for those filters instead of the ones here because those other filters are generally more sophisticated in their controls.

QuickTime	
Name	**Description**
Blur	Simple blur filter with single pop-up menu to control the amount of blur.
Brightness and Contrast	Works exactly the same as the filter of the same name in the Image Control bin.
Color Style	Allows you to both solarize and posterize your image.
Color Tint	This filter tints the black and white values of a clip according to the colors you choose.
ColorSync	This filter allows you to display your clip according to the ColorSync profile of your monitor.
Edge Detection	Similar to the find edges filter in the Stylize bin but with less control. The filter finds the edges, and you set the width of those edges and decide whether to colorize them.
Emboss	Similar to the emboss filter in the Stylize bin but with less control. There is one pop-up menu allowing for some control over the thickness of the embossed edge.
General Convolution	Using a mathematical process called convolution, you set the values of a brightness pattern throughout a clip. This filter works best if you experiment with the sliders and note your results. Descriptions are lacking in this case.
HSL Balance	Allows you to change color in the clip with hue, saturation, and lightness settings as opposed to RGB settings.

Continued

QuickTime (continued)

Name	Description
Lens Flare	Creates the effect of a light source (such as the sun) being shone directly into the lens of a camera.
RGB Balance	Allows for control of a clip's color balance using red, green, and blue values as opposed to HSL settings.
Sharpen	Works in a similar fashion to the Sharpen filter in the Sharpen bin, only it has less control. Appears to sharpen an image by increasing the contrast of adjacent pixels.

Sharpen

Name	Description
Sharpen	Although you can't sharpen the focus of an image after it has been shot, you can apply this filter, which increases the contrast between adjacent pixels, thus making the clip appear sharper.
Unsharp Mask	This filter uses the same principle as the sharpen filter but allows for greater control in increasing the contrast between adjacent pixels with the addition of radius and threshold sliders.

Stylize

Name	Description
Anti-Alias	Takes high-contrast areas in a clip and blurs them, making the image appear softer.
Diffuse	You use this filter to offset pixels. This creates a rather extreme and very stylized look if applied with a radius above 1. You can also control the direction of the diffusion or randomize it.
Emboss	This filter takes areas of high contrast and makes them appear raised as though they were etched on a surface. You control the direction and depth of the edges as well as how much they contrast with the original image by setting the embossing amount.
Find Edges	Similar to the emboss filter, this one also accentuates the high contrast areas of a clip but makes the edges even more pronounced. Results are often dark so that you can opt to invert this filter as well.

Name	Description
Posterize	This filter forces the 255 possible values of each channel into a range reduced to an amount that you select. Selecting lower color ranges results in a cutout and extremely-high-contrast image.
Replicate	Converts the image into a composite of tiles. You select the number of tiles with horizontal and vertical sliders.
Solarize	This filter removes the midtones of an image and increases highlights and shadows, resulting in a look that can be described as an amplified inversion.

Video

Name	Description
Blink	Turns a clip's visibility on and off according to the on and off slider values you choose. The slider values represent the number of frames in which a clip is on or off. You can also control the opacity of the clip's off state.
De-Interlace	This filter takes a clip with separate fields and interpolates them into a full but less-sharp image. It can be useful when you've slowed down a clip containing a lot of fast motion.
Flicker Filter	This filter reduces flicker caused by thin horizontal lines that appear only during one field of a video frame, causing it to look like it's blinking, or flickering. This is basically a vertical blur filter with three preset amounts of blur. Choosing a higher setting will reduce apparent flicker more, but also add overall softness to the image.
Image Stabilizer	If you have jittery handheld footage or clips, this filter is a great solution as long as the contrast is high and the clip contains a clear shape whose motion the software can track. If these conditions are met, the filter stabilizes the footage after you define the area that the filter must follow.
Stop Motion Blur	This filter blends the frames of a selected clip within a range of time you specify. You can also dictate the number of steps between the blended frames, their opacity levels, and the type of blend.
Strobe	The strobe filter freezes frames in a clip at intervals that you select through the use of the strobe duration slider.
Timecode Print	This filter burns timecode onto a clip.
View Finder	This filter makes a clip appear as though it is being seen by a camera operator who's shooting while looking through a viewfinder.

Video Generators

As the Apple Final Cut Pro User's Manual rightly points out, video generators are not applied to clips; in fact, they *are* clips. As clips, however, video generators have not been acquired. They are created within Final Cut Pro, and most video generators need to be rendered after they are used. Examples include text, bars, and tone and black slugs. Generators can be called up by dragging them from the Video Generators bin on the Effects tab of the Browser, or any of the generators can be accessed by the pop-up menu in the lower-right corner of the Viewer. You can affect the properties of video generators by accessing them through the Controls tab in the View window.

The three real-time generators are Bars and Tone (NTSC), Bars and Tone (PAL), and Slug. The rest of the video generators might need to be rendered when applied to a given sequence.

Real-Time Generators

Name	Description
Bars and Tone (NTSC and PAL)	This generator enables you to create reference video color and tone. Obviously, this is a good thing to place at the head of tape layoffs so that others can calibrate their own playback devices when playing your tape.
Slug	Slug contains black video and two empty audio tracks. This is very useful as a timing placeholder if you lack media.

Graphical Generators

Name	Description
Color Matte	Color Matte generator creates a complete frame of solid color, which you can select with the color picker.
Custom Gradient	This generates a gradient built to your specification. You control whether the gradient is linear or radial, where it starts, its direction, its width, and its colors.
Gradient	The Gradient generator has far fewer controls than its custom counterpart. You control the color and the preset type of this particular gradient.

Name	Description
Highlight	This generates a high contrast band of simulated light. You control its angle, position, width, softness, and foreground and background colors. Dither and Gaussian switches smooth the appearance.
Noise	The Noise generator makes random pixel noise. It closely resembles video static. You can adjust its color.
Particle Noise	Particle Noise generates particle shapes you define along with their color, size, edge softness, and density.
Shapes (Circle, Oval, Rectangle, Square)	Creates selected shapes on black background. You can control the size of the shape, edge softness, and its color, however, you cannot select a different background color, nor is there an alpha channel with this generated clip.

Titling Generators

Name	Description
Crawl	Use of Crawl generates text that moves across the screen at the direction and speed you specify. You also select the font, size, style, spacing, color, and vertical location of the text.
Lower 3rd	As its name suggests, use of Lower 3rd generates two lines of text in the lower third of an image. You can select the background as well as all aspects of the type including the font, style, size, tracking, and color.
Outline Text	Creates static text with an outline that you can customize. This generator allows for multiple lines of text created by carriage returns. In addition to the full controls that you have over the text characters, you can also adjust the color, softness and width of characters' outline, even using a photo to fill the character or its outline.
Scrolling Text	Scrolling Text generates text in the style of film credits. You control the font, size, alignment, color, spacing, and leading as well as whether the text scrolls up or down. The clip's length determines the speed at which the text scrolls.
Text	Text generator is similar to the Lower 3rd generator except that the text is placed in the center of the frame by default. However, you can position it wherever you like. There are more controls in this generator than in the Lower 3rd variant. These include kerning and subpixel control.
Typewriter	As its name indicates, this creates text that appears to type across the screen. You can control all aspects of the text as well as the speed at which it types.

Audio Transitions

Only two audio transitions are included with Final Cut Pro, but they're extremely valuable. Use these when audio at an edit point changes too abruptly for your taste. Examples include audible pops at edit points or cutting to someone talking in mid-sentence. Circumstances such as these are well served by audio transitions that smooth out the audio of both the outgoing and incoming clips by fading them in at a duration that you set.

Audio Transitions	
Name	**Description**
Cross Fade (0db)	This transition fades the outgoing clip out and the incoming clip in simultaneously. In so doing, it creates a drop in volume at the middle of the transition.
Cross Fade (+ 3db)	This transition performs the same function while maintaining a constant audio level throughout the length of the transition.

Audio Filters

Apple has made some serious improvements to Final Cut Pro's audio editing capabilities, including its audio filters. In addition to the standard set of Final Cut Pro audio filters that you will find in the bin named Final Cut Pro in the Audio Filters bin, you now have a second bin labeled Apple, containing Audio Unit filters. Audio Unit filters are denoted with the letters AU preceding the filter's name and were created to work natively with OS X's new audio architecture, called Core Audio.

Note   Audio Unit plug-ins that don't support mono-to-mono processing won't work with Final Cut Pro 4. Also, custom Audio Units plug-ins are not supported.

Audio filters in Final Cut Pro can be dropped onto audio clips in the same manner that you drop video filters onto video clips. If the audio is a pair of linked stereo tracks, then the filter is applied to both tracks and altering settings in the Viewer affects both tracks equally. Experiment with the filters when applying them to clips.

Even though Final Cut Pro's audio filters are not organized in the Audio Filters bin as I have organized them here, the available filters can be divided into four general categories:

✦ Equalization

✦ Compression noise

✦ Reduction

✦ Effects

All of Final Cut Pro's equalizing filters share a combination of the following three slider controls:

✦ **Frequency Control:** Enables you to select the frequency you want to either boost or attenuate.

✦ **Q Control:** Lets you select a range of frequencies on either side of your initial frequency selection.

✦ **Gain Control:** Determines the desired boost or attenuation within your chosen frequency.

Note: When Audio Unit filters are identical in operation to the standard Final Cut Pro audio filters, they are listed together. AU and standard filters that differ in controls or function are listed and described separately.

Equalizing Filters	
Name	*Description*
3 Band Equalizer	Imagine that your clip has bass, mid-range, and treble knobs like on a home stereo receiver, except that you get to define what those three ranges are. That is essentially what this filter does.
AUGraphicEQ	Allows you gain control of 31 frequency bands of your audio. This is faster than applying multiple EQ filters to the same clip to control more frequency bands, not so good if you need to equalize only a few frequencies.
AUBandpass and Band Pass	These Band Pass filters give you control in boosting a single frequency.
DC Notch	DC Notch works on a preset frequency that matches a DC sound artifact caused by current leakage on the set of a shoot.
AUHpass and High Pass	These filters are essentially band pass filters that has been optimized for knocking out sound at the lower end of the audio spectrum. Examples include traffic or appliances such as a refrigerator or air conditioner.

Continued

Equalizing Filters (continued)

Name	Description
AUHighShelfFilter and High Shelf	High Shelf cuts off the higher frequencies quite sharply.
AULowpass and Low Pass	A Low Pass filter is another band pass filter that works best in optimizing sound at the lower end of the spectrum while knocking out the higher end. Examples include tape hiss or the high-pitched whine of a television set.
AULowShelfFilter and Low Shelf	These filters cut off the lower frequencies rather sharply.
Notch	The opposite of the band pass filter, this knocks out frequencies, attenuating them within your selected range.
AUParametricEQ and Parametric Equalizer	These filters are a hybrid of the Band Pass, Notch, and Shelf filters.

Compression and expansion filters give you control over an audio clip's dynamic range. The four controls you can adjust are the following:

✦ **Threshold:** Determines a volume level above which compression or expansion will be applied.

✦ **Ratio:** Determines the amount of compression.

✦ **Attack time:** Determines the filter's sensitivity to changes in the clip's volume levels.

✦ **Release time:** Determines how long the filter will apply to a clip after the change in volume has occurred

Note: When Audio Unit filters are identical in operation to the standard Final Cut Pro audio filters, they are listed together. AU and standard filters that differ in controls or function are listed and described separately.

Compression/Expansion Filters

Name	Description
AUPeakLimiter and Compressor/Limiter	These filters smooth out inconsistent volume levels that irregularly spike, and allow you to define a constant volume range.
Expander/Noise Gate	The opposite of the compressor, this filter picks up inconsistent drops in volume and allows you to define a constant volume range.

Noise reduction filters have controls similar to the equalizing filters. Once again, you select a frequency, a Q setting, and a gain setting.

Noise Reduction Filters	
Name	**Description**
Hum Remover	Hum Remover screens out certain frequencies that you define. It also enables you to remove five related harmonic frequencies that can be very useful when attempting to remove certain irritating hums that don't seem to respond to other attempts at getting rid of them.
Vocal DeEsser	This filter, as its name suggests, removes the *s* consonant sound in spoken dialog.
Vocal DePopper	The Vocal DePopper filter works in a manner similar to the DeEsser, but it zeroes in on the *p* consonant sound in spoken dialog.

Sound Effect Filters	
Name	**Description**
AUDelay Echo	Causes delayed repeat of audio, creating the illusion of being in a space that you can define by tweaking the sliders. With practice, you can create the perception of audio happening in a variety of spaces like a canyon, for example.
Reverb	The Reverb filter enables you to simulate audio as it may occur in a closed space. A pop-up menu lets you determine a range of spaces that include examples such as a small room or a large hall.

✦   ✦   ✦

Resources

This appendix contains list of resources that may be of interest to any Final Cut Pro user.

Apple Final Cut Pro Sites

Table D-1 provides a listing of Apple's Web sites related to Final Cut Pro and other technologies and Apple products that you may use as a video editor. It is a good idea to visit these sites on a regular basis to look for news and announcements.

Table D-1
Important Web Sites from Apple

Page	URL
Apple's main Final Cut Pro page	www.apple.com/finalcutpro/
Apple-approved devices	www.apple.com/finalcutpro/qualification.html
Apple's Support links for Final Cut Pro	www.info.apple.com/usen/finalcutpro/
Apple's Final Cut Pro discussion area	http://discussions.info.apple.com/
Apple's knowledge base link	http://kbase.info.apple.com/
Apple's main QuickTime page	www.apple.com/quicktime
Apple's information page on FireWire	www.apple.com/firewire
Apple's Web page for creative coverage	www.apple.com/creative
Apple's Web page for education coverage	www.apple.com/education

Information on Video Cards for Final Cut Pro

Table D-2 lists links to companies that make video capture cards for Final Cut Pro.

Table D-2
Video Capture Cards for Final Cut Pro

Card	URL
Aja Kona SD and HD	www.aja.com/kona.htm
Aurora Video Systems IgniterX	www.auroravideosys.com/
Digital Voodoo D1 64RT	www.digitalvoodoo.net/products/detail/default.asp?card=10

Card	URL
Pinnacle Systems Targa CinéWave	www.pinnaclesys.com/productpage.asp?templ=9&Product_ID=108
Black Magic Decklink	www.decklink.com
Matrox RTMac	www.matrox.com/video/products/rtmac/home.cfm

Apple Technical Information Sites

Table D-3 provides a list of some very useful Apple Web sites for technical information. These sites can help you find technical information on just about anything Apple-related.

Table D-3 Apple Technical Information Sites		
Title	**URL**	**Description**
Technical Information Library	http://kbase.info.apple.com/	The Apple Technical Information Information Library (TIL) is Apple's technical support database and is technical support database and is now named Apple Care Knowledge Base. The TIL contains over 15,000 articles related to product specifications, reference documentation, and Apple and third-party product technical issues. Updated daily with new information, it's the same database that Apple employees use to answer support questions. You can search volumes of ReadMe files and other documentation on Apple hardware and software. If you are struggling with troubleshooting the Mac OS or anything else related to Apple, this is a great place to begin your search.
Apple Software Updates page	www.info.apple.com/support/downloads.html	If you are having a software issue, it is always best to to see if there is a newer version availabe. Upgrading newer version available. Upgrading to a newer version of software will often resolve the problems that you are facing.
Apple Product Specs	www.info.apple.com/support/applespec.html	This page is incredibly helpful. It helps you locate the helps you locate the precise specifications of your Apple computer product. Listed here are computers, displays, and printers.

Continued

Table D-3 *(continued)*

Title	URL	Description
Apple Vendors Info Third-Party	`http://guide. apple.com/ index.html`	This site lists over 21,000 products made for Apple.
Mirror of Apple Sites	`http://mirror. apple.com`	This site is a not well known. It is a mirror site for Apple as well as numerous other Mac-related sites. If you can't reach the main Apple Web site, try this one instead.

Apple Manual Locations

The manuals Apple ships with their equipment are often simple documents to get you started. If you've lost any of your manuals, you can find online versions of them at the locations listed in Table D-4.

Table D-4
Apple TIL Articles on Final Cut Pro

Manual	URL
G4 manuals and G4 Cube Manuals	`http://docs.info.apple.com/article.html? artnum=50018` `http://docs.info.apple.com/article.html? artnum=50074`
G3 manuals and G3 Minie tower manual	`http://docs.info.apple.com/article.html? artnum=50122` `www.info.apple.com/kbnum/n50122`
PowerBook manuals (see the Power Book listing on the Manuals download page)	`www.info.apple.com/support/manuals.html`
Final Cut Pro manuals (for versions1.2.5 and 2.0)	`http://docs.info.apple.com/article.html? artnum=50034`

Non-Apple Final Cut Pro Sites

Apple isn't the only organization that maintains Web sites designed to serve Final Cut Pro and the user community. Table D-5 lists sites relating to Final Cut Pro that are maintained by people or organizations other than Apple. Table D-6 lists sites with general information on digital video (DV), Table D-7 lists sites with information on storage hardware, Table D-8 lists sites with information on the tape-to-film transfer process, and Table D-9 provides information on cameras.

	Table D-5 Non-Apple Final Cut Pro Web Sites	
Site	*URL*	*Description*
2-Pop	www.uemedia.com/ CPC/2-pop/	The top Web site for any and all Final Cut Pro–related issues. Discussion groups, FAQs, and numerous Final Cut Pro–related links can be found here.
Ken Stone's Final Cut Pro Site	http://kenstone.net/ fcp_homepage/fcp_ homepage_index.html	Ken Stone manages a first-rate Web site for Final Cut Pro. Tutorials and hints abound in this carefully prepared and maintained site.
World Wide Users Group Final Cut Pro Site	www.wwug.com/forums/ apple_final_cut/ index.htmz	The World Wide Users Group maintains discussion forums for every conceivable multimedia software. The Final Cut Pro forum is an active and lively discussion group.
About.com's Final Cut Pro Site	http://desktopvideo. about.com/cs/ finalcutpro/index.htm	Location for About.com's digital video information site.
Postforum Site	www.postforum.com/ forums/list.php?f=37	Postforum maintains a discussion group on Final Cut Pro.
Final Cut Pro Planet	www.finalcutproplanet. com/	A good place for looking up information on Final Cut Pro.
Neil Sadwelkar's Final Cut Pro Site	www.sadwelkar.com/ FCP.htm	Neil Sadwelkar has started a basic site for Final Cut Pro users.
QuickTime Information	www.judyandrobert.com/ quicktime/	This site is a great starting point for information on QuickTime. Judy and Robert have created a first-rate Web page for information on QuickTime.

Table D-6
DV-Related Web Sites

Site	URL	Description
Adam Wilt's DV Site	www.adamwilt.com/DV.html	Tons of DV information.
DV & FireWire Central	http://www.dvcentral.org/	Information on DV and FireWire.
DV Magazine Site	www.dv.com/	*DV Magazine* maintains this site for information on digital video–related issues.

Table D-7
Storage Hardware Web Sites

Site	URL	Description
Medea Corp	www.medeacorp.com	Medea drives are used by many Final Cut Pro users.
Seagate	www.seagate.com	Makers of the renowned Barracuda and Cheetah drives.
Micronet	www.micronet.com	Makers of rugged and extremely reliable storage drives.
Rorke Data	www.rorke.com	Makers of A/V-enhanced hard drives, RAIDS, and storage systems.
ATTO	www.attotech.com	Makers of Atto drives and SCSI interface.

Table D-8
Tape-to-Film Transfer Web Sites

Site	URL
Cinesite (Kodak)	www.cinesite.com
DuArt	www.duart.com
DVFilm	www.dvfilm.com
Tape House Digital	www.tapehousedigitalfilm.com

Table D-9
Camera and Optics Web Sites

Site	URL
Sony Digital Cameras	www.sel.sony.com/SEL/consumer/ss5/generic/digitalvideo
Canon DV Cameras	www.canondv.com/
The TRV-900 Information Site	www.bealecorner.com/trv900/index.html
The Xl-1 Information Site	www.dvinfo.net/xl1.htm
The Panasonic DVX-100	www.panasonic.com/PBDS/subcat/Products/cams_ccorders/f_ag-dvx100.html
Optics for 16:9	www.centuryoptics.com/

Great Free Stuff for Final Cut Pro Users

Table D-10 lists goodies that are available for free and may be of interest to Final Cut Pro users. Some of these are demo or trial versions of software, while others are just plain free.

Table D-10
Free Stuff for Final Cut Pro Users

Site	URL	Description
Test Pattern Maker	www.synthetic-ap.com/downloads/tpmmdown.html	This first-rate application allows you to create numerous video patterns such as color bars, luma steps, luma ramps, and more. Works under Classic mode in OS X.
VideoScope	www.evological.com/videoscope.html	A software-based application that works as a Waveform monitor and a Vectorscope.
OMF Tool	www.digidesign.com/download/omf/	The OMF tool allows you to convert OMF files to Pro Tools work sessions. By using the OMF tool, you can convert any OMF file you export from Final Cut Pro into a Pro Tools audio work session. To get Pro Tools (also free) see the following row. Will *not* operate on OS X or Classic.

Continued

Table D-10 *(continued)*		
Site	**URL**	**Description**
Pro Tools Free	`www.digidesign.com/ptfree/`	Pro Tools remains by far the most popular Digital Audio Workstation for any kind of audio post environment. You can now have this world standard for free. The free version of Pro Tools uses the Mac Processor (as opposed to the Digidesign hardware) and allows for 8 tracks of audio and 48 tracks of MIDI. With the OMF tool (see the preceding row) and Pro Tools Free you can have yourself a first-rate digital audio workstation to compliment your Final Cut Pro setup. All free, courtesy of Digidesign. Will *not* operate on OS X or Classic.
CGM Demo	`www.cgm-online.de/cgi-bin/dve_downloadcount.pl?name=11&digit=increment`	Demo versions of Final Cut Pro plug-ins.
Pixelan Spice for FCP	`www.pixelan.com/download/form.htm`	Trial versions of Final Cut Pro plug-ins.
Free Fonts from Macfonts.com	`www.macfonts.com/index.php`	Free fonts for your Mac. Make some fun text with these.
Free Sound Effects	`www.partnersinrhyme.com/pir/PIRsfx.html`	A Web site for downloading public domain sound effects.
Find Sounds	`http://findsounds.com/`	This Web site is an amazing search engine for sound effects.
Adobe Acrobat Reader	`www.adobe.com/support/downloads/main.html`	Adobe Acrobat Reader enables you to read Acrobat (PDF format) files.
Boris Script LTD	`www.borisfx.com/downloads/demos_mac.htm`	Boris makes numerous plug-ins that you can download as tryouts.
Cinema 4D R8	`www.maxoncomputer.com`	Cinema 4D R8 is a professional 3-D package. You can download a demo version.
After Effects 6.0	`www.adobe.com/support/downloads/main.html`	Download a trial version of this world-standard compositing and effects application. There is nothing quite like the beauty of After Effects.

Site	URL	Description
Photoshop 7.0	`www.adobe.com/support/` `downloads/main.html1`	A trial version of Photoshop is available here. Photoshop from Adobe Systems is the standard in image editing.

Troubleshooting

Table D-11 provides a list of some sites to search for troubleshooting information. Table D-12 lists troubleshooting tools and plug-ins that you can download.

Table D-11 Troubleshooting Resources		
Site	**URL**	**Description**
Apple Troubleshooting Site	`http://support.info.apple.com/` `te/troubleshooting/`	This site explains the basic logic of troubleshooting on a Mac. This is not specific to any application or hardware, but it is a great starting point when you are developing a troubleshooting strategy.
Apple Error Codes (not an Apple site)	`www.appleErrorCodes.com`	Description of Apple Error codes.
MacFixIt	`www.macfixit.com`	A great site for Mac-related problems. Numerous resources and discussion groups can be found here.
MacTech	`www.mactech.com`	A great site for advanced technical information.
VersionTracker	`www.versiontracker.com/` `index.shtml`	This site keeps track of an astonishing amount of software updates.
Sitelink	`www.sitelink.net`	At this site, there are many resources listed for all things Mac, including troubleshooting pages.

Table D-12
Troubleshooting Tools

Site	URL	Description
Dumpster	http://devworld.apple.com/quicktime/quicktimeintro/tools/	This site is a QuickTime tool that allows you to view and edit moov resources for a QuickTime file. You can use it on any QuickTime movie to see enormous amounts of information about it. Do not use this on your original files, however. Make copies of them and then use the Dumpster to view the information.
Macsbug v6.6.3	http://devworld.apple.com/tools/debuggers/MacsBug/	Macsbug is Apple's assembly-level debugger for the Mac OS. If you install Macsbug after any crash that would have otherwise frozen your computer, you end up in the Macsbug window, where typing **stdlog** generates a list of the current state of your computer and any and all contents of your RAM. (Type in **rs** to restart your computer.) This log is very useful if you are submitting bug reports for issues with your system.

✦　　✦　　✦

FXScript Commands and Syntax

Final Cut Pro contains a very powerful feature called FXBuilder. This feature enables you to create your own effects and transitions by writing and editing scripts with the FXScript language. Using FXBuilder and FXScript, you can also customize an existing effect, if the effect isn't encoded (locked).

Several important rules apply when working with FXScript:

+ Expressions are interpreted from left to right.

+ Multiplication and division are processed before addition and subtraction.

+ The contents of parentheses are processed before parts of an expression that are outside parentheses.

+ FXScripts require parameters when carrying out calculations. Parameters can be replaced with variables assuming that the variable is of the correct data type and has already been declared somewhere else in the script.

The following is an outline of commands, functions, parameters, expressions, and other types of syntax of the FXScript language you must use when writing your own scripts.

Operators

Operator	Meaning
+	Add. Also used to indicate a positive number.
-	Subtract. Also used to indicate a negative number.
*	Multiply
/	Divide
! or not	Logical NOT
~	Bitwise NOT
% or mod	Modulo
==	Equal
!=	Not equal
<	Less than
>	Greater than
<=	Less than or equal to
>=	Greater than or equal to
<<	Shift left
>>	Shift right
&	Bitwise AND
|	Bitwise OR
^ or xor	Bitwise XOR
&& or and	Logical AND
|| or or	Logical OR
? and :<conditional> ? <value1> : <value2>	If the conditional value is true, it will return value 1; if it is false, it will return value 2.

Compound Operators

In an assignment statement, you can use the following compound assignment operators:
+=, -=, *=, /=, %=, &=, |=, ^=

Operators and Regions

When defining regions, only the following operators can be used:

+ (add)

- (subtract)

& (and)

| (or)

^ (exclusive; that is, one or the other, not both)

Operators and Strings

+ is the only operator you can use when concatenating or appending strings together.

Data Types

Data Type	Syntax	Description
float	`float variablename`	Declares a floating-point variable
point	`point variablename`	Declares a variable that has a two-dimensional point coordinate
point3d	`point3d variablename`	Declares a variable that has a three-dimensional floating-point coordinate
image	`image variablename [width] [height]`	Declares a two-dimensional buffer of pixels to be operated on
region	`region variablename`	Declares a named region that is an arbitrary shape
string	`string variablename`	Declares a text string
color	`color variablename`	Declares a variable with the four fields that comprise an ARGB color value (A is for Alpha channel)
YUVcolor	`YUVcolor variablename`	Declares a variable with the four fields that comprise an AYUV color value (once again, A is for Alpha channel)
clip	`clip variablename`	Declares a variable that corresponds to a video clip
value	`value variablename`	Declares a non-modifiable parameter in a subroutine

Functions

Function	Syntax	Description
Sin	Sin(angle)	The sine of the specified angle (as a floating-point number in units of degrees)
Cos	Cos(angle)	The cosine of the specified angle (as a floating-point number also measured in degrees)
Tan	Tan(angle)	The tangent of the specified angle (as a floating-point number also measured in degrees)
ASin	ASin(value)	The arcsine of the value measured in degrees
ACos	ACos(value)	The arccosine of the value measured in degrees
ATan	ATan(value)	The arctangent of the value measured in degrees
Sqrt	Sqrt(value)	The square root of the value
Abs	Abs(value)	The absolute integer value of the value
Power	Power(value, exponent)	The value raised to the exponential power specified by the exponent
Exp	Exp(value)	The mathematical constant e raised to the power specified by the value
Log	Log(value)	The base e logarithm of the specified value
Log10	Log10(value)	The base 10 logarithm of the specified value
Integer	Integer(value)	Converts the specified value into an integer
Sign	Sign(value)	The sign of the value as defined by the following: −1 if the value is less than zero, 0 if the value is zero, and 1 if the value is greater than zero

Geometry

Command	Syntax	Description
DistTo	DistTo(p1, p2)	The distance between the two x and y coordinates defined by the values of p1 and p2
AngleTo	AngleTo (p1, p2)	The angle returned by a p1 to p2 vector
Interpolate	Interpolate(p1, p2, percent, result)	The x and y coordinate result of interpolating p1 and p2

Command	Syntax	Description
CenterOf	CenterOf(poly, point)	Places the center of a specified polygon defined by the poly variable at the point specified by the point variable
BoundsOf	BoundsOf(image, result)	Fills in the polygon defined by the "result" variable with a four-sided rectangle that is the bounds of the "image" variable. The result variable must be in the form of a four point array.
DimensionsOf	DimensionsOf(image, width, height)	The width and height values returned by the specified image
AspectOf	AspectOf(image)	The aspect ratio returned by the specified image
Grid	Grid(srcPoly, destPoly)	Splits the rectangular polygon "srcPoly," and divides it into a grid of rectangles based on the dimensions of "destPoly"
Mesh	Mesh(srcPoly, destPoly)	Takes the rectangular polygon "srcPoly," and converts it into a mesh based on the dimensions of "destPoly".
Convert2dto3d	Convert2dto3d(point/poly, point3d/poly3d, zvalue)	Fills in the values of either "point3d" or "poly3d" with the corresponding values from "point" or "poly," using the number defined in "zvalue" as the z-axis dimension of each point
Convert3dto2d	Convert3dto2d(point3d/poly3d, point/poly, eye3d)	Fills in the values of either "point" or "poly" with the corresponding values from "point3d" or "poly3d." Eye3d is the view point for the conversion. If it is zero, then parallel projection is used for the conversion.

Shapes

Command	Syntax	Description
Line	`Line(p1, p2, image, color, width)`	Draws a line from p1 to p2 in the buffer corresponding to "image," with the specified color (expressed as an RGB value) and width (measured in pixels)
MakeRect	`MakeRect(result, left, top, width, height)`	Makes a rectangular polygon, "result," with the dimensions specified. Left and top are pairs of x and y coordinates, and width and height are distances measured in pixels.
MakeRegion	`MakeRegion(poly, rgn)`	Turns the specified polygon into a region, "rgn."
OvalRegion	`OvalRegion(poly, rgn)`	Makes an oval from the upper-left and lower-right corners of the specified polygon, "poly." This is stored in the region, "rgn."
RegionIsEmpty	`RegionIsEmpty(rgn)`	Returns "true" if the region defined in "rgn" contains no pixels. "True" has a value of 1.
FrameRegion	`FrameRegion(rgn, image, color, width)`	Draws a line around the specified region, "rgn," with specified color (RGB value) and width (measured in pixels) in the image buffer.
FillRegion	`FillRegion(rgn, image, color)`	Fills the defined region, "rgn," with the specified color (RGB value) and stores the result in the specified image buffer.
FramePoly	`FramePoly(poly, image, color, width)`	Draws a frame around the bounds of the polygon defined by "poly" with the specified color (RGB value) and width (measured in pixels). Stores the result in the specified image buffer.
FillPoly	`FillPoly(poly, image, color)`	Fills the polygon defined in "poly" with the specified color (RGB value). Stores the result in the specified image buffer.
DrawSoftDot	`DrawSoftDotdest, point/poly, shape, size, softness, subSteps, color(s), opacity(s), aspect)`	Draws one or more sub-pixel positioned shapes in a buffer. Can be used to draw circles, squares, and diamonds in the specified color, size, softness, positioning accuracy, and opacity. Both the color and opacity values can be an array or a single value.

Command	Syntax	Description
FillOval	FillOval(poly, dest, color)	Fills the oval defined in "poly" with the specified color (RGB value) and stores the result in the specified image buffer
FrameOval	FrameOval(poly, dest, color, width)	Draws a frame around the bounds of the oval polygon defined as "poly" with the specified color (RGB value) and the specified width (measured in pixels). Stores the result in the specified image buffer.
FillArc	FillArc(center, radius, startAngle, endAngle, dest, color, aspect)	Draws an arc from "startAngle" to "endAngle" to the "dest" output. The size of the arc is defined in "radius." The position is defined in "center." The arc is filled with the color defined in "color" (RGB value).
FrameArc	FrameArc(center, radius, startAngle, endAngle, sides, dest, dolor, width, aspect)	Draws a frame of the arc from "startAngle" to "endAngle" to the "dest" output. The size of the arc is defined in "radius" and the position is defined in "center." "color" and "width" define the color and the width of the frame. "sides" is a boolean operator. If true, it will draw two lines of the same color and width as the arc from the ends of the arc to the center point; if untrue, no lines are drawn.
CurveTo	CurveTo(startPt, tangentPt, endPt, dest, color, width)	Draws a curve from "startPt" to "endPt" to the "dest" output. The shape of the curve is defined by "tangentPt." The color and the width of the curve are defined by "color" and "width."

Transform

Command	Syntax	Description
Rotate	Rotate(point/poly, center, angle,aspect)	Rotates the point or polygon defined in "point" or "poly" by the specified angle around the defined center.
Rotate3d	Rotate3d(point3d/poly, center3d, xrotate, yrotate, zrotate)	Rotates the three-dimensional point or polygon defined in "point" or "poly" by the specified angles around the specified center. "Center3d" is composed of three fields: height, width, and depth.

Continued

Transform *(continued)*

Command	Syntax	Description
Scale	Scale(point/poly, center, hScale, vScale)	Scales a point or polygon around the defined center by the amounts defined in hscale and vscale.
Scale3d	Scale3d(point3d/poly3d, center3d, xscale, yscale, zscale)	Scales a three-dimensional point or polygon around the defined center by the three scale factors.
Offset	Offset(point/poly, hAmount, vAmount)	Moves a point or polygon by the amount defined in the two-dimensional values "hAmount" and "vAmount."
Offset3d	Offset3d(point3d/poly3d, xoffset, yoffset, zoffset)	Moves a three-dimensional point or polygon by the defined amount in each plane.
Outset3d	Outset3d(poly3d, center3d, amount)	Moves a four-sided polygon toward or away from the defined center in three dimensions.

Blit

Command	Syntax	Description
RegionCopy	RegionCopy(srcImage1, srcImage2, destImage, rgn, softness)	Copies the two source images into the destination image buffer using the defined region as a mask, softening the edges by the defined softness value.
Blit	Blit(sourceImage, sourcePoly, destImage, destPoly, opacity)	Copies the pixels inside "sourcepoly" and "sourceimage" into the values defined as "destpoly" and "destimage" at the defined opacity.
BlitRect	BlitRect(sourceImage, sourcePoly, destImage, destPoly)	Copies the pixels inside "sourcepoly" and "sourceimage" into the values defined as "destpoly" and "destimage." Both source and destination polygons must be four-sided, and the Alpha channel of the source is treated as opaque.
MeshBlit	MeshBlit(sourceImage, sourcePoly, destImage, destPoly, opacity)	Copies the pixels from "sourceImage" into "destImage," using two point meshes as the transformation and applying the defined "opacity."

Command	Syntax	Description
MeshBlit3D	MeshBlit3d(sourceImage, sourcePoly, destImage, destPoly3d, opacity, center3D)	Copies the pixels from "sourceimage" into "destimage," using two 3-D point meshes as the transformation and applying the defined "opacity."
MaskCopy	MaskCopy(sourceImage1, sourceImage2, maskImage, destImage, softness, amount)	Places the two source images into the destination image, using a gradient mask. "Softness" defines the threshold amount for the gradient, and "amount" defines the gradient percentage. The command is the same as RegionCopy, but the mask is derived from an image buffer.
PagePeel	PagePeel(srcImage1, srcImage2, destImage, centerPoint, radius, angle, peel, aspect)	Performs a "page peel" effect, using srcimage1 and 2 as the front and back of the page. The result is placed in "destImage." The center point and angle specify the location and angle of the "cut line" for the peel. "Radius" is the radius of the curvature for the peel. The value defined in "peel" determines the appearance of the peel: If it is zero, the image is rolled up along one side, like a scroll, and if it is any value other than zero, the image peels upward and away, starting at one corner, from the image below.

Process

Command	Syntax	Description
Blur	Blur(srcImage, destImage, radius, aspect)	Blurs the source image and places the result in the destination image. "Radius" defines the blur's radius or intensity.
BlurChannel	BlurChannel(srcImage, destImage, radius, doAlpha, doRed, doGreen, doBlue, aspect)	Blurs the specified channels of the source image and places the result in the destination image. "Radius" defines the blur's radius or intensity. The doChannel values are Boolean numbers, either known numbers or variables.

Continued

Process (continued)

Command	Syntax	Description
Diffuse	Diffuse(srcImage, destImage, repeatEdges, hMin, hMax, vMin, vMax)	Each pixel in the destination image is filled with a pixel from the source image, which is offset spatially by a random number. The range for this random number is defined by the values assigned to "hmin" and "hmax" on the horizontal axis, and "vmin" and "vmax" on the vertical axis. "RepeatEdges" is a Boolean operation that determines whether pixels that would be beyond the bounds of the source image are filled with either copies of the nearest edge pixel or transparent black pixels.
DiffuseOffset	DiffuseOffset(srcImage, destImage, repeatEdges, hMin, hMax, vMin, vMax, hTable[width], vTable[height])	This is similar to the Diffuse command, but the horizontal and vertical offset for each pixel is added to the hTable and vTable values, which contain the horizontal and vertical position for each pixel.
MotionBlur	MotionBlur(srcImage, destImage, hDist, vDist, steps)	Copies the source image into the destination image, adding a motion blur, the intensity of which is defined by "hdist" and "vdist." "Steps" define how many intermediate steps are added.
RadialBlur	RadialBlur(srcImage, destImage, centerPt, amount, spin, steps, aspect)	Copies the source image into the destination image, adding a radial blur, the intensity of which is defined by "amount," around the center defined in "centerPt." "Steps" specifies how many intermediate steps are added. "Spin" is either true or false. If true, "amount" is a rotation angle. If false, "amount" is the distance that the blur extends from the center point.
Blend	Blend(srcImage1, srcImage2, destImage, amount)	Blends the two source images and places the result in the destination image. "Amount" defines the blend percentage.

Command	Syntax	Description
ColorTransform	`ColorTransform(srcImage, destImage, matrix, float[3], float[3])`	Performs color transformation from the source image to the destination image, based on the specified 3x3 float matrix. The two float arrays define the offsets to be added to the source and destination images during the operation. If the matrix is an RGB to RGB transformation, the arrays should be filled with zeros.
LevelMap	`LevelMap(src, dest, alphaMap[256], redMap[256], greenMap[256], blueMap[256])`	Maps the source image into the destination image, passing each component of the source image through a 256-entry floating-point lookup table composed of alpha, red, green, and blue channels, in that order.
ChannelCopy	`ChannelCopy(src, dest, copyAlpha, copyRed, copyGreen, copyBlue)`	Copies a set of channels from the source image to the destination image. Each channel is copied from the channel specified by its corresponding parameter. The "copy" parameters are the predefined variables kalpha, kred, kgreen, and kblue.
Convolve	`Convolve(srcImage, destImage, kernel, divisor, offset)`	Performs a 3x3 convolution from the source image to the destination image. The sum of the contents of the 3x3 array defined as "kernel" is divided by the specified divisor, and "offset" is added in.
ChannelFill	`ChannelFill(destImage, alphaValue, redValue, greenValue, blueValue)`	Fills the channels of the destination image with the defined color values.
ChannelMultiply	`ChannelMultiply(srcImage, destImage, alphaValue, redValue, greenValue, blueValue)`	Copies the source image into the destination image, multiplying each channel by the corresponding color value. If any of these is set to 1.0, the channel value remains unchanged.
Desaturate	`Desaturate( image )`	This converts the image to black and white.

Distort

Command	Syntax	Description
Cylinder	`Cylinder(srcImage, destImage, center, radius, amount, vertical)`	Copies the source image into the destination image, distorting the pixels so that they appear to have been mapped onto the surface of a cylinder. "Center" defines the two-dimensional center point for the cylinder; "radius" defines the width of the affected area. Vertical is a Boolean number that defines whether the cylinder is horizontal or vertical. "Amount" defines the intensity of the effect.
Fisheye	`FishEye(srcImage, destImage, centerPt, radius, amount, aspect)`	Copies the source image into the destination image and distorts the image outward or inward depending on the value defined in "amount," creating a fisheye lens effect. "Radius" specifies the effect's radius from the center point in pixels. If you use a negative value for "amount," the distortion works inward.
Whirlpool	`Whirlpool(srcImage, destImage, repeatEdges, centerPt, amount, aspect)`	Copies the source image into the destination image, distorting the image outward from the center point by spinning the pixels around by the defined "amount." If "RepeatEdges" is true, then the edge pixels are repeated; otherwise transparent black pixels will be placed at the edges.
Ripple	`Ripple(srcImage, destImage, repeatEdges, centerPt, amplitude, wavelength, aspect)`	Copies the source image into the destination image, distorting the image by creating waves at the edges. "Amplitude" and "wavelength" define the size and number of waves in the ripple.
Wave	`Wave(srcImage, destImage, repeatEdges, centerPt, amplitude, wavelength, vertical, aspect)`	Copies the source image into the destination image, distorting the image outward from the center point in such a way that the image appears horizontally or vertically rippled. "Amplitude" and "wavelength" define the size and number of waves in the ripple. The Boolean number defined by "vertical" determines whether the waves are arranged horizontally or vertically. If "RepeatEdges" is true, then the edge pixels are repeated; otherwise transparent black pixels will be placed at the edges.

Command	Syntax	Description
PondRipple	PondRipple(srcImage, destImage, centerPt, radius[n], thickness[n], amplitude, luminance, aspect)	Copies the source image into the destination image, distorting the image outward from the center point in a pond ripple pattern. The two parameters must be floating-point arrays of the same size. "n" ripples are created, with radius and thickness corresponding to "n."
Displace	Displace(srcImage, destImage, mapImage, repeatEdges, xScale, yScale, lumaScale, aspect)	Takes the red and green channel values of a clip to offset the source clip's pixels both horizontally and vertically.
BumpMap	BumpMap(srcImage, destImage, mapImage, repeatEdges, angle, scale, lumaScale, aspect)	Takes the luminance value of a clip to offset the source clip's pixels.
OffsetPixels	OffsetPixels(srcImage, destImage, repeatEdges, hDisplace[width], vDisplace[height], aspect)	Performs a row and column operation by using two arrays to offset the source clip.

Composite		
Command	Syntax	Description
Matte	Matte(overImage, baseImage, destImage, amount, type)	Composites the image buffer specified as "overImage" onto the buffer specified as "baseImage," and places the result in the destination image. "Type" can be one of the predeclared variables kAlpha, kWhite, or kBlack. These allow Alpha channel compositing or black or white matte Alpha channel compositing. "Amount" defines the opacity of the image being overlaid.
Screen	Screen(srcImage1, srcImage2, destImage, amount, type)	Mixes the white areas of source image 1 into source image 2, placing the result in the destination image. "Amount" defines the percentage of the blend.

Continued

Composite *(continued)*

Command	Syntax	Description
Multiply	Multiply(srcImage1, srcImage2, destImage, amount, type)	Mixes the black areas of source image 1 into source image 2, placing the result in the destination image. "Amount" defines the percentage of the blend.
Overlay	Overlay(srcImage1, srcImage2, destImage, amount, type)	Mixes the white areas of source image 1 into source image 2, where the color values of pixels in source image 1 are over 127, and mixes the black areas of source image 1 into source image 2 elsewhere. The result is placed in the destination image. "Amount" defines the percentage of the blend.
Lighten	Lighten(srcImage1, srcImage2, destImage, percent, type)	For each pixel in the destination image, this function chooses the corresponding pixel in the source image that has the lighter grayscale value.
Darken	Darken(srcImage1, srcImage2, destImage, percent, type)	For each pixel in the destination image, this function chooses the corresponding pixel in the source image that has the darker grayscale value.
Difference	Difference(srcImage1, srcImage2, destImage, type)	Each pixel in the destination image is filled with a color value corresponding to the absolute value of the difference between each of the channels in the two source images.
Add	Add(srcImage1, srcImage2, destImage, percent, type)	Each pixel in the destination image is filled with a color value corresponding to the sum of the pixels in source image 1 and the fraction of source image 2 defined in "percent."
AddOffset	AddOffset(srcImage1, srcImage2, destImage, offset)	Each pixel in the destination image is filled with a color value corresponding to the sum of the pixels in source image 1 and source image 2. The amount of offset is defined by adding or subtracting a value.
Subtract	Subtract(srcImage1, srcImage2, destImage, percent, type)	Each pixel in the destination image is filled with a color value corresponding to that for the same pixel in source image 1 minus the values of the matching pixels in the portion of source image 2 defined by "percent."

Command	Syntax	Description
ImageAnd	ImageAnd(srcImage1, srcImage2, destImage)	Fills the destination image with a logical AND of all the pixels in the two source images.
ImageOr	ImageOr(srcImage1, srcImage2, destImage)	Fills the destination image with a logical OR of all the pixels in the two source images.
ImageXor	ImageXor(srcImage1, srcImage2, destImage)	Fills the destination image with a logical "Exclusive or" of all the pixels in the two source images.
Invert	Invert(srcImage, destImage)	Inverts the image.
InvertChannel	InvertChannel(srcImage, destImage, doAlpha, doRed, doGreen, doBlue)	Inverts one or more channels selectively.
UnMultiply	UnMultiply(srcImage, srcImagetype)	Removes black or white pre-multiplication.

Key		
Command	**Syntax**	**Description**
BlueScreen	BlueScreen(srcImage, destImage, min, max, fillRGB)	This command creates a mask from the source image, extracting the blue areas of the image. "Min" and "max" control the range of color extraction. If "fillRGB" is 1, the RGB channels are filled with a grayscale mask. Otherwise only the Alpha channel is filled.
GreenScreen	GreenScreen(srcImage, destImage, min, max, fillRGB)	This command creates a mask from the source image, extracting the green areas of the image. "Min" and "max" control the range of color extraction. If "fillRGB" is 1, the RGB channels are filled with a grayscale mask. Otherwise only the Alpha channel is filled.
BGDiff	BGDiff(srcImage, destImage, min, max, fillRGB)	This command creates a mask from the source image, extracting the areas of maximum difference between the blue and green channels. "Min" and "max" control the range of color extraction. If "fillRGB" is 1, the RGB channels are filled with a grayscale mask. Otherwise only the Alpha channel is filled.

Continued

Key *(continued)*

Command	Syntax	Description
RGBColorKey	`RGBColorKey(srcImage, destImage, redTarget, redPass, greenTarget, greenPass, blueTarget, bluePass, softness, fillRGB)`	Fills either the Alpha or RGB channels of the destination image with a mask created by comparing the values of the pixels in the source image to the defined "pass" and "target" values. "Softness" defines the softness of the mask. "FillRGB" defines whether or not the Alpha or RGB channels are filled with the results.
YUVColorKey	`YUVColorKey(srcImage, destImage, yTarget, yPass, uTarget, uPass, vTarget, vPass, softness, fillRGB)`	Fills either the Alpha or RGB channels of the destination image with a mask created by comparing the YUV values of the pixels in the source image to the defined "pass" and "target" values. "Softness" defines the softness of the mask. "FillRGB" defines whether or not the Alpha or RGB channels are filled with the results.

External

Command	Syntax	Description
Filter	`Filter("name", source, dest, frame, duration, fps, ["parmName", parmValue, ...])`	This command calls another script, which must be a filter. It passes one source and one destination image, as well as values corresponding to the frame where the filter is to begin, the frames per second for the video where the frame is found, and the duration of the filter effect. You can also opt to set the inputs for the called filter using the parameters in the square brackets that follow. These should correspond to the variable names declared to hold the inputs in the filter script being called.

Command	Syntax	Description
Transition	Transition("name", src1, src2, dest, frame, duration, fps, ["parmName", parmValue, ...])	This command calls another script, which must be a transition. It passes two source images and one destination image, as well as values corresponding to the frame where the transition is to begin, the frames per second for the video where the frame is found, and the duration of the transition effect. You can also opt to set the inputs for the transition using the parameters in the square brackets that follow. These should correspond to the variable names declared to hold the inputs in the transition script being called.
Generator	Generator("name", dest, frame, duration, fps, ["parmName", parmValue, ...])	This command calls another script, which must be a generator. It passes one destination image, as well as values corresponding to the frame where the generator is to begin, the frames per second for the video where the frame is found, and the duration of the generator effect. You can also opt to set the inputs for the generator using the parameters in the square brackets that follow. These should correspond to the variable names declared to hold the inputs in the generator script being called.

String

Command	Syntax	Description
NumToString	NumToString(number, string, format)	Converts a number into a string of text, using the defined format. The format can be any one of the constants used to describe text formatting.
StringToNum	StringToNum(string)	Converts a string into a series of numbers.
Length	Length(string)	Returns a number corresponding to the number of characters in the specified string.
CharsOf	CharsOf(sourceString, first, last, destString)	Places a subset corresponding to the "first" through the "last" characters of the source string into the destination string.

Continued

String *(continued)*

Command	Syntax	Description
ASCIIOf	ASCIIOf(string, index)	Returns the ASCII value of the character at the index in the string.
ASCIIToString	ASCIIToString (ASCIIValue, destString)	Converts the "ASCIIvalue" into the character it represents and places this character into the defined destination string.
CountTextLines	CountTextLines (string)	Returns a number corresponding to the number of lines of text in the string specified.
FindString	FindString (sourceString, startOffset, findString)	Finds the characters in "Findstring" within "sourceString," starting from "startOffset."

Text

Command	Syntax	Description
DrawString	DrawString(string, h, v, spacing, image, color, aspect)	Draws the specified text string in the defined image, starting in the position defined in the "h" and "v" values. "Spacing" defines the kerning distance between the characters in pixels. "Color" defines the color value for the text. Can be used with double-byte characters.
DrawStringPlain	DrawStringPlain (string, poly, image, color, aspect)	A faster string routine which does not feature auto-kerning. Can be used with double-byte characters.
MeasureString	MeasureString (string, spacing, width, height, ascent, descent, aspect)	Takes the specified string and returns numbers based on its dimensions. "Spacing" defines the kerning distance between the characters in pixels. Can be used with double-byte characters.
Measure StringPlain	MeasureStringPlain (string, width, height, ascent, descent, aspect)	Takes the specified string without an auto-kerning calculation and returns numbers based on its dimensions. Can be used with double-byte characters.
SetTextFont	SetTextFont(string)	Used to select a font for the text from the available system fonts.

Command	Syntax	Description
SetTextJustify	SetTextJustify (justification)	Used to select right, left, or center justification for a text string.
SetTextStyle	SetTextStyle(style)	Used to select plain, bold, italic, or bold italic, for the text type used in a text string.
SetTextSize	SetTextSize(size)	Used to select the point size for a text string.
ResetText	ResetText	Resets the text to the default defined by plain style, black text color, 24-point size, Times(r) font, and left-alignment.

Clip

Command	Syntax	Description
GetVideo	GetVideo(srcClip, timeOffset, destImage)	Puts a frame from the clip specified in "srcClip" into the destination image starting at the specified time offset.
GetTimeCode	GetTimeCode (srcClip, timeCode, frameRate, dropFrame)	Gets the timecode for the defined frame.
GetReelName	GetReelName (srcClip, string)	Puts the reel name for the source clip into the specified string.
GetLimits	GetLimits(srcClip, duration, offset)	Put the time duration of the specified clip into the variable defined in "duration."

Utility

Command	Syntax	Description
SysTime	SysTime	Returns the computer's current clock setting.
Random	Random(min, max)	Returns a random number no less than "min" and no greater than "max."
RandomTable	RandomTable (array[n])	Fills the specified float array with unique random values between 0 and n-1.
RandomSeed	RandomSeed(value)	Initializes the random number generator. If "value" is set to zero, the random numbers generated will be in a different sequence every time.

Continued

Utility *(continued)*

Command	Syntax	Description
MatrixConcat	`MatrixConcat (srcMatrix1, srcMatrix2, destMatrix)`	Concatenates two 3x3 matrices and places the result into the destination matrix.
ColorOf	`ColorOf(image, point, color)`	Places the color value of the specified point in the specified image buffer into the variable specified for "color."
Truncate	`Truncate(srcRect1, srcRect2)`	Takes the two source rectangles defined in "srcRect1" and "srcRect2" and truncates them into two equal-sized rectangles. This is used right before Blit commands to improve speed if sub-pixel accuracy is not required.
PointTrack	`PointTrack (fromImage, srcPoint, toImage, guessPoint, range, deltaPoint)`	Scans a rectangle of the size defined in "range" around the source point defined in the "from" image, looking for a match in the "to" image. This assesses the difference in position between the two images. The offset of the matching image data in the "to" image is placed in "deltapoint."
Highlight	`Highlight(destImage, centerPoint, angle, width, softness, dither, gaussian, foreColor, backColor, aspect)`	Paints a specular highlight band in the destination image, using the defined center point and angle as the highlight line. "Width," "softness" and "color" define the size and color of the highlight band. If the value for "dither" is true, a random dither is applied to the highlight gradient, making it smoother over large areas. If "gaussian" is true, the gradient will have a Gaussian fall-off, which looks more natural when used for specular highlight, or when two highlights are screened together.
CircleLight	`CircleLight (destImage, centerPoint, width, softness, aspect, dither, gaussian, foreColor, backColor)`	Creates a circular highlight outward from "centerPoint."

Command	Syntax	Description
RandomNoise	RandomNoise (destImage, alphaMin, alphaMax, redMin, redMax, greenMin, greenMax, blueMin, blueMax, makeColors)	Randomizes the color of all the pixels in the destination image according to the bounds set by the "_min" and "_max" values defined in each channel.
Assert	Assert(value)	Stops the script with an error.
GetPixelFormat	GetPixelFormat (image)	Takes and image and returns the pixel format of the image. For example, kFormatRGB255, kFormatRGB219, kFormatYUV219.
SetPixelFormat	SetPixelFormat (image, format)	Sets the pixel format of an image buffer without changing the contents of the image buffer. Thus, it should generally only be used on empty image buffers.
GetConversion Matrix	GetConversionMatrix (srcFormat, destFormat, matrix, srcOffsets, destOffsets)	Returns a matrix and the "srcOffsets" and "destOffsets" which would be used with ColorTransform to convert a buffer from "srcFormat" to "destFormat."
ConvertImage	ConvertImage (srcImage, destImage, format)	Performs a color space conversion from the source image's color space, which can be obtained by GetPixelFormat(srcImage) into the defined format. It copies the data into "destImage" with the color space conversion and sets the pixel format of "destImage" to "format."

Constants and Predeclared Variables
General

Constant	Description
kUndefined	Most static variables start with this value
kAlpha	Defines the Alpha channel
true	Boolean — anything except 0
false	Boolean — 0

Color

Constant	Description
kBlack	Defines black color
kWhite	Defines white color
kGray	Defines gray color
kRed	Defines red color or the R channel value
kGreen	Defines green color or the G channel value
kBlue	Defines blue color or the B channel value
kCyan	Defines cyan color
kYellow	Defines yellow color
kMagenta	Defines magenta color

Formatting

Constant	Description
kInteger	Defines the integer numerical format
kFloat2	Defines the real numerical format with two decimal places
kFloat4	Defines the real numerical format with four decimal places
kFloat6	Defines the real numerical format with six decimal places
kSize	Defines the data storage format
k24fps	Defines the 24 fps timecode format
k25fps	Defines the 25 fps timecode format
k30fps	Defines the 30 fps timecode format
k60fps	Defines the 60 fps timecode format
k30df	Defines the 30 fps drop-frame timecode format
k60df	Defines the 60 fps drop-frame timecode format
k16mm	Defines the 24 fps timecode format
k35mm	Defines the 24 fps timecode format

Shapes

Constant	Description
kRound	Defines an oval shape
kSquare	Defines a rectangle shape
kDiamond	Defines a diamond shape

Text

Constant	Description
kleftjustify	Defines left text alignment
kcenterjustify	Defines center text alignment
krightjustify	Defines right text alignment
kplain	Defines plain text style
kbold	Defines bold text style
kitalic	Defines italic text style
kbolditalic	Defines bold italic text style

Key

Constant	Description
kKeyNormal	Defines the Normal composite mode
kKeyAdd	Defines the Add composite mode
kKeySubtract	Defines the Subtract composite mode
kKeyDifference	Defines the Difference composite mode
kKeyMultiply	Defines the Multiply composite mode
kKeyScreen	Defines the Screen composite mode
kKeyOverlay	Defines the Overlay composite mode
kKeyHardLight	Defines the HardLight composite mode
kKeySoftLight	Defines the SoftLight composite mode
kKeyDarken	Defines the Darken composite mode
kKeyLighten	Defines the Lighten composite mode

Continued

Key *(continued)*	
Constant	**Description**
kFormatRGB255	Used as a label for "RGB" image buffers where white is set at (255,255,255) and black is set (0,0,0).
kFormatRGB219	Used as a label for "RGB-219" image buffers where white is set at (219,219,219), "CCIR superwhite" is set at (238,238,238) and black is set at (0,0,0).
kFormatYUV219	Used as a label for YUV buffers. A Y value of 0 is black, 219 is "CCIR white" and 238 is "CCIR superwhite."

Variables	
Constant	**Description**
fps	Defines the frame rate
frame	Defines the current frame number
duration	Defines the length of an effect
ratio	Defines the ratio between the current frame to the duration
src1	Defines the current frame buffer from the source clip in a filter and the outgoing source clip in a transition
clip1	Defines the source clip in a filter and the outgoing source clip in a transition
srcType1	Defines the source clip's alpha type
src2	Defines the current frame buffer from the incoming source clip in a transition
clip2	Defines the incoming source clip in a transition
srcType2	Defines the incoming source clip's alpha type
dest	Defines the current buffer for video output
exposedBackground	Defines the background visibility
previewing	Defines the rendering mode, frame render or sequence render
renderRes	Defines the sequence's resolution quality
RGBtoYUV	Defines the matrix conversion from RGB to YUV color space
YUVtoRGB	Defines the matrix conversion from YUV to RGB color space
linearRamp	Defines a linear ramp from 0-255
srcIsGap1	Boolean—True if scr1 is a gap, otherwise false
srcIsGap2	Boolean—True if scr2 is a gap, otherwise false

Input

Statement	Syntax	Description
CheckBox	`input varName, "UIName", CheckBox, value`	Defines a check box. 0 results in not checked, 1 results in checked.
Slider	`input varName, "UIName", Slider, value, min, max [ramp value] [label "Units"] [detent/snap v1, v2, ...]`	Creates a slider bar control. You can define an initial default value, minimum and maximum values, ramp value, "Units" specified as the label, and optional detent and snap values.
Angle	`input varName, "UIName", Angle, value, min, max [label "Units"] [detent/snap v1, v2, ...]`	Creates an angle control.
Popup	`input varName, "UIName", Popup, value, label1, label2, ..., labelN`	Defines a pop-up menu with the specified labels, set to the default defined in "value."
RadioGroup	`input varName, "UIName", RadioGroup, value, label1, label2, ..., labelN`	Specifies a radio button or group of radio buttons with the defined label or labels.
Color	`input varName, "UIName", Color, alpha, red, green, blue`	Defines a color selection tool. The chosen color is placed in the "color" variable. The default color is defined by the "alpha," "red," "green" and "blue" values.
Clip	`input varName, "UIName", Clip`	Defines an input control that allows you to input a video clip or a still image.
Text	`input varName, "UIName", Text, "string" [TextHeight h]`	Creates a text box.
Point	`input varName, "UIName", Point, x, y`	Creates a point entry control.

Continued

Input *(continued)*

Statement	Syntax	Description
Label	`input varName, "UIName", Label, "string"`	Defines the static text in the Name column.
FontList	`input varName, "UIName", FontList [, "InitialFont", "TextFieldName"]`	Creates a pop-up list of TrueType fonts to choose from. The "TextFieldName" is the name of the text box to be associated with this font pop-up list. For example, when you change the font pop-up to Geneva, the text in the text box "TextFieldName" will be drawn in Geneva.

Definition

Statement	Syntax	Description
Filter	`Filter "name"`	Defines the script as a filter with the specified name, which makes it appear in the Filters bin in the Browser's Effects tab.
Transition	`Transition "name"`	Defines the script as a transition with the specified name, which makes it appear in the Transitions bin in the Browser's Effects tab.
Generator	`Generator "name"`	Defines the script as a generator with the specified name, which makes it appear in the Generators bin in the Browser's Effects tab.
Group	`Group "name"`	Defines the group the script should be placed in. Groups can be identified as the bins inside the first level of bins in the Effects tab. For example, the Dissolve bin in the Video Transitions bin represents a group, in this case the dissolve transitions.
WipeCode	`WipeCode(code, accuracy)`	Defines the transition's wipe code.
KeyType	`KeyType(type)`	Defines the transition's key type.
AlphaType	`AlphaType(type)`	Defines the alpha type. A variable can be knone (none/ignore), kalpha (straight), kblack (black), or kwhite (white).
QTEffect	`QTEffect("name")`	QTEffect defines the QT real-time effect name.
ProducesAlpha	`ProducesAlpha`	Specifies that the effect will produce an Alpha channel.

Statement	Syntax	Description
FullFrame	FullFrame	Input definition which states that the filter only works on a full frame. Final Cut Pro, when processing fields, will only pass the full frames. This flag is only valid for filter scripts.
EffectID	EffectID ("name")	Reserved for future use.
InvalEntireItem	InvalEntireItem	This identifies the effect as time-dependent, or the effect changes over time. Subsequently, the render cache of the effect is invalidated when the duration of the effect changes.
RenderEach FrameWhenStill	RenderEachFrame WhenStill	This identifies the effect as time-dependent, or the effect changes over time. Thus, even if the source is a still graphic or non-animated generator, each frame should be rendered. This can be used to indicate that the script needs to be run for each frame, even if the parameters are not changing. This is useful for still graphics and generators or filters which are non-animated or time-varying, such as the "Blink" filter.
InformationFlag	InformationFlag (string)	This is a general tool for supplying additional keywords to Final Cut Pro.

Parser		
Statement	**Syntax**	**Description**
BezToLevelMap	BezToLevelMap (array,leftPt, ctlPt1, ctlPt2, rightPt, startIndex, endIndex)	Fills in the array from startIndex to endIndex as defined by leftPt, ctlPt1, ctlPt2, and rightPt.
Chroma AngleKey	ChromaAngleKey(src, dest,doLuma, lumaMin, lumaMax, lumaSoft, doSaturation, satMin, satMax, satSoft, doAngle, centerAngle, angleWidth, angleSoftness, fillRGB)	Creates a luma, saturation, and/or a chroma key from src to dest based on values supplied. If fillRGB is not set, the dest alpha channel will contain the matte. If fillRGB is set, the dest color channel will also contain the matte.

Continued

Parser *(continued)*

Statement	Syntax	Description
IntializeArray	`InitializeArray (theArray, startPos, endPos, initializeValue)`	Quick method of initializing a parser array to a constant value by filling in array indices from startPos to endPos with value of initializeValue.
LevelAdjust	`LevelAdjust (src, dest, aAdjustSrc, aAdjustArray, rAdjustSrc, rAdjustArray, gAdjustSrc, gAdjustArray, bAdjustSrc, bAdjustArray)`	Allows adjustment of each channel to be based on the value of another channel. For example, the green channel could be increased or decreased using the value of the blue channel. Passing a zero array for a channel copies the channel without any change to it.

Assignment

Statement	Syntax	Description
Set	`Set variable to value`	Assigns a value to a variable. The values that can be assigned to a variable depend on its data type.
Set Field	`Set the field of variable to value`	Assigns a value to a specific field within a variable.
assign	`variable = value`	Assigns a value to a variable. The values that can be assigned to a variable depend on its data type.

Flow Control

Statement	Syntax	Description

If/Else	`If (condition1)`
	`Else if (condition2)`
	`Else End If`
		"If/Else" statements run different script code if the stated conditions are met. Each "If" statement isolates a single condition and directs the flow of the script to the statement immediately following it only if the condition is met. Optional "Else/If" statements isolate successive conditions and direct script flow to the code following them, if the condition attached to the statement is met. Finally, "Else" statements provide for any other circumstance. They literally mean "in any other event." These are also optional. The end of an If statement has to be indicated by an End If statement.

Repeat While	`Repeat While`
	`(condition)`
	`End Repeat`
		A "Repeat While" statement is a loop. The script lines between "Repeat While" and "End Repeat" are run repeatedly as long as the condition in the "Repeat While" statement is true. As soon as the condition is no longer true, the script moves out of the loop and onto the next line.

Repeat With Counter	`Repeat With`
	`Counter = start to`
	`finish [step amount]`
	`End Repeat`
		This type of loop runs the script lines between the "Repeat" and "End Repeat" statements for the number of times specified. Repeat with counter=1 to 10 repeats the lines of script 10 times.

Repeat With List	`Repeat With`
	`variable in [x1, x2,`
	`x3, ...] End Repeat`
		This repeats the script lines between "Repeat" and "End Repeat" once for each of the values specified in the list. At the same time, it assigns each value in turn to the variable.

Exit Repeat	`Exit Repeat`	This command directs the script flow to the lines immediately following the "End Repeat" statement. It can be structured as the result of a condition being met.

For/Next	`For variable =`
	`start to finish`
	`[step amount] Next`
		This type of loop runs the script lines between the "For" and "Next" statements for the number of times specified. Loop with counter=1 to 10 loops the lines of script 10 times.

Continued

Flow Control *(continued)*		
Statement	*Syntax*	*Description*
Exit For	`Exit For`	This command directs the script flow in the "For" loop to the lines immediately following the "Next" statement. It can be structured as the result of a condition being met.
Subroutine	`On subName(type parm1, type parm2, ...) End`	A subroutine is a part of a script that can be called by name from anywhere else in the script. Once the subroutine has been run, the flow of the script returns to the line immediately after the subroutine call. You can pass parameters to a subroutine. This means that information, such as numbers or text strings, is put into the subroutine from the part of the script that calls it. The subroutine runs the code between the "On" statement and the "End" statement.
Return	`Return Return(value)`	A Return command directs script flow back to the line immediately after the subroutine was called; it leaves the subroutine and goes back to the main script. A return statement may be the result of a particular condition being met. Return (value) can be used to return a numerical value.

✦   ✦   ✦

About the DVD-ROM

This appendix provides you with information on the contents of the companion DVD that accompanies this book. All of the versions are Mac products. Here is what you'll find:

+ Tutorial files for exercises shown throughout this book

+ Trial and demo versions of many useful software and plug-ins

+ Utilities for diagnostics and troubleshooting

System Requirements

Make sure that your computer meets the minimum system requirements listed in this section. Although individual items on this DVD may be able to play on a system of slower speed, or with software of earlier versions than those listed here, in order to take full advantage and get full use of the project and media designed for use with Final Cut Pro 4, the system requirements I provide are those for running Final Cut Pro 4. If your computer doesn't match up to these requirements, you may have problems using the contents of the DVD.

For Macintosh:

+ Macintosh computer with a G4/350MHz processor and an AGP graphics card

+ Mac OS 10.2.5 or later

+ QuickTime 6.1 or later

+ 384MB of available RAM

+ Approximately 1.0 GB of available hard disk

+ DVD drive, either internal or external

Using the DVD with the Mac OS

To install the items from the DVD to your hard drive, follow these steps:

1. **Insert the DVD into your computer's DVD-ROM drive.**

2. **Double-click the DVD icon to show the DVD's contents.**

3. **Double-click the Read Me First icon.**

4. **With the programs that come with installer programs, you simply open the program's folder on the DVD and double-click the icon with the words Install or Installer.**

What's on the DVD

The DVD-ROM contains the image files for the tutorials in the book, applications, plug-ins, accessories, and an electronic version of the book. Following is a summary of the contents of the DVD-ROM arranged by category.

Applications

The following applications are on the DVD-ROM:

✦ **Shareware programs** are fully functional, trial versions of copyrighted programs. If you like particular programs, register with their authors for a nominal fee and receive licenses, enhanced versions, and technical support.

✦ **Freeware programs** are free, copyrighted games, applications, and utilities. You can copy them to as many PCs as you like — free — but they have no technical support.

✦ **Trial, demo, or evaluation versions** are usually limited either by time or functionality (such as being unable to save projects).

Material for lessons in the book

The following material is used throughout the book for various exercises.

✦ **Mountain Biking Tutorial:** This folder contains media and Final Cut Pro files for the tutorial used in the QuickStart as well as throughout the book for many exercises.

✦ **Film Tutorial:** The Film Tutorial folder contains film media and Final Cut Pro files pertaining to film editing as shown in Chapter 27.

Software and plug-ins demo versions

Included are demo or trial versions of the following software:

✦ **Adobe After Effects 6.0:** Demo version of the industry standard compositing and special effects software from Adobe Systems. Chapter 26 details working between Final Cut Pro and After Effects.

✦ **Adobe Photoshop 7.0:** Demo version of the finest image editing program in the world. Chapter 26 details working between Final Cut Pro and Adobe Photoshop.

✦ **Video SpiceRack PRO/OrganicFX Sampler:** Plug-ins for Final Cut Pro from Pixelan Software.

✦ **Cinema 4D Release 8:** A first-rate 3-D modeling, animation, and rendering package from Maxon. Demo version.

Free plug-ins

The following material is used throughout the book for various exercises.

✦ **CGM ImageMask:** Plug-in for Final Cut Pro from Eiperle CGM tv. Freeware.

✦ **CGM Stretch:** Plug-in for Final Cut Pro from Eiperle CGM tv. Freeware.

Utilities

The following utility is meant to be of use to Final Cut Pro users:

✦ **Adobe Acrobat Reader 6.0:** Adobe Acrobat Reader is free software that lets you view and print Adobe Portable Document Format (PDF) files. Freeware.

Troubleshooting

If you have difficulty installing or using the DVD-ROM programs, try the following solutions:

✦ **Turn off any anti-virus software that you may have running.** Installers sometimes mimic virus activity and can make your computer incorrectly believe that a virus is infecting it. (Be sure to turn the antivirus software back on later.)

✦ **Close all running programs.** The more programs you're running, the less memory is available to other programs. Installers also typically update files and programs; if you keep other programs running, installation may not work properly.

If you still have trouble with the DVD, call the Wiley Publishing Customer Care telephone number: 800-762-2974. Outside the United States, call 317-572-3993. Wiley will provide technical support only for installation and other general quality control items; for technical support on the applications themselves, consult the program's vendor or author.

✦   ✦   ✦

Index

Continued

Continued

Continued

Continued

Continued

Continued

Continued

Continued

Continued

Continued

Continued

Continued

Continued